International Handbook of Personality and Intelligence

PERSPECTIVES ON INDIVIDUAL DIFFERENCES

CECIL R. REYNOLDS, *Texas A&M University, College Station*
ROBERT T. BROWN, *University of North Carolina, Wilmington*

Current Volumes in This Series

COGNITIVE ASSESSMENT
A Multidisciplinary Perspective
Edited by Cecil R. Reynolds

DEAFNESS, DEPRIVATION, AND IQ
Jeffery P. Braden

DEMENTIA
Allen Jack Edwards

EXPLORATIONS IN TEMPERAMENT
Edited by Jan Strelau and Alois Angleitner

FIFTY YEARS OF PERSONALITY PSYCHOLOGY
Edited by Kenneth H. Craik, Robert Hogan, and Raymond N. Wolfe

HANDBOOK OF CREATIVITY
Assessment, Research, and Theory
Edited by John A. Glover, Royce R. Ronning, and Cecil R. Reynolds

HANDBOOK OF MULTIVARIATE EXPERIMENTAL PSYCHOLOGY
Second Edition
Edited by John R. Nesselroade and Raymond B. Cattell

INDIVIDUAL DIFFERENCES IN CARDIOVASCULAR RESPONSE TO STRESS
Edited by J. Rick Turner, Andrew Sherwood, and Kathleen C. Light

INTERNATIONAL HANDBOOK OF PERSONALITY AND INTELLIGENCE
Edited by Donald H. Saklofske and Moshe Zeidner

LEARNING STRATEGIES AND LEARNING STYLES
Edited by Ronald R. Schmeck

PERSONALITY, SOCIAL SKILLS, AND PSYCHOPATHOLOGY
An Individual Differences Approach
Edited by David G. Gilbert and James J. Connolly

SCHIZOPHRENIC DISORDERS
Sense and Nonsense in Conceptualization, Assessment, and Treatment
Leighton C. Whitaker

A Continuation Order Plan is available for this series. A continuation order will bring delivery of each new volume immediately upon publication. Volumes are billed only upon actual shipment. For further information please contact the publisher.

International Handbook of Personality and Intelligence

Edited by

Donald H. Saklofske

University of Saskatchewan
Saskatoon, Saskatchewan, Canada

and

Moshe Zeidner

University of Haifa
Mount Carmel, Israel

Plenum Press • New York and London

Library of Congress Cataloging-in-Publication Data

International handbook of personality and intelligence / edited by
Donald H. Saklofske and Moshe Zeidner.
p. cm. -- (Perspectives on individual differences)
Includes bibliographical references and index.
ISBN 0-306-44749-5
1. Personality and intelligence. I. Saklofske, Donald H.
II. Zeidner, Moshe. III. Series.
BF698.9.I6I57 1995
153.9--dc20 95-1086
CIP

ISBN 0-306-44749-5

A Division of Plenum Publishing Corporation
233 Spring Street, New York, N. Y. 10013

10 9 8 7 6 5 4 3 2 1

Printed in the United States of America

To our beautiful children
Jon and Alison
and
Omer and Yair

In memory of
Jeffrey Brian Cullum

Contributors

Phillip L. Ackerman
Department of Psychology
University of Minnesota
Minneapolis, Minnesota 55455

Norman E. Amundson
Department of Counselling Psychology
University of British Columbia
Vancouver, British Columbia V6T 1Z4, Canada

Michael Bar-Eli
Ribstein Center for Research and Sport Medicine Sciences
Wingate Institute for Physical Education and Sport
Netanya 42902, Israel

Ernest S. Barratt
Department of Psychiatry and Behavioral Sciences
University of Texas Medical Branch
Galveston, Texas 77550-0443

David J. Baxter
University of Ottawa and Ministry of Correctional Services
Rideau Treatment Centre
Merrickville, Ontario K0G 1N0, Canada

Benjamin Beit-Hallahmi
Department of Psychology
University of Haifa
Mount Carmel, Haifa 31999, Israel

Monique Boekaerts
Leiden University
Centre for the Study of Education and Instruction
2300 RB Leiden, The Netherlands

William A. Borgen
Department of Counselling Psychology
University of British Columbia
Vancouver, British Columbia V6T 1Z4, Canada

Gregory J. Boyle
School of Humanities and Social Sciences
Bond University
Gold Coast, Queensland 4229, Australia

Thomas J. Bouchard, Jr.
Department of Psychology
University of Minnesota
Minneapolis, Minnesota 55455

Jeffrey P. Braden
Department of Educational Psychology
University of Wisconsin-Madison
Madison, Wisconsin 53706

John Brebner
Department of Psychology
University of Adelaide
Adelaide, South Australia 5005, Australia

Nathan Brody
Department of Psychology
Wesleyan University
Middletown, Connecticut 06457

Raymond B. Cattell
Department of Psychology
University of Hawaii
Honolulu, Hawaii 96844

Robert C. Calfee
School of Education
Stanford University
Stanford, California 94305

M. R. Cox
Department of Educational Psychology
University of Georgia
Athens, Georgia 30602

Michael J. Crowley
Department of Psychology
Wesleyan University
Middletown, Connecticut 06457

Robert G. Curley
College of Education
San Jose State University
San Jose, California 95192

Ian J. Deary
Department of Psychology
University of Edinburgh
Edinburgh EH8 9JZ, Scotland

Lisa Dorn
School of Education
University of Birmingham
Birmingham B15 2TT, England

Norman S. Endler
Department of Psychology
York University
North York, Ontario M3J 1P3, Canada

Hans J. Eysenck
Institute of Psychiatry
University of London
London SE5 8AF, England

Martin E. Ford
Graduate School of Education
George Mason University
Fairfax, Virginia 22030-4444

Sylvie Fortin
School of Psychology
University of Ottawa
Ottawa, Ontario K1N 6N5, Canada

Adrian Furnham
Department of Psychology
University College London
London WC1H OAP, England

Reuven Gal
The Israeli Institute for Military Studies
Zikhron Ya'akov 30900, Israel

Maynard Goff
Department of Psychology
University of Minnesota
Minneapolis, Minnesota 55455

Elena L. Grigorenko
Department of Psychology
Yale University
New Haven, Connecticut 06520

Michael Houlihan
School of Psychology
University of Ottawa
Ottawa, Ontario K1N 6N5, Canada

R. W. Kamphaus
Department of Educational Psychology
University of Georgia
Athens, Georgia 30602

Ruth Kanfer
Department of Psychology
University of Minnesota
Minneapolis, Minnesota 55455

Paul Kline
Department of Psychology
University of Exeter
Exeter EX4 4QG, England

David F. Lohman
Psychological and Quantitative Foundations
University of Iowa
Iowa City, Iowa 52242-1529

Richard Lynn
Department of Psychology
University of Ulster
Coleraine BT52 1S1, Northern Ireland

Gerald Matthews
Department of Psychology
University of Dundee
Dundee DD1 4HN, Scotland

A. W. Morgan
Department of Educational Psychology
University of Georgia
Athens, Georgia 30602

Robert B. Most
Mind Garden
P.O. Box 60669
Palo Alto, California 94306

Laurence L. Motiuk
Department of Psychology
Carleton University and Correctional Service of Canada
Ottawa, Ontario K1A 0P9, Canada

Todd Murtha
Department of Psychology
University of Minnesota
Minneapolis, Minnesota 55455

Gregory R. Pierce
Department of Psychology
Hamilton College
Clinton, New York 13323

R. M. Powell
Department of Educational Psychology
University of Georgia
Athens, Georgia 30602

Cecil R. Reynolds
Department of Educational Psychology
Texas A&M University
College Station, Texas 77843-4225

Thomas Rocklin
Psychological and Quantitative Foundations
Univeristy of Iowa
Iowa City, Iowa 52242-1529

Donald H. Saklofske
Department of Educational Psychology
University of Saskatchewan
Saskatoon, Saskatchewan S7N 0W0, Canada

Barbara R. Sarason
Department of Psychology
University of Washington
Seattle, Washington 98195

Irwin G. Sarason
Department of Psychology
University of Washington
Seattle, Washington 98195

Vicki L. Schwean
Department for the Education of Exceptional Children
University of Saskatchewan
Saskatoon, Saskatchewan S7N 0W0, Canada

Margaret Semrud-Clikeman
Department of Educational Psychology
University of Washington
Seattle, Washington 98195

Dean Keith Simonton
Department of Psychology
University of California at Davis
Davis, California 95616-8686

Richard E. Snow
School of Education
Stanford University
Stanford, California 94305

Lazar Stankov
Department of Psychology
University of Sydney
Sydney, New South Wales 2006, Australia

Robert M. Stelmack
School of Psychology
University of Ottawa
Ottawa, Ontario K1N 6N5, Canada

Robert J. Sternberg
Department of Psychology
Yale University
New Haven, Connecticut 06520

Con Stough
Cognitive Psychophysiology Laboratory
Medical School
University of Queensland
Herstin, Queensland 4006, Australia

Laura J. Summerfeldt
Department of Psychology
York University
North York, Ontario M3J 1P3, Canada

Phyllis Anne Teeter
Department of Educational Psychology
University of Wisconsin-Milwaukee
Milwaukee, Wisconsin 53201

Elizabeth Tench
Department of Counselling Psychology
University of British Columbia
Vancouver, British Columbia V6T 1Z4, Canada

Gershon Tenenbaum
Department of Psychology
University of Southern Queensland
Toowoomba, Queensland 4350, Australia

Moshe Zeidner
School of Education
University of Haifa
Mount Carmel 31999, Israel

Foreword

This volume brings together many distingushed theorists, as well as many young investigators and a range of important viewpoints, to address a central problem of integration for psychology. As the editors note, the terms *personality* and *intelligence* label two grand but heretofore distinct domains of theory and research. The distinction is of course artificial—a convenient fiction adopted early on to divide the scientific problems of psychology into hopefully simpler, more manageable chunks. Unfortunately, despite admonitions to the contrary in much of the early work, the message received by subsequent generations of psychological scientists seems to have been that the person, as well as the research and researcher, can be similarly divided.

New research is now beginning to test this distinction, to look for relations across the domains of personality and intelligence, and even to imagine integrations that might be designed for particular theoretical or practical purposes. Many of the possibilities and also the myriad theoretical and methodological problems faced by this research are delineated in the contents of this book. No foreword can hope to reflect this complex array, even in abstract form. Rather, I have chosen in this small space to identify briefly four overarching problems that appear relevant to all of the present chapters, and to much of future research as well. Each chapter touches on one or another of these issues, in one way or another, in its own terms. Therefore, I identify these problems here only in abstract form, and I presume to offer no solutions. Some supporting literature outside of the present book is noted in passing.

The four problems, expressed as needs for different kinds of action, are:

1. Modeling the complexity of person–situation interactions;
2. Building a comprehensive and useful taxonomy of personality constructs;
3. Learning to use the complementarities among different research methods, measures, and approaches;
4. Finding the interrelations among individual differential and developmental structures, functions, and processes.

PERSON–SITUATION INTERACTIONS

Person–situation interactionist perspectives have now largely superseded the old person versus situation debates. It is clear that some situation characteristics are sometimes powerful enough to produce consistency of behavior across many persons, and also that some personal characteristics are sometimes powerful enough to produce consistency of behavior across many situations. But I think most researchers agree that most behavior most of the time is a function of interaction among person and situation characteristics. The research aim therefore is to partition the matrix of persons × situations into subsets in which generalizations hold (Cronbach & Snow, 1977).

However, person–situation interaction can take many forms and thus can be modeled in different ways. Different researchers emphasize different kinds of interaction, and may even use the same terms to refer to quite different phenomena. There seem to be especially important differences between reseachers operating in the biological versus cognitive-intelligence versus personality-social spheres in this respect (see, e.g., Hettema & Kenrick, 1992; Pervin & Lewis, 1978; Snow, 1994; Wachs & Plomin, 1991). Particularly, as we consider interactions involving intelligence-personality compounds, we need to be clear on the model(s) being used and interpreted. Following Hettema and Kenrick (1992), at least six types of interaction can be identified:

1. Person–environment matching, wherein relatively consistent characteristics of persons are assumed to suit them for relatively consistent characteristics of situations, and vice versa, to provide a mesh;
2. Choice of environments by persons to suit their own personality characteristics;
3. Choice of persons by environments, as in most selection systems;
4. Transformation of environments by persons to suit their own characteristics and personal goals (including changing goals);
5. Transformation of persons by environments, as in learning, adaptation, and development; and
6. Person–environment transaction—reciprocal interactions over time that change both persons and situations to attain a mesh.

There are also variations on each of these themes.

It is noteworthy that modern interactionist research on both intelligence and personality began with studies of statistical interaction among assumedly independent person and situation variables, as in Hettema and Kenrick's first type, but each has moved of late to address particularly the sixth type. The variations here range from reciprocal interactionist research on ability and strategy shifting in relation to task changes, through transactionist conceptions of learning in apprenticeships, to purely social constructivist definitions of personality. These approaches differ in the degree to which the individual histories of person and situation are deemed relevant to understanding the transaction system (see Snow, 1994, for relevant references). Perhaps the most challenging problem, for the philosophy of psychological science, as well as for theory and research on intelligence and personality, arises from these reciprocal interactionist or transactionist perspectives. It is the problem of how to conceptualize and study intelligence and personality as properties not of person or situation independently but of person–situation unions (i.e., as relational properties of persons-in-situations).

TOWARD TAXONOMY

A second problem is taxonomy construction, an important early activity in any science. Even quite loose and provisional classification structures can help guide exploration and provide a framework on which to pin individual findings as they accumulate. One of psychology's principal taxonomy-building tools has been factor analysis, which has been used to advantage in both intelligence and personality domains. Unfortunately, its use has been limited mainly to the person side or to the description of situations as perceived by persons. The situation side per se has rarely been addressed (but see Frederiksen, 1972; Van Heck, 1989). However, even on the person side, the coalescence of evidence favoring a hierarchical structure of cognitive ability factors (Carroll, 1993) and a five superfactor model of personality (John, 1990) hardly completes the taxonomic work. Many questions remain. Among the most important of these concern whether evidence based on methods other than factor analysis supports similar distinctions, or suggests other distinctions, and whether the constructs provided by factor analysis, even if hierarchical, are both molar and molecular enough to cover all the important theoretical needs. For short, these problems are here termed "coverage" and "grain size."

The coverage problem can be tested by casting the lists of defined personality and intelligence factors onto other kinds of category systems to see what may be left out. For example, taking the Aristotelian categories of affection, conation, and cognition, and then dividing affection into temperament and emotion, conation into motivation and volition, and cognition into declarative knowledge and procedural skills yields a fairly comprehensive six column array not derived from factor analysis (see Snow, Corno, & Jackson, in press). Mapping known personality and intelligence factors onto this array suggests at least one empty space. Personality factors seem to represent much of temperament, characteristic emotional moods, and sources of motivation and interest. Ability factors seem to reflect much of cognitive knowledge and skill. But the column representing volition (or will) seems poorly covered. It would appear to contain constructs of action control and self-regulation, metamotivational knowledge and social intelligence, and beliefs about one's own knowledge and skill, that so far at least do not seem well-represented in the factor structures typically used. Perhaps here is an important interface between cognition and conation, or between intelligence and personality, that deserves further exploration.

The grain-size problem is represented at several levels of intelligence and personality hierarchy. It is seen in the degree to which the whole-person-in-situation is not well described by combinations of ability or personality superfactors. Above the superfactors there may also be need for compound or syndrome constructs at the level of types. Below the superfactors, the grain-size problem appears when lower-order factors carry certain specialized and situated meanings that are not captured in the higher-order factors. It is becoming clear that both broad, higher-order, and narrow, lower-order factors need to be represented in studies of individual differences; each helps the interpretation of the effects of the other (Gustafsson, 1989). Other kinds of units, such as habitual responses, behavior episodes, or styles, strategies, and tactics similarly beg the grain-size question. Finally, the interface between behavioral and biological levels of description poses perhaps the most formidable grain size problem—the question is how to integrate variables defined in quite different grain sizes into a coherent biosocial model of person–situation interaction. There are significant differences of opinion on whether or not this will be possible (see, e.g., Gibson, 1979; Hettema, 1989; Hettema & Kenrick, 1992; Michaels & Carello, 1981).

COMPLEMENTARITIES OF METHOD

It is now commonplace to hear that nomothetic and idiographic designs, or quantitative and qualitative data analyses, or experimental, correlational, and naturalistic descriptions are (or should be) complementary. And lip service is paid to the power of multitrait-multimethod reasoning for convergent and discriminant construct validation in many parts of the research field beyond the kinds of correlation matrices in which it was first applied. Yet there are few discussions and even fewer concrete demonstrations of how to understand and capitalize upon these complementarities in actual research. Moreover, examinations of contrasting methodologies often lapse into philosophical arguments wherein one is forced to take a stance, pro or con, about a particular methodology fitting one's basic assumptions and goals. As examples, it seems one must choose among behavioral, cognitive, and projective assessments, or normative, ipsative, and idiothetic measurement models; experiments must be rejected if one rejects logical positivism. If one accepts phenomenological views, there is no point in attempting to characterize "real" or "objective" situations. (For further discussion, see Rorer, 1990.)

There is no denying the importance of considering the philosophical foundations from which particular methodologies arise. One can also agree that there are no theory-neutral methods or measures. Yet one can examine alternative methods and measures from a utilitarian and eclectic perspective, seeking to identify and exploit the functional complementarities that the deeper philosophical debates often obscure.

Interestingly, this kind of multimethod approach may be most readily built in practice-oriented fields removed a bit from research on personality and intelligence theory per se. Educational research is a case in point. When understanding educational problems or processes is the target, rather than theory for its own sake, the focus can be on whatever combination of methods illuminates the phenomena. Thus educational research, including research on intelligence and personality in education, seems to be developing this "disciplined eclectic" perspective (Shulman, 1988), and generating examples of some of the possibilities (Jaeger, 1988; Miles & Huberman, 1984). Important lessons for broader application might be learned by following and promoting this progress.

INDIVIDUAL DIFFERENCES AND DEVELOPMENT

Finally, a way needs to be found to integrate research on individual differences with research on the development of individuals. For a long time there has been not just a two-way split between intelligence and personality, but a four-way split in which research in each of these domains is divided between differentialists and developmentalists. Differentialists usually focus on measures taken at only one or two points in time and can only speculate on developmental trends. Developmentalists focus on the developmental trends but usually measure no individual difference except age. Yet it may be that the best way to understand both individual differences and individuality is in the context of development, whereas developmental pathways both general and unique may best be interpreted in the context of differential distributions.

There are already the beginnings of work in both these directions, in both personality and intelligence domains. Case and Edelstein (1993) have collected examples of Neopiagetian research on intellectual development in which different clusters or webs of ability may be traced along different developmental pathways, and for individuals who differ in some basic processing functions. Demetriou and Efklides (1994) have also brought together examples, and in their own work have explicitly combined developmental and psychometric theory and method. Weinert and Schneider (in press) have studied individual differences in cognitive, social, and emotional development. Magnusson (1990; Magnusson & Allen, 1983) has done the same for personality development within a person–situation interactionist perspective. And Bereiter (1990) has proposed the study of what he calls "acquired contextual modules," such as "public speaking ability" or "intentional learning style." Presumably, such constructs integrate intellectual and personality aspects, over development and individualization, of characteristic performance in a specialized type of situation.

It is too early to tell whether research on constructs of this sort will really allow us to weave all of these separate strands together. But this volume leads in taking at least the important first steps toward coalescence. It is exemplary of the best research and researchers currently in the field. Hopefully, it will encourage new and old investigators alike to join in, and other such volumes will follow.

RICHARD E. SNOW
Stanford University

REFERENCES

Bereiter, C. (1990). Aspects of an educational learning theory. *Review of Educational Research, 60*, 603–624.
Carroll, J. B. (1993). *Human cognitive abilities.* New York: Cambridge University Press.

Case, R., & Edelstein, W. (Eds.). (1993). *The new structuralism in cognitive development: Theory and research on individual pathways. Contributions to human development* (Vol. 23). Basel: Karger.

Cronbach, L. J., & Snow, R. E. (1977). *Aptitudes and instructional methods: A handbook for research on interactions*. New York: Irvington.

Demetriou, A., & Efklides, A. (Eds.). (1994). *Intelligence, mind, and reasoning: Structure and development*. Amsterdam: North-Holland.

Frederiksen, N. (1972). Toward a taxonomy of situations. *American Psychologist*, *27*, 114–123.

Gibson, J. J. (1979). *The ecological approach to visual perception*. Boston: Houghton Mifflin.

Gustafsson, J. E. (1989). Broad and narrow abilities in research on learning and instruction. In R. Kanfer, P. L. Ackerman, & R. Cudeck (Eds.), *Abilities, motivation, and methodology* (pp. 203–237). Hillsdale, NJ: Erlbaum.

Hettema, P. J. (Ed.). (1989). *Personality and environment: Assessment of human adaptation*. Chichester, UK: Wiley.

Hettema, P. J., & Kenrick, D. T. (1992). Models of person–situation interactions. In G. V. Caprara & G. L. Van Heck (Eds.), *Modern personality psychology: Critical reviews and new directions* (pp. 393–417). New York: Harvester Whestsheaf.

Jaeger, R. M. (Ed.). (1988). *Complementary methods for research in education* Washington, DC: American Educational Research Association.

John, O. P. (1990). The "Big Five" factor taxonomy: Dimensions of personality in the natural language and in questionnaires. In L. A. Pervin (Ed.), *Handbook of personality theory and research* (pp. 693–720). New York: Guilford Press.

Magnusson, D. (1990). Personality development from an interactional perspective. In L. A. Pervin (Ed.), *Handbook of personality theory and research* (pp. 193–222). New York: Guilford Press.

Magnusson, D., & Allen, V. L. (Eds.). (1983). *Human development: An interactional perspective*. New York: Academic Press.

Michaels, D. F., & Carello, C. (1981). *Direct perception*. Englewood Cliffs, NJ: Prentice-Hall.

Miles, M. B., & Huberman, A. M. (1984). *Qualitative data analysis: A sourcebook of new methods*. Newbury Park, CA: Sage.

Pervin, L. A., & Lewis, M. (1978). Overview of the internal–external issue. In L. A. Pervin, & M. Lewis. (Eds.), *Perspectives in interactional psychology* (pp. 1–22). New York: Plenum.

Rorer, L. G. (1990). Personality assessment: A conceptual survey. In L. A. Pervin (Ed.), *Handbook of personality theory and research* (pp. 693–720). New York: Guilford.

Shulman, L. S. (1988). Disciplines of inquiry in education: An overview. In R. M. Jaeger (Ed.). *Complementary methods for research in education* (pp. 3–17). Washington, DC: American Educational Research Association.

Snow, R. E. (1994). Abilities in academic tasks. In R. J. Sternberg & R. K. Wagner (Eds.), *Mind in context: Interactionist perspectives on human intelligence*. New York: Cambridge University Press.

Snow, R. E., Corno, L., & Jackson, D. N. III. (in press). Individual differences in affective and conative functions. In D. C. Berliner & R. Calfee (Eds.), *Handbook of Education Psychology*. New York: Macmillan.

Van Heck, G. L. (1989). Situation concepts: Definitions and classification. In P. J. Hettema (Ed.), *Personality and environment: Assessment of human adaptation* (pp. 53–69). Chichester, UK: Wiley.

Wachs, T. D., & Plomin, R. (Eds.). (1991). *Conceptualization and measurement of organism–environment interaction*. Washington, DC: American Psychological Association.

Weinert, F. E., & Schneider, W. (in press). Congitive, social, and emotional development. In D. Magnusson (Ed.), *The european network on longitudinal studies on individual development* (Vol. 8). Cambridge: Cambridge University Press.

Preface

For more than a century, psychologists have researched intelligence and personality in an effort to develop models of human behavior. The tendency, however, has been to examine the many variables described within each of these broad areas more or less separately. To date there have been few efforts to explore the potential avenues for integrating these two key constructs from a theoretical, empirical, and applied perspective. Consequently, there is a need to summarize current findings and further examine potential areas of the personality-intelligence interface.

This handbook is an attempt to address these purposes and is further guided by several considerations. First, these two broad constructs are linked and have much in common by virtue of being key sources of individual and group differences in behavior. The field of personality itself is frequently viewed as the combination and organization of all relatively enduring dimensions of individual differences, across time and situations, on which a person can be measured. Second, intelligence is often construed as the cognitive part of personality, so the two constructs are in effect mutually intertwined. Third, personality and intelligence variables may influence each other and therefore interact with respect to their development, manifestation, and measurement. These considerations attest to the critical importance of examining the interface between intelligence and personality in order to develop more comprehensive descriptions of human behavior. Some of these integrative efforts—drawn from psychological theory, research, assessment, and practice—are briefly noted below.

From a theoretical and conceptual perspective, earlier works by such influential figures in the field of differential psychology as Binet, Terman, Wechsler, and Anastasi recognized the inextricable web of interrelationships between personality and intelligence constructs. One of the more contemporary positions views intelligence as the cognitive part of the overall structure of human personality (Eysenck & Eysenck, 1985). Here personality is the superordinate construct, which can be further divided into two complementary categories: noncognitive components, such as affect and motivation; and cognitive components, including intelligence. In Cattell's (1971) theory of personality, intelligence is one of the 16 basic source traits. The "big five" (Costa & McCrae, 1992) describes a fifth factor labeled "openness to experience" or "intellect." Further examples range from Gough's (1987) conceptualization of personality to include an intellectual factor and Lazarus's (1991) theory of emotion, where intelligence is viewed as a major personal coping resource, to Gardner's (1983) theory of multiple intelligences, which identifies two personal components.

Among the many examples of research findings that can be cited are the considerable efforts directed at determining the relative genetic and environmental contributions for both personality and intelligence. There is a convergence of research data that supports a strong genetic component in personality and intelligence traits, although the heritability estimates are slightly higher for the latter. Using reliable data, large samples, and correlational methods, it is estimated that genetic influences account for at least 60% of the variance underlying individual differences in IQ (Vernon, 1979) and about 50% for personality factors (Bouchard & McGue, 1990). The meaningful remaining variance, excluding residual error, is attributable to such environmental factors as child-rearing practices and opportunities for language development and education. Further examples include research on the cognitive components of depression and anxiety (e.g., worry and cognitive interference), as well as the impact of affective states on intelligence and achievement test performance. Recent models of stress and coping have emphasized the mediating role of cognitive factors, including appraisals and rational problem-focused coping, in influencing adaptive outcomes (Zeidner & Saklofske, in press).

Many facets of measuring personality and intelligence (e.g., domain specification, procedures for item generation, test formats) have developed separately. This follows the psychometric tradition of striving for measures that maximize true score variance and minimize error variance that may be caused by any factor unrelated to the construct under consideration (i.e., nuisance variables). Clearly, confounding the measurement of well-established psychological variables will not further integrative efforts. Although contemporary test and measurement experts will continue developing valid and reliable measures of operationally defined constructs of intelligence (e.g., spatial reasoning, verbal fluency) and personality (e.g., extraversion, hostility), it is at the theoretical, research, and finally the clinical levels that the integration of the data from these measures will occur.

By necessity the greatest amount of integration of cognitive and affective variables takes place in clinical and applied settings. For example, the clinical or school psychologist may assess a child's poor school achievement by gathering data (tests, observations, interviews) on the child's intelligence, learning style, motivation, self-concept, anxiety, and social behavior, as well as physical and health status and home environment, in order to arrive at a diagnosis and prescription of the most appropriate intervention program. Thus the psychological practitioners' task is to develop a comprehensive and integrated description of the person by employing precise measurement strategies and continuously referencing the theory and research that describes the interrelationships among the various examined factors. Given that such an integration is not always explicit from theory or from the available research literature, clinicians may be required to make this integration on their own (i.e., at an intuitive level).

The relationship between cognitive and noncognitive constructs is best conceived of as one of reciprocal determinism. Obviously, more complete models of human behavior are impossible without recognizing the dynamic interplay between cognitive, affective, and motivational variables—what Hilgard (1980) calls the "trilogy of the mind." Because there have only been a small number of concerted efforts to explore the multiple facets of the potential interface between personality and intelligence, it is of critical importance to assess and document the current status of the integration between these cardinal constructs.

This is not the first effort to examine the interface between personality and intelligence (e.g., Baron, 1982). It is unique, however, in bringing together a wide range of potential integrative links drawn from theory, research, measurement, and application. Respected authorities in the field of psychology were invited to examine these issues critically from the perspective of their own areas of specialization. Authors chose to describe either a narrow or more broadly based view of this interface. We hope this volume makes an important step forward in our scientific efforts to construct an interactive model of human behavior and individual differences.

The handbook should be of interest to all psychologists and professionals in the behavioral and health sciences who have a serious interest in the study of either or both personality and intelligence. The chapters are arranged to reflect five broad but overlapping categories.

Part I focuses on basic and theoretical issues. These chapters present historical and contemporary paradigms and critically assess ideological, genetic, longitudinal, social, and cultural factors underlying the study of personality and intelligence. The chapters in Part II reflect personality and intelligence "at the crossroads." Included here are contributions that present contemporary and evolving theoretical views on thinking, creativity, learning, literacy, social behavior, exceptional children, and adult psychopathology. Part III explores empirical links between personality and intelligence variables and includes chapters ranging from psychometrically described traits to more basic processes such as attention, reaction time, and event-related potentials. Part IV discusses measurement issues that are critical in linking personality and intelligence. The chapters cover measurement models, test construction procedures, current instruments, psychodiagnostic processes, and the psychometric problem of test bias. Part V describes applications of personality and intelligence in applied settings and specific contexts. Included here are examples from applied psychology, including industrial and organizational, counseling, school, and clinical neuropsychology. Additional chapters focus on the integrative role of personality and intelligence in relation to sports, criminal behavior, health, war heroes, and leadership.

We are grateful to many colleagues and friends for supporting us throughout this project. First, we are indebted to all of the distinguished authors who prepared chapters that appear in this handbook; we recognize the complexity of the task and congratulate them all for their critical contributions. Richard Snow graciously agreed to write the foreword that appears at the beginning of the book. The active interest and encouragement from Charles Spielberger is acknowledged. Eliot Werner and Plenum Publishing Corporation have been most helpful in all phases required to bring this project to publication. The University of Saskatchewan and Haifa University provided the academic environments necessary to undertake and complete this handbook. Finally, we both thank our respective partners, Vicki and Eti, for their personal and professional support throughout the preparation of this volume.

DONALD H. SAKLOFSKE
MOSHE ZEIDNER

REFERENCES

Baron, J. (1982). Personality and intelligence. In R. Sternberg (Ed.), *Handbook of human intelligence* (pp. 308–351). New York: Cambridge University Press.

Bouchard, T. J., & McGue, M. (1990). Genetic and rearing environmental influences in adult personality: Reanalysis of adopted twins reared apart. *Journal of Personality, 58*, 263–292.

Cattell, R. B. (1971). *Abilities: Their structure, growth and action.* New York: Houghton Mifflin.

Costa, P. T., Jr., & McCrae, R. R. (1992). *Revised NEO Personality Inventory (NEO PI-PR) and NEO Five-Factor Inventory (NEO-FFI) professional manual.* Odessa, FL: Psychological Assessment Resources.

Eysenck, H. J., & Eysenck, M. W. (1985). *Personality and individual differences.* New York: Plenum.

Gardner, H. (1983). *Frames of mind.* New York: Basic Books.

Gough, H. G. (1987). *California Psychological Inventory administrator's guide.* Palo Alto, CA: Consulting Psychologists Press.

Hilgard, E. R. (1980). The trilogy of mind: Cognition, affection, and conation. *Journal of the History of the Behavioral Sciences, 16*, 107–117.

Lazarus, R. S. (1991). *Emotion and adaptation.* New York: Oxford University Press.

Vernon, P. H. (1979). *Intelligence: Heredity and environment.* San Francisco: Freeman.

Zeidner, M., & Saklofske, D. H. (in press). Adaptive and maladaptive coping. In M. Zeidner & N. S. Endler (Eds.), *Handbook of Coping: Theory, research, applications.* New York: Wiley.

Contents

I. BASIC AND THEORETICAL ISSUES IN THE STUDY OF PERSONALITY AND INTELLIGENCE

1. **History of Personality and Intelligence Theory and Research: The Challenge** 3
   Ernest S. Barratt

2. **Models and Paradigms in Personality and Intelligence Research** 15
   Lazar Stankov, Gregory J. Boyle, and Raymond B. Cattell

3. **Ideological Aspects of Research on Personality and Intelligence** 45
   Benjamin Beit-Hallahmi

4. **Environmental (and Genetic) Influences on Personality and Intelligence** 59
   Nathan Brody and Michael J. Crowley

5. **Longitudinal Studies of Personality and Intelligence: A Behavior Genetic and Evolutionary Psychology Perspective** 81
   Thomas J. Bouchard, Jr.

6. **Cross-Cultural Differences in Intelligence and Personality** 107
   Richard Lynn

II. PERSONALITY AND INTELLIGENCE AT THE CROSSROADS

7. **Intelligence and Personality in Social Behavior** 125
   Martin E. Ford

8. **Intellective and Personality Factors in Literacy** 143
Robert C. Calfee and Robert G. Curley

9. **The Interface between Intelligence and Personality as Determinants of Classroom Learning** 161
Monique Boekaerts

10. **A Cognitive-Social Description of Exceptional Children** 185
Vicki L. Schwean and Donald H. Saklofske

11. **Thinking Styles** 205
Elena L. Grigorenko and Robert J. Sternberg

12. **Creativity as a Product of Intelligence and Personality** 231
Hans J. Eysenck

13. **Intelligence, Personality, Psychopathology, and Adjustment** 249
Norman S. Endler and Laura J. Summerfeldt

14. **Cognitive Interference: At the Intelligence–Personality Crossroads** ... 285
Irwin G. Sarason, Barbara R. Sarason, and Gregory R. Pierce

III. EMPIRICAL LINKS BETWEEN PERSONALITY AND INTELLIGENCE

15. **Personality Trait Correlates of Intelligence** 299
Moshe Zeidner

16. **Theoretical and Empirical Relationships between Personality and Intelligence** 321
John Brebner and Con Stough

17. **Event-Related Potentials, Personality, and Intelligence: Concepts, Issues, and Evidence** 349
Robert M. Stelmack and Michael Houlihan

18. **Cognitive and Attentional Processes in Personality and Intelligence** .. 367
Gerald Matthews and Lisa Dorn

19. **The Relationship of Personality and Intelligence to Cognitive Learning Style and Achievement** 397
Adrian Furnham

IV. MEASUREMENT AND ASSESSMENT OF PERSONALITY AND INTELLIGENCE

20. **Measurement and Statistical Models in the Study of Personality and Intelligence** 417
Gregory J. Boyle, Lazar Stankov, and Raymond B. Cattell

21. **Current and Recurring Issues in the Assessment of Intelligence and Personality** 447
David F. Lohman and Thomas Rocklin

22. **Constructing Personality and Intelligence Instruments: Methods and Issues** 475
Robert B. Most and Moshe Zeidner

23. **A Critical Review of the Measurement of Personality and Intelligence** 505
Paul Kline

24. **Personality and Intelligence in the Psychodiagnostic Process: The Emergence of Diagnostic Schedules** 525
R. W. Kamphaus, A. W. Morgan, M. R. Cox, and R. M. Powell

25. **Test Bias and the Assessment of Intelligence and Personality** 545
Cecil R. Reynolds

V. APPLICATIONS AND CLINICAL PARAMETERS

26. **Personality and Intelligence in Industrial and Organizational Psychology** 577
Ruth Kanfer, Phillip L. Ackerman, Todd Murtha, and Maynard Goff

27. **Counseling and the Role of Personality and Intelligence** 603
Norman E. Amundson, William A. Borgen, and Elizabeth Tench

28. **Intelligence and Personality in School and Educational Psychology** ... 621
Jeffrey P. Braden

29. **Personality, Intelligence, and Neuropsychology in the Diagnosis and Treatment of Clinical Disorders** 651
Margaret Semrud-Clikeman and Phyllis Anne Teeter

30. **Intelligence and Personality in Criminal Offenders** 673
David J. Baxter, Laurence L. Motiuk, and Sylvie Fortin

31. **Personality and Intellectual Capabilities in Sport Psychology** 687
Gershon Tenenbaum and Michael Bar-Eli

32. **Intelligence, Personality, and Severe Hypoglycemia in Diabetes** 711
Ian J. Deary

33. **Personality and Intelligence in the Military: The Case of War Heroes** 727
Reuven Gal

34. **Personality and Intellectual Predictors of Leadership** 739
Dean Keith Simonton

Index 757

I

Basic and Theoretical Issues in the Study of Personality and Intelligence

1

History of Personality and Intelligence Theory and Research

The Challenge

Ernest S. Barratt

Personality theory has been aimed primarily at developing an inclusive description of persons, while intelligence theory has been aimed at a more specific question: What is a person's cognitive potential to adapt to environmental demands? Both subdisciplines developed within the context of individual-differences research, especially in their early history. Individual-differences research has been contrasted with studies in what often has been labeled experimental or hardcore psychology, characterized by controlled experiments with independent and dependent variables. Individual-differences research used primarily correlational procedures and descriptive statistics. It is obvious from a review of the history of psychology that the "two psychologies" differentiation (Cronbach, 1957) did not accurately characterize all of psychological research, although there was a fairly pervasive methodological split at one time. As personality theory evolves, it would be expected to increasingly integrate data from all branches of psychology and other disciplines into an inclusive scientific model of persons. This is the challenge that this chapter addresses.

This book is focused on the integration of personality and intelligence theory and research. This chapter will not be a historical survey of the topic in the conventional sense of a chronological sequence of events and the role of prominent persons. Rather, it will present selected examples in four areas: where personality and intelligence theory and research have overlapped (these examples will involve interrelationships based on techniques, constructs, and, within the factor analytic research, how research on the structure of personality has included intelligence factors); what problems have been encountered in attempts to arrive at an integrated view of persons (the emphasis here will be primarily on personality theory because of the assumption that *personality theory* is a more inclusive term; the examples will be aimed at posing problems that provide meaningful—that is, testable—hypotheses for research at the interface of intelligence and personality); a brief look at personality theory and research within the context of the general history of psychology (and related disciplines) and the philosophy of science; and suggestions to help personality theory achieve an integrated view of persons.

As noted, the goal of this chapter is not to provide a complete history of the interface between personality and learning theory and research. Rather, it is slanted

Ernest S. Barratt • Department of Psychiatry and Behavioral Sciences, University of Texas Medical Branch, Galveston, Texas 77550-0443.

International Handbook of Personality and Intelligence, edited by Donald H. Saklofske and Moshe Zeidner. Plenum Press, New York, 1995.

toward the above four goals, and sources were selected accordingly. Because this review involves a selective bibliography, the next section will refer readers to more complete historical reviews of personality and intelligence theory and research that are more general and provide a less biased view.

SELECTED SOURCES OF HISTORICAL OVERVIEWS OF PERSONALITY AND INTELLIGENCE THEORY AND RESEARCH

There are many excellent sources of the history of personality and intelligence theory and research. The history from 1950 until 1993 is chronicled in the *Annual Review of Psychology* (e.g., Sears, 1950; Thorndike, 1950) as well as selected journal articles and books. For history prior to 1950, there are textbooks of the history of psychology (e.g., Heidbreder, 1933; Murphy, 1949; Peters, 1953) and history chapters within personality and individual-difference textbooks that provide good overviews. Many textbooks on personality have an initial chapter or two that briefly outline either the history of personality theory or the techniques used in personality and intelligence theory and research. For example, the first two chapters of Guilford's (1959) *Personality* review a wide range of personality theories and some of the bases for the diverse elements that are still relevant to defining personality.

There are biases in going to any source for history. However, certain contributions represent milestones in providing a model of persons that integrates intelligence and the constructs of personality theory. One example is Allport's (1937) *Personality: A Psychological Interpretation*. He anticipated many of the later conflicts and advances in personality theory. Pervin (1985) notes, for example, that the "person-situation" controversy in personality theory generated by Mishel (1968) was not a new issue, as evidenced by Allport's discussion of the "generalists" (traits) versus "specifists" (situations). Murphy's (1947) *Personality: A Biosocial Approach to Origins and Structures* is another example. His attempt to integrate what was known at that time from the single cell to cultural influences into an understanding of a person marks an important step forward in the history of personality theory.

Murray's (1938) *Explorations in Personality* (or "Explorations," as it often labeled) has also occupied an important place in personality theory. Smith and Anderson (1989) noted that Murray's colleague Gordon Allport "gave personality its first great book in 1937 and in the following year, *Explorations in Personality* by Murray and his co-workers got the field fairly-launched." Kluckhon and Murray's (1949) *Personality in Nature, Society and Culture* was valuable because of the attempt by the editors to provide a "field" or integrated approach to understanding the individual in "nature, society and culture," and it illustrated the progress made after Murray and Allport's books had been published. These early attempts to provide a widely accepted theory of personality failed—as evidenced in Hall and Lindzey's (1985) *Introduction to Theories of Personality*, in which the authors list 20 major personality theories.

The current trend toward the study of the biological bases of personality traits was illustrated in the early writings of Hans Eysenck (1947, 1952). Eysenck's theory has led to extensive research on the biological correlates of personality. Zuckerman (1991) reviewed much of this research from the past three decades in his book on the "psychobiology of personality," which "combines the top down approach of Eysenck and the bottoms up approach of Gray" (1971). A top-down approach to personality starts with personality dimensions (e.g., defined primarily by self-report questionnaires or rating scales) and then searches for biological bases for the dimensions. A bottoms-up approach starts with biological and behavioral data from lower animal and human studies as a basis for identifying psychometric measures that define personality traits. If one includes the temperament research of eastern European personality theorists (e.g., Strelau, 1983) with that of Eysenck, Gray, and Zuckerman, it is evident that personality theory has made great strides toward integrating biological, behavioral, and personality trait concepts, even though no one theory has been accepted by all.

From an applied perspective, psychopathology or psychodiagnostics often provide a different view than the more psychometric orientations of research personality theorists. The early scope of clinical research involving projective tests and structured interviews is illustrated by Rapaport's (1946) two-volume work, *Diagnostic Psychological Testing*. The second volume contains the results of personality testing research, with a primary emphasis on projective tests; the interrelationship of personality and intelligence constructs is discussed from a practical viewpoint. A more recent book by Megargee and Spielberger (1992) provides another overview of the history of personality assessment in America. They reviewed 16 articles that span the period 1938 to 1990, including Meehl's (1979) paper on the need for taxonomy in diagnosis and his "eight reasons why diagnosis has benefitted more from clinical insight and acumen than from statistical methods of discovery."

The history of intelligence research and theory is more circumscribed and chronologically sequenced. An excellent overview of intelligence theory and research is Carroll's chapter in Sternberg's (1982) *Handbook of Human Intelligence*. Carroll (1982) divides the history of intelligence testing into two periods: from Galton's (1869) *Hereditary Genius* to the founding of the Psychometric Society in 1935; and from 1935 to 1982. Each period is discussed under six topics: what is being measured; theories of measurement and scaling; statistical theory and computational technology; psychological measurement theory; procedures of test construction, standardization, and application; and practices in the use of tests and research in such uses.

Examples of books or monographs that had a significant impact on intelligence testing include Thurstone's *The Nature of Intelligence* (1924) and *Primary Mental Abilities* (1938), Guilford's (1967) *The Nature of Human Intelligence*, Cattell's (1971) *Abilities: Their Structure, Growth and Action*, Eysenck's (1973) *The Measurement of Intelligence*, Sternberg's (1985) *Beyond IQ: A Triarchic Theory of Human Intelligence*, Gardner's (1983) *Frames of Mind*. From a developmental viewpoint, a number of creative approaches to understanding intelligence have been formulated (e.g., Piaget, 1947).

THE INTERRELATIONSHIP OF PERSONALITY AND INTELLIGENCE THEORY AND RESEARCH

Technique Interrelationships

This section assumes that personality and intelligence theory are really separate domains. Examples of overlap in these domains in the research and applications of techniques used to measure intelligence and personality will be briefly reviewed.

Wechsler (1944), in the *Measurement of Adult Intelligence*, discussed the "diagnostic and clinical features" of the Wechsler-Bellevue scales, and he listed clinical groups that generally score higher on verbal or performance subtests. For example, he suggested that "psychopaths" usually score higher on performance than verbal subtests, and current data appear to support this suggestion (Hare, Williamson, & Harpur, 1986). Wechsler also proposed profiles of intelligence subtests that were related to organic brain disease, schizophrenia, neuroticism, and mental retardation. Rapaport (1946) discussed in greater depth the use of the Wechsler-Bellevue intelligence scales to diagnose clinical disorders.

Matarazzo (1972) presented an overview of the Gittinger (1964) Personality Assessment System (PAS), which is based on subtest profiles of Wechsler's intelligence tests. Parenthetically, Matarazzo notes that Mayman, Schafer, and Rapaport (1951) presented a "conceptual framework relating intelligence and personality which can serve as a beginning (stimulative) theoretical model into which may fit the material presented throughout the whole of this book." He presents Mayman's proposition as an introduction to the PAS. The PAS is outlined in fair detail by Matarazzo (1972, pp. 467–480), and only highlights will be presented here.

The early stages of the PAS research involved applied empirical observations in a clinical setting. The early concepts were developed between 1945 and 1972 when more than 20,000 Wechsler Bellevue-I (WB-1) and Wechsler Adult Intelligence Scale (WAIS) subtest profiles were assessed, along with other clinical data in the form of personality and behavioral assessments. On the basis of these clinical data, the PAS outlined three dimensions of personality structure that were present at birth and changed as persons went through various developmental stages; each of the three personality dimensions at birth were assessed by deviation scores for WB-I or WAIS subtests. The three initial personality dimensions and their subtest measures were (a) the Externalizer–Internalizer (E–I) dimension, measured by the primary digit-span subtest deviation from normal; (b) a regulated–flexible dimension, measured by the block design subtest; (c) the Role Adaptive–Role Uniform dimension, measured by the picture-arrangement subtest.

As persons moved through various life stages, other WAIS subtest scores were used to describe how development was progressing. For example, the arithmetic and information subtests were used to assess further progress along the E–I dimension as the individual moved through life. As Matarazzo (1972) noted, this is a complicated system, and one that was not well known at that time. The PAS was typical of a number of attempts within clinical psychology to use intelligence tests as personality measures, but these models had no enduring effect on the personality assessment of persons.

Overlap between intelligence and personality theory was also evident in the use of projective tests to estimate intelligence. Rorschach (1942) described responses to his inkblot test that characterized "intelligent" subjects, including "a large percentage of clearly visualized forms, many kinesthetic influences acting in the receptive process, a large number of whole responses, good conceptive types, . . . orderly, small percentage of animal answers, neither too large or too small percentage of original answers" (p. 56). He discussed these concepts in depth with regard to why they measured intelligence. A *W* (whole) response, for example, represents a good conceptive type and relates to intelligence. He noted that the quality of *W* depends on the percentage of *D*s and *Dd*s (varying segments of blots in terms of area included or detail, respectively) related to personality or emotions. Rorschach noted that "from the comparison of the extremes, it may be concluded that the quality of the apperceptive type is determined primary by emotional factors" (p. 60). The interface between intelligence and personality thus takes place at the perceptual level.

Subsequent scoring systems for the Rorschach technique follow a similar pattern of reasoning but in much greater detail and with more objectivity (e.g., see Klopfer & Kelley, 1946). Exner (1986) discussed research efforts to relate *W* responses to intelligence tests such as the Wechsler-Bellevue. He noted that age is an important factor in these relationships; at best, the relationship appears equivocal at the adult level and not significant at younger ages. The interrelationship of personality and intelligence using Rorschach inkblots is still being pursued (Meyer, 1992; Wagner, Young, & Wagner, 1992). The Holtzman Inkblot Technique has also been used to measure personality and estimate intelligence, with form dominance (*FD*), form appropriateness (*FA*), and the level of integration (*I*) used to estimate superior intelligence (Hill, 1972, p. 147). Another projective technique, spontaneous or directed drawings, has also been used to measure intelligence. Goodenough (1926) discussed the early history of this research.

Construct Interrelations

The above examples of the interrelationships of intelligence and personality were primarily technique oriented. There have also been more focused attempts to link intelligence and personality theory within the same paradigm or model using constructs such as perception and other cognitive processes. Baron (1982) discussed the relationship of personality and intelligence from the viewpoint of the construct of cognition, using Dewey's (1933) concept of reflective thought as a starting point. Baron drew a distinction between "the rules that good thinkers follow" and "the factors that cause them to follow or not follow the rules." With regard to the latter he discussed learned helplessness and impulsiveness, suggesting some of their possible causes and stating that, "any cause of learned helplessness could also cause impulsiveness when the task used to measure impulsiveness involves repeated trials with feedback" (p. 319). This is an example of a personality dimension (impulsiveness) being related to learned behaviors (learned helplessness) and also affecting the ability to think clearly (intelligence). Baron further discussed the implications of the reciprocal effects of intelligence and personality; the main constructs involved in his approach are perception, cognitive style, values, and expectations.

Within the trait approach to individual differences, there are varying degrees to which researchers have kept personality and intelligence in separate domains. Cattell (1957) discussed the role of intelligence in personality, drawing a distinction between the relative contributions of culture-fluid and culture-crystallized general aptitude tests. He approaches the relationship of intelligence and personality from the standpoint of *g*, or a general ability, and not that of primary mental abilities (which is more characteristic of Thurstone and Guilford's approaches to intelligence). He defended retaining the concept of general ability and noted that "general ability is so potent and ubiquitous a source trait that our correlation studies with personality variables have produced the pattern as an invariable accompaniment to the other dimensions, even when we were not seeking it" (p. 872).

Cattell suggested that general abilities are second-order factors in Guilford and Thurstone's research and concluded that the primary mental abilities hypothesized by those authors must therefore be one degree lower than the primary personality traits in his own theory. He discussed specific relationships between intelligence and personality, noting that there are causal reciprocal effects between them. For example, Cattell's factor structure identified intelligence with dominance and radicalism, which, he noted, "may express a *causal* role of intelligence, producing success and independence in most undertakings, and so reacting back upon personality formation"; moreover, "the relation-perceiving power of intelligence *directly* aids certain personality developments, e.g., the growth of conscientiousness" (p. 873). He suggested that crystallized ability (or the "sum of particular relation-perceiving skills acquired in specific fields") and fluid ability (or "a general relation perceiving capacity" that operates in all fields) have different roles in personality development.

Guilford (1959) defined personality as an individual's "unique pattern of traits," with a trait defined as "any distinguishable, relatively enduring way in which one individual differs from others." Guilford included seven classes of traits that make up the personality of an individual, one class being aptitudes or ability. He viewed these classes of traits as fairly distinct (in line with his general penchant for orthogonality), noting that "although classification of traits in these categories is not always certain, there are not many whose class membership is in doubt." Guilford viewed most personality traits as dimensions in a hierarchical model. Intelligence, however, was defined by him within a morphological model or a "logical matrix" that had three orthogonal parameters: operations, products, and content. His "structure of intellect" (SI) model, with 120 hypothesized abilities, was more complex and extensive than his model of personality factors. Among the tasks used to measure these various abilities were selected ones that loaded on several of Cattell's personality factors. It appeared in general that Guilford was not as concerned about interrelating intelligence and personality theory.

The current debate about the number of dimensions needed to define personality structure (e.g., Digman, 1990; Eysenck, 1991) also involves the interrelationship of intelligence and personality. For example, the "big five" personality structure (Digman, 1990) includes intellect as one of the traits, although it has not been interpreted in the same way by all investigators. The problem of the item content of factors and the appropriate labeling of factors plays an important role in interrelating personality and intelligence dimensions" (p. 5). The semantic problems involved often cloud the interpretation of factors. In a monumental study, Sells, Demaree, and Will (1968) did a factor analysis of 300 Guilford and 300 Cattell personality items (600 by 600 matrix) and concluded that 400 of the 600 items needed to be reclassified with regard to personality dimensions. This study indicates the complexity of problems that can be encountered when one looks beneath the surface of factor or trait labels and does an analysis of items within complex personality factors and then attempts to relate them to intelligence.

Many other trait or factorial studies have attempted to interrelate personality and intelligence. Eysenck and Eysenck (1985) note:

> Current terminology sometimes contrasts personality and intelligence and sometime regards intelligence as part of personality. This is largely a semantic question; obviously we can define a term like *personality* so as to either include or exclude intelligence. H. J. Eysenck (1970) has included it and would prefer to use the term *temperament* to denote those aspects of personality that are non-cognitive. We would thus have a superordinate term, *personality*, subdivided into temperament, the non-cognitive aspects of personality, and *intelligence*, the cognitive parts of personality. (p. 159)

The Eysencks go on to discuss "the cognitive dimension" of temperaments and intelligence as components of personality. They define intelligence in this context as a general factor, much as Cattell did (and not in terms of primary mental abilities, as Thurstone or Guilford proposed).

SELECTED OBSTACLES IN ACHIEVING AN INTEGRATED VIEW OF PERSONS

The purpose of this section is to review some of the reasons that personality theory has not achieved more universal acceptance as a superordinate unifying concept that includes intelligence. Examples of selected problems that relate to the nature of personality and intelligence will be used to illustrate the importance of contexts and definitions in viewing data. Because these problems center around verbal descriptions of concepts, it is helpful to distinguish three levels of the use of language as reviewed by Stevens (1951): syntactics, or the "relation of signs to signs" (e.g., algebra, a system of rules that relates symbols to each other in a consistent way); semantics, or the "relationship of signs to objects" (as in making explicit the referents for words); and pragmatics, or "the relation of signs to the users of the signs."

It will be seen that most of the problems related to personality theory occur at the semantic or pragmatic level. Eysenck and Eysenck (1985) were quoted above with regard to whether intelligence is considered part of personality or a separate construct; they suggested that this is a semantic problem. It could also be considered a pragmatic problem, however, because the Eysencks viewed personality and intelligence within the context of Hans Eysenck's model of persons. Rarely are the debates in this area centered at a syntactical level, although mathematics has been used extensively in developing, for example, factor analytic or latent variable models.

Debates about models occur primarily at the semantic or pragmatic level. It is necessary that criteria for evaluating theories or models be agreed upon before there will be general acceptance of a model or theory (Eysenck, 1991; Hilgard, Leary, & McGuire, 1991; Kuhn, 1970). As long as the problems are primarily at the level of semantics or pragmatics it will be next to impossible to get a majority consensus on a model or theory of personality. Thus far, however, the attempts to arrive at a mathematical or comparable model of personality have not been widely accepted. Game theory made some progress in this regard (Singleton & Tyndall, 1974) and is making its appearance again among ethologists who are interested in comparative neural systems related to human behavior. The examples presented in this section will be primarily at the pragmatic or syntactical level of inquiry.

The debates about personality and intelligence theory range from fairly general to fairly specific topics and revolve around age-old themes. Mind/body Cartesian dualism and nature-versus-nurture debates are still present in one form or another. In some instances the starting point for a debate is clear, as in the following example. The far-reaching social implications of these debates are often not appreciated but are obvious in this example.

Primary Mental Abilities versus *g*: Example of Social Policy Applications

One of the classic debates about intelligence has centered on whether there is a general ability, or *g*, or whether intelligence is better defined in terms of primary mental abilities. (See Carroll, 1982, for the general context of this debate; also see Fruchter, 1954, for an explanation of Spearman's concept of *g* and specific abilities, *Ss*). Spearman considered *g* to be primarily genetically determined and *Ss* to be more related to environment and psychosocial learning opportunities. In 1927, Spearman hypothesized that black children scored lower than white children on ability tests that had a large *g* component. Jensen (1985) reviewed and reanalyzed the data from 11 large-scale studies related to black-white ability differences and concluded that "in accord with Spearman's hypothesis, the average black-white difference on diverse mental tests may be interpreted as mainly a difference in *g*." He further concluded that the data suggest that these differences were related to the "speed and efficiency of certain basic information-processing capacities" (p. 193). Comments on Jensen's article ran the usual gamut from supportive to almost completely negative; most of the criticism centered on his assessment of *g*.

Within the above discussion of Jensen's and Spearman's research, one can clearly see the need to differentiate among the syntactic, semantic, and pragmatic levels of inquiry. Commentaries are based in varying degrees on arguments within each of these levels of inquiry. What might have been helpful in evaluating this research would have been a broader syntactical context for considering the results. For example, if intelligence had been discussed more as a part of a personality model like Eysenck's (where his three types of intelligence are one large segment of personality, along with temperament), the concepts of reaction time and event-related potentials as discussed by Jensen could have taken on a broader meaning. It could have been shown that reaction time and selected event-related potentials are significantly related to personality traits (e.g., impulsiveness) that also have a genetic component. This would have resulted in a convergence of data from a broader source of studies to indicate that reaction time and efficiency of information processing are related to brain functions and are more basic characteristics of humans than is implied in their relationship to either intelligence or personality measures per se.

There have been a number of debates in the literature that, although not directly related to the interrelationship of intelligence and personality, have had an indirect influence on our understanding of the interrelationship. In the area of personality structure, the current debate about the number of second-order factors (or broad dimensions) of personality involves indirect relationships between intelligence and personality through constructs that relate to both. As has been alluded to several times, there are personality factors that appear to be directly or indirectly related to intellect. Costa and McCrae (1985) report a significant relationship between education and the WAIS Vocabulary subtest with their global domain scale of "openness":

> Openness is moderately related to both vocabulary and education. . . . The fact that curious, imaginative, literal men are a bit better educated than others is not surprising, although it does lead to the important question of whether intelligence promotes openness or vice versa. In any case, it is clear that the correlations are not so high that openness should be seen as an aspect of intelligence . . .

> or that relations between openness and other criteria are likely due to the influence of intelligence as a third variable. . . .
>
> Research using adjective measures of agreeableness and conscientiousness . . . shows that conscientious people describe themselves and are described by others as "intelligent," but that they score no higher on intelligence tests. It seems likely that conscientious men and women may be better able to utilize their intellectual capacities. (p. 10)

Costa and McCrae's personality structure is an example of a "big five" model (Digman, 1990) that has global dimensions that overlap with intelligence. They maintain however, that these results are complementary and represent different domains of individual differences.

Similar examples of other debates can be cited. Mishel's (1968) emphasis on situations as determinants of personality, the Eysenck-Guilford exchange about the "real" personality factors (Eysenck, 1977; Guilford, 1975; 1977), or the Cattell-Guilford exchanges about orthogonal versus oblique factors are all implicitly related to a better understanding of the interrelationship of personality and intelligence because they emphasize the need to study characteristics of persons at a more basic level. For example, studies of cognition (and, more specifically, perception) relate to both personality and intelligence measures. Beyond the examples already presented, there are many instances of biological or cognitive descriptors of persons having inherent relationships to both personality and intelligence. Cognitive style and personality measures (Kirton & de Ciantis, 1986), projective tests and perception (Spivack, Levine, Fuschille, & Tavernier, 1959), and the use of verbal behavioral analyses in the study of defense mechanisms (Weintraub & Aronson, 1964) are but a few cases of studies that share implicit descriptors of both intelligence and personality. In the last section of this chapter, we will propose one approach to solving these problems.

PERSONALITY AND INTELLIGENCE THEORY AND RESEARCH WITHIN THE CONTEXT OF THE GENERAL HISTORY OF PSYCHOLOGY

As noted at the beginning of the chapter, personality and intelligence theory and research currently draw heavily on all branches of psychology, as well as other disciplines. The separation of the "two psychologies" as proposed by Cronbach and others is less accurate now than it was in 1957. As biological correlates of personality and intelligence traits become more clear, this trend toward an integrated view of persons should continue (Matarazzo, 1992). One discipline that is truly multidisciplinary in its own right and that complements the personality and intelligence research is neuroscience. Kandel, Schwartz, and Jessell (1991) devote many chapters to topics directly relevant to understanding personality and intelligence. For example, Kandel (1991) discusses learning and the biological basis of individuality, along with the extent to which biological and behavioral disciplines will merge to produce a better understanding of mentation:

> As we have tried to illustrate in this book, the merger of biology and cognitive psychology is more than a showing of methods and concepts. The joining of these two disciplines represents the emerging conviction that scientific descriptions of mentation at several different levels will all eventually contribute to a unified biological understanding of behavior. (p. 1030)

Neural networks and models of the nervous system (e.g., parallel distributed processing) have interrelated cognition with personality and intelligence variables. Baars (1988) summarized one such approach:

> Our theoretical framework has really only a few entities: specialized unconscious processors, a global workspace, and contexts. Indeed, contexts are defined as stable coalitions of specialized processors that have over time gained privileged access to the global workspace. Thus, contexts reduce to sets of specialized processors. Further, there are only a few processing principles: competition through the global workspace, which can be viewed as lowering activation levels of global messages, and cooperation, which raises those activation levels. "Lowering and raising activation levels" is of course analogous to excitation and inhibition in neurons. There is also local processing within unconscious specialized processors, which does not require the global workspace; but this may also work by means of spreading activation (cooperation) and inhibition (competition) (e.g., Rumelhart, McClelland, and the PDP Group, 1986). In sum, three entities and two processing principles together can explain a vast range of evidence about consciousness, volition, and the organization of self. (pp. 359–360)

Within neuropsychology (Filskov & Boll, 1981; Lezak, 1976), there is a merging of the use of techniques and concepts to measure individual characteristics that overlap both personality and intelligence. Again, this should not be surprising, because there were historical precedents for this merger. Lashley (1929) discussed the biological basis of intelligence early in his research. In a seminal paper (Lashley, 1951), he proposed a view of the neural basis of serial order behavior that is consistent with what is being learned today about brain functions and behavior: "Every bit of evidence available indicates a dynamic, constantly active system, or, rather a composite of many interacting systems, which I have tried to illustrate at a primitive level by rhythm and space coordinates" (p. 135).

Another predecessor of current neuropsychology was Halstead's (1947) basic work on the relationship of brain functions to both personality and intelligence. In three background chapters, Halstead presents an insightful overview of the status of intelligence theory in 1947, demonstrating clearly the close parallel between personality and intelligence theory. Halstead isolated four factors of "biological intelligence": a central integrative field factor (C); an abstraction factor (A); a power factor (P); and a directional factor (D). In discussing the significance of these factors, he noted a similarity between his structure of the intellect and that of Lashley. More importantly for the interrelationship of personality and intelligence, he felt that his model of the four factors of intelligence were "the nuclear structure of the ego." He even suggested that these four factors might relate in different ways to selected psychopathologies:

> While the ego is always involved in psychopathology, are all components equally involved? What of the A factor in schizophrenia, the P factor in hypomanic and manic states or in severe depressions, the C factor in the post traumatic syndrome? These and many similar problems now become amenable to objective exploration with the results of such investigations specifiable in operational terms. Only the merest beginning—but, nevertheless, a beginning—has been made. (p. 100)

The interrelationship of research in other areas of psychology to individual-differences research on intelligence and personality can be seen from a number of perspectives. One example in learning theory is Taylor's (1953) development of the Manifest Anxiety Scale (MAS) based on Hull and Spence's learning theory. The MAS was theoretically a measure of habit strength and drive and was shown to relate to performance on a wide range of laboratory tasks, as well as everyday life coping measures. Another example is the Pavlovian influence evident in the work of European personality theorists such as Strelau (1983). Strelau draws a distinction between temperament and personality, with biological variables being primarily related to temperaments and psychosocial variables to personality traits. Biological variables were initially defined on the basis of Pavlov's nervous system typologies.

To the extent that personality is considered a superordinate concept, one would expect (as noted earlier) that it would overlap extensively with theories in other areas of psychology. Related to this observation, Piaget (1979) suggested that psychology per se "occupies a key position in the family of sciences in that it depends upon each of the others, to different degrees, and in turn illuminates them all in distinct ways." Personality theory accomplishes these goals for psychology.

On a related point, Rorer and Widiger (1983) called for new approaches to personality theorizing. They noted the heavy emphasis on attempts to mimic other sciences and observed that "psychologists seem to suffer from a pathological fear of being unscientific." They discussed widely ranging philosophical bases for psychological research, including personality theory and research, and questioned firmly held beliefs in causality and the need for operational definitions. The relevancy of their discussions to the topic at hand is clear. If personality is a superordinate concept, it will have to encompass intelligence in some manner other than a superficial lumping together of factors. This will require a new approach to understanding the interrelationships of intelligence and personality.

INTEGRATING PERSONALITY AND INTELLIGENCE THEORY AND RESEARCH: IS THERE AN APPROPRIATE MODEL?

Where do we go from here? Considering the many attempts to provide bases (models) for integrating psychology in general and personality theories in particular, it is probably foolhardy to suggest another approach. I have addressed this problem elsewhere (Barratt, 1985, 1991, in press), and a brief outline of my approach to synthesizing data within a personality model will be presented below. First, however, there are a few historical points that are relevant.

Sears (1950), in the first *Annual Review of Psychology*, noted that there are three main perspectives for viewing personality theory: structure (e.g., traits and trait structure), dynamics (e.g., defense mechanisms and psychoanalytically related concepts like projection and repression); and development (creating motives and traits). Within psychoanalytic theory, these three categories were broached in an inclusive theory. Within individual-differences research, however, these three facets of personality have not been generally integrated.

This lack of integration can be seen if one compares the titles of the *Annual Review of Psychology* chapters starting in 1950. The first chapter on "personality dynamics" appeared in 1960. For a few years after that, personality structure and dynamics alternated yearly as chapter topics, with subsequent larger time gaps in the appearance of these chapters. Personality was often discussed in chapters on "development"; intelligence was discussed in chapters focusing on individual differences, human abilities, or mental retardation. This history teaches us is that subsequent to psychoanalytic theories, with all of their problems, there were no theories that synthesized Sear's three categories of personality concepts. One requirement for a model of personality must be the inclusion of these three categories in some form.

Personality theories must also address other problems. The mind/body and nature/nurture problems are still evident, although different terms may be used in describing them (as noted previously). Cognitive research really addresses the "mind" issue, and cognitive psychophysiology addresses the mind/body problem. It has been difficult to abandon as data the private events that are always inferential, but may give some insight into how the brain works.

Another necessary characteristic of a personality model is the need to be discipline neutral. The model should be a framework that allows data and concepts from all disciplines to be integrated into a single view of a person. It is possible that if Allport (1937) had stopped with his first definition of personality (i.e., as the study of persons), personality theory may have advanced more along the lines of a general systems theory and less in the direction of eclecticism. There have been many inclusive and discipline-neutral models of persons that have been proposed by scientists other than psychologists; Weiss's (1973) systems model of persons is an excellent example.

Fiske (1971) outlined the process of going from natural observations to concepts and then to measurements. He discussed in clear terms how personality variables are defined and measured. One of the problems in developing personality theories has been the reliance on a semantic level of inquiry without considering the number of basic categories of quantified descriptors of persons that exist in nature. That is, how many domains of measurements and constructs that describe persons are there? If one were to list the minimum number of categories of natural observations about persons, how many would there be? What are the classes of characteristics of person that are integrated into a personality model?

I have suggested (Barratt, in press) that there are four such classes: biological, behavioral, environmental, and cognitive. It is at the level of measurement within these four categories that variables are defined and integrated into a trait personality theory. To understand extraversion as a second-order trait, for example, one has to analyze data from these four perspectives. To define first-order personality traits (including intelligence), one must address these four domains for each trait. One of the four categories of concepts may be more important in characterizing selected traits than others. The changes in the relationship of traits over time will define *processes* and *developmental patterns* (see Barratt, 1985, 1991, in press). Where attempts have been made to integrate intelligence and personality, for example, the syntheses took place within one of these four domains (e.g., see Eysenck & Eysenck, 1985). It is at the syntactical level that intelligence and personality will be meaningfully interrelated by developing a discipline-neutral model. Quite often the research pendulum swings too far in one direction with regard to these four categories without reaching a balance among them (Lipowski, 1989). Mischel (1979) notes in a discussion of the person-situation debate mentioned earlier that there is a common theme among recent diverse lines of personality research, namely, "the increasing integration of cognitive and personological constructs in the study of persons." I have suggested (Barratt, in press) that there is evidence of integration of all four categories (e.g., Zuckerman, 1991).

It should be noted that there is a difference between "eclecticism" (Yager, 1977) and an integrated model that forms a basis for a multidisciplinary approach. In a model, one looks for convergence of a wide range of data around constructs. It does not simply look at a person from different perspectives, but instead integrates data from these perspectives. The integration of personality and intelligence into one model should involve more that merely having an "intelligence" factor as part of a five-factor of personality structure.

There are many theories and research efforts that were not covered in this review. The goal was not to be inclusive. Duke (1986) proposed that a "personality science" should be developed, suggesting that such a science could "clear from our paths some of the built-up debris of disciplinary provincialism" (p. 385). This would certainly be a step forward in understanding normal behavior, as well as psychopathology. This is the challenge.

REFERENCES

Allport, G. W. (1937). *Personality: A psychological interpretation*. New York: Holt.

Baars, B. J. (1988). *A cognitive theory of consciousness*. New York: Cambridge University Press.

Baron, J. (1982). Personality and intelligence. In R. J. Sternberg (Ed.), *Handbook of human intelligence*. New York: Cambridge University Press.

Barratt, E. S. (1985). Impulsiveness defined within a systems model of personality. In C. Spielberger & J. Butcher (Eds.), *Advances in personality assessment* (Vol. 5). Hillsdale, NJ: Erlbaum.

Barratt, E. S. (1991). Measuring and predicting aggression within the context of a personality theory. *Journal of Neuropsychiatry, 3*, 535–539.

Barratt, E. S. (in press). Impulsivity: Integrating cognitive, behavioral, biological, and environmental data. In W. McCown & M. Shure (Eds.), *The impulsive client: theory, research, and treatment*. Washington, DC: American Psychological Association.

Carroll, J. B. (1982). The measurement of intelligence. In R. J. Sternberg (Ed.), *Handbook of human intelligence*. New York: Cambridge University Press.

Cattell, R. B. (1957). *Personality and motivation structure and measurement*. New York: World.

Cattell, R. B. (1971). *Abilities: Their structure, growth, and Action*. Boston: Houghton-Mifflin.

Cattell, R. B. (1985). Intelligence and *g*: an imaginative treatment of unimaginative data. *Behavioral and Brain Sciences, 8*, 227–228.

Costa, P. T., Jr., and McCrae, R. R. (1985). *The NEO Personality Inventory Manual*. Odessa, FL: Psychological Assessment Resources.

Cronbach, L. J. (1957). The two disciplines of scientific psychology. *American Psychologist, 12*, 671–684.

Dewey, J. (1933). *How do we think: A restatement of the relation of reflective thinking to the educative process*. Boston: Heath.

Digman, J. M. (1990). Personality structure: Emergence of the five-factor model. *Annual Review of Psychology, 41*, 417–440.

Duke, M. P. (1986). Personality science: A proposal. *Journal of Personality and Social Psychology, 50*, 382–385.

Exner, J. E. (1986). *The Rorschach: A comprehensive system* (Vol. 1). New York: Wiley.

Eysenck, H. J. (1947). *Dimensions of personality*. London: Routledge and Kegan Paul.

Eysenck, H. J. (1952). *The scientific study of personality*. London: Routledge and Kegan Paul.

Eysenck, H. J. (1970). *The structure of human personality* (3rd ed.). London: Methuen.

Eysenck, H. J. (Ed.). (1973). *The measurement of intelligence*. Baltimore, MD: Williams and Wilkins.

Eysenck, H. J. (1977). Personality and factor analysis: A reply to Guilford. *Psychological Bulletin, 84*, 405–411.

Eysenck, H. J. (1991). Dimensions of personality: 16, 5, or 3? Criteria for a taxonomic paradigm. *Personality and Individual Differences, 12*, 773–790.

Eysenck, H. J., & Eysenck, M. W. (1985). *Personality and individual differences*. New York: Plenum.

Filskov, S. B., & Boll, T. J. (1981). *Handbook of clinical neuropsychology*. New York: Wiley.

Fiske, D. W. (1971). *Measuring the concepts of personality*. Chicago: Aldine.

Fruchter, B. (1954). *Introduction to factor analysis*. New York: Van Nostrand.

Galton, F. (1869). *Hereditary genius: An inquiry into its laws and consequences*. London: MacMillan.

Gardner, H. (1983). *Frames of mind*. New York: Basic Books.

Gittinger, J. W. (1964). *Personality Assessment System* (2 vols.). Washington, DC: Psychological Assessment Associates.

Goodenough, F. L. (1926). *Measurement of intelligence by drawings*. Chicago: World.

Gray, J. A. (1971). *The psychology of fear and stress*. New York: Cambridge University Press.

Guilford, J. P. (1959). *Personality*. New York: McGraw-Hill.

Guilford, J. P. (1967). *The nature of human intelligence*. New York: McGraw-Hill.

Guilford, J. P. (1975). Factors and factors of personality. *Psychological Bulletin, 82*, 802–814.

Guilford, J. P. (1977). Will the real factor of extraversion–introversion please stand up? A reply to Eysenck. *Psychological Bulletin, 84*, 412–416.

Hall, C. S., & Lindzey, G. (1985). *Introduction to theories of personality*. New York: Wiley.

Halstead, W. C. (1947). *Brain and intelligence*. Chicago: University of Chicago Press.

Hare, R. D., Williamson, S. E., & Harpur, T. J. (1986). Psychopathology and language. In T. E. Moffitt & S. A. Mednick (Eds.), *Biological contributions to crime causation*. Boston: Martinus Nijhoff.

Heidbreder, E. (1933). *Seven psychologies*. New York: Appleton-Century-Crofts.

Hilgard, E. R., Leary, D. E., & McGuire, G. R. (1991). The history of psychology: A survey and critical assessment. *Annual Review of Psychology, 42*, 79–107.

Hill, E. F. (1972). *The Holtzman Inkblot Technique*. London: Jossey-Bass.

Jensen, A. R. (1985). The nature of black-white differences on various psychometric tests: Spearman's hypothesis. *Behavioral and Brain Sciences, 8*, 193–263.

Kandel, E. R. (1991). Cellular mechanisms of learning and the biological basis of individuality. In E. R. Kandel, J. H. Schwartz, & T. M. Jessell (Eds.), *Principles of Neural Science* (3rd. Ed.). New York: Elsevier.

Kirton, M. J., & de Ciantis, S. M. (1986). Cognitive style and personality: The Kirton Adaptation-Innovation and Cattell's Sixteen Personality Factor Inventories. *Personality and Individual Differences, 7*, 141–146.

Klopfer, B., & Kelley, D. M. (1946). *The Rorschach technique*. New York: World.

Kluckhon, C., & Murray, H. A. (Eds.). (1949). *Personality in nature, society, and culture*. New York: Knopf.

Kuhn, T. S. (1970). *The structure of scientific revolutions* (2nd ed.). Chicago: University of Chicago Press.

Lashley, K. S. (1929). *Brain mechanisms and intelligence*. Chicago: University of Chicago Press.

Lashley, K. S. (1951). The problem of serial order in behavior. In L. A. Jeffress (Ed.), *Cerebral mechanisms in behavior*. New York: Wiley.

Lezak, M. (1976). *Neuropsychological assessment*. New York: Wiley.

Lipowski, Z. J. (1989). Psychiatry: Mindless or brainless, both or neither? *Canadian Journal of Psychiatry, 34*, 249–259.

Matarazzo, J. D. (1972). *Wechsler's measurement and appraisal of adult intelligence* (5th ed.). Baltimore, MD: Williams and Wilkins.

Matarazzo, J. D. (1992). Psychological testing and assessment in the 21st century. *American Psychologist, 47*, 1007–1018.

Mayman, M., Schafer, R., & Rapaport, D. (1951). Interpretation of the Wechsler-Bellevue intelligence scale in personality appraisal. In H. H. Andersen & G. L. Andersen (Eds.), *An introduction to projective techniques*. New York: Prentice-Hall.

Meehl, P. E. (1979). A funny thing happened to us on the way to the latent entities. *Journal of Personality Assessment, 44*, 569–577.

Megargee, E. I., & Spielberger, C. D. (1992). *Personality assessment in America*. Hillsdale, NJ: Erlbaum.

Meyer, G. J. (1992). The Rorschach's factor structure: A contemporary investigation and historical review. *Journal of Personality Assessment, 59*, 117–136.

Mischel, U. (1979). On the interface of cognition and personality: Beyond the person-situation debate. *American Psychologist, 34*, 740–754.

Mishel, W. (1968). *Personality and assessment*. New York: Wiley.

Murphy, G. (1947). *Personality: A biosocial approach to origins and structure*. New York: Harper.

Murphy, G. (1949). *Historical introduction to modern psychology*. New York: Harcourt Brace.

Murray, H. A. (1938). *Explorations in personality*. New York: Oxford University Press.

Pervin, L. A. (1985). Personality: Current controversies, issues, and directions. In M. R. Rosenzweig & L. W. Porter (Eds.), *Annual Review of Psychology* (Vol. 36). Palo Alto, CA: Annual Reviews.

Peters, R. S. (1953). *Brett's history of psychology*. New York: Macmillan.

Piaget, J. (1947). *The psychology of intelligence*. New York: Harcourt Brace.

Piaget, J. (1979). Relations between psychology and the other sciences. *Annual Review of Psychology, 30*, 1–8.

Rapaport, D. (1946). *Diagnostic psychological testing*. Chicago: Yearbook.

Rorer, L. G., & Widiger, T. A. (1983). Personality structure and assessment. *Annual Review of Psychology, 34*, 431–463.

Rorschach, H. (1942). *Psychodiagnostiks: A diagnostic test based on perception*. New York: Grune and Stratton.

Rumelhart, D. E., McClelland, J. E., and the PDP Research Group. (1986). *Parallel distributed processing: Explorations in the microstructure of cognition. Vol. 1. Foundations*. Cambridge: Bradford/MIT Press.

Sears, R. R. (1950). Personality. *Annual Review of Psychology, 1*, 105–118.

Sells, S. B., Demaree, R. G., & Will, D. P., Jr. (1968). *A taxonomic investigation of personality on joint factor structure of Guilford and Cattell trait markers. Final report*. Fort Worth: Institute of Behavioral Research, Texas Christian University.

Singleton, R. R., & Tyndall, W. F. (1974). *Games and programs: Mathematics for modeling*. San Francisco: Freeman.

Smith, M. B., & Anderson, J. W. (1989). Henry A. Murray (1893–1988). *American Psychologist, 44*, 1153–1154.

Spearman, C. (1927). *The abilities of men*. London: MacMillan.

Spivack, G., Levine, M., Fuschille, J., & Tavernier, A. (1959). Rorschach movement responses and inhibition processes in adolescents. *Journal of Projective Techniques*. (Published as a separate by the Devereux Foundation, Devon, PA.)

Sternberg, R. J. (Ed.). (1982). *Handbook of human intelligence*. New York: Cambridge University Press.

Sternberg, R. J. (1985). *Beyond IQ: A triarchic theory of human intelligence*. New York: Cambridge University Press.

Stevens, S. S. (1951). Mathematics, measurement, and psychophysics. In S. S. Stevens (Ed.), *Handbook of experimental psychology*. New York: Wiley.

Strelau, J. (1983). *Temperament, personality, and arousal*. London: Academic Press.

Taylor, J. A. (1953). A personality scale of manifest anxiety. *Journal of Abnormal and Social Psychology, 48*, 285–290.

Thorndike, R. L. (1950). Individual differences. *Annual Review of Psychology, 1*, 87–104.

Thurstone, L. L. (1924). *The nature of intelligence*. London: Harcourt Brace.

Thurstone, L. L. (1938). Primary mental abilities. *Psychometric Monographs, 1*, 121.

Wagner, E. E., Young, G. R., & Wagner, C. F. (1992). Rorschach blends, IQ, and the effect of R. *Journal of Personality Assessment, 59*, 185–188.

Wechsler, D. (1944). *The measurement of adult intelligence*. Baltimore, MD: Williams and Wilkins.

Weintraub, W., & Aronson, H. (1964). The application of verbal behavior analysis to the study of psychological defense mechanisms. II. Speech patterns associated with impulsive behavior. *Journal of Nervous and Mental Disease, 139*, 75–82.

Weiss, P. A. (1973). *The science of life: The living system—a system for living*. Mt Kisco, NY: Futura.

Yager, J. (1977). Psychiatric eclecticism: A cognitive view. *American Journal of Psychiatry, 134*, 736–741.

Zuckerman, M. (1991). *Psychobiology of personality*. New York: Cambridge University Press.

2

Models and Paradigms in Personality and Intelligence Research

Lazar Stankov, Gregory J. Boyle, and Raymond B. Cattell

CENTRAL POSITION OF PERSONALITY AND INTELLIGENCE RESEARCH IN PSYCHOLOGY

Psychology is distinguished from its brethren sciences of biology and sociology in that its main concern is with behavioral and mental processes of the individual (Zimbardo, 1992). Traditional study of personality and intelligence has focused on individual differences—searching for traits or relatively stable characteristics along which people differ (H. J. Eysenck & Eysenck, 1985; Howard, 1993). This line of research is based on the assumption that an improved scientific understanding of the nature of psychological functions can be achieved only by taking into account information about overall levels of performance *and* between-subjects variability and covariability. Whereas the emphasis in individual-differences research has been on multivariate procedures, experimental psychology has been almost exclusive in its focus on univariate designs. Multivariate research is closely linked to the development of psychological measuring instruments that are widely used in educational, industrial, and clinical settings. More recently, psychobiological explanations of personality and ability constructs have been sought (e.g., Zuckerman, 1991), and the resulting hypotheses have opened the way for a more sophisticated understanding of the neuropsychological and neuroendocrinological mechanisms underlying personality and ability traits. Hence it is possible to claim that studies of intelligence and personality based on these combined approaches have made a more significant contribution to our social life in general than many other areas of psychological research (see Goff & Ackerman, 1992).

Cognitive tests are good predictors of many real-life criteria (Cattell, 1982, 1987a; Cronbach, 1990; Hunter & Schmidt, 1981; Jensen, 1980). Recent work, for example, has shown the validity of intelligence tests as predictors of death rates among males during the prime years (ages 20 to 40) of their adult lives. Personality instruments, in contrast, have been viewed as less adequate predictors of real-life criteria (O'Toole & Stankov, 1992). Kline (1979) argued that correlations with personality traits (measured via instruments such as the 16PF, California Personality Inventory [CPI] and Eysenck's Personality Questionnaire [EPQ]) seldom exceed about .30, accounting therefore for only a small proportion of the predictive variance. Boyle (1983), though, has demonstrated that under conditions of emotional arousal, the proportion of predictive variance accounted for by personality traits increases markedly.

Lazar Stankov • Department of Psychology, University of Sydney, Sydney, New South Wales 2006, Australia. Gregory J. Boyle • School of Humanities and Social Sciences, Bond University, Gold Coast, Queensland 4229, Australia. Raymond B. Cattell • Department of Psychology, University of Hawaii, Honolulu, Hawaii 96844.

International Handbook of Personality and Intelligence, edited by Donald H. Saklofske and Moshe Zeidner. Plenum Press, New York, 1995.

Need to Study Personality and Intelligence from Diverse Viewpoints

Personality and intelligence are studied from several different perspectives today. Approaches range from those with a biological basis to those that emphasize sociocultural influences; the central position is occupied by the traditional multivariate (see Boyle, 1991) and experimental cognitive approaches (see Stankov, 1989). Toward the biological end of the spectrum (see Zuckerman, 1991), there is a large body of research on the role of mental speed in intelligence (e.g., Jensen, 1980). Toward the anthropological and sociological end, studies have emerged in reaction to aspects of social policies, fashions, and other influences within our society. In regard to personality assessment, ratings (L-data), self-report questionnaires (Q-data), and objective tests (T-data) have all been utilized. For example, in the Q-data medium, significant intercorrelations between 16PF personality factors and cognitive abilities and real-life events have been reported (Boyle, in press).

Only T-data personality measures (e.g., Objective-Analytic Battery; Cattell & Schuerger, 1978), however, avoid the problems of item transparency and motivational response distortion (see Boyle, 1985). Ability-personality interactions are shown most clearly using such measures (Schmidt, 1988). Performance tests (as opposed to questionnaires or ratings) place greater demands on cognitive functioning. Schuerger (1986, p. 280) and Cattell (1987a, p. 452) reported several significant correlations between cognitive abilities and objective (T-data) personality measures.

Dangers of Oversimplifying Personality and Intelligence Models

Some recent theories have taken the principles of parsimony too far. In the intelligence domain, researchers (e.g., Miller & Vernon, 1992) not only have endorsed the single (general) factor model but also are searching for the "basic process" that underlies intelligence. Jensen (1987), for example, attributes an important role to mental speed. In the personality area, H. J. Eysenck (1991) has argued for three rather than five or eight major dimensions. Several investigators (e.g., Deary & Mathews, 1993) have focused on the "big five" personality dimensions, whereas Mershon and Gorsuch (1988) have shown that these dimensions measure but a fraction of the total personality trait sphere.

While we acknowledge the principle of parsimony and endorse it whenever applicable, the evidence points to relative complexity rather than simplicity. Insistence on parsimony at all costs can lead to bad science. Consider, for example, the assumption that frequency discrimination is the cause of individual differences on measures of intelligence. To test this assumption one might obtain scores on either Raven's Progressive Matrices test (Raven, Court, & Raven, 1984) or Cattell's Culture Fair Intelligence Tests (Cattell & Cattell, 1977), and a measure of frequency discrimination—for example, the smallest difference a person can detect between two tonal frequencies (Raz, Willerman, & Yama, 1987). A statistically significant correlation between these two measures provides supportive evidence for the assumption. If however, one remembers that tonal memory is one of several primary factors that define intelligence at some higher order of analysis, the study may lead to a different conclusion. Since it is likely that new Raz et al. measures will correlate mainly with tonal memory ability, not with intelligence test scores, the role of frequency discrimination in intelligence will appear less impressive. Within the hierarchical structure of abilities (Boyle, 1988a; Cattell, 1987a; Horn & Stankov, 1982; Stankov & Horn, 1980), the highest-order factor may exhibit negligible loadings on auditory frequency discrimination measures. Clearly, an overly simplified view of individual differences in personality and intelligence may attribute a greater than deserved role to a lower-order process because some of the nodes within the causal path have been omitted.

RECENT RESEARCH MODELS WITHIN THE MULTIVARIATE PSYCHOMETRIC TRADITION

Multivariate Structure of Human Abilities and Personality

There have been only a few attempts during the past two decades to develop a comprehensive new theory about the multivariate structure of human abilities. For example, Jensen (1982) emphasized so-called Level I and Level II abilities. The main difference between these resides in the amount of transformation and mental manipulation required. This is minimal in tasks that measure Level I abilities (digit-span tests are prototypical examples). Level II abilities, however, require a large amount of mental manipulation; marker tests of fluid intelligence (Gf; see Cattell, 1963, 1971) are good examples of these. The usefulness of this distinction was debated with some proponents of the theory of fluid and crystallized intelligence (Gf/Gc theory; Horn & Cattell, 1982; Horn & Stankov, 1982; Jensen, 1982; Stankov, 1987b; Stankov, Horn, & Roy, 1980), described below. A central issue was whether the Level I/Level II distinction could account for the richness and complexity of the cognitive domain. This debate strengthened the argument that short-term acquisition and retrieval (SAR) function is distinct from Gf. More recently, Jensen (Kranzler & Jensen, 1991) has abandoned his original interpretation: He now contends that a general factor loads on both levels, but that Level I abilities exhibit smaller loadings than Level II abilities. Nevertheless, a large body of data suggests broad ability factors additional to the general factor, and at least some of the controversies surrounding Jensen's work can be attributed to the inherent simplicity of his model (see Stankov, 1987b).

Carroll (1976) classified primary mental abilities in terms of the then-prevailing views within experimental cognitive psychology about the architecture of the mind. Reminiscent of Guilford's theory about the structure of abilities, it was called the "new structure of intellect" model—the three dimensions of Guilford's (1981) SOI model (contents, operations, products) corresponding to input, central processing, and output in information-processing theories of cognition. Carroll's model assumed several memory stores (sensory buffers and short-term, intermediate, and long-term memories) and provided a list of operations, studied by cognitive psychologists, that was salient in measures of intelligence. He showed that each primary ability from the French, Ekstrom, and Price (1963) list involves a unique combination of memory stores and operations. Because this model provides a taxonomic starting point, Stankov (1980) used it as an input to a clustering procedure. The resulting tree diagram indicated several clusters of abilities that correspond to the broad factors of Gf/Gc theory. The fact that subjective analysis of the processes involved in primary factors leads to the same groups of abilities as obtained through hierarchical factor analysis was interpreted as support for Gf/Gc theory.

Carroll's work alerted researchers to the richness and relevance of cognitive theories (see Carroll, 1993). Both Jensen's Level I/Level II theory and Carroll's model have strengthened the position of Gf/Gc theory. Messick (1992) compared factor analytic theories of abilities with two widely popularized theories of intelligence proposed by Gardner (1983) and Sternberg (1985), respectively. His conclusions favored the multivariate theories of intelligence—in particular, Gf/Gc theory. Indeed, Gf/Gc theory has become the most widely accepted psychometric paradigm of intelligence.

In the personality area, only the 16PF has been based on a comprehensive sampling of the trait domain, as expressed in the lexicon (see Boyle, 1990a). Krug and Johns (1986) reported six second-stratum dimensions (extraversion, neuroticism, independence, tough poise, control, and intelligence). This finding was then cross-validated separately for the subsamples of 9,222 males and 8,159 females. In comparison, the work of McCrae and Costa (1987) was derived from a restricted sampling of the normal trait domain—a subset of only 20 of Cattell's original 36 trait clusters served as the starting point for the Norman "big five," which ultimately were incorporated into Costa and McCrae's (1992) NEO Personality Inventory (NEO-PI) and Goldberg's (1992) 50-Bipolar Self-Rating Scales (50-BSRS). Thus the big five cover only 20/36 (56%) of the normal trait sphere as measured in 16PF second-order factors (see Boyle, 1989a), and H. J. Eysenck's (1991) argument for three dimensions is even less convincing (see also the chapter by Boyle, Stankov, & Cattell).

Role of Personality in Fluid and Crystallized Intelligence (Gf/Gc Theory)

Both Cattell (1987a) and Horn (1985, 1988) have reviewed recent literature on the Gf/Gc theory. The broad factors involve different cognitive processes that exhibit differential predictive validities and different genetic influences and are susceptible to different sets of personality-learning influences (see Goff & Ackerman, 1992; Snow, 1989). Factor analyses of a representative sample of cognitive tasks known to be good measures of primary abilities have revealed several broad factors (see Boyle, 1988a): fluid intelligence (Gf); crystallized intelligence (Gc); short-term acquisition and retrieval function (SAR); tertiary (long-term) storage and retrieval (TSR); broad visualization (Gv); broad auditory function (Ga); and broad speediness function (Gs).

Both Gf and Gc are characterized by processes of perceiving relationships, reasoning, abstracting, concept formation, and problem solving. They can be measured by speed and power tests based on pictorial-spatial, verbal-symbolic, and verbal-semantic material. The main difference is that Gf (in contrast to Gc) depends relatively little on the effects of formal education, acculturation, and interaction with personality. For the measurement of Gc, elements of the problems (or operations performed on these elements) are transmitted to the individual through formal societal means. Separate scores on Gf and Gc indicate an individual's potential for learning, as well as amount of learning accumulated. This is more informative for many practical purposes than a single general ability score. Results (e.g., Goff & Ackerman, 1992) reveal that personality measures of typical intellectual engagement (as opposed to measures of maximum intellectual engagement and associated performance) correlate significantly with both Gf and Gc. Goff and Ackerman predicted that personality-intelligence correlations would be greater in relation to Gc than to Gf. They found that measures of typical intellectual engagement, extraverted intellectual engagement, absorption (in task), interest in arts and humanities, openness (to new experiences), hard work, and interest in technology all exhibited significantly higher correlations with Gc than with Gf, as predicted.

Whereas Gf depends on the size and efficiency of working memory, Gc depends on size of the long-term store, organization of information within that store, and efficiency in retrieving information needed for problem solution (Horn, 1988; Horn & Hofer, 1992; Myors, Stankov, & Oliphant, 1989). Evidence of broad abilities additional to Gf and Gc suggests that performance on cognitive tasks depends not only on higher mental processes but also on lower level cognitive processes, including visual and auditory perceptual processes (Gv and Ga). These abilities capture parts of Gf and Gc that are perceptual in nature and are sufficiently different and independent from Gf and Gc. The finding of separate factors suggests that some individuals are more efficient in processing auditory information, others visual information, and so on. Memory abilities (SAR and TSR) reflect storage areas useful for the operation of Gf and Gc and indicate the relative independence of memory from the higher mental processes of Gf and Gc. Finally, broad speediness (Gs) reflects individual differences in speed of mental operations (i.e., individuals vary in their speed of cognitive functioning).

Gf/Gc theory shares certain features with other major theories of intelligence, including those of Thurstone, Burt, and Vernon (see Brody, 1992), as well as with the measurement of intelligence via such standard tests as the Wechsler scales (WAIS-R, WISC-R, WPPSI) or the Stanford-Binet (SB-IV) as revised by Thorndike, Hagen, and Sattler (1986; see Boyle, 1989b, 1990c). Gf/Gc theory is both more comprehensive and better supported by empirical evidence than alternative models and paradigms (Boyle, 1990b). The Gf/Gc distinction has provided an impetus for much of the life-span developmental research (see Horn, 1988; Stankov, 1986a, 1988a). These two broad abilities show distinct age-related changes. Performance on measures of Gc remain relatively stable or even increase during adulthood, whereas Gf measures show a decline starting around 30 years of age. This decline varies from study to study, ranging from 3 to 7 IQ points per decade of age, with the median estimate between 4 and 5 IQ points for cross-sectional studies and somewhat less for longitudinal studies (Brody, 1992). From among the remaining broad abilities, the long-term storage and retrieval function (TSR) behaves like Gc. All other broad factors (SAR, Gv, Ga, and Gs) decline in a fashion similar to Gf.

Cattell's (1987a) triadic theory of intelligence is an attempt to organize human abilities in terms of not only structure and development but also their action. Cattell (1971) proposed that cognitive abilities can be divided into three main categories. First, *general capacities*—Gf, Gs, and TSR—represent limits to psychophysiological and neuroendocrinological brain action as a whole (Gf may represent the neural substrate; see Zuckerman, 1991). Second, *provincial powers* or capacities correspond to each of the various sensory modalities (e.g., Gv, Ga). Third, *agencies* represent abilities that function in different areas of cultural content. Agencies correspond to Gc and primary abilities. According to triadic theory, these three kinds of cognitive abilities jointly influence any actually observed behavior.

Meta-Analysis of 20th-Century Psychometric Data

Carroll (1993) reanalyzed more than 400 data sets from important psychometric studies of intelligence conducted during the 20th century. The general conclusion from all these studies is in substantial agreement with Gf/Gc theory, the seven broad second-stratum factors have been supported by Carroll's analyses. He does, however, list new broad factors. For example, a factor of processing speed that appears in simple reaction time (RT) tasks is distinct from broad cognitive speediness (Gs). Measures of mental speed obtained with the Hick's and inspection time paradigms (to be discussed later) load on this factor. Emergence of this new factor is a reflection of the increased interest in the role of mental speed in intelligence, an interest spurred by developments in computer technology during the past decade. Further work will probably provide additional broad factors, particularly in relation to other sensory modalities (e.g., touch, smell, taste). Horn (1988) claims that there is already sufficient evidence to show that a broad quantitative ability (Gq) should be included in the list of second-stratum factors (see also Horn & Hofer, 1992).

Reemergence of Guttman's Radex Model

Rudiments of Guttman's theory about the structure of human abilities appeared in his methodological papers on radex (radical expansion of complexity) in the 1950s, but the first "mapping sentence" that defines the main facets of his theory of intelligence appeared a decade later (Guttman, 1965). His latest version of the model has arisen from attempts to interpret the results of multidimensional scaling of data collected with the WISC-R (Guttman, 1992).

Guttman's radex model has three facets (see the description of facet theory in Chapter 22). The rule-task facet refers to the kind of task to be performed. It has two major elements: inference, where the subject infers a rule from examples or hints (e.g., a test of analogical reasoning), and application, where a previously learned or explicitly presented rule is to be applied (e.g., "Who is the president of Israel?"). These two correspond to what was previously called analytical ability. Achievement is still retained with a changed name, learning, that refers to the rule-application items based on short-term memory. In terms of a tree-trunk analogy, the three elements of this facet represent concentric circles like yearly growth, with inference being the middle circle. The format-of-communication facet represents the medium of the test items (verbal, numerical, and geometrical-pictorial); this corresponds to vertically divided slices more similar in shape to a triangular piece of a pie. Last is the mode of expression facet, representing the way subjects respond to test items and consisting of three elements—oral, manual manipulation, and paper and pencil. This facet corresponds to horizontal tree-trunk slices (i.e., thin cylinders).

It is easy to link the five elements from this model to the seven broad Gf/Gc factors. If Gf corresponds to inference and Gc to application, then SAR corresponds to learning of the rule-task facet. Also, if Gv corresponds to the geometrical-pictorial and Ga corresponds in part to verbal, then Horn's (1988) Gq factor corresponds to the numerical element of the format-of-communication facet. There are no apparent links, however, between the broad factors of Gf/Gc theory and the mode-of-expression facet. This is probably because Guttman's recent model derives from the WISC-R battery, which contains three modes, whereas most other theories of intelligence have used one element—the paper-and-pencil mode of expression. Nevertheless, Horn and Knapp (1974) have shown that Guilford's products dimension, which roughly corresponds to Guttman's mode-of-expression facet, has very poor empirical support—suggesting that this facet is not needed.

Two broad abilities from Gf/Gc theory, TSR and Gs, are not present in Guttman's model. The TSR (or broad fluency ability) is likely to reside close to the periphery of the slice representing verbal mode of communication. The place of Gs within the radex is unknown at present. Finally, some aspects of Ga (e.g., perceptual auditory tests) suggest it may be necessary to include a fourth medium of test items (e.g., tonal-musical) to the format-of-communication facet.

Hierarchical Factor and Radex Models: Importance of the Concept of Complexity

Snow, Kyllonen, and Marshalek (1984) point to substantial agreement between hierarchical and radex models. Snow's model contains two facets. One corresponds to Guttman's mode of communication (verbal, numerical, and figural content), which can be visualized as pie slices within a circular arrangement of tests. The second is represented by concentric circles for the task-rule facet, but rather than labeling each circle as Guttman did (i.e., inference, application, and achievement), Snow acknowledged the variety of processes that coexist within each concentric circle. He was still able to point, however, to the essential feature—increase in task complexity as one moves toward the central circle. Furthermore, Snow et al. reported a high correlation between the loadings of the highest-order factor on tests and the distance between the test's position and the center of the circle (i.e., between a test's complexity and its variance on the general factor).

Figure 1 presents an idealized radex model, synthesized from the Guttman and Snow accounts, that shows their similarities and differences. The concentric circles in the top shaded section are labeled in

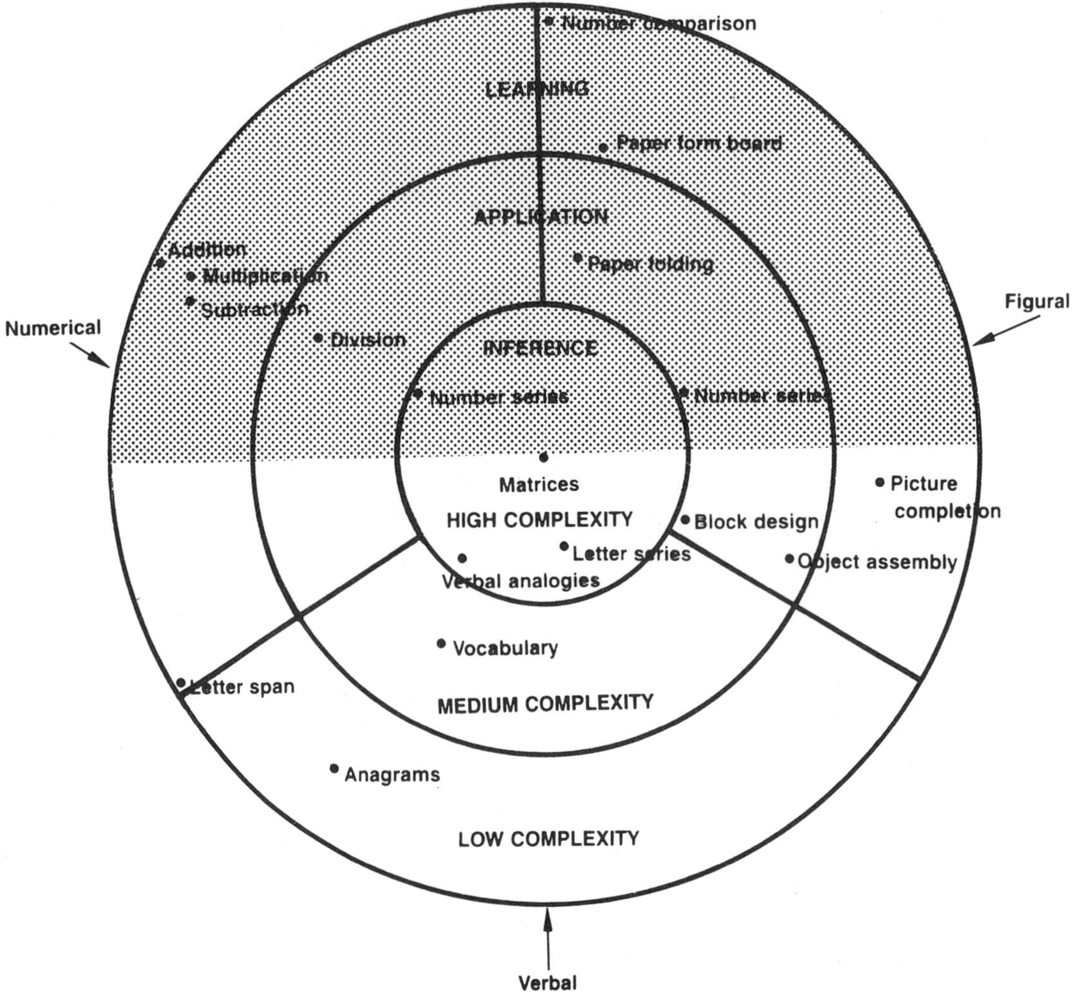

Figure 1. Illustration of the radex structure. Both Guttman and Snow agree about the main elements of the mode of expression facet (verbal, figural, and numerical), represented by the slices of the pie. They also agree on the location of the different tests. Their disagreement is with respect to the nature of the processes captured by the concentric circles: the shaded area contains labels suggested by Guttman (learning, application, inference), and the unshaded area is labeled in accordance with Snow's interpretations.

accordance with Guttman's rule-task facet; the unshaded half of the circle is labeled in terms of Snow's interpretation. Guttman's labeling of the circles is rather restrictive—a process within the inner circles may be more complex than one in the outer circle, even though one may hesitate to use the label *inference* or *application* to describe it. Snow's account thus is preferable. The positions of the tests are in general agreement with both accounts; there is no difference between the two models with respect to slices of the pie (i.e., verbal, numerical, and figural). We depart slightly from Guttman and Snow, however, leaving the middle circle intact in accord with Gustafsson (1992)—within the center of the circle it makes little sense to distinguish between different formats of communication. This is closely linked to the well-known factor analytic result that the mode of test presentation is of secondary importance for tests loaded highly by the general factor.

Snow (1989) examined task characteristics that lead to changes in complexity. He arrived at the conclusion that simple tasks "require relatively few component processes and relatively little reassembly of processing from item to item. . . . More complex tasks

. . . not only require more components but also more flexible and adaptive assembly and reassembly of processing from item to item." (p. 37). Snow's answer was based mainly on analysis of the psychological processes of tasks that led to the center of the circle. Several other investigators have addressed the same question using experimental manipulations.

Even though evidence for the broad factors of Gf/Gc theory is convincing, some researchers argue for an overriding general factor (Spearman's *g*). Gustafsson (1992) points out that the highest-order factor appears rather similar to the Gf second-order factor that is located in the center of the radex representation of abilities. Work with the Wechsler scales suggests that vocabulary plays the central role (Mattarazzo, 1972). Evidently, the center of the radex—or the apex of the hierarchy—can shift depending on the nature of the test battery. Using a single marker test of Gf for the measurement of intelligence can perhaps be justified under the assumption that a representative sampling from the cognitive domain has been accomplished. As Zuckerman (1991) has rightly pointed out, however, "A single average score on a nomothetic trait test offers little predictability" (p. 54). Clearly, what is needed is multidimensional measurement across a range of factor analytically verified trait dimensions (Boyle, 1991). In this respect, Cattell's (1987b) *Depth Psychometry* has much to offer. For example, quantitative differences on the second-order 16PF factors can be investigated qualitatively in terms of their specific factor loadings on the primary trait factors. Use of Cattellian instruments such as the 16PF or Clinical Assessment Questionnaire (CAQ) therefore provides greater flexibility with respect to interpretation of both the primary and secondary factor scales.

Another Old Issue: Mental Energy versus "Bonds"

Two contemporary investigators emphasize the role of *g* rather than broad factors but take the traditionally opposing views of its nature. Jensen (1979) takes a neo-Spearmanian view, arguing that *g* is a single theoretical entity that determines correlation between cognitive tests. L. G. Humphreys (1979) takes a neo-Thomsonian position and assumes that there are many different facets of a large number of potential measures of cognitive ability. Humphreys believes that it is possible to define an indefinitely large number of relatively homogenous tests that differ in only one facet. These tests should exhibit positive intercorrelations.

Although Willerman and Bailey (1987) argued in favor of a unitary mental energy view, their arguments remain unconvincing (Brody, 1992). There is no empirical test yet that can help decide what theory should be endorsed. Cognitive psychology, however, seems to favor neo-Thomsonian views, because the work within this tradition has produced a large number of elementary cognitive tasks (ECTs) easily linked to Thomson's concept of bonds. Some of these tasks have been used in recent work on intelligence. Kranzler and Jensen (1991), for example, employed a battery of 11 psychometric tests and five cognitive tasks; The tasks were scored for 37 different ECT measures. The study investigated whether psychometric *g* represents a unitary process or a number of independent processes. Because the general factor from the psychometric battery shared significant amounts of variance with four principal components obtained from the ECT measures, Kranzler and Jensen concluded that *g* is not a unitary process, and Jensen apparently has shifted away from his former strict neo-Spearmanian position. Carroll (1991) questioned Kranzler and Jensen's methodology, however, reanalyzing their data to show that it was premature to reject the unitary *g* conclusion.

Different broad ability factors of the Gf/Gc theory are likely to call upon different sets of ECTs. If *g* is as important as these broad factors, what is its nature? Though an indefinite number of facets or bonds may exist that can account for emergence of a general factor, we have to admit that Kranzler and Jensen had only a relatively small sample of tasks, and it is not clear that these ECTs have properties assumed by Thomson's bonds. We agree with Carroll that Kranzler and Jensen's methodology was inadequate to answer their question, even though, in theory at least, we can accept the interpretation of *g* in terms of an indefinite and large number of bonds.

STUDIES OF MATERIAL AND BIOLOGICAL SUBSTRATA OF PERSONALITY AND INTELLIGENCE

An increasingly popular paradigm explores relationships between various bodily measurements and tests of cognitive abilities. These measurements range from rather crude physical assessments of body size to sophisticated recordings of cellular metabolic changes that take place while the brain carries out mental operations. Neuropsychological investigators are still searching for a reliable network of correlations among physical, personality, and cognitive domains in hope of discovering causes of individual differences in cognitive abilities and personality structure within the brain itself (see Boyle, 1986; Powell, 1979; Stankov & Dunn, 1993). Even though it is premature to make strong causal inferences at present, some interesting new results have appeared in the literature (see Zuckerman, 1991).

Anatomical Correlates of Intelligence and Personality

Jensen and Sinha (1992) have reviewed the literature about the relationship between various physical measures and intelligence. A particularly large and reliable data base exists for the correlation with stature (i.e., general body size, height, and weight). That correlation is around .20, attributable both to assortative mating for stature and intelligence and to shared nutritional and health factors within families.

Another anatomical measure studied extensively is brain size (Jensen & Sinha, 1992). Intelligence test scores correlate between .10 and .20 with external head measurements, between .25 and .30 with intercranial volume, and about .35 with direct in-vivo assessment based on magnetic resonance imaging techniques. Rushton (1991) compared average cranial capacities of Mongoloids (1,460 cc) and Caucasoids (1,446 cc), and it has been reported (see Lynn, 1987) that Mongoloids tend to obtain somewhat higher (about 3 to 5 IQ points) scores in intelligence tests than Caucasoids. Given the very small within-race correlation of brain size and intelligence, however, and very small (trivial) Mongoloid-Caucasoid differences in IQ and in brain capacity, it would be irresponsible to draw any strong conclusions. More recently, Rushton (1993) has revised his work on race and sex differences in brain size and intelligence. There are many problems with this line of research; for example, all the above correlations are for brain measurements statistically corrected for overall body size. Willerman (1991) has questioned the appropriateness of this correction, because body weight differences between the subject samples studied by Rushton account for most of the variance in cranial capacity. Cain and Vanderwolf (1990) also argued that racial differences in brain size have no necessary implications for intelligence, especially because there are no significant sex differences in overall intelligence levels, even though men on average have larger brains than women (see Ankney, 1992).

Biochemistry and Intelligence: Role of Serological, Mineral, and Vitamin Imbalance

Jensen and Sinha (1992) observed that intelligence exhibits a low negative correlation (less than −.20) with the age at which girls first menstruate, and that hormonal factors therefore are possibly involved in intelligence. They also reported that individuals whose blood contains a greater than normal amount of serum uric acid (SUA; e.g., sufferers from gout) tend to be high achievers, and that this may be linked to the caffeine-like effects of SUA. Its correlation with intelligence per se is very low and trivial (less than .10), however, accounting for no more than 1% of the predictive variance. Because 99% of variance is not accounted for, it seems unlikely that SUA has any substantial impact on intellectual functioning.

There have been reports of successful attempts to increase intelligence using nutritional means. For example, Schoenthaler, Amos, Eysenck, Peritz, and Yudkin (1991) studied 615 primary school children, showing that supplementary vitamin intake over a period of four weeks can increase scores on Gf but not Gc. Using U.S. guidelines for recommended daily allowances of minerals and vitamins, this study tested the effects of several different intakes; the lowest dose was 50% of recommended daily allowance. Subjects within treatment groups exhibited a statistically significant, slight increase over placebo controls. On average, a maximum of only 4 IQ points was gained through intervention that assured a normal daily intake of vitamins and minerals.

Brain Glucose Metabolism in Personality and Intelligence

Diabetes mellitus is associated with impairment of memory, retrieval efficiency, abstract reasoning, problem solving, and ability to cope with complexity (Dunn, 1992). Performance on simple RT tasks and on forward (but not backward) digit-span tests is similar between diabetic patients and normal controls. Diabetic patients perform worse than normal subjects on measures of Gf (i.e., complex abstract reasoning tasks) but do not differ from normal controls on measures of Gc. Langan, Deary, Hepburn, and Frier (1991) reported a significant correlation between frequency of severe hypoglycemia and performance IQ, but this relationship did not emerge with verbal fluency and auditory learning scores. Also, Deary (1992) demonstrated the critical role of frequent severe hypoglycemia in development of cognitive deficits.

Aerobic glucose metabolism is the source for almost 95% of cerebral energy, with the synapse being the major location for consumption. The human body is protective of the brain's operation; if there is metabolic disturbance, all other organs are depleted of glucose before the brain shows any sign of a lack. Because glucose metabolism is important for brain functioning it is logical to expect disturbances as a result of prolonged or severe diabetes mellitus. Grill (1990) reported a significantly lower global cerebral blood flow in diabetic patients, and that the ratio of oxygen to glucose uptake is lower in diabetics. Moreover, a small but significant release of two by-products of the nonoxidative metabolism of glucose—lactate and pyruvate—are present to a larger extent in diabetics. Fox, Raichle, Mintun, and Dance (1988) reported that the oxygen/glucose metabolic ratio fell markedly in healthy subjects in areas of the brain with acutely increased neural activity. The decrease was associated with increased cerebral blood flow and with the regional uptake of glucose, but only a slight increase in oxygen uptake. The important role vitamin C plays in glucose metabolism may partly explain the slight improvement in intelligence test performance as a result of vitamin and mineral supplementation (Schoenthaler et al., 1991).

These findings indicate that the oxygen-glucose ratio may relate to the difficulty/complexity level of a cognitive task. Grill (1990) suggests that the increase in nonoxidative metabolism of glucose could reflect a state of brain overnutrition. Thus the diabetic state, as well as causing acute increases in neural activity, may lead to an oversupply of nutrients to the brain. Such inefficient functioning at a physical level may be responsible for the reduced ability of diabetics to cope with complex problems. Indeed it may be related to poor performance on intelligence tests even in nondiabetic individuals (Stankov & Dunn, 1993).

Although the effects of diabetes on personality have been studied for at least 50 years, there is still a disagreement about the nature of these effects and if they are due to chronic sickness in general or to diabetes in particular (see Dunn, 1992). Thus, depression has been seen as a characteristic of diabetes in adults since last century but Robinson, Fuller & Edmeades (1988) reported similar rates of depression in diabetics and normals. On the other hand, Lustman, Griffiths, and Clouse (1988) carried out a 5-year follow-up study of depression symptoms in a sample of adult non-insulin-dependent diabetes mellitus patients and reported that the course of depression in diabetes is malevolent and possibly more so than the course of depression in the medically well.

Neural Efficiency Hypothesis

Brain-imaging techniques such as positron emission tomography (PET) and cerebral blood flow (CBF; see Vernon, 1991) depend on the use of nuclear isotopes—a by-product of glucose metabolism is the tracer in PET research, and oxygen provides a tracer in CBF studies. For example, Metz, Yasillo, and Cooper (1987) carried out PET scanning as subjects performed a Wisconsin Card Sorting Test, as well as during a simple control task. Traditionally the frontal cortex has been assigned a special role in attention and in dealing with complex tasks, but Metz et al. (1987) reported a uniform global (rather than localized) metabolic increase in cortical activation, almost 30% above the control level. Frontal lobe impairment diminishes associational, relation-perceiving powers in the emotional control and impulse deferment-inhibition processes (Cattell, 1987a). This "frontal lobe" projection of intelligence into personality partly suggests how intelligence modifies personality (see Zuckerman, 1991).

Haier et al. (1988) did not find significant differences in absolute cerebral metabolic rate for glucose among three levels of task complexity. Several localized regions of the brain showed more activity when subjects worked through the complex Raven's Progressive Matrices test than when doing a visual search task (pressing a key whenever "O" appeared on the computer screen, or simply attending to a changing series of digits without responding). Particularly affected were the occipital posterior areas of the brain. Haier et al. reported that simple visual search and other control tasks (i.e., tasks of low complexity) showed nonsignificant correlations with measures of metabolic activity. Raven's test, in contrast, exhibited highly significant correlations with cerebral metabolic glucose rate (ranging from $-.44$ to $-.84$, depending on the locus of brain activity). This suggests that subjects with higher Raven's scores took up less glucose than those with low scores. Vernon (1990) reviewed the literature on speed of mental processing, EEG, and PET and concluded there is sufficient support for the neural efficiency hypothesis (see Vernon & Mori,

1992). If higher intelligence is associated with less energy-demanding, faster neural systems, this hypothesis suggests that intelligence is a function not of more brain activity but of efficiency of brain processes relevant to a particular task.

Health Issues in Relation to Intelligence, Personality, and Aging

Severe and prolonged illness may affect personality and intellectual functioning, yet there is a scarcity of information about the impact of less severe illness. For example, we do not know much about prolonged psychological effects of the common flu, which affects much of the population. We also know little about the prevalence of some conditions that influence personality and cognitive performance (e.g., chronic fatigue syndrome). These illnesses are part and parcel of everyday living.

There is a dearth of theories about the effects of health and physical well-being on personality and cognitive abilities. Birren and Cunningham's (1985) Cascade Hypothesis is one of the few attempts to operationalize chronological age in terms of primary and secondary aging and to relate these to cognitive function. The authors propose that primary aging (innate maturational processes captured by sensorimotor tests) causes a decline in perceptual speed; secondary aging (disease) is causally related to a decline in perceptual speed and reasoning. The "terminal drop" (decline in intellectual functioning about 5 years prior to death) is causally related to diminished verbal comprehension, reasoning abilities, and perceptual speed. The assumption that decline in perceptual speed occurs prior to decline in fluid abilities is not supported by Kaufman (1990). When perceptual speed is controlled statistically, residual age-related differences remain in inductive reasoning and spatial orientation. The effects of poor physical health on personality and intellectual functioning remain somewhat equivocal: Perlmutter and Nyquist (1990) demonstrated a relationship between self-reported health and intellectual performance, whereas Salthouse, Kausler, and Saults (1990) found no such association (see Fernandez, 1986; Fernandez & Turk, 1989).

Anstey, Stankov, and Lord (1993) measured health, physical activity, education, and chronological age in 100 community-dwelling women aged 65 through 90 years. The subjects were also given a battery of cognitive tests of fluid intelligence, as well as a wide-ranging battery of sensorimotor tasks. As expected, health had a significant negative effect on sensorimotor variables; older people have more difficulty with sensory tasks and tasks requiring motor activity. Although sensorimotor processes affected Gf, the indirect effect of health on Gf was not significant, nor was physical activity related to Gf. Again, chronological age did show a significant negative relationship to Gf. These data supported the findings of Salthouse et al. (1990) that higher mental functions seem to be largely spared the effects of transitory physical illness.

Another outcome of the work of Anstey et al. (1993) is the apparent unitary nature of sensorimotor abilities during the latter stages of life. This finding may have important theoretical implications, because it suggests that a modified version of the de-differentiation hypothesis may indeed have some empirical support. In other words, even though broad cognitive abilities may be relatively differentiated during old age (see Horn & Hofer, 1992), diverse sensorimotor abilities appear to be more closely related to each other and to define a single factor. This may indicate a common cause, in that sensorimotor abilities may be more sensitive to age-related physical changes than higher-order mental processes.

Among the many personality dimensions related to health, perhaps the most important is neuroticism, which is predictive of a variety of mental health indicators (Wistow, Wakefield, & Goldsmith, 1990). Neuroticism involves anxiety, stress, depression, regression, and guilt components (Boyle, 1989c). Deary and Mathews (1993) have reported that neuroticism is directly implicated in "dysthymic" neuroses, including anxiety, stress and depression, drug addiction, certain types of criminality, sexual difficulties, poor body image, disease proneness, and poor cognitive performance (see also Davis, Elliott, Dionne, & Mitchell, 1991; H. J. Eysenck, 1976; H. J. Eysenck & Eysenck, 1985; Friedman & Booth-Kewley, 1987; Gossop & Eysenck, 1983; Mathews, Coyle, & Craig, 1990; Ormel & Wohlfarth, 1991; Stone & Costa, 1990; Suls & Wan, 1989; Watson & Pennebaker, 1989).

Given that the major intellectual abilities show distinct life-span developmental curves, it is logical to ask if similar trends can be observed with respect to personality traits. Although cross-sectional data are more prevalent in the literature, the results from several large-scale longitudinal studies have become available recently. The data are remarkably consistent in showing that, by and large, there is a considerable continuity in personality traits during the later stages of life. Nevertheless, some changes have been reported; only one of five traits studied by Field proved to be neither stable nor constant. The trait in question "energetic" is correlated with health and is most affected by environmental circumstances.

VARIETIES OF SPEED MEASURES AND INDIVIDUAL DIFFERENCES

Mental speed can be defined operationally in many different ways. Measures of speed can be divided into three main groups. First, most studies employ speed as a dependent measure. Because many theories in experimental cognitive psychology deal with processes that are too short to be captured by crude accuracy (i.e., number correct) scores, speed of doing a task (or parts of a task) is used as a sensitive measure of components of the thinking process. This approach allows for measurement of elementary cognitive tasks or ECTs (see below). Other studies view speed as a property of an organism: Usually a very simple task is chosen, and subjects have to perform it as quickly as possible. The computer analogy is often used—the assumption being that the main cause of individual differences is the difference in "ticking of the internal clock." Most work deals with measures of both simple and choice RT, as well as inspection time (IT). The third group of studies focuses on speed in carrying out complex cognitive tasks. Interpretation of results is not solely in terms of mental speed as an expression of some physical property of the organism, but also in terms of stylistic factors associated with working through cognitive tasks.

Reaction Time Studies Related to Hick's Law

The measurement of speed of cognitive processes in relation to personality, using RT, has aroused much interest among researchers (see Robinson & Zahn, 1988). New technology and theoretical developments within experimental cognitive psychology are the main reasons for this renewed interest. In what ways has our knowledge improved because of this flurry of activity?

Simple and choice RT measured with the Roth-Jensen apparatus and Crossman's card-sorting task have provided the largest body of data. In both procedures, amount of information processed is systematically increased. The Roth-Jensen apparatus consists of a panel with a "home" button and eight small lights arranged in a semicircle around it. Next to each light is a "turn-off" button. The subject holds a finger on the home button; when a light comes on, he or she raises the finger (decision time) and quickly moves to extinguish the light (movement time). (The most commonly used numbers of visible lights are one, two, four, and eight.) In the Crossman task, the subject sorts ordinary playing cards into varying numbers of piles (typically two, four, or eight). In the two-pile version, the subject may have to sort all red cards into one pile and all black cards into another pile; in the four-pile version, piles may be defined with respect to suit, and so forth. Speed of sorting indicates both decision time and movement time. There is usually another two-pile version in which subjects sort cards consecutively into two piles without any concern about the nature of cards; speed in this case is interpreted as movement time.

Reaction times measured with these procedures show a pattern described by Hick's law—there is a linear relationship between decision time and the natural logarithm of the number of piles or visible lights in the display (i.e., number of "bits," where 1 bit corresponds to two alternatives, 2 bits to four alternatives, and 3 bits to eight alternatives). As tasks become more complex, it takes longer to reach a decision. For each subject, median RT for each bit, intercept and slope RT measures is obtained. With the Roth-Jensen procedure, the variability score is also available, and in both tasks, separate movement time scores exist.

Since the first report of noteworthy correlations (Jensen, 1979), many studies based on the Roth-Jensen apparatus have been published. Although speed plays a role in intelligence, a dispute exists about its relative importance. There are also theoretical problems. For example, different reaction time measures exhibit noteworthy correlations with intelligence; even in Jensen's original study, the highest correlation with intelligence was not for the slope measure but for the variability score. Individuals with lower intelligence tend to exhibit greater differences between their highest and lowest speeds, and RT scores from the five slowest trials suggest that individuals with low intelligence cannot maintain their performance at optimal level (Larson & Alderton, 1990). Because the slope measure reflects the time needed to process an additional bit of information (increase in complexity), the slope should exhibit a higher correlation with intelligence than with RT variability. In fact, choice RT measures often do not correlate more highly with intelligence than do simple RT measures. In most studies, the intercept measure does not correlate highly with intelligence, whereas movement time does (Jensen, 1987). Explanations of the discrepant results have acquired a very strong ex post facto quality, and it is hard to see how further work could serve a useful purpose.

Correlations between intelligence and speed measures from the Roth-Jensen choice RT apparatus rarely exceed −.30 (Jensen, 1987). This correlation is not higher than that obtained with many other cognitive or psychobiological measures (Boyle, 1988b; Hunt, 1980). Furthermore, as pointed out by Cattell (1987a), the correlation between the higher-order speed factor (Gs) and fluid intelligence (Gf) was .39 (accounting for only 16% of variance). Jensen's (1979) attempt to measure intelligence using RT cannot hope to exceed this value. Consequently, our substantive knowledge has improved little as a result of all this activity.

Performance on Crossman's task was also correlated with measures of intelligence. The emphasis has been on examining correlations between speed of card sorting and intelligence as the number of piles increases from two to eight. The feasibility of Hick's law has been examined at the group level, but little emphasis has been placed on estimates of the individual's slope and intercepts. Analogous data have been reported for the Roth-Jensen procedure (see Jensen, 1987)—correlations between median RT and intelligence increase with the number of bits of information processed. Nevertheless, as shown in Table 1, the increase in size of correlations for the Roth-Jensen apparatus is not dramatic.

Roberts, Beh, and Stankov (1988) used Crossman's card-sorting task and reported a pronounced increase in correlations between the 0- and 2-bits levels, but a drop at the 3-bit level, attributed to processing capacity limitations (this drop in correlation at the 3-bit level was not replicated by Roberts, Beh, Spilsbury, & Stankov, 1991). Another feature of the Roberts et al. (1988) study was the requirement to sort cards not only under the typical single condition but also together with a word classification task (i.e., under a competing condition). Table 1 shows that correlations of the competing condition exhibit the same pattern as the single condition across bit levels. Additionally, competing conditions also exhibit higher overall correlations with intelligence. This finding points to the importance of complexity in intelligence and to the possibility of using experimental manipulations in studies of the relationship between task complexity and intelligence.

Table 1. Correlations between Measures of Intelligence and Hick's Paradigm Tasks at Different Levels of Complexity

Number of bits	Roth-Jensen[a]	Card sorting[b]	Single	Competing
0	−.19	Alternative piles	.03	−.07
1	−.21	Color (2 piles)	−.21	−.65
2	−.24	Suite (4 piles)	−.49	−.71
3	−.26	Number (8 piles)	−.30	−.59

[a]From Jensen (1987)
[b]From Roberts et al. (1988)

Visual and Auditory Inspection Time

Another measure of speed that correlates with personality and intelligence is inspection time (IT). There are two versions of this paradigm: visual and auditory. In both versions, an aspect of exposure time is varied using some accepted psychophysical procedure, and the score is the minimum time needed to detect the difference between two simple stimuli. In the visual IT task, the stimuli consist of two simultaneously presented lines that differ in length (see Nettelbeck & Lally, 1976); the task is to state which line is longer. In the auditory task of Deary (1992), the stimuli to be discriminated are two square wave tones (870Hz and 770Hz) presented at 80 dB. Both tones last for equal time periods, and there is no gap between tone pairs. The time interval for presentation of the pair varies, however, so that tones are heard as increasingly shorter sounds. The aim is to establish the shortest time interval (i.e., tone duration) for which the subject can (with 90% accuracy) state whether the order of tones within a pair is "high-low" or "low-high."

Kranzler and Jensen (1989) reported a correlation between IT and Gf measures of −.29, although some other studies report higher values. There are problems with IT research (Levy, 1992). First, because IT measurement is time-consuming, many studies have employed only a small number of subjects; higher correlations with intelligence are obtained when extreme groups (mentally retarded versus university students) are used. Second, because of problems with the psychophysical methods used and with experimental procedures, up to 40% of subjects do not produce valid data that can be correlated with personality or intelligence. Third, there are serious problems with theoretical accounts of IT measures and their correlation with personality and intelligence (Mackintosh, 1986). The latest interpretation is that a higher IT threshold is associated with lapses of attention characteristic of individuals with lower intelligence. At this stage, there is no firm evidence to support this hypothesis. Again, it appears that our substantive knowledge has not improved much as a result of considerable research activity involving inspection time.

Primary Abilities of Mental Speed

At least two factors capture different aspects of mental speed. They are usually considered to be more complex than RT and IT measurements (see Buckhalt & Jensen, 1989).

Natural Tempo

It is assumed that individuals have a natural speed of thinking. One way to measure speed is to give a task with the instruction to work at one's "most comfortable pace." An approximation to this approach is provided by the tempo test in which a subject is induced to count a particular beat; after a period of time, the count is compared with that of a metronome. Some individuals overestimate the beat of the metronome, whereas others underestimate it—the amount of discrepancy may provide information about the subject's natural tempo. Traditionally scored tests of tempo measure ability to maintain and judge rhythm (MaJR) at the first order of analysis, and Ga at the second order. Stankov (1986a) reported a pronounced effect of aging on MaJR, amounting to a loss of about 5 IQ points per decade of age. It is possible that a changed scoring procedure for the tempo test will show correlations with RT and IT tasks and define a different factor.

Perceptual-Clerical Speed

Tests of perceptual-clerical speed have gained in importance in part because of an increased emphasis on speed in studies of aging (Cornelius, Willis, Nesselroade, & Baltes, 1983), as well as a realization that these tests measure selective attention processes. Recent interpretations of attention are akin to Spearman's mental energy and, as mentioned earlier, to Thomson's bonds (Stankov, 1983 a, b; 1988b). One interesting finding has been that impulsive individuals tend to be fast but inaccurate in visual pattern matching tasks (Dickman & Meyer, 1988), implicating the important role of personality dispositions in relation to speed and accuracy. Future research into perceptual-clerical speed tasks will need to examine their relationships with other types of speed measures. Recent findings (e.g., Robinson & Zahn, 1988) suggest that RT and IT measures exhibit significant correlations with this factor.

Test-Taking Speed, Personality, and Intelligence

Computerized test administration provides an easy way to measure the time needed to answer each item as well as detailed information about the speed of test taking. Speed scores from batteries of diverse personality and intelligence tests tend to exhibit somewhat higher average intercorrelations than accuracy scores, a finding supportive of a broad speediness function (Gs). Moreover, if we correlate accuracy scores from a test of Gf with speed of test-taking scores from a variety of cognitive tests, the size of correlations will depend on the nature of the tests. In general, speed in doing easy tasks shows higher correlation (in the .30s) with intelligence, whereas speed in doing difficult (power) tests shows zero correlation (Spilsbury, Stankov, & Roberts, 1990; Stankov & Cregan, 1993). Personality factors such as extraversion-introversion may play an important role, in that the more introverted individual may work more slowly but also more carefully and thoroughly (double-checking all answers, etc.). Speed scores may represent different things depending on the perceived difficulty of the task. At an easy level they may be measuring aspects of Gf, but other non-ability intrapersonal factors—maybe stylistic or perhaps related to self-esteem, confidence, or introversion—may come into play when the task becomes difficult. Boyle (1983) demonstrated that under nonemotive conditions, intelligence accounted for most variance in academic learning, whereas under stressful conditions, personality factors accounted for most of the predictive variance.

Composite Scores

A composite of speed and accuracy divides the number of correctly answered items by the time needed to take the test. Spilsbury (1992) and Spilsbury et al. (1990) employed such an "efficiency" score with a deductive reasoning test. The efficiency score had several properties (e.g., a significantly higher correlation with Gf) that make it superior to both accuracy and speed scores alone. This result, however, was not replicated with an inductive reasoning test used by Stankov and Cregan (1993). Perhaps the usefulness of the efficiency score may vary across different tasks and/or samples of subjects.

Individuals performing cognitive tasks operate at different levels depending on their understanding of the instructions and general requirements of the task. Some work quickly and sacrifice accuracy, and vice versa. According to Lohman (1989), this trade-off can be substantial. This was of particular concern to experimental cognitive psychologists who adopted the practice of using only data from subjects who showed a very high accuracy level (e.g., 90% to 95% correct). At that level, the trade-off is small and measures of speed are sensitive to task manipulations. Lohman has argued that individual differences in speed-accuracy trade-off can affect performance on intelligence tests. One way to reduce this problem is through explicit instructions that emphasize either speed or accuracy. Stankov and Crawford (1993) studied the effects of variations in instructions on a test's correlation with external measures of Gf; the same task was given twice so that accuracy and speed scores were available on both occasions. Results showed that there were no significant changes in correlation between this task and Gf attributable to differences in instructions. Thus the effects of speed-accuracy trade-off may be relatively unimportant.

Speed Measures and Personality

Although different measures of cognitive speed tend to have varying levels of correlation with traditional measures of intelligence, the reported correlations between personality measures and cognitive speed seem to be generally low (see Vernon, 1987). In several studies by Roberts (Roberts et al., 1991; Roberts et al., 1988) zero correlations were obtained between a variety of speed measures and Eysenck's Personality Questionnaire (EPQ). The only scale from the EPQ that had a reliable nonzero correlation with speed has been the Lie scale.

CONTRIBUTIONS FROM EXPERIMENTAL COGNITIVE PSYCHOLOGY

Hunt (1980) listed three areas of research in contemporary cognitive psychology that contribute to our understanding of intelligence. These are cognitive strategies, ECTs, and limited-capacity constructs (e.g., working memory and attentional resources).

Every task, even the simplest one, is assumed to have an associated set of cognitive strategies—often unique to the task—that can be employed for its solution. It is assumed that more intelligent individuals have a greater variety of strategies at their disposal, and that they can choose the most appropriate one for the task in question. Strategies are sometimes hard to distinguish from ECTs (Ferretti & Butterfield, 1992); the term *strategy* may be employed in the sense of "cognitive style." In other cases, an "executive" or homunculus that makes a choice from among the available ways of solving a problem is postulated. The most successful use of the construct of strategy has been in the attempt to teach borderline or mentally retarded individuals how to improve their performances on intelligence tests (Ferretti & Butterfield, 1992). In other areas, however, ECTs and limited capacity constructs seem to provide a sufficient explanation of individual differences.

Traditional Information-Processing Framework: Elementary Cognitive Tasks (ECTs)

Several hundred ECTs have been investigated. They can be used, as in Thomson's bonds, to provide an account of the general factor. Because the traditional information-processing framework assumes various stages of processing (i.e., sensory buffer, central processor, and output system), the nature of these ECTs varies. ECTs associated with peripheral functions are likely to differ in relation to intelligence and personality, as compared with ECTs from the center. Hunt (1980) listed ECTs associated with retrieval of information from the long-term store using a "name-versus-physical-identity" task, a short-term memory search task, and processes associated with verbal abilities. Sternberg (1985) constructed ECTs derived from the analogical reasoning tasks, such as preparation encoding, inference, mapping, application, justification, and response. Salthouse (1985) listed 45 ECTs studied in relation to aging. Hunt was not impressed with the size of correlations of ECTs with measures of intelligence (maximum around .30); he therefore turned his attention toward attentional resources, which seemed to hold promise of producing higher correlations.

Role of Capacity in Individual Differences

Individuals differ in their cognitive capacity. Two theoretical constructs—working memory and attentional resources—have both been linked to intelligence.

Working Memory

Because working memory has two parts—passive or storage, and active or manipulative—digit-span tests, visual sequential memory tests (e.g., as in the WAIS-R and ITPA tests, respectively), and other measures of short-term memory are viewed as an inadequate means of capturing its full meaning.

Although working memory seems particularly involved in Gf, there have been attempts to study it in relation to Gc. For example, Daneman (1982) assumed that working memory was important for successful reading comprehension. Her test of working memory consisted of a series of long sentences, from which subjects had to recall the last few words. Daneman expected poor readers would devote so much capacity to producing sentences that they would have less residual capacity for storing and producing the final words, and her results supported this hypothesis. At present we do not know the extent of her test's correlation with a variety of intelligence and personality measures.

Working memory is of major importance in two primary Gf abilities. Several types of tests define the temporal-tracking primary factor (Stankov & Horn, 1980), but mental counting tests seem to capture its essence best. The task is to count the number of times a particular stimulus is presented. Stimuli can be names, words, pictures, sounds, or combination of all these; typically, three or four different categories of stimuli are employed. Mental counting requires keeping in mind the tally for every stimulus (storage) and updating the counter (manipulation of new and stored stimuli).

Working memory is also present in the inductive-reasoning primary ability of Gf (e.g., the series completion tests developed by Thurstone; see French et al., 1963). Computer models of both letter- and number-series tests can produce the series employed in Thurstone's tests by manipulating a number of parameters. Holzman, Pellegrino, and Glaser (1983) demonstrated that the most critical aspect is the parameter known as number of working memory placekeepers (WMPs). To illustrate what is meant by WMPs, consider the following examples of letter-series items:

One-operator rule: $[X_1, X_1, + N(X_1)]$ Example: P, P, R, R, T, T, V (Answer: V)

Two-operators rule: $[X_1 + N(X_1), X_2, + N(X_1)]$ Example: V, L, X, N, Z, P, B (Answer: R)

The rules consist of variables—denoted X—and operators—denoted +N(X)—enclosed between square brackets that correspond to the cycle length of the item. The values of variables, once initialized, change from one cycle to the next according to the operator. In the above examples, N(X) equals 2. It is easy to generate analogous series by choosing different values for X. Number of WMPs can be increased at will by the experimenter. The difficulty of series completion items depends almost entirely on the number of operators used (i.e., number of WMPs) rather than other parameters derived from the rule (number of variables, length of series, etc.). Also, the test's correlation with other measures of Gf depends more on number of WMPs than on any other parameter (Myors et al., 1989; Stankov & Crawford, 1993; also see Table 3 below from Stankov & Cregan, 1993). Individuals who obtain higher intelligence test scores can keep track of a greater number of things that can change in the series completion problems. In addition, there is evidence that personality affects working memory performance (M. W. Eysenck, 1983), suggesting a likely interaction between cognitive and personality factors.

Attentional Resources

The construct of attentional (or processing) resources is also linked to capacity. It differs from working memory in that it is not restricted to central processes within immediate awareness. Processes involved in long-term memories and central processes that closely interact with peripheral sensory activities are also part of the conglomerate. The construct of attentional resources resembles Spearman's ideas about mental energy.

Measurement operations developed for assessment of available resources involve the use of dual tasks and typically employ either the primary-secondary task paradigm (Halford, 1989; Hunt & Lansman, 1982) or the competing task paradigm (Fogarty & Stankov, 1982, 1988). Because two concurrent tasks require more attentional resources than a single task, decrement in performance in dual tasks is an indication of demand for resources. And because individuals differ in available resources, dual tasks should exhaust individuals' resources more quickly, with resultant changes in correlation of the task with measures of intelligence. M. W. Eysenck (1979) has shown that depletion of attentional and cognitive resources can be severe under anxiety-inducing conditions. Anxious individuals can be highly sensitive in dual-task situations and suffer larger decrements in cognitive performance than less anxious persons.

In the primary-secondary task paradigm, subjects respond to an intelligence test with items of increasing difficulty (primary task). Simultaneously, they perform a simpler secondary task (e.g., pressing a button upon hearing a tone). The expectation is that individuals with lower intelligence and fewer attentional resources will show signs of disruption in secondary task performance while working at relatively easy levels of an intelligence test. Many assumptions have to be satisfied, however, before one can test this theory (Stankov, 1987a).

Role of Complexity in Individual Differences

Recent studies of complexity in relation to intelligence have used competing tasks and single tasks with carefully graded levels of increasing complexity.

Competing Tasks

The competing task paradigm differs from the primary-secondary task paradigm in that both components are subtests from intelligence test batteries, are of about equal difficulty, and receive equal emphasis. These tests are given as single tests and again simultaneously—as in dichotic listening experiments, or one through earphones and the other on a computer screen. If performance declines under the dual condition, tests are competing for attentional resources. If they also show higher correlation with IQ measures under competing conditions, attentional resources theory can provide an account of individual differences. Studies have investigated about 50 different competing tasks involving marker tests for primary abilities of Gf, Gc, SAR, Ga, and Gv (see Fogarty & Stankov, 1982, 1988; Myors et al., 1989; Roberts et al., 1991; Roberts et al., 1988; Spilsbury, 1992; Stankov, 1983a, b, 1986b, 1988b, 1989; Stankov, Fogarty, & Watt, 1988; Stankov & Myors, 1990; Sullivan & Stankov, 1990). Overall, evidence indicates that (a) intercorrelations within a battery of competing tasks tend to be higher than intercorrelations of the same tests given singly; (b) competing tasks tend to have higher correlations with external measures of intelligence than do the same tests given singly; (c) changes in the magnitude of correlation coefficients do not necessarily parallel changes in arithmetic means (i.e., correlations can increase even though single and competing tasks may be of equal difficulty); and (d) it has also been reported that extraverted individuals perform better, exhibiting greater selective recognition of attended-to information in dichotic listening tasks (Dunne & Hartley, 1985).

Processes involved in competing tasks include dividing attention, ability to resist interference, and higher-order planning. An account of individual differences in intelligence in terms of the attentional resources theory is threatened by point (c) above. If performance initially is below ceiling levels and there is no further reduction, competing tasks do not demand more attentional resources than single tests, and therefore attentional resources theory cannot account for the increase in correlation. Multiple resources theory (Wickens, 1980) may explain the findings with mean scores but cannot provide a parsimonious explanation of the general increase in correlations between cognitive tasks.

Single Tasks

Ceci (1990), Guttman (1992), Larson, Merritt, and Williams (1988), Snow (1989), Spilsbury (1992) and many others highlight the importance of complexity in personality and intelligence research (e.g., M. W. Eysenck & Eysenck, 1979, demonstrated that extraverted individuals work more rapidly than introverted persons in dual-task memory scanning experiments). Some of our studies employed the Triplet Numbers and Swaps tests (Stankov, 1983a, 1993; Stankov & Crawford, 1993). The most complex versions of these tests measure fluid intelligence. Each more complex version of the task has everything that the lower version has, plus something else. This important feature was not present in the componential approaches that searched for ECTs of intelligence.

Stimuli for the Triplet Numbers test consist of a randomly chosen set of three different digits that are presented simultaneously on the computer screen and change after each response. Four versions differ with respect to instructions given to subjects. The "two-rules" version is similar to those used in previous psychometric work, whereas all other versions were used for the first time in the Stankov and Crawford

Table 2. COSAN Solution for Swaps and Triplet Numbers Tasks and Seven Intelligence Tests (Stankov, 1993)

Psychological tests	Common factors: Gf	Swaps	Triplets	Unique factor loadings
1. Number span forward	.65	.0	.0	.57
2. Number span backward	.73	.0	.0	.47
3. General knowledge	.34	.0	.0	.88
4. Matrices	.67	.0	.0	.55
5. Letter counting	.68	.0	.0	.54
6. Letter series	.76	.0	.0	.42
7. Hidden words	.54	.0	.0	.71
8. Swaps: One swap	.48	.56	.0	.47
9. Swaps: Two swaps	.51	.68	.0	.28
10. Swaps: Three swaps	.53	.76	.0	.14
11. Swaps: Four swaps	.53	.71	.0	.21
12. "Search" triplets	.26	.0	.05	.92
13. "Half-rule" triplets	.26	.0	.51	.68
14. "One-rule" triplets	.48	.0	.67	.32
15. "Two-rule" triplets	.54	.0	.62	.33
Factor intercorrelations				
Gf	1.00	—	—	
Swaps	.00	1.00	—	
Triplets	.00	.37	.100	

(1993) study. Stimuli for all versions of the Swaps test consist of a set of three letters (J, K, L) presented simultaneously (letter order is varied from item to item) together with instructions to interchange, or "swap," the positions of pairs of letters. The four versions of the task differ in the number of such instructions. After completing all required mental swaps, the subject has to type the final resulting order on the computer keyboard.

Performance on these tests was correlated with measures of Gf, and the resulting COSAN confirmatory factor analytic solution (see McDonald, 1978) is displayed in Table 2. The pattern of loadings of Gf on the two tasks is important; in both cases, there is a nondecreasing pattern for Gf loadings, and the more complex task is somewhat more closely related to intelligence in these data. There is a less pronounced increase in size of loadings within the two task-specific factors as well. Overall, if we assume that complexity means that many different cognitive processes of Gf are involved, then whatever aspect of processing changes in the two experimental tasks captures that complexity as well.

Experimental manipulations inherent in the Swaps and Triplet Numbers tests can be understood in terms of capacity theory (either working memory or attentional resources), or in terms of Snow's (1989) interpretation of radex structure. Mental speed seems rather unimportant in these tasks. Clearly, these manipulations have nothing to do with the "novelty" or "non-entrenchment" emphasized in Sternberg's (1985) experiential subtheory. A salient feature is the ability to work through a series of steps required for problem solution. The larger the number of steps, the more likely the less intelligent person is to obtain an incorrect solution. This interpretation accords with the finding of significant correlations between Gf and several trail-making tests (Vernon, 1993).

Measurement Problem: Personality and Intelligence as a Quantitative Variable

Developments in measurement theory suggest new ways of examining what types of scales are involved in personality and intelligence tests. Conjoint measurement theory suggests a set of conditions that need to be satisfied by a quantitative variable (see Michell, 1990). One way to test the quantitative properties of a variable involves arranging experimental conditions in a two-way ANOVA layout. Thus, if we have two independent variables with three levels each, there are nine cells, and conjoint measurement assumptions can be tested. For a 3×3 cross, two tests of conjoint measurement need to be carried out. These "independence" and "double cancellation" conditions are illustrated in Figure 2.

Single cancellation means that for any two rows, if a cell in a row is greater than or equal to a corresponding cell in the other row, then all cells in the first row should be greater than or equal to corresponding cells in the other row. Similarly, orderings between columns of a conjoint matrix should be the same regardless of row. In the top of Figure 2, a single-line arrow indicates that a given cell is greater than another cell. Double-line arrows imply that the same relationship should hold for all other cells in a given row or column; otherwise, the independence condition of conjoint measurement is not satisfied. The double-cancellation condition is illustrated in the lower part of Figure 2: If the single-line arrows point in a particular direction, the double-line arrow should point as shown.

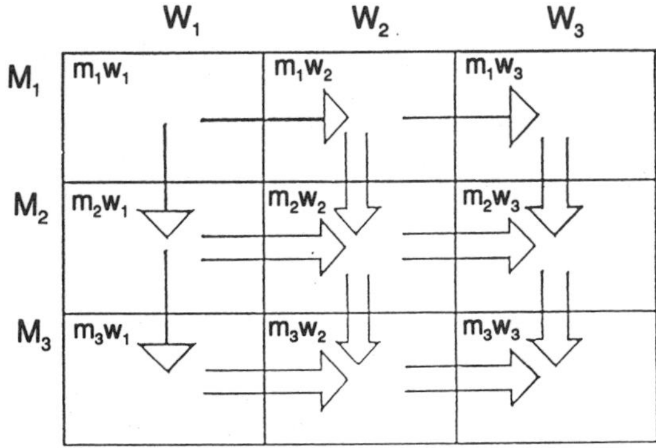

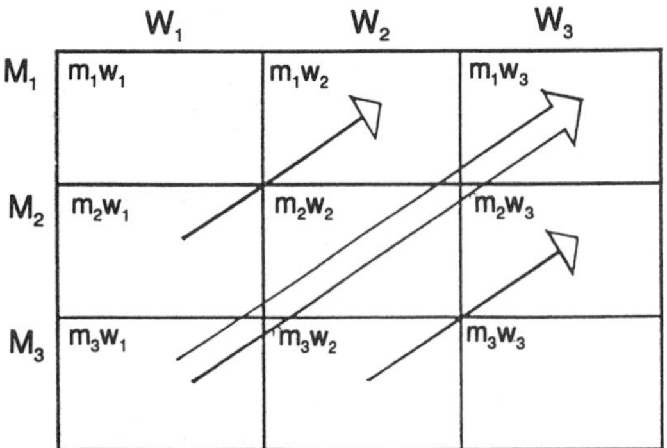

Figure 2. *Upper panel*: Single-cancellation conditions. Column labels W_1 to W_3 represent levels of the working-memory placekeepers (WMP) factor, and row labels M_1 to M_3 stand for the motivation (M) factor. Cells within the cross are defined in terms of the marginal labels. Lines with arrowheads within the cross of W and M illustrate tests of single cancellation. Premises are indicated by the single lines and the conclusion is represented by a double line. Basically, satisfaction of the single-cancellation condition establishes that cells in all rows and in all columns are ordered in exactly the same way. *Lower panel*: Double-cancellation condition. Column labels W_1 to W_3 represent levels of the working memory placekeepers (WMP) factor, and row labels M_1 to M_3 stand for the motivation (M) factor. Lines with arrowheads within the cross of W and M illustrate a test of double cancellation. Premises are indicated by the single lines, and the conclusion is represented by a double line.

If both conjoint measurement conditions are satisfied, we cannot reject the assumption that the dependent variable and the two independent variables are quantitative. Satisfaction of conjoint measurement conditions suggests that intelligence tests belong to a scale type higher than a simple ordinal scale. It is difficult to classify the IQ scale as either ordinal or interval, and it is better regarded as a quasi-interval scale. Likewise, personality inventories with Likert-type response scales are at best ordinal measures, whereas those with dichotomous (e.g., true-false) scales provide categorical measurement, so that statistical analyses of such personality data are necessarily restricted. However, Michell (in press) has used Coombs' theory of unidimensional unfolding to show that quantitative assumptions common to Thurstone's and Likert's scales can be tested and appear, in fact, to have empirical support.

In our work, the dependent variables were accuracy and speed scores from the letter-series test (Myors, Stankov, & Oliphant, 1989; Stankov & Cregan, 1993). The two independent variables were the number of WMPs and motivational instructions: Subjects had to work faster the second time (75% of the original time) and even faster the third time (50% of initial time). Both independence and double-cancellation conditions of conjoint measurement were satisfied by the structure on means, for both accuracy and time scores. Therefore, we cannot reject the assumption that intelligence measured by the letter-series test is a quantitative variable. What happens to the correlation between the scores on the letter-series test and another test of Gf (Raven's Progressive Matrices) under these treatment conditions? These correlations are presented in Table 3.

Because the pattern of correlations supports both the double-cancellation and independence conditions, the relationship between the two measures may be a quantitative variable as well. We may speculate that factor loadings on these two tests (see Table 2 above) have quantitative properties. Their measurement properties may be stronger than previously realized. As the most systematic increase in correlation is present across rows (Table 3), the increase is in number of WMPs, which leads to higher correlations with Raven's test. The pattern is similar to that with the Swaps and

Table 3. Correlations between Raven's Progressive Matrices Test and Scores on the Letter-Series Test under Different Levels of Working-Memory Placekeepers (WMP) and Motivation (M)

	WMP_1	WMP_2	WMP_3
Motivation:			
Normal speed (m_1)	.125	.457	.567
75% time (m_2)	.224	.423	.559
50% time (m_3)	.299	.459	.447

Source: Stankov & Cregan (1993).

Triplet Numbers tests in the previous section. The same explanation (i.e., an increase in number of steps required by the letter-series tasks at higher WMP levels) may be responsible for the increase. Yet only the first column shows systematic increase in correlations; the other two columns show about the same size of correlations across rows. Motivation, or asking individuals to work faster, is therefore a poor example of complexity manipulation.

The Effects of Anxiety and Mood on Cognitive Processes

Although it is obvious to most psychologists that mood and personality factors must affect cognitive processes, typical experimental studies of these processes tend to emphasize their "rational" side. An increasing number of studies during the past several years have looked at the role of personality factors in cognition. We shall mention two areas of interaction.

One line of research follows from the observation that highly anxious subjects exhibit performance decrements in comparison to less anxious subjects on tasks that are highly capacity demanding. M. Eysenck (1979) has proposed that the locus of the effect of anxiety on cognitive task performance lies in the working memory system—that is, high-anxiety subjects engage in significantly more task-irrelevant processing (worry) than their low-anxiety counterparts. This hypothesis found support in a series of experiments involving both fluid and crystallized intelligence inductive reasoning tasks (Darke, 1988). A theory linking personality, motivation, and cognitive performance was also suggested by M. Humphreys and Revelle (1984).

Another area of recent interaction between cognition and personality involves the effects of mood states on cognitive performance. For example, Forgas (1987) studied the role of mood in impression formation and memory. His findings indicate that happy people tend to form more favorable impressions and made more favorable judgments of others. Also, positive mood had a more pronounced effect on judgments and memory than did negative mood.

CONTRIBUTIONS FROM SOCIOLOGICAL AND ANTHROPOLOGICAL PERSPECTIVES

In addition to cross-cultural comparisons of performances on traditional psychometric tests of abilities and personality traits, there has been renewed interest in social and so-called "practical" intelligence. Some studies have suggested the concept of "wisdom" may be more relevant than that of intelligence in accounting for adaptive behavior in old age. New theoretical work has delineated complex cultural factors that influence the development and expression of intelligence (Irvine & Berry, 1988). Impetus for continuing interest in this interaction was provided by Sternberg's (1985) triarchic theory of intelligence, which emphasizes that intelligence is purposively directed toward pursuit of three goals: adaptation to, shaping of, and selection of one's physical and social environment. Despite Margaret Mead's anthropological studies (see Freeman, 1983) being exposed to criticism (e.g., information provided for Mead's *Coming of Age in Samoa* was in fact a joke manufactured by the native teenagers), some cross-cultural psychologists have embraced an extreme environmental position on intelligence.

Cross-Cultural Differences in Traditional Tests of Personality and Abilities

Studies have compared national, cultural, and racial groups with respect to mean IQ scores and factor structure of cognitive abilities and personality traits. The validity of these comparisons critically depends on adequate subject selection and test translation. Because these are rarely if ever satisfactory, comparisons are always open to criticism on methodological grounds. Even if there is no need to translate from one language into another (e.g., Cattell's Culture Fair Intelligence Test; or the Queensland Test, designed for testing nonverbal intelligence in desert aborigines), the nature of the test may change depending on the culture in question, and we can therefore talk only about grades of culture-fairness, rather than culture-free tests (see Cattell, 1982).

There are three main findings from these comparative studies. First, the factor structure of abilities and personality is remarkably similar across different racial and ethnic groups (Cattell, 1987a; Jensen, 1980). The structure of auditory abilities has been replicated in the United States (Stankov & Horn, 1980), Yugoslavia (Stankov, 1978), and Australia (Stankov & Spilsbury, 1978). Likewise, the 16PF personality structure has been replicated cross-culturally (see Cattell, 1973). To some extent, this finding is attributable to basic similarities in knowledge and educational practices across the world; the similarity in factor structures breaks down when the focus is on preliterate societies. Second, Cattell and Brennan (1984) gathered data on 80 variables from 110 countries. The variables were indices of integrated national behaviors, such as mortality rates, average income, number of Nobel Prize Winners, etc. Factor analysis of these data produced several so-called *syntality* factors. One of these factors—Vigorous Adapted Development—exhibited a correlation of .34 with the estimated average population intelligence (culture fair); it loads on such variables as level of industrial development, number of patented inventions, and Nobel prize winners per 100,000 of population. Third, small differences between various national-cultural groups are invariably evident, and often the pattern of mean differences reflects the emphasis on particular abilities within the culture.

Practical and Social Intelligence

Wagner and Sternberg (1986) developed a theory of behavior in occupational settings. The theory concerns tacit knowledge about managing oneself, others, and a career. This knowledge is not explicitly taught, even though it is important for success in many different work settings. Wagner and Sternberg constructed a measurement instrument that describes work-related situations and asks employees to choose among alternative courses of action. The instrument has high face validity and may appeal to users of psychological services. Although the test can discriminate between students and professionals and between successful and less successful individuals within the same field, we know little about its predictive validity. Reported correlations of the test with intelligence measures, however, are rather low.

The theory of tacit knowledge incorporates ideas that are considered part of social intelligence (see Brown & Anthony, 1990). Overall, there is no clear evidence of noteworthy correlations between different measures of social intelligence. These measures do not correlate better than ordinary intelligence measures with various real-world competencies, and it is not clear how social intelligence differs from certain personality traits such as sensitivity (16PF Factor I), and/or shrewdness (16PF Factor N).

Wisdom

According to Baltes and Smith (1989), *wisdom* refers to an expert knowledge system—a highly developed body of factual and procedural knowledge and judgment dealing with the "fundamental pragmatics of life." These concern such important but uncertain matters as the course, variations, conditions, conduct, and meaning of life. Wise people are said to have insight into human development and exceptionally good judgment about difficult life problems. This view can be traced to the theory of intelligence proposed by Baltes and associates in the early 1980s, which distinguishes between "mechanics" and "pragmatics" (or wisdom). On closer scrutiny, pragmatics appears to reduce to the processes of crystallized intelligence (Gc), and mechanics to fluid intelligence (Gf). Although various personality factors (e.g., surgency/16PF Factor F) appear to relate directly to cleverness and wit, there seems to be no necessary relationship with wisdom per se. Moreover, there is a lack of convincing empirical studies showing the usefulness of distinguishing wisdom from crystallized intelligence.

The Radical Cultural Relativism Hypothesis

Berry (1974) proposed a "radical cultural relativism" hypothesis that rejects the idea of psychological universals across cultural systems. Any behavioral concept applied within the culture, Berry argues, is unique to that culture; we can use only indigenous ideas about cognitive competence to describe and assess cognitive capacity. Literal interpretation of this position denies the possibility of cross-cultural comparisons. Echoes of this hypothesis can be found in studies within our own culture. For example, Ceci (1990) shows that highly competent behavior based on a rather complex knowledge within a subculture (e.g., successful betting at horse races) may not necessarily correlate significantly with intelligence test scores; other factors, including personality dispositions and learned behavior patterns, may also play an important role. As pointed out by Brody (1992), Berry's empirical work does not appear too radical—he has studied cognitive styles, as well as the so-called differentiation hypothesis that is closely related to visualization (Gv) spatial abilities. Berry shows that the type of society (e.g., agricultural, hunter-gatherer) relates to the degree of differentiation achieved by individuals living within a given cultural context. Overall, the work within sociological and anthropological perspectives that has criticized use of traditional intelligence and personality tests for cross-cultural comparisons has not produced a successful alternative way of measuring competencies. Crosscultural psychologists, however, have contributed to improvements in our understanding of cultural effects on intelligence and personality.

INDIVIDUAL DIFFERENCES AND SOCIAL POLICIES, FASHIONS, AND EPIDEMICS

Societal Changes and Increases in IQ Test Scores

The first large-scale data linking demographic trends and measured intelligence became available between the two world wars (see Cattell, 1987a). A more recent study by Vining (1982) supported early findings. Of major concern was the realization that different strata of society exhibit different natality rates, with the most educated producing disproportionately fewer offspring than poorly educated groups; this was coupled with improved health care and increased survival rates. These demographic changes, it was feared, could reduce overall levels of national intelligence, even though available data did not show significant reductions in intelligence between two generations.

In the 1980s, large-scale post-World War II data from the United States and Europe became available. Flynn (1984, 1987) reported that scores on Gf tests of intelligence administered in successive years to young people enlisted into the armed services showed systematic improvements (in excess of 13 IQ points) over the 40-year period (Cattell also obtained a slight increase in IQ scores when he retested the same population 15 years later). Presumably, early predictions did not allow for the differential death rate with intelligence (see O'Toole & Stankov, 1992) and the fact that not all people form families. There are two proposed explanations for the reported results. Biologically inclined researchers attribute improvements in intelligence scores to better nutrition in the second half of this century (Schoenthaler et al., 1991). Those who prefer socioenvironmental explanations emphasize improvements in educational interventions among disadvantaged groups. The latter explanation is supported by the work of Kvashchev in Yugoslavia (see Stankov, 1986b; Stankov & Chen, 1988).

Interaction of Personality and Abilities in Academic Achievement

Although traditional concepts of under- and over-achievement suggest it is feasible to predict academic achievement from intelligence test scores alone, there is no doubt that personality traits interact with cognitive abilities in influencing learning outcomes (Boyle, 1990b). This interaction is probably more important than the role of either abilities or traits alone. The first two 16PF second-stratum dimensions (Eysenck's extraversion and neuroticism factors) are particularly influential (see Birkett-Cattell, 1989). As M. W. Eysenck and Eysenck (1979) have shown, introverted individuals condition more rapidly than extraverts, and their decay of conditioned behaviors is slower than that of extraverts. At elementary school, extraverted students perform better, whereas at college level, introverted students outperform their extraverted classmates. Though neuroticism (anxiety) may attenuate learning in less intellectually able students or in those who do not know their work well, it may facilitate performance (serving as a drive) in more intelligent students and/or those who have more comprehensive knowledge. Thus anxiety may serve as both a debilitating influence and a facilitating factor on performance outcomes. As compared with written take-home assignments, examinations tend to produce a wider range of scores among students. In one study, under conditions of heightened emotionality, no fewer than seven of the 16PF factors were found to exhibit significant correlations with academic performance, whereas only Factor Q_2 (self-sufficiency) correlated significantly with learning under neutral emotional conditions (Boyle, 1983). Whereas intelligence (as measured via the ACER-AL test) correlated .35 with performance under neutral conditions, its magnitude dropped to .21 under heightened emotional activation, and several personality traits predominated over cognitive abilities in influencing learning outcomes. Other non-ability intrapersonal characteristics, including motivational dynamic traits and emotional states, also contribute significantly to the prediction of academic performance (e.g., Boyle & Start, 1989a, b; Boyle, Start, & Hall, 1989).

Sex Differences in Personality and Intelligence

Despite attempts by the feminist movement to minimize sex differences in cognitive abilities and personality, Sandra Scarr (1988) has called for objective scientific research into such differences. Feingold (1988) compared performances of males and females on the Differential Aptitude Test in successive years between 1947 and 1980. For two subtests (spelling and language), differences between males and females have remained relatively constant with successive generations. For three abilities (verbal reasoning, abstract reasoning, and numerical reasoning) these differences were not significant in 1980, even though some had shown significant differences in the past. For two abilities (clerical and mechanical reasoning) there was a significant reduction of sex differences over the years, but that difference remained significant in 1980. In all our work at the University of Sydney (Stankov, 1978, 1983b, 1986b, 1988a, 1994) with both student and nonstudent populations, sex differences on a battery of marker tests of fluid and crystallized intelligence have been insignificant. Brody (1992, p. 320) points out that the results "appear to implicate secular changes in our culture. These might plausibly include a decline in sex stereotyping of activities, interests, and curricular choices among high school students."

There is evidence for the existence of a relationship between sex-role identity, field independence, and scholastic intelligence. In a study by Bernard, Boyle, and Jackling (1990), subjects (140 males and 181 females in grades 11 and 12) completed the Witkin Group Embedded Figures Test, the Otis Higher Test C of intelligence, and a shortened version of the Bem Sex Role Inventory. Measurement of sex-role identity enables assessment of whether higher performance on a test of field independence and intelligence is more a function of masculinity or of reversed sex-role identity. Results showed significant differences in intelligence and field independence among different sex-role groups. Males performed significantly better on the Witkin and Otis tests than did females, and males with lower masculinity scores performed better on the Otis than those with higher scores on masculinity. Females with low femininity scores performed better on the Witkin and Otis tests than did those with high femininity scores. When subjects were allocated by sex into one of four sex-role identity groups, the most significant difference in intelligence was obtained between the high masculine–low feminine and low masculine–high feminine female groups, with the former group outperforming the latter. In contrast, highly androgynous (high masculine–high feminine) females did not perform as well as high masculine–low feminine groups. As Bradshaw and Nettleton (1983) pointed out, relationships between mental ability and social, biological, and hormonal factors among different sex-role groups require further exploration.

On mechanical reasoning ability, males are superior to females (about 11 IQ points) in dealing with mechanical and spatial problems. Stanley and Benbow (1986) summarized a large number of studies showing a consistently reported superiority of males over females in spatial ability; Benbow (1988) has discussed the role of environmental and genetic factors in accounting for sex differences in spatial abilities. According to Moir and Jessel (1989), sex differences in spatial/mechanical abilities cannot be accounted for by explanations in terms of cultural factors. Current biological explanations are in terms of either a sex-linked gene for spatial ability or differences in the degree of cerebral lateralization (i.e., males are more lateralized than females; Kimura, 1992; Kimura & Hampson, 1992). It is assumed the parietal lobe of the right cerebral hemisphere, which is responsible for performance on spatial tasks, is better specialized in males than in females. Females use a more "integrated" mode of thinking than males (the corpus callosum, which connects the two cerebral hemispheres, is larger in females; see Bradshaw & Nettleton, 1983; Moir & Jessel, 1989). Another biological explanation is hormonal differences, especially androgen/estrogen ratio.

Sex differences on some types of tasks exist in samples that are above or below average in general ability. Even though there is a small overall mean difference between males and females in performance on numerical and mathematical tasks—a difference that can be explained in terms of environmental effects (see Held, Alderton, Foley, & Segall, 1993)—there is a disproportionate number of males who show high mathematical ability. One explanation is that mathematical ability is dependent on spatial/mechanical abilities; because males are superior on such abilities, they tend to obtain higher scores on tests of mathematical ability. Another explanation is that small differences in central tendency imply large differences at the extremes of the distribution, given larger standard deviations for males than for females. Though there may be an insignificant difference in favor of males in overall level of performance in mathematics, there will be a disproportionately large number of males with high and low scores. The difference is therefore attributable to a greater spread of scores among males, not to a manipulation of social conditions in their favor.

With respect to non-ability intrapersonal psychological variables, Boyle and Start (1989b) examined the relationships between motivational dynamic traits (measured in the Children's Motivation Analysis Test) and both reading and mathematics performance among sixth-grade children (cf. Boyle & Start, 1989a). Results revealed several sex differences. Boyle (1989c), however, found few differences in reported mood states among male and female undergraduates. Cohn (1991), in a meta-analysis of 65 studies on sex differences throughout the course of normal personality development, reported substantial advantages for female adolescents on verbal abilities, ego development, moral judgments, aggression, and empathy. According to Cohn (p. 252), "The greater maturity displayed by adolescent girls is not an artifact of superior verbal abilities: Sex differences in ego development were more than twice the magnitude of differences in vocabulary skills (Hyde & Linn, 1988)."

Clearly there is greater variability among males than females in many respects; there are more males in jails, in psychiatric institutions, in special schools, and so on. At the same time, there is a larger proportion of males than of females among higher achievers. In many personality traits, the range of scores for males is greater than for females. The variance of males on general intelligence tests is about 10% larger than that of females. Thus, even though means for these two groups do not differ significantly, the spread of scores is clearly different—and, as a consequence, one finds more males than females among the high- and low-achieving groups.

Effects of AIDS on Personality and Cognitive Abilities

The AIDS epidemic that swept through many Western countries during the 1980s has increased awareness of the possible role of immunological factors in psychological functioning. Particularly noticeable at first was the deterioration in cognitive processes among AIDS sufferers, but it quickly became apparent that personality changes and motor disturbances were also an aspect of what is now called the AIDS dementia complex. Cognitive changes remain the most salient, and it is now accepted that the presence of severe dementia is sufficient to make a definite diagnosis of AIDS in a person known to be infected by the human immunological virus (HIV).[1]

Because it is known that soon after the HIV infection the virus enters the central nervous system and often penetrates the blood–brain barrier (see Resnick, Berger, Shapshak, & Tourttellotte, 1988), it has been suggested that mild cognitive changes associated with the HIV infection may be detected even at the very early stages of the disease. A battery of psychological tests was suggested for neuropsychological assessment purposes (see Butters et al., 1990). Apart from the commonly employed measures of premorbid intelligence, memory, abstraction, language, and measures of constructural and motor abilities and perceptual abilities, the battery included a psychiatric assessment. In recognition of the recent changes in studies of cognitive functioning, the battery placed a particular emphasis on measures of divided and sustained attention, as well as speed of processing and retrieval from working and long-term memory.

The usefulness of psychological measures for the detection of HIV infection is still being debated. This is partly because of uncertainty about the nature and timing of alterations in cognitive functions that result from HIV infection. It is also attributable to inadequate design aspects of the reported studies (i.e., differences between patients and controls in terms of educational or premorbid psychological status, history of drug use, and coexisting medical conditions) and to a difficulty in distinguishing between psychological states that result from organic as opposed to nonorganic factors. Indeed, recent reports based on HIV-positive drug users in Edinburgh indicate that although there is evidence of reduced capacity for concentration, speed of thought, and memory in these patients, the reductions in function may not be helpful for the early detection of the AIDS dementia complex (see Egan, Brettle, & Goodwin, 1992; Egan, Crawford, Brettle, & Goodwin, 1990).

Studies of personality changes in HIV-positive subjects are less common in the literature than studies of cognitive dysfunction. HIV-infected people show pronounced depression symptoms in the advanced stages of AIDS, however, the effects may be small and hard to detect prior to the onset of defining symptoms. A recent Australian study of hemophiliacs who became infected with HIV through blood transfusion prior to the availability of successful blood screening procedures reports that those who eventually developed AIDS tended to have somewhat higher state anxiety scores than controls (Jones, Garsia, Wu, Job, & Dunn, 1993). The effects are relatively small. The authors discuss several explanations of this relationship, including the possibility that state anxiety relates to the resistance to infection or exposure to HIV or that hemophiliacs have greater anxiety in general because

[1]See Centers for Disease Control. (1987). Revision of the CDC surveillance case definition for acquired immune deficiency syndrome. *Mortality and Morbidity Weekly Report*, *36*(Suppl. 1), 1–15.

they are likely to suffer from other infectious diseases. Jones et al. believe that infection with HIV has subtle but measurable effects on psychological state. Egan et al. (1992) question this interpretation; they report that self-ratings of mood do not change with time and stage of HIV illness.

The AIDS epidemic has alerted researchers to the possible role of immunological factors in many physical illnesses and in the development of certain types of psychological disorders. The most popular model assumes that psychosocial factors (e.g., stress, depression) are associated with the onset, course, or outcomes of physical illness, and a large body of research since the 1980s has considered the possibility that immunological alterations may be associated with depressive symptoms accompanying stressful life events. Initial studies of this link were encouraging, but more recent studies show that evidence for the role of the immune changes in depressive disorder has been far less clear than the early studies suggested (see Stein, Miller, & Trestman, 1991).

SUMMARY AND CONCLUSIONS

The multivariate psychometric model remains the main avenue for studying personality and intelligence today. The Cattell-Horn theory of fluid and crystallized intelligence provides a meaningful organization of the body of knowledge on individual differences in human abilities. Although other approaches have gained supporters during the past two decades, none has achieved the status of the Gf/Gc theory. Both normal and abnormal personality traits are important in influencing behavior, and both interact with other non-ability intrapersonal variables (motivation and mood-state factors) and cognitive abilities. A fresh and renewed effort to study the interaction between personality and cognitive abilities in their effects on behavior needs to be launched in the light of recent advances in both these fields.

New approaches and models have also enriched our understanding of personality and intelligence by adding concepts not available through traditional approaches, as well as by asking new questions. On the biological side, exciting avenues have been opened by technological advances in brain imaging and biochemistry. These advances will allow for a better description of the physical and psychobiological correlates of personality and intelligence (see Zuckerman, 1991) and therefore enable more precise theories about mind-body dualism. Also, there is a prospect for using nutritional and pharmaceutical interventions to improve overall cognitive performance. In research on cognitive aging health, physical activity, and various lifestyle variables have gained a prominent place. This work is likely to improve our understanding of intelligence.

Given the strength of reported relationships, it appears that studies relating mental speed to intelligence have been overemphasized; a large number of empirical studies since the late 1970s has not enabled us to pass through the "correlation of .30 barrier" (see Hunt, 1980). Although these studies have shown that mental speed is one of the important aspects of cognitive functioning, further work needs to be done to establish the actual correlations among different measures of speed and between speed measures and accuracy scores from broad abilities of the Gf/Gc theory. Little can be gained if we retain global measure of *g* as a sole indicant of cognitive ability.

Experimental cognitive studies of intelligence have left a significant impact. They have forced multivariate psychologists to look at the microstructure of their tasks and, in the process, have reawakened important questions about the nature of human abilities and the role of complexity. This area will continue to flourish, producing fresh views of intelligence when cognitive sciences reach the next stage of their development. Clearly, however, such developments must take into account the important role of personality effects on cognitive functioning.

Studies of intelligence from sociological and anthropological perspectives have been somewhat disappointing. Apart from defining what we mean by culture in its relation to intelligence, these studies have produced relatively little improvement in our understanding of intelligence. They have continued to provide a reminder about the dangers of rampant sociobiological interpretations and little truly new information about human cognitive functioning.

Clearly, social forces act in setting the agenda for research in personality and intelligence. Societal changes, including the rise of feminism, have affected our research and challenged some of the entrenched views of individual differences, as have concerns about aging populations and the effects of new diseases. These changes are partly responsible for the increase in the IQ test scores over the past several decades and the decrease in gender differences in many cognitive performances. These changes have also been instrumental in alerting us that disturbances in hitherto neglected systems of our bodily functions (e.g., immunological changes) can cause profound psychological changes in both intelligence and personality.

Substantial evidence exists that personality traits and cognitive abilities interact appreciably in modifying human behaviors. These combined effects are most discernible within the objective test (T-data) arena. In the future, considerably greater emphasis should be placed on the objective measurement of personality traits, enabling the nature and extent of complex personality–ability interactions to be clarified. Undoubtedly, further research based on new models and paradigms of personality and intelligence will result in considerable new insights.

REFERENCES

Ankney, C. D. (1992). Sex differences in relative brain size: The mismeasure of woman, too? *Intelligence, 16*, 329–336.

Anstey, K., Stankov, L., & Lord, S. (1993). Primary aging, secondary aging and intelligence. *Psychology and Aging, 8*, 562–570.

Baltes, P. B., & Smith, J. (1989). Toward a psychology of wisdom and its ontogenesis. In R. J. Sternberg (Ed.), *Wisdom: Its nature, origins, and development*. New York: Cambridge University Press.

Benbow, C. P. (1988). Sex differences in mathematical reasoning ability in intellectually talented preadolescents: Their nature, effects and possible causes. *Behavioral and Brain Sciences, 11*, 169–232.

Bernard, M. E., Boyle, G. J., & Jackling, B. F. (1990). Sex-role identity and mental ability. *Personality and Individual Differences, 11*, 213–217.

Berry, J. W. (1974). Radical cultural relativism and the concept of intelligence. In J. W. Berry & P. R. Dasen (Eds.), *Culture and cognition: Readings in cross-cultural psychology* (pp. 225–229). London: Methuen.

Birkett-Cattell, H. (1989). *The 16PF: Personality in depth*. Champaign, IL: Institute for Personality and Ability Testing.

Birren, J. E., & Cunningham, W. (1985). Research on the psychology of aging: Principles, concepts and theory. In J. E. Birren & W. Schaie (Eds.), *Handbook of the psychology of aging* (2nd ed.). New York: Van Nostrand Reinhold.

Boyle, G. J. (1983). Effects on academic learning of manipulating emotional states and motivational dynamics. *British Journal of Educational Psychology, 53*, 347–357.

Boyle, G. J. (1985). Self-report measures of depression: Some psychometric considerations. *British Journal of Clinical Psychology, 24*, 45–59.

Boyle, G. J. (1986). Clinical neuropsychological assessment: Abbreviating the Halstead Category Test of brain dysfunction. *Journal of Clinical Psychology, 42*, 615–625.

Boyle, G. J. (1988a). Contribution of Cattellian psychometrics to the elucidation of human intellectual structure. *Multivariate Experimental Clinical Research, 8*, 267–273.

Boyle, G. J. (1988b). Elucidation of motivation structure by dynamic calculus. In J. R. Nesselroade & R. B. Cattell (Eds.), *Handbook of multivariate experimental psychology* (rev. 2nd ed.; pp. 737–787). New York: Plenum.

Boyle, G. J. (1989a). Re-examination of the major personality-type factors in the Cattell, Comrey, and Eysenck scales: Were the factor solutions by Noller et al. optimal? *Personality and Individual Differences, 10*, 1289–1299.

Boyle, G. J. (1989b). Reliability and validity of the Stanford-Binet Intelligence Scale (fourth edition) in the Australian context: A review. *Australian Educational and Developmental Psychologist, 6*, 21–23.

Boyle, G. J. (1989c). Sex differences in reported mood states. *Personality and Individual Differences, 10*, 1179–1183.

Boyle, G. J. (1990a). A review of the factor structure of the Sixteen Personality Factor Questionnaire and the Clinical Analysis Questionnaire. *Psychological Test Bulletin, 3*, 40–45.

Boyle, G. J. (1990b, June). *Integration of personality and intelligence measurement within the Cattellian psychometric model*. Paper presented at the Symposium on Personality and Intelligence, Fifth European Conference on Personality, University of Rome.

Boyle, G. J. (1990c). Stanford-Binet Intelligence Scale: Is its structure supported by LISREL congeneric factor analyses? *Personality and Individual Differences, 121*, 1175–1181.

Boyle, G. J. (1991). Experimental psychology does require a multivariate perspective. *Contemporary Psychology, 36*, 350–351.

Boyle, G. J. (in press). Intelligence and personality measurement within the Cattellian psychometric model. In G. L. Van Heck, P. Borkenau, I. Deary, & W. Nowack (Eds.), *Personality Psychology in Europe* (Vol. 4).

Boyle, G. J., & Start, K. B. (1989a). Comparison of higher-stratum motivational factors across sexes using the Children's Motivation Analysis Test. *Personality and Individual Differences, 10*, 483–487.

Boyle, G. J., & Start, K. B. (1989b). Sex differences in the prediction of academic achievement using the Children's Motivation Analysis Test. *British Journal of Educational Psychology, 59*, 245–252.

Boyle, G., Start, K. B., & Hall, E. J. (1989). Prediction of academic achievement using the School Motivation Analysis Test. *British Journal of Educational Psychology, 59*, 92–99.

Bradshaw, J. L., & Nettleton, N. C. (1983). *Human cerebral asymmetry*. Englewood Cliffs, NJ: Prentice-Hall.

Brody, N. (1992). *Intelligence*. New York: Academic Press.

Brown, L. T., & Anthony, R. G. (1990). Continuing the search for social intelligence. *Personality and Individual Differences, 11*, 463–470.

Buckhalt, J. A., & Jensen, A. R. (1989). The British Ability Scales speed of information processing subtest: What does it measure? *British Journal of Educational Psychology, 59*, 100–107.

Butters, N., Grant, I., Haxby, J., Judd, L. L., Martin, A., McClelland, J., Pequegnat, W., Schacter, D., & Stover, E. (1990). Assessment of AIDS-related cognitive changes: Recommendations of the NIMH workshop on neuropsychological assessment approaches. *Journal of Clinical and Experimental Neuropsychology, 12*, 963–978.

Cain, D. P., & Vanderwolf, C. H. (1990). A critique of Rushton on race, brain size, and intelligence. *Personality and Individual Differences, 11*, 777–784.

Carroll, J. B. (1976). Psychometric tests as cognitive tasks: A new "Structure of Intellect." L. Resnick (Ed.), *The nature of intelligence*. Hillsdale, NJ: Erlbaum.

Carroll, J. B. (1991). No demonstration that "*g*" is not unitary, but there is more to the story: Comment on Kranzler and Jensen. *Intelligence, 15*, 423–436.

Carroll, J. B. (1993). *Human cognitive abilities*. New York: Cambridge University Press.

Cattell, R. B. (1963). Theory of fluid and crystallized intelligence: A critical experiment. *Journal of Educational Psychology, 54*, 1–22.

Cattell, R. B. (1971). *Abilities: Their structure, growth and action*. Boston: Houghton-Mifflin.

Cattell, R. B. (1973). *Personality and mood by questionnaire*. San Francisco: Jossey-Bass.

Cattell, R. B. (1982). *The inheritance of personality and ability*. New York: Academic Press.

Cattell, R. B. (1983). *Structured personality-learning theory: A wholistic multivariate research approach*. New York: Praeger.

Cattell, R. B. (1987a). *Intelligence: Its structure, growth and action*. Amsterdam: North Holland.

Cattell, R. B. (1987b). *Psychotherapy by structured learning theory*. New York: Springer.

Cattell, R. B., & Brennan, J. (1984). Population intelligence and national syntality. *Mankind Quarterly, 21*, 327–340.

Cattell, R. B., & Cattell, A. K. S. (1977). *Culture Fair Intelligence Tests*. Champaign, IL: Institute for Personality and Ability Testing.

Cattell, R. B., & Schuerger, J. M. (1978). *Personality theory in action: Handbook for the Objective-Analytic (O-A) Test Kit*. Champaign, IL: Institute for Personality and Ability Testing.

Ceci, S. J. (1990). *On intelligence . . . more or less*. Englewood Cliffs, NJ: Prentice-Hall.

Cohn, L. D. (1991). Sex differences in the course of personality development: A meta-analysis. *Psychological Bulletin, 109*, 252–266.

Cornelius, S. W., Willis, S. L., Nesselroade, J. R., & Baltes, P. B. (1983). Convergence between attention variables and factors of psychometric intelligence in older adults. *Intelligence, 7*, 253–269.

Costa, P. T., & McCrae, R. R. (1992). *The NEO Personality Inventory (Revised) manual*. Odessa, FL: Psychological Assessment Resources.

Cronbach, L. J. (1990). *The essentials of psychological testing* (5th ed.). New York: Harper & Row.

Daneman, M. (1982). The measurement of reading comprehension: How not to trade construct validity for predictive power. *Intelligence, 6*, 331–345.

Darke, S. (1988). Effects of anxiety on inferential reasoning task performance. *Journal of Personality and Social Psychology, 55*, 1–7.

Davis, C., Elliott, S., Dionne, M., & Mitchell, I. (1991). The relationship of personality factors and physical activity to body satisfaction in men. *Personality and Individual Differences, 12*, 689–694.

Deary, I. J. (1992). Diabetes, hypoglycemia and cognitive performance. In K. R. Boff, L. Kaufman, & J. P. Thomas (Eds.), *Handbook of human performance* (Vol. 2). New York: Wiley.

Deary, I. J., & Mathews, G. (1993). Personality traits are alive and well. *Psychologist, 6*, 299–311.

Dickman, S. J., & Meyer, D. E. (1988). Impulsivity and speed-accuracy trade-offs in information processing. *Journal of Personality and Social Psychology, 54*, 274–290.

Dunn, S. M. (1992). Psychological aspects of adult onset diabetes. In S. Maes, H. Leventhal, & M. Johnston (Eds.), *International review of health psychology*. New York: Wiley.

Dunne, M. P., & Hartley, L. R. (1985). The effects of scopolamine upon verbal memory: Evidence for an attentional hypothesis. *Acta Psychologia, 58*, 205–217.

Egan, V. G., Brettle, R. P., & Goodwin, G. M. (1992). The Edinburgh cohort of HIV-positive drug users: Pattern of cognitive impairment in relation to progression of disease. *British Journal of Psychiatry, 161*, 522–531.

Egan, V. G., Crawford, J. R., Brettle, R. P., & Goodwin, G. M. (1990). The Edinburgh cohort of HIV-positive drug users: Current intellectual function is impaired, but not due to early AIDS dementia complex. *AIDS, 4*, 651–656.

Eysenck, H. J. (1976). *Sex and personality*. London: Open Books.

Eysenck, H. J. (1991). Dimensions of personality: 16, 5, 3. *Personality and Individual Differences, 12*, 773–790.

Eysenck, H. J., & Eysenck, M. W. (1985). *Personality and individual differences: A natural science approach*. New York: Plenum.

Eysenck, M. W. (1979). Anxiety, learning, and memory: A reconceptualization. *Journal of Research in Personality, 13*, 363–385.

Eysenck, M. W. (1983). Anxiety. In G. R. J. Hockey (Ed.), *Stress and fatigue in human performance*. Chichester, England: Wiley.

Eysenck, M. W., & Eysenck, H. J. (1979). Memory scanning, introversion-extraversion, and levels of processing. *Journal of Research in Personality and Individual Differences, 13*, 305–315.

Feingold, A. (1988). Cognitive gender differences are disappearing. *American Psychologist, 43*, 95–103.

Fernandez, E. (1986). A classification system of cognitive coping strategies for pain. *Pain, 26*, 141–151.

Fernandez, E., & Turk, D. C. (1989). The utility of cognitive coping strategies for altering pain perception: A meta-analysis. *Pain, 38*, 123–135.

Ferretti, R. P., & Butterfield, E. C. (1992). Intelligence-related differences in the learning, maintenance, and transfer of problem-solving strategies. *Intelligence, 16*, 207–223.

Flynn, J. R. (1984). The mean IQ of Americans: Massive gains 1932–1978. *Psychological Bulletin, 95*, 29–51.

Flynn, J. R. (1987). Massive IQ gains in 14 nations: What IQ tests really measure. *Psychological Bulletin, 101*, 171–191.

Fogarty, G., & Stankov, L. (1982). Competing tasks as an index of intelligence. *Personality and Individual Differences, 3*, 407–422.

Fogarty, G., & Stankov, L. (1988). Abilities involved in performance on competing tasks. *Personality and Individual Differences, 9*, 35–49.

Forgas, J. P. (1987). Mood effects on person-perception judgments. *Journal of Personality and Social Psychology, 53*, 53–60.

Fox, P. T., Raichle, M. E., Mintun, M. A., & Dance, C. (1988). Nonoxidative glucose consumption during focal physiologic neural activity. *Science, 241*, 462–464.

Freeman, D. (1983). *Margaret Mead and Samoa: The making and unmaking of an anthropological myth*. Cambridge, MA: Harvard University Press.

French, J. W., Ekstrom, R. B., & Price, L. A. (1963). *Manual for reference tests for cognitive factors*. Princeton, NJ: Educational Testing Service.

Friedman, H. S., & Booth-Kewley, S. (1987). The "disease-prone" personality: A meta-analytic view of the construct. *American Psychologist, 42*, 539–553.

Gardner, H. (1983). *Frames of mind: The theory of multiple intelligences*. New York: Basic Books.

Goff, M., & Ackerman, P. L. (1992). Personality-intelligence relations: Assessment of typical intellectual engagement. *Journal of Educational Psychology, 84*, 537–552.

Goldberg, L. R. (1992). The development of markers of the big-five factor structure. *Psychological Assessment, 4,* 26–42.

Gossop, M. R., & Eysenck, S. B. G. (1983). A further investigation into the personality of drug addicts in treatment. *British Journal of Addiction, 75,* 305–311.

Grill, V. (1990). A comparison of brain glucose metabolism in diabetes as measured by positron emission tomography or by arteriovenous techniques. *Annals of Medicine, 22,* 171–176.

Guilford, J. P. (1981). Higher-order structure-of-intellect abilities. *Multivariate Behavioral Research, 16,* 411–435.

Gustafsson, J. E. (1992, July). *General intelligence and analytical ability.* Paper presented at the International Congress of Psychology, Brussels.

Guttman, L. (1965). A faceted definition of intelligence. *Studies in Psychology, Scripta Hierosolymitana* (Jerusalem: Hebrew University), *14,* 166–181.

Guttman, L. (1992). The irrelevance of factor analysis for the study of group differences. *Multivariate Behavioral Research, 27,* 175–204.

Haier, R. J., Siege, B., Jr., Huecheterlein, K. H., Hazlett, E., Wu, J., Browning, H. L., & Buchsbaum, M. S. (1988). Cortical glucose metabolic rate correlates of abstract reasoning and attention studied with positron emission tomography. *Intelligence, 12,* 199–217.

Halford, G. (1989). Cognitive processing capacity and learning ability: An integration of two areas. *Learning and Individual Differences, 1,* 125–153.

Held, J. D., Alderton, D. L., Foley, P. P., & Segall, D. O. (1993). Arithmetic reasoning gender differences: Explanations found in the armed services vocational battery. *Learning and Individual Differences, 5,* 171–186.

Holzman, T. G., Pellegrino, J. W., & Glaser, R. (1983). Cognitive variables in series completion. *Journal of Educational Psychology, 75,* 603–618.

Horn, J. L. (1985). Remodeling old models of intelligence. In B. Wollman (Ed.), *Handbook of intelligence: Theories, measurements and applications.* New York: Wiley.

Horn, J. L. (1988). Thinking about human abilities. In J. R. Nesselroade & R. B. Cattell (Eds.), *Handbook of multivariate experimental psychology.* New York: Plenum.

Horn, J. L., & Cattell, R. B. (1982). Whimsy and misunderstandings of Gf-Gc theory: A comment on Guilford. *Psychological Bulletin, 91,* 623–633.

Horn, J. L., & Hofer, S. M. (1992). Major abilities and development in the adult period. In R. Sternberg & C. Berg (Eds.), *Intellectual development* (pp. 44–99). New York: Cambridge University Press.

Horn, J. L., & Knapp, J. R. (1974). On the subjective character of the empirical base of Guilford's structure-of-intellect model. *Psychological Bulletin, 80,* 33–43.

Horn, J. L., & Stankov, L. (1982). Comments about a chameleon theory: Level I/Level II. *Journal of Educational Psychology, 74,* 874–878.

Howard, R. W. (1993). On what intelligence is. *British Journal of Psychology, 84,* 27–37.

Humphreys, L. G. (1979). The construct of general intelligence. *Intelligence, 3,* 105–120.

Humphreys, M. S., & Revelle, W. (1984). Personality, motivation and performance: A theory of the relationship between individual differences in information processing. *Psychological Review, 91,* 153–184.

Hunt, E. (1980). Intelligence as an information-processing concept. *British Journal of Psychology, 71,* 449–474.

Hunt, E., & Lansman, M. (1982). Individual differences in attention. In R. J. Sternberg (Ed.), *Advances in the psychology of human intelligence.* Hillsdale, NJ: Erlbaum.

Hunter, J. E., & Schmidt, F. L. (1981). Fitting people to jobs: the impact of personnel selection on national productivity. In E. A. Fleishman (Ed.), *Human performance and productivity.* Hillsdale, NJ: Erlbaum.

Hyde, J. S., & Linn, M. C. (1988). Gender differences in verbal ability: A meta-analysis. *Psychological Bulletin, 104,* 53–69.

Irvine, S. H., & Berry, J. W. (1988). *Human abilities in cultural context.* Cambridge, England: Cambridge University Press.

Jensen, A. R. (1979). "*g*": Outmoded theory or unconquered frontier? *Creative Science and Technology, 11,* 16–29.

Jensen, A. R. (1980). *Bias in mental testing.* New York: Free Press.

Jensen, A. R. (1982). Level I/Level II: Factors or categories? *Journal of Educational Psychology, 74,* 868–873.

Jensen, A. R. (1987). Individual differences in the Hick paradigm. In P. A. Vernon (Ed.), *Speed of information-processing and intelligence.* Norwood, NJ: Ablex.

Jensen, A. R., & Sinha, S. N. (1992). Physical correlates of human intelligence. In P. A. Vernon (Ed.), *Biological approaches to the study of human intelligence.* Norwood, NJ: Ablex.

Jones, Q. J., Garsia, R. J., Wu, R. T. M., Job, R. F. S., & Dunn, S. M. (1993). *A controlled study of anxiety and morbid cognitions at initial screening for HIV in a cohort of hemophiliacs.* Paper under review.

Kaufman, A. S. (1990). *Assessing adolescent and adult intelligence.* Boston: Allyn & Bacon.

Kimura, D. (1992). Sex differences in the brain. *Scientific American, 267,* 119–125.

Kimura, D., & Hampson, E. (1992). Neural and hormonal mechanisms mediating sex differences in cognition. In P. A. Vernon (Ed.), *Biological approaches to the study of human intelligence.* Norwood, NJ: Ablex.

Kline, P. (1979). *Psychometrics and psychology.* London: Academic Press.

Kranzler, J. H., & Jensen, A. R. (1989). Inspection time and intelligence: A meta-analysis. *Intelligence, 13,* 329–347.

Kranzler, J. H., & Jensen, A. R. (1991). The nature of psychometric "*g*": Unitary process of a number of independent processes? *Intelligence, 15,* 379–422.

Krug, S. E., & Johns, E. F. (1986). A large scale cross-validation of second-order personality structure defined by the 16PF. *Psychological Reports, 59,* 683–693.

Langan, S. J., Deary, I. J., Hepburn, D. A., & Frier, B. M. (1991). Cumulative cognitive impairment following recurrent severe hypoglycaemia in adult patients with insulin-treated diabetes mellitus. *Diabetologia, 34,* 227–344.

Larson, G. E., & Alderton, D. L. (1990). Reaction time variability and intelligence: "Worst performance" analysis of individual difference. *Intelligence, 14,* 309–325.

Larson, G. E., Merritt, C. R., & Williams, S. E. (1988). Information processing and intelligence: Some implications of task complexity. *Intelligence, 12,* 131–147.

Levy, P. (1992). Inspection time and its relation to intelligence: Issues of measurement and meaning. *Personality and Individual Differences, 13,* 987–1002.

Lohman, D. F. (1989). Individual differences in errors and latencies on cognitive tasks. *Learning and Individual Differences, 1,* 179–202.

Lustman, P. J., Griffiths, L. S., & Clouse, R. E. (1988). Depression in adults with diabetes. Results of 5-year follow-up study. *Diabetes Care, 11,* 605–612.

Lynn, R. (1987). The intelligence of the Mongoloids: A psychometric, evolutionary and neurological theory. *Personality and Individual Differences, 8*, 813–844.

Mackintosh, N. (1986). The biology of intelligence. *British Journal of Psychology, 77*, 1–18.

Mathews, G., Coyle, K., & Craig, A. (1990). Multiple factors of cognitive failure and their relationships with stress vulnerability. *Journal of Psychopathology and Behavioral Assessment, 12*, 49–65.

Mattarazzo, J. D. (1972). *Wechsler's measurement and appraisal of adult intelligence* (5th ed.). Baltimore, MD: Williams and Wilkins.

McCrae, R. R., & Costa, P. T. (1987). Validation of the five-factor model of personality across instruments and observers. *Journal of Personality and Social Psychology, 52*, 81–90.

McDonald, R. P. (1978). A simple comprehensive model for the analysis of covariance structures. *British Journal of Mathematical and Statistical Psychology, 31*, 161–183.

Mershon, B., & Gorsuch, R. L. (1988). Number of factors in the personality sphere: Does increase in factors increase predictability of real-life criteria? *Journal of Personality and Social Psychology, 55*, 675–680.

Messick, S. (1992). Multiple intelligence or multilevel intelligence? Selective emphasis on distinctive properties of hierarchy: On Gardner's "Frames of Mind" and Sternberg's "Beyond IQ" in the context of theory and research on the structure of human abilities. *Psychological Inquiry, 3*, 365–384.

Metz, J. T., Yasillo, N. J., & Cooper, M. (1987). Relationship between cognitive functioning and cerebral metabolism. *Journal of Cerebral Blood Flow and Metabolism, 7*(Suppl. 1), 305.

Michell, J. (1990). *An introduction to the logic of psychological measurement*. Hillsdale, NJ: Erlbaum.

Michell, J. (in press). Measuring dimensions of belief by unidimensional unfolding. *Journal of Mathematical Psychology*.

Miller, L. T., & Vernon, P. A. (1992). The general factor in short-term memory, intelligence, and reaction time. *Intelligence, 16*, 5–29.;

Moir, A., & Jessel, D. (1989). *Brainsex: the real difference between men and women*. London: Mandarin.

Myors, B., Stankov, L., & Oliphant, G. W. (1989). Competing tasks, working memory and intelligence. *Australian Journal of Psychology, 41*, 1–16.

Nettelbeck, T., & Lally, M. (1976). Inspection time and measured intelligence. *British Journal of Psychology, 647*, 17–22.

Ormel, J., & Wohlfarth, T. (1991). How neuroticism, long-term difficulties, and life situation change influence psychological distress: A longitudinal model. *Journal of Personality and Social Psychology, 60*, 744–755.

O'Toole, B. I., & Stankov, L. (1992). Ultimate validity of psychological tests. *Personality and Individual Differences, 13*, 699–716.

Perlmutter, M., & Nyquist, L. (1990). Relationships between self-reported physical and mental health and intelligence performance across adulthood. *Journal of Gerontology, 45*, 145–155.

Powell, G. E. (1979). *Brain and personality*. Farnborough, UK: Saxon House.

Raven, J. C., Court, J. H., & Raven, J. (1984). *A Manual for Raven's Progressive Matrices and Vocabulary tests*. New York: Psychological Corporation.

Raz, N., Willerman, L., & Yama, M. (1987). On sense and senses: Intelligence and auditory information processing. *Personality and Individual Differences, 8*, 201–210.

Resnick, L., Berger, J. R., Shapshak, P., & Tourttellotte, W. W. (1988). Early penetration of the blood-brain barrier by HIV. *Neurology, 38*, 9–14.

Roberts, R., Beh, H., Spilsbury, G., & Stankov, L. (1991). Evidence for an attentional model of human intelligence using the competing task paradigm. *Personality and Individual Differences, 12*, 445–555.

Roberts, R. D., Beh, H. C., & Stankov, L. (1988). Hick's law, competing tasks, and intelligence. *Intelligence, 12*, 111–131.

Robinson, N., Fuller, J. H., & Edmeades, S. P. (1988). Depression and diabetes. *Diabetic Medicine, 5*, 583–591.

Robinson, T. N., Jr., & Zahn, T. P. (1988). Preparatory interval effects on the reaction time performance of introverts and extraverts. *Personality and Individual Differences, 9*, 749–762.

Rushton, J. P. (1991). Mongoloid-Caucasoid differences in brain size from military samples. *Intelligence, 15*, 351–359.

Rushton, J. P. (1993). Corrections to a paper on race and sex differences in brain size and intelligence. *Personality and Individual Differences, 15*, 229–231.

Salthouse, T. A. (1985). *A theory of cognitive aging*. Amsterdam: North Holland.

Salthouse, T. A., Kausler, D. H., & Saults, J. S. (1990). Age, self-assessed health status, and cognition. *Journal of Gerontology, 45*, 156–160.

Scarr, S. (1989). Constructivism and socially sensitive research. *American Psychologist, 44*, 849.

Schmidt, L. R. (1988). Objective personality tests: Some clinical applications. In K. M. Miller (Ed.), *The analysis of personality in research and assessment: In tribute to Raymond B. Cattell*. London: Independent Assessment and Research Centre.

Schoenthaler, S. J., Amos, S. P., Eysenck, H. J., Peritz, E., & Yudkin, J. (1991). Controlled trial of vitamin-mineral supplementation: Effects on intelligence and performance. *Personality and Individual Differences, 12*, 351–362.

Schuerger, J. M. (1986). Personality assessment by objective tests. In R. B. Cattell & R. C. Johnson (Eds.), *Functional psychological testing: Principles and instruments*. New York: Brunner/Mazel.

Snow, R. E. (1989). Aptitude-treatment interaction as a framework for research on individual differences in learning. In P. L. Ackerman, R. J. Sternberg, & R. Glaser (Eds.), *Learning and individual differences: Advances in theory and research*. New York: Freeman.

Snow, R. E., Killonen, P. C., & Marshalek, B. (1984). The topography of ability and learning correlations. In R. J. Sternberg (Ed.), *Advances in the psychology of human intelligence* (Vol. 2). Hillsdale, NJ: Erlbaum.

Spilsbury, G. (1992). Complexity as a reflection of the dimensionality of a task. *Intelligence, 16*, 31–45.

Spilsbury, G., Stankov, L., & Roberts, R. (1990). The effects of a test's difficulty on its correlation with intelligence. *Personality and Individual Differences, 11*, 1069–1077.

Stankov, L. (1978). Fluid and crystallized intelligence and broad perceptual factors among the 11 to 12 year olds. *Journal of Educational Psychology, 70*, 324–334.

Stankov, L. (1980). Psychometric factors as cognitive tasks: A note on Carroll's "new structure of intellect." *Intelligence, 4*, 65–71.

Stankov, L. (1983a). Attention and intelligence. *Journal of Educational Psychology, 75*, 471–490.

Stankov, L. (1983b). The role of competition in human abilities revealed through auditory tests. *Multivariate Behavioral Research Monographs, 83*(1).

Stankov, L. (1986a). Age-related changes in auditory abilities and in a competing task. *Multivariate Behavioral Research, 21*, 65–75.

Stankov, L. (1986b). Kvashchev's experiment: Can we boost intelligence? *Intelligence, 10*, 209–230.

Stankov, L. (1987a). Competing tasks and attentional resources: Exploring the limits of primary-secondary paradigm. *Australian Journal of Psychology, 39*(2), 123–137.

Stankov, L. (1987b). Level I/II: A theory ready to be archived. In S. Modgil & C. Modgil (Eds.), *Arthur Jensen: Consensus and controversy*. London: Falmers.

Stankov, L. (1988a). Aging, intelligence and attention. *Psychology and Aging, 3*, 59–74.

Stankov, L. (1988b). Single tests, competing tasks, and their relationship to the broad factors of intelligence. *Personality and Individual Differences, 9*, 25–33.

Stankov, L. (1989). Attentional resources and intelligence: A disappearing link. *Personality and Individual Differences, 10*, 957–968.

Stankov, L. (1994). The complexity effect phenomenon in aging is an epiphenomenon. *Personality and Individual Differences, 16*, 265–288.

Stankov, L., & Chen, K. (1988). Can we boost fluid and crystallized intelligence? A structural modeling approach. *Australian Journal of Psychology, 40*, 363–376.

Stankov, L., & Crawford, J. D. (1993). Ingredients of complexity in fluid intelligence. *Learning and Individual Differences, 5*(2), 73–111.

Stankov, L., & Cregan, A. (1993). Quantitative and qualitative properties of an intelligence test: Series completion. *Learning and Individual Differences, 5*(2), 137–169.

Stankov, L., & Dunn, S. (1993). Physical substrata of mental energy: The number of neurons and efficient cerebral metabolic processes. *Learning and Individual Differences, 5*, 241–257.

Stankov, L., Fogarty, G., & Watt, C. (1989). Competing tasks: Predictors of managerial potential. *Personality and Individual Differences, 9*, 295–302.

Stankov, L., & Horn, J. L. (1980). Human abilities revealed through auditory tests. *Journal of Educational Psychology, 72*, 19–42.

Stankov, L., Horn, J. L., & Roy, T. (1980). On the relationship between Gf/Gc theory and Jensen's Level I/Level II theory. *Journal of Educational Psychology, 72*, 796–809.

Stankov, L., & Myors, B. (1990). The relationship between working memory and intelligence: Regression and COSAN analyses. *Personality and Individual Differences, 11*, 1059–1068.

Stankov, L., & Spilsbury, G. (1978). The measurement of auditory abilities of sighted, partially sighted and blind children. *Applied Psychological Measurement, 2*, 491–503.

Stanley, J. C., & Benbow, C. P. (1986). Youths who reason exceptionally well mathematically. In R. J. Sternberg & J. E. Davidson (Eds.), *Conceptions of giftedness*. Cambridge, England: Cambridge University Press.

Stein, M., Miller, A. H., & Trestman, R. L. (1991). Depression, the immune system, and health and illness. *Archives of General Psychiatry, 48*, 171–177.

Sternberg, R. J. (1985). *Beyond IQ: A triarchic theory of human intelligence*. New York: Cambridge University Press.

Stone, S. V., & Costa, P. T. (1990). Disease-prone personality or distress-prone personality? In H. S. Friedman (Ed.), *Personality and disease*. Chichester, England: Wiley.

Sullivan, L., & Stankov, L. (1990). Shadowing and target detection as a function of age: Implications for attentional resources theory and general intelligence. *Australian Journal of Psychology, 42*, 173–185.

Suls, J., & Wan, C. K. (1989). The relationship between Type A behavior and chronic emotional distress: A meta-analysis. *Journal of Personality and Social Psychology, 57*, 503–512.

Thorndike, R. L., Hagen, E. P., & Sattler, J. M. (1986). *Stanford-Binet Intelligence Scale: Guide for administering and scoring the fourth edition*. Chicago, IL: Riverside.

Vernon, P. A. (1987). Relationship between speed-of-processing, personality and intelligence. In P. A. Vernon (Ed.), *Speed of information processing and intelligence*. Norwood, NJ: Ablex.

Vernon, P. A. (1990). The use of biological measures to estimate behavioral intelligence. *Educational Psychologist, 25*, 293–304.

Vernon, P. A. (1993). Der Zahlen-verbindungs-test and other trail-making correlates of general intelligence. *Personality and Individual Differences, 14*, 35–40.

Vernon, P. A., & Mori, M. (1992). Intelligence, reaction times, and peripheral nerve conduction velocity. *Intelligence, 16*, 273–288.

Vining, D. (1982). On the possibility of the reemergence of a dysgenic trend with respect to intelligence in American fertility differentials. *Intelligence, 6*, 241–264.

Wagner, R. K., & Sternberg, R. J. (1986). Tacit knowledge and intelligence in everyday life. In R. J. Sternberg & R. K. Wagner (Eds.), *Practical intelligence*. Cambridge, England: Cambridge University Press.

Watson, D., & Pennebaker, J. W. (1989). Health complaints, stress and distress. *Psychological Review, 96*, 324–354.

Wickens, C. D. (1980). The structure of attentional resources. In R. Nickerson (Ed.), *Attention and performance* (Vol. 8; pp. 239–257). Hillsdale, NJ: Erlbaum.

Willerman, L. (1991). Commentary on Rushton's Mongoloid-Caucasoid differences in brain size. *Intelligence, 15*, 361–364.

Willerman, L., & Bailey, J. M. (1987). A note on Thomson's sampling theory for correlations among mental tests. *Personality and Individual Differences, 8*, 943–944.

Wistow, D. J., Wakefield, J. A., & Goldsmith, W. M. (1990). The relationship between personality, health symptoms and disease. *Personality and Individual Differences, 11*, 717–724.

Zimbardo, P. G. (1992). *Psychology and life* (13th ed.). New York: HarperCollins.

Zuckerman, M. (1991). *Psychobiology of personality*. New York: Cambridge University Press.

3

Ideological Aspects of Research on Personality and Intelligence

Benjamin Beit-Hallahmi

DEFINING A FRAME OF REFERENCE

In a volume filled with research findings and incisive, state-of-the-art theoretical analysis, is this chapter necessary? In a volume such as this one, the presence of a chapter on ideology has to be justified, or at least explained. Would the presentation of the field not have been complete without it? Do we really need this kind of reflection from the sidelines of actual research? At the outset, I also need to define (and possibly justify) my terms of reference.

In his novel *La Peau de Chagrin*, published in 1832, Honore de Balzac describes a scene where a young man, entering a casino, hands his hat to the doorman. While doing that, the young man muses that maybe some researcher is doing a study of gamblers' cranial capacity by measuring their hat sizes. Does this sound familiar? How did Balzac get these ideas? And how did we?

Psychologists do not often like to speak about their conceptions of human nature, but in the area of intelligence and personality—a subfield of differential psychology—we may be ready to discuss the ultimate causes of human individuality. As we have searched for these causes, the most vociferous basic debate has been about the biological substrate of what we measure. The recognition of biological causation has seemingly been subject to historical ebb and flow, but this chapter will attempt to show that biological determination has ruled the field during most of its history. There was a short period when social determinism was dominant, but this was the exception.

The viewpoint presented in this chapter is largely that of an external spectator, observing historical developments in order to arrive at a conception of an invisible layer below the surface. Writing about the ideological background behind research publications on intelligence and personality is reminiscent of the work of the literary critic, discovering hidden meanings and patterns in literary creations. But literature may be enjoyed without the contributions of literary critics, and the same is true of research in psychology, which can be discussed and debated without reference to ideology. Analyzing value preferences and biases is an added dimension to normal academic work, exposing a hidden (or not so hidden) message.

To use a bit of fashionable literary jargon, the ideological content of any academic work is its subtext, which may be even unconscious in a cognitive sense. Nevertheless, it is still there. Recognizing such a subtext is necessary to the appreciation of wider and deeper meanings in historical trends.

Ideology is defined here as a set of beliefs that promotes a particular way of life or a particular social

Benjamin Beit-Hallahmi • Department of Psychology, University of Haifa, Mount Carmel, Haifa 31999, Israel.

International Handbook of Personality and Intelligence, edited by Donald H. Saklofske and Moshe Zeidner. Plenum Press, New York, 1995.

system. An ideology is "that part of culture which is actively concerned with the establishment and defense of patterns of beliefs and value" (Geertz, 1964, p. 64). It is an identifiable system of shared beliefs, values, and justifications that organizes cognitions, interpretations, and behavior. Each ideology asserts that its way of thinking is the best way for society as a whole; each one also involves a program of action designed to bring about the kind of ideal future it promotes. Our decisions are not always purely technical; our ideological biases are reflected in what we take for granted. Within the context of research, ideology consists of unstated value preferences behind the interpretation of findings (Kurtines, Gewirtz, & Azmitia, 1992). Typically, academic presentations separate findings (which are visible) and values (which are hidden). One may speak, and we often read, of "implicit value assumptions," which here should be made more explicit (see Beit-Hallahmi, 1974). Without much research on the psychology of bias, it is easy to observe that we are often blind to our own presuppositions and biases. Experiments on "confirmation bias," "belief perseverance," and "schema-driven processing" prove that preconceptions do matter.

Very often the term *ideology* is used in the context of partisan accusations, where it is regarded as something which has no place in science or in technology, a violation of the positivist ideal. There is a common distinction in the academic subculture between hard science and the humanities in relation to their contexts. According to Bruner (1986), scientists build a context-independent worldview, characterized by an invariance of things and events across transformations in their life experiences. Humanists understand the world in a context-sensitive way—that is, in terms of the particular shifting requirements for living in it.

The human sciences are considered the area in which ideology can and does play a clear role, whereas the "real" sciences are context free. Most psychologists, wanting to see themselves as close as possible to natural scientists, treat the issue of ideology with a deafening silence. The goal of any research on ideological trends is to disturb this silence and create historical and contemporary awareness. Looking at ideological factors is another level of historical review, and it should be undertaken to give a complete and coherent picture of the field—especially in this field, where much of the work done attracts debate and controversy. The free-market model of ideas and interest groups should lead to an acceptance of differing ideologies as competing actors. Under capitalism, there is open admission and discussion of competition, conflict, and opposing interests; in the politics of liberal capitalism, competition among interest groups is open and legitimate. Competition (through debate) in the marketplace of ideas should be similar. In the world of ideas, pluralism and ecumenism are the claimed ideal, and it is dissension and debate that are supposed to bring about progress.

Another objection to the discussion of ideology may be the perception that such discussions are inappropriate in a climate of greater conformity and ideological hegemony. The "end of ideology" was first announced in the late 1950s. More recently the "end of history" has been declared following the elimination of the USSR as a competitor to the global dominance of the United States. This chapter will go back to the so-called classical questions, showing that there is always an ideological subtext.

One may suggest that there is much ideological awareness in psychology today, thanks to the literature of the past three decades (Beit-Hallahmi, 1981). The writings summarized in this volume often prove that many psychologists are only too well aware of the social implications of their theoretical claims. At the same time, there is not enough collective awareness of the culture and ideologies of psychology itself. Discussions of ideology are usually ghettoized in "state of psychology" essays (Bevan, 1991) or in specialized history publications. Only rarely are they considered essential to a complete survey of any field in psychology.

HISTORICAL CHANGES IN PSYCHOLOGY

One view of science, known as internalism, claims that scientific knowledge is socially neutral and is divorced from considerations of economics or politics (see Merton, 1973). Such knowledge is presumed to possess a privileged status and to be independent of the subjective observer and the context of discovery. The scientific realm is insulated from intrusions and interventions by political forces. The natural, intuitive impression of scientists is that scientific activity is autonomous of its cultural origins and its social environment. We are naturally given to seeing ourselves as hardworking, pure scholars interacting with colleagues in a joint effort guided by reason and self-criticism. Bevan (1980) referred to the Cartesian view of research as an individualistic, competitive, esoteric, and intrinsically satisfying activity. The individual researcher enjoys academic freedom and follows his or her own interests in deciding on what is to be studied and by what means. The goal is achieving theory-based knowledge to be published in esoteric, highly technical journals; disinterested knowledge is, however, the claim and the ideal. The objectivity endeavor means that we try to eliminate our prejudices from the search for truth. When objectivity is followed, our truth claims are separated, as much as possible, from personal values, prejudices, and emotions.

The externalist school of the history of knowledge asserts that factors outside the research process itself explain its particular course. This view is tied to the academic field of the sociology of knowledge. Its intellectual roots go back to Karl Marx and several historians who dared to suggest correlations between the most esoteric creations of the human mind and grand historical trends. One of the most amazing (and least known) claims along these lines was made by Spengler (1926), who suggested that even the development of mathematics—the most abstract of human endeavors—reflected the historical growth and decline stages of all human civilizations.

Why ask externalist questions? There is a natural resistance to this kind of historical-social analysis. Science likes to emphasize its independence from other institutions in society, and scientists consider themselves as autonomous in their pursuits and decisions. Scientists like to see themselves as individualistic and nonconformist, if not self-critically as prima donnas. They are supposed to be counterdependent and antiauthoritarian, and originality, after all, is the hallmark of progress in science. But the viewpoint that describes scientists as independent creators of ideas is narrow and unimaginative.

The reality of science as social process is expected to transform subjectivity (in the individual researcher) into objectivity (in multiple independent observers), but it may lead to less desirable and unintended effects. Research takes place in a sociopolitical milieu that may exert pressure on hypothesis formation and subsequently on data collection. "Behind all scientific studies there is not only the drive to understand but the compulsion to persuade. All scholarship, including science, uses argument, and argument uses rhetoric" (Bevan, 1991, p. 478).

To explain historical developments in psychology we need to use the concept of zeitgeist (i.e., nonsubstantive influences that make up the historical and psychological context of research; Boring, 1929). The idea of the zeitgeist does not imply ideological exclusivity or uniformity. Different schools and approaches may coexist during the same era, but there are changes in their relative importance, as we shall observe below.

All scientific research expresses in various nontrivial ways the cultural context in which it appears and the sociopsychological characteristics of those responsible for developing it (e.g., Haraway, 1989; Latour & Woolgar, 1979; Traweek, 1988). Even in the case of creative artists—who, according to the universal stereotype, are truly individualistic or even narcissistic—more and more philosophers and sociologists are claiming that art is always institutional rather than individual, created by social networks and defined by cultural ideologies (Aagaard-Mogensen, 1976). The working model presented here is a realistic zeitgeist model, combining internal and external factors. Group and individual behaviors are multidetermined, and manifest or stated reasons can be only a subset of the total causes. Psychologists will accept these claims about all groups and individuals; why not about themselves as researchers? Why are latent reasons denied? Are they really illegitimate? We might follow a sociological or anthropological vantage point and look at psychology as a human culture, characterized by dominant beliefs and ideologies, undergoing struggle and change. When a certain viewpoint is hegemonic or central, or when the spirit of the times may be changing, our zeitgeist model is challenged to offer explanations.

Left and Right in Social Science and in Psychology

For most of its history, modern psychology has been dominated by theories originating in the United States and the English-speaking world. Its ideology has thus reflected the liberal biases of North American social science (Ladd & Lipset, 1975). This ideological liberalism is made up of five elements (see Hogan & Emler, 1978):

1. There is no innate human nature, and personality is a reflection of social environments.
2. There are no innate differences among people, especially of the kind that might lead to differential social status.
3. People are rational.
4. Given the above, human beings are perfectible and progress unlimited. Differences in status will be eliminated by equalizing opportunities.

5. Existing social institutions are to be changed or eliminated to ensure progress.

The conservative ideology, held by a minority among social scientists during this same period, is expressed in the following alternative assumptions:

1. There is an innate human nature.
2. Differences in innate endowments lead to differences in status.
3. Individuals are often irrational and behave in self-defeating ways.
4. Social progress may be an illusion.
5. Social engineering is detrimental to historical group and individual identities.

The debate is about human nature as it is and as it should be, about our ideal human and our ideal society: What kind of world do we want to see? The left and right ideologies imply two views of remodeling humanity; one favors radical changes, and the other a return to earlier historical structures. We are always guided by an image of humans (a) as they are, and more importantly, (b) as they should be. Our conception of human nature leads to our conception of the human future. The right philosophical position is that (a) is equal to (b). The left view is that (a) and (b) are far apart, but could be moved closer.

The liberal-left worldview states that destiny is determined by social structure, not genes and capacities. Social reality is not natural or given, but ordered. Our "objective" descriptions or objectivizing way of looking at social reality serve to legitimize social arrangements. As suggested by social constructionists, "Legitimations explain the institutional order by ascribing cognitive validity to its meanings . . . and justify the order by giving normative dignity to its practical imperatives" (Berger & Luckmann, 1967, p. 93). We should be watchful and suspicious of conservative interests masquerading as objective descriptions.

For the conservative ideology, the starting point is a natural science view of social reality and humanity. This viewpoint tells us that generally speaking, social institutions are pretty much the way they should be, and individuals get what they deserve. Thus observers may regard victims as deserving their state, a common illusion in modern society (Lerner, 1980). "Nature" is often the model for human society, and what is "natural" is conceived to be necessary and deserving. Such a biologistic view tends to imply that what is, ought to be. The goal is not social change and human betterment, but a reflection of social realities.

LOOKING AT DIFFERENTIAL PSYCHOLOGY

The area of intelligence and personality is special because of the history of intelligence testing, an area mired in heated debates since its inception. Many topics in this area simultaneously represent basic, applied, and policy questions.

One cannot escape the memory of such historical debates and debacles as that concerning the IQ measurements of immigrants and soldiers in the United States before 1920. It would be naive or hypocritical to suggest that the area of intelligence and personality is in some way immune to the ideological undercurrents that have characterized differential psychology. Any doubts about the relevance and importance of ideological debates in this area should be dispelled by the following research illustration.

Testing Group Differences and Item Bias in Rats

The debate over group differences in IQ scores led to an ingenious study by Harrington (1988) that addressed a psychometric problem through the use of an animal model. Laboratory rats from six genetic strains were trained in standard mazes and then tested on their performance. Tests were constructed by selecting representative maze behavior; the items selected for the tests were shown to have a clear majority bias, which was considered to be inevitable. The methodological and operational details of this study are not of interest here. What is significant is psychology's preoccupation with the issues of "cognitive competence" and its validity within the context of the nature-nurture debate. A look at the history of experimental psychology shows that Harrington was not the first to use the rat as an animal model for issues having to do with human intelligence. Selective breeding of maze-dull and maze-bright laboratory rats started soon after World War I and eventually led to the appearance of behavior genetics as a research field (Innis, 1992). Some outside observers may use this line of research to criticize psychology for its emblematic use of rats to address serious human issues. A more sympathetic observer (like this one) will regard this as a reflection of serious concern, and even a collective self-questioning, on the part of the field.

It has been suggested that belief biases are dominant in the psychology of religion (Beit-Hallahmi, 1989). Can we say that there is always a hidden (or not so hidden) political agenda in differential psychology?

Pastore (1949) convincingly demonstrated the primacy of politics in the nature-nurture controversy, stating that "the sociopolitical allegiance of the scientists were a significant determinant of their position on nature-nurture questions. . . . These allegiances had a marked effect upon the formulation of a hypothesis and the method of its verification, the conclusions drawn from an investigation, and the statement of implications of these conclusions for society" (p. 181). In other words, psychologists have ideologies and value commitments, and these are among several determinants of findings and theories.

Sherwood and Nataupsky (1968) even showed that psychologists' positions regarding black-white intelligence differences were related to biographical characteristics of the investigator. Samelson (1978) suggested that the growing number of "ethnics," especially of Jewish descent, entering psychology as students and researchers in the 1930s was closely related to changes in ideological climate: "In the subsequent shift from race psychology to concern with prejudice, one finds names like Klineberg, Herskovits, Feingold, Viteles, Lasker, Katz, Lehman, Horowitz, Fukuda, and Yeung" (p. 273). The views of such "ethnics" reflected not their genetics but their social situation and history (Beit-Hallahmi, 1992).

Interests: Declared and Hidden

Scientists do not like to have their actions explained based on considerations that are other than intrinsic. Psychologists have developed a theoretical expertise, and they are proud of it. They want discussions to be technically "pure" or reduced to "apolitical," technical issues. We point to a conflict of interest when an economist or politician has stock in a certain corporation and is involved in decisions or recommendations affecting that stock. We demand disclosure of any financial interests for a politician, and we expect a partisan point of view from an expert witness hired by one side in a dispute. Can we claim that psychologists may have conscious or unconscious interests as members of social groups? We represent science, but we also represent our respective social group, class, race, or sex. Can we move beyond these collective or individual concerns?

A class-interest analysis looks for those who benefit from a particular position. Harwood (1982) suggested that the U.S. behavioral science establishment in the 1960s was committed to environmentalism in large part because of its involvement in early intervention programs. As one witness recalls: "Those were heady days as scores of programs were concocted in Washington, social scientists were accorded an importance akin to what the atomic scientists has once been given" (Sarason, 1978, p. 832). Once so many researchers had become publicly engaged in promoting Head Start and similar programs—and became the financial beneficiaries of such programs—they could not have been expected to accept hereditarian criticism of the whole enterprise (Jensen, 1969), even when faced with disappointing results.

Differential Psychology, History, and Ideology

Every field in psychology must reflect dominant theoretical and ideological biases in the discipline as whole, as well as its own hegemonic bent. The ideological questions in this area are naturally tied to the history of work on individual differences, where the ideological substrate of work has never been hidden. Although experimental psychology for most of the twentieth century has been dominated by behaviorism, which has disregarded the relevance of heredity and attempted to discover the laws of learning in a malleable organism, the tradition of mental testing was always biased in the opposite direction. As opposed to the liberal ideology described above, one might say that this tradition has always had a clearly illiberal bent.

The individual-differences tradition has not been developed in a social vacuum. Differential psychology has always been oriented toward application, either at the individual (e.g., clinical) level or at the level of policy recommendations. Historically and ideologically, the individual-differences tradition in psychology was committed, starting with Francis Galton, to individualization rather than equality as a social ideal (A. R. Buss, 1976). Galton was not only the founder (in 1865) of differential psychology but also the man who coined the term *eugenics*, having in mind not only "improving stock" but also helping more "suitable races" prevail over the less suitable ones (Galton, 1883, 1907).

This emphasis on heredity was typical of the English-language testing movement. When Alfred Binet was developing intelligence tests for the first time, he argued quite clearly that intelligence represented not a fixed characteristic of the individual but a score on a test that could be improved with training (Cairns & Ornstein, 1979). It was only when Binet's technology crossed the English Channel (and then the

Atlantic Ocean) that it became identified with hereditarianism and a nature-nurture distinction.

It is fair to claim that the mental testing movement in the English-speaking world was born under the sign of eugenics and scientific racism; however, this was part of the general zeitgeist that very few escaped at the time. Eugenic views were quite common among early 20th-century intellectuals. For example, H. G. Wells believed in "social engineering" that would eliminate undesirable humans (about 50% of the world's population) and promote racial homogeneity (Coren, 1992).

Today some of us might be shocked by such ideas, but let us remember the days of imperialism and colonialism. A term such as *racial hygiene*, which may seem horrifying to us, was not unheard of in social science literature before World War II. Both positive and negative judgments regarding "national character" and race—considered beyond the pale today—were acceptable then, before decolonization and the rise of the Third World. Scientists did not create the climate of opinion of their time; they simply reflected it. Thus it is sobering to read what Karl Pearson (founding director of the Eugenics Laboratory in 1907 and Galton Professor of Eugenics in London in 1911) wrote in the 1890s: "It is a false view of human solidarity, a weak humanitarianism, not a true humanism, which regrets that a capable and stalwart race of white men should replace a dark-skinned tribe which can neither utilize its land for the full benefit of mankind, nor contribute its quota to the common stock of human knowledge" (Pearson, 1937, p. 310). Galton's British disciples, starting with Pearson and continuing with R. A. Fisher, Charles Spearman, Cyril Burt, Raymond B. Cattell, and Hans J. Eysenck, have all been tied to the eugenics tradition.

In the United States, Davenport (1920) presented an actual research and policy program regarding inherited disorders and undesirable behaviors and personality traits within the eugenics framework, which was at the time quite respectable. As we all know, eugenics in the United States reached a degree of practical influence. Involuntary sterilization programs were in existence in most states, were approved by the courts, and continued to function even after the decline of eugenics in public opinion in the 1930s (Reilly, 1991). Between 1907 and 1965, more than 60,000 men and women in the United States were subjected to court-ordered sterilization in an effort to reduce the number of children born to "mental defectives." The development of vasectomy in 1898 and tubal ligation in the 1920s led some policymakers to the belief that there were modern and efficient solutions to the problems of "degenerates"—individuals whose heredity predisposed them to crime, idleness, insanity, idiocy, alcoholism, and poverty. Such ideas were in evidence in the budding social sciences of the time. In 1930 the *American Sociological Review* published an article advocating eugenic measures, and in 1935 an article in *American Anthropologist* predicted that the use of sterilization would eliminate 90% of all crime, insanity, mental debility and deficiency, and abnormal sexuality within 100 years (Biervliet et al., 1980).

Robert M. Yerkes, Carl C. Brigham, Lewis M. Terman, and Henry H. Goddard, leaders and pioneers in IQ testing, were all members of eugenics organizations set up in the United States after World War I. L. M. Terman (1947) published research reports in the official mouthpiece of the Eugenics Society. Moreover, psychologists in Great Britain and in the United States have turned to the general public with great alarms stemming from IQ findings indicating an overall decline in mental abilities. Nothing of the kind has ever happened in any other area of research in psychology, because no other area of research seemed to have such implications.

TECHNOLOGY AND POLICY

Why would psychological research in a certain area be contentious or controversial? Answers to this question seem to be determined by the relation of the area to social and political power, its potential to affect people's lives, and its inherent complexity for the researcher in light of the above factors. Even in contemporary physics, political and financial considerations are recognized as having a major impact on research directions (Dyson, 1993). Ideological commitments may affect research on two levels: through external influences in the form of research support, and through the researchers' own positions on issues. All ideological positions have social engineering implications and are reflected in advocacy of public policy.

Bevan (1980) suggested that technology in psychology is guided by the Baconian view of research as a social, collaborative means for contributing to the general public welfare, where any specific area of study is guided by a mission orientation. The emphasis is on the pragmatic payoff of reducing high-priority social and psychological problems, as well as on communicating with lay decision makers concerning programs and policies.

Liberals often express misgivings that the search for certainty is likely to lead to tenacious prejudices. They hope that all prejudices can be subject to revision in the light of evidence, favor openness to discussions and self-criticism, or even hold up continuous debate as an ideal. This laudable ideal certainly fits the academic world, but what are we to do when applied psychology is forced to make decisions and affect human lives?

The public is looking over our collective shoulder in some areas of research because the issues seem relevant to life and nontechnical. Both theoretical and technical questions that refer to "applied" issues of reliability and validity—and the appropriate use of measuring instruments, even when they seem quite narrow—are tied to a broader perspective on humanity and individual destiny. Beyond that is ideology, with implications for social issues such as education. Our beliefs about an unchanging human nature or about the impact of history and culture are related to specific theoretical and practical choices.

Following the presentation of research findings, psychologists may sometimes be called upon to suggest policies and even interventions. (An intervention is defined here as a well-defined procedure for correcting a specified deficiency in the recipient.) Some psychologists have been eager to advocate such policies and interventions. It not just that psychologists recognize the implications of their work and offer social commentary, but that they become advocates. Using their privileged position, they may choose to address not only the sophisticated audience of their peers, but also the lay public. Other psychologists may decide that their work should not have any practical uses or policy consequences, and they may not want to get involved in conflicts between opposing interest groups (i.e., politics) out of a desire to avoid undue criticism and confrontations. Such researchers should be well advised to stay away from research in personality and intelligence.

The field of intelligence and personality grew out of testing, which has developed as a technology, growing out of psychology as a science. When we observe technology, we have to realize that it follows a different set of objectives than science does. Every textbook on the history of psychology tells us that testing is the greatest achievement and the foremost social presence of psychology as a discipline. We have concepts that are clearly important and intriguing, and we have ways of measuring them. Whether the latter are called tests of cognitive skills, intelligence, or IQ, they are an applied instrument for classifying individuals according to ability as well as for collecting data on such theoretical questions as nature versus nurture, the structure of intelligence, or the interaction of intelligence and personality. We have data that we, as psychologists, find quite exciting. We have theoretical and practical questions that we find challenging. This derivation of technology from science is usually viewed as a major scientific achievement. Another way of looking at the same history, though, is to define it as a mental testing movement, an individual-differences movement equipped with ideology as well as technology.

There are implicit human ideals in the intelligence and personality literature. The whole enterprise is part of the individual-differences tradition and follows the latter's traditional ideology. Theories about individual or group differences may in reality be expressions of concern or ideological attempts to promote or subvert political goals. Our beliefs about an unchanging human nature, or about the impact of history and culture, are related to specific theoretical and practical choices.

DECLINE OF BIOLOGY

One common expression of biological determinism in recent generations has been racism. The ideology of racism is a system of beliefs that ascribes central importance to presumed racial differences. Racism asserts that psychological qualities are racially characteristic and that they are transmitted, along with physical traits, by heredity. These assertions are used as explanations for historical and social processes. Such theories were quite influential in the Western world between 1840 and 1940. In one popular racist theory, humanity was divided into the Negroid, Nordic, Alpine, Mediterranean, and Asiatic races, and this division was widely accepted among some of the psychologists who pioneered IQ testing (Yerkes, 1923).

Scientific attempts to prove racist hypotheses developed in the 19th century and reached a point of major influence in the early 20th century. Scientific racism was widely accepted by the intellectual elite of the Western world until the 1930, then declined sharply toward midcentury. In the 1920s one could witness the rise of environmental approaches that emphasized the roles of learning, culture, and social factors rather than race. In addition to the major economic and political upheavals that constituted the crisis of global capitalism between 1920 and 1945, there were also more immediate influences in the social sciences that helped the trend away from racism. We should not underestimate the effects of psychoanalysis, which emphasized early childhood experiences—rather than hereditary factors—as determining both normal and pathological personality development.

The tradition of social determinism flourished between the 1930s and the 1960s. It emphasized the importance of cultural factors, transmitted through membership in social classes and illustrated the lingering effects of economic disadvantage (e.g., Beilin, 1956; Blau, 1981; Bond, 1981; Havighurst, 1976; Kohn, 1963; Lesser, Fifer, & Clark, 1965; Rutter & Madge, 1977; Swinehart, 1962; Tuma & Livson, 1960). Social class background was tied to not only intelligence but also personality (Rosenberg & Pearlin, 1978), the achievement motive (the personality variable considered crucial for status attainment; Rosen, 1956), and serious psychological problems, including schizophrenia (Hollingshead & Redlich, 1958; Schwab & Schwab, 1978).

This academic enterprise of liberalism in the United States is linked to such political changes as the founding of the U.S. Commission on Civil Rights and the creation of various "affirmative action" programs, including those related to admissions at higher educational institutions. The 1954 U.S. Supreme Court *Brown v. Board of Education* decision, which ended school segregation, referred to social science research as part of its background and justification. Most of the research cited in the "social science statement" presented to the Court had been done long before the issue was litigated, and so reflected a dominant and longstanding liberal viewpoint (Clark, 1979; Cook, 1979; Gerard, 1983).

The environmental-sociological tradition has generated a discourse on equity that has focusing on education as giving access to power and privilege (e.g., Chesler & Cave, 1981). This discourse included debates about compensatory programs, multicultural classroom strategies, and the equalization of educational outputs. Compensatory education, and affirmative action in general, follows the assumption that achievement differences among social groups are circumstantial and will disappear under more favorable conditions. This concern, which started historically with African-Americans and the poor in the United States, has spread to other minorities and all those defined as disadvantaged (e.g., the handicapped).

The liberal position has been criticized for not really challenging the conservative worldview (deLone, 1979). As part of this radical critique within psychology, a literature dealing with "primary prevention"—meaning the structural-societal prevention of individual psychopathology and social problems—appeared in the 1960s. Primary prevention calls for nothing less than the restructuring of society in order to achieve better personal adjustment (Joffe & Albee, 1981).

THE BIOLOGICAL RENAISSANCE

Recent history, however, shows a remarkable rise of biological determinism in several forms. More studies have emphasized genetic factors in intelligence (e.g., Scarr & Weinberg, 1978) and in personality (e.g., Tellegen et al., 1988). We have observed the return of genetic theories of criminal tendencies (Mednick & Christiansen, 1977) as well as biological theories of alcoholism and psychosis. This has paralleled the rise of biological psychiatry, as schizophrenia (among other psychoses) is almost universally viewed now as biological and genetic in origin (Gottesman, 1991).

The appearance of sociobiology in the 1970s is part of this historical wave. Sociobiology combines population genetics, evolutionary theory, and ethology to explaining seeming generalities in human behavior (e.g., Symons, 1980). Wilson (1975) described as "personality differences" (p. 549) unique characteristics that lead to deviations from the biological norm, but sociobiological ideas have been borrowed even in the field of personality. The impact of sociobiology has been quite noticeable, as all the human sciences in their turn responded to the new challenge with either surrender or defiance (Losco & Baird, 1982; Rosenberg, 1980). Evolutionary psychological studies of human behavior have become more common even in ways that are not connected to sociobiology (Gangestad & Simpson, 1990).

There has been a biologization of personality theory (D. M. Buss, 1984, 1990), as hereditarian and nativist viewpoints regarding both personality and psychopathology are now more popular than ever (Gazzaniga, 1993; Gorenstein, 1992). Brain mechanisms and physiological processes are investigated more ambitiously and more broadly than ever in connection with both normal and pathological functioning (Hollandswort, 1990; Thompson, Crinella, & Yu, 1990), and this trend is likely to lead to a psychobiology of intelligence and personality (Zuckerman, 1991).

Any discussion of intelligence and personality seeks to end in a broader integration. The biological model seems to be a good organizing principle for this field. In terms of political implications, the biological determinist view insists that the presumed natural equality in traits do not exist. Biological determinism views observed economic, intellectual, and social inferiorities in particular groups as the result of innate and inherited qualities.

If this volume had been published in 1960, there would have been almost no mention of biological approaches. Biological notions were then almost beyond the pale. The remarkable change over the past three decades needs to be discussed within our zeitgeist framework. The enormous progress in the life sciences since 1945 has naturally affected the zeitgeist of psychology.

As indicted above, liberalism dominated the U.S. academic world from 1945 until the 1960s, a period of unprecedented economic productivity and unparalleled optimism. Paralleling the New Left of the 1960s, though, there was a New Right that was becoming quite visible in psychology (Beit-Hallahmi, 1984). The rise of the New Right has coincided with the slowdown (and eventual crisis) that has affected the world economy since the late 1960s and has been most pronounced since 1973.

If the New Left was created through its rejection of the old Left (i.e., communism), the new right has tried to disassociate itself from the old Right (i.e., fascism). Theoretical issues tied to the traditional right—among them genetic influences, racism, and inequality—have been discredited by their association with Nazism. Nevertheless, ties between the New Right and the old can still be found. A cursory examination of neofascist publications in Europe will discover the names of some leading psychologists in our field. Hans J. Eysenck, a major hereditarian, is a member of the honorary advisory board of the racist *Mankind Quarterly* (where the U.S. segregationist Henry A. Garrett served on the editorial board), a journal published since 1960. Arthur R. Jensen is an honorary adviser and active contributor to the neofascist German journal *Neue Anthropologie*, which has been published since 1973.

Connections to the eugenics movement of the early twentieth century also can be found. Burt (1969) is clearly a eugenics enthusiast, stating that "the overall efficiency of the citizens who make up a nation or a state must in the last resort depend on what has been called its 'chromosomal pool' " (p. 84). Jensen (1973) notes explicitly that "current welfare policies, unaided by genetic foresight, could lead to the genetic enslavement of a substantial segment of our population" (p. 179).

The gap between the Old Right and the New Right in the United States is only an illusion. The Old Right in differential psychology consisted of groups and theories supporting hereditarianism, eugenics, and racial segregation as social policy. The post-1960s New Right is directly connected to the old segregationists. Moreover, the neo-hereditarian campaign started soon after the 1954 U.S. Supreme Court *Brown* decision, not merely as a reaction to the events of the 1960s.

A typical link between the old and new right is suggested by funding sources (Mehler, 1983). The Pioneer Fund was founded in 1937 by Frederick Osborn, secretary of the American Eugenics Society, and Harry Laughlin, director of the Eugenics Record Office, to promote "practical education in racial constitution and family-stock qualities" (Laughlin received an honorary doctorate in medicine from the Nazis in 1936.) Since the 1930s, the fund has been directed by well-known conservative U.S. politicians and academics, and it has provided funds for anti-integration activities. In the 1960s and 1970s, it supported psychologists Audrey Shuey and Arthur R. Jensen. In the 1980s, it has become a major benefactor of psychological research on the heredity of personality characteristics.

The Ideology: A Return to the 19th Century

A broader historical perspective reminds us that biological determinism actually ruled human thought from the days of ancient Greece to the early 20th century. Social determinism thus may have been only a brief detour from biological thinking. Similarly, scientific racism and eugenics were dominant in social science literature well into the 1930s. To characterize the current biologistic zeitgeist, we may look at similar ideas a hundred years ago.

The 19th century was characterized by numerous biological theories of personality and conduct. One major example is the concept of degeneracy, which denoted a hereditary state of nervous, physical, and moral decay and was tied to so-called race and group differences. In Europe at the time, Jews were considered to suffer from higher rates of such "degenerative psychoses" as depression, schizophrenia, and paranoia. Jean-Martin Charcot, the leading neurologist at the time, was a believer in heredity as the cause of mental illness and developed the concept of a "famille nevropathique." He also argued that there was a particular propensity among Jews for certain types of inherited mental disorders (Gelfand, 1989). Sigmund Freud, an ardent admirer of Charcot, also adopted this hereditarian viewpoint in his earliest writings on hysteria before developing the theory of psychoanalysis.

Starting in the early 19th century, measurements of the human skull were thought to be related to many psychological variables. Cranial measures of different racial groups were collected and studied for many decades by anthropologists, who considered them to be genetically caused and to reflect "racial" differences and qualities. The 19th century saw the rise of an "anthropometric" movement based on the notion of measuring individual differences in physical features (e.g., cranial size) considered to be related to psychological features. Craniometry and the anthropometry movement followed the 18th-century popularity systematic physiognomy and were connected to the phrenology movement, which was the predecessor of many later developments in academic psychology. The emphasis on objective, physical measurements and on individual differences paved the way for the appearance of the psychometry movement later on.

Brigham (1923), in interpreting his findings regarding group differences in intelligence, quoted approvingly statements by the well-known racist Madison Grant regarding the superiority of the "Nordic race . . . a race of soldiers, sailors, adventurers, and explorers, but above all of rulers, organizers, and aristocrats. . . . Chivalry and knighthood . . . are peculiarly Nordic traits, and feudalism, class distinctions, and race pride among Europeans are traceable . . . to the north. . . . The pure Nordic peoples are characterized by a greater stability and steadiness than are mixed peoples such as the Irish" (p. 182). As history seems to be repeating itself, are we to expect such quotations in the differential-psychology literature soon? Will it become fashionable again to speak about races? Will there be a return to anthropometry and craniometry?

Indeed, we can encounter these ideas in the literature already. In the late twentieth century, we can observe a return to "cranial capacity" (Willerman, Schultz, Rutledge, & Bigler, 1991) and reports on differences in such capacity as related to IQ differences among races (Rushton, 1991). Is this a new scientific racism? Yes, it is. In the 1980s, claims of the innate superiority of racial groups reappeared, with North American authors viewing Asians as superior—apparently because of the outstanding scholastic achievements of Asian immigrants in the United States and the remarkable economic growth of Japan since World War II. Rushton (1988) suggested a "phylogenetic" ranking on which "Orientals" (i.e., Japanese and Chinese) are superior to Caucasoids, who in turn are superior to Africans on IQ scores, as well as in many positive social behaviors. Rushton, as well as Lynn in Chapter 6 of this volume, seems to recapitulate the 19th-century racial theories of Arthur de Gobineau, with a slight theoretical change (the anointing of Orientals as the master race).

Following these recent changes, is there now a chance for the return of eugenics? Indeed there is. Herrnstein (1989) warned the U.S. public against an impending decline of "four-to-five points in IQ over the coming five to six generations. . . . Because parents and children tend to have comparable levels of measurable intelligence, the average intelligence of the population will decline across generations to the extent that reproduction shifts towards the lower end of the scale (assuming no other influence on the average level)" (p. 76). According to Herrnstein, "differential fertility" is a major threat to North American society as it competes with other nations, especially the Japanese, whom he presents as having a higher average IQ. Thirty years ago, one might have proposed the return of craniometry or eugenics as a fantasy or joke, but these ideas are a serious reality in the literature of academic psychology today. Are to expect a rediscovery of Cesare Lombroso, with his original ideas about genius, insanity, and criminality?

Explaining the New Zeitgeist

Naturally, we do not have a complete (or even partial) explanation for these recent changes. The internalist explanation suggests that research findings helped to change psychologists' minds. The zeitgeist model, though, leads us to ask about changes in the world beyond academic psychology. If such ideas reappear, there must have been a recurrence of the social conditions responsible for the old-new ideological climate. Psychologists may have followed their data more than political developments and ideological fads, but a new climate of opinion made it possible to ask new questions. And although the War on Poverty indeed ended in defeat (or in the victory of poverty and related ills), this probably had little to do with anybody's genes (Sarason, 1978). The historical decline of socialism is connected to the resurgence of biological determinism. At the same time, though, the continuing crisis of capitalism—involving hundreds of millions all over the world who cannot find productive work, leading to cynicism and pessimism—may be tied to biologism.

HAS BIOLOGY WON?

Is this the end of environmentalism? Not yet. The opposition to biologism is not likely to disappear, for reasons that are both theoretical and practical. Research based on the social determinist model continues to be widely published (e.g., Belle, 1990; Capron & Duyme, 1989; Duyme, 1988), and radical critiques of IQ testing still abound (Seligman, 1992). On a basic theoretical level, severe criticisms of the application of biological concepts to human populations have come from biologists who claim that such concepts as heritability—which is now a technical term of quantitative genetics—cannot be used in behavior genetics (Hirsch, McGuire, & Vetta, 1980; Layzer, 1974). The conceptual (using biological terms properly) and practical (using equivalent testing procedures) challenges involved have not been met by researchers. This kind of critique is not environmentalist by any means; one of the vociferous critics is Jerry Hirsch, an antienvironmentalist who is opposed to the application of biological concepts in psychology (Hirsch, 1978).

Some critics of recent work emphasize the threats to privacy and civil liberties growing out of the use of genetic predictions (Hubbard & Wald, 1993). Though psychologists like Herrnstein call for eugenics policies to preserve the "national IQ," one can imagine totally different policy recommendations coming from benevolent psychologists, such as welfare and affirmative action for the "biologically challenged" and genetically impaired.

A new theoretical challenge to a biological view of group differences comes from a cultural-historical approach. Group comparisons often focus on persistent problems among underachieving and disadvantaged groups. In the United States attention has focused on one such group: underclass African-Americans. But white Appalachians, who also display a picture of extreme underachievement and numerous social problems, have attracted much less attention. These whites in the Cumberland mountain area are of pure British ancestry; nowhere else can one find a more homogeneous group genetically or culturally. This group of pure WASPs seem to belie many of the assumptions of neoracist models, while it fits the idea of cultural patterns transmitted (not via DNA) across generations. Psychologists are rediscovering cultural transmission as the importance of persistent cultural traditions is being recognized more often (Nisbett, 1993). This kind of research should provide more insights into persistent patterns of achievement or underachievement.

CONCLUSION

As was pointed out above, any discussion of this area is overshadowed by its history of controversy and by the real social and educational problems echoed in the academic literature.

> Every point of view in the social sciences, every theoretical model, every hypothesis, will have value implications—because that is the way nature is constructed and the human mind operates. Thus ultimately it is not a question of being careful, of using only operational definitions, of employing an objective data language. The problem of ideology is a problem from which there is no escape (Hogan & Emler, 1978, p. 530).

The internalist view of changes in the intelligence and personality area (which combines both science and technology) naturally describes progress toward an ideal, in this case the dream of having a unified field under a clear theoretical umbrella. Rushton (1988, 1990) offers us a clear theoretical integration of this area based on evolutionary principles and genetic factors, including the notion of race differences along a phylogenetic scale of development. Shall we adopt this model?

The great questions about world historical changes remain unanswered. The rise and fall of global empires, revolutions, upheavals—these are the question that historians tackle. When it comes to the history of psychology, the questions are easier to answer because we only mirror bigger trends. Psychology is only the surf on the breaking waves of social forces. Research is a reflection, not a cause, of public opinion, and we are influenced rather than influencing others. This was the case in 1954, where social science evidence was presented to the U.S. Supreme Court with great effect to support a liberal decision in favor of school desegregation, as well as in 1924, when IQ findings were presented to the U.S. Congress without much effect to support immigration restrictions (Samelson, 1975). The liberal, environmentalist hiatus between the 1930s and the 1960s in the United States was but a reflection of social changes (Samelson, 1978). With the end of mass immigration after 1924, claims about the IQ inferiority of southern European "races" disappeared; concern with domestic conflicts led to studies on how to reduce prejudice.

The consequences of discussing ideological implications should be more awareness on the part of psychologists to the clearly predictable effects of their work. There is always a human social message in what we write and say as psychologists, in research or in practice. We are all human beings first and scientists later. Our identity in terms of gender, ethnicity, and class—which is a reflection of real interests—must have an impact on our research work and policy decisions. Our opinions as citizens should be expressed, and our interests declared. As these are reflected in our writings themselves and in our nonacademic affiliations, they are likely to lead to public reactions. If you accept money from the Pioneer Fund, don't be surprised if your decision is discussed critically. If you associate with Nazis (which is your perfect right in a democracy), don't be surprised if such an affiliation is mentioned.

The problem is that measurement and classification always have a moral or judgmental aftereffect. Any mental measurement is a ranking of someone's self, and few people like to be measured and evaluated. There are serious consequences when we define somebody as "retarded" or assign a child to a "special education" class. The nature-nurture debate will not disappear from the scene any more than discussions of the mind-body problem will. The difference is that although the mind-body debate may seem purely philosophical in terms of social consequences, the former issue will forever remain political in every sense.

REFERENCES

Aagaard-Mogensen, L. (Ed.). (1976). *Culture and art.* Atlantic Highlands, NJ: Humanities Press.

Beilin, H., (1956). The pattern of postponability and its relation to social class mobility. *Journal of Social Psychology, 44,* 33–48.

Beit-Hallahmi, B. (1974). Salvation and its vicissitudes: Clinical psychology and political values. *American Psychologist, 24,* 36–42.

Beit-Hallahmi, B. (1981). Psychology and ideology. In R. Solo & C. H. Anderson (Eds.), *Value judgment and income distribution.* New York: Praeger.

Beit-Hallahmi, B. (1984). *The new right in contemporary psychology.* Unpublished manuscript.

Beit-Hallahmi, B. (1989). *Prolegomena to the psychological study of religion.* Lewisburg, PA: Bucknell University Press.

Beit-Hallahmi, B. (1992). *Original sins.* London: Pluto.

Belle, D. (1990). Poverty and women's mental health. *American Psychologist, 45,* 385–389.

Berger, P. L., & Luckmann, T. (1967). *The social construction of reality.* Garden City, NY: Doubleday.

Bevan, W. (1980). On getting in bed with a lion. *American Psychologist, 35,* 779–789.

Bevan, W. (1991). Contemporary psychology: A tour inside the onion. *American Psychologist, 46,* 475–483.

Biervliet, H., et al. (1980). Biologism, racism and eugenics in the anthropology and sociology of the 1930s. *Netherlands Journal of Sociology, 16,* 69–92.

Blau, Z. S. (1981). *Black children/white children: Competence, socialization, and social structure.* New York: Free Press.

Bond, G. C. (1981). Social economic status and educational achievement: A review article. *Anthropology and Education Quarterly, 12,* 227–257.

Boring, E. G. (1929). *A history of experimental psychology.* New York: Century.

Brigham, C. C. (1923). *A study of American intelligence.* Princeton, NJ: Princeton University Press.

Bruner, J. (1986). *Actual minds, possible worlds.* Cambridge, MA: Harvard University Press.

Burt, C. (1969). The inheritance of mental ability. In D. Wolfle (Ed.), *The discovery of talent.* Cambridge, MA: Harvard University Press.

Buss, A. R. (1976). Galton and the birth of differential psychology and eugenics: Social, political, and economic forces. *Journal of the History of the Behavioral Sciences, 12,* 47–58.

Buss, D. M. (1984). Evolutionary biology and personality psychology: Toward a conception of human nature and individual differences. *American Psychologist, 39,* 1135–1147.

Buss, D. M. (1990). Toward a biologically informed psychology of personality. *Journal of Personality, 58,* 1–16.

Cairns, R. H., & Ornstein, P. A. (1979). Developmental psychology. In E. Hearst (Ed.), *The first century of experimental psychology.* Hillsdale, NJ: Erlbaum.

Capron, C., & Duyme, M. (1989). Assessment of effects of socio-economic status on IQ in a full cross-fostering study. *Nature, 340,* 552–554.

Chesler, M. A., & Cave, W. M. (1981). *A sociology of education: Access to power and privilege.* New York: Macmillan.

Clark, K. B. (1979). The role of social scientists 25 years after *Brown. Personality and Social Psychology Bulletin, 5,* 477–481.

Cook, S. W. (1979). Social science and school desegregation: Did we mislead the Supreme Court? *Personality and Social Psychology Bulletin, 5,* 420–437.

Coren, C. (1992). *The invisible man: The life and liberties of H. G. Wells.* London: Bloomsbury.

Davenport, C. B. (1920). Heredity of constitutional mental disorders. *Psychological Bulletin, 17,* 300–310.

deLone, R. H. (1979). *Small futures: Children, inequality, and the limits of liberal reform.* New York: Harcourt Brace Jovanovich.

Duyme, M. (1988). School success and social class: An adoption study. *Developmental Psychology, 24,* 203–209.

Dyson, F. (1993). *From Eros to Gaia.* New York: Pantheon.

Galton, F. (1907). *Inquiries into human faculty and its development.* London: Dent. (Original work published in 1883)

Gangestad, S. W., & Simpson, J. A. (1990). Toward an evolutionary history of female sociosexual variation. *Journal of Personality, 58,* 123–150.

Gazzaniga, M. S. (1993). *Nature's mind: The biological roots of thinking, emotions, sexuality, and intelligence.* New York: Basic Books.

Geertz, C. (1964). Ideology as a cultural system. In D. E. Apter (Ed.), *Ideology and discontent.* New York: Free Press.

Gelfand, T. (1989). Charcot's response to Freud's rebellion. *Journal of the History of Ideas, 50,* 293–307.

Gerard, H. B. (1983). School desegregation: The social science role. *American Psychologist, 38,* 869–877.

Gorenstein, E. E. (1992). *The science of mental illness.* New York: Academic Press.

Gottesman, I. I. (1991). *Schizophrenia genesis: The origins of madness.* New York: Freeman.

Haraway, D. J. (1989). *Primate visions: Gender, race and nature in the world of modern science.* London: Routledge, Chapman and Hall.

Harrington, G. M. (1988). Two forms of minority-group test bias as psychometric artifacts with an animal model (*Ratus norvegicus*). *Journal of Comparative Psychology, 102,* 400–407.

Harwood, J. (1982). American academic opinion and social change: Recent developments in the nature-nurture controversy. *Oxford Review of Education, 8,* 41–67.

Havighurst, R. J. (1976). The relative importance of social class and ethnicity in human development. *Human Development, 19,* 56–64.

Herrnstein, R. J. (1989). IQ and falling birth rates. *Atlantic Monthly, 246,* 72–79.

Hirsch, J. (1978). Evidence for equality: Genetic diversity and social organization. In W. Feinberg (Ed.), *Equality and social policy.* Urbana: University of Illinois Press.

Hirsch, J., McGuire, T. R., & Vetta, A. (1980). Concepts of behavior genetics and misapplications to humans. In J. S. Lockard (Ed.), *The evolution of human social behavior.* New York: Elsevier.

Hogan, R. T., & Emler, N. P. (1978). The biases in contemporary social psychology. *Social Research, 45,* 478–534.

Hollandswort, J. G., Jr. (1990). *The physiology of psychological disorders: Schizophrenia, depression, anxiety, and substance abuse.* New York: Plenum.

Hollingshead, A. B., & Redlich, F. C. (1958). *Social class and mental illness.* New York: Wiley.

Hubbard, R., & Wald, E. (1993). *Exploding the gene myth.* Boston: Beacon.

Innis, N. K. (1992). Tolman and Tryon: Early research on the inheritance of the ability to learn. *American Psychologist, 46,* 190–197.

Jensen, A. R. (1969). How much can we boost IQ and scholastic achievement? *Harvard Educational Review, 39,* 1–123.

Jensen, A. R. (1973). *Educability and group differences.* New York: Harper & Row.

Joffe, J. M., & Albee, G. W. (1981). *Prevention through political action and social change.* Hanover, NH: University Press of New England.

Kohn, M. L. (1963). Social class and parent-child relationships: An interpretation. *American Journal of Sociology, 68,* 471–480.

Kurtines, W. M., Gewirtz, J. L., & Azmitia, M. (1992). *The role of values in psychology and human development.* New York: Wiley.

Ladd, E. C., & Lipset, S. M. (1975). *The divided academy: Professors and politics.* New York: McGraw-Hill.

Latour, B., & Woolgar, S. (1979). *Laboratory life: The social construction of scientific facts.* Beverly Hills, CA: Sage.

Lerner, M. J. (1980). *The belief in a just world.* New York: Plenum.

Lesser, G., Fifer, G., & Clark, D. H. (1965). Mental abilities of children from different social-class and cultural groups. *Monographs of the Society for Research in Child Development, 30,* 1–87.

Losco, J., & Baird, D. D. (1982). The impact of sociobiology on political science. *American Behavioral Scientist, 25,* 335–360.

Mednick, S. A., & Christiansen, K. O. (1977). *Biosocial bases of criminal behavior.* New York: Gardner.

Mehler, B. (1983). The new eugenics: Academic racism in the U.S. today. *Science for the People, 15*(3), 18–23.

Merton, R. K. (1973). *Sociology of science.* Chicago: University of Chicago Press.

Nisbett, R. E. (1993). Violence and U.S. regional culture. *American Psychologist, 48,* 441–449.

Pastore, N. (1949). *The nature-nurture controversy.* New York: King's Crown.

Pearson, K. (1937). *The grammar of science.* New York: Dutton.

Reilly, P. R. (1991). *The surgical solution: A history of involuntary sterilization in the United States.* Baltimore, MD: Johns Hopkins University Press.

Rosen, B. C. (1956). The achievement syndrome: A psychocultural dimension of social stratification. *American Sociological Review, 21,* 203–211.

Rosenberg, A. (1980). *Sociobiology and the preemption of social science.* Baltimore, MD: Johns Hopkins University Press.

Rosenberg, M., & Pearlin, L. I. (1978). Social class and self-esteem among children and adults. *American Journal of Sociology, 84,* 53–77.

Rushton, J. P. (1988). Race differences in behavior: Testing an evolutionary hypothesis. *Personality and Individual Differences, 2,* 1009–1024.

Rushton, J. P. (1990). Sir Francis Galton, epigenetic rules, genetic similarity theory, and human life-history analysis. *Journal of Personality, 58,* 117–140.

Rushton, J. P. (1991). Mongoloid-Caucasoid differences in brain size from military samples. *Intelligence, 15,* 351–359.

Rutter, M., & Madge, N. (1977). *Cycles of disadvantage: A review of research.* Atlantic Highlands, NJ: Humanities Press.

Samelson, F. (1975). On the science and politics of the IQ. *Social Research, 42,* 467–488.

Samelson, F. (1978). From "race psychology" to "studies in prejudice": Some observations on the thematic reversal in social psychology. *Journal of the History of the Behavioral Sciences, 14,* 265–278.

Sarason, S. (1978). An unsuccessful War on Poverty? *American Psychologist, 33,* 831–839.

Scarr, S., & Weinberg, R. A. (1978). The influence of "family background" on intellectual attainment. *American Sociological Review, 43,* 674–692.

Schwab, J. J., & Schwab, M. E. (1978). *Sociocultural roots of mental illness.* New York: Plenum.

Seligman, D. (1992). *A question of intelligence: The IQ debate in America.* New York: Carol.

Sherwood, J. J., & Nataupsky, M. (1968). Predicting the conclusions of Negro-white intelligence research from biographical characteristics of the investigator. *Journal of Personality and Social Psychology, 8,* 53–58.

Spengler, O. (1926). *The decline of the West.* New York: Knopf.

Swinehart, J. W. (1962). Socio-economic level, status aspiration, and maternal role. *American Sociological Review, 28,* 391–399.

Symons, D. (1980). *The evolution of human sexuality.* New York: Oxford University Press.

Tellegen, A., et al. (1988). Personality similarity in twins reared apart and together. *Journal of Personality and Social Psychology, 54,* 1031–1039.

Terman, L. M. (1947). Psychological approaches to the biography of genius. *Papers on Eugenics, 4,* 3–20.

Thompson, R., Crinella, F. M., & Yu, J. (1990). *Brain mechanisms in problem solving and intelligence: A lesion survey of the rat brain.* New York: Plenum.

Traweek, S. (1988). *Beamtimes and lifetimes: The world of high energy physics.* Cambridge, MA: Harvard University Press.

Tuma, E., & Livson, N. (1960). Family socioeconomic status and adolescent attitudes to authority. *Child Development, 31,* 387–399.

Willerman, L., Schultz, R., Rutledge, J. N., & Bigler, E. D. (1991). In vivo brain size and intelligence. *Intelligence, 15,* 223–228.

Wilson, E. O. (1975). *Sociobiology: The new synthesis.* Cambridge, MA: Harvard University Press.

Yerkes, R. M. (1923). Testing the human mind. *Atlantic Monthly, 131,* 358–370.

Zuckerman, M. (1991). *Psychobiology of personality.* New York: Cambridge University Press.

4

Environmental (and Genetic) Influences on Personality and Intelligence

Nathan Brody and Michael J. Crowley

Environmental and genetic influences both overlap and permeate each other. To discuss one in the absence of the other is likely to lead to error. Accordingly, environmental influences will be examined in this chapter within the context of behavioral genetic research designed to consider genetic and environmental influences simultaneously. Studies of presumed environmental influences on personality and intelligence have rarely been conducted with appropriate controls for genetic influences. We shall argue that we know relatively little about the influence of the environment on intelligence and personality.

The chapter will present an analysis of environmental influences on general intelligence and the "big five" personality traits that may be construed as the foundation of a descriptive taxonomy of personality (Digman, 1990; John, 1990; McCrae & Costa, 1990). General intelligence and the five personality traits do not exhaust all of the variance in the domains of intelligence and personality; variations in intelligence encompass many specialized abilities (Carroll, 1993), and personality traits may contain several facets (McACrae & Costa, 1990). In addition, there may be innumerable idiosyncratic forms of expression of broad traits. Environmental influences on narrowly construed dimensions may be quite different than those on broad dispositions such as the big five and *g*. In order to reduce the length of the chapter, this issue will not be dealt with here. Attempts will be made to contrast and compare environmental influences on intelligence and personality traits (for additional comparisons, see Brody, 1988, 1993a, b). The chapter should be construed as a theoretical analysis of environmental influences rather than as a compendium of established empirical relationships between environmental variables and personality and intelligence.

THE PARTITIONING OF VARIANCE: DOES $E^1 = 1 - H^1$?

Behavioral genetic analyses may be used to partition the total variance in a trait into several distinct sources of variance. The total phenotypic variance may be partitioned into environmental and genetic sources, and genetic variance may be partitioned into nonadditive and additive sources of variance. Nonadditive sources of variance reduce relationships between individuals who are genetically similar but not

Nathan Brody and Michael J. Crowley • Department of Psychology, Wesleyan University, Middletown, Connecticut 06457.

International Handbook of Personality and Intelligence, edited by Donald H. Saklofske and Moshe Zeidner. Plenum Press, New York, 1995.

identical; these influences occur as a result of dominance effects and epistasis interactions among genes at different loci. Nonadditive genetic influences contribute to similarities between monozygotic twins more than they do to similarities between siblings and between parents and children. Similarly, environmental sources of variance may be partitioned into shared and nonshared sources of variance. Shared sources of variance are environmental influences that are shared by individuals reared in the same family and lead to phenotypic similarity for such individuals reared together. Nonshared sources of variance are those that are not shared by individuals reared together and lead these individuals reared in the same family to differ from one another.

Two additional sources of variance involve combinations between genetic and environmental influences. Genetic-environmental covariance influences are created when genetic characteristics and environmental characteristics are correlated. A classic example exists for intelligence: Individuals likely to provide their biological offspring with genotypes that lead to the development of high intelligence are also likely to provide their offspring with environments that lead the same way. Genetic × environmental interactions occur when there is a nonadditive combination of genetic and environmental influences such that the effects of genotypes vary in different environments. In the most extreme case of a crossover interaction, particular genotypes may predispose individuals to develop high scores on a phenotype in one environment and low scores in a second environment.

The variance-partitioning approach to phenotypes has two advantages for our purposes. First, when we subtract values for H′ (the total genetic influence on a phenotype) from 1, the residual provides an upper-bound value for E′—the total environmental influence on a phenotype. Second, behavioral genetic analyses provide clues about the relative magnitude of different kinds of environmental influences. In particular, we shall argue that most of the environmental influences on traits are nonshared; therefore it is necessary to study the environment by examining differences in the experiences of siblings reared together. The variance-partitioning approach to understanding environmental influences, however, also has a major limitation: It does not inform us about processes of influence. It provides no information about how the environment works other than informing us about what may not be important (differences between families in socialization practices that have a common impact on children reared together).

Do H′ values provide an upper-bound estimate of the magnitude of environmental influences? In order to justify this claim, it is necessary to defend the validity of H′ values. Wahlstein (1990) challenged the validity of such estimates on grounds that they do not take account of interaction variance. In addition, he argued that many traditional designs used in behavioral genetic research have little power to detect interactions. Wahlstein and several commentators on his article also argued that current estimates for the heritability of intelligence and personality traits are suspect. If this is correct, we cannot derive upper-bound estimates for the magnitude of environmental influences by subtracting H′ values from 1.

Whether or not Wahlstein and other critics of the calculation of heritability values are correct, it is necessary to qualify the meaning of heritability estimates before they may be used to indicate the magnitude of environmental influences. Heritability is a property of a population, not a property of a trait. Estimates of heritability of a trait for a particular cohort do not consider secular influences on the trait that might be attributable to environmental effects. So, too, age corrections on measures will remove environmental influences on aging as a source of phenotypic variance. And limitations of sampling (e.g., the ubiquitous underrepresentation of the least privileged members of our society in twin and adoption studies) may result in estimates for the heritability of traits that are not representative for the population.

Systematic exclusion of sources of environmental variance in contemporary estimates of heritability may not only yield inflated heritability estimates but also lead to a failure to detect genetic × environmental interactions. For example, IQ is increasing in most industrialized societies (Flynn, 1984, 1987), and at least for some countries where the data have been examined, the effect appears to be larger for individuals with low intelligence than for those with high intelligence (Teasdale & Owen, 1989). That is, the mean has increased because of an increase in the scores of low-scoring individuals, despite little or no change among high-scoring individuals. It is unlikely that these effects are attributable to genetic influences. If the population distribution of genotypes has not changed, this pattern of results is compatible with a genetic × environmental interaction. Some environmental variations have differential impact on individuals with genotypes that predispose toward the development of low phenotypic intelligence. Behavioral genetic analyses of intelligence use IQ or some other age-corrected index of intellectual performance; environmental and genetic × environmental interactions attributable to cohort effects are removed, and the resulting estimates of heritability may be inflated. This example indicates just one of the many ways in which heritability estimates for a trait may be contingent.

Wahlstein (1990) considered research on phenylketonuria as paradigmatic for a consideration of genetic × environmental interactions. Phenylketonuria is a genetically influenced disease that leads to mental retardation if untreated. If phenylketonuria is diagnosed at birth (as it now routinely is) and treated by placing the individual on a phenylalanine-restricted diet, the genotype does not lead to mental retardation. The different outcomes of genotypes for phenylketonuria that are associated with variations in nutritional environments provide evidence for a dramatic genotype × environmental interaction. Wahlstein argued that environmental interventions may exist that serve to modify the heritability of many human phenotypes. Although this position is correct in principle, it may be difficult to discover the appropriate environments that will reduce the influence of genotypes on phenotypes in practice.

Heritability estimates for traits in a given population may be thought of as setting an upper bound for the magnitude of environmental influences for individuals in the defined population who encounter particular environmental variations. As long as no attempt is made to generalize to populations that have not been studied, or to environmental variations that either have not been encountered by members of the population or are excluded from consideration, heritability estimates do provide a basis for deriving upper-bound estimates of the magnitude of environmental influences.

Heritability of Intelligence

Biometric analyses of kinship data summarized by Bouchard and McGue (1981) are compatible with heritability estimates for intelligence of .50 (Chipuer, Rovine, & Plomin, 1990). Virtually all of the data reported in Bouchard and McGue's summary, which forms the basis for most of the heritability estimates for intelligence, are derived from studies of children or individuals below age 20 (McGue, Bouchard, Iacono, & Lykken, 1993). Several sources of evidence imply that the heritability of intelligence increases with age. Wilson (1983, 1986) obtained monozygotic (MZ) and dizygotic (DZ) twin correlations for intelligence in a longitudinal study; the correlation for MZ twins increased from infancy to age 15, and the correlation for DZ twins declined and did not reach an asymptote. McCartney, Harris, and Bernieri (1990) reported a meta-analysis of the influence of age on correlations for MZ and DZ twins for intelligence. They found that the magnitude of the obtained correlations for DZ twins was inversely related to the age of the sample studied, whereas MZ twin correlations did not decline with age. These data suggest that the heritability of intelligence increases as individuals grow older. McGue, Bouchard, et al. (1993) argued that estimates for the heritability of intelligence in adult samples based on MZ and DZ twin correlations are close to .8.

Comparable evidence for an increase in heritability is also obtained in adoption studies. Postadolescent biologically unrelated siblings reared together tend to have near-zero correlations in IQ (McGue, Bouchard, et al., 1993; Plomin & Daniels, 1987). Correlations between the IQ scores of adoptive parents and those of their adopted children decrease from early childhood to postadolescence in longitudinal studies. Loehlin, Horn, and Willerman (1989) obtained intelligence data on a large sample of adoptees and members of their families in a 10-year longitudinal study. The IQs of the adopted children when they were between 3 and 14 were related to the IQs of their biological mothers and of their adoptive parents, as well as those of biologically unrelated siblings who were reared in the same adoptive family. Ten years later, the IQs of adopted children continued to be related to the IQs of their biological mothers (the r values increased from .23 to .26 for a sample with some restriction in range of talent for IQ). The relationships between the IQs of adopted children and the IQs of members of their adoptive families declined: From .13 to .05 for the children and their adoptive mothers, from .17 to less than zero between biologically unrelated siblings reared in the same adoptive homes.

Studies of twins reared apart that are based on adult samples provide additional data on the effects of adoption. Correlations for MZ twins reared apart provide a direct estimate of H′. Data are available from two contemporary studies—the Minnesota study (Bouchard, Lykken, McGue, Segal, & Tellegen, 1990) and the Swedish Adoption Study of Aging (Pedersen, Plomin, Nesselroade, & McClearn, 1992). Correlations for MZ twins reared apart for the Minnesota and Swedish studies are .69 and .78, respectively. Both studies report that degree of separation and measures of within-pair variations in social class background have little or no influence on the magnitude of the correlation for MZ twins reared apart. The Swedish study, which is based on a systematically ascertained sample of all separated twins rather than on a volunteer sample, obtained correlations for MZ twins reared together of .80, for DZ twins reared apart of .32, and for DZ twins reared together of .22. These data were compatible with a heritability for intelligence of .80.

All of the available data provide consistent evidence for a monotonic relationship between age and estimates of the heritability of intelligence. These data imply that the heritability of intelligence for adult samples is approximately 50% larger than the value derived by Chipuer et al. (1990) based substantially on data derived from younger samples. In addition, these data imply that the value for the influence of the shared family environment on adult intelligence is close to zero.

What do these data tell us about the magnitude of the influence of the environment on intelligence? Much of this research is based on samples that are not completely representative of the population; they tend to omit individuals from the least privileged segments of society (e.g., the homeless, the addicted, the "underclass"). Nevertheless, they do provide information relevant to the heritability of intelligence for a relatively large subset of the population of modern industrialized societies. And for this segment of the population, environmental influences are weak relative to the magnitude of genetic influences. If heritability is .75, for example, the magnitude of the environmental influence cannot exceed .25; this latter value also includes error variance. Test-retest correlations for tests of intelligence do not exceed .90. Behavioral genetic analyses do not include phenotypes based on aggregated scores (derived from several administrations of a battery of tests of intelligence) that would eliminate short-term perturbations in performance. Environmental influences on adult intelligence might well account for less than 20% of the variance in the phenotype, and only a small part of this influence might be attributable to shared family influences determined by variations in the families in which individuals are reared.

The increase in the heritability of intelligence may be explained in several different ways. Genetic influences not expressed at an earlier age may be expressed in adulthood. Correlations between the intelligence test scores of biological parents and their children who have been adopted are a function of three parameters—the heritability of the measure of intelligence for biological parents, the heritability of intelligence for the children, and the degree to which genetic influences on intelligence are the same for both parents and children. DeFries, Plomin, and LaBuda (1987; see also Phillips & Fulker, 1989) obtained correlations between the IQs of biological mothers and those of their children who had been adopted. The investigators used these data to estimate the degree to which genes contributed to the stability of IQ between age 4 and adulthood. Their analysis indicated that approximately 50% of the test-retest stability in IQ for this time stretch was attributable to the influence of genes that contributed to both adult and childhood IQ. The remaining stability covariance was attributable to either genetic influences not expressed in childhood or environmental influences. Loehlin, Horn, and Willerman (1989) interpreted their longitudinal data on changing relationships between the intelligence of biological and adoptive parents and the IQs of adopted children as indicating that genetic influences not expressed at the initial assessment (when the adopted children were between 3 and 14) affected scores on IQ tests administered 10 years later.

Changes in the heritability of intelligence may also be attributable to changes in the environment. Prior to school entry, and perhaps for the first several years of education, shared environmental influences contribute to the intellectual socialization of the child. Over time, though, the intellectual socialization of the child is increasingly determined by formal schooling. Schooling may provide a relatively uniform environment that counteracts the influence of variations in the intellectual socialization practices of different families.

Nonshared family influences may contribute to the similarity of IQ of DZ twins during the years they live together. The twin who has lower intelligence may be the target of special compensatory efforts by parents; after adolescence, when twin pairs are separated, individuals may select their own environments. Scarr and McCartney (1983) suggested that genetic influences change from passive influences on how individuals respond to the environment to active influences ("niche selection") in which individuals learn to select environments that are compatible with their genetic characteristics. This theory implies that the way in which genes influence phenotypes changes over time. Genetic influences change to genetic-environmental covariance influences; that is, the influence of the genotype is contingent on the ability of individuals to select environments that are compatible with their genotypes. MZ twins are more similar than DZ twins in personality and interest as well as intelligence. The similarity of MZ twins may lead them to select environments and activities that increasingly create a constant environmental influence on intelligence over the adult life span. DZ twins, who are relatively dissimilar, may select divergent environmental experiences in adulthood, and these may contribute to an increasing divergence in their intelligence over the adult life span.

Behavioral genetic analyses of intelligence use age-corrected phenotypes. Changes in intelligence construed as a non-age-corrected score are not studied in the standard analyses. General intelligence declines over the adult life span (see Brody, 1992, Chapter 9); the decline may be as large as two standard deviations from age 20 to age 80. Because MZ correlations for intelligence remain constant or increase slightly over the adult life span, this implies that changes in intelligence reflect the unfolding influence of genotypes. These analyses imply that MZ twins tend to change (and decline) in intelligence in tandem; declines in the intelligence of DZ twins tend to be unrelated to the timing and rate of decline of the intelligence of their co-twins.

Heritability of Personality

Loehlin (1992) analyzed twin and adoption data for each of the "big five" personality traits. He reported H′ values ranging from .29 to .50 for the five traits. H′ values varied depending on assumptions that were made about the role of nonadditive genetic influences. Shared environmental influences for these traits ranged from .00 to .11. Nonshared environmental influences were substantial for each of the five traits.

Behavioral genetic analyses for both personality traits and intelligence lead to the conclusion that shared environmental influences are small. The analyses for personality differ from those obtained for intelligence: Heritability values for personality traits are dramatically lower than those for adult intelligence, and environmental influences on personality traits are larger than similar influences on intelligence.

Virtually all of the behavioral genetic research on adult personality traits relies on self-report measures. Such analyses are deficient in two respects. First, they rely on self-reports as a surrogate index for more conceptually relevant measures. Measures of intelligence and measures of personality traits are fundamentally different. Intelligence is measured behaviorally: We do not ask individuals to rate the size of their vocabulary; we present them with words to define. It is relatively easy to obtain behavioral indices of performance on a diverse set of intellectual tasks that may be aggregated to obtain an estimate of a person's general intelligence. Personality traits, in contrast, may be thought of as latent dispositions that are manifested in tendencies to behave in a consistent manner in different situations. Because it is virtually impossible to obtain cross-situational aggregate measures of an individual's trait-relevant behaviors, we rely on self-reports or acquaintance ratings as surrogate measures of personality traits.

Second, self-report trait measures conflate method variance and trait variance. Heteromethod analyses can, in principle, separate method variance from true-score latent trait variance. Phenotypic measures of personality traits based on heteromethod aggregate indices have rarely been used in behavioral genetic research.

Because nonshared environmental influences are a residual, method-specific sources of variance inflate estimates of these influences. Estimates of the heritability of personality traits would probably increase if method-specific variance were removed from phenotypic trait measures. Heath, Neale, Kessler, Eaves, and Kendler (1992) obtained self-report and co-twin measures of extraversion and neuroticism for a large sample of adult female twins, deriving phenotypic trait measures based on aggregate indices that controlled for method-specific variance. The authors obtained heritabilities of .73 for extraversion and .63 for neuroticism, values approximately 50% larger than those obtained by Loehlin (1992) based on analyses of self-report measures. Because we do not have an adequate body of research on adult personality based on heteromethod aggregate trait measures that include cross-situational behavioral observations, we do not have really good measures of the heritability of adult personality traits. It is probably safe to assume that heritability is larger than current estimates based on self-report measures.

Behavioral genetic analyses of personality traits differ from those of intelligence in a second major way: The heritability of personality does not increase over the adult life span. McCartney et al.'s (1990) meta-analysis of twin correlations for personality trait measures, based on cross-sectional age comparisons, indicated that both MZ and DZ twin correlations declined as a function of age. These data suggest that the heritability of personality traits remains more or less constant over the adult life span (i.e., the MZ-DZ difference remains approximately constant) but the influence of nonshared environmental influences may increase, leading to a gradual drift apart in correlations for MZ twins with common genotypes.

There is a dearth of longitudinal research on adult personality using genetically controlled designs. McGue, Bacon, and Lykken (1993) obtained longitudinal data on two occasions 10 years apart from a sample of twins ranging in age from 17 to 30 at initial assessment. These data may be used to explicate genetic and environmental influences on change and stability in adult personality. The authors used the Multidimensional Personality Questionnaire (Tellegen, 1982), which provides measures of three higher-order factors that correspond to three of the "big five" personality traits—Positive Emotionality (extraversion), Negative Emotionality (neuroticism), and Constraint (conscientiousness or impulsivity).

Their analysis of stability and change within the context of a behavioral genetic analysis is complicated by somewhat different results for each of the three factors; there are, however, some common patterns. First, the heritability of personality declined from time 1 to time 2. Second, a substantial portion of the stability of personality was attributable to genetic continuity. McGue et al. estimate that the heritability of a stability component for their data is close to .8. The nonstable or change component of personality is influenced by nonshared environmental effects; this component of variance accounted for approximately 60% of the residual variance in personality at time 2 after removing the influence of the stable component of personality. The residual or change component of personality was heritable, with heritabilities ranging from .33 to .43 for the three major personality factors. This last result contrasts with earlier findings by Eaves and Eysenck (1976), who reported results for a 2-year longitudinal study of twins and found that change scores for neuroticism were not heritable. It is possible that genetic influences on personality change require longer time periods to be manifested. McGue and his colleagues also studied a younger sample. Changes from the postadolescent to the young-adult period may be attributable to different influences than those that influence change in adult personality.

Loehlin, Willerman, and Horn (1987), using data from the Texas Adoption Project, found that adopted children exhibited increases in neuroticism relative to biological children reared in the same family from an initial to a second assessment ten years later. Because the biological mothers of the adopted children had higher neuroticism scores than the adoptive parents of these children, Loehlin et al. interpreted the changes that they obtained as being attributable to a genetic influence on personality change.

It is obvious that we know relatively little about the magnitude of genetic and environmental influences on change and stability in personality. The data obtained by McGue, Bacon and Lykken (1993) probably provide our best initial guess about these matters, with the important caveat that these results are restricted to an analysis of self-report measures of personality traits. Personality traits over the adult life span are relatively stable (McCrae & Costa, 1990), and much of that stability is attributable to stable genetic influences. Changes in personality traits are partially attributable to genetic influences and are more substantially affected by the cumulative impact of nonshared environmental events. Neither the stable component of personality trait scores nor changes in personality are influenced by experiences shared by individuals reared in the same family. In contrast, analyses of environmental influences on general intelligence imply that the genetic contribution to the stable component is larger, and that the environmental contribution to the change component is (over relatively large segments of environmental variation encountered by individuals in modern societies) vanishingly small. Changes in intelligence are largely attributable to increases in the magnitude of genetic influences.

GENOTYPE ENVIRONMENT COMBINATIONS OF ENVIRONMENTAL AND GENETIC INFLUENCES

Environmental Influences on Genetic Influences

Genetic influences cannot be actualized in the absence of at least some (usually unspecified) environmental conditions. Genetic influences on intelligence, for example, would not be manifest if a child either was not fed or was not exposed to individuals who provided linguistic models. Nevertheless, relatively little is known about the boundary conditions for the actualization of genetic influences. Scarr (1992) suggested that generalizations about the minuscule influence of shared environments hold within the range of what she calls "the average expectable environment." Environments that fall outside this range (e.g., those provided by "violent, abusive, and neglectful families") do not promote normal developmental patterns. Bronfenbrenner and Ceci (1993) characterize the necessary conditions for the actualization of genetic potentials as "processes of progressively more complex reciprocal interaction between an active evolving biopsychological human organism and the persons, objects, and symbols in its immediate environment" (p. 317).

Although there is widespread agreement that some dysfunctional environments do not provide sufficient nurturance for the development of psychological capacities, relatively little is known about the exact specifications of such environments. Scarr's (1992) concept of the average expectable environment implies that there are nonlinear influences of the shared family environment. Though most individuals reared in widely differing families (in terms of psychological characteristics) are not detectably influenced by these experiences as adults, some unknown subset of individuals who are reared outside the range of average expectable family environments are strongly influenced by these conditions. We are not aware, however, of any empirical findings that demonstrate the existence of such nonlinear influences in studies allowing for possible genetic effects. Some evidence suggests that the range of the average expectable environment encompasses wide variations. Gottesman and Bertelsen (1989) found a 17% risk for schizophrenia in the offspring of MZ twins who were discordant for the disease. The risk was virtually identical for offspring of MZ twins with and without the disease. These data indicate that exposure to a schizophrenic parent is not an etiological influence on the development of schizophrenia, although the example does not deal with the influence of unusual environments on personality and intelligence.

Differences in heritability in disparate populations may also provide information about the nature of the environment that is necessary for the actualization of genetic potentials. As more individuals in a population are exposed to average expectable environments, heritability should increase. If large numbers of individuals are exposed to environments that depress intelligence, then the heritability of intelligence would be positively related to IQ. By this analysis, individuals with low IQ include those who have not actualized their potential, as well as those who have genotypes that predispose them to develop low IQ. By contrast, individuals with high IQ are those who have actualized their genetic potentials. The available research on this issue is inconsistent. Detterman, Thompson, and Plomin (1990), and Reed and Rich (1982) found that heritability was inversely related to intelligence; Bailey and Revelle (1991) found evidence for a positive relationship between intelligence and heritability; and Volger and DeFries (1983) and Cherny, Cardon, Fulker, and DeFries (1992) found no evidence for a relationship between level of intelligence and heritability. These studies provide little support for the assumption that the absence of an average expected environment results in a failure to nurture the development of intelligence among large numbers of individuals.

Secular changes in heritability provide indirect evidence for changes in the environment that affect the actualization of genetic influences. Although studies of the heritability of intelligence have been conducted for several decades, it is not possible to form a clear conclusion about changes in heritability. Cohort comparisons in heritability typically are confounded by differences in samples and methods of analysis. Sundet, Tambs, Magnus, and Berg (1988) studied secular changes in the heritability of intelligence for a sample of Norwegian male twins who were tested at the same age for their selective service exams. The heritability of intelligence exhibited a complex wave form for cohorts born between 1932 and 1960; heritability tended to increase for cohorts born between 1954 and 1960. There is no obvious explanation of changes in Norwegian society that can be related to these changes in heritability. We have little systematic information about secular changes in heritability that could be related to social changes that would provide clues for a description of the kinds of environments necessary for the actualization of genetic influences on intelligence or personality.

Genetic Influences on Environmental Influences

What is an environmental measure? Plomin and Bergeman (1991) argued that many presumed measures of the environment are heritable, raising the possibility that relationships between such measures and outcome variables may be genetically mediated. Braungart, Fulker, and Plomin (1992) found higher correlations on the Home Observation and Measure of the Environment (HOME) scale (Caldwell & Bradley, 1978) for nonadoptive than for adoptive siblings. Their analyses suggested heritabilities of .40 on this "environmental" measure. In addition, they found that approximately 50% of the covariance between scores on the HOME scale and measures of 2-year-olds' mental ability was mediated genetically.

Chipuer, Plomin, Pedersen, McClearn, and Nesselroade (1993) used data from an adult sample of twins reared together and apart to study genetic influences on a measure of the family environment (Moos & Moos, 1981). They found that each of the three second-order factors derived from the perception of the family environment measure was heritable—and there were no shared environmental influences on these measures—implying that the perception of the family environment was not common to children reared together. There were significant relationships between two of the three dimensions of the environmental measure and extraversion and neuroticism; the covariances between personality and these two dimensions were heritable. These results indicate that relationships between family environmental variables and personality characteristics may be mediated by genetic characteristics that influence both personality traits and the nature of the family environment that an individual encounters (or the perception of that environment).

Genetic influences may exist for many kinds of events. For example, Plomin, Corley, DeFries, and Fulker (1990) found that the amount of time a child spent watching television was heritable. Relationships between television watching and some outcome variable could be attributable to genetic covariance. Without genetically controlled designs, it is difficult to know if one is studying an environmental influence on an outcome variable or a genetic influence.

Genetic × Environmental Interactions

It is a reasonable hypothesis that genetic × environmental interactions exist. Adoption designs may be used to search for such interactions. Characteristics of the biological parents may be used as surrogates for the genotypes of their children, and characteristics of the adoptive home may be used as indices of the environmental exposures of individuals with different genotypes. Plomin, DeFries, and Fulker (1988) used data from the Colorado Adoption Project in order to search for the presence of genetic × environmental interactions. Despite numerous tests for such influences for measures of personality and intelligence, however, virtually none were found.

Complete cross-fostering designs have rarely been used in behavioral genetic, studies and it is rare to find formal tests of interaction effects for personality and intelligence. Where such tests have been conducted, often additive (as opposed to interactive) effects have been obtained. For example, Capron and Duyme (1989) used a cross-fostering design to study the influence of parental social class on the IQs of adopted children. They found that the IQs of these children were related to the social class of both biological and adopted parents. The influences were additive; there was no evidence of an interaction. It is possible to speculate about possible interactions involving outcomes for individuals with different genotypes who encounter environments with different features. Nevertheless, there is little or no formal evidence that personality and intelligence are determined by genetic × environmental interactions.

In an adoption study, Cadoret, Troughton, Merchant and Witters (1990) found a significant genetic × environment interaction for the development of depression. The authors found that adopted children were at increased risk for the development of depression and manic symptoms if they were late adoptees or if they had biological parents with affective disorders. Adoptees whose biological parents had affective disorders (a genetic risk factor) *and* who were late adoptees (an environmental risk factor) had a greater risk for the development of the disorders than that derived from the additive effects of the two factors.

Cannon and his colleagues (Cannon, Mednick, & Parnas, 1990; Cannon et al., 1993) obtained evidence for a possible genetic × environmental interaction in a study of the children of schizophrenics. They used computed tomographic scans of these children to ascertain morphological brain abnormalities and found a monotonic relationship between ventricular enlargement and genetic risk for schizophrenia (as determined by the presence of schizophrenia in one or both parents of the subjects). Moreover, individuals who had high genetic risks for the development of schizophrenia and also encountered birth complications exhibited greater ventricular enlargement of the brain than would be expected from an additive combination of the two risk factors. Cannon et al. hypothesized that the genetic vulnerability toward schizophrenia might include increased risk for the development of brain abnormalities following exposure to birth complications, and the resulting abnormality could be of etiological significance in the development of schizophrenia. The Cadoret et al. (1990) and Cannon et al. (1990, 1993) studies suggest that genetic × environmental interactions that influence psychological development may occur early in life.

A number of possible influences of prenatal events and birth complications that may also affect personality involve genetic × environmental interactions. Moffitt (1993) argued that influences on the development of antisocial behavior extend from the prenatal period. She reviewed evidence indicating that anomalies of physical development related to prenatal events are elevated in individuals who exhibit enduring antisocial behavior. Individuals who have problems with impulse control and who exhibit neurological abnormalities are likely to exhibit antisocial behavior. Moffitt asserted that vulnerability to neurological insult may be heritable, and that the enduring effects of these insults may be reinforced by genetic environmental covariances or covariances between the biological and social environments. Individuals who are at increased risk to develop neurological anomalies for either genetic or environmental reasons are likely to encounter social environments that do not counteract the effects of these anomalies. Moffitt's analysis of antisocial behavior implicates genetic influences, biological insults following conception, genetic × environmental interactions, and the covarying influences of the social environment in the development of antisocial behavior.

Jacobsen (1988) found that individuals who committed suicide were more likely than case controls to have experienced asphyxia at birth. The influence of variables like asphyxia on subsequent development may be dependent on genetic vulnerabilities to biological insults; that is, the effects of such variables and of the kinds of neurological damage studied by Cannon and his colleagues may best be understood in terms of genetic × environmental interactions. It is also possible that the effect of such pre- and perinatal influences may be contingent on the kinds of social environments that individuals encounter. In order to understand the development of personality it may be necessary to study interactions between genes and the biological environment beginning with conception, as well as interactions of genes with the social environment.

Genetic-Environmental Covariance

There are several ways in which correlations between genetic and environmental influences could occur and affect individual differences. In families in which individuals are biologically related, children and parents share both genes and environments. These shared influences may jointly contribute to phenotypes. For example, biological parents who have high intelligence may contribute both genetic and environmental characteristics to their children that lead them to develop high intelligence. Similarly, parents who are high in neuroticism may also contribute genes and environments to their children that predispose them to develop neuroticism. Genetic-environmental correlations attributable to shared influences derived from parents are described as passive correlations. Do such effects exist? Loehlin and DeFries (1987) estimated that as much as 20% of the variance in intelligence might be attributable to the influence of genetic-environmental covariance, although these analyses are not based on data obtained from adults. As the heritability of intelligence increases, this influence probably declines.

Loehlin (1992) used the statistical methods applied to IQ phenotypes to study genetic environment covariances to search for comparable effects for personality traits. He found little evidence for their presence in two adoption studies. There is little formal evidence that implicates passive genetic-environmental covariances as a source of influence on personality trait phenotypes.

There are other kinds of genetic-environmental covariances. Scarr and McCartney (1983; Scarr, 1992) argued that development is characterized by a process in which passive genetic-environmental covariances are replaced by active covariances as individuals select environments that are compatible with their genotypes. This theory implies that individuals may transform potential genetic influences into phenotypes that are stabilized by virtue of the selection of reinforcing environments. From this perspective, it is important to conceptualize environments in terms of the variety of possible selections they permit. It is not hard to imagine that some individuals may be unable to create genetically compatible environments. For example, individuals with genes that predispose them to develop high intelligence may be denied access to books, libraries, and employment that enables them to continue to develop their intellectual abilities as adults. Neurotic individuals who might prefer to structure their environments to minimize interpersonal stress may unavoidably be placed in stressful interpersonal situations. There is relatively little formal research that examines the environment by considering whether it affords the development of optimal genetic-environmental covariances.

REFLECTIONS ON THE NONSHARED ENVIRONMENT

Are Environmental Influences Nonshared?

Although the preponderance of behavioral genetic research on personality and adult intelligence suggests that shared family environments do not influence these traits, this generalization may need to be qualified in three respects.

1. Some studies that indicate that shared family environments are important, although it is rare to find any that deal with adult intelligence or the big five personality traits. One of the few studies that obtained evidence for an influence of the shared environment is based on results for a brief measure of agreeableness administered to MZ and DZ twins (reared together and apart) participating in the Swedish study of aging. Bergeman et al. (1993) failed to find strong evidence for the heritability of agreeableness for these data; they also found that 21% of the phenotypic variance on this measure was attributable to the influence of the shared environment.

Some studies indicate that the shared environment may be important for a number of variables related to personality. For example, Gatz, Pedersen, Plomin, Nesselroade and McClearn (1992) found that depression in older adults was not highly heritable and was influenced by shared family environments; MZ and DZ twins reared apart had lower correlations for depression than MZ and DZ twins reared together. Mednick, Gabrelli, and Hutchings (1987), using a complete cross-fostering design to study criminality in a cohort of male adoptees, found that criminality was inversely related to the social class of both the biological and the adoptive parents. This finding suggests the presence of additive genetic and shared environmental influences associated with social class. Cloninger and Gottesman (1987) reviewed literature suggesting that juvenile delinquency was influenced by shared family environments. Although these studies provide some clear exceptions to statements about the lack of influence of shared family environments on personality and adult intelligence, it should be realized that results indicating a strong influence of shared environmental influences occur infrequently in behavioral genetic analyses of traits.

2. Failures to obtain evidence of shared environmental effects may be attributable to failures to include specific measures of the environment. Kendler, Neale, Kessler, Heath, and Eaves (1992) obtained information about parental loss (through either divorce or death) for a large sample of female twins, as well as about several nonpsychotic forms of psychopathology from the adult twins in their sample. They found that the experience of parental loss was predictive of adult psychopathology and contributed to the tendency of various forms of psychopathology to exhibit sibling concordances. Parental loss accounted for slightly less than 2% of the variance in depression. This study illustrates the possibilities of determining specific environmental influences in a genetically controlled design, as well as some of the difficulties involved in the use of this procedure. Although total environmental influences on traits may be large, specific environmental influences are probably small—in this instance, genetic influences account for more than 25 times as much variance as parental loss. Large samples are necessary to detect such small influences.

It is not at all clear that parental loss should be understood as an environmental influence. McGue and Lykken (1992) found that divorce is heritable and is not influenced by shared environments. If divorce is a heritable event, it is theoretically possible that children whose parents have experienced divorce are genetically different than children whose parents have not experienced divorce. There are several plausible hypotheses that involve genetic influences as mediators of the relationship between parental loss during childhood and adult psychopathology. Kelly and Conley (1987) found that divorce was related to neuroticism. Neuroticism has been found to be genetically comorbid with the experience of depressed states (Martin & Jardine, 1986), and anxiety disorders that are related to neuroticism are also genetically comorbid with depression (Kendler et al., 1992). Individuals whose parents are divorced therefore may be genetically predisposed to develop depressive states.

A similar analysis may be extended to the influence of premature death, the other cause of parental loss studied by Kendler et al. Allgulander and Lavori (1991) found that individuals who were anxiety neurotics had excess mortality. Because neuroticism is heritable, parental loss in childhood as a result of premature death might be associated with genetic characteristics linked to adult depression. It is also possible that premorbid childhood symptoms related to adult psychopathology may contribute to family discord and the divorce of parents. These speculations are meant not to suggest that an environmental interpretation of the effects of parental loss is wrong, but to establish the difficulty of forming unambiguous inferences about environmental influences from this research.

3. Generalizations about the lack of influence of the shared family environments refer to what Caspi, Herbener, and Ozer (1992) call the family of origin. They noted that many individuals have one or more additional family experiences associated with their families of destination (i.e., spouses/partners and children). Caspi and Herbener (1990) studied changes in personality in married couples in an 11-year longitudinal study. They obtained Q-sort ratings of their subjects on two occasions and computed test-retest stability correlations; they also obtained indices of mate similarity by correlating Q-sort ratings obtained for marriage partners. The authors found a positive relationship between personality stability and degree of similarity of marriage partners: Those individuals who were married to similar individuals changed least, whereas those who were married to dissimilar individuals changed most.

Caspi and Herbener's data suggest that shared environments created within the context of a person's family of destination influence personality. Their results suggest that there is a disjunction between influences of the shared environment created by families of origins as opposed to families of destination. Why might this be so? Perhaps shared environments created by families of destination are more influential because their effect occurs during adulthood, when individuals have more opportunity to structure their own environments (niche selection) and thus create possible covariances between genetic and environmental influences. Marriage partners may structure the environment from which niches are selected. Living with someone who is different from oneself may limit the ability of individuals to create micro-environments that are compatible with their genetic characteristics, and this may disrupt genetic contributions to stability in personality. For example, an introverted person married to someone who is extremely extraverted might find it difficult to choose an environment that provides some degree of social isolation, and this might interfere with crystallization of the tendency for introversion.

What Do We Know about Nonshared Environmental Influences?

If shared environmental influences are close to zero, most of the variables that have typically been studied by developmental psychologists have little or no influence on personality and adult intelligence. Social class background (within the range studied), marital conflict, personality characteristics of parents, and the intellectual atmosphere of the home are shared environmental influences. If the traditional socialization influences are excluded, though, what is left? Nonshared environmental influences encompass prenatal biological influences; illness and accidents not shared by siblings; differential experiences with siblings, parents, and peers; secular influences on siblings who differ in age; and the influence of adult role models (e.g., teachers and coaches). The range of potential influences is large.

Birth order is a nonshared environmental event that has been extensively investigated. Ernst and Angst (1983), summarizing this literature, concluded that there were virtually no reliable relationships between birth order and traits. Confluence theory, developed by Zajonc and Markus (1975), assumes that nonshared environmental characteristics related to birth order influence intelligence. The theory assumes that the impact of the family environment on a child is defined by the average intellect of all members of the family, including the child. Because absolute intellectual levels increase with age, parents tend to have higher absolute values of intelligence than young children. Depending upon parametric assumptions related to spacing and the growth of intelligence, later-born siblings thus tend to experience an environment that is less favorable for the development of intelligence than earlier-born siblings. The theory assumes that the impact of the relatively high intelligence of parents is diluted when one or more young siblings are present in the family.

Bouchard and Segal (1985) and Brody (1992) reviewed studies of confluence theory and concluded that predictions derived from the theory had not been empirically supported. For example, Brackbill and Nichols (1982) studied the influence of father absence on IQ in a large sample of black and white children. Confluence theory implies that children reared in father-absent homes should have lower IQs than children reared in two parent homes, because only one adult (rather than two) contributes her relatively high average intelligence in the former situations. After adjusting for social class, though, Brackbill and Nichols found that children in father-absent homes had slightly higher IQs than those in two-parent homes. Confluence theory also suggests that children reared in homes with extended families (i.e., where there are additional adults present) should have higher IQs than children reared in homes with two adults. Brackbill and Nichols found no support for this hypothesis.

Nonshared environmental influences encompass all environmental events that lead individuals reared in the same family to differ. In order to understand such influences, it is useful to study differences in the experiences of siblings reared together. Daniels and Plomin (1985) developed the Sibling Inventory of Different Experiences (SIDE) to assess such differences. If siblings in the same family are treated differently by their parents, or believe that they are treated differently, then these dissimilar experiences might be related to disparities in personality and intelligence.

Plomin and his colleagues (Dunn & Plomin, 1990, 1991; Dunn, Stocker, & Plomin, 1990; Hetherington, Reiss, & Plomin, 1994) have summarized research on this issue. Although a number of preliminary findings suggest lawful relationships between differences in sibling experiences and sibling differences in personality characteristics, these relationships are difficult to interpret. Baker and Daniels (1990) found that SIDE scores are heritable: MZ twins had smaller SIDE difference scores than DZ twins, and biological siblings had smaller SIDE difference scores on some dimensions of the SIDE than adoptive siblings. It is possible that relationships between the SIDE and individual differences may be mediated genetically. Baker and Daniels also found that within MZ pairs, twins who were more popular with peers were more likely to be extraverted, and that those who experienced greater maternal control were more likely to be depressed and scored lower on a measure of affective balance. Because these results involve differences between MZ twins, they cannot be attributable to genetic mediation.

It is difficult to determine the direction of relationships from these correlations. The results for extraversion, for example, might be interpreted as providing evidence that individuals who report being extraverted also report being popular with their peers; their interactions with their peers may not have caused them to be extraverted. It could be the case that environmental influences that contribute to the development of extraversion are independent of interactions with peers. Relationships between parental control and affective states of MZ twins might be attributable to parental responses to differences in the children's behavior caused by environmental influences that are independent of differential parental treatments. Longitudinal studies may help to disentangle the possible causal role of differential experience of siblings (Dunn & Plomin, 1991).

Reiss et al. (1994) reported preliminary results for the largest and most thorough study ever attempted of nonshared environmental influences. They obtained a systematic sample of 720 families with two adolescent children of the same gender. The families studied included those with MZ or DZ twins, blended families with biologically unrelated stepchildren, stepfamilies with full siblings, and nondivorced families with full siblings. Data were obtained from children and parents related to differences in their experiences; measures of individual differences in personality, psychopathology, and cognitive competence (based on parental and teacher ratings) were also obtained. Preliminary results for a subsample of 214 of the 720 families indicate that measures derived from parental reports about differences in their behavior toward their children had heritabilities as high as .78. Part of the reason that parents treat their children differently is that their children are genetically different. Measures based on children's reports about parental treatment were not heritable, and reports about the differential treatment they received from parents were substantially influenced by nonshared environmental influences.

Do these differential experiences (or perceptions of differential experiences) influence personality? Reiss et al. found that relative difference scores were not related to parental reports of psychopathology, but that correlations between absolute difference scores and parental ratings of pathology ranged from .02 to .19. (Absolute difference scores are measures of the extent to which children perceive differences in their treatment; if a child believes that he or she is treated less harshly than a sibling, the child might also infer that this treatment is temporary and that he or she is at risk for subsequent harsh treatment.) Because children's ratings were not substantially heritable, these results are not mediated by genetic influences. At the same time, it should be noted that the correlations are low and that it is not possible to predict accurately the rating of a child's psychopathology from knowledge of differences in sibling perceptions of parental treatment. Although the full analysis of the results from the Reiss et al. study is not available, the preliminary results do not provide evidence that differential sibling experiences within the context of the family are substantially related to individual differences in personality and intelligence.

If differential experiences within the context of the family are not major influences, though, where else would one look? Rowe, Woulbroun, and Gulley (1994) reviewed research on peer influences on individual differences. They noted that peer influences are subject to selection effects in which individuals may select peers who are similar to themselves. Selection may also be genetically influenced. Rowe et al. reviewed several sources of data indicating that peer influences are heritable and that the effects of selection appear to be larger than the independent influences of peers on individuals. They concluded "that the peer group is a non-shared environmental influence on siblings, but that its most important influence is not this, but is instead the reinforcement of existing genotypes" (p. 172). Rowe et al. view peer influences as an instance of niche selection in which genotypic influences are replaced by genetic-environmental covariance influences rather than solely environmental influences.

Nonshared environmental events that influence personality may be idiographic. Meehl (1972) developed a speculative scenario about the development of schizophrenia in discordant MZ twins that relied upon the occurrence of unique configurations of events in a genetically vulnerable individual. A confluence of mood, unpleasant interpersonal encounters, and emotionally laden thoughts might change the development of personality. Though no scientist ought to embrace enthusiastically a theory of random occurrences, it is possible that many critical environmental events that influence the development of personality and intelligence are chance encounters unlikely to be significant in the lives of more than a small subset of individuals.

We know that there must be environmental influences that cause individuals reared together to differ. At this early stage of systematic research on the problem, however, we do not know very much about what they are or even whether they predominantly derive from experiences within the context of the family, prenatal events, or complex configurations of events that constitute purely individual influences.

THE SEARCH FOR TRUE ENVIRONMENTAL INFLUENCES

At least three general approaches can be used to demonstrate the existence of specific environmental influences that are truly independent of genetic influences: (a) assume that any variable related to differences between MZ co-twins must be an environmental influence on a phenotype; (b) conduct true experiments with random assignment of individuals to conditions resulting in changes in a trait score; or (c) use statistical controls to eliminate genetic influences or to develop other relatively indirect evidence that a particular environmental event has an influence on intelligence or personality. In this section we shall examine studies exemplifying these approaches.

MZ Twin Differences

Because MZ twins are genetically identical, differences between MZ co-twins must be attributable to environmental influences. The presence of such differences provides evidence for environmental influences on a phenotype but does not indicate why the differences occur. Are there known environmental events that are related to differences among MZ twin pairs?

Intelligence

There are at least two variables that predict differences between MZ co-twins in intelligence. Lynn (1990, 1993) analyzed seven studies relating birth weight to intelligence in MZ twin samples. Each of these studies found that the heavier twin was likely to have a higher IQ than the lighter one; the mean within-pair difference in intelligence in these studies ranged from 1.9 to 9.0 IQ points. These results suggest that prenatal events (probably nutritional variations) influence the development of intelligence.

Beeckmans et al. (1993) studied differences in intelligence in a sample of 9- to 11-year-old monochorionic and dichorionic MZ twins. Dichorionic twins are believed to split 2 to 3 days after fertilization; whereas monochorionic twins are believed to split 4 to 7 days after fertilization. Beeckmans et al. found that dichorionic twins had significantly higher performance IQ scores (107.5 vs. 100.8). These results suggest that prenatal influences associated with chorionic status are associated with the development of intelligence. Dichorionic and monochorionic groups also exhibited within-pair differences in MZ correlations for performance IQ. The monochorionic twin correlation for performance IQ was .82, and the dichorionic twin correlation was .67. Because monochorionic MZ twins are more alike in performance IQ than dichorionic twins, intrauterine environmental influences associated with early and late splitting might contribute to the development of MZ within-pair differences in intelligence.

The research on the effects of birth weight differences in chorionic status on MZ twins implicates prenatal environmental influences as contributors to intelligence that are independent of genetics. Neither the Beeckmans et al. study nor any of the studies included in Lynn's (1990, 1993) summary of data on birth weight is longitudinal, nor do these studies deal with adult intelligence. Whether the effects noted persist over the adult life span or dissipate as individuals grow older is not known.

We are not aware of any research that relates postnatal environmental events to differences in intelligence in MZ twin pairs. Current research on separated MZ twins indicates that measures of variations in the social environment in which members of a separated twin pair are reared are not predictively related to within-pair differences in adult intelligence (Bouchard et al., 1990; Pedersen, Plomin, Nesselroade, & McClearn, 1992). McGue, Bouchard, et al. (1993), in their meta-analysis of kinship correlations for intelligence, reported a correlation of .86 for MZ twins reared together. The reliability of the tests used was estimated to be .87. Because the disattenuated MZ correlation for intelligence is close to 1.00, environmental influences contributing to within-pair differences in intelligence will be difficult to detect.

Personality

MZ correlations for self-report measures of personality are lower than MZ correlations for intelligence. Therefore, in principle, it should be easier to find environmental variables associated with within-pair differences in personality than in intelligence. What is true in principle, though, is not true in practice. Attempts to study within-pair differences among MZ twins that might have an impact on personality have yielded consistently negative findings. Plomin, Willerman, and Loehlin (1976), and Matheny, Wilson, and Dolan (1976) found that within-pair similarity of physical appearance was unrelated to trait similarity. Loehlin and Nichols (1976) were unable to find relationships in questionnaire data between degree of similarity of the shared environment and MZ twin correlations for either personality or intelligence. In addition, the authors were unable to find environmental events that correlated with personality trait differences within MZ twin pairs (see also Morris-Yates, Andrews, Howie, & Henderson, 1990). Scarr (1968; Matheny, 1979; Munsinger & Douglass, 1976; Scarr & Carter-Saltzman, 1979) compared MZ twins who were mistaken in their belief about their zygosity with MZ twins who were correct in their zygosity beliefs. (Mistaken zygosity might relate to differences in physical appearances or to differential treatments of children.) These studies all failed to find significant differences in MZ twin similarity for groups who differed in their beliefs about their zygosity. Other than the tentative findings based on the SIDE, there are no known environmental events that are predictively related to personality differences in MZ twins.

Experimental Interventions

In principle it is possible to assign individuals at random to different experimental groups that are exposed to some environmental manipulation, then measure the effects of that manipulation on a measure of individual differences. There is a literature on experimental interventions to increase intelligence, and it is possible to construe a subset of the psychotherapy outcome research as an experimental intervention to change neuroticism. We shall briefly consider these studies.

Intelligence

Several studies have randomly assigned young children to conditions that attempted to increase their intelligence. Many of these studies were designed to test the effects of Project Head Start, a federally funded program to provide an intellectually stimulating preschool environment to children from impoverished backgrounds. Most of these studies have yielded consistent results: moderately large increases in intelligence for a year or two after the intervention, followed by declines several years later. The Consortium for Longitudinal Studies (1983), which was formed to investigate the enduring effects of Head Start interventions, examined the subset of studies that used random assignment of subjects to a Head Start and a control condition and included at least 100 subjects for whom longitudinal information was available. Royce, Darlington, and Murray (1983) summarized the results of the seven interventions that also obtained IQ test scores for their subjects. The subjects included in these studies had an average initial IQ of 92 and had mothers whose average number of years of education was 10.4. At the conclusion of the intervention, the children in the experimental programs had IQs that averaged 7.42 points higher than those of children in the control groups. When the children were assessed in elementary school (3 or 4 years after the conclusion of the experimental interventions), the differences between experimental and control groups declined to 3.04 points. When the children were assessed at ages ranging from 10 to 17 (7 to 10 years after the completion of the programs), the differences between experimental and control groups declined to zero. These data indicate that Head Start interventions of 1 to 2 years in duration do not have detectable enduring influences on intelligence.

At least two studies initiated with preschool children provide evidence for somewhat larger increases in intelligence. Heber and Garber (1972, 1975; Garber, 1988) initiated an intensive intervention program for a group of 20 low-income children beginning prior to 6 months of age. The children lived in a publicly assisted low-income housing project; their mothers had IQs that averaged below 75. The intervention was one in which much of the intellectual socialization during the preschool period was provided by psychologists. Differences on IQ tests between children in the experimental group and those who were randomly assigned to the control group were as large as 2.92 standard deviations at age 6 (at the conclusion of the program). By age 14, the last age for which IQ test data are available, the differences had declined to .87 standard deviation units. This finding is somewhat difficult to interpret. Jensen (1989) attributed the effects of the intervention to specific training on items that were used in the IQ tests, compromising the validity of the tests. He noted that the differences in intelligence were not matched by differences in standardized tests of academic achievement. In the fourth grade, the 20 children in the experimental group had a mean score at the 11th percentile on a standardized test of achievement in math; the children in the control group had a mean score on the same test at the 9th percentile. Normally, differences of .87 standard deviations would be related to differences in academic achievement.

Ramey, Holmberg, Sparling, and Collier (1977) designed a comparable intervention that started at 3 months of age and continued throughout the preschool years. The mothers of the children in this study were all single parents who had not completed secondary school. Ramey et al. also found increases in intelligence for children in the experimental group, followed by declines. When the children were assessed at 36 months of age, the authors obtained differences in the Sanford-Binet of approximately one standard deviation. At age 12, the children in the experimental groups had IQs that were approximately one third of a standard deviation higher than children in the control groups (Ramey, 1992).

There are other studies of experimental interventions designed to increase intelligence for school-age children or older adults, but none demonstrates sustained significant increases in intelligence (Brody, 1992, Chapter 6; Spitz, 1986). Although the results of the Ramey et al. (1977) intervention lasted for several years after the conclusion of the experiment, it is not known whether they will endure into adulthood, when the phenotype for intelligence becomes more heritable and the influence of the shared environment declines.

Experimental research on nutrition also provides evidence for changes in intelligence. Rush, Stein, Susser, and Brody (1980) randomly assigned pregnant women to a control group or to groups receiving a liquid high-protein dietary supplement or a liquid high-calorie supplement. They tested the children of these women at age 1 and found that the children whose mothers had received the high-protein supplements exhibited more rapid visual habituation and larger response recovery when presented with a changed visual stimulus than children whose mothers were in either of the other two groups. Measures of habituation obtained in the first year of life correlated .5 with intelligence test performance for children as old as 8 (Colombo, 1993). Rush et al. (1980) obtained differences of approximately one-third of a standard deviation in their study. This finding suggests that prenatal nutritional interventions may have increased childhood intelligence by one sixth of a standard deviation. This is a speculative inference, however, and there is no basis to reach any conclusions about the influence of this intervention on adult intelligence.

Schoenthaler, Amos, Eysenck, Peritz and Yudkin (1991) administered vitamin and mineral supplements for 13 weeks to eighth-grade students in California with middle-class backgrounds. They found that subjects randomly assigned to the supplementation groups obtained performance IQ scores approximately .29 standard deviation units higher than subjects assigned to a placebo group. The enduring effects of the dietary intervention are unknown.

Personality

There are no studies of experimental interventions specifically designed to investigate the possibility of creating enduring changes in personality traits. It is possible, though, to construe some of the research on psychotherapy outcome as tests of experimental interventions to change neuroticism. Few therapy outcome studies provide ideal tests of this possibility. Many employ dependent variables that are specific to a particular manifestation, and few include long-term follow-ups. There is evidence, however, that neuroticism has an enduring influence on psychopathology. For example, Levenson, Aldwin, Bosse, and Spiro (1988) reported the results of a 10-year longitudinal study for a large sample of male subjects who were administered a brief version of the Eysenck Personality Questionnaire at initial assessment and the Hopkins Symptom Checklist (a measure used to diagnose a variety of DSM-III psychiatric conditions) at follow-up. Neuroticism scores accounted for close to 25% of the variance on the Hopkins measure.

Lewinsohn, Zeiss, and Duncan (1989) used a large community-based sample to study 10-year relapse rates for depression. Their data indicate that the probability of a person having one or more episodes of depression following the occurrence of a single episode of depression in a 10-year period is .89.

Many psychiatric conditions that are related to neuroticism are comorbid—that is, the occurrence of one increases the probability of occurrence of neuroticism (Cloninger, 1986; Klerman, 1990), and a broad impact of neuroticism on psychopathology has been demonstrated in longitudinal research. Convincing evidence for changes in neuroticism therefore should demonstrate that the effects of the intervention are enduring and of broad significance in reducing not only the symptomatic expression of a particular manifestation of neuroticism but also the probability of occurrence of comorbid psychopathological conditions (as well as the disposition to experience negative affect that may be construed as one of the important covarying psychological conditions related to, or defining of, neuroticism). From this perspective, the current literature on therapy outcomes does not provide convincing evidence of changes in neuroticism. Few studies of outcome include follow-ups that extend beyond a 6-month period. Recall that studies of experimental interventions designed to modify intelligence provide quite different results if outcomes are measured within a year of the conclusion of the intervention, as opposed to several years later. Moreover, few studies of therapy outcome include measures of outcome that extend across the spectrum of psychopathologically comorbid manifestations of neuroticism.

Contemporary meta-analyses of therapy outcome research aggregated across a range of therapies and outcome measures suggest that interventions yield changes of approximately .5 standard deviations relative to placebo groups (Smith, Glass, & Miller, 1980; see also Brody, 1983, 1990; Prioleau, Murdock, & Brody, 1983). For the reasons stated above, it is not possible to ascertain whether these studies provide evidence for enduring changes in neuroticism.

Inferred Environmental Influences

As we have seen, personal dispositions and genotypes may influence the likelihood of an individual encountering a particular environmental event. And environmental measures may be heritable. For these reasons, it is difficult to provide unambiguous evidence for environmental influences on a trait in the absence of genetically controlled designs or true experimental manipulations. Nevertheless, there are some studies in which the use of statistical controls likely to eliminate genetic mediation are sufficient to support the inference that a particular environmental variable has influenced a personal disposition.

Some well-controlled studies suggest that exposure to lead in the environment may have an impact on intelligence. Fulton et al. (1987) obtained measures of concentration of lead in the blood samples of 6- to 9-year-old children in Edinburgh, a city where many houses have lead plumbing. They used statistical controls for parental social background and found a linear dose-response effect of lead concentrations on intelligence. Children in the highest decile of lead concentration had IQs that were .43 standard deviation units lower than children in the lowest decile of lead concentrations (after adjustments for social background covariates of intelligence). McMichael et al. (1988) reported analogous results from a study in Port Pirie, Australia—a city with high levels of lead in the atmosphere attributable to the presence of a lead-smelting plant. They obtained blood samples from 4-year-old children and found, after adjusting for a variety of relevant social background covariates, a linear dose-response effect of lead concentrations in the blood. Children with the highest levels of lead concentration had IQs that were one standard deviation lower than children with the lowest levels of lead concentration.

Both the Fulton et al. (1987) and McMichael et al. (1988) studies controlled for the social and educational background of their subjects. The use of statistical control procedures in these studies undoubtedly eliminates some of the genetic variables that contribute to intelligence. At the same time, it should be realized that these studies measured lead concentrations in the blood, not lead exposure. The level of lead concentration in a person's blood may be related to genetic characteristics that influence the response to lead exposure; therefore, these studies' results may be attributable to an unknown degree to genetic influences. Lead concentrations in the blood may be a heritable phenotype, and the genes that influence this phenotype may contribute to the heritability of intelligence. There may be a genetic × environmental interaction involving lead exposure that contributes to variations in intelligence. There might be a main effect for lead exposure that is independent of genetic characteristics, and the presence of lead may be one of the environmental conditions that determines whether a particular subset of genetic influences affect intelligence. If lead were eliminated from the environment, possible genetic influences on lead metabolism would not contribute to variations in the IQ phenotype. This analysis demonstrates why it is difficult to obtain unambiguous evidence for an environmental influence on a phenotype even with studies that employ sophisticated statistical controls for possible genetic influences.

Are there influences of the social environment on intelligence? The adoption and twin studies reviewed in the first section of this chapter suggest that family influences over a relatively wide segment of environmental variations are not large and are difficult to detect in adult samples. If family influences are not important, though, where else would one look? Variations in schooling might be important. Cahan and Cohen (1989) studied variations in intelligence in fourth-, fifth-, and sixth-grade children in Jerusalem. Because the starting date for entry into elementary school is determined by age, children in the same grade may differ in age by 364 days; these data permit one to examine the influence of age and amount of education on intelligence. Cahan and Cohen found that amount of schooling was a stronger influence on performance on intelligence tests than age. Regression analyses indicated that 1 year of schooling led to an increase in intelligence of .275 standard deviations, whereas 1 year of age increased intelligence .15 standard deviations. These data provide clear evidence that school attendance influences intelligence (Ceci, 1990; see also Scribner & Cole, 1981, for an analysis of the influence of school attendance on intelligence in Third World countries).

Evidence also suggests that attendance in schools that provide extremely poor education can decrease intelligence. Jensen (1977) compared the IQ of siblings in a sample of black children attending public schools in rural Georgia. He found that older siblings had lower IQ than younger siblings, and his regression analyses suggested that IQ would decline in this sample by approximately one standard deviation between the ages of 6 and 16. A comparable study for a sample of black children attending schools in California failed to find evidence of a decline in intelligence. Jensen attributed the results he obtained in Georgia to the deleterious effects of inadequate schooling on the development of intelligence.

There is additional evidence that intelligence may be influenced by the curriculum of the public schools. Harnqvist (1968a, b; see also Lorge, 1945) studied changes in intelligence for students between the ages of 13 and 18 who were in secondary schools designed either to prepare them for additional education or to provide terminal educational experiences. After adjusting for initial differences in intelligence, Harnqvist found that students assigned to the more rigorous academic track increased in intelligence by .62 standard deviation units more than pupils assigned to the terminal educational track.

But to what extent do these studies provide evidence for enduring influences of schooling on intelligence? Though extreme variations in schooling undoubtedly affect intelligence, the dramatic effects of variations in schooling will probably decrease as technologically advanced societies move toward the provision of universal and partially egalitarian schooling. In contemporary studies of adult twins reared apart that exclude the least privileged members of society—but do include individuals who vary widely in social privilege and educational exposure—the effects appear to be vanishingly small. As for the variations in amount of education studied by Cahan and Cohen (1989), these effects are likely to be large in elementary school but of diminishing influence for older individuals who have longer exposure to schooling.

Harnqvist's data, which implicate tracking and the selection of curriculum, may also be difficult to interpret as an environmental influence that is independent of a person's genetic characteristics. The selection or assignment of individuals to different curricula may not be independent of a person's genetic characteristics. Selection and assignment of individuals to different educational tracks is probably related to academic achievement, and the covariance between ability (intelligence) and academic achievement is heritable. Thompson, Detterman, and Plomin (1991) obtained correlations between ability measures and academic achievement in a sample of 6- to 12-year-old twins. MZ twins had correlations between ability and achievement indices ranging from .32 and .40; the comparable correlations for DZ twins ranged between .18 to .23. A genetic covariance analysis of these data indicated that approximately 80% of the covariance between ability and achievement was attributable to genetic characteristics. The shared environmental influence was estimated to be zero.

It is possible that correlations between intelligence and academic performance are influenced by personality traits that influence the ways in which individuals respond to schooling. Because MZ twins are more concordant in personality than DZ twins, the significantly higher correlations they exhibit between ability and achievement may be mediated by personality characteristics that are heritable. These characteristics may contribute to changes in intelligence that are independent of educational experiences. Aggressive tendencies may be such a characteristic: Huesmann, Eron, and Yarmel (1987) obtained a correlation between IQ at age 8 and scores on the Wide Ranging Achievement test at age 30 of .49. When they added peer-rated aggression indices obtained at age 8 to the multiple regression, the correlation increased to .61; aggression at age 8 was inversely related to age 30 achievement scores. The assignment of individuals to different curricula that negatively affect the development of intelligence may be partially determined by dispositional characteristics of individuals that may themselves be heritable. Thus the influence of educational tracking on the development of intelligence may be attributable to genetic-environmental covariances, or possibly to genetic × environmental interactions. It is not unambiguously attributable to an environmental influence that is independent of a genetic effect.

The strongest evidence for an environmental influence on intelligence, apart from that derived from studies using genetic controls or true experimental interventions, comes from research on secular changes in intelligence (Flynn, 1984, 1987). This research includes studies of male selective-service registrants (constituting a virtually complete representation of the male population) from several countries. The effects are well documented but not fully understood—they may be attributable to nutritional influences (Lynn, 1990) or to educational influences. They are almost certainly independent of genetic influences; as indicated in the beginning of this chapter, though, they may involve interaction effects as well as a general environmental influence.

Studies of secular changes in personality cannot rely on systematic data from representative samples of the population to establish cohort effects. Few studies have data for representative cohorts that have been administered the same tests at the same age. There is evidence that the incidence of depression has increased over the last several decades, and some authorities estimate that risk for depression has increased by a factor of ten for cohorts born in the 1960s versus those born at the turn of the century (Klerman, 1988; Seligman, 1990). Increases of this magnitude in depression are probably associated with increases in neuroticism. In any case, like the secular increases in intelligence, they almost certainly represent an environmental influence. Klerman (1988) suggested that genetic × environmental interactions may also contribute to the secular increase in depression (i.e., secular changes may have increased the probability that individuals who are genetically vulnerable will become depressed). Studies of secular changes in personality traits using standard measures administered over time to comparable samples might provide a basis for understanding environmental influences on personality.

Are there specific environmental events that are predictably related to changes in adult personality traits? Exposure to stressful and unusual life events may increase neuroticism. Prolonged exposure to extreme levels of stress might define environments outside the average expected range and lead to enduring changes in personality. For several reasons, however, it is difficult to interpret this literature as providing unambiguous evidence for an enduring environmental influence on personality. Perceptions of stressful events (and even their occurrence) may be influenced by prior personality characteristics; for example, Hammen (1991) found in a prospective study that depressed women were more likely than normal women to encounter interpersonal stressors that were partially attributable to their own actions. Moreover, responses to stress are variable (Wortman & Silver, 1989). If the occurrence of stressors and the response to these events are variable and partially determined by neuroticism (McCrae, 1990), it is possible that the effects of stress are mediated by heritable personal characteristics. True et al. (1993) studied posttraumatic stress symptoms in a large sample of twins who were Vietnam-era veterans. The authors found that exposure to combat stress was heritable: MZ twins were more likely to be concordant for exposure to combat than DZ twins. Exposure to combat in turn led to a significant increase in symptoms of posttraumatic stress; these symptoms were heritable both for soldiers who were exposed to combat and for those who were not exposed to combat. These data indicate that genetic and environmental influences on posttraumatic stress symptoms are of two types—those that contribute to the exposure to the relevant stress, and those that contribute to the response to the stress. In each case, environmental influences were nonshared. There was little evidence of genetic × environmental interactions.

These data provide evidence that exposure to extreme stress is an environmental event likely to have an enduring influence on personality characteristics related to neuroticism. They also indicate that exposure to stress and the response to stress are heritable characteristics.

CONCLUSION

It is usually a mistake to study environmental influences on personality and intelligence without a consideration of possible genetic effects. An understanding of genetic influences will require a specification of the characteristics of the environment that permit the actualization of these influences on phenotypes. Future progress in the understanding of both genetic and environmental influences will be contingent on our ability to consider their overlapping and mutually permeating characteristics conceptually and empirically.

REFERENCES

Allgulander, C., & Lavori, P. W. (1991). Excess mortality among 3302 patients with pure anxiety neurosis. *Archives of General Psychiatry, 48*, 599–602.

Bailey, J. M., & Revelle, W. (1991). Increased heritability for lower IQ levels? *Behavior Genetics, 21*, 397–404.

Baker, L., & Daniels, D. (1990). Nonshared environmental influences and personality differences in adult twins. *Journal of Personality and Social Psychology, 58*, 103–110.

Beeckmans, K., Thiery, E., Derom, C., Vernon, P. A., Vlietinck, R., & Derom, R. (1993, July). *Relating type of placentation to later intellectual development in monozygotic twins*. Paper presented to the Behavior Genetics Association meeting in Sydney, Australia.

Bergeman, C. S., Chipuer, H. M., Plomin, R., Pedersen, N. L., McClearn, G. E., Nesselroade, J. R., Costa, P. T., Jr., & McCrae, R. R. (1993). Genetic and environmental effects on openness to experience, agreeableness, and conscientiousness: An adoption/twin study. *Journal of Personality, 61*, 159–179.

Bouchard, T. J., Jr., Lykken D. T., McGue, M., Segal, N. L., & Tellegen, A. (1990). Sources of human psychological differences: The Minnesota study of twins reared apart. *Science, 250*, 223–228.

Bouchard, T. J., Jr., & McGue, M. (1981). Familial studies of intelligence: A review. *Science, 212*, 1055–1059.

Bouchard, T. J., Jr., & Segal, N. (1985). Environment and IQ. In B. J. Wolman (Ed.), *Handbook of intelligence: Theories, measurements, and applications* (pp. 391–464). New York: Wiley.

Brackbill, Y., & Nichols, P. L. (1982). A test of the confluence model of intellectual development. *Developmental Psychology, 18*, 192–198.

Braungart, J. M., Fulker, D. W., & Plomin, R. (1992). Genetic mediation of the home environment during infancy: A sibling adoption study of the HOME. *Developmental Psychology, 28*, 1048–1055.

Brody, N. (1983). Where are the emperor's clothes? *Behavioral and Brain Sciences, 6*, 303–310.

Brody, N. (1988). *Personality: In search of individuality*. San Diego, CA: Academic Press.

Brody, N. (1990). Behavior therapy versus placebo: Comment on Bowers and Clum's meta-analysis. *Psychological Bulletin, 107*, 106–109.

Brody, N. (1992). *Intelligence* (2nd ed.). San Diego, CA: Academic Press.

Brody, N. (1993a). +.5 and −.5: Continuity and change in personal dispositions. In T. Heatherton & J. Weinberger (Eds.), *Can personality change*? Washington, DC: APA Books.

Brody, N. (1993b). Intelligence and the behavioral genetics of personality. In R. Plomin & G. E. McClearn (Eds.), *Nature nurture & psychology* (pp. 161–178). Washington, DC: APA Books.

Bronfenbrenner, U., & Ceci, S. J. (1993). Heredity, environment, and the question of "how"—a first approximation. In R. Plomin & G. E. McClearn (Eds.), *Nature, nurture, and psychology*. Washington, DC: APA Books.

Cadoret, R. J., Troughton, E., Merchant, L. M., & Witters, A. (1990). Early life psychosocial events and adult affective symptoms. In L. Robins & M. Rutter (Eds.), *Straight and devious pathways from childhood to adulthood*. Cambridge, England: Cambridge University Press.

Cahan, S., & Cohen, N. (1989). Age versus schooling effects on intelligence development. *Child Development, 60*, 1239–1249.

Caldwell, B. M., & Bradley, R. H. (1978). *Home observation and measurement of the environment*. Little Rock: University of Arkansas Press.

Cannon, T. D., Mednick, S. A., & Parnas, J. (1990). Antecedents of predominantly negative- and predominantly positive-symptom schizophrenia in a high-risk population. *Archives of General Psychiatry*, *47*, 622–632.

Cannon, T. D., Mednick, S. A., Parnas, J., Schulsinger, F., Praestholm, J., & Vestergaard, A. (1993). Developmental brain abnormalities in the offspring of schizophrenic mothers. *Archives of General Psychiatry*, *50*, 551–564.

Capron, C., & Duyme, M. (1989). Assessment of effects of socioeconomic status on IQ in a full cross-fostering design. *Nature*, *340*, 552–553.

Carroll, J. B. (1993). *Human cognitive abilities: A survey of factor-analytic studies*. Cambridge, England: Cambridge University Press.

Caspi, A., & Herbener, E. S. (1990). Continuity and change: Assortative marriage and the consistency of personality in adulthood. *Journal of Personality and Social Psychology*, *58*, 250–258.

Caspi, A., Herbener, E. S., & Ozer, D. J. (1992). Shared experiences and the similarity of personalities: A longitudinal study of married couples. *Journal of Personality and Social Psychology*, *62*, 281–291.

Ceci, S. J. (1990). *On intelligence . . . more or less: A bioecological treatise on intellectual development*. Englewood Cliffs, NJ: Prentice-Hall.

Cherny, S. S., Cardon, L. R., Fulker, D. W., & DeFries, J. C. (1992). Differential heritability across levels of cognitive ability. *Behavior Genetics*, *22*, 153–162.

Chipuer, H. M., Plomin, R., Pedersen, N. L., McClearn, G. E., & Nesselroade, J. R. (1993). Genetic influences on the family environment: The role of personality. *Developmental Psychology*, *29*, 110–118.

Chipuer, H. M., Rovine, M., & Plomin, R. (1990). LISREL modeling: Genetic and environmental influences on IQ revisited. *Intelligence*, *14*, 11–29.

Cloninger, C. R. (1986). A unified biosocial theory of anxiety and its role in the development of anxiety states. *Psychiatric Developments*, *3*, 167–226.

Cloninger, C. R., & Gottesman, I. I. (1987). Genetic and environmental factors in antisocial behavior disorders. In S. Mednick, T. Moffit, & S. Stack (Eds.), *The causes of crime* (pp. 92–109). New York: Cambridge University Press.

Colombo, J. (1993). *Infant cognition: Predicting later cognitive functioning*. Newbury Park, CA: Sage.

Consortium for Longitudinal Studies. (Ed.). (1983). *As the twig is bent . . . lasting effects of preschool programs*. Hillsdale, NJ: Erlbaum.

Daniels, D., & Plomin, R. (1985). Differential experience of siblings in the same family. *Developmental Psychology*, *21*, 747–760.

DeFries, J. C., Plomin, R, & LaBuda, M. C. (1987). Genetic stability of cognitive development from childhood to adulthood. *Developmental Psychology*, *23*, 4–12.

Detterman, D. K., Thompson, L. A., & Plomin, R. (1990). Differences in heritability across groups differing in ability. *Behavior Genetics*, *20*, 369–384.

Digman, J. M. (1990). Personality structure: Emergence of the five-factor model. *Annual Review of Psychology*, *41*, 417–440.

Dunn, J., & Plomin, R. (1990). *Separate lives*. New York: Basic Books.

Dunn, J., & Plomin, R. (1991). Why are siblings so different? The significance of differences in siblings experiences within the family. *Family Process*, *30*, 271–283.

Dunn, J., Stocker, C., & Plomin, R. (1990). Nonshared experiences within the family: Correlates of behavioral problems in middle childhood. *Developmental Psychology*, *2*, 113–126.

Eaves, L., & Eysenck, H. (1976). Genetic and environmental components of inconsistency and unrepeatability in twins' responses to a neuroticism questionnaire. *Behavior Genetics*, *6*, 145–160.

Ernst, C., & Angst, J. (1983). *Birth order: Its influence on personality*. New York: Springer-Verlag.

Flynn, J. R. (1984). The mean IQ of Americans: Massive gains 1932–1978. *Psychological Bulletin*, *95*, 29–51.

Flynn, J. R. (1987). Massive IQ gains in 14 nations: What IQ tests really measure. *Psychological Bulletin*, *101*, 171–191.

Fulton, M., Thomson, G., Hunter, R., Raab, G., Laxen, D., & Hepburn, W. (1987). Influence of blood lead on the ability and attainment of children in Edinburgh. *Lancet*, *1*, 1221–1226.

Garber, H., L. (1988). *The Milwaukee project: Preventing mental retardation in children at risk*. Washington, DC: American Association on Mental Retardation.

Gatz, M., Pedersen, N. L., Plomin, R., Nesselroade, J. R., & McClearn, G. E. (1992). Importance of shared genes and shared environments for symptoms of depression in older adults. *Journal of Abnormal Psychology*, *101*, 701–708.

Gottesman, I. I., & Bertelsen, A. (1989). Confirming unexpressed genotypes for schizophrenia. *Archives of General Psychiatry*, *46*, 867–872.

Hammen, C. (1991). Generation of stress in the course of unipolar depression. *Journal of Abnormal Psychology*, *100*, 555–561.

Harnqvist, K. (1968a). Relative changes in intelligence from 13–18: I. Background and methodology. *Scandinavian Journal of Psychology*, *9*, 50–64.

Harnqvist, K. (1968b). Relative changes in intelligence from 13–18: II. Results. *Scandinavian Journal of Psychology*, *9*, 65–82.

Heath, A. C., Neale, M. C., Kessler, R. C., Eaves, L. J., & Kendler, K. S. (1992). Evidence for genetic influences on personality from self-reports and informant ratings. *Journal of Personality and Social Psychology*, *63*, 85–96.

Heber, R., & Garber, H. (1972). An experiment in prevention of cultural-familial retardation. In D. A. A. Primrose (Ed.), *Proceedings of the Second Congress of the International Association for the Scientific Study of Mental Deficiency*. Warsaw: Polish Medical Publishers.

Heber, R., & Garber, H. (1975). Progress report II: An experiment in the prevention of cultural-familial retardation. In D. A. A. Primrose (Ed.), *Proceedings of the Second Congress of the International Association for the Scientific Study of Mental Deficiency* (Vol. 1). Warsaw: Polish Medical Publishers.

Hetherington, E. M., Reiss, D., & Plomin, R. (Eds.) (1994). *Separate social worlds of siblings: The impact of nonshared environment on development*. Hillsdale, NJ: Erlbaum.

Huesmann, L. R., Eron, L. D., & Yarmel, P. W. (1987). Intellectual functioning and aggression. *Journal of Personality and Social Psychology*, *52*, 218–231.

Jacobsen, B. (1988). Perinatal origin of eventual self-destructive behavior. *Pre- and Peri-Natal psychology*, *3*, 157–170.

Jensen, A. R. (1977). Cumulative deficit in IQ of blacks in the deep South. *Developmental Psychology*, *13*, 184–191.

Jensen, A. R. (1989). The Milwaukee Project: Preventing mental retardation in children at risk [Book review]. *Developmental Review*, *9*, 234–358.

John, O. P. (1990). The "big-five" factor taxonomy: Dimensions of personality in the natural language and questionnaires. In L. A. Pervin (Ed.), *Handbook of personality theory and research*. New York: Guilford.

Kelly, E. L., & Conley, J. J. (1987). Personality and compatibility: A prospective analysis of marital stability and marital satisfaction. *Journal of Personality and Social Psychology*, *52*, 27–40.

Kendler, K. S., Neale, M. C., Kessler, R. C., Heath, A. C., & Eaves, L. J. (1992). Major depression and generalized anxiety disorder: Same genes, (partly) different environments? *Archives of General Psychiatry, 49*, 716–722.

Klerman, G. L. (1988). The current age of melancholia: Evidence for increase in depression among adolescents and young adults. *British Journal of Psychology, 152*, 4–14.

Klerman, G. L. (1990). Approaches to the phenomena of comorbidity. In J. D. Maser & C. R. Cloninger (Eds.), *Comorbidity of mood and anxiety disorders*. Washington, DC: American Psychiatric Press.

Levenson, M. R., Aldwin, C. M., Bosse, R., & Spiro, A., III. (1988). Emotionality and mental health: Longitudinal findings from the Normative Aging Study. *Journal of Abnormal Psychology, 97*, 94–96.

Lewinsohn, P. M., Zeiss, A. M., & Duncan, E. M. (1989). Probability of relapse after recovery from and episode of depression. *Journal of Abnormal Psychology, 98*, 107–116.

Loehlin, J. C. (1992). Genes and environment in personality development. Newbury Park, CA: Sage.

Loehlin, J. C., & DeFries, J. C. (1987). Genotype-environment correlation and IQ. *Behavior Genetics, 17*, 263–277.

Loehlin, J. C., Horn, J. M., & Willerman, L. (1989). Modeling IQ change: Evidence from the Texas Adoption project. *Child Development, 60*, 993–1004.

Loehlin, J. C., & Nichols, R. C. (1976). *Heredity, environment, and personality*. Austin: University of Texas Press.

Loehlin, J. C., Willerman, L., & Horn, J. M. (1987). Personality resemblance in adoptive families when the children are late-adolescent or adult. *Journal of Personality and Social Psychology, 53*, 961–969.

Lorge, I. (1945). Schooling makes a difference. *Teachers College Record, 46*, 483–492.

Lynn, R. (1990). The role of nutrition in secular increases in intelligence. *Personality and Individual Differences, 11*, 273–285.

Lynn, R. (1993). Nutrition and intelligence. In P. A. Vernon (Ed.), *Biological approaches to human intelligence*. Norwood, NJ: Ablex.

Martin, N., & Jardine, R. (1986). Eysenck's contributions to behavior genetics. In S. Modgil & C. Modgil (Eds.), *Hans Eysenck: Consensus and controversy*. Philadelphia: Falmer.

Matheny, A. P., Jr. (1979). Appraisal of parental bias in twin studies: Ascribed zygosity and IQ differences in twins. *Acta Genetica Medica Gemmellologica, 28*, 155–160.

Matheny, A. P., Jr., Wilson, R. S., & Dolan, A. B. (1976). Relations between twins' similarity of appearance and behavioral similarity. *Behavior Genetics, 6*, 343–351.

McCartney, K., Harris, M. J., & Bernieri, F. (1990). Growing up and growing apart: A developmental analysis of twin studies. *Psychological Bulletin, 107*, 226–237.

McCrae, R. R. (1990). Controlling neuroticism in the measurement of stress. *Stress Medicine, 6*, 237–241.

McCrae, R. R., & Costa, P. T., Jr. (1990). *Personality in adulthood*. New York: Guilford.

McGue, M., & Lykken, D. T. (1992). Genetic influence on risk of divorce. *Psychological Science, 3*, 368–373.

McGue, M., Bacon, S., & Lykken, D. T. (1993). Personality stability and change in early adulthood: A behavioral genetic analysis. *Developmental Psychology, 29*, 96–109.

McGue, M., Bouchard, T. J., Jr., Iacono, W. G., & Lykken, D. T. (19930. Behavioral genetics of cognitive ability: A life-span perspective. In R. Plomin & G E. McLearn (Eds.), *Nature, nurture and psychology*. Washington, DC: APA Books.

McMichael, A. J., Baghurst, P. A., Wigg, N. R., Vimpani, G. V., Robertson, E. F., & Roberts, R. J. (1988). Port Pirie cohort study: Environmental exposure to lead and children's abilities at the age of four years. *New England Journal of Medicine, 319*, 468–475.

Mednick, S. A., Gabrelli, W. F., Jr., & Hutchings, B. (1987). Genetic factors in the etiology of criminal behavior. In S. A. Mednick, T. E. Moffitt, & S. A. Stack (Eds.), *The causes of crime: New biological approaches*. Cambridge, England: Cambridge University Press.

Meehl, P. E. (1972). A critical afterword. In I. I. Gottesman & J. Shields, *Schizophrenia and genetics: A twin study vantage point*. New York: Academic Press.

Moffitt, T. E. (1993). Adolescence-limited and life-course-persistent antisocial behavior: A developmental taxonomy. *Psychological Review, 100*, 674–701.

Moos, R. H., & Moos, B. S. (1981). *Family Environment Scale manual*. Palo Alto, CA: Consulting Psychologists Press.

Morris-Yates, A., Andrews, G., Howie, P., & Henderson, S. (1990). Twins: A test of the equal environments assumption. *Acta Psychiatrica Scandinavica, 8*, 322–326.

Munsinger, J., & Douglass, A., II. (1976). The syntactic abilities of identical twins, fraternal twins, and their siblings. *Child Development, 47*, 40–50.

Pedersen, N. L., Plomin, R., Nesselroade, J. R., & McClearn, G. E. (1992). A quantitative genetic analysis of cognitive abilities during the second half of the life-span. *Psychological Science, 3*, 346–353.

Phillips, K., & Fulker, D. W. (1989). Quantitative genetic analysis of longitudinal trends in adoption designs with application to IQ in the Colorado Adoption project. *Behavior Genetics, 19*, 621–658.

Plomin, R., & Bergeman, C. S. (1991). The nature of nurture: Genetic influences on "environmental" measures. *Behavioral and Brain Sciences, 14*, 373–427.

Plomin, R., Corley, R., DeFries, J. C., & Fulker, D. W. (1990). Individual differences in television viewing in early childhood: Nature as well as nurture. *Psychological Science, 1*, 371–377.

Plomin, R., & Daniels, D. (1987). Why are children in the same family so different from one another? *Behavioral and Brain Sciences, 10*, 1–16.

Plomin, R., DeFries, J. C., & Fulker, D. W. (1988). *Nature and nurture during infancy and early childhood*. New York: Cambridge University Press.

Plomin, R., Willerman, L., & Loehlin, J. C. (1976). Resemblance in appearance and the equal environments assumption in twin studies of personality traits. *Behavior Genetics, 6*, 43–52.

Prioleau, L., Murdock, M., & Brody, N. (1983). An analysis of psychotherapy versus placebo studies. *Behavioral and Brain Sciences, 6*, 275–310.

Ramey, C. T. (1992). High risk children and IQ: Altering intergenerational patterns. *Intelligence, 16*, 239–256.

Ramey, C. T., Holmberg, M. C., Sparling, J. H., & Collier, A. M. (1977). An introduction to the Carolina Abecedarian Project. In B. M. Caldwell & D. J. Stedman (Eds.), *Infant education: A guide for helping handicapped children in the first three years*. New York: Walker.

Reed, E. W., & Rich, S. S. (1982). Parent-offspring correlations and regressions for IQ. *Behavior Genetics, 12*, 535–542.

Reiss, D., Plomin, R., Hetherinton, E. M., Howe, G. W., Rovine, M., Tryon, A., & Hagan, M. S. (1994). The separate worlds of teenage siblings: An introduction to the study of the nonshared environment and adolescent development. In E. M. Hetherington, D. Reiss, & R. Plomin (Eds.), *Separate social worlds of siblings: The impact of nonshared environment on development*. Hillsdale, NJ: Erlbaum.

Rowe, D. C., Woulbroun, E. J., & Gulley, B. L. (1994). Peers and friends as nonshared environmental influences. In E. M. Hetherington, D. Reiss, & R. Plomin (Eds.), *Separate social worlds of siblings: The impact of nonshared environment on development*. Hillsdale, NJ: Erlbaum.

Royce, J. M., Darlington, R. B., & Murray, H. W. (1983). Pooled analyses: Findings across studies. In Consortium for Longitudinal Studies (Ed.), *As the twig is bent . . . lasting effects of preschool programs*. Hillsdale, NJ: Erlbaum.

Rush, D., Stein, Z., Susser, M., & Brody, N. (1980). Outcome at one year of age: Effects of somatic and psychological measures. In D. Rush, Z. Stein, & M. Susser (Eds.), *Diet in pregnancy: A randomized controlled trial of nutritional supplements*. New York: Liss.

Scarr, S. (1968). Environmental bias in twin studies. *Eugenics Quarterly, 15*, 34–40.

Scarr, S. (1992). Developmental theories for the 1990s: Development and individual differences. *Child Development, 63*, 1–19.

Scarr, S., & Cater-Saltzman, L. (1979). Twin method: Defense of a critical assumption. *Behavior Genetics, 9*, 527–542.

Scarr, S., & McCartney, K. (1983). How people make their own environments: A theory of gene-environment effects. *Child Development, 54*, 424–435.

Schoenthaler, S. J., Amos, S. P., Eysenck, H. J., Peritz, E., & Yudkin, J. (1991). Controlled trial of vitamin-mineral supplementation: Effects of intelligence and performance. *Personality and Individual Differences, 12*, 351–362.

Scribner, S., & Cole, M. (1981). *The psychology of literacy*. Cambridge, MA: Harvard University Press.

Seligman, M. E. P. (1990). Why is there so much depression today? The waxing of the individual and the waning of the commons. In R. E. Ingram (Ed.), *Contemporary psychological approaches to depression*. New York: Plenum.

Smith, M. L., Glass, G. V., & Miller, T. I. (1980). *The benefits of psychotherapy*. Baltimore, MD: Johns Hopkins University Press.

Spitz, H. H. (1986). *The rising of intelligence*. Hillsdale, NJ: Erlbaum.

Sundet, J. M., Tambs, K., Magnus, P., & Berg, K. (1988). On the question of secular trends in the heritability of intelligence test scores: A study of Norwegian twins. *Intelligence, 8*, 283–293.

Teasdale, T. W., & Owen, O. R. (1989). Continuing secular increases in intelligence and a stable prevalence of high intelligence levels. *Intelligence, 13*, 255–262.

Tellegen, A. (1982). *Brief manual for the Differential Personality Questionnaire*. Unpublished manuscript, University of Minnesota, Minneapolis.

Thompson, L. A., Detterman, D. K., & Plomin, R. (1991). Associations between cognitive abilities and scholastic achievement: Genetic overlap but environmental differences. *Psychological Science, 2*, 158–165.

True, W. R., Rice, J., Eisen, S. A., Heath, A. C., Goldberg, J., Lyons, M. H., & Nowak, J. (1993). A twin study of genetic and environmental contributions to liability for posttraumatic stress symptoms. *Archives of General Psychiatry, 50*, 257–264.

Volger, G. P., & DeFries, J. C. (1983). Linearity of offspring-parent regression for general cognitive ability. *Behavior Genetics, 13*, 355–360.

Wahlstein, D. (1990). Insensitivity of the analysis of variance to heredity-environment interaction. *Behavioral and Brain Sciences, 13*, 109–161.

Wilson, R. S. (1983). The Louisville twin study: Developmental synchronies in behavior. *Child Development, 54*, 298–316.

Wilson, R. S. (1986). Continuity and change in cognitive ability profile. *Behavior Genetics, 16*, 45–60.

Wortman, C. B., & Silver, R. C. (1989). The myths of coping with loss. *Journal of Consulting and Clinical Psychology, 57*, 349–357.

Zajonc, R. B., & Markus, G. B. (1975). Birth order and intellectual development. *Psychological Review, 82*, 74–88.

5

Longitudinal Studies of Personality and Intelligence

A Behavior Genetic and Evolutionary Psychology Perspective

Thomas J. Bouchard, Jr.

WHY STUDY LIVES OVER TIME?

Prediction

In 1882 Sir Francis Galton called for the creation of "anthropometric laboratories":

> The leading ideas of such a laboratory is I have in view, were that its measurement should effectually "sample" a man with reasonable completeness. It should measure absolutely where it was possible, otherwise relatively among his close fellows, the quality of each selected faculty. The next step would be to estimate the combined effect of these separately measured faculties in any given proportion and ultimately to ascertain the degree with which the measurement of sample faculties in youth justifies a prophecy of further success in life, using the word "success" in its most literal meaning. (Galton, 1885, p. 206)

This was one of the first calls for longitudinal research. The goal was the prediction of future success in life. Johnson et al. (1985) reanalyzed Galton's data a century after it was collected and reported as follows:

> The analyses we have described using the data that Galton did manage to acquire point out the value inherent in Galton's ideal and suggest that such a continuously maintained data bank and the historical perspectives it would provide may still be of considerable worth in contemporary psychology. The fact that his data–acquired a century ago–are the best and sometimes the only data available regarding some domains of individual differences is indicative of the uneven growth of different areas of psychology. (p. 892)

Fortunately the Murray Center now maintains longitudinal data files for secondary analysis (Young, Savola, & Phelps, 1991), and the problems involved in the archiving of longitudinal data are under active discussion (Colby & Phelps, 1990). Nevertheless, it is striking that for a long time the goal of most longitudinal studies remained the simple prediction of life outcome from earlier observations. As Block (1971) put it in his classic analysis of the Berkeley longitudinal studies, "Are there clues in the nature of their adolescent years and in their origins that can tell us why these men and women developed as they did?" (p. 3). At their simplest, longitudinal studies are descriptive studies carried out over more than on period of time. Unless they are couched in theoretical terms, and unless theoretically derived measures of both the trait and intervening experiences are obtained, the data are largely static. This does not mean that they are not

---

Thomas J. Bouchard, Jr. • Department of Psychology, University of Minnesota, Minneapolis, Minnesota 55455.

International Handbook of Personality and Intelligence, edited by Donald H. Saklofske and Moshe Zeidner. Plenum Press, New York, 1995.

useful. Knowledge of change or lack of change tells us what needs to be explained; description precedes explanation. Nevertheless, a sheer descriptive approach to the question in likely to be less informative than a well-formulated empirical approach embedded in a theory or perhaps metatheory. What theory might be useful?

Theory Testing

Most life-span psychologists would admit that they study lives over time not for descriptive reasons but rather in order to "understand life outcomes" (Funder, Parke, Tomlinson-Keasey, & Widaman, 1993). Many outcomes seem predictable. As Block (1971) points out, attendance at a high school reunion 20 years after graduation is an interesting experience that often confirms predictions made much earlier, but there are also many misses. Both the generality of the confirmations (the lazy and listless have become fatter) and the frequent misses (e.g., the average student who is now a university professor) tell us that we need a much more precise explanatory process.

Guidance can only be derived from theory, and in point of fact every study is theoretically biased. The choice of measures, the time of measurement, the characteristics of the individuals, the characteristics of significant others who supposedly influence the study participants, the reports on the environment or context of the lives of the participants, and so forth, all reflect theoretical presuppositions about how the world works. Investigators who conduct longitudinal studies expect to be able to "explain outcomes," otherwise they would not have carried out the study. Without a point of view, it is unlikely they would have persuaded anyone to provide financial backing or to commit part of their career to the data gathering enterprise. I make this point not to condemn any study—the comment applies evenhandedly to all of us—but rather to argue that every study must be judged both in terms of its frame of reference and by what it failed to do.

A Behavior Genetic Perspective

Psychologists have been overwhelmingly biased in their theorizing about what influences psychological traits over the course of development. They have almost universally assumed a stimulate-and-enhance environmental model for infancy, childhood, adolescence, and young adulthood and a wear-and-tear model of environmental influence for the latter years (Black, Isaacks, & Greenough, 1991). Brody (1993), for example, argues for the decreasing heritability of personality on the grounds that most of the environmental influence is not shared by individuals reared together and that such cumulative events will cause individuals to drift apart. If one assumes a dynamic model, however, and the individual organism is conceived of as constantly recreating his or her environment (seeking a level rather than simply suffering the accumulated slings and arrows of outrageous fortune), other explanations are possible.

Consider also the influence of stressful life experiences. Divorce is seen by many psychologists as an environmental influence (one of the "slings and arrows") with enormous impact on the developing personality of children (Hoffman, 1991). A recent review of longitudinal studies of divorce in Great Britain and the United States (Cherlin et al., 1991) concluded that "overall the evidence suggest that much of the effect of divorce on children can be predicted by conditions that existed well before the separation occurred" (p. 1388; see also Block, Block, & Gjerde, 1986). All of these authors provide an environmental interpretation of their results, but such a model is clearly much too simple. Divorce is now known to be influenced by genetic factors (McGue & Lykken, 1992; Turkheimer, Lovett, Robinette, & Gottesman, 1992) that are probably mediated by personality traits, all of which in turn are heavily influenced by genetic factors (Loehlin, 1992). It is worth noting that stressful life events in general (divorce being but one example) are sometimes used as correlates of trait change in longitudinal studies. Certain classes of stressful life events (i.e., controllable events) have now been shown to be partially under genetic influence (Moster, 1991; Plomin, Lichtenstein, Pedersen, McClearn, & Nesselroade, 1990).

It follows from these findings that longitudinal studies would be far more informative if they utilized human behavior genetic designs. Recent findings in behavior genetics simply overturn many of the assumptions underlying longitudinal studies that make use of children reared by their biological families. The standard longitudinal model (which typically studies one child per family within the context of biological families) is incapable of disentangling important genetic and environmental influences on behavioral development (Plomin, 1986; Plomin & Daniels, 1987; Scarr, 1992, 1993). To make this argument concrete, let us consider a modern highly sophisticated quantitative analysis of perhaps the most widely known longitudinal study in the history of psychology—the Terman longitudinal study of giftedness (Terman & Oden, 1959). The analysis was carried out by Tomlinson-Keasey and Little (1990). I have discussed this study elsewhere (Bouchard, Lykken, Tellegen, & McGue, in press), and the discussion below is taken from that source.

The Tomlinson-Keasey and Little (1990) paper is entitled "Predicting Educational Attainment, Occupational Achievement, Intellectual Skill and Personal Adjustment Among Gifted Men and Women." The title sounds quite neutral, speaking of prediction rather than explanation. The claims in the paper, though, are not neutral. Using teacher and parent ratings of children aged 11 or 12 years, the authors derived measures of three childhood personality characteristics that they called social responsibility (probably the higher-order personality trait of constraint or impulse control), intellectual determination (a rated IQ factor) and sociability (a personality trait). Two family-of-origin predictors, parents' education and family harmony were derived; the latter measure was based on eight retrospective items concerning the quality of the early family environment. Three outcome variables were created: educational attainment, intellectual skills (concept mastery test scores—straightforward measures of verbal IQ), and personal adjustment (from various mental health measures—perhaps comparable to neuroticism). A structural equation model was developed and tested to evaluate the role of the three childhood and two family variables as they related to the intermediate variables (educational attainment, intellectual skill, and personal adjustment) and the more distal outcome variable of occupational achievement.

These authors considered the variables they were studying to be proximal causes. "As educational psychologists, it behooves us to try to ascertain what factors promote the educational and occupational achievements that should accompany intellectual skill. Delineating the childhood variables critical to positive adult outcomes requires longitudinal information on individuals that spans a lifetime" (p. 442). They concluded as follows about the influence of their measures on intellectual skills:

> How well did these children, identified as gifted at age 11 or 12, maintain their intellectual superiority as adults, and what variables predicted their continuing interest in the intellectual sphere? For both sexes, three factors predicted Intellectual Skill in adulthood. Parental Education and Intellectual Determination were positively associated with maintaining Intellectual skills; Sociability was negatively associated with maintaining Intellectual skills. . . . Parental Education has appeared repeatedly in the literature as one of several indicators of the family's socioeconomic status and is often depicted as an indicator of the value parents place on education (see Henderson, 1981; White, 1982; Willerman, 1979). When parents place a premium on education, this attitude pervades the home environment and becomes part of the child's value structure. (p. 452)

It is worth emphasizing that Tomlinson-Keasey and Little did not measure parental values or the children's value structure, nor did they relate these value structures to adult intellectual skills. Their claim is based on the use of Parental Education as a proxy for Educational Values and goes well beyond the data. This claim, in our opinion, deserves a true test, as the authors' conclusion rests on an average correlation of only .15 (!) between Parental Education and the offspring's adult IQ. This is a within-family correlation in which genetic and environmental factors are confounded. If we take the model seriously, the authors have accounted for about 2.25% of the variance in adult IQ.

Not only is this a very modest amount of explanatory power, it is probably not even real. To truly test this claim we would need a comparable sample of adult adoptees. Such a sample is not available, but one can be approximated. In the Scarr and Weinberg (1978) adoption study (average age about 18 years), the correlation between parental education and IQ is .26 for biological offspring and .08 for adopted children (see Scarr, 1981, p. 395). The biological correlation is higher than for the Terman sample—a sample that is far from optimal for this type of analysis, because the Terman children were selected for extremeness on IQ and (as Keating, 1975, has shown) the sampling was peculiar—but extremely similar to those found in large sample surveys.

The Scarr and Weinberg (1978) adopted children, of course, still lived with their parents, and evidence suggests the correlation between parental education and adopted child's IQ will drop over time. In our study of adult adoptees (Bouchard, Lykken, McGue, Segal, & Tellegen, 1990a) the average correlation between IQ and parental education is .05. Consistent with a genetic interpretation of the Tomlinson-Keasey and Little (1990) data, in large-scale studies of biological families, mothers' education is seldom correlated more highly with child's IQ than fathers' education; the weighted mean values are .303 for fathers' education and .295 for mothers' education (n = 34, 714 from four studies; Bouchard & Segal, 1985). This is also true in both the Terman data and the Scarr and Weinberg data. We would argue that an environmental explanation along the lines suggested by Tomlinson-Keasey and Little would require at least a slightly higher correlation between mother and offspring than father and offspring. Genetic theory does not make this prediction. It is of interest to note that the same lack of a sex difference holds for the correlation between parents' IQ and offspring IQ (Bouchard & McGue, 1981). Again this outcome is expected on the basis of a genetic model but not an environmental one.

The Tomlinson-Keasey results are also incompatible with the essentially zero correlations for adult IQs of unrelated children reared together (McGue, Bouchard, Iacono, & Lykken, 1993). The specifics of the argument are unimportant. The Tomlinson-Keasey study employed a sample of individuals reared by their biological parents; correlations based on such samples confound heredity and environment. An adult sample of adoptees is mandatory if the authors wish to draw causal inferences. In this case all the relevant correlations between purported casual influences and targeted traits have been shown to be near zero in adoption families. Not mentioned to this point is the fact that all the traits in the model have been shown to be very significantly influenced by heredity.

The fundamental problem ignored by these authors was pointed out in 1869 by Galton, who proposed the adoption design to avoid it. Barbara Burks (1938), perhaps Louis Terman's most brilliant student, dealt with it quantitatively in the context of estimating genetic and environmental parameters for an adoption study. She was also one of the first psychologists to use the method of path analysis, which had been recently invented by Sewall Wright (1921, 1931). It is a sad commentary on our discipline that Tomlinson-Keasey and Little did not even see fit to cite her.

When studies utilize biological families, any measures of the environment confound heredity and environment, and correlations between these measures and offspring characteristics (intelligence, personality, etc.) are uninterpretable (Cardon & Cherney, 1994; Cavalli-Sforza, 1975; McGue & Bouchard, 1989; Neale & Cardon, 1992). Many modern studies continue in the same tradition, attaching the caveat that heredity and environment are confounded. Harrington (1993) refreshingly argues that

> longitudinal studies involving early parent-child interactions and subsequent personality development cannot disentangle causal chains. Although early child-rearing practices may influence personality development, it is also possible that child-rearing practices themselves are partly shaped by children's characteristics or by genetically influenced parental characteristics, either or both of which may influence children's later personality development. (p. 307)

Lytton (1977, 1990) has shown how children's behavior does drive parental behavior. The topic has been, however, seriously understudied. Some investigators attempt to leave the implication that heredity is unlikely to explain much variance; others reject heredity as a possible competing hypothesis, though, arguing that theoretical verisimilitude is sufficient support for environmental interpretations of findings (Baumrind, 1993). It is of interest that these authors repeatedly cite confounded studies (Hoffman, 1991; Steinberg, Lamborn, Dornbush, & Darling, 1992; see Bouchard, 1993a, for a detailed refutation).

An Evolutionary Psychology Perspective

One of the goals of this chapter is to review selected findings in the domain of longitudinal studies of personality and intelligence and attempt to show that there are alternative theoretical frames of reference for organizing the collection and interpretation of longitudinal data—frames of reference that conflict strikingly with what we call, following Tooby and Cosmides (1992), the "standard social science model" (SSSM). The evolutionary psychology model is quite new (Barkow, 1989; A. Buss, 1988; D.M. Buss, 1984, 1991; D.M. Buss & Schmidtt, 1993; Daly & Wilson, 1988). It is an approach for which there is much less evidence than the behavior genetic approach, but it is capable of linking longitudinal research with a rich, well-developed, and influential research tradition in the biological sciences (Cosmides, Tooby, & Barkow, 1992). In my own implementation of this model I see it primarily as a forthright extension of the ethological model (Eibl-Eibesfeldt, 1989). The ethological model has had some impact on developmental psychologists, but much less than one might have expected (Charlesworth, 1992). The evolutionary psychology approach argues that the human mind (I assume that personality and intelligence are embedded in human minds) is filled with numerous complex information-processing mechanisms that have evolved in response to repeated encounters with persistent problems to which our species has had to adapt (Fodor, 1983). The approach is explicitly adaptationist. As Symons (1979) has argued, the function of mind is to cause behavior: "A human being is a feeler, an assessor, a planner, and a calculator, that the proximate goal of mental activities always is the attainment of emotional states" (p. 207). The real question is what are the mechanisms and how has it come about that we have them (Barkow, 1989; Barkow, Cosmides, & Tooby, 1992; Buss, 1991; Buss & Schmidtt, 1993; Daly & Wilson, 1988).

Traditional life-span or life-course approaches (Caspi & Bem, 1990) conceive of the life course as "a sequence of culturally defined, age-graded roles that the individual enacts over time" (p. 549). Although correct as far as it goes, such an approach ignores the fact that life histories themselves are complex evolved adaptions (Betzig, Mulder, & Turke, 1988; Stearns, 1992). Parent-offspring conflict, for example, is a striking feature of everyone's life history; it expresses itself during adolescence and is a cross-cultural universal (Brown, 1991) with functional evolutionary roots (Trivers, 1985a). It is not—as claimed by adherents of the SSSM—an arbitrary result of culture, Margaret Mead notwithstanding (Freeman, 1983, 1992). As Trivers puts it,

> If this argument is valid, then it is clearly a mistake to view socialization in humans (or any other sexually reproducing species) as only or even primarily a process of "enculturation," a process by which parents teach their offspring their culture (e.g., Mussen, Conger, & Kagan, 1969, p. 259). . . . According to the theory presented here, socialization is a process by which parents attempt to mold each offspring in order to increase their own inclusive fitness, while each offspring is selected to resist some of the modeling and to attempt to mold the behavior of its parents (and siblings) in order to increase its inclusive fitness. (p.260)

Consider specifically the personality trait of authoritarianism (Adorno, Frenkel-Brunswick, Levinson, & Sanford, 1950). This dimension of personality has had a checkered history (Christie, 1991; Christie & Jahoda, 1954), but it is so powerful that it continues to appear in tests. Thus we see it as "traditionalism" in the Multidimensional Personality Questionnaire (Tellegen & Waller, in press) and "tolerance" in the California Psychological Inventory (Gough, 1987). The most sophisticated contemporary measure of this dimension of personality is the Right-Wing Authoritarian (RWA) scale (Altmeyer, 1988; Christies, 1991). Altmeyer and almost everyone else has treated this trait as environmental in origin (shaped by culture and socialization, in SSSM terminology). Altmeyer (1988) conducted a longitudinal study following up of college students 8 years after they left the university and 12 years after they had first taken the RWA as freshmen. The correlation between the 1974 scores and the 1986 scores was .62, indicating considerable change in ranking. The mean had gone from 152.5 as freshman to 145.5 in 1986; only about half the individuals were within half a standard deviation of their original score.

Altmeyer had already shown with other samples that RWA scores steadily declined over the course of a student's university education, a consistent finding in the attitude literature. Yet this difference in his own sample was much less than expected (these students had averaged 6 years at the university). What happened? When he examined the data in more detail Altmeyer found a subgroup of 48 cases (more than one-half of the sample) that had exactly the same scores as when they began their college education. Who were these people? They consisted of all of the individuals who were parents. Becoming a parent, in short, literally wiped out all the effects of 4 years of college experience on this trait; such an effect is a clear-cut prediction from parental investment models in sociobiology (Trivers, 1985b, chap. 9). The remainder of the cases scored just where they would be predicted to have scored given the continuous influence of the culture of higher education. The influence of parenthood has been studied repeatedly by developmentalists (Feldman & Aschenbrenner, 1983), but not from the point of view of parental investment models. Such an approach would put the research directly in the middle of a contemporary revolution in the behavioral and biological sciences.

The subtlety of the meaning of some RWA items and how they interact with life-course events is quite interesting. Consider item 13: "Rules about being 'well-mannered' and respectable are chains from the past which we should question very thoroughly before accepting." The antiauthoritarian response is to agree. But this response presumes that it is possible to figure out why particular "manners" make sense before accepting them. J. Q. Wilson (1993, p. 83), arguing from a sociobiological perspective, points out that manners and etiquette—while to some extent arbitrary in content—are near universals across cultures and represent an important set of processes for both teaching and signaling self-control. Most parents recognize this almost instinctively.

The history of authoritarianism in behavior genetics is also interesting. Scarr and Weinberg (1981) included a 20-item version of the F-Scale as a control variable in their large-scale adoption study. They expected it to show considerable similarity in adoptive families, thus demonstrating common family environmental influences. Sandra Scarr is a sophisticated developmental behavior geneticist who long ago had discarded an easy environmental approach to individual differences in intelligence and personality, but to her a simple common family environmental approach to attitudes had seemed reasonable. In fact, though, she and Weinberg demonstrated that the "differences in social-political attitudes, measured by the F-Scale, appear to be genetically transmitted from parents to their children in the form of verbal ability and personality and to show no effects of direct learning" (p. 400). A path analysis of the data also showed that "whatever is measured by the F-Scale, apart from verbal skills, is almost as 'heritable' as verbal skills," although the amount of the latter type of transmission was small. The authors admittedly failed to notice the strong correlation between IQ, SES, educational level, and the F-Scale and therefore not seeing the genetic link, via the strong genetic influence that they had already demonstrated underlay these variables (Scarr & Weinberg, 1978).

Scarr and Weinberg gave their results an "intellectual sophistication" interpretation, arguing that the strong correlation between the F-Scale and IQ reflects the product of social reasoning processes rather than social learning or modeling. More specifically, the items of a test like the F-Scale are a sample of conclusions that people have drawn based on their experiences in the world. This same interpretation was given by Himmelweit and Swift (1971) to the results of their longitudinal study of authoritarianism and Adelson (1975) based on his work on the development of political reasoning. Scarr has since developed a theoretical model that incorporates and elaborates these ideas as a fundamental explanation for most individual differences (Scarr, 1992; Scarr & McCartney, 1983), and we have elaborated on her theory (Bouchard et al., in press).

There are no longitudinal studies of this variable that extend over the entire life course. Cross-sectional studies of conservatism (a highly related variable), however, demonstrate dramatic age × level of education effects (Truett, 1993). An important point made by the Truett data is that real changes do not appear to occur before 30 or 40 years of age. The longitudinal studies that we have utilizing related constructs (authoritarianism, traditionalism) only cover earlier ages. The cross-sectional nature of the Truett data also confounds precisely the underlying relationships in which we are interested. Individuals with less education have lower IQs and bear more children than individuals with more education (Retherford, 1993); the former also have their children earlier. It would, however, have been very informative to see this data broken down within educational category by marital and reproductive status. Note also that older cohorts probably have more children. An even more important point made by the Truett data is that dramatic change that does appear to occur in later life (basically after the 5th decade, although this may be a cohort effect).

INTELLIGENCE

The Structure of Mental Abilities

In order to organize the findings from the intellectual domain, it is useful to place them in a frame of reference. The largest and most sophisticated review and re-analysis of the mental ability literature is that of Carroll (1993), and we will use his "structure of cognitive abilities." The structure is shown in Figure 1.

Carroll is confident that the overall evidence supports a factor of 'general intelligence' (or '*g*') along the lines suggested by Spearman and others. There is considerable evidence however, for what have long been called "group factors." Carroll identifies eight of them: fluid intelligence, crystallized intelligence, general memory and learning, broad visual perception, broad auditory perception, broad retrieval ability, broad cognitive speediness, and processing speed. The bottom stratum in Carroll's model consists of abilities measured with specific tests. In this chapter we will deal almost exclusively with '*g*.'

Continuity and Change in Cognitive Development in Early Childhood

How do the numerous special mental abilities in the Carroll model come about? Are all levels in place early in life? Is there differentiation from a general factor? To what extent are heredity and environment involved? These are all questions that have interested developmentalists from early on.

The Louisville Longitudinal Twin Study

The Louisville longitudinal twin study (R. S. Wilson, 1983) provides us with some basic observations that answer some of the questions. Figure 2 shows the mental development correlations for three sibling groups—monozygotic (MZ) twins, dizygotic (DZ) twins, and twin-sibling sets—as well as mid parent-offspring and the age-to-age correlations for the children.

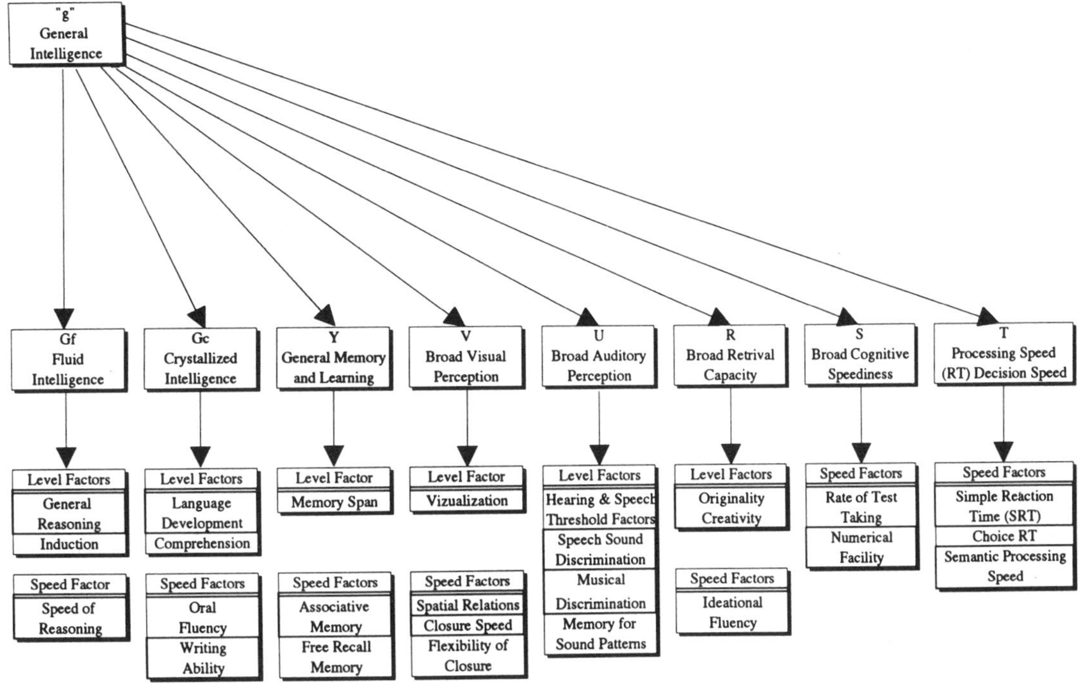

Figure 1. The Carroll structure of mental abilities (modified from Carroll, 1993).

These data tell us that environmental factors dominate as an explanation of the variance in mental development measures very early in life, but that genetic factors begin to express themselves soon afterward. Genetic expression is shown by the differentiation of the MZ and DZ correlations and the growth of the twin-sibling and parent-offspring correlations. Notice the strong tendency for all these effects to converge at about 5 to 6 years of age. Some of these effects, of course, are attributable to the changing nature of the instruments (basically what can be measured) and their increasing validity.

One of the remarkable findings in the Wilson study was the heritable nature of the trends in mental development. From ages 3 months to 6 years the individual children showed tremendous variability in their scores from one testing session to another. The MZ twins where highly concordant for these changes, and the DZ twins much less concordant. Figure 3 give some sample profiles. The top four panels show the remarkable similarity in patterns of change in MZ twins; the lower four panels show the lower concordance but not total discordance expected for DZ twins.

The Colorado Adoption Project

The Colorado Adoption Project (CAP) is a longitudinal prospective adoption study of behavioral development (DeFries, Plomin, & Fulker, 1994; Plomin & DeFries, 1985; Plomin, DeFries, & Fulker, 1988). Two recent reports from CAP (Fulker & Cardon, 1993; Fulker, Cherny, & Cardo, 1993) illustrate the enormous gain in conceptual power that occurs when twins and adoptees are added to a longitudinal design. The study is a multivariate one, and powerful modeling techniques are utilized.

> By entering the traits and correlated variables into such an analysis we can determine whether the causes of observed relationships among them are genetic or environmental in origin. By entering the same or similar measures at different ages we can determine whether the developmental process is driven by the genes or the environment. By breaking down general intelligence into its specific components we can determine whether genetic or environmental influences are responsible for the apparent organization of the specific traits into simpler entitles. Finally, if we have suitable data, we can combine these questions and ask what drives the developmental processes that organize specific abilities into more general components at different points in time (Fulker & Cardon, 1993, p. 36).

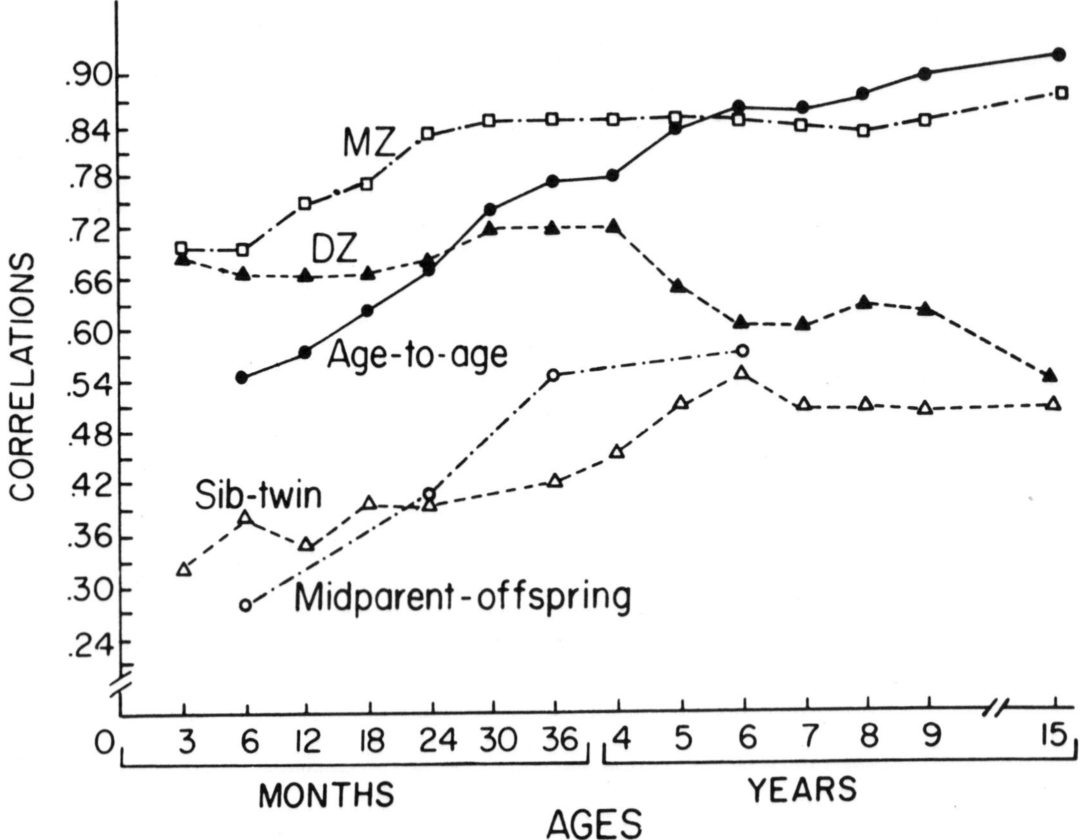

Figure 2. Mental development correlations for MZ twins, DZ twins, twin-sibling sets, parent-offspring sets, and individual children from age to age (from Wilson, 1983).

The analysis presented below makes use of twin (201 MZ, 175 same-sex DZ pairs) and sibling (102 biological, 87 adopted pairs) data (with the sample size dropping to about half at the last data point) gathered at 1, 2, 3, 4, and 7 years of age (Bayley Mental Development Index at ages 1 and 2, Stanford-Binet at ages 3 and 4, WISC-R at age 7). Specific cognitive abilities were available at ages 3, 4, 7, and 9. Figure 4 shows the results of fitting the so-called Cholesky decomposition model (often referred to in the factor analysis literature as a triangular factorization; Gorsuch, 1983) to the data from years 1 to 9 on the IQ measures. The boxes indicate the IQ phenotype at each age; sources of environmental variance are shown at the bottom and sources of genetic variance are shown at the top. The loadings are factor loading from common environmental influences (CE), genetic influences (G), and unique environmental influences (unlabeled). The following conclusions flow from the analysis and figure:

1. There is one continuous source of common family environmental influence across all ages. The remaining environmental influence is unique and transitory to each age; at no point does it even persist across even a single pair of years. Most of this influence is measurement error and state fluctuation (see discussion below of Moffitt, Caspi, Harkness, & Silva, 1993).
2. A common genetic factor existing at year 1 continues to influence IQ, but with diminishing impact, through year 9.
3. New genetic factors come into play, with continuing but diminishing influence, at years 2 and 3 but not at year 4.

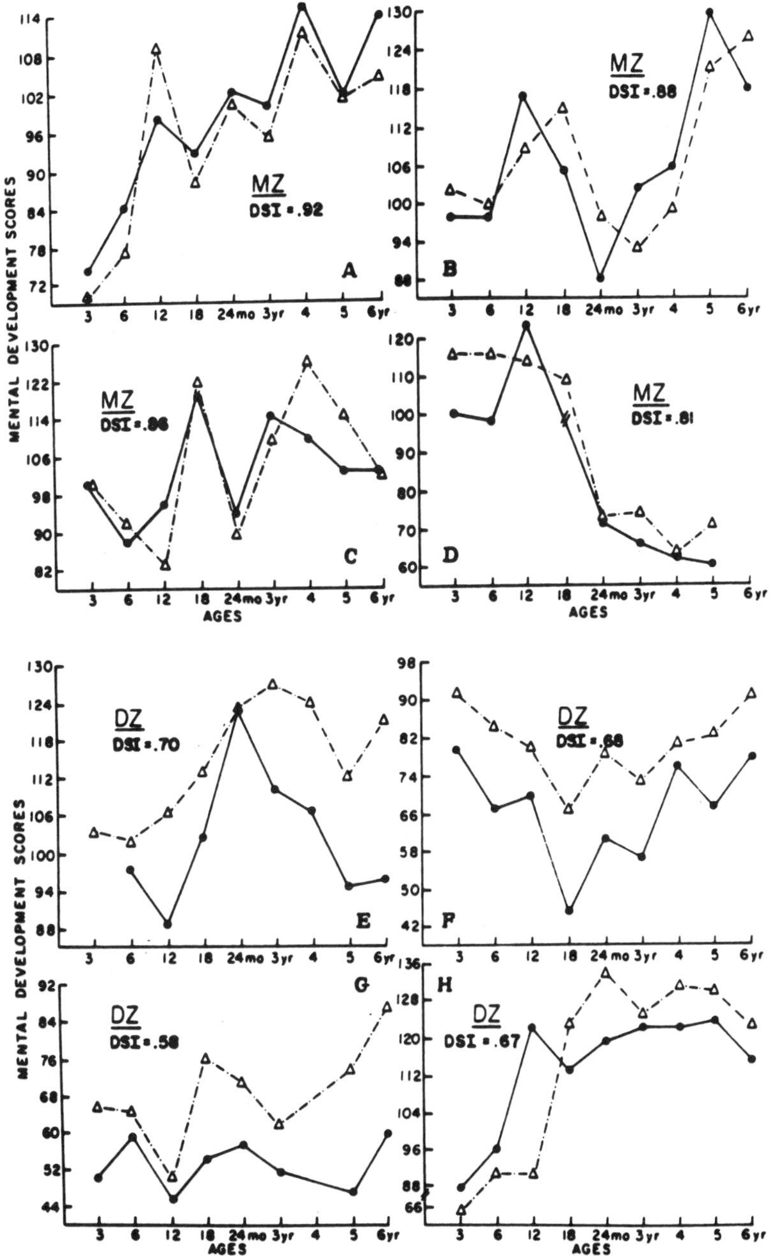

Figure 3. Trends in mental development during early childhood for four MZ and four DZ pairs (from Wilson, 1983).

4. A new genetic influence does arise at year 7 and persists to age 9.

Clearly we have a dynamic process at work. Fulker, Cherney, and Cardon (1993) speculate that the new genetic variance that expresses itself at age 7 may be in response to the "novel environmental challenge" of schooling. I would suggest that although this is possible, the observation of fundamental cognitive change at about this time goes back a long way, and one can ask why most societies send their children to school at about this age. In any event, in line with the R. S. Wilson (1983) findings, we clearly see that genetic factors are implicated in developmental change.

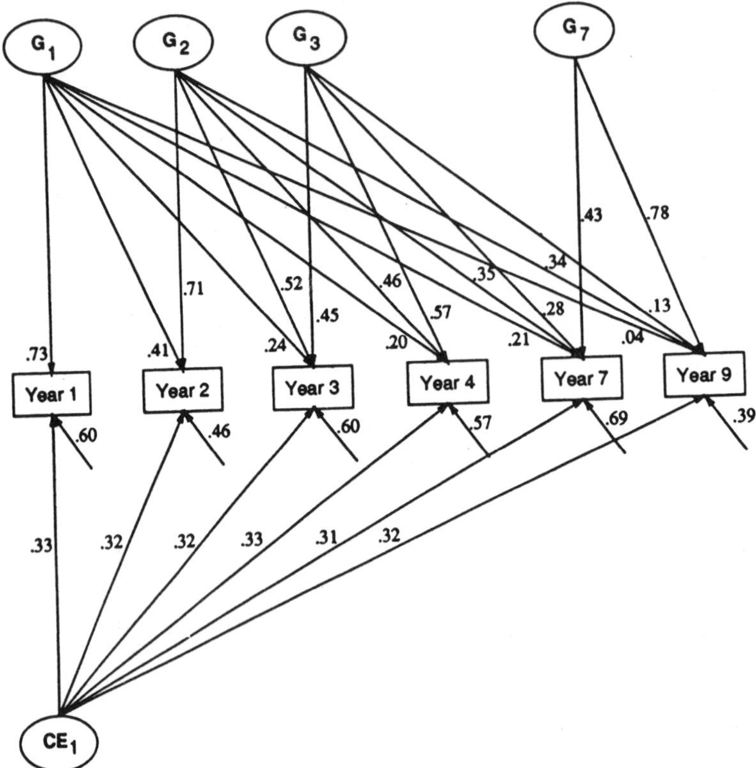

Figure 4. Final reduced model of cognitive development for years 1, 2, 3, 4, 7, and 9 (from Fulker, Cherney, & Cardon, 1993). The unlabeled factors are unique environmental time-specific influences. G = genetic influence; CE = shared environmental influence.

None of these findings can be inferred from phenotypic correlations alone; only a behavior genetic longitudinal design can bring them out.

I turn next to the issue of differentiation. As mentioned above, specific cognitive ability tests were administered at ages 3, 4, 7, and 9. Cardon and Fulker (1993) subjected the data to a hierarchical analysis conceptually quite similar to that of Carroll (1993), but including estimation of genetic and environmental parameters at each age and their correlations across time. There were sufficient tests to target four factors—verbal (V), spatial (S), perceptual speed (P), and memory (m)—with more than one test, thus allowing the investigators to cope directly with the reliability problem.[1] Both a static and a dynamic picture of the results are of interest. Table 1 below shows the heritable (h^2) and common family environmental influences on the four abilities at each age. I have added the results of a study by the Western Reserve Twin Project (Thompson, 1993; Thompson, Detterman, & Plomin, 1991) as a basis of comparison for a slightly older group. The latter data are very similar to adult data, where the average heritability is about .50 (Bouchard, Segal, & Lykken, 1990; DeFries, Vandenberg, & McClearn, 1976).

These data are interesting in many ways. First, they show dramatic changes in genetic and environmental influences from one measurement period to another. If the data were from different studies, it would be easy to ascribe the effect to different measurement techniques. In addition, in the Cardon and Fulker (1993) study estimates of nonshared environmental influence (e^2), though not shown in the table, are large; this is not attributable to measurement error, as multiple measures are used to estimate all effects in the model. These traits are clearly dynamic in their development, although this should not be misinterpreted to mean that they are highly malleable or easily thrown off course. The cross-sectional comparisons

[1]The tests were designed to be similar to those used in the Hawaii family study (DeFries, Vandenberg, & McClearn, 1976; DeFries, et al., 1974) and have also been used in the Minnesota study of twins reared apart (Bouchard, Segal, & Lykken, 1990), among others.

Table 1. Genetic and Environmental Estimates of Variance by Age for Four Specific Cognitive Abilities

		Verbal		Spatial		Perceptual speed		Memory	
Study	Age	h^2	c^2	h^2	c^2	h^2	c^2	h^2	c^2
Thompson (1993)[a]	7–12	.48	.12	.75	.03	.60	.11	.41	.02
Cardon and Fulker (1993)[b]	3	.56	.04	.17	.05	.66	.31	.97	.01
	4	.46	.03	.19	.02	.33	.03	.75	.01
	7	.65	.35	.97	.03	.34	.00	.82	.00
	9	.74	.06	.13	.26	.04	.64	.05	.00

[a]From Table 3.8
[b]From Table 1

and the adult data suggest that they eventually reach a common level of h^2 = .50. In terms used to describe longitudinal IQ change in the Dunedin study (described below), they are probably elastic rather than plastic.

This elasticity, which is influenced both by genes and environment, is also illustrated in the longitudinal hierarchical analysis of specific abilities shown in Figure 5. This figure illustrates the very first solid evidence "for genetic influences on specific abilities in childhood that are unrelated to those determining general cognition," and "the longitudinal outcomes extend the findings of genetic communality and specificity, which suggests that the ability-specific genes are pervasive throughout young childhood. In addition, the genetic persistence underlying observed continuity is accompanied by transitions in the genotype that lead to observed change" (Moffit et al., 1993, p. 117).

The figure is to be read as follows. The parameter estimates represent genetic influence, but are not heritability estimates. At year 3 the paths running from IQ to V, S, P, and M represent the full genetic effect attributable to IQ at that point in time. The residual genetic influences are shown underneath (.44 to V, .42 for S, .53 for P, .00 for M). The horizontal paths reflect the influence that carries over from year 3 to year 4; notice that the effects are sizable for the four specific abilities and much larger than for IQ. Except for V, there is very little new genetic influence (unique or from IQ) on the four specific abilities at year 4, although a considerable amount of new genetic variance in introduced in IQ at year 4 (.92). For all four abilities as well as IQ, genetic influence at year 4 is carried forward to year 7. A considerable amount of new genetic variance is introduced to IQ at year 7, and little is shared with the specific abilities (the loadings are negative, reflecting in part some instabilities in the model and/or data; the data seem strange, but remember that cross-multiplying negative numbers yields positive outcomes). At year 7 compared to year 4, a great deal of new genetic variance is introduced to all the specific abilities. From year 7 to year 9 there is considerable transmission of genetic influence for the special abilities but very little for IQ. At year 9 there is a large influx of new genetic variance for IQ and virtually none for the specific abilities. IQ also contributes little common genetic variance to the specific (again the loadings are negative).[2]

There are other reports from CAP (Cardon, DiLalla, Plomin, DeFries, & Fulker, 1990; Cardon & Fulker, 1993; Cardon, Fulker, DeFries, & Plomin, 1992; Fulker et al., 1993). Reports also are now appearing for participants in the MacArthur Longitudinal Twin Study (Plomin et al., 1993); these are discussed below.

A "Gold Standard" Longitudinal Study of IQ from Middle Childhood to Adolescence

The Dunedin longitudinal study (Silva, 1990) has recently reported on its IQ findings (Moffitt et al., 1993); this study, in both its execution and its data analysis, is so superior to all previous studies that it is almost not necessary to examine other longitudinal studies of this age span. The study consists of 794 children (constituting a nearly representative sample[3])

[2]Note that the IQ loadings at years 4, 7, and 9 are not what would be obtained if a cross-sectional analysis were carried out. They represent new contributions of IQ. Cross-sectional loadings would look more like the loadings at year 3.

[3]Not a high-IQ sample like the Berkeley-Oakland or Fels studies (Honzik, 1986; Sontag, Baker, & Nelson, 1958).

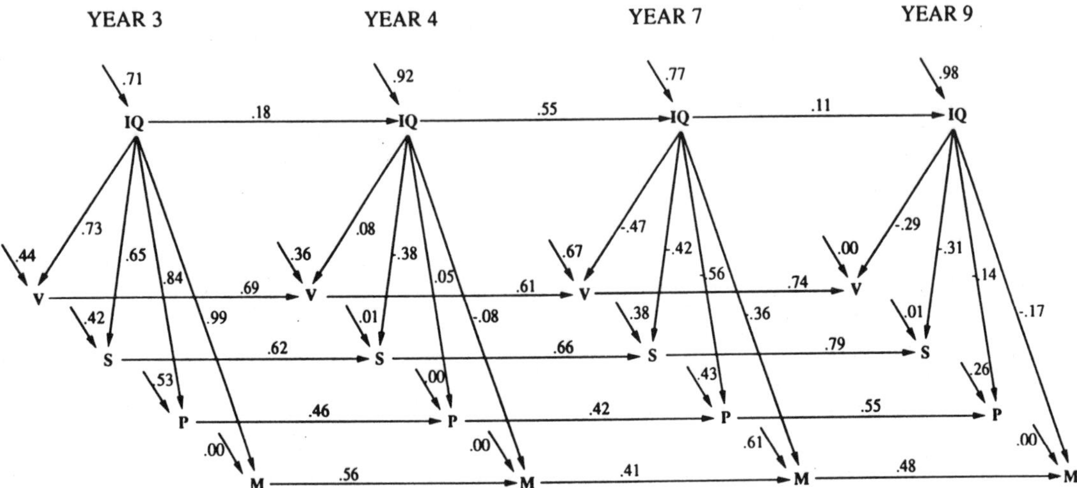

Figure 5. Genetic parameter estimates from reduced longitudinal hierarchical model. Measurement loadings and residuals have been omitted to simplify illustration. Symbols V, S, P, and M denote verbal, spatial, perceptual speed, and memory abilities respectively (from Cardon & Fulker, 1993).

and who are were assessed very close to their birthday with the WISC-R at ages 7, 9, 11, and 13. The study data set was analyzed to determine which children changed, how much, and whether the change was meaningful. The answers were that: it is difficult to tell who changes; there is not much change; and, the change that occurs is not very meaningful. These answers are disheartening to some, but they are coherent, have theoretical verisimilitude, and are based on powerful and sophisticated data analytic strategies. The authors, though, recognize that the study could have been improved very significantly had it incorporated behavior genetic design principles—most importantly, incorporating more than one child per family (Hetherington, Reiss, & Plomin, 1994; Plomin & Daniels, 1987) and including measures of within-family environmental differences. The addition of adoptees, twins, and measures of parental characteristics would certainly have been desirable, but these would have constituted a very different kind of study.

Moffitt et al. (1993) argue correctly that nearly all previous longitudinal studies of IQ assumed that the temporal profiles of intellectual performance were as reliable as the individual points. Indeed, until this study the reliability of profiles of intellectual development were unknown. Ordinary profiles can be described in terms of elevation, shape, and scatter (Cronbach & Gleser, 1953). As Moffitt et al. point out, it may be that once elevation is removed from a profile, the remainder (the pattern, which is made up of shape and scatter) is largely error saturated. They addressed this problem by subdividing the subtests of the WISC-R into two parallel forms, which allowed them to generate two profiles over the four testing periods for each child. This procedure is not as simple as it seems, and considerable psychometric sophistication was necessary to do it correctly.

Three different cluster analysis procedures were then used to determine types of profiles in the data base: average linkage, complete linkage, and wards. Moffitt et al. generated 11 different solutions via each method, and each method yielded 2 to 12 profile types. Using the method of co-capturability and taking into account change matches generated by the varying base rates of the different profiles, the authors determined the reliability of all the profiles with and without elevation. The findings are shown in Figure 6.

Removing elevation (compare the three IQ vs. the three IQ-E groups) radically reduced the reliability of the profiles. In addition, the reliability of profile also declined as the number of clusters increased. All the cluster analysis methods yielded fairly similar results; consequently, the remainder of the analysis made use of the wards clustering method, which is the most straightforward and probably the most widely used in the behavioral sciences (see Aldenderfer & Blashfield,

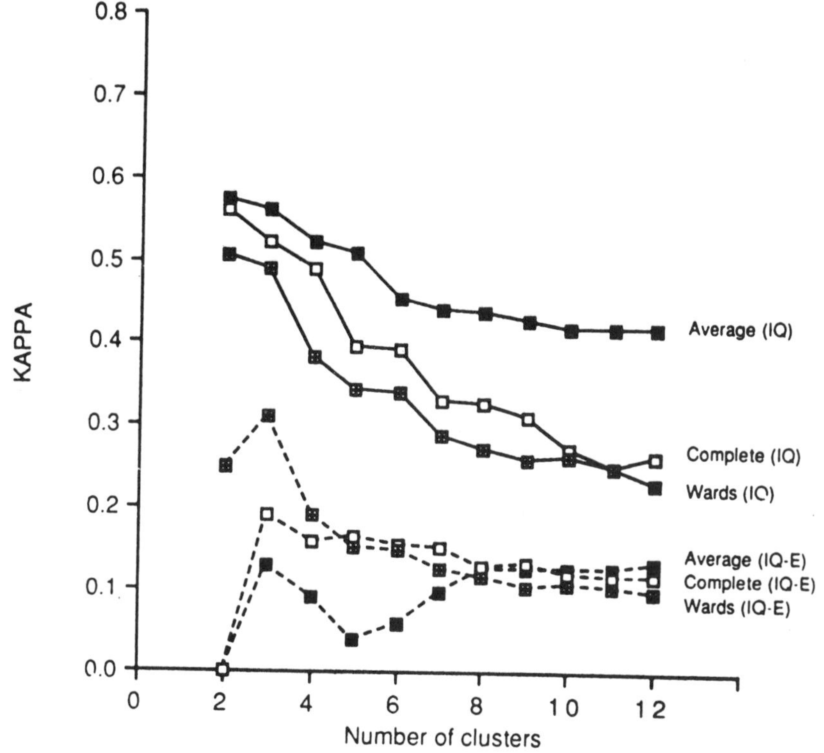

Figure 6. Reliability κ as a function of the number of clusters generated by three different clustering methods (from Moffitt, Caspi, Harkness, & Silva, 1993). The results are presented for IQ profiles that retain elevation (IQ) and for IQ profiles that refer to pattern without elevation (IQ-e).

1984). Using the Spearman-Brown formula, Moffitt et al. were able to project the reliability of IQ profiles constructed from the full complement of subtests on the WISC-R. The profiles were very unreliable, suggesting strongly "that the replicable fact that can be gleaned from the repeated assessment of IQ is the elevation." (p. 475). A second method of assessing the same question was also applied. The authors asked, "Does the variation across the years in our profiles coincide with the amount of change that classical psychometric tests theory would predict if each child's four observed IQ scores were randomly distributed about the child's true score?" (p. 475). To answer this question, they calculated the standard deviation of each child's four scores around his or her grand mean across the four testing occasions. The distribution is shown in Figure 7. Most of the children fell within one standard deviation of the standard error criterion and thus failed to show change in excess of expected measurement error. A third approach to this question was applied in which the variances of the children's deviations around their own mean was compared to the expected variance; there was very little difference.

In all of the above analyses, the majority of the children showed changes only consistent with the known reliability of the test. There were, however, children who fell outside this pattern—in other words, highly variable children. How reliable were their profiles? The authors selected the 107 children who demonstrated the greatest amount of variability. Using the procedures described earlier, they were able to show that these individuals did have more reliable profiles than the sample at large (average kappa of .60 vs .26 across the 11 clusters, using the Spearman-Brown correction to full test length). These data suggested that there were six quite reliable profile clusters in this group of children.

One of the more striking findings at this point (though one not discussed by the authors) is that among the six profile types, one showed a monotonic climb across the four periods, and two others showed monotonic climbs over three contiguous periods.

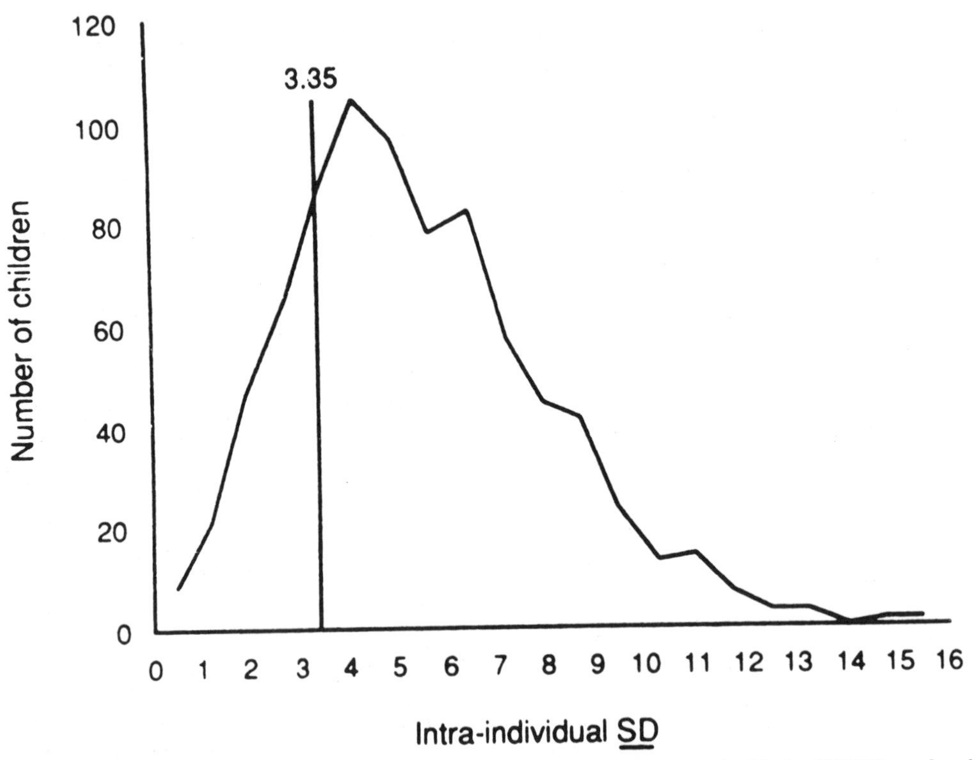

Figure 7. The distribution of intraindividual standard deviations for 794 children tested with the WISC-R on four biennial occasions (from Moffitt, Caspi, Harkness, & Silva, 1993). The standard error of measurement for the test was 3.35.

None, however, showed monotonic declines over either three or four contiguous periods. The preponderance of positive profiles and lack of negative ones seems to throw some doubt on one very common environmental hypothesis—namely, that although it is difficult to increase IQ via environmental means, negative environmental events can conspire (within the typical range of family environments) to inhibit its growth. This speculative interpretation is entirely consistent with the authors' conclusion that the profiles appear to represent level-maintaining and level-seeking phenomena rather than direct environmental influences. The authors did observe that although additive change (sum of changes regardless of direction) among these children was impressive (37.63 IQ points over 7 years), the cumulative and sequential amount of change (directional change) over the same period averaged only 5.3 IQ points.

It is tempting to suggest that these profiles of change might reflect genetic factors. The data from R. S. Wilson (1983), discussed earlier, demonstrated this phenomena in young children; I know of no comparable data for children in the 7- to 13-year-old range. The change that is occurring in these young children may reflect the expression of developmental genetic processes that cause them eventually to resemble their relatives (twins, siblings, and parents) to the degree that they share genes in common. This fact is illustrated in Figure 2. The important point to glean from this figure is the fact that much, but not all, of the resemblance is achieved by age 6. More likely we are seeing mostly level-seeking and level-maintaining change as a function of temporary perturbations. It should also be kept in mind that developmental processes within individuals may be expressing themselves in other domains (personality and interests) that have indirect effects on IQ.

The highly labile children did not differ from the large sample in ability, nor did they differ from the other children when compared on a wide variety of family characteristics (percentage reared by two biological parents, SES, maternal mental health, etc.) and own characteristics (e.g., perinatal problems, CNS syndromes, behavior problems). I cannot summarize this study better than the authors themselves;

> Our data have led us to the reluctant conclusion that there is very little measurable naturalistic change in IQ across middle childhood and early adolescence. Moreover, the reliable change that does take place appears to be idiosyncratic; it is not systematically associated with environmental changes. . . . Much to our chagrin, we (and many others) seem to have committed two fundamental errors in approaching this research: we overgeneralized from the unique and we imputed causation to correlation. (Moffitt et al., 1993, p. 499)

It is very important to recognize how common these errors are even among investigators who purport to have a genetic orientation. Consider the review of the Berkeley longitudinal studies by Honzik (1986). She clearly recognizes genetic changes early in life as the children increasingly come to resemble their parents, but other influences that could be genetic are interpreted by her as environmental. These results are striking and a genetic interpretation is consistent with the analysis of Figure 2. As R. S. Wilson (1983) puts it, "The cumulative effect of being raised together in the same home appears not to offset the developmental trend towards a level of similarity commensurate with the extent of shared genotype" (p. 312). This conclusion is also compatible with the finding that unrelated individuals reared together do resemble each other during early childhood, but show an essentially zero correlation when assessed in adulthood (McGue, Bouchard et al., 1993). There is, however, only one longitudinal study that measures such individuals at both ages (Loehlin, Horn, & Willerman, 1989).

Continuity and Change in Cognitive Functioning in Adulthood

There are few longitudinal twin studies of IQ in adulthood. Swan and his colleagues (Swan et al., 1990; Swan, LaRue, Carmelli, Reed, & Fabsitz, 1992) have studied small samples of MZ and DZ twins who are part of the National Heart, Lung, and Blood Institute twin study. They have shown that the heritability of performance on the digit-symbol subtest of the WAIS increases with age and that there is higher concordance for decline in performance in the MZ than the DZ sample, suggesting a possible role for genetic factors in any explanation of the decline. Jarvik and Bank (1983) have reported on a continuing study of a small sample of twins initially begun by Kallman (Kallman, Feingold, & Bondy, 1951). Contrary to what one might expect from a wear-and-tear perspective (Baltes, 1987) cross-sectional twin studies clearly support the view that heritability increases over the life span, even into old age (McGue, Bacon, & Lykken, 1993; Pedersen, Plomin, Nesselroade, & McClearn, 1992).

PERSONALITY

The Structure of Personality

Findings in the personality domain also should be placed in a frame of reference. The two major competing paradigms that specify the hierarchical structure of personality differ in the number of super factors (somewhat heterogeneous factors that subsume a larger number of more specific traits or facts) they specify. The Eysenck "big three"—Extraversion, Neuroticism, and Psychoticism (Eaves, Eysenck, & Martin, 1989, chap. 2; Eysenck & Eysenck, 1985)—has been an influential competitor for many years, and Eysenck continues to defend it against challengers, particularly the so-called big five (Eysenck, 1992, 1993). The "big five"—Extraversion, Neuroticism, Openness to Experience, Agreeableness, and Conscientiousness—have a long history but have taken center stage only recently. This model has been championed by a number of investigators (Goldberg, 1992b, 1993) but is often identified with the NEO PI-R (Costa & McCrae, 1992a, b). Table 2 shows the big five, sample bipolar scales often used to define the factors (Goldberg, 1992a), the Costa and McGrae facets, the California Psychological Inventory (CPI) regression equations for predicting the big five from the CPI (Gough, 1989, personal communication), and the highest loading Multidimensional Personality Questionnaire (MPQ) scales (Tellegen & Waller, in press).

It is obvious that there is agreement on Extraversion and Neuroticism. Eysenck argues that Psychoticism subsumes Agreeableness and Conscientiousness, and Zukerman and colleagues (Zukerman, Kuhlman, Joireman, Teta, & Kraft, 1993) have shown the same thing. With regard to the big five, Goldberg construes the Costa and McCrae Openness to Experience factor somewhat differently and calls it Intellect or Sophistication. There are also good grounds for dividing Extraversion into an Affiliative component and a Potency component (Hough, 1992; Waller, in press) and creating an Achievement (Hough, 1992) or Purpose-

Table 2. The "Big Five" Factors

Factor	Alternate names	Sample bipolar scales	Six NEO-PI-R facet scales	California Psychological Inventory regression equation	One or two highest loading Multidimensional Personality Questionnaires scales
Extraversion	Surgency Introversion-extraversion (−) Dominance	Introverted–extroverted Unenergetic–energetic Timid–bold	Warmth Gregariousness Assertiveness Activity Excitement-seeking Positive emotions	Extraversion = dominance + self-acceptance − self-control	Social closeness Social potency
Neuroticism	Adjustment Anxiety Emotional stability (−) Stress reactivity (−)	Angry–calm Nervous–at ease Emotional–unemotional	Anxiety Angry hostility Depression Self-consciousness Impulsiveness Vulnerability	Adjustment = well-being + work orientation − anxiety	Stress reaction Well-being
Conscientiousness	Conformity Dependability Authoritarianism (−)	Disorganized–organized Irresponsible–responsible Careless–thorough	Competence Order Dutifulness Achievement striving Self-discipline Deliberation	Conscientiousness = responsibility + achievement vis conformance − flexibility	Control Achievement
Agreeableness	Likability Friendliness Pleasant	Cold–warm Selfish–unselfish Distrustful–trustful	Trust Straightforwardness Altruism Compliance Modesty Tendermindedness	Agreeableness = socialization + tolerance − nacissism	Aggression
Openness	Culture Intellect Sophistication	Intelligent–unintelligent Reflective–unreflective Creative–uncreative	Fantasy Aesthetics Feelings Actions Ideas Values	Culture = empathy + achievement via independence + creativity	Absorption Harm avoidance

Source: Revised from Bouchard (1993a).

fulness (Cartwright & Peckar, 1993) factor from Extraversion and Conscientiousness.

Longitudinal Behavior Genetic Studies of Personality and Temperament in Infancy

The literature on genetic influence on personality development from infancy to adulthood (mostly cross-sectional) have been reviewed by Goldsmith (1983) and Plomin and Nesselroade (1990). Most behavior genetic studies carried on in this age range, excluding the Louisville longitudinal study (Matheny, 1989), have been severely limited by small sample sizes. The MacArthur Longitudinal Twin Study (MALTS; Plomin et al., 1993), however, is made up of 200 pairs of twins assessed both in the laboratory and at home at 14 and 20 months of age. The data gathered on these twins were analyzed in numerous ways. The results were similar regardless of the analytic techniques applied, and the estimated parameters from a model-fitting approach are shown in Figure 8.

There is far too much information from the study to discuss here, so I will focus on only a few variables. The dark bar in Figure 8 indicates the phenotypic correlation from 14 to 20 months of age. This is the extent to which the measures at the two ages covary and is what must be explained; this correlation does not need to be squared. The hatched section to the left of the dark bar indicates the genetic contribution to continuity. In the case of behavioral inhibition, continuity is explained entirely by genetic factors. Change, indexed on the right-hand side, is mediated in part by genetic factors but mostly by nonshared environmental factors (i.e., those unique to each individual) plus error. In the results for the Colorado Childhood Temperament Inventory (CCTI), Emotionality shows a cross-age correlation of about .5. About two-thirds of the continuity is genetic, a tiny portion is the result of shared environment, and the remainder is attributable to nonshared environment plus error. All change is attributable to nonshared environment plus error. CCTI Shyness shows strong continuity (about .65), and two-thirds of that is the result of genetic factors. Again, however, change is accounted for entirely by nonshared environmental factors plus error.

Because of the great variety of results, these findings are very difficult to summarize. Genetic factors are responsible for a very significant amount of the continuity for most variables from 14 to 20 months of age, and they also mediate change for some variables. One interesting pattern in the data is that most vari-

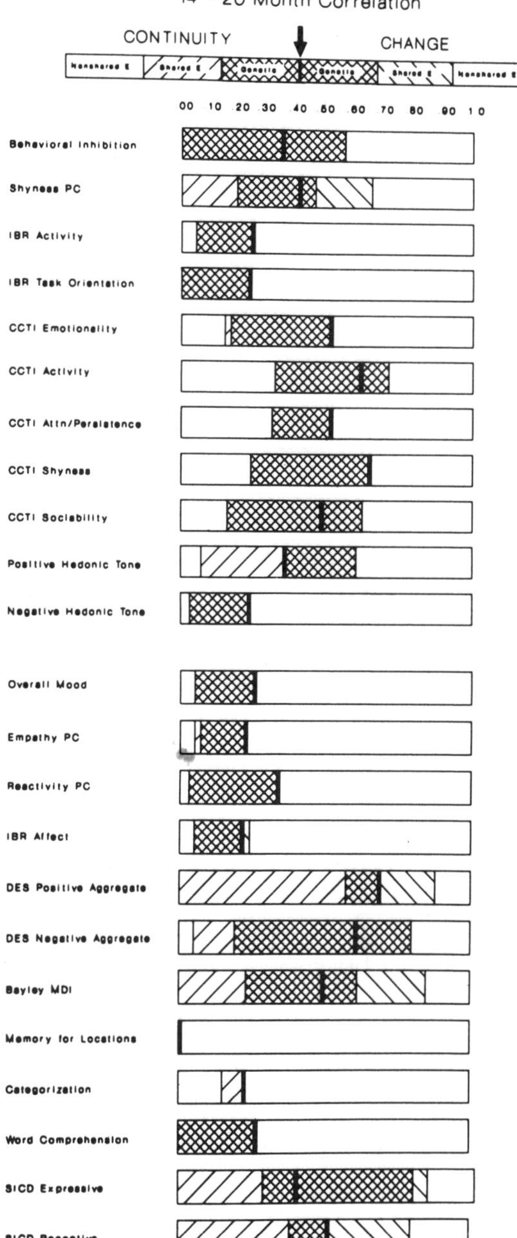

Figure 8. Summary of genetic and environmental components of continuity and change (from Plomin et al., 1993). As indicated in the key at the top of the figure, the vertical bar (marked with an arrow in the key) indicates the phenotypic correlation from 14 to 20 months. To the left of the bar are the genetic, shared environmental, and nonshared environmental components of the phenotypic correlation; to the right of the bar are the components of change. These components of continuity and change are derived from model-fitting parameter estimates.

ables show very little shared environmental influence for either continuity or change. Six or maybe seven variables show a reasonable amount of nonshared environmental influence; three of these—Bayley Development Index (BDI), Sequenced Inventory of Communication Development (SICD) Expressive, and SICD Receptive—involve the assessment of cognition or language. These results are very similar to what is found in adolescence—namely, shared environmental influence on cognition but little or no shared environmental influence on personality (Plomin & Daniels, 1987). As mentioned earlier, shared environmental influence on cognition appears to disappear in adulthood.

Longitudinal Behavior Genetic Studies of Personalty From Adolescence to Adulthood

The amount and quality of data in this age range are very limited. Dworkin and colleagues have analyzed Minnesota Multiphasic Personality Inventory (MMPI) and California Psychological Inventory (CPI) data gathered initially on high school twins (25 MZ and 17 DZ pairs) and then 12 years later (Dworkin, Burke, Maher, & Gottesman, 1976, 1977). They concluded that there was sufficient evidence of genetic influence on change for some traits (5 of 15 MMPI scales and 2 of 18 CPI scales) to recommend appropriate longitudinal twin and adoption studies. Pogue-Geile and Rose (1985) administered 6 MMPI scales (different scales than Dworkin et al., using some of the Wiggins scales as opposed to the clinical scales) to 71 MZ and 62 DZ twin pairs 5 years apart (20 to 25 years of age). Only one or two of the scales showed any genetic contribution to change.

Loehlin and his colleagues (Loehlin, Horn, & Willerman, 1990; Loehlin, Willerman, & Horn, 1987) have reported on personality change in a group of 229 adoptive and 83 biological children who participated in the Texas Adoption Project. The children were originally assessed between the ages of 3 and 14 and then reassessed 10 years later; because of the age span, only parent ratings were available at both ages. The data was organized into three dimensions—extraversion, socialization, and stability—and two different kinds of analyses were applied. The analysis of correlations suggested that most change in personality is nonfamilial (i.e., neither genes nor shared environmental influences are involved), a result consistent with the twin studies. The analysis of mean changes suggested that some change was taking place in the direction of making the children more like their genetic parents. The authors make it clear that the results from the correlation and means analyses are not quantitatively incompatible: There can be systematic changes in group averages while the bulk of change for individuals is idiosyncratic. Overall these studies suggest that there is genetic influence on change for some personality traits between adolescence and adulthood but that the amount is modest, with most change attributable to idiosyncratic environmental factors.

A Longitudinal Behavior Genetic Study of Personality in Early Adulthood

The only longitudinal behavior genetic study of personality in early adulthood was carried out by McGue, Bacon, and Lykken (1993) and included 79 MZ and 48 same-sex DZ twins who had completed the Multidimensional Personality Questionnaire (MPQ) at age 20 and again at age 30. Because the sample size is modest, the findings from this study should be interpreted tentatively. The MPQ has 11 primary scales that are somewhat correlated and yield three superfactors—Positive Emotionality, Negative Emotionality, and Constraint. These higher-order factors correspond to Eysenck's extraversion, neuroticism, and psychoticism, the last somewhat weakly. Figure 9 shows the mean changes for all scales, organized by superfactor, over the 10-year period. Scores on Positive Emotionality (extraversion) clearly remain constant, whereas scores on Negative Emotionality (neuroticism) decrease by about half a standard deviation. Constraint (impulse control, or reverse psychoticism) shows a more complex pattern: an increase on two scales, control and harm avoidance, but no change on traditionalism.

Some of this change is clearly normative. Alienation and aggression, for example, decrease as individuals pass from adolescence to adulthood. Cross-sectional studies show the same result: In a large twin study, Rushton, Fulker, Neale, Nias, and Eysenck, (1986) found a correlation of −.40 between aggression and age. It is surprising that the effect is not larger for the males in this sample as the normative effect for male is quite large (Sampson & Laub, 1990). Aggression is also known to be quite stable (Olweus, 1977; 1979). Huesmann, Eron, Lefkowitz, and Walder (1984) used several indices of aggression in a longitudinal study of males, and a latent trait analysis suggested a 20-year stability of .50.

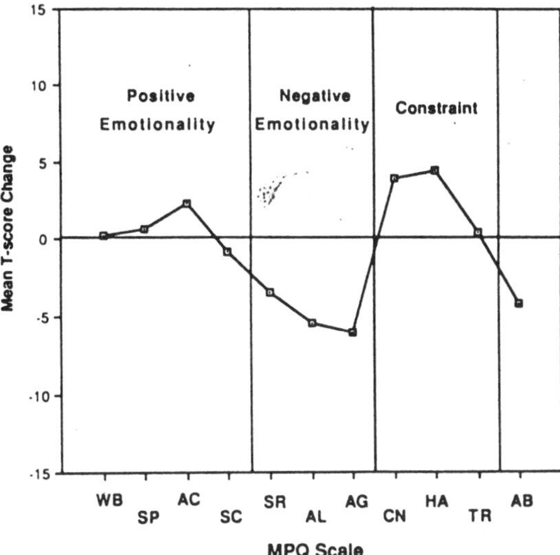

Figure 9. Longitudinal changes in the means of the 11 primary Multidimensional Personality Questionnaire (MPQ) scales pooled over sex (from McGue, Bacon, & Lykken, 1993). Mean changes are measured as time 1 score (in *T-score* units) minus time 2 scores (in *T-score* units). WB = well-being; SP = social potency; AC = achievement; SC = social closeness; SR = stress reaction; AL = alienation; AG = aggression; CN = control; HA = harm avoidance; TR = traditionalism; AB = absorption.

Table 3 gives some correlation information (cross-twin correlations and 10-year retest correlations) from the McGue, Bacon, and Lykken (1993) study and from other twin studies of the MPQ.[1] The correlations for MZ twins reared apart (MZA) estimate the broad heritability of a trait (Bouchard, Lykken, McGue, Segal, & Tellegen, 1990b), and these data show that the correlation for MZ twins raised together (MZT) is quite comparable. This is strong support for the argument that for many trait domains the MZT correlation alone is a good estimate of the broad heritability (Lykken, Bouchard, McGue, & Tellegen, 1993). The DZA and DZT correlations are quite comparable and somewhat less than half the MZ correlations; this finding suggests that there is nonadditive variance for a number of MPQ scales, a conclusion confirmed by a more thorough statistical analysis in the McGue, Bacon, and Lykken paper and previous analyses of the MPQ (Lykken, McGue, Tellegen, & Bouchard, 1992; Tellegen et al., 1988). The most striking finding in the table is that the cross-twin MZT correlations over 10 years (.41) fall only slightly short of the contemporaneous MZA and MZT correlations (.47 and .46). The DZT 10-year cross-twin correlations fall about where they should relative the MZT cross-twin correlations. The initial heritability of these traits, however, is considerably below the 10-year retest stability, a finding that suggests change has occurred. The next question is to what extent both the stability and change are due to genetic and/or environmental factors.

The genetic analyses are relatively complex and will not be described here. Table 4 summarizes the results of the analysis for the higher-order factors; we have already discussed the mean effects above. A question not discussed to this point is change in variances. This is an important question, because heritabilities could remain constant in the face of changes in variance if the changes for both environmental and genetic influences are proportional. For positive emotionality we see stable variances and stable genetic influences, but an increase in environmental influence. For negative emotionality we see decreases for the mean, the variance, and genetic influence, whereas environmental influence is stable. For constraint the pattern is different; the mean increases whereas the other components all remain stable. These results are similar to those found in adolescence: A modest genetic influence on change for some personality traits, but most change resulting from idiosyncratic environmental factors.

A behavior genetic analysis of adult CPI data scored to represent the "big five" shows heritabilities virtually identical to the MPQ data in this study. Further discussion of longitudinal behavior genetic designs can be found in Boomsma (1993), Hahn, Hewitt, Henderson and Benne (1990); Matheny (1990), Molenaar, Boomsma, and Dolan (1991), and Pedersen (1991, 1993).

SUMMARY AND IMPLICATIONS

Longitudinal twin studies of intelligence suggest that very early in life (prior to the age of 1 year), environmental factors are the primary determinant of individual differences. Between 1 and 6 years of age, though, genetic factors express themselves more and

[1]The MZA and DZA correlations are current data from the Minnesota study of twins reared apart. (Bouchard et al., 1990a) The MZT and DZT correlations are current data from the Minnesota twin registry (Lykken, Bouchard, McGue, & Tellegen, 1990). The 30-day reliability data are from the MPQ manual (Tellegen, 1982).

Table 3. Intraclass Correlations for Four Types of Twins, Interclass Cross-Twin Correlations over 10 years for Identical and Fraternal Twins Reared Together, and Within-Person Retest Correlations for the Multidimensional Personality Questionnaire Scales

Twin type:	MZA	MZT	MZTC	DZA	DZT	DZTC	Within-persons	
Testing Period:	Same time	Same time	10 years apart	Same time	Same time	10 years apart	30 days apart	10 years apart
Number of pairs:	52	553	79	33	459	74	75	254
Scales								
Well-being	.53	.44	.40	.18	.11	.07	.90	.50
Social potency	.52	.59	.54	.27	.24	.09	.82	.62
Achievement	.35	.40	.24	.07	.10	−.03	.88	.48
Social closeness	.33	.49	.47	.30	.26	.10	.92	.55
Stress reaction	.57	.45	.41	.27	.19	.01	.89	.53
Alienation	.46	.47	.27	.18	.18	.06	.87	.40
Aggression	.32	.41	.43	.06	.18	−.11	.82	.54
Control	.38	.38	.45	.03	.19	.01	.82	.55
Harm avoidance	.51	.48	.43	.24	.22	.30	.88	.64
Traditionalism	.54	.58	.30	.39	.35	.12	.90	.47
Absorption	.61	.40	.53	.21	.17	.40	.91	.69
Means	.47	.46	.41	.20	.20	.09	.87	.54

Note: MZA = monozygotic twins reared apart, MZT = monozygotic twins reared together, MZTC = monzygotic twins together cross-twin correlations between Twin A's (or B's) scores at time 1 with Twin B's (or A's) score at time 2. DZA = dizygotic twins reared apart, DZT = dizygotic twins reared together, DZTC = Same correlations as MZTC except for DZTs.

Table 4. Qualitative Summary of the Results from the Longitudinal Analysis

	Time 1 to Time 2 change				Heritability of Time 2 component	
Higher-order factor	M	Variance	Genetic effect	Environmental effect	Stability	Residual
Positive emotionality	Stable	Stable	Stable	Increases	Substantial	Modest
Negative emotionality	Decreases	Decreases	Decreases	Stable	Substantial	Moderate
Constraint	Increases	Stable	Stable	Stable	Substantial	Moderate

Note: Heritabilities were judged substantial if .60 or larger, moderate if between .40 and .60, and modest if between .20 and .40.
Source: McGue, Bacon, and Lykken (1993).

more strongly. During this period there can be dramatic changes in an individual child's level of mental development, changes that are often ascribed to environmental influences. Twin studies, however, strongly suggest that patterns of change themselves are under considerable genetic influence. Longitudinal studies employing twins, adoptees, and biological children extend these findings even further. The genetic influence present at age 1 carries through to age 9, but with diminishing influence from year to year. A strong level of genetic influence exists from year to year because new genetic influences come into play each year. These effects, though, are not smooth and continuous. For example, no new genetic influence comes into pay at year 4, but one does come into play at year 7 and persists to year 9 (there are no data for years 5 and 6).

Longitudinal behavior genetic studies have clearly revealed that the process of intellectual development is a far more dynamic process (involving both heredity and environment) than ordinary longitudinal studies had let us to believe. The process of ability differentiation is equally dynamic. Dramatic differences in the influence of heredity and environment can be detected from year to year, and there is reason to believe that these changes reflect the elasticity rather than plasticity of mental ability. The carefully conducted and analyzed Dunedin longitudinal study suggests that in ordinary middle-class families, there is not much meaningful change in intelligence from middle childhood to adolescence; the reliable change that does occur is highly idiosyncratic and is not systematically associated with measured environmental changes. The very few longitudinal studies of intelligence in adult and older twins suggest that heritability increase with age, a finding consistent with the cross-sectional studies. The heritability of intelligence in adulthood may be as high as .80. These studies also suggest that there is a possible role for genetic factors in the explanation of decline in intelligence in old age.

There are far fewer longitudinal behavior genetic studies of personality than of intelligence. Nevertheless, the available evidence suggests that very early in life (age 14 to 20 months), both genetic and environmental factors contribute to continuity and change. The relative proportions of each type of influence are dramatically different for the various traits that have been studied. Studies that cover the period from adolescence to adulthood are based on modest sample sizes. They suggest that there is a modest genetic influence on change for some personality traits, but that most change is the result of idiosyncratic environmental factors. The same is true for studies of early adulthood. The heritability of personality is about .45 to .50 in adolescence and adulthood.

Implications for Understanding the "Causes" of Behavioral Development

Contrary to the beliefs of many psychologists, the behavior genetic and evolutionary psychology approaches to explicating the processes underlying behavioral development do not underplay the role of the environment. What they do is recognize that our understanding of behavioral development is informed by processes at many levels, ranging from the distal processes of genes selected via natural selection, through the less distal process of family influence during social development, to the proximal processes called into play when an individual deals cognitively and/or emotionally with a contemporary situation (Bouchard, 1993b). In all of these instances the organism transacts with the environment, and if the environment is not above some threshold of adequacy (Scarr, 1992, 1993), development will be significantly interfered with. As I have argued elsewhere (Bouchard et al., 1990a), "The proximal cause of most psychological variance probably involves learning through experience, just as radical environmentalists have always believed. The effective experiences, however, to an important extent are self-selected, and that selection is guided by the steady pressure of the genome (a more distal cause)" (p. 227).

There is a growing consensus in behavior genetics and developmental psychology that nature accounts for a very sizable proportion of the variance in behavioral traits and that the mechanism by which this is accomplished is via behavior. Consider the following quotes:

> The alternative possibility is that geneticists and social scientists have misconceived the role of cultural inheritance and that individuals acquire little from their social environment that is incompatible with their genotype. In no way does our model minimize the role of learning and social interaction in behavioral development. Rather it sees humans as exploring organisms whose innate abilities and predispositions help them select what is relevant and adaptive from the range of opportunities and stimuli presented by the environment. The effects of mobility and learning, therefore, augment rather than eradicate the effects of the genotype on behavior. (Martin et al., 1986. p. 4368)

> [The above view is] "a modification of Heinz Hartmann's famous dictum that the infant is born adapted to survive in an average expectable environment. Hartmann's statement is undoubtedly correct as far as it goes, but we need to add that in the average expectable environment of all societal species, institutions or regulatory systems have arisen that take into account the essential needs of the young, including the need to grow up to be a typical and functional member of the group. These regulatory systems provide an *experiential* educational process which is calculated to realize, in the young growing up, the biological predispositions evolved through natural selection. In this way one learns what comes naturally. (Kaufman, 1975, p. 141; emphasis added)

> The classic opposition—genes versus the environment—now appears to be rather shopworn and empty. In reality, there never was a *versus* in this artificial dichotomy and there never were just two factors in the equation. Instead we see that early brain developments beget others, that the child is an active agent in the creation of its brain and neurolinguistic capacity, that environments are themselves the expression of genes which are also inherited by the infant,. . . . that behavior influences function and function influences structure, and that experience produces lasting changes in the architecture and function of the brain. (Locke, 1993, p. 423; emphasis in original)

> Intellectual performance that was reliably deflected across time was characterized by a self-righting tendency. IQ appeared to be elastic, rather than plastic.
>
> The observed patterns of change may be accounted for in terms of Scarr and McCartney's (1983) developmental theory of genotype-environment effects. According to their theory, two types of genotype-environment interactions may be involved in level-maintaining or level-seeking processes. As children begin to act on the environment in many different situation, they *evoke* responses that are matched to their abilities. Moreover, with the development of self-regulating capacities and skills, children begin to actively select experiences that are matched with their abilities and thereby create genotype-environment correlations. (Moffitt et al., 1993, p. 496; emphasis in original)

Implications for Future Longitudinal Studies

I believe that enough evidence has been presented in this chapter to convince the reader that although ordinary longitudinal studies can still contribute a great deal to our understanding of behavioral development (as demonstrated by Moffitt et al., 1993), they nevertheless confound most of the important influences we seek to understand. Far more will be learned about the processes that underlie normal development through the implementation of new longitudinal studies of twins and adoptees similar to CAP and MALT; the control groups in such studies will replace the ordinary longitudinal studies of the past. I conclude with another of Galton's prescient observations (Galton, 1875):

> It must be borne in mind that the divergence of development, when it occurs, need not be ascribed to the effect of different nurtures, but it is quite possible that it may be due to the appearance of qualities inherited at birth, though dormant (p. 569).

REFERENCES

Adelson, J. (1975). The development of ideology in adolescence. In S. E. Dragstin & G. H. Elder Jr. (Eds.), *Adolescence in the life cycle; Psychological change and social context.* New York: Wiley.

Adorno, T. W., Frenkel-Brunswick, E., Levinson, D. J., & Sanford, R. M. (1950). *The authoritarian personality.* New York: Harper.

Aldenderfer, M. S., & Blashfield, R. K. (1984). *Cluster analysis.* Newbury Park, CA: Sage.

Altmeyer, B. (1988). *Enemies of freedom.* San Francisco: Jossey-Bass.

Baltes, P. B. (1987). Theoretical propositions of life-span developmental psychology: On the dynamics between growth and decline. *Developmental Psychology, 23,* 611–626.

Barkow, J. H. (1989). *Darwin, sex, and status: Biological approaches to mind and culture.* Toronto: University of Toronto Press.

Barkow, J. H., Cosmides, L., & Tooby, J. (1992). *The adapted mind.* Oxford: Oxford University Press.

Baumrind, D. (1993). The average expectable environment is not good enough: A response to Scarr. *Child Development, 64,* 1299–1317.

Betzig, L., Mulder, M. B., & Turke, P. (Ed.). (1988). *Human reproductive behavior: A Darwinian perspective.* Cambridge, England: Cambridge University Press.

Black, J. E., Isaacks, K. R., & Greenough, W.T. (1991). Usual vs. successful aging: Some notes on experiential factors. *Neurobiology of Aging*, *12*, 325–328.

Block, J. (1971). *Lives through time*. Berkeley, C.A.: Bancroft.

Block, J. H., Block J., & Gjerde, P. S. (1986). The personality of children prior to divorce: A prospective study. *Child Development*, *57*, 827–840.

Boomsma, D. (1993). Current and future prospects in twin studies of the development of cognitive abilities: Infancy to old age. In T. J. Bouchard, Jr., & P. Propping (Eds.), *Twins as a tool of behavioral genetics*. Chichester, England: Wiley.

Bouchard, T. J., Jr. (1993a). Genetic and environmental influences on adult personality: Evaluating the evidence. In I. Deary & J. Hettema (Eds.), *Basic issues in personality*. Dordrecht, Netherlands: Kluwer Academic.

Bouchard, T. J., Jr. (1993b). The genetic architecture of human intelligence. In P.A. Vernon (Ed.), *Biological approaches to the study of human intelligence*. Norwood, NJ: Ablex.

Bouchard, T. J., Jr., Lykken, D. T., McGue, M., Segal, N. L., & Tellegen, A. (1990a). Sources of human psychological differences: The Minnesota study of twins reared apart. *Science*, *250*, 223–228.

Bouchard, T. J., Jr., Lykken, D. T., McGue, M., Segal, N. L., & Tellegen, A. (1990b). When kin correlations are not squared. *Science*, *250*, 1498.

Bouchard, T. J., Jr., Lykken, D. T., Tellegen, A. R., & McGue, M. (in press). Genes, drives, environment and experience: EPD theory revised. In C. P. Benbow & D. Lubinski (Eds.), *Psychometrics and social issues concerning intellectual talent*. Baltimore: Johns Hopkins University Press.

Bouchard, T. J., Jr., & McGue, M. (1981). Familial studies of intelligence: A review. *Science*, *212*, 1055–1059.

Bouchard, T. J., Jr., & Segal, N. L. (1985). Environment and IQ. In B. J. Wolman (Eds.), *Handbook of intelligence: Theories, measurements, and applications*. New York: Wiley.

Bouchard, T. J., Jr., Segal, N. L., & Lykken, D. T. (1990). Genetic and environmental influences on special mental abilities in a sample of twins reared apart. *Acta Geneticae Medicae et Gemellogiae*, *39*, 193–206.

Brody, N. (1993). Intelligence and the behavior genetics of personality. In R. Plomin & G. E. McClearn (Eds.), *Nature, nurture, and psychology*. Washington, DC: American Psychological Association.

Brown, D. E. (1991). *Human universals*. Philadelphia: Temple University Press.

Burks, B. (1938). On the relative contributions of nature and nurture to average group differences in intelligence. *Proceedings of the National Academy of Sciences*, *24*, 276–282.

Buss, A. (1988). *Personality: Evolutionary heritage and human distinctiveness*. Hillsdale, NJ: Erlbaum.

Buss, D. M. (1984). Evolutionary biology and personality psychology. *American Psychologist*, *39*, 1135–1147.

Buss, D. M. (1991). Evolutionary personality psychology. *Annual Review of Psychology*, *42*, 459–491.

Buss, D. M., & Schmidtt, D. P. (1993). Sexual strategies theory: An evolutionary perspective on human mating. *Psychological Review*, *100*, 204–232.

Cardon, L. R., & Cherney, S.S. (1994). Adoption design methodology. In J. C. DeFries, R. Plomin, & D. W. Fulker (Eds.), *Nature and nurture during middle childhood*. London: Blackwell.

Cardon, L. R., DiLalla, L. F., Plomin, R., DeFries, J. C., & Fulker, D. W. (1990). Genetic correlations between reading performance and IQ in the Colorado Adoption Project. *Intelligence*, *14*, 245–257.

Cardon, L. R., & Fulker, D. W., (1993). Genetics of specific cognitive abilities. In R. Plomin & G. E. McClearn (Eds.), *Nature, nurture and psychology*. Washington DC: American Psychological Association.

Cardon, L. R., Fulker, D. W., DeFries, J. C., & Plomin, R. (1992). Multivariate genetic analysis of specific cognitive abilities in the Colorado Adoption Project at age 7. *Intelligence*, *16*, 383–400.

Carroll, J. B. (1993). *Human cognitive abilities: A survey of factor-analytic studies*. New York: Cambridge University Press.

Cartwright, D., & Peckar, H. (1993). Purposefulness: A fourth superfactor? *Personality and Individual Differences*, *14*, 547–555.

Caspi, A., & Bem, D. J. (1990). Personality continuity and change across the life course. In L. Pervin (Eds.), *Handbook of personality: Theory and research*. New York: Guilford.

Cavalli-Sforza, L. L. (1975). Quantitative genetic perspectives: Implications for human development, In K. W. Schaie, V. E. Anderson, G. E. McClearn, & J. Money (Eds.), *Developmental human behavior genetics*. Lexington, MA: Lexington Books.

Charlesworth, W. R. (1992). Darwin and developmental psychology: Past and present. *Developmental Psychology*, *28*, 5–16.

Cherlin, A. J., Furstenberg, F. F., Chase-Lonsdale, P. L., Kiernam, K. E., Robins, P. K., Morrison, D. R., & Teitler, J. O. (1991). Longitudinal studies of effects of divorce on children in Great Britain and the United States. *Science*, *252*, 1386–1389.

Christie, R. (1991). Authoritarianism and related constructs, In J. P. Robinson, P. R. Shaver, & L. S. Wrightsman (Eds.), *Measures of personality and social psychological attitudes*. San Diego, CA: Academic Press.

Christie, R., & Jahoda, M. (Ed.). (1954). *Studies in the scope and method of "The authoritarian personality"*. New York: Free Press.

Colby, A., & Phelps, E. (1990). Archiving longitudinal data. In D. Magnusson & L. R. Bergman (Eds), *Data quality in longitudinal research* (pp. 249–262). Cambridge: Cambridge University Press.

Cosmides, L., Tooby, J., & Barkow, J. H. (1992), Introduction: Evolutionary psychology and conceptual integration. In H. Barkow, L. Cosmides, & J. Tooby (Eds.), *The adapted mind*. Oxford, England: Oxford University Press.

Costa, P. T., & McCrae, R. R. (1992a). Four ways five factors are basic. *Personality and Individual Differences*, *13*, 653–665.

Costa, P. T., & McCrae, R. R. (1992b). *NEO PI-R Professional manual*. Odesa, FL: Psychological Assessment Resources.

Cronbach, L. J., & Gleser, G. C. (1953). Assessing similarity between profiles. *Psychological Bulletin*, *50*, 68–80.

Daly, M., & Wilson, M. (1988). *Homicide*. Hawthorne, NY: Aldine de Gruyter.

DeFries, J. C., Plomin, R., & Fulker, D. W. (Eds.). (1994). *Nature and nurture during middle childhood*. London: Blackwell.

DeFries, J. C., Vandenberg, S. G., & McClearn, G. E. (1976). Genetics of specific cognitive abilities. *Annual Review of Genetics*, *10*, 179–207.

DeFries, J. C., Vandenberg, S. G., McClearn, G. E., Kuse, A. R., Wilson, J. R., Ashton, G. C., & Johnson, R. C. (1974). Near identity of cognitive structure in two ethnic groups. *Science*, *183*, 338–339.

Dworkin, R. H., Burke, B. W., Maher, B. A., & Gottesman, I. I. (1976). A longitudinal study of the genetics of personality. *Journal of Personality and Social Psychology*, *34*, 510–518.

Dworkin, R. H., Burke, B. W., Maher, B. A., & Gottesman, I. I.

(1977). Genetic influences on the organization and development of personality. *Developmental Psychology, 13,* 164–165.

Eaves, L. J., Eysenck, H. J., & Martin, N. G. (1989). *Genes, culture and personality: An empirical approach.* New York: Academic Press.

Eibl-Eibesfeldt, I. (1989). *Human ethology.* Hawthorne, NY: Aldine de Gruyter.

Eysenck, H. J. (1992). Four ways five factors are not basic. *Personality and Individual Differences, 13,* 667–673.

Eysenck, H. J. (1993). Comment on Goldberg. *American Psychologist, 48,* 1299–1300.

Eysenck, H. J., & Eysenck, M. W. (1985). *Personality and individual differences.* New York: Plenum.

Feldman, S. S., & Aschenbrenner, B. G. (1983). Impact of parenthood on various aspects of masculinity and femininity: A short term longitudinal study. *Developmental Psychology, 19,* 278–289.

Fodor, J. A. (1983). *The modularity of mind: An essay on faculty psychology.* Cambridge: MIT Press.

Freeman, D. (1983). *Margaret Mead and Samoa: The making and unmaking of an anthropological myth.* Cambridge, MA, Harvard University Press.

Freeman, D. (1992, October). *Paradigms in collision: The far-reaching controversy over the Samoan researches of Margaret Mead and it significance for the human sciences.* Research School of Pacific Studies, Australian National University.

Fulker, D. W., & Cardon, L. R. (1993). What can twin studies tell us about the structure and correlates of cognitive abilities? In T. J. Bouchard, Jr. & P. Proping (Eds.), *What are the mechanisms mediating genetic and environmental determinants of behavior? Twins as a tool of behavior genetics.* Chichester, England: Wiley.

Fulker, D. W., Cherny, S. S., & Cardon. L. R. (1993). Continuity and change in cognitive development. In R. Plomin & G. E. McClearn (Eds.), Nature, nurture and psychology. Washington, DC: American Psychological Association.

Funder, D. C., Parke, R. D., Tomlinson-Keasey, C., & Widaman, K. (Eds.). (1993). *Studying lives through time: Personality and development.* Washington, DC: American Psychological Association.

Galton, F. (1875, November), The history of twins, as a criterion of the relative powers of nature and nurture. *Fraser's,* 566–576.

Galton, F. (1885). On the anthropometric laboratory at the late International Health Exhibition. *Journal of the Anthropological Institute, 14,* 205–219.

Goldberg, L.R. (1992a). The development of markers for the big-five factor structure. *Psychological Assessment, 4,* 26–42.

Goldberg, L. R. (1992b). What the hell took so long? Donald Fiske and the big-five factor structure. In P. E. Shrout & S. T. Fiske (Eds.), *Advances in personality research, methods, and theory: A festschrift honoring Donald W. Fiske.* Hillsdale, NJ: Erlbaum.

Goldberg, L. R. (1993). The structure of phenotypic personality traits. *American Psychologist, 48,* 26–34.

Goldsmith, H. H. (1983). Genetic influence on personality from infancy to adulthood. *Child Development, 54,* 331–355.

Gorsuch, R. L. (1983). *Factor analysis* (2nd ed.) Hillsdale, NJ: Erlbaum.

Gough, H. G. (1987). *Californıa Psychological Inventory administrator's guide.* Palo Alto, CA: Consulting Psychologists Press.

Hahn, M., Hewitt, J., Henderson, J., & Benne, R. (Ed.). (1990). *Developmental behavior genetics: Neural, biometrical, and evolutionary approaches,* Oxford, England: Oxford University Press.

Harrington, D. M. (1993). Poisonous pedagogy and suboptimal development. In D. C. Funder, R. D. Parke, C. Tomlinson-Keasey, & K. Widaman (Eds.), *Studying lives through time: Personality and development.* Washington, DC: American Psychological Association.

Henderson, R. W. (1981). Home environment and intellectual performance. In R. W. Henderson (Eds.), *Parent-child interaction: Theory, research and prospects* (pp.3–32). New York: Academic Press.

Hetherington, E. M., Reiss, D., & Plomin, R. (1994). *The separate social worlds of siblings: The impact of nonshared environment on development.* Hillsdale, N.J.: Erlbaum.

Himmelweit, H. T., & Swift, B. (1971). Adolescent and adult authoritarianism reexamined: Its organization and stability over time. *European Journal of Social Psychology, 1,* 357–384.

Hoffman, L. W.(1991). The influence of the family environment on personality: Evidence for sibling differences. *Psychological Bulletin, 110,* 187–203.

Honzik, M. P. (1986). The role of the family in the development of mental abilities: A 50-year study. In N. Datan, A. L. Greene, & H. W. Reese (Eds.), *Life span developmental psychology: Intergenerational relations.* Hillsdale, NJ: Erlbaum.

Hough, L. (1992). The "big five" personality variables—construct confusion: Description versus prediction. *Human Performance, 5,* 139–155.

Huesmann, L. R., Eron, L., Lefkowitz, M. M., & Walder, L. O. (1984). The stability of aggression over time and generations. *Developmental Psychology, 20,* 1120–1134.

Jarvik, L. F., & Bank, L. (1983). Aging twins: Longitudinal psychometric data. In K. W., Schaie (Eds.), *Longitudinal studies of adult psychological adjustment* (pp. 40–63). New York: Guilford.

Johnson, R. C., McClearn, G. E., Yen, S., Nagoshi, C. T., Ahern, F. M., & Cole, R. E. (1985). Galton's data a century later. *American Psychologist, 40,* 875–892.

Kallman, F. J., Feingold, L. & Bondy, E. (1951). Comparative adaptational, social, and psychometric data on the life histories of senescent pairs. *American Journal of Human Genetics, 3,* 65–73.

Kaufman, I. C. (1975). Learning what comes naturally: The role of life experience in the establishment of species typical h-behavior. *Ethos, 3,* 129–142.

Keating, D. P. (1975). Possible sampling bias in genetic studies of genius. *Educational and Psychological Measurements, 35,* 657–662.

Locke, J. L. (1993). *The child's path to spoken language.* Cambridge, MA: Harvard University Press.

Loehlin, J. C., Horn, J. M., & Willerman, L. (1989). Modeling IQ change: Evidence from the Texas Adoption Project. *Child Development, 60,* 993–1004.

Loehlin, J. C. (1992). *Genes and environment in personality development.* Newbury Park, CA: Sage.

Loehlin, J. C., Horn, J. M., & Willerman, L. (1990). Heredity, environment, and personality change: Evidence from the Texas adoption project. *Journal of Personality, 58,* 221–243.

Loehlin, J. C., Willerman, L., & Horn, J. M. (1987). Personality resemblance in adoptive families: A 10-year follow-up. *Journal of Personality and Social Psychology, 53,* 961–969.

Lykken, D. T., Bouchard, T. J., Jr., McGue, M., & Tellegen, A. (1990). The Minnesota twins family registry: Some initial findings. *Acta Geneticae Medicae et Gemellogiae, 39,* 35–70.

Lykken, D. T., Bouchard, T. J., Jr., McGue, M., & Tellegen, A. (1993). The heritability of interests: A twin study. *Journal of Applied Psychology, 78,* 649–661.

Lykken, D. R., McGue, M., Tellegen, A., & Bouchard, T. J., Jr. (1992). Emergenesis: Genetic traits that may not run in families. *American Psychologist, 47*, 1565–1577.

Lytton, H. (1977). Do parents create, or respond to, differences in twins? *Developmental Psychology, 13*, 456–459.

Lytton H. (1990). Child effects—still unwelcome? Response to Dodge and Wahler, *Developmental Psychology, 26*(5), 705–709.

Matheny, A. (1990). Developmental behavior genetics: Contributions from the Louisville Twin Study. In M. Hahn, J. Hewitt, N. Henderson, & R. Benne (Eds.), *Developmental behavior genetics: Neural, biometrical, and evolutionary approaches*. Oxford: Oxford University Press.

Martin, N. G., Eaves, L. J., Heath, A. C., Jardine, R., Feingold, L. M., & Eysenck, H. J. (1986). Transmission of social attitudes. *Proceedings of the National Academy of Sciences, 83*, 4364–4368.

Matheny, A. P., Jr., (1989). Children's behavioral inhibitions over age and across situations: Genetic similarity for a trait during change. *Child Development, 57*, 215–236.

McGue, M., Bacon, S., & Lykken, D. T. (1993). Personality stability and change in early adulthood: A behavior genetic analysis. *Developmental Psychology, 29*, 96–109.

McGue, M., & Bouchard, T. J., Jr. (1989). Genetic and environmental determinants of information processing and special mental abilities: A twin analysis. In R. J. Sternberg (Eds.), *Advances in the psychology of human intelligence* (pp. 7–44). Hillsdale, NJ: Erlbaum.

McGue, M., Bouchard, T. J., Jr., Iacono, W. G., & Lykken, D. T. (1993). Behavior genetics of cognitive ability: A life-span perspective. In R. Plomin & G.E. McClearn (Eds.), *Nature, nurture and psychology* (pp. 59–76). Washington, DC: American Psychological Association.

McGue, M., & Lykken, D. T. (1992). Genetic influence on risk of divorce. *Psychological Science, 3*, 368–372.

Moffitt, T. E., Caspi, A., Harkness, A. R., & Silva, P. A. (1993). The natural history of change in intellectual performance: Who changes? How much? Is it meaningful? *Journal of Child Psychology and Psychiatry, 34*, 455–506.

Molenaar, P., Boomsma, D., & Dolan, C. (1991). Genetic and environmental factors in a developmental perspective. In D. Magnusson, L. Bergaman, G. Rudinger, & B. Torestad (Eds.), *Problems and methods in longitudinal research: Stability and change*, Cambridge, England: Cambridge University Press.

Moster, M. (1991) *Stressful life events: Genetic and environmental components and their relationship to affective symptomology*. Ph.D. dissertation, University of Minnesota.

Mussen, P. H., Conger, J. J., & Kagan, Jr. (1969). *Child development and personality* (3rd ed.). New York: Harper and Row.

Neale, M. C., & Cardon, L. R. (Ed.).(1992). *Methodology for genetic studies of twins and families*. Dordrecht, Netherlands: Kluwer Academic.

Olweus, D. (1977). Aggression and peer acceptance in adolescent boys: Two short term longitudinal studies of ratings. *Child Development, 48*, 1301–1313.

Olweus, D. (1979). Stability of aggressive reaction patterns in males: A review. *Psychological Bulletin, 86*, 852–875.

Pedersen, N. L. (1991). Behavioral genetic concepts in longitudinal analyses. In D. Magnusson, L. Bergman, G. Rudinger, & B. Torestad (Eds.), *Problems and methods in longitudinal research: Stability and change* (pp. 236–249). Cambridge, England: Cambridge University Press.

Pedersen, N. L. (1993). Genetic and environmental continuity and change in personality. In T. J. Bouchard, Jr., & P. Propping (Eds.), *What are the mechanisms mediating genetic and environmental determinants of behavior? Twins as a tool of behavior genetics* (pp. 147–162). Chichester, England: Wiley.

Pedersen, N. L., Plomin, R., Nesselroade, J. R., & McClearn, G. E. (1992). A quantitative genetic analysis of cognitive abilities during the second half of the life span. *Psychological Science, 3*, 346–353.

Plomin, R. (1986). *Development, genetics and psychology*. Hillsdale, NJ: Erlbaum.

Plomin, R., & Daniels, D. (1987). Why are children in the same family so different from one another? *Behavior and Brain Sciences, 10*, 1–60.

Plomin, R., & DeFries, J. C. (1985). *Origins of individual differences in infancy: The Colorado Adoption Project*. Orlando, FL: Academic Press.

Plomin, R., DeFries, J. C., & Fulkner, D. W. (1988). *Nature and nurture during infancy and early childhood*. New York: Cambridge University Press.

Plomin, R., Emde, R. N., Braungart, J. M., Campos, J., Corley, R., Fulker, D. W., Kagan, J., Reznick, J. S., Robinson, J., Zahn-Waxler, C., & DeFries, J. C. (1993). Genetic change and continuity from fourteen to twenty months: The MacArthur Longitudinal Twin Study. *Child Development, 64*, 1354–1376.

Plomin, R., Lichtenstein, P., Pedersen, N. L., McClearn, G. E., & Nesselroade, J. R. (1990). Genetic influences on life events during the last half of the life span. *Psychology and Aging, 5*, 25–30.

Plomin, R., & Nesselroade, J. R. (1990). Behavior genetics and personality change. *Journal of Personality, 58*, 191–220.

Pogue-Geile, M. F., & Rose, R. J (1985). Developmental genetic studies of adult personality. *Developmental Psychology, 21*, 547–557.

Retherford, R. D. (1993, August). *Demographic transition and the evolution of intelligence. Paper presented to the General Conference for the Study of Social Biology*, Pennsylvania State University.

Rushton, J. P., Fulker, D. W., Neale, M. C., Nias, D. K. B., & Eysenck, H. J. (1986). Altruism and aggression: The heritability of individual differences. *Journal of Personality and Social Psychology, 50*, 1192–1198.

Sampson, R. J. & Laub, J. H. (1990). Crime and deviance over the life course: The salience of adult social bonds. *American Sociological Review, 55* 609–627.

Scarr, S. (1981). *Race, social class and individual differences.* Hillsdale, NJ: Erlbaum.

Scarr, S. (1992). Developmental theories for the 1990's: Development and individual differences. *Child Development, 63*, 1–19.

Scarr, S. (1993). Biological and cultural diversity: The legacy of Darwin for development. *Child Development, 64*, 1333–1353.

Scarr, S., & McCartney, K. (1983). How people make their own environments: A theory of genotype → environment effects. *Child Development, 54*, 424–435.

Scarr, S., & Weinberg R. (1981). The transmission of authoritarianism in families: Genetic resemblance in social-political attitudes. In S. Scarr (Ed.), *Race, social class, and individual differences*. Hillsdale, NJ: Erlbaum.

Scarr, S., & Weinberg, R. A. (1978). The influence of family background on intellectual attainment. *American Sociological Review, 43*, 674–692.

Silva, P. A. (1990). The Dunedin multidisciplinary health and development study: A 15 year longitudinal study. *Paediatric and Perinatal Epidemiology, 4*, 96–127.

Sontag, L. W., Baker, C. T., & Nelson, V. L. (1958). Mental growth and personality development: A longitudinal study. *Monographs of the Society for Research in Child Development, 23* (Series No. 68).

Stearns, S. C. (1992). *The evolution of life histories.* Oxford, England: Oxford University Press.

Steinberg, L., Lamborn, S. D., Dornbush, S. M., & Darling, N. (1992). Impact of parenting practices on adolescent achievement: Authoritative parenting, school involvement, and encouragement to succeed. *Child Development, 63,* 1266–1281.

Swan, G. E., Carmelli, D., Reed, T., Harshfield, G. A., Fabitz, R. R., & Eslinger, P. J. (1990). Heritability of cognitive performance in aging twins: The National Heart, Lung, and Blood Institute twin study. *Archives of Neurology, 47,* 259–262.

Swan, G. E., LaRue, A., Carmelli, D., Reed, R. E., & Fabsitz, R. R. (1992). Decline in cognitive performance in aging twins: Heritability and biobehavioral predictions from the National Heart, Lung, and Blood Institute twin study. *Archives of Neurology, 49,* 476–481.

Symons, D. (1979). *The evolution of human sexuality.* New York: Oxford University Press.

Tellegen, A. (1982). *Brief manual for the Differential Personality Questionnaire.* Unpublished manuscript, University of Minnesota.

Tellegen, A., Lykken, D. T., Bouchard, T. J., Jr., Wilcox, K. J., Segal, N. L., & Rich, S. (1988). Personality similarity in twins reared apart and together. *Journal of Personality and Social Psychology, 54,* 1031–1039.

Tellegen, A., & Waller, N. G. (in press). Exploring personality through test construction: Development of the Multidimensional Personality Questionnaire. In S. R. Briggs & J. M. Cheek (Eds.), *Personality measures: Development and evaluation* Greenwich, CT: JAI.

Terman, L. M., & Oden, M. H. (1959). *Genetic studies of genius: Vol. 5. The gifted group at mid-life.* Stanford, CA: Stanford University Press.

Thompson, L. A., Detterman, D. K., & Plomin, R. (1991). Scholastic achievement and specific cognitive abilities in 7- to 12-year old twins. *Psychological Science, 2,* 158–165.

Thompson, L. E. (1993). Genetic contributions to intellectual development in infancy and childhood. In P. A. Vernon (Eds.), *Biological approaches to the study of human intelligence.* Norwood, NJ: Ablex.

Tomlinson-Keasey, C., & Little, T. D. (1990). Predicting educational attainment occupational achievement, intellectual skill and personal adjustment among gifted men and women. *Journal of Educational Psychology, 82,* 442–445.

Tooby, J., & Cosmides, L. (1992). The psychological foundations of culture. In J. H. Barkow, L. Cosmides, & J. Tooby (Eds.), *The adapted mind: Evolutionary psychology and the generation of culture.* Oxford, England: Oxford University Press.

Trivers, R. (1985a). Parent-offspring conflict. In R. Trivers (Eds.), *Social evolution.* Menlo Park, CA: Benjamin/Cummings.

Trivers, R. (1985b). *Social evolution.* Menlo Park, CA: Benjamin/Cummins.

Truett, K. R. (1993). Age differences in conservatism. *Personality and Individual Differences, 14,* 405–411.

Turkheimer, E., Lovett, G., Robinette, C. D., & Gottesman, I. I. (1992). *The heritability of divorce: New data and theoretical implications* Paper presented at the Behavior Genetics Association annual meetings, Boulder CO.

Waller, N. G. (in press). Evaluating the structure of personality. In C. R. Cloninger (Eds.), *Personality and psycholpathology.* Washington, DC: American Psychiatric Press.

White, R. K. (1982). The relation between socioeconomic status and academic achievement. *Psychological Bulletin, 91,* 461–481.

Willerman, L. (1979). Effects of families on intellectual development. *American Psychologist, 34,* 923–929.

Wilson, J. Q. (1993). *The moral sense.* New York: Free Press.

Wilson, R. S. (1983). The Louisville twin study: Developmental synchronies in behavior. *Child Development, 54,* 298–316.

Wright, S. (1921). Correlation and causation. *Journal of Agricultural Research, 20,* 557–585.

Wright, S. (1931). Statistical methods in biology. *Journal of the American Statistical Association, 26,* 155–163.

Young, C. H., Savola, K. L., & Phelps, E. (1991). *Inventory of longitudinal studies in the social sciences.* Newbury Park, CA: Sage.

Zukerman, M., Kuhlman, D. M., Joireman, J., Teta, P., & Kraft, M. (1993). A comparison of three structural models for personality: The big three, the big five, and the alternative five. *Journal of Personality and Social Psychology, 65,* 757–768.

6

Cross-Cultural Differences in Intelligence and Personality

Richard Lynn

Cross-cultural studies of intelligence and personality are concerned first with the measurement of the differences between peoples, and second with the explanation of the causes of these differences. The measurement largely takes the form of administering tests to representative samples of the populations in different societies and comparing the scores. Theoretical explanations look first for correlates of these differences and then postulate causes. For example, if it were found that national anxiety levels were strongly related to poverty it might be reasonable to propose that poverty is an important cause of differences in anxiety levels between nations.

There are three broad theoretical positions for explaining cross-cultural differences. These are designated the "absolutist," "universalist," and "relativist" theories by Berry, Poortinga, Segall, and Dasen (1992), but these labels are not properly self-explanatory. Better terms for these theories are (a) biological, (b) biological–cultural interaction, and (c) cultural. The *biological* position is that intelligence and personality differences between disparate peoples are solely the result of biological dissimilarities, although it is doubtful whether any one maintains this. The *biological-cultural interaction* position is that both biology and culture determine the differences, and there are disputes among those who back this theory about the strength of the contributions of biology and culture. The *cultural* position is that the differences are solely determined by culture. An example where the cultural position is clearly correct is the social convention in Western societies of people shaking hands when they meet—a convention that has gown up over centuries, but is not present in many other societies. No-one supposed that a gene for shaking hands is present among the peoples of Western societies, but absent in others. One of the major issues in this field is whether national and other group differences in intelligence and personality are entirely culturally conditioned, like shaking hands, or whether they have some biological basis (and, if so, how strong this biological basis is).

There is a further point that can usefully be made. There are certain features of intelligence and personality that are universal in the human species, and it is generally considered that these must be biologically programmed, although their strength and expression are influenced by culture. For instances, all humans can and do learn to speak, and all languages have similar grammatical structure. This has led Chomsky (1965) to propose that the propensity to acquire language is biologically programmed, although the kind of language acquired is determined by the particular cultures. Certain personality traits are probably also

Richard Lynn • Department of Psychology, University of Ulster, Coleraine BT52 1S1, Northern Ireland.

International Handbook of Personality and Intelligence, edited by Donald H. Saklofske and Moshe Zeidner. Plenum Press, New York, 1995.

universal in the human species and are therefore generally considered to have an element of biological programming. Two of the most striking examples are the greater aggressiveness of males as compared with females, and a tendency toward ethocentrism (i.e. hostility toward other groups). The general framework within which these problems are considered by cross-cultural psychologists has now been set out, and we are ready to consider the evidence and issues in more detail, starting with intelligence and proceeding to personality.

INTELLIGENCE

The central issue in cross-cultural studies of intelligence has been the problem of racial differences. There have been three phases in the consensus view of this problem during the last century and a half. In the first, which lasted until around 1930, it was generally accepted that the Caucasian (white or European) race was the most intelligent and the other races were characterized by varying degrees of inferiority. An early advocate of this view was the American anthropologist S. G. Morton (1849), who built up a collection of skulls from various locations around the world. He measured the size of these skulls, classified them by race, and concluded that European Caucasians had the largest average brain size, followed in descending order by East Asian Orientals and Africans. Morton believed that brain size is associated with intelligence and, therefore, that the races could be ranked for intelligence on the basis of their average brain size.

Similar views were being advanced in Britain around this time. Francis Galton (1869), in his book *Hereditary Genius*, asserted that intelligence was principally determined genetically and that racial differences in intelligence could be calculated from the numbers of intellectually outstanding individuals produced in relation to the size of the population. By using this method, Galton concluded that fifth-century B.C. Athens had the most intelligent population that ever existed. The lowland Scots scored high, followed by the English; Africans scored very low, and Australian aborigines even lower. Galton proposed a quantification for these differences that (in terms of contemporary intelligence scales) placed the English with a mean IQ of 100, Africans a mean of 79, and Australian aborigines a mean of 69.

With the invention of the intelligence test by Binet in the first decade of the twentieth century, it became possible to test samples of difference races for intelligence. A major source of data came from testing large numbers of conscripts with the American army during World War I. These tests showed that the mean IQ of blacks was 83 versus a white mean IQ of 100 (Loehlin, Lindzey, Spuhler, 1975). (IQs are typically based on a white mean of 100 and a standard deviation of 15). Numerous other studies in the United States have confirmed that this is about the magnitude of the intelligence gap between blacks and whites (Jensen, 1980; Loehlin et al. 1975; Shuey, 1966). One of the best relatively recent studies is that of the standardization sample of the WISC-R, which revealed precisely the same 17-point black-white IQ difference (Jensen & Reynolds, 1982).

Shortly after World War I, studies began to be published on the intelligence of American ethnic Japanese and Chinese. As these studies accumulated it became clear that American ethnic Orientals obtained mean IQs about the same as those of whites, or perhaps a little higher. A review of the literature was carried out by Vernon (1982), who concluded that their mean nonverbal and spatial IQ is about 110 and their verbal IQ about 97, the average of the two figures being 103.5. This conclusion has been disputed by Flynn (1991), who argues that American ethnic Orientals have virtually the same mean IQ as whites. The most recent and best study of the American ethnic Oriental IQ consists of an analysis of the data of the standardization of the Differential Abilities Scale, which showed that Orientals had a mean IQ of 104.7 (Stone, 1992).

Several studies were also made of the intelligence of Native Americans. The evidence up to 1930 was summarized by Garth (1931) and Pinter (1931) and indicated rather variable results, with means ranging from 69 to 97. One of the major reasons for this is the profile of abilities of Native Americans. They are strong on the visuospatial abilities (where they score about the same as Caucasians), but weak on the verbal abilities. Their average intelligence level, therefore, depended on the type of test used.

About the same time as the early results on the IQs of blacks, whites, Orientals, and American Indians were coming out in the United States, an Australian psychologist named Porteus was giving intelligence tests to the Australian Aborigines. Porteus constructed a paper-and-pencil test that required subjects to trace the correct route through a series of mazes. The work, continued over a period of some 30 years, indicated that Aborigines had an average IQ of around 70 (Porteus, 1965). Porteus took the same view of these intelligence differences as was generally held at this time in the United States—namely, that they reflected genetic differences between the races.

Garth (1931), in *Race Psychology*, initiated a reaction against the genetic interpretation of race differences in intelligence. He asserted that an environmentalist position that rapidly became the prevailing orthodoxy; this lasted for the next 40 years or so. The environmentalist view was asserted in an official statement issued by the United Nations Educational, Scientific and Cultural Organization (UNESCO; 1951): "According to present knowledge, there is no proof that the groups of mankind differ in their innate mental characteristics, whether in respect of intelligence or temperament. The scientific evidence indicates that the range of mental capabilities in all ethnic groups is much the same."

The environmentalist consensus was broken by Jensen (1969). His carefully phrased words on the issue were that it is "a not unreasonable hypothesis that genetic factors are strongly implicated in the average Negro-white intelligence difference." Jensen's paper attracted a great deal of attention and commentary. Several writers endorsed Jensen's view, including Eysenck (1971), Leohlin, Lindzey, and Spuhler (1975), and Vernon (1979). Others, such as Flynn (1980) and Brody (1992), have taken a contrary view. Many have opted to remain silent.

The state of contemporary opinion, however, was usefully ascertained by Snyderman and Rothman (1988), who conducted an anonymous survey of 661 experts on intelligence drawn from several disciplines, including psychology, sociology, genetics, and education. The survey consisted of a number of questions about intelligence, including "Which of the following best characterizes your opinion of the heritability of the black-white difference in IQ?" The percentages of experts selecting each of the five alternative answers were as follows: the difference is entirely due to environmental determination, 15%; the difference is entirely due to genetic variation, 1%; the difference is a product of both genetic and environmental variation, 45%; the data are insufficient to support any reasonable opinion, 24%; and no opinion, 14%. These results show that those who believe genetic factors are involved in the intelligence differences outnumber strict environmentalists by approximately three to one, but that nearly two out of five experts have no opinion. Thus, by the 1980s, there was no general consensus on the problem. I will discuss soon the principal arguments advanced by the two schools of thought, but first it is necessary to set out the evidence that the two schools argue about.

The Evidence on Race Differences in Intelligence

The evidence on racial differences in intelligence is set out in Table 1. This evidence consists of the results of intelligence tests administered to various racial groups in difference parts of the world. The figures given in Table 1, which is based on a detailed recent survey reported by Lynn (1991a), are median IQs derived from a number of studies. The races are designated in the anthropological terminology of Mongoloids (Oriental peoples, largely Chinese, Japanese, and Koreans from Northeast Asia), Caucasoids (Europeans), and so forth. The IQs are calculated in relation to a mean of 100 for American Caucasoids (whites) and standard deviation of 15. Shown first are the median IQs of the three numerically major races of Mongoloids, Caucasoids, and Negroids (103, 100, and 75, respectively). Negroids in the United States and Britain are entered separately because they are considered hybrids, with about 22% Caucasoid genes in the case of American blacks (Reed, 1968); their average IQs (84 to 87) are about midway between the two parent races. American Indians and Southeast Asians, who include Australian aborigines, New Zealand Maoris, and South Sea Islanders (Polynesians, Melanesians, etc.) obtain median IQs of 89 and 90, respectively.

There can be no real dispute about these figures, which are public and objective data. The problem lies in their interpretation. The theoretical interpretation of these differences are (a) the genetic interpretation, which holds that they reflect disparities in genetic capacity, either in whole or in part; and (b) the environmental interpretation, of which there are two schools—deficit theory, and difference theory.

Deficit theory holds that Western intelligence tests are universally valid instruments that can be given to peoples in a wide range of cultures to measure intelligence. The only restriction most deficit theorists would apply is that the peoples should have been to school for some years and learned—or have had the opportunity to learn—the basic concepts used in the tests (word meanings, logical relationships between concepts, progressions, arithmetical problems, etc.). Difference theory holds that all peoples and races have the same average intelligence, but intelligence is ex-

Table 1 Median IQs of the Races

Race	Location	Intelligence	Number of studies
Mongoloids	East Asia	103	23
Caucasoids	Europe	100	39
Caucasoids	United States	100	
Negroids	Africa	75	11
Caucasoid-Negroid hybrids	United States	84	169
Caucasoid-Negroid hybrids	Britain	87	3
American Indians	North America	89	15
South East Asians	South East Asia	90	5

pressed in different ways in different cultures. The two theories are sometimes designated the "emic" and "etic" theories, but it is doubtful whether these words do anything to clarify the distinction between the two schools of thought. In the next sections accounts are given in turn of deficit theory, difference theory, and the genetic theory.

Deficit Theory

A leading environmentalist of the deficit school is Flynn (1980, 1991, 1992). Deficit theorists like Flynn accept that intelligence is important for a wide variety of desirable real-life objectives (e.g., achieving a high standard of living), although personality and motivational traits are also important for the achievement of these objectives. They accept that intelligence is reasonably well—though perhaps not perfectly—measured by intelligence tests, and that the tests are not seriously biased against groups that perform poorly in them. The explanation for group and racial differences, according to this school of thought, lies in the social disadvantages suffered by the groups that perform poorly.

Flynn (1980) presents the fullest exposition of this theory to explain the IQ deficit of blacks in the United States. He argues that a number of factors may each account for a small IQ deficit. These adverse factors are the quality of verbal interaction between mother and child, prenatal factors, poor nutrition, lack of stimulation in early childhood, family dislocation, low self-image, poor schools, and the lack of an intellectual tradition. Each of these might adversely affect intelligence by 2 or 3 IQ points, so that taken together they can account for the 15 IQ point black-white gap. Flynn does not believe there is any test bias against blacks, a point argued in full by Jensen (1980).

The principal argument against this case is the theory of genotype-environment correlation first advanced by Plomin, DeFries, and Loehlin (1977) and elaborated by Scarr and McCartney (1983). This theory states that people largely make their own environments. For instance, pairs of brothers reared in the same families tend to rise or fall in the socioeconomic status system in accordance with their intelligence levels: Those born with high IQs rise, and those both with low IQs fall (Waller, 1971). Hence the environment may determine intelligence, but the environment is itself determined by the genes. Flynn's (1991) answer to this is that the adverse effect of slavery on the motivation and aspirations of blacks has endured for generations, but genetic theorists doubt whether fairly remote historical experience of this kind could have such persistent impact. The effect should diminish with time, yet the black-white difference first shown in World War I has not diminished over the subsequent 75 years.

Flynn also claims support from studies where black children have been raised in white families or in other matched environments. There have been two principal studies of this kind. The first (Eyferth, 1961) examined 181 children born between 1945 and 1953 to German mothers and black fathers who were soldiers in the US army of occupation, as well as a socially matched sample of 83 white children. The mean IQs of the two groups were 96.5 and 97.2, respectively, suggesting that drawing 50% of their genes from a black father had no disadvantageous effect on the intelligence of children raised in a white environment. Because nothing was known about the intelligence levels of the fathers, it may be possible to argue that they were highly intelligent blacks. Nevertheless, this study is probably the most compelling item of evidence for the environmentalist case. Possible explanations from the geneticist viewpoint are that the children, who were aged between 5 and 13 at the time of the testing, (a) were too young for the IQ deficit to appear or (b) displayed "hybrid vigor," the strengthening of characteristics often found in the progeny of cross-racial stocks in animals and plants.

The second study was an adoption study carried out in the United States by Weinberg, Scarr, and Waldman (1992) that examined 25 white, 68 black-white, and 29 black babies adopted by white graduate professional-class parents. The children were intelligence tested at average ages of 7 and 17 years. At the age of 7, their mean IQs were 111 (white), 109 (black-white), and 97 (black); at the age of 17, their mean IQs were 106 (white), 98 (black-white) and 89 (black). On the one hand, the black-white mean intelligence difference of 14 IQ points at age 7—virtually the same as the 15-point difference typically found in numerous studies—suggests that rearing black children in white families does nothing to diminish the black-white difference. On the other hand, (a) the black mean IQ of 97 is close to the white average; (b) the black children were adopted a little later than the white and interracial children, a situation that might have depressed their IQ; and (c) the interracial children's mean IQ (109) is virtually the same as that of white children (111).

Taking these points together, the results are inconclusive. But at age 17 the black-white difference is 17 IQ points, again suggesting that being reared in the same environments does nothing to diminish the black-white difference. Furthermore, (a) the black children's mean IQ of 89 is now indistinguishable from that of black children reared in their own families and environments (these children came from the northern states, where the mean black IQ is 89), and (b) the interracial children's mean IQ is now significantly lower than that of the white children (98 vs. 106), although they were adopted at a younger average age. The results taken as a whole indicate that being raised in white professional-class families has some advantageous effect on the intelligence of children at the age 7 but that this influence fades away to zero by age 17. This is in accordance with modern genetic theory and data, which find that genetic effects are stronger among adults than among children, and that being adopted by middle-class parents has no long-term effect on adopted children's intelligence (Plomin, 1986).

The upshot is that the two studies indicate contradictory results. The German study suggests that half-black children reared in white families have the same intelligence as white children. The American study indicates that being reared in a white environment has no beneficial effect on the intelligence of black or black-white children at that age of 17 years. Different readers will reach their own conclusions about what weight should be attached to each of the two studies.

Difference Theory

A more radical environmentalist account of group differences in intelligence is the so-called difference theory presented by Segall, Dasen, Berry, and Poortinga (1990). This hypothesis holds that the race differences in intelligence test scores occur because the tests are biased in favor of white populations by the white psychologists who construct the tests. Difference theorists believe that all peoples and races are equally intelligent, but that intelligence develops in different ways according to the ecological requirements of different cultures. For instance, Berry (1966) showed the Eskimo peoples have stronger spatial abilities than the Temne, an African people. Berry attributed this to the hunting and fishing lifestyle of Eskimos, which requires greater spatial abilities than the gathering lifestyle of the Temne. A similar theory has been applied to the Oriental peoples (Lynn, 1987). Sternberg (1988) attributes the superior early sensorimotor development of African infants to the more intense stimulation they receive, although he believes that this also has a genetic component.

There is no doubt that different peoples and races do have different patterns of cognitive abilities. This does not mean, however, that they cannot be measured for differences in general intelligence. This can be done most simply by averaging their scores for major verbal, reasoning, or spatial abilities. This is the method used to obtain the racial differences shown in Table 1. An alternative approach adopted by Jensen (1985) is to measure racial differences in Spearman's *g*—the general factor present in all cognitive tests but appearing more strongly in some tests than in others. When this is done, Jensen finds that the black-white difference is very largely a difference in *g*.

A second problem is that the differences in patterns of cognitive abilities are likely to have arisen genetically as adaptations to the ecological niche inhabited by various peoples, as argued in detail in Lynn (1987) with regard to the strong spatial abilities of the Oriental peoples. Thus, although difference theory is generally presented as an environmentalist theory, this is by no means the only possible explanation of the different patterns of cognitive abilities found in different peoples.

The Genetic Case

The genetic case has largely been advanced by Jensen (1969, 1973, 1980, 1992) and more recently by Rushton (1992). Jensen's principal arguments are outlined in the following paragraphs.

1. Intelligence has a high heritability. There is little dispute that individual differences in intelligence are genetically determined to a substantial extent. One of the lines of evidence comes from studies of identical twins who have been separated and brought up in different families. The correlation for intelligence for such pairs gives a direct measure of heritability. The average correlation is approximately .75, which gives a heritability of 75%; this could arguably be raised to about 80% to correct for unreliability of the tests. A second source of evidence comes from adopted children and adopting parents: The correlation for intelligence for these children and parents, approximately .15, represents the environmental contribution to intelligence (these figures are taken from Plomin, 1986).

The high heritability of intelligence is not confined to the United States and Europe. It is also present in Japan (Lynn & Hattori, 1990). Flynn (1980) and Scarr (1981), who are environmentalists on the issue of racial and ethnic differences in intelligence, accept that differences between individuals of the same race have a fairly high heritability. They also concede that there are probably genetic differences between the social classes. They are therefore in the slightly peculiar position of maintaining that it is only between racial and ethnic groups that genetic differences are absent. Jensen adopts the position that because genetic differences are so clearly present between individuals, they are also virtually certain to be present between groups.

2. It is often stated by environmentalists that the high heritability of intelligence within races does not necessarily imply genetic factors are involved in the differences in intelligence between races. This is strictly correct, but it does not follow that the high heritability of intelligence is irrelevant to the problem of racial differences. The problem for environmentalists is to specify what environmental factors could account for substantial differences in intelligence in blacks and whites in circumstances where the heritability of intelligence is high in both races. The high heritability means that the putative environmental factor depressing intelligence in blacks must be present among virtually all blacks (otherwise the heritability among blacks would be lower), yet largely confined to the black population (or else the white heritability would be lower).

It is not at all easy to find a plausible environmental factor that could fulfill these conditions. Suppose we were to postulate that the factor depressing the black IQ is the absence of vitamin X, a nutrient essential for the development of intelligence. It is impossible to imagine that such a nutrient could be present in the diet of virtually all whites and absent from the diet of virtually all blacks in a society like contemporary America, where everyone buys broadly the same kinds of foods from the same sorts of stores.

The same problem is present with virtually all of the environmental factors that have been advanced to explain the low black IQ (e.g., inferior schools, one-parent families, and low incomes). None of these is present for virtually all blacks and for very few whites. The only possible candidate for the factor is racism or racial prejudice because it can be argued that this does operate on the entire black population and not on the white. But does racial prejudice really stand up as the depressant of the black IQ? Many blacks in the United States of the present day live in cities where blacks are the majority and there are black mayors, officials, police officers, and teachers. The idea often advanced that blacks are an oppressed minority in a white majority culture bears little resemblance to the reality of the major American cities, which are more like ministates populated and run by black majorities. Other racial groups (e.g., Orientals and Jews) that have also been exposed to racism, and discrimination have not been adversely affected. It also is not easy to see how racism could impair the efficiency of the brain as a problem-solving organ. How would such an effect take place?

One of the most commonly advanced factors to account for the low mean IQ of blacks is low socioeconomic status (SES). But given the high heritability of intelligence, there would have to be very large SES differences between blacks and whites to account for the IQ differences. Vernon (1979, p. 267) estimated that if heritability is set at 0.8, blacks would have to be 3.66 standard deviations below whites in SES, and if heritability is set at 0.6, blacks would have to be 2.38 standard deviations below whites in SES. In fact, blacks are about 1.24 SDs below whites for SES (Jensen, 1973, pp. 166–169). These figures suggest that low socioeconomic status cannot provide an adequate explanation for the lower mean black IQ. Again, although the high heritability of intelligence is theoretically compatible with a solely environmental determination of racial differences in intelligence, it requires the identification of an environmental factor that acts almost uniquely on blacks, and it has not proved possible to find such a factor.

3. Another argument relates to controlling for SES. When blacks and whites in the United States are matched for SES, there remains a difference between them of 12 IQ points (Jensen, 1980). But even so, it is not legitimate to match blacks and whites for SES because it involves matching blacks with a subclass of whites that is likely to be genotypically lower for intelligence than the white average. This is because those with genotypically low IQ tend to drift to the bottom of the SES hierarchy and to transmit genotypically low IQs to their children. Matching the races for SES on the assumption that the matched groups are genotypically representative of their respective races is known as the "sociologists' fallacy."

4. As noted above, environmentalists frequently ascribe the lower mean black IQ to the lower average SES of blacks. But the pattern of abilities differentiating the socioeconomic classes is not the same as the pattern differentiating blacks from whites. This was shown by Humphreys, Fleishman, and Lin (1977) and has been confirmed by Jensen and Reynolds (1982). The higher socioeconomic classes have high verbal abilities but are less strong on visuospatial abilities; conversely, the lower socioeconomic classes are weaker on verbal abilities. This has long been known in the United States and Britain (e.g., Cattell, 1971) and has been confirmed by a study in France in which children adopted by middle-class parents showed greater superiority in verbal than in visuospatial ability, as compared with their siblings brought up in working-class families (Dumaret, 1988). Probably the reason for these SES differences is that verbal abilities (e.g., the meanings of words, readings) are taught by parents more frequently than visuospatial skills and middle-class parents tend to perform this teaching more effectively.

If low SES were the major factor depressing the mean black IQ, it would be expected that the black deficit would be greatest for the verbal abilities. It has been well established for many years that this is not the case, and that in fact blacks tend to be slightly stronger on the verbal than on the visuospatial abilities. These studies show that the effects of low SES on the pattern of intelligence cannot explain the black patterns and that the black deficit must be attributable to some other factor.

5. Comparisons with other racial and ethnic minorities strengthen the view that low socioeconomic status cannot provide an adequate explanation for the low black IQ. Mexican and Native Americans have lower average SES and earnings than blacks, but they have higher mean IQs. In these cases there must be other handicaps which retard their social advancement. Possibly these may be language difficulties, or in the case of the Mexicans their recent arrival in the United States.

One of the most striking contrasts is between black and Oriental Americans. When Orientals first arrived in the United States, they initially undertook work of low SES; many of them worked as laborers building the railways in California. Yet they have risen to achieve parity with the white majority and obtain similar or higher mean IQs. There can be little doubt that Oriental immigrants have been subject to prejudice and discrimination—large numbers of Japanese Americans were interned in concentration camps during World War II. Yet these experiences have not adversely affected their IQs or their socioeconomic advancement.

6. In his more recent work Jensen has been concerned with the relationship between reaction time (RT) and intelligence. RT can be measured for the mean speed of reaction and also for the variability of reactions over a number of trials. Both of these are related to intelligence such that more intelligent subjects have faster mean times and lower variability (i.e., more consistent times), with the order of magnitude of the correlations being around 0.2 to 0.3. Jensen argues that RT provides a measure of the neurological efficiency of the brain and that the mean speed and the variability of RT represent two independent neurophysiological processes. He finds that white children in California perform better than black children on both the speed and variability components, although the difference is more pronounced for variability (the difference in mean speed is only present on complex RT tasks). Similar differences are found in comparisons of Caucasian, Oriental, and Negroid children in Britain, Japan, Hong Kong, and South Africa (Lynn, 1991a).

The point of interest in these results is that they overcome the problems of cultural differences which environmentalists argue invalidate the evidence on race differences on intelligence tests. It may be argued that it is necessary to learn how to do arithmetical series problems in schools in order to perform on a test like the Progressive Matrices, but it cannot be so plausibly argued that culture determines the speed of pressing a button when a light comes on.

7. Recently the issue of race differences in brain size has been raised by Rushton (1992). As noted earlier, in the 19th century Morton (1849) claimed that significant racial disparities in brain size explained differences in intelligence. In the present century this claim has been generally rejected. Gould (1981) reworked the data from Morton's skull collection and calculated the following corrected values (in cubic inches): Mongolians, 87; modern Caucasians, 87; Native Americans, 86; Malays, 85; ancient Caucasians, 84; and Africans, 83. Although Gould concludes that Morton's data do not show significant racial differences in brain size, it is apparent that Mongoloids and modern Caucasians do have an advantage of 4 cubic inches over Africans in these corrected data.

More recent evidence has confirmed the existence of these differences. Beals, Smith, and Dodd (1984) collected data for approximately 20,000 crania and classified them in terms of geographical location, which in most cases can be used as an equivalent of racial group. Their findings were that Northeast Asians (Mongoloids) have a mean cranial capacity of 1,415 cubic centimeters; Europeans (Caucasoids), 1,362 cc; and Africans (Negroids), 1,276 cc. Rushton (1992), based on an analysis of 6,325 U.S. army personnel, presents comparable figures (adjusted for sex and rank) of Mongoloids, 1,416 cc; Caucasoids, 1,380 cc; and Negroids, 1,359 cc. He argues that brain size is correlated with intelligence at a magnitude of about 0.3 and therefore that race differences in brain size are a factor in the differences in intelligence.

8. It has sometimes been argued that the low average IQs obtained by people in economically underdeveloped cultures are attributable to attitude differences toward taking tests and, in particular, a lack of consciousness of the necessity to work quickly to perform well on some intelligence tests. The argument is that a less time-conscious attitude to life reduces intelligence test performance. Untimed intelligence tests, however, typically show the same differences as timed tests between peoples of economically undeveloped and developed cultures. For instance, Owen (1992) reports the differences between approximately 1,000 black and white 16-year-olds in standard secondary schools in South Africa tested untimed on Raven's Progressive Matrices. The blacks obtained a mean score of 2.8 standard deviations below the whites, mean IQ equivalent of 57 in relation to a mean white IQ of 100.

Conclusions on Intelligence

There is clear evidence that the races differ in intelligence as measured by Western intelligence tests, with Caucasian and Oriental peoples scoring higher than the other races. There are three principal explanations for these differences. The first theory is that various adverse environmental conditions depress the intelligence of some racial groups. The second is that the tests are invalid outside economically developed nations and for minorities within them who score poorly; these peoples are equally intelligent, but their intelligence is not shown by the tests. The third hypothesis is that genetic differences between the races are largely responsible for the intelligence differences. Hardly anyone argues for the wholly biological theory for these differences. The genetic theory is really a biological-cultural interaction theory maintaining that biological factors explain most of the differences, but cultural factors also have some effect.

PERSONALITY

Cross-cultural work on personality can be usefully considered in the same general framework as intelligence—namely, the collection of data on national and racial differences, and the biological, interactionist, and cultural theories advanced to explain the differences. The pioneering study in this area is that of Cattell and Scheier (1961). They administered the Cattell anxiety questionnaire to students in six countries and found the following rank order in the means (going from high anxiety to low): Poland, India, France, Italy, Britain, and the United States. The authors proposed that either a low standard of living (India) or a politically authoritarian regime (Poland) might generate high anxiety. Both a low standard of living and political totalitarianism can be envisaged as forms of stress, and because stress generates anxiety in individuals, it seems a sensible hypothesis that such social factors might be responsible for differences in anxiety or neuroticism between nations.

Lynn (1991) measured national differences in anxiety from demographic indices such as national rates of suicide, alcoholism, and accidents (for high anxiety) and the consumption of calories, caffeine, and tobacco (for low anxiety). It was shown that these indicators were strongly intercorrelated for the 18 most economically developed nations. Factor analysis showed the existence of a general factor identified as the anxiety level of the population; the nations were then scored on this factor. The results showed that the northern European nations scored lower on this factor than the southern and central nations and Japan. Further work on these demographic indices showed that in the nations that suffered stress during World War II anxiety levels rose during the war and subsequently declined (Lynn & Hampson, 1977). (Notice that in this work nations are treated as subjects, and the demographic indices as scores obtained on tests.)

Hofstede (1976) published a study of anxiety levels in 40 nations, using data obtained from a questionnaire given to employees in a multinational organization. The questionnaire yielded extensive normative data, with which it was possible to check measurements of national anxiety levels obtained from demographic indices. For the 18 most economically developed nations the correlation between the two measures was 0.57, showing a fairly close level of agreement.

The most extensive research program for the collection of data on national and racial differences in personality has been carried out in terms of the Eysenck and Eysenck (1976) personality theory, which posits three major traits: neuroticism (broadly, anxiety or emotionality), extraversion (sociability), and psychoticism (antisocial personality). The approach is strongly universalist (or "emic") in that is assumes that it is valid to construct a questionnaire for the measurement of these traits in Britain and then administer the questionnaire in other countries and cultures, score the respondents on the traits, and compare the means in the various cultures. The validity of this assumption has been checked by examining the factor structure of the questionnaire in different countries. When this has been done, it has universally been found that the factor structures are virtually identical (i.e., the same questions measure the same traits) except for a small number of questions. These are normally discarded in making cross-national and cross-cultural comparisons between means.

The first study to assemble a number of these cross-cultural investigations was carried out by the present author (Lynn, 1981). This study assembled means for 24 countries on the three traits. A number of regularities were observed, of which the most important was that the populations in the economically developed nations generally scored lower on neuroticism and psychoticism. The interpretations offered were that poverty (a) is a stress that raises the level of neuroticism, and (b) brutalizes individuals and raises their level of psychoticism.

Further extensive data on cross-cultural differences in these three personality traits were collated for 25 countries by Barrett and Eysenck (1984). Their results were descriptive only, but Rushton (1985b, 1988a,b) proposed that the national differences could be meaningfully analyzed in terms of the racial composition of the countries. He noted that Oriental peoples showed higher neuroticism and introversion than Caucasians, whereas Negroid peoples scored lower than both. Rushton proposed that these differences could be explained in terms of a more general theory positing racial differences in restraint, such that Oriental peoples show the greatest restraint and Negroids the least. This interpretation was criticized by Zuckerman and Brody (1988) on the grounds that there were too few Oriental and Negroid countries to make valid comparisons.

Another feature of these compilations of cross-cultural norms on the three Eysenck personality dimensions is that males invariably obtain higher means on psychoticism and females invariably obtain higher means on neuroticism. The universality of these sex differences probably means they have a biological basis. With regard to neuroticism, probably there was a selection advantage for males to be less timid, in order both to compete with other males to secure mates and to defend the group against competing groups and predators. The greater male psychoticism may reflect the same evolutionary requirements, because psychoticism has an aggression component.

Sex Differences in Aggression

The sex differences in neuroticism and psychoticism probably determine similar differences in aggression as a positive function of psychoticism and a negative function of neuroticism. There is a widespread agreement that males are more aggressive than females in all societies. In a review of cross-cultural studies of sex differences, Ember (1981) concluded that "the most consistent and most documented cross-cultural difference in interpersonal behavior appears to be that boys exhibit more aggression" (p. 551). Males also differ from girls on the related traits of dominance, competitiveness, and criminal behavior in nearly all societies. In the most comprehensive cross-cultural study of sex differences in competitiveness, carried out in 43 countries, males were significantly more competitive in the great majority of cases (Lynn, 1991c). In this survey it was also found that males value money more highly that females in virtually all countries; the reason for this is probably that money is a symbol of competitive success. The higher prevalence of crime among males can probably be understood as partly attributable to the stronger male aggressiveness.

Virtually all authorities agree that the greater male aggression has a biological basis. The reason for this is that aggression is partly determined by the male sex hormone testosterone. Manzur (1985) argues convincingly that testosterone production in boys in early adolescence motivates them primarily to strive for dominance (i.e., status or rank in relation to other males). One way of securing this is by aggression, but status can also be achieved by athletic and academic success or, in some social environments, by success in crime or as a gang leader. The most thorough recent survey of the effects of sex hormones on sex-role behavior (including aggression) was carried out by Reinisch, Ziemba-Davis, and Sanders (1991). They reviewed 19 studies in which sex hormones were administered to pregnant women, after which their children were tested for a number of sex-role behaviors. The general findings were that prenatal exposure to androgens had masculinizing effects on aggression, interest in competitive sports, assertiveness, and dominance, whereas the female hormone progesterone had feminizing effects. Even environmentally inclined writers like Seagall et al. (1990) admit that the greater male aggression and dominance has a biological basis: "There is good reason to consider biological (more specifically, hormonal) forces as being implicated in male adolescent aggression" (p. 278).

Ethnocentrism

A further characteristic that a number of authorities believe has a biological basis is ethnocentrism (loyalty to one's own group and hostility to outgroups). This theory was first set out authoritively by Darwin (1871) and was restated by the early sociologists Spencer (1882) and Sumner (1906). This approach was attacked by Margaret Mead (1935), who took the view that human social behavior is entirely culturally determined; in the middle years of the 20th century, the cultural determination theory became the orthodoxy. The biological view was revived by Wilson (1975), who gave it the name *sociobiology*, and since the late 1970s it has once more become a widely held position.

The biological case mobilizes five general arguments to establish that a type of social behavior is biologically determined: (a) It is universally present in the human species; (b) it is also present in a number of animal species, especially primates; (c) there is a plausible genetic theory to explain it; (d) it has had an adaptive advantage in evolution; and (e) it is under hormonal control. None of these criteria is present in purely socially conditioned behaviors (e.g., whether men open doors for women, whether individuals kiss or shake hands when they meet),

With regard to ethnocentrism, no hormonal or neurophysiological basis for the trait has been identified, but the other four conditions are fulfilled. The adaptive advantage of ethnocentrism was set out by Darwin (1871). He proposed that early humans, like most other primates, lived in social groups in possession of territories. Because the territories contained the food supply for the group, it was important to defend the borders against intrusions by neighboring groups, and it was even more advantageous to extend the territory at the expense of the neighbors. This involved attacking and defeating the neighbors because the latter would defend their territories. In these conflicts the more aggressive groups would tend to win, killing off the less aggressive groups and taking over their territories. After some hundreds of thousands of years, only aggressive groups would have survived.

This theory was extended by Spencer (1882), who proposed that human groups have a "dual ethical code" consisting of peaceful cooperation within the group and hostility to other groups. The term *ethnocentrism* for this dual code was coined by Sumner (1906), who extended the concept to explain the prevalence of group conflict and warfare among nations as well as tribal warfare among small groups of primitive peoples. The adaptive advantage of ethnocentrism and its expression in warfare was restated in sociobiological terms by Wilson (1975). He also noted that it is universal in the species, a second condition for inferring that the behavior is biologically based: "Throughout recorded history the conduct of war was been common among tribes and nearly universal among chiefdoms and states" (p. 572). The same conclusion is reached by Van Der Dennen (1987): "Ethnocentrism is very prevalent among primitive tribes, who either kill all strangers or regard them with suspicion" (p. 7).

A third condition for inferring a biological basis for ethnocentrism is that it should be widely present in other species, especially in primates. Van der Dennen (1987) cites numerous studies showing that aggression toward out-groups is very common among social species, including ants, bees, hamsters, gerbils, mice, rats, wolves, dogs, hyenas, and many species of monkeys and apes. He concludes that "xenophobia has apparently arisen in the course of natural selection and social evolution" (p. 22).

The remaining condition for inferring a biological basis for ethnocentrism is that there should be a plausible genetic theory to explain it. Such a theory has been supplied by Hamilton (1964, 1975). His first concept was kin selection and involved the idea that individuals can increase their biological fitness by assisting those with whom they have genes in common (e.g., brothers, cousins, nieces, and nephews). In small groups of primates and early humans many of the individuals would be fairly closely related and would therefore secure a biological advantage by mutual cooperation, self-sacrifice in defence of territory and aggression toward out-groups to extend territory. This concept provides a genetical theory for ethnocentrism in small genetically related groups but it does not provide such a plausible explanation for ethnocentrism in nations where the populations of millions are not closely related.

To explain nationalist ethnocentrism requires the addition of "inclusive fitness" to the concept of kin selection (Hamilton, 1975). According to this broadened theory, individuals can secure a significant fitness advantage by helping others with whom they have only weak genetic relationships so long as there are large numbers of them. An individual may see little fitness advantage in making a sacrifice for another who is perceived as sharing only 1/1000 of a relationship, but a sacrifice for 500 such individuals is genetically equivalent to helping the individual's own children, and a sacrifice for 1,000 such individuals is genetically equivalent to helping oneself. This concept provides a genetical theory for nationalist ethnocentrism, where individuals make sacrifices in warfare between nations for large numbers of others with whom they have low relationship coefficients. The theory has recently been restated by Alexander (1987).

The genetic theory of ethnocentrism has been further developed by Rushton (1989) into a more general "genetic similarity theory." This theory states that genetically similar people tend to like each other, seek each out, and form mutually supportive relationships of friendship, marriage, and group membership. Rushton (1989) proposes four possible ways by which people detect others who are genetically similar to themselves: (a) phenotypic matching (e.g., facial features, skin color); (b) familiarity (e.g., language, accent, and other learned behaviors), because children reared in social groups with common norms are likely to be more closely genetically related that those in other groups; (c) location, because people in the same or a nearby location are likely to be more closely related genetically than those in other locations; and (d) "recognition detectors" that can identify those who are genetically similar. Rushton's theory suggests a generalized tendency for people to associate with others who have many of the same genes as themselves, to cooperate with them in a variety of ways, and to display indifference or hostility toward other groups (including social classes, nationalities, and races) with whom they have relatively few genes in common.

How do environmentalists view ethnocentrism? The leading text by Segall et al. (1990) concludes that "people everywhere hold their own group in highest regard, and social distance increases as perceived similarity diminishes" (p. 339). This statement evidently concedes the first condition of the case for biological determination, namely, the universality of the phenomenon in all human societies. These authors have nothing to say on the issue of whether there may be a biological basis to ethnocentrism and, if so, how important it is. The prevalence and universality of group conflict suggest that there is a biological predisposition to ethnocentrism, although no doubt its strength and expression are affected by cultural conditions.

Race Differences in r-k Characteristics

Rushton (1985a, b, 1988a, b, 1992) posits that the common factor responsible for biologically based racial differences in a number of behaviors lies in what are called r-k characteristics. His concept is that species—and human races—vary in their reproductive strategies. One strategy (r) is to produce large numbers of offspring but devote little parental care to them; most of the offspring die young, but because there are so many of them enough reach maturity to assure species survival. The alternative strategy (k) is to produce few offspring but devote considerable parental care to rearing them, so that a much larger proportion survive. In general the first species to evolve (fish and reptiles) adopted r strategies, whereas later species (mammals, especially primates) adopted k strategies. For instance, frogs produce many hundreds of eggs, but female apes produce only one infant every 5 years or so. Species that adopt the k strategy—especially monkeys, apes, and humans—have larger brains and are more intelligent than r strategists.

The thesis advanced by Rushton is that racial differences have evolved such that the most strongly k are the Mongoloid peoples, and the least strongly k are the Negroids, whereas the Caucasoids are intermediate. Rushton assembles evidence that these differences are expressed in the following characteristics, which are greatest in Mongoloids, intermediate in Caucasoids, and lowest in Negroids: brain size, intelligence, late maturation, sexual restraint, fertility, rarity of dizygotic twins, martial stability, monogamy, mental health, law-abidingness, and anxiety.

There have been a number of criticisms of Rushton's theory, among which the most comprehensive is that of Zuckerman and Brody (1988). Their objections are that (a) not all the behavioral characteristics can be explained in terms of the r-k concept; (b) there is much contrary evidence; (c) there are no controls for social class in many of the racial differences (e.g., higher fertility is generally present in lower socioeconomic groups, in which Negroids are disproportionately represented); and (d) there is no evidence that fertility has any heritability. Rushton (1988b) has replied to these criticisms. Probably the strongest elements in his theory are the racial differences in brain size and in dizygotic twin rates, both of which are largely biologically determined and plausibly related to r-k differences. Rushton has presented a powerful challenge to those who believe that all racial differences are environmentally and culturally determined, but it will take some years before a consensus is likely to emerge on his theory.

Achievement Motivation and Economic Growth

One of the most ambitious studies to measure a personality trait in a number of countries was McClelland's (1961) work on national levels of achievement motivation and their relationship to rates of economic growth. The problem posed was why many nations in the course of history have displayed periods of strong economic growth that have been followed by absolute or relative economic decline. For instance, Britain was the leading economic power in the 19th century but in the following century slipped to being one of the less successful among the leading economic nations. McClelland's hypothesis to explain these national differences in rates of economic growth was that the populations differ in their levels of achievement motivation.

The motive to achieve excellence in tasks that are undertaken is considered to be acquired in childhood through independence training by parents. In initial studies in the United States, the strength of achievement motivation was measured by the projective Thematic Apperception Test, in which the subject is presented with pictures and asked to write stories about them. The stories were then scored for the degree to which they were concerned with achievement values and aspirations. Application of this method to a number of groups led to the discovery that achievement motivation is high in successful entrepreneurs (i.e., those who build their own businesses). McClelland suggested that the reason for this is that entrepreneurship provides a clear index of achievement in terms of the profitability of the firm.

Up to this point McClelland was working at the level of individual psychology: the conceptualization, analysis, and measurement of achievement motivation in individuals and its central role in the motivation of the entrepreneur. His next step was to move to the level of society. The work demonstrating the importance of high achievement motivation for individual entrepreneurs leads naturally to the thesis that where the average level of achievement motivation is high in a society—regarded simply as an aggregate of individuals—there will be relatively large numbers of entrepreneurially minded persons. This in turn will express itself in the various macro indices of a strong enterprise economy (e.g., fast rates of economic growth and a high rate of formation of small businesses). Hence McClelland turned his attention to determining whether a relationship could be demonstrated between the strength of achievement motivation in a society and its rate of economic growth.

There were two principal attacks on this problem. First, McClelland took four societies where the strength of the enterprise culture rose and then fell (classical Athens from 1000 to 900 B.C., 17-century Spain, England from A.D. 1400 to 1830, and the United States from A.D., 1800 to 1950) and endeavored to show that the pattern in the strength of the economy over time was preceded by a similar pattern in the strength of achievement motivation. The empirical problems were to obtain measures of the general level of achievement motivation in the populations of these societies, as well as measures of economic growth rates. The method adopted for the measurement of achievement motivation was to make assessments from samples of the societies' literature. (This employs the same rationale as was used for the measurement of achievement motivation in individuals, namely, the assumption that people express their values in the kinds of themes they write about.) The results showed that in all four cases achievement motivation was high in the early years of the society's rise. For instance, in the initial stage of classical Athens the writer Hesiod was extolling the virtues of competition between people for riches and success. Among later writers this preoccupation with achievement and success was absent.

McClelland employed various indices to measure rates of economic growth; the numbers and distribution of Athenian pottery finds at the various locations (Sicily, North Africa, etc.) where Athenian merchants carried on trade in the classical period. For all four of the societies studied McClelland was able to demonstrate the same pattern: initial high levels of achievement motivation sustained for a century or so and then undergoing a diminution, followed in time by a growth stabilization, and subsequent decline in economic strength. The temporal sequences in which high levels of achievement motivation precede the takeoff of strong economic growth, whereas the later falloff in achievement motivation presages the subsequent weakness of the economies, are persuasive evidence that the causal effect is from the psychological levels of motivation present in the population to the economic growth (and later decline) of the societies.

McClelland also tested the achievement motivation theory among nations of the 20th century. The method here was to test for correlations across countries between levels of achievement motivation and subsequent economic growth. Two data sets were obtained. First, achievement motivation levels for 1925 were quantified for 23 nations from an assessment of the themes present in children's reading books. Economic growth rates for the succeeding quarter century (1925 to 1950) were quantified by the use of Colin Clark's international units of per capita national income and by the per capita growth of electricity consumption. For both indices the predicted positive correlations (0.25 and 0.53, respectively) between levels of achievement motivation and subsequent economic growth were obtained. In the second data set, levels of national achievement motivation (again using children's readers) were assessed for 39 countries for the year 1950. Economic growth was indexed by the growth of electricity consumption between 1952 and 1958. The correlation between the two variables was 0.43, so that again the predicted positive correlation was present and substantial.

McClelland's work was a major creative effort, but there are certain criticisms that can be made of it. First, the concept of achievement motivation (consisting of a combination of the work ethic, a need for excellence and competiveness) needs more precise definition and measurement. Second, the use of growth of electricity consumption as an index of the general economic growth of nations is unsatisfactory, especially because better measures are available. Third, when conventional measures of economic growth are used, national levels of achievement motivation calculated by McClelland for 1950 failed to predict subsequent rates of economic growth (Finison, 1986). In spite of these criticisms, McClelland's work has stimulated a number of people to carry out further work on these problems.

Hoping to correct the weaknesses of McClelland's work, in the late 1980s I carried out a study of national differences in a number of "achievement motivations" and economic growth (Lynn, 1991c). The salient features of the study were (a) the use of 13 questionnaire measures of a spectrum of characteristics related to achievement motivation; (b) the administration of these questionnaires to samples of the population in 43 countries; (c) factor analysis of the questionnaires to reveal the underlying factors present in the concept of achievement motivation; (d) examination of the relationship between these factors and rates of economic growth (as conventionally measured by economists), as well as the standard of living (measured by per capita incomes). Two independent factors were found to underlie the concept of achievement motivation: work commitment (a moral commitment to work) and competitiveness (the motivation to perform better than others, expressed partly in the desire to make money). National rates of economic growth were found to be positively correlated across countries with competitiveness (at a magnitude of 0.52), but not with work commitment. In general, the countries with the highest levels of competitiveness were the Pacific rim nations of Japan, South Korea, Hong Kong, Taiwan and Singapore—the countries that have achieved the highest rates of economic growth in the post–World War II decades.

The study also revealed a negative relationship between competitiveness and per capita income, suggesting that as nations become more affluent, the competitiveness of the people declines. There was, however, no relationship between per capita income and work commitment. Certain sociologists, most notably Bell (1974), have maintained that as affluent nations evolved toward a postindustrial society, the commitment to work would decline in strength and be replaced by a commitment to leisure. The study showed no evidence that this was the case. Indeed, when the 20 most affluent nations were considered as a subgroup, the correlation between work commitment and per capita income was significantly positive. Thus people in affluent nations continue to feel a moral commitment to work, although their competiveness declines.

The Cultural View of Cross-Cultural Differences in Personality

The leading exponents of the cultural view of cross-cultural differences in personality are Segall et al. (1990) and Berry, Poortinga, Segall, and Dasen (1992). Their general view is that intelligence and personality differences among different peoples are brought about by dissimilar socialization and child-rearing practices. For instance, if people in economically developed nations tend to be more competitive than those in underdeveloped nations and traditional societies, this is because children in economically developed societies are brought up to compete. With regard to male-female differences in aggression, these authors concede that hormonal sex differences are involved, but they believe that cultural differences in child-rearing practices strongly modify the extent of the sex differences. Their judgments are generally approved by Monroe (1991) except in regard to ethnocentrism, for which the universality and selection advantage of the phenomenon are considered to favor a biological basis.

CONCLUSIONS

The debate on the determinants of cross-cultural differences in both intelligence and personality centers is largely between the positions of biological-cultural interaction and cultural determination. There are no exponents of the purely biological theory of differences between peoples, although a number of theorists hold that biological differences are the major factor, with some cultural determinants to solely or very largely cultural determination as well as (of course) those who do not claim to know. The debate has continued for more than a century, and theorists show little sign of reaching agreement.

REFERENCES

Alexander, R. D. (1987). *The biology of moral systems*. New York: Aldine de Gruyter.

Barrett, P., & Eysenck, S. B. G. (1984). The assessment of personality factors across 25 countries. *Personality and Individual Differences, 5*, 615–632.

Beals, K. L., Smith, C. L., and Dodd, S. M. (1984). Brain size, cranial morphology, climate, and time machines. *Current Anthropology, 25*, 307–330.

Bell, D. (1974). *The coming of post-industrial society*. London: Heineman.

Berry, J. W. (1966). Temne and Eskimo perceptual skills. *International Journal of Psychology. 1*, 207–229.

Berry, J. W., Poortinga, Y. H., Segall, M. H., & Dasen, P. R. (1992). *Cross-cultural psychology: Research and applications*. Cambridge, England, Cambridge University Press.

Brody, N. (1992). *Intelligence*. New York: Academic Press.

Cattell, R. B. (1971). *Abilities: Their structure, growth and action*. Boston: Houghton Mifflin.

Cattell, R. B., & Scheier, I. H. (1961). *Measurement of neuroticism and anxiety*. New York: Ronald.

Chomsky, N. (1965). *Aspects of the theory of syntax*. Cambridge, MIT Press.

Darwin, C. (1871). *The descent of man in relation to sex*. London: Murray.

Dumaret, H. (1988). IQ, scholastic achievement and behavior of siblings raised in contrasting environments. *Journal of Child Psychology and Psychiatry, 26*, 553–580.

Ember, C. R. (1981). A cross-cultural perspective on sex differences. In R. H. Monroe, R. L. Monroe, & B. B. Whiting (Eds.), *Handbook of cross-cultural human development*. New York: Garland.

Eyferth, K. (1961). Leistungen verschiedener gruppen von besatzungskindern im Hamburg—Wechsler Intelligenztest fur kinder. *Archiv fur die gesamte Psychologie. 113*, 222–241.

Eysenck, H. J. (1971). *Race, intelligence and education*. London: Temple Smith.

Eysenck, H. J., & Eysenck, S. B. G. (1976). *Psychoticism as a dimension of personality*. London: Hodder & Stoughton.

Finison, L. J. (1986). The application of McClelland's national development model to recent data. *Journal of Social Psychology, 98*, 55–59.

Flynn, R. J. (1980). *Race, IQ and Jensen*. London: Routledge and Kegan Paul.

Flynn, J. R. (1991). *Asian Americans: Achievement beyond IQ*. Hillsdale, NJ: Erlbaum.

Flynn, J. R. (1992). Cultural distance and the limitations of IQ. In J. Lynch, C. Modgil, & S. Modgil, (eds.), *Cultural diversity and the schools*. London: Falmer.

Galton. F. (1869). *Hereditary genius*. London; Macmillan.

Garth, T. R. (1931). *Race psychology*. New York: McGraw-Hill.

Hamilton, W. D. (1964). The genetical evolution of social behavior. *Journal of Theoretical Biology, 7*, 1–16, 17–52.

Hamilton, W. D. (1975). Innate social aptitudes of man: An approach from evolutionary genetics. In R. Fox (Ed.), *Biosocial anthropology*. London: Malaby.

Hofstede, G. (1976). *Nationality & organisational stress*. Brussels: European Institute for Research in Management.

Humphreys, L. G., Fleishman, A. I., & Lin, P. C. (1977). Causes of racial and socio-economic differences in cognitive tests. *Journal of Research in Personality. 11*. 191–208.

Jensen, A. R. (1969). How much can we boost IQ and scholastic achievement? *Harvard Educational Review, 39*, 1–123.

Jensen, A. R. (1973). *Education and group differences*. London: Methuen.

Jensen, A. R. (1980). *Bias in mental tests*. London: Methuen.

Jensen, A. R. (1985). The nature of the black-white difference on various psychometric tests: Spearman's hypothesis. *Behavioral Brain Sciences, 8*, 193–263.

Jensen, A. R. (1992). The importance of intraindividual variation in reaction time. *Personality and Individual Differences, 13*, 869–981.

Jensen, A. R., & Reynolds, C. F. (1982). Race, social class and ability patterns on the WISC-R. *Personality and Individual Differences, 3*, 423–438.

Loehlin, J. F., Lindzey, G., & Spuhler, J. N. (1975). *Race differences in intelligence*. San Francisco: Freeman.

Lynn, R. (1981). Cross-cultural differences in neuroticism, extraversion and psychoticism. In R. Lynn (Ed.), *Dimensions of personality*. Oxford, England: Pergamon.

Lynn R. (1987). The intelligence of the Mongolojds: A psychometric, evolutionary and neurological theory. *Personality and Individual Differences, 8*, 813–844.

Lynn R. (1991a). Race differences in intelligence: A global perspective. *Mankind Quarterly, 31*, 255–296.

Lynn R. (1991b). The evolution of racial differences in intelligence. *Mankind Quarterly, 32*, 99–121.

Lynn R. (1991c). *The Secret of the Miracle Economy*. London: Social Affairs Unit.

Lynn R., & Hattori, K. (1990). The heritability of intelligence in Japan. *Behavior Genetics, 20*, 545–546.

Lynn R., & Hampson, S. L. (1977). Fluctuations in national levels of neuroticism and extraversion. *British Journal of Social Clinical Psychology, 16*, 131–137.

McClelland, D. C. (1961). *The achieving society*. Princeton, NJ: Van Nostrand.

Mazur, A. (1985). A biosocial model of status in face to face primate groups. *Social Forces, 64*, 377–402.

Mead, M. (1935). *Sex and temperament in three primitive societies*. New York: Morrow.

Monroe, R. H. (1991). Culture permeates all. *Contemporary Psychology, 36*, 1040–1042.

Morton, S. G. (1849). Observations on the size of the brain in various races and families of man. *Proceedings of the Academy of Natural Sciences, 4*, 221–254.

Owen, K. (1992). The suitability of Raven's Standard Progressive Matrices for various groups in South Africa. *Personality and Individual Differences, 13*, 149–160.

Pinter, R. (1931). *Intelligence testing*. New York: Holt.

Plomin, R. (1986). *Development, genetics, and psychology*. Hillsdale, NJ: Erlbaum.

Plomin, R., DeFries, J. C., & Loehlin, J. C. (1977). Genotype-environment interaction and correlation in the analysis of human behavior. *Psychological Bulletin, 84*, 309–322.

Porteus, S. D. (1965), *Porteus maze test*. Palo Alto, CA: Pacific.

Reed, T. E. (1969). Caucasian genes in American negroes. *Science, 165*, 762–768.

Reinisch, J. M., Ziemba-Xavis, M., & Sanders, S. A. (1991). Hormonal contributions to sexually dimorphic behavioral development in humans. *Psychoneuroendocrinology, 16*, 213–278.

Rushton, J. P. (1985a). Differential theory: The sociobiology of individual and group differences. *Personality and Individual Differences, 6*, 441–452.

Rushton, J. P. (1985b). Differential theory and race differences. *Personalty and Individual Differences, 6*, 769–770.

Rushton, J. P. (1988a). Race differences in behavior: A review and evolutionary analysis. *Personalty and Individual Differences, 9*, 1009–1024.

Rushton, J. P. (1988b). The reality of racial differences: A rejoinder with new evidence. *Personality and Individual Differences, 9*, 1035–1040.

Rushton, J. P. (1989). Genetic similarity, human altruism and group selection. *Personality and Individual Differences, 12*, 503–559.

Rushton, J. P. (1992). Cranial capacity related to sex, rank and race in a stratified random sample of 6,325 U.S. military personnel. *Intelligence, 16*, 401–413.

Rushton, J. P., Russell, R. J. H., & Wells, P. A. (1984). Genetic similarity theory: Beyond kin selection. *Behavior Genetics, 14*, 179–192.

Scarr, S. (1981). *Race, social class and individual differences*. Hillsdale, NJ: Erlbaum.

Scarr, S., & McCartney, K. (1983). How people make their own environments: A theory of genotype-environment effects. *Child Development, 54*, 414–435.

Segall, M. H., Dasen, P. R., Berry, J. W., & Poortinga, Y. H. (1990). Human Behavior in Global Perspective. Oxford, England: Pergamon.

Shuey, A. M. (1966). *The testing of Negro intelligence*. New York: Social Sciences.

Spencer, H. (1882). *Principles of ethics*. London: Williams and Norgate.

Sumner, W. G. (1906). *Folkways*. Boston: Ginn.

Synderman, M., & Rothman, S. (1988). *The IQ controversy: The media and the public*. New Brunswick, NJ: Transaction Books.

Spencer, H. (1882). *The principles of ethics*. London: Williams and Norgate.

Sternberg, R. J. (1988). A triarchic view of intelligence in cross-cultural perspective. In S. H. Irvine & J. W. Berry (Eds.), *Human abilities in cultural context*. Cambridge, England: Cambridge University Press.

Stone, B. J. (1992). Prediction of achievement by Asian-American and white children. *Journal of School Psychology, 30*, 91–99.

Sumner, W. G. (1906). *Folkways*. Boston: Glinn.

United Nations Educational, Scientific and Cultural Organization. (1951). *Statement on the nature of race and race differences*. Paris: United Nations.

Van der Dennen, J. M. G. (1987). Ethnocentrism and in-group/out-group differentiation: A review and interpretation of the literature. In V. Reynolds, V. Falgar, & I. Vine (Eds.), *The sociobiology of ethnocentrism*. London: Croom Helm.

Vernon, P. E. (1979). *Intelligence: Heredity and environment*. San Francisco: Freeman.

Vernon, P. E. (1982) *The abilities and achievements of Orientals in North America,* New York: Academic Press.

Waller, J. H. (1971). Achievement and social mobility: Relationships among IQ score, education and occupation in two generations. *Social Biology, 18*, 252–259.

Weinberg, R. A., Scarr, S., & Waldman, I. D. (1992). The Minnesota transracial adoption study: A follow-up of IQ test performance at adolescence. *Intelligence, 16*, 117–135.

Wilson, E. O. (1975). *Sociobiology: The new synthesis*. Cambridge, MA: Harvard University Press.

Zuckerman, M., & Brody, N. (1988). Oysters, rabbits and people: A critique of race differences in behavior by J. P. Rushton. *Personality and Individual Differences, 9*, 1025–1033.

II

Personality and Intelligence at the Crossroads

7

Intelligence and Personality in Social Behavior

Martin E. Ford

The overall goal of this chapter is to provide the reader with an integrated conceptual framework for understanding human intelligence and personality as these qualities are reflected in dynamic, complex patterns of social behavior. To accomplish this rather broad and challenging objective, each of the three major constructs represented in this chapter—personality, intelligence, and social behavior—are defined and explicated in separate sections designed to build upon one another in an organized, systematic manner. The intended result is a rich, coherent framework of considerable practical utility (M. Ford & D. Ford, 1987).

Unfortunately, there is very little existing psychological theory and research that deals directly with the integrated functioning or joint impact of intelligence and personality in social contexts. The most relevant material resides in segments of the literatures on social intelligence and social motivation, both of which are relatively unconsolidated, emerging fields of study (e.g., Cantor & Kihlstrom, 1987; Csikszentmihalyi, 1990; Dweck & Leggett, 1988; Elliott & Dweck, 1988; M. Ford, 1986, 1992; Sternberg, Conway, Ketron, & Bernstein, 1981; Sternberg & Kolligian, 1990). Consequently, rather than trying to review isolated concepts and fragments of empirical evidence from a variety of disconnected sources, the basic strategy of this chapter is to introduce a framework of ideas that offers a coherent and practical way of thinking about intelligence and personality in social behavior. The Living Systems Framework (D. Ford, 1987), and one of its theoretical offspring, Motivational Systems Theory (M. Ford, 1992), provide the basis for this theoretical construction work. It is hoped that this approach will stimulate the efforts of scholars and practitioners to expand their own theories, research programs, and applied techniques for investigating and promoting effective social behavior.

THE NATURE AND ORGANIZATION OF HUMAN PERSONALITY

Personality is the core concept used by psychologists to refer to the content, meaning, or organization of a person's thoughts, feelings, perceptions, and actions. This concept is typically used to refer to broad patterns of functioning at the level of the whole person (e.g., a "well-adjusted" or "antisocial" personality). However, it has become commonplace in the increasingly fractionated literature in psychology (Bevan, 1991; Staats, 1991) to see this term applied to analyses of component psychological processes that have a powerful and pervasive impact on how and how well a person functions (e.g., "personality processes" repre-

Martin E. Ford • Graduate School of Education, George Mason University, Fairfax, Virginia 22030-4444.

International Handbook of Personality and Intelligence, edited by Donald H. Saklofske and Moshe Zeidner. Plenum Press, New York, 1995.

senting sets of self-regulatory strategies, coping skills, or social cognitive processes). It seems evident that what is needed is an approach that weds considerations of content and process to take advantage of the rich descriptions characteristic of the traditional approach and the explanatory power of the newer approach. The Living Systems Framework (LSF) offers such an approach (D. Ford, 1987; M. Ford & D. Ford, 1987). Before I offer a more precise definition of personality, though, it is necessary to introduce several core LSF concepts designed to represent the complexly organized functioning of the whole person-in-context.

The Principle of Unitary Functioning

The LSF begins with the basic premise that a person always functions as a unit in coordination with his or her environment (D. Ford, 1987). This assumption is regarded as so central and so essential to all psychological theorizing that it is given a formal label: the principle of unitary functioning. Because many personality theories—as well as most theories of intelligence—focus on component processes without a corresponding emphasis on how these processes are organized at the level of the whole person, insufficient attention has been given to this principle and its profound implications for research and practice (D. Ford & Lerner, 1992; M. Ford & D. Ford, 1987; Nesselroade & Ford, 1987). Although this sometimes reflects a well-intentioned effort to avoid overly ambitious theorizing, it still leaves scholars and professionals with little guidance in understanding the whole person in context.

Behavior Episodes: Organized Sequences of Goal-Directed Activity

To understand personality at the level of the whole person, one must be able to represent the coherent, organized flow of an individual's complex behavior patterns (e.g., an interpersonal encounter or social relationship) in a way that highlights the meaning and significance of those behavior patterns. In the LSF, the concept of behavior episodes is used to serve this purpose. A *behavior episode* is defined as a context-specific, goal-directed pattern of behavior that unfolds over time until one of three conditions is met: the goal organizing the episode is accomplished, or something less than full accomplishment is accepted (sometimes called "satisficing"); the person's attention is preempted by some internal or external event, and another goal takes precedence (at least temporarily); or the goal is evaluated as unattainable at least for the time being (D. Ford, 1987; Pervin, 1983; Simon, 1967). For example, a spousal-persuasion episode that begins with one partner's desire to have sex may continue until (a) the desired sexual activity has occurred; (b) the episode is disrupted by a telephone call, crying child, or some other compelling event; or (c) a lack of progress leads the initiator to wait for more promising circumstances.

A basic assumption of the LSF is that virtually all human activity—whether it involves work, play, social relationships, or solitary activity—is organized in behavior episode form. Thus behavior episodes are like stories on a television news show that is on all day, every day. Many episodes, like most news stories, are of only momentary interest (e.g., a brief encounter at a meeting or cocktail party); other episodes build upon one another to create an ongoing plot or saga (e.g., a dating, work, or family relationship). The latter episodes are of particular interest with respect to issues of personality and intelligence in social behavior.

The goal directing a behavior episode is a psychological phenomenon: namely, a cognitive representation of the state or outcome that the person would like to achieve or avoid (D. Ford, 1987). Such thoughts may take a variety of forms. Goals may range from the mundane to the grandiose, and they may represent desires or concerns that are realistic and immediate or merely wishful thinking (M. Ford, 1992). They may be private and idiosyncratic or widely shared among members of a social or cultural group. It is also commonplace for behavior episodes to be directed by multiple goals simultaneously (D. Ford, 1987). In such cases, the degree to which these goals are in conflict with one another or aligned in a synergistic ("win-win") fashion will greatly influence the productivity of and satisfaction derived from these episodes (M. Ford, 1992). Indeed, goal alignment is often an essential prerequisite for success in interpersonal and working relationships (Covey, 1990; Csikszentmihalyi, 1990; M. Ford, 1992; Slavin, 1981, 1984; Winell, 1987).

The goals directing a behavior episode serve a leadership function by triggering organized patterns of cognitive, emotional, biological, and perceptual-motor activity that, in coordination with facilitating and constraining conditions in the environment, are designed to attain those goals (D. Ford, 1987). Some goals that people think about, however, are too vague or transient to generate much activity. It is only when goals are "held in mind" and translated into *intentions* as a result of supporting evaluative thoughts and emotions that the motivational foundation for an effortful, productive episode can emerge (M. Ford, 1992). In some cases, prior learning enables this motivational processing to happen almost instantaneously, with minimal awareness that these cognitive and emotional processes are occurring. In other episodes, the translation of a goal into an intention may be a very deliberate or conflicted process characterized by a great deal of conscious thought processing.

The process of activating and evaluating goals is guided both by the person's enduring interests and concerns and by the opportunities and obstacles in the contexts influencing his or her activity. Contexts also facilitate and constrain the resulting efforts to accomplish whatever goals emerge as current intentions. Thus *goals and contexts are the anchors that organize and give coherence and meaning to the activities within a behavior episode* (D. Ford, 1987; M. Ford, 1992). Indeed, it is impossible either to understand the significance or judge the effectiveness of most human activities without understanding the goals and contexts that organize them (D. Ford, 1987; Schutz, 1991).

Behavior Episode Schemata: The Building Blocks of Human Personality

Like stories on a news program, behavior episodes are temporary phenomena with identifiable beginning and ending points. Yet although there are many "lost episodes" in each person's experience, people are capable of guiding their behavior in new episodes by using material from their past. Such experiences may include not only instrumental episodes (i.e., those in which the person was an active participant) but also observational and thought episodes in which the experiences were merely symbolic (what might be called "virtual" episodes in contemporary lingo; D. Ford, 1987). Thus behavior episodes provide the raw materials from which people can construct a complex repertoire of enduring behavior patterns.

The concept of a behavior episode schema (BES) is used in the LSF to represent the product of this self-construction process (D. Ford, 1987). A BES is an integrated internal representation of a particular kind of behavior episode experience or, more commonly, a set of similar behavior episode experiences (including episodes that have only been imagined or observed). Similarity is in the eye of the beholder, of course, but it is primarily a function of the degree to which different episodes involve the pursuit of similar goals in similar contexts. As with individual behavior episodes, goals and contexts are the anchors that organize a BES and give it coherence and meaning (D. Ford, 1987; M. Ford, 1992).

A BES represents the functioning of the whole person in context, not just some part of the behavior episode experiences from which they are derived. Thus although the BES concept is similar in many respects to those of motor (e.g., Schmidt, 1975), perceptual (e.g., Arbib, 1989), cognitive (e.g., Neisser, 1976), and self-schemata (e.g., Markus, Cross, & Wurf, 1990), it is broader in that it represents an integrated package of thoughts, feelings, perceptions, actions, biological processes, and relevant contexts. In other words, the BES concept is designed to provide scholars and practitioners with a clear and practical way to operationalize the principle of unitary functioning.

Functionally, a BES provides guidance about how to direct attention and effort in a specific behavior episode and how to think, feel, and act in those circumstances. The guidance provided, however, may vary tremendously in quality. A BES may be very specific and detailed or rather global and vague with respect to the information it conveys. Moreover, this information may or may not be accurate or appropriate for the situation at hand. Even if the activated BES is a good fit for the current episode, a great deal of attentional effort and conscious control may be needed to maintain effective functioning if the BES is not highly automatized (Sternberg, 1985a). The clarity, relevance, and organization of the BES guiding a behavior pattern are therefore primary factors in determining both the content and effectiveness of a person's activity.

For example, an experienced parent may be able to handle easily a wide array of child-rearing situations that would be very disorganizing to a new parent. Similarly, a career or substance abuse counselor with a rich and extensive repertoire of counseling schemata is likely to be able to proceed with great efficiency and confidence when a client presents a familiar profile or symptom pattern. Conversely, if the best available BES for a given situation is weak or disorganized, or a schema is activated that is a poor fit to a particular set of circumstances, the person's activity is likely to be erratic, tentative, self-defeating, or simply inappropriate. Such behavior patterns are typical of people who lack experience in dating or work episodes, who have an impoverished repertoire of relevant multicultural experiences, or who have a paranoid, arrogant, or highly egocentric view of their social surroundings.

Concepts and Propositions

The anchoring of a BES to particular goals and contexts greatly facilitates a person's capabilities for constructing effective guides to behavior, especially in familiar circumstances. This characteristic of BES organization, however, can also constrain the process of transferring a useful BES to new episodes. To overcome this limitation, humans have developed the capability for constructing cognitive representations of BES components and component relationships, typically called *concepts* (or constructs) and *propositions* (or rules, theories, or principles), respectively (D. Ford, 1987). Concepts and propositions are powerful tools in learning and communication because they are much less constrained by the goals, contexts, and activities embedded within the BES from which they were constructed. This "portability" allows them to be integrated into other schemata and combined with other concepts and propositions with relative ease, thus enabling learning and skill development to proceed much more efficiently and powerfully than would otherwise be the case. This capability also greatly facilitates the cultural transmission of knowledge and the development of cooperative relationships, because it is generally much easier to construct shared meanings from abstracted BES components (which tend to be relatively simple and general) than from whole BES units (which tend to be complex and closely tied to particular goals and contexts).

It is important to understand, though, that concepts and propositions by themselves lack meaningful content and personal significance precisely because they have been divorced from particular goals, contexts, and activities. It is only when concepts and propositions such as those communicated in a parental lecture, school lesson, or church doctrine are embedded back into a personalized BES that they become infused with personal meaning and utility. This is the missing link in much of education and socialization—information is taught in the form of abstract concepts and propositions to facilitate communication and generalization, but is too often left unconnected to the real-world contexts and purposes that make it evident why such information is important and useful. It is also a weak link in people's efforts to negotiate or interact effectively with individuals and groups from different cultural and socioeconomic backgrounds. Moreover, in an age when the amount and flow of information are expanding in dramatic fashion, there is increasing pressure to deal with this essential step in the learning and socialization process in a superficial way (i.e., so as to be inclusive and fully "cover" the information or social phenomena of interest). On a more encouraging note, one response to this pressure has been an increase in calls for authentic educational experiences—that is, experiences that engage students in observational and instrumental behavior episodes in which they apply concepts and propositions to significant problems in a personally meaningful context (e.g., Eisner, 1991).

Generative Flexibility and Scripts

Once a BES has been constructed from one or more behavior episode experiences, it can be elaborated, refined, or combined with other schemas and components. Over time, this can yield a very powerful BES encompassing a diverse repertoire of optional behavior patterns organized around a related set of goals and contexts. By combining a number of such schemata together, a qualitatively superior kind of expertise called *generative flexibility* can emerge (D. Ford, 1987). Generative flexibility represents a developed capability for creatively altering ongoing behavior patterns in response to varying circumstances. This ability to quickly and flexibly generate effective options for achieving a particular set of goals is characteristic of highly resourceful people (e.g., clever salespeople, master teachers, effective customer service personnel, and socially skilled young children; Shure & Spivack, 1980).

Schemata can also be elaborated and refined by linking them together in sequential fashion to produce a *script*. A script serves as a template for a stereotyped sequence of events (Abelson, 1981), as illustrated by the performance of a musician in an orchestra, a politician giving a speech, or a guest at a formal dinner party. Well-rehearsed scripts (also sometimes called habits) can greatly facilitate the execution of precise, efficient behavior patterns; however, they tend to be lacking in generative flexibility. Indeed, a primary benefit of "automatizing" certain kinds of BES into scripts or habits is to eliminate such variability! Scripts are therefore most useful in contexts that require close conformity to a set of rules or conventions (e.g., behaving properly in school or church), in emotionally challenging circumstances in which one can anticipate difficulty in maintaining organized functioning (e.g., a public performance), and in repetitive situations where efficiency is highly valued (e.g., classroom, office, and household routines).

Transfer of a BES to New Circumstances

Earlier the difficulty of transferring a BES to circumstances beyond those represented by the goals and contexts anchoring it was noted. When a BES is socially effective and desirable (e.g., is based on generosity or empathy), this lack of transfer can be a source of considerable frustration, as any parent can explain. Conversely, the tendency for a BES to be specific to goals and contexts can be a blessing when the episodes that produced it involve personally or socially damaging elements (e.g., inconsiderate or victimizing behavior). Understanding the processes that contribute to the isolation of a BES or its transfer to new circumstances is one of the keys to understanding the role of personality and intelligence in social behavior (Goldstein & Kanfer, 1979).

In humans, the content and effectiveness of social behavior patterns are largely a function of a person's history of observational and instrumental social learning experiences (Bandura, 1986). When behavior episode experiences with particular cognitive, emotional, behavioral, or interpersonal features begin to pile up over time, they are increasingly likely to become a pervasive part of an individual's BES repertoire. For example, when young women are continually bombarded by messages from the media, their peers, and perhaps even their parents regarding the importance of physical attractiveness in social and self-evaluations, it is easy for such messages to become embedded into a wide range of schemata. Similarly, individuals who observe and experience a large number and variety of violent or abusive episodes are likely to develop an extensive repertoire of schemata involving the use of aggression and/or strategies for coping with such behavior. The impact of such episodes can also be amplified through imagination and cognitive rumination (i.e., the repetition of thought episodes organized by the same goals and contexts).

Repetition, of course, is not the only factor contributing to the transferability of a BES to new circumstances. Informational and emotional salience are also key factors (M. Ford, 1992; Nisbett & Ross, 1980). Indeed, as many counselors and psychotherapists can attest, even one episode of sufficient personal meaning and emotional salience (e.g., being the victim of a crime or participating in a transformative religious experience) can have more impact on an individual's future functioning than hundreds of experiences of limited relevance (e.g., reading about crimes committed against others or hearing a weekly sermon). It follows, then, that the most powerful influences on social and personality development will be behavior episodes that (a) are anchored by "core" personal goals (Nichols, 1990, 1991); (b) generate high-amplitude emotions; and (c) are repeated in a diversity of contexts.

Personality Defined: One's Repertoire of Stable, Recurring Schemata

Personality theorists typically focus on the content and organization of enduring patterns of functioning, particularly those that transcend particular situations or component processes. Unfortunately, traditional means of representing such patterns (e.g., traits, dispositions, attitudes) have been of limited utility because they have failed to deal adequately with the goal and context specificity and functional variability characterizing most behavior patterns (Mischel, 1968). To address this problem, a number of contemporary theorists (e.g., Bandura, 1986; Carver & Scheier, 1981, 1982; Dweck & Leggett, 1988; Mischel, 1973) have focused on cognitive and social-cognitive processes that are variable in content but nevertheless may play a major role in organizing an individual's functioning (e.g., goal orientations, self-regulatory processes, coping strategies). This has been a useful and productive approach; however, because most such theories lack a broader conception of unitary functioning in which to anchor their major constructs, it has left many wondering what happened to the "person" in personality.

The LSF resolves this dilemma by defining personality as the person's repertoire of stable, recurring behavior episode schemata (M. Ford, 1992). Because goals and contexts are the organizing forces that define the meaning and significance of these schemata, the core of an individual's personality is understood to be the subset of stable, recurring schemata that are psychologically anchored by salient personal goals. In other words, if one can identify an individual's most important personal goals and the thoughts, feelings, actions, and contexts associated with the pursuit of those goals, that individual's personality will be clearly revealed.

Because a BES may be anchored to a very broad or very specific set of goals and contexts, this conceptualization of personality provides a way of resolving the long-standing debate between person-centered and situational determinants of behavior (i.e., both consistency and variability in functioning can be understood in BES terms). For example, people can be expected to manifest a high degree of temporal and situational consistency in their behavior patterns if their experiences tend to be organized around a narrow range of goal themes (or "current concerns") and they have well-developed habits for addressing those concerns. Conversely, individuals' behavior patterns may manifest a great deal of situational and temporal variability if they are involved in a diverse range of activities or social roles involving very different kinds of goals and contexts, or if they are unable to coordinate important subsets of their BES repertoire (as illustrated by identity crises, multiple personality disorders, etc.).

Because BES representations include all aspects of an individual's functioning, personality attributes or traits may be defined in terms of thought patterns (e.g., optimism, paranoia, or low self-esteem), emotional patterns (e.g., empathy, hostility, or depression), action patterns (e.g., shyness, aggression, or impulsiveness), or any other component process(es) that are particularly salient features of a stable, enduring set of schemata (e.g., a dysfunctional personality, Type A behavior pattern, or socially skilled individual). Because personal goals provide the psychological anchors for a BES, however, a particularly informative way to describe the central themes in a person's functioning (i.e., his or her personality) is through assessments that yield information about the most significant and meaningful goals in a person's life. Indeed, one of the most promising recent developments in the field of personality psychology is an emerging emphasis on goal content, goal hierarchies, and the use of goal assessments to represent the core features of personality (e.g., Cantor & Kihlstrom, 1987; Csikszentmihalyi, 1990; Emmons, 1986, 1989; M. Ford, 1992; M. Ford & Nichols, 1991; Lazarus, 1991; Markus & Nurius, 1986; Markus & Ruvolo, 1989; Nichols, 1991; Pervin, 1989; Winell, 1987).

LINKING CONCEPTIONS OF PERSONALITY AND INTELLIGENCE

The LSF focus on behavior episode schemata as the building blocks of personality leads very logically to an emphasis on *goal attainment* as the primary criterion for defining and assessing the effectiveness of human functioning (M. Ford, 1986, 1992). At the level of a particular behavior episode, this means successfully achieving the goal (or goals) of the episode within the circumstances and criteria defined by the context anchoring the episode. Thus *achievement* is the concept used to describe effective functioning at the behavior episode level of analysis. Achievement is defined as the attainment of a personally or socially valued goal in a particular context (M. Ford, 1992).

At the BES (i.e., personality) level of analysis, *competence* is the concept used in the LSF to describe effective functioning. Because evaluations of effectiveness at this level of analysis must consider possible consequences for a diversity of behavior episodes beyond the immediate episode, competence is defined by adding ethical and developmental boundary conditions to the anchoring criteria of goals and contexts. Specifically, competence is defined as the attainment of relevant goals in specified environments, using appropriate means and resulting in positive developmental outcomes (M. Ford, 1992).

Like competence, *intelligence* represents a pattern of effective functioning (or the potential for effective functioning) across a variety of behavior episodes. Indeed, intelligence is sometimes defined in essentially the same manner as competence—that is, in terms of criteria representing the attainment of relevant goals in specified environments (as in definitions emphasizing performance accomplishments or adaptation to the values and demands of a particular social-cultural context; e.g., M. Ford, 1986; M. Ford & Tisak, 1983; Kornhaber, Krechevsky, & Gardner, 1990; Sternberg & Wagner, 1986). Intelligence is also commonly used, however, to refer to organized sets of component processes (e.g., information-processing capabilities, reasoning and problem-solving skills, neural processes) that contribute to effective functioning in diverse contexts but do not actually represent such functioning (e.g., Eysenck, 1987; Sternberg, 1985a). Virtually all conceptions of intelligence pertain, at least indirectly, to the bottom-line issue of functioning effectively with respect to a broad range of goals and contexts. Thus intelligence can be defined, at least in very general terms, as a characteristic of a person's functioning associated with the attainment of relevant goals within some specified set of contexts and evaluative boundary conditions.

Intelligence Defined: Seven Variations on the Theme of an Effective BES Repertoire

By specifying more precisely the different characteristics of a BES repertoire that may be associated with effective functioning across a broad range of behavior episodes, it is possible to develop a taxonomy of the different prototypical meanings associated with the concept of intelligence. This taxonomy is presented in Table 1. Seven different qualities associated with broad patterns of effective functioning are described in this table, along with the prototypical conceptions of intelligence that correspond with each of these qualities. Consistent with the LSF principle of unitary functioning, each of the seven qualities refers not to specific component processes but to *patterns* of effective functioning at the level of the whole person in context.

The conceptions of intelligence outlined in Table 1 are applicable to virtually any content domain. The content that is appropriate for any particular assessment of intelligence may vary rather dramatically across groups and individuals, however, depending on the extent to which shared goals, contexts, and values (i.e., conceptions of ethical and developmental appropriateness) are involved. Thus the LSF weds a nomothetic understanding of intelligence with an idiographic conceptualization of personality.

Integrating Conceptions of Personality and Intelligence

It should now be clear that from the perspective of the LSF, the key to integrating the fields of personality and intelligence is linking evaluations of effectiveness to the content judged to be relevant for a particular individual or group of individuals. In other words, definitions and measures of intelligence must be anchored to content that is meaningful for a particular individual or group of individuals given their developmental history, cultural background, social and occupational roles, and personal circumstances—in short, their personality. This implies that intelligence tests should be regarded as evolving tools that should be changed whenever there is a significant change in the content that is regarded as appropriate or meaningful for some assessment purpose.

In some cases, content definitions may be broadly applicable to very large groups of people. This possibility is particularly well illustrated by assessments of infant intelligence (which focus largely on markers associated with biological maturation) and by the general dimensions identified in studies of experts' and laypersons' conceptions of intelligence and competence (e.g., verbal ability, practical problem-solving competence, prosocial behavior; M. Ford & Miura, 1983; Sternberg, 1985b; Sternberg, Conway, Ketron, & Bernstein, 1981). Nevertheless, to be maximally useful and informative, assessments of intelligence and personality must be tied together at the level of either the individual person or a relatively homogeneous group of people. This is an increasingly important principle to consider as the range of goals and

Table 1. A Living Systems Framework Conceptualization of the Variety of Meanings Associated with the Concept of Intelligence

Qualities associated with an effective BES repertoire	Prototypical meanings of intelligence
1. Quantity of accurate, useful information represented in the BES (and associated concepts and propositions) relevant to some general set of contexts (i.e., in some domain of human functioning)	Breadth of knowledge in a general domain of expertise
2. Quantity of accurate, useful information represented in the BES (and associated concepts and propositions) relevant to a relatively circumscribed set of contexts	Depth of knowledge in an area of specialization
3. Degree to which BES enactments (i.e., actual performances) meet objective standards representing mastery, excellence, or high levels of achievement	Performance accomplishments in a general domain or area of specialization
4. Degree to which BES enactments meet subjective criteria representing smooth, polished functioning (e.g., effortlessness, grace, elegance, etc.)	Automaticity or ease of functioning in a general domain or area of specialization
5. Probability of successfully enacting relevant BES under highly evaluative, arousing, difficult, or distracting conditions	Skilled performance under highly challenging conditions
6. Degree to which relevant BES are rich and varied with regard to potential combinations of optional components	"Generative flexibility"—ability to alter behavior patterns in response to varying circumstances
7. Degree to which existing BES can be incrementally improved in rapid fashion, or readily replaced in favor of more adaptive patterns	Speed of learning and behavior change

contexts in which targeted individuals can invest themselves becomes more variable and complex (e.g., as a result of increased capabilities for self-direction, increased opportunities for autonomous decision making, or increased variability produced by social-economic-political circumstances).

DOMAINS OF SOCIAL BEHAVIOR

To apply the LSF conceptualization of personality and intelligence to content involving social behavior, it is useful to have some way of categorizing the vast array of social episodes that might provide the basis for a meaningful assessment of social intelligence. The most common ways to do this are to focus either on different kinds of social *action patterns* (e.g., aggressive behavior, attachment behavior, prosocial behavior) or on the different kinds of *contexts* represented in patterns of social life (e.g., family contexts, school or work settings, dating situations). Another alternative, suggested by the LSF, is to focus on the different kinds of *social goals* represented in recurring social interactions and relationships.

Based on relevant theory, research, and clinical evidence, M. Ford and Nichols (1987, 1991) have constructed a comprehensive "taxonomy of human goals" that provides a useful starting point for classifying qualitatively distinct kinds of social behavior patterns. This 24-category taxonomy, which is described in Table 2, includes 10 goals that are particularly relevant to stable, recurring patterns of social behavior. These latter goals are italicized in Table 2.

Each of the 24 goals in the taxonomy is defined by a primary label and several additional words and phrases that help explicate the intended meaning of the label. At the highest level of abstraction, the taxonomy is divided into two types of goals based on where their desired consequences reside: within individuals, or in the relationship between people and their environments. These two categories are, by definition, exhaustive of all possible goals representing some outcome of person-in-context functioning.

There are three different kinds of within-person consequences that a person might desire: affective, cognitive, and "subjective organization" goals. Affective goals represent different kinds of feelings or emotions that a person might want to experience or avoid. Cognitive goals refer to different kinds of mental representations that people may want to construct or maintain. Subjective organization goals represent special or unusual states that people may seek to experience or avoid that involve a combination of different kinds of thoughts and feelings.

There are two broad categories of desired person–environment consequences in the taxonomy: social relationship goals and task goals. Within the former category, four goals represent the desire to maintain or promote the self (self-assertive goals), and four represent the desire to maintain or promote the well-being of other people or of social groups to which one belongs (integrative goals). Task goals represent desired relationships between the individual and various objects in the environment (including people when they are being conceived of in relatively impersonal terms).

Social behavior may function as a means of attaining goals representing any of the categories in the taxonomy, even those that are not intrinsically social. For example, one might develop a relationship with someone in order to get money (material gain), sex (arousal or bodily sensations), valued information (exploration or understanding), or simply to feel good about oneself (positive self-evaluations). Social behavior may also be designed to accomplish multiple social and/or nonsocial goals simultaneously. Nevertheless, the goals of greatest relevance to social behavior episodes and behavior episode schemata are the four self-assertive social relationship goals, the four integrative social relationship goals, and the task goals of management and safety.

Social Relationship Goals

In social relationships people try to accomplish (often simultaneously) two fundamental kinds of goals: maintenance or promotion of the self, and maintenance or promotion of other people or the social groups of which one is a part. These are manifestations of what Koestler (1967, 1978) calls the *self-assertive* and *integrative* tendencies of hierarchically organized living systems.

The eight goals listed in the taxonomy under the categories of self-assertion and integration are matched sets defined by four issues of critical importance to the functioning of living systems. Specifically, individuality and belongingness goals represent concerns about one's identity as an individual in social settings; self-determination and social responsibility goals focus on the issue of behavioral control; superiority and equity goals center on the issue of social comparison; and resource acquisition and resource provision goals deal with social exchange processes.

Table 2. The Ford and Nichols Taxonomy of Human Goals

	Desired within-person consequences
Affective Goals	
Arousal	Experiencing excitement or heightened arousal; avoiding boredom or stressful inactivity
Tranquility	Feeling relaxed and at ease; avoiding stressful overarousal
Happiness	Experiencing feelings of joy, satisfaction, or well being; avoiding feelings of emotional distress or dissatisfaction
Bodily sensations	Experiencing pleasure associated with physical sensations, physical movement, or bodily contact; avoiding unpleasant or uncomfortable bodily sensations
Physical well-being	Feeling strong, healthy, or physically robust; avoiding feelings of weakness or fatigue
Cognitive goals	
Exploration	Satisfying one's curiosity about personally meaningful events; avoiding a sense of being uninformed or not knowing what's going on
Understanding	Gaining knowledge or making sense out of something; avoiding misconceptions, erroneous beliefs, or feelings of confusion
Intellectual creativity	Engaging in activities involving original thinking or novel or interesting ideas; avoiding mindless or familiar ways of thinking
Positive self-evaluations	Maintaining a sense of self-confidence, pride, or self-worth; avoiding feelings of failure, guilt, or incompetence
Subjective organization goals	
Unity	Experiencing a profound or spiritual sense of connectedness, harmony, or oneness with people, nature, or a greater power; avoiding feelings of psychological disunity or disorganization
Transcendence	Experiencing optimal or extraordinary states of functioning; avoiding feeling trapped within the boundaries of ordinary experience
	Desired person–environment consequences
Self-assertive social relationship goals	
Individuality	Feeling unique, special, or different; avoiding similarity or conformity with others
Self-determination	Experiencing a sense of freedom from unwanted social obligations and commitments; avoiding feeling constrained or manipulated by others
Superiority	Comparing favorably to others in terms of winning, status, or success; avoiding losing or unfavorable comparisons with others
Resource acquisition	Obtaining approval, support, assistance, advice, or validation from others; avoiding social disapproval or rejection
Integrative social relationship goals	
Belongingness	Building or maintaining attachments, friendships, intimacy, or a sense of community; avoiding feelings of social isolation or separateness
Social responsibility	Keeping interpersonal commitments, meeting social role obligations, and conforming to social and moral rules; avoiding social transgressions and unethical or illegal conduct
Equity	Promoting fairness, justice, reciprocity, or equality; avoiding unfair or unjust actions
Resource provision	Giving approval, support, assistance, advice, or validation to others; avoiding selfish or uncaring behavior
Task goals	
Mastery	Meeting a standard of achievement, improving one's performance; avoiding incompetence, mediocrity, or decrements in performance
Task creativity	Engaging in activities involving artistic expression or creativity; avoiding tasks that do not provide ample opportunities for creative activity
Management	Maintaining order, organization, or productivity in daily life tasks; avoiding sloppiness, inefficiency, or disorganization
Material gain	Increasing the amount of money or tangible goods one has; avoiding the loss of money or material possessions
Safety	Being unharmed, physically secure, and free from risk; avoiding threatening, depriving, or harmful circumstances

Individuality goals represent a desire to maintain or enhance one's identity as a separate person by developing or expressing beliefs, values, self-concepts, behavior patterns, or stylistic characteristics that are uniquely personal or different from those of other relevant people. Nonconformists, adolescents, and people with very strong and definite values or belief systems are especially likely to be concerned with individuality goals.

Belongingness goals, in contrast, reflect a desire to create, maintain, or enhance the integrity of the social units of which one is a part. A person can experience a sense of belonging with any number of social groups, including families, friendships, clubs, communities, ethnic groups, political parties, and athletic teams. Because these groups provide a context for social exchange processes (i.e., resource provision and resource acquisition), belongingness goals are often associated with not only an altruistic desire to help and support significant others but also a self-enhancing desire to obtain social validation and approval. Nevertheless, belongingness goals per se are integrative concerns focused on the preservation or promotion of a group's existence or functioning. Such concerns are a central part of most people's goal hierarchies.

Self-determination goals reflect the human desire for freedom, independence, and choice in contexts that threaten to restrict or undermine these conditions. Because motivational patterns tend to be more robust and enduring when people believe they have the power to choose among options, this goal is at the core of several prominent motivation theories (e.g., Brehm & Brehm, 1981; deCharms, 1968; Deci & Ryan, 1985). It is clear, however, that the strength of this goal varies across people and contexts (Burger, 1989). For example, two-year olds, teenagers, and Type A individuals are notorious for their unusually strong self-determination goals.

Social responsibility goals represent a desire to avoid social and ethical transgressions and to facilitate smooth public functioning by behaving in accordance with rules, expectations, and obligations. Wanting to be socially responsible implies that some form of social control has been accepted as legitimate and necessary. Such acceptance is generally more likely to occur, however, in the context of self-determination. In other words, people are more likely to act in a socially responsible manner when social constraints are seen as personally chosen or collaboratively defined rather than externally imposed (Deci & Ryan, 1985). People who take rules and commitments seriously and who value such qualities as reliability, trustworthiness, and integrity are especially likely to give social responsibility goals high priority.

Superiority goals represent a desire to be better or higher than other people on some personally relevant dimension (e.g., academic or occupational achievement, income or material possessions, territorial coverage, athletic performance, popularity, beauty, moral virtue). Because people who are dissimilar in their developmental status, life circumstances, or social roles are unlikely to provide a meaningful basis for comparison, superiority goals are primarily relevant to relationships with peers (siblings, neighbors, classmates, athletic opponents, job-market competitors, etc.). Highly competitive individuals and those who view social relationships in terms of conquests and victories are among those who find superiority goals particularly attractive.

Equity goals also focus on social comparison concerns, but in this case the desired consequence is similarity among people on some relevant dimension. Like superiority, equity is a particularly salient issue in relationships with peers. It is also an important concern, however, of parents, employers, elected officials, and others in positions of authority who must be attentive to group members' demands for fair and unbiased treatment (Adams, 1965). Equity goals are prominent among people who are bothered by social injustice, unequal resource distribution, and the victimization of helpless or disadvantaged individuals.

Resource acquisition goals represent a desire to obtain valued emotional, informational, or material resources (from parents, friends, teachers, counselors, clergy, government agencies, etc.). Resource provision goals, conversely, reflect a desire to enhance other people's welfare by offering them resources (e.g., advice, instruction, emotional support, cognitive validation, task assistance, material aid). Resource acquisition and provision concerns are usually embedded in either social relationships involving reciprocal social exchange processes (e.g., friendship or spousal relationships) or asymmetrical social roles in which one person is responsible for providing resources to another (e.g., parent-child or teacher-student relationships). These goals are sometimes pursued, however, in situations that involve neither belongingness nor social responsibility goals. This is particularly likely for people who tend to be emotionally needy or insecure (with regard to resource acquisition goals) and for people who tend to be unusually caring and altruistic (with regard to resource provision goals).

Social Task Goals

Management goals represent a desire to maintain organization, efficiency, or productivity with respect to the relatively mundane tasks of everyday living. In social contexts, this typically involves organizing or influencing people to maintain or promote smooth social functioning and/or the attainment of particular task goals. People who value efficiency, order, neatness, and punctuality and dislike deviations from desired, expected, or planned outcomes (e.g., homemakers, event planners, office managers) are particularly likely to give management goals high priority.

Safety goals reflect a desire to protect oneself from physical harm or to avoid circumstances that may be risky or damaging to one's health. Social episodes directed by safety goals include those in which people must remain vigilant to the negative consequences of sexual activity, alcohol and drug abuse, and other forms of risky activity. Although safety goals are a prominent part of most people's goal hierarchies, they are especially salient concerns for cautious people and people who take a pragmatic approach to hazards and dangers.

PROCESSES CONTRIBUTING TO EFFECTIVE SOCIAL BEHAVIOR

There are four major prerequisites for effective functioning in any given behavior episode (M. Ford, 1992):

1. The person must have the motivation needed to initiate and maintain activity until the goal directing the episode is attained (this category includes the component processes of personal goals, emotional arousal patterns, and personal agency beliefs).
2. The person must have the skill needed to construct and execute a pattern of activity that will produce the desired consequence (this category includes transactional processes, information-processing and memory functions, attention and consciousness arousal processes, activity arousal processes, and control and performance evaluation cognitions).
3. The person's biological structure and functioning must be able to support the operation of the motivation and skill components.
4. The person must have the cooperation of a responsive environment that will facilitate, or at least not excessively impede, progress toward the goal.

In other words, effective functioning requires a motivated, skillful person whose biological and behavioral capabilities support relevant interactions with an environment that has the informational and material properties and resources needed to facilitate (or at least permit) goal attainment. If any of these components is missing or inadequate, achievements will be limited, and competence development will be thwarted (M. Ford, 1992).

In extreme cases of socially ineffective functioning (e.g., schizophrenic individuals, mass murderers, people with multiple personality disorders), it is commonplace to find gross biological and/or environmental deficiencies (e.g., neurological damage, abusive or neglectful parenting) in the individual's developmental history, with these deficiencies having a pervasive impact on his or her social behavior episodes and subsequent personality development (D. Ford & Lerner, 1992). The psychological impact of these deficiencies is typically manifested in the form of major skill deficits and/or pervasive motivational problems.

In cases where there are no major biological or environmental factors constraining an individual's behavior and development, the variability in personality development with respect to socially intelligent functioning is attributable primarily to motivational and skill-related factors within the person (which may be influenced both by biology and experience) operating in conjunction with stable features of his or her interpersonal and sociocultural environment. Research investigating the precise nature of these psychological and contextual processes, although sparse and inconclusive, has identified several processes that appear to be most closely linked to the development of effective social behavior patterns. These processes are briefly described next.

Motivational Processes associated with Social Intelligence

Goal Importance

Although the links between social goals and intelligent behavior are complex (M. Ford, 1986), it appears that one prerequisite for effective social functioning is interest in or concern about the attainment of such goals as social responsibility, resource provision, and safety (e.g., M. Ford, 1987; M. Ford, Chase, Love, Pollina, & Ito, 1994; Wentzel, 1991). This is presumably because prioritized goals direct attention and effort and activate thoughts, feelings, and actions that facilitate the attainment of these goals (Locke, Shaw, Saari, & Latham, 1981). Simply put, people are most likely to be socially intelligent in domains in which they invest their time, energy, and personal identity (Maehr, 1984; Maehr & Braskamp, 1986). Of course, trying hard is no guarantee of success with respect to a particular social goal. Nevertheless, effective social behavior is clearly much more likely under these circumstances than in cases where there is little intrinsic interest or concern.

Personal Agency Beliefs

Social motivation depends on more than simply having one's social priorities in order. People must also have a firm belief, or at least some hope, that they can attain their goals. Such beliefs are of two types: *capability beliefs*, which represent expectancies about whether one has the personal capabilities needed for effective action, and *context beliefs*, which represent expectancies about whether the environment will be responsive to one's goal attainment efforts (M. Ford, 1992). Of course, personal agency beliefs are no substitute for actual skills and a truly responsive environment. Nevertheless, people often fail to capitalize on their skills and opportunities because they underestimate what they can accomplish.

People who feel confident that good things will happen in their social interactions and relationships are much more likely to make the most of their existing capabilities and to maintain motivation in the face of obstacles to goal attainment (i.e., when new behavior patterns must be developed). Consequently, capability and context beliefs play a crucial role in social and personality development (Bandura, 1986; Deci & Ryan, 1985; M. Ford & Thompson, 1985; Seligman, 1971, 1991). They also play an important role in the development of social goals by suggesting what kinds of accomplishments one is most likely to be able to attain; people tend to invest themselves in domains in which they expect to succeed, and they avoid domains in which they expect to fail (Deci & Ryan, 1985; M. Ford, 1992).

Emotional Responsiveness

Emotions evolved to help people function effectively in circumstances requiring immediate or vigorous action in the context of a concrete problem or opportunity: for example, removal of an obstacle to goal attainment, investment in a rewarding relationship (or disengagement from an unproductive relationship), or inhibition of a socially damaging action (D. Ford, 1987). The tendency for people to respond emotionally to actual or anticipated social successes and failures appears to be an important factor in energizing efforts to be socially intelligent. For instance, people who are inclined to feel empathic concern when they encounter distress in others, guilt when they commit hurtful actions, and pride when they behave responsibly are much more likely to accomplish integrative goals than are those who do not experience such emotions (e.g., M. Ford et al., 1994; M. Ford, Wentzel, Wood, Stevens, & Siesfeld, 1989; Hoffman, 1982). Similarly, people who tend to experience strong feelings of satisfaction and pride when they successfully assert their individuality, self-determination, or superiority are likely to be particularly effective in attaining self-assertive goals (M. Ford et al., 1989).

Powerful goals often lead to strong emotions (Frijda, 1988). That is because the more one cares about achieving a goal, the more likely one is to activate emotions designed to facilitate achievement of that goal. Thus, to a large extent, emotional responsiveness is a reflection of goal importance. Nevertheless, emotions play a separate, crucial role in social motivation by helping to keep social interests and concerns from being forgotten or put aside. Indeed, unlike cognitive motivational processes (i.e., goals and personal agency beliefs), emotions cannot be kept out of consciousness once they are activated (M. Ford, 1992). In other words, the unique role of emotions is to press for action until some progress is made toward goal attainment (or some other goal takes precedence), thereby facilitating the development of an effective BES.

Skill-Related Processes associated with Social Intelligence

Behavioral Repertoire

As the entries in Table 1 clearly imply, a well-learned repertoire of social behavior patterns is an essential component of socially intelligent functioning (e.g., Goldstein, Sprafkin, Gershaw, & Klein, 1980). When such behavior patterns afford a high degree of automaticity, they allow one to behave with efficiency and ease in complex social situations (Sternberg, 1985a). This kind of expertise, however, does not come easily; it requires a serious investment of motivational resources and sufficient experience to enable one to develop stable, reliable behavior patterns. Consistent with the LSF emphasis on the interplay among observational, symbolic, and instrumental episodes, the social skills training literature suggests that the most effective way to develop a productive behavioral repertoire is to begin by observing and talking with experienced others, then follow that learning process with direct, guided practice in relevant contexts (Goldstein & Kanfer, 1979; Goldstein et al., 1980). Of particular interest is the fact that such procedures often place as much emphasis on removing motivational obstacles to social participation as they do on behavioral learning and practice.

Social Encoding Capabilities

Because there is a high degree of repetition and redundancy in most aspects of social life, social intelligence generally does not require a high degree of social perceptiveness or insight (M. Ford, 1986; Sternberg & Smith, 1985). There is a tendency, however, for people to develop habits of selective attention and encoding as a result of their personal goals and social experiences. For example, Dodge (1986) has demonstrated that highly aggressive children—who often use aggressive behavior very deliberately to accomplish self-assertive and social management goals—are more likely than their less aggressive peers to believe that others are acting in a hostile way toward them, as well as to miss relevant social cues to the contrary. Similarly, many ineffective parents selectively ignore evidence that their children may have committed certain kinds of social transgressions.

This is not to say that selective encoding of social information is intrinsically problematic. Attending to social cues that are particularly relevant to one's personal goals is natural and sensible, and in some cases a confirmatory bias may facilitate the maintenance of positive personal agency beliefs. Nevertheless, it seems clear that when selective biases become too discrepant with social reality, one's social interactions and social relationships are likely to suffer.

Social Planning and Problem-Solving Capabilities

In social situations characterized by a high degree of novelty or unpredictability, one must be able to create flexible plans of action that go beyond previously learned behavior patterns. Consequently, social-cognitive skills such as means-ends thinking (constructing step-by-step solutions to interpersonal problems) and consequential thinking (anticipating the consequences of one's actions) are among the best predictors of effective social behavior (M. Ford, 1982; Spivack, Platt, & Shure, 1976; Sternberg, 1985a). Such skills facilitate the development of generative flexibility, thereby increasing the probability that one will be able to adapt to new social situations and handle difficult interpersonal challenges quickly and effectively.

Contextual Processes associated with Social Intelligence

Congruence with Personal Goals

The social environments in which an individual functions must be congruent with his or her agenda of personal goals if those contexts are to facilitate the development of effective social behavior patterns. This means that social contexts must not block the attainment of personally valued outcomes (Maehr & Braskamp, 1986). It also implies, however, that these contexts must not overly control the defined menu of possible goals. Motivation is usually diminished when people experience a lack of ownership or personal commitment to the goals they are pursuing, or when they feel that they have no choice about what goals to pursue or how to pursue them (Deci & Ryan, 1985). Contexts may also be viewed as unresponsive if they are overly demanding, that is, if the agenda of "goal requirements" defined by the context is regarded as unreasonable in terms of time, effort, difficulty, or obstacles to goal attainment.

Congruence with Personal Capabilities

Social environments must also be congruent with an individual's biological, transactional, and cognitive capabilities if they are to facilitate the development of socially effective behavior patterns. For example, many social learning opportunities may be lost or truncated in social contexts that are crowded, noisy, or physically unsafe. Social environments may also be unresponsive in the sense that they fail to provide information about goals, standards, rules, procedures, or contingencies in a clear, consistent, or meaningful way. This kind of unresponsiveness is characteristic of many ineffective parents, teachers, administrators, and managers.

Material and Informational Resources

To facilitate effective functioning, social contexts must have the material and informational resources needed to facilitate goal attainment. For example, in order to function in an independent and socially responsible manner, people must have access to needed equipment, transportation, and supplies. Desired goods and services must also be available and affordable. In addition, people must be able to obtain sound guidance when they are unable to continue making progress toward their goals on their own. This latter kind of resource is particularly crucial to social and personality development. It is simply not realistic to expect people to be able to develop an effective repertoire of social behavioral schemata in environments that are developmentally impoverished in terms of informational resources such as those provided by effective parents, teachers, coaches, mentors, and so forth.

Positive Emotional Climate

An individual's social contexts must provide an emotional climate that supports social participation and learning if those contexts are to facilitate effective functioning. Concepts such as warmth, social support, and trust focus on this facet of environmental responsiveness. These variables have been linked with enhanced motivation, learning, and performance in a diversity of contexts, including home, school, work, and clinical settings (e.g., Baumrind, 1978; Bergin, 1987; Brophy, 1987; Cohen & Wills, 1985; Erickson, 1963; Zand, 1972). Conversely, contexts that fail to generate interest, commitment, or affection among participants are likely to contribute little to the development of socially intelligent functioning.

GENDER DIFFERENCES IN SOCIAL INTELLIGENCE AND PERSONALITY DEVELOPMENT

The topic of gender differences in social behavior presents one of the most mystifying dilemmas faced by psychologists. On the one hand, scholarly research on this topic suggests that with the apparent exception of males' greater propensity to commit physically aggressive and violent acts, there are few clear-cut areas of gender-differentiated social behavior at the personality level of analysis (e.g., Maccoby & Jacklin, 1974). On the other hand, as magazine writers and comedians are fond of illustrating, most people seem to believe that there are large and very obvious gender differences in a wide range of social behavior patterns. Is this discrepancy a tribute to researchers who refuse to accept blindly the validity of informal observations? Or have investigators in this area failed to appreciate the magnitude of real gender differences in everyday social behavior as a result of narrow conceptual, methodological, or perhaps even political aspects of their work?

From the perspective of the Living Systems Framework and Motivational Systems Theory, the most compelling explanation for this discrepancy is straightforward and substantive: the lack of emphasis in the research literature on social goals and their dramatic impact on personality development. In other words, one need not dismiss either the validity of everyday impressions or that of existing research, little of which can be explained away by serious methodological flaws or skewed political motives. Rather, the personality literature's preoccupation with gender differences in underlying skills, abilities, and traitlike personality characteristics, coupled with an apparent lack of appreciation for the organizing role of goals and contexts in personality development, has led to the discrepancy between research findings and everyday impressions. Whereas skill-related gender differences seem to be more the exception than the rule (and almost always of modest magnitude), motivational differences appear to provide a mechanism by which rather dramatic gender differences in social behavior patterns can emerge, at least in some sociocultural contexts (i.e., those that are organized along gender-differentiated lines). If accurate, this hypothesis would also help account for the considerable variation across cultures in the kind and degree of gender differences in social behavior patterns.

Consistent with this hypothesis, there is little evidence to suggest that males and females differ in consistent or meaningful ways with respect to the basic skills required for effective social behavior (e.g., social problem-solving skills, social reasoning skills, communication skills; M. Ford, 1986; Maccoby & Jacklin, 1974; Spivack, Platt & Shure, 1976). There appear to be substantial gender differences, however, in the importance of different kinds of social goals and in the motivational processes linked to these goals (i.e., personal agency beliefs and emotional responsiveness; M. Ford et al., 1992; M. Ford & Nichols, 1991; M. Ford et al., 1989). These differences manifest themselves, sometimes in dramatic fashion, with respect to both the processes involved in personality development and the outcomes associated with social intelligence. Such differences are possible even in the absence of significant skill differences because of the pervasive impact that goals have in organizing all aspects of human functioning—what people attend to, what they try to do, what they believe they can accomplish, the kinds of experiences they wish to repeat, the kinds of stimuli that arouse strong emotions, the time and effort devoted to personally relevant social episodes, and so forth. As Csikszentmihalyi (1990) explains, "More than anything else, the self represents the hierarchy of goals that we have built up, bit by bit, over the years" (p. 34).

How Small Differences Can Become Large Differences in Personality Development and Social Intelligence

A basic premise of most systems theories (including the LSF and MST) is that, through deviation-amplifying feedback and feedforward processes, small initial variations in system functioning can sometimes yield large differences in developmental outcomes over time (D. Ford, 1987; D. Ford & Lerner, 1992). In humans, such deviation-amplifying processes are typically most closely associated with the organizing influence of goals and contexts.

With respect to social goals, in many cultures there are strong, pervasive, and highly repetitive socialization influences that lead males and females to value and prioritize social goals in increasingly different ways. Whether there are intrinsic, traitlike properties (e.g., temperamental qualities) differentially influencing this developmental process in boys and girls is open to debate. It is clearly not necessary, however, for such properties to exist to produce gender differences in social behavior patterns given the behavior episode-based nature of personality development. All that is required is a set of early experiences that, on average, tend to produce at least some consistent differences in the kinds of social goals that are compelling and meaningful to boys and girls. Once such differences have emerged, the self-directing properties of human functioning will tend to amplify and elaborate these differences (assuming that the context continues to support such elaborations) as people selectively invest themselves in social domains of greatest interest and concern. As a result, certain kinds of behavior episodes will begin to pile up; prioritized social goals will become increasingly elaborated; the thoughts, feelings, and actions associated with these goals will become increasingly prominent aspects of an individual's personality; and before long the social BES repertoires of males and females may become as distinctive as two different Scrabble boards that started with the same set of words and letters (D. Ford, 1987).

Gender Differences in Social Goal Importance

Although there is currently very little empirical evidence directly focused on the topic of gender differences in social goal importance, M. Ford and Nichols (1991) have collected data from several different samples using their Assessment of Personal Goals (M. Ford & Nichols, 1995), a paper-and-pencil, behavior episode–based measure of the strength of the 24 goal categories represented in the taxonomy in Table 2. Although their results are constrained to the American context, Ford and Nichols found consistent, statistically significant differences in seven of the ten goals of greatest relevance to socially intelligent functioning. Indeed, most of the reliable gender differences were in socially relevant domains, with only three of the remaining goal categories yielding significant results across samples (positive self-evaluations, physical well-being, and happiness, with females scoring higher in all three of these categories).

Males had consistently higher goal importance scores than their female counterparts in only one category: superiority. Some men, but very few women, were attracted to this kind of self-assertive achievement. Males were also somewhat more likely to endorse self-determination goals, but this result was not consistent across samples. Females, in contrast, had substantially higher goal importance scores in six categories: one self-assertive goal (resource acquisition); three of the four integrative goals (belongingness, social responsibility, and resource provision), and both social task goals (safety and management). The only two social goal categories yielding no evidence of gender differences were individuality and equity.

The obvious implication of these results is that females are more likely than are males to invest themselves broadly and intensely in a diversity of social episodes, especially those associated with integrative concerns and safety and management goals. Such investments presumably result in more elaborated schemata in these domains, as reflected in a variety of component processes: increased selective attention to and mental preoccupation with interpersonal relationships and their consequences (with corresponding communicative and behavioral strategies for dealing with these anticipated consequences); enhanced attentional and emotional responsiveness to social problems and concerns; a more highly automatized repertoire of social behavior patterns; and a richer repertoire of social concepts and propositions. These are the kinds of qualities that are highlighted in everyday impressions and conversations concerning gender differences in social behavior.

On the positive side, men as a group are more likely to be seen as having a relatively straightforward, uncomplicated orientation to social life. Conversely, they are also more likely to be regarded as socially insensitive or incompetent, except when it comes to asserting their superiority or control. Women, in contrast, are more likely to be seen as having the expertise and concern about others needed to function effectively in challenging social situations. Many men, however, have trouble understanding why women care so much about so many different aspects and details of social life. Thus the question of which gender has the advantage with respect to social intelligence depends—just as in personality development—on the particular kinds of goals and accomplishments one values.

REFERENCES

Abelson, R. P. (1981). Psychological status of the script concept. *American Psychologist, 36*, 715–727.

Adams, J. S. (1965). Inequity in social exchange. In L. Berkowitz (Ed.), *Advances in experimental social psychology* (Vol. 2, pp. 267–300). New York: Academic Press.

Arbib, M. A. (1989). *The metaphorical brain: Vol. 2. Neural networks and beyond.* New York: Wiley.

Bandura, A. (1986). *Social foundations of thought and action: A social cognitive theory.* Englewood Cliffs, NJ: Prentice-Hall.

Baumrind, D. (1978). Parental disciplinary patterns and social competence in children. *Youth and Society, 9*, 239–276.

Bergin, C. A. C. (1987). Prosocial development in toddlers: The patterning of mother-infant interactions. In M. E. Ford & D. H. Ford (Eds.), *Humans as self-constructing living systems: Putting the framework to work* (pp. 121–143). Hillsdale, NJ: Erlbaum.

Bevan, W. (1991). Contemporary psychology: A tour inside the onion. *American Psychologist, 46*, 475–483.

Brehm, S., & Brehm, J. W. (1981). *Psychological reactance: A theory of freedom and control.* New York: Academic Press.

Brophy, J. (1987). Socializing students' motivation to learn. In M. L. Maehr & D. A. Kleiber (Eds.), *Advances in motivation and achievement: Vol. 5. Enhancing motivation* (pp. 181–210). Greenwich, CT: JAI.

Burger, J. M. (1989). Negative reactions to increases in perceived personal control. *Journal of Personality and Social Psychology, 56*, 246–256.

Cantor, N., & Kihlstrom, J. F. (1987). *Personality and social intelligence.* Englewood Cliffs, NJ: Prentice-Hall.

Carver, C. S., & Scheier, M. F. (1981). *Attention and self-regulation: A control-theory approach to human behavior.* New York: Springer-Verlag.

Carver, C. S., & Scheier, M. F. (1982). Control theory: A useful conceptual framework for personality-social, clinical, and health psychology. *Psychological Bulletin, 92*, 111–135.

Cohen, S., & Wills, T. A. (1985). Stress, social support, and the buffering hypothesis. *Psychological Bulletin, 98*, 310–357.

Covey, S. R. (1990). *The seven habits of highly effective people.* New York: Simon & Schuster.

Csikszentmihalyi, M. (1990). *Flow: The psychology of optimal experience.* New York: Harper & Row.

deCharms, R. (1968). *Personal causation.* New York: Academic Press.

Deci, E. L., & Ryan, R. M. (1985). *Intrinsic motivation and self-determination in human behavior.* New York: Plenum.

Dodge, K. A. (1986). A social information processing model of social competence in children. In M. Perlmutter (Ed.), *Minnesota Symposium in Child Psychology* (pp. 77–125). Hillsdale, NJ: Erlbaum.

Dweck, C. S., & Leggett, E. L. (1988). A social-cognitive approach to motivation and personality. *Psychological Review, 95*, 256–273.

Eisner, E. W. (1991). *The enlightened eye: Qualitative inquiry and the enhancement of educational practice.* New York: Macmillan.

Elliott, E. S., & Dweck, C. S. (1988). Goals: An approach to motivation and achievement. *Journal of Personality and Social Psychology, 54*, 5–12.

Emmons, R. A. (1986). Personal strivings: An approach to personality and subjective well-being. *Journal of Personality and Social Psychology, 51*, 1058–1068.

Emmons, R. A. (1989). The personal striving approach to personality. In L. A. Pervin (Ed.), *Goal concepts in personality and social psychology* (pp. 87–126). Hillsdale, NJ: Erlbaum.

Erickson, E. H. (1963). *Childhood and society* (rev. ed.). New York: Norton.

Eysenck, H. J. (1987). Speed of information processing, reaction time, and the theory of intelligence. In P. A. Vernon (Ed.), *Speed of information processing and intelligence* (pp. 21–67). Norwood, NJ: Ablex.

Ford, D. H. (1987). *Humans as self-constructing living systems: A developmental perspective on behavior and personality.* Hillsdale, NJ: Erlbaum.

Ford, D. H., & Lerner, R. M. (1992). *Developmental systems theory: A synthesis of developmental contextualism and the living systems framework.* Newbury Park, CA: Sage.

Ford, M. E. (1982). Social cognition and social competence in adolescence. *Developmental Psychology, 18*, 323–340.

Ford, M. E. (1986). A living systems conceptualization of social intelligence: Outcomes, processes, and developmental change. In R. J. Sternberg (Ed.), *Advances in the psychology of human intelligence* (Vol. 3, pp. 119–171). Hillsdale, NJ: Erlbaum.

Ford, M. E. (1987). Processes contributing to adolescent social competence. In M. E. Ford & D. H. Ford (Eds.), *Humans as self-constructing living systems: Putting the framework to work* (pp. 199–233). Hillsdale, NJ: Erlbaum.

Ford, M. E. (1992). *Motivating humans: Goals, emotions, and personal agency beliefs.* Newbury Park, CA: Sage.

Ford, M. E., Chase, C., Love, R., Pollina, S., & Ito, S. (1994). *Qualities associated with caring behavior in adolescence: Goals, emotions, and personal agency beliefs.* Manuscript submitted for publication.

Ford, M. E., & Ford, D. H. (Eds.). (1987). *Humans as self-constructing living systems: Putting the framework to work.* Hillsdale, NJ: Erlbaum.

Ford, M. E., & Miura, I. T. (1983). *Children's and adult's conceptions of social competence.* Paper presented at the annual meeting of the American Educational Research Association, New York.

Ford, M. E., & Nichols, C. W. (1987). A taxonomy of human goals and some possible applications. In M. E. Ford & D. H. Ford (Eds.), *Humans as self-constructing living systems: Putting the framework to work* (pp. 289–311). Hillsdale, NJ: Erlbaum.

Ford, M. E., & Nichols, C. W. (1991). Using goal assessments to identify motivational patterns and facilitate behavioral regulation and achievement. In M. L. Maehr & P. R. Pintrich (Eds.), *Advances in motivation and achievement* (Vol. 7, pp. 51–84). Greenwich, CT: JAI.

Ford, M. E., & Nichols, C. W. (1995). *Manual: Assessment of Personal Goals.* Palo Alto, CA: Consulting Psychologists Press.

Ford, M. E., & Thompson, R. A. (1985). Perceptions of personal agency and infant attachment: Toward a life-span perspective on competence development. *International Journal of Behavioral Development, 8,* 377–406.

Ford, M. E., & Tisak, M. S. (1983). A further search for social intelligence. *Journal of Educational Psychology, 75,* 196–206.

Ford, M. E., Wentzel, K. R., Wood, D., Stevens, E., & Siesfeld, G. A. (1989). Processes associated with integrative social competence: Emotional and contextual influences on adolescent social responsibility. *Journal of Adolescent Research, 4,* 405–425.

Frijda, N. H. (1988). The laws of emotion. *American Psychologist, 43,* 349–358.

Goldstein, A. P., & Kanfer, F. H. (Eds.). (1979). *Maximizing treatment gains: Transfer enhancement in psychotherapy.* New York: Academic Press.

Goldstein, A. P., Sprakfin, R. P., Gershaw, N. J., & Klein, P. (1980). *Skillstreaming the adolescent.* Champaign, IL: Research Press.

Hoffman, M. L. (1982). Development of prosocial motivation: Empathy and guilt. In N. Eisenberg (Ed.), *The development of prosocial behavior* (pp. 281–313). New York: Academic Press.

Koestler, A. (1967). *The ghost in the machine.* New York: Macmillan.

Koestler, A. (1978). *Janus.* New York: Random House.

Kornhaber, M., Krechevsky, M., & Gardner, H. (1990). Engaging intelligence. *Educational Psychologist, 25,* 177–199.

Lazarus, R. S. (1991). *Emotion and adaptation.* New York: Oxford University Press.

Locke, E. A., Shaw, K. N., Saari, L. M., & Latham, G. P. (1981). Goal setting and task performance: 1969–1980. *Psychological Bulletin, 89,* 125–152.

Maccoby, E. E., & Jacklin, C. N. (1974). *The psychology of sex differences.* Stanford, CA: Stanford University Press.

Maehr, M. L. (1984). Meaning and motivation: Toward a theory of personal investment. In R. Ames & C. Ames (Eds.), *Research on motivation in education: Vol. 1. Student motivation* (pp. 115–144). New York: Academic Press.

Maehr, M. L., & Braskamp, L. (1986). *The motivation factor: A theory of personal investment.* Lexington, MA: Lexington Books.

Markus, H., Cross, S., & Wurf, E. (1990). The role of the self-system in competence. In R. J. Sternberg & J. Kolligian, Jr. (Eds.), *Competence considered* (pp. 205–225). New Haven, CT: Yale University Press.

Markus, H., & Nurius, P. (1986). Possible selves. *American Psychologist, 41,* 954–969.

Markus, H., & Ruvolo, A. (1989). Possible selves: Personalized representations of goals. In L. A. Pervin (Ed.), *Goal concepts in personality and social psychology* (pp. 211–241). Hillsdale, NJ: Erlbaum.

Mischel, W. (1968). *Personality and assessment.* New York: Wiley.

Mischel, W. (1973). Toward a cognitive social learning reconceptualization of personality. *Psychological Review, 80,* 252–283.

Neisser, U. (1976). *Cognition and reality.* San Francisco: Freeman.

Nesselroade, J. R., & Ford, D. H. (1987). Methodological considerations in modeling living systems. In M. E. Ford & D. H. Ford (Eds.), *Humans as self-constructing living systems: Putting the framework to work* (pp. 47–79). Hillsdale, NJ: Erlbaum.

Nichols, C. W. (1990). *An analysis of the sources of dissatisfaction at work.* Unpublished doctoral dissertation, School of Education, Stanford University, Stanford CA.

Nichols, C. W. (1991). *Manual: Assessment of Core Goals.* Palo Alto, CA: Consulting Psychologists Press.

Nisbett, R. E., & Ross, L. D. (1980). *Human inference: Strategies and shortcomings of social judgment.* Englewood Cliffs, NJ: Prentice-Hall.

Pervin, L. A. (1983). The stasis and flow of behavior: Toward a theory of goals. In M. M. Page (Ed.), *Personality: Current theory and research* (pp. 1–53). Lincoln: University of Nebraska Press.

Pervin, L. A. (Ed.). (1989). *Goal concepts in personality and social psychology.* Hillsdale, NJ: Erlbaum.

Schmidt, R. A. (1975). A schema theory of discrete motor skill learning. *Psychological Review, 82,* 225–260.

Schutz, P. A. (1991). Goals in self-directed behavior. *Educational Psychologist, 26,* 55–67.

Seligman, M. E. P. (1975). *Helplessness: On depression, development, and death.* San Francisco: Freeman.

Seligman, M. E. P. (1991). *Learned optimism.* New York: Alfred A. Knopf.

Shure, M. B., & Spivack, G. (1980). Interpersonal problem solving as a mediator of behavioral adjustment in preschool and kindergarten children. *Journal of Applied Developmental Psychology, 2,* 211–226.

Simon, H. A. (1967). Motivational and emotional control of cognition. *Psychological Review, 74,* 29–39.

Slavin, R. E. (1981). When does cooperative learning increase student achievement? *Psychological Bulletin, 94,* 429–445.

Slavin, R. E. (1984). Students motivating students to excel: Cooperative incentives, cooperative tasks, and student achievement. *Elementary School Journal, 85,* 53–63.

Spivack, G., Platt, J. J., & Shure, M. B. (1976). *The problem-solving approach to adjustment.* San Francisco: Jossey-Bass.

Staats, A. W. (1991). Unified positivism and unification psychology: Fad or new field? *American Psychologist, 46,* 899–912.

Sternberg, R. J. (1985a). *Beyond IQ: A triarchic theory of human intelligence.* New York: Cambridge University Press.

Sternberg, R. J. (1985b). Implicit theories of intelligence, creativity, and wisdom. *Journal of Personality and Social Psychology, 49,* 607–627.

Sternberg, R. J., Conway, B. E., Ketron, J. L., & Bernstein, M. (1981). People's conceptions of intelligence. *Journal of Personality and Social Psychology, 41,* 37–55.

Sternberg, R. J., & Kolligian, J., Jr. (Eds.). (1990). *Competence considered.* New Haven, CT: Yale University Press.

Sternberg, R. J., & Smith, C. (1985). Social intelligence and decoding skills in nonverbal communication. *Social Cognition, 3*, 168–192.

Sternberg, R. J., & Wagner, R. K. (Eds.). (1986). *Practical intelligence: Nature and origins of competence in the everyday world.* Cambridge, England: Cambridge University Press.

Wentzel, K. R. (1991). Social and academic goals at school: Motivation and achievement in context. In M. L. Maehr & P. R. Pintrich (Eds.), *Advances in motivation and achievement* (Vol. 7, pp. 185–212). Greenwich, CT: JAI.

Winell, M. (1987). Personal goals: The key to self-direction in adulthood. In M. E. Ford & D. H. Ford (Eds.), *Humans as self-constructing living systems: Putting the framework to work* (pp. 261–287). Hillsdale, NJ: Erlbaum.

Zand, D. E. (1972). Trust and managerial problem solving. *Administrative Science Quarterly, 17*, 229–239.

8

Intellective and Personality Factors in Literacy

Robert C. Calfee and Robert G. Curley

INTRODUCTION AND DEFINITIONS

Few accomplishments are more critical for life in modern society than acquiring literacy: the capacity to use language to think and to solve problems in social settings. Handling print—reading and writing—is an important facet of literacy, but this capability is ancillary to the broader achievement of a *formal linguistic register*, the conventions and strategies governing discourse in traditional situations (de Castell, Luke, & Egan, 1986; Tuman, 1987; Freedman & Calfee, 1984). By this definition, literacy and its precursors are found in all cultures and societies, past and present.

On the surface, individuals differ greatly in literacy—in the rate at which they can process print, compose a written document, or respond to a complex question; in the accuracy with which they comprehend a passage or complete a questionnaire; and in their discourse preferences and styles. These differences appear in general surveys of adult illiteracy, in standardized test results, in research studies, and in everyday experience (Mullis, 1991).

Robert C. Calfee • School of Education, Stanford University, Stanford, California 94305. Robert G. Curley • College of Education, San Jose State University, San Jose, California 95192.

International Handbook of Personality and Intelligence, edited by Donald H. Saklofske and Moshe Zeidner. Plenum Press, New York, 1995.

The correlation of these differences with intellective and personality factors is the primary topic of this chapter. We underscore at the outset that the differences also reflect development (reading and writing take time to acquire), opportunity to learn (unlike the acquisition of natural language, literacy does not result from simple exposure), and value (literacy, because it requires a significant investment in time and energy from both the community and the individual, will be neither learned nor acquired without perceived benefit). Literacy requires investment, and so children from impoverished homes, uneducated families, and poor schools (or no school at all)—whose primary unmet needs may be food and shelter—are less likely to read and write as adults than are more advantaged youngsters (Kozol, 1991). Worldwide, poverty remains the single best predictor of reading achievement (Hladczuk & Eller, 1992).

To assist the reader in following our argument, Figure 1 displays the conceptual framework undergirding the chapter. The framework incorporates three significant assumptions: (a) oral literacy is on a par with print literacy; (b) intellective and personality variables are differentiable predictors of literacy; and (c) situational and cultural contexts significantly influence intellective and personality factors, as well as having direct effects on literacy.

Our framework also permits us to summarize the major conclusions from a review of the research on individual differences in literacy: (a) literacy is most

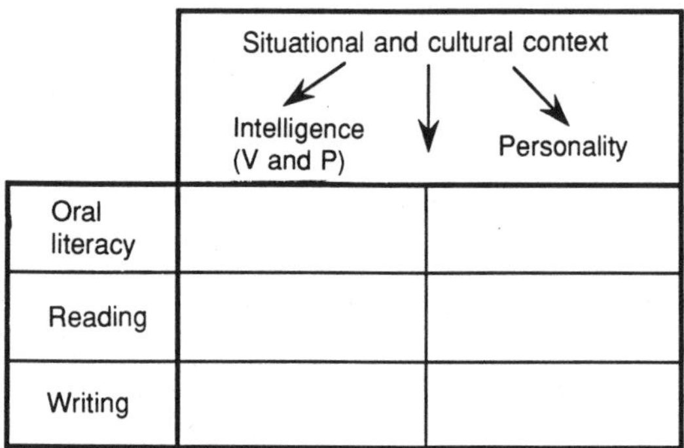

Figure 1. Conceptual framework showing relations among literacy achievements and predictive factors.

often equated with reading as a basic print skill; (b) relatively less is known about patterns of individual performance in writing and oral literacy; (c) verbal intelligence is a well-established predictor of reading achievement, but the meaning of this relation remains a mystery; and (d) the role of personality factors in literacy is frequently discussed but largely unexplored. In addition, literacy research is plagued by wide variations in definitions and methods, poor control over confounded individual-difference factors, and an astonishing disregard for the most critical variable influencing literacy—what and how students are taught.

This chapter focuses on conceptual issues in the study of literacy. Rather than attempting a comprehensive review of the extant literature, an impossible task in any event, we highlight significant questions for theory, research, and practice, relying on selected investigations to illustrate the issues. Our starting point is research from the United States, both because of our familiarity with this literature and because of its extensiveness and availability. We think that the main themes hold for most developed countries with democratic traditions; for developing nations and those under authoritarian rule, the conclusions may be less applicable. Knowledge is power, and the empowerment entailed in literacy as we define it challenges authority.

For readers interested in further information, a collection of handbooks published during the past decade offer both comprehensive and reflective reviews. The *Handbook of Research in Teaching the English Language Arts* (Flood, Jensen, Lapp, & Squire, 1991) has an entire section on "language learners" that deals with developmental differences, exceptionality, and multilinguality. The *Handbook of Research on Curriculum* (Jackson, 1992) likewise covers the differentiation of curriculum to accommodate demographic differences among students, along with a historical treatment of the evolution of the reading-writing curriculum in the United States. *The Handbook of Research on Teaching* (Wittrock, 1986) treats individual differences and literacy (including classroom discourse), but from different perspectives. The forthcoming *Handbook of Educational Psychology* (Berliner & Calfee, in press) likewise covers both the cognitive and motivational domains, as well as a chapter on literacy. Finally, the two volumes of the *Handbook of Research on Reading* (Barr, Kamil, Mosenthal, & Pearson, 1991; Pearson, 1984) both include chapters on individual differences in reading. These resources do have important limitations: (a) they lack any international perspective; (b) they emphasize cognitive factors but give little attention to personality factors; and (c) they provide virtually no information about adult literacy. Nonetheless, these resources constitute the basic foundation for this review, and we recommend them to others.

Defining Literacy

We assume a literate audience, which means that you have your own interpretation of what it means to be literate. Definitions of literacy span an enormous range, from the barest skill at decoding print and "making your mark" to the highest levels of interpreting and critiquing complex texts. Within the past generation, reflecting the movement toward an information-based society, the level of literacy necessary to gain employment and to act as a citizen has moved substantially upward in both developed and undeveloped nations. The United States in the 1970s established tests of "functional literacy" to ensure that high school graduates read and wrote at a minimum level. Twenty years later the country is engaged in a major effort to establish high national standards of literacy; in the judgment of policy analysts and politicians, the basics are no longer enough. In China, illiteracy dropped from 75% in the 1940s to 10% in the 1980s, but national policy in the 1990s calls for substantial enhancement in literacy achievement throughout the nation—once again, better is not good enough.

In this review, we adopt a social constructivist definition of literacy (Pearson, 1993), viewing comprehension and composition as two sides of the same coin. Garton and Pratt (1989) capture the essence of this position: "By the learning of literacy we mean the development of spoken and written language from their origins in early infancy to their mastery as systems of representation for communication with others" (p. 1). Sperling (1993) notes that "writing is a profoundly social act . . . the exercising of a voice, constructed out of experience in the social world" (p. 1). Literacy, viewed from this perspective, opens a window onto the human mind and society. As Huey (1908) noted, a complete theory of literacy will reveal "the most intricate workings of the human mind" (p. 6). Unfortunately, although the social-constructivist definition builds on a rich tradition (e.g., Moffett & Wagner, 1983), both research and practice have typically separated reading from writing, giving little attention to oral literacy. Therefore, we will often be forced to discuss reading apart from writing and oral language, although we will attempt to relate the domains as we proceed.

The social constructivist model, in contrast with a "basic skills" model, defines the competent reader as an active agent in dealing with texts, whether written or spoken. During comprehension, the social constructive reader rebuilds a passage much like a writer creating a text. Articulateness, or "meta-comprehension," is a hallmark of this capacity; the reconstructive reader employs explicit strategies for monitoring comprehension. Reading ability builds on three separable components (Calfee & Drum, 1986; Perfetti, 1985; Carr & Levy, 1990): decoding (translating print into the equivalent of speech), lexical access (word meaning) and text analysis (putting the parts together). Unfortunately, many studies of individual differences in reading have relied directly or indirectly on decoding indices, and we know less about vocabulary and comprehension. The studies of Yuill and Oakhill (1991) demonstrate the feasibility of investigating individual differences in text comprehension in a componential fashion with a combination of correlational and experimental methods.

From a social constructivist perspective, writing is likewise viewed not as a mechanical skill for placing words on paper according to conventions of spelling and grammar, but rather as a communicative act where the composer begins with a sense of purpose and audience, with a message and an intention. As for reading, conceptual analyses of writing tend to emphasize process components (Bereiter & Scardamalia, 1987; Scardamalia & Bereiter, 1986): prewriting (planning and organizing textual content and structure), drafting (translating the text into print), and reviewing/revising (polishing the text, syntax, and spelling). Describing writing as a process implies a seriality akin to many reading models, but the reality is undoubtedly more interactive and nonlinear. In addition, writing research has focused on purpose and audience, yielding insights without any parallel in reading research. For instance, Bereiter and Scardamalia (1987) distinguish between knowledge telling and knowledge transformation—that is, between regurgitating and constructing information.

Writing has a briefer research tradition than reading, with relatively few trustworthy investigations of individual differences. Flood et al. (1991), who provide arguably the most comprehensive account of writing research, discuss individual differences almost entirely from a reading perspective. Although national surveys of writing have begun to appear in the past decade (e.g., National Assessment of Educational Progress, 1990), the data are much less rich than for reading. Again, virtually no data are available for oral literacy.

Speech and Print: Reading and Writing

As we accentuate the concept of critical literacy as the literate use of all forms of language, we need to add a few caveats. First, although speech tends toward the natural end of the literacy register and writing the formal end, obvious exceptions come immediately to mind: Debaters take care in organizing and presenting their thoughts, whereas the writer of a love letter is more likely to take a devil-may-care attitude. The formal register—whatever the medium—is marked by greater explicitness and care in word choice, sentence construction, and the creation of a coherent text (or statement). Second, the print medium entails several inherent features that distinguish it from speech under virtually all purposes or conditions. For example, Perfetti (1985, p. 7) notes that (a) speech includes prosodic and paralinguistic information (e.g., gestures); (b) speech is transient, whereas print can be rescanned; (c) printed texts mark word, sentence, and paragraph boundaries; and (d) speech is social, whereas reading may be done in isolation. The essential distinctions, in short, are the physical design of the "signal" and the social context of the message. Printed text provides several advantages for explicit communication for those individuals who have learned to handle two obstacles: decoding and decontextualization.

Literacy learners, at least those in the United States, face a third obstacle: the separation of reading and writing as subject matters. Clifford-Jonich (1987) describes the historical roots of this dissociation: reading a topic for the elementary grades, writing for the secondary school; reading for the masses, writing for the elite; reading taught by generalists, writing by specialists; reading as phonics and narration, writing more as grammar and exposition. These contrasts and others created a chasm between practice in the two domains, frustrating both teachers and students.

The separation extends to scholarship in the two fields; the patterns are apparent in the Flood et al. (1991). Reading research typically springs from a psychological perspective, investigating performance in decontextualized laboratory-like settings, employing rigorous experimental designs, and relying on quantitative measures. Writing research springs more often from an anthropological/ethnographic perspective, investigating individual cases in natural settings and relying on qualitative outcomes. Given the dominance of psychologists in the field of intelligence and personality, it comes as no surprise that the study of individual differences in reading is far richer than for writing or oral literacy.

Individual Differences in Literacy

What is meant by individual differences in literacy? At one level the answer is obvious. Some adults read skillfully and voraciously; others cannot read at all or choose not to. Some can do little more than sign their name, whereas some (a relative few) write for the fun of it. Classroom teachers frequently comment on the challenge of adapting instruction to individual differences. On the testing front, a major accomplishment of psychometricians has been the measurement of reading and writing achievement, as well as the intellective and personality predictors of literacy. On closer examination, however, the nature of these differences is less obvious. The question is not whether individuals differ but how to interpret these differences; the issue, in short, centers around validity. And the debate about the validity of differences in reading and writing is at least as raucous as any other domain except, perhaps, intelligence.

The essence of the debate centers around the degree to which the achievement of literacy (both the rate of acquisition and the final level of competence) reflects either innate and immutable traits or the effects of external experiences. Unlike verbal intelligence, which is not officially part of the school curriculum, literacy is acquired through instruction, an explicit societal contract to create environments that foster literacy. Within this commitment, however, one policy aims to select children with a propensity toward literacy and to foster that trait, whereas another—assuming that virtually all students possess the basic prerequisites for literacy—aims to develop that capability to the fullest. The question, then, comes down to assumptions about human diversity and constancy.

Diversity and Constancy in Literacy

Individual differences in literacy build on constancies that pertain to (a) the functions of literate acts, (b) the nature of language, and (c) the abilities that undergird literacy (Calfee & Nelson-Barber, 1991). Variation is always based on some assumed common ground, even though differences often seem more salient than constancies. In a sociocultural domain such as literacy, comparisons can easily arise from false constancies—the presumption that the surface characteristics of one particular sociocultural context are the proper basis for comparison.

The first constancy is the functional nature of literacy: the notion that literacy is political and social as well as linguistic and psychological. Though researchers often define literacy by standardized tests, these measures cannot capture the broad range of this competence; thus we rely on a functional definition of literacy as the capacity to use language as a tool to think, communicate, and solve socially and culturally relevant problems. This definition encompasses oral language as well as reading and writing, and it presumes that in all cultural and social contexts, sophisticated language usage is needed to participate fully in the legal, religious, philosophical, moral, literary, historical, or political life and traditions of a culture. It is the existence of these formal language structures across social and cultural boundaries that we would take as a constant. In general, individuals adept in this formal register have an advantage over those who are not.

The second constancy pertains to the nature of language itself. Clark and Clark (1977) have argued that "a priori, every human language must be susceptible of (a) being learned by children, (b) being spoken and understood by adults easily and efficiently, (c) embodying the ideas people normally want to convey, and (d) functioning as a communication system in a social and cultural setting" (pp. 516–517). Because virtually all humans are capable of acquiring and using language as an instrument of thought and communication within familiar cultural and social settings, we believe that they are also capable of becoming literate.

The final constancy has to do with the cognitive

and motivational competencies that undergird language, which are characterized by certain similar features across individuals and cultures. The cognitive constancies include the availability of unlimited long-term memory capacity, the moderation of limited short-term memory, and the critical importance of organization in storing and retrieving information. The motivational constancies include reinforcement (people tend to repeat rewarded actions and avoid punishment) and interest/novelty (people tend to be attracted to activities that are engaging and attractive).

Sources of Diversity in Literacy

Our analysis of the individual differences within the preceding constancies contrasts literacy differences with predictor differences. Within literacy measures, the important distinction is between acquisition and performance. Within the predictors, we differentiate demographic from individual variance, with both sources moderated by cultural and situational influences.

Differences specific to literacy acquisition depend largely on the quality and quantity of what is acquired. These differences can be classified according to curriculum components: decoding, vocabulary, comprehension, and composition. In the primary years of schooling, decoding and vocabulary are emphasized in both instruction and assessment; in the later grades, comprehension and composition are emphasized. Adult performance, in contrast, is gauged by results on vocational and academic tasks across a range that extends from basic literacy to college grades and occupational accomplishments. In both domains, skill emphasis overrides assessment of strategies and preferences.

Turning to predictors, *demographic influences* include such factors as nationality, ethnic background, parent education and socioeconomic status, age, and sex. These variables are fixed in the sense that the individual cannot control them, nor do they usually fluctuate greatly during a person's life. The variance within the demographic categories comprises whatever is "left over." Intellective and personality factors differ as a function of demographic indicators; individual assessment of these factors accounts for literacy performance after demographic categories are taken into account. For a demographic population of Japanese males between 20 and 30 years old with middle-class college-educated parents, to what degree is individual variation in intellective and personality factors correlated with variation in literacy measures?

As Most and Zeidner (Chapter 22, Table 1; see also Cronbach, 1990; Messick, 1987) note, intellective and personality traits are distinctively different. Intellective traits—including intelligence, cognitive competence, and linguistic capability—all have a straightforward and predictable relation to literacy. Personality traits, in contrast, are conceptually diffuse, operationally obtuse, and situationally complex. They also tend to be magnetic in their attraction to reading and writing theorists; factors like intrinsic motivation, interest, and style must surely affect literacy! Our review of the available research shows that although these traits may appear promising, much work remains to realize the promise.

Finally, both literacy indicators and predictors are contextualized by environmental conditions, which have fundamental status as explanations for differences between individuals. Literacy reflects schooling, and schooling depends on cultural and socioeconomic conditions. The resources that support literacy include financing, social support (e.g., Japanese women ensure that their children have acquired the Hirigana script before they enter school), and societal canons (e.g., the conviction that all students can achieve, versus policies based on selection of the most capable for exceptional education). We begin with the assumption that virtually all students can acquire high levels of literacy if given effective instruction; inequalities in educational opportunity are sufficiently striking throughout the world that acting on this hypothesis will be worthwhile even if it is not totally true. Worldwide trends in female literacy during the past half century are just one reason for this conviction.

The critical issue here, of course, is nature versus nurture. When one adopts a trait approach to individual variations in cognition, language capacity, motivation, and volition, the underlying assumption is that these traits are inherent characteristics of an individual's potential and style, attributable to genetic or early environmental influences. Traits, which are generally assumed to be relatively stable or even immutable, depend on multiple assessments and factor analysis methods. A contrastive strategy begins with examination of cultural and situational effects on individual variability in cognition, language capacity, motivation, and volition. Research methods include case studies, ethnographic contextualization, and experimental variations; generalizability theory (Shavelson & Webb, 1991) is significant for both design and analysis.

Like other contrasts, the nature-nurture distinction in literacy is poorly framed as an all-or-none contrast. Men taller than 7 feet and women taller than 6 feet are inherently better prepared to excel on the basketball court than the average individual. Exceptional height, whether environmental or hereditary in cause, is immutable, predictive, and understandable. We lack comparably valid indicators of literacy excellence, but everyday experience suggests that some individuals possess preferences and proficiencies that predispose them to outstrip their fellows in the exercise of literate activities. Indeed, an argument can be made that many are capable of exceptionality with adequate assistance (Fowler, 1986; Howe, 1990). But the issue for present purposes is not transcendence but competence: the degree to which intellective and personality factors limit some children from attaining a level of literacy sufficient to thrive in modern society.

At the limiting end of the continuum are dyslexics, individuals (including notables like Nelson Rockefeller and Albert Einstein) who appear virtually incapable of acquiring literacy, despite adequate intelligence and motivation, because of unusual difficulty with decoding (Pavlidis & Fisher, 1986; Vellutino, 1979). Many students in the United States are classified as "learning disabled"; though decoding often appears to be their major limitation, social-emotional problems often appear in the background (Ekwall, 1985; McGuinness, 1985). Shortcomings are seldom attributed to writing and oral literacy, an error that probably reflects the use of administrative rather than educational categories.

In summary, one finds an incredible range of diversity, from the most accomplished readers and writers to those who struggle but can acquire this skill if given at least a modicum of encouragement. Especially puzzling are inner-city children who are surrounded by print but appear altogether lacking in literacy as young adults. The task in the remainder of this chapter is to explore the role of intellective and personality factors in explaining this diversity.

INTELLECTIVE PREDICTORS OF LITERACY

We begin this section by discussing how the formal register is manifest in reading, writing, and oral language in order to elaborate on the kinds of capabilities that underlie the exercise of literacy. As we have indicated, how well these capabilities are developed and used depends on many conditions—some experiential, some inherited, some grounded in cognitive and linguistic factors, some based on volitional factors. The emphasis in this section is on the manner in which intelligence and cognitive and linguistic factors appear to relate to the development and exercise of literacy.

At the outset, the formal language register is characterized by the use of vocabulary that is technical, abstract, precise, and uncommon: syntax that maps complex logical relationships among ideas, and discourse structures that support exposition, explanation, and argument. Literate use of vocabulary depends on semantic networks for technical terms and sensitivity to denotative and connotative distinctions, especially among otherwise similar words. Literate use of syntax entails the abilities to construct and parse complex sentences, to mark logical relationships among ideas, and to maintain in working memory the gist of sentences that contain numerous densely packed idea units. Finally, literate use of discourse depends on familiarity with the structural qualities of expositions, explanations, and arguments (and, depending on the social-cultural context, other forms as well) and the ability to take advantage of those structural qualities to support understanding and memory.

Special to reading is decoding, the task of translating visual symbols into the functional equivalent of spoken language. Decoding poses more of a challenge in some languages than in others. In English, for example, readers must be able to recognize spelling patterns that may differ in pronunciation depending on the linguistic origin of the word (Calfee & Drum, 1986). Until automaticity is reached in this decoding stage, readers are required to expend attention that might otherwise be allocated to other parts of the reading process (e.g., accessing lexical information, comprehending sentences, comprehending text). This attentional demand may be particularly problematic with formal texts because the special literacy requirements noted above for lexical, syntactic, and discourse levels all may be very demanding in terms of cognitive attentional resources. Individuals who have difficulty with decoding are often described as illiterate, or semiliterate; this condition may reflect their limited ability to acquire information from printed texts and not other impairments in language abilities.

There are several special demands involved in writing, particularly in writing formal, literate texts. Most obvious, perhaps, is the need to construct an argument (or exposition, explanation, etc.) that conveys a comprehensive, memorable message in a manner that holds up to public scrutiny. The final product, if it is to be regarded as literate, will be cast in a well-organized rhetorical form, build on syntactic structures that support the efficient and accurate representation of ideas, use vocabulary precisely, and, of course, be free of spelling errors. It will also be written in a style appropriate and accessible to its intended audience. By these criteria, a very high proportion of the population (certainly in the United States but probably elsewhere as well) might be regarded as marginally literate at best.

Oral language entails both speaking and listening, each of which makes its own literacy demands. Literate speech requires the same kind of text development as does writing, but (except in the case of a prepared speech read aloud) part or all of the development process occurs "on-line" as the speaker is talking. To be sure, the expectations may be less stringent than would be the case for a polished presentation, but the ability to compose a literate statement in situ imposes considerable cognitive and linguistic (and, in many cases, emotional) demands on individuals. Proficiency in formal speech is rare, and the incidence of fear of even attempting such performances is high. Even more so than writing, formal speech is an area of literacy that distinguishes the elite from commoners and stands as a barrier that inhibits many individuals from fully participating in public life.

Finally, listening is much like reading without the need to decode visual symbols, but with the added burden of processing verbal information on-line with only limited opportunities to preserve that information for future reference. Natural language tends to be highly redundant, supported by context, and limited in the amount of new information that is conveyed during any one "turn" in a conversation. Formal oral language contains fewer such built-in supports and thus places greater demands on a listener's ability to process, store, and (when appropriate) plan a response to the communication they are receiving.

What sorts of intellective factors might contribute to the development and exercise of literacy? The first major candidate, one of long-standing interest, is intelligence. The second source includes such perceptual and cognitive abilities as perceptual span, eye fixations, and working memory capacity, as well as psycholinguistic processes (e.g., lexical access and syntactic capability) and metacognitive and metalinguistic competencies (i.e., the capacity to reflect on thought and language). For both domains we will consider (a) the relations between these factors and literacy achievements, (b) the potential insights gained into the nature of thought and language gained from these relations, and (c) the contextualization of these variables with a broad conception of cultural and educational factors.

Intelligence and Literacy

That measures of intelligence correlate with measures of literacy should come as little surprise. The earliest intelligence tests were designed to predict success in school, and, of course, success in school depends to a large degree on proficiency with language. Bloom (1976), for example, found that a .40 correlation between achievement in science and literature approached zero when the effects of reading comprehension were partialed out. Correlations between standard intelligence tests and measures of reading proficiency are generally found to be in the neighborhood of .7 (Rayner & Pollatsek, 1989). In the early grades this association tends to be somewhat higher, in later grades somewhat lower. Schonell (1942) reports correlations on the order of .8 for second graders and between .4 and .5 for fifth graders. It is worth noting that the pattern of association between reading achievement and measures of intelligence is virtually identical to patterns found with respect to academic achievement overall (Snow & Yalow, 1982).

Do such associations suggest an important link between general intellectual abilities and the potential for developing high levels of literacy? Much of the literature on reading and reading instruction assumes that it does, particularly when the issue of poor readers is considered. Rayner and Pollatsek (1989), for example, discuss the distribution of poor readers in terms of their measured levels of intelligence: "Since the correlation between reading scores and IQ scores is pretty high, a large fraction of [readers 1 to 2 years behind] is accounted for in terms of low intelligence. . . . Of more interest are those whose IQ scores are such that they should be reading better than they are" (p. 401).

Historically, intelligence has been viewed as a limiting condition and used along with grade level to establish an expected level of achievement (Ekwall, 1985). Poor readers whose IQ scores are within expected levels (i.e., low) appear to do more poorly than good readers on virtually any measure of reading or reading-related processes that they are given. According to Rayner and Pollatsek (1989, pp. 401–402), poor readers when compared with good readers are less sensitive to orthographic structure, take longer to name words, are less effective in using the speech code for processing linguistic stimuli, do less well on tasks tapping phonemic awareness, are more reliant on context, do not use syntactic structure as effectively, are less efficient in the use of working memory, and have poorer verbatim recall of text and shorter memory spans. Poor readers with higher than expected IQs tend to do less well than good readers with comparable IQs on tasks requiring the ability to decode phonetic information, suggesting that their problems may be largely attributable to decoding deficiencies.

What might the pattern of association between measures of intellectual ability and reading achievement tell us about the nature of reading and, by extension, language and literacy? One possibility is that formal language draws on a wide range of relatively fixed thinking, reasoning, and information-processing skills, and that the abilities that undergird intellectual achievements in a variety of domains support the development of formal language as well. The lower a child's measured intelligence, the more likely he or she is to lack a wide range of skills necessary to become a proficient reader. A generation or two past, children were often "tagged" according to their potential development in reading and language based on IQ scores, the conviction being that those scores represented a fixed set of abilities established at birth or at a very early age. Indeed, such beliefs persist but are less commonly acted on by educators now because of less prevalent IQ testing and laws and policies that restrict the use of such data for placement and instructional decisions.

Recent thinking and research about the construct of intelligence paint a picture of aptitude that is more mutable, more sensitive to social and cultural constraints and influences, and as much a product of education and literacy as it is a constraint on them. Lohman (1993), for example, argues that "fluid abilities are important both as aptitudes for success in formal schooling and as outcomes of formal schooling. . . . The aptitude function has been overemphasized, and the outcome function ignored altogether, primarily because fluid abilities are often mistakenly thought to be innate" (p. 12). In support of this contention, Lohman notes the finding of negative correlations between age and IQ for children who are deprived of schooling, commenting that "abilities do not mature of their own accord" (p. 12). Howe (1990) observes that "there is firm evidence that even the most extraordinary human abilities do not justify our assuming that any person who displays them must have been born exceptional" (p. vii).

The point is that the intelligence brought to bear on the development of intellectual capabilities (of which formal language is certainly one) is a product of basic cognitive aptitudes, shaped by social, cultural, and family influences as well as by personal dispositions subject to the same kinds of influences. To be sure, prevailing evidence suggests that variance in intelligence is attributable to heredity as well as experience (Bouchard & Segal, 1985). Nonetheless, we note Cronbach's (1990) observation that intelligence is not a thing; it is a style of work. So too, we would argue, is formal language, and by extension, literacy. How innate and acquired abilities interact remains largely mysterious. Systematic study of the reciprocal relationship between the development of literacy and that of intelligence could shed considerable light on both constructs.

Perceptual, Cognitive, Linguistic, and "Meta" Differences

Earlier we proposed that for the vast majority of individuals, cognitive systems are more than adequate for the acquisition and use of natural language. We also indicated that although they are grounded in natural language, the formal registers of literacy make significant demands on language users. In this section we consider the extent to which the cognitive system and the processes it engages in while handling formal language are characterized by systematic individual differences. We limit our discussion to reading for the simple reason that this is where the research on cognitive/linguistic processing has been done. As indicated earlier, our intent is not to provide an exhaustive review of the literature, but rather to highlight research that suggests patterns for making sense of the kinds of individual cognitive and linguistic disparities that occur.

On the linguistic level, we might expect to find differences manifest in any of the component processes of reading, from decoding to establishing lexical meaning to parsing sentences and comprehending texts—and, of course, we do. On the cognitive level, we might expect to find differences in the manner in which perception and memory function in various kinds of linguistic subprocesses, and we do here as well. What we wish to highlight is that most differences appear to be rooted more in knowledge, strategy, and "metastrategy" than in elemental capacities or processing speeds.

We begin by considering differences related to

decoding. Decoding (in English and other alphabetic writing systems) entails transforming letters into a phonetic code. This may be done through recognition of an entire word or by a process of analysis that takes into account phonemic, orthographic, and/or morphological information. Readers typically must be able to identify words in order to assign accurate meanings to them, and fluency in reading is dependent on the ability to identify words quickly and accurately. Not surprisingly, good readers (those who do better on measures of comprehension) are faster and more accurate decoders than are poor readers. The advantage is greatest for low-frequency words and for words that follow conventional spelling patterns but are nonmeaningful. Speed differences persist, however, even when high-frequency words are read.

What factors seem to account for these differences in normal populations (i.e., those that exclude dyslexics)? On the one hand, the relative advantage gained by good readers in both speed and accuracy in the pronunciation of unfamiliar words suggests that the ready availability of knowledge concerning the implicit rules of English orthography plays a large role. Whether as a result of instruction or of inferences drawn from experience in reading, good readers demonstrate better awareness of how to utilize decoding principles available at the word level. Poor readers are much more likely to try to use lexical or syntactic context or to guess on the basis of a very limited amount of orthographic information. On the other hand, disparities in speed that persist for very high-frequency words (which are likely to be handled by sight) suggest at least the possibility that some differences in speed of processing for name retrieval are at work. Perfetti (1985) discusses a number of studies designed to examine this possibility and concludes that such differences, although they do appear to exist (at least for naming words and digits under some conditions, but not for pictures or colors) are probably not large enough to be of great consequence at least within normal populations.

Lexical access (or semantic encoding) entails the assignment of meaning to words and phrases. Readers may differ in two general ways in this process. They may differ in the availability of lexical items in semantic memory (the size of their vocabulary), as well as in how successfully they apply what they know in assigning meanings in context. Not surprisingly, good readers differ from poor readers on both counts. Good readers have larger vocabularies than do poor readers. This, of course, is of particular advantage in reading texts that contain a relatively high proportion of uncommon words. But the lexicons of good readers also are more richly elaborated—that is, there appear to be more connections and associations among semantic elements (Anderson & Freebody, 1979). Even for words that appear to be unknown to both good and poor readers based on standard vocabulary tests, good readers are more likely to come up with vague associations that demonstrate some sense of meaning (McKeown & Curtis, 1987).

With respect to the ability to infer meaning from context, good readers again demonstrate a significant advantage. In part, good readers are better able to infer meaning from context because they are more likely to maintain some information about the meaning of the word in question in semantic memory. As noted above, this may be little more than a vague association, but if this is combined with semantic and syntactic clues enough understanding may be gleaned to avoid a bottleneck in comprehension. A second part of the inference process has to do with knowledge that is more metalinguistic in nature—syntactic and semantic cues that support inferencing, and awareness of when and how to take advantage of those cues. As one might expect, good readers and highly verbal individuals are more proficient at using context clues (Sternberg, Powell, & Kaye, 1985), even though their superior word knowledge would seemingly make the application of this skill less critical to comprehension than it would be for poorer readers.

Comprehension at the sentence level involves the use of syntactic and semantic information to parse sentences and to combine the resulting propositions into meaningful "chunks" in working memory. Those chunks are kept active until such time as they are either moved into the long-term memory store or forgotten. Differences between good and poor readers could occur in their abilities to (a) parse sentences, (b) build accurate and efficient representations of meaning within and across sentences, (c) hold propositional information in short-term memory, or (d) transfer important information into long-term memory to prevent it from being lost and thus preserve working memory space for continued processing of upcoming text.

There is, indeed, evidence that such differences exist, but little certainty as to how such differences should be interpreted. Daneman (1991), for example, notes that poor readers are disadvantaged relative to good readers when it comes to such sentence-level processing activities as relating successive topics, integrating information to determine gist, making inferences (they make fewer, and those that they do make are less accurate), and determining pronomial referents. She goes on to indicate that two primary causal factors have been implicated: working memory capacity and background knowledge.

Whatever role working memory capacity plays in these processes, it is unlikely that passive capacity alone is an important factor. There is no significant relationship between conventional measures of short-term memory span (e.g., digit span, the ability to recall a random list of words) and sentence-level comprehension processes (Perfetti, 1985). Both Perfetti (1985) and Daneman (1991) cite evidence that good and poor readers differ on tasks that require attentional resources to be divided between storing some information in working memory and actively processing other information. With regard to background knowledge, the argument is that the more one knows about a topic, the easier it is to make inferences when the text is not explicit (Voss, Fincher-Kiefer, Greene, & Post, 1985). It is also likely that background knowledge (which good readers tend to have in greater measure than poor readers) facilitates the "chunking" of information in working memory, as well as the transfer of information to long-term memory.

A third factor, mentioned but not discussed by Daneman (1991), is metacognition. Poor readers appear less concerned than good readers when texts are inconsistent or incoherent, and they are less likely to detect or repair comprehension problems as they arise (Garner, 1980). They fail to monitor their comprehension and, thus, fail to read strategically. It may be that they do not know how to be strategic, and there is some evidence to support this hypothesis. Ann Brown and her colleagues, for example, have shown that poor readers can successfully be taught to monitor their comprehension, question themselves while reading, and generate appropriate summaries (Brown, 1987; Palincsar & Brown, 1984; Palincsar & Klenk, 1992). Readers can be taught to vary their reading speeds to adjust for the demands difficult texts impose on processing (Witty, 1969), and good readers seem to benefit from such instruction.

Text-level comprehension, finally, entails the meaningful representation of whole texts in long-term memory. This is the sine qua non of reading, and, by definition, good and poor readers differ in their abilities to carry out this process successfully. Good readers remember substantially more of what they read, and they understand it better. On one level, this too appears to be a function of background knowledge. As Perfetti (1985) notes, "A person comprehends a text only in relation to what he or she already knows" (p. 72). Ambiguous texts are interpreted to mesh with a reader's background experience (Bransford & Johnson, 1973). People who are more familiar with a topic will, on average, retain more of what they read on that topic than people who know less. As already noted, good readers tend to know more about more topics than do poor readers, in no small part because they read more.

Good and poor readers differ not only in how much they remember from what they read, but also in the way what they remember is structured. When information is divided into levels of importance to the overall message of the text, good readers tend to recall relatively more of the information rated high in importance. Poor readers, in contrast, are less likely to discriminate in their recall between more and less important information (Meyer, 1975). Poor readers also exhibit a tendency, especially when dealing with expository texts, to wander back and forth between one subtopic and another in their recall, whereas good readers tend to follow the author's structure and report completely on one subtopic before moving on to the next (Meyer, 1975). These patterns may be attributable to background knowledge and the manner in which related information is already structured in memory, but they show that good readers know something that poor readers do not about conventional rhetorical structures and about strategies for applying them in the comprehension process.

In examining the kinds of cognitive-linguistic differences that distinguish good and poor readers, one should note at least a heuristic distinction among those attributable to (a) basic cognitive abilities and processes, (b) metacognitive or metalinguistic processes, and (c) knowledge. To date, evidence of differences related to basic cognitive abilities is perhaps not as great as one might suspect given the strong association between intelligence and reading. There is some indication that speed of retrieval for names relates to decoding, but the association is weak. It has also been argued that the effective capacity of working memory is associated with processing at the sentence level. But this is not the same, of course, as a difference in short-term memory capacity.

More pervasive in the literature are indications of differences attributable either to knowledge or to the application of strategic metacognitive or metalinguistic processes. Such factors as knowledge of basic orthographic principles in decoding, depth and breadth of vocabulary, and the availability of appropriate content schemata in comprehension processes turn out to be significant in distinguishing good from poor readers. Similarly, good readers are distinguished by such "meta" skills as strategic use of knowledge about text structure and a predilection to monitor their comprehension processes. What seems clear is that all of these competencies are improved by explicit instruction.

PERSONALITY PREDICTORS OF LITERACY

Most and Zeidner (Chapter 22) characterize personality variables as bipolar, situationally dependent, and of limited practical utility. These features certainly mesh with the research in literacy. Our primary aim in this section is to give a sense of the work in this area, present a conceptual framework for thinking about issues, and point to possible areas for future research. At the outset, let us be clear about our convictions that personality variables, however construed, contribute substantially to literacy acquisition and achievement. The ease with which an individual learns to read and write, and the enthusiasm with which he or she then chooses to read and write—these are correlates of personality variables, both demographic and individual.

The challenge, of course, is how to define and assess personality variables effectively. This domain is plagued by debates about the number and nature of these traits, whether research studies are about words or reality, and the difficulty in establishing generalizability stability for any measure (see Goldberg, 1993)—and these debates rage among scholars whose specialization is personality! Within the field of literacy research, recent investigations of personality correlates are scattered and thin; even the most classical studies remain to be replicated (Ekwall, 1973, pp. 135–140, 187–198).

Accordingly, we propose a framework that we think will prove serviceable in organizing the theoretical and practical issues in the field. At the very least, the categories in this framework provide assembly points for the existing literature:

- *Motivation and conation* cover the broad domains of achievement motivation, efficacy, attribution, and self-regulation as related to the individual's pursuit of academic achievements: Why should a person want to acquire literacy and attempt tasks that entail literacy? How does the person express these wants?
- *Styles and preferences* refer to choices by the individual in particular contexts: Under what conditions and in what ways does the person most effectively acquire literacy skills and succeed in literacy tasks?
- *Attitudes and interests* encompass personal traits directed toward specific literacy activities: What texts and contexts tend to engage and sustain a person in the performance of literate activities?

Achievement motivation has been an active arena for the study of individual differences for decades, focusing most recently on the degree to which a student will pursue academic tasks because he or she has a sense of personal efficacy (Graham & Weiner, in press; Stipek, in press; Wigfield & Asher, 1984). Efficacy is enhanced when success is attributed to effort (an internal, controllable factor); motivation is lowest when a student attributes failure to an external, unstable factor (e.g., luck). Ability (internal but uncontrollable) and task difficulty (external and unstable) lead to intermediate levels of motivation. The chief finding in this field is that less capable learners attribute success to luck and failure to lack of ability, whereas high-achieving students see success as a product of effort and failure as a result of task difficulty. The consequence is a vicious spiral in which motivation decreases for the former group and increases for the latter.

Conation, a term resurrected by Snow and his colleagues (Snow, Corno, & Jackson, in press), can be thought of as meta-motivation, "a conscious striving" (Snow & Jackson, in press, p. 2). The concept also appears in the literature on self-regulation, a "mindful" control of motivation (Bandura, 1978; Zimmerman, 1990). Attributions, as they become more self-conscious, take shape as conative influences, as "personal and social epistemologies" about competence (Greeno, 1989).

Motivation and conation should be related to acquisition and performance of literacy. Indeed, textbooks on reading instruction and educational psychology encourage teachers to consider motivation as a factor, and studies of achievement motivation occasionally employ reading achievement as an indicator.

In the area of self-regulation—the practical side of conation—Meichenbaum (1986; also Harris, 1990; Schunk, 1990) has demonstrated the effectiveness for reading performance of teaching low-achieving students to monitor their purpose and intention during classroom reading. These studies demonstrate that motivation is modifiable; students who are apparently unmotivated can become self-motivated. But we have been unable to discover any systematic investigations of the relation of individual differences in motivation to reading in general, writing, or oral literacy.

The largest and most confusing domain of personality literature falls under the heading of *learning styles*. Several taxonomies have been proffered. The early "cognitive styles" which Messick (1987) defines as "consistency in manner or form within and across broad domains (p. 55) . . . and generalized habits of thought" (p. 56), contrast impulsive versus reflective, analytic versus synthetic, and field-dependent versus independent traits. Curry (1990) has proposed a more concrete set of contrasts not on the basis of empirical findings but as a way of categorizing the dozens of instruments available in this field: environmental preferences (light or dark, quiet or noisy), social-conditions preferences (work alone or with group), preferred level of engagement (slow or fast paced), and processing style (akin to the earlier cognitive styles). Carbo, Dunn, and Dunn (1986) have created an even more extensive list of styles, proposing that schooling should match the individual's profile as exactly as possible in order to optimize learning. Carbo et al. (1986) are chiefly interested in presenting instructional prescriptions based on this proposal; the research basis for their prescriptions is a collection of doctoral dissertations.

As Curry (1990) notes, "The learning styles field offers tantalizing possibilities" (p. 7) but it is plagued by "(1) confusion in definitions, (2) weaknesses in reliability and validity of the measurements, and (3) [lack of valid] identification of relevant characteristics in learners and instructional settings" (p. 1). A similar assessment colors virtually every review we have encountered (e.g., Globerson & Zelniker, 1989; Snow et al., in press). Globerson and Zelniker (1989), for example, concur with Curry's concerns but note further that style measures are weakly correlated with a diverse array of ability and achievement measures (general intelligence, problem solving, cognitive development, and school achievement), concluding that "styles and abilities are two distinct constructs, which can be either correlated or orthogonal" (p. 8).

Studies by Kagan (1965) and Robinson (1972) exemplify some of the better efforts to investigate the role of stylistic preferences on reading performance. Kagan (1965), for example, found that reflective first graders take more time and are more accurate in oral reading than impulsive ones. To be sure, skilled readers in the later grades become faster, and probably more adaptive, and the correlation of the reflective-impulsive dimension with verbal intelligence is a worrisome confounding. Robinson (1972) designed a careful experiment to investigate the widespread belief that so-called auditory and visual learners will acquire reading more effectively when instruction is matched to their style. The investigation covered a 3-year span of beginning reading instruction that stressed either phonics (auditory) or "look-say" (visual) techniques. Robinson found that (a) both style tests were correlated with verbal intelligence; (b) in first grade, the sight method led to significantly better oral reading than phonics for all groups; and (c) the phonics method led to higher reading comprehension in third grade. Intelligence correlates accounted for all of the variation associated with the style differences, and the predicted aptitude-treatment interactions (ATI) were nowhere in evidence (Cronbach & Snow, 1977). This landmark review of ATI research made no attempt to cover literacy achievement, though, because of the size (enormous) and quality (poor) of the literature.

Finally, interests and attitudes encompass personality-like variables that can be related to particular situations and tasks. Topic interest and familiarity are probably the most potent yet least investigated dimensions that affect reading comprehension and (we suspect) writing facility. Although Anderson, Shirey, Wilson, and Fielding (1986) identified interest as the most highly correlated factor influencing comprehension—substantially more so than readability and other such facets—the concept continues to pose both practical and definitional challenges (e.g., Hidi, 1992). In particular, it seems reasonable to assume that interest is partly reflected by personality factors, and yet it has proven difficult to identify systematic research along these lines. Ball (1992) and Francisco (1994) illustrate the type of work that we have in mind; both have shown that African-American students tend to prefer texts in which the writing style and structure mesh with culturally familiar patterns, and in which the protagonist is also African American. Under these conditions, students reported that they could identify with the characters, they read with greater engagement and comprehension, and they wrote about their reactions at greater length and with more substance.

In another example, Gilmore (1986) investigated "sub-rosa literacy" in Philadelphia schools, showing that in their out-of-class free time, girls preferred "doing steps" (rhymes and cheers accompanied by dance steps and hand claps), whereas boys played the game Dungeons and Dragons. Although the boys' game in particular called forth a wide array of technical skills in the creation of complex characters and plots, calling for comprehension of detailed rulebooks and evoking wide-ranging expository discourse, these talents were not observable in the classroom context. As Gilmore notes, "this finding raises a serious question for educators when a population that performs poorly in reading in a school context enthusiastically and voluntarily engages in more demanding, highly technical literacy texts for fun with friends" (p. 165).

As an example of attitudinal research, and in a marked departure from most standardized surveys of literacy assessment, the U.S. National Assessment of Educational Progress (NAEP, 1990) asks students to write essays and to indicate their preferences for various topics and genres. The findings show that most U.S. fourth and eighth graders do quite well when asked to write about informational topics (knowledge telling) but are less facile in constructing a persuasive essay. More than half the sample saw value in writing (endorsing the statement "Writing helps me think more clearly, understand my own feelings, share my ideas") as well as an appreciation of the functional value of writing ("Writing can help me get a good job, show people that I know something"). Interestingly, the value placed on writing was only slightly correlated with writing achievement. When asked for a self-assessment ("I like to write; people like what I write"), NAEP found a substantial decline in attitudes from fourth grade (50% to 60%) to eleventh grade (25% to 40%). A substantial proportion reported that they wrote in nonschool settings (e.g., notes and messages), and most disagreed with the statement, "If I didn't have to write for school, I wouldn't write anything."

This survey demonstrates the possibilities for informative research on personality factors in writing within the practical limits of a large-scale survey. Unfortunately, although the "report card" presents a detailed breakdown of achievement by demographic and regional factors, no parallel analyses are provided for the attitudinal factors. To be sure, the data base is in the public domain, and interested researchers can explore these questions on their own. Nonetheless, the official report reflects the policy priorities between attitudes and achievement.

CULTURAL AND CONTEXTUAL PREDICTORS OF LITERACY

What are the opportunities to acquire literacy, how valuable is this skill to the society and to individuals, and what are the competing demands? A complete account of this topic would take us far beyond the focus of the chapter, but it is important to connect the intellective and personality factors with their roots in culture and context. The most significant links, of course, are the opportunities for learning provided by family and school. Social policy affects these opportunities when it supports family well-being, when it offers pre- and postnatal care, and when it provides preschool programs. The most substantial programs for promoting literacy, unsurprisingly, are found in schools. Garton and Pratt (1989) note that "for both spoken and written language the child requires *assistance*—usually adult assistance" (p. 2), and they make it clear that they are referring to the acquisition of literate language, not language in general. Snow (1982) makes a similar point when he writes that "human intelligence is fundamentally a product of education, and education is fundamentally a product of the exercise of human intelligence" (p. 493). He might well have added that the literate use of language is the sine qua non in this equation.

Both the quantity and the quality of social support for the development of literacy in homes and schools are correlated with other demographic factors, including social stratification, socioeconomic status, race, and sex. Stanovich (1986) has described the "Matthew effect" in literacy: The rich become richer and the poor poorer. This effect is partly attributable to social policy that provides greater resources to the more influential, but it also reflects the mismatch between home and community circumstances and the expectations and conditions of school. The U.S. research literature is quite extensive on this point (e.g., Donmoyer & Kos, 1993), and the daily newspaper paints similar portraits. The schools for poor black students in South Africa, by all reports, are designed not to connect with children's backgrounds but to establish the challenges of entering middle-class, literate society (French, 1982).

Although it is possible to describe this mismatch by reference to the relation of intellective and personality variables to literacy acquisition, this conceptualization seems off the mark in mixing cause with effect. Moreover, the positive effects of accelerative and "high-expectation" schooling (e.g., Berrueta-Clement

& Weikart, 1984; Fowler, 1986) provide evidence of the benefits of early and sustained efforts to promote the literate use of language for children whose home, family, and community circumstances are not likely to provide the necessary support for this accomplishment. Family support for literacy development is likely to be far easier in Japan than in Zaire, in Helsinki than in Los Angeles. And local priorities and values must also be weighed; in poor nations such as Somalia, the essentials of physical survival take precedence over ensuring literacy. The basic questions have to do with the role of literacy within the culture, and the choice of educational systems that are selectional or adaptive in character.

Three brief case studies will serve to illustrate the interplay of cultural-contextual factors with the intellective-personality variables. The first builds on the investigations of Stevenson and his colleagues of literacy differences between the United States and Japan (Stevenson, Azuma, & Hakuta, 1986; Stevenson & Stigler, 1992). The prevailing beliefs hold that (a) the reading achievement of Japanese children is much higher than American youngsters, (b) "reading disability" is virtually unknown in Japan, and (c) these contrasts reflect the higher standards of effort and accomplishment prevalent in Japanese homes and schools. The third element can be viewed as a cultural-personality factor; Japanese mothers and teachers stress effort over ability and are less satisfied with "average" performance than their American counterparts. A closer examination of the data suggests other interpretations. For instance, mothers and teachers in both countries place effort at the top of their list and luck at the bottom; Americans judge effort and ability as more equal contributors to school success than Japanese, but the differences are actually quite small. In terms of the second point, the Japanese fifth graders studied by Stevenson actually performed less well on reading tests than the American students, and a substantial proportion were two or more grade levels below expectation. Finally, although Japanese first graders do outperform American children, virtually all Japanese preschoolers are taught the Hirigana syllabary by their mothers before they enter school.

Stevenson's analysis is that the increasing demands of *kanji* and *katagana* (Chinese- and foreign-based words, respectively) in the later grades places an substantial burden on Japanese readers; to be sure, American students confront a similar challenge in dealing with Romance words following basic training on Anglo-Saxon words. The point of this case study is that simple comparisons of literacy achievement between communities, cultures, and contexts are likely to be uninformative at best and misleading at worst. Correlational studies lacking in contextual grounding provide little trustworthy data for policy or understanding. Incidentally, these studies provide limited background on the effects of either intellective or socioeconomic factors.

Our second case study focuses on the literary achievement of boys and girls. Virtually every study in the United States shows the superiority of girls over boys in both language and its literate use, and reading disability is 10 times more likely for boys than for girls in most surveys. These trends can be attributed to a variety of intellective and personality factors, but for present purposes the pertinent fact is that this pattern is atypical of the rest of the world. Equally interesting are the trends in male-female literacy during the second half of the 20th century. Hladczuk and Eller (1992) report that 1982 illiteracy rates in China were 5% for males and 12% for females among the 12-year-olds; for 60-year-olds, the figures were 47% for males and 90% for females. Data from several other nations (e.g., Iran, South Africa) are comparable in showing a much larger proportion of females than males who are illiterate by UNESCO standards, but an incredible change over half a century in the absolute levels. Whatever intellective and personality factors distinguish males from females (and there are many), it seems reasonable to conclude that cultural and contextual variables play a much more significant role.

Our final case study relies on variations in schooling within the United States for children who are identified by demographic, intellective, or personality variables as at risk for academic failure. The prevailing pattern, once these children are so identified, is for teachers to offer a less rich, slower-paced, and less demanding curriculum (Allington, 1989; McGill-Franzen, 1993). Moreover, these decisions are moderated by individual teachers; those with a lower sense of self-efficacy about their capabilities as teachers are more likely to water down the curriculum, and students' literacy achievements suffer correspondingly (Ashton & Webb, 1986). The point of this example is that relations among literacy, intellective, and personality variables are linked by thoughts, beliefs, and actions as well as traits; whatever one might believe about the nature of traits, the thoughts, beliefs, and actions are subject to modification.

CONCLUSION

When we agreed to write this chapter, the task seemed straightforward enough, probably because our previous research interests focused on literacy rather than intellective and personality factors per se. To be sure, we were familiar with a broad range of the available literature, we found the creation of a conceptual framework an engaging task, and we were convinced that assembling the pieces of the puzzle would be relatively simple.

As it has turned out, the scholarly literature in this domain leaves much to be desired, largely because of the lack of comprehensive, multivariate, longitudinal research on a human endeavor of paramount importance. We knew in advance that our decision to take a broad perspective on literacy would lead to frustrations; we were surprised, though, at the dearth of information about the role of individual differences in reading achievement. We knew in advance that personality was much "fuzzier" than the intellective domain, but we were surprised at the lack of data on the contrast between verbal and performance intelligence on reading achievement. We knew in advance that social and situational factors were important moderators of individual-difference variables, but we were surprised that few investigations in the United States or elsewhere explored these relations, even when the data were apparently available.

From the melange that we have examined, certain conclusions do seem worthy of trust. One is that virtually all human beings are capable of exceptionality in a broad range of literacy achievements, regardless of the profile of intellective and personality indicators that they bring to the acquisition of these accomplishments. The weak relation of these indicators to achievement, the impact of educational programs, international trends in male-female literacy, and other findings all suggest that educational opportunity is a potent factor capable of overriding other considerations.

A second conclusion is the value of adaptive instruction. Although the strongest proposals for matching instruction to ability or personal style are less than convincing, rigid techniques aimed to select only those students who are unusually talented and interested in academics seem likely to waste an enormous amount of human potential. Ability grouping (the assignment of students to reading-writing instruction based on measured achievement) is clearly detrimental to low-ability students and provides little or no advantage to the high-ability students (Calfee & Brown, 1979; Oakes, 1992). The teacher whose students cover a broad range of achievement, however, faces the challenge of creating an instructional program that spans an equally broad range. Assignments based on learning styles seems equally questionable, given the unreliability of instruments and the lack of convincing evidence for such decisions. Nevertheless, it is probably worthwhile for teachers to determine student preferences in categories identified as significant by personality theorists, and to take these preferences into account in such practical matters as organizing cooperative groups and planning work assignments.

In short, though much remains to be understood about the conditions that foster the acquisition and performance of literacy, this achievement is of critical importance for the well-being of society. Moreover, both researchers and practitioners will do well to consider the personality and intellective factors that influence this achievement, along with the conditions and contexts that support it. Finally, we should set our sights high; basic literacy skills will be of little value for the future, and most youngsters are too smart and too motivated to spend much time and energy working toward a valueless end. They are likely to invest considerable effort, though, toward a more valued goal of critical literacy.

REFERENCES

Allington, R. L. (1989). School response to reading failure: Chapter 1 and special education students in grades 2, 4, and 8. *Elementary School Journal, 89*, 529–542.

Anderson, R. C., & Freebody, P. (1979). *Vocabulary knowledge* (Technical Report No. 146). Urbana: University of Illinois Center for the Study of Reading.

Anderson, R. C., Shirey, L., Wilson, P., & Fielding, L. (1986). Interestingness of children's reading material. In R. E. Snow & M. Farr (Eds.), *Aptitude learning and instruction*. Hillsdale, NJ: Erlbaum.

Ashton, P. T., & Webb, R. B. (1986). *Making a difference: Teachers' sense of efficacy and student achievement*. New York: Longman.

Ball, A. F. (1992). Cultural preference and the expository writing of African-American adolescents. *Written Communication, 9*, 501–532.

Bandura, A. (1978). The self system in reciprocal determinism. *American Psychologist, 33*, 344–358.

Barr, R., Kamil, M. L., Mosenthal, P. B., & Pearson, P. D. (1991). *Handbook of reading research* (Vol. 2). New York: Longman.

Bereiter, C., & Scardamalia, M. (1987). *The psychology of written composition*. Hillsdale, NJ: Lawrence Erlbaum Associates.

Berliner, D. C., & Calfee, R. C. (Eds.). (in press). *Handbook of educational psychology*. New York: Macmillan.

Berrueta-Clement, J. R., & Weikart, D. P. (1984). *Changed lives: The effects of the Perry preschool program on youths through age 19*. Ypsilanti, MI: High Scope.

Bloom, B. S. (1976). *Human characteristics and school learning*. New York: McGraw-Hill.

Bouchard, T. J., & Segal, N. L. (1985). Environment and IQ. In B. Wolman (Ed.), *Handbook of intelligence: Theories, measurements, and applications*. New York: Wiley.

Bransford, J. D., & Johnson, M. K. (1973). Considerations of some problems of comprehension. In W. G. Chase (Ed.), *Visual information processing*. New York: Academic Press.

Brown, A. L. (1987). Metacognition, executive control, self-regulated and other more mysterious mechanisms. In F. Weinert & R. Kluwe (Eds.), *Metacognition, motivation, and understanding* (pp. 65–116). Hillsdale, NJ: Erlbaum.

Calfee, R. C., & Brown, R. (1979). Grouping students for instruction. In D. L. Duke (Ed.), *Classroom management* (pp. 144–181, NSSE 78th Yearbook Part II). Chicago: University of Chicago Press.

Calfee, R. C., & Drum, P. A. (1986). Research on teaching reading. In M. C. Wittrock (Ed.), *Handbook of research on teaching* (3rd ed., pp. 804–849). New York: Macmillan.

Calfee, R. C., & Nelson-Barber, S. (1991). Diversity and constancy in human thinking: Critical literacy as amplifier of intellect and experience. In E. Hiebert (Ed.), *Literacy for a diverse society: Perspectives, programs, and policies* (pp. 44–57). New York: Teachers College Press.

Carbo, M., Dunn, R., & Dunn, K. (1986). *Teaching students to read through their individual learning styles*. Englewood Cliffs, NJ: Prentice-Hall.

Carr, T. H., & Levy, B. A. (1990). (Eds.) *Reading and its development: Component skills approaches*. San Diego, CA: Academic Press.

Clark, H. H., & Clark, E. V. (1977). *Psychology and language: An introduction to psycholinguistics*. New York: Harcourt Brace Jovanovich.

Clifford-Jonich, G. (1987). *A Sisyphean task: Historical perspectives on the relation between writing and reading instruction* (Technical Report No. 7). Berkeley: Center for the Study of Writing, University of California.

Cronbach, L. J. (1990). *Essentials of psychological testing* (5th ed.). New York: HarperCollins.

Cronbach, L. J., & Snow, R. E. (1977). *Aptitudes and instructional methods*. New York: Irvington.

Curry, L. (1990). *Learning styles in secondary schools: a review of instruments and implications for their use*. Madison: National Center on Effective Schools, University of Wisconsin.

Daneman, M. (1991). Individual differences in reading skills. In R. Barr, M. L. Kamil, P. B. Mosenthal, & P. D. Pearson (Eds.), *Handbook of reading research* (Vol. 2, pp. 512–538). New York: Longman.

de Castell, S., Luke, A., & Egan, K. (Eds.). (1986). *Literacy, society, and schooling: A reader*. Cambridge, England: Cambridge University Press.

Donmoyer, R., & Kos, R. (Eds.). (1993). *At risk students: Portraits, programs, and practices*. Albany: State University of New York Press.

Ekwall, E. E. (Ed.). (1973). *Psychological factors in the teaching of reading*. Columbus, OH: Merrill.

Ekwall, E. E. (1985). *Locating and correcting reading difficulties*. Columbus, OH: Merrill.

Flood, J., Jensen, J. M., Lapp, D., & Squire, J. R. (Eds.). (1991). *Handbook of research in teaching the English language arts*. New York: Macmillan.

Fowler, W. (1986). Editor's notes. In W. Fowler (Ed.), *Early experience and the development of competence*. San Francisco: Jossey-Bass.

Francisco, N. (1994). *No will, no skill: Combining motivation and cognition in reading comprehension of African American middle school students*. Unpublished doctoral dissertation, Stanford University.

Freedman, S. W., & Calfee, R. C. (1984). Understanding and comprehending. *Written Communication, 1*, 459–490.

French, E. (1982). *The promotion of literacy in South Africa*. Pretoria: Human Services Research Council.

Garner, R. (1980). Monitoring of understanding: An investigation of good and poor readers' awareness of induced miscomprehension of text. *Journal of Reading Behavior, 12*, 55–64.

Garton, A., & Pratt, C. (1989). *Learning to be literate: The development of spoken and written language*. Oxford, England: Basil Blackwell.

Gilmore, P. (1986). Sub-rosa literacy: Peers, play, and ownership in literacy acquisition. In B. B. Schieffelin & P. Gilmore (Eds.), *The acquisition of literacy: Ethnographic perspectives* (pp. 155–168). Norwood, NJ: Ablex.

Globerson, T., & Zelniker, T. (1989). *Cognitive style and cognitive development*. Norwood, NJ: Ablex.

Goldberg, L. R. (1993). The structure of phenotypic personality traits. *American Psychologist, 48*, 26–34.

Graham, S., & Weiner, B. (in press). Motivational theory and education. In D. C. Berliner & R. C. Calfee (Eds.), *Handbook of educational psychology*. New York: Macmillan.

Greeno, J. G. (1989). A perspective on thinking. *American Psychologist, 44*, 134–141.

Harris, K. R. (1990). Developing self-regulated learners: The role of private speech and self-instructions. *Educational Psychologist, 25*, 35–49.

Hidi, S. (1992). *The role of interest in learning and development*. Hillsdale, NJ: Erlbaum.

Hladczuk, J., & Eller, W. (1992). *International handbook of reading education*. Westport, CT: Greenwood.

Howe, M, J. A. (1990). *The origins of exceptional abilities*. Oxford, England: Basil Blackwell.

Huey, E. B. (1908). *Psychology and pedagogy of reading*. New York: Macmillan.

Jackson, P. W. (Ed.). (1992). *Handbook of research on curriculum*. New York: Macmillan.

Kagan, J. (1965). Reflection-impulsivity and reading ability in primary grade children. *Child Development, 36*, 609–628.

Kozol, J. L. (1991). *Savage inequalities*. New York: Crown.

Lohman, D. F. (1993). Teaching and testing to develop fluid abilities. *Education Researcher, 22*, 12–23.

McGill-Franzen, A. M. (1993). *Shaping the preschool agenda: Early literacy, public policy and professional beliefs*. Albany: State University of New York Press.

McGuinness, D. (1985). *When children don't learn*. New York: Basic Books.

McKeown, M. G., & Curtis, M. E. (1987). *The nature of vocabulary acquisition*. Hillsdale, NJ: Erlbaum.

Meichenbaum, D. (1986). Cognitive behavior modification. In F. H. Kanfer & A. P. Goldstein (Eds.), *Helping people change: A textbook of methods* (3rd ed., pp. 346–380). New York: Pergamon.

Messick, S. (1987). Structural relationships across cognition, personality, and style. In R. E. Snow & M. J. Farr (Eds.), *Aptitude, learning, and instruction: Vol. 3. Conative and affective process analyses* (pp. 35–75). Hillsdale, NJ: Erlbaum.

Messick, S. (1994). The matter of style: Manifestations of personality in cognition, learning, and teaching. *Educational Psychologist, 29*, 121–136.

Meyer, B. J. F. (1975). *The organization of prose and its effects on memory*. Amsterdam: North-Holland.

Moffett, J., & Wagner, B. J. (1983). *Student-centered language arts and reading. K–13: A handbook for teachers* (3rd ed.). Boston: Houghton-Mifflin.

Mullis, I. V. S. (1991). *Trends in academic progress*. Princeton, NJ: Educational Testing Service.

National Assessment of Educational Progress. (1990). *Writing report card*. Princeton, NJ: Educational Testing Service.

Palincsar, A. S., & Brown, A. (1984). Reciprocal teaching of comprehension-fostering and comprehension-monitoring activities. *Cognition and Instruction, 1*, 117–175.

Palincsar, A. S., & Klenk, L. (1992). Fostering literacy learning in supportive contexts. *Journal of Learning Disabilities, 25*, 211–225.

Pavlidis, G. T., & Fisher, D. F. (Eds.). (1986). *Dyslexia: Its neuropsychology and treatment*. New York: Wiley.

Pearson, P. D. (Ed.). (1984). *Handbook of reading research*. New York: Longman.

Pearson, P. D. (1993). Teaching and learning reading: A research perspective. *Language Arts*, 70, 502–511.

Perfetti, C. A. (1985). *Reading ability*. New York: Oxford.

Rayner, K., & Pollatsek, A. (1989). *The psychology of reading*. Englewood Cliffs, NJ: Prentice-Hall.

Robinson, H. M. (1972). Visual and auditory modalities related to methods for beginning reading. *Reading Research Quarterly, 8*, 7–39.

Scardamalia, M., & Bereiter, C. (1986). Research on written composition. In M. C. Wittrock (Ed.), *Handbook of research on teaching* (3rd ed., pp. 778–803). New York: Macmillan.

Schonell, F. J. (1942). *Backwards in the basic subjects*. Edinburgh, Scotland: Oliver and Boyd.

Schunk, D. H. (1990). Goal setting and self-efficacy during self-regulated learning. *Educational Psychologist, 25*, 71–86.

Shavelson, R. J., & Webb, N. M. (1991). *Generalizability theory: A primer*. Newbury Park, CA: Sage.

Snow, R. E. (1982). Education and intelligence. In R. J. Sternberg (Ed.), *Handbook of human intelligence* (pp. 493–585). New York: Cambridge University Press.

Snow, R. E., Corno, L., & Jackson, D. N., III. (in press). Individual differences in affective and conative functions. In D. C. Berliner & R. C. Calfee (Eds.), *Handbook of educational psychology*. New York: Macmillan.

Snow, R. E., & Jackson, D. N., III. (in press). Individual differences in conation: Selected constructs and measures. In H. F. O'Neill, Jr. (Ed.), *Motivation: Research and theory*. San Diego, CA: Academic Press.

Snow, R. E., & Yalow, A. (1982). Education and intelligence. In R. Sternberg (Ed.), *Handbook of human intelligence*. New York: Cambridge University Press.

Sperling, M. (1993). *The social nature of written text: A research-based review and summary of conceptual issues in the teaching of writing*. Urbana, IL: National Council of Teachers of English.

Stanovich, K. E. (1986). Matthew effects in reading: Some consequences of individual differences in the acquisition of reading. *Reading Research Quarterly, 21*, 360–406.

Sternberg, R. J., Powell, J. S., & Kaye, D. B. (1985). Teaching vocabulary building skills: A contextual approach. In A. C. Wilkinson (Ed.), *Classroom computers and cognitive science* (pp. 121–143). New York: Academic Press.

Stevenson, H., Azuma, H., & Hakuta, K. (Eds.). (1986). *Child development and education in Japan*. New York: Freeman.

Stevenson, H. W., & Stigler, J. W. (1992). *The learning gap*. New York: Summit.

Stipek, D. (in press). Motivation and instruction. In D. C. Berliner & R. C. Calfee (Eds.), *Handbook of educational psychology*. New York: Macmillan.

Tuman, M. (1987). *A preface to literacy: An inquiry into pedagogy, practice, and progress*. Tuscaloosa: University of Alabama Press.

Vellutino, F. R. (1979). *Dyslexia: Theory and research*. Cambridge: MIT Press.

Voss, J. F., Fincher-Kiefer, R. H., Greene, T. R., & Post, T. A. (1985). Individual differences in performance: The contrast approach to knowledge. In R. J. Sternberg (Ed.), *Advances in the psychology of human intelligence* (Vol. 3). Hillsdale, NJ: Erlbaum.

Wigfield, A., & Asher, S. R. (1984). Social and motivational influences on reading. In P. D. Pearson (Ed.), *Handbook of reading research* (pp. 423–452). New York: Longman.

Williams, J. P. (1992). Literacy writ large: Review of A. Garton & C. Pratt, *Learning to be literate: The development of spoken and written language. Contemporary Psychology, 37*, 366–367.

Wittrock, M. C. (Ed.). (1986). *Handbook of research on teaching* (3rd ed.). New York: Macmillan.

Witty, P. A. (1969). Rate of reading—a critical issue. *Journal of Reading, 13*, 102–106, 154–163.

Yuill, N. M., & Oakhill, J. V. (1991). *Children's problems in text comprehension: An experimental investigation*. Cambridge, England: Cambridge University Press.

Zimmerman, B. J. (1990). Self-regulated learning and academic achievement: An overview. *Educational Psychologist, 21*, 3–18.

9

The Interface between Intelligence and Personality as Determinants of Classroom Learning

Monique Boekaerts

THE INTERFACE BETWEEN INTELLIGENCE AND PERSONALITY AS DETERMINANTS OF CLASSROOM LEARNING

I find it helpful to consider the relationship between intelligence and personality as determinants of classroom learning in terms of three broad questions:

- What is meant by intelligence in a scholastic context?
- What is meant by personality when studied in a scholastic context?
- What is the effect of mental ability and induced personality states on learning outcomes?

In dealing with the first two questions, I will review the relevant literature. I will then address the third question by presenting a heuristic model of the interaction between mental abilities and personality states. This model provides a useful tool for organizing most of the empirical findings reported in the literature, for identifying gaps in our knowledge, and for generating research questions about the interplay between cognitive and affective variables in relation to scholastic learning. This chapter is not a comprehensive review; it presents different conceptual approaches, citing supporting empirical evidence.

Monique Boekaerts • Leiden University, Center for the Study of Education and Instruction, 2300 RB Leiden, Netherlands.

International Handbook of Personality and Intelligence, edited by Donald H. Saklofske and Moshe Zeidner. Plenum Press, New York, 1995.

WHAT IS MEANT BY INTELLIGENCE IN A SCHOLASTIC CONTEXT

Intelligence Tests versus Achievement Tests

Intelligence in a scholastic context is denoted in a variety of ways, including as general intelligence, general mental ability, crystallized intelligence, fluid intelligence, general cognitive ability, higher scholastic aptitudes, overall aptitude, and higher scholastic ability. Researcher use these terms interchangeably to refer to a quality of behavior that is considered to be determined largely by innate factors. A distinction is drawn between intelligence and achievement, with the latter denoting something that is acquired at school and reflected in grades and standardized achievement tests. Furthermore, intelligence is considered a product of natural development, whereas achievement is believed to be a result of both the effort exerted by the learner and the quality of instruction.

Content analyses of intelligence and achievement

tests reveal considerable resemblance both in test items and in the cognitive processes they call forth. This likeness may account for the fact that correlations between measures of general cognitive ability and achievement have been found to be moderately positive. Jensen (1980) reported correlations that range from .60 to .70 in elementary education, from .50 to .60 in high school, and from .40 to .50 at the college level. It is noteworthy that the association between general cognitive ability and achievement is only moderately strong, and it decreases as students progress through the educational system. This suggests that the cognitive processes elicited by intelligence tests bear more resemblance to the subject matter in elementary education than to that in subsequent education.

Close analysis of the items contained in standard intelligence tests reveals that some measure skills that children are taught at school (e.g., reading comprehension or mathematical problem solving) but that most draw on cognitive skills that are not taught directly (e.g., mental rotation, finding embedded figures, solving number-series problems). The correspondences and contrasts between the cognitive processes evoked by achievement tests and intelligence tests correspond to Cattell's (1963) distinction between crystallized and fluid intelligence. The former measures the student's capacity to assemble and allocate general cognitive skills to solve problems in specific subject areas, whereas the latter assesses capacity to generate rules for solving problems with which the student has had little or no prior experience, and to apply these newly derived rules to novel problems. In recent years, several authors have argued that intelligence test scores only weakly represent the complex trait we refer to as general mental ability, and that they are unstable across populations and generations (e.g., Flynn, 1987).

Intelligence Redefined in Terms of Information-Processing Activities

Since the 1980s the work of Sternberg has had considerable influence on researchers' conceptualizations of mental ability. Sternberg (1985) proposed a triarchic theory of human intelligence in which intelligent behavior is demystified and broken down into three types of components: metacomponents, performance components, and knowledge acquisition components. Metacomponents are higher-order control processes that steer and regulate our behavior, including performance and knowledge acquisition components. Performance components consist of execution processes such as encoding, inferring, mapping, comparing information, responding, and justifying the response. Knowledge acquisition components are processes for dealing with new information, including selective encoding, selective combination, and selective comparison. The advantage of Sternberg's theory is that these same three components specify the information-processing activities that intelligent people engage in when deriving answers to intelligence test items, yet they also enable us to explore the mental processes characteristic of problem solving by "unintelligent" people.

In addition to shedding light on the mental processes that different people use when answering test questions, Sternberg (1986) clarified the distinction between automatization and novelty. He demonstrated that the performance of many kinds of complex tasks is only feasible when numerous subskills have been automatized. He suggests that there is a trade-off between automatization and novelty in the sense that the automatization of subskills frees attentional resources to generate solutions that take novel aspects of the situation into account. Hence the ability to solve novel problems may be the most sensitive index of intelligence we have.

Sternberg (1986) also refers to "intelligence in context"—the ability to effectively adapt to, shape, and select real-world environments in view of one's life circumstances and abilities. He reported that tacit knowledge (i.e., knowledge and skills that individuals pick up from the physical or social environment without explicit instruction) can be measured at different levels of expertise and is a good predictor of real-life performance, despite the fact that it is uncorrelated with conventional intelligence test scores. This finding suggests that mental ability as measured through decontextualized problem solving is dissimilar to mental ability used to perform context-bound problems.

Snow, Kyllonen, and Marshalek (1984) integrated an information-processing account of individual differences in cognitive ability with correlational evidence gathered in factor analytic studies of cognitive ability organization. They analyzed the data with the aid of multidimensional-similarity structure analysis and found that a radex structure provided an adequate representation of these cognitive interrelations. The more complex and general ability constructs were located in the center of the radex structure, whereas the more simple, specialized, and domain-specific abilities were distributed around the periphery. Continua of increasing information-processing complexity could be situated along the arrays of the radex, with increasing information-processing activity as one moves from the periphery to the center.

Metacognition and Self-Regulation

As early as 1916, Binet and Simon pointed to the vital role of metacognition in general intellectual functioning. Sternberg reintroduced the same ideas more than 60 years later. In the educational literature, metacognitive learning theory developed in parallel with Sternberg's theory of human intelligence, reflecting consonant thinking about higher-order mental abilities. Metacognitive theory helps the educationalist understand how students deal with novel learning tasks and learning situations, as well as with complex learning tasks in which they have to combine many subskills.

Brown (1978) and Flavell (1976) drew a distinction between cognitive strategies that a student can use in a specific content area, on the one hand, and metacognition, on the other. Cognitive strategies are an integral part of adequate information processing. They are potentially conscious and can be elementary (e.g., attention, rehearsal, retrieval) or complex (e.g., paraphrase, summary, elaboration). Metacognition can be broken down into metacognitive knowledge and metacognitive skills. The former refer to the student's naive theory about how his or her own cognitive system works and about the cognitive strategies required for specific learning tasks (e.g., How can I determine the message of a text? What strategies do I know for committing this type of information to memory?). Having access to this sort of declarative knowledge facilitates, but does not guarantee, appropriate learning or problem-solving behavior. Appropriate problem-solving behavior depends on the student's capacity to regulate his or her own learning (using such skills as orientation, planning, execution, monitoring, assessment, and remediation), together with knowledge about the information processing system and how it works. Brown emphasized that what marks experts in a particular domain is that they have access to metacognitive knowledge and skills. Activation of this information permits them to select relevant knowledge and skills and to incorporate the latter in a strategy for learning or problem solving.

Brown and Palincsar (1989) emphasize that although metacognitive knowledge and skills may improve as students get older, the acquisition of such knowledge and skills is not part of natural development. Based on a review of the literature, they conclude that deficiencies in metacognition seem to be a problem of the novice, regardless of age. Students who have more metacognitive knowledge are better problem solvers. Access to metacognitive knowledge enables them to manage novel and challenging tasks by generating task-appropriate cognitive strategies; in turn, direct and indirect experiences during task performance (as well as explicit instruction) help them improve their metacognitive knowledge, leading to improved performance. Hence a bidirectional causal link is hypothesized between metacognition, on the one hand, and strategy acquisition and use, on the other.

Changed Perspectives on Ability

In parallel with cognitive psychologists' exploration of students' metacognitive knowledge and skills, motivational researchers (e.g., Dweck, 1986; Nicholls, 1984) have made it clear that a distinction should be made between students who view ability as a fixed trait and those who consider it an incremental property. It has been shown that children who regard ability as a fixed capacity view their performance, errors, and performance feedback as mirroring their mental abilities. Negative feedback, deficient performance, public evaluation, and social comparison produce anxiety in these children, who fear that such activities may demonstrate that their intelligence is low. High effort is also regarded as threatening by these children, because they believe that failure despite high effort would confirm to the outside world that their mental abilities are deficient. In learning situations, these students display an ego orientation—that is, they avoid situations in which they can make errors and seek out situations in which they can demonstrate their existing abilities. This goal orientation minimizes possibilities for expanding knowledge and increasing competence.

By contrast, students who view ability as acquirable and malleable harbor a different goal orientation. They seek situations that will foster expansion of their knowledge and skills, and they consider effort, errors and feedback as natural ingredients of the learning process. In short, they judge their ability in terms of their capacity to assemble and distribute their resources to achieve gains in competence. Changed perspectives on ability over the past decade have opened the floodgates to training programs for boosting intelligence and metacognition.

Attempts to Raise Intelligence and Metacognition

Several authors, including Feuerstein (1980) and Lazar and Darlington (1982), have argued that intellectual stimulation in the home, in the extended home, or at school can lead to improvements in students' IQ scores, grades, and performance on achievement tests. Feuerstein designed an enrichment program for culturally deprived adolescents in which perceptual and problem-solving skills were explicitly taught. Together with his coworkers (Feuerstein, Jensen, Hoffman, & Rand, 1985) he identified subskills necessary for problem solving and taught these subskills to students in regular sessions scheduled two or three times a week over an extended period of time (2 or 3 years). These subskills included mental abilities assessed in traditional intelligence tests, such as those needed to solve embedded figures, analogies, number-series problems, and spatial relations. The training emphasized self-regulatory skills. The teacher provided scaffolding when necessary, but the students had to monitor their own learning. Promising results have been reported, but the main problem with assessing the results of these programs is that there are as yet no standardized assessment procedures.

Brown and Campione (1984) drew attention to the fact that flexible access to and use of knowledge are crucial not only for responding to items on intelligence tests, but also for intelligent problem-solving in any domain of knowledge. They hypothesized—and found—that there are ability-related differences both in the ease with which the rules required for solving relatively decontextualized problems are learned and in the breadth of transfer. They presented fluid intelligence test items to individuals representing a wide range of ages, providing instruction as needed to ensure that each individual learned the rules necessary to meet a standard criterion. Their research findings suggest that younger and lower-ability students are less able to deal with problems that require flexible use of previously learned rules. They also found that the lower the ability level of the student, the smaller the change in complexity required to elicit a disruption of performance. These findings suggest that dynamic learning and transfer measures that assess the number of interventions required to reach a stable level of performance provide more valuable indices of the sort of problem-solving ability demanded in a scholastic context than do more static intelligence tests.

Another line of research has focused on teaching students discrete strategies to enhance learning and raise performance. Evidence from these studies indicates that students can be taught to execute many discrete strategies and that their performance can be elevated accordingly. For example, Borkowski and Peck (1986) demonstrated that the provision of complete strategy instructions led to comparable posttest performance by gifted and average students. The average students' strategy use, however, did not match that of gifted students on a far-transfer task. By contrast, when students were given only partial strategy instruction, prior metacognitive knowledge predicted strategy use on both the trained task and far-transfer tasks (even when IQ was partialed out). On the basis of these and similar findings, it was concluded that the teaching of discrete strategies does not guarantee either self-regulated learning or improved classroom learning.

The positive link between metacognition on the one hand, and strategy use and transfer on the other, has been widely accepted following the success of a number of instructional training programs, including Palincsar and Brown's (1984) reading intervention program, Scardamalia and Bereiter's (1986) writing program, and Schoenfeld's (1985) mathematic problem-solving program. These programs took as their starting point the finding that experts in a particular area use strategic behavior tacitly acquired through long experience to facilitate their problem solving. The basic elements of a cognitive apprenticeship were incorporated in the respective programs by means of modelling, coaching, and fading methods. The researchers in each of these programs hypothesized (a) that strategic behavior is generated on the basis of metacognitive knowledge and guided by metacognitive skills, and (b) that when the components of strategic behavior are identified and treated as explicit educational targets (together with the application of problem-solving procedures), students will become better problem solvers in the respective domain. In each program researchers identified elements of expert practice and made them explicit instructional targets. Students were encouraged to apply problem-solving procedures while reflecting on their own problem solution process. These three studies provide evidence that students can acquire metacognitive knowledge and skills in the course of instructional programs and that such knowledge may lead to effective strategic behavior, reflected in higher performance on curricular tasks in the same domain.

Veenman (1993) investigated whether the rate of progression in novice discovery learning is determined predominantly either by intelligence or by metacognition (the independence model). He also investigated the alternative hypothesis that these two factors jointly determine the rate of discovery learning (the mixed model). His results indicated that metacognitive knowledge and skills are stable characteristics of the student across domains, and he found support for the mixed model. He suggested that less intelligent novices differ from more intelligent novices in that the former acquire metacognitive habits (rules of thumb, e.g., "think before you act") that still need to be translated into appropriate learning strategies, whereas the latter acquire metacognitive strategies directly through their experience with the task.

Aptitudes for Learning

Snow (1992) has argued that if one wants to describe and explain observed individual differences in goal attainment, some construct of aptitude is needed. In his view, aptitude for learning should be regarded as a potential for learning, or an initial state of the student that affects later learning. Hence he views aptitudes not merely as correlates of learning, but as propaedeutic (i.e., preparatory and conditional) to learning in a particular learning situation. It is the unique combination of aptitude for learning and actual learning that is in turn propaedeutic to future learning in the same domain. In Snow's account, students must continually assemble Sternberg-like components into strategies for task performance and change them flexibly as task performance proceeds.

On the basis of a vast body of empirical research using eye movement analyses and Sternberg-style componential analyses, Snow (1992) concluded as follows:

> Our continuing hypothesis is that aptitude differences in learning appear in the person-task interface as differences in within-person adaptation to the stream of continuing changes in within-task demands and opportunities. Learners construct their performances in instructional situations by drawing on their resources and assembling, reassembling, and controlling them to adapt to perceived needs and opportunities in the situation. We also think there are thresholds of task novelty and complexity for each person-task interface near which learning is optimal and flexible assembly and control functions are most needed. (p. 21)

Conclusion

So far this review has focused on the effect of higher mental processes on performance. The main conclusions are as follows:

1. Intelligence as measured by traditional intelligence tests is closely associated with metacognitive knowledge and skills, these constructs exerting reciprocal influence on each other.
2. Both are propaedeutic to strategic behavior and subsequent task performance.
3. Students who score high on these overlapping constructs can create an optimal internal environment which will lead to better strategy use and higher performance.
4. Lack of this propaedeutic condition can be remedied by explicit teaching.
5. A simple extension of the student's repertoire of strategies, however, is not enough to promote better learning; other skills are also propaedeutic to transfer and generalization.

In the next section, the available literature will provide the basis for a discussion of how learning outcomes, conceived as complex skill acquisition and problem solving, may also be affected by other personality variables.

WHAT IS MEANT BY PERSONALITY WHEN STUDIED IN A SCHOLASTIC CONTEXT?

Personality Variables Measured at Three Different Levels

Personality theorists traditionally regarded motivation and other affective measures (e.g., anxiety, self-efficacy, need achievement, intrinsic motivation) as stable personality traits. They believed that personality questionnaires could reliably measure the degree to which students experience anxiety, feelings of self-efficacy, or motivation to engage in educational tasks. Furthermore, they were of the opinion that scores on these traitlike measures could be used to study the effects of motivation and other affective variables on classroom learning. Mischel (1973) questioned the idea that the individual can be expected to display consistent behavior across a wide range of situations, arguing that individuals do not behave as consistently as psychologists had assumed. It has since been demonstrated that scores on personality tests administered to the same individuals twice over a rather long interval show relatively low test-retest correlations, but that personality questionnaires repeated in similar circumstances show more consistency. Mischel argued that cross-situational consistency can be understood in terms of the individual's personal reward system. He posited that consistency in behavior across situations will arise when the actor perceives the personal consequences of his or her behavior in these situations as similar.

Most theorists in the field of motivation and emotion now assume that students' self-referenced cognitions are context and situation specific. There is a vast body of literature documenting the role of students' beliefs, motivation, attributions, anxiety, and concerns in actual performance. Various theoretical models use slightly different constructs to articulate the idea that goal-directed learning is heavily influenced by self-referenced cognitions. These models include attribution theory (Weiner, 1986), self-worth theory (Covington, 1992), achievement motivation (Atkinson, 1965; Heckhausen, 1980), intrinsic motivation (DeCharms, 1984; Deci & Ryan, 1985; Harter, 1985), goal orientation (Dweck, 1986; Nicholls, 1984), action control theory (Kuhl, 1984), self-efficacy theory (Bandura, 1986), and stress theory (Lazarus & Folkman, 1984). Despite the wide variety of constructs and theoretical models, there is striking agreement that self-referenced cognitions can be seen as strong motivators or inhibitors of behavior: They influence the student's intention to learn by giving meaning and valence to tasks and situations.

There is insufficient space here to explicate each of these models separately or to detail the similarities and differences among them. I will instead concentrate on a selection of important findings. My selection is based on the distinction Cantor (1981) has made between personality variables measured at three different levels: the superordinate level, the middle level, and the subordinate level. She maintains that self-reports about situations can best be obtained at the middle level. When situations are formulated at the superordinate level (i.e., very abstractly), it is unclear how individuals conceptualize them. When formulated at the subordinate or momentary level, situations are too rich in detail, which means that respondents may be overwhelmed by their thoughts and feelings. At the middle level, situations provide just enough information to elicit thoughts, feelings, and behavior that are characteristic for the respondent in that type of situation.

It is important to note that most personality variables can and should be measured at all three levels. Indeed, each one allows us to examine the intricate relations between a personality characteristic and scholastic learning from a different angle. For example, motivational variables measured at the superordinate level represent the student's overall inclination to engage in scholastic learning, which is fueled by general motives (achievement motives, need affiliation, intrinsic motivation) and behavioral commitments based on these motives. Instruments for assessing motivation at the middle level measure students' tendency to react in a favorable or unfavorable way to particular domains of knowledge, given their self-referenced cognitions about the various subject areas. Finally, at the subordinate level, researchers measure students' selective sensitivity to specific learning situations, given their general inclination to engage in scholastic learning and their tendency to react in favorable or unfavorable ways to the subject area in question. Selective sensitivity is assumed to be reflected in momentary readiness or willingness to do what is necessary to achieve mastery or complete a learning task. The subordinate level of measurement is focused on actual performance; at this level the quality of the student's subjective experience of a concrete learning situation can be measured.

In view of space limitations, I will not review the literature on the measurement of personality variables at the superordinate level. Following Cantor, I have argued that in an educational context academic subject areas should be seen as the middle level, and that this is the optimal level for formulating situations when one's objective is to elicit characteristic attitudes and beliefs or to study strategies (Boekaerts, 1987). Indeed, during the course of their school career, students develop a variety of beliefs about school, about learning and teaching, and about the various subject domains. These beliefs may be rather weak at the beginning of elementary education, yet strengthen considerably once students have discovered that the different academic subjects can be regarded as domains of knowledge. In secondary education, the various subjects are taught by specific teachers who may have different teaching methods and evaluation procedures. And most importantly, levels of performance in the different subject areas are represented by separate grades with their own consequences. Hence it stands to reason that when students come to view learning activities in the various subject areas as functionally equivalent, and as equivalently linked to their personal reward system (i.e., as similar in terms of the perceived personal consequences of their behavior), cross-situational consistency in cognition, affect, and behavior in relation to these domains may be expected. In other words it is assumed that students form subcategories of the self (see the discussion of "current selves" and "ideal selves" by Cantor, Markus, Niedenthal, & Nurius, 1986) related to the various subject areas.

Consonant with this line of argument, I will devote the remainder of this section to a discussion of self-referenced cognitions triggered at the middle level. These cognitions arise through the interaction of personality variables with subject areas. More specifically, the interaction between the student's personality variables and a particular subject domain results in self-referenced cognitions and feelings vis-à-vis that domain. In the literature, a distinction has been made between three different types or sets of self-referenced cognitions. The first includes beliefs and judgments about the self in relation to the different subject areas; the second consists of the values that are attached to various situations, tasks, activities, courses, and careers; and the third entails concerns about ability and control.

Self-Referenced Cognitions: Beliefs about the Self

Burns (1982) defined self-concept as the perception individuals have of themselves, including their attitudes, feelings, and knowledge about their appearance, social acceptability, abilities, and skills. Shavelson and colleagues (e.g. Byrne & Shavelson, 1986) made several attempts to operationalize self-concept and proposed a multifaceted model of the construct. They predicted and found that the more a particular subset of self-concept is linked to a specific situation, the stronger the association is between the student's score on that facet of self-concept and the behavior displayed in that situation.

The facet of self-concept that has been most intensively studied is the academic self-concept. This has been investigated under different headings, including self-concept of ability, self-efficacy, success expectation, perceived controllability, and attributions of success and failure. Bandura (1986, 1993) argued that there are two basic ways in which an individual can perceive and exercise control over his or her environment—namely, through perceived self-efficacy and outcome expectation. The first form of control concerns individuals' beliefs about their performance capabilities in a particular domain. The second form of control has to do with students' beliefs that there is a contingent relation between their actions (e.g., performing an activity or task) and the outcome or consequences of their actions (e.g., staying out of trouble, getting high grades). I will briefly review some of the literature demonstrating the effects of self-efficacy and outcome expectation on performance and achievement.

Perceived Self-Efficacy

Bandura (1986) argued that self-efficacy in relation to a field of study is a very powerful motivator and instigator of behavior. When an activity or task is unfamiliar, or when individuals have reason to believe that their personal or social resources have altered in relation to that activity, they make efficacy judgments. These self-conceptualizations are based on direct and vicarious experiences, on persuasion, and on self-attributions. Numerous studies have shown that individuals' beliefs about their competence and control in relation to a domain of knowledge play a major role in their performance. In an educational context, self-efficacy refers to students' beliefs that they can accomplish specific types of academic tasks and thus achieve the educational goals embodied by these tasks. In other words, self-efficacy beliefs are the basis of self-confidence in a domain of study (as distinguished from global judgments of one's capabilities).

Students' self-referenced cognitions about their abilities have been measured with the aid of various questionnaires. In a review of the literature, Schunk (1985, 1991) concluded that students with high self-efficacy—reflected in high perceived personal control in a domain of study—score higher on tests of intelligence and on achievement tests, and also earn better grades, than students with low self-efficacy. Additionally, a positive link between self-judgments of ability on the one hand, and the use of cognitive and metacognitive strategies on the other hand, was demonstrated at the elementary (Paris & Oka, 1986), secondary (Pintrich & De Groot, 1990) and college levels (Pintrich & Garcia, 1991; Volet, 1991) in different subject areas (reading and writing skills, and mathematics). The association between self-judgments of ability and achievement is moderately strong. For example, Fennema and Sherman (1978) reported correlations between .22 and .47 for math, and Taube (1988) mentioned correlations between .49 and .56 for native language.

Importantly, Schunk has pointed out that self-efficacy contributes to the development of cognitive skills through two paths of influence: a direct path from self-efficacy to cognitive skills, and an indirect path via affective variables such as goal setting and initiating and sustaining qualitative effort. Schunk (1989) reported further that students who score low on self-efficacy can be trained to change their efficacy beliefs and that such changed beliefs prompt the use of more adequate cognitive strategies and foster higher achievement in math, reading, and writing.

Yet several authors have reported that in certain age groups, self-concept of ability and scholastic achievement are not reciprocally related. For example, Skaalvik and Hagtvet (1990) found no such reciprocal relation in the third and fourth grades. On the basis of data from a German longitudinal classroom environment study, Weinert, Schrader, and Helmke (1989) reported that a bidirectional relationship between self-concept of math ability and math achievement emerged only in the middle of the sixth grade. In the fifth grade, self-concept of math ability was significantly influenced by math achievement but did not exert a significant effect on such achievement. There are several plausible reasons for the lack of a reciprocal relation before the age of 12: Younger children may misjudge their capacities because of incomplete information about what they need to learn, misunderstandings concerning the nature of appropriate cognitive strategies and metacognitive skills, or inconsistent recognition of their efforts or ability by parents and teachers.

Several other researchers (e.g., Harter, 1982; Taube, 1988) have shown that children's beliefs about their own competence develop during elementary school years and that correlations between these beliefs and achievement increase as students grow older and more skillful. Newman and Wick (1987) showed that children aged 7 to 9 tend to overestimate their ability to perform specific tasks, and that they do not automatically modify perceptions of their ability following feedback. In this respect they differed significantly from children aged 10 to 11; however, this difference disappeared when the younger children had adequate domain-specific knowledge to perform the tasks. Berenson and Dweck (1986) reported that students' self-judgments of their ability declined in the course of primary education and then dropped sharply during junior high school. By contrast, other studies (e.g., Zimmerman & Martinez-Pons, 1990) yielded evidence of an increase in students' verbal and math self-efficacy as they moved through elementary education, junior high, and high school. These contradicting results could be an artifact of the measurement instruments used in the different studies: The self-concept of ability questionnaires call for a social comparison between perceived self-competence and perceived peer competence, whereas the self-efficacy measures ask students to give an indication of perceived capacities in a domain of study without any judgment of their peers.

Perceived Controllability

Let us now turn to students' views about the degree of control they have over their environment. Weiner (1986) described how students causally interpret their success and failure in a scholastic context. He explained that there are three dimensions along which causal attributions can be classified: locus of control, stability, and controllability. For example, students who believe that they have done poorly on a math test may ascribe their failure to the type of test used (external, variable, uncontrollable) rather than to low ability (internal, stable, uncontrollable) or lack of effort (internal, variable, controllable).

There is a large body of research on the relations between controllability attributions and academic achievement. In literature reviews, Findley and Cooper (1983) and Whitley and Frieze (1985) concluded that students generally attribute success to internal factors (effort and ability) and failure to external factors (luck, task difficulty). In general, students who perceive their ability in relation to a domain of study as low tend to display avoidance behavior and are less likely to invest effort. There are also some studies demonstrating a positive link between beliefs about controllability on the one hand, and the use of cognitive and metacognitive strategies on the other. Borkowski and associates (e.g., Borkowski, Carr, Rellinger, & Presley, 1990; Schneider, Borkowski, Kurtz, & Kerwin, 1986) showed that successful students not only possess knowledge about efficient strategy use but also know when it will take effort to apply these strategies successfully. Students who attributed their memory performance to controllable factors (e.g., effort) not only showed better performance on various memory tasks than students who did not but also displayed more appropriate cognitive strategies and more metacognitive knowledge.

It is in fact strange that children in elementary school explain success and failure predominantly in terms of effort (or lack of it), and that as they grow older ability and lack of ability seem to become more dominant attributions. Nicholls (1984) called attention to this pattern and showed that effort and ability are not clearly differentiated from each other until the age of 11. Young children seem to view ability in a self-referenced manner as "learning through effort." A more mature conception of ability involves a social comparison in which the effort and time required to reach performance are taken into account. Adolescents conceive of ability as capacity relative to others; they determine their capacity within a subject area by direct experiences, by comparing their performance and effort expenditure with that of their peers, and by the presence or absence of physiological symptoms. Unlike primary school students, adolescents realize that effort may compensate for low ability, thus masking true ability. This belief may lead to hiding of effort, avoidance of effort, and a focus on external control.

The findings of Schneider et al. (1986) cast doubt on the universality of the positive influence of effort attribution on strategy use and achievement which has been demonstrated primarily by data from North American students. These researchers' investigation of the interrelations between performance, metacognition, strategy use, and attributions in German and American students indicated that there might be a critical level of perceived task complexity and difficulty below which German students do not consider effort a favorable attribution.

Self-Referenced Cognitions: Beliefs about Subject Areas

Students may develop a variety of beliefs about different tasks, activities, and subject areas. For example, they may value history not only because they find the subject interesting but also because they find it important and relevant to their everyday functioning or career. In addition, they may find that history texts help them gain a deeper understanding of their environment and of people's habits. Relevance or utility judgments focus on the instrumentality of an activity or situation for achieving valued goals; importance judgments have to do with priority in the student's goal structure; and interest refers to preference for a deeper understanding of some content area. In the literature on motivation, these aspects of task evaluation have been captured under four different headings: task value, goal orientation, interest, and attitudes. I will briefly discuss each of these constructs in the following sections.

Task Value

The construct of task value stems from expectancy × value theory (see Atkinson, 1965). It refers to the significance an individual attaches to success and failure, in view of task difficulty and the probability of success. Eccles (1983) extended this construct to include task characteristics as well as the goals and needs of the student. She proposed three components of task value: the utility value of the task for future goals, intrinsic interest in the task, and the student's perception of the importance of the task. Eccles describes utility value in terms of the student's perceptions of the usefulness of the task for future goals (e.g., career). She assumes that students who find a particular academic subject important for their career preparation will be more committed to that subject area and thus demonstrate greater effort.

Interest, in contrast, is viewed as the student's general attitude toward and degree of liking for learning tasks. Hence interest reflects both students' preferences for and their perceptions of learning tasks. Eccles assumes that students who are interested in specific tasks or courses will choose them and get involved in them more than students who are not interested. Finally, the student's perception of the importance of a task is related to his or her goal orientation. Given the same goal orientation, however, students who attach greater importance to a particular skill may select different tasks, perform them with more vigor, and persist longer in the face of difficulties than students who do not attach importance to that skill.

Goal Orientation

Goal orientation refers to the student's reason for learning, as reflected in his or her approach to the learning material. Two basic goal orientations have been identified, although they have been given different names by different research groups: for example, ego versus task orientation (Nicholls, 1984), performance versus learning orientation (Dweck, 1986), and extrinsic versus intrinsic orientation (Harter, 1981). This dichotomy distinguishes between students who prefer situations in which they can demonstrate their superior ability and avoid making errors and those who seek out situations that will enable them to expand their knowledge and skills.

It has been assumed that goal orientation guides and directs students' cognitions, affects, and behavior during learning episodes. More specifically, Pintrich and his coworkers (Pintrich & De Groot, 1990; Pintrich & Garcia, 1991; Pintrich & Schrauben, 1992) hypothesized that the two types of goal orientation are linked to different patterns of cognitive engagement. They predicted and found that students of various ages who demonstrated an intrinsic orientation toward learning selected deeper processing strategies and were more apt to select appropriate cognitive and metacognitive strategies. Similar results were reported by Meece, Blumenfeld, and Hoyle (1988) in the domain of science and by Nolen (1988) in the domain of text comprehension. Their results suggest that ego-oriented students who focus on themselves rather than on the learning activity use more superficial processing strategies than students who value learning and understanding.

As Pintrich and Garcia (1991) have demonstrated, however, students may simultaneously have both an ego and a task orientation. For example, some students may be inherently interested in the course material but also be concerned about the assessment techniques used by the teacher. Hence concerns about evaluation might lead these students to opt for a risk-avoiding surface strategy even though they might otherwise have selected deeper processing strategies.

Interest

Measures of extrinsic versus intrinsic motivational orientation are based on the assumption that students are either intrinsically or extrinsically motivated. Schiefele (1991) expressed doubt as to whether this is always the case. His research supports the idea that the student develops specific relationships with the various subject domains, and that each relationship is reflected in the student's specific interest in that domain. Hence, in his view, a content-specific intrinsic motivational orientation should be distinguished from general motivational orientation and from attitudes. Interest in a domain of study should therefore be defined in terms of both a value-related and a feeling-related component. The former reveals the personal significance of a specific topic or activity for the student; the latter refers to feelings of involvement and enjoyment. Schiefele (1992) found that college students who showed interest in text comprehension not only recalled more information but also used cognitive strategies that reflected deep-level processing (i.e., they reported using less rehearsal and more elaboration strategies, sought more information, and engaged more in critical thinking than students who showed less interest and displayed surface-level processing).

Hidi (1990), in a summary of the literature, concluded that interest has a profound effect on students' attentional and retrieval processes, their acquisition of knowledge, and their effort expenditure. Students who score high on interest want to become involved in a subject domain for its own sake; they do not necessarily spend more time on tasks and activities for which they show interest, but the quality of their interaction with the material is superior. Schiefele, Krapp, and Winteler (1992) conducted a meta-analysis on the relation between measures of interest in specific subject areas and achievement. Based on 121 independent samples, they found an average correlation coefficient of .31.

Attitudes

In the psychological literature, attitudes are defined as the individual's predisposition to respond in a favorable or unfavorable way to a particular person, object, event, idea, situation, or other stimulus. The construct consists of three interrelated components—cognitive, affective, and behavioral. In the educational literature, though, attitudes have been defined differently. Some authors use the construct in an overinclusive way, integrating such diverse constructs as like and dislike of an academic subject, anxiety aroused by the subject matter, self-confidence, perceived difficulty level, and perceived importance; other researchers measure attitudes only in terms of beliefs (the cognitive component) or emotional reactions (the affective component). Reyes (1984) studied attitudes toward mathematics and reported that of all the aspects that had been investigated, only confidence about learning and doing mathematics had been shown to be consistently related to achievement in mathematics.

Helmke (1993) reported the results of a longitudinal study in which the affective component of students' attitudes toward mathematics were measured from kindergarten to the end of elementary education. He reported that at the beginning of elementary education children have positive attitudes toward mathematics and learning their native language. In the beginning of the second year of formal schooling, however, a drop in the pleasure reported in doing arithmetic tasks was noted. This decrease was most evident for girls. The downward slope continued for boys as well as for girls in subsequent years, although boys showed a brief increase in reported pleasure at the end of the third year. It is interesting to note that students with negative attitudes toward math did not differ from their peers in their scores on standardized intelligence tests.

It was also observed that the association between attitude toward math and achievement in math became stronger from the second year onward. Further, students who had positive attitudes at the end of the second year had higher grades in the third year; conversely, successful performance at the end of the second year predicted attitudes toward math in the subsequent year. Helmke explains the sharp rise in the correlation between attitudes and achievement, as well as the simultaneous emergence of a bidirectional relationship between these variables, on the basis of his interview data: Once the taking home of school reports has become standard practice, success and failure experiences are seen by the children as consequential in nature. These experiences then start to affect their self-referenced cognitions, especially their attitudes.

Self-Referenced Cognitions and Feelings: Anxiety

A topic related to beliefs about the self and about specific subject areas is anxiety, or self-referenced concerns. Task-irrelevant cognitions (e.g., worry) and concomitant emotions (e.g., tension) have traditionally been studied in terms of the constructs of test anxiety, state and trait anxiety, and cognitive interference (see Covington & Omelich, 1984; Sarason, 1984). The effect of anxiety on student achievement has been researched extensively. Deffenbacher and Hazaleus (1985) assert that feelings of increased arousal occur in both high and low test-anxious students, although these groups may show differences in intensity and duration of the increased arousal. These researchers furthermore argued that students who experience low and high levels of test anxiety differ primarily in the way they interpret the increased level of arousal and in how they cope with physiological tension and intrusive thoughts. A vast amount of evidence attests to the detrimental effects that intrusive thoughts (task-irrelevant cognitions) during instruction and exams can have on cognitive functioning (for a meta-analysis, see Heembree, 1988).

Many researchers (Covington & Omelich, 1984; Eysenck, 1987; Sarason, 1984) have reported that concerns and intrusive thoughts about one's own incompetence may attenuate or block task-relevant information processing. Further, the fact that anxiety does not seem to affect grossly overlearned skills, yet usually does impair higher-order cognitive processes, suggests that self-referenced concerns affect strategy use (e.g., impair the encoding and retrieval of information). Many researchers have postulated that self-referenced concerns about ability and control compete with task-relevant information for processing capacity in working memory, and that this competition impedes performance.

There are, however, some puzzling effects. For example, Pintrich and De Groot (1990) found that test anxiety (conceptualized as a high level of concern about test-taking skills) was negatively related to self-efficacy, exam performance, and grades, but not to seatwork or essay writing. They also reported that test anxiety was not significantly related, in either a linear or a nonlinear fashion, to strategy use or metacognitive skills. These findings were taken as an indication that, at least for seventh-grade students, self-referenced concerns during a test impair retrieval rather than encoding or self-regulation skills. In a dissimilar vein, Wieland (1984) reported that anxious individuals increased their efforts following failure, exerting more effort (as measured by physiological activity, behavioral involvement, and subjective ratings) than nonanxious subjects with equal or inferior performance. Increased speed of performance produced an increase in the quantity, but not the quality, of the output. This finding can be interpreted in the light of Leventhal's (1980) parallel response model, which draws a distinction between anxiety control and danger control in response to threatening stimuli or events. Anxiety control is primarily based on internal information and is geared toward the reduction of tension and discomfort; danger control is based on environmental information and seeks to limit or control the threat through increased effort.

In a longitudinal study conducted by Meece, Wigfield, and Eccles (1990), increased anxiety was found to be a consequence of negative self-perceptions of ability. Perceived ability measured in the seventh grade directly and positively predicted both mathematics expectancies and importance ratings in ninth grade. Students' initial perceptions of their mathematical ability also had both a direct and an indirect effect on anxiety in the ninth grade (the latter effect was mediated by importance and expectancy ratings; see also Helmke, 1989, cited below).

Conclusion

In the second part of this review, it was argued that personality variables interact with subject areas and that students gradually form subcategories of the self (both current and ideal selves) in relation to the various academic subjects. In view of space limitations, the main focus was on the effect of self-referenced cognitions on strategy use and performance. (I use the term *self-referenced cognitions* to refer to the student's skill to react in a favorable or unfavorable way to the different domains of knowledge, based on beliefs and feelings about the self and about the various subject areas.) The main conclusions are as follows:

1. Several overlapping key constructs referring to self-referenced cognitions and feelings have been identified. These overlapping constructs include self-efficacy, self-concept of ability, perceived controllability, task value, goal orientation, intrinsic motivation and interest, attitudes, and concerns.
2. Favorable beliefs about the self are associated with higher achievement and better grades, and positively affect strategy use.
3. Favorable beliefs about a subject matter are propaedeutic to the quality of the interaction with learning materials (surface vs. deep level of processing), for strategy use, and for the selection of metacognitive skills.
4. Favorable self-referenced cognitions create an optimal internal milieu that leads to higher achievement and better grades.
5. Unfavorable self-referenced cognitions can be changed, and such changed beliefs prompt the use of more appropriate cognitive strategies.
6. Anxiety is negatively associated with self-efficacy, exam performance, and grades but is not related to strategy use and metacognitive skills.

WHAT IS THE EFFECT OF MENTAL ABILITY AND PERSONALITY STATES ON LEARNING OUTCOMES?

Research on higher mental processes and metacognition has clarified many aspects of cognitive functioning in a classroom context. The cognitive model that has emerged from this research allows us to describe student learning as it happens in real classroom situations. There is abundant evidence that students with high general cognitive ability have the potential to regulate their own learning process and are, as such, less dependent on scaffolding procedures provided by the teacher than are students with lower general cognitive ability. A second line of research suggests that ability to learn is only half of the story: Willingness or inclination to learn also comes into play in complex learning. Once students have come to see tasks and activities in a particular subject domain as functionally equivalent and have linked them to their personal reward system, cross-situational consistency in cognitions and behavior in relation to that domain may be expected. More specifically, favorable beliefs about a subject area (reflected in high interest, positive attitude, or task involvement) and favorable self-perceptions of ability (high scores on self-concept of ability, self-efficacy, or perception of control) are propaedeutic to learning.

Until the middle of the 1980s few attempts had been made to study the joint effects of cognitive and affective variables on learning outcomes. The first large-scale attempts to study the integration and interface of self-referenced cognitions and mental ability as determinants of learning outcomes were inspired by changed conceptualizations of ability (entity vs. incremental property), which led to revised ideas about goal orientation and about the nature of learning. Rapid progress in our understanding of the separate and joint effects of mental ability and self-referenced cognitions was stimulated by reports from many research groups that much of the knowledge children acquire in school remains inert, and that taking a skill from one domain to another requires deliberate effort on the part of teachers and students. Teachers need to provide powerful learning environments in which students can apply new skills in many different contexts (see Resnick, 1987; Salomon & Perkins, 1990). Students, for their part, need to make willful attempts to regulate their learning process. These types of self-regulatory skills include not only metacognitive skills but also the selection and coordination of multiple strategies (cognitive, emotional, motivational, and social), the maintenance of these strategies in the face of difficulties, and strategy modification when desired outcomes are not achieved (Corno & Mandinach, 1983; Kuhl, 1984).

In order to integrate the hitherto separately developed lines of research, new models had to be designed. A good starting point for many research groups was the influential work of Bandura (1986), who views self-referenced cognitions as strong motivators or inhibitors of self-regulatory behavior. He holds (see also Bandura, 1993) that all purposeful human behavior is regulated by anticipatory scenarios that are constructed and rehearsed. Students who have favorable self-referenced cognitions in relation to a specific domain may visualize success scenarios that serve to guide and support their performance. Such students are confident that they can achieve self-set and teacher-set goals by making use of their capabilities and resources. By contrast, students who doubt their efficacy in a particular domain of study visualize failure scenarios and dwell on the many things that can go wrong. Because of self-doubts about their capabilities, these students also think that effort will not influence their learning. In the same vein, Masterpasqua (1989) wrote that a history of failure to acquire important competencies will mean few possibilities and few favorable "possible selves."

The Interface between Objective and Subjective Competence

According to Masterpasqua (1989) individuals differentiate between their competencies in various domains. These self-conceptualizations of competence depend on the recognition of possibilities. Masterpasqua made a distinction between objective competence and subjective competence: The former refers to "personal characteristics (knowledge, skills and attitudes) which lead to adaptive pay-offs in significant environments" or "learned attitudes and aptitudes, manifested as capacities for confronting, actively struggling with and mastering life problems through the use of cognitive and social skills"; the latter entails "the emotional and motivational significance of an individual's appraisals and expectations of his or her adaptive abilities rather than . . . the abilities themselves" (p. 1366). The significance of these concepts in education depends on their power to predict academic achievement. In the following pages, I will review some recent studies investigating the interplay between objective and subjective competence and their effect on performance and grades.

Kurtz and Weinert (1989) conducted a study of fifth- and seventh-grade German students who had been identified as either gifted or average students. The authors found that average students differ from their gifted peers in that they possess less advanced metacognitive knowledge, independent of age. Further, they are less likely to attribute success to ability, attributing it instead more often to effort. Kurtz and Weinert studied the separate and joint effects of three exogenous variables—intelligence, metacognition, and beliefs about effort control—on the students' strategy use and performance on a novel task (a word-sorting task followed by recall under time pressure). Causal modeling procedures on the entire sample showed metacognition to be a much stronger predictor of performance (word recall with time constraints) than either control beliefs or scores on traditional intelligence tests. Metacognition influenced recall both directly and indirectly via strategy use (i.e., the type of clustering procedures used in the card-sorting task). No significant paths were detected from either intelligence or effort control to the endogenous constructs (strategy use and recall performance).

This study is especially interesting because separate models were constructed for data from the gifted and average samples. Comparison of these models reveals more of the underlying mechanism linking strategy use to performance. It was found that metacognition remained an important predictor of strategy use in both samples, yet there were interesting differences as well. For the average students, performance on the recall task was not predicted by strategy use; in this group there was only a direct path leading from metacognition to performance. For the gifted students, there was no direct path from metacognition to performance, but a strong path from strategy use to performance.

These results suggest that students who have appropriate metacognitive knowledge about the skills required to perform a novel task can deal better with the task. In the case of gifted students, this is because they can generate task-appropriate cognitive strategies during task performance. The fact that a direct link between strategy use and performance was only evident among the gifted suggests that these students can profit more than their average peers from their experience with clustering strategies. I would suggest that simply generating appropriate cognitive strategies during task performance does not guarantee their efficient use in recall. Gifted students, more so than their average peers, may be capable of acquiring cognitive strategies directly from their experience with a task *and* integrating them into their repertoire of available strategies (see Veenman, 1993, and Borkowski & Peck, 1986, quoted above). An alternative hypothesis is that the average students could have been hindered more by the time limit on recall; self-referenced concerns could have impaired their retrieval (see Pintrich & De Groot, 1990, quoted above). It remains to be demonstrated that retrieval in the absence of time limits would yield the same results.

From these findings it may also be inferred that the influences of both intelligence and effort attribution are relatively weak in comparison with that of metacognitive knowledge. This implies that mental ability as measured by intelligence tests is less powerful in predicting learning outcomes than are metacognitive skills that bear directly on learning tasks. The findings do not, however, imply that self-referenced cognitions are less powerful predictors of performance and strategy use than metacognitive knowledge. Kurtz and Weinert (1989) examined only one aspect of self-referenced cognitions—namely, effort control—and it is not clear that the students they studied perceived the target task as difficult and requiring effort. Hence generalizations to other forms of self-referenced cognitions are not in order. It would be informative if future studies investigated the separate and joint effects of metacognitive knowledge, on the one hand, and self-perceptions of self-regulation, on the other, on recall measured with and without time constraints.

In this respect, Zimmerman, Bandura, and Martinez-Pons (1992) have pointed out that knowledge about appropriate strategy use will not contribute much to performance if students cannot convince themselves that these strategies should be applied persistently and flexibly, even in the face of distractions and stressors. Zimmerman and Martinez-Pons (1990) studied youngsters who attended a separate high school for the gifted and compared their performance and their self-efficacy judgments with age peers who attended a high-quality regular high school. The results indicated that students' perceptions of both their verbal and mathematics efficacy were associated with their use of self-regulated learning strategies. As expected, the gifted students displayed higher levels of self-efficacy in the verbal and math domains, and different developmental patterns in their verbal and math efficacy, than the regular students. The gifted students also displayed greater organizing and transforming skills, relied more heavily on self-recorded notes for reviewing procedures, and took greater advantage of peer and adult (teacher and parental) resources than the regular students.

Zimmerman et al. (1992) studied the impact of prior achievement and self-referenced cognitions on grade level in high school students. They distinguished between two types of self-referenced cognitions: self-efficacy for self-regulated learning, and self-efficacy for academic tasks. The former was defined in terms of perceived efficacy to structure environments that are conducive to learning, to plan and organize one's own learning activities, to use internal (strategies) and external (social) resources, to motivate oneself for schoolwork, and to show persistence and commitment. Causal modeling procedures showed that the higher students' perceptions of self-efficacy were for regulated learning, the more self-confident they were about their ability to master academic subjects. In turn, these favorable perceptions led to higher grades both directly and indirectly (by raising the student's grade goals). The students' past grades, which can be seen as a rough indication of their prior knowledge (objective competence) in an academic subject, affected their present grades only indirectly via parental grade goals, which in turn influenced the students' grade goals. In this sample of high school students no direct effect of prior grades on current grades was found, whereas the students' beliefs about their self-regulatory and academic skills did affect their grades both directly and indirectly (via their goals). These results suggest that in high school students who have the resources to succeed in school, self-referenced cognitions about their capacity to guide and direct their own learning are more powerful predictors of academic achievement than is previous academic achievement.

In the German longitudinal classroom environment study, Helmke, Schneider, and Weinert (1986) also investigated causal direction and causal predominance in the relation between academic achievement and affective variables. Helmke (1989) reported on the relative impact of math achievement on self-concept of math ability in the beginning of the fifth grade and again 2 years later. With the aid of LISREL analyses, he found a direct effect of earlier on later math achievement, but no confirmation of a direct effect of self-concept on math achievement. Several indirect effects, however, were demonstrated. First, positive self-concept of math ability promoted math achievement by reducing self-referenced concerns during test taking (cognitive interference). Second, students with a positive self-concept of their math ability invested more qualitative effort, which led to higher achievement on the math posttest. More specifically, these students exerted more mental effort during the instruction process, which was reflected in higher perseverance and engagement. By contrast, students with an unfavorable self-concept in math spent more quantitative effort (time on homework). Quantitative effort increased self-referenced concerns during test taking and exerted a negative effect on math achievement.

These results, which have been endorsed by several authors (Oka & Paris, 1987; Pintrich & De Groot, 1990; Skinner, Wellborn & Connell, 1990), suggest that the influence of self-concept on later achievement is mediated by effort expended on the task, and to a lesser degree by the absence of self-referenced concerns. It is also interesting to note that in addition to a direct effect, there were indirect effects of pretest math achievement on posttest math achievement; these effects strongly resembled those found for self-concept. More specifically, students who scored high on the math pretest invested more qualitative effort, which led to higher achievement on the math posttest, whereas students with low math self-concept spent more quantitative effort, which increased self-referenced concerns and thereby produced a negative effect on math achievement. Like positive self-concept, then, high pretest math achievement reduced cognitive interference.

In sum, the data from the German longitudinal classroom environment study reveal that objective competence is a more powerful predictor of later math achievement than subjective competence. The total effect (direct and indirect) of the former variable on achievement was .62, whereas the total effect of the latter variable was .12. This was not the case in the study reported by Zimmerman et al. (1992), where the total impact of self-referenced cognitions on later grades was .19, whereas that of objective competence (as reflected in prior grades) was only .04. Obviously, more research is needed to gain insight into the developmental aspects of these relations. The findings that have been discussed, which reflect samples from different age groups, together suggest that once the reciprocal relationship between self-perception of ability and achievement has emerged (at about the age of 11), learning outcomes and self-referenced cognitions will continue to fuel one another. From this age onward, current self-conceptions will be continuously elaborated and restructured, and new ones will be added. Hence well-elaborated self-concepts of ability in various domains will gradually take shape and become available in encounters with new learning tasks.

The research discussed so far explored the interaction between objective and subjective competence at the middle level. Objective competence was defined as either prior achievement, intelligence, or metacognitive knowledge; subjective competence was operationalized as students' beliefs about an academic subject, about their academic studies, or about their efficacy concerning the use of self-regulatory skills. It is important to note, however, that a student's perceptions of learning tasks and learning situations, and the dominant emotions they elicit, may change drastically both over a student's academic career and in the course of skill development. It can be assumed that any learning opportunity finds the learner not only at a certain stage of skill development but also with a certain degree of confidence in relation to that skill. This means that the favorableness of students' beliefs about a topic or course, and about their ability in that topic or course, may vary depending on the exact timing of questionnaire administration. Or, to put it differently, the measurement instrument that registers the students' self-perceptions concerning subject areas at the middle level provides only a glimpse of a complex and continually changing network of connotations.

If we want to gain insight into the dynamics of the interaction between objective and subjective competence, we ought to measure this interaction at the subordinate level as well. This level focuses on actual performance and thus allows for the measurement of selective sensitivity to particular aspects of the learning environment as reflected in the quality of the subjective experience, as well as situation-specific learning intention and effort expenditure.

Experiential States

Csikszentmihalyi and Nakamura (1989) used the signal-contingent method of sampling to study the effect of experiential variables on student achievement. They asked gifted secondary school students to carry an electronic pager and to answer a set of questions about their cognitions, moods, and activities whenever they were beeped during the day. For example, intrinsic motivation or involvement was measured with the question, "Do you wish you had been doing something else at this moment?" A negative answer to this question was seen as an indication of task involvement at the time of paging. A number of basic dimensions of experiential state were distinguished: potency, affect, cognitive efficiency, and involvement. By aggregating repeated self-reports on the same activities over a 1-week period, the students' experiential state was determined. The results displayed that doing homework or working in class are, in general, nonrewarding experiences compared to other activities in daily life. Most adolescents reported that the former activities made them feel bored, sad, lonely, passive, constrained, and detached. Those students who showed involvement in an academic subject, however, earned better grades for that subject.

Schiefele and Csikszentmihalyi (in press) studied the quality of subjective experience in class. They asked students attending a high-quality high school to carry a pager for 1 week and to complete a set of questions on their experiential state whenever they were paged. Five dimensions of experiential state were distinguished: potency (an active/excited vs. passive/bored state of mind), concentration, intrinsic motivation or involvement, self-esteem/satisfaction, and perception of skill level (high/low). In addition, they measured the students' interest in four different academic subjects; students were asked to indicate on 5-point rating scales the extent to which each subject was their favorite. Ability (Scholastic Aptitude Test, measures of basic mathematical reasoning skills and verbal skills, including knowledge of grammar, understanding of sentence structure, and rhetorical skills) was the strongest predictor of grades, followed by interest and achievement motivation (measured at the superordinate level). Interest contributed significantly to the explained variance in grades for mathematics, biology, and history, but not for native language. The interest-achievement relation proved to be independent of level of ability and achievement motivation.

Contrary to the researchers' hypothesis, not a single dimension of experience was affected by scholastic ability, which was an even weaker predictor than achievement motivation. Interest significantly predicted the quality of experience, and controlling for achievement motivation and for ability did not decrease the strength of the association. On the basis of these findings, it was suggested that students' experiential states in academic settings, as reflected in their subjective perceptions of their skills and in their induced motivational and emotional states at the time of learning, are governed mainly by motivational variables (subjective competence). Objective competence did not play a role of any importance. These findings suggest that interest in a specific content area can only be maintained as long as learning activities provide positive experiential states (see also Helmke, 1993, quoted above).

Induced Motivational States

Selective sensitivity to learning situations is reflected not only in the quality of the subjective experience but also in momentary readiness or willingness to engage in a task. Elsewhere (Boekaerts, 1992) I have argued that by studying student cognitions, feelings, and behavior in context, one can gain insight into the person-environment transactional units that form the basis for goal-directed behavior. This information can in turn elucidate the mechanisms of motivated behavior. These principles underlie my model of the adaptable learning process, which I have presented and elaborated elsewhere (Boekaerts, 1987, 1992, 1993). The model is hierarchically structured in the sense that objective and subjective competence measured at the superordinate and middle levels are believed to exert an indirect effect on the student's learning intention and experiential state via appraisals. Learning intention may be defined as willingness to invest effort to accomplish learning goals.

The model of adaptable learning draws heavily on the work of several leading psychologists, including Bandura, Kuhl, Lazarus and Folkman, and Cantor. I will briefly describe the model here, because it clarifies the relationship between objective and subjective competence and links them to two parallel information-processing systems—the learning system, and the well-being system. Although the model is used to study the interface between cognitive and affective variables at the subordinate or momentary level, I also find it a useful tool for organizing the empirical literature discussed in this review and for identifying gaps in our current knowledge.

Adaptable learning, or self-regulated learning, may be regarded as an ideal form of learning. Students are said to be learning in an adaptable way when they have found a balance between two parallel priorities: enlarging their available personal resources (competence and social resources), and preventing loss of resources and distortions of well-being. Appraisals assume a central position in the model (component 4) because they are seen as steering mechanisms directing the student's attention and energy either to adaptive payoffs in significant environments (increase in competence) or to the prevention of losses of resources (pathways 5 and 6, respectively).

Further, the model posits that learning activities trigger a network of highly specific connotations because they impinge on a learner's personal strivings and vulnerabilities. This is represented in the model by the link between appraisals and the contents of a dynamic internal working model (WM) that is constantly fed information from three main sources. The first source of information is the perception of the task and the physical, social, and didactic context in which it is

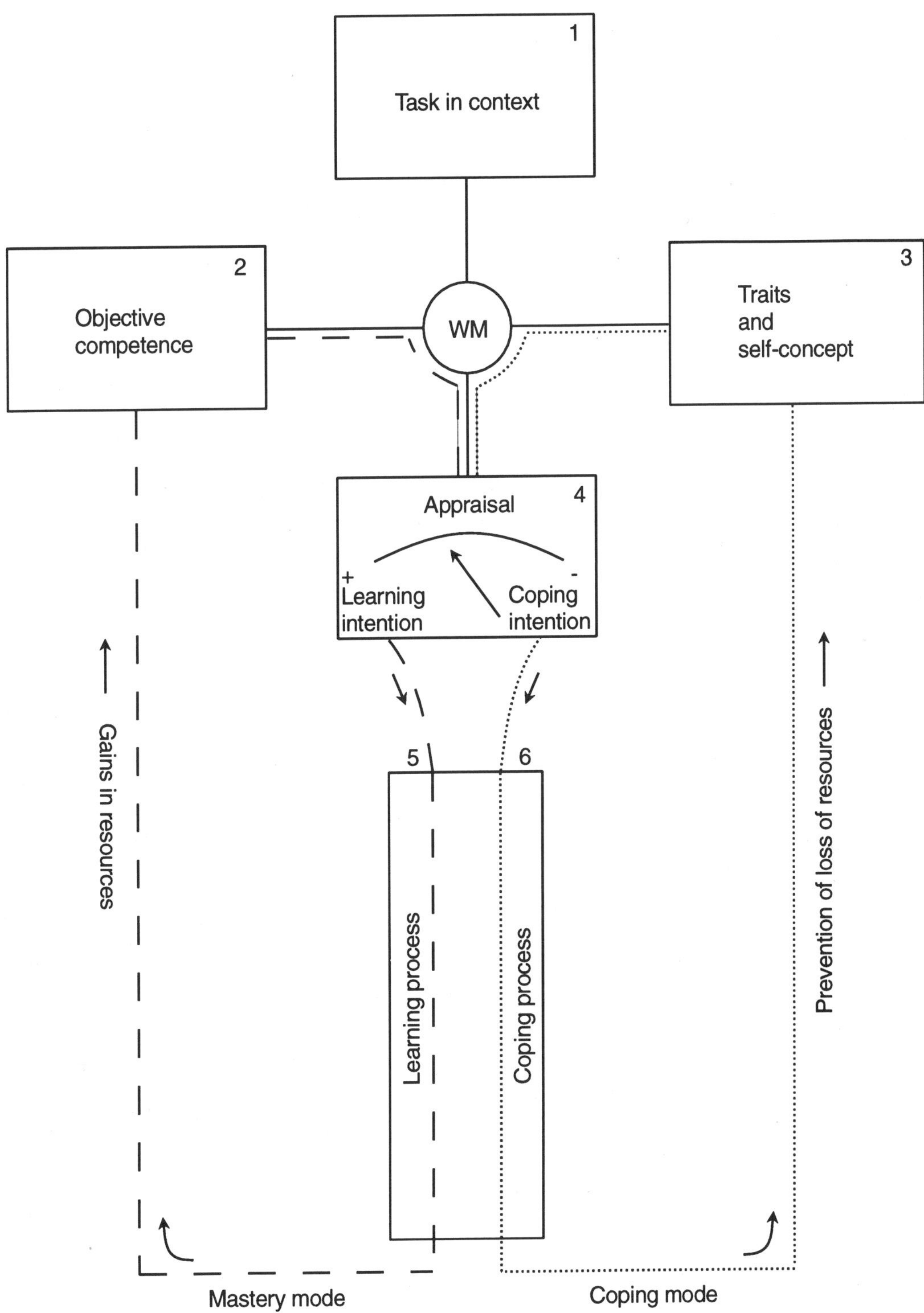

Figure 1. Heuristic model of the affective learning process.

embedded (component 1). The second source of information is activated domain specific knowledge and skills, including cognitive strategies and metacognitive knowledge relevant to the task (component 2). The third source consists of manifest personality traits, together with a subset of the self-concept derived from a particular collection of self-perceptions made salient and dominant by the prevailing physical and social context. Cantor et al. (1986) proposed a dynamic view of the self-concept as a collection of images and cognitions about the self, including "good," "bad," "hoped-for," "feared," "ideal," and "ought" selves. The authors argued that these selves, which are elaborated by plans and strategies for realization or avoidance, are not all available for thinking about the self at any one time. For this reason, it is preferable to speak about "current selves," or about the "working self-concept" that is currently "on-line" in information processing. This construct is akin to Bandura's favorable and unfavorable scenarios (Bandura, 1993).

Students' appraisals of particular learning situations (e.g., of a mathematics assignment or history task) are unique because the information stemming from the three sources (subject-matter specific competence, self-referenced cognitions, and perception of the task and the context within which it is embedded) differs depending on the task and acts as a frame of reference for appraisals. These unique appraisals may be regarded as steering mechanisms that stimulate or impede ongoing and upcoming behavior. They elicit specific experiential states (positive and negative emotions, states of mind) and behavioral intentions. It was theorized that when the information in the dynamic working model is basically positive (i.e., bears on the student's personal strivings and predicts personal gains), positive appraisals of the learning situation are elicited; this is referred to as benign or challenge appraisal. By contrast, when negative scenarios are dominant in the working model (i.e., when the activated information bears on personal vulnerabilities or predicts personal loss), negative or threat appraisal of the learning situation is evoked. Following Lazarus and Folkman (1984), a task or learning situation is said to be appraised as irrelevant for well-being (null operation) when there is no match between the input and personal strivings or vulnerabilities.

The model postulates that predominantly favorable appraisals lead to a strong learning intention and a positive experiential state, which initiate activity in the learning or mastery mode (this pathway is symbolized by the broken lines in Figure 1). In contrast, predominantly unfavorable appraisals are believed to result in weak learning intention and a negative experiential state. The latter are in turn linked to a "coping intention," which starts activity in the coping mode. This non-learning-oriented pathway is symbolized by dotted lines in Figure 1. It is furthermore assumed that the mastery and coping modes coexist, but that at any given time one of the two will assume priority in the student's goal structure.

Evidence for Two Modes of Processing

Seegers and Boekaerts (1993) proposed a structural model for explaining the processes mediating between subjective and objective competence measured at the middle level and learning intention, experiential state, and task performance measured at the momentary level. They conducted a study with sixth-grade students in order to investigate causal direction in the relation between affective variables and math performance. At the middle level, four variables were measured: goal orientation in relation to math learning, attribution of success and failure on math tasks, self-perception of math ability, and fluid intelligence. At the momentary level, the students' appraisals of a concrete set of math tasks on two successive occasions were assessed with the On-Line Motivation Questionnaire (Boekaerts, 1987), which elicits students' appraisals of task attraction, self-confidence and task value. Furthermore, experiential state (positive and negative emotions), learning intention, and task performance were assessed. LISREL analyses confirmed the hypotheses that subjective competence measured at the middle level influences task appraisals, and that only the latter directly affects learning intention, experiential state, and task results. As a measure of objective competence, intelligence had a direct effect on math performance but not on appraisals.

The direct and indirect paths leading from self-referenced cognitions to appraisals and to the outcome variables provide evidence for the two modes of information processing proposed in the model of adaptable learning (i.e., the mastery and coping modes). It was clear that favorable self-referenced cognitions measured at the middle level (especially task orientation) positively affected the students' ratings of task attraction and task value. These positive appraisals were in turn linked to learning intention and to experiential state (positive emotions), both directly and indirectly. Strong activity in these direct and indirect paths leading to learning intention symbolizes the dynamics of ongoing cognitions (appraisals) that motivate students to assemble available learning resources for mastering a task. In terms of the model of adaptable learning, strong activity in these pathways indicates that a student is in the mastery mode.

Conversely, unfavorable self-referenced cognitions measured at the middle level (especially ego orientation, low perception of control, and low self-efficacy) influenced the students' self-confidence appraisals. This negative appraisal was in turn linked to experiential state (negative emotions) both directly and indirectly via low task attraction. Strong activity in these direct and indirect paths leading to experiential state symbolizes the dynamics of ongoing cognitions (appraisals) that motivate students to assemble available coping resources for protecting their well-being (see Boekaerts, 1993). In terms of the model of adaptable learning, strong activity in these pathways suggests that a student is concerned with well-being and that the coping mode is in operation.

Both learning intention and experiential state had relatively little influence on task performance. The latter outcome variable was affected directly—and with equal strength—by intelligence (objective competence measured at the middle level) and situation-specific self-confidence (subjective competence measured at the momentary level). The model was cross-validated and showed good fit, and it was replicated in another study with students (aged 12 to 14) in their first year of secondary education.

These findings suggest that prior affect-laden experiences in the math domain influence self-confidence at the time of learning math, which in turn affects students' math performance and experiential state but not their learning intention. In other words, self-confidence is positively associated with math achievement and as such is propaedeutic to good performance. Yet high self-confidence by itself is no guarantee that students will put in effort, nor does low self-confidence lead automatically to low effort. Self-confidence seems to influence task attraction jointly with task orientation (at the middle level) and task value (at the momentary level). It is the total effect of task attraction stemming from different sources that determines learning intention.

CONCLUSIONS AND IMPLICATIONS FOR EDUCATION

This chapter began with an attempt to define intelligence and personality as they are relevant in a scholastic context. On the basis of a review of the literature, the former construct was defined in terms of objective competence, or the student's skill in handling task-relevant, item-relevant, or problem-relevant information. This regulatory skill is reflected to a certain degree in intelligence test scores but also in metacognitive knowledge and skills and, to a lesser extent, in prior achievement or grades. Personality variables were restricted to subjective competence, or the student's skill in handling self-referenced cognitions. This regulatory skill pertains to the student's ability to activate and generate favorable beliefs about subject areas and tasks, as well as about personal competence in relation to these domains.

Evidence was presented that objective and subjective competence are complementary, and that their integration forms an effective and dynamic internal environment for learning. From Helmke's (1989, 1993) research and review of the literature, it may be inferred that objective competence is the most potent predictor of math achievement in elementary education. Nevertheless, very early in a student's academic career (i.e., second grade), failures in connection with important competencies may start building up and feed back on attitudes toward mathematics. It is likely that such negative attitudes will be part of the self-referenced cognitions that are activated when learning situations are appraised. Helmke also demonstrated that at the end of the sixth grade, the effects of self-perceptions of mathematics ability on achievement are mediated by the type of effort expended on the task and by the degree of cognitive interference. Seegers and Boekaerts (1993) studied the same age groups and reported that self-confidence measured in the learning situation is equally as strong a predictor of math performance as intelligence.

At the high school level, the most powerful predictor of current achievement is still higher mental ability, followed by interest (Schiefele et al., 1992). Prior grades seem to be less powerful predictors than self-referenced cognitions (Zimmermann et al., 1992). The learner's experiential state and learning intention are not affected by objective competence. Subjective competence measured at either the middle or the momentary level are better predictors (Schiefele et al., 1992; Seegers & Boekaerts, 1993).

In sum, subjective competence contributes—beyond what can be explained by objective competence—to the prediction of subsequent achievement. Hence both objective and subjective competence should be regarded as important aspects of learning aptitude because they prompt learners to regulate their own learning in concrete learning situations. Or, as Snow (1992) aptly puts it, differences in learning appear in the person-task interface as differences in within-person adaptation to the stream of continuing changes in within-task demands and opportunities. Learners seem to fashion their performances in instructional situations by drawing on their resources and by assembling, reassembling, and controlling these resources to adapt to perceived needs and opportunities in the situation.

Several researchers have argued that when students are not (yet) capable of active, self-regulated learning, the teacher can remedy the suboptimal internal learning environment by providing optimal instructional support (i.e., scaffolding). There is a vast literature demonstrating that optimal instructional support can reduce the correlation between general mental ability and learning. For example, Snow and Lohman (1984) reported that low-ability learners perform better when provided with individually adjusted instruction rather than conventional teaching methods, and that these learners also profit from training in specific cognitive strategies. High-ability learners, however, suffer rather than profit from such manipulations, and extra teacher support and guidance may even interfere with their own learning strategies, thus producing lower motivation and decrements in performance.

Weinert and Helmke (1993) drew attention to the apparent paradox between studies that demonstrate superior effects of direct instruction and those that show superior effects of active, self-regulated learning. In the German longitudinal classroom environment study, they found that direct instruction—which is characterized by efficient classroom management and a strong focus on academic work and evaluation—had a positive effect on math achievement, on self-concept of ability and on cognitive interference; however, it negatively influenced the students' attitudes toward both school and math after a period of 2 years. Why does direct instruction have negative effects on motivation and positive effects on achievement?

Specialists in the field of intrinsic motivation (e.g., Deci & Ryan, 1985, 1992; Malone & Lepper, 1987; Ryan, 1982) have suggested that different instructional methods and evaluation procedures may change students' perceptions of control. A longitudinal study conducted by Boggiano et al. (1989) revealed that teachers who made frequent use of controlling techniques (e.g., a great deal of surveillance, evaluations, and verbal expressions using *ought* and *must*) had students who saw themselves as dependent on the teacher (i.e., as pawns) and were extrinsically motivated. In contrast, teachers who did not make use of such controlling techniques had students in their classes who found learning intrinsically motivating, and this motivational orientation predicted higher achievement.

Ryan's (1982) distinction between informational events and controlling events is quite helpful in interpreting the apparent paradox raised by the findings of the German study. Informational events are perceived by students as supports to their autonomy, rather than as controls on their behavior, whereas controlling events are experienced as pressure to answer, think, or behave in a specific way. Many specialists in intrinsic motivation defend the view that the perception of an event as controlling undermines the student's sense of self-determination and may at best result in compliance or defiance. In contrast, the perception of an event as informational fosters purposeful accomplishment, a major factor influencing learning outcome. The latter sort of perception, together with the beliefs it activates, makes students more apt to select effective cognitive strategies, which in turn fosters higher achievement.

Valås and Søvik (1993) tested this hypothesis, predicting that students who perceived their teachers as less controlling would show higher achievement in mathematics. The authors conducted a longitudinal study with students from the lower grades of secondary education (grades seven and eight) and measured two aspects of self-referenced cognitions: the students' aggregated math self-efficacy, and their intrinsic motivation. In addition, Valås and Søvik assessed the students' perceptions of teacher control and their achievement in math (using scores on a norm-referenced national mathematics achievement test). Teacher control was measured in terms of two observed variables: control math and emotional tune. The former variable measured the teacher's controlling behavior as perceived by the student (the teacher's emphasis on grades, tests, willingness to give students choices); the latter measured the student's perception of the teacher's warmth, involvement, and care. Gender, intelligence, and socioeconomic status were investigated as exogenous variables. Path analysis revealed that the students' self-referenced cognitions and performance varied in relation to the teacher's controlling strategies. More concretely, students who perceived their math teacher as more supportive of autonomy than controlling considered themselves more competent in mathematics and were more intrinsically motivated than students who perceived their teacher as controlling. High self-efficacy in mathematics was linked to high intrinsic motivation, even when the math teacher was perceived as controlling. Flink, Boggiano, Main, Barrett, and Katz (1992) reported similar results and suggested that intrinsically oriented students may be more tolerant of external control and pressure than students who are extrinsically oriented.

It must be concluded that the most appropriate form of instruction for a particular group of students depends not only on their aptitudes for learning (i.e., their subjective and objective competence and associated self-regulatory skills) but also on the stage of the learning process in which the students find themselves. Every learning opportunity finds the learner at a particular stage of skill development (in terms of conceptual structures, procedural skills, cognitive strategies, and metacognition) and with a particular degree of confidence in relation to that skill (subjective competence). It is the unique combination of these two aspects of learning aptitude with actual learning that determines the degree of support and autonomy that is needed at a given moment, and that is in turn propaedeutic to future learning in the same domain. More research in the actual learning situation will be necessary to elucidate the interface between the two aspects of learning aptitude and the opportunities provided to the student. The interested reader is referred to two excellent reviews dealing with these and related issues: Pintrich, Marx, and Boyle (1993) and Wang, Haertel, and Walberg (1990).

REFERENCES

Atkinson, J. W. (1965). *An introduction to motivation.* New York: Van Nostrand.

Bandura, A. (1986). *Social foundations of thought and action: A social cognitive theory.* Englewood Cliffs, NJ: Prentice-Hall.

Bandura, A. (1993). Perceived self-efficacy in cognitive development and functioning. *Educational Psychologist, 28*(2), 117–148.

Berenson, J., & Dweck, C. (1986). The development of trait explanations and self-evaluations in the academic and social domains. *Child Development, 57,* 1179–1187.

Boekaerts, M. (1987). Die Effekte von state- und trait-motivationaler Orientierung auf das Lernergebnis. *Zeitschrift für Pädagogische Psychologie, 1*(1), 29–43.

Boekaerts, M. (1992). The adaptable learning process: Initiating and maintaining behavioural change. *Journal of Applied Psychology: An International Review, 41*(4), 377–397.

Boekaerts, M. (1993). Being concerned with well-being and with learning. *Educational Psychologist, 28*(2), 149–167.

Boggiano, A. K., Main, D. S., Flink, C., Barrett, M., Silvern, L., & Katz, P. A. (1989). A model of achievement in children: The role of controlling strategies in helplessness and affect. In R. Schwarzer, H. M. van der Ploeg, & C. D. Spielberger (Eds.), *Advances in test anxiety research* (Vol. 6, pp. 13–26). Amsterdam: Swets & Zeitlinger.

Borkowski, J., Carr, M., Rellinger, E., & Pressley, M. (1990). Self-regulated cognition: Interdependence of metacognition, attributions, and self-esteem. In B. Jones & L. Idol (Eds.), *Dimensions of thinking and cognitive instruction* (pp. 53–92). Hillsdale, NJ: Erlbaum.

Borkowski, J. G., & Peck, V. A. (1986). Causes and consequences of metamemory in gifted children. In R. J. Sternberg & J. Davidson (Eds.), *Conceptions of giftedness* (pp. 182–200). Boston: Cambridge University Press.

Brown, A. L. (1978). Knowing when, where, and how to remember: A problem of meta-cognition. In R. Glaser (Ed.), *Advances in instructional psychology* (Vol. 1, pp. 77–165). Hillsdale, NJ: Erlbaum.

Brown, A. L., & Campione, J. C. (1984). Three faces of transfer: Implications for early competence, individual differences and instruction. In M. E. Lamb, A. L. Brown & B. Rogoff (Eds.), *Advances in developmental psychology* (pp. 143–192). Hillsdale, NJ: Erlbaum.

Brown, A. L., & Palincsar, A. S. (1989). Guided, cooperative learning and individual knowledge acquisition. In L. B. Resnick (Ed.), *Knowing, learning and instruction: Essays in honor of Robert Glaser* (pp. 393–451). Hillsdale, NJ: Erlbaum.

Burns, R. (1982). *Self-concept development and education.* London: Holt, Rinehart & Winston.

Byrne, B. M., & Shavelson, R. J. (1986). On the structure of adolescent self-concept. *Journal of Educational Psychology, 78,* 474–481.

Cantor, N. (1981). Perceptions of situations. In D. Magnusson (Ed.), *Toward a psychology of situations: An interactional perspective* (pp. 229–244). Hillsdale, NJ: Erlbaum.

Cantor, N., Markus, H., Niedenthal, P., & Nurius, P. (1986). On motivation and the self-concept. In R. M. Sorrentino & T. Higgins (Eds.), *Handbook of motivation and cognition: Foundation of social behavior* (pp. 96–111). Chichester, England: Wiley.

Cattell, R. B. (1963). Theory of fluid and crystallized intelligence: A critical experiment. *Journal of Educational Psychology, 54,* 1–22.

Corno, L., & Mandinach, E. (1983). The role of cognitive engagement in classroom learning and motivation. *Educational Psychologist, 18,* 88–100.

Covington, M. V. (1992). *Making the grade: A self-worth perspective on motivation and school reform.* New York: Cambridge University Press.

Covington, M. V., & Omelich, C. L. (1984). An empirical examination of Weiner's critique of attribution research. *Journal of Educational Psychology, 76,* 1199–1213.

Csikszentmihalyi, M., & Nakamura, I. (1989). The dynamics of intrinsic motivation: A study of adolescents. In C. Ames & R. Ames (Eds.), *Research on motivation in education* (Vol. 3, pp. 45–72). Orlando, FL: Academic Press.

DeCharms, R. (1984). Motivation enhancement in educational settings. In R. E. Ames & C. Ames (Eds.), *Research on motivation in education: Vol. 1. Student motivation.* London: Academic Press.

Deci, E. L., & Ryan, R. M. (1985). *Intrinsic motivation and self-determination in human behavior.* New York: Plenum.

Deci, E. L., & Ryan, R. M. (1992). The initiation and regulation of intrinsically motivated learning and achievement. In A. K. Boggiano & T. S. Pittman (Eds.), *Achievement and motivation: A social-developmental perspective* (pp. 9–36). New York: Cambridge University Press.

Deffenbacher, J. L., & Hazaleus, S. L. (1985). Cognitive, emotional and physiological components of test anxiety. *Cognitive Therapy and Research*, 9(2), 169–180.

Dweck, C. S. (1986). Motivational processes affecting learning. *American Psychologist*, *41*, 1040–1048.

Eccles, J. (1983). Expectancies, values and academic behaviors. In J. T. Spence (Ed.), *Achievement and achievement motives* (pp. 75–146). San Francisco: Freeman.

Eysenck, M. (1987). Anxiety and attention. *Anxiety Research*, *1*, 9–15.

Fennema, E., & Sherman, J. (1978). Sex-related differences in mathematics achievement and related factors: A further study. *Journal for Research in Mathematics Education*, *9*, 189–203.

Feuerstein, R. (1980). *Instrumental enrichment: An intervention program for cognitive modifiability*. Baltimore: University Park Press.

Feuerstein, R., Jensen, N., Hoffman, N. B., & Rand, W. (1985). Instrumental enrichment, an intervention program for structural cognitive modifiability: Theory and practice. In J. W. Segal, S. F. Chipman, & R. Glaser (Eds.), *Thinking and learning skills* (Vol. 1). Hillsdale, NJ: Erlbaum.

Findley, M., & Cooper, H. (1983). Locus of control and academic achievement: A review of the literature. *Journal of Personality and Social Psychology*, *44*, 419–427.

Flavell, J. H. (1976). Metacognitive aspects of problem solving. In L. B. Resnick (Ed.), *The nature of intelligence* (pp. 231–236). Hillsdale, NJ: Erlbaum.

Flink, C., Boggiano, A. K., Main, D. S., Barrett, M., & Katz, P. A. (1992). Children's achievement-related behaviors: The role of extrinsic and intrinsic motivational orientations. In A. K. Boggiano & T. S. Pittman (Eds.), *Achievement and motivation: A social-development perspective* (pp. 189–214). New York: Cambridge University Press.

Flynn J. R. (1987). Massive IQ gains in 14 nations: What IQ tests really measure. *Psychological Bulletin*, *101*, 171–191.

Harter, S. (1981). A model of mastery motivation in children: Individual differences and developmental change. In A. Pick (Ed.), *Minnesota Symposium on Child Psychology* (Vol. 14). Hillsdale, NJ: Erlbaum.

Harter, S. (1982). A developmental perspective on some parameters of self-regulation in children. In P. Karoly & F. H. Kanfer (Eds.), *Self-management and behavior change: From theory to practice* (pp. 165–204). New York: Pergamon.

Harter, S. (1985). Processes underlying self-concept formation in children. In J. Suls & A. Greenwald (Eds.), *Psychological perspectives on the self.* Hillsdale, NJ: Erlbaum.

Heckhausen, H. (1980). *Motivation und Handeln: Lehrbuch der Motivation psychologie*. Berlin: Springer-Verlag.

Heembree, R. (1988). Correlations, causes, effects and treatment of test anxiety. *Review of Educational Research*, *58*, 47–77.

Helmke, A. (1989). The impact of student self-concept of ability and task motivation on different indicators of effort at school. *International Journal of Educational Research*, *13*(8), 281–295.

Helmke, A. (1993). Die Entwicklung der Lernfreude vom Kindergarten bis zur 5. Klassenstufe [Development of affective attitudes towards learning from kindergarten to grade five]. *Zeitschrift für Pädagogische Psychologie*, *7*(2/3), 77–86.

Helmke, A., Schneider, W., & Weinert, F. E. (1986). Quality of instruction and classroom learning outcomes: Results of the German contribution to the Classroom Environment Study of the IEA. *Teaching and Teacher Education*, *2*, 1–18.

Hidi, S. (1990). Interest and its contribution as a mental resource for learning. *Review of Educational Research*, *60*, 549–571.

Jensen, A. R. (1980). *Bias in mental testing*. New York: Free Press.

Kuhl, J. (1984). Volitional aspects of achievement motivation and learned helplessness: Toward a comprehensive theory of action control. In B. A. Maher & W. B. Maher (Eds.), *Progress in experimental personality research* (Vol. 13, pp. 99–171). New York: Academic Press.

Kurtz, B. E., & Weinert, F. E. (1989). Metamemory, metaperformance, and causal attributions in gifted and average children. *Journal of Experimental Child Psychology*, *48*, 45–61.

Lazar, I., & Darlington, R. (1982) Lasting effects of early education. *Monographs of the Society of Research in Child Development* 17(2/3), Series No. 195.

Lazarus, R. S., & Folkman, S. (1984). *Stress, appraisal and coping*. New York: Springer.

Leventhal, H. (1980). Toward a comprehensive theory of emotion. In L. Berkowitz (Ed.), *Advances in experimental social psychology* (Vol. 13, pp. 140–228). New York: Academic Press.

Malone, T., & Lepper, M. (1987). Making learning fun: A taxonomy of intrinsic motivations for learning. In R. Snow & M. Farr (Eds.), *Aptitude, learning, and instruction: Vol. 3. Cognitive and affective process analyses* (pp. 223–253). Hillsdale, NJ: Erlbaum.

Masterpasqua, F. (1989). A competence paradigm for psychological practice. *American Psychologist*, *44*(11), 1366–1371.

Meece, J. L., Blumenfeld, P. C., & Hoyle, R. H. (1988). Students' goal orientation and cognitive engagement in classroom activities. *Journal of Educational Psychology*, *80*, 514–523.

Meece, J. L., Wigfield, A., & Eccles, J. S. (1990). Predictors of math anxiety and its influence on young adolescents' course enrollment intentions and performance in mathematics. *Journal of Educational Psychology*, *82*, 60–70.

Mischel, W. (1973). Toward a cognitive social learning reconceptualization of personality. *Psychological Review*, *80*, 252–283.

Newman, R. S., & Wick, P. L. (1987). Effect of age, skill and performance feedback on children's adjustment of confidence. *Journal of Educational Psychology*, *79*(2), 115–119.

Nicholls, J. (1984). Achievement motivation: Conceptions of ability, subjective experience, task choice, and performance. *Psychological Review*, *91*, 328–348.

Nolen, S. B. (1988). Reasons for studying: Motivational orientations and study strategies. *Cognition and Instruction*, *5*, 269–287.

Oka, E. R., & Paris, S. G. (1987). Pattern of learning and motivation among underachieving children. In S. Ceci (Ed.), *Handbook of cognitive, social, and neuropsychological aspects of learning disabilities*. Hillsdale, NJ: Erlbaum.

Palincsar, A. S., & Brown, A. L. (1984). Reciprocal teaching of comprehension-fostering and comprehension-monitoring activities. *Cognition and Instruction*, *1*, 117–175.

Paris, S. G., & Oka, E. R. (1986). Children's reading strategies, metacognition, and motivation. *Developmental Review*, *6*, 25–56.

Pintrich, P. R., & De Groot, E. V. (1990). Motivational and self-regulated learning components of classroom academic performance. *Journal of Educational Psychology*, *82*, 33–40.

Pintrich, P. R., & Garcia, T. (1991). Student goal orientation and self-regulation in the college classroom. In M. Maehr & P. R. Pintrich (Eds.), *Advances in motivation and achievement: Goals and self-regulatory processes* (Vol. 7, pp. 371–402). Greenwich, CT: JAI.

Pintrich, P. R., Marx, R. W., & Boyle, R. A. (1993). Beyond cold conceptual change: The role of motivational beliefs and classroom contextual factors in the process of conceptual change. *Review of Educational Research*, *63*, 167–199.

Pintrich, P. R., & Schrauben, B. (1992). Students' motivational beliefs and their cognitive engagement in academic tasks. In

D. Schunk & J. Meece (Eds.), *Students' perceptions in the classroom: Causes and consequences* (pp. 149–183). Hillsdale, NJ: Erlbaum.

Resnick, L. B. (1987). Learning in school and out. *Educational Researcher, 16*(9), 13–20.

Reyes, L. H. (1984). Affective variables and mathematics education. *Elementary School Journal, 84*, 558–581.

Ryan, R. M. (1982). Control and information in intrapersonal sphere: An extension of cognitive evaluation theory. *Journal of Personality and Social Psychology, 43*, 450–461.

Salomon, G., & Perkins, D. N. (1990). Rocky roads to transfer: Rethinking mechanisms of a neglected phenomenon. *Educational Psychologist, 24*, 113–142.

Sarason, I. G. (1984). Stress, anxiety and cognitive interference: Reaction to tests. *Journal of Personality and Social Psychology, 46*, 929–938.

Scardamalia, M., & Bereiter, C. (1986). Research on written composition. In M. C. Wittrock (Ed.), *Handbook of research on teaching* (3rd ed., pp. 778–803). New York: Macmillan.

Schiefele, U. (1991). Interest, learning and experience. *Educational Psychologist, 26*, 299–323.

Schiefele, U. (1992). Topic interest and levels of text comprehension. In K. A. Renninger, S. Hidi, & A. Krapp (Eds.), *The role of interest in learning and development* (pp. 151–182). Hillsdale, NJ: Erlbaum.

Schiefele, U., & Csikszentmihalyi, M. (in press). Interest and the quality of experience in classroom. *European Journal of Psychology of Education.*

Schiefele, U., Krapp, A., & Winteler, A. (1992). Interest as a predictor of academic achievement: A review of research. In K. A. Renninger, S. Hidi, & A. Krapp (Eds.), *The role of interest in learning and development* (pp. 183–212). Hillsdale, NJ: Erlbaum.

Schneider, W., Borkowski, J. G., Kurtz, B. E., & Kerwin, K. (1986). Metamemory and motivation: A comparison of strategy use and performance in German and American children. *Journal of Cross-Cultural Psychology, 17*, 315–336.

Schoenfeld, A. H. (1985). *Mathematical problem solving*. Orlando, FL: Academic Press.

Schunk, D. H. (1985). Self-efficacy and school learning. *Psychology in the School, 22*, 208–223.

Schunk, D. H. (1989). Self-efficacy and cognitive skill learning. In C. Ames & R. Ames (Eds.), *Research on motivation in education* (Vol. 3, pp. 13–41). Orlando, FL: Academic Press.

Schunk, D. H. (1991). Self-efficacy and academic motivation. *Educational Psychologist, 26*, 207–231.

Seegers, G., & Boekaerts, M. (1993). Task motivation and mathematics achievement in actual task situations. *Learning and Instruction, 3*, 133–150.

Skaalvik, E. M., & Hagtvet, K. A. (1990). Academic self-concept: An analysis of causal predominance in a developmental perspective. *Journal of Personality and Social Psychology, 58*, 292–307.

Skinner, E. A., Wellborn, J. G., & Connell, J. P. (1990). What it takes to do well in school and whether I've got it: A process model of perceived control and children's engagement and achievement in school. *Journal of Educational Psychology, 82*(1), 22–33.

Snow, R. E. (1992). Aptitude theory: Yesterday, today, and tomorrow. *Educational Psychologist, 27*, 5–33.

Snow, R. E., Kyllonen, P. C., & Marshalek, B. (1984). The topography of ability and learning correlations. In R. J. Sternberg (Ed.), *Advances in the psychology of human intelligence* (Vol. 2, pp. 47–104). Hillsdale, NJ: Erlbaum.

Snow, R. E., & Lohman, D. F. (1984). Toward a theory of cognitive aptitude for learning from instruction. *Journal of Educational Psychology, 76*, 347–376.

Sternberg, R. J. (1985). Instrumental and componential approaches to the nature and training of intelligence. In S. F. Chipman, J. W. Segal, & R. Glaser (Eds.), *Thinking and learning skills* (Vol. 2, pp. 392–490). Hillsdale, NJ: Erlbaum.

Sternberg, R. J. (1986). A triarchic theory of human intelligence. In S. E. Newstead, S. H. Irvine, & P. L. Dann (Eds.), *Human assessment: Cognition and motivation* (pp. 43–47). Dordrecht, Netherlands: Martinus Nijhoff.

Taube, K. (1988). *Reading acquisition and self-concept*. Doctoral dissertation, University of Umea.

Valås, H., & Søvik, N. (in press). Variables affecting students' intrinsic motivation for school mathematics: Two empirical studies based on Deci and Ryan's theory on motivation. *Learning and Instruction.*

Veenman, M. V. J. (1993). *Intellectual ability and metacognitive skill: Determinants of discovery learning in computerized learning environments*. Doctoral dissertation, University of Amsterdam, Amsterdam.

Volet, S. E. (1991). Modelling and coaching of relevant metacognitive strategies for enhancing university students' learning. *Learning and Instruction, 1*, 319–336.

Wang, M. C., Haertel, G. D., & Walberg, H. J. (1990). What influences learning? A content analysis of review literature. *Journal of Educational Research, 84*(1), 30–43.

Weiner, B. (1986). *An attributional theory of motivation and emotion*. New York: Springer.

Weinert, F. E., & Helmke, A. (1993, September). *Learning from wise Mother Nature or Big Brother instructor: The wrong alternative for cognitive development*. Paper presented at the conference of the European Association for Research on Learning and Instruction, Aix-en-Provence, France.

Weinert, F. E., Schrader, F. W., & Helmke, A. (1989). Quality of instruction and achievement outcomes. *International Journal of Educational Psychology, 13*(8), 895–912.

Whitley, B. E., Jr., & Frieze, I. H. (1985). Children's causal attributions for success and failure in achievement settings: A meta-analysis. *Journal of Educational Psychology, 5*, 608–616.

Wieland, R. (1984). Temporal patterns of anxiety: Towards a process analysis of anxiety and performance. In R. Schwarzer (Ed.), *The self in anxiety, stress and depression* (pp. 133–150). Amsterdam: North Holland.

Zimmerman, B. J., Bandura, A., & Martinez-Pons, M. (1992). Self-motivation for academic attainment: The role of self-efficacy beliefs and personal goal setting. *American Educational Research Journal, 29*, 663–676.

Zimmerman, B. J., & Martinez-Pons, M. (1990). Student differences in self-regulated learning: Relating grade, sex, and giftedness to self-efficacy and strategy use. *Journal of Educational Psychology, 82*, 51–59.

10

A Cognitive-Social Description of Exceptional Children

Vicki L. Schwean and Donald H. Saklofske

There is considerable evidence through the works of early and contemporary philosophers, scientists, educators, and artists, that humankind is most fascinated by itself. Our history is replete with descriptions of both individual and group differences in human behavior. Exceptionalities have been the focus of much of this interest, ranging from the gifted mathematician and the idiot savant to the great political leader and the schizophrenic. Human similarities, differences, and exceptionalities have frequently been viewed and even defined in relation to intelligence and personality.

This chapter will briefly introduce the reader to childhood exceptionality, noting the limitations of earlier psychological efforts in arriving at comprehensive and integrative descriptions of various exceptionalities. We present the basic tenets of cognitive-social theories in recognition of the recent contributions these frameworks have made toward enhancing our understanding of exceptionalities. We will then apply these paradigms to an examination of two areas of exceptionality in children—learning disabilities and emotional and behavioral disorders. Here we contend that attempts to explore the possible interface between personality and intelligence are likely to be furthered by a careful analysis of recent cognitive-social theory and research.

DEFINITION AND INCIDENCE OF EXCEPTIONALITY IN CHILDREN

Marked by significant differences in intellectual, emotional, physical, or social characteristics, exceptional individuals have occupied positions of either reverence or derision in societies from ancient to modern times. Although considerable heterogeneity may be found within any category of exceptionality, contemporary educational nomenclature defines primary handicapping conditions to include physical and health impairments, communication disorders, hearing or visual impairments, behavioral disorders, learning disabilities, and mental retardation. The nosology also refers to gifted and talented individuals, who are differentiated on the basis of ability rather than disability.

Though there are clearly a number of difficulties in arriving at accurate prevalence data, Winzer, Rogow, and Charlotte (1987) suggest that approximately one eighth of the world's population can be regarded as

Vicki L. Schwean • Department for the Education of Exceptional Children, University of Saskatchewan, Saskatoon, Saskatchewan S7N 0W0, Canada. Donald H. Saklofske • Department of Educational Psychology, University of Saskatchewan, Saskatoon, Saskatchewan S7N 0W0, Canada.

International Handbook of Personality and Intelligence, edited by Donald H. Saklofske and Moshe Zeidner. Plenum Press, New York, 1995.

disabled. It is estimated that 9.4% of the school-age population in the United States present as "special needs" students, with learning disabilities, communication disorders, mental retardation, and emotional and behavioral disorders accounting for 94% of this disabled group. Gifted and talented students make up another 5% of school-age children (Heward & Orlansky, 1992). These figures can and do vary as a function of social and economic conditions, political decisions, and measurement criteria. Further, the estimated incidence can fluctuate because of comorbidity between exceptionalities, as well as the complexities in defining and assessing any condition.

EXCEPTIONALITY, PERSONALITY, AND INTELLIGENCE

Exceptionality has often been attributed to or linked with personality and intelligence constructs, both of which have a lengthy history that predates the founding of scientific psychology. Historical evidence indicates that human "mentality" has been in the forefront of individual-differences descriptions. Rogers (1995) and Sattler (1992) have presented in table form some of the more important contributions to cognitive and educational assessment over the centuries. In the 19th century, Esquirol, Itard, and Seguin developed methods of assessing intellectual functioning that attempted to distinguish between different levels of retardation or to contrast mental retardation with mental illness. The writings of Sir Francis Galton (1883, 1892) and the founding of his anthropometric laboratory toward the end of the century firmly established the basis for the study of individual differences and the measurement of human intelligence. When the Binet scales were introduced in the United States in 1908—initially to assess mental retardation in school-age children—the testing movement rapidly gained momentum, and intelligence tests became one of the trademarks of psychology.

Similarly, personality descriptions of human behavior and exceptionality are not new. Four "humors" or bodily fluids were suggested by Hippocrates and Galen to underlie the full range of human temperament. This model has served as a basis for the more recently hypothesized personality traits of extraversion, neuroticism, and psychoticism, which have been linked to behaviors ranging from creativity, anxiety, and aggression to various psychiatric disorders in both children and adults (Eysenck & Eysenck, 1985). The numerous personality theories, including psychodynamic, behavioral, trait, phenomenological, and (more recently) cognitive-social paradigms, have provided a rich basis for exploring the full range of typical to exceptional behavior.

ASSESSMENT OF EXCEPTIONALITY

Historically, the assessment of exceptional children has been entangled with the measurement of intelligence (Swanson & Watson, 1989). Only among children who are emotionally or behaviorally disordered has the assessment of personality been accorded any significance, despite substantive evidence for the powerful impact of personality factors on learning and mounting evidence confirming coexisting psychological and behavioral problems with all disabling conditions.

Norm-referenced construct measures of intelligence and personality typically have been employed in the assessment of exceptional children whose disabilities are manifested primarily in achievement or social and emotional competence. These tests may aid in initial identification, classification, and placement decisions but are also expected to provide information relevant to the development and evaluation of individual educational or behavioral programs. In recent years, concerns have been expressed about whether tests grounded in construct or attribute models can serve these latter educational assessment needs (Swanson & Watson, 1989).

These criticisms have led to alternative techniques for measuring intelligence and personality in children. For example, newer measures of intelligence seek to provide data on learning potential (Feuerstein, Haywood, Rand, Hoffman, & Jensen, 1984) and cognitive processes (e.g., Das, Naglieri, & Kirby, 1994; Kaufman & Kaufman, 1983) in children. The Behavior Assessment System for Children (Reynolds & Kamphaus, 1992) is an example of the newer multimethod, multidimensional approach to "facilitate the differential diagnosis and educational classification of a variety of emotional and behavioral disorders of children and to aid in the design of treatment plans" (p. 1). Personality and intelligence, however, have yet to be married at the theoretical level underlying these assessment approaches. It is left up to the practitioner to assess the relationship between the many measured psychological variables, based either on an awareness of the published research or on clinical intuition. Recent calls have surfaced in the literature on exceptionality for an integrative reconceptualization of the constructs of intelligence and personality so as to promote an increased understanding of the interrelationships between the processes subserving intelligence, on the one hand, and social and behavioral competence, on the other (e.g., T. Bryan, 1991).

THE NEED FOR AN INTEGRATIVE DESCRIPTION OF EXCEPTIONALITY

Psychology may be both advanced and limited by a reliance on any particular theory and methodology. This realization is the basis for the paradigm shifts witnessed in the brief history of psychology. To illustrate this point, one can refer to the progress in the study of personality that has resulted from Eysenck and Wilson's (1973) critical appraisal of psychoanalysis, Szasz's (1961) hypothesis regarding the "myth of mental illness," Bandura's (1973) demonstration that aggression may be a result of observational learning and imitation, and Mischel's (1968) argument that personality traits by themselves are insufficient descriptors of human behavior, which is also not very consistent. Debates about the causes and structure of intelligence, accusations of fraud in research on intelligence (e.g., Kamin, 1977), and concern over possible cultural bias in IQ tests (e.g., Jensen, 1980; Larry P. v. W. Riles, 1984) were certainly catalysts in stimulating continued research in these areas. From a methodological perspective, Cronbach (1957) distinguished between the two disciplines of psychology—correlational and experimental—aimed at either elaborating individual differences or discovering general laws. His call for an interactionist position was intended to allow both disciplines to thrive. Journals such as *Personality and Individual Differences* support the view that it is the integration of correlational and experimental psychology that gives promise of a "unitary science."

These developments have taken us in the direction of creating models and conducting research studies that promote a more integrated explanation of human behavior. Learning disabilities, behavior disorders, and even creativity cannot be fully understood in a singular way. Identifying learning-disabled children as those who are not achieving in school in spite of adequate general mental ability does little more than identify a heterogeneous group of special-needs children. By elaborating on the emotional and behavioral correlates of learning disabilities, we allow for potential causal hypotheses about the children's academic deficiencies. Studies of intellectually gifted children (identified by high intelligence test scores) have recently focused on defining concomitant social and emotional problems potentially associated with advanced cognitive abilities (Hillyer & Kearney, 1988). The role of personality, temperament, and motivational factors in creativity has also been explored (Cattell & Drevdahl, 1955; Rossman & Horn, 1972).

Increased recognition of the determinative influence of motivation, self-concept, and other personality factors on learning has also affected studies focusing on children with mental retardation (defined by low intelligence; Landesman-Dwyers & Butterfield, 1983). Tendencies toward oversimplification of concepts and ideas, poor transfer and generalization skills, attentional problems, overfocusing on one aspect of a problem, less well-developed problem-solving skills, and difficulty in generating hypotheses are now seen as factors that are important not only in the school learning of children with retardation but also in their social and interpersonal interactions. Each of these examples demonstrates the complexity of human behavior and the necessity of creating models that permit an examination of the interface between behavioral and intellectual components.

Simply noting the correlations among various personality and intelligence factors, however, is not sufficient to complete our understanding of exceptional individuals. Cognitive psychology has evolved as a major force in contemporary intelligence theories such as those advocated by Sternberg (1986) and Das and colleagues (Das, Naglieri, & Kirby, 1994). The influence of cognitive-social theories has also been evident since the 1970s as an alternative to psychoanalytic, strict behaviorist, and trait models of personality. Here researchers may find a rich basis for examining the personality-intelligence interface and expanding their knowledge of human exceptionalities. Models articulating the cognitive processes and mediational patterns that may be operative in social learning promise to advance our theoretical understandings of the mechanisms underlying emotional and behavioral competence. These understandings should, in turn, inform and guide assessment and intervention practices. A brief overview of the theoretical underpinnings of cognitive-social theories is provided below.

COGNITIVE-SOCIAL THEORY: AN INTEGRATION OF PERSONALITY AND INTELLIGENCE

> Stimulated by developments in the analysis of cognitive processes, a new perspective on personality is emerging under the label cognitive social theories. . . . They are united in their belief that conceptions and methods dealing with persons both as cognitive and as social beings are essential elements in an adequate psychological theory of individuality. (Mischel, 1993, p. 396)

Cognitive-social theories comprise a heterogeneous grouping of formulations that draw heavily from several disciplines, including cognitive psychology, learning, the neurosciences, developmental psychology, and social psychology. Still in their formative years and lacking a parenting model, they are characterized by much conceptual and terminological variation. Despite diversity, however, they share several core principles, summarized as follows by Kendall (1985):

> 1. The human organism responds primarily to cognitive representations of and experiences in its environment rather than to the environments and experiences per se.
> 2. Most human learning is cognitively mediated.
> 3. Thoughts, feelings, and behaviors are causally interrelated.
> 4. Cognitive events, processes, products, and structures . . . are important in understanding and predicting . . . behavior.
> 5. Cognitive events, processes, products, and structures can be cast into testable formulations that can be integrated with behavioral paradigms. (p. 358)

In contrast to traditional conceptualizations of personality as a reflection of underlying and stable traits, cognitive-social theories reconceptualize the construct as a set of person variables. Such variables are idiographic, contextually sensitive, active cognitive processes that interact with affective and environmental variables to determine behavior. Congruent with information-processing paradigms, the primary focus of cognitive-social formulations is how the cognitive strategies individuals use to perceive, retain, and transform social information affect the internal and external determinants of behavior (Mischel, 1993). Although a detailed exposition of cognitive-social theory is beyond the scope of this chapter, the reader is referred to thorough presentations in Mischel (1968, 1973) and Bandura (1969, 1977, 1991).

The application of cognitive-social theories to childhood psychopathology is a relatively recent phenomenon. Butterfield and Cobb (1994) note that the success of behavioral methods with childhood behavior disorders overshadowed the development and use of cognitive-social theories. In the last few years, however, there has been increasing emphasis on viewing the child as part of a larger network of interacting social systems and on the important role of cognition (Mash & Terdal, 1988). A number of factors led to the incorporation of cognitive elements into developmental behavioral theory. Craighead, Meyers, and Craighead (1985) succinctly summarize these influences into three categories: the applications and findings of cognitive psychology, the development of self-control procedures, and the developments in cognitive therapy itself.

Bandura's (1969, 1977) elaboration of personal agency (i.e., the ability of individuals to use symbols for communication, to anticipate future events, to learn from observation or vicarious experience, to evaluate and regulate themselves, and to be reflectively self-conscious; Kauffman, 1993) and triadic reciprocality (i.e., the operation of behavior, cognitive and other personal factors, and environmental events as interacting determinants that exercise a bidirectional influence) was to have a profound influence on the ontogenesis of developmental cognitive-social theories. In Bandura's framework, person variables—in particular, the self-regulatory processes—are accorded a central role. Self-regulatory processes are conceptualized as multifaceted phenomena that operate through a number of subsidiary cognitive processes (e.g., self-observation, standard setting, affective self-reaction) and are indexed by self-beliefs of efficacy, personal goal setting, self-evaluation, and quality of analytic thought (Bandura, 1991).

Additional impetus for weaving cognitive elements into developmental behaviorism stems from the literature on interpersonal cognitive problem solving (ICPS). According to Spivack, Platt, and Shure's (1976) and Spivack and Shure's (1974) developmental hypothesis, ICPS is explicitly linked to social competence and adjustment. These authors have provided data to demonstrate that cognitive deficiencies, as manifested in an inability to engage in systematic interpersonal problem solving, presage inter- and intraindividual failure. Another stream of influence has been studies within the metacognitive tradition. Spawned largely by the research of Flavell (1970) and Brown (1978), a burgeoning literature has emerged on how children develop the ability to organize their activities such that they utilize various cognitive skills and mediational devices spontaneously and appropriately (Wertsch, 1985). Finally, models of social competence (e.g., Dodge, Pettit, McClaskey, & Brown, 1986) represent a recent addition to the cognitive-social assemblage; these attempt to mirror information-processing models in cognitive psychology by specifying the sequence of processes that are implemented in the reception, perception, storage, and recall of social information.

The self-control literature has also exercised significant influence on the emergence of developmental cognitive-social theories. According to Harris (1990), the theoretical substrates of this work are threefold: the behavioral perspective; the perspectives of the Soviet researchers Vygotsky (1934/1962) and Luria (1959, 1961); and the mediational perspective. Behavioral studies led the way in recognizing the role of induced self-speech in the implementation of self-control. Reasoning that self-speech was subject to the principles of operant conditioning, researchers (e.g., Kanfer, Karoly, & Newman, 1975) devised techniques for altering children's behavior by modifying self-statements and environmental antecedents and consequences. The developmental theories of Vygotsky and Luria, outlining the role of language in the self-regulation of behavior, formed the conceptual basis for self-instructional training, as elaborated on by Meichenbaum and Goodman (1977). The early work of mediational theorists—Kuenne (1946), Kendler, Kendler, and Wells (1960), and Reese (1962), who elucidated the role of developmental factors as determinants of verbally mediated behavior, and Flavell, Beach, and Chimsky's (1966) elaboration of production deficiencies (i.e., the failure to invoke task-relevant verbalizations)—was to have substantive impact on studies evaluating children's self-regulated learning.

Cognitive therapy itself served to stimulate interest in developmental cognitive paradigms. The early work of Ellis (1962), focusing on irrational statements, and Beck (1976), outlining negative cognitive schemata in depression, was extended to describe populations of depressed and "helpless" children (e.g., Diener & Dweck, 1978; Kaslow, Rehm, & Siegel, 1984) and has recently formed the conceptual basis for studying passivity in exceptional children (e.g., Borkowski, Estrada, Milstead, & Hale, 1989).

There have been several recent attempts to construct integrative developmental cognitive-social models for diverse child psychopathologies (e.g., the social exchange model of aggression of Dodge et al., 1986). The current state of the art, however, could best be described as embryonic. For example, a thorough consideration of developmental considerations has been notably absent in contemporary cognitive formulations of childhood psychopathology (e.g., Craighead et al., 1985; Kendall, 1985; Mahoney & Nezworski, 1985). Mash (1989) argues that a reasoned application of developmental considerations calls for recognition not only of age, gender, and normative issues but of more complex dimensions, such as developmental processes as they unfold and interact with and within one or more dynamic and changing social situations (p. 8). Citing data showing that maternal cognitions are predictive of childhood adjustment, Mash (1989) also underscores the need for formulations that are sensitive to the interrelationships among child behavioral, emotional, and cognitive response systems and family and ecological response systems. The relative absence of affective considerations in earlier conceptualizations has also been observed (Craighead et al., 1985), although more contemporary frameworks attempt to give an integrative account of the emotional and cognitive determinants of behavior (e.g., Kazdin, 1989). Studies documenting that biological determinants may represent significant vulnerability factors in child psychopathology (e.g., Offord & Boyle, 1989) further suggest a need for integration of organismic factors into cognitive-social formulations.

We now turn to two categories of exceptionality to examine the contributions of developmental cognitive-social theories to advancing understanding of personal variables and their impact on behavioral and emotional competence. Our first category, emotional and behavioral disorders, is given only cursory treatment, as the literature is expansive and diverse and this category is discussed (using clinical nomenclature) in other chapters of this book. A more thorough treatment is accorded to the category of children with learning disabilities, as cognitive-social theories have only recently been introduced as explanatory hypotheses of their behavioral and emotional problems.

EMOTIONAL OR BEHAVIORAL DISORDERS: A COGNITIVE-SOCIAL DESCRIPTION

Over the years, children and youths exhibiting significant deviations in behavior and/or emotion have been variously referred to by special educators as "emotionally handicapped," "emotionally impaired," "emotionally disturbed," "behaviorally disordered," "socially and emotionally maladjusted," "psychologically disordered," and "personally and socially maladjusted," among other labels. Although considerable terminological confusion has plagued the field, professionals appear to be approaching consensus in describing these individuals as "children and youths with emotional or behavioral disorders." Efforts to reach agreement on a definition have been equally contentious. The most contemporary definition proposed in the United States by the National Mental Health and Special Education Coalition reads as follows:

> (i) The term emotional or behavior disorder means a disability characterized by behavioral or emotional responses in school programs so different from appropriate age, cultural, or ethnic norms that they adversely affect educational performance, including academic, social, vocational or personal skills, and which:
> (A) is more than a temporary, expected response to stressful events in the environment;
> (B) is consistently exhibited in two different settings, at least one of which is school-related; and
> (C) persists despite individualized interventions within the education program, unless, in the judgment of the team, the child or youth's history indicates that such interventions would not be effective.
>
> (ii) Emotional or behavioral disorders can coexist with other disabilities.
>
> (iii) This category may include children or youth with schizophrenic disorders, affective disorders, anxiety disorders, or other sustained disturbances of conduct or adjustment when they adversely affect educational performance. (Kauffman, 1993, p. 32)

Within the clinical literature, psychiatric systems of classification have been the standard for categorizing emotionally and behaviorally disordered children and youths. The most widely endorsed system—that of the *Diagnostic and Statistical Manual of Mental Disorders* (American Psychiatric Association, 1987, 1994), founded on clinical observation and developed by committee consensus—provides diagnostic criteria for developmental disorders (e.g., mental retardation, pervasive developmental disorders, specific developmental disorders), disruptive behavior disorders (e.g., attention-deficit hyperactivity disorder, conduct disorder, oppositional-defiant disorder), anxiety disorders (e.g., separation anxiety disorder, avoidant disorder, overanxious disorder), eating disorders (e.g., anorexia nervosa, bulimia nervosa, pica, rumination disorder), gender identity disorders (e.g., gender identity disorder, transsexualism), tic disorders (e.g., Tourette's disorder, chronic motor or vocal tic disorder, transient tic disorder), elimination disorders (e.g., functional encopresis, functional enuresis), and speech disorders (e.g., cluttering, stuttering), among others.

A number of problems inherent in psychiatric classification systems (e.g., empirical inadequacy, questionable etiological assumptions, prescriptive limitations; see Mash & Terdal, 1988, for discussion) have prompted educators to endorse dimensional approaches to classification of emotional and behavioral disorders. Empirically derived dimensional systems provide descriptions of behavioral symptoms that statistically cluster and constitute a syndrome. A number of syndromes are generated by these techniques, and it is anticipated that children fall along the continuum of each of the syndromes. Multivariate statistical procedures that yield dimensional classifications have consistently identified two broad-band dimensions of child behavior: overcontrolled and undercontrolled. More specific narrow-band syndromes generated through statistical approaches include academic disability, aggressive, anxious, delinquent, depressed, hyperactive, immature, obsessive-compulsive, schizoid, sexual problems, sleep problems, social withdrawal, somatic complaints, and uncommunicative (Achenbach & Edelbrock, 1989). Though there remain attendant problems with dimensional systems (e.g., determination of constituent behavior, interactions between methods and informants; again see Mash & Terdal, 1988), educators argue that issues of reliability, validity, and utility render these systems more conducive to pedagogical practice.

A number of researchers have embraced cognitive-social theories as explanatory frameworks for varied narrow-band syndromes. For example, with regard to depression, Beck's (1976) model emphasizing the importance of the "cognitive triad" (a negative view of oneself, the world, and the future), Seligman's (1975) learned-helplessness model, Rehm's (1977) self-control model, and paradigms emphasizing the primacy of deficits in interpersonal problem-solving skills (e.g., D'Zurilla & Nezu, 1982) have all been applied to the study of depressive symptomatology in children (e.g., Fielstein et al., 1985; Leitenberg, Yost, & Carroll-Wilson, 1986). Models outlining the cognitive features of anxiety (e.g., Ingram & Kendall, 1987) have recently surfaced in studies evaluating cognitive-behavioral approaches to treating anxiety in children (e.g., Kane & Kendall, 1989). Current cognitive (e.g., Douglas, 1983) and cognitive-functional (e.g., Barkley, 1990) conceptualizations of hyperactivity as principally a disorder of self-regulation have generated substantive research examining cognitive processing and ecological determinants (e.g., Hamlett, Pellegrini, & Conners, 1987; Voelker, Carter, Sprague, Gdowski, & Lachar, 1989).

Aggression is the most frequently occurring behavioral disorder, not only in terms of referrals to child mental health clinics and special education services but in the general population as well (McMahon & Wells, 1989). The salience and prevalence of this disorder have led to a substantial amount of work aimed at elucidating etiological factors, conceptualizations, correlates, assessment, and interventions. Cognitive-social theories have played a pivotal role in this research. Though a comprehensive review of this literature is again beyond the scope of this chapter, for illustrative purposes we would like briefly to revisit historical descriptions of aggression. We will then examine selected studies elaborating on the cognitive/mediational correlates of aggression.

Aggression

History is laden with evidence of human aggression. Even before recorded civilization, there is ample archaeological evidence of individual and collective aggression. Though it is recognized that low intelligence represents a vulnerability factor in early aggression (Huesmann & Eron, 1987), there is substantive data to show that aggression does not respect intellectual boundaries. Indeed, aggression may be observed across all ability levels. Psychologists were quick to study aggression, and various theoretical views have been posited during this century. Freud initially described aggression as an impulse but later—in *Beyond the Pleasure Principle* (1920/1955)—elevated it (as Thanatos) to one of two major instincts (the other being the life instinct, or Eros). Freud was convinced that aggression was our greatest obstacle to civilization; with Einstein, he examined human aggression in an exchange of letters on the question of "Why war?" Various other dynamic positions range from seeing aggression as an instinct (e.g., Alexander, 1949; Hartmann, Kris, & Lowenstein, 1949) to describing it as the result of disturbed parent-child relationships (e.g., Bowlby, 1969). In contrast was Adler's later formulation (see Ansbacher & Ansbacher, 1956) in which aggression resulted from hostile environments and faulty upbringing. Karen Horney (1945) suggested that basic anxiety was responsible for supplying the core motivation for all tendencies, including aggression; aggressive personalities adapt only the single approach of moving against others in response to this basic anxiety.

A variety of behavioral interpretations have also been offered to explain human aggression. Dollard, Doob, Miller, Mowrer, and Sears (1939) argued that frustration (interference of a goal response) was the instigator of aggression. The operant-learning position described aggression as a learned behavior that was influenced by both antecedent and consequent conditions. Buss (1961) stated that aggressiveness was a personality variable composed of a class of enduring and pervasive responses. In his theory, aggressiveness is a habit system in which four key variables are involved in determining the strength of aggressive responses: antecedents of aggression, reinforcement history, social facilitation, and temperament. No description of aggression would be complete without mentioning Bandura's studies of social learning and the effects of observing aggression on later manifestations of aggression in children (Bandura, Ross, & Ross, 1963).

More eclectic views were developed in response to the limited progress in the study of human aggression. Kahn and Kirk (1968) stated that "consideration of definitional problems, the contributions and limitations of the drive position, frustration-aggression, learning and a variety of phylogenetic antecedents point to the need for a more comprehensive and integrated model" (p. 559). They defined aggression as a biologically based drive that serves to energize and direct behavior and is elicted by frustration. The physiological basis of a drive explanation has been examined in both animal and human studies (e.g., Delgado, 1969; Lorenz, 1966). Other studies have further probed the role of hormones such as testosterone and alcohol (Hull & Bond, 1986; Moyer, 1976) on aggressive behavior. Although Kahn and Kirk (1968) attempted to reconcile and integrate descriptions of aggression as a drive, as a means of gratifying other basic drives, as a result of frustration, and as modifiable through learning and the "law of effect," the greatest progress in the psychological study of aggression has come from more recent cognitive-social models.

Contemporary cognitive-social theory argues that behavior is influenced by cognitive processes. An understanding of the aggressive behavior of children is effectively articulated within a framework that examines how they perceive their world (including cause-and-effect attributions) and evaluate the outcomes of their actions. Though it would be wrong to ignore the potential importance of models that describe aggression as a latent trait, or ascribe causes of aggression to genetic, social, or cultural explanations, there is strong research evidence that the cognitive processes and mediational patterns of aggressive children are instrumental in behavior production. A brief examination of this literature follows.

Cognitive Correlates of Aggression

A substantive body of literature has documented mediational biases among socially rejected and aggressive children. A number of studies report that aggressive children and youths display a bias toward attributing hostile intentions to peers (Dodge, Murphy, & Buchsbaum, 1984; Dodge & Somberg, 1987; Dodge & Tomlin, 1987; Lochman, 1987; Milich & Dodge, 1984; Nasby, Hayden, & DePaulo, 1980; Steinberg & Dodge, 1983). Other work documents that such hostile attributional biases may be sensitive to affective and processing factors and dimensionally specific. For example, Dodge and Coie (1987) found attributional biases characterize reactive (but not proactive) aggression, but that reactive biases vary as a function of perceptions of threat. Dodge and Price (1990) report further that attributional biases were implicated in interpersonal reactive aggression involving anger but not in socialized delinquency. Dodge and Newman (1981) and Dodge and Frame (1982) demonstrated that biases were mediated by tendencies toward impulsive responding.

Self-efficacy for aggressive responding has also been the subject of several studies. Aggressive children often report that it is easier to perform aggression and more difficult to inhibit aggressive impulses (Deluty, 1979, 1981a,b; Perry, Perry, & Rasmussen, 1986). In related work, response-outcome biases have been documented. Research examining beliefs about the reinforcing and punishing consequences of aggression converge on the finding that aggressive children express more confidence that aggressive versus assertive responding produces tangible rewards and reduces aversive treatment by others (Asarnow & Callan, 1985; Milich & Dodge, 1984; Perry et al., 1986). Lochman and Wayland (1993) elaborate on this finding by showing that relative to socially competent peers, aggressive subjects place a higher value on social goals of dominance and revenge and lower values on goals for affiliation. Recent work (e.g., Dodge & Siegmund, 1993; Dodge & Tomlin, 1987; Huesmann, 1987) has focused on the knowledge structures that guide cognitive processing, characterizing the social schemata of aggressive children as emphasizing self-versus social referents.

Processing deficiencies in aggression have also been amply documented. Several studies have confirmed selectivity in attending to social cues. Dodge and Newman (1981), Dodge and Frame (1982), Dodge and Tomlin (1987), and Milich and Dodge (1984) have shown that aggressive children (a) fail to utilize appropriate situational cues and (b) demonstrate selective recall of hostile cues. Deficits in determination of the intentions of self and others are also substantiated in a number of studies (Dodge & Coie, 1987; Dodge & Somberg, 1987; Lochman, 1987). Dodge and Somberg (1987), for example, report that aggressive subjects exhibit a deficit in interpreting others' intentions accurately, as well as in linking interpretations to behavioral responses. Lochman (1987) found that aggressive children presented with a perceptual bias, manifested through minimizing their perceptions of their own aggression.

In other processing research, constituent elements of problem solving have been investigated. French and Waas (1987), Richard and Dodge (1982), Hairns and Herrman (1989), and Gouze (1987) have each shown that aggressive children are less likely to generate effective prosocial alternatives to social problem situations. Deficits in perspective taking and interpersonal awareness have also been found (Gurucharri, Phelps, & Selman, 1984; Minde, 1992).

Dodge et al. (1986) conducted one of the few studies of the cognitive-processing correlates of aggression within a theoretical context that takes into consideration ecological variables. These authors proposed a model of social exchange in which social behavior was conceptualized as a function of the child's processing of a set of social environmental cues. This processing was posited to occur in five separable sequential steps: the encoding of social cues, the mental representation of those cues, the accessing of potential behavioral responses, the evaluation and selection of an optimal response, and the enactment of that response. Dodge et al. hypothesized that skillful processing at each step would increase the probability that a child would behave in a manner judged to be competent by peers and adults, and that increments in prediction would accrue from measures of processing at each step. Further, they speculated that peers' judgments of a child would be based on their processing of that child's behavior, and that such processing would influence their behavior toward that child.

A total of 96 children (48 aggressive children and 48 average children matched for age and gender, with aggression levels assessed by teachers and peers) were measured on the five steps of processing for each of two social domains (peer-group entry and responding to a provocation). Children participated in a peer-group entry task and were exposed to an actual provocation by a peer; observations of children's naturally occurring peer-group entry and aggressive behavior in the classroom and on the playground were also conducted. Results indicated significant differences between groups on each of the processing steps: Relative to average children, aggressive children were less likely to use presented cues, were less accurate at detecting prosocial intentions (but more accurate at detecting hostile intentions), generated a higher proportion of aggressive responses, were less likely to endorse competent responses, and were less skilled at enacting a competent response to a provocation. Of particular interest is that several measures of domain-specific processing predicted a child's success in provocation and peer-entry encounters, whereas processing patterns in each domain were related to general social behavioral adaptation in a natural peer setting.

This study is exemplary in that through careful task analysis of processing components and by contextualizing the study, Dodge et al. were able to delineate the specific nature of maladaptive processing, as well as the situational specificity of these processing patterns. In contrast to structural or attribute descriptions of aggression, the findings of this research have direct prescriptive application.

LEARNING DISABILITIES: A COGNITIVE-SOCIAL DESCRIPTION

Traditionally, the term *learning disabilities* has been used as a categorical label for children exhibiting academic performance problems that are the result of inherent and specific difficulties in performing some of the psychological processes required for learning (Torgeson, 1991). For example, the National Joint Committee on Learning Disabilities (1981) defined learning disabilities as

> a generic term that refers to a heterogeneous group of disorders manifested by significant difficulties in the acquisition and use of listening, speaking, reading, writing, reasoning, or mathematical abilities. These disorders are intrinsic to the individual and presumed to be due to central nervous system dysfunction. Even though a learning disability may occur concomitantly with other handicapping conditions . . . or environmental influences . . . , it is not the direct result of those conditions or influences. (p. 1)

Such definitions emphasize the achievement correlates of learning disabilities while according the emotional and behavioral concomitants a secondary role. Torgenson (1991) and T. Bryan (1991), however, note that in response to a substantial body of literature documenting the social problems of children with learning disabilities, arguments have been advanced for formal recognition of deficits in emotional-behavioral competence as a potentially defining characteristic of learning disabilities. To date, this recognition has not occurred.

Emotional and Behavioral Correlates

Although legislatively mandated definitions have not been responsive to calls for primary inclusion of emotional and behavioral criteria (Gresham & Elliott, 1989; Torgeson, 1991), empirical support for such a position continues to mount. Reviews of research literature addressing the social competence of children with learning disabilities converge on the view that this population is vulnerable to emotional and behavioral problems (e.g., T. Bryan, 1991; Pearl, 1986). A sampling of independent comparative studies documents deficits ranging from maladaptive cognitive and affective responses (Axelrod, 1982; Ayres, Cooley & Dunn, 1990; Chapman, 1988a,b; Garrett & Crump, 1980; Gerber & Zinkgraf, 1982; Horowitz, 1981; Jackson, Enright, & Murdock, 1987) to contextually inappropriate behavioral actions (Center & Wascom, 1986; Gresham & Reschly, 1986). Factorial studies of the behavioral problems of children with learning disabilities (Cullinan, Epstein, & Dembinski, 1979; Cullinan, Epstein, & Lloyd, 1981; McConaughy & Ritter, 1986) report significantly more behaviors indicative of anxiety, depression, uncommunicativeness, social withdrawal, hyperactivity, aggressiveness, and delinquency among children with learning disabilities relative to normal peers. Longitudinal data (Cantwell & Baker, 1991) provide confirmatory evidence for the stability of emotional and behavioral disorders in the learning-disabled population.

Reliance upon the comparative paradigm to document emotional and behavioral problems in children with learning disabilities has come under significant criticism. Ackerman and Howes (1986), for example, argue that this framework obscures the equally important issue of the within-group variability of the learning-disabled population. They, along with others (e.g., Merrell, 1990; Schumaker & Hazel, 1984; Weener, 1981), underscore the heterogeneity of children with learning disabilities with regard to emotional and behavioral deficits and suggest that categorical inferences drawn from mean differences may encourage conclusions that overemphasize differences and minimize similarities between groups.

Comorbidity with other disorders is also a factor that must be considered when reviewing studies reporting on emotional and behavioral impairments in children with learning disabilities. A number of researchers, for example, have documented the high prevalence of hyperactivity in learning disabilities (Holborow & Berry, 1986; Shaywitz & Shaywitz, 1988). Other studies (e.g., McKinney, 1984; McKinney, McClure, & Feagans, 1982) have shown the presence of hyperactivity in learning disabilities to be associated with poorer behavioral and academic outcomes, suggesting hyperactivity may represent the vulnerability factor in emotional and behavioral disorders in some children with learning disabilities. Cantwell and Baker (1991), citing research studies showing considerable comorbidity of conduct disorders and learning disabilities in children, present evidence to show that for at least a subgroup of children who have both conditions, the onset of conduct problems precedes learning disabilities about half the time. Other work documenting similar behavioral abnormalities in learning-disabled, low-achieving, and mildly handicapped children has led to speculation that behavioral impairments may accrue more from intellectual and experiential factors than from impaired information processing (e.g., Merrell, 1990; McKinney & Forman, 1982). Unfortunately, examination of subject-selection criteria reveals the need for more rigorous sampling procedures if we are to disentangle the complex relationships between learning disabilities and other comorbid behavioral and emotional problems.

Classification research on learning disabilities has also confirmed the need for more rigorous methodology, particularly with reference to emotional and behavioral constituents. McKinney et al. (1982) identified six different overt behavioral patterns in learning-disabled children and found differential outcomes over a 3-year period with respect to emotional and behavioral well-being. Rourke, Young, and Leenaars (1989) describe a particular subtype of learning disabilities, nonverbal learning disabilities, which is at particular risk for the development of internalized socioemotional pathology, including withdrawal, anxiety, and depression. Bender and Golden (1990) report on a visual problem subgroup that exhibited significant acting-out behavior.

Etiology of Emotional and Behavioral Problems in Children with Learning Disabilities

The focus within the field of learning disabilities has shifted from simply cataloguing the emotional and behavioral deficits exhibited by learning-disabled children to searching for an explanatory hypothesis for emotional-behavioral differences (Perlmutter, 1986). Over the years, numerous factors have been cited as causal in the emotional and behavioral problems of children with learning disabilities. Early theories attributed inappropriate emotional reactions, hyperactivity, conceptual disorders, distractibility, and faulty perceptions to nonspecific exogenous neurological impairment (e.g., Strauss & Lehtinen, 1947). Others argued for inadequate development of ego functions as a result of an impaired central nervous system and failure experiences (e.g., Rappaport, 1966). Still others posited that there are several specific types of learning disabilities, with social deficiencies forming a separate syndrome, likely involving dysfunctions principally on the right hemisphere (e.g., Johnson & Myklebust, 1964).

Language Conceptualization

Studies on subtypes of learning disabilities have consistently classified language disorder as the largest subtype (Doehring & Hoshko, 1977; Doehring, Hoshko, & Bryans, 1979; Fish & Rourke, 1979; Lyon & Watson, 1981; McKinney, 1984). A recent conceptualization posits that deficiencies in language contribute significantly to the emotional and behavioral difficulties of children with learning disabilities (e.g.,

Spafford & Grosser, 1993). A number of studies have shown that such linguistic problems are not limited to deficits in the structural aspects of language but also encompass impairments in pragmatic competence. Research exploring such diverse pragmatic skills as code switching, presuppositional knowledge, referential communication, speech act knowledge, and discourse skills has demonstrated subtle communication problems in learning-disabled children (Boucher, 1984; T. Bryan, Donahue, Pearl, & Sturn, 1981; Donahue, Pearl, & Bryan, 1982; Knight-Arest, 1984; Pearl, Donahue, & Bryan, 1986; Schwean Kowalchuk, 1991; Schwean Kowalchuk & Nostbakken, 1991). Studies have also pointed to nonverbal communicative impairments in this population (J. Bryan, Bryan, & Sonnefeld, 1982; J. Bryan & Perlmutter, 1979; J. Bryan & Sherman, 1980).

Whether or not such pragmatic impairments play a significant role in the emotional and behavioral difficulties of children with learning disabilities remains a thorny theoretical question. At issue is the relationship of social cognition to language. The Piagetian assumption that language is not a separate innate characteristic but rather only one of several abilities that result from cognitive maturation (Berko Gleason, 1993) argues for cognitive impairments as central in language and social deficits. The neo-Piagetian position that language, social, and cognitive knowledge are both interrelated and independent but stem from common structural underpinnings (e.g., Bates & MacWhinney, 1982) affords language a contributing but not causal role. In contrast, arguments that language attainments may predate cognitive concepts (e.g., Vygotsky, 1934/1962) allow for the possibility that language deficits may play a principal role in the social difficulties of children with learning disabilities. Regardless, it would appear that given the current state of the art, pragmatic competencies should be included in attempts to understand the emotional and behavioral profile of children with learning disabilities (T. Bryan, 1991).

Cognitive Conceptualization

The position that the psychological subprocesses responsible for the inadequate academic performances of children with learning disabilities are instrumental in their emotional and behavioral difficulties has attained prominence in the field of learning disabilities. Termed the "social cognition hypothesis" by Pearl (1986), this proposal underscores the centrality of information processing and mediational factors in the development of emotional and behavioral difficulties in learning-disabled children.

During the past 15 years, considerable debate has been waged over the nature of the "psychological subprocesses responsible for inadequate academic performance" in the learning disabled (e.g., Vellutino, 1986). Perceptual-motor impairments; disorders of attention, language, memory, and thinking; distractibility, impulsivity, and emotional lability; poor motivation and self-concept; deficiencies in basic academic skills; and equivocal neurological signs have all been implicated as causal (McKinney, 1984). In the past few years, however, congruent with the current zeitgeist in psychology, accounts have become more cognitively focused.

> It is also clear that the early and more traditional conceptualizations of learning disabilities . . . have lost much of their popularity and have been challenged, not only by theories postulating deficiencies in language as the major source of difficulty in school learning, but also by those postulating deficiencies in higher order cognitive processes. (Vellutino, 1986, p. 327)

Two contemporary hypotheses—the deficiency hypothesis and the inactive-learner hypothesis, both deriving from Flavell's (1970) concept of a production deficiency—have been invoked to account for generalized learning disabilities (Borkowski et al., 1989; Torgeson, 1991). Though many proponents of the deficiency hypothesis acknowledge the contributory role of lower-level information processing deficits, they accord primary causal status to deficits or developmental delays in higher order metacognitive processes. Metacognitive functioning, as defined by Reeve and Brown (1985), comprises the self-regulatory activities of the cognitive system and includes planning, monitoring, checking, and regulating problem-solving behavior. Meichenbaum (1976) hypothesizes that such self-regulatory activities are under the control of inner speech and, utilizing a cognitive-functional approach, explains the deficiency in learning disabilities as follows:

> If one had to summarize this diagnostic process under one rubric, then perhaps the summary term "cognitive strategies deficiency syndrome" could be applied with learning disabled children. This label places immediate emphasis on cognitive strategies: the means by which the subject manages his own thinking. The term "deficiency" underscores the failure of the child with learning disabilities to produce and emit task-relevant cognitions and his likelihood to emit task-irrelevant cognitions and behaviors that contribute to inadequate performance. It is suggested that children with learning disabilities signifi-

> cantly differ from normals in their thinking processes, cognitive strategies, and in the quantity and quality of their inner speech. (p. 440)

The inactive-learner hypothesis argues that children with learning disabilities are less intrinsically motivated to perform well or to expend effort on various tasks (Deshler, Schumaker, Alley, Warner, & Clark, 1982). Subscribed to by a number of researchers (e.g., Borkowski et al., 1989; Douglas, 1980; Licht, 1983; Torgeson & Licht, 1983), this formulation places primary emphasis on the self-systems (i.e., self-efficacy, self-esteem, attributions) of children with learning disabilities. Studies within the tradition of social learning theory have documented the substantive influence that self-beliefs have on how much effort individuals mobilize in a given endeavor, how long they persevere in the face of difficulties and setbacks, and whether their thought patterns are self-hindering or self-aiding (Bandura, 1991). This work has provided the impetus for researchers to speculate that aberrant learning experiences are causal in producing expectations of failure, impaired perception of personal adequacy, lack of persistence, and impaired intrinsic motivation in children with learning disabilities. Wong (1991) elaborates on the maladaptive attributional patterns of children with learning disabilities, arguing that they underlie impoverished motivation and self-esteem and give rise to metacognitive deficits:

> The unwholesome self-systems of learning disabled students lead them to avoid challenging tasks, to give up readily at difficult tasks after initial setbacks. Hence, they rob themselves of opportunities in generating problem-solving strategies and fail to apply and modify learned strategies flexibly to suit the task demands. The net result of such poorly developed self-systems is to restrict learning disabled students' development in self-efficacy and self-regulation and make them into passive learners. (p. 249)

In keeping with Bandura's (1991) notion that beliefs about the self function are an important set of proximal determinants of human self-regulation, Borkowski et al. (1989) and Douglas (1983) underscore the interactive relationship between maladaptive self-beliefs and impaired self-regulation or metacognitive functioning in children with learning disabilities. These authors construct a sequelence of actions in which deficient cognitive subprocesses, aberrant learning experiences, self-deprecating motivational states, impoverishment of higher-order metacognitive processes, and decrements in strategic behavior and intellectual development are mutually interactive.

As explanatory hypothesis of the achievement problems of children with learning disabilities, both the deficiency and inactive-learner formulations have received correlational support. Stone and Michals (1986), in a review of the literature on the metacognitive skills of children with learning disabilities, segment metacognitive activities into three elements: goal establishment (planning), data gathering (selection of relevant information, monitoring, use of feedback), and information integration (reasoning). They cite studies documenting that although task content and complexity are confounding variables, there is evidence of deficits in all three components. There is also ample evidence to support the contention that the maladaptive belief systems of children with learning disabilities are important determinants of achievement outcomes. Various studies have shown that children with learning disabilities are more likely to make maladaptive academic attributions (attributing failure to stable factors beyond their personal control; e.g., Ayres et al., 1990; Jacobsen, Lowery, & DuCette, 1986), report lower academic self-concepts than peers whose achievement is satisfactory (e.g., Ayres et al., 1990; Jacobsen et al., 1986; Marsh, 1988), articulate lower expectations for future academic success (e.g., Chapman, 1988b), and fail to persist with difficult academic tasks (e.g., Ayres et al., 1990; Licht, Kistner, Ozkaragoz, Shapiro, & Clausen, 1985; Palmer, Drummond, Tollison, & Zinkgraff, 1982). Other research underscores the powerful mediating effect that ability belief patterns have on instructional responsivity (e.g., Chapman, 1988b; Kistner, Osborne, & LeVerrier, 1988).

Methodological and conceptual problems have led a number of authors to argue for caution in interpreting information-processing/mediational studies of children with learning disabilities. Particularly germane to the present discussion is the potentially confounding effect that intelligence may exercise on such processes. Although learning disabilities are defined on the basis of average intellect, relatively few studies have taken the necessary steps to establish equality of normally achieving and learning-disabled samples on measures of intelligence. Where such methodological rigor has been ensured, there is some indication that among samples of children with generalized learning disabilities, IQs are often depressed relative to normally achieving peers (e.g., Aponik & Dembo, 1983). Indeed, there is considerable controversy about whether achievement, intellectual, and behavioral correlates reliably discriminate children with learning disabilities from underachievers (e.g., Merrell, 1990; Shepard, Smith, & Vojir, 1983).

Research on the mediational patterns of children with learning disabilities adds further fuel to the controversy, as studies have not always yielded differential affective and task-oriented responses in learning-disabled and low achievers. For example, Friedman and Medway (1987) report learning-disabled boys tended to attribute academic outcomes to external forces. However, like low achievers, learning-disabled boys did not evidence lower performance expectations or greater expectancy shifts following outcome information and exhibited greater persistence with difficult tasks relative to normally achieving peers. These results led the authors to conclude that a hypothesis referencing achievement motivation (e.g., Atkinson, 1964) rather than passivity has greater explanatory power for both underachieving and learning-disabled children. Information-processing research suggests further than metacognitive deficits may not always differentiate between children with learning disabilities and those with depressed IQs (Borkowski, Johnston, & Reid, 1986).

Interface of Metacognition and Behavior

Given these caveats, there remains good reason to hypothesize that the kind of metacognitive or self-regulatory deficits some learning-disabled children exhibit would have substantive impact on behavioral and emotional functioning. Although there is clearly a need for researchers to articulate models of the cognitive processes underlying social and emotional competence, there is enough information to propose that "realistic rational, and flexible cognitive styles are desirable over unrealistic, irrational, and rigid styles and that having access to and engaging in the cognitive processes necessary for problem resolution is superior to deficient processing" (Kendall, 1985, p. 361).

At issue here, though, is the generalizability of the information-processing/mediational deficits purported to be causal in academic failure to behavioral and emotional problems. Dodge et al. (1986) point to the substantive work that has been undertaken by cognitive researchers on the processing of nonsocial information and eschew the relative absence of understanding regarding the processing of social information. They note that

> empirical work is simply not far enough along to be able to articulate the major differences between the social and the nonsocial information-processing systems. It has been suggested that affect plays a major role in social cognition, in contrast with the "cold" and rational processes of nonsocial cognition. Still, it is quite possible that the major features of each system are similar. (p. 60)

Dodge and colleagues go on to argue that in addition to affect, a number of other factors may differentiate social and nonsocial processing, including source of information (i.e., rules acquired from past experience in nonsocial processing, direct experience in social processing), object of processing (i.e., enduring rules in nonsocial processing, highly changeable and unpredictable stimuli in social processing), and task (i.e., interpretation of "intent" which is idiosyncratic to social processing).

Cognitive-Social Skills of Children with Learning Disabilities

A brief review of studies assessing the cognitive-social skills of children with learning disabilities may serve to illuminate the specificity of cognitive processes and mediational patterns. Although diverse methodologies have been used to explore the cognitive/mediational determinants of emotional and behavioral problems in children with learning disabilities, norm-referenced measures of self-concept and self-esteem represent the preferred methodology in assessing the self-systems. Research examining self-concept has yielded mixed results. Though a number of studies suggest global self-concept deficits (e.g., Jones, 1985; Kistner & Osborne, 1987; Margalit & Zak, 1984; Rogers & Saklofske, 1985), other reports argue for the academic specificity of self-concept differences (e.g., Silverman & Zigmond, 1983; Winnie, Woodlands, & Wong, 1982).

Research evaluating differences in self-esteem is more consistent in reporting no differences between normally achieving and learning-disabled children (e.g., Lincoln & Chazan, 1979; Tollefson et al., 1982; Winnie et al., 1982), although there is evidence to suggest developmental decrements (Gregory, Shanahan, & Walberg, 1986). Although there is a substantive body of literature examining self-efficacy and attributions in children with learning disabilities, studies have unfortunately only explored patterns within the context of academic concerns. Whether such maladaptive belief patterns generalize to social spheres remains an issue for future research, although studies showing high comorbidity between learning disabilities and affective disorders (e.g., Cullinan et al., 1979; Cullinan et al., 1981) hint at generalized effects.

Various tasks (again mostly of a structuralist nature) have been used to probe the cognitive-social skills of children with learning disabilities. Role taking, for example, has been examined in affective, cognitive, and perceptual domains. The findings can be described as equivocal at best. Bruck and Hebert (1982), Dickstein and Warren (1980), Horowitz (1981), and Wong and Wong (1980) report that learning-disabled children performed more poorly than their normally achieving peers, but Ackerman, Elardo, and Dykman (1979) and Fincham (1979) found no differences. Studies examining the perception of nonverbal cues (e.g., Axelrod, 1982; Hall & Richmond, 1985; Jackson et al., 1987; Sisterhen & Gerber, 1989) report that children with learning disabilities are less accurate in their interpretation of nonverbal behavior, but a study by Stone and leGreca (1984) suggests differences may be attributable to attention factors.

The understanding of social and moral conventions has also been assessed in several studies, with mixed results. Whereas Derr (1986) found learning-disabled subjects are less sophisticated in their understanding of moral principles, data presented by Fincham (1977) suggest age-appropriate understandings. Using diverse methodology, studies assessing the social problem-solving skills of children with learning disabilities converge on the conclusion that these children exhibit deficits but that they vary as a function of the salience and familiarity of cues (e.g., Maheady, Maitland, & Sainato, 1984; Pearl, Donahue, & Bryan, 1990; Schneider & Yoshida, 1988; Silver & Young, 1985; Toro & Weisberg, 1990).

Given these equivocal findings, what kind of summative statement can we make regarding the viability of the social cognition hypothesis in relation to furthering our understanding of children with learning disabilities? Our analysis of this literature leads us to the position that the hypothesis remains tenable, but that methodological considerations preclude one from drawing any robust conclusions. We have made reference to the almost exclusive use of structural measures to assess the cognitive-social skills of children with learning disabilities. Though such structural measures fuel interesting conjecture, they operate within the parameters imposed by attribute models, focusing on constructs whose direct relationship to behavior is often poorly defined. Knowing, for example, that children with learning disabilities perform poorly on an inferencing task does little to illuminate if or how these skills are related to emotional and behavioral competence. Similarly, revealing that children with learning disabilities present with negative self-concepts provides no direction in terms of the specific inner-speech patterns that sustain maladaptive beliefs. Moreover, by focusing on the outcome product rather than the constituent processes, we fail to arrive at an understanding of the specific cognitive processes that may underlie impaired performance; this absence limits the prescriptive utility of our findings. Finally, exclusive use of construct models imposes severe constraints on advancing theoretical understandings of the interactive relationships between and within cognitive and environmental determinants of behavior and emotion in children with learning disabilities.

We argue that progress in this field rests on the application of models that take into consideration an understanding of the relationships among cognitive processes, mediational patterns, affective responses, and social and environmental determinants. At this point in time, affective considerations have received only peripheral attention (e.g., Goldstein & Dundon, 1986; Perlmutter, Crocker, Cordray, & Garstecki, 1983), and there is a notable paucity of studies examining the connection between ecological systems (e.g., family) and learning-disabled children's cognitions (but see Dishion, 1990).

SUMMARY

Individual differences and exceptionalities have been described throughout history, and current educational and psychological classification systems similarly recognize a diversity of abilities and disabilities. Until recently, our understanding of these categories of exceptionality was constructed largely from traditional conceptualizations of personality and intelligence. In the main, however, these approaches have failed to capture the complex interrelationships between individual-difference and situational variables, a failure that consequently limits their prescriptive utility. In recognition of these limitations, contemporary theorists in the fields of child and adolescent exceptionalities have called for an integrative reconceptualization of the constructs of personality and intelligence.

Cognitive-social theories marry personality and intelligence through the delineation of person variables, defined as idiographic, contextually sensitive, active processes that act in concert with affective and environmental variables to determine behavior. Influence on developmental cognitive-social models has come from the literature on social learning theory and self-control, interpersonal cognitive problem-solving, metacognition, information-processing, and cognitive therapies. Although developmental cognitive-social theories are still in the formative stage, they hold considerable promise for enriching our understanding of the role of cognition in the behavioral and emotional responses of exceptional children. By way of illustration, this chapter applied the extant research literature to an analysis of two categories of exceptionality in children: emotional and behavior disorders, and learning disabilities.

The category of emotional and behavior disorders includes children who exhibit pervasive and chronic deviations in their behavioral or emotional responses that negatively affect their school performance. Aggression is the most prevalent and salient syndrome within this category and has been the focus of considerable attention in cognitive-social studies. This work has advanced our understanding of the cognitive correlates of aggression and has enriched educational and psychological assessment and intervention practices. The model of social exchange proposed by Dodge et al. (1986), in which cognitive processing is viewed in relation to contextual factors, is exemplary of this approach.

Finally, our examination of the literature on learning disabilities underscores the integrative potential of cognitive-social paradigms. Learning disabilities have traditionally been defined as academic performance problems; however, substantive evidence points to emotional and behavioral deficits as primary defining characteristics. Recent cognitive conceptualizations of learning disabilities have stressed higher-order cognitive deficits and provide explanatory hypotheses for their emotional and behavioral problems. This research has been grounded mainly within structural models, though, with limited attention directed to examinations of situationally specific cognitive processes that may underlie emotional or behavioral disorders in children with learning disabilities.

REFERENCES

Ackerman, D., & Howes, C. (1986). Sociometric status and after-school social activity of children with learning disabilities. *Journal of Learning Disabilities, 19*, 416–419.

Ackerman, P. T., Elardo, P. T., & Dykman, R. A. (1979). A psychosocial study of hyperactive and learning disabled boys. *Journal of Abnormal Child Psychology, 7*, 91–99.

Achenbach, T. M., & Edelbrock, C. S. (1989). Diagnostic, taxonomic, and assessment issues. In T. H. Ollendick & M. Hersen (Eds.), *Handbook of child psychopathology* (2nd ed.). New York: Plenum.

Alexander, F. (1949). *Fundamentals of psychoanalysis.* New York: Norton.

American Psychiatric Association. (1987). *Diagnostic and statistical manual of mental disorders* (rev. 3rd ed.). Washington, DC: Author.

American Psychiatric Association. (1994). *Diagnostic and statistical manual of mental disorders* (4th ed.). Washington, DC: Author.

Ansbacher, H. L., & Ansbacher, R. B. (Eds.). (1956). *The individual psychology of Alfred Adler.* New York: Basic Books.

Aponik, D. A., & Dembo, M. H. (1983). LD and normal adolescents' causal attributions of success and failure at different levels of task difficulty. *Learning Disability Quarterly, 6*, 31–39.

Asarnow, J. R., & Callan, J. W. (1985). Boys with peer adjustment problems: Social cognitive processes. *Journal of Consulting and Clinical Psychology, 53*, 80–87.

Atkinson, J. W. (1964). *An introduction to motivation.* Princeton, NJ: Van Nostrand.

Axelrod, L. (1982). Social perception in learning disabled adolescents. *Journal of Learning Disabilities, 15*, 610–613.

Ayres, R., Cooley, E., & Dunn, C. (1990). Self-concept, attribution, and persistence in learning-disabled students. *Journal of School Psychology, 28*, 153–163.

Bandura, A. (1969). *Principles of behavior modification.* New York: Holt.

Bandura, A. (1973). *Aggression: A social learning analysis.* Englewood Cliffs, NJ: Prentice-Hall.

Bandura, A. (1977). *Social learning theory.* Englewood Cliffs, NJ: Prentice-Hall.

Bandura, A. (1991). Social cognitive theory of self-regulation. *Organizational Behavior and Human Decision Processes, 50*, 248–287.

Bandura, A., Ross, D., & Ross, S. (1963). Imitation of film mediated aggressive models. *Journal of Abnormal and Social Psychology, 69*, 1–9.

Barkley, R. A. (1990). *Attention-deficit hyperactivity disorder: A handbook for diagnosis and treatment.* New York: Guilford.

Bates, E., & MacWhinney, B. (1982). Functionalist approaches to grammar. In E. Wanner & L. R. Gleitman (Eds.), *Language acquisition: The state of the art* (pp. 173–218). Cambridge, England: Cambridge University Press.

Beck, A. T. (1976). *Cognitive therapy and the emotional disorders.* New York: International Universities Press.

Bender, W. N., & Golden, L. B. (1990). Subtypes of students with learning disabilities as derived from cognitive, academic, behavioral, and self-concept measures. *Learning Disabilities Quarterly, 13*, 183–194.

Berko Gleason, J. (1993). *The development of language* (3rd ed.). New York: Macmillan.

Borkowski, J. G., Estrada, M. T., Milstead, M., & Hale, C. A. (1989). General problem-solving skills: Relations between metacognition and strategic processing. *Learning Disability Quarterly, 12*, 57–70.

Borkowski, J. G., Johnston, M. B., & Reid, M. K. (1986). Metacognition, motivation, and controlled performance. In S. J. Ceci (Ed.), *Handbook of cognitive, social, and neurological aspects of learning disabilities* (Vol. 2, pp. 147–173). Hillsdale, NJ: Erlbaum.

Boucher, C. R. (1984). Pragmatics: The verbal language of learning disabled and nondisabled boys. *Learning Disability Quarterly, 7*, 271–286.

Bowlby, J. (1969). *Attachment and loss.* New York: Basic Books.

Brown, A. (1978). Knowing when, where and how to remember: A problem of mental cognition. In R. Glaser (Ed.), *Advances in instructional psychology* (Vol. 1, pp. 77–165). Hillsdale, NJ: Erlbaum.

Bruck, M., & Hebert, M. (1982). Correlates of learning disabled students' peer-interaction patterns. *Learning Disability Quarterly, 5*, 353–362.

Bryan, J. H., Bryan, T., & Sonnefeld, J. (1982). Being known by the company one keeps: The contagion of first impressions. *Learning Disability Quarterly, 5*, 288–294.

Bryan, J. H., & Perlmutter, B. (1979). Immediate impressions of LD children by female adults. *Learning Disability Quarterly, 2*, 80–88.

Bryan, J. H., & Sherman, R. (1980). Immediate impressions of non-verbal ingratiation attempts by learning disabled boys. *Learning Disability Quarterly, 3*, 19–28.

Bryan, T. (1991). Social problems and learning disabilities. In B. Y. L. Wong (Ed.), *Learning about learning disabilities* (pp. 195–229). San Diego, CA: Academic Press.

Bryan, T., Donahue, M., Pearl, R., & Sturn, C. (1981). Learning disabled children's conversational skills—the "T.V. talk show". *Learning Disability Quarterly, 4*, 250–259.

Buss, A. H. (1961). *The psychology of aggression.* New York: Wiley.

Butterfield, W. H., & Cobb, N. H. (1994). Cognitive-behavioral treatment of children and adolescents. In D. K. Granvold (Ed.), *Cognitive and behavioral treatment: Methods and applications* (pp. 65–89). Pacific Grove, CA: Brooks/Cole.

Cantwell, D. P., & Baker, L. (1991). Association between attention deficit-hyperactivity disorder and learning disorders. *Journal of Learning Disabilities, 24*, 88–95.

Cattell, R. B., & Drevdahl, J. E. (1955). A comparison of the personality profile (16PF) of eminent researchers with that of eminent teachers and administrators, and the general population. *British Journal of Psychology, 46*, 248–261.

Center, D. B., & Wascom, A. M. (1986). Teacher perceptions of social behavior in learning disabled and socially normal children and youth. *Journal of Learning Disabilities, 19*, 420–425.

Chapman, J. W. (1988a). Cognitive-motivational characteristics and academic achievement of learning disabled children: A longitudinal study. *Journal of Educational Psychology, 80*, 357–365.

Chapman, J. W. (1988b). Learning disabled children's self-concepts. *Review of Educational Research, 58*, 347–371.

Craighead, W. E., Meyers, A. W., & Craighead, L. W. (1985). A conceptual model for cognitive-behavior therapy with children. *Journal of Abnormal Child Psychology, 13*, 331–342.

Cronbach, L. J. (1957). The two disciplines of scientific psychology. *American Psychologist, 12*, 671–684.

Cullinan, D., Epstein, M. H., & Dembinski, R. J. (1979). Behavior problems of educationally handicapped and normal pupils. *Journal of Abnormal Child Psychology, 7*, 495–502.

Cullinan, D., Epstein, M. H., & Lloyd, J. (1981). School behavior problems of learning disabled and normal girls and boys. *Learning Disability Quarterly, 4*, 163–169.

Das, J. P., Naglieri, J. A., & Kirby, J. (1994). *Assessment of cognitive processes.* New York: Allyn & Bacon.

Delgado, J. M. R. (1969). *Physical control of the mind.* New York: Harper & Row.

Deluty, R. H. (1979). Children's Action Tendency Scale: A self-report measure of aggressiveness, assertiveness, and submissiveness in children. *Journal of Consulting and Clinical Psychology, 47*, 1061–1071.

Deluty, R. H. (1981a). Adaptiveness of aggressive, assertive, and submissive behavior for children. *Journal of Clinical Child Psychology, 10*, 149–155.

Deluty, R. H. (1981b). Alternative-thinking ability of aggressive, assertive, and submissive children. *Cognitive Therapy and Research, 5*, 309–312.

Derr, A. M. (1986). How learning disabled adolescent boys make moral judgments. *Journal of Learning Disabilities, 19*, 160–164.

Deshler, D. D., Schumaker, J. B., Alley, G. R., Warner, M. M., & Clark, F. L. (1982). Learning disabilities in adolescent and young adult populations: Research implications. *Focus on Exceptional Children, 15*, 1–12.

Dickstein, E. B., & Warren, D. R. (1980). Role-taking deficits in learning disabled children. *Journal of Learning Disabilities, 13*, 33–37.

Diener, C. I., & Dweck, C. S. (1978). An analysis of learned helplessness: Continuous changes in performances, strategy and achievement cognitions following failure. *Journal of Personality and Social Psychology, 36*, 451–462.

Dishion, T. J. (1990). The family ecology of boys' peer relations in middle childhood. *Child Development, 61*, 874–892.

Dodge, K. A., & Coie, J. D. (1987). Social-information-processing factors in reactive and proactive aggression in children's peer groups. *Journal of Personality and Social Psychology, 53*, 1146–1158.

Dodge, K. A., & Frame, C. L. (1982). Social cognitive biases and deficits in aggressive boys. *Child Development, 53*, 620–635.

Dodge, K. A., Murphy, R. R., & Buchsbaum, K. C. (1984). The assessment of intention-cue detection skills in children: Implications for developmental psychology. *Child Development, 55*, 163–173.

Dodge, K. A., & Newman, J. P. (1981). Biased decision-making processes in aggressive boys. *Journal of Abnormal Psychology, 90*, 375–379.

Dodge, K. A., Pettit, G. S., McClaskey, C. L., & Brown, M. M. (1986). Social competence in children. *Monographs of the Society for Research in Child Development, 51*, 1–85.

Dodge, K. A., & Price, J. M. (1990). Hostile attributional biases in severely aggressive adolescents. *Journal of Abnormal Psychology, 99*, 385–392.

Dodge, K. A., & Siegmund, L. (1993). Social-cognitive mechanisms in the development of conduct disorder and depression. *Annual Review of Psychology, 44*, 559–584.

Dodge, K. A., & Somberg, D. R. (1987). Hostile attributional biases among aggressive boys are exacerbated under conditions of threats to the self. *Child Development, 58*, 213–224.

Dodge, K. A., & Tomlin, A. M. (1987). Utilization of self-schemas as a mechanism of interpretational bias in aggressive children. *Social Cognition, 5*, 280–300.

Doehring, D. G., & Hoshko, I. M. (1978). Classification of reading problems by the 2-technique of factor analysis. *Cortex, 13*, 281–294.

Doehring, D. G., Hoshko, I. M., & Bryans, S. (1979). Statistical classification of children with reading problems. *Journal of Clinical Neuropsychology, 1*, 5–16.

Dollard, J., Doob, W., Miller, N. E., Mowrer, O. H., & Sears, R. (1939). *Frustration and aggression.* New Haven, CT: Yale University Press.

Donahue, M., Pearl, R., & Bryan, T. (1982). Learning disabled children's syntactic proficiency on a communicative task. *Journal of Speech and Hearing Disorders, 47*, 397–403.

Douglas, V. I. (1980). Higher mental processes in hyperactive children: Implications for training. In R. M. Knights & D. J. Bakker (Eds.), *Treatment of hyperactive and learning disordered children* (pp. 65–91). Baltimore, MD: University Park Press.

Douglas, V. I. (1983). Attention and cognitive problems. In M. Rutter (Ed.), *Developmental neuropsychiatry* (pp. 280–330). New York: Guilford.

D'Zurilla, T. J., & Nezu, A. (1982). Social problem solving in adults. In P. C. Kendall (Ed.), *Advances in cognitive-behavioral research and therapy* (Vol. 1, pp. 202–274). New York: Academic Press.

Ellis, A. (1962). *Reason and emotion in psychotherapy*. New York: Stuart.

Eysenck, H. J., & Eysenck, M. (1985). *Personality and individual differences: A natural science approach*. New York: Plenum.

Eysenck, H. J., & Wilson, C. D. (1973). *The experimental study of Freudian theories*. London: Methuen.

Feuerstein, R., Haywood, H., Rand, Y., Hoffman, M., & Jensen, B. (1984). *Examiner manuals for the Learning Potential Assessment Device*. Jerusalem: Hadassah-WIZO-Canada Research Institute.

Fielstein, E., Klein, M. S., Fisher, M., Hanon, C., Koburger, P., Schneider, M. J., & Leitenberg, H. (1985). Self-esteem and causal attributions for success and failure in children. *Cognitive Therapy and Research, 9*, 381–398.

Fincham, F. A. (1977). Comparison of moral judgment in learning disabled and normal achieving boys. *Journal of Psychology, 96*, 153–160.

Fincham, F. A. (1979). Conservation and cognitive role-taking in learning disabled boys. *Journal of Learning Disabilities, 12*, 34–40.

Fisk, J. L., & Rourke, B. P. (1979). Identification of subtypes of learning disabled children at three age levels: A neuropsychological, multivariate approach. *Journal of Clinical Neuropsychology, 1*, 289–310.

Flavell, J. H. (1970). Developmental studies of mediated memory. In H. Reese & L. Lipsitt (Eds.), *Advances in child development and behavior* (Vol. 5, pp. 182–211). New York: Academic Press.

Flavell, J. H., Beach, D. R., & Chimsky, J. M. (1966). Spontaneous verbal rehearsal in a memory task as a function of age. *Child Development, 37*, 283–299.

Freud, S. (1955). Beyond the pleasure principle. In J. Stachey (Ed. and Trans.), *Standard edition* (Vol. 18). London: Hogarth. (Original work published 1920)

Friedman, D. E., & Medway, F. J. (1987). Effects of varying performance sets and outcome on the expectations, attributions, and persistence of boys with learning disabilities. *Journal of Learning Disabilities, 20*, 312–316.

Galton, F. (1883). *Inquiries into human faculty and its development*. New York: Dutton.

Galton, F. (1892). *Hereditary genius* (2nd ed.). New York: Macmillan.

Garrett, M. K., & Crump, D. W. (1980). Peer acceptance, teacher preference, and self-appraisal of social status among learning disabled students. *Learning Disability Quarterly, 3*, 42–48.

Gerber, P. J., & Zinkgraf, S. A. (1982). A comparative study of social-perceptual ability in learning disabled and nonhandicapped students. *Learning Disability Quarterly, 5*, 374–378.

Goldstein, D., & Dundon, W. D. (1986). Affect and cognition in learning disabilities. In S. J. Ceci (Ed.), *Handbook of cognitive, social, and neuropsychological aspects of learning disabilities* (Vol. 2, pp. 233–249). Hillsdale, NJ: Erlbaum.

Gouze, K. R. (1987). Attention and social problem solving as correlates of aggression in preschool males. *Journal of Abnormal Child Psychology, 15*, 181–197.

Gregory, J. F., Shanahan, T., & Walberg, H. J. (1986). A profile of learning disabled twelfth-graders in regular classes. *Learning Disability Quarterly, 9*, 33–42.

Gresham, F., & Elliott, S. N. (1989). Social skills deficits as a primary learning disability. *Journal of Learning Disability, 22*, 120–124.

Gresham, F. M., & Reschly, D. J. (1986). Acceptance of mainstreamed learning disabled children. *Learning Disability Quarterly, 9*, 23–32.

Gurucharri, C., Phelps, E., & Selman, R. (1984). Development of interpersonal understanding: A longitudinal and comparative study of normal and disturbed youths. *Journal of Consulting and Clinical Psychology, 52*, 26–36.

Hairns, A. A., & Herrman, L. P. (1989). Social cognitive skills and behavioural adjustment of delinquent adolescents in treatment. *Journal of Adolescence, 12*, 323–328.

Hall, C. W., & Richmond, B. O. (1985). Non-verbal communication, self-esteem and interpersonal relations of LD and non-LD students. *Exceptional Child, 32*, 87–91.

Hamlett, K. W., Pellegrini, D. W., & Conners, C. K. (1987). An investigation of executive processes in the problem-solving of attention deficit disorder-hyperactive children. *Journal of Pediatric Psychology, 12*, 227–240.

Harris, K. R. (1990). Developing self-regulated learners: The role of private speech and self-instructions. *Educational Psychologist, 25*, 35–49.

Hartmann, H., Kris, E., & Lowenstein, R. (1949). Notes on the theory of aggression. *Psychoanalytic Studies of the Child, 3*, 9–36.

Heward, W. L., & Orlansky, M. D. (1992). *Exceptional children: An introductory survey of special education* (4th ed.). New York: Macmillan.

Hillyer, K., & Kearney, C. J. (1988). Problems of gifted children. *Journal of the Association for the Study of Perception, 21*, 10–26.

Holborow, P. L., & Berry, P. S. (1986). Hyperactivity and learning difficulties. *Journal of Learning Disabilities, 19*, 426–431.

Horney, K. (1945). Our inner conflicts. New York: Norton.

Horowitz, E. C. (1981). Popularity, decentering ability and role-taking skills in learning disabled and normal children. *Learning Disability Quarterly, 4*, 23–30.

Huesmann, L., & Eron, L. D. (1987). Intellectual functioning and aggression. *Journal of Personality and Social Psychology, 52*, 232–240.

Huesmann, L. R. (1987). An information processing model for the development of aggression. *Aggressive Behavior, 14*, 13–24.

Hull, J. G., & Bond, C. F., Jr. (1986). Social and behavioral consequences of alcohol consumption and expectancy: A metanalysis. *Psychological Bulletin, 99*, 347–360.

Ingram, R. E., & Kendall, P. C. (1987). The cognitive side of anxiety. *Cognitive Therapy and Research, 11*, 523–536.

Jackson, S. C., Enright, R. D., & Murdock, J. Y. (1987). Social perception problems in learning disabled youth: Developmental lag versus perceptual deficit. *Journal of Learning Disabilities, 20*, 361–364.

Jacobsen, B., Lowery, B., & DuCette, S. (1986). Attributions of learning disabled children. *Journal of Educational Psychology, 78*, 59–65.

Jensen, A. R. (1980). *Bias in mental testing*. New York: Free Press.

Johnson, D. J., & Myklebust, H. R. (1964). *Learning disabilities: Educational principles and practices*. New York: Grune & Stratton.

Jones, C. J. (1985). Analysis of the self-concepts of handicapped students. *Remedial and Special Education, 6*, 32–36.

Kahn, M., & Kirk, W. (1968). The concepts of aggression: A review and reformulation. *Psychological Record, 18*, 559–573.

Kamin, L. (1977). Burt's IQ data. *Science, 195*, 246–248.

Kane, M. T., & Kendall, P. C. (1989). Anxiety disorders in children: A multiple-baseline evaluation of a cognitive-behavioral treatment. *Behavior Therapy, 20*, 499–508.

Kanfer, F. H., Karoly, P., & Newman, A. (1975). Reduction of children's fear of the dark by competence-related and situational threat-related verbal cues. *Journal of Consulting and Clinical Psychology, 43*, 251–259.

Kaslow, N. J., Rehm, L. P., & Siegel, A. W. (1984). Social-cognitive and cognitive correlates of depression in children. *Journal of Abnormal Child Psychology, 12*, 605–620.

Kauffman, J. M. (1993). *Characteristics of emotional and behavioral disorders of children and youth* (5th ed.). New York: Macmillan.

Kaufman, A. S., & Kaufmann, N. L. (1983). *K-ABC: Kaufman Assessment Battery for Children*. Circle Pines, MN: American Guidance Service.

Kazdin, A. E. (1989). Childhood depression. In E. J. Mash & R. A. Barkley (Eds.), *Treatment of childhood disorders* (pp. 135–166). New York: Guilford.

Kendall, P. C. (1985). Toward a cognitive-behavioral model of child psychopathology and a critique of related interventions. *Journal of Abnormal Child Psychology, 13*, 357–372.

Kendler, T. S., Kendler, H. H., & Wells, D. (1960). Reversal and nonreversal shifts in nursery school children. *Journal of Comparative and Physiological Psychology, 53*, 83–88.

Kistner, J. A., & Osborne, M. (1987). A longitudinal study of LD children's self evaluations. *Learning Disability Quarterly, 10*, 258–266.

Kistner, J. A., Osborne, M., & LeVerrier, L. (1988). Causal attributions of learning-disabled children: Developmental patterns and relation to academic progress. *Journal of Educational Psychology, 80*, 82–89.

Knight-Arest, I. (1984). Communicative effectiveness of learning disabled and normally achieving 10- to 13-year-old boys. *Learning Disability Quarterly, 7*, 237–245.

Kuenne, M. K. (1946). Experimental investigation of the relation of language to transposition behavior in young children. *Journal of Experimental Psychology, 36*, 471–490.

Landesman-Dwyers, S., & Butterfield, E. C. (1983). Mental retardation: Developmental issues in cognitive and social adaptation. In M. Lewis (Ed.), *Origins of intelligence, infancy and early childhood* (2nd ed., pp. 479–519). New York: Plenum.

Larry, P. v. Riles, 793 F.2d 969 (9th Cir. 1984).

Leitenberg, H., Yost, L. W., & Carroll-Wilson, M. (1986). Negative cognitive errors in children: Questionnaire development, normative data, and comparisons between children with and without self-reported symptoms of depression, low self-esteem, and evaluation anxiety. *Journal of Consulting and Clinical Psychology, 54*, 528–536.

Licht, B. G. (1983). Cognitive-motivational factors that contribute to the achievement of learning disabled children. *Journal of Learning Disabilities, 16*, 483–490.

Licht, B. G., Kistner, J. A., Ozkaragoz, T., Shapiro, S., & Clausen, L. (1985). Causal attributions of learning disabled children: Individual differences and their implications for persistence. *Journal of Educational Psychology, 77*, 208–216.

Lincoln, A., & Chazan, S. (1979). Perceived competence and intrinsic motivation in learning disability children. *Journal of Clinical and Child Psychology, 8*, 213–216.

Lochman, J. E. (1987). Self- and peer perceptions and attributional biases of aggressive and nonaggressive boys in dyadic interactions. *Journal of Consulting and Clinical Psychology, 55*, 404–410.

Lochman, J. E., & Wayland, K. K. (1993). Social goals: Relationship to adolescent adjustment and to social problem solving. *Journal of Abnormal Child Psychology, 21*, 135–151.

Lorenz, K. (1966). *On aggression*. New York: Harcourt.

Luria, A. R. (1959). The directive function of speech in development. *Werd, 18*, 341–352.

Luria, A. R. (1961). *The role of speech in the regulation of normal and abnormal behaviors*. New York: Liveright.

Lyon, R., & Watson, B. (1981). Empirically derived subgroups of learning disabled readers: Diagnostic characteristics. *Journal of Learning Disabilities, 14*, 256–261.

Margalit, M., & Zak, I. (1984). Anxiety and self-concept of learning disabled children. *Journal of Learning Disabilities, 17*, 537–539.

Marsh, H. W. (1988). Causal effects of academic self-concept on academic achievement: A reanalysis of Newman (1984). *Journal of Experimental Education, 56*, 100–103.

Mash, E. J. (1989). Treatment of child and family disturbance: A behavioral-systems perspective. In E. J. Mash & R. A. Barkley (Eds.), *Treatment of childhood disorders* (pp. 3–36). New York: Guilford.

Mash, E. J., & Terdal, L. G. (1988). Behavioral assessment of child and family disturbance. In E. J. Mash & L. G. Terdal (Eds.), *Behavioral assessment of childhood disorders* (2nd ed., pp. 3–65). New York: Guilford.

Maheady, L., Maitland, G., & Sainato, D. (1984). The interpretation of social interactions by mildly handicapped and nondisabled children. *Journal of Special Education, 18*, 151–159.

Mahoney, M. J., & Nezworski, M. T. (1985). Cognitive-behavioral approaches to children's problems. *Journal of Abnormal Child Psychology, 13*, 467–476.

McConaughy, S. H., & Ritter, D. R. (1986). Social competence and behavioral problems of learning disabled boys aged 6–11. *Journal of Learning Disabilities, 19*, 39–45.

McKinney, J. (1984). The search for subtypes of specific learning disability. *Journal of Learning Disabilities, 17*, 43–50.

McKinney, J., & Forman, S. (1982). Classroom behavior patterns of EMH, LD and EH students. *Journal of School Psychology, 20*, 271–279.

McKinney, J. D., McClure, S., & Feagans, L. (1982). Classroom behavior of learning disabled children. *Learning Disability Quarterly, 5*, 45–52.

McMahon, R. J., & Wells, K. C. (1989). Conduct disorders. In E. J. Mash & R. A. Barkley (Eds.), *Treatment of childhood disorders* (pp. 73–132). New York: Guilford.

Meichenbaum, D. (1976). Cognitive-functional approach to cognitive factors as determinants of learning disabilities. In R. M. Knights and S. J. Bakker (Eds.), *The neuropsychology of learning disorders: Theoretical approaches* (pp. 423–442). Baltimore, MD: University Park Press.

Meichenbaum, D. H., & Goodman, J. (1977). Training impulsive children to talk to themselves: A means of developing self-control. *Journal of Abnormal Psychology, 77*, 115–126.

Merrell, K. W. (1990). Differentiating low achieving students and students with learning disabilities: An examination of performances on the Woodcock-Johnson Psycho-Educational Battery. *Journal of Special Education, 24*, 296–305.

Milich, R., & Dodge, K. A. (1984). Social information processing in child psychiatric populations. *Journal of Abnormal Child Psychology, 12*, 471–489.

Minde, K. (1992). Aggression in preschoolers: Its relation to socialization. *Journal of the American Academy of Child and Adolescent Psychiatry, 31*, 853–862.

Mischel, W. (1968). *Personality and assessment.* New York: Wiley.

Mischel, W. (1973). Toward a cognitive social learning reconceptualization of personality. *Psychological Review, 80*, 252–283.

Mischel, W. (1993). *Introduction to personality* (5th ed.). Fort Worth, TX: Harcourt Brace Jovanovich.

Moyer, K. E. (1976). *The psychobiology of aggression.* New York: Harper & Row.

Nasby, W., Hayden, B., & DePaulo, B. M. (1980). Attributional bias among aggressive boys to interpret unambiguous social stimuli as displays of hostility. *Journal of Abnormal Psychology, 89*, 459–548.

National Joint Committee on Learning Disabilities. (1981). *Definitions.* Washington, DC: Author.

Offord, D. R., & Boyle, M. H. (1989). Ontario Child Health Study: Correlates of disorder. *Journal of the American Academy of Child and Adolescent Psychiatry, 28*, 856–860.

Palmer, D. J., Drummond, F., Tollison, P., & Zinkgraff, S. (1982). An attributional investigation of performance outcomes for learning-disabled and normal-achieving pupils. *Journal of Special Education, 16*, 207–219.

Pearl, R. (1986). Social cognitive factors in learning-disabled children's social problems. In S. J. Ceci (Ed.), *Handbook of cognitive, social, and neuropsychological aspects of learning disabilities* (Vol. 2, pp. 273–294). Hillsdale, NJ: Erlbaum.

Pearl, R., Bryan, T., & Herzog, A. (1990). Resisting or acquiescing to peer pressure to engage in misconduct: Adolescents' expectations of probable consequences. *Journal of Youth and Adolescence, 19*, 43–55.

Pearl, R., Donahue, M., & Bryan, T. (1986). Social relationships of learning-disabled children. In J. K. Torgesen & B. Y. L. Wong (Eds.), *Psychological and educational perspectives on learning disabilities* (pp. 194–224). New York: Academic Press.

Perlmutter, B. F. (1986). Personality variables and peer relations of children and adolescents with learning disabilities. In S. J. Ceci (Ed.), *Handbook of cognitive, social, and neurological aspects of learning disabilities* (Vol. 1, pp. 339–359). Hillsdale, NJ: Erlbaum.

Perlmutter, B. F., Crocker, J., Cordray, D., & Garstecki, D. (1983). Sociometric status and related personality characteristics of mainstreamed learning disabled adolescents. *Learning Disability Quarterly, 6*, 20–30.

Perry, D. G., Perry, L. C., & Rasmussen, P. (1986). Cognitive social learning mediators of aggression. *Child Development, 57*, 700–711.

Rappaport, S. (1966). Personality factors teachers need for relationship structure. In W. Cruikshank (Ed.), *The teacher of the brain-injured children.* Syracuse, NY: Syracuse University Press.

Reese, H. W. (1962). Verbal mediation as a function of age level. *Psychological Bulletin, 59*, 502–509.

Reeve, R. A., & Brown, A. L. (1985). Metacognition reconsidered: Implications for intervention research. *Journal of Abnormal Child Psychology, 13*, 343–356.

Rehm, L. P. (1977). A self-control model of depression. *Behavior Therapy, 8*, 787–804.

Reynolds, C. R., & Kamphaus, R. W. (1992). *Behavior Assessment Schedule for Children.* Circle Pines, MN: American Guidance Service.

Richard, B. A., & Dodge, K. A. (1982). Social maladjustment and problem solving in school-aged children. *Journal of Consulting and Clinical Psychology, 50*, 226–233.

Rogers, H., & Saklofske, D. H. (1985). Self-concept, locus of control and performance expectations of learning disabled children. *Journal of Learning Disabilities, 18*, 273–278.

Rogers, T. B. (1995). *The psychological testing enterprise: An introduction.* Pacific Grove, CA: Brooks/Cole.

Rossman, B. B., & Horn, J. C. (1972). Cognitive, motivational and temperamental indicants of creativity and intelligence. *Journal of Educational Measurement, 9*, 265–286.

Rourke, B. P., Young, G. C., & Leenaars, A. A. (1989). A childhood learning disability that predisposes those afflicted to adolescent and adult depression and suicide risk. *Journal of Learning Disabilities, 22*, 169–175.

Sattler, J. M. (1992). *Assessment of children* (3rd ed.). San Diego, CA: Author.

Schneider, M., & Yoshida, R. K. (1988). Interpersonal problem-solving skills and classroom behavioral adjustment in learning-disabled adolescents and comparison peers. *Journal of School Psychology, 26*, 25–34.

Schumaker, J. B., & Hazel, J. S. (1984). Social skills assessment and training for the learning disabled: Who's on first and what's on second? *Journal of Learning Disabilities, 17*, 422–431.

Schwean Kowalchuk, V. L. (1991). Stylistic variations in requesting: How does the language/learning disabled adolescent fare? *Canadian Journal of Special Education, 7*, 61–75.

Schwean Kowalchuk, V. L., & Nostbakken, M. A. (1991). Help seeking: How successful is the learning disabled adolescent? *Canadian Journal of Special Education, 6*, 1–11.

Seligman, M. E. P. (1975). *Helplessness: On depression, development and death.* San Francisco: Freeman.

Shaywitz, S. E., & Shaywitz, B. A. (1988). Attention deficit disorder: Current perspectives. In J. F. Kavanagh & T. J. Truss, Jr. (Eds.), *Learning disabilities: Proceedings of the National Joint Conference* (pp. 369–546). Parkton, MD: York.

Shepard, L., Smith, M. L., & Vojir, C. (1983). Characteristics of pupils identified as learning disabled. *American Educational Research Journal, 20*, 309–331.

Silver, D. S., & Young, R. D. (1985). Interpersonal problem-solving abilities, peer status, and behavioral adjustment in learning disabled and non-learning-disabled adolescents. *Advances in Learning and Behavioral Disabilities, 4*, 201–223.

Silverman, R., & Zigmond, N. (1983). Self-concept in learning disabled adolescents. *Journal of Learning Disabilities, 16*, 478–482.

Sisterhen, D. H., & Gerber, P. J. (1989). Auditory, visual, and multisensory nonverbal social perception in adolescents with and without learning disabilities. *Journal of Learning Disabilities, 22*, 245–249, 257.

Spafford, C. S., & Grosser, G. S. (1993). The social misperception syndrome in children with learning disabilities: Social causes versus neurological variables. *Journal of Learning Disabilities, 26*, 178–189, 198.

Spivack, G., Platt, J. J., & Shure, M. B. (1976). *The problem solving approach to adjustment.* San Francisco: Jossey-Bass.

Spivack, G., & Shure, M. B. (1974). *Social adjustment of young children: A cognitive approach to solving real-life problems.* San Francisco: Jossey-Bass.

Steinberg, M. D., & Dodge, K. A. (1983). Attributional bias in aggressive adolescent boys and girls. *Journal of Social and Clinical Psychology*, *1*, 312–321.

Sternberg, R. J. (1986). *Intelligence applied: Understanding and increasing your intellectual skills.* San Diego, CA: Harcourt Brace Jovanovich.

Stone, A., & Michals, D. (1986). Problem-solving skills in learning-disabled children. In S. J. Ceci (Ed.), *Handbook of cognitive, social, and neurological aspects of learning disabilities* (Vol. 1, pp. 291–315). Hillsdale, NJ: Erlbaum.

Stone, W. L., & leGreca, A. M. (1984). Comprehension of nonverbal communication: A reexamination of the social competencies of learning-disabled children. *Journal of Abnormal Child Psychology*, *12*, 505–518.

Strauss, A. A., & Lehtinen, L. (1947). *Psychopathology and education of the brain-injured child. Vol. 2. Progress in theory and clinic.* New York: Grune & Stratton.

Swanson, H. L., & Watson, B. L. (1989). *Educational and psychological assessment of exceptional children: Theories, strategies, and applications* (2nd ed.). Columbus, OH: Merrill.

Szasz, T. S. (1961). *The myth of mental illness: Foundations of a theory of personal conduct.* New York: Harper & Row.

Tollefson, H., Tracy, D. B., Johnsen, E. P., Buenning, M., Farmer, A., & Barke, C. R. (1982). Attribution patterns of learning disabled adolescents. *Learning Disability Quarterly*, *5*, 14–20.

Torgesen, J. K. (1991). Learning disabilities: Historical and conceptual issues. In B. Y. L. Wong (Ed.), *Learning about learning disabilities* (pp. 3–37). San Diego, CA: Academic Press.

Torgesen, J. K., & Licht, B. G. (1983). The learning disabled child as an inactive learner: Retrospect and prospects. In J. D. McKinney & L. Feagans (Eds.), *Current topics in learning disabilities* (pp. 184–197). Norwood, NJ: Ablex.

Toro, P. A., & Weisberg, R. P. (1990). A comparison of children with and without learning disabilities on social problem solving skill, school behavior, and family background. *Journal of Learning Disabilities*, *23*, 115–120.

Vellutino, F. R. (1986). Commentary: Linguistic and cognitive correlates of learning disability: Reactions to three reviews. In S. J. Ceci (Ed.), *Handbook of cognitive, social, and neurological aspects of learning disabilities* (Vol. 1, pp. 317–335). Hillsdale, NJ: Lawrence Erlbaum Associates.

Voelker, S. L., Carter, R. A., Sprague, D. J., Gdowski, C. L., & Lachar, D. (1989). Developmental trends in memory and metamemory in children with attention deficit disorder. *Journal of Pediatric Psychology*, *14*, 75–88.

Vygotsky, L. S. (1962). *Thought and language.* Cambridge: MIT Press. (original work published 1934)

Weener, P. (1981). On comparing learning disabled and regular classroom children. *Journal of Learning Disabilities*, *14*, 227–232.

Wertsch, J. V. (1985). Adult-child interaction as a source of self-regulation in children. In S. K. Yussen (Ed.), *The growth of reflection in children* (pp. 69–97). Orlando, FL: Academic Press.

Winnie, P. H., Woodlands, M. H., & Wong, B. Y. L. (1982). Comparability of self-concept among learning disabled, normal and gifted students. *Journal of Learning Disabilities*, *15*, 470–475.

Winzer, M., Rogow, S., & Charlotte, D. (1987). *Exceptional children in Canada.* Scarborough, Ontario: Prentice-Hall.

Wong, B. Y. L. (1991). The relevance of metacognition to learning disabilities. In B. Y. L. Wong (Ed.), *Learning about learning disabilities* (pp. 231–258). San Diego, CA: Academic Press.

Wong, B. Y. L., & Wong, R. (1980). Role-taking skills in normally achieving and learning disabled children. *Learning Disability Quarterly*, *3*, 3–11.

11

Thinking Styles

Elena L. Grigorenko and Robert J. Sternberg

THE CONCEPT OF STYLE

What Are Styles?

If someone says to you, "Tell me about yourself," your responses will probably include a number of statements about your likes and dislikes. Most people refer to their preferences when describing themselves: for example, "I prefer to work alone," "I'm a people person," or "I like to do creative things." All of these statements are references to favorite ways of behaving—that is, to styles.

Imagine a pair of identical twins reared together. They look so much alike that they often get mixed up by their teachers and friends; sometimes they even answer for each other in class. They do equally well at school (i.e., the level of their abilities is approximately the same). One, Twin A, is very good at solving problems that require detailed and scrupulous work. She likes to use existing rules and ways of completing tasks, and she will sometimes spend hours searching for existing paths to a goal rather than creating new ones. Her homework is usually perfect, and she does very well on school tests. The other, Twin B, hates tests. She would rather write essays and design projects, because she prefers to do everything her own way. She favors school assignments that allow her to deal with the "big picture" and forget about details. Their teachers say that even though they cannot distinguish A from B by looking at them, they always know whose test or whose essay they are reading.

These short descriptions illustrate some of the different ways people use their intelligence. It is intuitively obvious that the way people approach tasks does not depend only on their level of intelligence, their personality traits, and the difficulty of the task. Another variable affecting task performance is style. A style is neither a level of intelligence nor a personality trait, but rather an interaction of intelligence and personality. Gordon Allport (1937) introduced the idea of style to psychology when he referred to "styles of life" as a means of identifying distinctive personality types or types of behavior. The term has since been used to refer to patterns of behavior that are consistent over long periods of time and across many areas of activity.

Although styles influence many types of activity, in this chapter we will focus on *thinking styles*—a concept introduced by Sternberg (1988; Sternberg & Lubart, 1991a,b) in his theory of mental self-government. Thinking styles refer to the ways in which people choose to use or exploit their intelligence as well as their knowledge. Thus styles are not abilities, but rather how these abilities (and the knowledge acquired through them) are used in day-to-day interactions with the environment. Simply put, styles are not how much intelligence we have, but how we use it. Although the concept of thinking styles is relatively new, a number of related constructs have been developed in the psychology of personality and cognitive psychology. Be-

Elena L. Grigorenko and Robert J. Sternberg • Department of Psychology, Yale University, New Haven, Connecticut 06520.

International Handbook of Personality and Intelligence, edited by Donald H. Saklofske and Moshe Zeidner. Plenum Press, New York, 1995.

low we review some of these related definitions and approaches to studying styles.

Nature and Definition of Style

Regardless of the specific approach or theory, the term *style* usually refers to an habitual pattern or preferred way of doing something. According to *Webster's New World Dictionary* (Guralnik, 1976), "A style is a distinctive or characteristic manner . . . or method of acting or performing" (p. 1415). The more specific term *cognitive style* refers to an individual's way of processing information. The term was developed by cognitive psychologists conducting research into problem solving and sensory and perceptual functions. This research provided some of the first evidence for the existence of styles. More recently, attention has turned to styles in learning and teaching. Goldman (1972), for example, classified students' study practices into "logical" and "mnemonic" styles. Reissman (1964) also argues for the concept of styles in learning, defining a learning style as a "more wholistic (molar) or global dimension of learning operative at the phenomenal level" (p. 485).

But support for the notion of styles has not been limited to cognitive psychology. The broad and flexible nature of the concept has made it attractive to a number of researchers in widely differing areas of psychology and related fields. For example, Conway (1992), in discussing the philosophy of science, stated that philosophical differences among psychologists may be related to individual differences in their personality factors and cognitive styles. Liddle (1987) utilized the concept of style in the area of psychopathology by relating three mental-processing styles to specific schizophrenic syndromes: a psychomotor-poverty syndrome, a disorganizational syndrome, and a reality-distortion syndrome. Furthermore, Hogarty and Flesher (1992) have suggested that these three broad cognitive styles may provide a point of entry for the cognitive retraining of schizophrenics.

Fortunately, the increasing volume of published material on styles has included a number of excellent review papers. Vernon (1973) examines the historical roots of cognitive styles in early twentieth-century German typological theories and then critically analyzes contemporary approaches. Bieri (1971), Goldstein and Blackman (1978), and Kagan and Kogan (1970) consider the diverse theoretical orientations that have distinguished the cognitive-style domain. Kogan (1976) offers a review of research on cognitive styles from the point of view of their implications for intellectual functioning and academic achievement. Wardell and Royce (1978) analyze problems related to the definition of *style* in the current literature.

Although there is fairly extensive disagreement throughout these reviews on preferred approaches and measurement of styles, there is considerable agreement as to the empirical and conceptual problems related to the concept of style (see, e.g., Goldstein & Blackman, 1978; Kogan, 1976; Wardell & Royce, 1978). The empirical problems go beyond the usual inadequacies of methodology and fragmented research. More important is the observation that empirical generalizability is limited because the findings are so instrument bound: Whatever is measured by a particular test or questionnaire is called a "style of . . . ," and there are only a few examples in the literature of replications in which the same latent constructs were studied with measures created by different authors.

The conceptual problems derive from the proliferation of interpretations of style as a theoretical construct. Two specific conceptual weaknesses have been mentioned in the literature. The first is related to the way in which different authors use the concepts of "strategies" and "styles" (Luchins & Luchins, 1970); each concept has different theoretical foundations and encompasses functional differences. Cognitive styles are "adaptational control mechanisms of the ego that mediate between the need states and the external environment" (Wallach & Kogan, 1965, p. 17). Strategies, in contrast, usually imply operations followed to minimize error during the decision-making process. At a basic level, styles and strategies can be distinguished by the degree of consciousness involved: Styles operate without individual awareness, whereas strategies involve a conscious choice of alternatives. The two terms are used interchangeably by some authors (Cronbach & Snow, 1977), but in general, *strategy* is used for task- or context-dependent situations, whereas *style* implies a higher degree of stability (falling midway between *ability* and *strategy*).

The second conceptual weakness is related to the nature of styles themselves. Many theorists locate styles at the interface of intelligence and personality, in a sense belonging to both domains. But there are exceptions. Gustafson and Kallen (1989), for example, distinguish cognitive styles from personality styles, and P. L. Myers (1988) refers to a hierarchy of styles of cognition (e.g., perceptual, verbal, and cognitive) and assumes that personality is a source of individual variability within styles. As noted, much of this confusion is attributable to the nature of styles, because although styles have been viewed primarily in the context of cognition, they have always included a heavy element of affect.

In the 1970s, the concept of style developed further as it gained popularity among educators. As a result, the notion of styles expanded in two directions through research in educational psychology. The first direction was primarily one of application: Investigators attempted to apply traditional cognitive styles to school settings, seeking explanations for students' individual differences in achievement and performance. The second direction was an effort to create new frameworks for studying learning and teaching styles based on empirical observations rather than theoretical background. These researchers have provided a number of domain-specific theories of styles, including theories of learning styles (Dunn & Dunn, 1978; Gregorc, 1979, 1985; Renzulli & Smith, 1978), teaching styles (Fischer & Fischer, 1979), and even styles relevant to choosing career opportunities (Holland, 1973).

Overview of the Chapter

The goal of this chapter is both to provide the reader with a background in the literature on style research and to discuss more recent developments in this area. The chapter focuses primarily on a hypothesis of thinking styles called "the theory of mental self-government" (Sternberg, 1988; Sternberg & Lubart, 1991a).

The chapter contains three major parts. The first part consists of a review of a variety of theories of styles, followed in the second part by a more detailed discussion of the theory of mental self-government. The rationale for this approach is best explained by analogy. Consider the difficulties facing a photographer who wants to capture a sweeping and complex vista on film. No single photo will do justice to the scene, because each photo will only capture fragments of the larger picture. The photographer has two options. The first is to take many pictures from different angles and vantage points; the photos can then be combined to form a collage that reflects the scene. The second option is to take a single photo using a wide-angle lens. In this chapter we will use both approaches to depict the broad and complex panorama of styles.

In the review section of the chapter we explore the different aspects of styles emphasized in different areas of psychology. The researchers studying cognitive processes focus on the relation between styles and cognition; we will call this approach "a cognition-centered approach." We will refer back to the pioneer approaches to styles in cognitive psychology as well as to more recent developments. Personality psychologists study styles in relation to other individual personality characteristics; we refer to this approach as the "personality-centered approach." Another type of research we will discuss is the "activity-centered" approach, which focuses on styles in relation to various activities, settings, and environments. This approach is primarily found in educational settings and includes theories of learning and teaching styles.

Then we will change the lens and present the theory of mental self-government (Sternberg, 1988) in the second part of the chapter. Sternberg's theory acts as a wide-angle lens as it combines the thinking of the cognition-centered, personality-centered, and activity-centered traditions.

THE TRADITION OF STYLISTIC APPROACHES IN PSYCHOLOGY AND EDUCATION

Cognition-Centered Studies of Styles

Cognitive Styles

Interest in styles developed in part because traditional psychometric research on abilities and IQ had failed to elucidate the processes generating individual differences. Disappointment in IQ as a construct was prominent in the 1960s in both cognitive and developmental psychology. As a result, psychologists started looking for new ways to describe cognitive functioning, and the stylistic approach was born. Almost simultaneously, in the framework of the "new look," a school of thought in cognitive psychology developed in the late 1950s and 1960s that gave way to a number of stylistic constructs. Among the cognitive styles identified and investigated in the early new-look days were constricted-flexible control (G. Smith & Klein, 1953), leveling-sharpening (Klein, 1954), equivalence range (Gardner, 1953), tolerance for unrealistic experience (Klein & Schlesinger, 1951), and field dependence-independence (Witkin, 1973). Later entries include reflection-impulsivity (Kagan, 1958) and category width (Pettigrew, 1958), among many others (see Table 1 for details). These approaches were based loosely on a definition of cognitive styles as "the characteristic, self-consistent modes of functioning which individuals show in their perceptual and intellectual activities" (Witkin, Oltman, Raskin, & Karp, 1971, p. 3). All of these styles were used to identify and explain individual differences in a way that did not involve IQ scores.

Although more than a dozen different approaches to cognitive styles originated under the new-look framework, it is likely that the list could be expanded by including other dimensions of individual variation in cognitive functioning that are stylistic in nature. The diverse theoretical backgrounds of the various cognitive styles were discussed in a number of reviews (e.g., see Kagan & Kogan, 1970; Vernon, 1973; Wolitzky & Wachtel, 1973) and need not be presented in detail here. Table 1 displays short definitions of a variety of cognitive styles studied in the new-look framework.

It is interesting to note that cognitive styles differ markedly not only in their definitions and the instruments used in their measurement but also in the level of empirical attention that has been directed toward them. At one extreme, hundreds—if not thousands—of articles pertaining to the field dependence-independence construct have been published since the appearance of *Personality Through Perception* (Witkin et al., 1954). At the opposite extreme, the construct of

Table 1. Styles in the Cognition-Centered Approach

Author(s)	Styles	Definitions
Pettigrew (1958)	Category width	"the degree to which subjects are impelled to act on or ignore an awareness of differences"
Kagan, Moss, & Sigel (1963)	Conceptual styles	"stable individual preferences in mode of perceptual (analytical versus relational organization and conceptual categorization of the external environment categorization) distinction between persons and events"
Kagan (1966)	Reflection-impulsivity	"refers to the degree to which a subject considers alternative hypotheses with minimal consideration of their probable validity"
Witkin (1964)	Field dependence-independence	"the individual differences . . . in terms of degree of dependence on the structure of the prevailing visual field, ranging from great dependence, at one extreme, to great ability to deal with the presented field analytically, or to separate an item from the configuration in which it occurs, at the other"
Messick & Kogan (1963)	Compartmentalization	"a tendency to compartmentalize ideas . . . in discrete categories . . . a possible limitation in the production of diverse ideas"
Gardner & Schoen (1962)	Conceptual (cognitive) differentiation (equivalence range)	a way of "spontaneous differentiation of heterogeneous items into a complex of related groups"
Harvey, Hunt, & Schroder (1961)	Abstract versus concrete	"preferred level of and capacity for abstraction"
Klein (1954)	Leveling versus sharpening	"tendency to be hypersensitive to minutiae, to respond excessively to the fine nuances and sharpening small differences (sharpening) versus tendency to maximize assimilization effects in such a way that the fine shades of distinctions among individual elements are lost (leveling)"
Gardner & Schoen (1962)	Cognitive complexity	"persons of great 'cognitive complexity' presumably make more, and more complex, associations between groups"
Harvey, Hunt, & Schroder (1961)	Conceptual integration	"the relating or hooking of parts (concepts) to each other and to previous conceptual standards"
Klein & Schlesinger (1951)	Tolerance for unrealistic experiences	"the subject's readiness to accept and report experiences at variance with conventional reality or with what they knew to be true"
G. Smith & Klein (1953)	Constricted-flexible control	"an ability to disregard one of the two conflicting cues"
Gardner & Moriarty (1968)	Scanning	"the extent to which an individual attempts to verify the judgments he/she makes"
Klein (1970)	Physiognomic versus literal	"a preference for the dynamic and emotive rather than for the static and literal"

"tolerance for unrealistic experiences" has generated only a loose handful of studies since Klein and Schlesinger (1951) introduced this particular cognitive style to the psychological community.

The various cognitive-styles theories, however, are not as disparate as they may appear at first glance. The common denominator underlying all these approaches is the authors' belief that the perceptual system can be a window into the person's cognition (Gardner, 1953). This view accounts for why the majority of instruments evaluating cognitive styles use perceptual tasks. According to Gardner (1953), perceptual tasks offer unique opportunities for observing in action individuals' styles of adaptation to the world around them.

In the following section we will analyze three major conceptualizations of cognitive styles developed in the framework of the new look: field dependence-independence (Witkin, 1973), cognitive styles in categorization behavior (Gardner, 1959, 1962, 1970; Kagan, Moss, & Sigel, 1963; Klein, 1954; Pettigrew, 1958), and reflection-impulsivity (Kagan, 1958). These particular constructs were chosen because, in addition to being the most widely used approaches, each illustrates some of the conceptual and empirical difficulties surrounding cognitive styles.

Field Dependence-Independence

The principal work on field dependence-independence was directed by Witkin. Field dependence-independence is usually measured by scores on the Embedded Figures Test (EFT; Witkin et al., 1971) or on performance tests such as the Rod and Frame Test (RFT; Witkin, Dyk, Faterson, Goodenough, & Karp, 1962). Both the EFT and the RFT are perceptual tests. In the EFT, the subject must locate a previously seen simple figure within a larger, more complex figure that has been designed to obscure or embed the simple figure. In the RFT, subjects must ignore a visual and/or postural context to locate a true vertical. Strictly speaking, scores on the EFT and the RFT reflect the subject's competence at perceptual disembedding; however, Witkin (1973) has claimed that individual differences in test performance reflect differences in cognitive style—specifically, field dependence-independence (Witkin et al., 1971). The subject who is able to locate a simple figure or a vertical position in a complex context is said to be *field-independent* or *analytic*; one who has difficulty with such tasks is said to be *field-dependent* or *global*. In general, in a field-dependent mode of perceiving, perception is strongly dominated by the overall organization of the surrounding field, and parts of the field are experienced as "fused," whereas in a field-independent mode of perceiving, parts of the field are experienced as discrete from the organized background.

Because the concept of field dependence-independence was created to overcome the failure of IQ to explain individual differences in cognitive task performance, many researchers attempted to determine the relation between these two constructs. In a number of studies (see, e.g., Witkin, 1975), researchers demonstrated that field-dependent and field-independent individuals are not predictably different in tasks calling for the particular verbal skills tapped by tests such as the verbal-comprehension triad of the Wechsler scales, nor do they differ in their ability to acquire new information (Eagle, Goldberg, & Breitman, 1969).

There is reason to believe, however, that field independence is at least in part a "fluid ability," defined by Cattell (1963) as an ability to deal with essentially new problems. Fluid ability is probably best seen as a combination of intellectual skills and strategies. Therefore, complex tasks such as the Matrices and Block Design tasks used as tests of intelligence combine to provide the best measure of fluid ability. Witkin stated that of "the three main factor components" of the Wechsler, the one centered on Block Design, Object Assembly, and Picture Completion "happens to be essentially identical with the field dependence-independence dimension" (Witkin, 1973, p. 7). Witkin's comment raises the possibility, though, that field dependence-independence is an indicator of intellectual strength and weakness rather than style. This is reminiscent of Binet's definition of intelligence, which included the observation that weakness in analysis or self-discipline is a cause of poor intellectual performance. From this point of view, field dependence is a deficit rather than a style.

As Cronbach and Snow (1977) pointed out, there is a lack of evidence supporting the claim that a stylistic construct must be added to the concept of fluid ability in order to explain the results of Witkin's research. They assert that the notion of styles in this case is superfluous, and empirical evidence has been gathered to support this contention. Goldstein and Blackman (1978), in their review of 20 studies, found generally consistent indications that various measures of field independence are related to both verbal and performance aspects of intelligence; the correlations between field independence and intelligence were mostly in the .40 to .60 range. In addition, MacLeod, Jackson, and Palmer (1986) questioned whether field independence and spatial ability are different labels for a common underlying psychological dimension. These results called into question the usefulness of the field dependence-independence construct in relation to different types of intelligence. In summary, it is doubtful that field dependence-independence constitutes a set of cognitive styles.

Cognitive Styles in Categorizing Behavior

Several investigators studying stylistic aspects of cognition and personality (Bruner, Goodnow, & Austin, 1956, Gardner, 1953; Gardner & Schoen, 1962) have assessed individual modes of categorizing perceived similarities and differences in stimuli. These studies have suggested that (a) individuals differ consistently in categorizing behavior; (b) the consistencies persist over time; (c) the consistencies are most apparent when categorizing occurs under relatively "free" conditions; and (d) the consistencies are largely independent of the level of abstraction at which the person chooses to function. In this section, three approaches to cognitive styles in categorizing behavior are surveyed—specifically, cognitive controls, category width, and conceptual styles.

Cognitive Controls. Klein (1954) introduced the term *cognitive control* to refer to a hypothetical construct that directs the expression of need in socially acceptable ways, as required by the situation. Gardner and Long (1962) noted that cognitive controls were conceived within the framework of psychoanalytic ego psychology: "Controls are viewed as enduring cognitive structures that, like defense mechanisms, presumably emerge in the course of development from the interaction of genetics and experiential determinants" (p. 48). The evolution of terms used to denote this set of styles parallels the evolution of the construct itself. Gardner (1962) noted that in early work, Klein and his associates used the term *perceptual attitudes*, which was later replaced by *cognitive attitudes* and *cognitive system principles*. The terms *cognitive controls* and *cognitive control principles* were then adopted to denote that a delaying, controlling function was involved in cognition.

Gardner, Jackson, and Messick (1960) differentiated cognitive controls from cognitive style. According to these authors, the former refers to the specific dimensions (e.g., leveling-sharpening, scanning, field articulation, conceptual differentiation, and constricted-flexible control), whereas the latter refers to the organization of these dimensions within an individual. As Kagan and Kogan (1970) noted, however, the distinction between cognitive control and cognitive style has not been strictly adhered to by other researchers investigating these concepts. Table 1 includes the definitions of the dimensions of cognitive control that have been explored; reviews of the work on cognitive control are outlined in Gardner (1959, 1970).

The Free Sorting Test (Gardner, 1953) has been widely used to measure equivalence range, one of the dimensions of cognitive control. The test is used to assess consistent preferences for broad versus narrow equivalence ranges and consists of an individually administered task in which a subject is given 73 common objects and instructed to sort into groups the objects that seem to belong together. Those few objects that, after careful consideration, do not seem to belong with any of the others are to be placed into groups by themselves. The subject's score is the total number of groups formed, with lower scores presumably implying a preference for broad equivalence classes and higher scores a preference for narrow classes. The final score also depends on whether a subject groups objects according to either functional or abstract properties or superficial qualities and associations.

Conceptual Styles. The construct of conceptual style is defined as "stable individual preferences in mode of perceptual organization and conceptual categorization of the external environment" (Kagan et al., 1963, p. 5). Here, too, the focus of analysis is on how individuals group objects. Kagan et al. postulated that individuals could be dimensionalized on the basis of their proclivity "to analyze and to differentiate the stimulus environment" (p. 6).

To measure this type of categorizing behavior, Kagan et al. (1963) developed the Conceptual Style Test (CST). This test initially consisted of 44 triads of pictures, but shorter versions are more commonly used. The subject is asked to select from each triad the two pictures that could go together. The reasons for the grouping are considered in terms of analytic, relational, and inferential styles. An individual whose style is *analytic-descriptive* groups pictures on the basis of common elements (e.g., people without shoes). An individual whose style is *relational* utilizes functional, thematic relationships in his or her grouping (e.g., two people are grouped together because they are married). An individual whose style is *inferential-categorical* makes groupings on the basis of a more abstract similarity between the pictures (e.g., two individuals may be seen as poor).

Category Width. Pettigrew (1958) cited research by Bruner et al. (1956) as evidence for intra-individual consistencies in the range in which individuals consider events likely to occur—for example, individuals who estimate a wide range for the width of windows are likely to estimate wide ranges for other phenomena. Pettigrew developed a paper-and-pencil measure of category width, the C-W Scale, to measure this stylistic dimension. In its final form, the 20-item test offers a central-tendency value for a variety of categories (e.g., annual rainfall, width of windows, length of whales), and the subject is required to choose the upper and lower boundaries for the category from among the multiple-choice options provided.

Pettigrew gave two explanations for the observed consistency in judgments of category width. An explanation in terms of risk-taking properties suggests that broad categorizers are willing to risk being overinclusive. The second explanation uses the cognitive-control concept of equivalence range and posits that narrow categorizers make fewer differentiations. Research on these two points of view has been reviewed by Bieri (1969) and is not conclusive.

The major findings of studies of categorizing styles indicate that individual consistencies in categorization are demonstrable in a wide variety of activities, such as learning and teaching, in addition to tests administered in experimental settings (Beller, 1967; Gardner & Schoen, 1962). The preferred level of abstraction apparent over a brief period of time in a variety of situations, however, may fluctuate considerably over longer periods depending on the emotional condition of the subject (Glixman, 1965; Palei, 1986). In addition, although conceptual differentiation and preferred level of abstraction are independent of IQ (Gardner & Schoen, 1962), teaching instructions similar in style to that of the learner have been shown to increase task performance (Beller, 1967).

Reflection-Impulsivity

The third approach to cognitive styles was termed *reflection-impulsivity* by Kagan (1958, 1965a,b,c, 1966). Kagan (1965a) defines reflectivity as the tendency to reflect on alternative solution possibilities. Operationally, reflectivity is defined as a long-response latency with few errors. Conv
sivity is defined as the tendency to dem
tion impulsivity and is operationally s
short-response latency with frequent [...] Researchers have used a variety of tasks in trying to differentiate reflective individuals from impulsive individuals; the tasks are all presumed to measure the same construct. Kagan (1965a) used a tachistoscopic recognition task in which subjects are expected to recognize pictures shown at exposures ranging from 18 milliseconds to 3 seconds. A picture-story task required subjects to generate a story from a picture displayed by the experimenter (Eska & Black, 1971).

The instrument that has been most typically used to measure reflection-impulsivity is the Matching Familiar Figures Test (MFFT; Block, Block, & Harrington, 1974; Butter, 1979; Das, 1983; Kagan, 1966). In the MFFT, a person is required to select, from among several alternatives, the one that exactly matches a standard. The number of errors and the time latency are measured, and a median point is determined as a cutoff for categorizing a subject. People with faster reaction times and relatively more errors are called *impulsive*; those with longer latencies and relatively fewer errors are called *reflective*; those with faster reaction times and fewer errors are called *quick*; and those with more errors and longer latencies are called *slow* (Eska & Black, 1971). Investigators of reflection-impulsivity have generally tended to ignore the latter two categories, however, and focus only on the reflective and impulsive categories.

A series of investigations of reflection-impulsivity in children has demonstrated impressive stability over both time and tasks. In addition, the construct has produced meaningful findings concerning IQ (Bryant & Gettinger, 1981; Camara & Fox, 1983; Eska & Black, 1971), modifiability (Butter, 1979; Laval, 1980), fluid ability (Cronbach & Snow, 1977), and a variety of problem-solving and decision-quality exercises (Kagan, 1966; Mann, 1973). Impulsive subjects, in contrast to reflective subjects of similar age and verbal skills, make more errors in reading prose when in the primary grades, make more errors of commission on serial recall tasks, and are more likely to offer incorrect solutions on inductive reasoning problems and visual discrimination tasks (Stahl, Etickson, & Rayman, 1986). Furthermore, impulsives do not appear concerned about making mistakes. They offer answers quickly and without sufficient consideration of the probable accuracy of their solutions.

The research findings on reflective subjects are commonly the opposite of those obtained with impulsives. In general, reports describe the reflective child as one who pauses before beginning a task or making a decision, and as one who spends time evaluating the differential validity of alternatives (Kagan, 1965a,c). The reflective subject tends to make fewer errors in word recognition tests, serial learning, and inductive reasoning (Zelniker & Oppenheimer, 1973). Researchers also have found that a number of personality factors tend to contribute to the impulsive cognitive style—specifically, minimal anxiety over committing errors, an orientation toward quick success rather than avoiding failure, low performance standards, low motivation to master tasks, and less careful attention to and monitoring of stimuli (Kagan, 1966; Messer, 1970; Paulsen, 1978).

These latter findings have provoked controversy as to the meaning of this construct for child development (Victor, Halverson, & Montague, 1985). Kagan has argued (see Kagan & Messer, 1975) that the definition of reflection-impulsivity should be highly specific and restricted to cognitive situations of high response uncertainty, such as in the MFFT. In contrast, Block et al. (1974) support a broader definition of reflection-impulsivity, interpreting the dimension as it relates to everyday life. Investigators interested in the second view have conducted considerable research on reflection-impulsivity and its relation to behavioral impulsivity, hyperactivity, and attention-deficit disorder (Borden, Brown, Wynne, & Schleser, 1987; Das, 1983; DeHaas & Young, 1984; Finch, Saylor, & Spirito, 1982; Smith and Kemler, 1988; Victor et al., 1985). The controversy is far from resolved. Cognitive impulsiveness, as measured by the MFFT, has come to be regarded as a traitlike construct (Block, Block, & Harrington, 1974), although some theorists view this approach as an overgeneralization (Victor et al., 1985).

One attempt (Glow, Lange, Glow, & Barnett, 1983) to challenge this trait characterization was to assess the appropriateness of the "impulsive" label for fast-inaccurate MFFT performers by measuring MFFT performance along with responses to questionnaire items traditionally used to measure impulsiveness via the Eysenck Personality Questionnaire (EPQ) (Eysenck & Eysenck, 1975). The authors found no strong associations between the scores on the MFFT and those on the EPQ, and thus the value of the reflection-impulsivity style was called into question.

Furnham and Kendall (1986) performed a study in which the MFFT was administered to 6- to 11-year-olds and the Child Behavior Checklist (CBCL; Achenbach & Edelbrocker, 1983) was completed by their parents. Fast, inaccurate, impulsive responses on the MFFT were associated with attentional deficit, as measured by the CBCL, but not with 11 other behavioral problems (e.g., aggressiveness, social withdrawal, delinquency). Contrary to a previous report by Schwartz, Friedman, Lindsay, and Narrol (1982), reflection-impulsivity was found to have no relation to childhood depression. Furnham and Kendall (1986) discuss their findings in terms of a distinction between cognitive deficiency (which reflects a lack of cognitive self-control among hyperactive children) and cognitive distortion (which reflects faulty or irrational thinking in children with other behavioral disorders). Their findings suggest that fast-inaccurate MFFT performance should be regarded as a measure of cognitive style, not of impulsiveness as a behavior problem. Furnham and Kendall assert that impulsiveness as a general personality characteristic does not have to be associated with an impulsive mode of responding on the MFFT.

Attempts at Integration

As we have shown above, numerous approaches to the study of cognitive style have been attempted. Some researchers (Goldstein & Blackman, 1978; Kogan, 1973; Messick, 1970; Wardell & Royce, 1978) have tried to conceptualize the work involving cognitive styles into a number of schemes. Messick (1970) identified a total of 9 cognitive styles from the range of those proposed. The first 4—scanning, leveling-sharpening, constricted-flexible control, and tolerance for incongruous or unrealistic experience—were derived from the work on cognitive controls by Gardner, Klein, and their colleagues (Gardner & Moriarty, 1968; Klein, 1954; Klein & Schlesinger, 1951; G. Smith & Klein, 1953). The remaining categories were field dependence-independence (Witkin et al., 1971), cognitive complexity (Harvey, Hunt, & Schroder, 1961; Kelly, 1955), reflection-impulsivity (Kagan, 1966), styles of categorization (Pettigrew, 1958), and styles of conceptualization (Kagan et al., 1963). In 1976, Messick modified and expanded these 9 categories, eventually listing a total of 19 cognitive styles.

Kogan (1973) offered a threefold classification based on the distance of a style from the domain of abilities. A Type I style is closest to the ability domain, because performance on the operational index of the style can be described as more or less veridical. For example, an individual described as field-independent is more proficient in setting the rod to the vertical in the rod-and-frame test than the field-dependent person. Because the task requirement is to set the rod at the true vertical, field independence necessarily implies a superior level of performance.

In Type II cognitive styles, the question of veridicality of performance does not arise. Nevertheless, the investigator places greater value on one specific kind of performance relative to another. Such a value choice is sometimes made on purely theoretical grounds—one style is postulated to be developmentally more advanced than another. The value aspect may also derive from observed correlations of the styles in question with ability measures. If one style correlates with ability indexes, whereas an alternative style does not, the former tends to be endowed with greater value. Typical of the Type II category are the conceptual styles described by Kagan et al. (1963). Although an analytic style in no sense represents a higher level of performance than a thematic-relation style, the investigators place greater value on the former.

Type III is the only category in which styles are neither ranked nor synonymous with ability. For example, a broad-versus-narrow style of categorization (Pettigrew, 1958) was initially advanced in largely value-neutral terms. Since that time, investigators have not found a consistent pattern of correlations to suggest that either broad or narrow categorizers have a consistent cognitive advantage (Kogan, 1971).

In the 1970s, Wardell and Royce (1978) attempted to summarize the vast literature on styles in the framework of one multifactorial theory. Before we can discuss this approach, however, it is necessary to specify the definitions used in developing the theory. Royce (1973) defined style as "a characteristic mode or way of manifesting cognitive and/or affective phenomena" (p. 178). This definition suggests that styles are essentially stable traits, designating consistent modes of cognitive and affective processings. Furthermore, the combination of styles of any individual constitutes that individual's style subsystem. Royce defined the style subsystem as "a multidimensional, organized subsystem of processes (that includes cognitive, affective, and cognitive-affective styles) by means of which an organism manifests cognitive or/and affective phenomena" (p. 330). According to this definition, styles can be seen as higher-Order traits in that they influence the way cognitive abilities and affective traits are related to individual behavior. Based on this definition, Royce's analysis distinguishes among the three major types of stylistic constructs: cognitive styles, affective styles, and cognitive-affective styles. The first two are concerned with functional consistencies in the relationship between styles and ability factors or affective traits, respectively. Cognitive-affective styles are concerned with consistent ways in which styles simultaneously integrate ability and affective traits.

The multifactorial theory of styles proposed by Wardell and Royce (1978) was developed to incorporate the range of cognitive styles in one theory by specifying three ways cognition and affect may be integrated. The basic units of this theory are identified primarily via the theory and methodology of factor analysis (Royce, 1973). Wardell and Royce describe three higher-order constructs or "general styles": rational, empirical, and metaphoric. Through meta-analysis, Wardell and Royce identified seven cognitive and four affective styles corresponding to the general styles. The cognitive and affective styles reflect some degree of construct validity based on extensive empirical research performed mostly in the new-look framework. Table 2 displays the three higher-order constructs and cognitive and affective styles corresponding to the general styles.

The multifactorial theory illustrates the need for better operationalizations of stylistic constructs, a need emphasized by a number of researchers (Goldstein & Blackman, 1978; Klein, Barr, & Wolitsky, 1967; Kogan, 1976; Vernon, 1973). The multifactor theory of styles, however, needs to be supported by empirical research. It is not known, for example, whether all 11 cognitive styles presented in the theory represent mutually distinct processes, or how they are psychologically different. In addition, though cognitive styles appear to have some generality across cognitive domains, research is needed to determine the extend to which individuals shift styles in accordance with situational demands or in the context of different activities (Peterson & Scott, 1975).

Limitations of the Cognition-Centered Theories of Styles

Despite these attempts to generalize the theories of cognitive styles, the area remains problematic. First of all, these studies were more empirically driven than theory driven. Investigations of cognitive styles have often used correlational and experimental data to sketch networks of relations that characterize a given style as a construct; the result has been to make it even

Table 2. Royce and Wardell's Higher-Order Constructs and Corresponding Affective and Cognitive Styles

General styles	Cognitive styles	Affective styles
Rational	Cognitive complexity (Gardner & Schoen, 1962) Conceptual differentiation (Gardner & Schoen, 1962) Category width (Pettigrew, 1958) Abstract versus concrete (Harvey, Hunt & Schroder, 1961) Analytical versus relational categorizing (Kagan, Moss, & Sigel, 1963)	Constricted versus flexible control (Klein, 1954; Gardner, Holzman, Klein, Linton, & Spence, 1959)
Empirical	Compartmentalization (Messick & Kogan, 1963) Leveling versus sharpening (Klein, 1951) Abstract versus concrete (Harvey, Hunt & Schroder, 1961) Analytical versus relational categorizing (Kagan, Moss, & Sigel, 1963)	Tolerance for the unconventional (Klein, Gardner, & Schlesinger, 1962) Reflection versus impulsivity (Kagan, 1965)
Metaphoric	Conceptual integration (Harvey, Hunt & Schroder, 1961) Compartmentalization (Messick & Kogan, 1963)	Physiognomic versus literal (Klein, 1951)

more difficult to see the forest for the trees. There has been an ever-increasing accumulation of detail without the presentation of the general principles needed to organize it.

Second, the classification of subjects as field-dependent or -independent, analytical or relational, and reflective or impulsive inevitably depends upon the validity of the measures used in the study. Correlations of stylistic variables with ability and personality measures and with other stylistic variables have not been assembled systematically. A systematic organization is needed to clarify the overlap among stylistic variables, intelligence, and traitlike parameters of personality. Because the validity of the measures is unknown, it is difficult to determine the validity of the studies.

Third, there has often been an implicit bias in the interpretation of the results, with some of the styles considered good (e.g., field independence, reflection), and the others considered bad (e.g., field dependence, impulsivity). This characterization clearly does not correspond to the general definition of a style as a preferred way of doing things, in which there is no implication of ability-dependent quality of performance. Instead we are left with good preferences that are good because they lead to superior performance on a test that is supposed to measure preference rather than ability!

Finally, to date there have been no studies that assess styles in an ecologically natural environment. Measuring a child's tendency toward reflection or impulsivity, field dependence or independence, or styles of categorization in a mobile van unit complete with sophisticated equipment may not be a valid method of assessing cognitive styles (Butter, 1979; Laval, 1980). Studying the relationship between cognitive style and performance in various environments seems to be one particularly worthwhile endeavor. The one exception to the tendency to rely entirely on artificial environment is the work on integrative complexity; here low and high environmental complexity appear to have differential effects on subjects who vary in levels of integrative complexity (Harvey et al., 1961). In sum, although researchers of cognitive styles have found a wide variety of interesting and, in some instances, important associations between cognitive styles and different psychological variables, this wide range of results has still not come together to form a single, comprehensive picture.

Personality-Centered Studies of Styles

In their search for psychological constructs at the interface of intelligence and personality, scientists also have looked at personality styles related to cognition. In the context of the personality-centered approach, styles are conceived not as personality traits but as "deep-seated individual differences exercising a wide, but somewhat loose control over the domains of cognitive function, interest, values, and personality development" (Ross, 1962, p. 76). In this section we will discuss two major theories of personality styles: the Myers-Briggs theory of psychological types and Gregorc's model of styles.

The Theory of Psychological Types

The need for stylistic constructs led some investigators to look to much earlier work for clues as to the nature of styles. Jung (1923; I. Myers & Myers, 1980), in his theory of psychological types, proposed a set of orientations and attitudes to describe basic individual preferences accompanying a person's interaction with the environment. The typology Jung developed to characterize typical differences among individuals consists of two attitudes (extraversion and introversion), two perceptual functions (intuition and sensing), and two judgment functions (thinking and feeling).

The attitudes of extraversion and introversion describe our basic stance in dealing with other people we encounter. Extraversion characterizes those who are outgoing, with an interest in people and the environment; introversion describes people whose interests are more inwardly focused. Sensing and intuition are used in Jung's typology to describe preferences in perceiving stimuli. An intuitive person tends to perceive stimuli holistically and to concentrate on meaning rather than details, whereas a sensing individual perceives information realistically and precisely. Thinking and feeling represent two distinct modes for judging or understanding perceived stimuli. Judgments made in the thinking mode tend to be logical, analytical, and impersonal; those made in the feeling mode are usually based upon values rather than logic.

Because the Myers-Briggs theory, a contemporary theory of styles, was based on Jung's theory of types, there is a close similarity between its variables and those outlined by Jung. There are also, however, some obvious differences. Jung does not refer to the perceptive-judging distinction directly, although he does refer to the function of feeling as "a king of judging" (Jung, 1923). More importantly, the functions of sensation, intuition, thinking, and feeling are not as tightly organized in Jung's typology as in the Myers-Briggs scheme.

The main assumption of the Myers-Briggs theory is that "the many aspects of conscious mental activity can be subsumed under one of these four categories" (I. Myers & McCaulley, 1985, p. 12). According to Myers (1981), there are 16 types of personality styles, resulting from all possible combinations of the four different functions, each of which has two categories. The theory proposes two ways of perceiving (sensing and intuition), two ways of judging (thinking and feeling), two ways of dealing with self and others (introversion and extraversion), and two ways of dealing with the outer world (judgment and perception). A brief description of the styles is displayed in Table 3. Sensing, intuiting, thinking, and feeling are always present to various degrees in every individual, but one function tends to be dominant and the other subordinate.

This theory has been applied to a variety of professional fields, such as business (Corman & Platt, 1988), law (Hennessy, 1992), and education (Bargar & Hoover, 1984). Because the educational findings are the most relevant to the content of this chapter, we will discuss them in more detail. According to Bargar and Hoover (1984), the styles defined by the theory are not equally represented in the general population of school children. Extraversion and sensing are often cited as most common (I. Myers, 1981; Lawrence, 1982). Lawrence (1982) recommends developing teaching strategies for the majority group of extraverted-sensing children, then creating more individualized approaches for the smaller number of introverted and intuitive children. In addition, extraversion, sensing, and feeling appear to be prominent among teachers, particularly at the elementary level (I. Myers, 1981). It may be that intuitive persons, particularly those with an intuitive-feeling orientation, tend to self-select out of teaching. Huelsman (1983) found that whereas preferred learning styles were fairly evenly distributed among psychological types, preferred teaching styles were not. Teachers who report intuitive-thinking and feeling as the preferred learning styles of their students tended to prefer teaching with sensing-feeling and sensing-thinking styles. Huelsman concluded that this lack of congruity could be detrimental to teacher effectiveness and might be a factor in teachers' stress, job dissatisfaction, and decisions to leave the profession.

Gregorc's Energic Model of Styles

A second theory of cognitive styles that originated in personality psychology is Gregorc's (1985) energic model of styles. Gregorc (1984) defines style as being "superficial, consisting of surface behaviors, characteristics, outward features, and mannerisms" (p. 51). The energic model is based on two principal dimensions: space and time. Space refers to perceptual categories for acquiring and expressing information and is divided into concrete (or physical) and abstract (or metaphorical) space. Time is divided into two different ways of ordering facts and events: sequential (i.e., in a step-by-step or branchlike manner) and random ordering (i.e., in a weblike or spiral manner). In

Table 3. Characteristics Frequently associated with Myers-Briggs Styles

Sensing types-introverts-judging-with thinking
Serious, quiet, earn success by concentration and thoroughness. Practical, orderly, matter-of-fact, logical, realistic and dependable. Live their outer life more with thinking, inner more with sensing.

Sensing types-introverts-judging-with feeling
Quiet, friendly, and conscientious. Work devotedly to meet their obligations. Thorough, painstaking, accurate. Live their outer life more with feeling, inner more with sensing.

Sensing types-introverts-perceptive-with thinking
Cool onlookers, quiet, reserved, observing and analyzing life with detached curiosity and unexpected flashes of original humor. Interested in impersonal principles, cause and effect. Live their outer life more with sensing, inner more with thinking.

Sensing types-introverts-perceptive-with feeling
Retiring, quiet, friendly, sensitive, modest about their abilities. Shun disagreements, do not force their opinions or values on others. Live their outer life more with sensing, inner more with feeling.

Sensing types-extraverts-judging-with thinking
Practical realists, matter-of-fact, with a natural head for business or mechanics. Like to organize and run activities. Live their outer life more with thinking, inner more with sensing.

Sensing types-extraverts-judging-with feeling
Warm-hearted, talkative, popular,. conscientious, born cooperators, active committee members. Live their outer life more with feeling, inner life more with sensing.

Sensing types-extraverts-perceptive-with thinking
Matter-of-fact, do not worry or hurry, enjoy whatever comes along. Adaptable, tolerant, generally conservative in values. Live their outer life more with sensing, inner more with thinking.

Sensing types-extraverts-perceptive-with feeling
Outgoing, easygoing, accepting, friendly, fond of a good time. Live their outer life more with sensing, inner more with feeling.

Intuitives-introverts-judging-with thinking
Have original minds and great drive, which they use only for their own purposes. Skeptical, critical, independent, determined. Live their outer life more with thinking, inner more with intuition.

Intuitives-introverts-judging-with feeling
Succeed by perseverance, originality and desire to do whatever is needed or wanted. Put their best efforts into their work. Live their outer life more with thinking, inner more with intuition.

Intuitives-introverts-perceptive-with thinking
Quiet, reserved, impersonal. Enjoy especially theoretical or scientific subjects. Interested mainly in ideas, with little liking for parties or small talk. Live their outer life more with intuition, inner more with thinking.

Intuitives-introverts-perceptive-with feeling
Full of enthusiams and loyalties. Care about learning, ideas, language, and independent projects of their own. Live their outer life more with intuition, inner more with feeling.

Intuitives-extraverts-judging-with thinking
Hearty, frank, decisive, leaders in activities. Good in anything that requires reasoning and intelligent talk. Live their outer life more with thinking, inner more with intuition.

Intuitives-extraverts-judging-with feeling
Responsive and responsible. Feel real concern for what others think and want, and try to handle things with due regard for other people's feelings. Live their outer life more with feeling, inner more with intuition.

Intuitives-extraverts-perceptive-with thinking
Quick, ingenious, good at many things. Stimulating company, alert and outspoken, argue on either side of a question for fun. Live their life with intuition, inner more with thinking.

Intuitives-extraverts-perceptive-with feeling
Warmly, enthusiastic, high-spirited, ingenious, imaginative. Quick with a solution for any difficulty and ready to help anyone with a problem. Live their outer life more with intuition, inner more with feeling

combination, these two dimensions form four qualitatively different styles that mediate individuals' interactions with their environments (concrete-sequential, abstract-sequential, abstract-random, and concrete-random). Short descriptions of these styles are given in Table 4.

Gregorc's four styles describe thinking patterns, mind-sets, and modes of self-expression. Although it is possible for individuals to obtain equal scores in each of the styles, most people tend to have one or two dominant styles that describe their most effective way of interacting with the environment.

Limitations of Personality-Centered Approaches

In spite of differences in the styles proposed by Myers-Briggs and Gregorc, they have similar limitations. First, even though the theories may have empirical utility and importance, the Myers-Briggs and Gregorc questionnaires are often criticized because the overall measurement models (defined through confirmatory factor analysis) are incongruent with the underlying theoretical models, and because the factor structures of these questionnaires are not supported by the empirical findings (Goldsmith, 1985; Keller & Holland, 1978; Kirton & de Ciantis, 1986; Mulligan & Martin, 1980; O'Brien, 1990). Joniak and Isaksen (1988), analyzing the Gregorc questionnaire, showed that an instrument with only two subscales (sequential-random and concrete-abstract) based on two orthogonal dimensions (ordering, perception) would give a more parsimonious representation of Gregorc's styles. Ross (1962) found a mismatch between the Myers-Briggs scales and the factors resulting from the analysis he performed.

Table 4. Gregorc's Styles and Brief Descriptions

Styles	Descriptions
Concrete-sequential	Refers to a preference for the ordered, the practical, and the stable. Individuals who are primarily concrete-sequential have a tendency to focus their attention on concrete reality and physical objects and to validate ideas via the senses.
Abstract-sequential	Refers to a preference for mentally stimulating environments. Individuals who are primarily abstract-sequential have a tendency to focus their attention on the world of the intellect. They are characterized by a preference for logical and synthetic thinking and for validating information via personal formulae.
Abstract-random	Refers to a preference for emotional and physical freedom. Individuals who are primarily abstract-random have a tendency to focus their attention on the world of feeling and emotion. They are also characterized by a tendency to validate ideas via inner guidance.
Concrete-random	Refers to a preference for a stimulus-rich environment that is free from restriction. Individuals who are primarily concrete-random tend to prefer intuitive and instinctive thinking and to rely on personal proof for validating ideas. They rarely accepting outside authority.

Second, there have been no systematic studies of the relationship between similar styles originating in different theories—for example, Gregorc's abstract-sequential style and Myers-Briggs sensing-introvert-judging-thinking type. Some studies found a significant amount of overlap between different styles (Joniak & Isaksen, 1988), whereas others noted the lack of correspondence (Ross, 1962). Joniak and Isaksen (1988) performed a correlation analysis of scores on the Gregorc Style Delineator (Gregorc, 1982) and the Kirton Adaptation-Innovation Inventory (Kirton, 1977). Kirton's (1976) theory of cognitive style specifies a bipolar dimension with the innovator and the adaptor on opposite ends. When confronted with a problem, the adaptor turns to traditional or conventional procedures in order to find solutions; in contrast, the innovator will typically redefine the problem and approach it using a novel perspective. The results indicated that Gregorc's sequential stylists were adaptors on the Kirton scale, and Gregorc's randoms were innovators; however, the concrete-abstract dimension did not correlate with Kirton's measure. The results suggest that five styles rather than six are sufficient to describe the dimensions of these two theories. Clearly, further research and comparison of this type would be useful in organizing the numerous theories of styles. Messick (1984) made a similar observation, noting that "sometimes quite disparate measures are used to assess ostensibly the same style in different studies, while on other occasions, highly similar instruments serve to tap purportedly distinct styles" (p. 59).

The third problem with the personality-centered approach is the difficulty of distinguishing between styles and personality traits. Ross's (1962) suggestion that styles relate to the cognitive domain of personality has not been thoroughly explored. Moreover, authors use such terms as *types* (I. Myers & Myers, 1980) and *channels* (Gregorc, 1985) as synonyms for *style*, which brings us close to the point where the definition of *style* becomes too flexible for the concept to be of much use.

Finally, the lack of clarity in the definition of the styles concept leads to a question of domain generality and specificity. If style is a traitlike concept, one can assume that a person who is concrete-sequential would demonstrate this pattern in all types of activities. If styles are more flexible patterns of behavior, however, a person demonstrating a concrete-sequential style in learning may demonstrate an abstract-sequential style in managing. It is also plausible that personality styles are relatively stable and traitlike, whereas the behavioral styles that correspond to these personality styles only appear in specific contexts. The next class of theories we will discuss is in large part an attempt to address the issue of domain specificity of styles—that is, to describe styles in the context of different types of activities.

Activity-Centered Theories of Styles

The activity-centered theories of styles were developed primarily in the late 1960s and early 1970s, when the notion of styles was becoming popular among educators. At that time, educators and school psychologists found themselves caught between a theoretical understanding of individual differences and the practical problem of dealing with such differences in their schools and classrooms. They needed new psychological instruments (tests, questionnaires, etc.) that might provide new insights into their students' individual differences. Because of their disappointment with intelligence tests and the need for new measures of individual differences, the concept of style attracted the attention of many theorists. The learning styles that were the focus of educators' attention are described in detail in the following section.

Learning Styles

Many attempts have been made to describe learning styles, ranging from simple definition statements to elaborate taxonomies. Perhaps the most striking aspect of the literature on learning styles is the range of definitions that have been adopted to describe these constructs. For example, Hunt (1979) believes that a student's learning style can be described in terms of those educational conditions under which he or she is most likely to learn. Gregorc (1979, 1985) defines a learning style as those distinctive behaviors that serve as indicators on how a person learns from, and adapts to, his or her environment. Some theorists focus on the learning styles of children suffering from psychological problems (e.g., adolescent delinquents; Meltzer, 1984). The available theories of learning styles show considerable variation in focus, ranging from an emphasis on preferred sensory modalities (Renzulli & Smith, 1978) to descriptions of personality characteristics that have implications for behavioral patterns in learning situations (Bargar & Hoover, 1984). Taken together, the descriptions suggest that learning styles have both cognitive and affective dimensions that serve as relatively stable indicators of how learners perceive, interact with, and respond to the learning environment (Kuerbis, 1988). Although the presentation of the full range of theories of learning styles is beyond the scope of this chapter, in the following section we will discuss a number of approaches to learning styles that represent a variety of definitions and theories.

The research goal of Kolb (1974) is to gain a better understanding of the various ways in which people can learn and solve problems. He refers to learning style as the way people "emphasize some learning abilities over others" (p. 29) and suggests that individuals could benefit by being aware of the consequences of their learning style and of the alternative learning modes available to them. The Learning Style Inventory (LSI; Kolb, 1978) is designed to measure an individual's strengths and weaknesses as a learner. More specifically, it measures an individual's relative emphasis on four learning abilities: concrete experience, reflective observation, abstract conceptualization, and active experimentation. Based on the results of the LSI, Kolb (1974) has identified four dominant types of learning styles: converging, diverging, assimilating and accommodating.

Convergers' dominant learning abilities are abstract conceptualization and active experimentation. Their knowledge is organized in such way that, through hypothetical-deductive reasoning, they can focus it on specific problems. Divergers have the opposite learning strengths of convergers. Divergers are best at concrete experience and reflective observation; they are interested in people, and they tend to be imaginative and emotional. Assimilators' dominant learning abilities are abstract conceptualization and reflective observation. Their greatest strength lies in their ability to create theoretical models; they excel in inductive reasoning and assimilating disparate observations into an integrated explanation. Assimilators are less interested in people than in abstract concepts. Just as the converger's strengths are opposite those of the diverger, the accommodator excels in the areas in which the assimilator might feel uncomfortable. Accommodators are best at concrete experience and active experimentation; they tend to take more risks than people with the other learning styles.

A very different approach to learning styles is a theory based on the specialized functions of the cerebral hemispheres (Reynolds, Riegel, & Torrance, 1977). Applying their research in hemispheric specialization, Reynolds et al. defined learning styles as preferred modes of information processing. Three styles were specified: left-dominant (or active, verbal, analytic, and logical), right-dominant (or receptive, nonverbal, spatial, and intuitive), and whole-brained (or complementary, integrated, simultaneously left and right) information processing. Thus students with left-dominant learning styles may be better able to generate logical relationships among alternative scientific constructs than those with right-dominant learning styles, whereas the latter may have the intrinsic capacity to understand abstract ideas.

Perhaps one of the most influential and widely known theories of learning styles is the theory proposed by Dunn, Dunn, and Price. Dunn and Dunn (1978) discuss in detail many different learning styles yielded by their own learning-styles inventory. These authors define learning style as "a biologically and developmentally imposed set of personal characteristics that make the same teaching method effective for some and ineffective for others" (Dunn, Beaudry, & Klavas, 1989, p. 50). The Dunn Learning Style Inventory (Dunn, Dunn, & Price, 1979) measures 18 elements divided into four main categories: environmental (sound, light, temperature, design), emotional (motivation, persistence, responsibility, structure), sociological (peers, self, pair, team, adult, varied), and physical (perceptual, intake, time, mobility). But in spite of its popularity among educators, the Dunns' definition of learning styles seems to raise more questions than it answers. There is little information regarding the reasons for the choice of the 18 elements, nor is there any explanation given of possible interactions of the elements.

The greatest problem with the theory, however, may be its lack of attention to the learning process. Specifically, the Dunns' definition does not address the issue of how the student learns, instead focusing exclusively on what elements affect a person's ability to learn. As Hyman and Rosoff (1984) noted, according to the Dunns' definition, a learning style is a matter of ability, not of a behavioral preference or process. This definition seems to be of limited use if the purpose of determining style is to aid teachers in their understanding of the processes involved in learning and the ways in which students differ on process dimensions. Unfortunately, this criticism is not limited to the Dunns' theory of learning styles. As Hyman and Rosoff indicate, most theories of learning styles fail to provide a clear and readily usable definition of learning style.

Teaching Styles

Despite years of searching for the definitive teaching method, educators have come to realize that in fact there is no single best method. Every technique has its advantages and disadvantages and will be differentially effective depending on many factors, including the topic being addressed, the students being taught, and the teacher doing the teaching. Given the number of variables involved in good teaching, a likely conclusion is one suggested by Joyce and Hodges (1966): "A teacher who can purposefully exhibit a wide range of teaching styles is potentially able to accomplish more than a teacher whose repertoire is relatively limited" (p. 411). Simply put, adjusting teaching styles to fit the materials and the students leads to more effective teaching. This insight led educators to start discussing the need to understand the range of teaching styles used in the classroom. Furthermore, it became clear that students would benefit if teaching styles were varied. These observations led to the development of a number of different theories of teaching styles. Each theorist who has investigated teaching styles has noted the variety teachers bring to the classroom and the impact of that variety on their students.

Fischer and Fischer (1979) differentiated between teaching styles and methods of instruction. They define teaching style as "a pervasive way of approaching the learners that might be consistent with several methods of teaching" (p. 251). They also note that two teachers may both use such methods as lectures, audiovisual materials, and discussion groups but still differ in their teaching styles. Kuchinskas (1979), using the term *cognitive style* to define the manner in which an individual acts, reacts, and adapts to the environment, suggests that a teachers' cognitive style has a significant impact on students. According to Kuchinskas, if we are to exploit the key role a teacher plays in the learning process, then his or her cognitive style—as well as the resulting teaching style—needs to be closely examined to determine the effect it has on classroom activities.

In an important article on the theories of teaching, B. O. Smith (1963) points out the need to consider the interaction of subject matter and teaching style. Specifically, the teacher must determine how best to teach the differing facts, concepts, principles, skills, and values that are commonly associated with such subjects as social studies, language arts, science, mathematics, fine arts, and physical education. The determining factor for the teacher is not the "whom" but the "what"—in other words, the subject matter. This is what Smith means when he says that teaching is "controlled" by the subject matter. Teachers think of themselves as teachers of history, or mathematics, or writing, and so on, but "while the teacher's behavior is influenced by his understanding of the student—by his perception and diagnosis of the student's behavior—still the determining factor in the teacher's behavior is not his understanding of the student but his comprehension of the subject matter and the demands which clear instruction in the subject matter make upon him" (p. 296). Clearly teachers need more than one approach if they are to achieve a good fit with subject material.

Henson and Borthwick (1984) suggested six different categories of teaching styles, giving teachers a range of options that vary according to their emphasis on teacher- versus student-directed planning. In a *task-oriented* approach, planned tasks associated with some appropriate materials are prescribed. In a *cooperative-planner* approach, an instructional venture is planned by teacher and students, though the teacher is in charge. The task structure in the *child-centered* approach is provided by the teacher, with the students choosing from options according to their interests. In *subject-centered* teaching, the content is planned and structured to the extent that students are nearly excluded. In *learning-centered* teaching, equal concern is shown by the teacher for both the student and for subject content; a teacher who favors this approach attempts to guide students in their development. *Emotionally exciting* teachers try to make their teaching as stimulating as possible. The notion of fitting teaching style to both student and subjects suggests that although teachers may have a preferred approach, using a variety of approaches will make for more effective teaching.

Limitations of Activity-Centered Approaches

The positive result of studying learning and teaching styles was that practical definitions were adopted. Furthermore, these approaches have strong empirical support. The strength of these theories is in their relevance for the school setting. Yet these approaches, like those discussed earlier, seem to have their limitations.

First, like the approaches described earlier, the activity-centered framework suffers from the lack of a clear definition of style. Thus it is difficult to find a correspondence between different approaches developed in this framework, and it is even more problematic to relate them to work outside of the activity-centered tradition.

Second, the activity-centered approaches do little about the development of styles. The fact that we can diagnose the learning style of a student does not tell us anything about how this style was developed or if a teacher can revise it. Cognition-centered and personality-centered theories, in contrast, do discuss the development of styles in the context of overall intellectual and personality development.

THE THEORY OF MENTAL SELF-GOVERNMENT

A style of thought is a preferred way of thinking. Sternberg (1994) defines it more specifically as a preferred way of expressing or using one or more abilities. One might view a style as a personality attribute (although not a fixed one) for the utilization of abilities. Sternberg (1986, 1988; Sternberg & Lubart, 1991a,b) has proposed a model of mental self-government that addresses the question of how intelligence is organized or directed (see Figure 1). When applied to intelligence, the metaphor of mental self-government generates 13 thinking styles, or stylistic ways of approaching the world.

Governments have different forms, functions, levels, scopes, uses, and leanings. A government in its form may be monarchic, anarchic, hierarchic, or oligarchic, and it may act legislatively, executively, or judicially. It may also function at either a global or local level. In addition, government may assume either an internal (domestic) or external (foreign) scope of

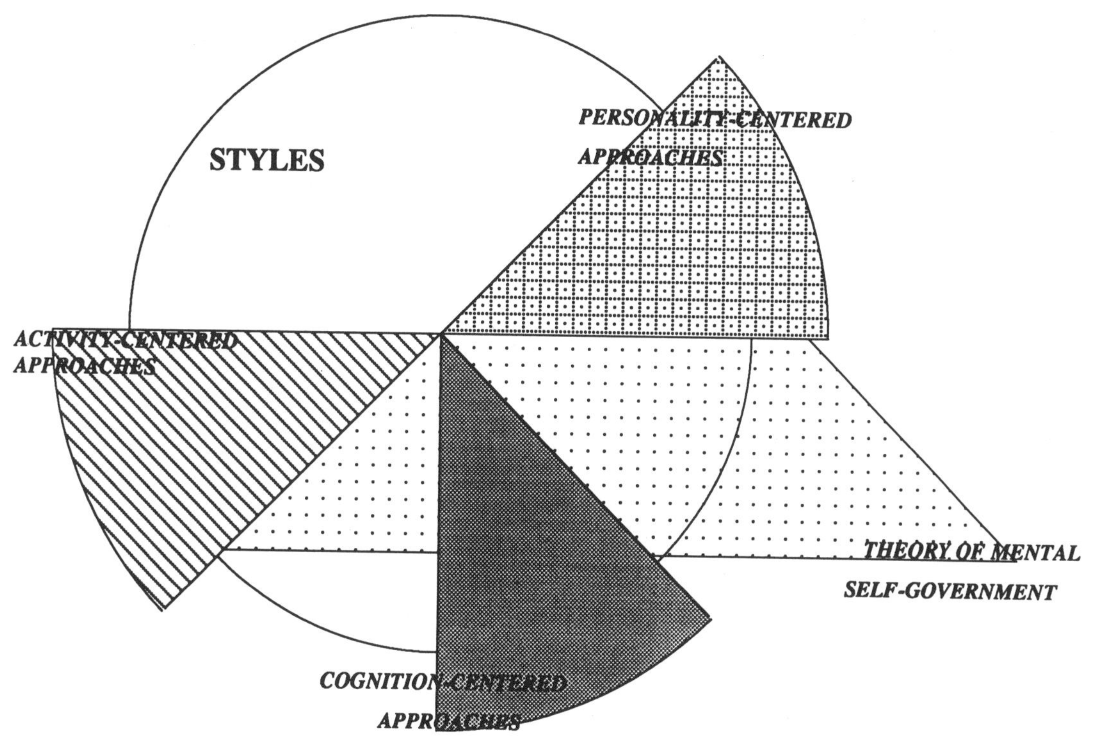

Figure 1. A schematic representation of studies of styles. Historically, styles have been studied in psychology of personality, cognitive psychology, and in areas of applied psychology (e.g., educational psychology and organizational psychology). The frequent development of new approaches to styles suggests that the concept and its limitations have not been determined. Various approaches merge in the center of the "styles circle," symbolizing the studies done at the intersection of different approaches. The theory of mental self-government incorporates both original aspects and aspects drawn from the earlier theories of styles.

affairs, and it may tend to lean toward either the liberal or conservative end of the spectrum. According to the theory of mental self-government, the various styles of government we see in the world are external reflections of the styles that we can find in the mind. Thus, in order to understand the styles of thought, we can look at aspects of government for a sense of what is internally (as well as externally) possible.

The Functions of Mental Self-Government

Just as governments carry out legislative, executive, and judicial functions, so does the mind. The legislative function of the mind is concerned with creating, imagining, and planning; the executive function is concerned with implementing and doing; and the judicial function is concerned with judging, evaluating, and comparing. It is very important to notice that mental self-government involves all three functions. In many people, however, one of the functions tends to be dominant.

The *legislative* style characterizes people who enjoy creating and formulating. Such individuals like to create their own rules, do things in their own way, and build their own structures when deciding how to approach a problem. They prefer tasks that are not prestructured or prefabricated. Legislative people prefer creative and constructive planning-based activities, such as writing papers, designing projects, and creating new business or education systems.

Individuals with an *executive* style are implementers. They prefer to follow rules, and they often rely on existing methods to master a situation. Executive people prefer tasks that are prefabricated and prestructured. Such people prefer activities that are already defined for them, such as solving word problems, ap-

Figure 2. This figure illustrates the thinking styles constituting the functions of mental self-government. One can imagine a tsar-legislator, who gives orders and points to new ways of doing things, an executer, who implements these orders and follows the advice of a wiseman-advisor, who judges, evaluates, and analyzes the words and actions of others.

plying rules to already structured engineering problems, giving talks or lessons based on others' ideas, and enforcing rules.

The judicial style is seen in those people who like to evaluate rules and procedures, who like to judge things, and who like tasks in which one analyzes and evaluates existing rules, ways, and ideas. People with a judicial style prefer activities that exercise the judicial function, such as writing critiques, giving opinions, judging people and their work, and evaluating programs. Figure 2 illustrates the thinking styles constituting the functions of mental self-government.

The Forms of Mental Self-Government

Just as there are four main forms of government, there are four major ways that describe how individuals govern themselves: oligarchic, monarchic, hierarchic, and anarchic. The *oligarchic* form allows for multiple goals, all of which are equally important. A student who has an oligarchic style of thinking will do well in a course that includes several tasks weighted equally (e.g., a major paper that will count just as much as the final exam). Oligarchic individuals like dealing with multiple and often competing goals of perceived equal importance, but they tend to experience conflict and tension when they are forced to assign priorities. Competing goals keep oligarchic individuals from completing tasks, because everything seems equally important to them.

The *monarchic* form of mental self-government is characterized by a preference for tasks and situations that allow a person to focus on one item or aspect of that item until it is completed. People with a monarchic style tend to focus single-mindedly on one goal or need at a time.

Figure 3. Think of medieval astronomers approaching the task of observing stars in different ways. The astronomer with an oligarchic style treats all stars he or she can see as equally important. The monarchic astronomer focuses on a favorite star to study it completely, paying little attention to the rest of the sky. The stargazer with the hierarchic style studies a number of stars, rating their importance based on his or her own sense of priorities. Finally, the anarchic stargazer, enjoying sparkles from many different stars, observes each of them as he or she wishes, but does not really analyze any of them.

The *hierarchic* form allows for multiple goals, each of which may have a different priority. People with a hierarchic style enjoy dealing with many goals, though they recognize that some goals are more important than others. They have a good sense of priorities, and they tend to be systematic in their approach to solving problems. When a student needs to allocate time to several homework assignments of varying importance, that student will benefit from having a hierarchic style.

Finally, the *anarchic* thinking style is characterized by a preference for activities that lend themselves to great (sometimes too great) flexibility of approaches. Anarchic stylists tend to be motivated by a potpourri of needs and goals that are often difficult for themselves, as well as for others, to sort out. They are often simplifiers who are intolerant, and too flexible, in that they may believe that anything goes. People with an anarchic thinking style have trouble setting priorities because they have no firm set of rules upon which to base these priorities. Figure 3 illustrates these different styles.

Levels of Mental Self-Government

Government exists at multiple levels: federal, state, county, city, and so on. In essence, the levels of government suggest that individuals may vary in their concern for detail. Thus one can distinguish between global and local styles.

The *local* style refers to a preference for tasks, projects, and situations that require engagement with specific, concrete details. The person with this style relishes the very small matters that the global person eschews, and he or she likes to work on problems that require precision. Localists are often down-to-earth and oriented toward the pragmatics of a situation.

In contrast, the *global* style refers to a preference for problems that are likely to be general in nature and to require abstract thinking. The global person likes to conceptualize and work in the world of ideas. Metaphorically, he or tends to see the forest, but does not always consider the trees that constitute it. Figure 4 illustrates the difference between a globalist and a localist.

Scope of Mental Self-Government

Governments need to deal with both internal (or domestic) and external (or foreign) affairs. Similarly, mental self-government needs to deal with internal and external issues. The *internal* style refers to a preference for projects, tasks, or events that allow one to work independently from others. Internalists tend to be introverted, task oriented, aloof, and both less socially sensitive and less interpersonally aware than externalists. Essentially, their preference is to apply

Figure 4. This figure illustrates the difference between a globalist and a localist. A globalist can spend his life looking at the sky and not paying any attention to celestial details, whereas a localist can open the world under the microscope.

their intelligence to problems or ideas in isolation from other people.

In contrast, the *external* style refers to a preference for activities that allow working and interacting with others at different stages of progress. Externalists tend to be extroverted, people oriented, outgoing, socially more sensitive, and more interpersonally aware than internalists. They seek problems that either involve working with other people or are related to these other people in some way. Figure 5 illustrates the difference between these styles.

The Leanings of Mental Self-Government

Governments can have various political leanings. Optimally, these leanings are represented on a continuum from right wing to left wing, but for our purposes, two major regions of leanings will be distinguished: conservative and liberal. The two leanings of government suggest that individuals vary in their degree of adherence to preexisting rules or structures—that is, in their degree of mental liberalism and conservatism. The *liberal* thinking style refers to a preference for tasks and projects that require going beyond existing rules and procedures, as well as situations that allow substantial change. The person with this style seeks ambiguous and uncertain stimuli and becomes bored when things never seem to change.

In contrast, the *conservative* thinking style refers to a preference for tasks, projects, and situations that require adherence to existing rules and procedures. Conservative stylists prefer familiarity in life and

Figure 5. The internalist shown prefers to think and to create in solitude, whereas the externalist enjoys working and sharing ideas with people.

work. The characters shown in Figure 6 illustrate the difference between the liberal and conservative styles.

These 13 thinking styles delineate a cognitive profile of how people direct their intelligence. Individuals vary in their relative preference for these stylistic ways of adapting to and interacting with the environment, independent of their level of intelligence. Also, it is important to note that individuals can use more than one style, but some find it easier to switch among styles than others. Applying this approach in practice, we have collected some evidence regarding the utility of the theory. Our data are described elsewhere (Grigorenko & Sternberg, 1993; Sternberg, 1994; Sternberg & Grigorenko, 1994).

CONCLUSION

Having pointed out in our introduction the weaknesses in the concept of style as presented in the current literature, can we argue that the theory of thinking styles points to some new direction in stylistic research? We believe that the theory does. First of all, it gives a definition of a style as a dynamic structure, playing the role of a communicator between intelligence and personality. Style is neither intelligence nor personality, but rather what brings the two psychological structures together. A thinking style, in short, is the personal way in which someone uses his or her intelligence.

As was shown above, the theory of thinking styles has the potential to be applied in a variety of different areas. Using the categories of thinking styles, we can describe people's preferred ways of using their intelligence in a variety of domains and professions. In our studies, we showed how the theory of thinking styles can be applied to school settings (Grigorenko & Sternberg, 1993; Sternberg & Grigorenko, 1994). The advantage of such an application is that the same constructs and terminology can be used for studying both teaching and learning styles, as well as interactions between them.

The model of the mind functioning as a mental self-government seems to have potential to further the study of both human intelligence and individual stylistic differences. The theory of thinking styles that

Figure 6. The characters shown illustrate the difference between the liberal and conservative styles. Some of us prefer more traditional ways of doing things while others seek to develop new ones.

this model generates leads to questions about the nature of the mind that are not addressed by other theories. In particular, the theory may contribute to a better understanding of stylistic ways of adapting to and interacting with the environment and of the relation between intelligence and personality. The theory may be especially important in its educational applications. Because various forms of evaluation in school differentially benefit students with dissimilar style profiles, evaluation should be varied so as to avoid bias. The practical application of Sternberg's theory of mental self-government gives educators and psychologists an opportunity to understand the ways in which students use their intelligence and may also help students to develop and manage their own intelligence better. In any case, considering the role of styles in school settings is worthwhile because it encourages professionals to question educational practices and, particularly, whether some styles are more rewarded in school settings than others.

Acknowledgments. Research for this chapter was supported under the Javits Act Program (Grant No. R2O6R00001) as administered by the Office of Educational Research and Improvement of the U.S. Department of Education. Grantees undertaking such projects are encouraged to express freely their professional judgments; this chapter, therefore, does not necessarily represent positions or policies of the government, and no official endorsement should be inferred. Elena L. Grigorenko was supported by a fellowship from Yale University. Copies of the instruments may be obtained at cost from the authors. Figures 2 through 6 were drawn by V. Shpitalnik.

REFERENCES

Achenbach, T. M., & Edelbrock, C. (1983). *Manual for the Child Behavior Checklist and Revised Child Behavior Profile.* Burlington: Department of Psychiatry, University of Vermont.

Allport, G. W. (1937). *Personality, a psychological interpretation*. New York: Holt.

Bargar, R. R., & Hoover, R. L. (1984). Psychological type and the matching of cognitive styles. *Theory Into Practice*, *23*(1), 56–63.

Beller, E. K. (1967). *Methods of language training and cognitive styles in lower-class children*. Paper presented to the American Educational Research Association.

Bieri, J. (1969). Category width as a measure of discrimination. *Journal of Personality*, *37*, 513–521.

Bieri, J. (1971). Cognitive structures in personality. In H. M. Schroder & P. Suedfeld (Eds.), *Personality theory and information processing*. New York: Ronald.

Block, J., Block, J. H., & Harrington, D. M. (1974). Some misgivings about the Matching Familiar Figures Test as a measure of reflection-impulsivity. *Developmental Psychology*, *11*, 611–632.

Borden, K. A., Brown, R. T., Wynne, M. E., & Schleser, R. (1987). Piagetian conservation and response to cognitive therapy in attention deficit disordered children. *Journal of Child Psychology and Psychiatry and Allied Disciplines*, *28*(5), 755–764.

Bruner, J. S., Goodnow, J., & Austin, G. A. (1956). *A study of thinking*. New York: Wiley.

Bryant, N., & Gettinger, M. (1981). Eliminating differences between learning disabled and nondisabled children on a paired-associate learning task. *Journal of Educational Research*, *74*, 342–346.

Butter, E. (1979). Visual and haptic training and cross-modal transfer of reflectivity. *Journal of Educational Psychology*, *72*, 212–219.

Camara, R. P. S., & Fox, R. (1983). Impulsive versus inefficient problem solving in retarded and nonretarded Mexican children. *Journal of Psychology*, *114*(2), 187–191.

Cattell, R. B. (1963). The theory of fluid and crystallized intelligence: A critical experiment. *Journal of Educational Psychology*, *54*, 1–22.

Conway, J. B. (1992). A world of differences among psychologists. *Canadian Psychology*, *33*(1), 1–24.

Corman, L. S., & Platt, R. G. (1988). Correlations among the Group Embedded Figures Test, the Myers-Briggs Type Indicator and demographic characteristics: A business school study. *Perceptual and Motor Skills*, *66*(2), 507–511.

Cronbach, L. J., & Snow, R. E. (1977). *Aptitudes and instructional methods*. New York: Wiley.

Das, P. (1983). Impulsive behavior and assessment of impulsivity with hospitalized adolescents. *Psychological Reports*, *53*(1), 764–766.

DeHaas, P. A., & Young, R. D. (1984). Attention styles of hyperactive and normal girls. *Journal of Abnormal Child Psychology*, *12*(4), 531–545.

Dunn, R., Beaudry, J. S., & Klavas, A. (1989). Survey of research on learning styles. *Educational Leadership*, *46*(6), 50–58.

Dunn, R., & Dunn, K. (1978). *Teaching students through their individual learning styles*. Reston, VA: Reston Publishing.

Dunn, R., Dunn, K., & Price, G. E. (1979). Identifying individual learning styles. In *Student learning styles: Diagnosing and prescribing programs* (pp. 39–54). Reston, VA: National Association of Secondary School Principles.

Eagle, M., Goldberger, L., & Breitman, M. (1969). Field dependence and memory for social vs. neutral and relevant vs. irrelevant incidental stimuli. *Perceptual and Motor Skills*, *29*, 903–910.

Eska, B., & Black, K. N. (1971). Conceptual tempo in young grade-school children. *Child Development*, *45*, 505–516.

Eysenck, H. J., & Eysenck, S. B. G. (1975). *Manual of the Eysenck Personality Questionnaire*. San Diego, CA: Digits.

Finch, A. J., Saylor, C. F., & Spirito, A. (1982). Impulsive cognitive style and impulsive behavior in emotionally disturbed children. *Journal of Genetic Psychology*, *141*(2), 293–294.

Fischer, B. B., & Fischer, L. (1979). Styles in teaching and learning. *Educational Leadership*, *36*(4), 245–254.

Furnham, M. J., & Kendall, P. C. (1986). Cognitive tempo and behavioral adjustment in children. *Cognitive Therapy and Research*, *10*(1), 45–50.

Gardner, R. (1953). Cognitive style in categorizing behavior. *Perceptual and Motor Skills*, *22*, 214–233.

Gardner, R. W. (1959). Cognitive control principles and perceptual behavior. *Bulletin of the Menninger Clinic*, *23*, 241–248.

Gardner, R. W. (1962). Cognitive controls in adaptation: Research and measurement. In S. Messick & J. Ross (Eds.), *Measurement in personality and cognition*. New York: Wiley.

Gardner, R. W. (1970). Cognitive structure formation, organismic equilibration, and individuality of conscious experience. *Journal for the Study of Consciousness*, *3*, 119–136.

Gardner, R. W., Holzman, P. S., Klein, G. S., Linton, H., & Spence, D. P. (1959). Cognitive control: A study of individual consistencies in cognitive behavior. *Psychological Issues*, *1*(4).

Gardner, R. W., Jackson, D. N., & Messick, S. J. (1960). Personality organization in cognitive controls and intellectual abilities. *Psychological Issues*, *2*(4).

Gardner, R. W., and Long, R. I. (1962). Cognitive controls of attention and inhibition: A study of individual consistencies. *British Journal of Psychology*, *53*, 381–388.

Gardner, R. W., & Moriarty, A. (1968). Dimensions of cognitive control at preadolescence. In R. Gardner (Ed.), *Personality development at preadolescence*. Seattle: University of Washington Press.

Gardner, R. W., & Schoen, R. A. (1962). Differentiation and abstraction in concept formation. *Psychological Monographs*, *76*.

Glixman, A. F. (1965). Categorizing behavior as a function of meaning domain. *Journal of Personality and Social Psychology*, *2*(3), 370–377.

Glow, R. A., Lange, R. V., Glow, P. H., & Barnett, J. A. (1983). Cognitive and self-reported impulsiveness: Comparison of Kagan's MFFT and Eysenck's EPQ Impulsiveness measures. *Personality and Individual Differences*, *4*(2), 179–187.

Goldman, R. D. (1972). Effects of a logical versus a mnemonic strategy on performance in two undergraduate psychology classes. *Journal of Educational Psychology*, *63*, 347–352.

Goldsmith, R. E. (1985). The factorial composition of the KAI Inventory. *Educational and Psychological Measurement*, *45*, 245–250.

Goldstein, K. M., & Blackman, S. (1978). *Cognitive style*. New York: Wiley.

Gorham, J., & Self, L. (1987). Developing communication skills: Learning style and the educationally disadvantaged student. *Communication Research Reports*, *4*(1), 38–46.

Gregorc, A. F. (1979). Learning/teaching styles: Potent forces behind them. *Educational Leadership*, *36*(4), 234–236.

Gregorc, A. F. (1982). *Gregorc Style Delineator*. Maynard, MA: Gabriel Systems.

Gregorc, A. F. (1984). Style as a symptom: A phenomenological perspective. *Theory Into Practice*, *23*(1), 51–55.

Gregorc, A. F. (1985). *Inside styles: Beyond the basics*. Maynard, MA: Gabriel Systems.

Grigorenko, E. L., & Sternberg, R. J. (1993). *Thinking styles in school settings*. Unpublished manuscript.

Guralnik, D. B. (Ed.). (1976). *Webster's new world dictionary, second college edition: Classics edition*. Akron, OH: William Collins.

Gustafson, R., & Kallen, H. (1989). Alcohol effects on cognitive and personality style in women with special reference to primary and secondary process. *Alcoholism: Clinical and Experimental Research, 13*(5), 644–648.

Harvey, O. J., Hunt, D. E., & Schroder, H. M. (1961). *Conceptual systems and personality organization*. New York: Wiley.

Hennessy, S. M. (1992). A study of uncommon Myers-Briggs cognitive styles in law enforcement. *Dissertation Abstracts International, 52*(12-A), 4308.

Henson, K. T., & Borthwick, P. (1984). Matching styles: A historical look. *Theory Into Practice, 23*(1), 3–9.

Hogarty, G. E., & Flesher, S. (1992). Cognitive remediation in schizophrenia: Proceed . . . with caution. *Schizophrenia Bulletin, 18*(1), 51–57.

Holland, J. L. (1973). *Making vocational choices: A theory of careers*. Englewood Cliffs, NJ: Prentice-Hall.

Huelsman, J. (1983). *An exploratory study of the interrelationships of preferred learning styles, psychological types, and other selected characteristics of practicing teachers*. Unpublished doctoral dissertation. Ohio State University, Columbus.

Hunt, D. E. (1979). Learning style and students needs: An introduction to conceptual level. In *Diagnosing and prescribing programs* (pp. 27–38). Reston, VA: National Association of Secondary School Principals.

Hyman, R., & Rosoff, B. (1984). Matching learning and teaching styles: The jug and what's in it. *Theory and Practice, 23*(1), 35–43.

Joniak, A. J., & Isaksen, S. G. (1988). The Gregorc Style Delineator: Internal consistency and its relationship to Kirton's adaptive-innovative distinction. *Educational and Psychological Measurement, 8*, 1043–1049.

Joyce, B. R., & Hodges, R. E. (1966). Instructional flexibility training. *Journal of Teacher Education, 17*, 409–416.

Jung, C. (1923). *Psychological types*. New York: Harcourt Brace.

Kagan, J. (1958). The concept of identification. *Psychological Review, 65*, 296–305.

Kagan, J. (1965a). Individual differences in the resolution of response uncertainty. *Journal of Personality and Social Psychology, 2*, 154–160.

Kagan, J. (1965b). Information processing in the child. In P. M. Mussen, J. J. Conger, & J. Kagan (Eds.), *Readings in child development and personality*. New York: Harper and Row.

Kagan, J. (1965c). Reflection-impulsivity and reading ability in primary grade children. *Child Development, 36*, 609–628.

Kagan, J. (1966). Reflection-impulsivity: The generality and dynamics of conceptual tempo. *Journal of Abnormal Psychology, 71*, 17–24.

Kagan, J., & Kogan, N. (1970). Individual variation in cognitive processes. In P. A. Mussen (Ed.), *Carmichael's manual of child psychology* (Vol. 1). New York: Wiley.

Kagan, J., & Messer, S. B. (1975). A reply to "Some misgivings about the Matching Familiar Figures Test as a measure of reflection-impulsivity." *Developmental Psychology, 11*, 244–248.

Kagan, J., Moss, H. A., & Sigel, I. E. (1963). Psychological significance of styles of conceptualization. *Monographs of the Society for Research in Child Development*.

Keller, R. T., & Holland, W. E. (1978). A cross-validation of the KAI in three research and development organizations. *Applied Psychological Measurement, 2*, 563–570.

Kelly, G. A. (1955). *The psychology of personal constructs* (2 vols). New York: Norton.

Kirton, M. J. (1976). Adaptors and innovators: A description and measure. *Journal of Applied Psychology, 61*, 622–629.

Kirton, M. J. (1977). *Research edition: Kirton Adaptation-Innovation inventory*. London: National Federation for Educational Research.

Kirton, M. J., & de Ciantis, S. M. (1986). Cognitive styles and personality: The Kirton Adaption-Innovation and Cattell 16 Personality Factors Inventory. *Personality and Individual Differences, 7*(2), 141–146.

Klein, G. S. (1954). Need and regulation. In M. R. Jones (Ed.) *Nebraska Symposium of Motivation*. Lincoln: University of Nebraska Press.

Klein, G. S. (1970). *Perception, motives, and personality*. New York: Knopf.

Klein, G. S., Barr, H. C., & Wolitsky, D. (1967). Personality. *Annual Review of Psychology, 18*, 467–560.

Klein, G. S., Gardner, R. W., & Schlesinger, H. J. (1962). Tolerance for unrealistic experience: A study of the generality of a cognitive control. *British Journal of Psychology, 53*, 41–55.

Klein, G. S., & Schlesinger, H. J. (1951). Perceptual attitudes toward instability: I. Prediction of apparent movement experiences from Rorschach responses. *Journal of Personality, 19*, 289–302.

Kogan, N. (1971). Educational implications of cognitive styles. In G. S. Lesser (Ed.), *Psychology and educational practice*. Glenview, IL: Scott, Foresman.

Kogan, N. (1973). Creativity and cognitive style: A life span perspective. In P. Baltes & K. W. Schaie (Eds.), *Life span developmental psychology: Personality and socialization*. New York: Academic Press.

Kogan, N. (1976). *Cognitive styles in infancy and early childhood*. New York: Wiley.

Kolb, D. A. (1974). On management and the learning process. In D. A. Kolb, I. M. Rubin, & J. M. McIntyre (Eds.), *Organizational psychology*. Englewood Cliffs, NJ: Prentice-Hall.

Kolb, D. A. (1978). *Learning Style Inventory technical manual*. Boston: McBer.

Kuerbis, P. J. (1988). Learning styles and science teaching. *Newsletter of the National Association for Research in Science Teaching, 30*(1).

Kuchinskas, G. (1979). Whose cognitive style makes the difference? *Educational Leadership, 36*(4), 269–271.

Laval, C. (1980). *Modification of impulsivity in male adolescent delinquents*. Unpublished doctoral dissertation, University of South Carolina, Columbia.

Lawrence, G. W. (1982). *People type and tiger stripes*. Gainesville, FL: Center for the Application of Psychological Type.

Liddle, P. F. (1987). Schizophrenic syndromes, cognitive performance and neurological disfunction. *Psychological Medicine, 17*(1), 49–57.

Luchins, A. S., & Luchins, E. H. (1970). Effects of preconceptions and communications on impressions of a person. *Journal of Social Psychology, 81*(2), 243–252.

MacLeod, C. M., Jackson, R. A., & Palmer, J. (1986). On the relation between spatial ability and field dependence. *Intelligence, 10*(2), 141–151.

Mann, L. (1973). Differences between reflective and impulsive children in tempo and quality of decision making. *Child Development, 44*, 274–279.

Meltzer, L. J. (1984). An analysis of the learning styles of adolescent delinquents. *Journal of Learning Disabilities, 17*(10), 600–608.

Messer, S. (1970). The effect of anxiety over intellectual performance on reflection-impulsivity in children. *Child Development, 41*, 353–359.

Messick, S. (1970). The criterion problem in the evaluation of instruction: Assessing possible, not just intended, outcomes. In M. C. Wittrock & D. Wiley (Eds.), *The evaluation of instruction: Issues and problems*. New York: Holt Rinehart & Winston.

Messick, S. (1984). The nature of cognitive styles: Problems and promises in educational practice. *Educational Psychologist, 19*, 59–74.

Mulligan, D. G., & Martin, W. (1980). Adaptors, innovators and promises in educational practice. *Educational Psychologists, 19*, 59–74.

Myers, I. B. (1981). *Gifts differing*. Gainesville, FL: Center for the Application of Psychological Type.

Myers, I. B., & McCaulley, M. H. (1985). *Manual: A guide to the development and use of the Myers-Briggs Type Indicator*, Palo Alto, CA: Consulting Psychological Press.

Myers, I. B., & Myers, P. B. (1980). *Gifts differing*. Palo Alto, CA: Consulting Psychologists Press.

Myers, P. L. (1988). Paranoid pseudocommunity beliefs in a sect milieu. *Social Psychiatry and Psychiatric Epidemiology, 23*(4), 252–255.

O'Brien, T. P. (1990). Construct validation of the Gregorc Style Delineator: An application of Lisrel 7. *Educational and Psychological Measurement, 50*, 631–636.

Palei, A. I. (1986). Modal'nostnaya structura emotsional'nosti i cognitivnyi stil' [Emotionality and cognitive style]. *Voprosy Psikhologii, 4*, 118–126.

Paulsen, K. (1978). Reflection-impulsivity and level of maturity. *Journal of Psychology, 99*, 109–112.

Peterson, C., & Scott, W. A. (1975). Generality and topic specificity of cognitive styles. *Journal of Research in Personality, 9*, 366–374.

Pettigrew, T. F. (1958). The measurement of category width as a cognitive variable. *Journal of Personality, 26*, 532–544.

Reissman, F. (1964). The strategy of style. *Teachers College Record, 65*, 484–489.

Renzulli, J. S., & Smith, L. H. (1978). *The learning styles inventory: A measure of student preference for instructional techniques*. Mensfield Center, CT: Creative Learning Press.

Reynolds, C. R., Riegel, T., & Torrance, E. P. (1977). Bibliography on R/L hemisphere function. *Gifted Child Quarterly, 28*, 121–126.

Ross, J. (1962). Factor analysis and levels of measurement in psychology. In S. Messick & J. Ross (Eds.), *Measurement in personality and cognition*. New York: Wiley.

Royce, J. R. (1973). The conceptual framework for a multi-factor theory of individuality. In J. R. Royce (Ed.), *Contributions of multivariate analysis to psychological theory*. London: Academic Press.

Schwartz, M., Friedman, R. J., Lindsay, P., & Narrol, H. (1982). The relationships between conceptual tempo and depression in children. *Journal of Consulting and Clinical Psychology, 50*(4), 488–490.

Smith, B. O. (1963). A conceptual analysis of instructional behavior. *Journal of Teacher Education, 14*, 294–298.

Smith, G. J. W., & Klein, G. S. (1953). Cognitive controls in serial behavior patterns. *Journal of Personality, 22*, 188–213.

Stahl, S. A., Erickson, L. G., & Rayman, M. C. (1986). Detection of inconsistencies by reflective and impulsive seventh-grade readers. *National Reading Conference Yearbook, 35*, 233–238.

Sternberg, R. J. (1986). Intelligence is mental self-government. In R. J. Sternberg & D. K. Detterman (Eds.), *What is intelligence? Contemporary viewpoints on its nature and definition*. Norwood, NJ: Ablex.

Sternberg, R. J. (1988). *The triarchic mind: A new theory of human intelligence*. New York: Viking.

Sternberg, R. J. (1994). Thinking styles and testing: Bridging the gap between ability and personality assessment. In R. J. Sternberg & P. Ruzgis (Eds.), *Intelligence and personality* (pp. 169–187). New York: Cambridge University Press.

Sternberg, R. J., & Grigorenko, E. L. (1994). Thinking styles and the gifted. *Roeper Review, 16*, 122–130.

Sternberg, R. J., & Lubart, T. I. (1991a). Creating creative minds. *Phi Delta Kappan*, 608–614.

Sternberg, R. J., & Lubart, T. I. (1991b). An investment theory of creativity and its development. *Human Development, 34*, 1–31.

Sternberg, R. J., & Wagner, R. K. (1991). *MSG Thinking Styles Inventory Manual*. Unpublished manuscript.

Vernon, P. (1973). Multivariate approaches to the study of cognitive styles. In J. R. Royce (Ed.), *Contributions of multivariate analysis to psychological theory*. London: Academic Press.

Victor, J. B., Halverson, C. F., & Montague, R. B. (1985). Relations between reflection-impulsivity and behavioral impulsivity in preschool children. *Developmental Psychology, 21*(1), 141–148.

Wallach, M., & Kogan, N. (1965). *Modes of thinking in young children*. New York: Holt Rinehart & Winston.

Wardell, D. M., & Royce, J. R. (1978). Toward a multi-factor theory of styles and their relationships to cognition and affect. *Journal of Personality, 46*(3), 474–505.

Witkin, H. A. (1964). Origins of cognitive style. In C. Sheerer (Ed.), *Cognition: Theory, research, promise*. New York: Harper & Row.

Witkin, H. A. (1973). *The role of cognitive style in academic performance and in teacher-student relations*. Unpublished report, Educational Testing Service, Princeton, NJ.

Witkin, H. A. (1975). Some implications of research on cognitive style for problems of education. In J. M. Whitehead (Ed.), *Personality and learning*. London: Hodder and Stoughton.

Witkin, H. A., Dyk, R. B., Faterson, H. F., Goodenough, D. R., & Karp, S. A. (1962). *Psychological differentiation*. New York: Wiley.

Witkin, H. A., Lewis, H. B., Hertzman, M., Machover, K., Meissner, P. B., & Wapner, S. (1954). *Personality through perception*. New York: Harper.

Witkin, H. A., Oltman, P. K., Raskin, E., & Karp, S. A. (1971). *Embedded Figures Test, Children's Embedded Figures Test, Group Embedded Figures Test* [manual]. Palo Alto, CA: Consulting Psychologists Press.

Wolitzky, D. L., & Wachtel, P. L. (1973). Personality and perception. In B. B. Wolman (Ed.), *Handbook of general psychology*. Englewood-Cliffs, NJ: Prentice-Hall.

Zelniker, T., & Oppenheimer, L. (1973). Modification of information processing of impulsive children. *Child Development, 44*, 445–450.

12

Creativity as a Product of Intelligence and Personality

Hans J. Eysenck

Creativity has always been a problem in the well-tended garden of cognitive ability, and though its empirical study has flourished, a recent handbook (Glover, Ronning, & Reynolds, 1989) has characterized it as "a large-scale example of a 'degenerating' research program" (p. xi). The reasons for such a disparaging estimate are not hard to find: Research in this area has been largely descriptive, full of anecdotal evidence, and without close links with the two disciplines of scientific psychology (Cronbach, 1957)—the experimental and the psychometric. Admittedly there have been many attempts to measure creativity along psychometric lines (Runco, 1991), but these have not been linked theoretically or experimentally with the large body of the psychological literature, and thus they have remained resolutely isolated.

I have tried to support a theory of creativity that attempts to bridge this gap (Eysenck, 1993). I shall try here to continue this process, demonstrating links with experimental constructs (e.g., latent inhibition and negative priming) that may give a solid foundation to observations of "differential associative hierarchies" (Mednick, 1962). This attempt to construct a nomological network in order to provide proper construct validity for the measurement of creativity is an assertion of my belief in the correctness of Lewin's famous saying: "There is nothing as practical as a good theory." It is, of course, a moot point whether the theory here developed deserves to be called good; at least it is testable, and hence it fulfills the minimum requirement of a scientific theory in a field that has notoriously been lacking in such theories.

THE NATURE AND DEFINITION OF CREATIVITY

It is well known that there are two major definitions of the term *creativity*, and these are quite different in many ways. *Trait creativity* is conceived as a latent trait underlying creative behavior, normally distributed in the population, and a necessary but not sufficient cause of creative productivity. *Achievement creativity* is defined in terms of novel and socially useful/acceptable products; it is the *product* of trait creativity, intelligence, and many other components, as suggested in Figure 1. It is distributed as a J-curve, like many socially nonconformist behaviors (Allport, 1934). This type of distribution is characteristic of behaviors that are determined by several causal agents acting synergistically (i.e., their effects are multiplicative rather than additive; Eysenck, 1993).

Trait creativity has been measured in several ways (Runco, 1991), but most usually and characteristically in terms of tests of fluency (i.e., the number

Hans J. Eysenck • Institute of Psychiatry, University of London, London SE5 8AF, England.

International Handbook of Personality and Intelligence, edited by Donald H. Saklofske and Moshe Zeidner. Plenum Press, New York, 1995.

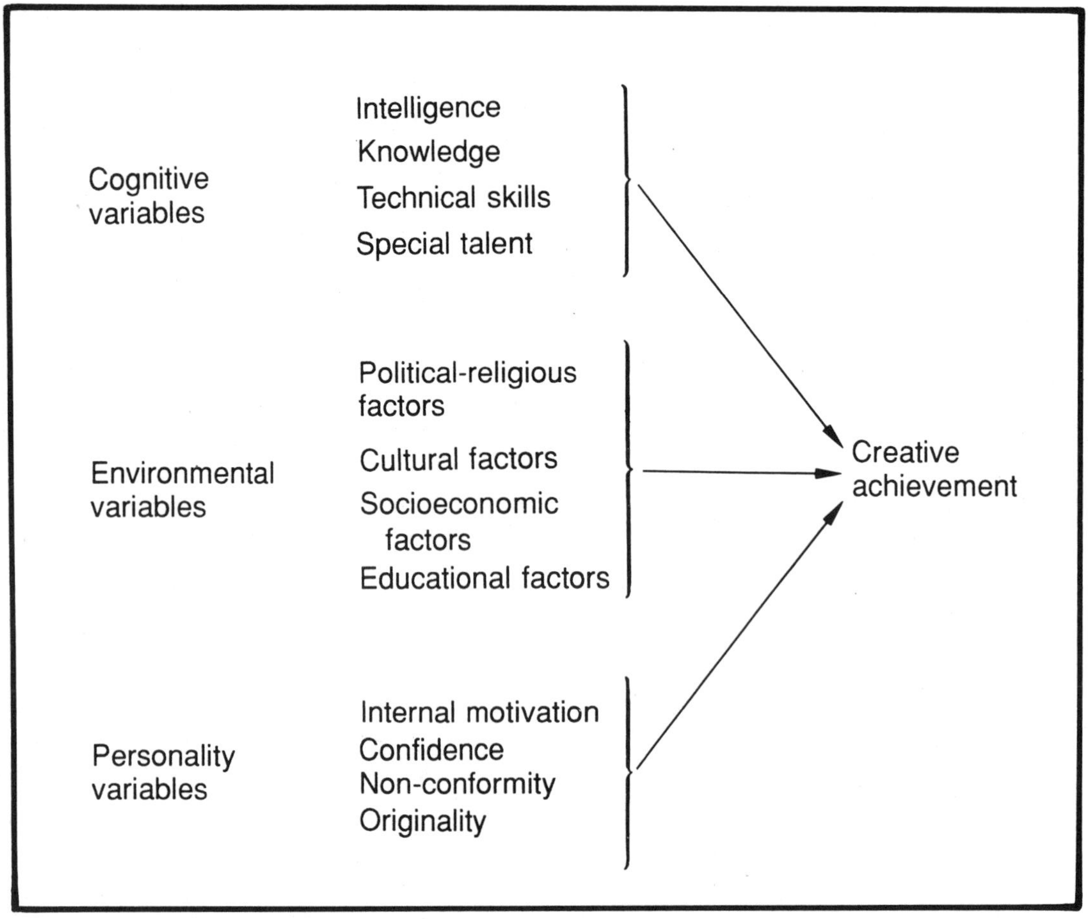

Figure 1. Relation between creative achievement and originality (trait creativity). From Eysenck (1993).

and/or originality of items produced in response to a problem having multiple solutions); an alternative and more recent name is *divergent* (as opposed to *convergent*) problem solution (Guilford, 1950). The foundations for work along this line were laid by Hargreaves (1927) in his studies of "the faculty of imagination," suggested and supervised by Spearman. Hargreaves found that a number of tests calling for a large number of imaginative responses tended to correlate together, with an average intercorrelation of .3. These correlations fulfilled the demands of the tetrad criterion (matrix rank = 1), and were shown not to be identical with intelligence ("*g*"). The tests included were number of things seen in an inkblot, number of words written, number of different completions to an incomplete picture, and so forth; other early workers in this field followed Hargreave's lead (Eysenck, 1970).

These early findings are mentioned because there is little if any mention of this early work by Glover et al. (1989), although they laid down the major laws according to which creativity may be conceptualized: (a) Creativity correlates with intelligence overall, but (b) is also something independent of intelligence. Also, (c) creativity is correlated with personality; the trait usually mentioned is extraversion. Traits correlated with fluency on the Fells Child Behavior Scales were curiosity, gregariousness, originality, aggressiveness, competitiveness, and cheerfulness, together with an absence of social apprehensiveness and patience (Benassy & Chauffard, 1947; Gewirtz, 1948). Later studies of "divergent ability" added the important point that intelligence only correlated with creativity measures up to IQ values of approximately 120; when this value was reached or exceeded, no correlations were found. We may interpret this to mean that a certain amount of intelligence is needed to lay a foundation in knowledge that enables trait creativity to make a genuine contribution—to understand the fundamentals of the problem, interpret the rules, and give solutions that are socially acceptable. Most of the work done on trait creativity has accordingly been done with bright children and adults.

CREATIVITY AND PERSONALITY

There is a large body of evidence linking creativity and genius with psychopathology (Lange-Eichbaum, 1931; Lombroso, 1901; Prentky, 1980); though others have emphasized a link with psychological health (Kessel, 1989; Kubie, 1958; Maslow, 1976; Rogers, 1961). A good summary of the debate is provided by Ochse (1991) and Richards (1981). The evidence, both historical and from more recent empirical studies, demonstrates quite clearly that (a) there is a definite link between creativity/genius and psychopathology, but (b) actual psychosis is negatively related to these traits, and (c) certain favorable personality traits (e.g., ego strength) are usually found positively correlated with creativity and/or genius.

A few examples will illustrate the kind of evidence that links psychological abnormality with creativity and genius. Karlsson (1970), on the basis of biographical material, claimed to have found the rate of psychosis to be 30% for great novelists, 35% for great poets, 35% for great painters, 25% for great mathematicians, and 40% for great philosophers; these values are well above those for ordinary people (roughly 2%). Similarly, Andreasen (1987), in a controlled study of 30 eminent writers, 30 matched control subjects, and first-degree relatives of both groups, found that no fewer than 80% of the writers had experienced an episode of affective disorder, whereas only 30% of the controls had done so. In addition, "the families of writers were riddled with both creativity and mental illness, while in the families of the control subjects much of the illness and creativity seems to be randomly scattered" (p. 1290). Ochse (1991) cites an unpublished study in which 38% of 47 eminent British writers had been treated for manic-depressive illness or recurrent depression, whereas 50% of the poets in the sample had received psychiatric treatment. In addition to these studies, it has been found quite generally that when highly creative subjects are given personality questionnaires, their answers (e.g., on the MMPI) have been similar to those of neurotic or psychotic individuals, although usually at a lower level (e.g., see Barron, 1968; Cattell, 1971; Goetz & Goetz, 1979a,b; McKinnon, 1965; Mohan & Tiwana, 1987; Roe, 1953).

Yet the presence of psychopathology does not make the appearance of positive personality characteristics impossible. Dellas and Gaier (1970), who evaluated more than two dozen studies, conclude that "evidence points up a common pattern of personality traits among creative persons, and also that these personality factors may have some bearing on creativity in the abstract, regardless of field" (p. 65). They found major 13 traits to be associated with creativity: independence in attitude and social behavior; dominance, introversion, openness to stimuli, wide interests, self-acceptance, intuitiveness, flexibility, social presence and praise, an asocial attitude, concern for social norms, radicalism, and rejection of external constraints.

Similarly, Welsh (1975), on the basis of his own work, gives a list of the personality characteristics (including both socially positive and negative items) of creative and noncreative students not having any overt psychopathology. Creative students were unstable, irresponsible, disorderly, rebellious, uncontrolled, self-seeking, tactless, intemperate, rejecting of rules, uncooperative, impulsive, and careless—surely all negative traits socially, and positively indicative of psychopathology. But they were also original, adventurous, liberal, refined, tolerant, candid, subtle, spontaneous, interesting, flexible, and artistic—all rather positive variables. Perhaps one side of the coin implies the other; it is impossible to possess all of a number of contradictory virtues.

McKinnon (1962, 1965, 1978), whose group's very large-scale research into creativity extended over many years and included external criteria of achievement as well as internal ratings, repeatedly draws attention to the high scores of his creative subjects on some MMPI scales related to psychosis (e.g., Schizophrenia, Depression, Psychopathic Deviate, Paranoia): "On the eight scales which measure the strength of these descriptions in the person, our creative subjects earn scores which, on the average, are some 5 to 10 points above the general population's average score of 50" (MacKinnon, 1962, p. 488). A difference of 10 points is equal to a whole standard deviation and is certainly not negligible, particularly when it is remembered that his sample (successful architects) came from a socioeconomic and educational group whose mean scores on these scales is usually well below 50

(Dahlstrom, Lachar & Dahlstrom, 1986; Friedman, Webb, & Lewak, 1989). MacKinnon adds that "in the self-reports and in the MMPI profiles of many of our creative subjects, one can find rather clear evidence of psychopathology, but also evidence of adequate control mechanisms, as the success with which they live their productive and creative lives testifies" (p. 488). Ego strength in particular has been found to be above average in these highly creative people, although in the general population ego strength correlates −.50 to −.60 with the MMPI psychopathological variables. Possibly it is the creative tension set up by these contradictory personality traits that is responsible for the outstanding success of MacKinnon's subjects.

CREATIVITY/GENIUS AND PSYCHOTICISM

I have suggested that a possible answer to the obvious paradox of genius and psychopathology may be found in the concept of psychoticism, conceived as a latent trait underlying a variety of functional psychotic disorders (schizophrenia, manic-depressive illness, schizoaffective illness, unipolar depression), as well as schizoid, psychopathic and other borderline or "spectrum" disorders (Eysenck, 1952; Eysenck & S. Eysenck, 1976). I have recently summarized the large body of empirical and experimental work that has gone into establishing the concept as a useful complement to neuroticism (N) and extraversion (E) among the major dimensions of personality. Figure 2 illustrates the nature of psychoticism (P). The abscissa runs from low-P characteristics (altruism, socialization, empathy, conformity) to the high-P characteristics (impulsivity, hostility, aggression) and through criminality and schizoid personality to the various functional psychoses (Eysenck, 1992a). P_A in the figure indicates the probability of an individual developing an actual psychosis, given his or her score on the abscissa.

There is good evidence to show that (a) different psychotic illnesses are not categorically differentiated from each other, but are closely connected and run into each other; (b) genetic relations fail to show *specific* heritability for assumed specific illnesses; and (c) diagnoses change over time from one illness to another. These and many other types of evidence make it impossible to accept the ancient Kraepelinian division, although it is equally impossible to return to the even more ancient concept of the "Einheitspsychose" as apparently advocated by Crow (1986, 1990). It seems safe to accept that a general trait of psychoticism (proneness to psychosis) underlies nonneurotic psychopathology, but that there are also specific genes or groups of genes related to specific symptomatologies. Psychoticism is a dispositional trait making it more likely for a P^+ person to develop psychotic illness under stress (the diathesis-stress model), but P is not to be identified with psychosis.

Some of the individual traits that correlate together to produce the higher-order concept of P are shown in Figure 3. Clearly they are not the only ones; others (e.g., Machiavellianism) have been identified (Allsop, Eysenck, & Eysenck, 1991), as well as such components of the "big five" system as agreeableness (negative) and conscientiousness (negative; Eysenck, 1991, 1992b).

The construct of psychoticism is based on the factor analytic study of questionnaire responses, but a special technique has been used to make the identification of the dimension with psychotic-proneness more objective. Consider a test, *T*, which on theoretical grounds is predicted to differentiate significantly between a group of psychotics and a group of nonpsychotic, normal people. If P is colinear with psychotic-proneness, then we would predict that P+ normals would be distinguished from P− normals in their *T* scores in the same way that psychotics are distinguished from normals. Similarly, P+ psychotics should be distinguished from P− psychotics along similar lines.

Experiments of this kind have been reported extensively in the literature, mostly with positive results (Eysenck, 1992a). Several classes of variables have been so studied. One class dealt with biological variables (H2A B27, MAO, serotonin) of various kinds. A second dealt with laboratory behavior (eye tracking, dichotic listening, sensitivity levels). A third was concerned with learning-conditioning variables (latent inhibition, negative priming). Yet another group dealt with physiological variables (EMG, autonomic-perceptual inversion). Finally, a fifth group was concerned with psychological variables (hallucinatory activity, word association, creativity). For obvious reasons, it is the role of creativity in this list that will mostly concern us.

We have already seen that psychopathology is directly related with creativity-genius; it is required to show that P is also thus related, both with trait creativity and with achievement creativity. I will discuss the former first.

Some of the early studies linking psychoticism

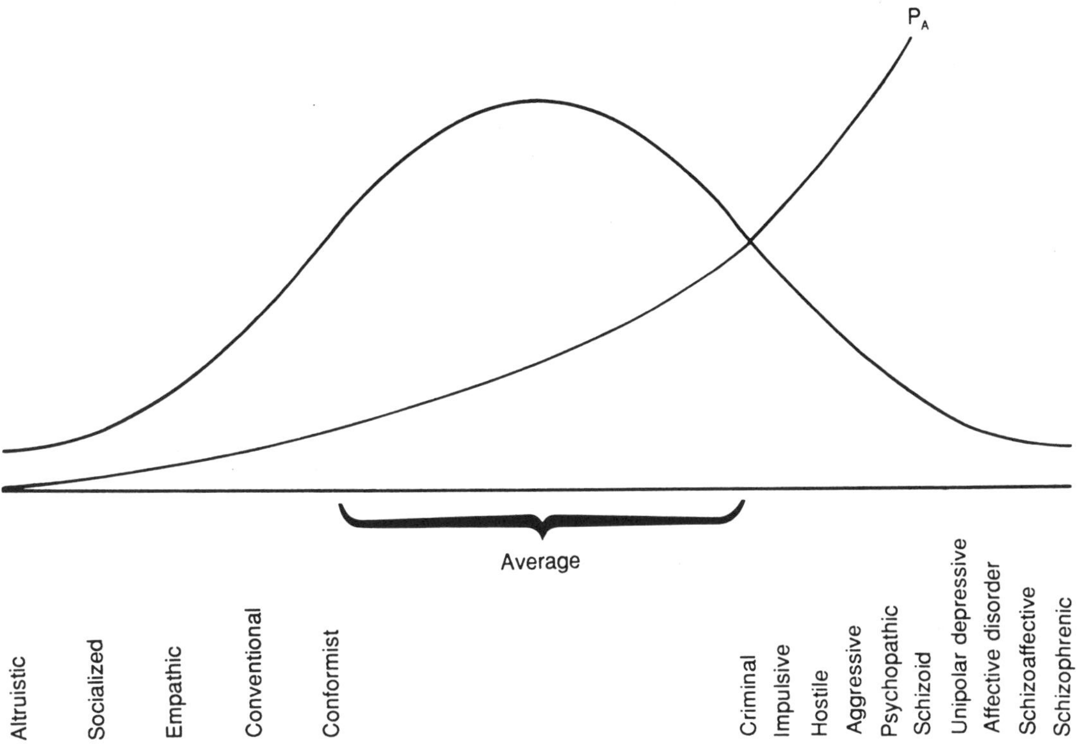

Figure 2. Psychoticism as a personality variable. P_A indicates probability of psychopathology at various levels of P. From Eysenck (1992a).

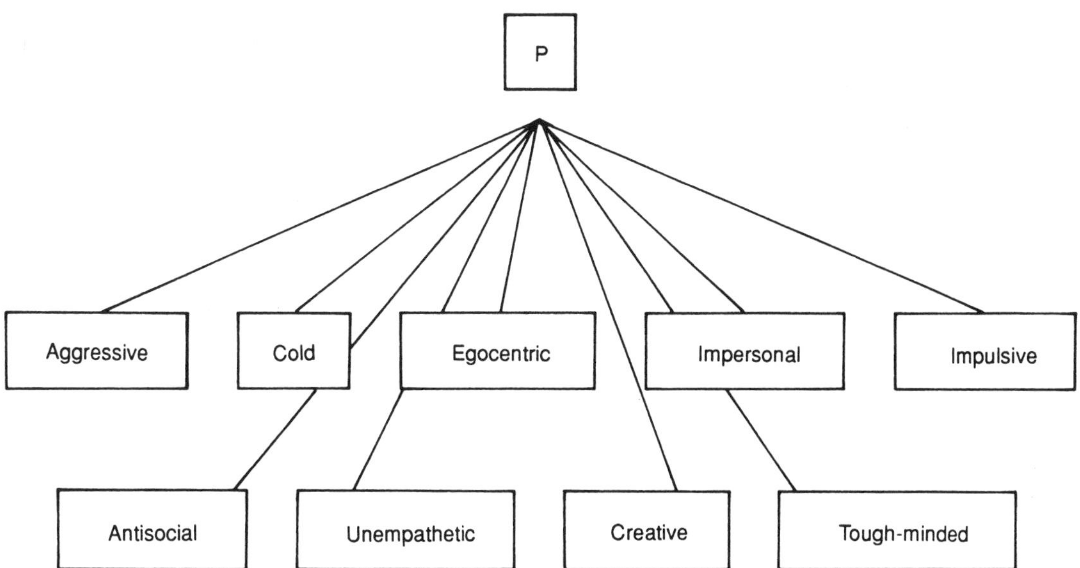

Figure 3. Number of primary traits combining to identify psychoticism (P). From Eysenck and M. Eysenck (1989).

and creativity have been discussed elsewhere (Eysenck & S. Eysenck, 1976). Farmer (1974) found two factors, fluency and originality, in a factor analysis of correlations between divergent-thinking tests. P had a small loading of .24 on fluency, but a very high one on originality (r = .74). Kidner (1978; see Eysenck & S. Eysenck, 1976, pp. 186–187) used IQ and divergent-thinking tests, creating an "index of creativity" by subtracting the standardized sum of the IQ tests from that of the creativity tests; this correlated .31 with P and .21 with E (extraversion). In another experiment Kidner replicated the correlation of P with creativity and also found P to be correlated with over-inclusiveness of thinking and slowness in categorization; these aspects of schizophrenic thinking are discussed in later sections.

Much more important and impressive is a study by Woody and Claridge (1977), which was designed especially to test the hypothesis of a strong relationship between creativity and psychoticism. The tests used were the Eysenck Personality Questionnaire (Eysenck & S. Eysenck, 1975), the Wallach-Kogan (Wallach & Kogan, 1965) creativity tests, and the Nufferno Speed Test as a measure of intelligence (Furneaux, 1960). The subjects were 100 Oxford University students, sampled widely from the various fields of specialization; the mean age of the group was 20 years (SD = 2 years).

Consider first the correlation of P with the 5 tasks constituting the creativity test—instances, pattern meanings, uses, similarities, and line meanings. For each of these divergent tests, there are two scores, one for numbers of suggestions (fluency) and the other for consequences (originality); correlations with P were .32, .37, .45, .36, and .38 for number score and .61, .64, .66, .68, and .65 for uniqueness. Overall the correlations with extraversion and neuroticism were quite insignificant, but those for the Lie scale (L) were significant and in the −.20 region. (For groups such as this, L probably measures social conformity rather than lying, and it correlates negatively with P.) It is worth noting that the 10 indices of creativity were all highly intercorrelated, with correlations ranging from .37 to .83; thus it appeared that the tests were tapping a unitary factor. Correlations between the creativity and personality variables, on the one hand, and intelligence, on the other, were insignificant.

Using all ten tests of creativity predicted P at a high level (multiple R = .84). Although replications no doubt would give a lower value for R, using the same prediction formula, the fact that R is higher than the reliability of P does suggest an astonishingly close relationship between the two variables and thus supports the original theory.

Of course, these results refer only to creativity as a trait; they say nothing about creativity in terms of achievement. This problem has been tackled by Goetz and Goetz (1979a,b), two internationally known German painters who were successful, because of their inside position, in getting 147 male and 110 female artists of renown to return completed forms of the EPQ. Painters and sculptors were included in this sample; the mean age was 47 years, with a range of 29 to 78 years. 300 male and 300 female controls with a similar age range (mean 41 years, range 21 to 79 years) were also tested. Testing was done individually or in small groups.

Male but not female artists were more introverted (perhaps women need more dominance and surgency to compete!) and more neurotic than respective controls. Most important from our point of view, male artists had higher P scores than male controls (6.53 vs. 5.79), and female artists had higher P scores than female controls (6.18 vs. 4.32); the standard deviations were around 3.00. Both differences were highly significant and are in the predicted direction. Note the exceptionally high P score of the female artists; this is expected on the basis of the double-threshold hypothesis (Eysenck & Gudjonsson, 1988) and is similar to findings concerning P scores for male and female criminals. For L, there is no difference for males, but a large one for females (negative; $p < .001$). It should be noted that comparisons between artists and controls as stated may appear less significant than they really are, because P declines with age (Eysenck, 1987) and the artists were significantly older (by 6 years).

In a second study (Goetz & Goetz, 1979b), 60 well-known artists were divided by experts into 37 more and 23 less successful ones. The more successful ones had significantly higher P scores. Some artists who were successful had low P scores, but these tended to be in the high age group, where P scores tend to drop. Altogether, being a successful artist correlates well with P, and P distinguishes artists from nonartists. This is very much in line with our theory. These studies are thus complementary in linking P with both definitions of creativity.

What is the position with respect to psychosis? Hebeison (1960), Kidner (1978), and Soueif and Farar (1971) have found significantly *depressed* performance of schizophrenics on tests of creative thinking. As I have argued, creativity demands a combination of high P and high ego strength; there is considerable evidence for the necessity of combining these two apparently antithetical properties. Rawlings (1985) has suggested a theoretical resolution to this problem, using an experiment involving dichotic listening. As he points out, the problem is similar to that of reaction time, where P correlates with quick reactions, whereas psychotics are generally slow. Psychosis adds a new element to high psychoticism, eliminating individuals with high ego strength (who would not succumb to actual psychotic illness) and influencing performance in a negative direction. Psychosis should never be identified with psychoticism; the former is an illness, the latter a predisposition.

It may be more illuminating to consider persons within the psychotic Erbkreis, but who are not themselves psychotic. This can be done by looking at relatives of psychotics to see if they show unusual amounts of creativity (Eysenck, 1983). Heston (1966) studied offspring of schizophrenic mothers raised by foster parents and found that although about half showed psychosocial disability, the remaining half were certainly successful adults, pursuing artistic talents and demonstrating imaginative adaptations to life to a degree not found in the control group. In Iceland, Karlsson (1970) found that among relatives of schizophrenics there was a high incidence of individuals of great creative achievement. McNeil (1971) studied the occurrence of mental illness in highly creative adopted children and their biological parents, discovering that the mental illness rates in the adoptees and in their biological parents were positively and significantly related to the creativity level of the adoptees. Such findings give powerful support to a link between psychoticism and creativity.

CREATIVITY AS A MENTAL PROCESS

What has been said so far suggests that psychotics, high P scorers in normal populations, and creative people generally share certain mental processes or cognitive styles, and any theory of creativity must be able to identify the nature of these styles. Measurement always implies a theory and a model, however primitive, and the only model to lend itself to scientific testing—and to have received such testing—is the one that views creativity as an associative process (Mednick, 1962). According to Mednick, the creative thinking process may be defined as "the forming of associative elements into new combinations which either meet specified requirements or are in some way useful. The more mutually remote the elements of the new combination, the more creative the process or solution" (p. 221). Mednick postulated an "associative hierarchy" (i.e., a way in which people produce associations to words or problems) in which creative people have a shallow gradient, extending much further than the steep gradients of less creative people.

Mednick was concerned with the steepness of the associative gradient, or what I would call the extent of the associative horizon (Eysenck, 1993). But that has to be set in a more inclusive associative framework, such as that provided by the Campbell (1960) and Simonton (1984) and the Furneaux (1960) and Eysenck (1953) models. Both postulate something like a chance-configuration theory, according to which random variations in associate formation occur in response to a perceived problem, with certain successful combinations being selected for retention. I have suggested that both formulations make the unlikely assumption that the production of associates is truly random (Eysenck, 1993); this is inherently unlikely and contradicted by a wealth of experimental studies. I have postulated instead that associations are restricted to a class that may be considered relevant, although it is also postulated that the criterion of relevance varies from person to person, with creative people having a less stringent criterion. This, in turn, gives rise to the less steep association gradient (or wider association horizon) of the creative person.

How does creativity fit into this model, which is here only sketched in most inadequately? The answer may lie in considering the nature of psychotic (mainly schizophrenic) thinking. If the theory is correct, or at least along the right lines, then there should be some connection between what characterizes such thinking and creative cognition. It may be useful to start with a well-established theory, namely, Cameron's notion of overinclusion (Cameron, 1947; Cameron & Magaret, 1950, 1951). Cameron believes that schizophrenics' concepts are overgeneralized. Schizophrenics are unable to maintain the normal conceptual boundaries, and thus they incorporate into their concepts elements—some of them personal—that are merely associated with the concept but not an essential part of it. Cameron (1939) used the term *overinclusion* to describe this abnormality; he reported that in solving problems on the Vygotsky test and a sentence completion test, schizophrenics "included such a variety of categories at one time, that the specific problems became too extensive and too complex for a solution to be reached"

(Cameron, p. 267). A fair number of experiments have been carried out to investigate this theory (for reviews, see Payne, 1960; Payne & Hewlett, 1960; Payne, Matussek, & George, 1959). The results obtained have consistently supported the theory (e.g., Epstein, 1953; Moran, 1953; see also Chapman, 1956; Chapman & Taylor, 1957).

Payne et al. (1959) have suggested that it is possible to reformulate Cameron's theory of overinclusion in a slightly more general way so that a number of predictions follow from it. Concept formation can be regarded as largely the result of discrimination learning. When a child first hears a word in a certain context, the word is associated with the entire situation (stimulus compound). As the word is heard again and again, only certain aspects of the stimulus compound are reinforced. Gradually the extraneous elements cease to evoke the response (the word), having become inhibited through lack of reinforcement. This inhibition is in some sense an active process, as it suppresses a response that was formerly evoked by the stimulus. Overinclusive thinking may be the result of a disorder (failure) of the process whereby inhibition is built up to circumscribe and define the learned response (the word or concept). In short, such thinking could be an extreme degree of stimulus generalization.

The same theory can be expressed in different terms. All purposeful behavior depends for its success on the fact that some stimuli are attended to and some other stimuli are ignored. It is a well-known fact that when concentrating on one task, normal people are quite unaware of most stimuli irrelevant to the task. It is as if some filter mechanism cuts out or inhibits the irrelevant stimuli, both internal and external, to allow the most efficient processing of incoming information. Overinclusive thinking might be only one aspect of a general breakdown of this filter mechanism.

A similar concept to overinclusion is that of allusive thinking, which is characteristic of many schizophrenics on object-sorting tests. McConaghy and Clancy (1968) demonstrated that this type of thinking exists widely in less exaggerated forms in the normal population, shows similar familiar transmission in schizophrenics and nonschizophrenics, and is akin to creative thinking. Dykes and McGhie (1976) actually demonstrated that highly creative normals score as highly on the Lovibond object-sorting test as do schizophrenics. In their study, less creative normals tended to produce conventional, unoriginal sortings, whereas the highly creative normals and the schizophrenics tended to give an equal proportion of unusual sortings. "This supports strongly [the hypothesis] that a common thinking style may lead to a controlled usefulness in normals and an uncontrollable impairment in schizophrenics" (Woody & Claridge, 1977).

The notion of overinclusion and allusive thinking as being characteristic of normal as well as schizophrenic thinking ultimately derives from Rapaport's (1945) suggestion that at least two quite different types of formal thought disorder contributed to the disturbances of thinking found in schizophrenics, neither of which was in fact specific to schizophrenia. One of these defects, demonstrated clearly in object-sorting tests, consisted in a tendency to function more at a concrete than an abstract level (Vygotsky, 1934). The other consisted of a loosening of the concept span, in that schizophrenics included objects in various groups of the test to which those objects did not strictly belong. This "looseness" of thinking is what others have called overinclusive or allusive thinking, and it occurs in normal people as well as in schizophrenics. Looseness of thinking, as measured by sorting tests, correlates well with clinical assessments of that behavior (Lovibond, 1954). Looseness thus may be suggested to be a normal type of thinking related to psychoticism and fundamental to creativity; concrete thinking is characteristic rather of psychosis and has no link with creativity, but rather precludes it.

An interesting study that demonstrates the dependence of creativity (as shown by fluency and unusualness of word associations) on psychosis, as well as the relevance of bipolar disorders, was done by Shaw, Mann, and Stokes (1986), who found that lithium decreases both the number of productions and the idiosyncracy of production. Thus the link with creativity may be via psychotic depression rather than schizophrenia.

Whatever may be the most appropriate name for the thinking characteristics that link schizophrenics and highly creative normals (overinclusiveness, allusive thinking, etc.), there clearly is a marked similarity. Furthermore, this view supports the notion of schizophrenia as a genetic morphism (Huxley, Mayr, Hoffer, & Osmond, 1964) whose frequency results from a balance between selectively favorable and unfavorable properties. The term *overinclusion* has long since been replaced, and new theories and experiments developed to include what are essentially similar ideas and conceptions: I have discussed these in some detail elsewhere (Eysenck, 1993).

Our theory would thus demand that some good and appropriate measure of overinclusion should

(a) be commonly found in schizophrenics and/or in other psychotic patients, (b) correlate with measures of psychoticism in normal people, and (c) correlate with creativity. The obvious choice for such a test must be one of word association, because it has been known for a long time that unusual associations are highly characteristic of schizophrenic patients; I have reviewed the literature elsewhere (Eysenck, 1993). Does the giving of unusual word associations correlate with creative performance? An excellent test of this hypothesis comes from the work of MacKinnon (1962, 1965), who has described the study in detail.

MacKinnon (1962) starts his account with a reference to a study by Bingham (1953), who tested the poet Amy Lowell with (among other tests) the word association test and found that "she gave a higher proportion of unique responses than those of anyone outside a mental institution" (p. 11). With groups of creative, somewhat creative, and noncreative architects (n = 124), MacKinnon found the same. The unusualness of responses correlated .50 with the rated creativity of the architects: Group 1 (the most creative) scored 204, group 2 scored 128, and group 3 (the least creative) scored 114. The postulated association between creativity and overinclusion, at least as measured by this test, was thus clearly demonstrated.

Gough (1976) has reported on a similar study done with 60 engineering students and 45 industrial research scientists. The subjects were rated for creativity and given two word association tests: one a general test, and the other using a scientific word list. Both correlated with creativity, but the scientific word list gave rather higher correlations. This is an intriguing finding that ought to be followed by in future research.

Similar results have also been reported by Miller and Chapman (1983) using the Chapman and Chapman (1980) scales as measures of schizotypal behavior. Using a continuous word association test, Miller and Chapman found that subjects with high scores in perceptual aberration/magical ideation gave a larger number of idiosyncratic responses. It is also relevant with Griffiths, Mednick, Schulsinger, and Diderichsen (1980) reported more deviant associations in the children of schizophrenic parents.

Finally, we come to the predicted association between unusual word associations and psychoticism. In the most relevant study (Upmanyu & Kaur, 1986), 140 university students were tested on the Kent- Rosanoff Word Association Test (WAT) and the Eysenck Personality Questionnaire (Eysenck & S. Eysenck, 1975). Unique responses correlated .32 with P; E, N, and L failed to show any correlation, as did intelligence. The reliability of the WAT was .72, and that of the P scale was .68; correcting for attentuation gives us a correlation between P and unique responses of .46. Ward, McConaghy, and Catts (1991) reported similar results; this requirement of our theory seems to be fulfilled.

THE CAUSES OF OVERINCLUSIVENESS

Negative Priming

What has been said so far is merely a brief summary of what has been discussed at much greater length in earlier presentations (Eysenck, 1983, 1993). It has been suggested that creativity is closely related to psychoticism, and that underlying both is a cognitive style loosely identified as overinclusiveness (i.e., a tendency to have a flat associative gradient, which allows the individual a wider interpretation of relevance as far as responses to stimuli are concerned). This overinclusiveness may be attributed to a failure of inhibition characteristic of psychotics, high P scorers, creative people, and geniuses. Clearly, though, there must be further characteristics of the cognitive apparatus that makes the difference between a psychotic patient and a genius; presumably these include high intelligence (and the other variables associated with creative achievement listed in Figure 1) and an ability to reject responses that are too far removed from the stimulus to make a genuine contribution to solving the problem under consideration.

In this section and the next, I shall discuss two candidates for the role of inhibitor of remote associations: negative priming and latent inhibition. Both fulfill this role to an extent indicated by a great deal of experimental work; both have been shown to be linked with schizophrenia (by their absence, or at least weakness); and both have been shown to be equally related to psychoticism. Both sections are theoretical in nature; there has not been any direct study of these variables in creative as opposed to noncreative people, as far as I know. The theory underlying negative priming and latent inhibition, however, presents a possible answer to our problem, as well as an experimental paradigm that can be used to test the theory presented here. It is hoped that this may encourage readers to carry out the necessary experiments to disprove or support the theory.

Among experimental paradigms used to investigate the stages and selectivity of processing information, the concept of cognitive inhibition is only one of many that have recently been applied to the assessment of possible creative dysfunction in mental health (Power, 1991). Incoming information has to be narrowed down and irrelevant information selectively excluded, a process that is postulated to occur through a balancing of facilitatory processing of task-relevant stimuli and the inhibition of task-irrelevant ones. Schizophrenia is postulated to be characterized by a breakdown of this balance, in that the failure of inhibitory processes produces over inclusiveness (Beech, Powell, McWilliam & Claridge, 1989; Bullen & Hemsley, 1986; Frith, 1979). This line of argument originated with Treisman (1964), who suggested that selecting certain specific stimuli for analysis might involve the exclusion or alternation of others. Keele and Neill (1978) produced a similar argument for the activation of memory traces; activated memory inappropriate to the task in hand had to be actively inhibited. An experimental paradigm for such cognitive inhibition is that of *negative priming*.

Negative priming may be defined in terms of the experimental paradigm in which a distractor object that had previously been ignored is subsequently represented as the target object to be named, classified, or otherwise dealt with. These processes take longer than if there had been no prior presentation; because the subject has associated the prime with negative salience, it is more difficult (i.e., takes longer) to make it salient when required. A typical defining experiment is the Stroop color-naming task, in which a color word (e.g., *red*) is presented, written in ink of a different color (e.g., green); the task is to disregard the word and state the color of the ink. If now the next word in the above example is printed in red ink, the response of normal subjects is significantly slowed; the previously ignored word *red* has acquired negative salience, which inhibits cognition associated with it. Hence the term *negative priming*, as the irrelevant stimulus word acts as a negative prime for later recognition and meaning by inhibiting reaction.

Frith (1979) suggested that schizophrenia is associated with a weakening of the inhibitory selection mechanisms that are active in the early phases of information processing, giving rise to some of the positive symptoms of schizophrenia, including hallucinations, delusions, and formal thought disorders such as overinclusiveness. Cognitive inhibition is vital for normal thought processes to occur; its absence (lack of negative priming) would therefore characterize—and be causally related to—the vagaries and excesses of schizophrenic thinking. Beech, Powell, et al. (1989) used a negative priming task to differentiate a group of schizophrenics from a matched group of mixed diagnosis psychiatric patients; as predicted, the schizophrenics shared reduced inhibition. We would expect that high-P (or schizotypal) normal subjects would show a similar lack of cognitive inhibition, and this has been shown to be so (Beech, Baylis, Smithson, & Claridge, 1989b; Beech & Claridge, 1987; Beech, McManus, Baylis, Tipper, & Agar, 1991). High schizotypes not only showed failure of negative priming but even *positive* primary effects; in other words, the supposedly negative prime had facilitatory rather than inhibitory effects for this group.

Curiously enough, the failure of negative priming was less noticeable in the schizophrenic subjects studied in these experiments than in the (normal) high schizotypes. This may be explained in terms of the medication effects shown by the schizophrenics. As Beech, Powell, McWilliam, and Claridge (1990) have shown, a small dose of chlorpromazine in normal subjects significantly increased the negative priming effect, as compared to placebo.

The nature and definition of the negative priming effect are fairly clear, but the actual processes involved are still a matter of debate. Neill (1977) has put forward the view that priming effects occur as a result of active inhibition of the irrelevant stimulus, making possible an efficient response to the target stimulus. The need to undo the inhibition produces a response cost on the subsequent trial, measured in terms of increased reaction time. In an alternative theory, Tipper (1985) has suggested that what is inhibited is the access of the activated structure to the mechanisms required for an overt response, an effect that decouples the representations from the construct of action. For the purpose of this section, we need not prefer one theory over the other.

In general terms, what makes the negative priming paradigm applicable to our problem? It is based on the view that both facilitatory and inhibitory processes are involved in selectivity determining attention to relevant information input, relevance being decided by prior experience. Marked individual differences exist in the degree of cognitive inhibition, measured by negative priming, with schizophrenics/schizotypes failing to show such inhibition and consequently becoming overinclusive. In other words, the flat associative gradient characteristic of creative people may be the result of lack of cognitive inhibition, as measured by negative priming. At present this is clearly only an hypothesis, there being no direct evidence on the assumed relation between creativity and negative priming. The fact that high P scorers have been shown to be creative and also to have low negative priming scores, however, is at least indirect evidence to firm up the general theory.

Latent Inhibition

The theories of Tipper (1985) and Neill (1977), mentioned in the previous section as explaining negative priming effects, are clearly cognitive theories. Yet these phenomena may also be explained along the lines of classical conditioning theory. As far as I know this line of argument has not previously been followed, but the theory and phenomena of latent inhibition bear a remarkable similarity to negative priming. (Lubow, 1989, in a book on latent inhibition, does not mention negative priming.)

Latent inhibition (LI) is defined by an experimental paradigm that requires, as a minimum, a two-stage procedure. The first stage involves stimulus preexposure (i.e., the to-be-CS is exhibited without being followed by any UCS); this leads theoretically to the CS acquiring a negative salience (i.e., it signals a lack of consequences, and thus acquires inhibitory properties). The second stage is one of *acquisition*: The CS is now followed by an UCS, and it acquires the property of initiating the UC response. Latent inhibition is shown by increasing difficulties of acquiring this property, as compared with lack of preexposure. As with negative priming, there is a masking task during preexposure to the CS. For instance, the masking task might be the auditory presentation of a series of syllable pairs, whereas the CS would be a white noise randomly superimposed on the syllable reproduction. The LI group would be exposed to this combined recording, with the control group was exposed only to the syllable pairs without the white noise. In the test phase the white noise is reinforced, and subjects are given scores according to how soon they discover the rule linking CS with reinforcement. LI would be indicated by the group with preexposure to the white noise discovering the rule later than the control group. There are more complex, three-stage procedures, but these complications are not crucial to our argument (Lubow, 1989).

Is it possible to classify negative priming as a variant of latent inhibition? There are obviously close similarities. Conditioning of performance is preceded by the exhibition of the to-be-CS (or action stimulus) under conditions that endow it with negative salience; the subject either is instructed to disregard it (negative priming) or learns independently that the to-be CS does not signal anything specific. Hence in both cases the sign-significate (S-S) link is counterindicated, and the establishment of such a link is made more difficult.

Applying the nomenclature of conditioning to the negative priming paradigm is permissible in the recent climate of S-S theorizing and inclusion of cognitive elements in the conditioning process (Gray, 1975; Macintosh, 1974, 1983). The cognitive elements in latent inhibition theory are emphasized by Lubow (1989) in terms of his conditioned attention theory. According to this theory, nonreinforced preexposure to a stimulus retards subsequent conditioning to that stimulus, because during such preexposure the subject learns not to attend to it. The theory is based on the use of attention as a hypothetical construct with the properties of a Pavlovian response, and on the specification of reinforcement conditions that modify attention.

The same theory may be used to explain negative priming effects. Nonreinforced preexposure in this case is the not-to-be-reacted-to part of the red-green Stroop combination, which retards subsequent conditioning to that stimulus because during preexposure the subject learns not to attend to it. The general view of the importance of changes in attention to stimuli, which underlies this theory, goes back to Lashley (1929) and Krechewsky (1932), and may be traced through Lawrence (1949) to MacIntosh (1975), Frey and Sears (1978), and Pearce and Hall (1980). Granted the similarities, we would expect (a) less latent inhibition in schizophrenics, and (b) less latent inhibition in high P scores. The evidence supports both deductions.

Baruch, Hemsley, and Gray (1988) found an abolition of latent inhibition in acute schizophrenics, but not in chronic schizophrenics or normals. Lubow, Weiner, Schlossberg & Baruch (1987) also failed to find such abolition in chronic cases, presumably because such patients are on a dopaminergic antagonist, neuroleptic drug regime that would normalize attentional processes (e.g., Braff & Saccuzzo, 1982; Oltmans, Otayon & Neale, 1978). There is a large body of evidence to show that LI can be attentuated or abolished in rats by dopamine agonists (e.g., amphetamines) and can also be increased with dopamine antagonists (e.g., haloperidol, chlorpromazine; see discussion by Lubow, Ingberg-Sacks, Zalstein-Orda,

& Gewirtz, 1992). In this respect, then, latent inhibition closely resembles negative priming.

Regarding their high-versus-low psychoticism group, Baruch et al. (1988) found the expected negative correlation between LI and P: the greater the proneness to psychosis, the less latent inhibition. Similar results have been reported by Lubow et al. (1992) using two different experimental procedures; again, high-P subjects showed an attentuated latent inhibition effect compared with subjects with low P scores. Both auditory and visual stimulus preexposure resulted in slower acquisition of new associations as compared with a lack of preexposure to the test stimulus, but to a much lesser extent in high-P than in normal and low-P subjects. Lubow et al. (1992) argue that "the idea that schizophrenics fail to filter out irrelevant stimuli is congruent with the phenomenology of schizophrenics, and with a considerable variety of data on the differential effects of distractors on the behavior of schizophrenics and normals. Frith (1979) cogently and succinctly described this type of result as reflecting an inability to limit the contents of consciousness." (p. 570).

This, of course, is precisely what is characteristic of the mechanism needed to explain the overinclusiveness of schizophrenics and high P scorers. The failure of negative priming and/or latent inhibition to limit associationist spreading (flat associationist gradient) would appear to account for the prominent symptoms of psychotic cognition and the major feature of creativity. Accordingly, this may be the missing link between psychopathology and genius. Of course, as already explained, a flat associative gradient produced by an absence of cognitive inhibition is not enough by itself to produce creative achievement; other components, such as those listed in Figure 1, are needed. Among these, the ability to weed out unsuitable and unusuable associations must be the distinguishing mark between the word salad of the schizophrenic and the utterances of the poet.

Latent inhibition and negative priming have a biological basis, of course, and this seems firmly related to dopamine levels. As reported, dopamine agonists (e.g., amphetamines) attenuate or abolish LI, while dopamine antagonists (e.g., haloperidol, chlorpromazine) increase LI, just as they affect psychotic behavior. As Lubow et al. (1992) say, "these data are in accord with the premise that schizophrenia has a major attentional deficit component . . . and that the disorder is mediated by a dopamine system dysfunction. While other neurotransmitter involvements in schizophrenia have been proposed . . . the dopamine hypothesis remains a leading component in understanding schizophrenia (Gray, Feldman, Rawlins, Hemsley & Smith, 1991) (p. 503).

The suggested relevance of LI to creativity is, of course, similar to that suggested for negative priming. Cognitive inhibition characteristic of most people is lessened or removed in creative individuals, and hence the associationist gradient is flattened, criteria for relevance are reduced, and "overinclusiveness" appears. Again, it should be emphasized that there is no *direct* evidence in favor of the theory; it is based essentially on the strong association between creativity and psychoticism, the finding that psychoticism (like schizophrenia) is characterized by low degrees of LI and negative priming, and that LI and negative priming account for the lack of cognitive inhibition apparent in schizophrenia and high P scorers. Direct evidence is needed before the theory can be accepted as a true, rather than merely possible, account of the observed relation between personality and creativity.

CREATIVITY, AROUSAL, AND PERSONALITY

An additional psychological variable that has been connected both with creativity and personality is *cortical arousal*. Theoretically this link between creativity and (lack of) arousal dates back to Hull (1943), who postulated a "behavioral law" according to which increases in drive (arousal) make the dominant response to a stimulus even more dominant (i.e., increase the steepness of the associative gradient). Anxiety, acting as a drive, has a similar effect (Eysenck, 1973). Easterbrook (1959) similarly put forward the hypothesis that arousal causes attentional narrowing, again suggesting an increase in the steepness of the associative gradient. Martindale (1981, 1989) has rephrased this general law, stating that in the information network more nodes will be activated and to a more equal degree in a state of low as compared with high arousal.

Martindale (1981) has provided some empirical evidence that defocused attention, flat associative hierarchies, and "primary process thought" are indeed associated with states of low cortical activation. This law would imply that anything that increases arousal impairs performance on tests of creativity. Positive evidence for such a deduction from the general principle has been found for stress (Dentler & Mackler, 1964), the simple presence of other people (Lindgren

& Lindgren, 1965), noise (Martindale & Greenough, 1973), extremes of temperature (Lombroso, 1901), and even reward (extrinsic motivation; Amabile, 1983a).

There is an apparent contradiction here: It would not be true to say that generally creative people are in a state of low arousal. Maddi and Andrews (1966) found that creative people are more anxious than uncreative people; they also tend to show slightly higher levels of resting (basal) arousal on physiological measures. Similarly, creative people like scientists tend to be introverted (Eysenck, 1973) as do artists (Goetz & Goetz, 1979a,b). Introversion, of course, is linked with *high* levels of arousal (Eysenck & M. Eysenck, 1989; Strelau & Eysenck, 1987); Goetz and Goetz (1979a,b) also found successful artists to be high on neuroticism. Clearly there is a paradox here.

Martindale has suggested the solution: As compared with less creative people, those who are more creative do show low levels of cortical arousal while performing creative tasks (Martindale & Hines, 1975). Martindale and Hasenfus (1978) found that low levels of arousal were found precisely where they were expected to occur—during creative inspiration, rather than during the elaboration stage. Martindale goes on to suggest that creative people may be more *variable* in their level of arousal, and thus they show more extreme fluctuations. This is a psychophysiological restatement of Kris's (1952) contention that creative people are more variable on the primary process–secondary process continuum. Although there is no direct evidence for this hypothesis, Gooding and Jamison (1990) have shown that highly creative people tend to fluctuate between states of excessive energy and excessive apathy, abulia, and depression; this variance is perhaps the effect of high P (manic-depressive abnormality).

Quite generally, people tend to influence their level of arousal by choosing activities that raise or lower arousal to approach optimum levels. Hence introverts seek solitude, and extraverts look for company (Wilson, 1990). Though anecdotal, the evidence of supreme acts of intuition/creativity on the part of scientific geniuses suggests that very frequently these acts occur in states of low arousal—dreamy pre-sleep, sitting on a train or bus, or during a vacation. High arousal accompanied the elaboration stage (when creative people attempt to prove their intuitive insights, search the literature, argue with skeptics, etc.).

Although the evidence is less strong than in the case of introversion, it seems clear that P is related to low arousal or arousability (Zuckerman, 1991); the physiological mediators are again dopamine and monoamine oxydase (MAO). There has been less study of the low arousal-P connection than of the low arousal-E connection. In particular, the possibility of rapid change from high to low arousal, suggested by Martindale, has not been investigated in relation to personality, although Pavlov's notion of excitation-inhibition equilibrium may be relevant. Here, as in so many other aspects of this theory, future research must come to the aid of Martindale's view and support it (or not, as the case may be). That there is a connection between arousal and creativity is very likely; whether this connection is similar to that suggested by Martindale remains to be seen. He has certainly made an important beginning in the direction of testing it.

I may add one further point here. The concept of arousal has many similarities with the concept of drive in the Hullian sense, and an attempt has been made to see if schizophrenics are characterized by low drive, as has often been suggested in explanation of their frequently poor performance on various tasks. I have reported an experiment to test this hypothesis (Eysenck, 1961), using as a measure of drive the amount of reminiscence on a pursuit-rotor task. (Eysenck and Frith, 1977, have summarized the evidence that reminiscence can be used as a good measure of drive.) The results showed no evidence of low drive in schizophrenics, but did show that they had a low rate of dissipation of inhibition. If this is true of (normal) high P scorers, too, then we may have to consider slow dissipation of inhibition as a possible causal factor for creativity. Another, more appealing explanation of the observed retarded appearance of reminiscence in schizophrenics and manic-depressives may be a slow process of consolidation of the memory trace (Eysenck & Frith, 1977). This might lead to a comparative failure in psychotics (and possibly high-P subjects) to form firm memory structures, which might in turn impede the use of flat associationist gradients. Unfortunately, little work has been done in this field, so this possibility must remain a suggestion.

SUMMARY AND CONCLUSIONS

Creativity clearly is a complex concept, defined at two very different levels as a personality trait or creative style and as an achievement-oriented behavior. Because of the multiple determination of creative behavior by synergistically acting causes of which trait creativity is only one, we would not expect (and do not find) high correlations between trait and achievement creativity (Eysenck, 1993). This does not lessen the importance of or lower our interest in trait creativity; although the latter does not carry all the burden of creative achievement, it is one indispensable condition for such achievement.

Creativity is best conceived in terms of an associative paradigm—namely, in terms of being the product of a flat associative gradient that allows remote associations to influence cognitive processes of problem-solving. Flat associative gradients in general lead to overinclusiveness, which is a characteristic feature of schizophrenia and functional psychoses generally (Eysenck, 1992a); this may explain the close connection between creativity and psychoticism. The latter concept differs from psychosis by not being pathological and hence enabling people to use remote associations in a constructive way, whereas psychotics are overwhelmed by overinclusive thoughts and cannot cope with them in a critical manner.

If we do conceptualize creativity as being closely linked with personality through the cognitive style just specified, we have the added opportunity of being able to explain the reasons for a flat associative gradient in terms of reasonably well understood processes like negative priming, latent inhibition, and low arousal—processes that have been theoretically and empirically linked with both psychoticism and psychosis. Such a link with experimental psychology and learning theory is essential if we are ever to go beyond a purely descriptive effort and attempt a causal analysis of creativity and genius. This emphasis on personality-related mechanisms has always been prominent in theories about creativity and genius, linking "great wits" and "madness," as in Dryden's famous poem. Modern thinking insists more on the "thin partitions" that "their bounds divide": the distinction between psychoticism as a dispositional trait and psychosis as an active illness, where the characteristics pertaining to the illness overwhelm the positive features of the disposition (Eysenck, 1993).

REFERENCES

Allport, F. H. (1934). The J-curve hypothesis of conforming behavior. *Journal of Social Psychology*, *5*, 141–143.

Allsop, J., Eysenck, H. J., & Eysenck, S. (1991). Machiavellianism as a component in psychoticism and extraversion. *Personality and Individual Differences*, *12*, 29–41.

Amabile, T. M. (1983). *The social psychology of creativity*. New York: Springer-Verlag.

Andreasen, N. C. (1987). Creativity and mental illness: Prevalence rates in writers and their first-degree relatives. *American Journal of Psychiatry*, *144*, 1288–1292.

Barron, F. (1968). *Creativity and psychological health*. New York: Van Nostrand.

Baruch, I., Hemsley, D. R., & Gray, J. (1988). Differential performance of acute and chronic schizophrenics in a latent inhibition task. *Journal of Nervous and Mental Diseases*, *170*, 598–606.

Beech, A. R., Baylis, G. C., Smithson, P., & Claridge, G. S. (1989). Individual differences in schizotypy as reflected in cognitive measures of inhibition. *British Journal of Clinical Psychology*, *28*, 117–129.

Beech, A. R., & Claridge, G. S. (1987). Individual differences in cognitive priming: Relation with schizotypal personality traits. *British Journal of Clinical Psychology*, *78*, 349–356.

Beech, A. R., McManus, D., Baylis, G. S., Tipper, S. P., & Agar, K. (1991). Individual differences in cognitive processes: Towards an explanation of schizophrenic symptomatology. *British Journal of Psychology*, *82*, 417–426.

Beech, A. R., Powell, T., McWilliam, J., & Claridge, G. (1989). Evidence of reduced cognitive inhibition in schizophrenia. *British Journal of Clinical Psychology*, *28*, 109–116.

Beech, A. R., Powell, T., McWilliam, J., & Claridge, G. (1990). The effect of a small dose of chlorpromazine as a measure of cognitive inhibition. *Personality and Individual Differences*, *11*, 1141–1145.

Benassy, M., & Chauffard, C. (1947). Le test F de Cattell est-il un test objectif de temperament? *L'Annee Psychologique*, *43*, 200–230.

Bingham, M. T. (1953). Beyond psychology. In M. T. Bingham (Ed.), *Homosapiens audubonìensis: A tribute to Walter van Dyke Bingham* (pp. 5–29). New York: National Audubon Society.

Braff, D. L., & Saccuzzo, D. P. (1982). Effects of antipsychotic medication on speed of information processing in schizophrenic patients. *American Journal of Psychiatry*, *139*, 1127–1130.

Bullen, J. G., & Hemsley, D. R. (1986). Schizophrenia: A failure to control the content of consciousness. *British Journal of Clinical Psychology*, *26*, 25–33.

Cameron, N. (1939). Deterioration and regression in schizophrenic thinking. *Journal of Abnormal and Social Psychology*, *34*, 265–270.

Cameron, N. (1947). *The psychology of behavior disorders*. Boston: Houghton Mifflin.

Cameron, N., & Magaret, A. (1950). Experimental studies in thinking: I. Scattered speed in the response of normal subjects to incomplete sentences. *Journal of Experimental Psychology*, *39*, 617–627.

Cameron, N., & Magaret, A. (1951). *Behavior pathology*. Boston: Houghton Mifflin.

Campbell, D. T. (1960). Blind variation and selective retention in creative thought as in other knowledge processes. *Psychological Review*, *67*, 380–400.

Cattell, R. B. (1971). *Abilities: Their structure, growth, and action*. Boston: Houghton Mifflin.

Chapman, J. (1956). Distractibility in the conceptual performance of schizophrenia. *Journal of Abnormal and Social Psychology*, *53*, 286–291.

Chapman, L. J., & Chapman, J. P. (1980). Scales for rating psychotic and psychotic-like experiences as continua. *Schizophrenia Bulletin*, *6*, 476–489.

Chapman, L. J., & Taylor, J. (1957). Breadth of deviate concepts used by schizophrenics. *Journal of Abnormal and Social Psychology, 54*, 108–123.

Cronbach, L. J. (1957). The two disciplines of scientific psychology. *American Psychologist, 12*, 671–684.

Crow, T. J. (1986). The continuum of psychosis and its implication for the structure of the gene. *British Journal of Psychiatry, 179*, 419–429.

Crow, T. J. (1990). The continuum of psychosis and its genetic origins. *British Journal of Psychiatry, 156*, 788–797.

Dahlstrom, W. G., Lachar, D., & Dahlstrom, L. (1986). *MMPI patterns of American minorities*. Minneapolis: University of Minnesota Press.

Dellas, M., & Gaier, E. L. (1970). Identification of creativity: The individual. *Psychological Bulletin, 73*, 55–73.

Dentler, R. A., & Mackler, B. (1964). Originality: Some social and personal determinants. *Behavioral Science, 9*, 1–7.

Dykes, M., & McGhie, A. (1976). A comparative study of attentional strategies of schizophrenic and highly normal subjects. *British Journal of Psychiatry, 128*, 509–56.

Easterbrook, J. A. (1959). The effect of emotion as cue utilization of behavior. *Psychological Review, 66*, 183–201.

Epstein, S. (1953). Overinclusive thinking in schizophrenics and a control group. *Journal of Counseling Psychology, 17*, 384–388.

Eysenck, H. J. (1952). *The scientific study of personality*. London: Routledge & Kegan Paul.

Eysenck, H. J. (1953). *Uses and abuses of psychology*. London: Penguin.

Eysenck, H. J. (1961). Psychosis, drive and inhibition: A theoretical and experimental account. *American Journal of Psychiatry, 118*, 198–204.

Eysenck, H. J. (1970). *The structure of human personality*. London: Methuen.

Eysenck, H. J. (1973). Personality, learning and "anxiety." In H. J. Eysenck (Ed.), *Handbook of abnormal psychology* (2nd ed., pp. 390–419). London: Pitman.

Eysenck, H. J. (1983). The roots of creativity: Cognitive ability or personality trait? *Roeper Review, 5*, 10–12.

Eysenck, H. J. (1987). Personality and aging: An exploratory analysis. *Journal of Social Behavior and Personality, 3*, 11–21.

Eysenck, H. J. (1991). Dimensions of personality: 16, 5 or 3—criteria for a taxonomic paradigm. *Personality and Individual Differences, 12*, 773–790.

Eysenck, H. J. (1992a). The definition and measurement of psychoticism. *Personality and Individual Differences, 13*, 757–785.

Eysenck, H. J. (1992b). Four ways five factors are *not* basic. *Personality and Individual Differences, 13*, 667–673.

Eysenck, H. J. (1993). Creativity and personality: A theoretical perspective. *Psychological Inquiry, 4*, 147–246.

Eysenck, H. J., & Eysenck, M. W. (1989). *Personality and individual differences: A natural science approach*. New York: Plenum.

Eysenck, H. J., & Eysenck, S. B. G. (1975). *Manual of the Eysenck Personality Questionnaire*. London: Hodder & Stoughton.

Eysenck, H. J., & Eysenck, S. B. G. (1976). *Psychoticism as a dimension of personality*. London: Hodder & Stoughton.

Eysenck, H. J., & Frith, L. D. (1977). *Reminiscence, motivation and personality*. New York: Plenum.

Eysenck, H. J., & Gudjonsson, G. (1988). *The causes and cures of criminality*. New York: Plenum.

Farmer, E. W. (1974). *Psychoticism and place-orientation as general personality characteristics of importance for different aspects of creative thinking*. Unpublished thesis, University of Glasgow, Scotland.

Frey, P. W., & Sears, R. J. (1978). Model of conditioning incorporating the Rescorda-Wagner associated axiom, a dynamic attention process, and a catastrophe scale. *Psychological Review, 85*, 321–340.

Friedman, A. F., Webb, J. I., & Lewak, R. (1989). *Psychological assessment with the MMPI*. Hillsdale, NJ: Erlbaum.

Frith, C. (1979). Consciousness, information processing and schizophrenia. *British Journal of Psychiatry, 134*, 225–235.

Furneaux, W. D. (1960). Intellectual abilities and problem-solving behavior. In H. J. Eysenck (Ed.), *Handbook of abnormal psychology* (pp. 167–192). London: Pitman.

Gewirtz, J. L. (1948). Studies in word fluency. I. Its relation to vocabulary and mental age in young children. *Journal of Genetic Psychology, 72*, 165–176.

Glover, J. A., Ronning, R. R., & Reynolds, C. P. (Eds.). (1989). *Handbook of creativity*. New York: Plenum.

Goetz, K. O., & Goetz, K. (1979a). Personality characteristics of professional artists. *Perceptual and Motor Skills, 49*, 327–334.

Goetz, K. O., & Goetz, K. (1979b). Personality characteristics of successful artists. *Perceptual and Motor Skills, 49*, 919–924.

Gooding, F., & Jamison, K. (1990). *Manic depressive illness*. New York: Oxford University Press.

Gough, H. C. (1976). Studying creativity by means of Word Association Tests. *Journal of Applied Psychology, 61*, 348–353.

Gray, J. A. (1975). *Elements of a two-process theory of learning*. New York: Academic Press.

Gray, J. A., Feldon, J., Rawlins, J. N. P., Hemsley, D. R., & Smith, A. D. (1991). The neuropsychology of schizophrenia. *Behavioral and Brain Sciences, 14*, 77–88.

Griffiths, J. J., Mednick, S. I., Schulsinger, F., & Diderichsen, B. (1980). Verbal associative disturbances in children at high risk for schizophrenia. *Journal of Abnormal Psychology, 89*, 125–131.

Guilford, J. P. (1950). Creativity. *American Psychologist, 5*, 444–454.

Hargreaves. H. L. (1927). The "faculty" of imagination. *British Journal of Psychology, 10*(Monograph Suppl.), 74.

Hebeison, A. A. (1960). The performance of groups of schizophrenic patients in a test of creative thinking. In E. P. Torrance (Ed.), *Creativity: Third Minnesota Conference on Gifted Children*. Minneapolis: University of Minnesota.

Heston, I. I. (1966). Psychiatric disorders in foster-home-reared children of schizophrenic mothers. *British Journal of Psychiatry, 112*, 819–825.

Hull, C. (1943). *Principles of behavior*. New York: Appleton-Century-Crofts.

Huxley, J., Mayr, E., Hoffer, H., & Osmond, A. (1964). Schizophrenia as a genetic morphism. *Nature, 204*, 220–221.

Karlsson, J. I. (1970). Genetic association of giftedness and creativity with schizophrenia. *Heredity, 66*, 171–182.

Keele, S. W., & Neill, W. T. (1978). Mechanisms of attention. In E. C. Carberette (Ed.), *Handbook of Perception* (Vol. 9, pp. 3–47). New York: Academic Press.

Kessel, N. (1989). Genius and mental disorder: A history of ideas concerning their conjunction. In P. Murray (Ed.), *Genius: The history of ideas* (pp. 196–212). Oxford, England: Basil Blackford.

Kidner, D. W. (1978). Personality and conceptual structure: An integrative model. Unpublished Ph.D. thesis, University of London, England

Krechewsky, D. (1932). "Hypotheses" in rats. *Psychological Review, 39,* 516–532.

Kris, E. (1952). *Psychoanalytic exploration in art.* New York: International University Press.

Kubie, L. S. (1958). *Neurotic distortions of the creative process.* New York: Noon Lay.

Lange-Eichbaum, W. (1931). *The problem of genius.* London: Kegan Paul.

Lashley, K. S. (1929). *Brain mechanisms and intelligence: A quantitative study of injuries to the brain.* Chicago: University of Chicago Press.

Lawrence, D. N. (1949). Acquired distinctiveness of cues: I. Transfer between disorientations on the basis of familiarity with the stimulus. *Journal of Experimental Psychology, 39,* 770–784.

Lindgren, H. C., & Lindgren, F. (1965). Brainstorming and orneriness as facilitators of creativity. *Psychological Reports, 16,* 572–583.

Lombroso, C. (1901). *The man of genius.* (6th ed.). New York: Scribner's.

Lovibond, S. N. (1954). The Object Sorting Test and conceptual thinking in schizophrenics. *Australian Journal of Psychology, 6,* 52–70.

Lubow, R. E. (1989). *Latent inhibition and conditional attention theory.* New York: Cambridge University Press.

Lubow, R. E., Ingberg-Sacks, Y., Zalstein-Orda, N., & Gewirtz, J. C. (1992). Latent inhibition in low and high "psychotic-prone" normal subjects. *Personality and Individual Differences, 13,* 563–572.

Lubow, R. E., Weiner, I., Schlossberg, A., & Baruch, I. (1987). Latent inhibition and schizophrenia. *Bulletin of the Psychonomic Society, 25,* 464–467.

MacIntosh, N. J. (1974). *The psychology of animal learning.* London: Academic Press.

MacIntosh, N. J. (1975). A theory of attention: Variations in the associability of stimuli with reinforcement. *Psychological Revue, 82,* 276–298.

MacIntosh, N. J. (1983). *Conditioning and associative learning.* Oxford, England: University Press.

MacKinnon, D. W. (1962). The nature and nurture of creative talent. *American Psychologist, 17,* 484–495.

MacKinnon, D. W. (1965). Personality and the realization of creative potential. *American Psychologist, 20,* 273–281.

MacKinnon, D. W. (1978). *In search of human effectiveness.* New York: Creative Education Foundation.

Maddi, S. R., & Andrews, S. (1966). The need for variety in fantasy and self-description. *Journal of Personality, 34,* 610–625.

Martindale, C. (1981). *Cognition and consciousness.* Homewood, IL: Dorsey.

Martindale, C. (1989). Personality, situation, and creativity. In J. A. Glover, R. R. Ronning, & C. R. Reynolds (Eds.), *Handbook of creativity.* New York: Plenum.

Martindale, C., & Greenough, J. (1973). The differential effect of increased arousal on creative and intellectual performance. *Journal of Genetic Psychology, 123,* 329–335.

Martindale, C., & Hasenfus, N. (1978). EEG differences as a function of creativity, stage of the creative process, and effort to be original. *Biological Psychology, 6,* 157–167.

Martindale, C., & Hines, D. C. (1975). Creativity and cortical activation during creative, intellectual, and EEG feedback tasks. *Biological Psychology, 3,* 71–80.

Marlow, A. C. (1976). Creativity in self-analyzing people. In A Rottenberg & C. R. Haussman (Eds.), *The creative question* (pp. 86–92). Durham, NC: Duke University Press.

McConaghy, N., & Clancy, M. (1968). Familial relationships of allusive thinking in university students and their parents. *British Journal of Psychiatry, 114,* 1079–1087.

McNeil, T. F. (1971). Prebirth and postbirth influence on the relationship between creative ability and recorded mental illness. *Journal of Personality, 39,* 391–406.

Mednick, S. A. (1962). The associative basis of the creative process. *Psychological Review, 69,* 220–232.

Miller, E. N., & Chapman, L. J. (1983). Continued word association in hypothetically psychosis-prone college students. *Journal of Abnormal Psychology, 92,* 408–478.

Mohan, J. L., & Tiwana, M. (1987). Personality and alienation of creative writers: A brief report. *Personality and Individual Differences, 8,* 449.

Moran, L. J. (1953). Vocabulary knowledge and usage among normal and schizophrenic subjects. *Psychological Monograph, 67* (Whole No. 370).

Neill, W. T. (1977). Inhibitory and facilitatory processes in selective attention. *Journal of Experimental Psychology: Human Perception and Performance, 3,* 444–450.

Ochse, R. (1991). The relation between creative genius of psychopathology: An historical perspective and a new explanation. *South African Journal of Psychology, 21,* 45–53.

Oltmans, T. F., Otayan, J., & Neale, J. M. (1978). The effects of antipsychotic medication and diagnostic criteria on distractibility in schizophrenics. *Journal of Psychiatric Research, 14,* 81–91.

Payne, R. W. (1960). Cognitive abnormalities. In H. J. Eysenck (Ed.), *Handbook of abnormal psychology.* London: Pitman.

Payne, R. W., & Hewlett, J. H. G. (1960). Thought disorder in psychotic patients. In H. J. Eysenck (Ed.), *Experiments in personality* (pp. 3–104). London: Routledge & Kegan Paul.

Payne, R. W., Matussek, P., & George, E. I. (1959). An experimental study of schizophrenic thought disorder. *Journal of Mental Science, 105,* 627–652.

Pearce, J. M., & Hall, G. (1980). A model of Pavlovian learning: Variations in the effectiveness of conditioned but not of unconditioned stimuli. *Psychological Review, 87,* 532–552.

Power, M. J. (1991). Cognitive science and behavioral psychotherapy: Where behaviour was, there shall co-operation be? *Behavioral Psychotherapy, 19,* 20–41.

Prentky, R. A. (1980). *Creativity and psychopathology.* New York: Praeger.

Rapaport, D. (1945). *Diagnostic clinical testing.* Chicago: Year Book.

Rawlings, D. (1985). Psychoticism, creativity and dichotic shadowing. *Personality and Individual Differences, 6,* 737–742.

Richards, R. L. (1981). *Relationships between creativity and psychopathology: An evaluation and interpretation of the evidence. Genetic Psychology Monographs, 103,* 261–324.

Roe, A. (1953). A psychological study of eminent psychologists and anthropologists, and a comparison with biological and physical scientists. *Psychological Monographs: General and Applied, 67*(Whole No. 352).

Rogers, C. R. (1961). *On becoming a person.* Boston: Houghton & Mifflin.

Runco, M. A. (1991). *Divergent thinking.* Norwood, NJ: Ablex.

Shaw, E. R., Mann, J. J., & Stokes, P. E. (1986). Effects of lithium carbonate in creativity in bipolar outpatients. *American Journal of Psychiatry, 143,* 1166–1169.

Simonton, D. K. (1984). *Genius, creativity and leadership.* Cambridge, MA: Harvard University Press.

Soueif, M. I., & Farag, S. E. (1971). Creative thinking aptitudes in schizophrenics: A factorial study. *Scientific Aesthetics, 8,* 51–60.

Strelau, J., & Eysenck, H. J. (Eds.). (1987). *Personality dimension and arousal.* New York: Plenum.

Tipper, S. R. (1985). Negative priming effect: Inhibitory priming by ignored objects. *Quarterly Journal of Experimental Psychology, 37A*, 571–590.

Treisman, A. (1964). Verbal cues, language and meaning in selective attention. *American Journal of Psychology, 77*, 205–219.

Upmanyu, V. V., & Kaur, K. (1986). Diagnostic utility of word association emotional indicator. *Psychological Studies, 32*, 71–78.

Vygotsky, L. S. (1934). Thought in schizophrenics. *Archives of Neurology and Psychiatry, 31*, 1063–1077.

Wallach, M. A., & Kogan, N. (1965). *Modes of thinking in young children: A study of the creativity and intelligence distinction.* New York: Holt, Rhinehart, & Winston.

Ward, P. B., McConaghy, N., & Catts, S. V. (1991). Word association and measures of psychosis-proneness in university students. *Personality and Individual Differences, 12*, 473–480.

Welsh, G. (1975). *Creativity and intelligence: A personality approach.* Chapel Hill: University of North Carolina.

Wilson, G. D. (1990). Personality, time of day and arousal. *Personality and Individual Differences, 11*, 153–168.

Woody, E., & Claridge, G. (1977). Psychoticism and thinking. *British Journal of Social and Clinical Psychology, 16*, 241–248.

Zuckerman, M. (1991). *Psychobiology of personality.* New York: Cambridge University Press.

13

Intelligence, Personality, Psychopathology, and Adjustment

Norman S. Endler and Laura J. Summerfeldt

What has been termed the "cognitive revolution" (Gardner, 1985) has had a profound impact throughout all areas of psychology. Though it has been suggested that much of this trend is better regarded as a "rediscovery" (Sternberg, 1990; Sternberg & Frensch, 1990), it is clear that the 1980s and 1990s have seen a surge of interest in the cognitive aspects of the three topics with which this chapter primarily concerns itself: intelligence, personality, and psychopathology. We will explore the integrative potential of a cognitive approach for the understanding of these three constructs, as revealed in both theory and research.

The criteria that define any given condition as psychopathological have historically been the topic of considerable debate in clinical and taxonomic circles (see Achenbach, 1985; Blashfield, 1984; Buss, 1966; Millon, 1987). Statistical, historical, and phenomenological factors have all been considered (see McReynolds, 1989; Sims, 1988). Despite the many approaches taken to the delineation of psychopathology, according to the fourth edition (DSM-IV) of the diagnostic manual of the American Psychiatric Association (APA, 1994), its basic unit is the *mental disorder*. This is conceptualized as a clinically significant behavioral or psychological syndrome or pattern that is associated with present distress, impairment, or risk. This includes the symptom syndromes, located on Axis I, and the Axis II disorders, those of personality. The inclusion of the latter represents an attempt to provide context for more transient symptom states; it "emphasizes the realization that all of the Axis I disorders exist in the psychological milieu we call personality" (Shea, 1991, p. 33).

Personality researchers have failed to come to any consensus regarding the best answer to their discipline's most fundamental ontological question: What is personality? As with any construct, definitions and emphases reflect the theoretical frameworks adopted by those offering them (Endler & Parker, 1990). For the purposes of the present discussion, we would conceptualize personality in the following way:

> Behavior is a function of a continuous multidirectional process of person-by-situation interactions; cognitive, motivational and emotional factors have important determining roles on behavior, regarding the person side, and the perception or psychological meaning that the situation has for the person is an essential determining factor of behavior. (Endler, 1983, p. 160)

Thus what has been regarded as personality is the ongoing and constructive process of the individual's engagement with his or her world (see Magnusson &

Norman S. Endler and Laura J. Summerfeldt • Department of Psychology, York University, North York, Ontario M3J 1P3, Canada.

International Handbook of Personality and Intelligence, edited by Donald H. Saklofske and Moshe Zeidner. Plenum Press, New York, 1995.

Törestad, 1993). In this process, a primary integrative role is played by the cognitive system in both the inner and outer life of the individual.

Our decision to emphasize cognitive factors reflects our perception of a common theme running through the three relatively self-contained literatures on personality, intelligence, and psychopathology. As Endler and Parker (1992), Magnusson and Törestad (1993), and many others have noted, the field of personality has been in a state of fragmentation almost since its inception. We do not wish to contribute to this trend by suggesting that patterns of information processing alone are the sole determinants of an individual's adjustment. Cognitive dimensions are closely tied to affective, temperamental, and motivational structures as part of total personality configuration. Current trends in cognitive psychology, particularly in clinical contexts, stress the interdependence of cognitive and emotional subsystems (e.g., Barnard & Teasdale, 1991; G. Bower, 1981; Mandler, 1984; Oatley & Johnson-Laird, 1987). Similarly, a large empirical literature has arisen on the topic of mechanisms of self-regulation, conceptualized by Karoly (1993) as "those processes, internal and/or transactional, that enable an individual to guide his or her goal directed activities over time and across changing circumstances" (p. 25). The constructs of *self-monitoring* (Ford, 1987) and *self-efficacy* (Bandura, 1986), increasingly recognized in the personality field, are hypothesized as variables mediating between intentional activity and an individual's mental, emotional, and sensory states. Similar trends are apparent in the literature on intelligence. Illustratively, Sternberg (1990) has suggested that intelligence should be regarded as "mental self-government," as it provides "a means to govern ourselves so that our thoughts and actions are organized, coherent, and responsive to both our internally driven needs and to the needs of the environment" (p. 49).

An understanding of current and premorbid intellectual functioning has long been considered a valuable part of clinical assessment and treatment planning. The methods used in its determination, however, may be particularly unsuited to this task. The equation of intelligence with academic aptitude, IQ, or general intelligence (g) is particularly problematic, because of both its explanatory limitations (Ceci, 1990) and the rationale it provides for the use of most standardized intelligence tests in clinical contexts. As Kay (1989) has indicated, "The meaning of a defective IQ score is essentially ambiguous; it tells little about the nature of the cognitive disorder, that is, the sources and processes involved" (p. 183). Though profile analyses for clinical groups and idiographic interpretive strategies (e.g., Sattler, 1982) attempt to remedy this problem, they are still reliant upon the same basic test materials. These materials, as Kay (1989) has stressed, are neither developed nor standardized with psychiatric populations foremost in mind. Such psychometric tools may then be of limited utility in attempts to understand the cognitive structures and processes associated with particular diagnostic categories.

Interest in the relationship between cognition and psychopathology is not new (see Neisser, 1976). As Monroe and Roberts (1991) have indicated, however, until relatively recently clinical researchers have relied on self-report measures as an indirect index of structural and process components of cognition. This introspective approach to the investigation of patterns in information processing suffers from a number of problems of interpretation, including response biases and the confounding influence of features of the disorders themselves (Dagleish & Watts, 1990; Kay, 1989). Consequently, there has been growing interest in the application of information-processing paradigms to the investigation of the role of cognition in the genesis and maintenance of psychopathology.

This chapter seeks to explore classic and recent research findings in this literature, as well as the models associated with them. These will be discussed in terms of their consequences for intellectual adjustment, their clinical significance, and their expression in the more general pattern of functioning known as personality. Although statements about causality are premature, the implicit assumption throughout this field is that many psychiatric disorders represent the behavioral and emotional consequences of underlying distortions, biases, and restrictions in the processing of information. It is not unlikely that a number of factors, including genetic, biochemical, and physiological mechanisms, may contribute to the etiology of many disorders. Cognitive theories, however, maintain that it is their manifestation in particular patterns of thought that ultimately serve to elicit psychopathology (see MacLeod, 1991). Such biological variables, in conjunction with social factors, also play a role in personality (see Endler, 1993). This chapter, however, will focus on psychological factors, primarily cognitive processes. Three diagnostic categories will be discussed: personality, mood, and anxiety disorders. Others, for which neurological conceptualizations are often useful, such as schizophrenia and the organic mental syndromes, will not be addressed.

THE INTELLIGENCE CONSTRUCT AND PERSONALITY

As in the case of personality, there is a lack of general agreement on the best definition of intelligence. This pervasive conceptual uncertainty is apparent in summary statements such as that of R. W. Howard (1993):" a concept of intelligence thus consists of information about a general category labelled by the word intelligence" (p. 27). Detailed accounts of this construct are offered elsewhere in this volume; for the purposes of the present discussion, it suffices to note that research and theory regarding the role of intellectual functioning in psychopathology have traditionally been guided by the psychometric tradition, in which the term *intelligence* is often used synonymously with IQ. Illustratively, standard intelligence measures such as the revised Wechsler Adult Intelligence Scale (WAIS-R, Wechsler, 1981) are still standardly administered as part of clinical diagnostic assessment (see Wetzler & Katz, 1989).

In recent years there has been a growing tendency to view intelligence in terms of the concepts and mechanisms hypothesized by the field of cognitive psychology (see Sternberg & Detterman, 1986; Sternberg & Frensch, 1990). Thus the intellectual adjustment of the individual is seen as reflective of total cognitive functioning and the coordinated interaction of structural components (e.g., knowledge domains) with cognitive processes. The latter, in the words of Ceci (1990), are "mechanisms involved in the translation and interpretation of sensory information into mental representations . . . and in bringing previously translated information back into consciousness" (p. 24). Thus attention, encoding, inferential reasoning, interpretation, and all forms of memory play roles in one's ability to synthesize both internal and external experience. These and structural components act symbiotically, with efficient and relatively accurate processing adding to the complexity of cognitive structures, and with existing structures helping to guide and shape the processes that mediate between the environment and themselves. In this view, intelligence represents the flexibility, accuracy, and complexity of the total cognitive configuration.

Recognition of the importance of cognitive processes by intelligence theorists may be found throughout the field's history (Sternberg & Frensch, 1990). Nonetheless, it is only in recent years that clinical conceptual and empirical accounts have begun to be guided more by cognitive considerations than by those that drove the IQ literature. When general intellectual functioning is conceptualized in this way, the task of delineating the interrelationships among intelligence, personality, and psychopathology becomes infinitely less difficult. Personality, as we have seen, is a reflection of the way the individual organizes and integrates both internal (i.e., emotional) and environmental information, then expresses this in behavior. The cognitive system, then, plays an active constructive role in the individual's general adjustment (Been-Zeev, 1988; Ceci, 1990; Endler & Magnusson, 1976). In this regard, Magnusson and Törestad (1993) have maintained that "the individual's selection, interpretation, and use of information from the environment plays a basic role in the way in which he/she functions and develops" (p. 429). *Intelligence*, interpreted broadly, is a term used to describe one's general competence in these endeavors.

In the works of the most influential figures in the fields of personality and intelligence, one finds repeated reference to the inextricable web of interrelationships among these two constructs and cognition. Binet, who was never satisfied with his efforts to define intelligence precisely (Matarazzo, 1979), regarded intellect as a collection of internal events representative of the individual's characteristic modes of organizing experience. As J. C. Howard (1989) has indicated, "Binet never attempted to remove intelligence from the total personality" (p. 158). Similarly, Terman (1916) conceptualized intelligence in terms of a complex system of intellectual functions that could not be considered apart from the context provided by personality. A strikingly similar approach was taken by Allport (1937): "A person's pattern of intelligence is idiographic . . . partly because intelligence is blended inextricably with the total personality" (p. 65). All of these orientations have referred to both intelligence and personality in terms of the person's synthesis and coordination of experience as expressed in behavior, emotion, thought, and communication. It is unfortunate that this view was lost in the flurry of psychometric activity inspired by these, and other authors', methodological innovations. Hans Eysenck (1970), by comparison, has used the superordinate term of *personality* to describe the coordination of two separate psychological components: noncognitive, emotional elements, or temperament, and intelligence (see also H. Eysenck & Eysenck, 1985). Even Wechsler, in his failed efforts to establish the "Hold versus Don't Hold" components of IQ, sought to determine those relatively enduring forms of intellectual functioning that changed little over the life span (see Lezak, 1983).

The implications of these views of both intelligence and personality for adjustment are quite clear. The coordinated system of cognitive structures and processes, operating together with emotions, motives, values, and goals, serves to determine a number of adaptive capacities of clinical significance. These include the ability to learn from experience (or integrate novel information), to exhibit cognitive flexibility (or adapt one's characteristic modes of processing information to changing environmental demands), and to use abstract thought and insight to solve problems. These themes and others will arise throughout our discussion of the role of cognitive factors in the experience of both (a) enduring patterns of personality pathology and (b) the more transient symptom states found in anxiety and mood disorders.

Social and Emotional Intelligences

The notion that there are different forms of intelligence has long been present in the field and is a primary feature of contemporary "systems" approaches to the concept (see Sternberg, 1990). For the purposes of the present discussion, two constructs are particularly noteworthy: social and emotional intelligence. The former (and older) of the two has been traditionally conceptualized in terms of interpersonal astuteness (see Thorndike, 1920), often with manipulative connotations (Weinstein, 1969). More recently, Sternberg (1985; Wagner & Sternberg, 1986) has maintained that a key component of what he has termed "practical intelligence" is tacit knowledge—knowledge about the social environment that is acquired through implicit cues, or "what one needs to know to adapt to a given context that is not explicitly taught and that often is not even verbalized" (Sternberg & Frensch, 1990, p. 91). A less instrumental conceptualization is found in Gardner's (1983; Walters & Gardner, 1986) notion of "interpersonal intelligence," which entails one's understanding of the moods, intentions, and motives of others.

Thus, in more recent formulations, the individual's insight regarding the nonverbal and emotional cues provided by others is given recognition. Here we see the overlap with the emotional intelligence construct. Emotional intelligence has been defined by Salovey and Mayer (1990) as "a subset of social intelligence that involves the ability to monitor one's own and others' feelings and emotions, to discriminate among them, and to use this information to guide one's thinking and actions" (p. 189). Like Gardner's (1983) concept of "interpersonal intelligence," emotional intelligence represents a capacity to have full access to one's own emotional life and to synthesize and integrate the experiences found there. Emotional regulation, both in oneself and in others, constitutes a major feature of this general competence.

Both of these intelligences are highly pertinent to any understanding of psychopathology; similarly, features of both (e.g., empathy and expressiveness) have long been regarded as aspects of personality. Deficits in the general areas of social and emotional adjustment constitute a central feature of almost all the clinical disorders, including pervasive personality disorders and more transient symptom states. We maintain that the form and expression of these psychopathological conditions is reflective of more general ways of organizing and processing both internal and external experience. Social and emotional adjustment, in this view, is inextricably linked with more fundamental cognitive tendencies (see also Barnard & Teasdale, 1991).

Cognitive Schemata

The schema construct, perhaps best conceptualized as a hypothetical cognitive structure that determines the seeking and organizing of all new information, figures prominently in accounts of cognitive factors in psychopathology. There is little agreement on a precise definition, however, although a useful conceptualization has been offered by Ingram and Wisnicki (1991): "A schema consists of an organized, prototypical abstraction of complex concepts that are induced from past experience with the concepts represented, and that guides the acquisition of information through purposeful processing of input" (p. 197). This seems to be the most common understanding of the term, and despite criticisms that its clinical usage has been guided by obsolete models (MacLeod, 1990), its heuristic value must be recognized. The most familiar analogue of this construct in the field of personality is George Kelly's (1955) "personal construct" formulation.

Cognitive Styles

In our attempt to integrate the literatures on personality, intelligence, and psychopathology, perhaps the most valuable bridging concept has been that of cognitive style. This term is used to describe self-consistent modes of perceiving, focusing attention, organizing information and thought, and remembering, and has been thought by Millon (1990b) to be "among the most useful indices to the clinician of the patient's distinctive way of functioning" (p. 146).

Cognitive styles may influence the form of both symptoms and highly adaptive traits, and a number of specific stylistic dimensions have traditionally been thought to reflect their influence (see Hashway & Duke, 1992, for a review). "Tolerance for ambiguity and novelty," for example, represents the individual's need for precision, definition, and the concordance of new experiences with preconceived notions (see Frenkel-Brunswick, 1949). The degree to which an individual prefers to organize information into discrete and clearly defined categories is thought to indicate their degree of "conceptual differentiation" (Gardner, Jackson, & Messick, 1960; Gardner & Moriarty, 1968). The cognitive style dimension of "scanning"—a term used frequently in this chapter—refers to the extensiveness and breadth of one's deployment of attention to all features, both relevant and irrelevant, of the stimulus field (see Messick, 1989). The individual's proclivity for organizing experience into narrow and minimally related bundles of information is referred to as the cognitive variable of "category width."

All of these dimensions of cognitive style are useful in the understanding of how manifestations of psychopathology reflect underlying modes of processing information. By the same token, they help reveal how general intellectual functioning—the synthesis and adaptive coordination of experience (Ingram & Kendall, 1987)—may be impaired by the availability to the cognitive system of a highly restricted and frequently biased range of information about the environment. As Sternberg (1990) has indicated, intelligence involves the interaction of both existing knowledge bases and ongoing cognitive processes. The cognitive-style construct serves to explain the form and content of both of these contributing variables. When such cognitive styles become inflexible, and when they are used in situations to which they are poorly suited, the individual is unable to adapt effectively to a wide range of life circumstances.

PERSONALITY DISORDERS AND COGNITION

The adoption of a multiaxial format in the third edition of the *Diagnostic and Statistical Manual of Mental Disorders* (DSM-III; APA, 1980) marked a significant turning point in approaches to clinical diagnosis. The inclusion of disorders of personality on the separate and crucial Axis II represented an acknowledgement that a diagnosis based on manifest symptoms is often incomplete without consideration of the context provided by more enduring personality patterns (see Millon, 1990a).

We have already discussed personality and its complexities. According to DSM-IV (APA, 1994), it is only when the associated characteristics (or traits) are inflexible and maladaptive, and cause either substantial impairment or subjective distress, that they may be considered personality disorders. The point on the continuum at which a coordinated constellation of traits constitutes a disturbance is far from clear. Millon (1969, 1990a), a recognized authority in this area, has proposed three chief differentiating features. The first, *functional inflexibility*, describes the rigid imposition of characteristic modes of relating, thinking, and perceiving upon even those situations not amenable to such an approach. It represents a basic inability to adjust one's strategies to contextual demands. The genesis and maintenance of *vicious circles* is the second distinguishing feature. Habitual modes of thought and action may restrict experience in such a way that one's problems are continually reinforced and reactivated: "Personality disorders are themselves pathogenic. . . . (They) set into motion self-defeating sequences that cause their already established difficulties not only to persist, but to be further aggravated" (Millon, 1990a, p. 342). Finally, Millon has proposed *structural instability*, or these personality patterns' lack of structural integrity under conditions of stress, to be a feature distinguishing normal functioning from pathology.

It is clear that the effects of disordered personality are evident in all areas of experience, including interpersonal, emotional, and intellectual domains. Similarly, the primary determinant of such pathology can in no way be regarded as a single deficit. It is reflective of a synchronized configuration of psychological structures and functions, as well as the control systems that regulate both internal and external experience (see Karoly, 1993). Nonetheless, characteristic ways of organizing and processing information and experience—in other words, cognitive styles—appear to play primary roles in the genesis and perpetuation of personality disorders. Self-consistent modes of perceiving, remembering, thinking, and problem solving are evident in each of the patterns identified in DSM-IV. Their primacy has been acknowledged in this work: "personality traits are enduring patterns of perceiving, relating to, and thinking about the environment and oneself, and are exhibited in a wide range of important social and personal contexts" (APA, 1994, p. 630).

In our discussion we will address cognitive and intellectual expressions of personality and their implications for the general functioning of the individual. A specific theoretical orientation to the origins of these cognitive consistencies will not be taken; the reader is referred to Millon (1981) for an extensive review of explanatory models. A cognitive account of these patterns is not incompatible with any of these orientations. As Shapiro (1965) has maintained, a person's "general style of thinking may be considered a matrix from which the various traits, symptoms, and defense mechanisms crystallize" (p. 2). It is possible that regardless of the etiological factors involved, it is the manifestation of particular cognitive styles that serves ultimately to shape the clinical features of personality disorders. The distinction between proximal (immediate) and distal (ultimate) causes, in this case, is particularly useful (see Massaro & Cowan, 1993).

Many of the constructs already discussed (e.g., cognitive schemata, social and emotional intelligence) figure prominently in clinical and theoretical accounts. An inability to synthesize internal experience and deficits in the regulation of affect, key components of emotional intelligence, have long been associated with schizoid, borderline, and obsessive-compulsive patterns. Similarly, the interpersonal awareness and empathy associated with social intelligence appear to be the source of considerable difficulties in almost all the recognized personality disorders. We have chosen to emphasize the role of cognitive styles and schemata in the individual's patterns of engagement with the world. These concepts may serve to explain, in part, the higher-order social and emotional dysfunction associated with Axis II disorders. Our conceptual organization of these categories will mirror that of the DSM-IV classificatory framework.

Cluster A

Paranoid, schizoid, and schizotypal personality disorders may be grouped together according to the shared features of oddness or eccentricity (APA, 1994). Though such a descriptive criterion offers little insight into more meaningful shared causal or functional characteristics (see Million, 1990b, for a general discussion of this topic), it is highly consistent with specified diagnostic criteria (Marshall & Barbaree, 1991). As with all the personality disorders, these conditions represent relatively enduring patterns of behaving, integrating emotional experience, thinking, and perceiving. As such, cognitive tendencies form only a part of a complex pattern of interrelated systems that determines ultimate maladjustment. Despite this, their pervasive influence is evident in the way the individual processes information in a wide variety of domains—a fact underscored in diagnostic criteria, clinical and theoretical accounts, and the few empirical investigations that have been made of them. Our discussion will be limited to the schizotypal and paranoid patterns.

Schizotypal Personality Disorder

The defining characteristic in this case is an enduring and pervasive pattern of odd behaviors and cognitions, many of which are shared with schizophrenia, but not of sufficient severity to warrant that diagnosis. Among these eccentricities, DSM-IV has included odd beliefs, magical or superstitious thought, disturbed ideas of reference, and oddities in speech and perceptual experience. The foremost presenting feature is eccentricity of thought (Marshall & Barbaree, 1991).

It has been suggested that relative to other Axis II categories, the cognitive mechanisms associated with this disorder have received the greatest amount of empirical attention, perhaps because of their value as neurocognitive markers for vulnerability to schizophrenia (Morey, 1993). The significance of these observations for the understanding of the specific mechanisms involved in the personality disorder itself has been proposed by Morey (1993), who notes that they "provide an assessment of sensory input regulation and attentional functioning" (p. 159). Although such indices of low-level cognitive functioning as resting EEGs may help to identify signs of vulnerability to the more florid symptoms of schizophrenia, they provide little insight into the patterns of thought and association observed in individuals with the personality disorder. Millon (1986, 1990a) has conceptualized these as "cognitively autistic," a label descriptive of their blurring of reality boundaries and the constant intrusion of tangentially related material into thought and communication.

It is implicit in Millon's formulation that the difference between this personality disorder and schizophrenia is one of degree and not of kind. In a content analysis of clinical vignettes, Sternbach, Judd, Sabo, McGlashan, and Gunderson (1992) found considerable evidence for cognitive and perceptual distortions associated with this personality pattern. Relevantly, research with normal subjects has suggested the relationship between such eccentricities of thought and the loss of cognitive integration associated with severe psychopathology. In one such study, Allen, Chapman, and Chapman (1987) found that undergraduates who scored deviantly high on a measure of perceptual aberration and magical thinking (both key components of DSM-IV diagnostic criteria) were also found to exhibit significant cognitive slippage, evidenced in idiosyncratic word associations and disturbances of referential communication.

Empirical support also exists for clinical impressions regarding schizotypal patients' problems with the regulation of irrelevant cognitive material. In a study of the relationship between schizotypal characteristics in nonclinical subjects and cognitive inhibition, Beech, McManus, Baylis, Tipper, and Agar (1991) found that "high schizotypes" exhibited significantly less ability to selectively ignore irrelevant stimuli than did low schizotypes. Similarly, one index of one's capacity to attend selectively to target stimuli while screening out distractors is sustained attention. Recently, Obiols, Garcia-Domingo, De Trinchería and Doménech (1993) have reported that subjects high in schizotypic traits have a higher proportion of missing responses to target trials on a sustained attention task than do control subjects. Such results provide compelling evidence for the role of information-processing deficits in this personality pattern, in both normal and clinical populations.

Paranoid Personality Disorder

Patients classified with paranoid personality disorder (PPD) exhibit an enduring tendency to interpret a wide variety of occurrences, particularly in interpersonal contexts, as having negative and threatening intent. This overpersonalization has been described in the DSM-IV in terms of pervasive suspiciousness and a proclivity to read negative meanings into even the most benign of remarks or events.

The basic cognitive feature then appears to be interconnected schemata, or a coherent belief system, regarding hostile self-reference. Such structures serve to guide the acquisition of new information through purposeful and restricted processing of input (Ingram & Wisnicki, 1991). This is particularly true of PPD, in which an ever larger circle of events is incorporated into the cognitive web of perceived interrelatedness. Efforts to maintain the integrity of these schemata make this personality disorder among the most difficult to treat. In the words of Millon (1981), "Therapeutic work with paranoids is a touchy proposition at best. . . . Excessive friendliness and overt sympathies often connote deceit to these patients" (p. 398). Such cognitive tendencies are self-perpetuating; by provoking discomfort in others through their hostility and distrust, the individual virtually guarantees the negative outcome that he or she has come to expect.

In one of the few existing studies of this subject, Thompson-Pope and Turkat (1988) investigated responses of individuals with paranoid personalities and normal controls to ambiguous experimental stimuli. Subjects were asked to match picture content with a list provided by the investigators. Paranoid personalities were distinguished by their accurate identification of stimuli in the earliest, most ambiguous stages, and by their voiced suspiciousness that correct answers were intentionally missing from the provided rating list. Some evidence was therefore provided of such individuals' interpersonal assumptions, as well as their vigilant efforts to find meaning in ambiguous contexts.

Hypervigilance regarding information congruent with their belief systems is a recognized clinical feature of individuals with this disorder: "In a new situation [they] intensely and narrowly search for confirmation of their expectations" (APA, 1987, p. 337). Though little empirical investigation has been made of this phenomenon, an interesting conceptualization has been offered of its origination in basic information-processing tendencies. *Focused scanning*, as a general cognitive orientation to both external perceptual fields and internal knowledge structures, entails broad coverage of stimulus fields with a highly restricted attentional focus. Messick (1989) has proposed that the paranoid cognitive style entails such extensive scanning of a broad range of fields with a highly selective attentional strategy. In this way, schema-congruent "evidence" might be collected in a number of domains while permitting ongoing alertness for potential threats to the self. Furthermore, information not consistent with the paranoid belief system may be screened out, effectively guaranteeing the confirmatory nature of acquired information (Wachtel, 1967). Messick has likened this general processing style to continuous "signal detection," an observation markedly similar to one made by Cameron (1963): "The paranoid personality must be vigilant in order to safeguard himself" (p. 645). This feature played a central role in DSM-III diagnostic criteria, which included "hypervigilance, manifested by continual scanning of the environment for signs of threat" (APA, 1980, p. 309).

In summary, despite the lack of empirical findings, clinical and theoretical accounts offer compelling evidence for the central role of cognitive styles in the maladjustment associated with PPD. Well organized schemata serve to restrict the information available to the cognitive system to only that material most consistent with the existing framework. In this way, the paranoid style is reinforced and perpetuated (Beck & Freeman, 1990). Impoverishment in interpersonal, emotional, and intellectual functioning is the inevitable consequence.

Cluster B

In DSM-IV, antisocial, borderline, histrionic, and narcissistic personality disorders are grouped together on the basis of the shared features of dramatic, emotional, or erratic behaviors, appearance, and expressed thoughts. The arbitrariness of this grouping has been noted elsewhere (Marshall & Barbaree, 1991). Nonetheless, a general underdevelopment of cognitive resources, although manifested in different ways, seems to characterize all of these patterns. This feature of the dramatic cluster has been broadly identified by Burgess (1992) as an impaired capacity for cognitive planning or integrative operations that is particularly evident in future-oriented tasks requiring multiple steps and simultaneous considerations. Investigations of such cognitive features have been particularly fruitful in the case of antisocial and histrionic personality disorders. The remaining classifications, although the focus of vast literatures, are surrounded by theoretical controversy, little of it guided by cognitive models. The antisocial, histrionic, and narcissistic patterns will be discussed in this section.

Antisocial Personality Disorder

The constellation of traits and behaviors characteristic of individuals diagnosed with antisocial personality disorder (APD) includes insensitivity and indifference to the rights of others; an enduring pattern of irresponsible, antisocial, and frequently unlawful activity; and a general tendency to disregard the implications of one's actions (APA, 1994). In the words of Marshall and Barbaree (1991), "Their behavior is often impulsive, irresponsible or reckless, and they show little regard for future consequences" (p. 365). It has been suggested that current diagnostic approaches overemphasize the criminal aspects of this disorder, to the neglect of more general personality traits (Hare, Hart, & Harpur, 1991; Kernberg, 1989; Millon, 1981, 1983; Rogers & Dion, 1991; see also Widiger & Corbitt, 1993). Nonetheless, investigations of underlying cognitive features have revealed general patterns with implications for the understanding of both of these phenomena.

In their discussion of cognitive therapy objectives for such patients, Beck and Freeman (1990) have identified the following cognitive distortions: self-serving beliefs that emphasize immediate gratification and disregard future consequences, concrete thought processes, and a loss of future time perspective. Such cognitive characteristics, targeted by these authors as key therapeutic foci (see Salama, 1988, for alternative considerations), have received considerable empirical attention. In an authoritative discussion of cognitive features of APD, Gorenstein (1991) reviews the research literature. Although many of the paradigms and interpretations associated with this body of work show the influence of classical learning theory, the growing consensus appears to be that distortions or deficits in mental representations of environmental contingencies may play a primary role. This may be particularly evident in the case of response perseveration, a characteristic thought to reflect inadequate abstract mental representations and an incapacity for cognitive evaluation of the advantages and disadvantages of a given action in the absence of explicit situational cues.

In one illustrative study, Newman, Patterson, and Nathan (1987) sought to investigate the perseveration of a dominant reinforcement-linked behavior even in the face of punishment. In a computer-simulated card-turning exercise, subjects were rewarded for revealing face cards and were punished (i.e., lost money) when number cards were turned up. Following the first round, during which the probability of being rewarded was intentionally increased in order to elicit a dominant card-turning response, the reward/punishment ration was gradually reversed, so that by the last trial every card turned resulted in punishment. Subjects were free to cease playing at any point. In accordance with expectation, subjects high in psychopathy (a construct similar to antisocial personality; Hare, 1980) continued to play significantly longer than normal controls, with the majority continuing to the point of almost continual punishment. Gorenstein (1991) has interpreted the results of this and a number of other studies (e.g., Gorenstein, 1982; Newman & Kosson,

1986; Newman, Widom, & Nathan, 1985) as evidence for these individuals' weak capacity for symbolic, anticipatory mental representation and their consequent reliance on established patterns of stereotyped response. In this author's words, "Cognitive mediating processes—the central nervous system's means of representing events that are not immediately available to the senses—are weak in antisocial individuals" (Gorenstein, 1991, p. 115).

Research confirming the value of such a model provides systematic evidence of the lack of sustained insight regarding future consequences, and the strong governing influence of concrete needs, long associated with this disorder. Although contradictory findings have been reported (e.g., Brown & Gutsch, 1985), a growing body of literature points to the primary influence of such cognitive tendencies, as does work on impulsivity, a related psychopathology construct (see Dickman, 1990; Matczak, 1990). Such a basic lack of cognitive autonomy will inevitably be maladaptive, and it serves to trap the individual in a ceaseless cycle of drive satisfaction. Intellectual impairment at a higher level of abstract cognitive functioning would seem to be a chief source of the impairment in societal functioning definitive of this disorder.

Narcissistic Personality Disorder

This clinical pattern has received a great deal of attention in recent years, with little of it guided by cognitive perspectives. An exception to this has been the topic of social cognition and narcissistic personality disorder (NPD), a small but growing field (see Watson, Sawrie, & Biderman, 1991). Allusions to a characteristic mode of processing information may be found throughout the literature. Olden (1946), for example, described the following intellectual characteristics: "gathering catchwords or headlines in one dashing glance, a certain ability to combine the few and superficially collected bits . . . [and being] incapable of thorough studying and learning in any one field" (p. 263).

The defining feature of NPD is egocentricity. Associated features include self-absorption and minimal interest in events not directly reinforcing of one's grandiose self-image, which may serve to explain in part the superficial processing of information commented upon by Olden (1946). Millon (1986) has emphasized the expansiveness of narcissistic cognitions and their relative independence from the constraints of objective reality. The associated imaginativeness and inflated confidence in one's opinions often result in others' initial impressions of these individuals as knowledgeable, decisive, and articulate. As Akhtar (1989) has indicated, however, the covert features of this cognitive style include knowledge of only the most shallow and trivial details (or "headline intelligence") and general impairment in the cognitive capacities required for in-depth learning and abstract, balanced knowledge about the world and oneself.

In short, the role played by cognitive factors in general intellectual and social adjustment is evident in clinical and conceptual accounts. The extent to which these tendencies occupy a causal role is unclear; the widely held view is that they represent defensive manifestations of a more primary disturbance in one's sense of self (see Akhtar, 1989; Robbins, 1989). Further investigation from a cognitive point of view may be informative.

Histrionic Personality Disorder

The most salient clinical features of individuals with histrionic personality disorder (HPD) are emotional overresponsiveness, attention seeking, and general insincerity. The relationship between clinical manifestations of this pattern and underlying cognitive styles has long been recognized. Illustratively, Shapiro (1965) has observed that "hysterical cognition in general is global, relatively diffuse, and lacking in sharpness. . . . It is impressionistic. . . . the hysterical person tends cognitively to respond quickly and is highly susceptible to what is immediately impressive, striking, or merely obvious" (pp. 111–112). Despite the nosological revision, little has been added to this description in the nearly three decades since it was offered.

Andrews and Moore (1991), in their thorough discussion of cognitive aspects of HPD, have identified global, diffuse cognitive style as a chief characteristic. Empirical support, these authors have suggested, may be found in studies using a variety of approaches. For example, McMullen and Rogers (1984), found nonclinical subjects with this histrionic traits to score higher on the Comprehension subtests of the Wechsler Adult Intelligence Scale (WAIS) than on its Information or Vocabulary subtests. High scores on the latter tests are thought to reflect concentrated, detail-oriented cognitive functioning, a feature antithetic to clinical impressions of the processing styles associated with HPD. Similar patterns on tests of intellectual functioning have been reported by Howard (1989): "General factual information is not important, and the global, impressionistic style does not provide a context that facilitates discrete memory" (p. 167).

Evidence of this style of processing information may also be found in the results of studies of HPD and field dependence-independence (Andrews & Moore, 1991). Field dependence is associated with a relative inability to differentiate important elements of information from the distracting stimuli in the surrounding field. More broadly, it is indicative of a global style of categorization and reliance on external cues rather than internal representations (Witkin, Dyk, Fattuson, Goodenough, & Karp, 1962). A number of studies have demonstrated that subjects high in histrionic characteristics also show heightened field dependence (e.g., Lawrence & Morton, 1980; Magaro & Smith, 1981). These findings support the conceptualization offered by Millon (1986, 1990b), in which overattentiveness to fleeting and trivial external events figures prominently.

The lack of cognitive integration implicit in these observations has been addressed by Messick (1989) in a different way. Referring to the histrionic individual's attentional processing strategies, he has noted that they are "responsive to the striking and obvious features of the environment, with thinking and judgement dominated by quick impressions, hunches, and vagueness" (p. 9). The consequences of this cognitive style, as we have seen, are apparent in a number of domains, including perceptions of self and others, intellectual functioning, and social adjustment.

Cluster C

According to DSM-IV, avoidant, dependent, obsessive-compulsive, and passive-aggressive personality disorders may be grouped together according to their shared features of anxiety and fearfulness. Although these characteristics are manifested in different ways, for each of these patterns they are associated with relatively inflexible patterns of cognition and behavior, the effects of which are apparent in almost all areas of functioning. It is clear that dysfunctional beliefs and interpretive distortions play an important role in dependent and passive-aggressive personality disorders (see Beck & Freeman, 1990). Nonetheless, the investigation of these disorders has focused more on interpersonal strategies and self-schemas than on general cognitive or intellectual functioning (see Bornstein, 1992; Small, Small, Alig, & Moore, 1970). Consequently, and in view of space limitations, our discussion of this cluster will be restricted to the avoidant and obsessive-compulsive patterns.

Avoidant Personality Disorder

The primary feature of this disorder is a pervasive and enduring pattern of sensitivity to the disapproval of others, social insecurity, and overestimation of the probability of failure and rejection. As the appellation suggests, such individuals also tend to avoid situations—particularly interpersonal ones—where their fears might be realized (APA, 1994). The general lack of an empirical basis for statements about underlying causal mechanisms and definitive features has been lamented elsewhere (Millon, 1991); however, a considerable body of literature has arisen surrounding this pattern's utility in the understanding of agoraphobia and forms of phobic disorder (e.g., Hoffart & Martinsen, 1992; Mattick & Newman, 1991; Renneberg, Chambless, & Gracely, 1992; Starcevic, 1992). Implicit in such efforts is the belief that characteristic strategies for processing information about one's experience may be associated with the development of debilitating patterns of behavior.

Beck and Freeman (1990) have proposed that avoidant patients have several dysfunctional beliefs, or what these authors have considered to be schemata, concerning self and others. All of these are variations on the theme of personal inefficacy and probable rejection. The expression of these in characteristic information-processing styles was alluded to by Millon (1969) in his introduction of the construct to the literature: "[The patient] has learned to be watchful . . . to be on guard against the ridicule and contempt he anticipates from others. . . . He must be ever-alert" (p. 237). Unfortunately, no empirical investigation has been made of this characteristic, perhaps because of the recency of the disorder's inclusion in widely used diagnostic frameworks.

One suggestive study, however, has been made of the role of cognitive style in agoraphobia, an Axis I classification frequently associated with avoidant personality disorder (APD; e.g., Renneberg et al., 1992). Fitzgerald and Phillips (1991), in an attempt to clarify the attentional components of agoraphobic avoidance, administered tests of field dependence-independence to agoraphobics and two groups of controls (clinical and normal). It was found that agoraphobics showed enhanced levels of field dependence, a result interpreted by the investigators in terms of an inability to distinguish threatening stimuli from their context and a predisposition for the development of diffuse cognitive "fear networks." The subjects used in this study were not diagnosed with APD, but the results, interpreted cautiously, suggest some of the topics that researchers should address. As frequent references to specific attentional and interpretive strategies are made in clinical accounts of this disorder, it is clear that cognitive factors may be a fruitful area of study.

Obsessive-Compulsive Personality Disorder

An all-encompassing striving for control and absolute completion characterizes individuals diagnosed with this disorder. This is manifested in a pattern of perfectionism and inflexibility evident in all areas of functioning (APA, 1994). The influence of cognitive factors, perhaps more evident in this than in any other personality disorder, has been acknowledged in clinical and theoretical accounts since the turn of the century (e.g., Abraham, 1921; Fenichel, 1945; Janet, 1903; Rado, 1959; Salzman, 1973, 1980). These authors, despite their divergent theoretical orientations, have all remarked upon the pervasive influence of characteristic modes of perceiving and arranging experiences in the obsessional individual's engagement with the world.

The rigidity of obsessional cognition in such individuals has been described by Millon (1986): "[He or she] constructs the world in terms of rules, regulations, time schedules, and social hierarchies" (quoted in Millon, 1990a, p. 366). Beck and Freeman (1990) analogously have emphasized globally dichotomous thinking as the cognitive distortion most characteristic of this disorder (see also Mollinger, 1980). These features have been given consideration by Reed (1985, 1991), who has proposed that all of the classic obsessional traits—conscientiousness, pedantry, moral rigidity, valuation of routines, regulations and established codes of conduct—represent active attempts by the individual to impose structure on experience.

If, as Reed (1985) suggested, obsessionals "strive for clarity, definition, and clear-cut boundaries" (p. 46), few experiences will be compatible with their perceptual and cognitive style, a characteristic sharing many features with what Sorrentino and his associates (e.g., Sorrentino & Hewitt, 1984; Sorrentino, Short, & Raynor, 1984) have termed a "certainty-orientation." Thus, although these individuals will seek to include as much material as possible in their cognitive operations, the need to structure such information carefully will result in its encoding in terms of exceedingly discrete, rigidly delineated details and ideas, with little attention given to relationships (Wachtel, 1967). This style, termed "non-inclusive all-inclusiveness" by Mollinger (1980), precludes the possibility of integrative cognitive functioning. Reed (1991) has reported a number of research findings congruent with this conceptualization. The same general theme is apparent in Messick's (1989) discussion of information-processing styles: "the obsessive-compulsive style is characterized by extensive scanning of stimulus fields using a narrow, high-fidelity attentional bandwidth" (p. 9). This argument has been lent credence by empirical demonstrations of the obsessional cognitive style and its manifestations in particular behavioral tendencies. Rosenberg (1953), for example, found that following tachiscopic presentation of ambiguous designs, such individuals tended to prefer symmetrical, orderly choices. Similarly, Rosenwald (1972) concluded that highly obsessional persons spend more time imposing order on a disordered, unstructured situation than do those low in obsessional traits.

Their meticulousness and attention to detail often results in others' perception of obsessionals as conscientious and intelligent. Regarding these individuals' actual performance on the WAIS-R, J. C. Howard (1989) has observed that they typically display high scores on tests that assess acquired information and concept formation. Frequently, however, their preoccupation with detail will result in poor Performance scores, reflective of an impaired ability to distinguish between essential and nonessential details. In short, although the cognitive characteristics discussed may be quite adaptive in a number of contexts, they leave the individual ill-prepared to deal with experiences not amenable to the imposition of absolute boundaries and clearly defined categories. It is because a great many of life's tasks take this form that obsessive-compulsive personality disorder may be associated with the onset of more severe forms of psychopathology (Millon, 1981).

Summary

Clinical and theoretical accounts, as well as the few existing empirical studies, all point to the role of cognitive factors in the patterns which constitute personality disorders. Consistencies in the ways that such individuals organize and process information and experience appear to be determinant of general maladjustment in a number of areas. These cognitive styles, in moderation, may be adaptive in a limited range of contexts. Nonetheless, the breadth and richness of the information available to the individual may be profoundly restricted. General intellectual functioning, defined in terms of flexibility of thought and the availability to the cognitive system of an extensive range of internal representations, is necessarily affected. Impoverished social and emotional functioning may be similarly predicted.

A number of symptom syndromes, or Axis I disorders, have been associated with the personality patterns that have been discussed (see Millon, 1981, for a summary). The direction of causality in these relationships is not clear. Personality patterns may render an individual vulnerable to particular clinical disorders (Klerman, 1973), or to certain environmental stressors that, in interaction with such predispositions, result in clinical syndromes. Alternatively, both characterological features and such clinical states as depression may share a common cause or third factor (Doherty, Feister, & Shea, 1986).

Despite this ambiguity, it is apparent that habitual modes of processing information play a role in many Axis I disorders. The rest of this chapter will address this issue as it pertains to two broad diagnostic categories: anxiety and mood disorders. The cognitive biases and styles associated with Axis II disorders are pervasive and enduring; they appear to be in operation on a relatively continuous basis in almost all areas of functioning. The growing consensus among cognitive theorists seems to be that the processing tendencies associated with Axis I disorders are more circumscribed and transient, but that they nonetheless play a crucial role.

MOOD DISORDERS AND COGNITION: DEPRESSION

Depressive psychopathology, subsumed under the category of mood disorders in DSM-IV (APA, 1994), includes major depression, dysthymia, and the more temporally limited category of major depressive episode. These syndromes share a common feature of depressed affect, characterized by feelings of sadness, disappointment and despair. Co-occurring features include reduced interest, feelings of guilt and worthlessness, and impairment in concentration. Dysthymia, which has received much attention in the work of Akiskal (e.g., 1983), is used to describe a form of minor depression evidenced in habitual gloominess, overconscientiousness, and preoccupation with personal inadequacy. Such patients, whom Akiskal has described as "ambulatory depressives," rarely achieve the diagnostic criteria for major depressive illness but tend to be perpetually handicapped by their mood disturbance. This category may be likened to what has long been conceptualized as "depressive personality"—a term that does not currently have formal classificatory status, though it is familiar to many clinicians (see Phillips, Hirschfeld, Shea, & Gunderson, 1993). In short, the salient clinical feature of depressive disorders is mood disturbance. Despite this, the cognitive features of these disorders have received more attention from both theorists and researchers than those of any other form of psychopathology.

The cognitive dysfunction characteristic of the depressed patient influences the accurate and efficient acquisition of new information, as well as the ability to use such information to guide adaptive behavior. As such, it has profound implications for the individual's level of adjustment in a number of domains. This disordered cognitive functioning is found (as we discuss in detail below) in bias and impairment in the processes involved in attention, comprehension, and memory. Before addressing empirical findings, a brief review will be made of two cognitive models thought to have explanatory value: Beck's schema theory, and the semantic network model of G. H. Bower.

Models of Cognition in Depression

Interest in cognitive factors contributing to the etiology and perpetuation of depression was first prompted by the information-processing model of Beck (1967, 1976). This model suggested that depressed individuals possess a negative self-schema that is responsible for consistently negative views of self, the world, and the future (the "cognitive triad"). More recent revisions have adopted a more complex diathesis-stress orientation (e.g., Beck, 1984), which maintains that interrelated webs of depressive schemata may be seen as "deep" cognitive structures or vulnerabilities activated, indirectly, by events perceived as stressors.

Relevantly, several studies have reported increased levels of depression associated with the interaction of dysfunctional attitudes and negative life events (see Kuiper, Olinger, & Air, 1989). Such findings may be congruent with Beck's (1976) proposal that depressive schemata are dormant cognitive structures that remain relatively uninfluential in processing until activated by elevations in depressed mood associated with specific negative events. Segal and Shaw

(1986) have explained the vulnerability of certain individuals to depression in terms of the "operation of latent but potentially reactive cognitive structures that are activated by events idiosyncratically interpreted as personally significant" (p. 674). Such formulations have prompted an increased interest in the types of stressors serving to activate these dormant structures (see Beck, 1983). Most important for the present discussion is the proposal that once active, these schemata give rise to processing biases throughout the cognitive system, influencing attention, interpretation, and memory for emotionally toned information.

Conceptualizations of biasing schemata in depressives as latent factors in operation only at particular times have led a number of researchers to suggest that therapeutic improvement reflects these factors' return to dormancy (e.g., Simons, Murphy, Levine, & Wetzel, 1986); others have proposed that therapy effects actual structural changes in schemata (Winfrey & Goldfried, 1986). Though such interpretations are congruent with suggestions that individuals may draw from a number of domain-specific schemata, depending upon situation requirements (G. Bower, 1981), they stand at marked odds with approaches emphasizing cross-domain cognitive styles (e.g., Messick, 1989). They also conflict somewhat with Beck's own emphasis upon the active nature of cognition. As Strauman (1991) has indicated, current approaches assign the construction of meaning a central and presumably causal role in the etiology and maintenance of emotional disorders. Objective assessment of potentially "activating" situational contingencies may be somewhat problematic.

In summary, Beck's information-processing model of depression presents a framework for understanding many of the cognitive biases frequently observed in clinical practice and research with depressed patients. This model predicts the presence of affect-congruent cognitive biases that enhance the processing of negative information. In this way, all stages of cognitive processing, including attention, interpretation, and memory, may be influenced. Thus the individual's accurate acquisition of information will be functionally impaired, and a downward spiral of depressive experiences may be predicted.

Learning and memory impairment have long been considered key components of depressive disorders, and the majority of the vast research literature that has resulted has focused on the identification of general cognitive deficits (Wright & Salmon, 1990). It has been observed, however, that these deficits often are not found in the case of emotionally congruent material, and that depressed subjects may actually exhibit facilitated processing of negative information (G. Bower, 1981). Some explanation is enabled by Beck's schema construct, with its high-level guidance of selective processing; other models, however, are also of particular relevance.

In an early network model of memory (Anderson & Bower, 1973), it was proposed that information in long-term memory is stored as network "nodes" that share associative connections with related nodes; access to stored information is enabled through the activation of appropriate nodes. As described by MacLeod (1990), the consequent spread of activation throughout the network "primes" related information, which then also becomes more easily accessible. G. Bower (1981), in an elaboration of this model, suggested that network nodes specific to particular emotional states share associated connections with nodes containing information causally related with past experiences of the same emotion. As the model emphasizes the spread of activation through associative connections, mood-congruent processing biases across a wide range of cognitive operations thus may be predicted. MacLeod (1990) has contrasted this approach with schema models, suggesting that in contrast to the latter's top-down model of idiosyncratic biases, "mood-congruency effects may percolate up through the processing system, but have their origins in low-level priming effects located within long-term memory" (p. 14).

An interesting complement to this model may be found in Barnard and Teasdale's (1991) discussion of interacting cognitive subsystems and their role in the persistence of depressive disorders. In an early network model based in part upon Bower's formulations, Teasdale (1988) suggested that the severity of depression following an initial experience of depressed mood depends upon the extent to which the individual's cognitive networks are organized to process and synthesize depressive information. The self-perpetuating function of these predisposed cognitive networks leads to a downward spiral into clinical depression (see Ingram & Wisnicki, 1991).

More recently, in the context of a systemic model of cognitive operations (Barnard, 1985), Barnard and Teasdale (1991) have suggested that emotions may progress from being innate responses to triggering stimuli, to having a highly elaborated and associatively laden form as a result of repeated life experiences. In this way, situations sharing certain symbolic features with those initially eliciting the affective response may come to have the same effect. Furthermore, the persistence of depression in the absence of objectively depressing external events may arise from reciprocal interactions among processing subsystems, so that the continued processing of depression-linked codes, their affective concomitants, and propositional (interpreted) significance become essentially self-maintaining. The code itself serves as the triggering stimulus. The overrepresentation of depressogenic cognitive material and the pattern-sensitive aspects of cognitive processes posited by this model may serve to explain some of the anomalies observed in both clinical and experimental contexts.

A related approach has been recently adopted by Sedikides and Skowronski (1991). In light of the wealth of empirical evidence for biases in processing ambiguous stimuli in terms of structures most highly active in memory, these authors have proposed a general "law of cognitive structure activation." They have suggested that the many studies indicating the more efficient processing of negative information by depressed subjects provide support for the proposition that negative thoughts are easily activated in such individuals. A critical analysis of the implications of this "law" for the investigation of psychopathology has been offered by Strauman (1991), who has cited the failure of studies using nonclinical samples to support associative network assumptions. He has particularly emphasized the importance not of semantic characteristics of material (a key component of network models), but of their personal significance to the individual.

In summary, though they exhibit a number of differences in terms of complexity and their capacity to explain the range of depressive symptoms and characteristics, schema and network models serve to predict the existence of pervasive processing biases that affect attention and memory for (and interpretation of) emotionally valenced material. The consequences of these operations for the accurate and efficient processing of information have been the focus of a considerable research literature.

Cognitive Deficits and Depression

A large empirical literature exists concerning general cognitive deficits associated with depressed states. As Wright and Salmon (1990) have indicated, impairment in concentration and memory has long been considered a key feature of this disorder. This is recognized in both diagnostic criteria and clinical accounts of intellectual markers of depression. In her discussion of clinical interpretation of intelligence assessment using the WAIS-R, J. C. Howard (1989) has observed that "the major mark of the depressive is a significant drop on the performance subtest" (p. 167). As this subscore is thought to be reflective of perceptual organization skills, such observations are suggestive of a general inefficiency in information-processing abilities. In a relevant longitudinal study of intellectual functioning both during depressive episodes and following clinical improvement, Sackeim, Freeman, McElhiney, Coleman, et al. (1992) reported that depressives showed a normal verbal ability but pronounced performance deficits, even following treatment. These results were interpreted as evidence for a general trait-like processing deficit that may be exacerbated by more transient symptom states.

This pattern is supported by recent findings from tests of neurocognitive performance, which suggest impairment in planning and sequencing operations but not in language ability, as assessed by tests of verbal repetition, naming of common objects, and verbal comprehension (Burgess, 1991). Interestingly, though such dysfunction was associated with acute symptoms in subjects with major depressive disorder, subjects diagnosed with personality disorders who scored high on measures of both acute and chronic depression exhibited the same pattern. This finding is suggestive of a relatively permanent cognitive deficit in individuals predisposed to depression that may become aggravated by symptom states. Interestingly, it has recently been suggested that a lack of awareness of one's own cognitive skills and performance, rather than the performance itself, is a salient cognitive feature of depression. Slife and Weaver (1992), in a study using a mood induction procedure with normal subjects, found that metacognitive abilities (i.e., knowledge about cognition and self-monitoring) varied systematically with manipulated depression, whereas cognitive skill itself did not.

In summary, a number of cognitive deficits in depression have been demonstrated empirically. Such studies, however, have not yet determined the primary points in the cognitive process where such impairments may originate. Lack of original attention, response bias, inefficient encoding, and inaccurate retrieval may all be implicated (Wright & Salmon, 1990), and it is also not unlikely that general fatigue plays a role. Nonetheless, some degree of agreement exists regarding the difficulty that depressed individuals have with complex material requiring "deep-level" cognitive operations. In a test of this hypothesis, Tancer et al. (1990) reported that a sample of depressed subjects exhibited significantly more impairment in effort-demanding tasks than in relatively effortless, automatic ones. Such findings may be explained, in part, by the distinction made by Williams, Watts, MacLeod, and Matthews (1988) between passive/automatic and active/strategic cognitive processes, with the latter being primarily influenced by depression. Also heuristically valuable is Ellis and Ashbrook's (1988) resource allocation model, which suggests that depression and other strong emotional states divert finite cognitive resources. Thus tasks requiring increased processing capacity, as opposed to effortless automatic responses, will be most impaired.

Though this body of research has identified clinically significant cognitive deficits, its findings, and the models generated to account for them, do not address a distinctive cognitive feature of depression—the biased processing of emotionally valenced information (the reader is referred to Ingram & Wisnicki, 1991, for a pertinent discussion of cognitive specificity). This feature, which has implications for the individual's psychological, intellectual and social adjustment, may reflect characteristic ways of schematizing and organizing information. Schema and network models predict biases favoring the processing of depressive material throughout the cognitive system. Despite this, quite different patterns are apparent in attention, interpretation, and memory. As our discussion will make clear, the most compelling evidence exists for an association between depression and memory bias. This stands in contrast to findings with anxious subjects, for whom attentional bias appears to be dominant; this topic will be discussed later.

Cognitive Biases in Depression

A striking clinical feature of the depressed individual is his or her preoccupation with negative, depressive events and experiences. This characteristic, which may serve to restrict the field of available information to only that material most reinforcing of a depressive outlook, may be implicated in the disorder's self-perpetuating nature. Though it is not impossible that depressives simply experience a greater number of negative life events (Dagleish & Watts, 1990), considerable consensus exists regarding the likelihood that biases in certain aspects of cognitive processing are a key factor. A vast research literature has arisen from this approach, and recent comprehensive reviews may be found elsewhere (see Dagleish & Watts, 1990; Ingram & Wisnicki, 1991; MacLeod, 1990; Mineka & Sutton, 1992). The present discussion will focus on a few representative studies that indicate the roles played by processing biases in the areas of attention, interpretation, and, most significantly, memory.

Attentional Bias

As MacLeod (1990) has indicated, research findings in this area must be interpreted with caution, as alternative explanations (e.g., response bias, the confounding influence of anxiety) might be offered. Mogg, Matthews, May, et al. (1991), for example, reported that attentional bias in their nonclinical depressed sample was more closely associated with state anxiety than with depression. Nonetheless, some evidence does exist for attentional biases in this disorder. Powell and Helmsley (1984), in a study with clinical depressives using tachistoscopically presented emotionally valenced words, found depressed subjects to be significantly superior to controls in their ability to identify negative material. These authors have suggested that such effects are unique to clinical samples, an observation congruent with Challis and Krane's (1988) failure to find any evidence of emotional-congruency effects in lexical decision latencies associated with induced depressed mood in nonclinical subjects. Results, however, may depend on the investigative paradigm employed.

Using a Stroop methodology, with its assumptions about limited attentional resources and the interference in processing of task-irrelevant material, Gotlib and McCann (1984) showed that mildly depressed students took longer than nondepressed controls to name the colors of emotionally negative words in comparison to positive or neutral ones. In a later study, however, using tachistoscopically presented words with depressed, manic, and neutral content, Gotlib, McLachlan, and Katz (1988) found that depressed undergraduates attended equally to all three groups of words. Nondepressed subjects, by comparison, selectively attended to manic-content words. The authors interpreted this as evidence of "even handedness" in depressives' cognitive processing, as opposed to the self-serving bias of nondepressed individuals.

Interestingly, this finding is congruent with older conceptualizations (e.g., Mischel, 1979) of "depressive realism," according to which depressed subjects have a balanced and realistic picture of the world (see

Alloy & Abramson, 1988). Taylor and Brown (1988) have also commented upon the unrealistically positive views of self held by so-called healthy individuals. Relevantly, in a study using a lexical decision task, Caballero and Morena (1993) have reported that unlike their nondepressed and elation-induced peers, mildly depressed subjects' decision times were not differentially affected by the hedonic tone (positive or negative) of words. In contrast, partial support was recently found for the hypothesis that visual attention in subjects with depressed mood, as operationalized by eye fixation, would be focused on sad themes more than would that of nondepressed controls (Matthews & Antes, 1992). These results were interpreted as evidence of a depressive dysfunction of a visual attentional defense mechanism. In short, this literature is fraught with inconsistencies.

A different but related line of attentional research is that on self-focus. Although inward-directed attention may be adaptive for self-regulation (see Carver & Scheir, 1981; Karoly, 1993), dysfunction may also arise. A number of studies have found self-focused attention to be related to depression in both clinical and nonclinical samples (Ingram, Lumry, Cruet, & Sieber, 1987; Ingram & Smith, 1984). Pyszczynski, Hamilton, Herring, and Greenberg (1989) have investigated the regulatory function of self-focus as a mediator in the relationship between depression and negative memory bias. They reported that for subclinically depressed students, the manipulation of degree of self-focused attention was highly predictive of subsequent recall of recent negative events; this was true primarily for self-referent events. An interesting variation on such findings has been offered by Rothkopf and Blaney (1991), who have suggested that the completion of self-report depression measures (a necessary part of studies with nonclinical subjects) is itself sufficient to induce a certain degree of self-focus and mood-congruent processing bias.

In summary, the evidence for attentional bias in depression is rather sparse and inconsistent. Alternative explanations and minimal success with replications suggest the need for cautious interpretation of existing findings. It is noteworthy, however, that work on the content-specificity hypothesis (e.g., Greenberg & Beck, 1989) has indicated that arbitrary material, such as the adjective lists frequently used, may be less revealing of attentional bias than material more personally meaningful to subjects. Support for this is found in work on ruminations, or selective self-focus, and the perpetuation of depressive cognitions (e.g., Greenberg, Pyszczynski, Burling, & Tibbs, 1992; Nolen-Hoeksema, 1991). Findings regarding memory biases in depression appear much more straightforward.

Interpretive Biases

The preoccupation of depressives with negative life experiences perceived to confirm their own general feelings of worthlessness may be explained in terms of both interpretive and memory biases favoring negative material. Though interpretive biases in this disorder have not received an overwhelming amount of empirical attention, several studies using self-report measures are suggestive of depressives' tendency to impose negative interpretations on ambiguous stimuli (e.g., Butler & Mathews, 1983; Norman, Miller, & Dow, 1988). Wenzlaff, Wegner, and Roper (1988) found that in a sentence-unscrambling task, depressed subjects unscrambled stimuli to form the negative sentence solution more frequently than the positive one, unlike their nondepressed peers.

As MacLeod (1990) has indicated, existing investigations of interpretive bias (particularly those relying on mood induction with nonclinical subjects) are vulnerable to a number of explanatory confounds, particularly in the form of demand characteristics. A recent clinical study, however, has illustrated that these results may not always be attributed to perceived experimenter demands. White, Davison, Haaga, and White (1992) reported that cognitive biases were evident in the unstructured, articulated thoughts of depressives, in the absence of explicit cues. In summary, a modest amount of support exists for a negative interpretive bias in depression; valid and reliable conclusions, however, will require more extensive experimental investigation (MacLeod, 1990).

Memory Biases in Depression

The same cannot be said of the topic of memory biases, around which a vast literature has evolved. In light of clinical observations of depressives' construal of their present state as the consequence of an unbroken series of personal inadequacies, much empirical attention has been given to the association of depression with selective memory biases for emotionally congruent material. A selected number of representative studies will be considered here; for more detailed discussions of the mood and memory literature, the reader is referred to Dagleish and Watts (1990), Ellis and Ashbrook (1988), MacLeod (1990), and Williams et al. (1988). This literature focuses on three different areas: naturally occurring mood in clinically depressed subjects, this mood in nonclinical samples, and on the consequences of mood induction. Generally these studies have demonstrated the clear association of depression with superior recall for emotionally negative material in a number of forms, ranging from life experiences (e.g., Nolen-Hoeksema, 1991; Pyszczynski et al., 1989; Rholes, Riskind, & Lane, 1987) to such manipulated stimuli as emotionally valenced words (e.g., Bellew & Hill, 1991; Bradley & Mathews, 1983, 1988; Dobson & Shaw, 1987; Caballero & Moreno, 1993) and emotional phrases (e.g., Forgas & Bower, 1987).

Clinical accounts have received support from research on depressives' selective autobiographical memory. Using the conventional manipulation of a cue word to prompt memories, Clark and Teasdale (1982) found clinical depressives to respond to a neutral cue initially with more negative than positive memories, a trend opposite to that observed with nondepressed controls. Such findings, though suggestive, have a number of possible interpretations. These include the possible depressive imposition of negative meaning, in recall, on objectively neutral stimuli, or a greater tendency to report selectively the most negative of a number of available emotional memories (see Dagleish & Watts, 1990; MacLeod, 1990). This interpretive problem has been solved in part by studies measuring response latencies between presentation of both positive and negative emotional cue words and the required recall of emotionally congruent memories. Williams and Broadbent (1986), in one of the first of these studies, reported that a sample of depressed suicide attempters exhibited shorter latencies for negative memories than positive, a pattern opposite to that of nondepressed subjects. Williams and Scott (1988) have reported similarly that patients with major depressive disorder took longer to recall positive cue-congruent autobiographical material than did controls.

The biasing effect of mood on the recall of autobiographical memories appears to be relatively robust. Further support comes from studies reporting that such memory biases decline when levels of depression are reduced (e.g., Clark & Teasdale, 1982; Fogarty & Helmsley, 1983), from findings suggestive of the role of primary memory biases in vulnerability to subsequent depression (e.g., Bellew & Hill, 1991), and from replications using mood induction procedures with nonclinical subjects (e.g., Teasdale & Taylor, 1981). Thus facilitated recall of negative events, rather than a heightened tendency to report such events, does seem to be a feature of depression. The mechanisms responsible for such enhanced selective processing, however, are not made clear by such studies. It is possible, for example, that initial encoding of that material was elaborated, thus making the events more accessible in memory; subjects' mood at encoding, though, cannot be determined (see Dagleish & Watts, 1990). Investigations in which emotionally valenced material is provided for subjects in a controlled setting, and recall is subsequently tested, address this problem of interpretation.

A number of studies have examined memory for lists of emotionally valenced words in clinical populations (e.g., Dunbar & Lishman, 1984; McDowall, 1984). Such studies have generally demonstrated the relationship between enhanced recall or recognition of negative material and depression. Much recent work has focused on the mediating influence of such stimuli's personal relevance; self-referent negative semantic material has been found to be particularly associated with recall bias (e.g., Bellew & Hill, 1991; Blaney, 1986). In one such study, Bradley and Mathews (1988) reported that a negative bias in recall of self-referent trait adjectives was exhibited by current depressives but not recovered subjects. The personal meaningfulness of experimental stimuli is also implicated in a study of selective recall in chronic pain and depression by Edwards, Pearce, Collett, and Pugh (1992), who demonstrated that depressed pain patients showed enhanced recall of both sensory and emotionally negative semantic material.

Beck's cognitive theory, in which depressive schemata pertaining to the self play a central role, has explanatory value in such empirical cases. Further understanding is provided by such conceptualizations of specific mechanisms as that of Watkins, Mathews, Williamson, and Fuller (1992). Watkins et al. maintain that mood-congruent memory biases in depression involve the elaborative mechanisms involved in explicit (strategic) memory, and that such biases are highly specific to depressive material rather than to negative material per se. Implicit memory, reflective of ease of activation, is not so affected. This approach is congruent with suggestions that the effects of depression are most evident in strategic cognitive processes, rather than automatic ones (e.g., Williams et al., 1988).

Summary

There is some evidence not only for general decrements in cognitive performance associated with depression, but for specific characteristic biases in the processing of a wide variety of information. Schema and network models predict biases in such areas of processing as attention, interpretation, and memory. This breadth of explanatory coverage may in fact be problematic, as the most robust experimental findings point to the relationship between memory biases and this form of psychopathology.

Such biases may be seen as general cognitive styles that limit the range of information available to the individual. As such, they influence intellectual functioning as well as one's characteristic way of approaching a variety of life experiences, including person perception (Bradley & Mathews, 1983) and interpersonal relationships (Forgas & Bower, 1987). Processing advantages for affect-congruent material may reflect the impact not only of relatively enduring cognitive tendencies but of elevated state depression as well. This possibility is supported by numerous studies that have elicited such biases using mood induction with nondepressed subjects (see Blaney, 1986, for a brief summary). Though such results clearly demonstrate the impact of current dysphoric mood, there is also evidence for the role of trait depression, or a general vulnerability to experience recurrent depressive episodes. Much of this is found in studies reporting processing biases in recovered depressives. One such study (Bradley & Mathews, 1988) found support for the role of both transient mood states and more stable cognitive structures. It is also noteworthy that Bellew and Hill (1991) found that a number of subjects in their nondepressed control group exhibited depressive recall bias for emotionally negative nouns; these subjects were also those most susceptible to the induction of depressed mood states.

The interactive effects of these two classes of variables have been addressed by Williams et al. (1988), whose model suggests that certain individuals have an enduring predisposition to process negatively toned information in a highly elaborative manner (see Graf & Mandler, 1984). This process, in the words of MacLeod (1990), "involves the formation and strengthening of associative linkages between the representation currently being processed and other existing representations in memory" (p. 45). Given this stable tendency, state emotion associated with a stimulus will increase its degree of associated aversiveness, thus prompting biased processing. Refinements of diathesis-stress models of depression, which hypothesize the existence of latent cognitive structures activated by events perceived as negative, reflect such approaches. As Dagleish and Watts (1990) have indicated, the distinction between vulnerability to severe and persistent depression and vulnerability to onset of depression is an important one. In this regard, differential activation theories (e.g., Teasdale, 1988; see also Barnard & Teasdale, 1991) suggest that transient mood disturbances activate spreading patterns of cognitive activity that result in severe and persistent depression. This conceptualization, like schema and network models, serves to explain how enduring, latent modes of processing experience—in interaction with "depressogenic" stressors—result in the self-maintaining downward spiral characteristic of this disorder.

COGNITIVE FACTORS AND MANIC DISORDERS

Our discussion of depression and its cognitive characteristics addressed only some of the classifications included under the DSM-IV general heading of mood disorders (APA, 1994). Also included are a group of disorders that have mania (either primary or alternating with depression) as a defining feature: manic episode, hypomanic episode, and the bipolar disorders. Our exclusion of these from the more extensive treatment given depressive disorders reflects a long tradition in both psychiatry and clinical psychology of regarding the two as qualitatively different in both form and content (e.g., Angst, 1966; Leonhard, 1957). There is some consensus regarding the genetic and neurochemical foundations of bipolar illness (see Smith & Winokur, 1991, for a summary). Furthermore, and relevant to the present discussion, although mania manifests itself as fluctuations in temperament (Goodwin & Jamison, 1990), there is little evidence of the influence of personality factors on either the onset or course of the illness (Tyrer, 1989).

The manic phase of bipolar illness is divided into two levels of severity: hypomania and mania. The persistent, abnormally elated mood found in both of these is associated in hypomania with increased overall activity, a loss of judgment, and an accelerated rate of thought. All of these characteristics are increased in severity in manic episodes. Though this psychopathology is classified according to manifest disturbances in affect, its cognitive characteristics have received much attention. Foremost among these, in recent years, has been the formal thought disorder classically associated with schizophrenia (Grossman & Harrow, 1991). This dysfunction, characterized by associative disturbance, a failure in abstract conceptualizations, and general cognitive disorganization, is now recognized as a common feature of the manic phase of bipolar disorder (Goodwin & Jamison, 1990). In a recent study of the prognostic value of thought disorder in affective syndromes, Wilcox (1992) reported that formal thought disorder at the onset of illness was the most significant of a number of predictors of poor outcome and chronic dysfunction.

For purposes of the present discussion, which has expressly avoided the topic of psychosis, a more interesting form of manic disorder is the hypomania evident in cyclothymia, defined by DSM-IV as a chronic mood disturbance involving numerous hypomanic and dysthymic periods. As Tyrer (1989) has noted, this disorder was historically included among the personality disorders, and it is still found in the tenth edition of the International Classification of Diseases (ICD-10; World Health Organization [WHO], 1992a) under the heading of "affective personality disorder." Hypomania is there defined in terms of a "persistent mild elevation of mood . . . increased energy and activity, and usually marked feelings of well-being and both physical and mental efficiency" (WHO, 1992b, p. 113). Akhtar (1988) has offered a similar discussion of "hypomanic personality." Despite these conceptualizations, most cyclothymics perceive their mood episodes as transient disruptions in their normal personalities. This has led to the widespread clinical recognition of these episodes as a disturbance in mental state associated with bipolar disorder, rather than a personality disturbance (Akiskal, Djenderedjian, & Rosenthal, 1977).

Despite the nosological debate, it is worth noting that one characteristic frequently associated with clinically significant elated mood has traditionally been considered in terms of both personality and general intellectual functioning. The relationship between creativity and mania has long been a topic of some interest among clinicians and biographers (Goodwin & Jamison, 1990); for example, Holden (1987) has noted the frequency of bipolar illness among writers and poets. This account is congruent with the interesting empirical finding that clinicians, asked to rate thought-disordered content in proverb interpretations and writing samples, were unable to distinguish between creative writers and manic patients (Andreason, Tsuang, & Canter, 1974). In a study of British writers and artists, Jamison (1989) found a high incidence of affective disorders and considerable overlap between mood changes and self-reported periods of "intense creativity." Frosch (1987) has investigated the disorder's role in musical creativity and the possibility that symptoms are central to both exceptional innovation and productivity. Interestingly, he concludes that there is no compelling evidence for a relationship between psychopathology and musical creativity (see, by comparison, H. Bower, 1989).

Creativity as a personality factor has been defined in terms of the substitutability of diverse plans and actions in the attainment of higher order goals (Klinger, 1987), as well as general flexibility (Gullwitzer & Wicklund, 1985; Steele, 1988). It is also a central feature of one of the dimensions of the big-five model of personality (see Digman, 1990). Costa and McCrae (1992), in their measurement attempts, have defined their "openness to experience" factor in terms of imagination, intellectual curiosity, and willingness to entertain novel ideas and experiences and unconventional values. Creativity as a facet of intelligence has long been seen in terms of divergent thinking (e.g., Guilford, 1967) and flexibility in finding unconventional solutions to challenges. McCrae (1987) has discussed the relationship between the openness-to-experience factor and both divergent thinking and general creativity.

It appears that specific features of manic states may be implicated in both everyday and exceptional creativity. The energy, increased sensory awareness, accelerated thought, and heightened self-confidence associated with this form of psychopathology all contribute to this. The loosened and idiosyncratic associations found in more severe manic episodes may also explain its association with literary genius (Holden, 1987). Nonetheless, one must recognize the degree of impairment associated with the transient formal thought disorder found in bipolar illness (see Grossman & Harrow, 1991). Richards and Kinney (1990) have reported that the majority of bipolar patients experience the greatest creativity when in hypomanic, or mildly elevated, mood states. Such observations should be qualified by a recognition that many of the true symptoms of hypomania may be counterproductive (Andreason, 1980).

In short, though severe forms of mania are often associated with impairments in cognition and reality testing similar to those found in schizophrenia, hypomania may sometimes be associated with forms of creativity. There is some consensus that although such episodes are marked by specific ways of framing experience, behaving, and expressing oneself, they are more a disturbance of mental state than one of personality. Creativity, defined as both a personality and intellectual characteristic and a correlate of hypomania, would seem to reflect shared features rather than any degree of causality (Richards & Kinney, 1990).

ANXIETY DISORDERS AND COGNITION

Anxiety is a feature of both adaptive functioning and a number of forms of psychopathology. It is generally defined in terms of its cognitive and emotional features, including elevated negative affect and pronounced apprehensiveness regarding the possibility of threat or danger (e.g., Barlow, 1991; Ingram & Kendall, 1987). Avoidance, as its behavioral component, has also been emphasized (Lang, 1977). Anxiety is accompanied by enhanced vigilance; as such, it may have a highly adaptive function, putting the individual into a state of psychological and physiological readiness to meet possible challenges and avoid harm (Beck & Emery, 1985; Endler, 1980). The classic literature on performance and optimal levels of anxious arousal attests to this benefit (e.g., Yerkes & Dodson, 1908). Anxiety often occurs with such severity or frequency, though, that it significantly interferes with one's ability to function. In such cases, it is considered a clinically significant form of psychopathology. Anxiety disorders (the relevant DSM-IV classification), include panic disorder with or without agoraphobia, agoraphobia, social and simple phobias, obsessive-compulsive disorder, and generalized anxiety disorder.

Though there is some consensus regarding the defining features of anxiety, there have been a number of refinements in its conceptualization. One of these is the primary distinction between state and trait anxiety (Endler, 1980, 1983; Spielberger, 1972). The latter represents a relatively enduring predisposition to respond anxiously to stressors (e.g., Costa & McCrae, 1992; Eysenck, 1967, 1981). Endler, Edwards, and Vitelli (1991) have proposed that trait anxiety has four distinct facets—social evaluation, physical danger, ambiguous, and daily routines—that reflect the type of perceived situational context in which the individual is predisposed to experience anxiety. State anxiety, in contrast, is the transient reaction most commonly referred to as anxiety. Conceptual elaboration of anxiety as a dispositional construct has prompted much interest in its role in personality and the individual's adaptive functioning. An additional development has been the anxiety-sensitivity construct (Reiss & McNally, 1985). This stylistic variable, distinct from trait anxiety, is defined by a tendency to interpret bodily arousal as threatening and to respond anxiously (Reiss, 1987). This construct has been particularly useful in the explanation of why certain individuals engage in the dramatic misinterpretations of bodily sensations thought to underlie panic attacks.

As in depression, the affective and behavioral aspects of anxiety are its most compelling features. There is increasing recognition, however, that its cognitive components represent not just concomitant but perpetuating and potentially causal features. As mentioned, a salient clinical feature of anxious individuals is their hypervigilance for, and preoccupation with, potentially threatening events (APA, 1987; Tyrer, 1989). The possibility that this is evidence of mood-congruent biases in information processing has generated a great deal of research activity (see MacLeod, 1990; Mineka & Sutton, 1992, for summaries). A number of operations may be implicated in these observations: increased attentional focus, biased interpretation of ambiguous events, and rumination about and elaboration of negative events (and their subsequent enhanced accessibility in memory; Dagleish & Watts, 1990).

It is worth noting that anxiety, phenomenologically, is a future-oriented, anticipatory state; in view of this, Barlow (1991) has suggested that a more precise term might be "anxious apprehension." The adaptive function of anxiety in the history of the species has been discussed elsewhere (e.g., Beck & Emery, 1985; Mathews, 1988). It is sufficient to note that anxiety may facilitate the detection of harmful stimuli in the environment. Elaborate processing of this information, or enhanced recall ability, is likely associated with mechanisms other than the psychological and physiological readiness specific to anxiety. Accordingly, a growing number of studies indicate the primary role played in anxiety by attentional bias. Specific research findings will be summarized below, following a brief discussion of the models that provide a conceptual framework for them.

Models of Cognition in Anxiety

The schema and network models discussed earlier in the context of depression are nonspecific to emotion, and thus they posit the same mechanisms for anxiety. Both of these cognitive models are able to accommodate the important distinction between state and trait anxiety, and they predict facilitated processing of affect-congruent information at all levels of cognitive functioning. This breadth of coverage, however, may be an explanatory flaw. As MacLeod (1990) and others (Dagleish & Watts, 1990; Strauman, 1991) have indicated, this generality renders these models almost unfalsifiable, and it fails to account adequately for the differential pattern of empirical findings for these two forms of psychopathology. Nonetheless, both models offer heuristically useful frameworks for the understanding of the cognitive mechanisms underlying processing biases in anxiety.

On the basis of clinical observations, Beck has maintained that anxious individuals are characterized by idiosyncratic danger schemata, which serve to facilitate the processing of threat- and danger-relevant information. These schemata, which Beck (1967, 1976) has described as basic structural components of cognitive organization, are developed in early life to accommodate experience involving danger. Drawing on the traditional concept of "cognitive set," Beck (1984) proposed that cognitive constellations are subsets of schemata organized to adapt to diverse life situations; these direct the individual's filtering of pertinent information from the environment and enhance the likelihood of certain responses. Under ordinary conditions, these subsets of schemata remain latent in the cognitive system until activated by an appropriate environmental threat.

In pathological states, however, a cognitive feedback loop results in prolonged activation of danger schemata and their cognitive, affective, and behavioral concomitants. "If the resultant behavioral and affective mobilization is sufficiently intense or prolonged, then a variety of symptoms associated with anxiety disorder appear" (Beck & Emery, 1985, p. 59). Elevations in state anxiety thus may serve to activate latent idiosyncratic danger schemata, which are associated with a wide range of processing biases throughout the cognitive system. The facilitated processing of affect-congruent threatening information restricts feedback to only that material most reinforcing of an individual's current state of anxious arousal. In this way, danger schemata and the resulting organismic activation are self-perpetuating. This account also accommodates the state/trait distinction by proposing a mediating interaction whereby activation of danger schemata in individuals high in trait anxiety is mediated by levels of state or manifest anxiety (MacLeod, 1990). In this view, threat stimuli that are particularly relevant to the dominant danger schemata of anxious individuals are the most cognitively disruptive (see also Endler, 1983).

The network model most frequently referred to in the literature on anxiety and cognition is that initially proposed by Anderson and Bower (1973) and elaborated by G. H. Bower (1981; see Johnson-Laird, Herrmann, & Chaffin, 1984, for a review of alternative models). Like the schema account, Bower's associative network model predicts processing biases for threatening material in anxiety analogous to those operating in depression, reflecting similar underlying mechanisms. Bower has suggested that anxiety, as an emotional state, is represented by a node within memory space. This acts as a focusing point for associative connections with propositional nodes containing information associated with past experiences of anxiety. Thus the activation of this emotion node, corresponding with the experience of state anxiety, will result in a spreading activation throughout all associated propositional nodes. This emotionally congruent information, as MacLeod (1990) has indicated, "thus becomes disproportionately available to the cognitive system" (p. 14), thereby exerting a dominant influence on the processing of currently available information.

The state/trait distinction is accommodated by the model's emphasis upon cognitive structural correlates of experience. Individuals high in trait anxiety will have had a history of more frequent and contextually varied experiences of elicited state anxiety. The associative networks between the nodal focusing point and congruent information will be similarly elaborated; thus extensive processing biases will be evident when individuals high in dispositional anxiety experience elevated levels of state anxiety. Other conceptualizations, such as Barnard and Teasdale's (1991) systemic approach to cognitive-affective interaction, similarly acknowledge the combined effects of transient anxious arousal and dispositional tendencies. Barlow (1991), in an interesting variation on this theme, has proposed that certain anxiety disorders (e.g., panic attacks) are a consequence of spontaneous "misfirings" of transient arousal interacting with a stable psychological vulnerability to experience such inappropriate expressions of emotion as threatening. This model, however, is not able to explain the specific processing tendencies associated with anxiety, a task to which the other models are well suited.

Attentional Biases and Anxiety

The late 1980s and early 1990s have witnessed a surge of empirical interest in the role of cognitive factors in anxiety; this is particularly true of the topic of attentional biases for threatening material. A vast investigative literature has resulted, and a number of comprehensive research programs have addressed themselves to the specific mechanisms involved. The work of MacLeod and his colleagues (e.g., MacLeod & Mathews, 1988, 1991; MacLeod, Mathews, & Tata, 1986; MacLeod, Tata, & Mathews, 1987) and of Mogg and collaborators (e.g., Mogg, Mathews, Bird, & MacGregor-Morris, 1990; Mogg, Mathews, & Eysenck, 1992; Mogg, Mathews, Eysenck, & May, 1991; Mogg, Mathews, & Weinman, 1989) are illustrative of these studies. The following section will provide a summary of frequently cited and more recent cognitive experimental research of the connection between anxiety and attention to emotionally valenced information; it will attempt to address those studies most representative of current conceptualizations of this relationship.

The study of attentional biases in anxiety has revolved around two basic approaches: those that seek to identify performance impairment resulting from selective focus on salient stimuli, and those that attempt to understand how the same process enhances performance (Dagleish & Watts, 1990). As MacLeod (1990) has indicated, the most common experimental strategy has been to present subjects with emotionally toned stimuli under conditions where their identification is difficult. An enhanced ability to detect threatening material (relative to neutral or emotionally noncongruent material) is a characteristic predicted by both schema and network models. In general, this body of research has found a consistent relationship between facilitated attention for threatening stimuli and anxiety (Mineka & Smith, 1992).

Several studies have used Stroop-type methodologies, which seek to assess the degree of cognitive interference evoked by emotionally valenced words by measuring latencies in the naming of the ink colors in which the words are printed. Mathews and MacLeod (1986) have reported that patients diagnosed with generalized anxiety disorder took longer to name a selected group of threat-relevant words than nonthreatening ones, a trend not exhibited by matched controls. Mogg et al. (1989), in a replication of this study with a clinically anxious sample, also sought to determine the consequences for processing of including threat words congruent with the dominant worries reported by subjects (i.e., physical or social threat versus nonthreat). The validity of the replicated study's general findings was confirmed. Also reported, however, was the substantial interference effect associated with worry-congruent stimulus items. Comparable findings have been obtained with alternative methodologies for presenting salient semantic material, such as dichotic listening tasks (e.g., Mathews & MacLeod, 1986). In summary, the finding that anxiety is characterized by enhanced attention for threatening stimuli has received considerable empirical support. A detailed discussion of these results is presented by MacLeod (1990, 1991).

Findings obtained with the Stroop paradigm, though, may be difficult to interpret. It is possible that the observed differences in color naming between anxious and nonanxious subjects reflect a response bias, with the former group showing a tendency to output emotional words rather than selectively attend to them (see Dagleish & Watts, 1990). In an effort to address this, MacLeod et al. (1986) used a visual probe paradigm, in which subjects were asked to indicate as quickly as possible when a small dot (probe) on a VDU screen replaced one of a pair of stimulus words. Anxious subjects appeared to allocate attentional resources selectively toward the location where threat had occurred; this facilitated responses to probe replacements of threat words and impaired responses when neutral stimuli were replaced. Control subjects, in contrast, tended to shift attentional resources away from threat stimuli (see also Broadbent & Broadbent, 1988).

The finding that anxiety is associated with a shift in attentional focus toward threatening features of the environment appears to be a robust one, and it may be readily accommodated by both schema and network models of anxious cognition. The latter model, for example, suggests that attentional operations are mediated by an enhanced accessibility of threat-relevant information from memory stores. One would then expect the pattern of findings to be quite straightforward. Nonetheless, MacLeod and his colleagues have reported that in a number of studies with anxious subjects where mood-congruent processing biases were predicted, null results were obtained (see MacLeod, 1990; MacLeod & Mathews, 1988). In an effort to explain this pattern, these investigators have noted that each of the experimental tasks that successfully demonstrated the predicted processing bias shared a common feature: more than one source of information was simultaneously presented (Eysenck, MacLeod, & Mathews, 1987; MacLeod & Mathews, 1991). In the words of MacLeod and Mathews (1991), the task "explicitly offers two distinctly differed processing options, and [the subject is] required to allocate and/or maintain processing priorities for these competing alternatives" (p. 601). Thus mood-congruent attentional biases in anxiety may only be evident when there is competition for cognitive resources. In this way, null findings from recognition threshold studies and lexical decision manipulations (see Mathews, 1988) may be explained in terms of their sequential rather than simultaneous presentation of stimulus items.

In short, attentional biases in anxiety may reflect the operation of cognitive control mechanisms involved in the allocation of processing resources to given tasks. In an effort to test this competition hypothesis, MacLeod and Mathews (1991) used a lexical decision task with a sample of generalized anxiety disorder patients, manipulating the degree to which conditions required the assignment of processing priorities. Only in double-string trials (which involved simultaneous presentation of a stimulus word with a nonword) were anxious subjects differentiated from controls in their decision times for threat rather than neutral words. These findings were interpreted as evidence that anxiety selectively facilitates the processing of threat-relevant stimuli under conditions that demand the allocation of processing priorities to different stimulus alternatives.

Although MacLeod and Mathews's study provided compelling evidence for the mediation of processing biases by mechanisms other than the simple increased accessibility of information posited by dominant models, a potential confound existed. A main effect was found for word valence, with all subjects exhibiting faster decision times for threat- rather than neutral-stimulus words. These findings may have reflected the greater semantic similarity of words in the threat list (e.g., *palpitation*, *coronary*, *disease*) than those in the neutral category (e.g., *facilitate*, *powdered*, *activities*). In an attempt to replicate the original findings while accounting for word categorization, Mogg, Mathews, Eysenck, and May (1991) used a lexical decision task with the two original word lists. A categorized neutral word list was also included. As predicted, a strong main effect for word categorization was observed. Furthermore, though an anxiety-related attentional bias was evident in the presence of competition for processing resources, this was only true when target words appeared below the fixation point on the presentation screen. Thus the position of threatening stimuli was an important determinant.

Though the investigators concurred with MacLeod and Mathews's conclusion that competition for processing resources is important, they have suggested that it is not a sufficient cause of selective bias. The results may have reflected a selective shift of attention toward threat stimuli similar to the one implicated in MacLeod et al.'s (1986) visual probe manipulation. As there was a general trend for all subjects to preferentially attend to stimuli in the upper portion of the screen, the appearance of a threat-related word in a lower position would require an active attentional search. As MacLeod et al. suggested, this task was associated with an attentional shift away from threat material for nonanxious subjects and a selective shift of attention toward such stimuli on the part of anxious subjects. Mogg, Mathews, Eysenck, and May (1991), in consideration of similar findings (e.g., Mathews, May, Mogg, & Eysenck, 1990), have interpreted these results as evidence for the role of attentional search strategies in the allocation of processing resources to threatening stimuli. Such findings, despite their experimental origins, have considerable ecological validity. In daily functioning, the individual is required to scan the environment for information; the selective threat-related attentional bias characteristic of anxious individuals is only one of a number of possible search strategies adopted to perform this task.

Although considerable evidence exists for the relationship between attentional biases and anxiety, the relative contributions made by state and trait variables are difficult to disentangle. Use of clinically anxious subjects, for example, implicates the influence of both current elevations in state anxiety and more enduring predispositions to experience these states. The role of state anxiety is particularly evident in studies comparing the responses of anxious patients before and after recovery (e.g., Foa & McNally, 1986; Watts, 1986). A pattern has emerged of processing biases decreasing with reduced manifest anxiety. Illustratively, in a study of interpretive biases in clinically anxious patients and normal controls, Eysenck, Mogg, May, Richards, and Mathews (1991) reported that patients high in state anxiety were more likely than both recovered and normal control subjects to interpret ambiguous sentences in a threatening way. The authors considered this to be evidence for the minimal influence of more enduring dispositional anxiety, which is presumably a feature of subjects who are currently experiencing (as well as those who have recovered from) clinically significant anxiety states.

With respect to attentional biases in particular, however, the opposite pattern has been observed. In the replication study by Mogg et al. (1989) discussed previously, it was found that clinical patients' trait (not state) anxiety, as assessed by a self-report measure, was the only predictor of the color-naming latencies exhibited for threat-related words. Comparable results were found in an investigation of the effects of distractor word manipulation on attentional focus or selective search (Mathews et al., 1990). Though state anxiety was determinant of general impairment associated with distractors, both currently anxious and recovered subjects showed attentional disruption when threat-related distractors were used. "A bias favouring threat cues during perceptual search is an enduring feature of individuals vulnerable to anxiety, rather than a transient consequence of current mood state" (p. 166). In a study comparing the attentional tendencies of highly trait-anxious normal subjects and those who primarily employ repressive coping styles, Fox (1993) has found that subjects high in trait anxiety were more likely to shift visual attention toward socially threatening information. As state anxiety levels were not elevated in this study, this may have reflected habitual strategies for processing information.

As MacLeod (1990) has indicated, the extremely high correlation found in clinical samples between state and trait anxiety makes it somewhat difficult to partial out their unique effects. In an interesting attempt to circumvent this problem, MacLeod and Mathews (1988) identified medical students high and low in trait anxiety and used a repeated-measures design to assess attentional biases associated with a naturally occurring increase in state anxiety (determined by the proximity of a major examination). Subjects high in trait anxiety exhibited not only an overall greater allocation of attentional resources to threat-related stimuli but an increased tendency to do so when state anxiety was elevated. Subjects low in this trait, by comparison, showed an increased selective diversion of attention away from threatening stimuli.

In short, there is empirical evidence for the roles of both state and trait variables in the attentional biases associated with anxiety. Further complication has been provided by suggestions that the interaction between the two is in fact only evident under prolonged periods of stress (Mogg et al., 1990). Nonetheless, there is some consensus that processing biases are mediated by the interacting influence of both trait and state anxiety. The general vulnerability characteristic of the former has been discussed by MacLeod (1991). In light of an extensive literature review, this author has suggested that the predisposition alone may reflect a tendency to attend selectively to, or encode, threatening information in the environment. Thus anxiety proneness may be associated, in a causal and perhaps reciprocal way, with an enduring cognitive style.

Interpretive and Memory Biases in Anxiety

The roles played by biases of interpretation and memory in anxiety appear to be minimal; the amount of recent empirical attention given these two topics reflects this. Nonetheless, there is some evidence for bias associated with anxiety both in the interpretation of ambiguous stimuli and in memory for mood-congruent material.

If one study investigating the role of anxiety in the interpretation of homophones having both neutral and threat-related meanings, Eysenck, MacLeod, and Mathews (1987) reported suggestive results. The ambiguous words were imbedded in a list of unambiguous buffer items; subjects were directed to listen to a tape of these recorded words and record them as a form of spelling list. The frequency with which subjects reported the threat-relevant spelling of these words (e.g., *pain* versus *pane*, *die* versus *dye*) was highly correlated with their scores on a self-report measure of trait anxiety. Although state anxiety had a negligible impact, Mathews, Mogg, May, and Eysenck (1989) have reported evidence for the role of both trait and state variables. In a study with current and recovered anxious patients and normal controls, it was found that currently anxious patients (high state anxiety) were more likely than subjects in either control group to report the threatening interpretation of the stimuli. Nonetheless, recovered patients (presumably high in trait anxiety, but not currently anxious) showed a level of threat-oriented interpretive bias neither as extreme as that of the experimental groups nor, importantly, as neutral as that of the normal controls. The authors interpreted this as evidence for the mediating role of the interaction between state and trait anxiety. Only partial support for this conclusion was provided by Eysenck et al. (1991), in whose study the chief role of state anxiety was emphasized.

In summary, there is some evidence for a mood-congruent bias operating at the level of interpretation, similar to that observed for attention. A program of research with the goal of determining the subtleties of this bias has been initiated by MacLeod and his colleagues (see MacLeod, 1990). Evidence for memory biases in anxiety, however, is not very compelling. Currently anxious, recovered anxious, and normal control subjects have commonly not been shown to exhibit hypothesized differences in the recall or recognition of emotionally valenced words (MacLeod, 1990; Mineka & Sutton, 1992). In fact, experiments have often found patterns of results exactly contrary to what was expected, with anxious subjects showing disproportionately poorer memory for threat-related or negative information (e.g., Mogg, Mathews, & Weinman, 1987; Watts, Trezise, & Sharrock, 1986).

In one such study, unique in its use of state anxiety induction, Foa, McNally, and Murdock (1989) used a self-referent encoding task and assessed incidental free recall. It was found that neither of the two indices of state anxiety—the induction manipulation and measured heart rate—were associated with any facilitated recall of anxiety-related self-referent adjectives; in fact, the latter index had a strong negative correlation with relative recall scores. These results were interpreted as evidence for selectively impaired memory in anxiety, something dramatically inconsistent with the affect-congruent retrieval hypothesis. More recently, Mogg, Gardiner, Stavrou, and Golumbek (1992) have obtained comparable results in a study of recognition memory with clinically anxious subjects. Anxiety was not found to be associated with an implicit memory bias for threat-related words. Nor, however, was it found to be related to an explicit (conscious or strategic) memory bias against threat, a frequent cognitive feature of nonanxious, nonclinical control subjects.

Synthesis

The cognitive biases associated with anxiety appear to take place at a relatively low level in the processing system. It seems that underlying anxiety vulnerability, as reflected in the individual-differences variable of trait anxiety, is a selective attentional bias that operates to facilitate the intake of threatening information. The presence of this systematic bias was indicated by the many studies discussed, as were the important roles played by (a) the personal meaningfulness of threatening stimuli and (b) the simultaneous presence of alternative processing options. Nonetheless, anxious individuals, when engaged in an attentional search and required to assign processing priorities to a small proportion of the information available in the environment, will selectively favor the most threatening material. This appears to reflect the mediating influence of an interaction between state and trait variables. In the words of MacLeod (1991), "High trait anxious individuals are people who respond to state anxiety, or arousal, with an increased tendency to selectively encode threatening information" (p. 284). By comparison, less trait-anxious individuals exhibit a tendency to avoid such stimuli.

Although schema and network models partially account for these tendencies, they do not explain their more active features, such as the assignment of priorities when faced with processing options (see MacLeod & Mathews, 1991). These authors have suggested that a more suitable conceptualization is found in Oatley and Johnson-Laird's (1987) model of the cognitive system as a flexible "plan-oriented" system of organizations unique to specific basic emotions. Evidence for biases in other areas of processing is less compelling. Though there does appear to be a mood-congruent processing bias in interpretation of stimuli, memory processes are not similarly affected. It appears that the bias favoring threat stimuli may not operate at later stages of information processing, such as those involved in memory. Anxiety may in fact preclude the subsequent elaborated processing of stimuli, a phenomenon termed "cognitive avoidance" by Foa and Kozak (1986).

Anxious individuals may make an active cognitive effort to minimize extensive processing of relevant information in order to maintain their selective attentional focus (see Harvey, 1984). This account is congruent with formulations of processing biases in terms of their functional value (Mathews, 1988; Oatley & Johnson-Laird, 1987). Though anxiety facilitates an anticipatory (and often adaptive) attentional vigilance for potentially harmful environmental stimuli (Ingram & Kendall, 1987), its primary function is not to process them more extensively. The exact mechanisms involved, however, are far from clear. The extent to which processing biases operate outside awareness has been addressed elsewhere (e.g., Mathews & MacLeod, 1986; Mogg et al., 1989) and has been alluded to in empirical manipulations. For example, Mathews et al. (1989) compared the effects of anxiety on a strategic memory task (cued recall) with those on a form of implicit memory that involves more passive, automatic operations (word completion). The effects of anxiety were only apparent in the implicit memory task, thus providing support for the suggestion that anxiety operates on processes that occur without deliberate intention, as opposed to the strategic processes involved in memory.

This distinction echoes Graf and Mandler's (1984) conceptualizations of the cognitive operations of integration and elaboration. Whereas integration serves to make mental representations more accessible to the cognitive system—and more available to subsequent operations—it does not involve the strengthening of associative linkages between current representations and former ones existing in memory (see MacLeod, 1990). The latter is the function of elaboration, which renders representations more easily retrievable. The different cognitive biases associated with depression and anxiety may be thus explained (MacLeod, 1990; Williams et al., 1988). In the case of anxiety, although threat-related information is highly accessible and determinant of attention, the detected information will not be highly elaborated; mood-congruent processing biases are therefore not to be expected. The opposite pattern is predicted in depression, wherein cognitive characteristics may reflect biases in elaborative processing.

The models and empirical findings presented provide a framework for understanding the mechanisms involved in specific cognitive features of people high in trait anxiety—unrealistically threatening thoughts regarding the probability of future harm, and the hypervigilance associated with them. Such individuals are highly vulnerable to the development of a number of clinical anxiety disorders (Eysenck & Mathews, 1987; MacLeod, 1991). We have reviewed general features of anxiety as found in individuals high in this trait or in generalized (or undifferentiated) anxiety disorders. One must ask about these models' value in explaining unique defining features both of the constellation of problems identified as anxiety disorders, and of their relationship with particular environmental and internal cues. The latter task is complicated by the fact that once mobilized, a vicious cycle of anxiety may operate relatively independent of apparent contextual stressors (Dagleish & Watts, 1990). MacLeod (1991) has referred to this as a "feed-forward" cycle; in predisposed individuals, "state anxiety elevations will elicit a biased pattern of encoding that results in a further increase in state anxiety, in turn exaggerating the encoding bias, and so on" (p. 284).

Nonetheless, the relatively circumscribed nature of such clinical anxiety classifications as panic disorder and phobias may in part be accounted for by findings regarding the central role in processing played by personally relevant fears. The anxiety-linked attentional biases that appear to play both causal and perpetuating roles in these disorders exhibit some specificity, in that they seem to be restricted to particular stimulus domains. Illustrative findings have been obtained with panic disorder patients (Ehlers, Margraf, Davies, & Roth, 1988; see also Zinbarg, Barlow, Brown, & Hertz, 1992), spider phobics (Watts, McKenna Sharrock, & Trezise, 1986), and social phobics (Hope, Rapee, Heimberg, & Dombeck, 1990; Mogg, Mathews, & Eysenck, 1992). In all of these cases, anxiety has been associated with a bias, operating at a relatively low level of processing, that favors personally threatening material. The cognitive features of obsessive-compulsive disorder, whose unusual qualities have prompted suggestions that it be differentiated from the anxiety disorders classification, may not fit so neatly into this framework. An alternative conceptualization will be addressed.

Obsessive-Compulsive Disorder

The origin and maintenance of a number of the categories in the anxiety disorders classification may be explained quite readily in terms of the models and mechanisms discussed thus far. There is some consensus that although the content of the disorders may vary, the general form remains constant (Craske, 1991). The cognitive features of obsessive-compulsive disorder (OCD), however, have been the focus of quite different conceptualizations. The defining characteristics of this syndrome are obsessions (persistent recurrent thoughts, images, or impulses that are experienced as invasive and senseless) and compulsions (repetitive stereotyped behaviors performed in response to an obsession). The presence of either or both, coupled with an effort to resist them and significant impairment in functioning and/or subjective distress, warrants a diagnosis (APA, 1994). Though manifest compulsions are the most dramatic feature of this disorder, it would seem that cognitive characteristics—as seen in the obsessions and phenomenological reports of obsessionals—have a primary role in the disorder's genesis and maintenance.

The characterization of OCD in terms of an habitual style of thinking and approaching information has historically been a feature of clinical accounts (see Reed, 1985, for a review). It has been suggested that OCD, like other anxiety disorders, may be explained in terms of the low-level processing biases already discussed (MacLeod, 1991). Some support for this hypothesis has been provided by Foa and McNally (1986), who have described obsessional patients' enhanced ability to detect experimental words associated with their own unique preoccupations. In an earlier study, Persons and Foa (1984) found that in a card-sorting task, OCD subjects took for far longer to sort fear-relevant cards than neutral ones. This finding was thought to reflect interference in task-relevant cognition by task-irrelevant selective processing (analogous to that proposed for other anxiety disorders); however, it may also have reflected cognitive tendencies unique to OCD. Explanation of this possibility may be found in the line of research that prompted this study.

Drawing on a conceptual tradition dating back to Janet (1903), Reed (e.g., 1985, 1991) has proposed that the defining cognitive feature of OCD is an impairment in the spontaneous organization and integration of experience. In this view, clinical markers of the disorder—obsessions and the related compulsive activity—represent compensatory attempts to impose the structure that is otherwise unobtainable. In a program of research spanning almost two decades, Reed obtained empirical support for this basic cognitive deficit's expression in such areas of functioning as reasoning and problem solving in both clearly delineated and open-ended tasks, decision making, memory, imagery, and conceptual structuring of categories of meaning. With regard to this last domain, for example, Reed (1969b) hypothesized that the overstructuring cognitive style of obsessionals should be reflected in rigid and highly restricted conceptual limits. He asked OCD subjects and matched controls to sort blocks into "classes" according to shared features, and to do so into the smallest number of groups. As predicted, obsessionals allocated fewer stimulus items to each class and required more "overly precise" classes to do so. These and similar findings (e.g., Reed, 1969a) prompted Reed's conclusion that in their efforts to impose structure on experience, obsessionals' conceptualizations are "under-inclusive"—that is, overly precise and maladaptively restrictive (see also Mollinger, 1980).

Reed's work has stood rather alone, and despite supporting evidence from other investigators' accounts (e.g., Frost, Lahart, Dugas, & Sher, 1988; Hamilton, 1957a,b; Makhlouf-Norris & Jones, 1971; Sher, Frost, & Otto, 1983; Sher, Mann, & Frost, 1984), it has been cited as a conceptual innovation but not adopted as an investigative framework. This is unfortunate, as it was unique in its effort to account for the feature of OCD most frequently referred to by patients themselves: pervasive feelings of doubt and uncertainty in all areas of functioning (see McNally & Kohlbeck, 1993). The idiosyncratic subject matter of obsessive thoughts, which studies on worry-congruent biases commonly emphasize, was considered secondary by Reed. Regarding this, he made a crucial distinction: "the cognitive style is employed in processing the material; the material does not engender the style. In other words, the style is a matter of form, whereas the material being processed is content" (Reed, 1991, pp. 79–80). Though other authors have concurred with Reed's appraisal of the primacy of processing tendencies in OCD, their work, on the whole, has reflected the influence of more mainstream models (e.g., Enright & Beech, 1993a,b; Rachman, 1993).

In short, more than one approach may be taken to obsessional phenomena. It is worth noting that Reed's conceptualization, in contrast to those most frequently cited in the context of anxiety research, explicitly adopted a top-down model of cognitive operations; the influence of classical information-processing models is very apparent (e.g., Bartlett, 1932; see also Neisser, 1976). Reed has expressed less interest in the precise mechanisms involved in these cognitive characteristics (the focus of more mainstream approaches) than in their expression in a wide array of domains. The latter may help to explain why features of OCD display considerable overlap with other anxiety disorders. Clarification of OCD's more unique cognitive characteristics, though, will likely require a more tailored approach.

Comment

We have discussed mainstream approaches to the relationship between anxiety and cognition, as well as the value of such alternative perspectives as Reed's approach to OCD. Anxiety, like most psychological factors, exists on a continuum of severity extending from normal, adaptive responses and predispositions to the pathological states discussed. An important direction for future study derives from this fundamental recognition.

A number of explanations might be offered for the differing cognitive processes and degrees of impairment between these clinical disorders and the high trait anxiety found in nonclinical populations. Three interesting suggestions have been offered by MacLeod (1991). First, it is possible that in clinical patients there is simply a stronger association of state anxiety with selective attentional biases; minimal elevations would then result in the self-perpetuating hypervigilance referred to previously. Alternatively, whereas these biases may remain latent in individuals predisposed toward high trait anxiety until mobilized by elevated state anxiety, this may not be true in clinical anxiety disorders. Patients may in fact exhibit these processing tendencies chronically, quite independently of levels of state anxiety. Some support for this possibility is provided by findings that recovered patients exhibit biases similar to those found in currently anxious patients (e.g., Mathews et al., 1990). Finally, although similar patterns of automatic processing may be shown by both highly trait-anxious and clinical patients, the differences between the two may reflect the latter group's continuing increased tendency to process threatening information, even in the case where conscious strategies are possible (see also Beck & Emery, 1985). Clearly, the delineation of differential processing patterns among individuals high in trait vulnerabilities and those experiencing clinically significant anxiety states is a topic worthy of future investigation. It is also worth noting that much existing research, though stressing personally relevant fears, has failed to make explicit the fundamental multidimensionality of trait anxiety (see Endler et al., 1991); treating it as a unidimensional global vulnerability may limit the generalizability of findings.

CONCLUSION

We have attempted to survey and evaluate models, constructs, issues, and empirical findings in cognitive research in psychopathology. All of these have implicated the inadequacy of standardized psychometric approaches for the understanding of intelligence, a construct that we have conceptualized in terms of an individual's capacity to acquire and use information from the environment in an efficient, accurate, and flexible way. This research has provided considerable support for the existence of a number of processing biases associated with personality, mood, and anxiety disorders. These modes of selection, interpretation, and organization of information all influence intellectual adjustment, as well as the more general pattern of purposeful adaptation known as personality. The literature points to highly selective processing biases in anxiety and depression, primarily in the respective areas of attention and memory. Personality disorders, by comparison, appear to be associated with pervasive and enduring consistencies in the organization of information and experience. Both lower-level operations (e.g., attention) and higher-level integrative functions are involved in this form of psychopathology.

In the case of anxiety and depression, the distinction between state and trait variables has proven to be a valuable one. As Dagleish and Watts (1990) have suggested, the refinement of diathesis-stress models of psychopathology—which emphasize the ongoing interactions among contextual subjective stressors, state elevations, and enduring vulnerability factors—has been among the most important contributions of this line of research. In light of this, MacLeod (1991) has devoted considerable attention to the factors that differentiate nonclinical subjects high in trait anxiety from those who succumb to clinically significant depressive states. This is an area particularly worthy of further study.

Characteristic ways of organizing and processing information and experience, rather than transient states or latent vulnerabilities, appear to play a primary role in the development, maintenance, and expression of personality disorders. As we have noted, despite the amenability of this form of psychopathology to the application of cognitive frameworks, empirical investigations have been few. This may in part reflect concerns about the reliability and validity of existing approaches to their diagnosis. As these and other Axis II disorders occupy a comparably significant position in DSM-IV (see Millon & Frances, 1991a,b, 1993), it is perhaps time for an application of the well-delineated methodologies adopted in cognitive research on depression and anxiety to personality pathologies. In doing so, investigators may help clarify the relationships of these pathologies to more transient symptom syndromes (e.g., Burgess, 1991).

The limitations of the approaches and findings here discussed must be recognized. The price paid for scientific precision may be the dubious ecological validity of cognitive experimental paradigms. An individual is constantly collecting, transforming, and using information that has personal relevance beyond that encompassed by most experimental stimuli. Motivation, goal orientations, and regulatory mechanisms all play a role in adaptive functioning (see Karoly, 1993). Any parsimonious explanation of the relationships among thought, emotion, and behavior runs the risk of oversimplifying this dynamic process. Similarly, one must be vigilant regarding the tendency to shape one's conceptual frameworks to suit popular methodologies. For example, the paradigms that have been used so successfully with a number of anxiety disorder categories may be minimally informative regarding the unique cognitive characteristics of obsessive-compulsive disorder. Comparable results, in this case, may require quite different explanations (see Reed, 1985, 1991).

The need for this line of research to pay increasing attention to the distinction between cognitive factors true of any one disorder and those common in psychopathology generally has been stressed by Ingram and Wisnicki (1991). Comorbidity is problematic, both theoretically and in an applied sense. These authors have noted that the use of heterogeneous experimental groups (i.e., those with multiple co-occurring disorders other than that targeted) may considerably cloud interpretation. Similarly, the practice of selecting "normal" control groups with low levels of the targeted variable being the sole exclusion criteria leaves one vulnerable to the possibility that these groups may exhibit a heterogeneous array of other forms of psychopathology. The latter is an important issue, and researchers have begun to recognize the need for clinical comparison groups; a number of the studies discussed have adopted this approach. Increased understanding of the specificity of certain processing patterns to particular disorders will rely on a continuation of this trend. It may also reveal categorical commonalities among disorders in terms of cognitive-structural similarities, a conceptual framework considered by Blatt (1991) to be more meaningful and heuristically useful than current descriptive symptom-based taxonomies.

Finally, a traditional criticism of this literature has concerned its failure to determine whether biased information processing temporally precedes (i.e., plays a causal role in) or is a consequence of psychopathological states. This issue cannot be clarified via the predominant use of cross-sectional designs (see Monroe & Roberts, 1991), but recent trends have begun to remedy this explanatory flaw. Examples, as discussed, include studies of processing associated with both trait vulnerabilities and state manifestations, as well as investigations comparing the responses of individuals following recovery with those of individuals currently experiencing symptoms. Although short-term follow-up studies are informative, longitudinal prospective designs are needed. If cross-sectional methods are going to continue to be utilized in the investigation of the dynamic interplay among intelligence, personality, and psychopathology, simple linear models must be abandoned, as their assumptions may not be justified by the data (e.g., Costello, 1992; Fergusson, Horwood, & Lawton, 1989).

All of the limitations discussed have suggested directions for future research. A number of other possibilities are associated with the potential application of these findings in clinical contexts. For example, few attempts have been made to use experimental cognitive paradigms in the evaluation of treatment efficacy. Not only are such methods less vulnerable to response bias over repeated assessments than self-report measures (Dagleish & Watts, 1990), but their sensitivity to low levels of variation and validity are well established. Such an approach would enable comparison of different therapeutic models and help to determine the mechanisms involved in the relapse rates associated with them.

The research and models discussed have been quite successful in identifying the mechanisms involved in the processing biases that perpetuate a number of disorders. The next logical step may be to identify the ways in which these mechanisms may be modified. In the words of MacLeod (1990, p. 49), "Specifically, can we directly induce in high trait vulnerable subjects those patterns of information processing that characterize low trait subjects?" One particularly relevant finding is that of the consequences of mood induction on processing biases, particularly those of memory (see Dagleish & Watts, 1990). The use of such procedures might be developed into specific clinical interventions, with interference in the self-perpetuating cycle of processing bias leading to more enduring benefits for clinical patients. More generally, the proclivity of individuals diagnosed with personality disorders to force a wide array of experiences into particular schematic frameworks may be of particular relevance to attempts at therapeutic intervention.

In summary, the theme that has run throughout this chapter has been the inextricable web of interrelationships among psychopathology, personality, and intelligence. Cognitive processes such as attention, encoding, interpretation, and all forms of memory play crucial roles in the individual's ability to synthesize both internal and external experiences. These processes and structural components act symbiotically. In this view, intelligence represents the flexibility, accuracy, and complexity of the total cognitive configuration; personality reflects its manifestation in the expression of thought and emotion, interpersonal activity, and general adaptive functioning. Emotional, motivational, and purposive factors play an indisputable role in both of these psychological activities, as well as in failures of adjustment (i.e., psychopathology). As Magnusson and Törestad (1993) have indicated, psychology as a discipline must be guided in its choice of models and paradigms by a consideration of the individual as a purposeful agent, capable of constructing and influencing the psychological situations within which he or she acts (see also Lewin, 1935). Cognitive frameworks acknowledging this dynamic complexity provide theorists, researchers, and clinicians with a powerful conceptual and methodological tool. We have explored only a portion of its potential for the understanding of human adjustment, and we have sought to underscore its value for future attempts to integrate the many psychological processes involved.

Acknowledgments. The authors would like to acknowledge the general support provided during the writing of this chapter by the Social Sciences and Humanities Research Council of Canada (SSHRC), both in the form of a research grant to the first author (No. 418-91-1150), and a doctoral fellowship to the second.

REFERENCES

Abraham, K. (1923). Contributions to the theory of the anal character. *International Journal of Psycho-Analysis, 4*, 400–418.

Achenbach, T. M. (1985). *Assessment and taxonomy of child and adolescent psychopathology*. Newbury Park, CA: Sage.

Akhtar, S. (1988). Hypomanic personality disorder. *Integrative Psychiatry, 6*, 37–52.

Akhtar, S. (1989). Narcissistic personality disorder: Descriptive features and differential diagnosis. *Psychiatric Clinics of North America, 12*, 505–529.

Akiskal, H. S. (1983). Dysthymic disorder: Psychopathology of proposed depressive subtypes. *American Journal of Psychiatry, 26*, 315–317.

Akiskal, H. S., Djenderedjian, A. H., & Rosenthal, R. H. (1977). Cyclothymic disorder: Validating criteria for inclusion in the bipolar affective group. *American Journal of Psychiatry, 134*, 1227–1233.

Allen, J. J., Chapman, L. J., & Chapman, J. P. (1987). Cognitive slippage and depression in hypothetically psychosis-prone college students. *Journal of Nervous and Mental Disease, 175*, 347–353.

Alloy, L. B., & Abramson, L. Y. (1988). Depressive realism: Four theoretical perspectives. In L. B. Alloy (Ed.), *Cognitive processes in depression* (pp. 223–265). New York: Guilford.

Allport, G. M. (1937). *Pattern and growth in personality*. Toronto: Holt, Rinehart & Winston.

American Psychiatric Association. (1980). *Diagnostic and statistical manual of mental disorders* (3rd ed.). Washington, DC: Author.

American Psychiatric Association. (1987). *Diagnostic and statistical manual of mental disorders* (rev. 3rd ed.). Washington, DC: Author.

American Psychiatric Association. (1994). *Diagnostic and statistical manual of mental disorders* (4th ed.). Washington, DC: Author.

Anderson, J., & Bower, G. H. (1973). *Human associative memory*. Washington, DC: Winston.

Andreason, N. C. (1980). Mania and creativity. In R. H. Belmaker & H. M. van Praag (Eds.), *Mania: An evolving concept* (pp. 377–386). New York: Spectrum.

Andreason, N. C., Tsuang, M. T., & Canter, A. (1974). The significance of thought disorder in diagnostic evaluations. *Comprehensive Psychiatry, 15*, 27–34.

Andrews, J. D. W., & Moore, S. (1991). Social cognition in the histrionic/overconventional personality. In P. A. Magaro (Ed.), *Cognitive bases of mental disorders* (pp. 11–76). London: Sage.

Angst, J. (1966). *Zur Ätiologie und Nosologie endogener depressiver Psychosen*. Berlin: Springer.

Bandura, A. (1986). *Social foundations of thought and action: A social cognitive theory*. Englewood Cliffs, NJ: Erlbaum.

Barlow, D. H. (1991). Disorders of emotion. *Psychological Inquiry, 2*, 58–71.

Barnard, P. (1985). Interacting cognitive subsystems: A psycholinguistic approach to short-term memory. In A. Ellis (Ed.), *Progress in the psychology of language* (Vol. 2, pp. 197–258). London: Erlbaum.

Barnard, P. J. & Teasdale, J. D. (1991). Interacting cognitive subsystems: A systemic approach to cognitive-affective interaction and change. *Cognition and Emotion, 5*, 1–39.

Bartlett, F. C. (1932). *Remembering: A study in experimental and social psychology*. Cambridge, England: Cambridge University Press.

Beck, A. T. (1967). *Depression: Clinical, experimental, and theoretical aspects*. New York: Hoeber.

Beck, A. T. (1976). *Cognitive therapy and the emotional disorders*. New York: International University Press.

Beck, A. T. (1983). Cognitive therapy of depression: New Perspectives. In P. J. Clayton & J. E. Barrett (Eds.), *Treatment of Depression: Old controversies and new approaches* (pp. 265–290). New York: Raven Press.

Beck, A. T. (1984). Cognition and therapy. *Archives of General Psychiatry, 411*, 1112–1114.

Beck, A. T. (1987). Cognitive models of depression. *Journal of Cognitive Psychotherapy, 1*, 5–37.

Beck, A. T., & Emery, G. (1985). *Anxiety disorders and phobias: A cognitive perspective*. New York: Basic Books.

Beck, A. T., & Freeman, A. (1990). *Cognitive therapy of personality disorders*. New York: Guilford.

Beech, A. R., McManus, D., Baylis, G., Tipper, S. P., & Agar, K. (1991). Individual differences in cognitive processes: Towards an explanation of schizophrenic symptomatology. *British Journal of Psychology, 82*, 417–426.

Been-Zeev, A. (1988). The schema paradigm in perception. *Journal of Mind and Behavior, 9*, 487–514.

Bellew, M., & Hill, A. B. (1991). Schematic processing and the prediction of depression following childbirth. *Personality and Individual Differences, 12*, 943–949.

Blaney, P. H. (1986). Affect and memory: A review. *Psychological Bulletin, 99*, 229–246.

Blashfield, R. K. (1984). *The classification of psychopathology*. New York: Plenum.

Blatt, S. J. (1991). A cognitive morphology of psychopathology. *Journal of Nervous and Mental Disease, 179*, 449–458.

Bornstein, R. F. (1992). The dependent personality: Developmental, social, and clinical perspectives. *Psychological Bulletin, 112*, 3–23.

Bower, G. H. (1981). Mood and memory. *American Psychologist, 36*, 129–148.

Bower, H. (1989). Beethoven's creative illness. *Australian and New Zealand Journal of Psychiatry, 23*, 111–116.

Bradley, B., & Mathews, A. (1983). Negative self-schema in clinical depression. *British Journal of Clinical Psychology, 22*, 173–182.

Bradley, B., & Mathews, A. (1988). Memory bias in recovered clinical depressives. *Cognition and Emotion, 2*, 235–246.

Broadbent, D., & Broadbent, M. (1988). Anxiety and attentional bias: State and trait. *Cognition and Emotion, 2*, 165–183.

Brown, H. J., & Gutsch, K. U. (1985). Cognitions associated with a delay of gratification task: A study with psychopaths and normal prisoners. *Criminal Justice and Behavior, 12*, 453–462.

Burgess, J. W. (1991). Neurocognition in acute and chronic depression: Personality disorder, major depression, and schizophrenia. *Biological Psychiatry, 30*, 305–309.

Burgess, J. W. (1992). Neurocognitive impairment in dramatic personalities: Histrionic, narcissistic, borderline, and antisocial disorders. *Psychiatry Research, 42*, 283–290.

Buss, A. H. (1966). *Psychopathology*. New York: Wiley.

Butler, G., & Mathews, A. (1983). Cognitive processes in anxiety. *Advances in Behaviour Research and Therapy, 5*, 51–62.

Caballero, J. A., & Moreno, J. B. (1993). Depressed mood, mood-simulation and congruent recall. *Personality and Individual Differences, 14*, 365–368.

Cameron, N. (1963). *Personality development and psychopathology*. Boston: Houghton Mifflin.

Carver, C. S., Scheier, M. F. (1981). *Attention and self-regulation: A control theory approach to human behavior*. New York: Springer-Verlag.

Ceci, S. J. (1990). *On intelligence . . . more or less: A bioecological treatise on intellectual development*. Englewood Cliffs, NJ: Prentice-Hall.

Challis, B. H., & Krane, R. V. (1988). Mood induction and the priming of semantic memory in a lexical decision task: Asymmetric effects of elation and depression. *Bulletin of the Psychonomic Society, 26*, 309–312.

Clark, D. M., & Teasdale, J. D. (1982). Diurnal variations in clinical depression and accessibility of memories of positive and negative experiences. *Journal of Abnormal Psychology, 91*, 87–95.

Costa, P. T., & McCrae, R. R. (1992). *Revised NEO Personality Inventory (NEO PI-R) and NEO Five-Factor Inventory (NEO-FFI): Professional manual*. Odessa, FL: Psychological Assessment Resources.

Costello, C. G. (1992). Conceptual problems in current research on cognitive vulnerability to psychopathology. *Cognitive Therapy and Research, 16*, 379–390.

Craske, M. G. (1991). Phobic fear and panic attacks: The same emotional states triggered by different cues? *Clinical Psychology Review, 11*, 599–620.

Dagleish, T., & Watts, F. N. (1990). Biases of attention and memory in disorders of anxiety and depression. *Clinical Psychology Review, 10*, 589–604.

Dickman, S. J. (1990). Functional and dysfunctional impulsivity: Personality and cognitive correlates. *Journal of Personality and Social Psychology, 58*, 95–102.

Digman, J. M. (1990). Personality structure: Emergence of the five-factor model. *Annual Review of Psychology, 41*, 417–440.

Dobson, K. S., & Shaw, B. F. (1987). Specificity and stability of self-referent encoding in clinical depression. *Journal of Abnormal Psychology, 96*, 34–40.

Doherty, J. P., Feister, S. J., & Shea, T. (1986). Syndrome diagnosis and personality disorder. In A. Frances & R. E. Hale (Eds.), *American Psychiatric Association annual review* (Vol. 5, pp. 315–355). Washington, DC: American Psychiatric Association.

Dunbar, D. C., & Lishman, W. A. (1984). Depression, recognition-memory, and hedonic tone: A signal detection analysis. *British Journal of Psychiatry, 144*, 376–382.

Edwards, L., Pearce, S., Collett, B. J., & Pugh, R. (1992). Selective memory for sensory and affective information in chronic pain and depression. *British Journal of Clinical Psychology, 31*, 239–248.

Ehlers, A., Margraf, J., Davies, S., & Roth, W. T. (1988). Selective processing of threat cues in subjects with panic attacks. *Cognition and Emotion, 2*, 201–220.

Ellis, H. C., & Ashbrook, P. W. (1988). Resource allocation model of the effects of depressed mood states on memory. In K. Fiedler & J. Forgas (Eds.), *Affect, cognition and social behavior* (pp. 25–43). Toronto: Hogrefe.

Endler, N. S. (1980). Person-situation interaction and anxiety. In I. L. Kutash & L. B. Schlesinger (Eds.), *Handbook on stress and anxiety: Contemporary knowledge, theory and treatment* (pp. 241–266). San Francisco: Jossey-Bass.

Endler, N. S. (1983). Interactionism: A personality model, but not yet a theory. In M. M. Page (Ed.), *Nebraska Symposium on Motivation 1982: Personality—current theory and research* (pp. 155–200). Lincoln: University of Nebraska Press.

Endler, N. S. (1993). Personality: An interactional perspective. In J. Hettema & I. Deary (Eds.), *Foundations of personality* (pp. 251–268). Dortrecht: Kluwer Academic Publishers.

Endler, N. S., Edwards, J. M., & Vitelli, R. (1991). *Endler Multidimensional Anxiety Scales: Manual*. Los Angeles: Western Psychological Services.

Endler, N. S., & Magnusson, D. (1976). Toward an interactional psychology of personality. *Psychological Bulletin, 83*, 956–979.

Endler, N. S., & Parker, J. D. A. (1990). Personality research: Theories, issues and methods. In M. Hersen, A. E. Kazdin, & A. S. Bellack (Eds.), *The clinical psychology handbook* (2nd ed., pp. 258–275). Toronto: Pergamon.

Endler, N. S., & Parker, J. D. A. (1992). Interactionism revisited: Reflections on the continuing crisis in the personality area. *European Journal of Personality, 6*, 177–198.

Enright, S. J., & Beech, A. R. (1993a). Further evidence of reduced cognitive inhibition in obsessive-compulsive disorder. *Personality and Individual Differences, 3*, 387–395.

Enright, S. J., & Beech, A. R. (1993b). Reduced cognitive inhibition in obsessive-compulsive disorder. *British Journal of Clinical Psychology, 32*, 67–74.

Eysenck, H. (1967). *The biological basis of personality*. Springfield, IL: Thomas.

Eysenck, H. (1970). *The structure of human personality* (3rd ed.) London: Methuen.

Eysenck, H. (1981). *A model for personality*. New York: Springer.

Eysenck, H., & Eysenck, M. W. (1985). *Personality and individual differences: A natural science approach*. New York: Plenum.

Eysenck, M. W., & Mathews, A. (1987). Trait anxiety and cognition. In H. J. Eysenck & I. Martin (Eds.), *Theoretical foundations of behavior therapy*. New York: Plenum.

Eysenck, M. W., MacLeod, C., & Mathews, A. (1987). Cognitive functioning in anxiety. *Psychological Research, 49*, 189–195.

Eysenck, M. W., Mogg, K., May, J., Richards, A., & Mathews, A. (1991). Bias in interpretation of ambiguous sentences related to threat in anxiety. *Journal of Abnormal Psychology, 100*, 144–150.

Fenichel, O. (1945). *The psychoanalytic theory of neurosis*. New York: Norton.

Fergusson, D. M., Horwood, L. J., & Lawton, J. M. (1989). The relationships between neuroticism and depressive symptoms. *Social Psychiatry and Psychiatric Epidemiology, 24*, 275–281.

Fitzgerald, T. E., & Phillips, W. (1991). Attentional bias and agoraphobic avoidance: The role of cognitive style. *Journal of Anxiety Disorders, 5*, 333–341.

Foa, E. B., & Kozak, M. J. (1986). Emotional processing of fear: Exposure to corrective information. *Psychological Bulletin, 99*, 20–35.

Foa, E. B., & McNally, R. J. (1986). Sensitivity to feared stimuli in obsessive-compulsives: A dichotic listening analysis. *Cognitive Therapy and Research, 10*, 477–486.

Foa, E. B., McNally, R. J., & Murdock, T. B. (1989). Anxious mood and memory. *Behaviour Research and Therapy, 27*, 141–147.

Fogarty, S. J., & Helmsley, D. R. (1983). Depression and the accessibility of memories. *British Journal of Psychiatry, 142*, 232–237.

Ford, D. H. (1987). *Humans as self-constructing living systems: A developmental perspective on behavior and personality*. Hillsdale, NJ: Erlbaum.

Forgas, J. P., & Bower, G. H. (1987). Mood effects in person perception. *Journal of Personality and Social Psychology, 53*, 53–60.

Fox, E. (1993). Allocation of visual attention and anxiety. *Cognition and Emotion, 7*, 207–215.

Frenkel-Brunswick, E. (1949). Intolerance of ambiguity as an emotional and perceptual personality variable. *Journal of Probability, 18*, 103–143.

Frosch, W. A. (1987). Moods, madness, and music: I. Major affective disease and musical creativity. *Comprehensive Psychiatry, 28*, 315–322.

Frost, R. O., Lahart, C. M., Dugas, K. M., & Sher, K. J. (1988). Information processing among non-clinical compulsives. *Behaviour Research and Therapy, 26*, 275–277.

Gardner, H. (1983). *Frames of mind: The theory of multiple intelligences*. New York: Basic Books.

Gardner, H. (1985). *The mind's new science: A history of the cognitive revolution*. New York: Basic Books.

Gardner, R. W., Jackson, D. N., & Messick, S. J. (1960). Personality organization in cognitive controls and intellectual abilities. *Psychological Issues, 2*, 1–45.

Gardner, R. W., & Moriarty, A. (1968). Dimensions of cognitive control in preadolescence. In R. Gardner (Ed.), *Personality development at preadolescence* (pp. 118–148). Seattle: University of Washington Press.

Goodwin, F. K., & Jamison, K. R. (1990). *Manic-depressive illness*. New York: Oxford University Press.

Gorenstein, E. E. (1982). Frontal lobe functions in psychopaths. *Journal of Abnormal Psychology, 91*, 368–379.

Gorenstein, E. E. (1991). A cognitive perspective on antisocial personality. In P. A. Magaro (Ed.), *Cognitive bases of mental disorders* (pp. 100–133). London: Sage.

Gotlib, I. H., & McCann, C. D. (1984). Construct accessibility and depression: An examination of cognitive and affective factors. *Journal of Personality and Social Psychology, 47*, 427–439.

Gotlib, I. H., McLachlan, A. L., & Katz, A. N. (1988). Biases in visual attention in depressed and nondepressed individuals. *Cognition and Emotion, 2*, 185–200.

Graf, P., & Mandler, G. (1984). Activation makes words more accessible, but not necessarily more retrievable. *Journal of Verbal Learning and Verbal Behavior, 23*, 553–568.

Greenberg, M. S., & Beck, A. T. (1989). Depression versus anxiety: A test of the content-specificity hypothesis. *Journal of Abnormal Psychology, 98*, 9–13.

Greenberg, M. S., Pyszczynski, T., Burling, J., & Tibbs, K. (1992). Depression, self-focused attention, and the self-serving attributional bias. *Personality and Individual Differences, 13*, 959–965.

Grossman, L. S., & Harrow, M. (1991). Thought disorder in mania. In P. A. Magaro (Ed.), *Cognitive bases of mental disorders* (pp. 134–186). London: Sage.

Guilford, J. P. (1967). *The nature of human intelligence*. New York: McGraw-Hill.

Gullwitzer, P. M., & Wicklund, R. A. (1985). The pursuit of self-defining goals. In J. Kuhl & J. Bechmann (Eds.), *Action control: From cognition to behavior* (pp. 61–85). New York: Springer-Verlag.

Hamilton, V. (1957a). Conflict avoidance in obsessionals and hysterics, and the validity of the concept of dysthymia. *Journal of Mental Science, 103*, 666–676.

Hamilton, V. (1957b). Perceptual and personality dynamics in reactions to ambiguity. *British Journal of Psychology, 48*, 200–215.

Hare, R. D. (1980). A research scale for the assessment of psychopathy in criminal populations. *Personality and Individual Differences, 1*, 111–119.

Hare, R. D., Hart, S. D., & Harpur, T. J. (1991). Psychopathy and the DSM-IV criteria for antisocial personality disorder. *Journal of Abnormal Psychology, 100*, 391–398.

Harvey, N. (1984). The Stroop effect: Failure to focus attention or failure to maintain focusing? *Quarterly Journal of Experimental Psychology, 36*, 89–108.

Hashway, R. M., & Duke, L. I. (1992). *Cognitive styles: A primer to the literature*. San Francisco: EmText.

Hoffart, A., & Martinsen, E. W. (1992). Personality disorders in panic with agoraphobia and major depression. *British Journal of Clinical Psychology, 31*, 213–214.

Holden, C. (1987). Creativity and the troubled mind. *Psychology Today, 21*, 9–10.

Hope, D. A., Rapee, R. M., Heimberg, R. G., & Dombeck, M. J. (1990). Representation of the self in social phobia: Vulnerability to social threat. *Cognitive Therapy and Research, 14*, 177–189.

Howard, J. C. (1989). Clinical interpretation of intelligence assessment. In S. Wetzler & M. M. Katz (Eds.), *Contemporary approaches to psychological assessment* (pp. 157–176). New York: Brunner/Mazel.

Howard, R. W. (1993). On what intelligence is. *British Journal of Psychology, 84*, 27–37.

Ingram, R. E., & Kendall, P. C. (1987). The cognitive side of anxiety. *Cognitive Therapy and Research, 11*, 523–536.

Ingram, R. E., Lumrey, A., Cruet, D., & Sieber, W. (1987). Attentional processes in depressive disorders. *Cognitive Therapy and Research, 11*, 351–360.

Ingram, R. E., & Smith, T. W. (1984). Depression and internal versus external focus of attention. *Cognitive Therapy and Research, 8*, 139–152.

Ingram, R. E., & Wisnicki, K. (1991). Cognition in depression. In P. A. Magaro (Ed.), *Cognitive bases of mental disorders* (pp. 187–230). London: Sage.

Jamison, K. R. (1989). Mood Disorders and season patterns in British writers and artists. *Psychiatry, 52*, 125–134.

Janet, P. (1903). *Les Obsessions et la psychasthénie* (Vol. 1, 2nd ed.). Paris: Alcan.

Johnson-Laird, P. N., Herrmann, D. J., & Chaffin, R. (1984). Only connections: A critique of semantic networks. *Psychological Bulletin, 96*, 292–315.

Karoly, P. (1993). Mechanisms of self-regulation: A systems view. *Annual Review of Psychology, 44*, 23–52.

Kay, S. R. (1989). Cognitive diagnostic assessment. In S. Wetzler & M. M. Katz (Eds.), *Contemporary approaches to psychological assessment* (pp. 177–200). New York: Brunner-Mazel.

Kelly, G. A. (1955). *The psychology of personal constructs*. New York: Norton.

Kernberg, O. F. (1989). The narcissistic personality disorder and the differential diagnosis of antisocial behavior. *Psychiatric Clinics of North America, 12*, 553–570.

Klerman, G. L. (1973). The relationship between personality and clinical depressions: Overcoming the obstacles to verifying psychodynamic theories. *International Journal of Psychiatry, 11*, 227–233.

Klinger, E. (1987). Current concerns and disengagement from incentives. In F. Halisch & J. Kuhl (Eds.), *Motivation, intention and volition* (pp. 337–347). New York: Springer-Verlag.

Kuiper, N. A., Olinger, L. J., & Air, P. A. (1989). Stressful events, dysfunctional attitudes, coping styles, and depression. *Personality and Individual Differences, 10*, 229–237.

Lang, P. J. (1977). Physiological assessment of anxiety and fear. In J. D. Cone & R. P. Hawkins (Eds.), *Behavioral assessment: New directions in clinical psychology* (pp. 178–195). New York: Brunner/Mazel.

Lawrence, D., & Morton, V. (1980). Associating embedded figures test performance with extreme hysteria and psychasthenia MMPI scores in a psychiatric population. *Perceptual and Motor Skills, 50*, 432–434.

Leonhard, K. (1957). *Aufteilung der Endogenen Psychosen*. Berlin: Akademie-Verlag.

Lewin, K. (1935). *A dynamic theory of personality*. New York: McGraw-Hill.

Lezak, M. (1983). *Neuropsychological assessment* (2nd ed.). New York: Oxford University Press.

MacLeod, C. (1990). Mood disorders and cognition. In M. W. Eysenck (Ed.), *Cognitive psychology: An international review* (pp. 9–56). Toronto: Wiley.

MacLeod, C. (1991). Clinical anxiety and the selective encoding of threatening information. *International Review of Psychiatry, 3*, 279–292.

MacLeod, C., & Mathews, A. (1988). Anxiety and the allocation of attention to threat. *Quarterly Journal of Experimental Psychology: Human Experimental Psychology, 38*, 659–670.

MacLeod, C., & Mathews, A. (1991). Biased cognitive operations in anxiety: Accessibility of information or assignment of processing priorities. *Behaviour Research and Therapy, 29*, 599–610.

MacLeod, C., Mathews, A., & Tata, P. (1986). Attentional bias in emotional disorders. *Journal of Abnormal Psychology, 95*, 15–20.

MacLeod, C., Tata, P., & Mathews, A. (1987). Perception of emotionally valenced information in depression. *British Journal of Psychology, 26*, 67–68.

Magaro, P., & Smith, P. (1981). The personality of clinical types: An empirically derived taxonomy. *Journal of Clinical Psychology, 37*, 796–809.

Magnusson, D., & Törestad, B. (1993). A holistic view of personality: A model revisited. *Annual Review of Psychology, 44*, 427–452.

Makhlouf-Norris, F., & Jones, H. G. (1971). Conceptual distance indices as measures of alienation in obsessional neurosis. *Psychological Medicine, 1*, 381–387.

Mandler, G. (1984). Consciousness, imagery, and emotion—with special reference to autonomic imagery. *Journal of Mental Imagery, 8*, 87–94.

Marshall, W. L., & Barbaree, H. E. (1991). Personality, impulse control, and adjustment disorders. In M. Hersen & S. M. Turner, *Adult psychopathology and diagnosis* (2nd ed., pp. 360–391). Toronto: Wiley.

Massaro, D. W., & Cowan, N. (1993). Information processing models: Microscopes of the mind. *Annual Review of Psychology, 44*, 383–425.

Matarazzo, J. D. (1979). *Wechsler's measurement and appraisal of adult intelligence* (5th ed.). New York: Oxford University Press.

Matczak, A. (1990). Reflection-impulsivity, need for stimulation, and intellectual potentialities. *Polish Psychological Bulletin, 21*, 17–25.

Mathews, A. (1988). Anxiety and the processing of threatening information. In V. Hamilton, G. Bower, & N. Frijda (Eds.), *Cognitive perspectives on emotion and motivation*. Dordrecht, Netherlands: Kluwer.

Mathews, A., & MacLeod, C. (1986). Discrimination of threat cues without awareness in anxiety states. *Journal of Abnormal Psychology, 95*, 131–138.

Mathews, A., & MacLeod, C. (1987). An information-processing approach to anxiety. *Journal of Cognitive Psychotherapy, 1*, 105–115.

Mathews, A., May, J., Mogg, K., & Eysenck, M. (1990). Attentional bias in anxiety: Selective search or defective filtering? *Journal of Abnormal Psychology, 99*, 166–173.

Mathews, A., Mogg, K., May, J., & Eysenck, M. (1989). Implicit and explicit memory bias in anxiety. *Journal of Abnormal Psychology, 98*, 236–240.

Mathews, G. R., & Antes, J. R. (1992). Visual attention and depression: Cognitive biases in the eye fixations of the dysphoric and the nondepressed. *Cognitive Therapy and Research, 16*, 359–371.

Mattick, R. P., & Newman, C. R. (1991). Social phobia and avoidant personality disorder. *International Review of Psychiatry, 3*, 163–173.

McDowall, J. (1984). Recall of pleasant and unpleasant words in depressed subjects. *Journal of Abnormal Psychology, 93*, 401–407.

McCrae, R. R. (1987). Creativity, divergent thinking, and openness to experience. *Journal of Personality and Social Psychology, 52*, 1258–1265.

McMullen, L. M., & Rogers, D. L. (1984). WAIS characteristics of nonpathological obsessive and hysteric styles. *Journal of Clinical Psychology, 40*, 577–479.

McNally, R. J., & Kohlbeck, P. A. (1993). Reality monitoring in obsessive-compulsive disorder. *Behaviour Research and Therapy, 31*, 249–253.

McReynolds, P. (1989). Diagnosis and clinical assessment: Current status and major issues. *Annual Review of Psychology, 40*, 83–108.

Messick, S. (1989). *Cognitive style and personality: Scanning and orientation toward affect*. Princeton, NJ: Educational Testing Service.

Millon, T. (1969). *Modern psychopathology*. Philadelphia: Saunders.

Millon, T. (1981). *Disorders of personality: DSM-III, Axis II*. New York: Wiley-Interscience.

Millon, T. (1983). The DSM-III: An insider's perspective. *American Psychologist, 38*, 804–814.

Millon, T. (1986). Personality prototypes and their diagnostic criteria. In T. Millon & G. L. Klerman (Eds.), *Contemporary directions in psychopathology*. New York: Guilford.

Millon, T. (1987). On the nature of taxonomy in psychopathology. In C. G. Last & M. Hersen (Eds.), *Issues in diagnostic research* (pp. 3–85). New York: Plenum.

Millon, T. (1990a). The disorders of personality. In L. A. Pervin (Ed.), *Handbook of personality* (pp. 339–369). New York: Guilford.

Millon, T. (1990b). *Toward a new personology: An evolutionary model*. Toronto: Wiley.

Millon, T. (1991). Classification in psychopathology: Rationale, alternatives, and standards. *Journal of Abnormal Psychology, 100*, 245–261.

Millon, T., & Frances, A. J. (Eds.). (1991a). DSM-IV personality disorders: I [Special series]. *Journal of Personality Disorders, 5*(2).

Millon, T., & Frances, A. J. (Eds.). (1991b). DSM-IV personality disorders: II [Special series]. *Journal of Personality Disorders, 5*(4).

Millon, T., & Frances, A. J. (Eds.). (1993). DSM-IV personality disorders: III [Special series]. *Journal of Personality Disorders, 7*(1).

Mineka, S., & Sutton, S. K. (1992). Cognitive biases and the emotional disorders. *Psychological Science, 3*, 65–69.

Mischel, W. (1979). On the interface of cognition and personality: Beyond the person-situation debate. *American Psychologist, 34*, 740–754.

Mogg, K., Gardiner, J. M., Stavrou, A., & Golumbek, S. (1992). Recollective experience and recognition memory for threat in clinical anxiety states. *Bulletin of the Psychonomic Society, 30*, 109–112.

Mogg, K., Mathews, A., Bird, C., & MacGregor-Morris, R. (1990). Effects of stress and anxiety on the processing of threat stimuli. *Journal of Personality and Social Psychology, 59*, 1230–1237.

Mogg, K., Mathews, A., & Eysenck, M. (1992). Attentional bias to threat in clinical anxiety states. *Cognition and Emotion, 6*, 149–159.

Mogg, K., Mathews, A., Eysenck, M., & May, J. (1991). Biased cognitive operations in anxiety: Artefact, processing priorities, or attentional search? *Behaviour Research and Therapy, 29*, 459–467.

Mogg, K., Mathews, A., May, J., Grove, M., Eysenck, M., & Weinman, J. (1991). Assessment of cognitive bias in anxiety and depression using a colour perception task. *Cognition and Emotion, 5*, 221–238.

Mogg, K., Mathews, A., & Weinman, J. (1987). Memory bias in clinical anxiety. *Journal of Abnormal Psychology, 96*, 94–98.

Mogg, K., Mathews, A., & Weinman, J. (1989). Selective processing of threat cues in anxiety states: A replication. *Behaviour Research and Therapy, 27*, 317–323.

Mollinger, R. N. (1980). Antitheses and the obsessive-compulsive. *Psychoanalytic Review, 67*, 465–477.

Monroe, S. M., & Roberts, J. E. (1991). Psychopathology research. In M. Hersen, A. E. Kazdin, & A. S. Bellack (Eds.), *The clinical psychology handbook* (2nd ed., pp. 276–292). Toronto: Pergamon.

Morey, L. C. (1993). Psychological correlates of personality disorder. *Journal of Personality Disorders, 7* (Suppl.), 149–166.

Neisser, U. (1976). *Cognition and reality: Principles and implications of cognitive psychology.* San Francisco: Freeman.

Newman, J. P., & Kosson, D. S. (1986). Passive avoidance learning in psychopathic and nonpsychopathic offenders. *Journal of Abnormal Psychology, 95*, 252–256.

Newman, J. P., Patterson, C. M., & Nathan, S. (1987). Response perseveration in psychopaths. *Journal of Abnormal Psychology, 96*, 145–148.

Nolen-Hoeksema, S. (1991). Responses to depression and their effects on the duration of depressive episodes. *Journal of Abnormal Psychology, 100*, 569–582.

Norman, W. H., Miller, I. W., & Dow, M. G. (1988). Characteristics of depressed patients with elevated levels of dysfunctional cognitions. *Cognitive Therapy and Research, 12*, 39–52.

Oatley, K., & Johnson-Laird, P. (1987). Towards a cognitive theory of emotions. *Cognition and Emotion, 1*, 29–50.

Obiols, J. E., Garcia-Domingo, M., De Trinchería, I., & Doménech, E. (1993). Psychometric schizotypy and sustained attention in young males. *Personality and Individual Differences, 14*, 381–384.

Olden, C. (1946). Headline intelligence. *Psychoanalytic Study of the Child, 2*, 263–269.

Persons, J. B. & Foa, E. B. (1984). Processing of fearful and neutral information by obsessive-compulsives. *Behaviour Research and Therapy, 22*, 259–265.

Phillips, K. A., Hirschfeld, R. M. A., Shea, M. T., & Gunderson, J. G. (1993). Depressive personality disorders: Perspectives for DSM-IV. *Journal of Personality Disorders, 7*, 30–42.

Powell, M., & Helmsley, D. R. (1984). Depression: A breakdown of perceptual defence? *British Journal of Psychiatry, 145*, 358–362.

Pyszczynski, T., Hamilton, J. C., Herring, F. H., & Greenberg, J. (1989). Depression, self-focused attention, and the negative memory bias. *Journal of Personality and Social Psychology, 57*, 351–357.

Rachman, S. (1993). Obsessions, responsibility and guilt. *Behaviour Research and Therapy, 31*, 149–154.

Rado, S. (1974). Obsessive behavior: A. So-called obsessive-compulsive neurosis. In S. Arieti (Ed.), *American handbook of psychiatry* (Vol. 3, 2nd ed.). New York: Basic Books.

Reed, G. F. (1969a). "Under-inclusion"—a characteristic of obsessional personality disorder: I. *British Journal of Psychiatry, 115*, 781–785.

Reed, G. F. (1969b). "Under-inclusion"—a characteristic of obsessional personality disorder: II. *British Journal of Psychiatry, 115*, 787–790.

Reed, G. F. (1985). *Obsessional experience and compulsive behaviour: A cognitive-structural approach.* Toronto: Academic Press.

Reed, G. F. (1991). The cognitive characteristics of obsessional disorder. In P. A. Magaro (Ed.), *Cognitive bases of mental disorders* (pp. 77–99). London: Sage.

Reiss, S. (1987). Theoretical perspectives on the fear of anxiety. *Clinical Psychology Review, 7*, 585–596.

Reiss, S., & McNally, R. J. (1985). Expectancy model of fear. In S. Reiss & R. R. Bootzin (Eds.), *Theoretical issues in behavior therapy* (pp. 107–121). New York: Academic Press.

Renneberg, B., Chambless, D. L., & Gracely, E. J. (1992). Prevalence of SCID-diagnosed personality disorders in agoraphobic outpatients. *Journal of Anxiety Disorders, 6*, 111–118.

Rholes, W. S., Riskind, J. H., & Lane, J. W. (1987). Emotional states and memory biases: Effects of cognitive priming and mood. *Journal of Personality and Social Psychology, 52*, 91–99.

Richards, R., & Kinney, D. K. (1990). Mood swings and creativity. *Creativity Research Journal, 3*, 202–217.

Robbins, M. (1989). Primitive personality organization as an interpersonally adaptive modification of cognition and affect. *International Journal of Psycho-Analysis, 70*, 443–459.

Rogers, R., & Dion, K. (1991). Rethinking the DSM-III diagnosis of antisocial personality disorder. *Bulletin of the American Academy of Psychiatry and Law, 19*, 21–31.

Rosenberg, C. M. (1953). Compulsiveness as a determinant in selected cognitive-perceptual performances. *Journal of Personality, 21*, 506–516.

Rosenwald, G. C. (1972). Effectiveness of defenses against anal impulse arousal. *Journal of Consulting and Clinical Psychology, 39*, 292–298.

Rothkopf, J. S., & Blaney, P. H. (1991). Mood congruent memory: The role of affective focus and gender. *Cognition and Emotion, 5*, 53–64.

Sackeim, H. A., Freeman, J., McElhiney, M., Coleman, E., Prudic, J., & Devanand, D. P. (1992). Effects of major depression estimates of intelligence. *Journal of Clinical and Experimental Neuropsychology, 14*, 268–288.

Salama, A. A. (1988). The antisocial personality. *Psychiatric Journal of the University of Ottawa, 13*, 149–153.

Salovey, P., & Mayer, J. D. (1990). Emotional intelligence. *Imagination, Cognition and Personality, 9*, 185–211.

Salzman, L. (1973). *The obsessive personality: Origins, dynamics and therapy* (2nd ed.). New York: Aronson.

Salzman, L. (1980). *Treatment of the obsessive personality*. New York: Aronson.

Sattler, J. M. (1982). *Assessment of children's intelligence and special abilities*. Boston: Allyn & Bacon.

Sedikides, C., & Skowronski, J. J. (1991). The law of cognitive structure activation. *Psychological Inquiry, 2*, 169–184.

Segal, Z. V., & Shaw, B. F. (1986). Cognition in depression: A reappraisal of Coyne & Gotlib's critique. *Cognitive Therapy and Research, 10*, 671–694.

Shapiro, D. (1965). *Neurotic styles*. New York: Basic Books.

Shea, S. (1991). Practical use of the DSM-III-R. In M. Hersen & S. M. Turner, *Adult psychopathology and diagnosis* (2nd ed., pp. 23–46). Toronto: Wiley.

Sher, K. J., Frost, R. O., & Otto, R. (1983). Cognitive deficits in compulsive checkers: An exploratory study. *Behaviour Research and Therapy, 21*, 357–363.

Sher, K. J., Mann, B., & Frost, R. O. (1984). Cognitive dysfunction in compulsive checkers: Further explorations. *Behaviour Research and Therapy, 21*, 498–501.

Simons, A. D., Murphy, E. E., Levine, J. L., & Wetzel, R. D. (1986). Sustained improvement one year after cognitive and/or pharmacotherapy of depression. *Archives of General Psychiatry, 43*, 43–48.

Sims, A. (1988). *Symptoms in the mind: An introduction to descriptive psychopathology*. Toronto: Balliere Tindall.

Slife, B. D., & Weaver, C. A. (1992). Depression, cognitive skill, and metacognitive skill in problem solving. *Cognition and Emotion, 6*, 1–22.

Small, I. F., Small, J. G., Alig, V. B., & Moore, D. F. (1970). Passive-aggressive personality disorder: A search for a syndrome. *American Journal of Psychiatry, 126*, 973–983.

Smith, R. E., & Winokur, G. (1991). Mood disorders (bipolar). In M. Hersen & S. M. Turner (Eds.), *Adult psychopathology and diagnosis* (2nd ed., pp. 208–225). Toronto: Wiley.

Sorrentino, R. M., & Hewitt, E. C. (1984). The uncertainty-reducing properties of achievement tasks revisited. *Journal of Personality and Social Psychology, 47*, 884–899.

Sorrentino, R. M., Short, R. A. C., & Raynor, J. O. (1984). Certainty orientation: Implications for affective and cognitive views of achievement behavior. *Journal of Personality and Social Psychology, 47*, 189–206.

Spielberger, C. D. (1972). Anxiety as an emotional state. In C. D. Spielberger (Ed.), *Anxiety: Current trends in theory and research* (Vol. 1). New York: Academic Press.

Starcevic, V. (1992). Comorbidity models of panic disorder/agoraphobia and personality disturbances. *Journal of Personality Disorders, 6*, 213–225.

Steele, C. (1988). The psychology of self-affirmation: Sustaining the integrity of the self. In L. Berkowitz (Ed.), *Advances in experimental social psychology* (Vol. 21, pp. 261–302). New York: Academic Press.

Sternbach, S. E., Judd, P. H., Sabo, A. N., McGlashan, T., & Gunderson, J. G. (1992). Cognitive and perceptual distortions in borderline personality disorder and schizotypal personality disorder in a vignette sample. *Comprehensive Psychiatry, 33*, 186–189.

Sternberg, R. J. (1985). *Beyond IQ: A triarchic theory of human intelligence* (Vol. 1). New York: Cambridge University Press.

Sternberg, R. J. (1990). *Metaphors of mind: Conceptions of the nature of intelligence*. New York: Cambridge University Press.

Sternberg, R. J., & Detterman, D. K. (Eds.). (1986). *What is intelligence? Contemporary viewpoints on its nature and definition*. Norwood, NJ: Ablex.

Sternberg, R. J., & Frensch, P. A. (1990). Intelligence and cognition. In M. W. Eysenck (Ed.), *Cognitive psychology: An international review* (pp. 57–103). Toronto: Wiley.

Strauman, T. J. (1991). Psychopathology and the construction of meaning: Comments on a proposed law of cognitive structure activation. *Psychological Inquiry, 2*, 208–210.

Tancer, M. E., Brown, T. M., Evans, D. L., Ekstrom, D., & Elkind, J. (1990). Impaired effortful cognition in depression. *Psychiatry Research, 31*, 161–168.

Taylor, S. E., & Brown, J. E. (1988). Illusion and well-being: A social psychological perspective on mental health. *Psychological Bulletin, 103*, 193–210.

Teasdale, J. D. (1988). Cognitive vulnerability to persistent depression. *Cognition and Emotion, 2*, 247–274.

Teasdale, J. D., & Taylor, R. (1981). Induced mood and accessibility of memories: An effect of mood state or induction procedure? *British Journal of Clinical Psychology, 20*, 39–48.

Terman, L. M. (1916). *The measurement of intelligence*. Boston: Houghton Mifflin.

Thompson-Pope, S, K., & Turkat, I. D. (1988). Reactions to ambiguous stimuli along paranoid personalities. *Journal of Psychopathology and Behavioral Assessment, 10*, 21–32.

Thorndike, E. L. (1920). Intelligence and its uses. *Harper's, 140*, 227–235.

Tyrer, P. (1989). *Classification of neurosis*. Toronto: Wiley.

Wachtel, P. L. (1967). Conceptions of broad and narrow attention. *Psychological Bulletin, 68*, 417–429.

Wagner, R. K., & Sternberg, R. J. (1986). Tacit knowledge and intelligence in the everyday world. In R. K. Wagner & R. J. Sternberg (Eds.), *Practical intelligence: Nature and origins of competence in the everyday world* (pp. 51–85). New York: Cambridge University Press.

Walters, J., & Gardner, H. (1986). The crystallizing experience: Discovering an intellectual gift. In R. J. Sternberg & J. E. Davidson (Eds.), *Conceptions of giftedness* (pp. 306–331). New York: Cambridge University Press.

Watkins, P. C., Mathews, A., Williamson, D. A., & Fuller, R. D. (1992). Mood-congruent memory in depression: Emotional priming or elaboration? *Journal of Abnormal Psychology, 101*, 581–586.

Watson, P. J., Sawrie, S. M., & Biderman, M. D. (1991). Personal control, assumptive worlds, and narcissism. *Journal of Social Behavior and Personality, 6*, 929–941.

Watts, F. N. (1986). Cognitive processing in phobias. *Behaviour Psychotherapy, 14*, 295–301.

Watts, F. N., McKenna, F. P., Sharrock, R., & Trezise, L. (1986). Colour naming of phobia-related words. *British Journal of Psychology, 77*, 97–108.

Watts, F. N., Trezise, L., & Sharrock, R. (1986). Processing of phobic stimuli. *British Journal of Clinical Psychology, 77*, 97–108.

Wechsler, D. (1981). *Manual for the Adult Intelligence Scale—Revised*. New York: Psychological Corporation.

Weinstein, E. A. (1969). The development of interpersonal competence. In D. A. Goslin (Ed.), *Handbook of socialization theory and research*. Chicago: Rand McNally.

Wenzloff, R. M., Weger, D. M., & Roper, D. W. (1988). Depression and mental control: The resurgence of unwanted negative thoughts. *Journal of Personality and Social Psychology, 55*, 882–892.

Wetzler, S., & Katz, M. M. (Eds.). (1989). *Contemporary approaches to psychological assessment.* New York: Brunner/Mazel.

White, J., Davison, G. C., Haaga, D. A., & White, K. (1992). Cognitive bias in the articulated thoughts of depressed and nondepressed psychiatric patients. *Journal of Nervous and Mental Disease, 180,* 77–81.

Widiger, T. A., & Corbitt, E. M. (1993). Antisocial personality disorder: Proposals for DSM-IV. *Journal of Personality Disorders, 7,* 63–77.

Williams, J. M. G., & Broadbent, K. (1986). Autobiographical memory in attempted suicide patients. *Journal of Abnormal Psychology, 95,* 144–149.

Williams, J. M. G., & Scott, J. (1988). Autobiographical memory in depression. *Psychological Medicine, 18,* 689–695.

Williams, J. M. G., Watts, F. N., MacLeod, C., & Mathews, A. (1988). *Cognitive psychology and the emotional disorders.* Chichester, England: Wiley.

Wilcox, J. A. (1992). The predictive value of thought disorder in manic psychosis. *Psychopathology, 25,* 161–165.

Winfrey, L. L., & Goldfried, M. R. (1986). Information processing and the human change process. In R. E. Ingram (Ed.), *Information processing approaches to clinical psychology* (pp. 241–260). Orlando, FL: Academic Press.

Witkin, H., Dyk, R., Fattuson, H., Goodenough, D., & Karp, S. (1962). *Psychological differentiation: Studies of development.* New York: Wiley.

World Health Organization (1992a). *ICD-10: International classification of diseases and related health problems.* Geneva: Author.

World Health Organization (1992b). *The ICD-10 classification of mental and behavioral disorders: Clinical descriptions and diagnostic guidelines.* Geneva: Author.

Wright, J. H., & Salmon, P. G. (1990). Learning and memory in depression. In C. D. McCann & H. S. Endler (Eds.), *Depression: New directions in theory, research, and management* (pp. 211–236). Toronto: Wall & Emerson.

Yerkes, R. M., & Dodson, J. D. (1908). The relation of strength of stimulus to rapidity of habit-formation. *Journal of Comparative and Neurological Psychology, 18,* 459–482.

Zinbarg, R. E., Barlow, D. H., Brown, T. A., & Hertz, R. M. (1992). Cognitive-behavioral approaches to the nature and treatment of anxiety disorders. *Annual Review of Psychology, 43,* 235–267.

14

Cognitive Interference

At the Intelligence–Personality Crossroads

Irwin G. Sarason, Barbara R. Sarason, and Gregory R. Pierce

Cognitive interference occupies territory on the border between personality and intelligence. Intelligence is inferred from how people perform on certain kinds of tasks. Poor performance, however, does not necessarily mean low intellective potential; it could be because the individual was upset, thinking about something else, or unmotivated. All of these circumstances can contribute to *cognitive interference*: thoughts that intrude on task-related activity and serve to reduce the quality and level of performance. Some cognitive intrusions can be thought of as aspects or products of personality, because they involve personal preoccupations that interfere with attention to the task at hand. Personality can facilitate performance (e.g., through high motivation and the ability to become absorbed in tasks), but it can also debilitate it (e.g., through worrying about the consequences of failure and being uncooperative with the tester).

This chapter describes this border territory and reviews measures for assessing cognitive interference and its effects on performance. An important need for future research is exploration of how cognitive interference affects behavior in situations beyond the one that has been studied the most—performance in academic-type testing situations. For example, what role does such interference play in interpersonal relationships? Other research needs include identification of the causes of cognitive interference and classification of the types of thoughts that interfere with performance. We know that thoughts stemming from low self-esteem can be attentionally demanding and interfere with task focus (e.g., "I'm no good"; "People don't like me"). We know much less about other personality characteristics and other domains of self-preoccupation.

Attention-demanding task-irrelevant thoughts can have negative influences on problem solving and behavior. In this chapter we review evidence related to the role of cognitive interference in intellective performance and social relationships, particularly under evaluative conditions. People who focus their attention on the task at hand in an evaluative situation (e.g., a test) are likely to be successful. This probably holds also for situations, like a job interview, that involve both performance and interpersonal relationships. Those who are generally concerned about negative evaluation are prone to worry about this possibility and as a result experience both degradation of their performance and an increase in dysphoric mood.

When a task requires any kind of problem-solving and performance criteria, self-oriented thoughts create cognitive interference because these thoughts interfere with task-related thinking and activity. Eysenck and Calvo (1992) have hypothesized that these self-oriented

Irwin G. Sarason and Barbara R. Sarason • Department of Psychology, University of Washington, Seattle, Washington 98195. Gregory R. Pierce • Department of Psychology, Hamilton College, Clinton, New York 13323.

International Handbook of Personality and Intelligence, edited by Donald H. Saklofske and Moshe Zeidner. Plenum Press, New York, 1995.

thoughts reduce the storage and processing capacity of the working memory system available for a concurrent task. Cognitive interference can be thought of as a joint product of (a) exposure to situations that increase the likelihood of self-oriented peremptory cognitions and (b) vulnerability to such cognitions. Theoretical and research challenges posed by cognitive interference include the definition of classes of cognitions that lower personal effectiveness, identification of situations that bring them above threshold, and specification of pertinent risk factors.

ASSESSING COGNITIVE INTERFERENCE

Various assessment strategies can be used to provide information about thoughts that precede, accompany, or follow performance. Cognitive assessment can be carried out in a variety of ways, but all methods have in common a reliance on self-report of thoughts. Pertinent methods include think-aloud procedures, retrospective reports of thoughts in particular situations, and posttask questionnaires (Sarason, Sarason, & Pierce, 1990). Each of these methods has advantages and disadvantages and requires the subject's cooperation in giving self-reports regarding cognitive activity.

We have developed several measures to assess the degree to which intrusive cognitions occur during task performance. Together, two of these instruments provide measures of cognitive interference occurring in specific situations (i.e., a state measure), and as a general tendency to experience preoccupations in evaluative situations (i.e., a trait measure). A third instrument focuses on four broad categories of cognitive, affective, and physiological responses to evaluative situations, of which the worry component is especially pertinent to cognitive interference.

The Cognitive Interference Questionnaire (CIQ; Sarason & Stoops, 1978; Sarason, Sarason, Keefe, Hayes, & Shearin, 1986) was designed to measure, following performance on a task, the degree to which people report experiencing various types of thoughts while working on that task, and the extent to which these thoughts are viewed as interfering with concentration on it. The CIQ consists of 22 items, the first 21 of which are rated for frequency of occurrence of particular types of thoughts. Each type of thought is rated on a scale from 1 (*never*) to 5 (*very often*). The first 10 items provide postperformance reports of the frequency of occurrence of task-related thoughts that intruded while working on the task (e.g., worries over the adequacy of one's performance). Eleven additional items refer to thoughts whose contents do not refer to the task (e.g., thinking about other activities). The final item provides a global rating (on a 7-point scale) of the degree of mental wandering experienced while working on the task. Table 1 presents the CIQ items, together with mean values for 712 undergraduates.

The Thought Occurrence Questionnaire (TOQ; Sarason, Sarason, Keefe, et al., 1986) was designed as an indicator of the habitual tendency to have extraneous thoughts in evaluative situations. The TOQ was based on the idea that people who are generally able to maintain a task focus should be better than those who are less focused at meeting the demand of a particular assigned task. The 28 items of the TOQ, rated on the same 5-point scale used for the CIQ, provide an index of individuals' general tendency to misappropriate attention off-task. Table 2 presents the TOQ items, together with mean item values for a large group of college students.

The Reactions to Tests questionnaire (RTT; Sarason, 1984) assesses four broad classes of responses that individuals may experience in evaluative situations: worry, tension, test-irrelevant thinking, and bodily symptoms. These categories of responses correspond to the four 10-item subscales of the RTT. Items are rated on a scale from 1 (*not at all typical of me*) to 4 (*very typical of me*).

In combination, these three measures assess, in increasingly general terms, people's responses to evaluative situations. The CIQ provides an index of the frequency of specific cognitions experienced while working on a particular task; the TOQ measures the degree to which people generally experience preoccupation while completing tasks; and the RTT assesses a broad range of indicators of test anxiety, two key elements of which are cognitive interference (i.e., test-irrelevant thinking) and worry. The Worry subscale of the RTT has proved particularly promising because it has highlighted the need to investigate debilitating affective (as well as cognitive) responses in stressful circumstances.

The CIQ and TOQ were conceived as general measures of misappropriated attention applicable to virtually any situation. Because much of the research on cognitive interference has been linked with test anxiety, which is usually regarded as a risk factor for degraded performance, the RTT was constructed so as to build cognitive interference into a multidimensional instrument for the assessment of test anxiety. Table 3

Table 1. Cognitive Interference Questionnaire Items and Mean Values for 712 Undergraduates

Instructions: This questionnaire concerns the kinds of thoughts that go through people's heads at particular times, for example, while they are working on a task. The following is a list of thoughts, some of which you might have had *while doing the task on which you have just worked.* Please indicate approximately how often each thought occurred to you while working on it by placing the appropriate number in the blank provided to the left of each question.

1 = Never
2 = Once
3 = A few times
4 = Often
5 = Very often

		Mean
____	1. I thought about how poorly I was doing.	1.44
____	2. I thought about what the experimenter would think of me.	2.33
____	3. I thought about how I should work more carefully.	2.03
____	4. I thought about how much time I had left.	1.74
____	5. I thought about how others have done on this task.	1.59
____	6. I thought about the difficulty of the problems.	1.82
____	7. I thought about my level of ability.	1.92
____	8. I thought about the purpose of the experiment.	3.08
____	9. I thought about how I would feel if I were told how I performed.	1.61
____	10. I thought about how often I got confused.	1.67
____	11. I thought about other activities (for example, assignments, work).	2.07
____	12. I thought about members of my family.	2.08
____	13. I thought about friends.	1.93
____	14. I thought about something that made me feel guilty.	1.34
____	15. I thought about personal worries.	1.85
____	16. I thought about something that made me feel tense.	1.67
____	17. I thought about something that made me feel angry.	1.28
____	18. I thought about something that happened earlier today.	1.60
____	19. I thought about something that happened in the recent past (last few days, but not today).	1.64
____	20. I thought about something that happened in the distant past.	1.51
____	21. I thought about something that might happen in the future.	1.99

Please circle the number on the following scale which best represents the degree to which you felt your mind wandered *during the task you have just completed.*

Not at all	1	2	3	4	5	6	7	Very Much	2.86

Source: Sarason et al. (1986), p. 226.

presents the items of the RTT and indicates the subscales on which they loaded most highly.

TEST ANXIETY AND COGNITIVE INTERFERENCE

Sarason and Stoops (1978) used the CIQ in a study in which college students who differed in test anxiety performed on a series of tasks presented to them as measures of intelligence. The dependent measures were performance, estimates the subjects made of how long they had worked on the tasks, and postperformance reports of task-relevant and irrelevant thoughts that passed through their minds during performance. Sarason and Stoops found that highly test-anxious subjects under achievement-orienting conditions reported high levels of interfering thoughts, judged the time they spent on the tasks to be longer than did other subjects, and performed at relatively low levels.

Sarason, Sarason, Keefe, et al. (1986) verified through a factor analysis that the CIQ measures two types of thoughts—task-oriented worries, and off-task thoughts. They found that individuals who describe their customary reactions to testing situations in terms

Table 2. Thought Occurrence Questionnaire and Item Means

Instructions: This questionnaire concerns the kind of thoughts that go through people's heads when they have to concentrate on something, such as working, reading directions, or reading a book. The following is a list of thoughts, which, in your past experience, you may have had while working on various types of tasks. Please estimate how often each thought has occurred to you by placing the appropriate letter to the left of each item.

A = Never
B = Once
C = A few times
D = Often
E = Very often

	Item	*Mean*
____	1. I think about how poorly I am doing.	2.53
____	2. I think about what someone will think of me.	2.74
____	3. I think about how I should be more careful.	2.73
____	4. I think about how well others can do on what I am trying to do.	2.63
____	5. I think about how difficult what I am doing is.	2.74
____	6. I think about my level of ability.	3.00
____	7. I think about the purpose of what I am doing.	3.15
____	8. I think about how I would feel if I were told how I performed.	2.39
____	9. I think about how often I get confused.	2.08
____	10. I think about other activities (for example, assignments, work).	3.05
____	11. I think about members of my family.	2.48
____	12. I think about friends.	2.85
____	13. I think about something that makes me feel guilty.	1.92
____	14. I think about personal worries.	2.81
____	15. I think about something that makes me feel tense.	2.19
____	16. I think about something that makes me feel angry.	1.98
____	17. I think about something that happened earlier in the day.	2.81
____	18. I think about something that happened in the recent past (for example, in the last few days).	2.69
____	19. I think about something that happened in the distant past.	2.14
____	20. I think about something that might happen in the future.	2.82
____	21. I think about stopping.	2.42
____	22. I think about how unhappy I am.	1.84
____	23. I think about how hard it is.	2.54
____	24. I think about how I can't stand it anymore.	2.02
____	25. I think about quitting.	2.01
____	26. I think about running away.	1.44
____	27. I think about taking something (e.g., pills, a drink) to make it easier.	1.54
____	28. I think about going to bed/or to sleep.	2.84

Source: Sarason et al. (1986), p. 226.

of worry and arousal reported high levels of interfering cognitive activity while performing on a demanding task. The authors also found that the CIQ scores (particularly for task-relevant interfering thoughts) correlated significantly with performance on intellective tasks administered under testlike conditions. Blankenstein, Toner, and Flett (1989) reported that highly test-anxious students had more interfering thoughts and mental wandering while performing on a task than did less test-anxious students. Highly test-anxious students had especially high scores on CIQ items dealing with self-deprecatory and worry-laden thoughts. Blankenstein, Flett, and Watson (1992) also found that test-anxious students felt less self-confident and less in control of their lives than did other students.

These findings are consistent with theories that describe the active ingredients of test anxiety as self-preoccupying thoughts (Sarason, 1978, 1980; Wine, 1982). According to these theories, attention to self and self-involvement are defining features of anxiety states. The theories are also consistent with Carver and Scheier's (1986) expectancy model, which emphasizes the role played by anticipations of outcomes on performance, and Cooley and Klinger's (1989) analysis of

Table 3. Reactions to Tests Questionnaire

Almost everybody takes tests of various types and there are differences in how people react to them. The purpose of this survey is to gain a better understanding of what people think and feel about tests.

In filling out this survey, for each item please fill in the appropriate letter on your mark-sense form that reflects your typical reaction to the situation described.

1. I feel distressed and uneasy before tests. (T)
2. The thought, "What happens if I fail this test?" goes through my mind during tests. (W)
3. During tests, I find myself thinking of things unrelated to the material being tested. (I)
4. I become aware of my body during tests (feeling itches, pain, sweat, nausea). (B)
5. I freeze up when I think about an upcoming test. (T)
6. I feel jittery before tests. (T)
7. Irrelevant bits of information pop into my head during a test. (I)
8. During a difficult test, I worry whether I will pass it. (W)
9. While taking a test, I find myself thinking how much brighter the other people are. (W)
10. I feel the need to go to the toilet more often than usual during a test. (B)
11. My heart beats faster when the test begins. (B)
12. My mind wanders during tests. (I)
13. After a test, I say to myself, "It's over and I did as well as I could." (W)
14. My stomach gets upset before tests. (B)
15. While taking a test, I feel tense. (T)
16. I find myself becoming anxious the day of a test. (T)
17. While taking a test, I often don't pay attention to the questions. (I)
18. I think about current events during a test. (I)
19. I get a headache during an important test. (B)
20. Before taking a test, I worry about failure. (W)
21. While taking a test, I often think about how difficult it is. (W)
22. I wish tests did not bother me so much. (T)
23. I get a headache before a test. (B)
24. I have fantasies a few times during a test. (I)
25. I sometimes feel dizzy after a test. (B)
26. I am anxious about tests. (T)
27. Thoughts of doing poorly interfere with my concentration during tests. (W)
28. While taking tests, I sometimes think about being somewhere else. (I)
29. During tests, I find I am distracted by thoughts of upcoming events. (I)
30. My hands often feel cold before and during a test. (B)
31. My mouth feels dry during a test. (B)
32. I daydream during tests. (I)
33. I feel panicky during tests. (T)
34. During tests, I think about how poorly I am doing. (W)
35. Before tests, I feel troubled about what is going to happen. (T)
36. The harder I work at taking a test, the more confused I get. (W)
37. I sometimes find myself trembling before or during tests. (B)
38. During tests I think about recent past events. (I)
39. During tests, I wonder how the other people are doing. (W)
40. I have an uneasy feeling before an important test. (T)

Source: Sarason (1984).
Note: RTT scales are Tension (T), Worry (W), Test-Irrelevant Thinking (I), and Bodily Symptoms (B).

the role attributional processes play in cognitive interference. In their study, Blankenstein et al (1989) also employed a quantified thought-listing indicator of cognitive activity. They asked students to write down their thoughts and feelings while working on a test and found that this method yielded results well correlated with the CIQ. Highly test-anxious college students were differentiated from less test-anxious students by their negative, self-deprecatory cognitions and a failure to engage in task-facilitative thinking.

Research employing the TOQ has demonstrated a clear link between the general predisposition to experience high levels of interfering thoughts and individuals' subpar performance on specific tasks. Those individuals describe themselves who on the TOQ as customarily being worriers and having a high level of task-irrelevant thoughts show these same tendencies in their CIQ reports of cognitive activity after performance on a complex intellective task. All types of thoughts, however, did not have the same effect: Task-related worries as measured by the CIQ ("I thought about how poorly I was doing") were more predictive of performance on the task than were task-irrelevant thoughts ("I thought about friends"). This is consistent with other findings that generalized tendencies toward self-deprecatory thoughts and test-related worries are negatively related to intellective task performance under testlike conditions and positively related to cognitive interference (Bruch, Kaflowitz, & Kuethe, 1986; Sarason, 1984). Hunsley (1987), using the CIQ, found this relationship to be particularly strong for performance on mathematics tasks. Nichols-Hoppe and Beach (1990) found cognitive interference related to test anxiety to have an especially detrimental effect on decision making and the use of predecisional information, and Cervone (in press) has summarized similar relationships for goal setting.

These studies have provided considerable evidence that cognitive interference has negative consequences on task performance; in addition, these intrusive cognitions appear to stem in part from traitlike characteristics of the individuals. For example, using instruments such as the TOQ, it has been possible to identify individuals who will later be at high risk for experiencing debilitating preoccupations when confronting the challenges posed by particular situations. Yet to what extent might these intrusive thoughts be subject to situational parameters? Evidence suggests that cognitive interference can be increased by emphasizing the evaluative aspects of the performance situation (Hammermaster, 1989; Sarason, Sarason, & Shearin, 1986). Can it be decreased through certain types of preperformance communications to subjects? In other words, can interventions be designed to enable individuals to maintain a high level of task focus and to ward off unwanted thoughts that may impede efficient processing of task-related information?

COGNITIVE-BASED INTERVENTIONS FOR COGNITIVE INTERFERENCE

Some interventions have successfully increased the performance of highly test-anxious individuals, only to have a negative effect on the performance of others who have less extreme places in the test-anxiety distribution. For example, in one study, reassuring subjects that they did not have to worry about the level of their performance facilitated the performance of those who were highly test anxious, but negatively affected the performance of less test-anxious college students (Sarason, 1958). It appeared that although reassurance increased the ability of highly test-anxious subjects to direct their attention to the task at hand, the motivation of less test-anxious subjects may have been lowered by the same communication.

Some other preperformance interventions have not yielded this type of interaction. Sarason and Turk (1983) studied 180 undergraduates differing in test anxiety who performed in groups of 15 to 20 on a difficult anagrams task. The subjects were told that performance on the anagrams task was a measure of the ability to do college-level work. After this communication, one third of the subjects were given attention-directing instructions and one-third were given reassurance, whereas a control group received no additional communication. For the reassurance condition, the subjects were told not to be overly concerned about their performance on the anagrams (e.g., "Don't worry"; "You will do just fine"). Under the attention-directing condition, subjects were told to absorb themselves as much as possible in the anagrams task and to avoid thinking about other things (e.g., "Concentrate all your attention on the problems"; "Think only about the anagrams"; "Don't let yourself get distracted from the task").

Highly test-anxious subjects under the control condition performed poorly compared to the other subjects, but those in the attention-directing and reassurance groups performed well. Consistent with previous evidence, however, the study showed that reassuring instructions have a detrimental effect on people who are not test anxious. Subjects under the reassurance condition who were low in test anxiety performed poorly, perhaps because they took the reassuring communication at face value (i.e., they took the task lightly and lowered their motivational level). In contrast, the performance levels of all groups that received the attention-directing instructions were high. The attention-directing approach seems to have all of the advantages of reassurance for highly test-anxious subjects, with none of the disadvantages for less test-anxious subjects.

After the anagrams task, Sarason and Turk's subjects responded to the CIQ, which provided a measure of the number and type of interfering thoughts experienced under each condition. Cognitive interference at the end of the anagrams task was relatively low under the attention-direction condition for subjects at all levels of test-anxiety. Under the control condition, however, the highly test-anxious group showed a high level of cognitive interference. It would seem, then, that cognitive interference can be not only assessed but also experimentally manipulated. People who are low in test anxiety and/or who feel satisfied with their perceived level of social support may not benefit from efforts to increase the comfort level of the performance situation, but the performance of people with certain types of insecurities may be significantly facilitated by these efforts. Further research is needed to develop effective interventions for those whose personal characteristics may put them at high risk for cognitive interference and poor performance.

Taking different approaches to fostering task-relevant thought, Naveh-Benjamin (1991) used a desensitization technique to increase the information-processing skills of highly test-anxious students, and Sedikides (1992) created a happy mood in college students in an effort to decrease self-focused attention. Both of these attempts were successful. Naveh-Benjamin found that the desensitization training program helped students relax various muscles of the body under testlike conditions and that this led to improved performance, including the ability to retrieve pertinent information from memory. Sedikides's study showed that both happy and neutral (as contrasted with sad) moods promoted the ability to maintain an attentional focus.

Another promising approach to influencing task focus, modeling, has grown out of social learning theory. Observational opportunities can provide a person not only with demonstrations of overt responses but, if the model thinks through problems and tactics aloud, covert ones as well. Observing a credible, effective model prepare for a test can influence someone's views and expectancies concerning self and others. Whereas exposure to models who have failure experiences can have a negative effect on performance, exposure to models displaying adaptive behavior might play a salutary role in facilitating a problem-solving approach and performance. Subjects differing in test anxiety have been given opportunities to observe a model who demonstrated effective ways of performing an anagram task (Sarason, 1972, 1973); using a talk-out-loud technique, the model displayed several types of facilitative thoughts and cognitions. Highly test-anxious subjects benefited more from the opportunity to observe a cognitive model than did those low in test anxiety. Such formal and informal cognitive modeling plays a role in many instructional programs through demonstrations for students of the differences between adaptive and maladaptive cognitions.

SOCIAL SUPPORT–BASED INTERVENTIONS FOR COGNITIVE INTERFERENCE

Sarason and Sarason (1986) investigated the effects of experimentally administered social support on cognitive interference and task performance. Support was manipulated by the experimenter's communication to the subject of interest in him or her and of being available to assist the subject if help should be needed. Subjects who received the experimenter's communication of interest and who had previously indicated low levels of perceived available social support in their personal lives reported reduced levels of interfering thoughts and solved more anagrams than did subjects with low social support in the control condition. In addition, low-social-support subjects in the treatment condition performed at levels comparable to the high-social-support subjects in both the control and support conditions. The performance of subjects high in social support did not benefit from the experimenter's communication.

Although most interventions aimed at reducing cognitive interference have been directed toward individuals, Sarason (1981) has described a promising group approach based on the concept of social support. Social support was provided by a group discussion in which students shared concerns and solutions regarding problems with stress and anxiety in evaluative situations. Several confederates in the group were used to heighten social association by suggesting a meeting after the experimental session to discuss common interests further. The group discussion was followed by an anagrams task that was presented as an unrelated study being conducted by another experimenter. The results showed that anagram performance and self-preoccupation (as measured by the CIQ) were affected by this specially created opportunity for social association and acceptance by others. Performance on the anagrams task increased and self-preoccupation decreased as a function of the social support manipulation. This change, however, was pronounced only in subjects who were initially high in test anxiety; the performance of those low in test anxiety was essentially unchanged by the support manipulation. Thus a supportive intervention may change the content of subjects' cognitions from worry to task-relevant thoughts.

PERSONALITY AND SUPPORTIVE PROCESSES IN COGNITIVE INTERFERENCE

One recurring theme in these studies is the interaction between individuals' personality characteristics and properties of the situations in which they find themselves. For example, research suggests that individuals who are prone to experience high levels of anxiety in evaluational settings benefit from instructional and supportive communications, whereas those low in anxiety appear not to gain from such interventions. These person × situation interactions have led us to focus on the interplay between personal vulnerabilities and the opportunities and challenges afforded by various situations. To what extent does anxiety about test situations correspond to concerns about other types of situations, such as those involving significant social ties? Might the general tendency to experience preoccupation reflect a personality characteristic that is transituational? We have been investigating the relationship between perceived social support and cognitive interference as part of an effort to identify clues to the mechanisms by which social support exerts its influence. Goldsmith and Albrecht (1993) have pursued this possibility and shown that pre-exam supportive communications to students have a positive impact on exam grades for all students, not only those high in test anxiety.

People low in social support have been found to have relatively low self-esteem, high anxiety, and identifiable deficits in their social relationships (Sarason, Levine, Basham, & Sarason, 1983; Sarason, Sarason, & Shearin, 1986). Lakey and Heller (1988) showed that people high in social support generally believe that they are accepted by others, whereas those who are low in assessed social support are less likely to believe that they are interesting, worthy people, and appropriate stimuli for the attention of others. Sarason and Sarason (1990) have found a negative relationship between perceptions of social support and social anxiety.

It is possible that self-oriented social and evaluational self-preoccupations have important cognitive commonalities. Highly test-anxious students worry excessively about failure and its consequences, and these worries are often maladaptive because they interfere with task-relevant cognitive activity. Johnson and Glass (1989) found similar results for socially anxious high school boys whose interfering thoughts were related to negative evaluations of their social qualities. People who see themselves as being low in social support often worry about their social isolation and unlikability, and this may have undesirable consequences in social situations. Research is needed to determine the generality with which cognitive interference is associated with various types of personally perceived weaknesses and deficits.

As a step in that direction, Miller, Sarason, and Sarason (1987) showed that when faced with a challenging task, low-social-support subjects experience self-preoccupying thoughts (e.g., worry) that interfere with task-relevant activity. These researchers assessed cognitive interference after subjects had completed a personality questionnaire. Cognitive interference items that were especially characteristic of subjects low in perceived social support included "I thought about how others have done on this task"; "I thought about how I would feel if I were told how I performed"; and "I thought about how often I got confused." A negative relationship was found between satisfaction with perceived social support and cognitive interference. Though evidence concerning the association between social support and cognitive interference is not nearly as extensive as that for the association between test anxiety and cognitive interference, the former evidence provides impetus for further inquiry into the relationships among social perceptions, social behavior, and cognitive interference. Because social support deficits are linked with morbidity and mortality and with indices of maladjustment (Cohen & Syme, 1985), the finding that social support is negatively correlated with cognitive interference might provide clues concerning the role of cognitive events in health and maintenance of social ties.

One other study has explored the correlation between social support and cognitive interference reported by subjects as having occurred while completing a packet of personality questionnaires (Sarason et al., 1983). In addition to the SSQ, the packet included measures of test anxiety and stressful life events. Test anxiety and cognitive interference, as assessed with the CIQ, were positively correlated. This is consistent with evidence reviewed earlier in this chapter showing that the test-anxious person experiences self-preoccupying worry, insecurity, and self-doubt in situations that seem personally evaluative. The test anxiety–cognitive interference association was stronger for task-related interfering thoughts than for unrelated thoughts. Interestingly, although social support and cognitive interference were negatively correlated, this association was greater for task-unrelated than for task-related thoughts. Four CIQ items showed especially strong relationships with satisfaction with social support. All of these items were among the task-unrelated thoughts assessed by the CIQ; two are the only CIQ items that refer specifically to interpersonal relationships (the other two might be linked to interpersonal relationships, but their referents are ambiguously specified).

This study, then, showed that social support and cognitive interference are negatively related and that the content of the interfering thoughts may be interpersonal in character for subjects with low satisfaction scores on the SSQ. These findings suggest the importance of specifying the content of intrusions reported by groups differing along particular personality dimensions. People who are not satisfied with their social support may dwell more on interpersonal aspects of their lives (e.g., interpersonal sources of unhappiness) than do people who are satisfied with their available support. A study by Sarason, Sarason, and Pierce (1993) showed that test anxiety was more strongly related than social support to both cognitive interference and performance on an anagrams task. Social support was also related to cognitive interference, but unlike for test anxiety, the biggest SSQ correlations were with CIQ items that have interpersonal overtones (specifically, items 12, 13, 15, and 18 of Table 1).

It might be said that the cognitive interference of highly test-anxious students comes about because of worries and preoccupations concerning their ability to perform adequately and excessive awareness of the possibility of failure. These types of thoughts loom large in the thinking of highly test-anxious people, and this interferes with effective performance. From this perspective, cognitive interference results from evaluative concerns that compete with task-relevant cognitions. The content of these evaluative concerns, however, will vary depending on the nature of the situation. For example, the content of interfering thoughts reported by those with high test anxiety and those with low perceived social support are unlikely to be identical. A profitable path for future research would be attempts to identify the classes of interfering cognitions that characterize or derive from particular personality characteristics. Each person may have certain types of critical cognitions, whether they are fears, fantasies, or assumptions about the self and how the world works. For one person, perceived social support deficits might be especially associated with anticipation of rejection by others; for another, the deficits might be taken as confirmation of the meager trust that can be placed in other people.

COGNITIVE PEREMPTORINESS

Peremptory thoughts tend to dominate an individual's thinking and to direct her or his behavior. People whose thoughts are dominated by ideas such as "I'm no good" or "People don't like me" have peremptory thoughts related to low self-esteem. Other cognitive themes can also have a peremptory quality. These thoughts tend to take on a life of their own and to be maladaptive (e.g., self-oriented thoughts that are not task-relevant lead to poor performance; Schwarzer, 1986).

Though we do not know whether cognitive interference is directly or indirectly associated with peremptory thinking, it is known that peremptory thought can play a controlling role in a person's life (Katakis, 1990). This role is most evident in instances of clearly abnormal behavior: the fears of the homebound agoraphobic individual, the commanding voices heard by someone who is psychotic, and the compulsive person who is continually vigilant for dirt that must be removed. Kazdin (1990) found uncontrollable automatic thoughts to play an important role in childhood depression, and Clark (1992) has reported similar results for depressed adults. Test anxiety and concerns related to one's social support network might seem minor compared to the above problems, which seriously reduce well-being and distort personal effectiveness. They serve to suggest, however, the diverse forms of peremptoriness in everyday life that serve to reduce the ability to focus on tasks, as well as the need to help people gain control over their cognitive lives.

Individuals who are depressed, test anxious, or unloved may share in common the belief that they lack the ability to meet certain situational demands; yet these schemas also differ in significant ways (e.g., the class of situations in which feelings of hopelessness, frustration, and a sense of personal insecurity become paramount). Thus it seems likely that peremptory thoughts may do more than interfere with task-oriented behavior in particular situations. They may also decrease the likelihood that individuals will encounter situations that, although anxiety provoking, may produce personal successes, which in the long term may lead to significant revisions in their schemas.

Sometimes peremptory thinking can be beneficial to both performance and adjustment. A scientist who cannot let go of an intriguing question and a composer in pursuit of just the right melody are preoccupied, but their preoccupations are (a) related to events and phenomena outside themselves, and (b) have the potential of contributing to personal happiness and the social good. Both serious and less serious self-preoccupations (e.g., worry over performance and social evaluations), however, often keep individuals from becoming involved in positive ways in important aspects of the real world. As Mathews, May, Mogg, and Eysenck (1990) have noted, future research is needed to determine to what degree self-preoccupation exerts its influence by selectively directing attention or through defective filtering of informational inputs. Personal schemas and peremptory thoughts may play important roles in information processing. Is cognitive interference caused by the peremptoriness of schemas that intrude on ongoing activities (e.g., tests and social encounters)? We need a fuller, more well-rounded picture of where self-preoccupations fit with regard to personal schemas and the situations that evoke them.

Research on goal orientations and performance suggests the potential importance of this relationship for an understanding of cognitive interference (Nicholls, 1984). Several writers have discussed the influence that specific goal orientations might have on the interference process and performance. For example, a *learning* goal orientation (which emphasizes the individual's wanting to learn and master skills) might be less evocative of cognitive interference than a *performance* goal orientation (which emphasizes worrying about failure to achieve a goal; Dweck, 1986, 1989; Dweck & Leggett, 1988). Certain types of superordinate goals might be especially dysfunctional on certain kinds of tasks. Hofmann (1992) recently found that students with performance goal orientations had generally high CIQ scores and poorer performance than students with learning goal orientations. The results for the task-related CIQ items were particularly strong.

The concept of cognitive interference as a product of peremptory thinking raises some important questions. What are the origins of different types of peremptory thinking? Is cognitive peremptoriness caused by the linkage of certain thoughts with strong emotions? How does peremptoriness influence learning and problem solving? Can the cognitive interference caused by peremptory thoughts be reduced or eliminated? We have seen that there is some evidence that modeling, reassurance, and other interventions facilitate the performance of highly test-anxious subjects. This facilitation might be conceptualized as the result of a weakening of maladaptive schemas and peremptory thoughts. From this perspective low perceived social support could be attributed to beliefs and schemas about interpersonal relationships that drive other people away. Alternatively, perceptions of unsatisfying support could be caused by unfortunate life experiences that reduce opportunities for desired social contact. In any case, a clearer picture is needed of the beliefs and schemas that contribute to social support levels and the behaviors that influence them.

As we just mentioned, cognitive interference may be related to experience of certain emotions. But to what extent are the observed decrements in performance caused by intrusive thoughts versus emotions? In this regard, and it might prove worthwhile to investigate "affective" as well as cognitive interference. It may prove difficult to separate the two, however, it may also be misleading. We suspect that individuals experience a large number of thoughts in a wide range of situations; many of these thoughts prove to be distracting, whereas others do not. Those cognitions that contribute most to distraction may be those that lead to affective arousal. We believe that the study of cognitive interference—whether focused on intrusive thoughts occurring in academic, athletic, or social situations—will profit most by attending to those cognitions that are upsetting or emotionally charged for the individual. In this sense, we see the situation as analogous to the task encountered by the psychotherapist, who must attend to and synthesize a wide range of disclosures during her or his client's free associations. The challenge is to identify the thoughts that lead to maladaptive behavior. Research efforts that focus on affect-laden intrusive thoughts are likely to prove most profitable.

THE ROLE OF COGNITIVE INTERFERENCE IN INTELLIGENCE AND SOCIAL ADJUSTMENT

The concept of intelligence refers to individual differences in the ability to acquire knowledge, to think and reason effectively, and to deal adaptively with the environment. The concept of social adjustment, though perhaps less well specified, seems equally central because so much of our lives involves other people. In both cases, cognitive interference can cause attentional dysfunction that has unfortunate consequences (Mogg, Mathews, & Eysenck, 1992). Further research related to cognitive interference could have important theoretical and practical implications. More information is needed concerning the personality characteristics of individuals who are prone to experience cognitive interference, as well as about the types of interfering thoughts that play salient roles in the person's life. Are certain self-preoccupations more likely to occur in certain personality constellations than others? More information is also needed concerning the situations that elicit cognitive interference.

The concept of stress is likely to play a role in theoretical analyses of cognitive interference. Stress can be understood in terms of perceived performance demands—a person's awareness of the need to do something about a given state of affairs. These demands are evoked by situational challenges and can lead to either task-relevant or -irrelevant cognitions. From this point of view, the most adaptive response to stress should be thinking that directs the individual's attention to the task at hand. The task-oriented person is able to set aside unproductive worry and preoccupations; the self-preoccupied person, in contrast, becomes absorbed in the implications and consequences of failure to meet situational challenges. Anxious people worry about their perceived personal incompetence and possible difficulties they may be called upon to confront. Their negative self-appraisals are unpleasant and, because they are self-preoccupying, detract from task concentration. Given that many anxious people describe themselves as being tense and feeling that something terrible will happen, even though they cannot specify the cause of their worry, these self-preoccupations are likely to create cognitive interference that precludes an orderly, task-oriented approach to situational requirements.

The situational challenges to which people react may be either real or imagined. It seems clear that an understanding of the effects of stress and the prediction of behavior must take into account an individual's perceptions of the nature of a challenge and his or her ability to meet it, as well as the self-preoccupations that influence these perceptions.

We believe research on cognitive interference offers a particularly promising avenue by which to link personality processes occurring in a wide range of situations. An important challenge for research and theory on cognitive interference is to specify its developmental antecedents, cross-situational influences, and role in interpersonal behavior. In addition, affect-laden preoccupations may also have important implications for health. Efforts to uncover the mechanisms by which intrusive thoughts exert their impact on a wide range of outcomes are likely to yield a good harvest.

REFERENCES

Blankenstein, K. R., Flett, G. L., & Watson, M. S. (1992). Coping and academic problem-solving ability in test anxiety. *Journal of Clinical Psychology*, *48*, 37–46.

Blankenstein, K. R., & Toner, B. B., & Flett, G. L. (1989). Test anxiety and the contents of consciousness: Thought-listing and endorsement measures. *Journal of Research in Personality*, *23*, 269–286.

Bruch, M. A., Kaflowitz, N. G., & Kuethe, M. (1986). Beliefs and the subjective meaning of thoughts: Analysis of the role of self-statements in academic test performance. *Cognitive Therapy and Research*, *10*, 51–69.

Carver, C. S., & Scheier, M. F. (1986). Self and the control of behavior. In L. M. Hartman & K. R. Blankenstein (Eds.). *Advances in the study of communication and affect: II. Perception of self in emotional disorder and psychotherapy* (pp. 5–35). New York: Plenum.

Cervone, D. (in press). The role of self-referent cognitions in goal setting, motivation, and performance. In M. Rabinowitz (Ed.), *Applied cognition*. New York: Ablex.

Clark, D. A. (1992). Depressive, anxious and intrusive thoughts in psychiatric inpatients and outpatients. *Behavioral Research Therapy*, *30*, 93–102.

Cohen, S., & Syme, S. L. (Eds.) (1985). *Social support and health*. New York: Academic Press.

Cooley, E. J., & Klinger, C. R. (1989). Academic attributions and coping with tests. *Journal of Social and Clinical Psychology*, *8*, 359–367.

Dweck, C. S. (1986). Motivational processes affecting learning. *American Psychologist, 41*, 1040–1048.

Dweck, C. S. (1989). Motivation. In A. Lesgold & R. Glaser (Eds.), *Foundations for a psychology of education* (pp. 87–136). Hillsdale, NJ: Erlbaum.

Dweck, C. S., & Leggett, E. L. (1988). A social-cognitive approach to motivation and personality. *Psychological Review, 95*, 256–273.

Eysenck, M. W., & Calvo, M. G. (1992). Anxiety and performance: The processing efficiency theory. *Cognition and Emotion, 6*, 409–434.

Goldsmith, D., & Albrecht, T. (1993). The impact of supportive communication networks on test anxiety and performance. *Communication Education, 42*, 142–158.

Hammermaster, C. S. (1989). Levels of performance and cognitive interference in test-anxious subjects. *Alberta Journal of Educational Research, 35*, 164–170.

Hofmann, D. A. (1992). *The influence of goal orientation on task performance: A substantively meaningful suppressor variable*. Unpublished manuscript, Purdue University.

Hunsley, J. (1987). Cognitive processes in mathematics anxiety and test anxiety: The role of appraisals, internal dialogue, and attributions. *Journal of Educational Psychology, 79*, 388–392.

Johnson, R. L., & Glass, C. R. (1989). Heterosocial anxiety and direction of attention in high school boys. *Cognitive Therapy and Research, 13*, 509–526.

Katakis, G. (1990). The self-referential conceptual system: Towards an operational definition of subjectivity. *Systems Research, 7*, 91–102.

Kazdin, A. E. (1990). Evaluation of the Automatic Thoughts Questionnaire: Negative cognitive processes and depression among children. *Psychological Assessment: A Journal of Consulting and Clinical Psychology, 2*, 73–79.

Lakey, B., & Heller, K. (1988). Social support from a friend, perceived support, and social problem solving. *American Journal of Community Psychology, 16*, 811–824.

Mathews, A., May, J., Mogg, K., & Eysenck, M. (1990). Attentional bias in anxiety: Selective search or defective filtering? *Journal of Abnormal Psychology, 99*, 166–173.

Miller, G., Sarason, I. G., & Sarason, B. R. (1987). *Social support and cognitive interference*. Paper presented at the Western Psychological Association Convention, Long Beach, CA.

Mogg, K., Mathews, A., & Eysenck, M. (1992). Attentional bias to threat in clinical anxiety states. *Cognition and Emotion, 6*, 149–159.

Naveh-Benjamin, M. (1991). A comparison of training programs intended for different types of test-anxious students: Further support for an information-processing model. *Journal of Educational Psychology, 83*, 134–139.

Nicholls, J. G. (1984). Achievement motivation: Concepts of ability, subjective experience, task choice, and performance. *Psychological Review, 91*, 328–346.

Nichols-Hoppe, K. T., & Beach, L. R. (1990). The effects of test anxiety and task variables on predecisional information search. *Journal of Research in Personality, 24*, 163–172.

Sarason, I. G. (1958). The effects of anxiety, reassurance, and meaningfulness of material to be learned on verbal learning. *Journal of Experimental Psychology, 56*, 472–477.

Sarason, I. G. (1972). Test anxiety and the model who fails. *Journal of Personality and Social Psychology, 22*, 410–413.

Sarason, I. G. (1973). Test anxiety and cognitive modeling. *Journal of Personality and Social Psychology, 28*, 58–61.

Sarason, I. G. (1978). The Test Anxiety Scale: Concept and research. In C. D. Spielberger & I. G. Sarason (Eds.), *Stress and anxiety* (Vol. 5, pp. 193–216). Washington, DC: Hemisphere.

Sarason, I. G. (Ed.). (1980). *Test anxiety: Theory, research, and applications*. Hillsdale, NJ: Erlbaum.

Sarason, I. G. (1981). Test anxiety, stress, and social support. *Journal of Personality, 49*, 101–114.

Sarason, I. G. (1984). Stress, anxiety, and cognitive interference: Reactions to tests. *Journal of Personality and Social Psychology, 46*, 929–938.

Sarason, I. G., Levine, H. M., Basham, R. B., & Sarason, B. R. (1983). Assessing social support: The Social Support Questionnaire. *Journal of Personality and Social Psychology, 44*, 127–139.

Sarason, I. G., & Sarason, B. R. (1986). Experimentally provided social support. *Journal of Personality and Social Psychology, 50*, 1222–1225.

Sarason, I. G., & Sarason, B. R. (1990). Test anxiety. In H. Leitenberg (Ed.), *Handbook of social and evaluation anxiety*. New York: Plenum.

Sarason, I. G., Sarason, B. R., Keefe, D. E., Hayes, B. E., & Shearin, E. N. (1986). Cognitive interference: Situational determinants and traitlike characteristics. *Journal of Personality and Social Psychology, 51*, 215–226.

Sarason, I. G., Sarason, B. R., & Pierce, G. R. (1990). Anxiety, cognitive interference and performance. *Journal of Social Behavior and Personality, 5*, 1–18.

Sarason, I. G., Sarason, B. R., & Pierce, G. R. (1993). *Social support, cognitive interference, and performance*. Unpublished manuscript, University of Washington, Seattle.

Sarason, I. G., Sarason, B. R., & Shearin, E. N. (1986). Social support as an individual difference variable: Its stability, origins, and relational aspects. *Journal of Personality and Social Psychology, 51*, 215–226.

Sarason, I. G., & Stoops, R. (1978). Test anxiety and the passage of time. *Journal of Consulting and Clinical Psychology, 46*, 102–109.

Sarason, I. G., & Turk, S. (1983). *Test anxiety and the direction of attention*. Unpublished manuscript, University of Washington, Seattle.

Schwarzer, R. (Ed.). (1986). *Self-related cognitions in anxiety and motivation*. Hillsdale, NJ: Erlbaum.

Sedikides, C. (1992). Mood as a determinant of attentional focus. *Cognition and Emotion, 6*, 129–148.

Wine, J. D. (1982). Evaluation anxiety: A cognitive-attentional construct. In H. W. Krohne & L. Laux (Eds.), *Achievement, stress, and anxiety*. Washington, DC: Hemisphere.

III

Empirical Links between Personality and Intelligence

15

Personality Trait Correlates of Intelligence

Moshe Zeidner

For more than half a century now, psychologists have explored the avenues linking human intelligence to a wide array of personality traits. Psychologists have longed to unravel the theoretical and practical interface between personality and intelligence, hoping to shed light on how these two key constructs affect one another (and other variables) in the course of development, day-to-day behavior, and adaptive functioning. Indeed, personality and intelligence are linked by virtue of being key sources of individual differences in behavior, and would seem to share many parameters in common and various conceptual links between these concepts do appear in the literature, as discussed in Chapter 1 of this handbook (see also H. J. Eysenck & Eysenck, 1985). Although some of the most influential figures in the field of intelligence and personality allude repeatedly to the inextricable web or nexus of interrelations among these two constructs (see Chapter 13), researchers have traditionally treated them as relatively independent factors in their analyses.

This chapter sets out to review and assess critically the literature focusing on key personality trait correlates of intelligence. Given the various conceptual links commonly claimed for personality and intelligence, a meaningful pattern of relationships would be expected between measures of intelligence and a wide array of personality traits. If these relationships are found to be negligible, however, we might need to rethink the conceptual links posited between these two constructs.

The material presented in this chapter aims at being illustrative rather than comprehensive, concentrating on a select number of personality variables that have been investigated in relation to intelligence and seem to be of some theoretical interest and/or practical importance. Because the interface between intelligence and cognitive styles and related variables (mindfulness, intellectual engagement) has been covered elsewhere in this volume (see Chapters 11, 19, and 21), these variables will not be addressed here. Similarly, because the relationship between personality factors and lower-level theories and corresponding physiological measures of intelligence is addressed in Chapter 16 (see also Chapter 17), I will limit the discussion in this chapter to the relationship between personality and intelligence as assessed by conventional psychometric measures.

Before embarking on a systematic survey of the evidence bearing on the magnitude of the personality-intelligence relationship, it may be useful to make two distinctions that may help the reader appraise the evidence relating personality traits to intelligence. First, because this chapter focuses on personality traits, one should keep in mind the distinction between person-

Moshe Zeidner • School of Education, University of Haifa, Mount Carmel 31905, Israel.

International Handbook of Personality and Intelligence, edited by Donald H. Saklofske and Moshe Zeidner. Plenum Press, New York, 1995.

ality *traits* and *states*. Traits are broad determining tendencies or propensities to behave, whereas states are temporary states of mind and mood determined by the interaction between a person's traits and present situation (Spielberger, 1972; Spielberger, Gonzales, Taylor, Algaze, & Anton, 1978). States and traits are typically correlated, because a trait is actually defined as a disposition for behavior to be manifested in particular situations. For example, evaluative trait anxiety refers to an individual's disposition to respond with worry, tension, and physiological arousal across a variety of evaluative conditions (e.g., tests, mathematics exercises, social encounters, sports events), whereas state anxiety refers to the specific level of anxiety experienced in a particular situation, such as an important college examination or athletic competition. Two people may have the same level of trait anxiety but differ in their anxiety elevations in a particular state.

Second, the majority of the studies available are correlational in nature, assessing the relationship between specific personality traits and intelligence at one point in time (see Baron, 1982). As is true of all correlational research, these studies allow statements that personality trait A is related to ability B but preclude causal statements to the effect that A causes B, as A is not experimentally manipulated (see Darlington, 1990). This ties in with the previous point, in that whenever a personality variable is experimentally manipulated (e.g., experimentally aroused anxiety), we may make some causal statement about the relationship between the personality *state* (e.g., state anxiety) and the ability assessed. No causal inference, however, may be clearly made about the relationship between the *trait* (e.g., trait anxiety) and the ability assessed.

NEGATIVE AFFECTIVITY

Anxiety and Test Anxiety

Anxiety is perhaps the most intensively studied variable in personality research, and more reliable data seem to be available about its relationship to intelligence than for any other personality construct. Anxiety has received particular attention because it has long been recognized that beyond an optimal level it may negatively affect a wide array of performances, from intelligence test scores and school achievement (Sarason, 1980) to dating (Hope & Heimberg, 1990). Thus, aside from the aversive emotional experience associated with the tension, arousal, and worrisome thoughts constituting the anxiety experience, anxiety has been repeatedly shown to be detrimental to the performance of individuals on a variety of complex cognitive tasks.

Anxiety is a signal that the individual is under threat. The threat evokes a "fight or fight" reaction that includes such somatic reactions as increased heart rate, sweating, stomachaches, and trembling. Although anxiety is believed to be intrinsic to mankind, the stimuli evoking the anxiety reaction have changed over the years. For example, tests and evaluative situations are one class of anxiety-evoking stimuli that have become particularly salient in modern industrial and achievement-oriented society, where success on a variety of tests may have important consequences for the individual's academic and occupational careers.

Matarazzo (1972) reviews studies suggesting that the relationship between intelligence and trait anxiety is negligible. Neither pattern nor scatter analysis approaches to the Wechsler scales showed any relation to a trait measure of anxiety; however, studies utilizing situationally induced anxiety (i.e., state anxiety) did reveal decrements in performance on the same measures of intellectual functioning. Matarazzo concludes that only when we separate the currently anxious (state anxious) from the chronically anxious (trait anxious) can we show a decrement in intellectual performance as a result of anxiety. Siegman (1956) found that highly trait-anxious individuals did poorer on the timed WAIS subtests (type of situational stress) relative to their own performance on the nontimed tests (nonstress condition); subjects low in trait anxiety did equally well on both timed and untimed tests.

Anxiety is particularly relevant to intelligent test performance, as research has indicated that state anxiety has a more adverse effect on difficult or complex tasks than on simple tasks (M. W. Eysenck, 1982; Sarason, 1975). Tasks that test maximum performance (e.g., intelligence tests) often provide more failure experiences and feelings of anxiety than easy tasks because they take longer to perform and lead to a greater incidence of error. It stands to reason that how easy a task is perceived to be depends on the examinee's intelligence level. According to the law proposed by Yerkes and Dodson (1908), there is an optimal level of drive for any given task; drive levels above or below that optimal level will lead to less efficient performance. For highly intelligent subjects, cognitive tasks are often perceived to be sufficiently easy that the anxiety level is still in the optimum range, thereby facilitating performance for these students.

Test anxiety is typically construed as a situation-specific personality trait characterized by the individual's disposition to react with extensive worry, intrusive thoughts, mental disorganization, tension, and physiological arousal when exposed to evaluative situations (Spielberger, 1972; Sarason & Sarason, 1990). In this section I will focus on this particular form of anxiety, which appears to be the type most intrinsically related to intelligence and intelligence test performance.

Test-anxious students tend to view examinations or evaluative situations as personally threatening, and they respond with elevated levels of state anxiety, self-derogatory cognitions, anticipatory failure attributions, and more intense emotional reactions and arousal. The self-critical thoughts experienced by test-anxious students have been linked to general anxiety, fear of failure, and extraordinarily high aspirations and needs for achievement. Indeed, test anxious students appear to have a particularly low response threshold for test anxiety and tend to react with threat perceptions, reduced feelings of self-efficacy, and elevated levels of test anxiety at the very first hint of failure. In particular, test-anxious students have been shown to have more negative thoughts and higher arousal during an exam in contrast to nonanxious peers and even report more trouble sleeping the night before the exam (Blankstein, Flett, Watson, & Koledin, 1990).

Whereas early research was concerned with the negative impact of test anxiety on academic performance, more recent research has differentiated between so-called debilitating and facilitating effects of anxiety (Alpert & Haber, 1960). Although feelings of arousal may actually occur in subjects both high and low in test anxiety, they may be interpreted differentially, and this self-labeling may either facilitate or disturb behavior on cognitive tasks such as intelligence tests. In addition, researchers have differentiated between different anxiety reactions as cognitive (worry, task-irrelevant thinking) or affective (tension, bodily reactions; Sarason & Sarason, 1990; Spielberger, 1972). Whereas worry refers to the cognitive side of test anxiety (e.g., concern for one's performance, negative task expectations, and negative self-evaluations), emotionality refers to the person's awareness of physiological changes and bodily arousal and accompanying feelings of tension, uneasiness, and nervousness while being tested.

Test Anxiety and Cognitive Performance

Interference with cognitive performance can occur in virtually any domain in which people strive to do well with achievement goals at stake. Because intelligence test results have important practical implications for a students' academic and vocational career, test anxiety is commonly claimed to be an important factor influencing test scores. Although the findings are sometimes contradictory, it has been repeatedly demonstrated that students who are high in test anxiety may experience decrements in performance in evaluative situations (Gaudry & Speilberger, 1971; Zeidner, Klingman, & Papko, 1988; Zeidner & Nevo, 1992). The higher the reported test anxiety scores, the greater the problems reported in the processing of information (Tobias, 1986). Recent meta-analytic studies of the literature bearing on anxiety and cognitive performance (see Hembree, 1988; Seipp, 1991) have shown average correlations of about −.20.

The worry (W) and emotionality (E) components of test anxiety have been found to be very strongly related but distinguishable by virtue of their different patterns of correlations with aptitude test scores (Deffenbacher, 1980; Liebert & Morris, 1967; Zeidner et al., 1988). This supports the notion that in evaluative situations, highly test-anxious individuals direct their attention away from the task at hand to self-related cognitions, which serve to debilitate performance.

In theory, anxiety may affect cognitive performance at each of the stages involved in processing information (i.e., encoding of new information, short- and long-term storage, elaboration and processing of encoding material, retrieval of content from long-term memory, and problem solving). Thus anxiety may produce a narrowing of attention and increased distractibility, affecting encoding of intelligence test information and test items particularly sensitive to distractibility (e.g., digit-symbol coding). Anxiety may impair the efficiency of short-term storage, thus affecting tasks requiring considerable short-term storage capacity. Working memory may be particularly affected in the concurrent processing of task-relevant and -irrelevant information, thus affecting intelligence test tasks that require large amounts of working memory (e.g., arithmetic calculations performed without paper and pencil). At the processing stage, elevations in test anxiety may reduce performance by absorbing a large proportion of information-processing capacity, leaving a reduced amount for task solution. Anxiety has been shown to lead to reduced processing, with fewer stimulus attributes processed in highly anxious examinees (Mueller, 1980). Anxiety may also affect students' long-term memory, with highly anxious subjects showing a greater retention loss over time (H. J. Eysenck & Eysenck, 1985).

It is also useful to differentiate between a person's performance *effectiveness* (i.e., quality of performance) and processing *efficiency* (i.e., quality of performance relative to effort expended: H. J. Eysenck & Eysenck, 1985). Anxiety may have its major effect on the efficiency of performance. Thus highly anxious individuals, who have less spare processing capacity, invest more resources to obtain a given level of performance. Highly test-anxious individual may be compared to a car with a trailer hooked up to it, with additional acceleration needed to reach a given level of speed than for a car without a trailer (H. J. Eysenck & Eysenck, 1985).

It should be stressed that the whole process by which anxiety serves to debilitate cognitive performance is highly complex, with a variety of factors possibly mediating the effects (e.g., the perception of the situation, previous experience with the material being tested, task frustration, expectancies of success, effort and task perseverance, attributions, ability, and perceived cognitive resources). Test anxiety may also interact with both situational variables (e.g., task complexity, test atmosphere) and personal variables (e.g., optimism, personal resources, social support) in influencing cognitive test performance. The same level of anxiety can facilitate performance in one situation and depress performance in another, depending on the particular configuration of variables in the person × situation interaction. Thus there is considerable evidence that the performance of highly test-anxious individuals on complex tasks is detrimentally affected by evaluational stressors: the less complex the task, the weaker the effect. Furthermore, Sarason (1975) reports that the differences between anxious and nonanxious students in performance are realized mainly in the competitive atmosphere; under neutral conditions, the differences between anxious and nonanxious students are minimal.

According to self-control theory (Carver & Scheier, 1989), optimism is a key personal variable that may interact with test anxiety in affecting cognitive task performance. Thus anxiety is claimed to have its most debilitating effect on individuals who are relatively pessimistic about their changes of success, eventually leading to reduced self-confidence and physical or mental disengagement from the cognitive task at hand. By contrast, individuals optimistic about their chances of success will attempt to bridge the gap between entering behavior and goals, and the anxiety will become a facilitating motivational factor toward that goal. According to the process delineated by Carver and Scheier (1989), test-anxious individuals are those whose expectations for successful test outcomes are not very favorable. Given a stressful situation, they suffer from acute lack of confidence, low persistence, and mental disengagement and distress, thus debilitating their test performance.

How are we to make sense of the reported inverse correlation between test anxiety and cognitive performance? Evidently, the specific direction of the relationship is ambiguous in most cases and may come about for several different reasons. Most theories view test anxiety as the independent variable and intelligence as the dependent variable. Accordingly, test anxiety may either prevent or limit the use of personal wherewithal on cognitive tasks, or anxiety may aversely influence intellectual development. The fear-of-failure component of anxiety may inhibit the undertaking of achievement-related activities, with individuals high in anxiety avoiding activities that enhance intellectual growth. Conversely, persons low in academic ability may become anxious about the need to confront situations that produce failure, thus leading to feelings of helplessness and low self-efficacy. Accordingly, intelligence may affect the growth of motivational structures such as anxiety, with the effects of intelligence on adaptation serving to decrease anxiety in a demanding situation. A third interpretation is that individuals with low IQ are not really smart enough to mask their true feelings about the exams, and the negative relations are caused by shortcomings in use of self-report instruments (Weiner, 1973). Finally, the observed relationship of anxiety to intelligence may result from the artifactual influences of extraneous variables (e.g., social class, child-rearing patterns, test situation) affecting both variables.

Anger and Aggression

Anger is commonly described as a negative emotion—in terms of both subjective experiences and social evaluation—ranging in intensity from mild irritation to rage (Spielberger et al., 1985). It is often hailed as one of the most intriguing of human emotions and plays a central role in modern personality theory and research, with important implications for psychological practice in the clinical, health, occupational, and educational domains (Zeidner, 1990).

The distinction between anger as a trait (T-Anger) and as a state (S-Anger) has gained wide recognition among personality researchers (Spielberger, Jacobs, Russell, & Crane, 1983). Accordingly, T-Anger is defined in terms of relatively stable individual differences among people in the proneness to perceive a wide range of situational stimuli as frustrating or annoying, and the tendency to respond to such stimuli with marked elevations in state anger. Thus individuals who are chronically angry may have certain maladaptive cognitive styles that predispose them to perceive events as more frequently and intensely anger arousing than do their nonangry counterparts. By contrast, S-Anger is subjectively experienced as an emotional state; it varies in intensity and may fluctuate over time as a function of the amount of frustration and annoyance resulting from perceived injustice or the blocking of goal-directed behavior in a given context. Another useful distinction is between anger suppressed (anger-in) and anger directed outward (anger-out). Anger-in is subjectively experienced as an emotional state that varies in intensity and with time as a function of the specific provoking contextual stimuli and the individual's level of T-Anger (see Averill, 1982; Speilberger et al., 1983). Anger-out, by contrast, is expressed in physical acts and verbal manifestations both directly toward the source of provocation or indirectly toward objects closely associated with or symbolic of the provoking agent or stimuli.

Anger is typically evoked in response to perceived injustice or blocking of an individual's needs or goal-directed behavior. Anger may function as a "social role" aimed at upholding normative standards of conduct in social contexts and geared toward correcting some perceived injustice or wrong (Averill, 1982). As such, the manner in which each person fulfills this role may be dependent on his or her personality characteristics and abilities, as well as gender, age, and social and ethnic group membership. Although a flurry of recent research has studied anger in relation to a wide array of personality and health factors, there is little research directly relating various facets of anger (e.g., anger-in, anger-out) to cognitive ability or performance.

Based on the assumption that anger underlies much of aggressive behavior (Charles Spielberger, personal communication, 1986) and is an integral part of what Spielberger et al. (1983) call the "AHA" (i.e., anger, hostility, aggression) phenomenon, one way to get a handle on the anger-intelligence interface is to look at the relations between aggression and ability. Cattell (1971) points out that perhaps the most persistent dynamic relation for all periods of society is between low intelligence and personality difficulties. Accordingly, there is considerable evidence to support the contention that there is an increased degree of delinquency and crime, and even child and wife abuse, among individuals with lower IQs (see Cattell, 1971, for an extensive discussion). How can we account for the general tendency for low IQ to go with increased aggression, impulsive behavior, and delinquency? Although there are a number of causal links, the most popular explanation claims that the correlation may be attributable to the effects of low intelligence on frustration and the inability to control impulses, delay rewards, and calculate one's own interest.

Common sense dictates that intelligence is a requisite for ego control and the operation of the reality principle. Accordingly, the capacity for postponing immediate gratification has been conceptualized in developmental terms as involving a transition from immediate and wish-fulfilling types of behavior to those requiring delay and reality testing. Because learning to delay is related to cognitive capacity (Mischel & Metzner, 1962), it follows that as intelligence increases, delay of gratification should increase as well. The more intelligent person also is believed to seek further into consequences of his or her behavior, build up more inhibitions, and acquire more socially desirable traits. Thus high intelligence can aid a student in simultaneously learning the realities of general and school culture and of the physical world. By contrast, there is a statistical probability that the less intelligent person will experience more frustration in the learning process and will therefore be more provoked to impulsive and antisocial activities. For example, children of low ability who fail school or cannot acquire basic skills of reading and math become frustrated and develop an aggressive attitude. Furthermore, children with low IQs tend to have parents with low IQs who provide poorer social conditions and less discipline.

Kipnis (1971) found that impulsiveness moderated the influences of individual differences in intelligence on college success, thus serving as a moderator variable in the relation between ability and performance. Thus individuals high on impulsivity and high on scholastic ability (as assessed by SAT scores) tend to have lower grades than those high on SAT and low on impulsivity. Huesmann, Eron, and Yarmel (1987) present evidence that aggression may act over a long period of time to depress intellectual functioning. They studied the association between intelligence and aggression using a longitudinal design, with data on the two variables collected at age 8 and again at age 30. Aggression at age 8 added significantly to the prediction of intellectual attainment at age 30 beyond that contributed by IQ scores at age 8. By contrast, intelligence at age 8 did not add significantly to the ability to predict age 30 aggression beyond that contributed by age 8 aggression. The results suggest that whereas intellectual competence has little or no influence on differences in aggression after age 8, aggressive tendencies that exhibit continuity may act over a long period of time to depress intellectual performance.

According to Freudian psychoanalytic theory, a more developed culture demands greater instinctual restraints, which it rewards by greater security and opportunity for sublimated emotional satisfaction in the arts and sciences. As Cattell (1971) remarks, an individual with low IQ will find Bach or Boolean algebra a poor thrill compared to fighting and gambling. IQ may affect the way impulses are transformed and lead to divergent expression of personality. The fundamental frustrations of a complex society pressing hardest on those of lower intelligence is the perennial cause, according to Cattell, of the association of delinquency and lower IQ.

Conversely, the observed relationship may be attributable to the effects of impulsivity (and inability to delay impulses) on deficits in acquisition of knowledge or skills measured by ability tests. The relationship may also result from the effects of a third variable (e.g., strict parental rearing patterns or social class) on both intelligence and delinquency/aggression. It should also be remembered, however, that high intelligence may also serve as an aid to rationalization and evasion on the part of people with low moral principles (Cattell, 1971). Thus a person with dubious moral character but endowed with high intelligence may be more dangerous to society than a less intelligent delinquent.

COPING, ADJUSTMENT, AND INTELLIGENCE

Given the view that intelligence is a global form of adaptation to the environment, intelligent people might also be expected to be better adjusted, both socially and emotionally, than their less intelligent counterparts. Furthermore, intelligence may serve as a resource that can facilitate personal growth and adjustment and also serve as a buffer against the crippling effects of psychological stress and disease (see Lazarus, 1991; Lazarus & Folkman, 1984). If we assume for a moment that the essence of intelligence is rational thought and problem-solving ability that allows one to adapt to the environment, certain personality disorders and pathological states may be expected to affect intellectual performance and intelligence test scores. Unfortunately, although research in the stress domain has given lip service to the importance of intelligence as a coping resource (see Lazarus & Folkman, 1984), empirical research in this area has basically failed to assess directly and systematically the role of intelligence as a predictor of stress reactions or adaptational outcomes.

Stress and Coping Styles

Stress arises when the perceived demands of the environment tax or exceed the individual's perceived capacity to cope with these demands (Lazarus & Folkman, 1984). Thus it stands to reason that the more intellectual capacity one has, or perceives oneself to have, the less susceptible one should be to stress. Intelligence, as a personal resource, may also facilitate personal growth and adjustment, as well as possibly buffer the effects of environmental stress on stress reactions.

Intelligence may influence each of the phases of the stress process. In his cognitive-motivational-relational theory of emotion, Lazarus (1991) posits that if a person appraises his or her relationship to the environment in a particular way, then a specific emotion tied to the appraisal pattern always follows. In other words, once the appraisals have been made, the emotion is a foregone conclusion. Intelligence can affect the appraisal process by allowing more complex reasoning and consideration of alternatives during both primary and secondary appraisal of a given situation. It stands to reason that individuals with a higher intellectual level and greater problem-solving skills are more likely to diagnose accurately the causes of stress, collect information bearing on the situation from a variety of sources, examine the situation from different viewpoints, reason about the causes, and generate options about how to change themselves or their environment (see Payne, 1991 for an extensive discussion of these points). If, for example, two people have been treated inconsiderately in a social situation, one may interpret the other person's behavior as an unwarranted offense and get angry or become anxious. The other person, who is higher in intelligence, may take additional alternatives into consideration (e.g., the offending party may be under stress or may have suffered from a personal tragedy); that person may feel concern, compassion, or sympathy rather than anger (Lazarus, 1991).

Intelligence may also enter into the actual process of coping, affecting both the choice and implementation of particular coping strategies in a stressful situation. Though problem- and emotion-focused strategies will likely be used by people of both high and low intelligence, those lower in intelligence may use emotion-focused coping more frequently because they will assess more situations as being ones they can do very little about.

Haan (1963) has provided some empirical evidence that changes in intelligence from early adolescence to middle adulthood correlate positively with increased usage of coping mechanisms, but negatively with defense mechanisms. It is not clear from this research which particular experiences enhance and accelerate an individual's intellectual growth and freedom to cope with stress and which promote the development of defenses, thus closing off the individual from experience and intellectual growth. Overall, there is very little hard empirical evidence to back up the claims about the role of intelligence at various stages in the stress and coping process.

Mental Health

One of the key symptoms of mental disorder, by definition, is the inability to actualize one's mental and physical potential. Thus an individual's ability to function intellectually is predicted to decline when he or she is suffering from severe emotional distress, with most forms of psychological pathology expected to affect thought processes in some way.

One of the effects of severe stress is to lower one's overall adaptive efficiency and to increase the rigidity of cognitive processes (see Chapter 13). Under stress, it becomes difficult for the individual to assess the situation objectively, to differentiate rationally between relevant and irrelevant stimuli, to abstract crucial features, or to perceive and scan the range of available alternatives. It should be stressed that stress and situational anxiety affect *performance* on cognitive tasks, whereas *competence* (or ability) generally remains intact.

Neurosis

Although clinicians often claim to observe ongoing mental deterioration and irrational processing of information of some sort in pathological cases, milder levels of mental disorder generally have little impact on one's intelligence. Mildly disturbed neurotics often act in an irrational manner and fail to think rationally in conflict-laden areas (e.g., the obsessive individual who generally has difficulty in making decisions). In other areas their intelligence is not impaired, although their ability to apply intelligent behavior may be reduced. Thus their competence remains intact, and what appears to be influenced is a failure to use their intellectual capacity in an emotionally laden field. The general anxiety experienced by neurotics may aversely affect the intelligence test performance in a particular test situation but have little permanent affect on competence.

Psychosis

Although psychotic affective disorders chiefly involve a disturbance of mood, there are also frequent disturbances of perception and information-processing mechanisms (delusions and hallucinations) that interfere with the rational processes involved in intelligence. Much of the research has centered on intellectual decline in schizophrenia, the most prevalent of the psychoses. As Coleman, Butcher, and Carson (1984) point out, schizophrenics' thought and judgment are seriously impaired as mental health deteriorates, with a growing tendency to confuse wish and reality. The schizophrenic mind, although unselectively registering everything in its field of vision, is unable to distinguish between relevant and irrelevant cues. In fact, disturbances in thinking ("cognitive slippage") are thought to be the hallmark of schizophrenia. The intellectual abilities of manifest schizophrenia appear to fluctuate, and the same person may obtain different scores on mental tests.

A number of hypotheses exist in the literature with respect to the effects of schizophrenia on intellectual functioning: One common hypothesis is that all schizophrenics may go through a time-limited period of intellectual deteriorization after which intelligence stabilizes. A second hypothesis is that only some intellectual skills (e.g., numerical, spatial) deteriorate, whereas others (e.g., verbal) do not. A third hypothesis states that the intellectual performance of some diagnostic groups deteriorates, but that the performance of others do not; thus schizophrenics of high and low IQ may represent different subtypes, one of which is susceptible to intellectual deterioration and the other not. A fourth hypothesis states that intellectual skills do not decline but personalities decompensate, thus creating the illusion of decline. It is also hypothesized that decrements in performance may be attributed in part to the subject's low motivation to perform, minimal cooperation, and impaired contact with the examiner.

Unfortunately, the direct empirical evidence of whether the intellectual abilities of schizophrenics decline after the onset of psychosis is conflicting and often confusing. Although the intelligence of severely schizophrenic individuals may be below average, one is struck by the preservation of average or even remarkable intellectual superiority in many schizophrenics, especially those diagnosed as paranoid (Payne, 1973). A recent review of the literature (Watson, Herder, Kucala, & Hoodecheck-Schow, 1987) shows that some studies report substantial decline between high school (or military) and hospitalization, whereas some studies show that intellectual deficits among schizophrenics may be attributable to preexisting conditions and are not an inherent factor associated with the onset of schizophrenia. In one study (Watson et al., 1987), no significant decay in intelligence scores was observed for schizophrenics whose initial aptitude test scores (AGCT) were above average, with the observed decline in test scores largely attributable to a drop in a specific skill (arithmetic performance). Deterioration limited to certain skills is best interpreted as a loss in particular intellectual functions rather than a more generalized intellectual decay. Conversely, the failure to report intellectual loss in schizophrenia may often be the result of IQ deterioration long before the illness became apparent.

Some research shows that intelligence is adversely affected under acute schizophrenia attack but that during remission, performance on intelligence tests improves again (Schwartzman & Douglas, 1962). In schizophrenic inpatients with long histories of hospitalization, chronic patients manifest greater intellectual deficits than do those with recent onset or brief hospitalization. This finding, however, may be attributable to changes in the composition of hospitalized cohorts over time rather than to the effects of hospitalization or processes intrinsic to psychosis. Longitudinal studies of hospitalized patients fail to find progressive decline (Hamlin, 1963); in other words, chronics may be less bright than acutes because of an association between IQ and retention in and readmission to hospitals. In a study (Heffner, Strauss, & Grisell, 1975) based on the records of 91 schizophrenics aged 20 to 30, brighter patients were less often rehospitalized 3 and 5 years after discharge than patients of lower IQ. Thus there appears to be a prognostic significance for IQ that contributes to the differences in intelligence between acute and chronic schizophrenics.

The effects of psychosis on intellectual functioning for children may be more pernicious than those for adults, and children suffering from certain personality dysfunctions and disturbances have been reported to suffer from a severe deterioration of abilities. Sattler (1988) points out that children with disintegrative psychosis usually have a period of normal development for the first 3 to 4 years, after which profound regression and behavioral disintegration occurs, intelligence declines, speech and language abilities deteriorate, and social skills diminish. In addition, such children become restive, irritable, anxious, and overactive, and the overall prognosis is poor. One study (Rutter & Lockyer, 1967) found that only about 25% of psychotic children had IQs within normal range. A child's level of ability may be related to prognosis of childhood psychosis in a number of other ways (Sattler, 1988): (a) in families that are predisposed to schizophrenia, children with the lowest IQ are the most vulnerable, (b) psychotic children with nonorganic etiologies obtaining higher IQ scores than those with organic etiologies; and (c) the higher the intelligence of the child, the better the prognosis.

Intelligence and Therapy

Because intelligence is a measure of one's current overall level of organization and integrative functioning, it may play an important role in the prognosis of maladjusted individuals as well. Furthermore, on the assumption that intelligence involves the ability to understand relations (including social and emotional relations) adequately and to correct cognitions on the basis of evidence, it might be hypothesized that highly intelligent patients would profit more from psychotherapeutic relations compared to their less intelligent counterparts and also show a better prognosis. Thus, on purely theoretical grounds, it may be predicted that the greater effectiveness of intellectual functioning (as revealed in IQ tests) should also be associated with greater modifiability in personality structure. Furthermore, because traditional psychotherapy involves verbal exchanges between therapist and patient, its success entails some verbal learning (e.g., acquisition and elimination of responses). Thus success at psychotherapy should be related to general verbal learning ability and intelligence.

In fact, there is some research to support the claim that intelligence is a significant predictor of success in psychological treatment and therapy. Barron (1953) reported correlates of change in psychological morbidity in 33 adult neurotics after 6 months of therapy; improvement in therapy correlated about .46 with scores on the Wechsler Adult Intelligence Scale. Furthermore, clients who remain in therapy are found to be more intelligent than those who terminate prematurely: Most of those who remain are of average IQ (i.e., 100) or higher, and most of those who leave are below average (Hiler, 1958).

EXTRAVERSION AND DEALING WITH NOVELTY IN THE ENVIRONMENT

Dealing effectively with novelty in the environment and responding in a novel manner to stimuli are among the characteristics commonly attributed to intellectual performance of any age, whether for a bright preschooler, high school or college student, or a Nobel laureate.

Creativity

Creativity seems to hold an intermediate position between intelligence and personality, because creative productions imply both an *ability* to think fluently and flexibility and an *inclination* to do so. In the post-Sputnik era, when scientific ingenuity was valued most highly, educators began paying more attention to attributes such as creativity and called for the study of these abilities and for the development of measures to gauge them. Although the relationship between creativity and intelligence has engaged the interest of scholars for several decades now, however, there is still some dispute whether creativity is an independent ability, a part of general intelligence, or a personality correlate of intelligence (see various chapters in Glover, Ronning, & Reynolds, 1989).

The predominant conception in the literature is based largely on Guilford's (1959, 1967) "structure of intellect" model. Because intelligence covers the entire multifactorial domain of cognitive abilities, creativity is construed to be a component and proper subset of the intelligence domain. In fact, creativity is equated with a particular type of cognitive operation (termed *divergent thinking* in Guilford's model) assumed to underlie creative achievement. Divergent thinking is assessed by open-ended tasks asking for as many answers as possible (e.g., "Name all the square things you can think of"; "List all possible uses of shoes") and involving multiple solutions, with typically no one correct response (Guilford, 1967). Instead, responses are judged by their fluency, rarity, originality, and quality. By contrast, convergent tasks demand one correct response (e.g., "What is 3 to the third power?") and are typically judged by the correctness of the solution (e.g., 27 is correct; 9 is incorrect).

Scores of studies have compared more or less creative individuals on measures of personality, often with inconsistent and ambiguous results. Among the personality traits identified with creativity are aesthetic sensitivity, broad interests, and toleration of ambiguity (Barron & Harrington, 1981). Thus creative subjects may avoid premature closure or judgment that can limit the number of ideas produced. These traits may be interpreted as components of a broad trait termed "openness to experience," which includes intellectual curiosity, aesthetic sensitivity, liberal values, and emotional differentiation (McCrae, 1987).

It seems probable that a fairly high level of intelligence is necessary for creative achievements (Nicholls, 1972), and it is commonly held that a certain cutoff level of intelligence may be a prerequisite to creative performance. To be sure, individuals with average or low average IQs would have great difficulty competing successfully in some of today's most creative scientific and artistic professions. Research confirms that highly creative individuals (e.g., creative artists, writers, architects, scientists, and mathematicians) score very high on measures of intelligence (Barron & Harrington, 1981) and are also perceived as being highly intelligent by qualified observers (Barron & Harrington, 1981).

Although measures of intelligence and divergent thinking ability are partially distinct, they are substantially related, particularly when corrected for limited range of IQ and attenuation. When the full range of variables is assessed, there is considerable evidence that creativity is moderately associated with intelligence, with an average correlation of about .3 being a reasonable estimate (Barron & Harrington, 1981). These low to moderate correlations imply that a good many subjects fall in the "off-quadrants"—that is, some subjects are creative but not so intelligent, whereas others are intelligent but not so creative. In fact, different behavioral profiles may characterize such children. Wallach and Kogan (1965) have shown that children high in creativity and low in IQ tend to be in angry conflict with themselves and the school environment and are beset by feeling of inadequacy and unworthiness. By contrast, those high in intelligence and low in creativity appear to be addicted to school achievement, continually striving for excellence and doing exceptionally well.

Reviewers of the literature have concluded that whereas creativity is significantly related to IQ up to about 120 (the level of an average university undergraduate in the United States), after that creativity becomes independent of IQ, and the IQ-creativity relationship drops to near zero (Getzels & Jackson, 1962; Wallach & Kogan, 1965). These findings imply that beyond some minimum level of cognitive skill necessary for mastery of a particular field, nonintellective factors may determine creative performance, in that intellectual skills may be necessary but not sufficient for creative performance.

As critics have observed, however, the magnitude of the relationship between the two characteristics may be a function of the variability of the sample: In a fairly homogenous group in terms of IQ (whether high or low), creativity and intelligence are indeed not as meaningfully correlated as they are in a more heterogenous group. It is also possible that the relationship between the two constructs may be curvilinear, with intelligence becoming less influential in determining creativity as one moves into higher and lower levels of intelligence.

Wallach and Kogan (1965) have provided evidence showing that when both creativity and intelligence measures are administered under conventional testing conditions (time pressure, evaluative atmosphere) there is little evidence that creativity is distinct from general ability. When the creativity assessment situation is modified to optimize associational flow (e.g., freedom from time pressure, absence of evaluational pressures, a playful or gamelike context), however, a creativity dimension quite independent of intelligence does emerge. This unique factor concerns the child's ability to generate unique and plentiful associations in a playful context. Unfortunately, creativity tests are infrequently used these days, because their validity has never been adequately established. Thus there is considerable consensus among experts that creativity tests have not fulfilled their goals: Although they may show adequate reliability and may measure something different than IQ, they cannot predict which individuals will be creative in real-life situations (Wallach, 1985).

Curiosity

It is commonly assumed that intelligence and curiosity go together (Henderson & Wilson, 1991): The more intense the basic motive of curiosity is in a person, the greater the motivation is to acquire concepts, techniques, habits, and skills to gratify this motive. Whereas some people seem to prefer a relatively low level of stimulation input, others tend to require increased levels of input for optimal functioning. Because intellectual behaviors such as reading, questioning, and manipulating the environment are effective behavioral methods of gratifying one's curiosity, the curious child would be more likely to develop these skills and apt to gain in general knowledge and intelligence (Kagan, Sontag, & Nelson, 1958). It is commonly held that early learning behaviors might inhibit or enhance the child's exploratory tendencies.

This commonsense view has more sophisticated versions in a number of theories of intelligence and intellectual development. Thus Piaget's assimilation-accommodation model of intelligent adaptation assumes an active curiosity by children about their worlds. Also, the notion that curiosity influences intelligence would concur with recent theories suggesting that responses to environmental novelty may be a source of developmental continuity in intelligence from infancy through adulthood. Furthermore, in current theories of intelligence, response to novelty is viewed as having two aspects that are integral components of intelligence (Berg & Sternberg, 1985): (a) an energizing element linked to the individual's interest in and preference for novel stimuli as well as attention to discrepancies between existing schemas and novelty in the environment; and (b) the greater ability of intelligent individuals to extract information automatically, thus freeing cognitive resources for dealing with novel tasks.

Despite the potential theoretical importance of a relation between intelligence and curiosity, there is surprisingly little direct empirical evidence of concurrent correlations between these two variables. A review of the available studies relating IQ and curiosity shows generally low correlations (usually below .30), though teachers' ratings of curiosity correlate at a somewhat higher level with group intelligence scores (see Henderson & Wilson, 1991). One line of research has suggested that observed developmental changes in IQ may be accounted for in part by recourse to personality variables such as curiosity. Kagan et al. (1958) compared children who showed IQ increases over time with those showing decreases over the years; the authors found significantly more themes of curiosity about nature and fewer themes of passivity in the former group.

Prior research by Zuckerman (1979) reports a low correlation (about .20) between intelligence and sensation seeking, a trait akin to curiosity. Furthermore, recent research points to a greater attentional capacity among sensation seekers (see Ball & Zuckerman, 1992). Ball and Zuckerman (1992) speculate that focused attention is linked with high levels of sensation seeking because engaging in high-risk activities requires close attention to cues. Thus more focused attention on tasks may mediate the modest relationship found between sensation seeking and intelligence. Furthermore, there is some evidence that novel tasks arouse the attention and interest of high sensation seekers; such increased arousal may improve their ability to focus on and succeed on these tasks (including those often found on intelligence tests).

Introversion–Extraversion

Introversion–extraversion is a basic dimension of individual differences in human behavior and is often construed as a source trait with a strong biological basis (H. J. Eysenck & Eysenck, 1985). Extraverts tend to direct their psychic energy outward: They tend to be outgoing, quick at establishing contact and social relationships, impulsive, and able to venture confidently into unknown situations. By contrast, introverts tend to direct much of their psychic energy inward, being quite introspective, slow at establishing contacts, reliable, pessimistic, and moralistic.

Theories proposed by Eysenck (see H. J. Eysenck, 1967a) and Robinson (1986) have served as the major conceptual frameworks for research on intelligence and extraversion/introversion. According to Eysenck's theory of arousal (see Brody, 1988, for a clear exposition), the tonic or resting level of arousal for introverts is higher than that of extraverts. Thus introverts are viewed to be more responsive and physiologically affected by arousing stimuli than extraverts. Robinson (1986) further hypothesized that intraverts have inherited a nervous system that permits them to form learned connections between stimulus and response more rapidly. The more intense thalamocortical activity of introverts favors the development of "lateral connectivity"—the physiological basis of association learning. Thus, for introverts, any particular stimulus should have a greater number of associations than for extraverts, and it is possible for the former to access these associations more readily. The greater tonic level of activity sustained by thalamocortical processes of introverts, however, also results in a stronger inhibition of the brain-stem system (which is normally involved in elaboration of automatic motor sequences), thus impairing introverts' ability to acquire manipulative skills. Accordingly, introverts are predicted to have an advantage on any task where performance is facilitated by superior associative learning ability (i.e., verbal tasks); by contrast, extraverts a predicted to show better performance on tasks facilitated by ready acquisition of automatic motor sequences (i.e., performance tasks).

A review of the literature bearing on the relationship between extraversion and intelligence yields rather inconsistent results. Some authors (e.g., Wilson, 1977) have concluded that extraverts and introverts do not differ much in intelligence. In one study conducted among 398 male nurses, extraversion was uncorrelated with both verbal and nonverbal intelligence measures (H. J. Eysenck, 1971). More recently, Robinson (1985) showed that the extraversion did not correlate significantly with any of the IQ indices of the WAIS for an adult sample. These results were replicated on a sizable sample of Canadian children in grade 6 to 8 (Saklofske & Kostura, 1990). In direct contrast, Lynn, Hampson, and Magee (1982) using data collected among 711 adolescents in Northern Ireland, showed modest correlations between IQ and extraversion for both boys ($r = .21$) and girls ($r = .19$). Similar results were found in a study by Crookes, Pearson, Francis, and Carter (1981), who found a positive correlation between extraversion and IQ in 15- to 16-year-old boys and girls.

Furthermore, examination of the empirical evidence suggests that the relationship between intelligence and extraversion may be a bit more complex than it appears at first sight. Robinson (1985) provided data indicating that extraversion and introversion are intimately associated with different intellectual styles and intelligence profiles, but not with absolute levels of performance on intelligence tests. Accordingly, introverts and extraverts were found not to differ in overall IQ, only on profile: Introverts were found to do relatively better on verbal tests, and extroverts on performance tests.

H. J. Eysenck and Cookson (1969) further complicated the picture by suggesting a developmental or maturational link between intelligence and personality. Indeed, considerable research shows that mean extraversion scores in children rise steadily with increasing age, reach a peak at age 13 or 14, then fall slightly. At the peak age, there is a tendency for the correlation between extraversion and IQ to change from positive to negative. A number of alternative explanations for this shift have been suggested in the literature. It has been hypothesized that able students become more introverted and the less able more extraverted with time; it has also been suggested that extraverts fall behind in the development of ability, whereas the introverts make faster changes. Anthony (1973) provided evidence that intelligent children tend to become less extraverted over time. A further possible explanation is that because introverts mature more slowly, introversion in primary-school-age children is not advantageous to mental achievement, but by secondary school it becomes an assistance. Also, the shift in correlations could be caused by different rates of development of extraversion (Anthony, 1973): If the average peak of extraversion is about 14 years of age, the rapid developers would reach the peak, resulting in the positive IQ–extraversion correlation. But this trend would reverse after the age of 14 when the slower become more extraverted and the quicker more introverted.

To confuse matters even further, a number of studies hint at an interaction between extraversion-introversion and test conditions in their influence on ability test performance (see Revelle, Amaral, & Turriff, 1976). Under high arousal conditions, introverts are found to act slowly and accurately, whereas under low arousal conditions extraverts act rapidly and erroneously. Furthermore, it has been claimed that when performance on intelligence tests is broken down into independent components, extraverts are found to be faster, less accurate, and less persistent than introverts. In fact, one of the earliest findings was that extraverts opt for speed in experimental tasks whereas introverts opt for accuracy (H. J. Eysenck, 1967b). Thus Jensen (1964) found that extraversion correlated moderately with speed of solution of Raven's matrices, although extraverts made significantly more errors. Furthermore, there are a number of experiments demonstrating the superiority of extraverts over short intervals in learning tasks and the superiority of introverts over long intervals. As a result of greater cortical arousal, introverts manage to mediate learning better through the consolidation process, with higher arousal leading to better memory in the long run.

Revelle, Humphreys, Simon, and Gilliland (1980) hypothesized that introverts who are low in impulsiveness differ from extraverts not in their chronic levels of arousal but rather with respect to the time of day during which they are most aroused. Nonimpulsive subjects were hypothesized to be highly aroused in the morning but not in the evening; the opposite pattern was hypothesized for impulsive subjects. Subjects low in impulsivity showed a clear decrement in ability test performance when given caffeine (assumed to be a nonspecific energizer) in the morning, but showed improvements when given caffeine in the evening. The authors interpreted this rather complex pattern of interactions by appeal to the assumption that caffeine added to the arousal level of their subjects. Thus less impulsive subjects who were highly aroused in the morning became overaroused when given caffeine in the morning and this state caused their performance to deteriorate. The highly impulsive subjects given caffeine in the morning were underaroused, and addition of caffeine brought them to an arousal level optimal for cognitive task performance.

MOTIVATION

Motivation, much like anxiety, is an important variable in the assessment of intelligence. Unless the examinee taking an intelligence test cares about the results and is motivated to do his or her best, the results will not be a very accurate or reliable reflection of the person's ability. Thus *motivation* is a term frequently employed in intelligence test protocols or reports to account for the performance of clients.

Achievement Motivation

Achievement motivation is a learned motive, with the term designating a general striving to perform one's best when (a) the quality of one's performance is judged in terms of success or failure, and (b) a relevant standard of excellence applies (Weiner, 1973). According to achievement motivation theory (Atkinson, 1964), all individuals have both a basic motive to approach an achievement-related goal and a motive to avoid failure. The tendency to seek success (T_{as}) and approach an achievement-related goal is postulated to be a product of three factors: a relatively stable disposition to strive for success (i.e., need for achievement); the (subjective) probability that one will be successful; and the incentive value of success. If one of these values equals or approaches zero (e.g., the person feels his or her chances of success in a particular endeavor are nil, or there is little value or incentive in doing well) the resulting multiplicative value will also be zero, and no effort will be put forth by the individual to attain the goal. Similarly, the opposing force—the tendency to avoid failure (T_{af})—is posited to be multiplicatively determined by three factors: (a) the motive to avoid failure, (b) the probability of failure, and (c) the incentive value or negative affect (shame) associated with failure. Achievement striving is postulated to be the result of an approach-avoidance conflict between the two opposing tendencies, with the stronger of the two tendencies being expressed in action.

On the basis of Atkinson's theory, it is conceivable that only students of average intelligence should be strongly motivated to achieve or avoid failure, depending on the relative strengths of their motivations for success or motivation to avoid failure. The very bright or very dull would not be expected to have achievement-related dispositions aroused, because the conventional competitive classroom situation will be either too easy or too difficult for them. Very bright students are expected to perform well in school and dull students poorly regardless of motivation; hence performance differences as a function of motivation are relatively confined to groups intermediate in ability.

Achievement motivation may influence intellectual performance in one of several ways. First, achievement motivation may determine the level of interest and effort that persons invest in the development of their intellectual skills throughout all their life experiences prior to the test. Because school environment emphasizes competitive intellectual strivings, students with strong competitive needs would be highly motivated to acquire intellectual skills that result in successful competition with peers. Second, achievement motivation may help shape the level of attention, effort, concentration, and persistence applied in the test situation itself. Conversely, the hypothesized association of achievement motivation with intelligence may be attributable to the adaptation of one's motives to intelligence. Thus a person high in quantitative ability is likely to develop a motive to achieve in math. Furthermore, highly intelligent students develop a strong motivation to acquire or develop various intellectual skills tapped by IQ tests and to perform well in testing situations.

Unfortunately, reviews of the empirical research relating achievement motivation and intelligence have failed to yield consistent results. Some authors surveying the literature have concluded that the relationship is on the whole unsupported by empirical research, with most studies reporting statistically unreliable correlations between measures of achievement motivation and intelligence test scores (Heckhausen, 1967). Other reviews have reported modest positive relations between need for achievement and intelligence (Veroff, McClelland, & Marquis, 1971).

A well-cited study by Spielberger and Katzenmeyer (1959) yielded findings consistent with the hypothesis that achievement motivation may interact with ability in affecting scholastic performance. Student college grade point average (GPA) was not reported to differ between groups high and low in anxiety at the extreme ability levels, but it was moderately influenced at the intermediate levels. Achievement motivation theory can account for these results in that students of average ability have an intermediate subjective probability of doing well in school. Thus motivation should be maximally aroused for students low in anxiety but be maximally inhibitory among highly anxious students, resulting in the observed differences in GPA. At the extreme ability levels, where success or failure is nearly certain for high-ability and low-ability students, respectively, hopes of success and fears of failure are minimally aroused and therefore are not observed to affect GPA. Thus motivational differences, mediated by the subjective probability of success, may be responsible for the observed GPA differences among students differing in ability.

There is some evidence for a positive correlation between intelligence and *intellectual orientation*, a term that refers to emotional responses to the process and content of intellectual learning. Two basic orientations have been differentiated in the literature (Lloyd, 1984): (a) extrinsic orientation, in which the learning is for ulterior purposes (e.g., grades, material success) and (b) intrinsic orientation, in which learning is driven by a desire to know for the sake of knowing. Intrinsic intellectuality is thought to contribute to academic achievement because the learning process is supported primarily by immediate intrinsic rewards (i.e., delight in the very process of learning). Lloyd

(1984) found a correlation of .27 between IQ and intrinsic intellectual motivation and a correlation of .27 between IQ and need for achievement. Intrinsic intellectual motivation, however, accounts for only about a third as much variance in achievement as does IQ.

Attributions and Perceived Control

Locus of control is a factor often claimed to be related to cognitive ability. The term refers to decisions and beliefs about the origins of behavior and the assignment of credit and blame for its results. Internally controlled individuals assume that their own behaviors and actions are responsible for what happens to them, whereas externally controlled people believe that the locus of control is out of their hands and subject to the whims of fate.

Much of this line of work is based on Rotter's (1966) social learning theory. This theory views the likelihood of an individual to perform a given behavior to be a function of two factors: (a) the importance or value of the outcome (reinforcement value), and (b) the individual's expectancy that the behavior will result in a favorable outcome. If a person sees a contingency between behavior and attainment of a desirable outcome and believes that attaining the goal depends on the adequacy of his or her behavior, than he or she might be described as having an internal locus of control. Because internals typically see themselves to be effective, powerful, independent, and trusting of others, it may come as no surprise that they also view themselves as being more intelligent. The rationale is that those who feel at mercy of their environment and have little control over what happens to them would also have low adaptive capacity.

Some research has found the belief that the major events in one's life are outside of one's control to be negatively correlated with intelligence. Intelligence has been reported to be inversely correlated with external locus of control in a sizable sample of male (−.37) and female (−.36) junior and high school students (Samuel, 1980). Also, as reported by Coleman et al. (1966), the item "Good luck is more important than hard work for success," reflecting an external locus of control, was more frequently endorsed by blacks and was negatively related to test scores. Seligman (1975) specifically related deficits in mean IQ shown by black examinees to the phenomena of learned helplessness, in which their motivation to cope with environmental contingencies is drastically diminished by preliminary exposure to uncontrollable aversive stimuli.

The rationale underpinning this relationship is that people who believe they can control their own lives will put forth the effort to gain competencies and skills, thus enhancing their crystallized intelligence and abilities. Conversely, people who are successful at using their abilities come to believe in their capacity to control their destiny, so that locus of control may shape the development of intelligence. Thus we do not know for sure what the causal direction is: Does attribution affect cognitive test performance, or do less intelligent people tend to rely more on luck and accidental or external factors than on their own abilities?

BELIEF SYSTEMS OF SELF AND OTHERS

A number of belief systems related to oneself (i.e., self-concept) and to others (e.g., authoritarianism, superstition, paranormal beliefs, social desirability) have been found to be moderately related to intelligence. This section, bridging the gap between intelligence and social psychology, will examine some of these interesting relationships.

Self-Concept and Efficacy

Self-Concept

A need for a positive self-concept or self-regard develops universally. People's self-image (how they see themselves) and their self-esteem (to what degree they feel positive about themselves) are crucial in determining how they perceive the world, their goals and attitudes, the behaviors they initiate, the responses they make to others, and generally how they develop their potential. Both theory and past research suggest that a positive self-concept and high self-esteem are related to higher academic ability and attainment, whereas negative beliefs about the self are associated with lower ability, scholastic underachievement, and failure (Purkey, 1970). Children who think of themselves poorly are likely to underestimate their ability, to anticipate failure, and to stop trying when difficulties arise.

The major determinant of self-concept is generally held to lie in the early and enduring patterns of parent-child relations that underpin the emotional security of the growing child. The child's self-concept is formed by interactions with significant others, with the child coming to see himself or herself as others do (Byrne, 1974). Among the factors shaping positive self-esteem in the child are positive parental regard for the child, respectful treatment of him or her, and definition of clear boundaries and realistic expectations for his or her achievement. These factors produce high self-esteem by fostering personal concern for people important to the child and by providing standards to guide the child's progress and define what is acceptable. Children who grow up without boundaries or standards cannot develop high self-esteem, because they remain uncertain about how to determine capabilities and performance. But although the earliest and most general aspects of the self-concept develop in the interaction between the child and parent figures, continuing changes take place as a consequence of later interactions, so the self-concept is a dynamic and viable construct.

As with test anxiety, the causal dynamics in the assumed relationship between intelligence and self-concept are necessarily ambiguous. One commonly held view is that causality flows from intelligence to self-esteem, with a positive self-concept and adjustment only reflecting past achievement and intellectual ability. Thus the correlation of IQ and self-concept may reflect little more than a person's subjective appraisals of his or her own social or educational standing and scholastic aptitudes. A causal modeling study by Maroyama, Rubin, and Kingsbury (1981) reported that self-esteem at age 12 is significantly predicted by ability at age 7, suggesting that the causal direction does in fact flow from ability to self-esteem. If this hypothesis is correct, efforts to improve adjustment would have little effect on ability and achievement.

A second view is that a favorable self-image may lead to positive expectations of future success, which in turn produce increased effort and motivation to succeed and subsequent favorable outcomes on measures of both ability and achievement. Furthermore, measures of adjustment (including self-concept) may tap values and attributes that facilitate achievement and thus mediate the relation between ability and achievement (Coleman et al., 1966). Additional views hold that there is a bidirectional relationship between the two constructs or that the observed covariation between the two is simply an artifact resulting from some additional variable (e.g., social class).

The empirical evidence directly bearing on the relationship between self-esteem and ability is often contradictory. For example, one study employing the Coopersmith Self-Esteem Inventory, one of the more popular measures of self-esteem, reported significant correlations between self-concept and both verbal (about .30) and nonverbal (.32) test scores (Simon & Simon, 1975). By contrast, in the well-known Coleman report (Coleman et al., 1966) assessing the achievements of elementary school education in the United States, most of the items relating to self-concept showed nonsignificant relationships to ability. Much the same was attested to in the Israeli replication of the Coleman study (Minkowitch, Davis & Bashi, 1982).

Self-Efficacy

One belief system that has been claimed to affect cognitive functioning and performance is concerned with how people construe ability. It stands to reason that personal accomplishments require not only ability but also self-beliefs of efficacy to use these cognitive abilities well. Indeed, effective intellectual functioning requires much more than a simple understanding of the factual knowledge and reasoning operations for given tasks. There are also self-regulatory social, motivational, and affective contributions to cognitive functioning that have been recently addressed within the conceptual framework of the exercise of human agency (Bandura, 1993).

Among the mechanisms of self-agency, none may be more central or pervasive than people's beliefs about their capability to control their own level of functioning and events that affect their lives. Much purposive human behavior is regulated by forethought embodying known goals. Personal goal setting is influenced, among other things, by self-appraisal of capabilities, including intelligence. The stronger the perceived self-efficacy, the higher the goal challenges people set for themselves, and the firmer their commitment to them. Those who have a high sense of efficacy visualize success scenarios that provide positive guides and supports for performance.

Bandura (1983) surveys research suggesting that students who regard ability as an acquirable skill that can be increased by gaining knowledge and competencies tend to adopt a functional learning goal. These students seek challenges that provide opportunities to expand their knowledge and competencies. They regard errors as a natural part of the acquisition process; because one learns from errors, these students are not easily rattled by difficulties. Indeed, research by Bandura and colleagues shows that students who view ability as an acquirable skill fostered a resilient sense of self-efficacy. Furthermore, human functioning appears to also be affected by the beliefs people hold about how ability changes over time. Those who regard intelligence or ability as a skill to be developed and practiced achieve higher attainments compared to those who regard it as a biologically shrinking capacity with age.

Authoritarianism

Authoritarianism refers to an attitudinal system consisting of a set of interrelated antidemocratic sentiments, including ethnic prejudice, political conservatism, and moralistic rejection of the unconventional. Research on this construct was prompted toward the end of World Ward II by attempts to describe and understand potentially fascistic and anti-Semitic individuals and to seek the determinants of this pattern of behavior. The results were published by Adorno and his associates at the University of California, Berkeley, in a monumental work entitled *The Authoritarian Personality* (Adorno, Frenkel-Brunswick, Levinson, & Sanford, 1950). Individuals with an authoritarian personality were characterized by the following salient features: (a) conventional adherence to middle-class values; (b) uncritical submission to authority, particularly idealized moral authority of the in-group; (c) displacement of aggression from appropriate targets in the in-group onto appropriate targets in the out-group; (d) generalized hostility and cynicism and contempt for human nature; (e) an orientation toward power and toughness; (f) superstitious beliefs and stereotypic thinking; (g) a tendency to respond in concrete facts rather than rely on speculations, feelings, and fantasies; (h) projection of problems onto the external world; and (i) an exaggerated concern for sex.

Using a psychoanalytic frame of reference, researchers hypothesized authoritarians as individuals who use repressive defenses to control their sexual and aggressive needs. Their own repressed needs of aggression and sexuality are projected onto others and expressed in justifiable ways (e.g., against enemies of one's nation). The origins of such a belief system are attributed to the early interactions of an individual with his or her parents and others and may well reflect the norms of an underprivileged culture (Brown, 1965). Parents of authoritarians are presumably anxious about their status and therefore stress conventional values as a way for their children to succeed socially. Authoritarian traits in parents establish an autocratic family structure (e.g., punitiveness, restrictiveness, nonloving techniques), and this in turn leads to the development of the authoritarian personality in offspring.

Adorno et al. (1950) devote a chapter to the relationship between intelligence and ethnocentrism; the latter was assessed by the F scale, a well-known indirect measure of prejudice. The studies of these and other researchers show that authoritarianism scores are negatively correlated with scholastic ability. Overall correlations between intelligence and F-scale scores are generally quite strong, ranging between −.20 and −.50. The dogmatism (D) scale, a related scale developed as a measure of openness of individual belief systems regardless of the content of the belief, was also reported to correlate inversely with SAT scores (Thompson & Michel, 1972).

A number of explanations may account for the observed inverse relationship between authoritarian beliefs and intelligence. One possibility is that only individuals of relatively low intelligence are able to accept the kind of ideology represented by an extreme fascist orientation. Conversely, this hypothesis presumes that one's capacity to accept people whose values differ from one's own and to remain open in changing situations (i.e., be less dogmatic, rigid, or stereotypic) is enhanced by keen mental ability and intelligence (Thompson & Michel, 1972). It is also conceivable that more intelligent subjects see through the wording of the items of the F scale (or similar scales) and respond in the more open and less ethnocentric direction.

Another line of reasoning points out that intelligence, attaintment, and authoritarianism are all related to social class. Perhaps social class differences in child rearing mediate the relationship between IQ and F-scale scores. Also, it may be chiefly education or cultural sophistication rather than intelligence per se that reduces authoritarianism. Christie (1954) estimates that with education partialed out, the correlation between intelligence and F scores drops considerably. Thus those in society who are low in personal and social resources (e.g., social status, intelligence, education) feel threatened and frustrated and turn to authoritarian beliefs as a solution to problems.

Paranormal Belief and Superstitiousness

Paranormal phenomena include a wide range of beliefs and experiences concerning religion, psi (e.g., clairvoyance, precognition, telepathy, psychokinesis), the occult, witchcraft and superstition, the supernatural, and extraordinary life forms. Although there is little consensus about the definitional criteria of paranormal belief (see Jahoda, 1971), it is commonly agreed that these phenomena are not currently explicable in terms of current science and are incompatible with normative perceptions, beliefs, and expectations about reality.

The occult believer has often been characterized as female, misinformed, poorly educated, authoritarian, emotionally unstable, and of low intelligence (Zusne & Jones, 1982). A summary of the literature (Zusne & Jones, 1982) shows that intelligence is an established correlate of paranormal belief, with lower-IQ subjects having been found to be stronger believers in paranormal and occult phenomena. Believers also earn lower college grades, and intelligent students are much less likely to accept orthodox beliefs or to have proreligious attitudes or mystical experiences (Argyle & Beit-Hallahmi, 1975). In view of the reported inverse relationship between information and extent of belief about the paranormal (e.g., Zeidner & Beit-Hallahmi, 1988), a positive relationship is expected between intelligence and information about the paranormal, as such information is part of the general cultural knowledge. Furthermore, a survey of American studies of children and students (Argyle, 1961) found negative correlations between intelligence and religious beliefs, attitudes, and experiences. The correlations are generally higher for religious conservatism (−.15 to .55) than for attitudes and experiences (−.19 to −.27).

Also, research shows that although more intelligent children have a more accurate knowledge of both religious and parareligious concepts, they start questioning or disbelieving them earlier. High school students of higher intelligence who took a superstitiousness questionnaire (including such items as "It is bad luck for cats to cross one's path") were shown to be less superstitious than those of lower IQ (Killen & Wildman, 1974). Whereas most of the previous research on religious beliefs and intelligence is based on children or students, the same results would appear to hold for adults. Indeed, authoritarianism, which correlates strongly with religious conservatism, is also inversely correlated with IQ. The negative correlations are generally higher for those from a liberal background than for individuals from conservative backgrounds.

As pointed out by Argyle and Beit-Hallahmi (1975) in their extensive survey of the literature on the psychology of religion, a number of studies in the United States found negative correlations between intelligence and measures of religious conservatism. For example, Symington (1935) divided his subjects into those from liberal and conservative homes. The correlation of IQ and conservatism was higher for those from a liberal background (from −.42 to −.55) than for those with a conservative background (−.13 to −.29). This suggests that those from liberal homes had been more free to use their intellectual capacities to discard orthodox ideas. Rhodes and Nam (1970) arranged various categories of religious identification according to their degree of fundamentalism and anti-intellectualism, with Baptists ranking highest and Jews lowest. When the religious groups were ranked according to their distance from fundamentalism, there was a positive, though very modest, correlation with intelligence ($r = .17$).

The usual interpretation of the inverse relationship between intelligence and paranormal beliefs is straightforward: Higher intelligence renders an individual less vulnerable to the circular and ephemeral arguments put forth in defense of paranormal ideas (Zusne & Jones, 1982). Furthermore, intelligent people may be less amenable to social pressures and would be expected to be unorthodox in religious beliefs and other matters. Also, as noted above, subjects from a liberal background may simply be freer to use their brains to discard unorthodox ideas (Argyle, 1961). Because of the antirationalism and antiscientific attitudes typical of many intellectually superior students during the 1960s and the 1970s, however, the historical relationship may have changed, with the paranormal now associated with higher rather than lower intelligence (see Jones, Russel, & Nickel, 1977). It is unclear if intelligence per se directly influences a person's level of superstitiousness or has its effect through influencing the social group, which in turn influences belief.

Social Desirability

Social desirability is the belief that one should behave in a manner intended to make one attractive to others and is indicative of a strong need for approval in the individual. A general pattern of results suggests that higher social desirability is related to a variety of cognitive and social deficits; the negative correlations found with IQ are consistent with results from children (Crowne, 1979). A number of studies report an inverse correlation between social desirability and intelligence. For example, Fisher (1967) found a negative correlations between social desirability and the Army General Classification Test in a sample of prisoners. In a study by Evans and Forbach (1982), the Marlow-Crowne Social Desirability Scale was reported to be negatively correlated ($r = -.45$) with intelligence test scores, as assessed by a Quick test (brief picture vocabulary test).

Basic ability deficits may reinforce and maintain vulnerable self-esteem in high social desirability subjects. Crowne (1979) suggested that lower intelligence and a history of academic failure experience may contribute to the development of defensiveness and vulnerable self esteem which is characteristic of high social desirability adults.

SUMMARY

Because the bulk of the data relating intelligence to key personality traits are of a correlational nature, the direction of causality in the intelligence–personality association is indeterminate. The nature of the causal flow of direction in the observed relationships between intelligence and personality constructs has been conceptualized and interpreted in a variety of different ways, the most common of which are listed below:

1. Intelligence is the independent variable, whereas personality is the dependent variable.
2. Intelligence is the dependent variable, whereas personality is the independent variable.
3. Intelligence and personality show a bidirectional relationship, with reciprocal determinism existing between the two constructs.
4. The observed personality–intelligence relationship is artifactual, with a third extraneous variable responsible for the observed relationship between the constructs.
5. Personality is an intervening of "nuisance" variable intervening between the intelligence construct (as input) and manifest level of intelligence (as output, evidenced in intelligence test scores).
6. Personality is a moderator variable, moderating the relationship between intelligence and a criterion variable of interest.
7. Intelligence is a moderator variable, moderating the relationship between personality and a criterion outcome variable.

Although the relationship between personality and intelligence variables has generally been conceptualized and investigated as a linear one, there is a possibility of a nonlinear relation between IQ and certain personality qualities. Also, the magnitude (or direction) of the relationship may change across time, and there may be a shift in the nature of the relationship across time, contexts, and cultural groups. Furthermore, the extent of the relationship between intelligence and certain personality traits may vary with certain background variables such as social background or gender (see Hakstian & Cattell, 1978).

Overall, the present review points to rather modest relationships between intelligence and a wide variety of personality variables. Similarly, a survey of the relationship between broad personality factors and micro-level measures of intelligence (e.g., reaction time, evoked-related potentials; see Chapter 16) shows few meaningful relations—and thus few theoretical links—between personality traits and intelligence. As Mayer, Caruso, Zigler, and Dreyden (1989) observate "After a half-century of personality research, the evidence suggests that personality traits have, at best, small relations to intellect and intellectual achievement" (p. 120).

Overall, the line of research focusing on personality trait correlates of intelligence seems to add little to our theoretical understanding of either personality or intelligence traits. The body of research in this area is largely descriptive/correlational, often contradictory, and not easily integrated, thus showing some of the characteristics of a degenerating program of research. It should be kept in mind, however, that this survey covered only a small subset of key personality traits, and an exhaustive examination of all such traits has yet to be made. With more refined conceptualization, research methodology, and analyses, the above conclusions may need to be tempered.

From a theoretical point of view, the modest and often inconsistent associations reported between intelligence and key personality traits suggest that the links between these constructs may be weak. Perhaps the two constructs are really independent, and the research tradition of dealing with them separately has arisen for good reason. From a practical point of view, personality variables seldom bear such a sizable impact on intellectual performance that they invalidate intelligence assessments or test scores as a whole. The influences of various personality factors that do affect performance (e.g., anxiety, motivation, extraversion), may be fact be viewed as key aspects of the individual's global intellectual capacity (Matarazzo, 1972; Wechsler, 1944). Moreover, personality factors may actually enhance rather than detract from the validity of intelligence measures: Individuals who do poorly on intelligence tests because of the debilitating effects of certain personality factors (e.g., high test anxiety, low motivation) would most likely do poorly on the criterion measure of performance, for much the same reasons.

REFERENCES

Adorno, T. W., Frenkel-Brunswick, E., Levinson, D. J., & Sanford, R. N. (1950). *The authoritarian personality.* New York: Harper & Row.

Alpert, R., & Haber, R. N. (1960). Anxiety in academic achievement situations. *Journal of Abnormal and Social Psychology, 61,* 207–215.

Anthony, W. S. (1973). The development of extraversion, of ability, and of the relation between them. *British Journal of Educational Psychology, 43,* 223–227.

Argyle, M. (1961). *Religious behavior.* Chicago: Free Press.

Argyle, M., & Beit-Hallahmi, B. (1975). *The social psychology of religion.* London: Routledge & Kegan Paul.

Atkinson, J. W. (1964). *An introduction to motivation.* Princeton, NJ: Van Nostrand.

Averill, J. R. (1982). *Anger and aggression: An essay on emotion.* New York: Springer-Verlag.

Ball, S. A., & Zuckerman, M. (1992). Sensation seeking and selective attention: Focused and divided attention on a dichotic listening task. *Journal of Personality and Social Psychology, 63,* 825–831.

Bandura, A. (1993). Perceived self-efficacy in cognitive development and functioning. *Educational Psychologist, 28,* 117–148.

Baron, J. (1982). Personality and intelligence. In R. Sternberg (Ed.). *Handbook of human intelligence* (pp. 308–351). New York: Cambridge University Press.

Barron, F. (1953). Some test correlates of response to psychotherapy. *Journal of Consulting Psychology, 17,* 235–241.

Barron, F., & Harrington, D. M. (1981). Creativity, intelligence, and personality. *Annual Review of Psychology, 32,* 439–476.

Berg, C., & Sternberg, R. (1985). Response to novelty: Continuity vs. discontinuity in the development course of intelligence. In H. W. Reese (Ed.), *Advances in child development and behavior* (Vol. 19, pp. 1–47). New York: Academic Press.

Blankenstein, K. R., Flett, G. L., Watson, M. S., & Koledin, S. (1990). Test anxiety, self-evaluative worry, and sleep disturbance in college students. *Anxiety Research, 3,* 193–204.

Brody, N. (1988). *Personality: In search of individuality.* San Diego, CA: Academic Press.

Brown, R. (1965). *Social psychology.* Toronto: Collier-Macmillan.

Byrne, D. (1974). *An introduction to personality research: Theory and applications* (2nd ed.). Englewood Cliffs, NJ: Prentice-Hall.

Carver, C. F., & Scheier, M. F. (1989). Expectancies and coping: From test anxiety to pessimism. In R. Schwarzer, H. M. Van der Pleog, & C. D. Spielberger (Eds.), *Advances in test anxiety research* (Vol. 6, pp. 3–11). Lisse, Netherlands: Swets & Zeitlinger.

Cattell, R. B. (1971). *Abilities: Their structure, growth and action.* New York: Houghton Mifflin.

Christie, R. (1954). Authoritarianism re-examined. In R. Christie & M. Jahoda (Eds.), *Studies in the scope and method of "The Authoritarian Personality."* New York: Free Press.

Coleman, J. C., Butcher, J. N., & Carson, R. C. (1984). *Abnormal psychology* (7th ed.). Glenview, IL: Scott, Foresman.

Coleman, J. S., Coleman, J. S., Campbell, E. Q., Hobson, C. J., McPartland, J., Mood, A. M., Weinfeld, F. D., & York, R. L. (1966). *Equality of educational opportunity.* Washington, DC: Department of Education.

Crookes, T. G., Pearson, P. R., Francis, L. J., & Carter, M. (1981). Extraversion and performance on Raven's Progressive Matrices in 15–16-year-old children. *British Journal of Educational Psychology, 51,* 109–111.

Crowne, D. P. (1979). *The experimental study of personality.* Hillsdale, NJ: Erlbaum.

Darlington, R. B. (1990). *Regression and linear models.* New York: McGraw-Hill.

Deffenbacher, J. (1980). Worry and emotionality in test anxiety. In I. Sarason (Ed.), *Test anxiety: Theory, research and applications* (pp. 111–128). Hillsdale, NJ: Erlbaum.

Evans, R. G., & Forbach, G. B. (1982). Intellectual ability correlates of the Marlowe-Crowne Social Desirability Scale. *Journal of Personality Assessment, 46* 59–62.

Eysenck, H. J. (1967a). The biological basis of personality. Springfield, IL: Thomas.

Eysenck, H. J. (1967b). Intelligence assessment: A theoretical and experimental approach. *British Journal of Educational Psychology, 37,* 81–98.

Eysenck, H. J. (1971). Relation between intelligence and personality. *Perceptual and Motor Skills, 32,* 637–638.

Eysenck, H. J., & Cookson, D. (1969). Personality in primary school children—ability and achievement. *British Journal of Educational Psychology, 39,* 109–130.

Eysenck, H. J., & Eysenck, M. W. (1985). *Personality and individual differences.* New York: Plenum.

Eysenck, M. W. (1982). *Attention and arousal: Cognition and performance.* Berlin: Springer-Verlag.

Fisher, G. (1967). The performance of male prisoners on the Marlowe-Crowne Social Desirability Scale: II. Differences as a function of race and crime. *Journal of Clinical Psychology, 23,* 473–475.

Gaudry, E., & Spielberger, C. D. (1971). *Anxiety and educational achievement.* New York: Wiley.

Getzels, J. W., & Jackson, P. W. (1962). *Creativity and intelligence.* New York: Wiley.

Glover, J. A., Ronning, R. R., & Reynolds, C. P. (Eds.). (1989). *Handbook of creativity.* New York: Plenum.

Guilford, J. P. (1959). Three faces of intellect. *American Psychologist, 14,* 469–479.

Guilford, J. P. (1967). *The nature of human intelligence.* New York: McGraw-Hill.

Haan, N. (1963). Proposed model of ego functioning: Coping and defense mechanisms in relationship to IQ change. *Psychological Monographs: General and Applied, 77,* 3–23.

Hakstian, A. R., & Cattell, R. B. (1978). An examination of interdomain relationships among some ability and personality traits. *Educational and Psychological Measurement, 38,* 275–290.

Hamlin, R. M. (1963). The stability of intellectual functioning in chronic schizophrenia. *Journal of Nervous and Mental Disease, 136,* 360–364.

Heckhausen, H. (1967). *The anatomy of achievement motivation.* New York: Academic Press.

Heffner, P. A., Strauss, M. E., & Grisell, J. (1975). Rehospitalization of schizophrenics as a function of intelligence. *Journal of Abnormal Psychology, 84,* 735–736.

Hembree, R. (1988). Correlates, causes, effects and treatment of test anxiety. *Review of Educational Research, 58*, 47–77.

Henderson, R. B., & Wilson, S. E. (1991). Intelligence and curiosity in preschool children. *Journal of School Psychology, 29*, 167–175.

Hiler, E. W. (1958). Wechsler-Bellvue intelligence as a predictor of continuation in psychotherapy. *Journal of Clinical Psychology, 14*, 192–194.

Hope, D. A., & Heimberg, R. G. (1990). Dating anxiety. In H. Leitenberg (Ed.), *Handbook of social and evaluative anxiety* (pp. 217–246). New York: Plenum.

Huesmann, L. R., Eron, l. D., & Yarmel, P. W. (1987). Intellectual functioning and aggression. *Journal of Personality and Social Psychology, 52*, 218–231.

Jahoda, G. (1971). *The psychology of superstition*. Middlesex, England: Penguin.

Jensen, A. R. (1964). Individual differences in learning: Interference factors. U.S. Department of Health, Education, and Welfare. Co-op project no. 1867.

Jones, W. H., Russel, D. W., & Nickel, T. (1977). Belief in the Paranormal Scale: An objective instrument to measure belief in magical phenomena and causes. *JSAS Catalog of Selected Documents in Psychology, 7*, 100.

Kagan, J., Sontag, L. W., & Nelson, V. L. (1958). Personality and IQ change. *Journal of Abnormal and Social Psychology, 56*, 261–266.

Killen, P., & Wildman, R. W. (1974). Superstitiousness and intelligence. *Psychological Reports, 34*, 1158.

Kipnis, D. (1971). *Character structure and impulsiveness*. New York: Academic Press.

Lazarus, R. S. (1991). *Emotion and adaptation*. New York: Oxford University Press.

Lazarus, R. S., & Folkman, S. (1984). *Stress, appraisal and coping*. New York: Springer.

Liebert, R. M., & Morris, L. W. (1967). Cognitive and emotional components of test anxiety: A distinction and some initial data. *Psychological Reports, 20*, 975–978.

Lloyd, J. (1984). Intrinsic intellectuality: Its relation to social class, intelligence, and achievement. *Journal of Personality and Social Psychology, 46*, 646–654.

Lynn, R., Hampson, S. L., & Magee, M. (1982). Determinants of educational achievement at 16+: Intelligence, personality, home background and school. *Personality and Individual Differences, 4*, 473–481.

Matarazzo, J. D. (1972). *Wechsler's measurement and appraisal of adult intelligence* (5th ed.). Baltimore, MD: Williams & Wilkins.

Maroyama, G., Rubin, R. A., & Kingsbury, G. G.. (1981). Self-esteem and educational achievement: Independent constructs with a common cause. *Journal of Personality and Social Psychology, 40*, 962–975.

Mayer, J. D., Caruso, D. R., Zigler, E., & Dreyden, J. I. (1989). Intelligence and intelligence related traits. *Intelligence, 13*, 119–133.

McCrae, R. R. (1987). Creativity, divergent thinking, and openness to experience. *Journal of Personality and Social Psychology, 52*, 1258–1265.

Minkowitch, A., Davis, D., & Bashi, Y. (1982). *Success and failure in Israeli elementary education*. New Brunswick, NJ: Transaction Books.

Mischel, W., & Metzner, R. (1962). Preference for delayed reward as a function of age, intelligence, and length of delay interval. *Journal of Abnormal and Social Psychology, 64*, 425–436.

Mueller, J. H. (1980). Test anxiety and the encoding and retrieval of information. In I. Sarason (Ed.), *Test anxiety: Theory, research and applications* (pp. 63–86). Hillsdale, NJ: Erlbaum.

Nicholls, J. G. (1972). Creativity in the person who will never produce anything original and useful: The concept of creativity as a normally distributed trait. *American Psychologist, 27*, 717–727.

Payne, R. (1991). Individual differences in cognition and the stress process. In C. L. Cooper & R. Payne (Ed.), *Personality and stress: Individual differences in the stress process*. New York: Wiley.

Payne, R. W. (1973). Cognitive abnormalities. In H. J. Eysenck (Ed.), *Handbook of abnormal psychology* (pp. 420–483). San Diego: R. R. Knapp.

Purkey, W. W. (1970). *Self-concept and school achievement*. Englewood Cliffs, NJ: Prentice-Hall.

Revelle, W., Amaral, P., & Turriff, S. (1976). Introversion/extraversion, time stress, and caffeine: Effects on verbal test performance. *Science, 192*, 149–150.

Revelle, W., Humphreys, M. S., Simon, L., & Gilliland, K. (1980). The interactive effects of personality, time of day, and caffeine: A test of the arousal model. *Journal of Experimental Psychology: General, 109*, 1–31.

Rhodes, A. C., & Nam, C. B. (1970). The religious context of educational expectations. *American Sociological Review, 35*, 253–267.

Robinson, D. L. (1985). How personality relates to intelligence test performance: Implications for a theory of intelligence, ageing research, and personality assessment. *Personality and Individual Differences, 6*, 203–216.

Robinson, D. L. (1986). The Wechsler Adult Intelligence Scale and personality assessment: Towards a biologically based theory of intelligence and cognition. *Personality and Individual Differences, 7*, 153–159.

Rotter, J. B. (1966). Generalized expectancies for internal vs. external control of reinforcement. *Psychological Monographs, 80* (Whole No. 609).

Rutter, M., & Lockyer, L. (1967). A five-fifteen year follow up study of infantile psychosis—I. Description of sample. *British Journal of Psychiatry, 113*, 1169–1182.

Saklofske, D. H., & Kostura, D. D. (1990). Extraversion-intraversion and intelligence. *Personality and Individual Differences, 11*, 547–551.

Samuel, W. (1980). Mood and personality correlates of IQ by race and sex of subject. *Journal of Personality and Social Psychology, 38*, 993–1004.

Sarason, I. G. (1975). Test anxiety, attention, and the general problem of anxiety. In C. D. Spielberger & I. G. Sarason (Eds.), *Stress and anxiety* (Vol. 1, pp. 165–210). New York: Hemisphere/Halstead.

Sarason, I. G. (Ed.). (1980). *Test anxiety: Theory, research and applications*. Hillsdale, NJ: Erlbaum.

Sarason, I. G., & Sarason, B. R. (1990). Test anxiety. In H. Leitenberg (Ed.), *Handbook of social and evaluative anxiety* (pp. 475–496). New York: Plenum.

Sattler, J. M. (1988). *Assessment of children* (3rd ed.). San Diego: Author.

Schwartzman, A. E., & Douglas, V. I. (1962). Intellectual loss in schizophrenics. Part I. *Canadian Journal of Psychology, 16*, 1–10.

Seipp, B. (1991). Anxiety and academic performance: A meta-analysis of findings. *Anxiety Research, 4*, 27–41.

Siegman, A. W. (1956). The effect of manifest anxiety on a concept formation task, a nondirected learning task, and on timed and untimed intelligence tests. *Journal of Consulting Psychology, 20,* 176–178.

Seligman, M. E. P. (1975). *Helplessness.* San Francisco: Freeman.

Simon, W. E., & Simon, M. G. (1975). Self-esteem, intelligence, and standardized academic achievement. *Psychology in the Schools, 12,* 97–100.

Spielberger, C. D. (1972). Conceptual and methodological issues in anxiety research. In C. D. Spielberger (Ed.), *Anxiety* (Vol. 2, pp. 482–493). New York: Academic Press.

Spielberger, C. D., Gonzales, H. P., Taylor, C. J., Algaze, B., & Anton, W. D. (1978). Examination stress and test anxiety. In C. D. Spielberger & I. G. Sarason (Eds.), *Stress and anxiety* (Vol. 5, pp. 167–191). New York: Wiley.

Spielberger, C. D., Jacobs, G., Russell, S., & Crane, R. (1983). Assessment of anger: the State-Trait Anger Scale. In J. N. Butcher & C. D. Spielberger (Eds.), *Advances in personality assessment.* Hilsdale, NJ: Erlbaum.

Spielberger, C. D., Johnson, E. H., Russell, S. F., Crane, R. J., Jacobs, G. A., & Worden, T. J. (1985). The experience and expression of anger: Construction and validation of an anger expression scale. In M. A. Chesney & R. H. Rosenman (Eds.), *Anger and hostility in cardiovascular and behavioral disorders.* New York: Hemisphere/McGraw-Hill.

Spielberger, C. D., & Katzenmeyer, W. C. (1959). Manifest anxiety, intelligence, and college grades. *Journal of Consulting Psychology, 23,* 278.

Symington, T. A. (1935). *Religious liberals and conservatives.* New York: Columbia University Teachers College.

Tobias, S. (1986). Anxiety and cognitive processing of instruction. In R. Schwarzer (Ed.), *Self related cognitions in anxiety and motivation* (pp. 247–263). Hillsdale, NJ: Erlbaum.

Thompson, R. C., & Michel, J. B. (1972). Measuring authoritarianism: A comparison of the F and D scales. *Journal of Personality, 40,* 180–190.

Veroff, J., McClelland, L., & Marquis, K. (1971). *Measuring intelligence and achievement motivation in surveys.* Ann Arbor: University of Michigan.

Wallach, M. (1985). Creativity testing and giftedness. In F. Horowitz & M. O'Brien (Eds.), *The gifted and talented: Developmental perspectives.* Washington, DC: American Psychiatric Association.

Wallach, M. A., & Kogan, N. (1965). A new look at the creativity-intelligence distinction. *Journal of Personality, 33,* 348–369.

Watson, C. G., Herder, J., Kucala, T., & Hoodecheck-Schow, E. (1987). Intellectual deterioration and personality decompensation in schizophrenia. *Journal of Clinical Psychology, 43,* 447–455.

Wechsler, D. (1944). *The measurement of adult intelligence* (3rd ed.). Baltimore, MD: Williams & Wilkins.

Weiner, B. (1973). *Theories of motivation.* Chicago: Rand McNally.

Wilson, G. (1977). Introversion/extraversion. In T. Blass (Ed.), *Personality variables in social behavior* (pp. 179–218). Hillsdale, NJ: Erlbaum.

Yerkes, R. M., & Dodson, J. D. (1908). The relation of strength of stimulus to rapidity of habit-formation. *Journal of Comparative and Neurological Psychology, 18,* 459–482.

Zeidner, M. (1990). Some demographic and health correlates of trait anger in Israeli adults. *Journal of Research in Personality, 24,* 1–15.

Zeidner, M., & Beit-Hallahmi, B. (1988). Sex, ethnic and social class differences in para-religious beliefs among Israeli adolescents. *Journal of Social Psychology, 128,* 333–343.

Zeidner, M., Klingman, A., & Papko, O. (1988). Enhancing students' test coping skills: Report of a psychological health education program. *Journal of Educational Psychology, 80,* 95–101.

Zeidner, M., & Nevo, B. (1992). Test anxiety in examinees in a college admission testing situation: Incidence, dimensionality, and cognitive correlates. In K. Hagtvet (Ed.), *Advances in test anxiety research* (Vol. 7, pp. 288–303). Lisse, Netherlands: Swets & Zeitliner.

Zuckerman, M. (1979). *Sensation seeking: Beyond the optimal level of arousal.* Hillsdale, NJ: Erlbaum.

Zusne, L., & Jones, W. H. (1982). *Anomalistic psychology: A study of extraordinary phenomena, of behavior, and experience.* Hillsdale, NJ: Erlbaum.

16

Theoretical and Empirical Relationships between Personality and Intelligence

John Brebner and Con Stough

What theoretical relationships have been postulated between intelligence and personality? The short answer is that there are very few in the mainstream of Western personality research. Even books titled *Intelligence and Personality* (Heim, 1970) turn out to be more about intelligence than personality. Despite the separation that generally exists between psychologists working in these areas, there are some cases (e.g., Baron, 1982) where there is clearly a sufficient communality of interests for the different approaches to overlap. This is evident for areas of intellectual functioning like creativity or cognitive style (see Brody, 1972), but the prevailing tendency is to treat intelligence and personality as independent.

In this chapter we have necessarily adopted a selective approach. For instance, several approaches involve forms of intelligence that differ from the concept measured by current standard psychometric tests. Cantor and Kihlstrom (1987) discuss "social intelligence," which covers an area between personality, intelligence, and social psychology; they explain that "as cognitive personologists, we want to think about the intelligence that individuals bring to bear in solving their personal life tasks" (p. 47). Similarly, though Gardner's (1983) concept of "personal intelligences" might be considered particularly relevant in a chapter such as this one, these descriptions of the development of individuality within social and cultural influences lie largely outside the scope of our effort to find relationships between what intelligence and personality tests measure. Thus, we first discuss the relationship between intelligence and personality from a purely psychometric approach, reviewing key papers and results from recently conducted experiments. Second, we examine three recent correlates of intelligence and ask whether these measures are theoretically or empirically related to personality. Third, we investigate theories and measures of intelligence and personality that involve more planned, creative, and cognitive strategies.

Outside of the realm of intelligence testing, commonsense observations of relationships between intelligence and personality tend to be in terms of the speed or efficiency of information processing or of carefully considered, planful behavior. In other words, "intelligent" behavior is measured by many criteria, which are seen as appropriate in different situations. Education and experience tend to be confounded with intel-

John Brebner • Department of Psychology, University of Adelaide, Adelaide, South Australia 5005, Australia. Con Stough • Cognitive Psychophysiology Laboratory, Medical School, University of Queensland, Herstin, Queensland 4006, Australia.

International Handbook of Personality and Intelligence, edited by Donald H. Saklofske and Moshe Zeidner. Plenum Press, New York, 1995.

ligence in subjective judgments, and so may other factors (e.g., slowness or indecisiveness because of a lack of self-confidence). But with the exception of a few strategic forms of behavior that are likely to reduce the probability of reaching a correct answer—such as impulsively responding with the first available association (Stott, 1985), or ignoring some of the available information—there does not appear to be any popular link between intelligence and particular aspects of personality. This, taken together with the current trend in intelligence and personality research, should alert us to the likelihood that intelligence is only related to personality factors that reflect characteristic ways of dealing with information.

Within the domain of psychological inquiry, it is widely accepted by those studying intelligence or personality that both are biologically based and culturally influenced, and this is important because it raises the possibility of biologically based links between the two psychological constructs. In considering relationships that have been proposed by psychologists, it is worth starting by making an important distinction. Anderson (1992) distinguishes different theories in terms of whether intelligence is attributable to some low-level property of the nervous system or is a higher-level ability to perceive relationships and manipulate symbols, which may be affected by experience. As Eysenck and Barrett (1985) have indicated, these have been the two major approaches in intelligence research. Low-level theories, concerned mainly with the biological basis of intelligence, are often described as the Galtonian approach. High-level theories derive from Binet and Simon's (1905) attempt to construct a test that would alert school officials to learning disabilities in children (and which therefore focused on education and learning as determinants of intelligence). In personality research, low-level theories (which view personality as behavior resulting from features of central nervous system functioning) can also be easily distinguished from high-level theories (which regard personality as a complex interaction of traits, attitudes, and beliefs). When looking for connections between personality and intelligence, it is conceivable that research would support a high-level basis for personality but a low-level explanation for intelligence, or vice versa. Most studies concerned with an association between personality and intelligence, however, take a low-level approach to both. This may reflect a concern that high-level theories are more likely to confound presumed personality and intelligence factors as measured by standard psychological tests.

THE RELATIONSHIP BETWEEN PSYCHOMETRIC INTELLIGENCE AND PERSONALITY

Given the initial distinctions above, it might seem appropriate to contrast Eysenck's and Cattell's positions regarding the relationships between intelligence and personality. Eysenck's 3-factor theory of personality excludes intelligence, whereas Cattell includes intelligence as Factor B in his 16-factor approach. Cattell, Eber, and Tatsuoka (1970), however, are quite clear that the point of including intelligence "is not to add personality information as such, but to complete the supply of data on the range of source traits important in most predictions, for general ability is obviously an important dimension in individual differences" (p. 82). Even within his own approach, Cattell's Factor B is relatively independent of his other factors.

It is also worth noting that although Cattell names the factor as if it measures the capacity for abstract thought, its correlation with a measure of abstract thinking from the Differential Aptitude Test (DAT; Bennett, Seashore, & Wesman, 1989), turns out to be as low as .05 ($n = 67$), whereas significant correlations of +.34 ($p < .05$) were found with both verbal thinking and language usage. The only significant correlation obtained for Cattell's 16 personality factors in this study of Adelaide undergraduates was .26 ($p < .05$) with Factor C, which measures emotional lability-stability (Kirby, personal communication). Against this latter finding, Eysenck (1971) has reported the results from a larger sample of 398 English trainee male nurses, in which he found correlations ranging between zero and −.05 between extraversion and neuroticism (or emotional lability-stability) and two measures of intelligence, Raven's Progressive Matrices and the Mill Hill Vocabulary test. These results support Eysenck's position that intelligence and extraversion or neuroticism are independent theoretically, because the correlations are around zero. Nevertheless, a problem that such results expose—and which is inherent in personality and intelligence research—is that different measures produce different outcomes even when they purport to measure the same construct (e.g., emotional lability-stability). In fact, the shared variance between many intelligence tests may only be 30% to 40% when correlated.

Eysenck and Cookson (1969) suggested that there is an association in children between intelligence and extraversion that reverses with maturation, with the two being positively related in primary school but becoming negatively correlated by secondary school. Though extraversion and neuroticism were not related to intelligence in Eysenck's (1971) adult study, White (1973) reported negative correlations of the order of .30 between intelligence measures and the Psychoticism and Lie scales which represent the other Eysenckian personality factors. In a study using Adelaide University students (Brebner, Donaldson, Kirby & Ward, in press), however, this finding was not replicated; the Pearson correlation between psychoticism and intelligence (Cattell's Factor B) was not significant ($r = .14$; $n = 52$). The correlation between Factor B and the Lie scale was .03. Employing the Kaufman Assessment Battery for Children, the Woodcock-Johnson Brief Scale, and the junior version of the Eysenck Personality Questionnaire (JEPQ) in 105 children (aged 8.5 to 10.5 years), Saklofske (1985) also reported no evidence of a relationship between his two measures of intelligence and the JEPQ dimensions of extraversion and neuroticism.

D. L. Robinson (1982a, b, 1983, 1985, 1986) has examined extraversion-introversion differences in relation to performance on intelligence tests. The neurophysiological basis of his model is described later in the chapter, but he has provided evidence that introverts do better on verbal subtests and extraverts better on performance subtests of the Wechsler Adult Intelligence Scale (WAIS; Robinson, 1985, 1986). He has also studied performance on intelligence tests for ambiverts (i.e., those who fall midway between extraversion and introversion), relating arousal levels and the inverted-U relationship to intelligence in this subgroup. (Robinson's position is discussed in more detail later in this chapter, when the relationship between low-level measures of intelligence and personality is explored.) Saklofske and Kostura (1990) attempted to replicate Robinson's finding in a sample of 84 children who were classified into extraverts, ambiverts, and introverts; all children were administered the JEPQ and the revised Wechsler Intelligence Scale for Children (WISC-R). Analysis of variance revealed no significant differences on any measure of WISC-R IQ for the three groups, a finding that Saklofske and Kostura interpreted as supporting Eysenck's position that intelligence and personality are not related.

The studies reviewed are inconclusive on the existence or nature of any relationship between psychometric intelligence and personality. In an attempt to clarify whether personality and intelligence are related, Stough, Nettelbeck, and Cooper (1993) examined the correlations between psychometric intelligence scores from the revised Wechsler Adult Intelligence Scale (WAIS-R) and Raven's Advanced Progressive Matrices (APM) and the personality scales of the Eysenck Personality Questionnaire (EPQ) or the Strelau Temperament Inventory (STI); Brebner (unpublished material) has used the EPQ and the Structure of Temperament Questionnaire (STQ; Rusalov, 1989).

INTELLIGENCE, PERSONALITY, AND TEMPERAMENT TEST MEASURES

The WAIS-R is commonly regarded as the standard to which other tests of intelligence are compared; incorporating 11 subtests, it provides information on a wide range of abilities. Both the WAIS-R and the APM are considered to be good measures of general intelligence (Flynn, 1987; Jensen, 1987), although the WAIS-R also provides verbal, performance, full-scale, and subtest scores. Flynn (1987) has suggested that a combination of the Raven and Wechsler tests can be used as an adequate measure of general intelligence: "Raven's can be used as the marker of fluid *g* and the Wechsler tests as markers when a mix of both fluid and crystallized *g* is required." Fluid *g* (Gf) refers to tests that do not involve acquired knowledge, usually those that involve the manipulation of simple elements (e.g., nonverbal problem-solving tasks). Crystallized *g* (Gc) refers, in contrast, to tests that do tap acquired knowledge (e.g., information and vocabulary). Horn (1985) has discussed the constructs of fluid and crystallized intelligence in terms of the Wechsler subtests and demonstrated that fluid intelligence comprises of Picture Completion, Picture Arrangement, Block Design and Object Assembly. Crystallized *g* comprises the Information, Vocabulary, Comprehension, and Similarities subtests.

Table 1 displays the intercorrelations between the personality tests used in the Stough, Nettelbeck et al. (1993) study. The four dimensions of the STI—strength of excitation (Ex), strength of inhibition (In), balance (B), and mobility (M)—are all aimed at identifying personality dimensions based on Pavlovian principles. Strength of excitation refers to the level of excitation created by stimuli of given intensity, with greater excitatory strength indicating the nervous system's greater capacity to withstand strong and/or prolonged excitation (Strelau, 1987). In Pavlovian terms, the "top capability" of a group of cells is reached

Table 1. Intercorrelations between EPQ and STI Dimensions ($N = 93$) (Data from Stough, Nettelbeck et al., 1993)

	Extraversion (E)	Neuroticism (N)	Psychoticism (P)	Lie (L)
Excitation (Ex)	.30[b]	−.16	00	−.02
Inhibition (In)	−.04	−.25[a]	−.16	−.14
Mobility (M)	.52[b]	.11	00	−.13
Balance (B)	.19	.18	.17	−.17

[a]$p < .05$.
[b]$p < .01$.

when there is failure to continue to produce excitation as the intensity of stimulation is increased. The inhibitory state created in this way, termed transmarginal inhibition (TI), has been used as the major index of strength of the nervous system by researchers in the former Soviet Union and eastern Europe since Pavlov's experiments. Strength of inhibition describes the processes involved in the ability to maintain a state of conditioned inhibition (e.g., extinction and delay). Balance refers to the ratio between strength of excitation and strength of inhibition, representing the ability of the nervous system to adapt to changes in the environment. Mobility is the capacity to switch between excitatory and inhibitory states.

Brebner has recently correlated the EPQ and the STQ (Rusalov, 1989), and the results are shown in Table 2. Rusalov relates all behavioral acts to properties of individual differences in "systems generalization" of central nervous system properties mediating four basic functional states: motivation to interact with the environment, switching from one behavioral program to another, speed in executing a program, and a process that enables feedback to be gained about the success of execution of a program. He suggests that two subdimensions can be identified within each functional dimension relating to one's objective (impersonal) and communicative (interpersonal) aspects of interaction. In total, Rusalov proposes an eight-dimensional model of temperament, including both social- and object-related dimensions of ergonicity, plasticity, tempo, and emotionality. Though not identical with the dimensions in Strelau's STI, both derive from Pavlov's basic properties of the higher nervous system. The correlations between the EPQ and STQ scales shown in Table 2 support the existence of a speed as well as an excitatory-strength link with extraversion, as significant correlations are obtained for both plasticity and tempo in their object as well as social forms.

As noted, Table 1 reports Pearson correlations between the EPQ and STI dimensions. The results support previous findings linking strength of excitation and mobility with extraversion, and strength of inhibition with neuroticism (Carlier, 1979; Strelau,

Table 2. Intercorrelations between EPQ and STQ Dimensions ($N = 145$) (Data from Brebner)

	Extraversion (E)	Neuroticism (N)	Psychoticism (P)	Lie (L)
Ergonicity (Er)	.32[b]	.03	−.19[a]	.14
Social ergonicity (SEr)	.41[b]	−.05	−.25[b]	.27[b]
Emotionality (Em)	−.12	.53[b]	−.09	−.16[a]
Social emotionality (SEm)	−.10	.57[b]	.01	−.22[b]
Plasticity (Pl)	.20[b]	−.07	.01	.09
Social plasticity (SP)	.38[b]	.10	.15	−.10
Tempo (T)	.51[b]	−.08	.04	−.03
Social tempo (ST)	.35[b]	−.05	−.09	.05
Lie (K)	−.14	−.01	−.08	.10

[a]$p < .05$.
[b]$p < .01$.

1970), although the correlations account for little of the reliable variance. Mangan (1982) has suggested that the Eysenck and Strelau scales can be combined to produce the following major personality/temperament clusters: (a) extraversion, strength of excitation, and mobility; (b) stability, strength of excitation, and strength of inhibition; and (c) strength of inhibition and impulse control. Of particular interest to this chapter is the relatively high correlation between extraversion and mobility, because mobility may differ from the other three STI factors by involving the speed of switching between central states rather than being an intensity factor, and thus it may underlie introverts' tendency to be slower than more mobile extraverts (Brebner & Cooper, 1978).

Strelau (1987) argues that temperament traits are expressed in the dynamics of intellectual processes; he refers mainly to the importance of speed of mental processes and to the dynamics of mental activation. He has shown that mobility from the STI is related to flexibility and fluency of thinking from Guilford's tests. In Strelau's model, both efficiency and quality of thought processes are influenced by intellectual abilities. Kozcielak (1979) compared inventors and noninventors on tests of intellectual ability and creativity and STI dimensions; the inventor group scored significantly higher on both the inhibition and mobility dimensions from the STI, and on the intellectual ability and flexibility tests, than the noninventor group.

Lewicka (cited by Strelau, 1980) reported a relationship between extraversion from the EPQ and the development of crystallized intelligence. Table 3 presents the correlations between WAIS and APM intelligence measures and the EPQ and STI personality scales. The correlation shown in the table of −.03 between extraversion and WAIS-R verbal IQ does not confirm Lewicka's finding; in fact, no significant correlations were obtained between crystallized intelligence and any of the personality and temperament measures. Significant correlations were obtained between fluid intelligence and strength of excitation and mobility, raising the possibility that a speed index of central information processing may be implicated in both intelligence and in Pavlovian personality theory. If mobility relates to speed of response to information from the environment (e.g., Teplov, 1956) then more mobile individuals might be able to integrate more information within a given unit of time. Along the same lines, Jensen (1982) has suggested a relationship between IQ and reaction time (RT), arguing that individuals with quicker RTs are able to acquire information about the world more quickly and thus more information in general, which may lead to the development of higher IQ:[1]

> Individuals with greater speed of information processing acquire more cognitively integrated knowledge and skill per unit of time that they interact with the environment. Seemingly small individual differences in speed of information processes amounting to only a few milliseconds per bit of information, when multiplied by months or years of interaction with the environment, can account in part for the relatively large differences observed between individuals in vocabulary, general information and the other developed cognitive skills assessed by IQ tests. (pp. 98–99)

As can be seen from Table 3, there is little evidence for any strong relationship between WAIS subtest scores and most personality dimensions from the EPQ or the STI. Statistically significant relationships are found between measures of verbal IQ (digit span and vocabulary) and social desirability (L scale), as well as between measures of nonverbal IQ and mobility scores from the STI. In the case of L, those subjects with poorer verbal IQs were more likely to fake EPQ responses. Mobility scores are positively related to IQ tasks that are timed. Extraversion correlates positively with Block Design, whereas neuroticism correlates negatively with Block Design and Object Assembly; again, this points to the possible effect of timed tasks. Further analysis is provided later in the chapter of Robinson's position that moderate levels of arousal

[1]This hypothesis is examined later in this chapter when low-level measures of intelligence are correlated with personality dimensions. Here we note that Table 2 below shows small but significant correlations between mobility and fluid intelligence measures. However, tasks like Jensen's which are so simple as to be error-free are nor representative of the circumstances in which people perform under time-pressure. Even when all the relevant information is immediately available, integrating the same amount of information in a shorter time may not be acquiring "more cognitively integrated knowledge". In fact, if the period over which information can be integrated is limited, and this is characteristic of the person, then information arriving after that period, or requiring longer to be included, will not be integrated, resulting (on Jensen's argument) in less "cognitively integrated knowledge" rather than more. What would seem to be important is to process information purposively for as long as is needed to produce the integration(s) that information allows, and then start a new process. From the correlations obtained, mobility (and, by implication, other speed-related factors) may be involved in this. In this sense, satisfactory or correct integrations will tend to be produced earlier than failures by more mobile individuals, even if there are difficulties in reaching those integrations. This suggests a slightly different explanation for Jensen's findings.

Table 3. Pearson Correlations between WAIS-R and APM Scores and Personality Dimensions from the EPQ and the STI (Data from Stough, Nettelbeck et al., 1993)

	E	N	P	L	Ex	In	M	B
Arithmetic	−.12	−.07	.00	−.25[a]	.24[a]	.04	.14	.14
Comprehension	−.03	.18	−.15	.12	.12	.03	.11	.09
Similarities	−.03	.02	−.17	−.03	.16	.13	.18	−.01
Picture Completion	.08	.04	.20	−.14	.19	.17	.21	−.01
Picture Arrangement	.01	.00	−.05	−.14	.04	.17	.18	−.11
Block design	.23[a]	−.23[a]	.08	−.13	.26[a]	.13	.33[b]	.07
Object Assembly	−.01	−.25[a]	.01	−.06	.18	−.08	.28[b]	.07
Digit symbol	−.01	−.01	−.25[a]	.16	.01	−.04	−.03	.03
Information	−.21	−.01	.08	−.09	.12	.03	.09	.07
Digit span	.16	.06	.27[b]	−.51[b]	.13	−.10	.18	.15
Vocabulary	−.03	−.02	.02	−.32[b]	.08	.02	.05	−.05
Verbal IQ	−.03	−.20	−.03	−.29[b]	−.17	−.01	.21	.12
Performance IQ	.08	−.12	−.02	−.01	.27[a]	.09	.27[a]	.11
Full-scale IQ	.00	.04	.00	−.20	.26[a]	.03	.30[a]	.15
APM	.04	.02	−.05	−.26[a]	.22	.01	.22	.11
Gf	.08	.08	.07	−.18	−.24[a]	.16	.30[a]	.06
Gc	−.10	−.19	−.08	−.13	.16	.07	.10	.03

[a]$p < .05$.
[b]$p < .01$.
Note: See Table 1 and 2 for key to abbreviations.

linked to ambiverts) are optimal for the development of intelligence.

Table 4 reports correlations found by Pamula (1993) between STQ dimensions and measures of intelligence. Plasticity and tempo from the STQ correlate significantly with measures of convergent and divergent thinking derived from French, Exstrom, and Price (1963), and they show small correlations with spatial IQ as measured by the Comprehensive Ability Battery (Hakstian & Cattell, 1982). Ergonicity correlates significantly with convergent thinking, but all the intellectual measures are timed. Referring back to Table 3, it can be seen that the correlations for strength of excitation and mobility with PIQ are attributable to the Picture Completion and Block Design subtests. The general pattern is that small but significant positive correlations exist between measures of intellectual ability and speed-related personality measures. This speed factor may also be why neuroticism and emotionality are negatively correlated with verbal IQ in the table.

The correlations in Tables 3 and 4 show no strong, systematic relationship between intelligence test scores and the personality variables measured, although a small, significant effect of speed is supported by the results for mobility, for plasticity and tempo in relation to both convergent and divergent thinking, and for nonverbal IQ. In considering different theories of intelligence, we are therefore forced to consider different approaches. Brebner et al. (in press) investigated possible relationships between measures of intellectual performance and personality. A group of 52 second-year psychology students at the University of Adelaide completed six tests: Cattell's 16PF, the Differential Aptitude Test (DAT; Bennett et al., 1989), the Self-Directed Search (Holland, 1985), the EPQ, the STQ, and a measure of happiness—the Oxford Happiness Inventory (OHI; Argyle, Martin, & Crossland, 1989).

The matrix of correlations (Table 5) showed no consistently high correlations between any of the personality scales and the various intellectual measures. Small positive correlations were found between plasticity, social plasticity, tempo, and social tempo and abstract reasoning, language usage, and enterprising. A slight tendency for measures of emotional lability

Table 4. Pearson Correlations between Spatial and Verbal IQ, Divergent and Convergent Thinking, the EPQ-R ($N = 70$) and the STQ ($N = 63$) (Data from Pamula, 1993)

	E	N	P	L	Er	Em	Pl	T
Divergent thinking	−.04	.23	−.16	−.19	−.02	−.09	.29[a]	.28[a]
Convergent thinking	−.09	−.13	−.02	−.07	.28[a]	.02	.34[b]	.40[b]
Spatial IQ	−.10	.08	−.15	.15	.18	.13	.21	.29[a]
Verbal IQ	−.09	−.25[a]	.15	−.19	−.09	−.29[a]	.13	.09

[a]$p < .05$.
[b]$p < .01$
Note: See Tables 1 and 2 for key to abbreviations.

(N, Em, and SEm) again to be negatively related to intellectual measures could be suspected from the data. K, the STQ equivalent of the EPQ Lie (L) scale, correlates negatively with almost all of the intellectual measures, echoing the findings in Table 3, though the picture for L is not so clear. Happiness as measured by the OHI is positively related to E, L, Er, SEr, Pl, and T, but negatively related to N, Em, and SEm. In line with results from other intelligence measures, this study found no association between intellectual abilities and any of the major personality factors.

The absence of any clear association between performance on personality and intelligence test variables apart from speed-related measures like mobility, plasticity, or tempo suggests that we may expect to find a relationship between speed-related personality measures and low-level measures of intelligence that also involve speed. We consider this possibility in the next section.

LOW-LEVEL THEORIES OF INTELLIGENCE AND PERSONALITY

During the 1980s and 1990s a new approach has evolved in the study of human intelligence. Investigators following this new paradigm have used elementary measures—like averaged evoked potentials (AEPs), inspection time (IT), and reaction time (RT)—that do not depend on levels of acquired knowledge. The aim has been to observe the correlation between performance on these measures and performance on IQ tests; usually positive correlations have been found. Jensen (1987, p. 394) suggests that this approach may not have the same problems as the purely psychometric strategy. Although much information has been yielded by the latter approach, it is now clear that additional levels of analysis are required for further refinement of theories of intelligence. As Eysenck (1988) argues, theories based solely on IQ measurement have reached a theoretical cul-de-sac, and the use of IQ data will not be sufficient for the development of an adequate scientific explanation of intelligence.

In partial recognition of this fact, some investigators have advocated an approach involving adaptive intelligence (e.g., Guilford, 1959; Sternberg, 1985). This view may include many variables (e.g., personality, motivation, and adaptive behaviors) that may be thought of as influences on personality rather than on intelligence, although as Eysenck and Barrett (1985) described, the study of intelligence does not also necessarily equate to the study of the whole of human personality. Galtonian-type measures (i.e., RT, IT, and AEPs) have now been refined and developed through advances in technology and have been shown to correlate with measures derived from the Binet approach (i.e., IQ). It is of obvious interest to this chapter to examine the possibility that these correlates of psychometric intelligence may be related to measures of personality.

EEG

For low-level theories of intelligence, the problem of identifying some property of the nervous system as the basis of intelligence has two parts: first, identifying the psychological functions of neurophysiological events most often measured by EEG and evoked (or event-related) potentials, and second, identifying the psychological functions underlying the correct responses to widely disparate types of intelligence test. Both research areas are far from complete, and this may be the reason why low-level theories only

Table 5. Pearson Correlations (Decimals Omitted) between Personality and Intellectual Measures for 16PF, SDS, $n = 52$; DAT, $n = 47$; EPQ, STQ, and OHI, $n = 145$

	EPQ				STQ									
	E	N	P	L	Er	SEr	Pl	SPl	T	ST	Em	SEm	K	OHI
16PF														
A	25	02	18	−19	13	14	−05	22	05	−08	03	−05	−12	12
B	−15	−07	07	05	−10	−09	22	04	−06	09	−26	−24	−22	11
OHI	38[c]	−36[b]	−15	20[a]	30[c]	29[c]	23[b]	01	26[c]	12	−35[c]	−25[b]	−01	
DAT														
VR	00	−04	08	−02	−12	−12	17	20	−05	18	−22	−18	−08	10
NA	18	−30[a]	15	−12	−08	28	28	30[a]	43[b]	30[a]	−14	−20	−24	15
AR	24	05	20	−27	10	09	35[a]	38[b]	49[b]	21	00	−10	−23	02
CS	36[a]	−01	09	−18	−01	19	−11	25	25	33[a]	07	21	−15	−01
MR	−01	−33[a]	11	04	00	−04	26	16	32[a]	11	−14	−39[b]	−40[b]	18
SR	00	−35[a]	−08	06	18	05	27	10	30[a]	18	−30[a]	−29[a]	−24	34[a]
S	−12	−08	−16	−13	−21	04	05	05	−19	22	07	−06	02	−08
LU	19	−03	00	05	−02	17	45[b]	29[a]	18	27	02	−07	−23	29[a]
SDS														
REAL	−03	−19	16	−11	13	−19	11	02	10	−31[a]	07	−11	−15	−14
INV	12	−10	20	−29[a]	09	−00	01	15	30[a]	01	12	−06	−31[a]	−11
ART	07	15	−09	18	12	08	14	03	10	−06	09	05	−28[a]	05
SOC	28[a]	05	−08	02	20	05	20	40[b]	11	−10	12	22	07	18
ENT	21	−03	16	−19	22	08	32[a]	20	33[a]	−23	08	−12	−24	00
CON	−07	−12	09	−16	06	03	01	−05	−02	−26	06	−20	−10	−14

[a]$p < .05$.
[b]$p < .01$.
[c]$p < .001$.
Note: VR = Verbal Reasoning; NA = Numerical Ability; AR = Abstract Reasoning; CS = Clerical Speed; MR = Mechanical Reasoning; SR = Space Relations; S = Spelling; LU = Language Usage; REAL = Realistic; INV = Investigative; ART = Artistic; SOC = Social; ENT = Enterprising; CON = Conventional. See Tables 1 and 2 for key to abbreviations for personality dimensions.

postulate general features of brain function as relating to intelligence. Barrett, Daum, and Eysenck (1990), for example, found that the averaged variability of sensory nerve action potentials correlated negatively with intelligence measured by the Advanced Progressive Matrices (APM), suggesting that lack of variability of neural conduction may be an indicator of successful intellectual functioning. This is supported by the additional finding that the highest correlation for the APM was with the standard deviation of the choice RT component decision time − movement time. Velocity, however, correlated positively with psychoticism. Despite the significant correlations for speed-related personality measures discussed above, a high-speed nervous system may not predict intelligence; rather, low variability might lead to more accurate and therefore faster processing.

The explanation may not be so simple, though, given that some researchers (e.g., Zhang, Caryl, & Deary, 1989) have found the rise time of some components (P200) of the averaged evoked potential (AEP) to correlate with other measures that have been shown to correlate with IQ (P200 refers to a positive wave occurring around 200 msec poststimulus; see Figure 1). Figures 1 and 2 present in schematic form the process involved in obtaining a visual AEP and illustrates individual components.

Vernon (1990) has claimed a positive relationship among IQ, AEPs, and nerve conduction velocity. It is clear from these reports that there are electrophysiological measures that correlate with IQ, and with other correlates of IQ, so the important question is whether there is any evidence that such measures correlate with both personality and intelligence. This question is taken up in the following section after a consideration of Eysenck's (1982) theoretical position.

From a theoretical point of view, Eysenck and Cattell are both low-level theorists with respect to intelligence. Eysenck's position is perhaps best illustrated by his inclusion of the Hendricksons' (A. E. Hendrickson, 1982; D. E. Hendrickson, 1982) treatment of intelligence, and to some extent personality correlates, in his edited book. There, the Hendricksons reported a correlation of .72 between scores on the WAIS and their "string" measure. The correlation was obtained from a sample of 218 schoolchildren with a mean age of 15.6 years (SD = 1.13). The string measure is one of several attempts to find a biologically based and culture-free measure of intelligence.

The Hendricksons have based their neurophysiological model of intelligence on work by Fox and O'Brien (1965), who recorded the activity of single neurons in the cat cortex in response to large numbers of repetitive visual stimuli (4,000 total). Immediately after the presentation of the stimulus the pulse train activity of the neuron was measured, the time from stimulus onset to pulse activity at the single neuron was recorded, and a histogram of the number of pulse occurrences was determined. The close approximation between the histogram reported by Fox and O'Brien and their concordant AEP waveforms was interpreted by A. E. Hendrickson (1982) to correspond to the summation of the individual pulses. The AEP waveform represents electrical activity measured on the scalp; this measurement was assumed to reflect accurately the initial pulse activity and its subsequent propagation through the cortex. The AEP waveform thus is supposed to describe the individual pulse trains that are set off by the stimulus. Pulse trains are transmitted from one neuron to the next through synaptic transmission, with errors in propagation of the initial activity resulting in the AEP waveform showing degradation from one of complexity to simplicity.

A criticism of such an interpretation is that the relationship between scalp recorded potentials and underlying neuronal populations is more directly related to fluctuations of neuronal transmembrane potential levels than to action potentials. The model may therefore be susceptible to criticism that what the AEP waveform measures is somewhat ambiguous. Nevertheless, whatever the AEP is measuring, correlations with intelligence measures have been observed. A. E. Hendrickson (1982) proposed that "if high IQ people have high levels of R, it may be because their axonal-pulse train transmission has less error in it. If axonal pulse trains give rise to the AEP waveform, then we should be able to see differences between the AEP records of high-IQ people and low-IQ people" (p. 195).[2]

The full rationale for this measure is described in detail by D. E. Hendrickson and Hendrickson (1980). Briefly, their hypothesis was that people with high IQs would have longer string lengths because their lower error rates in axonal pulse train transmission would be reflected in the shape of the AEP. Against this, however, Bates and Eysenck (1993) have shown an inverse relationship between string length and inspection time.

[2]R refers to the probability that the information traveling throughout the cortex is accurately propagated at the neuronal level. If R is very high (i.e., approximates 1), then there is a very high probability that the information will be accurately propagated from neuron to neuron and throughout millions of cells in the cortex.

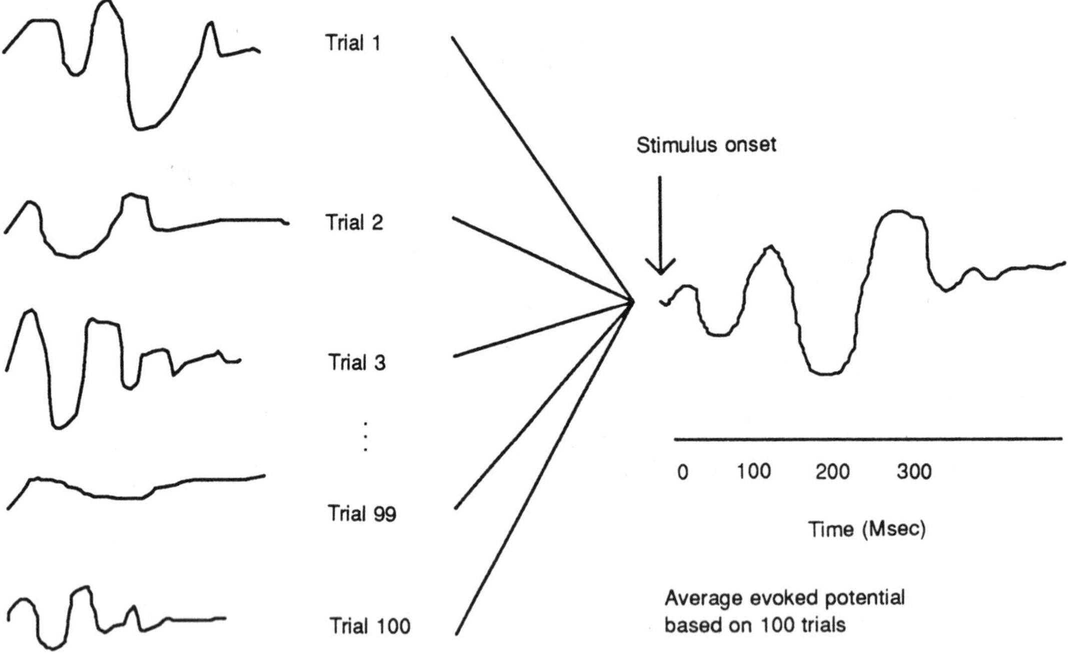

Figure 1. Diagram illustrating a hypothetical AEP based on 100 evoked potential trials.

Because inspection time and string length both correlate with intelligence (see below), it is interesting that under the high attentional demands during inspection time tasks, string length shortens in high-IQ subjects.

In the D. E. Hendrickson (1982) study, although the string measure correlated positively with WAIS-IQ (particularly when measured from stimulus onset to 256 msec poststimulus), correlations with Eysenck Personality Questionnaire (EPQ) factors were −.01 for neuroticism, −.03 for extraversion, −.05 for the Lie scale, and −.13 ($p < .05$) for psychoticism. This again supports the argument that intelligence is independent of these personality measures. The correlations between the personality factors and the WAIS scores showed the same pattern, with the correlations ranging from −.10 to .01. In fact, out of all of the WAIS subtests, the highest correlation with EPQ dimensions was −.18 (between neuroticism and digit span).

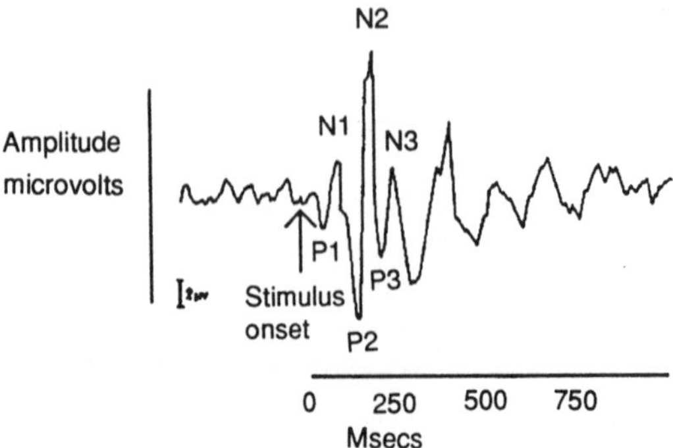

Figure 2. Diagrammatic representation of the visual AEP.

Eysenck's position with respect to extraversion is well known. According to his model, introversion-extraversion differences are largely determined by the reticular formation cortex arousal loop (specifically, the ascending reticular activating system): Given identical levels of stimulation, the theory postulates that introverts are more aroused than extraverts. This theory replaced Eysenck's earlier view that such differences were attributable to reactive inhibition. There is a possible theoretical relationship between intelligence and extraversion if arousability can be linked to string length; there have been various attempts to demonstrate the postulated relationship between extraversion and arousal, but the evidence is still not conclusive. EEG studies have shown some support for it. Most recently, Matthews and Amelang (1993) have reported one of the best controlled studies of EEG activity in relation to performance of introverts and extraverts on eight tasks, which were subdivided into perceptual, information-processing, ability and psychomotor tasks. None of the correlations between EEG measures and personality measures was greater than .19. Significant small correlations ranging from .16 to .19 were found between extraversion and averaged delta/theta activity and between impulsivity and both delta/theta and alpha activity.

Matthews and Amelang (1993) make the point that "correlations between extraversion, EEG measures and performance may well be quite small in magnitude, because of measurement difficulties, and because individual differences in arousal and behaviour probably reflect a variety of influences in addition to personality. Hence, it is essential that the reliability of measures is demonstrated, and that a reasonably large sample size is used" (p. 348). Bartussek, Diedrich, Naumann, and Collett (1993) make essentially the same point but suggest controlling the sample to include only extreme scorers to strengthen the expected effect. Though we sympathize with the difficulties inherent in electrophysiological research into personality, unless ways can be found to show that personality factors can account for reasonable amounts of the variance, the usefulness of electrophysiological studies for theory testing will necessarily be limited.

Matthews and Amelang (1993) found several interactions of extraversion and the EEG measures on performance tasks, including tracking, visual probe RT during a short-term memory task, and aspects of concentration and verbal comprehension. Their results are too detailed to review here, but they summarize this part of their study as follows: "The data support the view that extraversion modifies the relationship between arousal and performance, although alpha was the only EEG band to show an effect consistent with previous research" (p. 361). Their data showed little evidence of an inverted-U relationship between EEG and performance, which led them to conclude that "the present study . . . provides little support for the usefulness of traditional arousal theory as a unifying principle. Relationships between extraversion and EEG variables were small in magnitude, though suggestive in some respects of lower arousal in more extraverted or impulsive [subjects]. Support for arousal theory was strongest for narrow impulsivity, with the influences of N [neuroticism] and P [psychoticism] statistically controlled" (p. 361).

It had previously been argued (Gale, 1981) that under conditions of too much or too little stimulation, differences between introverts and extraverts will not be found. Matthews and Amelang's data, however, showed that under moderately stimulating visual conditions, impulsives were in the opposite direction to the lower arousal expected for extraverts. Earlier research had narrowed the nature of the relationship with arousal from broad extraversion down to narrow impulsivity. O'Gorman and Lloyd (1987) used a method involving opening and closing the eyes on instruction, which is recommended by Gale (1984) as moderately arousing and therefore likely to reveal introversion-extraversion differences. Their results clearly demonstrated that "impulsiveness (narrow not broad) rather than E [extraversion] is the significant correlate of EEG alpha activity" (p. 173). This result posed a problem, because O'Gorman and Mallise (1984) had previously established a correlation between extraversion and EEG. The suggestion was made by O'Gorman and Lloyd (1987) that extraversion scores in the EPQ may still be influenced by impulsiveness if the latter is evidenced by a high extraversion-neuroticism correlation within the particular sample, given that narrow impulsiveness relates to both these dimensions.

O'Gorman and Lloyd (1987) report in a footnote that in their data, psychoticism as a covariate functioned as a suppressor variable that, by taking up part of the variance not relevant to the correlation between impulsiveness and the EEG, served to strengthen that correlation. Correlations of .46 and .45 between impulsiveness and psychoticism for men and women, respectively, were found by Eysenck, Pearson, Easting, and Allsopp (1985), so it may be important to include psychoticism in further studies of impulsiveness and arousal. Stenberg (1992) confirmed lower arousal in impulsive subjects; in this case, lower arousal was defined by increased posterior theta activity, rather than the total alpha power measured by O'Gorman and Lloyd. It may be important to note that the relationship is between the EEG and impulsiveness rather than extraversion, given that impulsiveness is raised as a personality factor affecting cognitive performance when dealing with high-level theories of intelligence, but the theoretical link between impulsiveness and intelligence through arousal has only been the subject of a handful of studies.

If greater arousability is reflected in greater amplitude of evoked potentials, then AEP amplitude might be related to both extraversion and intelligence, because greater amplitude is associated with longer string lengths. Several studies have shown differences in evoked potentials for introversion and extraversion (e.g., Stelmack, Achorn, & Michaud, 1977; Stenberg, Rosen, & Risberg, 1988; see Eysenck, 1990), and a correlation between string length and IQ has been replicated in some studies since the Hendricksons' research. Haier, Robinson, Braden, and Williams (1983), however, found that string length–IQ correlations disappeared if N140–P200 amplitude scores were partialed out, suggesting that such correlations were only observed because of AEP amplitude–IQ correlations and raising the question of the relevance of specific components for intelligence. This finding was not replicated by Stough, Nettelbeck, and Cooper (1990), who report significant correlations between string length and IQ independent of N140–P200 amplitude. Table 6 shows the correlations obtained.

Table 6. Uncorrected Correlations between String Length, IQ Scores, and Raw APM Scores, Together with Correlations Corrected for Restriction in Range and Test Reliability (Adapted from Stough, Nettelbeck, & Cooper, 1990)

Duration of record	Verbal IQ	Performance IQ	Full-Scale IQ	APM
0–100	.36	.31	.36	.08
Corrected	.50[b]	.38	.50[b]	
100–200	.71[b]	.44[b]	.60[b]	.07
Corrected	.86[b]	.52[b]	.74[b]	
0–250	.37	.50[b]	.43[a]	.01
Corrected	.52[b]	.58[b]	.58[b]	
0–200	.45[a]	.37	.39	−.16
Corrected	.62[b]	.43[a]	.53[b]	
100–300	.45[a]	.40	.36	−.26
Corrected	.62[b]	.48[a]	.49[a]	
N140-P200	.14	.14	.02	−.03

[a] $p < .05$.
[b] $p < .01$.

Stough, Nettelbeck et al. (1993) have investigated the relationship between extraversion, string length, and psychometric intelligence in 50 student subjects (see Table 7). This study only differed from the Hendricksons' research in that a tone of more moderate intensity (70 rather than 85 dB) was used. String scores correlated negatively with extraversion: −.30 and −.27 when measured from 100–200 msec and 0–250 msec poststimulus, respectively. Significant correlations up to .62 (uncorrected for restriction in range) were also found between WAIS-R IQ and string scores. Although the correlations with extraversion are only about .30, these results do not support the D. E. Hendrickson (1982) finding that extraversion is not related to String scores. It is possible that the different results reflect different levels of arousal associated with the intensities of the tones used in the two studies. In the D. E. Hendrickson study, the more intense tone may have raised extraverts' level of arousal to the same level as that of introverts, thus giving rise to near-zero correlations. It is even possible that intense stimulation increases arousal in extraverts but decreases it in introverts if the latter's arousal

Table 7. Pearson Correlations between String Length and Variability Scores Measured at Different Temporal Epochs and Dimensions from the EPQ and STI (N = 50)

	E	N	P	L	Ex	In	M	B
String								
100–200	−.30[a]	.08	−.34[b]	−.06	.25	.08	−.02	.08
0–250	−.27[a]	−.02	−.28[a]	−.08	.36[a]	.23	.06	.05
0–100	−.22	−.16	−.20	−.02	.37[b]	.30[a]	.12	.00
0–200	−.11	.32[a]	−.33[b]	−.07	−.01	.13	−.10	−.11
100–300	−.09	.26	−.21	−.20	.12	.09	.01	.02
Variability								
100–200	−.13	.03	−.01	−.19	−.15	−.23	−.26	.08
0–250	−.02	−.05	.24	−.19	−.17	−.27[a]	−.22	.10
0–100	−.10	−.01	.10	−.24	−.18	−.24	−.26	.07
0–200	−.06	.03	.17	−.32[a]	−.19	−.12	−.11	−.03
100–300	−.07	−.04	−.06	.25	−.10	−.11	−.09	.07

[a] $p < .05$.
[b] $p < .01$.
Note: See Tables 1 and 2 for key to abbreviations.

passes the top of the inverted U-shaped curve usually postulated when arousal and stimulus intensity are plotted together. Partialing out extraversion from the string length–IQ correlation only reduces the correlation from .62 to .59, suggesting (if the smaller correlations between string length and extraversion are reliable) that extraversion and intelligence share different parts of the string length variance and correlate with string length for different underlying reasons.

These results allow the possibility that extraversion and string length are related through level of arousal, whereas intelligence and String length are related through other factors affecting the efficiency of processing information. String length was not found to be strongly related to personality variables, however, as Table 7 shows. Moreover, despite correlations between AEP measures and IQ, there have been arguments about whether the string measure is really measuring a biological basis of intelligence (see Mackintosh, 1986). This issue is made even more difficult by the results of further experiments that have failed to establish the relationship between string length and IQ (see Haier et al., 1983; Shagass, Roemer, Straumanis, & Josiassen, 1981; Stough et al., 1990).

As noted above, although some correlations in Table 7 between string measures and the EPQ dimensions were significant, they were small in magnitude. Moreover, the pattern of the correlations requires interpretation. The correlations between string length and extraversion are negative—possibly indicating higher amplitudes for introverts, as would be expected if their higher arousal levels increased amplitude—but the correlations between string length and strength of excitation are positive. To explain this, it could be argued that scores on strength of excitation relate to amplitude but in the opposite direction of extraversion. Though the relationship between extraversion and strength of excitation is highly equivocal, and some evidence does equate extraversion with weak nervous systems (see Strelau, 1980, chap. 4), the correlation of .30 for extraversion and strength of excitation in Table 1 for a different group of subjects does not support this.

If the amount of the variance explained by the correlations between string length and these personality measures was greater, it might be necessary to invoke another possible line of argument: The particular task is heavily biased toward stimulus analysis rather than response organization (Brebner & Cooper, 1974; Brebner, 1983b), so that introverts produce excitation (which is reflected in greater amplitudes and longer string lengths) whereas extraverts produce inhibition (smaller amplitudes and shorter string lengths). On this view, measures of the strength of excitation produced by stimulus analysis would correlate negatively with extraversion, but that produced by response organization would correlate positively because extraverts generate inhibition from stimulus analysis but excitation from response organization. This is potentially researchable, and even weak relationships can be theoretically important. But given the results in Table 7, and to avoid being charged with electronic phrenology, it should be said that these speculative interpretations warrant mentioning only because the purpose of this chapter is to canvass whether there are *any* theoretical relationships between personality and intelligence.

The small correlations in Table 7 might be attributable to the method adopted. If AEP amplitude correlates with personality only at particular parts of the waveform (a point elaborated upon later in this chapter), the variability of waveforms may mean that using fixed temporal epochs is not the most appropriate approach. Table 7 also reports correlations between personality and AEP variability, the other measure derived from the Hendricksons' neurophysiological theory taken to be an index of the variability between individual evoked potentials. EPQ dimensions and variability did not correlate significantly; this contrasts with the Hendricksons' theory that string length and variability measures should be closely correlated, since they are hypothesized to index the accuracy of transmission information through the cortex. Yet, string length and variability also were not significantly (negatively) related in this sample, suggesting that string length and variability scores may index different neurophysiological processes. Eysenck (1987) discussed the relationship between variability of information processing in the cortex and speed processes, suggesting that speed is a secondary factor related to accuracy in that inaccurate transmission of information within the cortex leads to slower transmission times.

Low-level theories of intelligence tend to rely on general features of central nervous system functioning, but as signaled earlier, it is possible to look at more specific features—for example particular components of the AEP. To take one example, it has been suggested (Ragot, 1984; Brebner, 1990b) that P300 is involved in the resolution of spatial uncertainty, so P300 might be studied in relation to the solution of Block Design problems. As shown in Table 3, extraversion correlated positively with Block Design (r = .23) but near zero with other PIQ subtests. P300 was not included in the study by Stough, Nettelbeck et al. (1993), but differences in the latency of P300 between introverts and extraverts have been reported under spatial compatibility-incompatibility conditions; Brebner (1990a), comparing the latencies of P300 and performed responses, showed that introverts recorded shorter P300 latencies but longer reaction times than extraverts under all conditions. More recently, Stelmack, Houlihan, and McGarry-Roberts (1993) found that extraversion was negatively related to movement time, but P300 latency was negatively associated with neuroticism rather than with extraversion, raising the possibility that the Brebner result was attributable to introvert subjects also being higher neuroticism scorers.

Various other studies have indicated links among P300, personality, and intellectual functioning. In line with O'Gorman's (1977) view of extraverts habituating quickly, Ditraglia and Polich (1991) found that the amplitude of P300 to target stimuli in a two-tone auditory discrimination task declined across trials for extraverts but not for introverts. This suggested that extraverts habituate to the task more quickly than introverts, a tendency reflected in the changes to their P300 amplitude. This finding is consistent with the theoretical position expressed by Brebner and Cooper (1974) and Brebner (1983b) that in conditions of stimulus analysis, extraverts generate central inhibition. There has also been continuing interest in relating personality to the augmenting or reducing of evoked potentials; Lolas, Etcheberrigaray, Elqueta, and Camposano (1989) are among those who have found evidence that extraverts are reducers. But, again, though effects such as reducing or the habituation observed by Ditraglia and Polich (1991) should be reflected in behavior, there is little evidence that they affect intelligence test performance in extraverts.

Strelau (1987) has also summarized the results of experiments relating psychophysiological parameters to personality dimensions. Of importance to this chapter is the correspondence between amplitude of AEP components and extraversion and strength of the nervous system dimensions. Typically, studies have shown that extraverts have lower AEP component amplitudes than introverts (Haier et al., 1983; Shagass & Schwartz, 1965) and that stronger nervous system types have lower AEP amplitudes than weaker nervous system types (Bazylevich, 1974; Strelau, 1983).

The amplitude of AEP components has been related to intellectual functioning in a range of other studies. Whipple, Parker, and Noble (1988) tested a group of 15 alcoholic and nonalcoholic fathers and their high-risk/low-risk sons (average age 10.1 years). During a complex visual discrimination task, high-risk children showed reduced amplitude of late positive components and significantly lower scores on the WISC Object Assembly, Block Design, and Picture Completion subtests. Raine and Venables (1988) compared 14 diagnosed psychopaths and 14 nonpsychopathic correctional service inmates. In line with clinical reports of enhanced short-term attentional ability in psychopaths, Raine and Venables found larger P300 amplitudes and longer recovery times to targets relative to nontargets for psychopaths at parietal (but not temporal) sites. Tested on the WAIS, the psychopaths also scored higher than nonpsychopaths on the Block Design and Object Assembly subtests, which are thought to be maximally sensitive to parietal lobe functioning (Warrington, James, & Maciejewski, 1986). These results may indicate that larger P300 amplitudes are associated with higher IQ scores.

The effect of cognitive load on P300 in pathological conditions has also been studied. In a study of aged probable Alzheimer's disease sufferers, DeToledo, Evers, Hoeppner, and Morrell (1991) found that when more than one item had to be remembered, the Alzheimer's group showed significantly reduced P300 amplitudes when compared to a healthy age-matched group who did not differ from young healthy control subjects. P300 latency, however, was increased relative to the young group in both older groups by approximately the same amount. Polich, Ladish, and Bloom (1990) also found smaller P300 amplitudes and increased latencies among Alzheimer's patients using a standard "oddball" discrimination task.

Returning to intelligence measures rather than on-line cognitive tasks, Josiassen, Shagass, Roemer, and Slepner (1988) have confirmed that higher intelligence test scores on Raven's Progressive Matrices are positively associated with AEP amplitudes. Rather than amplitude simply being greater (but consistent with the string measure correlating with IQ), however, Weiss (1989) has implicated P300 with memory span and argued that recordings from high-IQ people are more complex than those from people with low IQ because the upper harmonics are not expressed in the records from the latter individuals. Also, Stough et al. (1990), specifically investigating the relationship between string length and IQ, found moderate to high correlations which were sensitive to temporal events occurring within the AEP waveform. Analyzing the first 250 msec poststimulus revealed that high-IQ undergraduate subjects had significantly more early components in their waveforms than did lower-IQ undergraduate subjects. It would very satisfactory if intelligence was related to the complexity of the early components, but personality to their amplitude and that of later components (e.g., P300 amplitude); like many satisfactory solutions, though, it may be confounded by the evidence. It may be worth pointing out here that Hendrickson's string length measure based on the first 256 msec poststimulus correlated more highly with IQ than did the same measure based on 512 msec poststimulus. The question could also be asked whether the latency of P300 being longer under higher cognitive load (Polich, 1987) is attributable to greater complexity of the early part of the waveform.

As well as its being implicated in intellectual tasks, there are studies comparing the AEP of different personality types at different sites. Stenberg, Rosen, and Risberg (1990), for example, note the following in a study of augmenting/reducing of visual AEPs in introverts and extraverts:

> Assuming, then, that the occipital response is a concomitant of perceptual analysis, and the vertex response is part of an alerting reaction which includes motor preparation, the psychological significance of a disposition for one or the other becomes clearer. Brebner and Cooper (1974) have suggested, on the basis of RT data, that introverts are "geared to inspect" and extraverts "geared to respond." Along the same lines Stelmack and Plouffe (1983) concluded from physiological data that extraverts exhibit selective facilitation of motor processes, and introverts a corresponding facilitation of sensory processes. The findings concerning the relative strengths of the vertex responses and the occipital responses in the present study are compatible with this line of reasoning. (p. 1252)

The authors conclude as follows:

> It is worth noting that for the occipital, perceptual part of the visual response studied here the original conception of Petrie (1967) applies, according to which extraverts are reducers, i.e., disposed to attenuate the perceptual impact of stimulation. The tendency for introverts to carry out perceptual processing even in the face of aversive stimulation offers interesting resemblances to MacLeod, Mathews and Tara (1986) who showed that anxious subjects have a bias towards visual processing of threatening words, while non-anxious subjects have the opposite bias, towards innocuous stimuli. (p. 1253)

The first point seems to be in agreement with Brebner and Cooper (1974) that extraverts derive central inhibition from stimulus analysis, which shows itself in the tendency to attenuate or cease that activity, whereas introverts derive excitation from stimulus analysis, tending to continue or augment that activity. For example, although introverts tend to persist in stimulus analysis, in relation to aversive stimulation, introverts have lower pain thresholds than extraverts (Lynn & Eysenck, 1961), perhaps because of the inhibition produced by extraverts through stimulus analysis (Brebner, 1983a). Stenberg et al. (1990) were recording vertex N120 and P200 waves and occipital N140 to four light intensities under "attend" and "ignore" conditions. Their measures from the vertex showed clear separation in the amplitude of introverts' and extraverts' N120 and P200 responses, with extraverts eliciting enhanced amplitudes. For the occipital N140 response, higher amplitudes were obtained for the "attend" versus "ignore" condition for both groups, but within the conditions there was again separation (although in this case amplitude is greater for introverts).

Lukas (1987) related vertex augmenters to sensation seeking, but Zuckerman (1984) notes that augmenting-reducing is most strongly related to sensation-seeking items that measure "a hedonistic pursuit of extraverted activities." It is also possible that the higher sensory thresholds of extraverts and their greater behavioral activity (e.g., talkativeness, gesturing, voluntary movements) relate to stronger vertex amplitudes in these subjects. In addition, the tendency of vertex amplitudes to be inversely related to occipital activity has also been shown (Lolas et al., 1989), in this case for recordings of P115 to N147 and N147 to P180 occipitally and P98 to N127 and N127 to P178 from the vertex. Lolas, Camposano, and Etcheberrigaray (1989) demonstrated a positive association between extraversion and the amplitude of auditory evoked potentials from the vertex; they also found a relationship with psychoticism.

It would be wrong here to ignore criticisms of evoked potentials and their interpretation. There are negative comments by Connolly (1986) on the biological basis of sensation seeking, and by Juhel (1991) and Mackintosh (1986) on the correlation between biological measures and intelligence (though this has been countered by Nettelbeck & Rabbitt, 1992). Vogel, Kruger, Schalt, and Schnobel (1987) found no evidence for any relationship between AEPs and performance on intelligence tests. It should also be pointed out that there are criticisms of the above articles, however, and failure to find an association between relevant measures does not necessarily imply that there is no relationship between them. Indeed, as Eysenck and

Barrett (1985) have pointed out, the employment of peculiar methodologies has most likely resulted in some studies reporting no relationships between AEP measures and IQ. On the basis of the studies above, though, there is some evidence to relate intelligence scores to the amplitude of P300. IQ also relates to earlier components, and the P300 relationship is not stronger than that between IQ and AEP. Extraversion has been associated with the amplitude of later components like P300, or AEP components recorded from the vertex. But from this evidence a simple theoretical link between intelligence and extraversion through arousal-amplitude cannot be said to have been strongly supported.

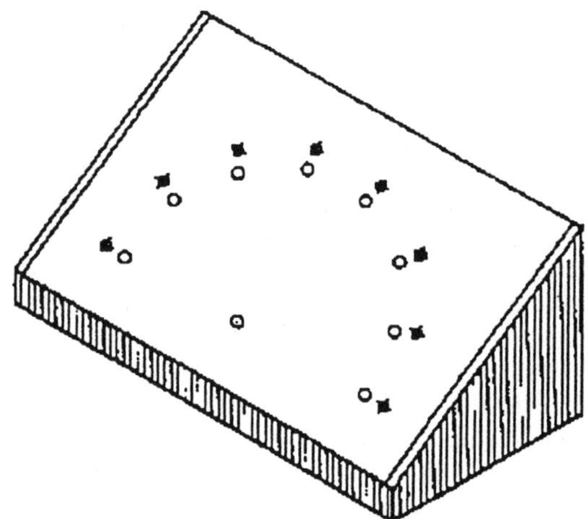

Figure 3. Jensen's reaction time apparatus. Adapted from A. R. Jensen (1987), Individual differences in the Hick paradigm. In P. A. Vernon (Ed.), *Speed of information processing and intelligence* (pp. 101–175). Norwood, NJ: Ablex.

Reaction Time

Not all low-level indices of intelligence are physiological measures. Several studies have demonstrated that measures of inspection time (IT) and reaction time (RT) correlate highly and significantly with psychometric intelligence (Anderson, 1992; Jensen, 1987; Nettelbeck, 1987; Stough & Nettelbeck, 1989). This has prompted some authors to suggest that IT and RT should be further examined as new measures of intelligence or used as an adjunct to intelligence tests. Flynn (1987), Matarazzo (1992), and Stough, Bates, Colrain, Mangan, and Pellett (in press) have suggested that both IT and RT may prove to be better measures of intelligence than standard psychometric tests of intelligence.

Jensen has provided evidence that mean decision time to complete a simple sensory discrimination is related to psychometric intelligence (e.g., Jensen, 1982, 1987; Jensen & Munro, 1979). The apparatus designed by Jensen (see Figure 3) uses eight lights presented in a semicircular arrangement. Adjacent to each light is a response button; a "home" button is located in the center of the panel. Subjects are required to press the home button until they see a light go on, at which point they are to release the home button as quickly as possible and press the response button adjacent to the stimulus light. Choice is manipulated in this paradigm by limiting the number of stimulus alternatives (i.e., the number of lights that may be turned on). Decision time (DT) is defined as the amount of time required by the subject to release the home button, and movement time (MT) is the time taken after the release of the home button to press the button adjacent to the stimulus. Thus RT in the Jensen paradigm separates two processes: the time taken to make a simple sensory discrimination, and the time taken to effect a response subsequent to the decision. Typically, mean DT rather than mean MT correlates with tests of intelligence.

Jensen (1982, 1987) has summarized work in this area, concluding that several parameters of DTs are related to psychometric intelligence. Eysenck (1967) has proposed that introverts are on average slower than extraverts, because the former are more careful and precise, taking longer to check their responses. It is not clear whether this trait may still hold in the Hick paradigm, in which subjects are instructed to respond as quickly as possible. Welford (1986) has criticized the Jensen paradigm on methodological grounds, pointing out that little can be learned from reaction times that do not include errors. Errors within this context are important because they enable the experimenter to allow for strategies such as speed-accuracy trade-off.

Stough, Nettelbeck et al. (1993) administered the Jensen RT procedure to 50 undergraduate psychology students, together with the EPQ and the STI. Correlations between these variables are reported in Table 8. Correlations between mobility and DT at 2 and 3 bits, and between mobility and MT at 2 bits, were significantly negatively related; all other correlations were statistically insignificant. Bits of information in this context refers to the level of stimulus choice: 0 bits refers to one choice (i.e., 1 light), whereas 3 bits refers

Table 8. Pearson Correlations between Median Decision Time Scores and EPQ-R and STI Dimensions

	E	N	P	L	Ex	In	M	B
DT0	.20	.21	−.16	−.06	.01	−.24	−.05	.19
DT1	.00	.01	−.04	.05	.13	−.01	−.11	.09
DT2	−.03	−.10	−.10	.06	−.10	−.16	−.32[a]	.08
DT3	−.11	.06	−.21	.06	−.02	.03	−.24	−.05
MT0	.13	.14	.03	.06	−.16	−.06	−.15	−.03
MT1	.03	.00	−.03	.06	−.02	−.07	−.16	.02
MT2	.01	.01	−.06	.05	−.11	−.09	−.28[a]	.01
MT3	−.04	−.04	−.22	.12	.08	−.15	−.07	.16

[a] $p < .05$.
Note: DT = mean decision time; MT = mean movement time; 0–3 = bits of information. See Tables 1 and 2 for key to abbreviations for personality dimensions.

to an eight-choice condition. The significant correlations between mobility from the STI and median DTs support Strelau's (1987) view that mobility is related to speed of mental activation processes.

It is interesting to note that mobility does not relate to IT (see Table 10) but to RT, suggesting that mobility is implicated in some psychophysical process in the latter that is not shared with the former. As IT measures input or perceptual speed and does not involve speeded responding, and RT involves responding as quickly as possible, it might be suggested that mobility is related to the speed to which a subject can make a decision to respond, independent of the stimulus recognition time. In other words, mobility may be related to response organization rather than stimulus analysis in this sort of task. This would be in line with the significant correlation between extraversion and mobility in Table 1 and higher AEP amplitudes for extraverts recorded from the vertex. But it must be stressed again that the small correlations for mobility in Table 3 do not explain much of the variance.

Apart from the small, significant correlations between Jensen's DT and mobility, there is no suggestion that other personality features are related to simple or choice DT. Stough, Mangan, Pellett, and Bates (1993), investigating personality dimensions on the Jensen-Hick paradigm, found negative correlations between APM IQ scores and DT parameters only in the introverted group; positive correlations were reported in the extraverted group (see Table 9). These results suggest that extraversion is related to DT parameters in Jensen's task and that extraversion may have been a confounding variable in past studies. Introverts recorded significantly faster mean DTs and fatigued less quickly across trials than extraverts. Although extreme care must be exercised in interpreting the results of this experiment because of the small sample size ($n = 15$), the authors concluded that extraverts and introverts may have differed in terms of the strategies they adopted for both the Jensen task and the

Table 9. Pearson Correlations (Corrected and Uncorrected) between IQ and DT variables

	APM	APM corrected	APM	APM corrected
Introverts (n = 15)				
Intercept	−.45	−.70[b]	−.28	−.48[a]
MSE	−.45	−.69[b]	−.49[a]	−.73[b]
Slope	.41	.65[b]	−.25	−.43
Mean1	−.52[a]	−.73[b]	−.35	−.51[a]
Mean2	−.26	−.45	−.33	−.55[a]
Mean3	−.32	−.54[a]	−.36	−.59[a]
Mean4	−.28	−.38	−.47	−.71[b]
SD1	−.39	−.62[a]	−.35	−.56[a]
SD2	.01	.02	−.29	−.48[a]
SD3	−.32	−.53[a]	−.58[a]	−.81[b]
SD4	−.44	−.69[b]	−.56[a]	−.80[b]
Extraverts (n = 15)				
Intercept	.34	.55[a]	.26	.44
MSE	.27	.46	.18	.32
Slope	.00	.00	−.06	−.11
Mean1	.47	.71[b]	.37	.59[b]
Mean2	.43	.67[b]	.34	.55[a]
Mean3	.51[a]	.73[b]	.44[a]	.68[b]
Mean4	.49[a]	.72[b]	.34	.55[a]
SD1	.11	.20	.22	.38
SD2	−.25	−.43	.15	.27
SD3	.31	.53[a]	.27	.46
SD4	.43	.67[b]	−.01	−.02

[a] $p < .05$.
Note: APM = Advanced Progressive Matrices.

AMP. Stough, Mangan et al. also discuss the results in terms of arousal theory. Eysenck might have suggested that introverts should perform better at discrimination tasks than extraverts because their characteristic greater arousal may lead to better concentration.

Inspection Time

The psychophysical measure of inspection time (IT) has emerged in the intelligence literature over the last two decades. According to Vickers, Nettelbeck, and Willson (1972), who first coined the term, IT refers to the minimum amount of time needed to make nearly error-free decisions about a simple sensory stimulus. IT is the shortest duration of presentation at which a person can reliably detect a difference between two stimuli or two features of one stimulus at a selected criterion level (note that it is neither a difference threshold, because it is the duration that is important, nor a reaction time task, because speed of responding is not the relevant measure). The procedure for measuring IT is relatively simple and involves the presentation of a simple sensory stimulus followed by a backward mask that prevents continued sensory sampling of the stimulus or aftereffects. Subjects are required to discriminate between two stimulus alternatives (commonly two vertical line lengths) at different exposure durations. IT is usually calculated at discriminations between 85% and 95% accuracy. The parameter resulted from the attempt to develop a measure of mental speed that was relatively elementary in nature and immune to the influence of higher-order cognitive abilities, motivation, and other environmental factors. As Vickers and Smith (1985) point out,

> The IT paradigm was designed as a way of measuring performance under certain boundary conditions, in which the effects of variations in decision rule, in sensory noise, threshold values and other parameters of the process became negligibly small, so that individual differences in performance could be ascribed with some confidence to differences in a single parameter. (p. 115)

The IT parameter is based upon the accumulator model of discriminative judgment described in detail by Vickers and Smith (1985). The model hypothesizes that the subject makes a number of independent samplings of the sensory information (with each sample taking a small and constant amount of time) until a critical amount is collected for either of the stimulus alternatives. Although the IT procedure has been used in several research areas, the most frequent use has been in the field of intelligence, where it has been employed to test the possibility that intelligence is related to the ability to utilize available information efficiently to make correct discriminations.

Several studies have now reported significant negative correlations between IT and various forms of IQ tests. Nettelbeck (1987) has summarized research on this topic and has concluded that IT and IQ most probably correlate at about the −.5 mark, a finding in close agreement with more recent studies (Anderson, 1992; Kranzler & Jensen, 1989; Stough & Nettelbeck, 1989).

Table 10 reports the correlation between two IT scores at 90% accuracy, tested with different methodologies, and personality dimensions from the EPQ and the STI. All correlations were small and insignificant, suggesting there is no relationship between IT and personality factors. IT1 scores were derived from a tachistoscope, whereas IT2 scores were derived employing a computer monitor. Brebner and Cooper (1986), however, found that extraverts were more likely to adopt a strategy of using an aftereffect of apparent movement to do the IT task than introverts were. This strategy use (normally precluded by backward masking) allows subjects to decrease their ITs without any commensurate decrease in their perceptual speed. In cases where such strategies can be adopted by subjects, personality may be related to IT, but where IT is free from higher-order influences there does not appear to be any relationship with the Eysenckian factors.

In a more recent experiment, Stough, Bates et al. (in press) compared subjects' ITs using three different masks (the standard penetrable mask and two new masks designed to prevent poststimulus strategies) and scores on the EPQ. Correlations between EPQ dimensions and ITs derived from all masks were small and statistically insignificant, although subjects scoring more highly on both the extraversion and psychoticism scales reported that one of the new masks (the flash mask; see Evans & Nettelbeck, 1993, for a

Table 10. Pearson Correlations between Inspection Time (IT) Scores and EPQ and STI Dimensions (N = 50)

	E	N	P	L	Ex	In	M	B
IT1	.09	.11	−.10	−.13	−.23	−.05	−.09	−.12
IT2	−.06	.07	−.02	.02	−.01	.03	−.18	−.03

Note: See Tables 1 and 2 for key to abbreviations for personality dimensions.

description) was the hardest in terms of target discrimination.

On the basis of this review and the present results, personality (at least in terms of the EPQ and the STI) does not relate to speed of information processing as indexed by IT. Though the above evidence is against any personality-IT relationship, significant negative correlations between the time required to make a simple sensory discrimination task and IQ scores have led some authors (see Jensen, 1987; Lehrl & Fischer, 1990; Nettelbeck, 1987) to postulate that IQ may be related to the speed of processing information from the environment. Presumably, theories that link speed of information-processing abilities to IQ postulate either quicker or more efficient neural processing of information, and Lehrl and Fischer (1990) suggest that intelligence may be reconstructed as a scientific concept using simple sensory discrimination tasks such as RT and IT. Further studies that include Strelau's mobility and Rusalov's tempo/social tempo measures may be indicated here.

Given the lack of evidence (apart from speed measures) to show that personality and intelligence are related, and the current Zeitgeist to consider the two constructs as theoretically independent, Robinson is one of very few researchers to link low-level measures of intelligence with arousal measures of personality. Robinson (1989) proposed a novel model of the neurophysiological basis of intelligence in which previous linear models (e.g., D. E. Hendrickson & Hendrickson, 1980) are replaced with a curvilinear model linking EEG parameters to intelligence at different levels of arousal. Linking behavioral data on the relationship between performance on cognitive tests and different levels of arousal (Corcoran, 1972), Robinson has suggested that the neurophysiological processes underlying the development of intelligence are best when operating at a moderate level of arousal. Robinson equates arousal level directly with Eysenck's concept of extraversion (i.e., extraverts are less aroused than introverts); he has also proposed that an intermediate degree of arousal is optimal for neural transmission of information.

Unfortunately, there is little evidence to support Robinson's theory, although to be fair there is also very little evidence to disprove it. Table 11 displays IQ, String length, IT and RT scores for extraverts, ambiverts, and introverts adapted from Stough, Brebner et al. (1993). These results support Robinson's position that moderate levels of arousal are optimum for information processing. Ambiverts' scores were significantly greater for full-scale and performance IQ and for other speed variables. This result is different from that reported by Stough, Mangan et al. (1993), who found that introverts recorded significantly faster DTs than extraverts. That study did not report mean scores for ambiverts because of the small sample size; it also differed by employing the EPQ-R instead of the EPQ and the APM rather than the WAIS-R. There was no significant difference between the two groups in the APM scores.

Table 11. Scores on Main Variables for Introverts, Ambiverts and Extraverts

	Introverts	Ambiverts	Extraverts
IQ tests			
Verbal	100	117	111
Performance	108	119	113
Full scale	109	120	112
APM	25	27	25
Decision time			
0 bits	277	255	265
1 bits	299	289	295
2 bits	331	311	314
3 bits	370	339	340
IT	64	60	64
String length (msec)			
0–100	1,624	1,267	1,163
100–200	1,323	958	945
0–250	1,119	677	668
0–200	9,91	972	869
100–300	1,155	963	1,012

An overall interpretation is difficult because there is evidence to support the following conclusions:

1. Ambiverts record significantly higher WAIS-R IQ and a commensurate enhancement in mean DTs in the Jensen-Hick paradigm.
2. Introverts matched for IQ with extraverts display significantly faster mean DTs than extraverts.

It is therefore unclear whether an intermediate level of arousal influences IQ and DT processes, or that the results from Stough, Mangan et al. (1993) are simply attributable to sampling error (selecting more intelligent ambiverts) and that the higher mean DTs reflect the fact that DT and IQ are correlated. To test Robinson's hypothesis more adequately it would be necessary to compare larger numbers of introverts, ambiverts, and extraverts on a wide battery of intelligence tests and related measures including IT and RT. Robinson's position may be upheld by future research—and perhaps by also studying impulsiveness, as would be suggested by O'Gorman and Lloyd's (1987) results—but studies investigating psychophysiological and psychophysical measures of intelligence and personality do not offer unequivocal support for his theoretical position.

In summary, researchers investigating low-level theories of intelligence find no strong link with either Eysenckian or Pavlovian personality dimensions. Personality theorists postulate an arousal mechanism mediating some personality dimensions (especially extraversion and strength of excitation), and intelligence researchers postulate an efficiency model of neuronal transmission largely independent of any ascending reticular activating system mechanisms. There appears to be no persuasive theory or body of evidence linking these two biological theories together. Despite some evidence relating personality to EEG components or aspects of evoked potentials, and other evidence relating intelligence to AEP and the complexity of early components, personality and intelligence still appear largely independent of each other. At best, rather weak relationships have been found with psychoticism or the Lie scale of the EPQ, or between personality and intellectual tasks that involve the speed of processing information. The significant correlations reported in Tables 3, 4, and 5 for mobility, tempo, and plasticity when predicting nonverbal ability, for example, are interesting, and suggest that those measures do weakly favor responding correctly within a time limit. But these measures did not predict verbal intelligence, and further research is needed to establish the strength and reliability of the nonverbal relationship.

HIGH-LEVEL THEORIES OF INTELLIGENCE AND PERSONALITY

Among high-level theories of intelligence, Jonathon Baron's (1982) is one of the best articulated. Baron derives his approach from Dewey's (1933) description of "good" or reflective thinking, which refers to reaching conclusions that are justified on the basis of evidence rather than beliefs or habits. Following Dewey, Baron suggests there are five stages or processes involved in reflective thought:

1. Problem recognition
2. Enumerating possibilities
3. Reasoning
4. Revision
5. Evaluation

Baron prefers the term *phase* to *stage*, because the timing of the processes can vary from seconds to years. For our present interest, however, it is more important that he accepts that there may be consistent individual differences in any of these processes that, therefore, represent different sorts of cognitive styles. Baron recognizes that the processes will be affected by education and experience, and believes that good thinking can be taught insofar as one can be told, for example, to enumerate as many possibilities as possible and to revise the list of possibilities after checking the available evidence.

He makes a distinction between capacities and propensities that are subject of voluntary control, which allows him to acknowledge that some individual differences in intellectual functioning may result from limitations in capacity that have a biological basis. But Baron's interest lies in the person's cognitive style, and he has suggested that the main parameters of thinking are as much part of the individual as other consistencies in behavior identified as personality traits. Cognitive style, he notes, emerged from psychoanalytic theory via ego psychology, and certainly Jung himself allowed that the four functions (thinking, emoting, socializing, and intuiting) were more or less inward or outward directed, a hypothesis that gave us the constructs of introversion and extraversion.

More recent cognitive styles, however, have tended to multiply to include, among others, measures of the characteristic riskiness of an individual's judgments (Kagan & Wallach, 1964; Pettigrew, 1958) and his or her sensitivity to change in the physical attributes of stimuli (Holzman, 1954). The variety of different cognitive styles and the tendency for many of those championed to become less precise in their conceptualization has tended to divorce studies on cognitive style from the mainstream theoretical literature on intelligence or personality. Nevertheless, there are some similarities. Baron (1982), for example, refers to a study by Johnson (1957) showing that speed was consistent for individuals across tasks and was positively related to confidence. He goes on to suggest that this may be related to a dimension of reflection-impulsivity (which, of course, sits well with introversion-extraversion) and that impulsivity "may result from overconfidence, that is, a bias toward positive evaluation of the result of the thinking done so far" (p. 322).

Three points may be worth making about this. First, whether confidence is positively or negatively related to speed of performance depends on the nature of the task, particularly its difficulty. (This could underlie the Eysenck and Cookson, 1969, suggestion that extraverted children's confidence at the simpler primary school level could advantage them.) Second, there is a considerable literature on speed—including what used to be called "personal tempo"—to support the notion that although speed of performance tends to be regarded as under voluntary control, individuals are characteristically speedy or slow. But, third, whether impulsiveness is attributable to overconfidence is less certain. If, for example, impulsive people responded quickly but with more than one answer or solution, that would imply a lack of confidence in the thinking done so far. Clearly, however, in tasks where there is a speed-accuracy trade-off, impulsive people will be disadvantaged; in intelligence tests that involve such a trade-off, intelligence and impulsiveness will be negatively related. A general bias toward negative or positive evaluation, though, has been related to introversion and extraversion, respectively, by both Gray (1972) and Brebner (1991), but without narrowing the link to impulsiveness.

Whether extraverts are "overconfident" is certainly arguable, insofar as Argyle et al. (1989) have shown them to initiate conversations, ask more questions, and joke more than introverts do when placed in social situations with strangers. Even more directly relevant, two simulated betting studies by Brebner (1991) showed that extraverts tended to generalize from a positive event (reinforced on 80% of trials) rather than a negative event (reinforced on 20% of trials). Rather than showing the opposite tendency, it is more accurate to describe introverts as having made a more realistic appraisal of changes in reinforcement probabilities, presumably through updating their estimates of population parameters more often. Though the two are not identical, the parallel between extraverts' behavior in this study and Baron's view that underlying impulsivity is a positive bias at the evaluation phase is worth pointing out.

At this point it is also worth bringing in the work of Bartussek et al. (1993), who used a task quite similar to Brebner (1991) to test Gray's theory while recording event-related potentials. Briefly, their subjects (who were high or low on extraversion and neuroticism) performed a betting task, winning or losing 0, 0.5, or 5 deutschmarks while auditory and visual evoked potentials were recorded. Extraverts showed larger amplitudes to signals indicating a win than to those indicating losses; introverts produced the opposite result. This interaction was found for the P200, N200, and an early P300 component(s) and supports Gray's view that introverts and extraverts are affected in opposite ways by signals for reward and punishment. This study may also provide evidence bearing on extraverts' and introverts' confidence in that extraverts showed more positive N200 and P300 amplitudes to the visual presentation of the amount that could be bet after a losing trial, whereas the amplitudes of introverts were more positive after a winning trial. Bartussek et al. assume that on average, all subjects expected a win to be followed by a loss, and vice versa. It appears that extraverts are more affected when expecting to win, introverts when expecting to lose. Impulsivity is not reported in this study, but extraverts could be regarded as overconfident in the sense of being optimistic.

Impulsivity has, however, been studied extensively in relation to criminal or delinquent behavior (Farrington, 1991), children's learning, and particularly hyperkinesis, and low-impulsive children have been shown to score higher than impulsives on the Attention-Concentration and Visual Organization subtests of the revised Wechsler Intelligence Scale for Children, but not on verbal ability (Brannigan, Ash, & Margolis, 1980).

Three studies have been performed relating impulsivity, intelligence, and arousal level. The first, by Gupta (1988), tested the effect of caffeine on the intelligence test performance of high- and low-impulsive students. Caffeine, particularly in higher doses, facilitated performance significantly for high impulsives but had no effect for low impulsives. This finding completes a link between arousal and intelligence test scores through impulsivity, although arousal was not directly measured. It suggests that high impulsives are lower on arousal and that increasing their arousal improves their performance at intellectual tasks. This study would also support Robinson's theory, mentioned earlier, relating arousal and IQ. The second study, by Matthews (1987), used a composite physiological (rather than self-report) measure of skin conductance and heart rate for arousal; impulsivity was measured by Cattell's F factor, and intelligence was also measured using a standard British test for senior school and university students. Subjects were tested at 9.30 a.m. or 7.30 p.m. A three-way interaction between time of day, arousal level, and intelligence test score was significant. Unlike Gupta, however, Matthews found that high impulsives' intelligence test scores *decreased* under high physiological arousal both in the morning and evening. Intelligence test scores for low impulsives decreased under high arousal in the morning, but increased under high arousal in the evening. None of the main effects or two-way interactions was significant, and more than half the subjects completed only one-third of the intelligence test items. It may also be worth noting that different tests were used in these studies.

The third study, by Revelle, Humphreys, Simon, and Gilliland (1980), showed that the administration of caffeine to high impulsives in the morning improved their verbal ability performance, but had the opposite effect for low impulsives. This is in line with a negative relationship between arousal and impulsivity, but the effects were reversed in the evening. This is explicable in terms of low impulsives being "morning people" (high on arousal early in the day but lower, relative to themselves, in the evenings), whereas high impulsives are "evening people." In absolute terms, however, the differences between groups in the evening were small with standard scores on the order of 0.2, whereas they were about twice that in the morning. Also, relative to themselves, high impulsives were affected much more by caffeine in the morning than were the low impulsives. Thus, the strongest difference found was that for high impulsives in the morning.

These few studies trying to unravel the theoretical connection between impulsivity, arousal, and performance are scarcely conclusive. What they do have in common is the demonstration that under some conditions, high impulsives achieve higher scores at intellectual tasks than low impulsives. The two groups therefore cannot be regarded as simply differing in intelligence, though under particular conditions of arousal, one or the other may perform below its potential. Just how general the tendency is for highly impulsive people to underperform is difficult to estimate, but Kipnis (1971; cited in Brody, 1982) found that individuals who reported being impulsive did not obtain grades as good as those who stated they were low on impulsiveness.

In thinking aimed at problem solving, there is, of course, a decision about the most appropriate strategy to adopt. This strategy choice may be made prior to the five phases of reflective thinking when dealing with a set of similar problems, or as part of the stage of identifying the problem. The assumption need not be made that one best possible solution is always required. In many cases, where penalties and payoffs either are the same across alternatives or are unimportant, the first workable possibility will do. There are often penalties (e.g., running out of time) for overdetermining the nature of the problem, enumerating more possibilities than necessary, or continuing the evaluation process beyond some optional stopping point. The ability to select the best strategy may be important for measures of intelligence but independent of personality variables related to the speed of performance, which may be why characteristically quick (if not impulsive) extraverts and cautious introverts are not as disadvantaged in power and speed tests of intelligence as their respective personalities might suggest they should be.

Selecting correct strategies could underlie the relationship between speed of performance and measures of intelligence, because the selection is accurate as well as selected quickly and ahead of less satisfactory strategies when subjects are attempting to be fast and accurate. The complexity of early components in the AEP waveform found to correlate with intelligence by Stough et al. (1990) could conceivably reflect the strategy for dealing with the information, and it may even be possible that it is at this stage that introverts' bias toward stimulus analysis and extraverts' bias toward response organization show themselves. A negative correlation between IQ and reaction time has often been postulated, and the reciprocal of the slope constant in a series of choice RT tasks has been offered as the natural successor to IQ (Edwards, 1964), but the well-documented speed-accuracy trade-off (Welford, 1980) needs to be controlled in such research.

The importance of which aspect of peri mance—speed or accuracy—is emphasized has bee. shown recently by Neubauer, Bauer, and Holler (1992) using simple and two-choice RT tasks. Intelligence and RT were only negatively correlated (as hypothesized) for those subjects who were not fast but inaccurate or were accurate but slow (i.e., only for subjects who were not trading speed or accuracy at the expense of the other). The personality characteristics of the different groups are not reported. If personality features like extraversion bias individuals to be fast at the expense of accuracy, however, or if introverts need to deal with intelligence test items very slowly and cautiously, any relationship with intelligence will be obscured unless these biases are controlled.

One study has linked cognitive style and extraversion. Furnham (1992) used Honey and Mumford's (1982) Learning Style questionnaire (LSQ), Whetten and Cameron's (1984) Cognitive Style Questionnaire (CSQ), and Kolb's (1976) Learning Style Inventory (LSI), in conjunction with the Eysenck Personality Questionnaire (EPQ), and found that extraversion correlated positively ($r = .52$, $n = 60$, $p < .01$) with the LSQ Activists scale and negatively with the Reflector scale ($r = -.51$, $n = 60$, $p < .01$). A similar result was obtained on the Active ($r = .44$, $n = 44$, $p < .01$) and Reflective ($r = -.44$, $n = 44$, $p < .01$) measures of the CSQ, which are described as tending to "execute a behaviour as the result of receiving information" and to "observe rather than actively participate," respectively. Significant correlations of .33 ($n = 35$, $p < .01$) were also found between extraversion and the LSI Converger and Accommodator styles of dealing with information, which rely primarily "on the dominant learning abilities of abstract conceptualisation and active experimentation" and "concrete experience and active experimentation," respectively. Most theoretical approaches to extraversion would predict these results (e.g., Brebner, 1983b).

Unfortunately for our purposes, Furnham did not also report the IQ of his subjects. Nevertheless, his study shows a definite link between personality and cognitive style. If sets of intelligence test items can be identified that require an active or a reflective approach, then, in principle at least, IQ could be related to selecting the appropriate strategy, and extraverts and introverts would be expected to be biased toward the active and reflective alternatives, respectively.

CONCLUSION

With the exception of speed related factors like mobility, tempo and plasticity, personality and intelligence are not related from the evidence presented here. There are some small negative correlations, between Eysenck's psychoticism and intelligence, which could simply mean that intelligent people are less likely to adopt or admit to the behavior of high psychoticism scorers. Alternatively, it has been suggested that psychoticism in normals is associated with arousal level, e.g. T. N. Robinson and Zahn (1985), and Matthews and Amelang (1993) found P and alpha correlated significantly ($r = .16$, $p < .05$, $n = 181$) but, apart from explaining only a trivial amount of the variance, the only significant performance effect of P was on a concentration task where high P scorers made fewer errors, a result which is in line with Raine and Venables (1988) study outlined above. P also correlated significantly with impulsivity but appeared to be predicting different parts of the variance in alpha.

Impulsivity and the speed-related personality measures mobility, plasticity, and tempo show some small statistically significant correlations with intellectual performance measures, but they do not explain much of the variance. Within a normal population, impulsivity might be viewed as a cognitive style capable of control in the light of studies showing the performance level of impulsives on intellectual tasks can be manipulated by caffeine administration or the time of day, but the nature of the manipulations implicates arousal level rather than voluntary control. A question raised by manipulating arousal is whether it affects both speed and accuracy of performance. It would be very interesting if increasing arousal affected only accuracy in impulsives, and only speed in low impulsives.

What the jig-saw of studies above seems to show is that the biological bases of intelligence and personality factors such as extraversion lie in separate aspects of nervous system functioning. Eysenck's theory of arousal differences underlying introvert-extravert differences, which has been the subject of numerous studies, continues to derive some support from electrophysiological studies (Gale, 1984; Matthews & Amelang, 1993) even though the latter authors found no support for the inverted-U relationship between electrophysiological arousal and performance. There may be a recurring problem for Western research of knowing where on the hypothesized inverted-U "scale" of arousal an individual is expected to be under particular experimental conditions since Kohn, Cowles and Lafreniere (1987) suggest from their results that psychometric and experimental indices of arousability form two solitudes since the psychometric measures correlate together, and so do the experimental indices, but the two do not intercorrelate. The Eastern European transmarginal inhibition measure provides one index but it is not widely used in Western research.

The possibility has been raised above that, while intelligence and extraversion are independent, they might possibly be reflected respectively by the complexity of early components, and the amplitude of early and late components of averaged evoked potentials, with complexity being related to strategies which determine how information is processed. Only further studies can determine the nature of any relationship between intelligence and early components of the AEP. On the personality side, evidence that the amplitude of evoked potentials recorded from different regions (occipital and vertex) differ for introverts and extraverts (Stenberg et al., 1990) also needs to be accounted for by any theory of extraversion, and this may be possible in some (Brebner & Cooper, 1974), but the difficulty in reliably discriminating electrophysiologically between processes concerned with stimulus-analysis and response-organization makes it difficult to test this view of extraversion adequately in this way.

To conclude, the studies looked at in this chapter offer support only for the existence of rather weak theoretical relationships between speed-related personality measures and intelligence, and a negative relationship between impulsivity and intelligence test performance that may be mediated through arousal level.

REFERENCES

Anderson, M. (1992). *Intelligence and development: A cognitive theory*. Oxford, England: Blackwell.

Argyle, M., Martin, M., & Crossland, G. (1989). Happiness as a function of social encounters. In J. P. Forgas & M. J. Innes (Eds.), *Recent advances in social psychology: An international perspective* (pp. 189–193). Amsterdam: Elsevier.

Baron, J. (1982). Personality and intelligence. In R. J. Sternberg (Ed.), *Handbook of intelligence*. Cambridge, England: Cambridge University Press.

Barrett, P. T., Daum, I., & Eysenck, H. J. (1990). Sensory nerve conduction and intelligence: A methodological study. *Journal of Psychophysiology, 4*, 1–13.

Bartussek, D., Diedrich, O., Naumann, E., & Collett, W. (1993). Introversion-extraversion and event-related potential (ERP): A test of J. A. Gray's theory. *Personality and Individual Differences, 14*, 565–574.

Bates, T., & Eysenck, H. J. (1993). String length, attention and intelligence: Focussed attention reverses the string length-IQ relationship. *Personality and Individual Differences, 15*, 363–371.

Bazylevich, T. F. (1974). The syndrome of strength of the regulative brain system. *Nauka, 8*.

Bennett, G. K., Seashore, H. G., & Wesman, A. G. (1989). *Differential aptitude tests*. Orlando, FL: The Psychological Corporation.

Binet, A., & Simon, T. (1905). Application des methodes nouvelles au diagnostic du niveau intellectual chez des enfants normal et anormaux d'hospice et d'ecole primiaire. *L'Annee Psychologique, 11*, 245–336.

Brannigan, G. G., Ash, T., & Margolis, H. (1980). Impulsivity-reflectivity and children's intellectual performance. *Journal of Personality Assessment, 44*, 41–43.

Brebner, J. (1983a). A comment on Paisey and Mangan's neo-Pavlovian temperament theory and the biological bases of personality. *Personality and Individual Differences, 4*, 229–230.

Brebner, J. (1983b). A model of extraversion. *Australian Journal of Psychology, 35*, 349–360.

Brebner, J. (1990a). Personality factors in stress and anxiety. In C. D. Spielberger, R. Diaz-Guerrero, and & J. Strelau (Eds.), *Cross-cultural anxiety* (Vol. 4). Washington, DC: Hemisphere.

Brebner, J. (1990b). Psychological and neurophysiological factors in stimulus-response compatibility. In R. W. Proctor & T. G. Reeve (Eds.), *Stimulus-response compatibility: An integrated perspective* (pp. 241–260). Amsterdam: Elsevier.

Brebner, J. (1991). Personality and generalization as a source of stress. In I. Sarason, C. D. Spielberger, J. Strelau, & J. Brebner (Eds.), *Stress and anxiety* (Vol. 14). Washington, DC: Hemisphere.

Brebner, J., & Cooper, C. (1974). The effect of a low rate of regular signals upon the reaction times of introverts and extraverts. *Journal of Research in Personality, 8*, 263–276.

Brebner, J., & Cooper, C. (1978). Stimulus or response-induced excitation: A comparison of the behavior of introverts and extraverts. *Journal of Research in Personality, 12*, 306–311.

Brebner, J., & Cooper, C. (1986). Personality factors and inspection time. *Personality and Individual Differences, 7*, 709–714.

Brebner, J., Donaldson, J., Kirby, N., & Ward, L. (in press). Happiness measures, psychoticism and intelligence. *Personality and Individual Differences.*

Brody, N. (1972). *Personality: Research and theory*. New York: Academic Press.

Brody, N. (1982). *Intelligence* (2nd ed.). New York: Academic Press.

Cantor, N., & Kihlstrom, J. F. (1987). *Personality and social intelligence*. Englewood Cliffs, NJ: Prentice-Hall.

Carlier, M. (1979). *An attempt to validate Strelau's questionnaire*. Paper presented at the International Conference on Temperament, Need for Stimulation, and Activity, Warsaw.

Cattell, R. B., Eber, H. W., & Tatsuoka, M. M. (1970). *Handbook for the Sixteen Personality Factor Questionnaire*. Champaign, IL: Institute for Personality and Ability Testing.

Connolly, J. F. (1986). Evoked potential augmenting-reducing: A weak link in the biology-personality chain. *Behavioral and Brain Sciences, 9*, 746–747.

Corcoran, D. W. (1972). Studies of individual differences at the Applied Psychology Unit. In V. D. Nebylitsyn & J. A. Gray (Eds.), *Biological bases of individual behavior* (pp. 269–290). New York: Academic Press.

DeToledo, L., Evers, S., Hoeppner, T. J., & Morrell, F. (1991). A "stress" test for memory dysfunction: Electrophysiological manifestations of early Alzheimer's disease. *Archives of Neurology, 48*, 605–609.

Dewey, J. (1933). *How we think: A restatement of the relation of reflective thinking to the educative process*. Boston: Heath.

Ditraglia, G. M., & Polich, J. (1991). P300 and introverted/extraverted personality types. *Psychophysiology, 28*, 177–184.

Edwards, E. (1964). *Information transmission: An introductory guide to the application of the theory of information to the human sciences*. London: Chapman and Hall.

Evans, G., & Nettelbeck, T. (1993). Notes and shorter communication. Inspection time: A flash mask to reduce apparent movement effects. *Personality and Individual Differences, 15*(1): 91–94.

Eysenck, H. J. (1967). *The biological basis of personality*. Springfield, IL: C. C. Thomas.

Eysenck, H. J. (1971). Relation between intelligence and personality. *Perceptual and Motor Skills, 32*, 637–638.

Eysenck, H. J. (1982). *A model for intelligence*. London: Springer-Verlag.

Eysenck, H. J. (1987). Speed of information processing, reaction time, and the theory of intelligence. In P. A. Vernon (Ed.), *Speed of information processing and intelligence*. Norwood, NJ: Ablex.

Eysenck, H. J. (1988). The concept of "intelligence": Useful or useless? *Intelligence, 12*, 1–16.

Eysenck, H. J. (1990). Biological dimensions of personality. In L. A. Pervin (Ed.), *Handbook of personality: Theory and research*. New York: Guilford.

Eysenck, H. J., & Barrett, P. (1985). Psychophysiology and the measurement of intelligence. In C. R. Reynolds & V. L. Wilson (Eds.), *Methodological and statistical advances in the study of individual differences*. New York: Plenum.

Eysenck, H. J., & Cookson, D. (1969). Personality in primary schoolchildren. *British Journal of Educational Psychology, 39*, 109–122.

Eysenck, S. B. G., Pearson, P. R., Easting, G., & Allsopp, J. B. (1985). Age norms for Impulsiveness, Venturesomeness, and Empathy in adults. *Personality and Individual Differences, 6*, 613–619.

Farrington, D. P. (1991). Psychological contributions to the explanation of offending. *Issues in Criminological and Legal Psychology, 1*, 7–19.

Flynn, J. R. (1987). The ontology of intelligence. In H. Forge (Ed.), *Measurement, realism and objectivity*. Dordrecht, Netherlands: Reidel.

Fox, S. S., & O'Brien, S. (1965). Duplication of evoked potential waveform by curve of probability of firing a single cell. *Science, 147*, 888–890.

French, J. W., Exstrom, R. B., & Price, L. A. (1963). *Kit of references for cognitive factors*. Princeton, NJ: Educational Testing Service.

Furnham, A. (1992). Personality and learning style: A study of three instruments. *Personality and Individual Differences, 13*, 429–438.

Gale, A. (1981). EEG studies of extraversion-introversion. In R. Lynn (Ed.), *Dimensions of personality: Papers in honour of H. J. Eysenck*. Oxford, England: Pergamon.

Gale, A. (1984). O'Gorman versus Gale: A reply. *Biological Psychology, 19*, 129–136.

Gardner, H. (1983). *Frames of mind: The theory of multiple intelligences*. New York: Basic Books.

Gray, J. (1972). The psychophysiological nature of introversion-extraversion: A modification of Eysenck's theory. In V. D. Nebylitsyn & J. A. Gray (Eds.), *Biological bases of individual behavior* (pp. 151–169). New York: Academic Press.

Guilford, J. P. (1959). Three faces of intellect. *American Psychologist, 17*, 459–479.

Gupta, U. (1988). Effects of impulsivity and caffeine on human cognitive performance. *Pharmacopsychologeia, 1*, 33–41.

Haier, R. J., Robinson, D. L., Braden, W., & Williams, D. (1983). Electrical potentials of the cerebral cortex and psychometric intelligence. *Personality and Individual Differences, 4*, 591–592.

Hakstian, A. R., & Cattell, R. B. (1982). *Manual for the comprehensive ability battery*. Champaign, IL: Institute for Personality and Ability Testing.

Heim, A. (1970). *Intelligence and personality*. Harmondsworth, England: Penguin.

Hendrickson, A. E. (1982). The biological basis of intelligence: II. Measurement. In H. J. Eysenck (Ed.), *A model for intelligence* (pp. 151–196). New York: Springer-Verlag.

Hendrickson, D. E. (1982). The biological basis of intelligence: I. Theory. In H. J. Eysenck (Ed.), *A model for intelligence* (pp. 197–228). New York: Springer-Verlag.

Hendrickson, D. E., & Hendrickson, A. E. (1980). The biological basis for individual differences in intelligence. *Personality and Individual Differences, 1*, 3–33.

Holland, J. L. (1985). *The self-directed search*. Hawthorn, Victoria: Australian Council for Educational Research.

Holzman, P. S. (1954). The relation of assimilation tendencies in visual, auditory, and kinesthetic time-error to cognitive attitudes of leveling and sharpening. *Journal of Personality, 22*, 375–394.

Honey, P., & Mumford, A. (1982). *The manual of learning styles*. Maidenhead, England: Honey Press.

Horn, J. L. (1985). Remodelling old models of intelligence. In B. B. Wolman (Ed.), *Handbook of intelligence* (pp. 462–503). New York: Wiley.

Jensen, A. R. (1982). Reaction time and psychometric g. In H. J. Eysenck (Ed.), *A model for intelligence*. New York: Springer-Verlag.

Jensen, A. R. (1987). Individual differences in the Hick paradigm. In P. A. Vernon (Ed.), *Speed of information processing and intelligence*. Norwood, NJ: Ablex.

Jensen, A. R., & Munro, E. (1979). Reaction time, movement time and intelligence. *Intelligence, 3*, 121–126.

Johnson, L. C. (1957). Generality of speed and confidence in judgment. *Journal of Abnormal and Social Psychology, 54*, 264–266.

Josiassen, R. C., Shagass, C., Roemer, R. A., & Slepner, S. (1988). Evoked potential correlates of intelligence in nonpatient subjects. *Biological Psychology, 27*, 207–225.

Juhel, J. (1991). Relationships between psychometric intelligence and information processing speed indices. *Cahiers de Psychologie Cognitive, 11*, 73–105.

Kagan, W., & Wallach, M. A. (1964). *Risk taking: A study in cognition and personality*. New York: Holt, Rinehart and Winston.

Kipnis, D. (1971). *Character structure and impulsiveness*. London: Academic Press.

Kohn, P. M., Cowles, M. P., & Lafreniere, K. (1987). Relationships between psychometric and experimental measures of arousability. *Personality and Individual Differences, 8*, 225–232.

Kolb, D. (1976). *Learning Style Inventory: Technical Manual*. Boston, MA: McBer.

Kozcielak, R. (1979). The role of the nervous system traits in inventive creativity. *Polish Psychological Bulletin, 10*, 225–232.

Kranzler, J. H., & Jensen, A. R. (1989). Inspection time and intelligence: A meta analysis. *Intelligence, 13*, 329–347.

Lehrl, S., & Fischer, B. (1990). A basic information psychological parameter (BIP) for the reconstruction of concepts of intelligence. *European Journal of Personality, 4*, 259–286.

Lolas, F., Camposano, S., & Etcheberrigaray, R. (1989). Augmenting/reducing and personality: A psychometric and evoked potential study in a Chilean sample. *Personality and Individual Differences, 10*, 1173–1176.

Lolas, F., Etcheberrigaray, R., Elqueta, D., & Camposano, S. (1989). Visual evoked potential reducing: A vertex feature of late components. *Research, Communications in Psychology, Psychiatry and Behavior, 14*, 173–176.

Lukas, J. H. (1987). Visual evoked potential augmenting-reducing and personality: The vertex augmenter is a sensation seeker. *Personality and Individual Differences, 8*, 385–395.

Lynn, R., & Eysenck, H. J. (1961). Tolerance for pain, extraversion and neuroticism. *Perceptual and Motor Skills, 12*, 161–162.

Mackintosh, N. J. (1986). The biology of intelligence? *British Journal of Psychology, 77*, 1–18.

MacLeod, C., Mathews, A., & Tara, P. (1986). Attention bias in emotional disorders. *Journal of Abnormal Psychology, 95*, 15–20.

Mangan, G. L. (1982). *The biology of human conduct*. Sydney: Pergamon.

Mattarazzo, J. D. (1992). Psychological testing and assessment in the 21st century. *American Psychologist, 47*, 1007–1018.

Matthews, G. (1987). Personality and multidimensional arousal: A study of two dimensions of extraversion. *Personality and Individual Differences, 8*, 9–16.

Matthews, G., & Amelang, M. (1993). Extraversion, arousal theory and performance: A study of individual differences in the EEG. *Personality and Individual Differences, 14*, 347–363.

Nettelbeck, T. (1987). Inspection time and intelligence. In P. A. Vernon (Ed.), *Speed of information processing and intelligence* (pp. 295–346). Norwood, NJ: Ablex.

Nettelbeck, T., & Rabbitt, P. (1992). Aging, cognitive performance, and mental speed. *Intelligence, 16*, 189–205.

Neubauer, A. C., Bauer, C., & Holler, G. (1992). Intelligence, attention, motivation and speed-accuracy trade-off in the Hick paradigm. *Personality and Individual Differences, 13*, 1325–1332.

O'Gorman, J. G. (1977). Individual differences in habituation of human physiological responses: A review of theory, method, and findings in the study of personality correlates in nonclinical populations. *Biological Psychology, 5*, 257–318.

O'Gorman, J. G., & Lloyd, J. E. M. (1987). Extraversion, impulsiveness, and EEG alpha activity. *Personality and Individual Differences, 8*, 169–174.

O'Gorman, J. G., & Mallise, L. R. (1984). Extraversion and the EEG: 2. A test of Gale's hypothesis. *Biological Psychology, 19*, 113–127.

Pamula, D. (1993). *Environmental attitudes, knowledge, and behavior, and their relationship with demographic variables and personality characteristics*. Unpublished honors thesis, University of Adelaide, South Australia.

Petrie, A. (1967). *Individuality in pain and suffering*. Chicago: Chicago University Press.

Pettigrew, T. F. (1958). The measurement and correlates of category width as a cognitive variable. *Journal of Personality, 26*, 532–544.

Polich, J. (1987). Task difficulty, probability, and interstimulus interval as determinants of P300 from auditory stimuli. *Electroencephalography and Clinical Neurophysiology, 68*, 311–320.

Polich, J., Ladish, C., & Bloom, F. E. (1990). P300 assessment of early Alzheimer's disease. *Electroencephalography and Clinical Neurophysiology, 77*, 179–189.

Ragot, R. (1984). Perceptual and motor space representation: An event-related potential study. *Psychophysiology, 21*, 159–170.

Raine, A., & Venables, P. H. (1988). Enhanced P3 evoked potentials and longer P3 recovery times in psychopaths. *Psychophysiology, 25*, 30–38.

Revelle, W., Humphreys, M. S., Simon, L., & Gilliland, K. (1980). The interactive effect of personality, time of day, and caffeine: A test of the arousal model. *Journal of Experimental Psychology: General, 109*, 1–31.

Robinson, D. L. (1982a). Properties of the diffuse thalamocortical system and human personality: A direct test of the Pavlovian/Eysenckian theory. *Personality and Individual Differences, 3*, 1–16.

Robinson, D. L. (1982b). Properties of the diffuse thalamocortical system, human intelligence, and differentiated vs. integrated modes of learning. *Personality and Individual Differences, 3*, 393–405.

Robinson, D. L. (1983). The diffuse thalamocortical system and Pavlovian/Eysenckian theory: A response to criticism. *Personality and Individual Differences, 4*, 535–541.

Robinson, D. L. (1985). How personality relates to intelligence test performance: Implications for a theory of intelligence, ageing research and personality assessment. *Personality and Individual Differences, 6*, 203–216.

Robinson, D. L. (1986). The Wechsler Adult Intelligence Scale and personality assessment: Towards a biologically based theory of intelligence and cognition. *Personality and Individual Differences, 7*, 153–159.

Robinson, D. L. (1989). The neurophysiological bases of high IQ. *International Journal of Neuroscience, 46*, 209–234.

Robinson, T. N., & Zahn, T. P. (1985). Psychoticism and arousal: Possible evidence for a linkage of P and psychopathy. *Personality and Individual Differences, 6*, 47–66.

Rusalov, V. M. (1989). Object-related and communicative aspects of human temperament: A new questionnaire of the structure of temperament. *Personality and Individual Differences, 10*, 817–827,

Saklofske, D. H. (1985). The relationship between Eysenck's major personality dimensions and simultaneous and sequential processing in children. *Personality and Individual Differences, 6*, 429–433.

Saklofske, D. H., & Kostura, D. D. (1990). Extraversion-introversion and intelligence. *Personality and Individual Differences, 11*, 547–551.

Shagass, C., Roemer, R. A., Straumanis, J. J., & Josiassen, R. C. (1981). Intelligence as a factor in evoked potential studies of psychopathology: I. Comparison of low and high IQ subjects. *Biological Psychiatry, 16*, 1007–1030.

Stelmack, R. M., Achorn, E., & Michaud, A. (1977). Extraversion and individual differences in auditory evoked response. *Psychophysiology, 14*, 368–374.

Stelmack, R. M., Houlihan, M., & McGarry-Roberts, P. A. (1993). Personality, reaction time, and event-related potentials. *Journal of Personality and Social Psychology, 65*, 399–409.

Stelmack, R. M., & Plouffe, L. (1983). Introversion-extraversion: the Bell-Magendie law revisited. *Personality and Individual Differences, 4*, 421–427.

Stenberg, G. (1992). Personality and the EEG: Arousal and emotional arousability. *Personality and Individual Differences, 13*, 1097–1113.

Stenberg, G., Rosén, I., & Risberg, J. (1988). Personality and augmenting/reducing in visual and auditory evoked potentials. *Personality and Individual Differences, 9*, 571–579.

Stenberg, G., Rosen, I., & Risberg, J. (1990). Attention and personality in augmenting/reducing of visual evoked potentials. *Personality and Individual Differences, 11*, 1243–1254.

Sternberg, R. J. (1985). *Beyond IQ: A triarchic theory of human intelligence*. Cambridge, England: Cambridge University Press.

Stott, D. H. (1985). Learning style or "intelligence"? *School Psychology International, 6*, 167–174.

Stough, C., Bates, T., Colrain, I., Mangan, G. L., & Pellett, O. (in press). Apparent motion, backward masking, inspection time and IQ. *Personality and Individual Differences*.

Stough, C., Mangan, G. L., Pellett, O. L., & Bates, T. C. (1993). *Jensen's reaction time–intelligence paradigm: Effects of extraversion and strategy*. Manuscript submitted for publication.

Stough, C., & Nettelbeck, T. (1989). Inspection time and IQ [Letter]. *Bulletin of the British Psychological Society, 2,* 341.

Stough, C. Nettelbeck, T., & Cooper, C. (1990). Evoked brain potentials, string length and intelligence. *Personality and Individual Differences, 11,* 401–406.

Stough, C., Nettelbeck, T., & Cooper, C. J. (1993). *The relationship between elementary information processing, personality and intelligence.* Manuscript submitted for publication.

Strelau, J. (1970). Nervous system type and extraversion-introversion: A comparison of Eysenck's theory with Pavlov's typology. *Polish Psychological Bulletin, 1,* 17–24.

Strelau, J. (1980). *Regulatory functions of temperament.* Wroclaw, Poland: Ossolineum.

Strelau, J. (1983). *Temperament-Personality-Activity.* London: Academic Press.

Strelau, J. (1987). Personality dimensions based on arousal theories: Search for integration. In J. Strelau & H. J. Eysenck (Eds.), *Personality dimensions and arousal* (pp. 269–286). London: Plenum.

Teplov, B. M. (1956). Problems in the study of general types of higher nervous activity in man and animals. In B. M. Teplov (Ed.), *Typological features of higher nervous activity in man* (Vol. 1). Moscow: Academy of Pedagogical Sciences.

Vernon, P. A. (1990). The use of biological measures to estimate behavioral intelligence. *Educational Psychologist, 25,* 293–304.

Vickers, D., Nettelbeck, T., & Willson, R. J. (1972). Perceptual indices of performance: the measurement of "inspection time" in the visual system. *Perception, 1,* 263–295.

Vickers, D., & Smith, P. (1985). *The rationale for the inspection time index.* Paper presented at meeting of the International Society for the Study of Individual Differences, Saint Feliu de Guixols, Catalonia, Spain.

Vogel, F., Kruger, J., Schalt, E., Schnobel, R., & Hassling, L. (1987). No consistent relationships between oscillations and latencies of visual and auditory evoked potentials and measures of mental performance. *Human Neurobiology, 6,* 173–182.

Warrington, E. K., James, M., & Maciejewski, C. (1986). The WAIS as a lateralizing and localizing diagnostic instrument: A study of 656 patients with unilateral cerebral lesions. *Neuropsychology, 24,* 223–239.

Weiss, V. (1989). From short-term memory capacity toward the EEG resonance code. *Personality and Individual Differences, 10,* 501–508.

Welford, A. T. (ed.). (1980). *Reaction times.* London: Academic Press.

Welford, A. T. (1986). Longstreth versus Jensen and Vernon on reaction time and IQ: An outsider's view. *Intelligence, 10,* 193–195.

Whetton, D., & Cameron, K. (1984). *Development Management Skills.* London: Scott, Foreman.

Whipple, S. C., Parker, E. S., & Noble, E. P. (1988). An atypical neurocognitive profile in alcoholic fathers and their sons. *Journal of Studies on Alcohol, 49,* 240–244.

White, P. O. (1973). Individual differences in speed, accuracy and persistence: A mathematical model for problem solving. In H. J. Eysenck (Ed.), *The measurement of intelligence.* Lancaster, England: Medical and Technical Press.

Zhang, Y., Caryl, P. G., & Deary, I. J. (1989). Evoked potentials, inspection time and intelligence. *Personality and Individual Differences, 10,* 1079–1094.

Zuckerman, M. (1984). Sensation seeking: A comparative approach to a human trait. *Behavioral and Brain Sciences, 7,* 413–471.

Zuckerman, M. (1990). The psychophysiology of sensation seeking. *Journal of Personality, 58,* 313–345.

17

Event-Related Potentials, Personality, and Intelligence

Concepts, Issues, and Evidence

Robert M. Stelmack and Michael Houlihan

Event-related potentials (ERPs) are records of the electrocortical activity that is evoked by physical stimuli and modulated by psychological processes such as attention, memory, and cognition. Since the mid-1960s, ERP methods have been used to explore the nature of individual differences in both personality and intelligence; often, the same ERP measures and experimental procedures were applied in these inquiries. In this chapter we examine the convergences and distinctions in the application of ERP methods to the study of personality and intelligence. The rationale and strategies guiding the research are briefly noted. In order to highlight the understanding provided by ERP methods, the functional significance of the ERP components relevant to personality and intelligence research is outlined. The ERP components and paradigms that have been most successful in demonstrating consistent or promising findings are illustrated, and the insights that this work offers are discussed.

Robert M. Stelmack and Michael Houlihan • School of Psychology, University of Ottawa, Ottawa, Ontario K1N 6N5 Canada.

International Handbook of Personality and Intelligence, edited by Donald H. Saklofske and Moshe Zeidner. Plenum Press, New York, 1995.

CONSTRUCTS AND MEASURES

There has been significant progress toward a consensus for a descriptive structure of mental ability and personality using psychometric methods. For intelligence, there is a strong case for a unitary structure composed of two major factors—fluid and crystallized intelligence—that converge in a substantial general factor (Brody, 1992; Carroll, 1993; Kline, 1991). For personality, there is broad agreement that lengthy lists of trait terms can be reliably subsumed to a small number of fundamental factors, notably sociability (also referred to as extraversion or positive affect) and emotional instability (neuroticism, anxiety, or negative affect; Costa, McCrae, & Dye, 1991; Eysenck & Eysenck, 1975). The identity of other fundamental personality factors is currently debated. Among the factors that have been proposed are psychoticism (Eysenck, 1992); impulsive unsocialized sensation-seeking (Zuckerman, 1989); and openness to experience, conscientiousness, and agreeableness (Costa & McCrae, 1992). Overall, this work constitutes an important step toward a comprehensive framework of descriptive constructs, which is a prerequisite for exploring the nature and determinants of variation in personality and intelligence.

The validity of intelligence and personality tests

has been established in educational, occupational, and mental health institutions. These descriptive measures are successfully exploited in academic and personnel selection and in predicting social and psychiatric behavior. The success in describing personality and intelligence, however, has not been matched in explaining the bases of the variation that is described. Notable exceptions here are the remarkable demonstrations of the heritability of intelligence and personality (Bouchard, Lykken, McGue, Segal, & Tellegen, 1990; Loehlin, 1989). This work suggests that constitutional factors, under the influence of genetic mechanisms, can contribute substantially to variation in both personality and intelligence. The nature of these constitutional factors has not been explicated, though some good progress has been achieved.

ERP recording procedures are among several methods used to provide measures of explanatory constructs for personality and intelligence. These constructs are drawn from various areas of inquiry into the nature of psychological processes, notably perception, motivation, learning, and cognition. Habituation, sensitization, arousal, inhibition, short-term memory, and information-processing speed are just a few examples of explanatory constructs that are exploited in research on intelligence and personality. It is often assumed that these constructs can be referred to biological substrates, but the references are not always explicit. ERP measures have been used to index variation in a broad range of these constructs.

In general, the explanatory constructs proposed to account for variation in personality are better established than they are for intelligence. In personality research, for example, the arousal construct has been extensively explored (Revelle & Anderson, 1992); it assumes a continuum of neuropsychological activation that has an inverted-U relationship with performance (Malmo, 1959). The validity of this construct has been endorsed in animal and human studies that recorded both behavioral and physiological (see Malmo, 1975) or psychophysiological measures (Smith, 1983). Moreover, there has been substantial progress in articulating the physiological systems that may compose arousal (Le Moal & Simon, 1991; Vanderwolf & Robinson, 1981). An inverted-U relation of performance with increasing arousal has been observed for both psychophysical and cognitive dimensions (Revelle, Anderson, & Humphreys, 1987), although consensus has not been achieved in this work (Neiss, 1988). In intelligence research, an important focus of interest is the construct of neural efficiency (Jensen & Munro, 1979), but it has not been investigated to the same extent as arousal. Evidence linking variation in personality or intelligence to discrete neural systems (e.g., sensory or motor processes) is extant, but direct evidence connecting it to specific neural mechanisms is limited. In addition to information concerning the functions of a construct, ERP measures provide some insight into the physiological substrates of individual differences. This information ranges from the general to the specific.

BASIC ERP CONCEPTS

Event-related potentials are derived by averaging ongoing EEG activity that is time-locked to specific stimulus events. It is assumed that random EEG activity emanating from neural sites not engaged in the repeated presentation of the stimulus is canceled out in the averaging; what remains is a signature of the neural activity that occurred during the processing of the stimulus. This signature is a result of the initial activation of peripheral nerves and nuclei in the brainstem and of the subsequent sequence of neural activity along the way to cortical projection pathways. Procedures are developed for examining segments of the time course of this activity in terms of brainstem, middle, and later ERP waveform components. The functional significance of these components has been explored within a wide variety of experimental paradigms. The neural generators of the early brainstem components are quite clearly determined, whereas the neural generators of the later components are not resolved.

ERPs and the Brain

Can ERPs provide biological measures of personality and intelligence that will replace conventional psychometric measures? This question has been raised, often dismissively, in discussions of the biological bases of individual differences, especially with respect to intelligence (Sternberg, 1991). The prospect of a biological measure of intelligence using ERP measures has been cast as a questionable "search for the holy grail"—that is, for a reliable biological index that can provide a culture-fair measure of intelligence (Brody, 1992). Indeed, in the early 1970s there was a failed attempt to market an ERP system that assessed intelligence on such a claim. In the context previously described, intelligence and personality constructs such as extraversion and neuroticism are descriptive factors that are measured by psychometric scales. ERP indices, in contrast, are measures of the constructs and processes used to explain variation in intelligence and personality. From this perspective, ERPs cannot substitute for psychometric measures any more than other correlates of intelligence (e.g., height or brain size) or personality (e.g., pain threshold or skin conductance) that are used as indices of explanatory constructs.

ERP recording techniques provide one of only a few ways to explore the relation of psychological processes (e.g., sensation, attention, decision making, and language) to neural activity in intact normal human brains. At the present time, research linking ERPs influenced by these processes to individual differences in intelligence and personality is clearly in the exploratory stage. Moreover, the relation of neural activity and ERPs is limited. The increases in electric potential that are detected by scalp electrodes, amplified and averaged in the ERP waveform, result from the firing of a large number of neurons in synchrony. Currently it is thought that ERPs emanate mainly from postsynaptic potentials, because the latter have a slower time course and are more likely to summate than are presynaptic potentials. For this summation to occur, it is necessary for the neurons to be organized in the same orientation, as in the cortical layers. From this perspective, it is clear that ERPs are an incomplete reflection of the electrical activity of the brain. Nevertheless, some reliable relations between ERP wave components and brain functions have been established. These relations have been examined with respect to variation in both personality and intelligence.

Sensory and Cognitive ERPs

It is useful to distinguish ERPs that are determined by physical stimulus characteristics from those that are determined by intrinsic psychophysiological processes. ERP waves that are primarily influenced by stimulus intensity, acoustic frequency, or wavelength are termed *sensory* or *exogenous* ERP waveform components. When evoked potential technology was first developed, it was the exogenous components that were the first to be explored; they were also the first to be applied to personality and intelligence research questions. ERP waveforms that develop while the subject is actively engaged in tasks that require attending, discriminating, naming, or understanding are referred to as *cognitive* or *endogenous* components. These components, which are relatively independent of the physical characteristics of the stimulus, have been recently used in research on personality and intelligence.

ERPs that develop at about 100 to 200 ms following repetitive visual, auditory, or somatosensory stimulation are sensory ERP components generated by primary sensory cortex and association areas. The morphology of these waveforms varies according to the modality of stimulation and the scalp location of the recording electrode. ERPs that are recorded from the midline electrode placement (vertex), however, are similar for visual, auditory, and somatosensory stimulation. Increases in the amplitude and decreases in the latency of this vertex response (labeled N1 and P2, respectfully) are affected by such factors as increases in stimulus intensity and slower stimulus presentation rates. Under some conditions, increases in attention and arousal also increase N1-P2 amplitude. A majority of research on personality and intelligence, especially the earlier work, has examined these sensory ERPs in response to series of simple light flashes or tones under conditions where attention or arousal demands are minimal.

PERSONALITY AND SENSORY ERPs

Several studies have used ERP methods to examine the hypothesis that introverts are characterized by higher levels of cortical arousal than extraverts (Eysenck, 1967). In general this ERP work complements research using psychophysical methods (Kohn, 1987; Stelmack & Campbell, 1974) and autonomic measures of arousal (Smith, 1983; Stelmack & Geen, 1992), showing that introverts exhibit greater reactivity to simple auditory and visual stimulation than extraverts. An enhanced ERP amplitude to simple tones for introverts has been observed with some consistency at fronto-central electrode placements, notably when the stimuli are of moderate intensity (80 dB SPL), of lower frequency (.5 KHz) and presented in mixed serial orders (Bruneau, Roux, Perse, & Lelord, 1984; Stelmack, Achorn, & Michaud, 1977; Stelmack & Michaud-Achorn, 1985). Similar effects under similar conditions have been observed with visual stimuli (Stenberg, Rosen, & Risberg, 1988). Also in the auditory modality, ERP amplitude at posterior left hemisphere sites was greater for introverts than extraverts to verbal stimuli (De Pascalis & Montirosso, 1988). The greater ERP amplitude for introverts than for extraverts appears pronounced for the P200 component at the vertex electrode site (Cz), and this effect is observed under both attend and ignore conditions (Stelmack & Michaud-Achorn, 1985; Stenberg, Rosen, & Risberg, 1990). Overall, this is an intensity effect that is indicative of the introverts' greater sensitivity to physical stimulation of moderate intensity and that is consistent with the arousal construct hypothesis. The larger ERP amplitude to auditory stimulation for introverts as compared to extraverts is illustrated in Figure 1.

There are no reports of differences in ERPs to simple physical stimulation for subjects who differ in degree of neuroticism/anxiety or psychoticism. Some reliable effects have been observed for the Sensation-Seeking Scale, however, especially the Social Disinhibition Scale, which has a modest correlation with extraversion (Zuckerman, 1979). High disinhibition has been associated with ERP augmenting (i.e., an increase in ERP amplitude with increasing stimulus intensity), whereas subjects with low disinhibition tend to exhibit a reducing effect (characterized by a constant or decreasing ERP amplitude with more intense stimulation). The augmenting-reducing phenomenon has been the subject of considerable controversy, as different methods of defining the effect and different electrode placements have resulted in inconsistent and contradictory data (e.g., Connolly & Gruzelier, 1982; Raine, Mitchell, & Venables, 1981). Nevertheless, the association of greater ERP augmenting with higher sensation-seeking scores has been reported with some consistency for both auditory (Como, Simons, & Zuckerman, 1984; Hegerl, Prochno, Ulrich, & Muller-Oelinghausen, 1989; Mullins & Lukas, 1984; Orlebeke, Kok, & Zeillemaker, 1989) and visual modalities (Buchsbaum, 1971; Lukas, 1987; von Knorring & Perris, 1981; Zuckerman, Murtagh, & Siegel, 1974). Overall, this ERP augmenting effect can be viewed in terms of greater tolerance (less sensitivity) to higher-intensity stimulation on the part of high sensation-seeking subjects, and it is consistent with greater pain tolerance, less hypochondriasis, and higher absolute sensory thresholds that have been reported for high sensation-seeking subjects (Goldman, Kohn, & Hunt, 1983; Kohn, Hunt, & Hoffman, 1982).

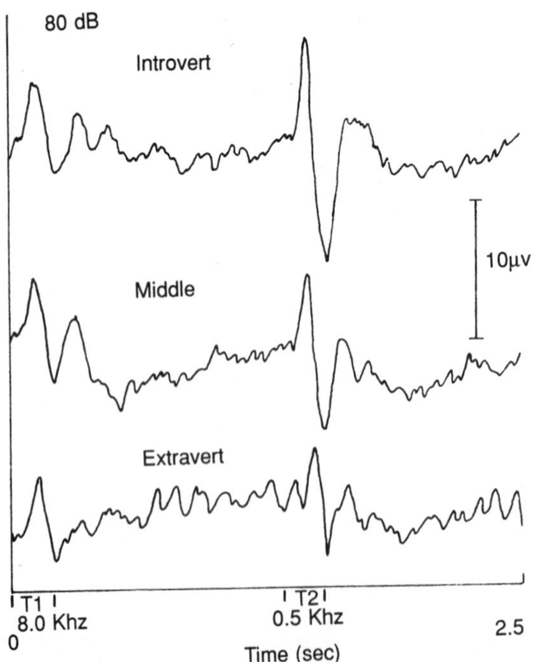

Figure 1. Introverts display larger N1-P2 amplitude than extraverts to 80dB tones of low frequency (.5KHz) but not high frequency (8.0KHz; Stelmack, Achorn, & Michaud, 1977).

INTELLIGENCE AND SENSORY ERPs

A negative correlation between intelligence and the latency of visual evoked potentials was first reported by Chalke and Ertl in 1965 and subsequently in a series of experiments at the University of Ottawa by this group (Ertl, 1968; Ertl & Schafer, 1969). In the initial work, the waveforms were derived using a zero-crossing method: The number of EEG deflections that crossed a baseline (or "zero") within 12 ms intervals were counted during a .5 sec analysis period for a series of 120 light flashes. An *evoked potential* to a stimulus was indicated when the zero-crossing count within an interval exceeded the number counted during intervals in which no stimuli were presented. This frequency method contrasts with conventional ERP techniques, which average absolute EEG voltage differences. The latency to the maximum modal deflections is, at best, a tentative approximation of the latency to maximum peak amplitude derived from EEG averaging following stimulation. Ertl also used a bipolar electrode montage with placements at two active sites. These waveform configurations differ markedly from records that are obtained using monopolar electrode placements, where an electrode is sited on the scalp at an active neural site that is referenced to a relatively inactive site (e.g., the earlobe). Among the few published studies that followed Ertl's procedure for electrode placement, there were two endorsements (Gucker, 1973; Shucard & Horn, 1972) and, notably, an exacting large-scale replication attempt that was unsuccessful (Davis, 1971).

Intelligence and ERP Latency

The challenge of predicting intelligence from ERP methods was taken up by many investigators who adapted the initial stimulus presentation procedures and used conventional voltage averaging techniques and monopolar electrode montages. The outcomes of studies exploring the relation between intelligence measures and the latency of an early visual ERP (prior to P200) are mixed. There are reports of negative associations (Osaka & Osaka, 1980; Rhodes, Dustman, & Beck, 1969), positive associations (Callaway, 1975; Callaway & Halliday, 1973; Vogel, Kruger, Schalt, Schnobel, & Hassling, 1987) and no significant associations (Engel & Henderson, 1973; Rust, 1975). The outcomes of a dozen studies examining the relation of intelligence and the latency of the P200 wave for brief visual and/or auditory stimuli are unequivocal; in nonclinical samples of healthy adults, there is no significant association between the two (Barnet & Lodge, 1967; Barrett & Eysenck, 1992; Callaway, 1975; Engel & Fay, 1972; Haier, Robinson, Braden, & Williams, 1983).

Intelligence and ERP Amplitude

Several authors reported that higher intelligence is associated with enhanced ERP amplitudes. These effects were observed for earlier waves (P100 and P200), primarily with visual stimulation (Haier et al., 1983; Josiassen, Shagass, Roemer, & Slepner, 1988; Osaka & Osaka, 1980; Rhodes et al., 1969; Shagass, Roemer, & Straumanis, 1981). In only one case was this effect observed with auditory stimulation (Callaway & Halliday, 1973). There are also several notable failures to observe any significant association between intelligence and ERP amplitude (Barrett & Eysenck, 1992; Callaway, 1975; Engel & Fay, 1972; Engel & Henderson, 1973; Robinson, Haier, Braden, & Krengel, 1984; Rust, 1975; Vogel et al., 1987).

Intelligence and the String Measure

A composite measure of ERP amplitude called the string measure was also applied in a number of studies. With this method, the full excursion of positive and negative waves are computed across the full EEG analysis period. The method was first applied by Hendrickson and Hendrickson (1980) to capture the greater complexity of waveforms for higher-intelligence subjects that were apparent in the Ertl and Schafer (1969) illustrations. Because the waveforms were selected to illustrate the effects reported, the correlations of the string measure with intelligence scores on these data ($r = .77$) were clearly inflated. In subsequent studies (Blinkhorn & Hendrickson, 1982; Hendrickson & Hendrickson, 1980), though, the string measure was applied to auditory ERPs with similarly outstanding results. An association between greater string length and higher intelligence was also endorsed in several independent investigations (Gilbert, Johnson, Gilbert, & McColloch, 1991; Haier et al., 1983; Rhodes et al., 1969; Stough, Nettelbeck, & Cooper, 1990). Failures to observe the effect (Bates & Eysenck, 1993; Shagass et al., 1981) and results in the opposite direction (Barrett & Eysenck, 1992) were also reported.

A detailed assessment of the string measure and the technical recording requirements proscribed by Hendrickson and Hendrickson (1980) was published by Barrett and Eysenck (1992). The lack of consistency across studies underscores the need to be sensitive to factors that are likely to influence the morphology of the waveform, especially filter settings, eye movements or other muscle artifacts, and instructions to subjects that could induce attention or arousal effects. The claim that the string measure captures the greater complexity of the ERP waveform is dubious. The morphology of the auditory ERP to tones, especially, is a rather simple form—N1, P2, N2—that is very consistent across subjects. From this perspective, the string measure would not seem to hold any particular advantage over component amplitude measures.

Intelligence and Neural Adaptability

A composite measure of ERP amplitude termed the neural adaptability (NA) index also showed some promise as a correlate of intelligence (Schafer & Marcus, 1973). The NA index is based on the assumption that higher-ability subjects are more adaptive (and invest greater neural energy) in response to novel stimulation and are more efficient in processing expected stimulation (e.g., habituate more readily) than lower-ability subjects. In this view, it was argued that higher-ability subjects should exhibit larger-amplitude ERPs to temporally unpredictable stimuli and smaller-amplitude ERPs to expected stimuli than lower-ability subjects.

In a series of experiments, temporal expectancy

was varied by presenting series of auditory stimuli (60 dB SL) with random, constant, and subject-controlled interstimulus intervals (ISI; Jensen, Schafer, & Crinella, 1981; Schafer, 1982; Schafer & Marcus, 1973). The NA index was calculated by determining the difference in integrated amplitude (disregarding the sign) across a 500 ms analysis period between random and subject-controlled auditory ERPs, then dividing this value by the average integrated amplitude across the three conditions. In the first report, mentally retarded subjects obtained smaller NA scores than technicians, who in turn had smaller NA scores than scientists with doctoral degrees (Schafer & Marcus, 1973). A correlation of 0.31 between NA and a measure of general intelligence in a sample of mentally retarded subjects was also reported (Jensen et al., 1981). Remarkably high correlations ($r = .66$) between an NA index and intelligence scores were also observed with a relatively large sample of bright normal adults ($n = 74$) for whom the range of intelligence scores was quite restricted (Schafer, 1982). In this case, NA was defined as the amplitude to tones with ISIs previously determined by the subject and divided by the average across all conditions. Average amplitudes and difference scores were not presented in any of the reports; from the information available, higher-ability subjects exhibited larger amplitude ERPs than lower-ability subjects to the stimuli presented in irregular serial order. The determination of the NA index for a subject is shown in Figure 2.

The NA index is a novel transformation of ERP response amplitude. Between-subject variability due to individual differences in the effect of intensity on response amplitude is reduced by expressing responses (or response differences) as a ratio of average response amplitude across all conditions. This trans-

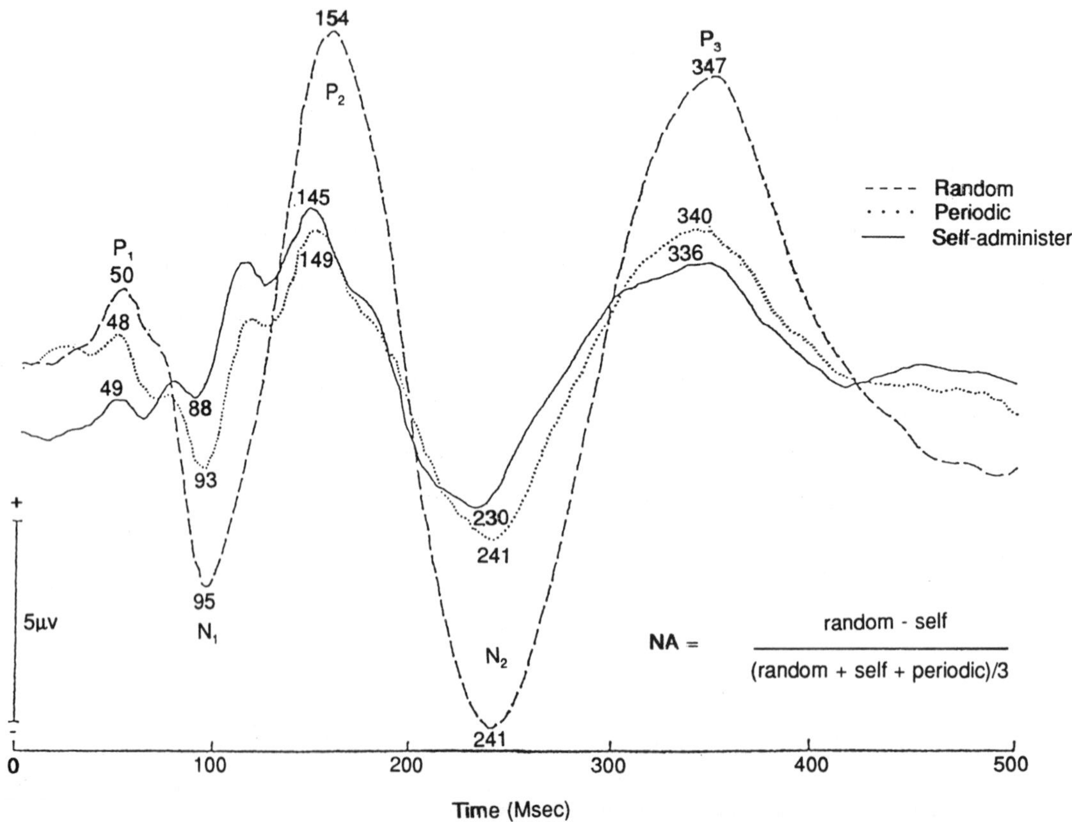

Figure 2. The neural adaptability index is illustrated with auditory event-related potential waveforms obtained from one subject during a random stimulus presentation condition, periodic stimulus presentation condition, and a self-initiated presentation condition (Schafer & Marcus, 1973).

formation shifts the emphasis of the ERP work from individual differences in absolute sensory responses to differential responding between conditions. At the present time, there are no independent replications of this work (Callaway, 1975).

OVERVIEW OF PERSONALITY, INTELLIGENCE, AND SENSORY ERPs

Overall, neither personality nor intelligence measures have shown any consistent relation to the latency of ERP waves that are derived from simple, repetitive visual or auditory stimulation. The personality dimensions of extraversion and sensation-seeking tend to be inversely related to ERP amplitude, while intelligence measures tend to be directly related. There appears to be less consistency, or greater confusion, in the association of ERP amplitude with intelligence than with personality. The string measure that has claimed remarkable associations with intelligence has received considerable scourging on technical grounds. The idiosyncrasy to intelligence research of the string measure as an ERP scoring procedure also contributes to the difficulty of evaluating the effect. The functional significance of the string measure has not been studied, and it is not used in other ERP applications; therefore the validity of the construct (neural efficiency) indexed by the string measure is not known.

Because of the passive nature of the tasks, the observed variation of ERP amplitude with personality and intelligence can be understood as an intensity effect with introverts, low sensation-seekers, and higher-ability subjects tending to respond as if the stimulus was more intense than for extraverts, high sensation-seekers, and lower-ability subjects. For the personality dimensions, such intensity effects are consistent with greater absolute sensory sensitivity, lower noise and pain thresholds, and greater autonomic nervous system responses to moderate-intensity stimuli that have been consistently observed for introverts and low sensation-seekers, as previously noted. These response dispositions are also consistent with the greater aversions to noise and excessive social stimulation, as well as with the ease of conditioning to aversive stimulation, that are characteristic of introverted behavior. For intelligence, similar corroboration with independent measures of variation in response to sensory stimulation (e.g., absolute thresholds, pain thresholds) or with behavioral characteristics (e.g., aversion to noise) is not extant.

In this respect, it is notable that the association, reported by Spearman and others, of intelligence and performance on simple sensory tasks invariably refers to tasks that require detecting relations between stimuli rather than merely reacting to stimulation. For Spearman, it is this grasping of relations that defines the general ability factor. The neural adaptability index described by Schafer minimizes intensity effects and to some extent involves detecting relations between stimuli. In the case of the neural adaptability index, it is claimed that the ERP amplitude measure (mainly a composite of N100 and P300) stems from attention processes that develop in unexpected (or random) sequences of stimulation. The individual variation in the apprehension of novel stimulation (detecting the relation between present and previous stimulation) can also be explored, perhaps more effectively, in several paradigms that were used to study the P300 ERP component.

COGNITIVE EVENT-RELATED POTENTIALS: THE P300 COMPONENT

A positive ERP wave that develops maximum peak latency at about 300 ms (P300) in simple stimulus discrimination tasks has proved to be a reliable index of endogenous cognitive activity. When the subject is actively engaged in detection or decision tasks, the amplitude and latency of the P300 wave are affected by such factors as the novelty, salience, or discriminability of the stimulus events. For example, in an extensively exploited procedure named the oddball paradigm, the P300 wave is elicited by a target stimulus that occurs infrequently among a series of standard stimuli. The amplitude of the P300 wave varies inversely with the sequential or temporal probability of occurrence of the target stimulus (Fitzgerald & Picton, 1981; Friedman, Hakerem, Sutton & Fleiss, 1973). When the difficulty of discriminating the target from the standard stimulus is increased, the amplitude of the P300 response decreases, and the latency of the response increases. Again, these effects on the P300 wave are shown to be largely the result of endogenous cognitive processes (e.g., attention and decision-making) that are independent of the effect of physical stimulation. Stimulus intensity, however, can contribute to the magnitude of P300 amplitude, with high-intensity target stimuli evoking larger amplitude responses than lower-intensity stimuli (Roth, Dorato, & Kopell, 1984).

On elementary cognitive tasks, P300 amplitude and latency vary systematically with task difficulty. In the Sternberg memory paradigm (S. Sternberg, 1969), P300 latency to the target stimulus increases and amplitude decreases when stimulus set size is increased (Gomer, Spicuzza, & O'Donnell, 1976; Ford, Roth, Mohs, Hopkins, & Kopell, 1979). P300 latency corresponds to reaction time on simple and choice reaction time tasks, particularly when accuracy instructions are assumed or emphasized (see Duncan-Johnson, & Donchin, 1982). It is notable, however, that speed and accuracy instructions have a marked effect on reaction time but a minimal effect on P300 latency. This disparity suggests that the variation of P300 latency with task difficulty is a consequence of stimulus evaluation that is independent of factors that influence response production (Kutas, McCarthy, & Donchin, 1977). Overall, there is a good deal of evidence that P300 latency and reaction time, although positively correlated on some tasks and under some conditions, are largely independent (Ragot & Renault, 19891; Ragot, 1984; Warren & Marsh, 1979). P300 amplitude and latency measures have been used extensively to explore attention, memory, and cognition. There are initial efforts to extend this work to examine individual variation in personality and intelligence.

INTELLIGENCE AND P300

In general, it is assumed that higher-ability subjects perform discriminations faster and with less difficulty than lower-ability subjects. Therefore it is expected that the former will exhibit faster P300 peak latency and larger maximum peak amplitude than the latter during the performance of simple discrimination tasks. At present, research that has examined individual differences in intelligence and variation in the P300 component falls into two categories. In the first case, the covariation is determined between ability measures and values for P300 latency and amplitude obtained during an auditory oddball task. In the second case, P300 values and reaction time measures are obtained concurrently during performance of elementary cognitive tasks that have been shown to covary with psychometric intelligence. The covariation is then determined for ability scores with both reaction time and P300 measures. An advantage of this latter approach is that the stimulus conditions from which the ERPs are derived can be shown, with behavioral measures concurrently recorded, to be directly relevant to intelligence.

Intelligence and P300 Latency with the Oddball Paradigm

A negative relation between ability measures and P300 latency to the infrequently occurring target stimulus in the auditory oddball paradigm has been reported by several investigators. This effect was observed both during passive conditions where the subject was instructed to ignore the stimuli, and active conditions where the subject was instructed to count the target stimuli (O'Donnell, Friedman, Swearer, & Drachman, 1992). Moreover, this relation was obtained for both dementia patients (primarily with Alzheimer's syndrome) and normal control subjects (O'Donnell et al., 1992). For the passive condition, P300 latency was negatively correlated to factors of Verbal Learning ($r = -.32$) and Verbal Fluency ($r = -.39$). For the counting condition, P300 latency was negatively correlated with a factor that they identified as intelligence, that appears to consist of items describing crystallized intelligence ($r = -.44$). In this active condition, P300 latency was also negatively correlated with a factor labeled Concentration ($r = -.33$). This Concentration factor had major loadings on digit-span and mental control tests.

In both of the reports by O'Donnell et al., all significant correlations between P300 latency and measures of intelligence were negative. In a recent study with a sample of HIV-positive drug users, P300 latency was also negatively correlated with intelligence (Egan, Chiswick, Brettle, & Goodwin, in press). These negative correlations with several different broad factors of cognitive ability suggest that P300 latency is related to a general factor of intelligence.

Faster P300 latency for the target stimulus in the auditory oddball paradigm was also associated with better performance on a digit-span task (Howard & Polich, 1985; Ladish & Polich, 1989; Polich, Ladish, & Burns, 1990), a global deterioration scale (Polich, Ehlers, Otis, Mandell, & Bloom, 1986) and self-reported grade-point average, but not Raven's matrices (Polich & Martin, 1992). Overall, these reports provide quite consistent evidence that mental ability is inversely related to P300 latency for the target stimulus on the oddball discrimination task. Perhaps because of the low difficulty level in these oddball discriminations, none of these studies report significant correlations between P300 amplitude and intelligence.

Intelligence and P300 Latency during Elementary Cognitive Tasks

There is a considerable body of work demonstrating a moderate inverse relation between intelligence and reaction time on a variety of cognitive tasks that assess speed of decision making and speed of retrieval from short- and long-term memory (Jensen, 1987; Vernon, 1983). In some recent research, the P300 component has been recorded concurrently with reaction time measures during the performance of some of these simple decision tasks. Specifically, ERPs were recorded during the performance of an auditory Sternberg memory scanning task (Pelosi et al., 1992a, b). Nineteen subjects were required to determine whether a single digit had been presented in a preceding set of 1 to 5 digits. The amplitude of a late positive wave (approximately 400 ms) decreased with increasing set size, but there was a good deal of individual variability in the morphology of the positive waves across the different set sizes. A negative correlation between intelligence and a P400 amplitude ratio of difficult to easy memory tasks was reported (i.e., the greater the amplitude difference between the responses to easy and more difficult tasks, the higher the ability scores).

In general, the waveforms for higher-ability subjects exhibited significantly smaller positive amplitude to the probe digit than did those for lower-ability subjects. These results cannot be explained in terms of individual differences in the effects of task difficulty on P300 amplitude. There is an inverse relation of P300 amplitude and task difficulty with smaller amplitude for the more difficult set size. One would expect the task to be more difficult for lower-ability subjects, and thus their P300 amplitude would be smaller than for higher-ability subjects—effects opposite to those observed here. The authors speculate that the waveforms of higher-ability subjects may be modulated by a prolonged negative wave that begins early in the processing of the target stimulus and that may be related to selective attention.

The relation between P300 and intelligence was examined by McGarry-Roberts, Stelmack, and Campbell (1992), who recorded ERPs from 30 subjects during the performance of six cognitive tasks. The tasks included simple reaction time, choice reaction time, physical similarity of words, category matching, Sternberg memory scanning, and synonym-antonym discrimination. With aggregate measures for intelligence and for P300 latency (factor scores from the first unrotated factor), general intelligence was inversely related to general P300 latency to the target stimulus. All of the correlations between full-scale intelligence on the Multiple Aptitude Battery (Jackson, 1984) and both P300 latency and amplitude during the six tasks were negative, but statistically significant effects for individual tasks were only observed with P300 latency in the category matching and digit memory task and with P300 amplitude in the synonym-antonym task.

Overall, this work clearly indicated that the ERP measures were sensitive to differences in degree of difficulty between the tasks. As in the work with the oddball paradigm, higher-ability subjects tended to exhibit faster P300 latency to the target stimuli than lower-ability subjects. Both reaction time and P300 amplitude measures for these tasks were negatively (but weakly) related to intelligence; the relation between P300 latency and reaction time was negligible. These results provide some evidence that P300 latency assesses a speed-of-stimulus-evaluation component of decision-making that is independent of response production and that varies inversely with general intelligence. Waveforms illustrating the increase in P300 latency with increasing task difficulty and the faster P300 latency for higher- relative to lower-ability subjects are shown in Figure 3.

PERSONALITY AND P300

Several authors have explored individual differences in extraversion using the auditory oddball paradigm. Larger P300 amplitude responses to the target stimulus for introverts as compared to extraverts is a result that is consistently reported (Daruna, Karrer, & Rosen, 1985; Polich & Martin, 1992; Pritchard, 1989; Wilson & Languis, 1990). Similarly, a smaller decrease in P300 amplitude was observed for introverts relative to extraverts in response to the infrequent stimuli across trial blocks (Ditraglia & Polich, 1991); opposite results, however, were indicated in a subsequent report (Cahill & Polich, 1992). In general, these effects are understood in terms of the greater amount of attentional resources that introverts invest in the processing of these simple target stimuli. The influence of individual differences in sensitivity to stimula-

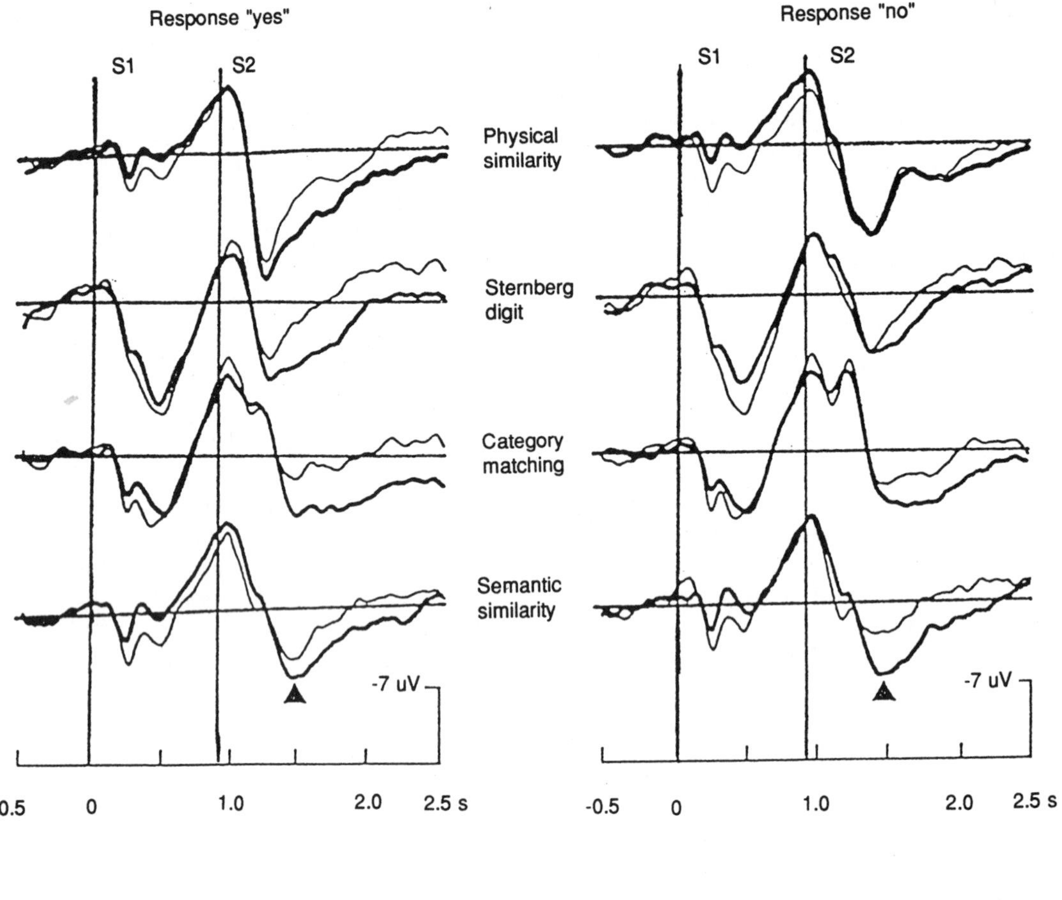

Figure 3. The event-related potential waveforms were obtained during the performance of elementary cognitive tasks, and they are arranged from top to bottom in order of increasing task difficulty. P300 latency increases and the amplitude decreases with increasing task difficulty. In general, higher-ability subjects exhibit faster P300 latency than lower-ability subjects (McGarry-Roberts, Stelmack, & Campbell, 1992).

tion, though, cannot be discounted entirely. In some of this work, for example, introverts also appeared to exhibit larger amplitude responses than extraverts to the standard stimuli (Daruna et al., 1985). It is also noteworthy that none of these studies observed correlations between extraversion and P300 latency. The greater P300 amplitude effect for introverts as compared to extraverts is illustrated in Figure 4.

A negative relation between P300 latency and neuroticism was observed by Pritchard (1989) in a simple oddball paradigm for a small sample of male subjects, but not for females. In studies using simple cognitive tasks, a negative relation between P300 latency and neuroticism scores has also been reported. In a choice reaction time task, subjects classified as anxiety neurotic with DSM-III criteria displayed faster P300 latency than control subjects who were matched for extraversion (Plooij-van Gorsel, 1981). In our own work, higher neuroticism scores were consistently associated with faster P300 latency (and with slower reaction time) for both "yes" and "no" response categories during the performance of the six cognitive tasks previously listed (Stelmack, Houlihan, & McGarry-Roberts, 1993). In this study, higher psychoticism scores were associated with smaller P300 amplitude. Introverts displayed faster P300 latency (and slower reaction time) than extraverts in a reaction time task that manipulated stimulus and response position (Brebner, 1990); however, neuroticism scores were not reported.

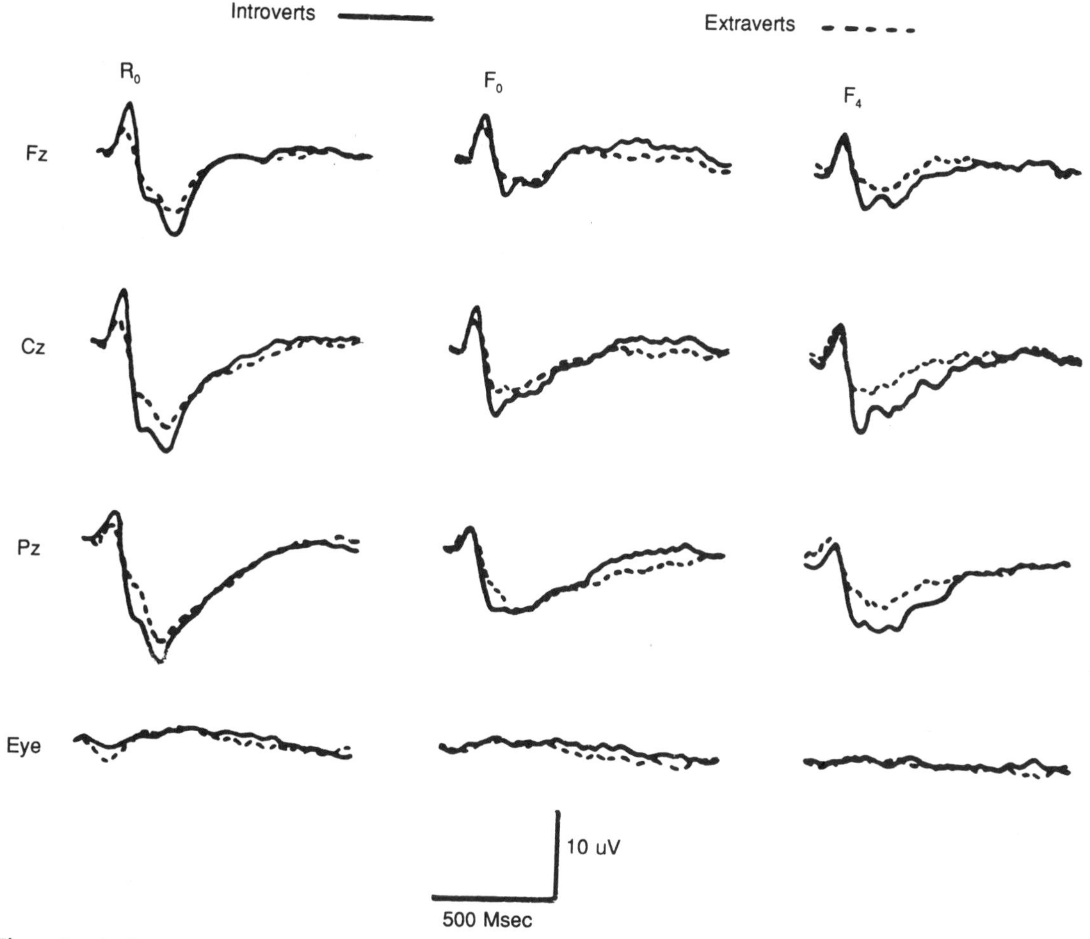

Figure 4. Auditory event-related potentials to rare tones (R_0), frequent tones immediately following rare tones (F_0), and frequent tones immediately preceding rare tones (F_4) that were recorded during an oddball task. Introverts display larger P300 amplitude than extraverts (Daruna, Karrer, & Rosen, 1985).

OVERVIEW OF INTELLIGENCE, PERSONALITY, AND P300

At this time, there is a clear and promising pattern of results in these early reports that examined the relation of P300 latency and amplitude to variation in intelligence and personality using the oddball paradigm. P300 latency to the target stimulus appears to be inversely related to intelligence measures, whereas P300 amplitude tends to be inversely related to extraversion. The strength of the association of faster P300 latency with higher intelligence seems somewhat greater when the target stimuli are of moderate (85 dB SPL) rather than lower intensity (60 dB). In order to consolidate this effect in future work, it will be important to take account of several subject factors that influence P300 latency, especially age and gender. The P300 ERP develops when the discrimination of a simple auditory target is required; the latency to maximum P300 peak amplitude is widely regarded as a measure of speed of stimulus evaluation that is relatively independent of response production processes. This work provides new evidence that refers individual differences in intelligence to the speed with which elementary sensory discriminations proceed; such findings complement behavioral research using reaction time measures.

In contrast to the association of P300 latency and intelligence, it is the P300 amplitude measure that shows a consistent association with personality (specifically, the extraversion dimension) when the oddball paradigm is used. In general, this work indicates smaller P300 amplitude (less attentional demand or lower arousal) for extraverts than for introverts, and the effect is consistent with similar results reported for orienting responses to novel stimulation using autonomic nervous system recording procedures (Smith, Concannon, Campbell, Bozman, & Kline, 1990; Stelmack & Geen, 1992).

Elementary cognitive tasks—in particular, such tasks as simple and choice reaction time—are fundamentally the same as the oddball task in regard to stimulus evaluation requirements. Thus faster P300 latency for higher-ability subjects would also be expected on these tasks. In our own work (McGarry-Roberts et al., 1992), faster P300 latency for higher-ability subjects was observed across a range of simple decision tasks. Recent research comparing different levels of difficulty on the Sternberg scanning task (Pelosi et al., 1992a), however, revealed a more complex picture in which P300 amplitude was inversely related to intelligence, an effect that was contrary to expectations. Overall, these preliminary inquiries suggest that ERP waves recorded in these elementary cognitive tasks may comprise of overlapping waves that stem from different neural processes. It will be a challenge for future work to devise strategies and procedures that will identify those component waves, which may vary with individual differences in intelligence.

Neuroticism, like intelligence, appears to exhibit a negative association with P300 latency. Thus neuroticism/anxiety, along with age and gender (which also covary with P300 values), should be taken into account in analyses of intelligence. In our own work with elementary cognitive tasks (Stelmack, Houlihan, & McGarry-Roberts, 1993), neuroticism was also positively correlated with reaction time. Though both intelligence and neuroticism exhibited faster stimulus evaluation speed (as indexed by P300 latency), response initiation (as indexed by reaction time) was facilitated with higher ability and inhibited with higher neuroticism. Analysis of the conjunction between P300 latency and reaction time may be helpful in articulating and distinguishing the component structure of information processing in intelligence and neuroticism.

BRAINSTEM AUDITORY EVOKED POTENTIALS

The brainstem auditory evoked potential (BAEP) is a reliable waveform that consists of a series of small vertex-positive waves occurring within the first 10 ms following the onset of an abrupt tone. There is a close correspondence between BAEP waves and specific neural sites; similar reliability and physiological correspondence has not been established for the visual system. For the BAEP, there is good evidence that wave I is generated from the action potentials of the auditory nerve. Waves II and III appear to originate in the lower medullary region. Wave V is generated in the pontine or midbrain regions (Chiappa, 1990). This evidence has made the BAEP a useful tool for assessing the integrity of the auditory brainstem pathway.

The latency of the BAEP components decreases, and the amplitude increases, with increases in acoustic intensity. There is also a good correspondence between intensity-loudness power functions and wave I intensity-amplitude power functions (Wilson & Stelmack, 1982). Thus larger amplitude and faster latency of BAEP peaks are indicative of greater auditory sensitivity. The interpeak latencies of BAEP waves provide reliable measures of central conduction time in the brainstem auditory pathways. The interpeak latencies are of constant magnitude across a wide range of stimulus intensities, indicating that the decrease in peak latency with increase in intensity occurs at the level of the auditory nerve (Chiappa, 1990).

An important feature of the BAEP waveform is that the amplitudes of BAEP components appear to be relatively invariant across states of attention, arousal, sleep, and even metabolic coma (Starr & Achor, 1975). The latency of BAEP peaks is somewhat slower during sleep than during wakefulness (Stelmack, Campbell, & Bell, 1993), an effect that may be attributed to lower body temperature during sleep (Bastuji, Larrea, Bertrand, & Mauguiere, 1988; Marshall & Donchin, 1981). There has been some debate whether voluntary attention effects that are apparent in the later ERP waveforms also influence the brainstem components (Connolly, Aubry, McGillivary, & Scott, 1989; Hirschorn & Michie, 1990; Lukas, 1980; Picton, Stapells, & Campbell, 1981). The weight of the evidence, however, seems to favor the view that attention and arousal demands do not influence the BAEP.

Brainstem Auditory Evoked Potentials and Extraversion

Several studies have examined extraversion and individual differences in BAEP. The research is important in a number of ways. First, faster-latency and greater-amplitude BAEPs for introverts as compared to extraverts would complement evidence of greater auditory sensitivity that has been observed with psychophysical, ERP, and other psychophysiological methods (Stelmack & Geen, 1992). With the BAEP, the neural generators of the waves are determined quite explicitly, so that rather precise information about the bases of introversion–extraversion differences can be offered. Such findings, however, would implicate differences in peripheral nervous system processes that are not determined by mechanisms in the reticular system, as proposed in the arousal hypothesis (Eysenck, 1967). The BAEP effects would require an elaboration of the neurological bases of extraversion to accommodate differences in neuronal transmission that are present in peripheral nervous system processes.

In an early report, no significant differences were observed between introvert, middle (or "ambivert"), and extravert groups for the BAEP recorded in response to a range of lower-intensity click stimuli (Campbell, Baribeau-Braun, & Braun, 1981). Lower-frequency and higher-intensity auditory stimuli that were successful in distinguishing introverts and extraverts on later ERP waves were manipulated in two subsequent studies (Stelmack & Wilson, 1982). In the first study, extraverts displayed somewhat faster wave V latencies than introverts at 0.5 kHz, whereas introverts tended to show faster latencies at 2 and 4 kHz. (Because BAEPs develop to the onset of stimulation, the slow rise times of low-frequency tones obscure the recording of early BAEP waves.) In the second study, subjects obtaining high, middle, and low scores on the extraversion scale were compared in their BAEP waves to square-wave click stimuli across eight intensity levels that ranged from 55 to 90 dB SPL. The mean wave V latency of extraverts was slower than for the middle and introvert groups across all intensity levels except at 90 dB. In addition, a significant positive correlation was observed between extraversion and power function exponents that were derived from wave I latency to click stimuli across the 55 to 90 dB intensity levels. This effect reflected relatively faster wave I latencies that were displayed by the introverts at the higher intensities (notably 75–85 dB).

Similar results were reported by Szelenberger (1983), who recorded the BAEP to 80 dB SPL click stimuli from 20 paranoid schizophrenic patients and 50 control subjects. The Extraversion (E), Neuroticism (N), and Psychoticism (P) scales were highly intercorrelated for both groups. Factor analysis of the data shows that P and E load on the first factor in the analysis for each group. For the control group, wave II, III, and V latencies and interpeak latency I–III and I–V had positive loadings on this first factor. For the patient group, wave I, II, and III latencies and interpeak latency I–II and I–III had positive loadings on the P/E factor. One can regard this P/E factor as an impulsivity factor, with high impulsives tending to display slower BAEP latencies than low impulsives.

In a recent report, the BAEP to 80 dB click stimuli was recorded under three levels of caffeine-induced arousal (Bullock & Gilliland, 1993). Faster wave V latency for introverts than for extraverts was observed in all three conditions, as was faster interpeak latency for introvert groups for waves I–III and I–V was also noted. Although there were no interactive effects on BAEP components that were attributable to arousal, the authors tend to favor an interpretation that attributed these latency effects to central neural mechanisms rather than peripheral sensitivity differences.

Although the case is far from certain, the evidence to date indicates faster BAEP latency to higher-intensity click stimuli for introverts relative to extraverts. In view of the anatomical and functional independence of the BAEP from the influence of central arousal processes, these effects can be referred to peripheral neuronal mechanisms. The olivo-cochlear bundle exercises an inhibitory influence on the auditory nerve, the cochlear nucleus, and the inferior colliculus (Desmedt, 1975). This inhibitory influence is reduced or absent for intensities above 75 dB, and according to Desmedt, these inhibitory effects are independent of the reticular system. As previously noted, interpeak conduction times (I–III; I–V) are constant across intensity levels. This means that variation in wave V latency (inferior colliculus) is in lock step with variation of wave I latency (auditory nerve). Even in the absence of statistically significant differences between groups at wave I (owing to the difficulty in recording this wave), faster wave V latency for introverts than for extraverts would implicate differential sensitivity of peripheral neuronal processes rather than central arousal mechanisms.

In our recent work, this issue of the peripheral and central origins of extraversion differences was pursued by recording the BAEP of introverts and extraverts during wakefulness and during sleep (Stelmack, Campbell, & Bell, 1993). Attention is absent and cortico-reticular influences on brainstem activity are minimized during sleep; BAEP effects during sleep thus cannot be attributable to central cortical arousal mechanisms. Although none of the comparisons were significant at the .05 level of confidence, introverts exhibited faster wave V latency than extraverts in all six conditions that were recorded. The effect sizes of the personality group contrasts were approximately half a standard deviation; on average, the power of these statistical tests was .30. Because the a priori probability of rejecting the null hypothesis was low, the negative results of this BAEP analysis must be regarded as inconclusive. Further research on this basic issue is clearly desirable.

BAEP measures have not been used in research on intelligence, but such work would be worthwhile. An important issue in research on intelligence concerns the bases of differences in the speed of processing of elementary cognitive tasks. Several studies have explored the possibility that the variation of intelligence with speed of processing on these simple tasks may involve fundamental differences in the speed of neural conduction. These studies used electromyographic recording to determine the speed of nerve conduction following electrical stimulation of the median nerve in the arm. Early reports associating higher intelligence with faster nerve conduction velocity have not been confirmed (Vernon & Mori, 1992). The interpeak BAEP latency measures would provide an alternative means to examine individual differences in speed of neuronal conduction, as they are reliable measures that are relatively independent of the intensity of stimulation.

SUMMARY AND CONCLUSIONS

In early research, sensory evoked potentials were used to explore individual variation in both intelligence and personality. In the intelligence work, these measures were used as indices of the construct of neural efficiency or information-processing speed. In the personality research, the measures were used as indices of such constructs as arousal and sensory augmenting/reducing. In both cases, the experimental paradigm consisted of the repeated presentation of tones or light flashes to a passive observer. For these sensory ERPs, latency decreases and amplitude increases with increasing stimulus intensity; thus individual variations in ERP amplitude and latency are regarded as intensity effects (or differences in sensitivity to stimulation). In the intelligence work, the implicit assumption was that intelligence could be referred to simple sensory processing and that this would be reflected in faster neural transmission. In the work reviewed, clearly there is no relation between intelligence and the latency of early ERP waves. The association of greater amplitude with higher ability is inconsistent and, in regard to the string measure, quite contentious. This gloomy reprise is also expressed in recent reviews on the subject (Barrett & Eysenck, 1992; Deary & Caryl, 1993). In our view, it is also important to note that variation in intelligence has not been associated with either behavioral or other psychophysiological measures of stimulus intensity that involve the repetitive presentation of simple lights and tones. On the whole, there is little support for the notion that intelligence is associated with faster speed of processing of simple punctate stimuli.

With respect to personality, there appears to be some consistency in the observation that introversion and low scores on social disinhibition are associated with larger ERP amplitudes to sensory stimulation. These ERP effects do converge with behavioral observations (e.g., lower pain and noise thresholds for introverts) and similar effects with other psychophysiological measures (e.g., larger skin conductance responses for introverts) under similar stimulus conditions. Moreover, there is some evidence from the BAEP work that these intensity effects are evident at the level of the auditory nerve, with introversion associated with faster BAEP latency.

The P300 ERP component is a reliable index of endogenous cognitive activity (e.g., selective attention and decision making). The amplitude of this component varies directly with increased novelty and subjective task demands and varies inversely with the difficulty of discrimination requirements. The latency to maximum P300 peak amplitude is a good index of stimulus discrimination time that is relatively independent of response production. There is some evidence that higher extraversion scores are associated with smaller P300 amplitude to the target stimulus in the oddball paradigm. This effect is indicative of less attentional demand for extraverts than introverts; however, the contribution of intensity effects to these observations has not been ruled out. With the oddball paradigm, there is some evidence that higher ability is associated with faster P300 latency. This effect is consistent with the view that regards intelligence in terms of the ability to educe relations. Overall, the feasibility of applying the principles of P300 measurement to assess individual differences in the performance of elementary cognitive tasks has been demonstrated. Pursuing this line of inquiry promises to enrich our understanding of the determinants of mental ability.

Acknowledgment. This work was supported by grants awarded by the Social Science and Humanities Research Council of Canada (to Robert M. Stelmack; No. 410-93-0462) and the Natural Science and Engineering Research Council of Canada (to Michael Houlihan).

REFERENCES

Barnet, A. B., & Lodge, A. (1967). Click evoked EEG responses in normal and developmentally retarded infants. *Nature, 214*, 252–255.

Barrett, P. T., & Eysenck, H. J. (1992). Brain electrical potentials and intelligence. In A. Gale, & M. W. Eysenck (Eds.), *Handbook of individual differences: Biological perspectives* (pp. 255–285). New York: Wiley.

Bastuji, H., Larrea, L. G., Bertrand, O., & Mauguiere, F. (1988). BAEP latency changes during nocturnal sleep are not correlated with sleep stages but with body temperature variations. *Electroencephalography and Clinical Neurophysiology, 70*, 9–15.

Bates, T., & Eysenck, H. J. (1993). String length, attention and intelligence: Focused attention reverses the string length-IQ relationship. *Personality and Individual Differences, 15*, 363–371.

Blinkhorn, S. F., & Hendrickson, D. E. (1982). Averaged evoked responses and psychometric intelligence. *Nature, 295*, 596–597.

Bouchard, T. J., Jr., Lykken, D. T., McGue, M., Segal, S., & Tellegen, A. (1990). Sources of human psychological differences: The Minnesota study of twins reared apart. *Science, 250*, 223–228.

Brebner, J. (1990). Psychological and neurophysiological factors in stimulus-response compatibility. In R. W. Proctor & T. G. Reeves (Eds.), *Stimulus-response compatibility*. Amsterdam: Elsevier.

Brody, N. (1992). *Intelligence* (2nd ed.). San Diego, CA: Academic Press.

Bruneau, W., Roux, S., Perse, J., & Lelord, G. (1984). Frontal evoked responses, stimulus intensity control, and the extraversion dimension. In R. Karrer, J. Cohen, & P. Teuting (Eds.), Brain and information: Event-related potentials. *Annals of the New York Academy of Sciences, 425*, 546–550.

Buchsbaum, M. (1971). Neural events and the psychophysical law. *Science, 172*, 502.

Bullock, W. A., & Gilliland, K. (1993). Eysenck's arousal theory of introversion-extraversion: A converging measures investigation. *Journal of Personality and Social Psychology, 64*, 113–123.

Cahill, J. M., & Polich, J. (1992). P300, probability, and introverted/extroverted personality types. *Biological Psychology, 33*, 23–35.

Callaway, E. (1975). *Brain electric potentials and individual psychological differences*. New York: Grune & Stratton.

Callaway, E., & Halliday, R. A. (1973). Evoked potential variability: Effects of age, amplitude and methods of measurement. *Electroencephalography and Clinical Neurophysiology, 34*, 125–133.

Campbell, K. B., Baribeau-Braun, J., & Braun, C. (1981). Neuroanatomical and physiological foundations of extraversion. *Psychophysiology, 18*, 263–267.

Carroll, J. B. (1993). *Human cognitive abilities*. New York: Cambridge University Press.

Chalke, F. C. R., & Ertl, J. P. (1965). Evoked potentials and intelligence. *Life Sciences, 4*, 1319–1322.

Chiappa, K. H. (Ed.). (1990). *Evoked potentials in clinical medicine* (2nd ed.). New York: Raven.

Como, P. G., Simons, R., & Zuckerman, M. (1984). Psychophysiological indices of sensation seeking as a function of stimulus intensity. *Psychophysiology, 21*, 572–573.

Connolly, J. F., Aubry, K., McGillivary, N., & Scott, D. W. (1989). Human brainstem evoked responses fail to provide evidence of efferent modulation of auditory input during attentional tasks. *Psychophysiology, 26*, 292–303.

Connolly, J. F., & Gruzelier, J. H. (1982). Amplitude and latency changes in the visual evoked potential to different stimulus intensities. *Psychophysiology, 19*, 599–608.

Costa, P. T., & McCrae, R. R. (1992). Four ways five factors are basic. *Personality and Individual Differences, 13*, 653–666.

Costa, P. T., McCrae, R. R., & Dye, D. A. (1991). Facet scales for Agreeableness and Conscientiousness: A revision of the NEO personality inventory. *Personality and Individual Differences, 12*, 887–898.

Daruna, J. H., Karrer, R., & Rosen, A. J. (1985). Introversion, attention and the late positive component of event-related potentials. *Biological Psychology, 20*, 249–259.

Davis, F. B. (1971). *The measurement of mental capability through evoked-potential recordings* (pp. 1–171). Greenwich, CT: Educational Records Bureau.

De Pascalis, V., & Montirosso, R. (1988). Extraversion, neuroticism and individual differences in event-related potentials. *Personality and Individual Differences, 9*, 353–360.

Deary, I., & Caryl, P. (1993). Intelligence, EEG, and evoked potentials. In P. A. Vernon (Ed.), *Biological approaches to human intelligence*. Norwood, NJ: Ablex.

Desmedt, J. E. (1975). Physiological studies of the efferent recurrent auditory system. In W. D. Keidel & W. D. Neff (Eds.), *Handbook of sensory physiology* (Vol. 5). Berlin: Springer.

Ditraglia, G. M., & Polich, J. (1991). P300 and introverted/extraverted personality types. *Psychophysiology, 28*, 177–184.

Duncan-Johnson, C. C., & Donchin, E. (1982). The P300 component of the event-related brain potential as an index of information processing. *Biological Psychology, 14*, 1–52.

Egan, V. G., Chiswick, A., Brettle, R. P., & Goodwin, G. M. (in press). The Edinburgh cohort of HIV-positive drug users: The relationship between auditory P3 latency, cognitive function and self-rated mood. *Psychological Medicine, 23*.

Engel, R., & Fay, W. (1972). Visual evoked responses at birth, verbal scores at three years, and IQ at four years. *Developmental Medicine and Child Neurology, 14*, 283–289.

Engel, R., & Henderson, N. B. (1973). Visual evoked responses and IQ scores at school age. *Developmental Medicine and Child Neurology, 15*, 136–145.

Ertl, J. P. (1968). Evoked potentials, neural efficiency, and IQ. In L. D. Proctor (Ed.), *The proceedings of an international symposium on biocybernetics of the central nervous system* (pp. 419–433). London: Little, Brown.

Ertl, J. P., & Schafer, E. W. P. (1969). Brain response correlates of psychometric intelligence. *Nature, 223*, 421–422.

Eysenck, H. J. (1967). *The biological basis of personality*. Springfield, IL: Thomas.

Eysenck, H. J. (1992). The definition and measurement of psychoticism. *Personality and Individual Differences, 13*, 757–785.

Eysenck, H. J., & Eysenck, S. B. G. (1975). *Manual of the Eysenck Personality Questionnaire*. London: Hodder and Stoughton Educational.

Fitzgerald, P. G., & Picton, T. W. (1981). Temporal and sequential probability in evoked potential studies. *Canadian Journal of Psychology*, *35*, 188–200.

Ford, J. M., Roth, W. T., Mohs, R. C., Hopkins, W. F., & Kopell, B. S. (1979). Event-related potentials recorded from young and old adults during a memory retrieval task. *Electroencephalography and Clinical Neurophysiology*, *47*, 450–459.

Friedman, D., Hakerem, G., Sutton, S., & Fleiss, J. L. (1973). Effect of stimulus uncertainty on the pupillary dilation response and the vertex evoked potential. *Electroencephalography and Clinical Neurophysiology*, *34*, 475–485.

Gilbert, D. G., Johnson, S., Gilbert, B. O., & McColloch, M. A. (1991). Event-related potential correlates of IQ. *Personality and Individual Differences*, *12*, 1183–1184.

Goldman, D., Kohn, P. M., & Hunt, R. W. (1983). Sensation seeking, augmenting-reducing and absolute auditory threshold: A strength-of-the-nervous-system perspective. *Journal of Personality and Social Psychology*, *45*, 405–419.

Gomer, F. E., Spicuzza, R. J., & O'Donnell, R. D. (1976). Evoked potential correlates of visual item recognition during memory-scanning tasks. *Physiological Psychology*, *4*, 61–65.

Gucker, D. K. (1973). Correlating visual evoked potentials with psychometric intelligence, variation in technique. *Perceptual and Motor Skills*, *37*, 189–190.

Haier, R. J., Robinson, D. L., Braden, W., & Williams, D. (1983). Electrical potentials of the cerebral cortex and psychometric intelligence. *Personality and Individual Differences*, *4*, 591–599.

Hegerl, U., Prochno, I., Ulrich, G., & Muller-Oelinghausen, B. (1989). Sensation seeking and auditory evoked potentials. *Biological Psychiatry*, *25*, 179–190.

Hendrickson, A. E., & Hendrickson, D. E. (1980). The biological basis of individual differences in intelligence. *Personality and Individual Differences*, *1*, 3–33.

Hirschorn, T. N., & Michie, P. T. (1990). Brainstem auditory evoked potentials (BAEPs) and selective attention revisited. *Psychophysiology*, *27*, 495–512.

Howard, L., & Polich, J. (1985). P300 latency and memory span development. *Developmental Psychology*, *21*, 283–289.

Jackson, D. (1984). *The Multidimensional Aptitude Battery manual*. Port Huron, MI: Research Psychologists Press.

Jensen, A. R. (1987). Individual differences in the Hick paradigm. In P. A. Vernon (Ed.), *Speed of information processing and intelligence* (pp. 101–175). Norwood, NJ: Ablex.

Jensen, A. R., & Munro, E. (1979). Reaction time, movement time, and intelligence. *Intelligence*, *3*, 121–126.

Jensen, A. R., Schafer, E. W. P., & Crinella, F. M. (1981). Reaction time, evoked brain potentials, and psychometric *g* in the severely retarded. *Intelligence*, *5*, 179–197.

Josiassen, R. C., Shagass, C., Roemer, R. A., & Slepner, S. (1988). Evoked potential correlates of intelligence in nonpatient subjects. *Biological Psychology*, *27*, 207–225.

Kline, P. (1991). *Intelligence: The psychometric view*. London: Routledge.

Kohn, P. M. (1987). Issues in the measurement of arousability. In J. Strelau & H. J. Eysenck (Eds.), *Personality dimensions and arousal*. New York: Plenum.

Kohn, P. M., Hunt, R. W., & Hoffman, F. M. (1982). Aspects of experience seeking. *Canadian Journal of Behavioral Science*, *14*, 13–23.

Kutas, M., McCarthy, G., & Donchin, E. (1977). Augmenting mental chronometry: The P300 as a measure of stimulus evaluation time. *Science*, *197*, 792–795.

Ladish, C., & Polich, J. (1989). P300 and probability in children. *Journal of Experimental Child Psychology*, *48*, 212–223.

Le Moal, M., & Simon, H. (1991). Mesocorticolimbic dopaminergic network: Functional and regulatory roles. *Physiological Reviews*, *71*, 155–234.

Loehlin, J. C. (1989). Partitioning environment and genetic contributions to behavioral development. *American Psychologist*, *44*, 1285–1292.

Lukas, J. H. (1980). Human auditory attention: The olivocochlear bundle may function as a peripheral filter. *Psychophysiology*, *17*, 444–452.

Lukas, J. H. (1987). Visual evoked potential augmenting-reducing and personality: The vertex augmenter is a sensation seeker. *Personality and Individual Differences*, *8*, 385–396.

Malmo, R. B. (1959). Activation: A neurophysiological dimension. *Psychological Review*, *66*, 367–386.

Malmo, R. B. (1975). *On emotions, needs, and our archaic brain*. New York: Holt, Rinehart & Winston.

Marshall, N. K., & Donchin, E. (1981). Circadian variation in the latency of brainstem responses: Its relation to body temperature. *Science*, *212*, 356–358.

McGarry-Roberts, P. A., Stelmack, R. M., & Campbell, K. B. (1992). Intelligence, reaction time, and event-related potentials. *Intelligence*, *16*, 289–313.

Mullins, L. F., & Lukas, J. H. (1984). Auditory augmenters are sensation seekers—if they attend the stimuli. *Psychophysiology*, *21*, 589.

Neiss, R. (1988). Reconceptualizing arousal: Psychobiological states in motor performance. *Psychological Bulletin*, *10*, 345–366.

O'Donnell, B. F., Friedman, S., Swearer, J. M., & Drachman, D. A. (1992). Active and passive P3 latency and psychometric performance: Influence of age and individual differences. *International Journal of Psychophysiology*, *12*, 187–195.

Orlebeke, J. F., Kok, A., & Zeillemaker, C. W. (1989). Disinhibition and the processing of auditory stimulus intensity: An ERP study. *Personality and Individual Differences*, *10*, 445–452.

Osaka, M., & Osaka, N. (1980). Human intelligence and power spectral analysis of visual evoked potentials. *Perceptual and Motor Skills*, *50*, 192–194.

Pelosi, L., Holly, M., Slade, T., Hayward, M., Barrett, G., & Blumhardt, L. D. (1992a). Event-related potential (ERP) correlates of performance of intelligence tests. *Electroencephalography and Clinical Neurophysiology*, *84*, 515–520.

Pelosi, L., Holly, M., Slade, T., Hayward, M., Barrett, G., & Blumhardt, L. D. (1992b). Wave form variations in auditory event-related potentials evoked by a memory-scanning task and their relationship with tests of intellectual function. *Electroencephalography and Clinical Neurophysiology*, *84*, 344–352.

Picton, T. W., Stapells, D., & Campbell, K. B. (1981). Auditory evoked potentials from the human cochlea and brainstem. *Journal of Otolaryngology*, *10*, 1–41.

Plooij-van Gorsel, E. (1981). EEG and cardiac correlates of neuroticism: A psychophysiological comparison of neurotics and controls in relation to personality. *Biological Psychology*, *13*, 141–156.

Polich, J., Ehlers, C. L., Otis, S., Mandell, A. J., & Bloom, F. E. (1986). P300 latency reflects the degree of cognitive decline in dementing illness. *Electroencephalography and Clinical Neurophysiology*, *63*, 138–144.

Polich, J., Ladish, C., & Burns, T. (1990). Normal variation of P300 in children: Age, memory span and head size. *International Journal of Psychophysiology*, *9*, 237–248.

Polich, J., & Martin, S. (1992). P300, cognitive capability, and personality: A correlational study of university undergraduates. *Personality and Individual Differences*, *13*, 533–543.

Pritchard, W. S. (1989). P300 and EPQ/STPI personality traits. *Personality and Individual Differences, 10*, 15–24.

Ragot, R. (1984). Perceptual and motor space representation: An event-related potential study. *Psychophysiology, 21*, 159–170.

Ragot, R., & Renault, B. (1981). P300 as a function of S-R compatibility and motor programming. *Biological Psychology, 13*, 289–294.

Raine, A., Mitchell, D. A., & Venables, P. H. (1981). Cortical augmenting-reducing: Modality specific? *Psychophysiology, 18*, 700–708.

Revelle, W., & Anderson, K. J. (1992). Models for the testing of theory. In A. Gale & M. W. Eysenck (Eds.), *Handbook of individual differences: Biological perspectives* (pp. 81–114). New York: Wiley.

Revelle, W., Anderson, K. J., & Humphreys, M. S. (1987). Empirical tests and theoretical extensions of arousal-based theories of personality. In J. Strelau & H. J. Eysenck (Eds.), *Personality dimensions and arousal* (pp. 17–36). New York: Plenum.

Rhodes, L. E., Dustman, R. E., & Beck, E. C. (1969). The visual evoked response: A comparison of bright and dull children. *Electroencephalography and Clinical Neurophysiology, 27*, 364–372.

Robinson, D. L., Haier, R. J., Braden, W., & Krengel, M. (1984). Psychometric intelligence and visual evoked potentials: A replication. *Personality and Individual Differences, 5*, 487–489.

Roth, W. T., Dorato, K. H., & Kopell, B. S. (1984). Intensity and task effects of evoked physiological responses to noise bursts. *Psychophysiology, 21*, 466–481.

Rust, J. (1975). Cortical evoked potential, personality and intelligence. *Journal of Comparative and Physiological Psychology, 89*, 1220–1226.

Schafer, E. W. P. (1982). Neural adaptability: A biological determinant of behavioral intelligence. *International Journal of Neuroscience, 17*, 183–191.

Schafer, E. W. P., & Marcus, M. M. (1973). Self-stimulation alters human sensory brain responses. *Science, 181*, 175–177.

Shagass, C., Roemer, R. A., & Straumanis, J. J. (1981). Intelligence as a factor in evoked potential studies of psychopathology: II. Correlations between treatment-associate changes in IQ and evoked potentials. *Biological Psychiatry, 16*, 1031–1040.

Shucard, D. W., & Horn, J. L. (1972). Evoked cortical potentials and measurement of human abilities. *Journal of Comparative and Physiological Psychology, 78*, 59–68.

Smith, B. D. (1983). Extraversion and electrodermal activity: arousability and the inverted-U. *Personality and Individual Differences, 4*, 411–420.

Smith, B. D., Concannon, M., Campbell, S., Bozman, A., & Kline, R. (1990). Regression and criterion measures of habituation: A comparative analysis in extraverts and introverts. *Journal of Research in Personality, 24*, 123–132.

Starr, A., & Achor, L. J. (1975). Auditory brainstem responses in neurological disease. *Archives of Neurology, 32*, 761–768.

Stelmack, R. M., Achorn, E., & Michaud, A. (1977). Extraversion and individual differences in auditory evoked response. *Psychophysiology, 14*, 368–374.

Stelmack, R. M., & Campbell, K. B. (1974). Extraversion and auditory sensitivity to high and low frequency. *Perceptual and Motor Skills, 38*, 875–879.

Stelmack, R. M., Campbell, K. B., & Bell, I. (1993). Extraversion and brainstem auditory evoked potentials during sleep and wakefulness. *Personality and Individual Differences, 14*, 447–453.

Stelmack, R. M., & Geen, R. G. (1992). The psychophysiology of extraversion. In A. Gale & M. W. Eysenck (Eds.), *Handbook of individual differences: Biological perspectives* (pp. 227–254). New York: Wiley.

Stelmack, R. M., Houlihan, M., & McGarry-Roberts, P. A. (1993). Personality, reaction time, and event-related potentials. *Journal of Personality and Social Psychology, 65*, 399–409.

Stelmack, R. M., & Michaud-Achorn, A. (1985). Extraversion, attention, and habituation of the auditory evoked response. *Journal of Research in Personality, 19*, 416–428.

Stelmack, R. M., & Wilson, K. G. (1982). Extraversion and the effects of frequency and intensity on the auditory brainstem evoked response. *Personality and Individual Differences, 3*, 373–380.

Stenberg, G., Rosen, I., & Risberg, J. (1988). Personality and augmenting/reducing in visual and auditory evoked potentials. *Personality and Individual Differences, 9*, 571–580.

Stenberg, G., Rosen, I., & Risberg, J. (1990). Attention and personality in augmenting/reducing of visual evoked potentials. *Personality and Individual Differences, 11*, 1243–1254.

Sternberg, R. J. (1991). Death, taxes, and bad intelligence tests. *Intelligence, 15*, 257–269.

Sternberg, S. (1969). Memory scanning: Mental processes revealed by reaction time experiments. *American Scientist, 57*, 421–457.

Stough, C. K. K., Nettelbeck, T., & Cooper, C. J. (1990). Evoked brain potentials, string length and intelligence. *Personality and Individual Differences, 11*, 401–406.

Szelenberger, W. (1983). Brain stem auditory evoked potentials and personality. *Biological Psychiatry, 18*, 157–174.

Vanderwolf, C., & Robinson, T. (1981). Reticulo-cortical activity and behavior: A critique of the arousal theory and a new synthesis. *Behavioral and Brain Sciences, 4*, 459–514.

Vernon, P. A. (1983). Speed of information processing and general intelligence. *Intelligence, 7*, 53–70.

Vernon, P. A., & Mori, M. (1992). Intelligence, reaction times, and peripheral nerve conduction velocity. *Intelligence, 16*, 273–288.

Vogel, F., Kruger, J., Schalt, E., Schnobel, R., & Hassling, L. (1987). No consistent relationships between oscillations and latencies of visually and auditory evoked EEG potentials and measures of mental performance. *Human Neurobiology, 6*, 173–182.

von Knorring, L., & Perris, C. (1981). Biochemistry of the augmenting-reducing response in visual evoked potentials. *Neuropsychobiology, 7*, 1–8.

Warren, L. R., & Marsh, G. R. (1979). Changes in event-related potentials during processing of Stroop stimuli. *International Journal of Neuroscience, 9*, 217–223.

Wilson, K. G., & Stelmack, R. M. (1982). Power functions of loudness magnitude estimations and auditory brainstem evoked responses. *Perception & Psychophysics, 31*, 561–565.

Wilson, M. A., & Languis, M. L. (1990). A topographic study of differences in the P300 between introverts and extraverts. *Brain Topography, 2*, 269–274.

Zuckerman, M. (1979). *Sensation seeking: Beyond the optimum level of arousal*. Hillsdale, NJ: Erlbaum.

Zuckerman, M. (1989). Personality in the third dimension: A psychobiological approach. *Personality and Individual Differences, 10*, 391–418.

Zuckerman, M., Murtagh, T. M., & Siegel, J. (1974). Sensation seeking and cortical augmenting-reducing. *Psychophysiology, 11*, 535–542.

18

Cognitive and Attentional Processes in Personality and Intelligence

Gerald Matthews and Lisa Dorn

INTRODUCTION

The aim of this chapter is to discuss progress in relating intelligence and personality to constructs based on information-processing theory. There has been extensive research on correlations between indices of information-processing functions and psychometric intelligence and personality measures, although it is relatively rare for intelligence and personality to be assessed within the same study. Because of the correlational nature of the evidence, we must tread carefully in drawing conclusions from it, and so we begin with an outline of the interpretative problems involved.

A useful starting point is the distinction between Intelligences A, B, and C (Vernon, 1969), where Intelligence A refers to the individual's genotype, Intelligence B to the hypothesized (but not directly observable) phenotype, and Intelligence C to specific measures or tests of intelligence. We suppose that the genotype influences an array of specific processing functions, such as speeds of encoding particular types of stimuli and short-term memory (STM) capacity. Both elementary and more complex strategic functions may be sensitive to the genotype. The efficiency of these functions will also be affected by environmental factors, as well as by genes unrelated to general intelligence (*g*). There are two important distinctions to be made between qualitatively different types of functions that may be sensitive to these various influences. First, functions may be basic processes, or they may be more complex strategic operations. Second, we must distinguish discrete processes (e.g., a specified encoding operation) from more general properties of processing (e.g., overall mental speed or attentional resource availability). We assume that we cannot identify Intelligence B with any single processing function, but as Sternberg (1985) has claimed, phenotypic *g* is distributed across a wide range of elementary and strategic processes. In addition, processes differ in their centrality of importance to *g*. Some processes—for example, speed of processing simple stimuli (Jensen, 1987) and STM (Kyllonen & Christal, 1990)—may be of special importance, whereas others may be only slightly related to *g*. Performance of any given intelligence-related task (Intelligence C) depends on a multiplicity of individual processes, some largely unrelated to Intelligence B.

We assume also that any given personality trait (e.g., extraversion or neuroticism) is associated with a largely separate set of genetic and environmental influences on *g*, on the grounds that associations between estimates of phenotypic personality variables

Gerald Matthews • Department of Psychology, University of Dundee, Dundee DD1 4HN, Scotland. Lisa Dorn • School of Education, University of Birmingham, Birmingham B15 2TT, England.

International Handbook of Personality and Intelligence, edited by Donald H. Saklofske and Moshe Zeidner. Plenum Press, New York, 1995.

and *g* are generally small (e.g., Saklofske & Kostura, 1990). Furthermore, just as with intelligence, there seems to be no single key behavioral or cognitive construct underlying each one of the major personality dimensions (Matthews, 1992). It has been claimed that broad personality dimensions reflect underlying individual differences in psychobiology; for example, extraversion might be a function of individual differences in arousability of a reticulo-cortical activation circuit (H. J. Eysenck & Eysenck, 1985). Just as correlations between intelligence test performance and single task measures rarely exceed 0.3 or so (e.g., Hunt, 1980), however, correlations between personality and psychophysiological measures taken in samples large enough for estimating correlation magnitude are generally modest (see Zuckerman, 1991). For example, Matthews and Amelang (1993) found no correlations exceeding 0.2 between extraversion and power in three bandwidths of the EEG across three different measurement situations ($n = 180$). At best, we may suppose that genes influence psychobiological functions, which in turn are one of several independent influences on phenotypic personality. Information-processing correlates of personality are also less stable than those of *g*, in that personality effects frequently vary with such environmental factors as level of stimulation and motivational signals (Matthews, 1992).

Hence there may be a subset of processes associated with both phenotypic intelligence and personality. For example, STM tends to correlate with both *g* and extraversion (Matthews, 1992). Processes are not directly observable, and inferences concerning them are always theory-dependent; for example, theories of STM differ in the number of component processes involved. Correlational data alone will not suffice to identify the role of information-processing in personality and intelligence. Consider a correlation between some intelligence test and P, a particular processing measure. Jensen (1980) distinguishes several distinct causes of correlations, including the *part-whole relationship* (such that P indexes a subset of the skills required for the test), and the *functional relationship* (where P is a prerequisite for test performance). For example, if the test is one of mental arithmetic, P might be a working memory measure. In these two cases, we might reasonably say that efficiency of the specific process is a direct contributory cause of the measured level of Intelligence C.

Two further causes that may be grouped together as *common antecedents* are genetic and environmental correlation. P and the test may be influenced by common genetic or environmental influences, although P is not among the processes required for test performance. Lastly, an additional cause might be termed the *ontogenetic prerequisite*, where the development of a process is contingent upon other, preexisting processes. M. Anderson (1992) proposes that basic information-processing speed constrains development of complex, high-level knowledge acquisition routines or algorithms. Hence processing speed may continue to correlate with test performance, even if the efficiency of the complex processing routine is the direct causal influence. The upshot of the multiple causation of correlations is that any given association is ambiguous. The larger empirical correlations between *g* and processing measures are possibly inflated by independent contributions from antecedent, ontogenetic, and direct causal influences on the association.

Either experimental work or sophisticated modeling of data are needed to determine the causal role of specified processes. One such technique is Sternberg's (1985) componential analysis, which decomposes test performance into elementary components and strategic metacomponents. Correlations between comparable component measures obtained from different tasks are often modest, however, whereas theoretically unrelated components do tend to intercorrelate positively (Brody, 1992). The first finding implies inadequacies of the models tested, the second that common influences on components (e.g., mental speed) are being neglected. The weakness of componential analysis as usually applied is its neglect of nonlocalized influences on performance at both the lower level (network parameters associated with mental speed) and the upper level (attentional resource availability).

Attentional and Cognitive Frameworks

This review is organized within a multilevel framework for information processing (Matthews & Dorn, 1989; Norman & Shallice, 1985), with upper and lower levels of control. Lower-level processing comprises a network of simple units that must be activated to process information. Conventional cognitive psychological models see each unit as performing a single elementary function, such as short-term storage of information. Connectionist models of processing (e.g., Rumelhart, Hinton, & McClelland 1986) see elementary functions as emergent properties of the spread of activation between units responsive to specific types of stimulus attributes. Hence verbal STM may be associated with the residual activation of lexical (word) units resulting from verbal processing, rather than a discrete short-term store (Brown & Hulme, in press). Lower-level networks may have general parameters associated with individual differences; for example, we might naively relate mental speed to rate of spread of activation between units. (We shall switch between the metaphors of discrete component processes and of distributed network processes as convenient.)

Performance at the lower level is automatic in the sense of being involuntary, inaccessible to consciousness, and requiring little attentional capacity; it is reflexively triggered by suitable stimulus inputs (Schneider, Dumais, & Shiffrin, 1984). In contrast, upper-level processing is controlled in that it depends on voluntary plans and strategies, requires capacity, and is partly conscious. It operates by biasing lower-level processing, so that many tasks depend on both automatic and controlled processing. Automaticity is best conceived of as a continuum, in that the operation of any given processing unit may be influenced both by direct stimulus input and voluntary attention (see Cohen, Servan-Schreiber, & McClelland, 1992). Given some consistency of stimulus-response mapping, task performance becomes more automatic and less strategic with practice as the person develops stable procedures (J. R. Anderson, 1982). Ackerman (1988) relates *g* to performance at the early, cognitive stage of skill acquisition; perceptual speed to the intermediate, and autonomous stage of skill; and psychomotor speed to full automaticity. Quantitative and qualitative aspects of upper-level functioning must be distinguished. Overall efficiency is limited by availability of attentional resources, seen as a metaphorical pool of energy or fuel for controlled processing (Hirst & Kalmar, 1987). It is important also to assess specific executive functions (e.g., setting speed-accuracy trade-offs that correspond to task strategy.

Psychometric and Conceptual Issues

We shall primarily be concerned with general ability—*g*—although we shall introduce data on primary abilities, particularly verbal ability, where relevant. The starting point for the structure of personality is the well-known "Big Five" model (McCrae & Costa, 1987), which is becoming increasingly accepted as the paradigm for personality assessment, although there are still some theoretical (H. J. Eysenck, 1992) and psychometric (Matthews & Oddy, 1993) problems with it. In fact, the great majority of performance studies are concerned with the two Eysenckian (1967) factors of extraversion (E) and neuroticism (N) that the Big Five preserves. There is increasing interest in the Big Five dimension of conscientiousness (C), or its achievement striving component, as a predictor of performance (e.g., Hough, 1992), but the studies conducted to date make too little reference to information processing to be reviewed here. Performance correlates of the remaining Big Five factors of openness and agreeableness have hardly been explored at all. Self-rated intelligence and intellectual interest may be a central part of openness (e.g., McCrae & Costa, 1987), or a personality factor additional to the Big Five (Brand & Egan, 1989).

Broadly, we wish to explain the performance correlates of extraversion and neuroticism in terms of adaptations to particular information-processing environments. We discuss the adaptation hypotheses briefly next, then elaborate on them in subsequent sections. In a previous review, Matthews (1992) identified a variety of fairly reliable correlates of extraversion that could not be reduced to any single processing function. Performance changes associated with extraversion included facilitation of STM and attentionally demanding performance, together with impairment of vigilance and complex problem-solving. Extraversion is associated with a complex *patterning* of strengths and weaknesses in information processing. Presumably, extraversion is associated also with items of social knowledge, processes supporting social skills, and other elements of social cognition. The purely cognitive analysis of effects of extraversion does not explain why the trait should be associated with a particular patterning of performance. A possible explanation is that extraversion may be associated with an *adaptation* to environments of high information flow, in which successful action requires high attentional capacity and immediate memory capacity, the ability to monitor multiple input channels, resistance to distraction, and tolerance of stress. Conversely, introverts may be well equipped cognitively to deal with environments that provide only occasional stimulation and opportunities for reflective thought. (The adaptation could be either genetically or environmentally caused, or both.)

It is possible that impulsivity and sociability are differentially related to performance (Amelang & Ullwer, 1991; Revelle, Humphreys, Simon, & Gilliland, 1980). We can relate impulsivity to adaptation to time-pressuring environments, where rapidity of action is at a premium. Dickman (1990) has discriminated separate dimensions of functional and dysfunctional impulsivity, of which the former is more strongly correlated with the broad trait of extraversion. Sociability may be associated with coping with social stimuli; its close relationship to extraversion may derive from the high attentional demands that social settings often impose, particularly when interaction with strangers is required. Other people deliver information on multiple channels (words, facial expressions, behaviors) that may conflict (e.g., when someone is being insincere). Verbal information requires high-level semantic analysis and is often complex and ambiguous; the textbook example of the cocktail party for informational overload is well chosen.

On the basis of the high correlations between various measures of "negative affectivity" (Watson & Clark, 1984), we shall treat trait anxiety and neuroticism as interchangeable. There is some uncertainty over the respective contributions of trait and state anxiety, but we shall not tackle this issue in detail here. Worry states seem particularly associated with general performance decrement (e.g., Morris, Davis, & Hutchings, 1981), but there is some evidence that trait anxiety is more strongly correlated with attentional bias (see M. W. Eysenck, 1992). M. W. Eysenck (1992) describes a variety of correlates of trait anxiety, including distractibility, scanning for threat, and biases toward threat in attention and memory. M. W. Eysenck reviews various instances of enhanced selective attention for threatening stimuli shown by trait-anxious subjects. These subjects are distracted by threat-related words on the Stroop test, direct their attention to the spatial locations of threatening words, and tend to encode preferentially threatening meanings of ambiguous words. As M. W. Eysenck (1992) points out, the complexity of the findings seems to require a number of different explanatory principles at the level of information-processing theory. We can plausibly account for the overall pattern of correlates of trait anxiety by supposing that, jointly, they support an adaptation to threatening environments. The anxious individual shows a generalized heightened sensitivity to threats, particularly those of a social or evaluative nature. Presumably threat sensitivity is adaptive when the environment is genuinely threatening, though the association between neuroticism and affective disorder implies that it is often maladaptive. An adaptation to threatening environments might be supported either by psychobiological processes (Gray, 1982), or by cognitive stress processes (Lazarus & Folkman, 1984)—that is, the negative beliefs, evaluations, and coping strategies associated with neuroticism (Wells & Matthews, 1994). McCrae and Costa (1986) show that neurotics' reactions to threat are characterized by coping strategies directed toward altering internal perceptions and reactions (emotion-focused coping), rather than toward changing the external situation (problem-focused coping).

Aims and Scope of the Chapter

The remainder of the chapter reviews intelligence and personality effects on several qualitatively different types of information processing: "basic" information-processing associated with overall mental speed, resource-limited attention, STM, and strategy use. Each area of research is linked with the information-processing theory which provides a framework for integrating intelligence and personality effects within the overall levels-of-control model. Basic information processing is linked to lower-level network function, and performance of demanding attentional tasks to resource theory. Short-term retention depends on several processes and structures, any or each of which might be related to individual differences. Individual differences in strategy use are related to the executive functions of the upper level of control. We shall in part consider the role of strategies in the context of the other research areas, particularly where strategies are considered mainly as a nuisance factor, obscuring relationships between individual-difference variables and information-processing functions. Studies in which strategy use itself is the central issue, however, are reviewed as a separate area. Within each research area we review the correlational evidence relating *g* to information-processing theory, the causal significance of any correlations, empirical studies of personality, and the adaptive significance of relationships between personality and cognition.

BASIC INFORMATION PROCESSING

Contemporary *network models* of lower-level information processing have been developed most explicitly within connectionist approaches to human cognition. Stimulus inputs generate activation in a network of nodes or units connected by excitatory and inhibitory links of varying degrees of associative strengths. Different sets of units are sensitive to different kinds of information. So, when the stimulus is a word, word recognition takes place as follows: The stimulus activates letter feature units, which in turn activate letter units, which in turn activate to some threshold level a unit corresponding to the word (see Rumelhart et al., 1986). Although the scope of models of this kind is continually increasing, they are best suited to explaining performance of fairly simple tasks. Network models are thus of most relevance in explaining correlations between *g* and tasks such as reaction time (RT) and inspection time (IT), although no formal models appear to have been developed yet. Network models have a variety of different parameters, connection strengths between different types of units, decay rates, random noise levels, and other characteristics that all affect network performance, however, so that detailed simulation work is required to explain experimental results (Matthews & Harley, 1993). This type of model concerns not so much discrete processes as the network parameters that control the efficiency of various functions.

Intelligence

The impetus for relating IQ to the speed and/or efficiency of basic information processing is provided by its correlations with speed of performance on simple tasks (e.g., choice RT) that appear to have little to do with the higher-level qualities of intelligence, described by Spearman (1923) as the education of relations and correlates. Jensen (1987) reports *N*-weighted RT correlates of *g* ranging from −.18 for simple RT to −.23 for choice RT ($N = 1129$). Kranzler and Jensen (1989) report an uncorrected mean correlation between IT and IQ of .29 ($N = 1120$). Correlations of this kind can be raised to above .5 by correcting for unreliability of measures and restriction of range, and/or by combining several parameters from the same task in a multiple correlation (e.g., Kranzler & Jensen, 1989). Rabbitt and Maylor (1991) present evidence suggesting that IQ often acts as a simple multiplicative scaling factor for response times, although this relationship seems to break down when qualitative features of the task are changed (Matthews & Dorn, 1989).

Data of this kind are suggestive of a correlation between *g* and some parameter of low-level network function that controls speed of response. They are also conducive to neuropsychological speculation: *g* may relate to neuronal processes such as synaptic transmission (H. J. Eysenck, 1986), but there is little direct evidence that any such process plays a direct causal role in mediating the *g*–RT correlation (Brody, 1992). It is also unclear whether there are one or several mental speeds. Several studies have derived two or more speed measures independently and related them to *g*. Nettelbeck and Rabbitt (1992) derived indices of speed from RT, IT and coding tasks. Although the speed measures intercorrelated positively, they made significant independent contributions to the prediction of psychometric IQ measures, implying that different speed measures partially index different processing functions. McGarry-Roberts, Stelmack, and Campbell (1992) suggest similarly that individual differences in speeds of stimulus evaluation and response production may be independently related to *g*.

Several objections to the hypothesis of a correlation between *g* and speed of mental processing have been raised. Longstreth (1984) suggested that the *g*–RT correlation might be mediated by higher-level processes associated with practice, visual attention and response biases. In general, subsequent research has failed to sustain these objections (Brody, 1992). For example, Matthews and Dorn (1989) used a battery of RT tasks in which each task version added a single specific information-processing function (e.g., short-term storage) to a simple 3-choice continuous reaction task. The strongest correlations with *g* were found mainly with unmodified control tasks, implying that the *g*–RT correlation was not mediated by processes of feature extraction, short-term retention, response selection, or flexibility of strategy use. A measure of conscious attention, indexed in a cueing paradigm, did predict *g* over and above the simple RT task but could not statistically explain the *g*–RT relationship. The correlation between *g* and RT might also be confounded by strategies such as trading off speed and accuracy, or decision time and movement time (Smith, 1989). In fact, controlling for strategy use or modifying RT tasks to reduce higher-level influences seems to increase the *g*–RT correlation (Neubauer, 1991).

As with RT tasks, IT tasks provide scope for strategies, such as using apparent motion cues. Mackenzie and Cumming (1986) reported that the IT–IQ correlation holds for strategy users but disappears in the strategy-using group, implying that the association between IT and IQ cannot be explained by use of the apparent motion strategy. Further work by Egan and Deary (1992), who used a superior method to assess IT, obtained negative relationships between IT and IQ in groups of both strategy users and nonusers. Egan and Deary point out that perception of apparent motion cues does not seem to be under voluntary control, and the strategy may simply augment automatic perceptual intake. Consistent with this view, they showed that the IT–IQ correlation was unaffected by controlling statistically for individual differences in performance of an attentionally demanding mental arithmetic task.

It is difficult to assess the extent to which measures of RT index processes contribute directly to performance of specific tests. It is plausible that speed of processing might contribute directly to performance of a great many intelligence tests (Mackintosh, 1986), but there are some difficulties. Simple speed measures correlate with IQ irrespective of whether tests are timed or untimed (Nettelbeck & Rabbitt, 1992), a result inconsistent with Mackintosh's (1986) hypothesis. Another possibility is that high processing speed is necessary to overcome capacity constraints of the system (Necka, 1992). A complex skill (e.g., solving a particular type of problem) may require a number of items to be activated in working memory simultaneously (see J. R. Anderson, 1982), which may only be possible if each individual item can be rapidly activated. Resolution of the causal role of simple speed measures in IQ test performance probably requires the more complex analyses of component processes developed by Sternberg (1985), although, as discussed previously, the componential approach has perhaps not fulfilled its initial promise. In the present context, what is required is the comparison of models based on (a) independent components and (b) components mutually correlated through an association with mental speed, but analyses of this type have yet to be done for tasks strongly associated with *g*.

Two important studies by Geary and Widaman (1987, 1992) on a componential model of numerical cognition partially meet the gap in existing research. Of particular interest is their identification of a speed or intercept factor in mental arithmetic associated with rate of executive basic processes (e.g. encoding integers). The speed factor was distinct from factors representing more complex arithmetic processes and working memory capacity; it related to a perceptual-speed trait factor—defined by tasks such as "finding A's" and "number comparison"—rather than to a general reasoning factor (Geary & Widaman, 1992). Geary and Widaman (1987) suggest that their results differ from those of Sternberg (1985) in emphasizing a role for mental speed because component processes are simpler in mental arithmetic than in the reasoning tasks studied by Sternberg. These studies provide evidence for a direct contribution of mental speed to a specific primary ability, but evidence on the causal role of mental speed in performance of power tests more representative of *g* is lacking. Arguably, the correlation between *g* and mental speed is indirect, mediated by common environmental and genetic antecedents and by the developmental processes discussed by M. Anderson (1992).

Extraversion: Empirical Data

Considered in isolation, neither extraversion nor neuroticism seems very reliably correlated with speed of performance on simple cognitive tasks, such as RT. Several large-scale studies (e.g., Amelang & Ullwer, 1990, 1991; Matthews, Jones & Chamberlain, 1989) suggest that there is no reliable general relationship between either personality factor and speed of response, although, as described later, both factors may relate to speed-accuracy trade-off in some circumstances. There may also be correlations between personality and RT in specific task paradigms (e.g., Stelmack, Houlihan, & McGarry-Roberts, in press). It is unclear whether there are any consistent relationships between personality and IT. Nettelbeck (1973) obtained U-shaped relationships between IT and both extraversion and neuroticism. In contrast, Egan and Deary (1992) found a negative relationship between extraversion and IT only in subjects not using apparent motion strategies, and no relationship between N and IT.

The strongest personality effects on basic information processing are associated with interactive effects of extraversion and arousal on performance. (We shall not discuss effects of neuroticism further, because of the lack of evidence to support a coherent story.) In a series of studies, Matthews (1992) found that in the morning, aroused extraverts and dearoused introverts show faster or more accurate performance than dearoused extraverts and aroused introverts on tasks dependent on simple encoding (e.g., letter detection, five-choice serial reaction, letter cancellation, and probe RT). In most of these studies, arousal was indexed with the UWIST Mood Adjective Checklist (UMACL), an adjective checklist measure validated against autonomic arousal measures and stress manipulations (Matthews, Jones, & Chamberlain, 1990). Thayer (1989) has proposed that feelings of energy and vigor are associated with a reticulo-cortical arousal system. Matthews and Amelang (1993) showed that the effect also generalized to an EEG alpha measure, across a variety of simple information-processing tasks. In the evening, the interaction seems to reverse: Extraverts benefit from low arousal, but introverts perform better under high arousal (Matthews, Jones, & Chamberlain, 1989). An analysis of error types in letter detection suggested the effect was associated with the lower rather than the upper level of control (Matthews,

1989). More demanding or complex attentional tasks, such as those that require attentional resources, fail to show the interactive effect (Matthews, Davies, & Lees, 1990).

The information-processing basis for the interaction is a matter of some debate. Humphreys and Revelle (1984) propose that extraversion (or impulsivity) and time of day interactively affect arousal, which in turn affects the availability of multiple attentional and STM resources. The restriction of the interaction to relatively undemanding tasks not limited by resource availability (Matthews, Davies, & Lees, 1990), however, implies that the underlying mechanism is associated with individual differences in low-level processing rather than in resources. Matthews and Harley (1993) have proposed alternatively that extraversion and arousal influence the spread of activation in a connectionist network: In the morning, increasing levels of cortical arousal decrease levels of random noise in extraverts, but increase noise in introverts. In other words, extraversion and time of day together regulate whether increases in cortical arousal enhance or degrade the sensitivity of the network. Matthews and Harley used a connectionist network simulation to show that individual differences in noise level may affect semantic priming of lexical decisions.

Experiments confirmed that extraversion and arousal are associated with individual differences in priming, as shown in Figure 1. Priming magnitude indicates the speed advantage resulting from prior presentation of a word semantically associated with the target word. Extraverts tend to show enhanced priming in high arousal states in the morning, but low arousal states in the evening. Together, the simulation and experimental data imply that extraversion and arousal may interactively affect a specific parameter of basic information processing related to random noise level. Comparison of simulation and experimental data ruled out other possible parameters, such as decay rate and strengths of excitatory connections between lexical and semantic processing units. Harley and Matthews (1992) ran a further experiment that replicated the personality effect on priming and showed that it was not attributable to postlexical processes associated with checking of responses. Priming was affected as predicted when nonwords were easily distinguished from words (so that lower-level activation processes were sufficient as a basis for response) but not when words and nonwords were confusable, forcing response checking after initial lexical access.

If extraversion and arousal interactively affect basic processing, they should affect intelligence test performance, particularly on tests on which speed is important as well as power. Several studies manipulating arousal by stimulant drugs (e.g., Gilliland, 1980) have confirmed that extraverts (or high impulsives) performed better when aroused. The most extensive series of studies (Revelle et al., 1980) also found that the interaction reversed in the evening, as in the later studies of simple attentional tasks (e.g., Matthews, 1989). Extraversion and arousal also interactively affect creativity test performance (Matthews, 1986), an effect that may be linked to individual differences in speed of retrieval from semantic memory (M. W. Eysenck, 1982). Revelle et al.'s (1980) data also provide some indication of the generality of effects on ability test performance. Most of their tests were of verbal ability, but in their Experiment 5 significant effects were also found on numerical and abstract tests. In most of these studies time pressure was considerable (5 minutes to answer 68 questions in the most extreme case). In the only study to approximate the conditions of a standard power test (Experiment 2; see Revelle et al., 1980, p. 24), personality effects were weaker than the norm and nonsignificant.

Verbal intelligence test performance is also sensitive to interactive effects of extraversion and arousal measured directly by self-report (Matthews, 1985) or by EEG alpha (Matthews & Amelang, 1993). Matthews (1983) performed a direct test of the role of subjective task difficulty in the Matthews (1985) study, by having subjects rate their confidence in their solution of each item. The time of day × extraversion × arousal interaction was significant only for items in which subjects were confident they were correct, and not for solutions of which subjects were uncertain. The interaction appears to be associated with failure of largely routine and unconscious lower-level processes, and not with impairment of the ability to solve complex, difficult problems. In Ackerman's (1988) terms, it may be perceptual speed rather than *g* that is sensitive to individual differences in network noise.

Extraversion: Adaptive Significance

Considered solely in terms of information-processing theory, the research reviewed presents a consistent picture. Time of day, extraversion, and arousal interactively affect spreading activation in a lower-level network controlling simple encoding and priming processes; both routine attentional tasks and speeded intelligence test performance are influenced by these network processes. The puzzle is why this rather complex interactive effect on performance

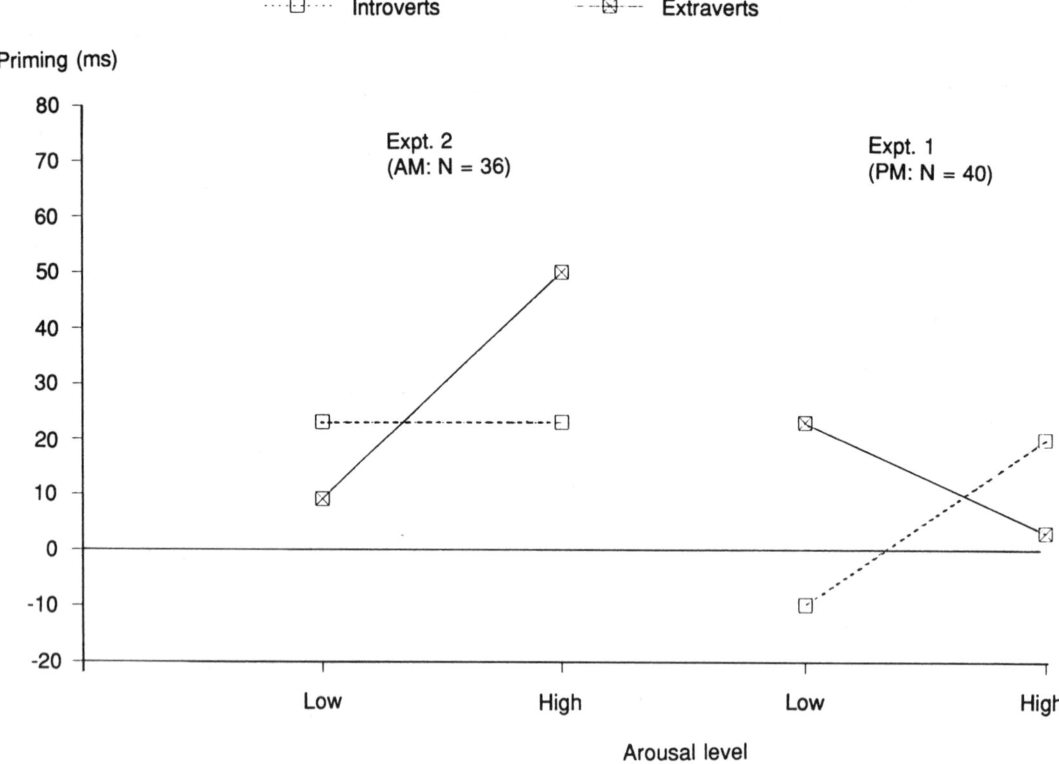

Figure 1. Priming magnitude as a function of extraversion and arousal level in studies run at two times of day (data from Matthews & Harley, 1993).

should be related to the central qualities associated with the extraversion trait (sociability, impulsivity, etc.). Humphreys and Revelle (1984) suggested that the interaction varies with time of day because extraversion/impulsivity is correlated with the circadian rhythm in arousal: extraverts/high impulsives tend to be evening types, whereas introverts/low impulsives tend to be morning types. Extraversion and impulsivity, however, are both too weakly linked to morningness-eveningness for this hypothesis to be convincing (Matthews, 1988).

Matthews and Harley (1993) advanced a different hypothesis: that the interaction is associated with the regulation of daily activities. Energetic arousal—the self-report dimension that interacts with extraversion—shows a pronounced diurnal rhythm, with a midday peak and low arousal in the early morning and in the evening (Thayer, 1989). The form of the diurnal arousal curve is similar in both extraverts and introverts. Hence a consequence of the interactive effect of extraversion on performance is that extraverts will tend to perform poorly during the early morning episode of low arousal, whereas introverts will be impaired during the low arousal of the evening. If introverts in fact tend to avoid social interaction, their performance impairment coincides with the time at which they are liable to be inactive (i.e., when parties and other social events typically take place). Conversely, at the time extraverts are most impaired (in the early morning), social events are relatively rare. Hence the performance interaction may be associated with the timing of daily activities to avoid or coincide with times of maximum social interaction. We can do no more than speculate about the more distal causes of the interaction. Possibly the performance effect is one of many biological and cognitive factors that influence phenotypic extraversion. If the cognitive system is unable to handle the processing demands of lively evening gatherings well, the person may be somewhat disposed to introversion.

DEMANDING ATTENTIONAL TASKS AND RESOURCES

The general idea of attentional resource models is that resource-limited processing requires input from a metaphorical energy or fuel supply to run successfully (Hirst & Kalmar, 1987). According to Townsend and Ashby (1983), resource limitation is a *macro* feature of the processing system that can be operationalized in terms of change in performance as processing load is varied; hence detailed knowledge of the *micro*-level processing architecture central to the network approach is not required (though, in practice, it may be useful). Resource usage is studied experimentally by varying task demands or, especially, by investigating performance of two or more concurrent tasks. There are, however, three major complications. First, resources may well be multiple, so that different types of processing draw on different energy supplies (Wickens, 1984). Humphreys and Revelle (1984) have discriminated resources for sustained throughput of information, required for many attentional tasks, from resources for STM. Second, some processing requires rather little allocation of resources for maximal performance; peripheral sensory and motor processes often have this characteristic of *data limitation* (Norman & Bobrow, 1975). Third, there are difficulties with most of the experimental techniques used to assess resource usage (Navon, 1984). Decrement in dual-task performance (i.e., interference) may be caused not just by an insufficiency of resources for combining the two tasks, but also by competition for specific processing structures and by overload of executive processes. Wickens (1984) points out that there is a "cost of concurrence" of dual-task performance believed to be associated with an executive time-sharing mechanism that coordinates sampling of stimuli and responses and also controls allocation of resources. Cost of concurrence is particularly associated with unpracticed performance at J. R. Anderson's (1982) cognitive state: People are often able to learn how to combine two tasks as a specific skill (Hirst & Kalmar, 1987).

Intelligence

The attraction of resource theory for the individual-differences researcher is the resemblance of the metaphor to Spearman's (1923) conception of *g* as a kind of intellectual energy. Ackerman (1988) proposes that *g* is associated with availability of resources for processing at the cognitive stage of skill learning, and presents evidence showing that correlations between *g* and performance decline when the task is sufficiently consistent for automatization to take place. The difficulty with this hypothesis is the assumption that a resource mechanism is involved; an alternative possibility is that *g* is associated with the efficiency of the executive functions involved in cognitive learning (Matthews, Jones, & Chamberlain, 1992). With respect to models of dual-task performance, we might expect *g* to be related to handling cost of concurrence as much as to resource availability. In any case, there is little psychometric evidence for a general attentional resource factor: Correlational studies of time sharing have generally failed to identify any consistent individual differences in concurrent performance of two tasks (Davies, Jones, & Taylor, 1984). There are more specific time-sharing factors associated with particular tasks (e.g., tracking; Braune & Wickens, 1986), but such task-specific factors do not appear to relate to *g* (Brookings, 1990).

Intelligence is only weakly related to many attentional tasks, such as vigilance and selective attention (Davies & Parasuraman, 1982; Davies et al., 1984). The relationship between *g* and attentional resources, however, can be assessed only within the specialized paradigms reviewed by Wickens (1984). A recent program of research on correlations between IQ and dual-task performance reported by Stankov (e.g., 1989), Spilsbury (e.g., 1992) and others sheds new light on the role of attentional resources. (Studies of working memory in this program are reviewed in the next section.) Several studies showed that competing tasks were more highly *g*-loaded than single tasks. For example, Roberts, Beh, and Stankov (1988) found that the correlation between card-sorting speed and Raven's matrices was stronger when the sorting task was combined with a secondary word-categorization task. Superficially, results of this kind suggest a correlation between *g* and resource availability, because dual-task performance presumably requires more resources than single task performance. Other studies, however, showed that the competing-task effect did not in fact seem to be mediated by individual differences in resource availability. A good example is provided by Sullivan and Stankov (1990), whose subjects combined "shadowing" (repeating aloud words presented visually) with a secondary task of detecting aurally presented target words. Although crystallized intelligence was associated with accuracy of shadowing, the main measure of resource availability provided by speed of secondary target detection was unrelated to measures of intelligence.

Spilsbury (1992) offers the general conclusion that increasing task difficulty or adding a competing task does not necessarily increase the correlation between *g* and performance. The critical factor seems to be task complexity: that is, the qualitative change in task demands associated with combining two tasks (Spilsbury, Stankov, & Roberts, 1990). A plausible interpretation of the dual-task data is that *g* is associated with the executive processes that sequence and interleave the components of the two tasks. In terms of Wickens's (1984) analysis, *g* may affect the cost of concurrence rather than resources.

Neuroticism: Empirical Data

It is well-established that neuroticism and related traits (e.g., trait anxiety, test anxiety) are associated with general performance decrements, particularly on more difficult tasks (Mueller, 1992). Depression, which tends to correlate with neuroticism, has also been related to a deficit in resources and controlled processing (Ellis & Ashbrook, 1987). Detrimental effects of anxiety are primarily associated with states of worry, rather than with the trait per se. Several resource theory accounts of the decrement have been proposed. Sarason et al. (1990) suggest that worry over evaluation diverts attentional resources that could otherwise be allocated to task performance. Humphreys and Revelle (1984) claim similarly that state anxiety reduces resources associated with on-task effort, which in turn impairs performance on tasks requiring sustained throughput of information. Test anxiety research has shown perceptual sensitivity decrement on a purely attentional sensory vigilance task under evaluative conditions (Geen, 1985), although vigilance is insensitive to neuroticism in neutral testing conditions (Davies & Parasuraman, 1982).

There have been surprisingly few rigorous dual-task studies of the relationship between anxiety and resources, although M. W. Eysenck (1992, p. 141) cites two studies showing slower secondary probe RT in trait-anxious subjects. Several studies show that anxiety tends to impair secondary rather than primary task performance (M. W. Eysenck, 1982), a result that could be attributed either to lack of resources or a strategy of increased selectivity of attention, or both. These findings provide some support for the resource hypothesis, but lack of control over the subject's strategy for allocating resources across primary and secondary tasks makes these results somewhat inconclusive. The greater distractibility of anxious subjects may also be attributable to a lack of resources for processing irrelevant stimuli, although it might also reflect a strategy of hypervigilant scanning for threat (M. W. Eysenck, 1992). Wells and Matthews (1994) point out that existing research often fails to discriminate between lack of resources and reluctance to exert executive control. For example, traits correlated with neuroticism (e.g., anxiety, mild depression) are associated with reduced use of elaborative strategies in memory (Mueller, 1992) and reduced use of probability information in vigilance (Griffin, Warm, & Dember, 1986). In general, though, the sheer range of performance functions sensitive to anxiety is suggestive of a resource mechanism.

Neuroticism: Adaptive Significance

Traditionally, anxiety related decrements on performance of demanding tasks have simply been taken as an indication of the dysfunctional nature of anxiety. There is a growing realization, however, that the loss of resources and executive efficiency may be accompanied by benefits if the situation is genuinely threatening. M. W. Eysenck (1992) suggests that state anxiety has an alarm function (in introducing a threat into conscious awareness), a prompt function (in accessing threat-related thoughts and images), and a preparation function (assisting anticipation of future situations). According to Wells and Matthews (1994), worry is useful for accessing information about discrepancies between the current state of the self and desired or socially normative states, and so plays a central role in self-regulation; it is only when worry is excessive or prolonged that it is liable to be maladaptive. The trade-off of increased self-related processing for reduced functional resources associated with neuroticism may be advantageous when threats to self-esteem are infrequent or disguised. For example, the neurotic individual may be better at detecting indirect criticism or early signs that all is not well with an intimate relationship. The low neurotic person may lack sensitivity to others in such contexts. However, when the threat is salient, the typical coping style of neurotics may disrupt effective threat processing. Consistent with these speculations, it appears that neurotic individuals (particularly neurotic introverts) are more accurate at identifying the feelings of others in neutral settings, but are impaired in their perceptions of others when subjected to interpersonal stress (Cunningham, 1977; Duckworth, 1975).

One expression of the neurotic adaptation may be impaired intelligence test performance because of overlap between the executive functions sensitive to *g* and to neuroticism. Relationships between *g* and neuroticism, however, tend to be weak: Trait anxiety measures associated with worry seem to be more strongly related to creativity test performance than to intelligence (Matthews, 1986). In general, neuroticism should maximally impair those tests that require strategy development and coping with novelty (i.e., fluid rather than crystallized intelligence). Leon and Revelle (1985) provide a demonstration of state-anxiety deficits on a task of this kind (a geometric analogical reasoning test presumably unfamiliar to subjects), although the strength of the effect did not vary with task difficulty. Effects of anxiety are much more context dependent than those of *g*, an effect that generalizes to intellectual tasks. Anxious subjects are particularly impaired by time stress on intelligence test performance (Morris & Liebert, 1969), possibly because time pressure prevents anxious subjects from dividing attention between processing task stimuli and self-evaluative processing. We might also expect particularly poor intelligence test performance in subjects low in *g* and high in neuroticism, an effect found for academic achievement by Spielberger (1966).

Extraversion: Empirical Data

M. W. Eysenck's (1982) review of extraversion effects on performance concluded that extraverts typically have more resources available than introverts, as evidenced by the former's greater resistance to distraction and response competition and faster retrieval of information from memory. M. W. Eysenck and Eysenck (1979) provided relatively direct evidence for the hypothesis, using a memory search task. Extraversion had little effect on single-task performance, but extraverts were faster when two searches had to be conducted simultaneously. In contrast, extraverts are reliably poorer in performance of "traditional" vigilance tasks (i.e., those in which events and signals are infrequent), although this effect may reflect the low arousal engendered by tasks of this kind. Koelega's (1992) meta-analysis of the vigilance data showed modest but significant relationships between extraversion and lower detection rate, lower perceptual sensitivity, and greater decrease in detection rate over time. The effect on detection rate was significant for visual but not for auditory tasks.

The conflict between extraverts' superiority on demanding attentional tasks and their poorer vigilance is resolved by recent vigilance research. In fact, so-called traditional vigilance tasks are not strongly resource limited (Parasuraman, Warm & Dember, 1987); individual differences in resources are important only for tasks that have high event rates or are otherwise demanding (Matthews, Davies, & Holley, 1993). Matthews, Davies, and Lees (1990) and Matthews, Davies, and Holley (1990) found some evidence for superior performance of extraverts on high-event-rate symbolic processing tasks, consistent with the resource hypothesis, although the effect was not very strong. A more reliable advantage is found for subjects high in energetic arousal (Matthews, Davies, & Holley, 1990); this is consistent with Humphreys and Revelle's (1984) multiple resource theory, which proposes that arousal is positively correlated with availability of resources for sustained information transfer. Matthews, Davies, and Holley (1990) tentatively suggest that extraverts may tend to perform better on attentionally demanding tasks with symbolic stimuli, but worse on perceptually demanding tasks with visual stimuli. Extraverts' advantage in dual-task performancc may, in Spilsbury et al.'s (1990) terms, be on difficult rather than complex tasks, because extraverts appear to be poorer than introverts at complex problem-solving tasks requiring insight (Kumar & Kapila, 1987) and at perceptual maze tasks (Weinman, 1987). Possible strategic explanations for such effects are discussed in a later section.

Extraverts may also exhibit superior skilled performance to introverts when the task is both resource-demanding and symbolic in nature. Matthews et al. (1992) showed that extraversion predicted greater speed and accuracy of performance on a simulated mail-sorting task in a sample of 53 post office trainees selected on the basis of ability tests similar to the digit-symbol substitution task, but not in a sample of 158 unselected members of the public. Further analyses suggested that correlates of skilled performance varied with ability level. In low-ability subjects (thought to be at the early, cognitive stage of skill development), elementary information processing measures were the main predictors of performance; in high-ability subjects (believed to be at the later, autonomous stage), personality was more predictive than elementary processing measures. In other words, extraverts' higher resource availability may only have been beneficial in those subjects who found the task relatively simple and so had developed stable procedures for performing it.

Extraversion: Adaptive Significance

As discussed previously, greater availability of attentional resources (particularly for symbolic or verbal processing) is likely to be adaptive for dealing with time-pressuring or social environments, such as the giddy whirl of social events that extraverts profess to enjoy. The introvert seems better adjusted to unspeeded, but possibly more complex activities such as problem solving, in which the quality of strategy choice is more important than resource availability. On these grounds we might expect superior performance by extraverts on speeded and relatively simple IQ tests, and more accurate performance by introverts on unspeeded power tests. The former hypothesis receives some support in that extraverts do indeed tend to solve intelligence test items faster than introverts (e.g., Goh & Farley, 1977). There is little evidence from the studies cited for greater accuracy in introverts, however, so there is a degree of conflict between these data and those on problem solving—possibly because of neglect of the exact information-processing demands of the tests used.

SHORT-TERM MEMORY: PASSIVE STORAGE AND ACTIVE CONTROL

The psychology of short-term retention is dauntingly complex. Within the levels-of-control framework, information can be retained in an accessible state in several ways. First, as in connectionist models reviewed by Brown and Hulme (in press), persistent activation of network units preserves information at the lower level. Memory may be conceptualized as those long-term memory nodes that are currently active (J. R. Anderson, 1982), or as a set of "traces" that decay or are over-written with time. Second, retention is also influenced by the upper level of control, through strategies such as active rehearsal, reorganization of material, and chunking. Implementation of such strategies may in turn require that general-purpose or specialized STM resources are voluntarily allocated to retention (Humphreys & Revelle, 1984). One of the most influential theories of STM, Baddeley's (1986) working memory model, describes how upper-level controlled processes work in concert with specialized lower-level processes. The core of the working memory system is the central executive that controls a variety of strategic functions. These include relaying information to two "slave" systems—the articulatory loop, which uses subvocal rehearsal to maintain information, and the visuospatial scratchpad, which holds spatially coded material (we will not consider the scratchpad further here). The central executive has some independent temporary storage capacity, but its nature is poorly specified. Verbal information has privileged status in that it also enters (in syntactically processed form) a passive verbal input register where it is insensitive to control processes. It follows that individual differences in retention may be derived from a variety of sources, and the careful experimental techniques developed by Baddeley and others are necessary to distinguish them.

Intelligence

Two diametrically opposed trends are evident in the literature on STM correlates of intelligence: the psychometric identification of general STM factors that correlate with *g*, and attempts to establish relationships of differing strength between specific components of STM and *g*. The first approach is exemplified in work reported by Kyllonen and Christal (1990). In four studies (*N*s = 412 to 723), they fitted correlational data to a structural model with a single factor of working memory capacity (defined by four to six measures) and additional intellectual factors (e.g., reasoning). Correlations between working memory and reasoning factors varied from .8 to .9; working memory was more weakly correlated with general knowledge and intelligence-speed factors. The authors conclude that reasoning ability may reflect little more than working memory capacity, and they suggest that Baddeley's (1986) central executive may control both types of performance. Tasks of this kind, however, are poorly suited to discriminating the role of specific components. The working memory tasks used by Kyllonen and Christal in fact are so complex that they overlap with the reasoning tasks; both sets of tasks included grammatical reasoning tasks, mental arithmetic tasks, and tasks requiring rule-based recoding of character strings. It is possible that all or most of Kyllonen and Christal's memory tasks sampled a range of components whose influence on *g* is conflated in the memory factor. Kyllonen and Christal did not in any case test the single-memory-factor model against multiple-factor models, which would have required additional, component-based measures.

There are several reasons for testing for the roles of specific components, in addition to the theoretical distinctions outlined previously. First, different measures of short-term retention do not always correlate. Martin (1978) has shown that ordered recall tasks such as digit span are largely independent of free-recall tasks, where items may be recalled in any order. Horn (1986) claims that there are two well-replicated primary STM factors (associative memory and span memory) and three additional primaries of uncertain reliability. He also identifies a second-order short-term acquisition and retrieval factor distinct from other secondaries (e.g., fluid and crystallized intelligence). Second, studies of individual differences implicate a variety of distinct processing and storage elements of STM (although not all sources of individual differences in STM are necessarily associated with individual differences in ability). Studies of individual differences in digit span illustrate the complexity of data and theory in this area. Dempster's (1981) comprehensive review suggests that the strongest individual-difference factor related to span is item identification, indexed by measures such as item-recognition time and naming speed. Item identification could plausibly be related to the basic or lower-level information-processing correlates of *g* previously described (see Rabbitt & Maylor, 1991). Naming speed also depends on speed of subvocal rehearsal or articulation rate. Baddeley (1986) sees this factor as critical in determining the capacity of the articulatory loop, but Dempster (1981) argues that digit span is unrelated to individual differences in articulation rate. Dempster (1981) also claims that span is not associated with either capacity limitations or strategic processes, but that strategies such as rehearsal, grouping, and chunking may contribute to other ordered short-term retention tasks. Direct evidence for the role of strategic factors was obtained by Geiselman, Woodward, and Beatty (1982), who used structural modeling of free-recall data to show that the ratio of maintenance rehearsal to elaborative rehearsal predicted better STM and poorer LTM.

In summary, there are at least four components of STM that may contribute directly to the performance of intelligence tests and are potentially conflated in measures of complex working memory tasks:

- Item identification
- Specialized stores within the working memory model (e.g., the verbal input register and articulatory loop)
- Resources (which may be general or specific to STM)
- Executive control processes (e.g., those controlling strategy use)

Item Identification

Next we consider evidence relating to the roles of these processes in intelligence, although such evidence is scarce because of the reluctance of individual-difference researchers to decompose short-term retention into theoretically meaningful elements. The role of item identification is a case in point. If such processes explain individual differences in digit span (Dempster, 1981), and digit span correlates with *g*, does item identification mediate the correlation? Such a hypothesis gains credibility from the associations discussed previously between speed of basic information processing and *g*. In addition, Kyllonen and Christal's (1990) structural model show a path of .3 to .4 between the general working memory factor and a processing-speed factor. Ideally, we could use regression or structural modeling approaches to test whether item identification predicts variance in *g* over and above that predicted by measures of passive store usage, resource availability, and specific strategies. No such test has been conducted, though, and the hypothesis must remain conjectural.

Specialized Stores: Verbal Input Register

Rate of forgetting seems to be independent of *g* (Rabbit & Maylor, 1991), but studies of the specific stores posited by Baddeley (1986) are rather lacking. The relationship between ability and the verbal input register can be assessed from studies of the recency effect (the tendency for the last few items in a sequence to be recalled better than earlier items). Although there are a variety of explanations for such effects, the recency effect in short-term free recall is satisfactorily explained by positing a separate passive store, because it is insensitive to secondary task manipulations and the subject's intentions (Glenberg et al., 1980; Hitch, 1980). Early studies of free recall suggested that intelligence effects were largely a function of rehearsal strategy (M. W. Eysenck, 1977, pp. 286–288). For example, Fagan (1972) found that intelligence was related mainly to free recall of words presented early and in the middle of the list (rather than to the later words associated with the recency effect) and Hitch's (1980) verbal input register. More intelligent children rehearsed material more strongly, and they were more likely to rehearse present and previous items concurrently. Intelligence is more strongly related to free recall of lists on which the person can choose to reorganize the words around semantic categories than to lists on which there is no scope for a reorganization strategy (Jensen & Frederiksen, 1973).

In a study of particular interest, Crawford and Stankov (1983) have shown significant correlations between intelligence and recency in free recall. They assessed a variety of other STM measures, including forward and backward digit span and free recall of the initial words in a list, which also tends to be enhanced (the primacy effect) as a result of rehearsal processes (Glenberg et al., 1980). The correlational data provided by Crawford and Stankov (1983) thus allow partial correlations to be computed between these STM measures and psychometric factors related to verbal comprehension (V), cognitive speed (S), and inductive reasoning (I). Controlling for item identification and rehearsal by controlling the digit-span measures and free recall of primary items, free-recall recency is significantly positively correlated with V ($r = .32$, $p < .01$), negatively correlated with S ($r = -.25$, $p < .05$), and nonsignificantly correlated with I ($r = .16$), probably the closest equivalent to *g*. With recency and primacy in free recall controlled, forward digit span is positively related to I ($r = .30$, $p < .01$), and backward digit span to S ($r = .30$, $p < .01$). These data suggest that different components of memory may be associated with different ability dimensions. Enhanced passive verbal storage seems to be an advantage only for verbal comprehension tasks, consistent with the use of the verbal input register in speech comprehension (Hitch, 1980).

Specialized Stores: Articulatory Loop

Cantor, Engle, and Hamilton (1991) investigated the role of Baddeley's (1986) articulatory loop in verbal ability. They showed that ability was independently predicted by both word span and probe recall (conceptualized as measures of passive storage in STM) and a complex working memory task (conceptualized as a measure of the central executive). Digit span did not predict ability, implying that item identification speed (Dempster, 1981) and articulation rate (Baddeley, 1986) may not have contributed to the correlations with ability. Cantor et al. (1991) also review evidence suggesting that increased dependence of recall on maintenance rehearsal reduces the relationship between ability and *g*. They conclude that verbal ability relates to both passive storage and executive control in STM, but not to articulatory rehearsal. Given the data discussed in the previous section, it may be the verbal input register that contributes the passive storage component. Given considerable evidence that digit span relates to *g* (e.g., Kyllonen & Christal, 1990), it would be premature to conclude that articulatory loop capacity is unrelated to ability, but it may not correlate with verbal ability.

Resource Limitations of STM

More recent studies run by Stankov and his colleagues have investigated whether individual differences in intelligence are associated with working memory capacity limitations. As described above, this research program has shown that correlations between task performance and *g* increase with complexity, an effect that might be attributed to working memory load increasing with complexity (Spilsbury, Stankov, & Roberts, 1990). Myors, Stankov, and Oliphant (1989) and Spilsbury et al. (1990), however, have shown that although problem-solving performance relates both to the working memory load of the task and to psychometric intelligence, there is no interaction between the two factors, implying that the *g*-loading of the task does not vary with working memory load. Hence complexity is not reducible to working memory and probably relates to qualitative changes in the nature of the task. Spilsbury (1992) showed that the correlation between fluid intelligence and a mental counting task placing high demands on working memory increased from .18 to .53 when counting performance had to be combined with a word-meanings task. The correlation of intelligence with counting task performance, however, did not vary with the memory load of the task. Further analysis showed that the interaction between intelligence and complexity was accounted for by recency and primacy measures taken from an ordered-digit recall task (considered to reflect active strategic processes rather than memory capacity per se). A variety of attentional measures failed to explain the interaction.

STM and g: Conclusions

Despite the complexity of the evidence, it seems that some of the various components of STM are more strongly related to ability than others. Figure 2 summarizes the major components discussed within the context of the working memory model (omitting the visuospatial scratchpad; Baddeley, 1986) and their relationships with operational measures. Tentatively, we may conclude that it is individual differences in the control processes associated with active working memory (Baddeley's central executive) that are the strongest single influence on correlations between *g* and STM tasks. The strength of the relationship between factorial measures of working memory and ability in Kyllonen and Christal's (1990) study may reflect the importance of executive control in their rather complex working memory tasks. The central executive is notoriously difficult to characterize, but it may be especially concerned with the dynamic updating of the contents of memory (N. Morris & Jones, 1990). Individual differences in STM resources appear to be a minor influence at most.

There also appears to be some involvement of specific lower-level processing functions in individual differences in ability. Reanalysis of Crawford and Stankov's (1983) data implies that passive storage in Hitch's (1980) verbal input register may contribute to verbal ability independently of other components of STM; Baddeley's (1986) visuospatial scratchpad might relate to spatial ability. There is also some evidence for links between item identification, STM, and general ability, but detailed proof is lacking. Mental speed might be associated with several lower-level components of working memory, including item identification and the rate of recycling information through lower-level networks. As yet, there is no strong evidence that either articulation rate or articulatory loop capacity influences ability, but more research is needed. All the memory components discussed might plausibly contribute directly to the performance of intelligence tests, and so might mediate correlations between intelligence and personality.

Neuroticism: Empirical Data

The overall performance decrement associated with anxiety generalizes to STM tasks, although there is some uncertainty over the exact roles of state and trait anxiety. In reviewing studies of digit span, M. W. Eysenck (1982) concludes that only state anxiety is reliably correlated with memory impairment; however, more demanding tasks (e.g., competitive paired-associate learning) do appear to show trait-anxiety deficits, though anxiety may enhance learning of easy paired associates. M. W. Eysenck (1985) found that trait anxiety was negatively associated with letter transformation speed when memory load was high: A further experiment showed the effect was attributable to rehearsal and storage processes rather than letter access or transformation. Darke (1988) found a detrimental effect of trait test anxiety on digit span, but the anxiety decrement on a more complex sentence verification task was stronger.

One explanation for these effects is the general deficit in resources associated with anxiety discussed previously: We might reasonably expect Darke's (1988) sentence verification task to require more attentional resources than digit span. The restriction of anxiety effects to memory-related components in M. W. Eysenck's (1985) study might simply result from the tasks's attentional components being insufficiently demanding to be strongly resource limited. Although a resource explanation based on the cognitive interference associated with neuroticism and anxiety remains plausible, however, resource limitations may not be the whole story. Anxiety may also impair control processes in memory over and above any effect on resources. In a series of studies, Mueller has shown that trait anxiety is associated with a reduction in the use of active and elaborative rehearsal strategies. For example, Mueller (1976) used a free-recall task to show that anxiety did not affect passive storage of information, but anxiety was associated with reduced clustering in recall of semantically or phonemically related items. Clustering is usually seen as an indication of the subject's voluntary reorganization of material between encoding and retrieval.

Neuroticism: Adaptive Significance

Effects of neuroticism on memory appear to be similar to those on demanding attentional tasks, and may reflect a similar adaptive trade-off. Again, upper-level processing effort appears to be diverted from external task performance to self-regulative activities. Under some circumstances, the anxious person may be capable of compensating for this loss of task-available memory capacity through increased effort (M. W. Eysenck, 1992), although the relationship between anxiety and effort seems somewhat unstable (Geen, 1987). Taking the attention and memory studies together, there is stronger evidence for linking processing resources to anxiety than to intelligence, consistent with the hypothesis that anxious subjects tend to time-share task processing with self-regulative processing. Low anxiety and intelligence, however, appear to be broadly comparable in their association with more efficient use of control processes, such that both char-

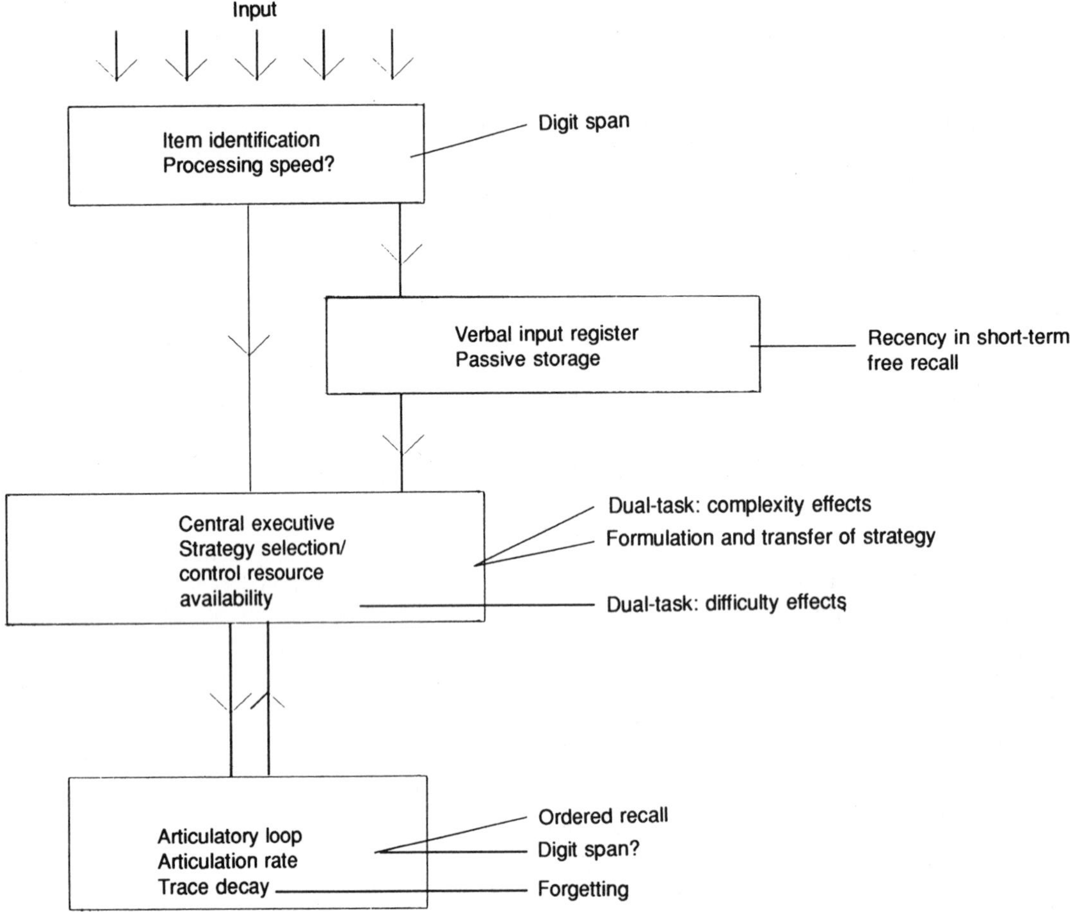

Figure 2. Some components of working memory, and their relationship to performance measures used in studies of individual differences.

acteristics are likely to be most advantageous on complex tasks. It is unclear how much overlap there is in the specific control processes affected. Both factors seem to affect clustering strategies in free recall (Jensen & Frederiksen, 1973; Mueller, 1976), but their strategic effects may well differ in detail.

Extraversion: Empirical Data

Studies of extraversion show a fairly reliable association between extraversion and superior STM, and a less reliable negative correlation between extraversion and LTM (M. W. Eysenck, 1982; Matthews, 1992). Again, the relationship between extraversion and STM may be mediated by factors not directly associated with short-term storage. As with neurotic subjects, introverts' decrement on STM seems to be especially marked on more demanding tasks, such as paired-associate learning under conditions of response competition (M. W. Eysenck, 1982). As Eysenck infers, results of this kind can be plausibly linked to personality differences in resource availability; however, the effect may be limited to verbal tasks. In two fairly large-scale studies of tasks requiring short-term retention of single characters, Matthews, Davies, and Lees (1990; N = 100) and Matthews et al. (1989; N = 116) found no effect of extraversion on demanding working memory tasks requiring combined visual and memory search, or memory search alone.

Extraversion appears to have weaker effects on strategy use in STM than does neuroticism: Matthews (1992) reviews studies of extraversion and semantic clustering in free recall that provide extremely inconsistent results. There is also some direct evidence for an association between extraversion and passive verbal storage. As discussed previously, demonstrations of superior free recall in extraverts are ambiguous because a variety of processes contribute to free recall; the variation of the personality effect with serial position, and its sensitivity to experimental manipulation, provide more direct evidence. Matthews (1992) presents data on free recall as a function of extraversion and serial position in the word list. Recall probability was not much affected by extraversion in the early and middle parts of the list, but extraverts showed a greater recency effect, as shown in Figure 3. In terms of Hitch's (1980) analysis of working memory, this finding provides fairly direct evidence for extraverts storing more information in the verbal input register. As Baddeley (1986) describes, the role of other components of STM may be tested by secondary task manipulations. The role of the articulatory loop is tested by requiring the subject to articulate a meaningless phrase out loud, and the role of the central executive is investigated by adding an additional, concurrent memory load. In the Matthews (1992) study, these manipulations had no effect on individual differences in recency, implying that extraversion effects on recency are not related to either the articulatory loop or the central executive.

The correlation between extraversion and digit span appears to be weak (Blake, 1971). Ordered-recall tasks similar to digit span, however, are sensitive to interactive effects of time of day, extraversion, and arousal in the same way as the simple attentional tasks discussed earlier in relation to basic information processing. Matthews et al. (1989) obtained similar triple interactions with five-choice serial reaction (a purely attentional task) and ordered recall of a nine-digit sequence. A study of EEG arousal (Matthews & Amelang, 1983) showed that extraverts low in EEG alpha power (high arousal) showed better short-term ordered recall of strings of eight consonants and, consistent with the attentional hypothesis, faster probe RT during retention. Introverts performed better on both tasks when high in EEG alpha (low arousal). These data are consistent with Dempster's (1981) hypothesis that individual differences in digit span are associated with item identification processes.

Individual differences in noise within lower-level

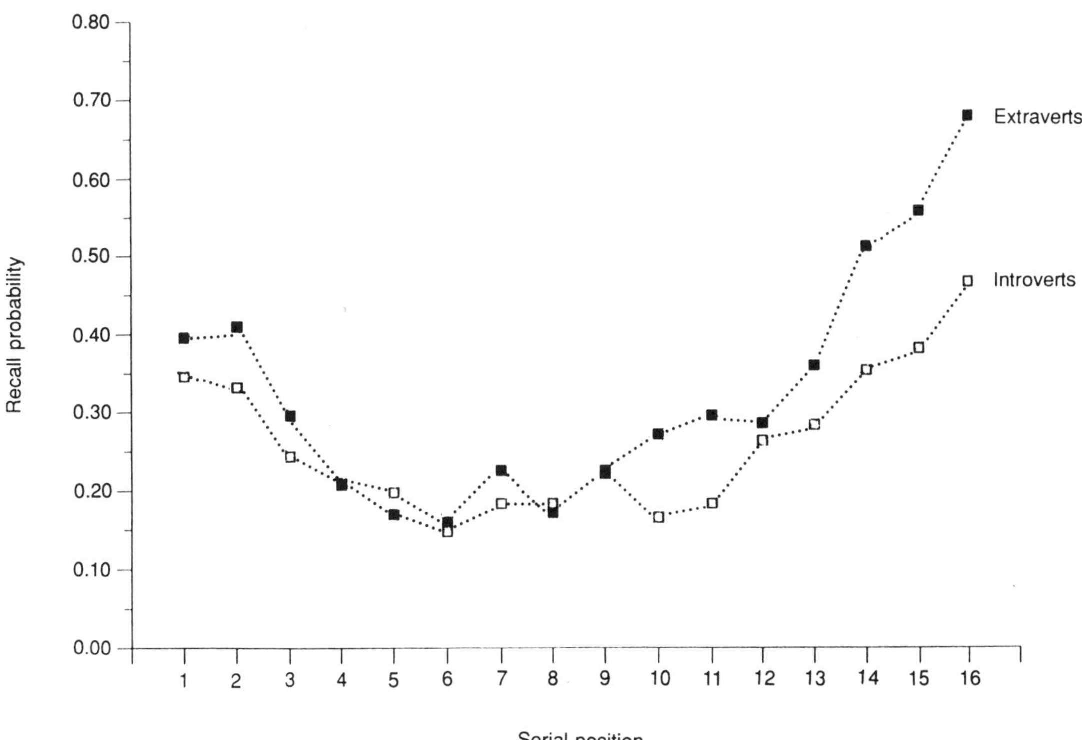

Figure 3. Recall probability in free recall of word lists as a function of extraversion and serial position (Matthews, 1992; copyright Academic Press).

processing networks may influence ordered recall, as well as attentional tasks such as lexical decision (Harley & Matthews, 1992). Matthews (1987) showed that the extraversion × arousal interaction (assessed in the morning) generalized to a working memory task used by Baddeley, Logie, Nimmo-Smith, and Brereton (1985) that required ordered recall of words embedded in sentences. Recall was reduced by both articulatory suppression and concurrent memory load manipulations, consistent with the hypothesis that the articulatory loop and the central executive contribute to performance on this task. There was no further interaction between these manipulations and extraversion and arousal, however, implying that the interactive effect was associated with the low-level attentional demands of encoding the words rather than with the memory structures posited by Baddeley (1986).

Extraversion: Adaptive Significance

Studies of extraversion contrast with studies of neuroticism and of *g* in that the low-level mechanism of passive, automatic verbal storage appears to be the main vehicle for extraverts' superiority in STM, although other mechanisms may possibly contribute to the effect. This individual difference may help to support verbal skills that facilitate adaptation to social interaction. Hitch (1980) proposes that the verbal input register is used to provide backup storage in speech comprehension. Extraverts may have an advantage in processing complex or ambiguous utterances in that they can refer back to a more extensive record of what the speaker has just said. To the extent that active STM processes are the primary correlate of *g*, we would not expect that extraversion should correlate strongly with typical intelligence tests, which seems to be the case. Because recency in free recall seems to be implicated in verbal ability (Crawford & Stankov, 1983), we might expect that some verbal intelligence tests would correlate with *g*, although the empirical data are inconsistent on this point (Saklofske & Kostura, 1990).

It is possible that extraversion would be positively related to verbal ability in naturalistic settings (where the problem had to be encoded from speech) rather than being available for reference throughout the period of problem solution (as in an IQ test). Alternatively, verbal ability may be mainly sensitive to interactive effects of extraversion and arousal (Matthews, 1985), so that individual differences in speed of lower-level processing are the primary influence on this test category. These individual differences may affect test performance through their effects on ordered short-term recall (Matthews et al., 1989), as well as through verbal encoding. A study of WAIS performance conducted by Rawlings and Carnie (1989) showed that extraverts were superior on a verbal processing test (WAIS Information) only under conditions of time pressure. Conversely, introverts were superior to extraverts on digit span under timed but not untimed conditions.

STRATEGY SELECTION AND APPLICATION

Strategies may be defined as modifiable procedures for organizing cognitive processes in acquiring knowledge and solving problems (Baron, 1982), such as selecting a focus for attention, choosing the type of representation for a problem, and regulating various processing trade-offs (e.g., the relative importance of speed and accuracy). As such, strategies are the specific operations of the upper-level executive system. They can be modeled as high-level productions that require both triggering stimuli and specific goals as inputs (J. R. Anderson, 1982). At the cognitive stage of skilled performance, strategies are developed "on-line" from the person's declarative knowledge of the problem. With more practiced skills, the strategy is held in procedural form in LTM, while remaining sensitive to the person's immediate aims.

There are several dangers inherent in the strategy concept. There is a tendency in empirical work for strategies to be invoked as a post hoc "fudge factor" when data cannot be explained any other way. Strategy explanations also risk circularity; that is, they may be no more than a redescription of the phenomena for which an explanation is sought. Brand (1987) criticizes strategy hypotheses on grounds of lack of falsifiability and parsimony. It may also be difficult to distinguish strategies from lower-level processes. What is required are detailed specifications of specific control functions that can be measured independently of the other processes they influence (see Logan, 1985, for examples). In this section, we consider those studies of individual-difference factors that have investigated the role of strategies most directly.

Intelligence

General ability is correlated with some aspects of strategy selection, as demonstrated most clearly in Sternberg's work on metacomponents. Sternberg

(1985) lists a variety of metacomponents, but those subjected to empirical analysis are primarily concerned with time management in problem solving. Sternberg (1981) showed that ability was associated with greater time spent on global planning, planning solution of problems of varied format, and less time spent on local planning for problems of a specific type. Sternberg (1985) also points out that a "reflective" style of problem solving and slow problem encoding is associated with a higher quality of performance. It is not unreasonable to suppose that effective time management strategies contribute directly to test performance; such strategies, however, seem partially distinct from *g*. Wagner and Sternberg (cited in Sternberg, 1985) assessed strategies for time allocation and using adjunct information in reading. In some cases these strategies predicted reading performance, but as Brody (1992) points out, they were generally unrelated to verbal ability. Another strategy that may be associated with high *g* has been identified by Carpenter, Just, and Schell (1990) in a study comparing a simulation of Raven's Progressive Matrices performance with real subjects. To simulate more able subjects, they incorporated goal management procedures which implemented strategies such as control of the order in which procedures were run, and modification of the procedures which directly controlled task performance. The authors conclude that the decomposition of problems into manageable segments and management of a hierarchy of goals and subgoals are important elements of successful performance on this test.

Evidence of the kind discussed fails to deal with several important questions. First, it does not directly test whether *g* is solely or mainly associated with metacomponential function, because speed of information processing may contribute to ability over and above metacomponential effects. As discussed previously, strategy use does not explain correlations between *g* and simple basic processing tasks. Second, there are several different ways in which individual differences in strategy use might contribute to test performance, which have not been distinguished. More intelligent subjects might simply have a wider range of strategies available, or they might be more efficient in (a) strategy implementation in general, (b) implementation of complex strategies, (c) selecting the optimal strategy for a specific task, or (d) modifying strategies in response to task feedback.

There is some evidence that bears on these issues. Rabbitt and Maylor (1991) discuss evidence from their laboratory that *g* is unrelated to efficiency of simple strategies used for controlling speed-accuracy trade-off. For example, all subjects slow down following an error in speeded response, but there is no relationship between general ability and the amount of slowing. At a more molar level of analysis, *g* does not seem to relate to choice of speed-accuracy trade-off. Studies of error rate averaged across the task run show that, if anything, more intelligent subjects are more accurate as well as faster on RT tasks, although the relationship between *g* and error rate is frequently nonsignificant (Jensen, 1987).

Evidence on the availability and application of strategies comes from studies of mental retardation. There is extensive evidence that retardation is associated with difficulties in maintenance and transfer of strategies, effects attributed to executive processes that control and monitor subordinate processing operations (Belmont, Butterfield, & Ferretti, 1982). The role of executive processes is shown by demonstrations that the mentally retarded often can be taught the strategies for specific tasks, but such subjects seem to fail to realize spontaneously that the strategies can also be applied to novel tasks (Campione, Brown, & Ferrara, 1982). These studies largely avoid the difficulties inherent in correlational studies of strategy by manipulating strategy use through instruction. The exact skills involved are somewhat elusive: Ferretti and Cavalier (1991) point out that attempts to train specific strategic skills have met with mixed success. They also present evidence suggesting that there is more of a gradation in strategy use across mentally retarded and normal subjects than is sometimes appreciated.

Unfortunately, it is unclear whether strategy generalization is correlated with *g* in adults, although there are some data on children. Ferrara, Brown, and Campione (1986) showed that more intelligent children required fewer hints in acquiring rules to learn a series completion task and showed greater transfer of previously learned rules to new problems, particularly when previously learned rules had to be integrated with new rules. Ferretti and Butterfield (1992), however, showed that whereas mentally retarded children showed clear deficits in strategy transfer, there was no difference in transfer between average and gifted children. An earlier study using the same problem-solving task (Ferretti & Butterfield, 1989) did show that gifted children tended to adopt spontaneously more sophisticated strategies than average children, although transfer effects were not tested.

In summary, *g* may be correlated with availability and efficiency of some strategies, particularly complex strategies such as those for time and goal management. The importance of strategies of this kind for complex working memory tasks may explain the strong association between working memory and *g* (Kyllonen & Christal, 1990), although direct measurement of strategy use in working memory has been neglected. The evidence reviewed, though, does not suggest that strategy availability and use should be given special status. As with specific lower-level processes, there may simply be a modest tendency for measures of availability and efficiency of strategy use to correlate with *g*, with some correlations being quite large and others minimal. Where the strategies available are fairly simple, IQ appears to be more strongly associated with overall efficient lower-level functioning than with specific strategy use (e.g., Matthews & Dorn, 1989). Studies of mental retardation suggest that strategy generalization under executive control may be of special importance, but it is unclear whether it is central to normal, adult intelligence. It may be relevant that people do not normally receive much formal instruction in strategies for internal information management in task performance. The advantage of the more intelligent person in more complex tasks may in part reflect the need to develop information-handling strategies spontaneously. At a causal level, it is plausible that strategy use contributes directly to performance, but the relationship between strategy use and other elements of information processing remains unclear. Rapid processing may be a direct prerequisite for adopting a complex strategy if, for example, a number of lower-level processing units must be activated simultaneously to trigger a complex production. The relationship between low-level processing and strategy development might also be ontogenetic, as M. Anderson (1992) has suggested.

Neuroticism: Empirical Data

We have already discussed evidence that neuroticism may be characterized by reduced use of active, elaborative strategies in memory (Mueller, 1992). There is an unfortunate lack of research on neuroticism and learning and use of the high-level strategies implicated in intelligence test performance. One study by Weinman, Elithorn and Cooper (1985) does provide relevant evidence; these authors used a perceptual maze task to distinguish initial searching of the maze prior to response from time for checking the response pathway initially traced. Weinman et al. also varied whether an explicit criterion for the optimal solution was provided. Results showed that neuroticism was significantly positively correlated with search time when no criterion was provided, but there were no significant correlations with checking time, implying that neurotic subjects were not generally cautious. On the most complex mazes used, neurotic subjects were also slower overall on no-criterion trials. The dependence of the performance decrement in neurotics on lack of information about the problem is somewhat reminiscent of the special difficulties of low-intelligence subjects when exposed to novel tasks. It could plausibly be argued that absence of criterion made selection of a search strategy more difficult, and neurotic subjects were particularly disadvantaged under these circumstances.

In the main part of this section, we consider the relationship between neuroticism and the simpler strategic task of controlling speed-accuracy trade-off. Research on test anxiety (Geen, 1987) shows that under evaluative conditions, anxiety is associated with behavioral caution. For example, Geen (1985) showed that on a vigilance task, anxious subjects detected fewer signals but also tended to commit fewer false-positive errors. A signal detection theory analysis showed that anxious subjects given evaluative instructions adopted a conservative response criterion (i.e., they required a relatively high level of sensory evidence for response). Test anxiety did not affect response criterion when subjects were given reassuring instructions. Geen (1987) interprets results of this kind as showing that in situations carrying an evaluation threat, test anxiety is associated with a strategy of passive avoidance and, if the situation permits, actual escape. The effect seems to be at least partially cognitively mediated; Geen (1987) describes studies in which caution in responding was associated with worry. It should be noted that evaluative cues may be essential for effects of this kind. In Matthews's (1992) series of studies of personality and performance in neutral conditions, there has been no tendency for neuroticism or tense arousal to be associated with a more conservative speed-accuracy trade-off or raised response criterion.

Strategic caution, however, is not the whole story: Sometimes anxious impulsivity (Wallace, Newman, & Bachorowski, 1991) is observed. For example, Leon and Revelle (1985) found that state-anxious subjects adopted a riskier speed-accuracy trade-off on geometric analogy problems under time-pressuring instructions. Both psychobiological and cognitive explanations for this phenomenon have been advanced.

Wallace et al. (1991) suggest that the effect is associated with two brain mechanisms: the greater arousability of neurotic subjects (Eysenck & Eysenck, 1985), and the greater sensitivity to motor inhibition of trait anxious-individuals (Gray, 1981). In this formulation, anxiety and neuroticism are distinguished, with anxiety is seen as a mixture of introversion and anxiety (though the psychometric evidence for this hypothesis is not supportive; e.g., Rocklin & Revelle, 1981). Normally motor inhibition is dominant, leading to greater behavioral caution, but under some task and motivational conditions, modulatory control of response breaks down, so that response speed is enhanced by greater arousal. Zinbarg and Revelle (1989) offer an alternative explanation for anxious impulsivity that emphasizes cognitive factors. They follow Gray (1981) in arguing that anxious subjects are particularly sensitive to punishment cues (with anxiety seen as closer to neuroticism than to introversion). Response depends on expectancies, however, which depend on impulsivity and learning as well as anxiety. A series of studies obtained complex but replicable interactions among anxiety, impulsivity, and type of cue that were broadly consistent with this hypothesis.

Neuroticism: Adaptive Significance

Previously we suggested that neuroticism and *g* may have some commonality of effect on executive control processes, a hypothesis consistent with Weinman et al.'s (1985) finding that neurotics are slower at maze searching when information about the optimal solution is lacking. The data reviewed show that neuroticism is differentiated from *g* by its effects on speed-accuracy trade-off, which is normally insensitive to ability. In contrast to *g*, neuroticism may be associated with both simple and complex strategy effects. The evidence can be explained by supposing that performance effects are in part an expression of the coping strategies adopted by neurotic subjects to deal with perceived threat. Neuroticism tends to be correlated with increased use of emotion-focused coping strategies, and decreased use of problem-focused coping (McCrae & Costa, 1986). Emotion-focused coping leads to allocation of processing effort to internal self-regulation rather than to task performance, which in turn leads to specific performance effects (e.g., reluctance to respond, reluctance to engage in complex strategic processing, and overall performance impairment; Wells & Matthews, 1994). Implementation of the coping strategy, however, may depend on other factors, such as contextual cues. Anxious subjects may actually show greater task-directed effort if emotion-focused coping is blocked through instructions (see Sarason et al., 1990), if task performance is seen as directly instrumental in threat avoidance (see M. W. Eysenck, 1982), or if expectancies associated with other personality characteristics and task cues override the tendency toward emotional focus (e.g., Zinbarg & Revelle, 1989). In other words, neurotic subjects show a degree of adaptive flexibility in task strategy: They appear to be (consciously or unconsciously) biased toward adopting emotion-focused coping strategies, which tend to detract from task performance, but can sometimes adopt task-focused strategies associated with greater vigor of response.

Extraversion: Empirical Data

As with neuroticism, the nature of the research base constrains us to focus on the relationship between extraversion and speed-accuracy trade-off. Although there are sporadic reports of greater behavioral impulsivity in extraverts (e.g., H. J. Eysenck & Eysenck, 1985), the effect does not seem very strong. Koelega's (1992) meta-analysis of vigilance studies reports a small but significant effect of extraversion on response criterion, but not on RT. He points out that the majority of studies fail to show significantly lower response criterion in extraverts. Matthews's (1992) extensive studies of extraversion and information-processing tasks do not show any general tendency toward risky performance in extraverts under neutral testing conditions. These experiments do show that extraversion and arousal tend to affect riskiness interactively, although the effect is less reliable than the effect on performance efficiency already discussed (Matthews, Davies, & Lees, 1990).

There are three approaches (which may be combined) to identifying the conditions under which extraverts exhibit behavioral impulsivity. The first is to suppose that risk and caution depend on impulsivity rather than extraversion. Naively, we might expect impulsivity to be associated with a performance style of fast, spontaneous, and unplanned response, as opposed to the slow, cautious, and planned response of low-impulsive subjects. Although impulsivity sometimes affects speed-accuracy trade-off on simple tasks as expected (e.g., Edman, Schalling, & Levander, 1983), however, the effect is still not very consistent (e.g., Matthews et al., 1989; Matthews, Davies, & Lees, 1990). Barrett (1987) claims that the relationship between impulsivity and RT is complex: more impulsive subjects are actually slower when information-processing demands of the imperative stimulus are high. It may also be necessary to distinguish different dimensions of impulsivity: Dickman (1990) found that lack of caution in responding was related to functional impulsivity, but not to dysfunctional impulsivity.

The second approach is to investigate motivational or cognitive variables that moderate extraversion/impulsivity effects on risk. For example, Brebner and Cooper (1985) propose that extraverts are "geared to respond" and introverts "geared to inspect," but the behavioral expression of these sets seems to depend on the extent to which they are facilitated or inhibited by task demands. Extraverts' responsivity is particularly evident in a catch-trial paradigm, in which sequences of trials requiring fast responding are occasionally interrupted by trials where response must be withheld (at which extraverts are poor; Brebner & Flavell, 1978). Another possible influence is time at work: H. J. Eysenck and Eysenck (1985) claimed that extraverts respond faster only in the early part of the task run, although Koelega's (1992) review of vigilance found no evidence for extraversion affecting temporal change in RT or response criterion. Like neuroticism, impulsivity effects on response speed seem to vary with motivational cues. Wallace et al. (1991) define impulsivity as neurotic extraversion, hypothesizing that subjects of this kind are both arousable (because of neuroticism) and sensitive to reward signals (because of extraversion). Hence neurotic extraverts are particularly responsive under conditions that excite the neural activation system associated with reward, such as provisions of incentives or a clear goal.

Again, an alternative explanation is that responsiveness depends on expectancies, which are affected by extraversion/impulsivity in conjunction with other factors (Zinbarg & Revelle, 1989). An interesting twist to the data on behavioral impulsivity is provided by evidence that extraverts tend to respond faster following negative feedback on outcome of the previous trial, whereas introverts respond faster if positive feedback is provided (Derryberry, 1987), or if both punishment and reward signals are delivered (Nichols & Newman, 1986). This effect does not seem to be tightly bound to control of speed-accuracy trade-off because Derryberry's (1987) paradigm emphasized speed, whereas Nichols and Newman's (1986) stressed accuracy. Instead, extraversion seems to be associated with a general bias toward adjusting response speed in reaction to motivational signals.

The third approach to resolving the inconsistency of the data is to ascertain whether there are components of information processing that are especially sensitive to extraversion/impulsivity. Weinman et al. (1985) also tested for extraversion effects in the study of maze solution described in the previous section. Extraverts tended to spend less time on the search phase of the task and more on the checking phase, implying that behavioral impulsivity was restricted to the initial part of the task. The effect was stronger when subjects were not provided with a criterion for optimal performance, but less so than in the case of neuroticism. There were no significant correlations between extraversion and total solution time. A subsequent study (Weinman, 1987) in which mazes were completed under a time limit showed that extraverts committed more errors overall and, specifically, more errors associated with adopting an "impulsive exit strategy."

Two sets of studies reported by Dickman (1985; Dickman & Meyer, 1988) provide broadly comparable evidence for impulsivity. Dickman (1985) showed that impulsives were only impaired on a card-sorting task when local and global information had to be integrated. His hypothesis is that impulsives adopt a strategy of rapid intake of information that leads to response on the basis of one dimension of information only, and hence to performance deficit on the more complex task version. Dickman and Meyer (1988) report studies of a visual comparison task in which high impulsives were consistently faster and less accurate than other subjects. An additive-factors analysis indicated that high impulsives were faster and less accurate at a feature comparison stage, but impulsivity had no effect on speed-accuracy trade-off at a later response execution stage.

Extraversion: Adaptive Significance

Taken together, these studies show that both extraversion and impulsivity are associated with a strategy of time-limiting intake of information, particularly on relatively complex tasks, rather than with behavioral impulsivity in general. These results are generally consistent with the informational adaptation hypothesis, because in high-information environments the priority is to avoid inability to respond through information overload. Dickman and Meyer (1988) present evidence for the adaptive nature of impulsivity, in that high impulsives were actually more accurate than low impulsives when all subjects were required to process information extremely rapidly. The impulsive response style may sometimes be maladaptive, though, in that several studies have shown a higher incidence of accidents in extraverted drivers, an effect that seems to be associated with impulsivity (Loo, 1979). Conversely, introverts' more protracted stimulus analysis may be beneficial in the absence of high stimulation levels, particularly on the complex problem-solving tasks on which introverts show superior performance (Kumar & Kapila, 1987). Studies of motivational variables show that extraversion effects are controlled by reinforcement signals as well as by task parameters (see Gray, 1981).

The complexity of these data (which we have not reviewed in detail) precludes any simple conclusions. They do broadly suggest, however, that extraverts or high impulsives are more likely to maintain a high response rate and optimistic expectancies in the face of negative feedback but the possibility of reward. We can reasonably suppose that information flows that overload the person's processing capacities are likely to be stressful and to threaten appraisals of personal competence and self-efficacy. Hence extraverts' greater responsivity to negative feedback may also support adaptation to high information inflows.

CONCLUSIONS

Cognitive and Adaptational Levels of Explanation

Two kinds of conclusions may be drawn concerning (a) information-processing models of personality and intelligence, and (b) the wider implications of correlations between personality and information processing. The evidence reviewed demonstrates several points of contact between ability and personality regarding specific processes sensitive to both types of influence. Table 1 is a preliminary and tentative attempt to indicate how *g*, extraversion, and neuroticism may influence the processing functions reviewed in this chapter. A number of entries in the table are based on very limited and sometimes inconsistent evidence, and much empirical work remains to be done; some general conclusions, however, are possible. Lower-level information processing efficiency is associated both with *g* and with the conjoint effects of extraversion, arousal, and time of day, but not with neuroticism. Individual differences in attentional resources appear to be more strongly related to personality than to *g*. STM and strategy use show effects of *g*, extraversion, and neuroticism, but close examination of the data indicates that these effects are controlled by different mechanisms. Intelligence and neuroticism seem most strongly related to upper-level, strategic aspects of STM, whereas extraversion mainly correlates with lower-level passive retention of information.

Strategic correlates of personality and ability also differ in detail. The specificity of the processes jointly associated with *g* and personality implies that correlations between ability and personality depend on the exact information-processing demands of the ability test. Predicted relationships should concern Intelligence C rather than Intelligence B, because they may depend critically on processes contributing only to certain specific tests. Neglect of the role of task demands may explain the rather patchy nature of the correlational evidence on the relationship between ability, extraversion, and neuroticism. We have seen that reliable correlations can be obtained where the processing demands of the ability tests are congruent with the processing functions sensitive to personality. Relatively simple verbal ability tests are sensitive to interactive effects of extraversion and arousal because of their dependence on low-level verbal processing (see Matthews, 1985), but other types of ability test may not show the effect.

The weakness of a purely information-processing approach is that it does not explain the overall patterning of individual differences in cognitive functions associated with ability and personality factors. The balance of the evidence implies that both types of construct are independently associated with a variety of different processing functions. Moreover, these functions cannot be identified exclusively with either lower or upper levels of control. Both *g* and extraversion relate to basic information-processing speed and to high-level strategy use, though in somewhat different ways. A case might be made for neuroticism being primarily a property of the upper level of control, on the basis of the studies reviewed previously. Thus, although the cognitive approach is successful (and indispensable) descriptively, it take us no further than a somewhat arbitrary collection of cognitive correlates for each individual-difference variable.

The limitations of exclusively correlational data have been widely recognized within intelligence research, in at least three respects. First, intelligence cannot be understood without reference to iearning

Table 1. A Summary of Effects of Individual-Difference Factors on Various Processing Functions

	Individual-difference factor		
Processing function	*g*	E	N
Basic information processing	Yes—causation uncertain. Direct effect on perceptual speed only?	(i) No simple correlation (ii) Deficit in simple visual processing (iii) Interaction with time of day and arousal—consistent with network model	No general relationship
Attentional resource availability	No	Yes—relatively weak, and possibly restricted to verbal tasks	Yes—may affect wide range of tasks
STM			
Item identification	No direct evidence—conceptual link with basic information processing	Yes?—Interactive effect of E and arousal on digit span	Yes?—state anxiety effects on digit span
Verbal input register	Verbal ability only	Yes—recency in free recall	No?
Articulatory loop	No?	No?	No?
Resources for STM	No	No	Yes—but difficult to distinguish from attentional resources
Executive control	Yes—strategies for rehearsal and information management	No—inconsistent data	Yes—reduced executive control
Strategies			
Control of speed-accuracy trade-off	No simple relationship-associated with time management strategies	Yes—but highly task and context dependent	Yes—but highly task and context dependent
Complex strategic control	Yes-strategy selection and transfer and management of goals	Yes?—impairment of problem solving	Yes?—impairment of problem solving

Note: Each entry indicates whether there is a relationship, and indicates sources of evidence briefly where appropriate. Questionable relationships are mostly those based on limited evidence.

processes, as in M. Anderson's (1992) hypothesis that basic information-processing speed constrains the extent of knowledge elaboration. Second, there is reasonably persuasive evidence for a biological substrate for intelligence, although the causality of associations between cognitive and neural measures is poorly understood. Third, intelligence has an adaptive function, as expressed by Sternberg's (1985) "contextual" view of intelligence as purposive and active adaptation to the individual's environment.

Research on personality and performance has been slow to develop a comparable view of the wider relevance of empirically observed relationships between personality and cognition. Until recently, research on extraversion has been mainly concerned with testing somewhat naive physiological theories of personality whose predictions are poorly supported empirically (Zuckerman, 1991). Research on neuroticism, when not similarly constrained, has been overly concerned with anxiety as a factor disrupting performance. Revelle (1987) aptly points out that many personality effects are best conceptualized as trade-offs between different automatic components of performance and different strategic choices; these include speed-accuracy trade-off, allocation of effort and choice of activities over longer time scales. The identification of personality with performance trade-offs contrasts sharply with individual differences in ability, which are associated with overall efficiency of performance. Different trade-offs are likely to be controlled by different mechanisms, within as well as between Revelle's (1987) various levels of analysis. As we have seen, lower-level correlates of extraversion such as network processing efficiency (in conjunction with time of day and arousal) and passive short-term verbal recall cannot be reduced to any single information-processing function. It is not implausible that low-level trade-offs are controlled by biological mechanisms that in turn are influenced by genetic factors: The extraversion genotype may affect severally functionally independent parameters of processing. Higher-level trade-offs may be more dependent on learning.

Personality, Intelligence and Adaptation

In this review, we have argued that the patterning of performance change associated with extraversion and neuroticism is best explained as supporting adaptations to particular information-processing environments. In contrast, high-*g* individuals appear to be well adapted to fast and/or complex information handling regardless of factors such as time pressure, time of day, and stress. Specifically, the processing characteristics of extraverts may assist them in dealing with high information flows (particularly of verbal stimuli), time pressure, and the low arousal of the evening. These characteristics facilitate efficient performance in the environments favored by extraverts, such as social interaction (Furnham, 1981). For example, the liking for parties that figures so strongly in questionnaire extraversion items may be associated with competence in handling high rates of social signals, resistance to distraction, and efficient lower-level processing late into the evening. Conversely, the processing advantages of introverts (e.g., superior complex problem-solving and vigilance) may help to adapt them to a relatively solitary existence characterized by opportunity for reflective thought and infrequency of significant stimuli.

Figure 4 illustrates the levels of explanation necessary to account for some of the observed cognitive correlates of extraversion, such as high verbal resource availability and STM. (Performance advantages of introverts are omitted.) Each cognitive characteristic supports specific complex behaviors (e.g., good conversation skills), which together support the adaptation that provides the highest-level explanation. Testing these hypothesized relationships requires more ecologically valid research to investigate how extraverts compare with introverts in processing and behavior in relevant contexts (e.g., parties). We also wish to link processing to lower-level descriptions of individual differences in connectionist and neural mechanisms. For the majority of functions, such links remain conceptual (as illustrated by the open arrows), and no definite hypotheses may be proposed. In the case of extraversion × arousal interaction, we tentatively suggest that the performance effect may be supported by individual differences in network and neural noise. Finally, some of the psychobiological characteristics of extraversion may support the top-level adaptation without directly influencing cognitive performance. For example, the low autonomic arousability of extraverts (H. J Eysenck & Eysenck, 1985) and the insensitivity to punishment signals in conditioning paradigms noted by Gray (1981) may confer a degree of stress resistance to extraverts that assists in managing high-information environments.

The most straightforward view of neuroticism, viewed as an element of normal personality, is that it relates to a trade-off between awareness of social threat and insensitivity to criticism, which in turn influences the person's general strategy for dealing with potential threat. In general, the most adaptive setting for the trade-off will depend on the actual level of threat and the utility to the individual of processing negative feedback from others. The preponderance of detrimental effects of anxiety may arise because it tends to be associated with conflicts in adaptive goals. The test-anxious subject may be highly motivated to perform well, but performance goals tend to be overridden by self-regulative goals (Wells & Matthews, 1994).

The causal relationship between phenotypic personality and the corresponding pattern of cognitive strengths and weaknesses is a matter for conjecture. The simplest hypothesis might be that if a person has an extraverted genotype, it predisposes both physiological and cognitive adaptations to handling high information flows. We can equally well suggest an environmental or a mixed genetic/environmental hypothesis. Children reinforced for extraverted behavior or exposed to high-information environments may be more likely to develop adaptive processing routines and to learn adaptive strategies (e.g., impulsive exit). Both hypotheses assume that the individual's adaptation is largely set during childhood, resulting in stability of personality and adaptation subsequently. Alternatively, the adaptation may be more dynamic, such that the individual's collection of processing characteristics itself influences phenotypic personality. If a person has difficulty processing the content of conversations, cannot function efficiently in the evenings, and cannot time-limit processing when necessary, he or she may well be disposed toward introversion regardless of biological adaptations (e.g., arousability). Personality would then change with the individual's learning of processing routines and strategies throughout adulthood. The adaptive approach is of course

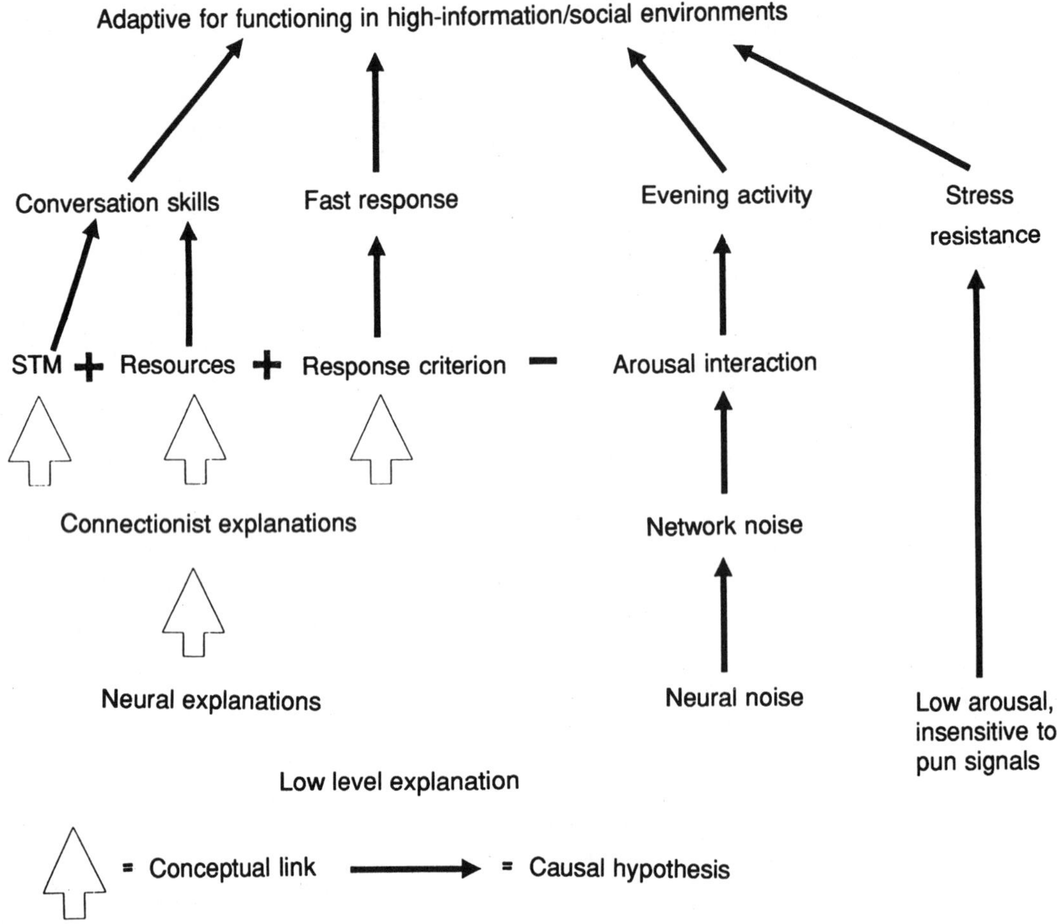

Figure 4. Levels of explanation for some elements of the cognitive patterning associated with extraversion.

somewhat speculative in the absence of direct evidence, but it is difficult to see how else the functional diversity of information-processing correlates of personality could be explained.

In general, the relationship between personality and intelligence may depend on the match within the testing context between the processing functions assessed and their adaptive relevance to the person concerned. For example, we might expect extraverts to perform better on *g*-loaded tests that tap the processes used in everyday conversation, when performance is tested late in the evening, or under stressful conditions. We look forward to research into whether the information-processing characteristics of personalty "types" actually facilitate performance of the activities central to the trait concerned.

REFERENCES

Ackerman, P. L. (1988). Determinants of individual differences during skill acquisition: Cognitive abilities and information processing. *Journal of Experimental Psychology: General, 117*, 288–318.

Amelang, M., & Ullwer, U. (1990). Untersuchungen zur experimentellen Bewahrung von Eysencks Extraversion-Theorie. *Zeitschrift fur Differentielle und Diagnostische Psychologie, 11*, 127–148.

Amelang, M., & Ullwer, U. (1991). Correlations between psychometric measures and psychophysiological as well as experimental variables in studies on extraversion and neuroticism. In J. Strelau & A. Angleitner (Eds.), *Explorations in temperament*. New York: Plenum.

Anderson, J. R. (1982). Acquisition of cognitive skill. *Psychological Review*, *89*, 369–406.

Anderson, M. (1992). *Intelligence and development: A cognitive theory*. Oxford, England: Blackwell.

Baddeley, A. (1986). *Working memory*. Oxford, England: Oxford University Press.

Baddeley, A. D., Logie, R. H., Nimmo-Smith, M. I., & Brereton, N. (1985). Components of fluent reading. *Journal of Memory and Language*, *24*, 119–131.

Baron, J. (1982). Personality and intelligence. In R. J. Sternberg (Ed.), *Handbook of human intelligence*. Cambridge, England: Cambridge University Press.

Barrett, E. S. (1987). Impulsiveness and anxiety: Information processing and electro-encephalograph topography. *Journal of Research in Personality*, *21*, 453–463.

Belmont, J. M., Butterfield, E. C., & Ferretti, R. P. (1982). To secure transfer of training instruct self-management skills. In D. K. Detterman & R. J. Sternberg (Eds.), *How and how much can intelligence be increased?* Norwood, NJ: Ablex.

Blake, M. J. F. (1971). Temperament and time of day. In W. P. Colquhoun (Ed.), *Biological rhythms*. London: Academic Press.

Brand, C. R. (1987). Strategy theories of IQ: Facile, false, or just unfalsifiable? A rejoinder to Pellegrino. In S. Modgil & C. Modgil (Eds.), *A. Jensen: Consensus and controversy*. Brighton, England: Falmer.

Brand, C. R., & Egan, V. (1989). The "Big Five" dimensions of personality? Evidence from ipsative, adjectival self-attributions. *Personality and Individual Differences*, *10*, 1165–1172.

Braune, R., & Wickens, C. D. (1986). Time-sharing revisited: Test of a componential model for the assessment of individual differences. *Ergonomics*, *29*, 1399–1414.

Brebner, J., & Cooper, C. (1985). A proposed unified model of extraversion. In J. T. Spence & C. E. Izard (Eds.), *Motivation, emotion and personality*. Amsterdam: North-Holland.

Brebner, J., & Flavell, R. (1978). The effect of catch-trials on speed and accuracy among introverts and extraverts in a simple RT task. *British Journal of Psychology*, *69*, 9–15.

Brody, N. (1992). *Intelligence* (2nd ed.). New York: Academic Press.

Brookings, J. B. (1990). A confirmatory factor analytic study of time-sharing performance and cognitive abilities. *Intelligence*, *14*, 43–59.

Brown, G. D. A., & Hulme, C. (in press). Connectionist models of human short-term memory. In O. Omidvar (Ed.), *Progress in neural networks*. Norwood, NJ: Ablex.

Campione, J. C., Brown, A. L., & Ferrara, R. A. (1982). Mental retardation and intelligence. In R. J. Sternberg (Ed.), *Handbook of human intelligence*. Cambridge, England: Cambridge University Press.

Cantor, J., Engle, R. W., & Hamilton, J. (1991). Short-term memory, working memory, and verbal abilities: How do they relate? *Intelligence*, *15*, 229–246.

Carpenter, P. A., Just, M. A., & Schell, P. (1990). What one intelligence test measures: A theoretical account of the processing in the Raven Progressive Matrices test. *Psychological Review*, *97*, 404–431.

Cohen, J. D., Servan-Schreiber, D., & McClelland, J. L. (1992). A parallel distributed approach to automaticity. *American Journal of Psychology*, *105*, 239–269.

Crawford, J. D., & Stankov, L. (1983). Fluid and crystallized intelligence and primacy/recency components of short-term memory. *Intelligence*, *7*, 227–252.

Cunningham, M. R. (1977). Personality and the structure of nonverbal communication of emotion. *Journal of Personality*, *45*, 564–584.

Darke, S. (1988). Anxiety and working memory capacity. *Cognition and Emotion*, *2*, 145–154.

Davies, D. R., Jones, D. M., & Taylor, A. (1984). Selective and sustained attention: Individual and group differences. In R. Parasuraman & D. R. Davies (Eds.), *Varieties of attention*. New York: Academic Press.

Davies, D. R., & Parasuraman, R. (1982). *The psychology of vigilance*. London: Academic Press.

Dempster, F. N. (1981). Memory span: Sources of individual and developmental differences. *Psychological Bulletin*, *89*, 63–100.

Derryberry, D. (1987). Incentive and feedback effects on target detection: A chronometric analysis of Gray's model of temperament. *Personality and Individual Differences*, *8*, 855–866.

Dickman, S. (1985). Impulsivity and perception: Individual differences in the processing of the local and global dimensions of stimuli. *Journal of Personality and Social Psychology*, *48*, 133–149.

Dickman, S. (1990). Functional and dysfunctional impulsivity: Personality and cognitive correlates. *Journal of Personality and Social Psychology*, *58*, 95–102.

Dickman, S. J., & Meyer, D. E. (1988). Impulsivity and speed-accuracy trade-offs in information processing. *Journal of Personality and Social Psychology*, *54*, 274–290.

Duckworth, D. H. (1975). Personality and perception of nonverbal communications. *Perceptual and Motor Skills, 40*, 325–326.

Edman, G., Schalling, D., & Levander, S. E. (1983). Impulsivity and speed and errors in a reaction time task: A contribution to the construct validity of the concept of impulsivity. *Acta Psychologica*, *33*, 1–8.

Egan, V., & Deary, I. J. (1992). Are specific inspection time strategies prevented by concurrent tasks? *Intelligence*, *16*, 151–168.

Ellis, H. C., & Ashbrook, P. W. (1987). Resource allocation model of the effects of depressed mood states on memory. In K. Fielder & J. Forgas (Eds.), *Affect, cognition, and social behavior*. Toronto: Hogrefe.

Eysenck, H. J. (1986). The theory of intelligence and the psychophysiology of cognition. In R. J. Sternberg (Ed.), *Advances in the psychology of human intelligence* (Vol. 3). Hillsdale, NJ: Erlbaum.

Eysenck, H. J. (1992). Four ways five factors are not basic. *Personality and Individual Differences*, *13*, 667–673.

Eysenck, H. J., & Eysenck, M. W. (1985). *Personality and individual differences: A natural science approach*. New York: Plenum.

Eysenck, M. W. (1977). *Human memory: Theory, research and individual differences*. Oxford, England: Pergamon.

Eysenck, M. W. (1982). *Attention and arousal: Cognition and performance*. London: Springer.

Eysenck, M. W. (1985). Anxiety and cognitive-task performance. *Personality and Individual Differences*, *6*, 579–586.

Eysenck, M. W. (1992). *Anxiety: The cognitive perspective*. Hillsdale, NJ: Erlbaum.

Eysenck, M. W., & Eysenck, M. C. (1979). Memory scanning, introversion-extraversion, and levels of processing. *Journal of Research in Personality*, *13*, 305–315.

Fagan, J. F. (1972). Rehearsal and free recall in children of superior and average intelligence. *Psychonomic Science, 28,* 352–354.

Ferrara, R. A., Brown, A. L., & Campione, J. C. (1986). Children's learning and transfer of inductive reasoning rules: Studies of proximal development. *Child Development, 57,* 1087–1099.

Ferretti, R. P., & Butterfield, R. C. (1989). Intelligence as a correlate of children's problem solving. *American Journal of Mental Retardation, 93,* 424–433.

Ferretti, R. P., & Butterfield, R. C. (1992). Intelligence-related differences in the learning, maintenance, and transfer of problem-solving strategies. *Intelligence, 16,* 207–223.

Ferretti, R. P., & Cavalier, A. R. (1991). Constraints on the problem solving of persons with mental retardation. *International Review of Research in Mental Retardation, 17,* 153–192.

Furnham, A. (1981). Personality and activity preference. *British Journal of Social Psychology, 20,* 57–68.

Geary, D. C., & Widaman, K. F. (1987). Individual differences in cognitive arithmetic. *Journal of Experimental Psychology: General, 116,* 154–171.

Geary, D. C., & Widaman, K. F. (1992). Numerical cognition: On the convergence of componential and psychometric models. *Intelligence, 16,* 47–80.

Geen, R. G. (1985). Test anxiety and visual vigilance. *Journal of Personality and Social Psychology, 49,* 963–970.

Geen, R. G. (1987). Test anxiety and behavioral avoidance. *Journal of Research in Personality, 21,* 481–488.

Geiselman, R. E., Woodward, J. A., & Beatty, J. (1982). Individual differences in verbal memory performance: A test of alternative information-processing models. *Journal of Experimental Psychology: General, 111,* 109–134.

Gilliland, K. (1980). The interactive effect of introversion-extraversion with caffeine induced arousal on verbal performance. *Journal of Research in Personality, 14,* 482–492.

Glenberg, A. M., Bradley, M. M., Stevenson, J. A., Kraus, T. A., Tkachuk, M. J., Gretz, A. L., Fish, J. J., & Turpin, B. A. M. (1980). A two-process account of long-term serial position effects. *Journal of Experimental Psychology: Human Learning and Memory, 6,* 355–369.

Goh, D. S., & Farley, F. H. (1977). Personality effects on cognitive test performance. *Journal of Psychology, 96,* 111–122.

Gray, J. A. (1981). A critique of Eysenck's theory of personality. In H. J. Eysenck (Ed.), *A model for personality.* London: Springer.

Gray, J. A. (1982). *The neuropsychology of anxiety: An enquiry into the functions of the septo-hippocampal system.* Oxford, England: Oxford University Press.

Griffin, J. A., Dember, W. N., & Warm, J. S. (1986). Effects of depression on expectancy in sustained attention. *Motivation and Emotion, 10,* 195–205.

Harley, T. A., & Matthews, G. (1992). Interactive effects of extraversion, arousal time and time of day on semantic priming: Are they pre-lexical or post-lexical? *Personality and Individual Differences, 13,* 1021–1029.

Hirst, W., & Kalmar, D. (1987). Characterizing attentional resources. *Journal of Experimental Psychology: General, 116,* 68–81.

Hitch, G. J. (1980). Developing the concept of working memory. In G. Claxton (Ed.), *Cognitive psychology: New directions.* London: Routledge.

Horn, J. L. (1986). Intellectual ability concepts. In R. J. Sternberg (Ed.), *Advances in the psychology of human intelligence* (Vol. 3). Hillsdale, NJ: Erlbaum.

Hough, L. M. (1992). The "big five" personality variables—construct confusion: Description versus prediction. *Human Performance, 5,* 139–155.

Humphreys, M. S., & Revelle, W. (1984). Personality, motivation and performance: A theory of the relationship between individual differences and information processing. *Psychological Review, 91,* 153–184.

Hunt, E. (1980). Intelligence as an information-processing concept. *British Journal of Psychology, 71,* 449–474.

Jensen, A. R. (1980). *Bias in mental testing.* New York: Free Press.

Jensen, A. R. (1987). Individual differences in the Hick paradigm. In P. Vernon (Ed.), *Speed of information processing and intelligence.* Norwood, NJ: Ablex.

Jensen, A. R., & Frederiksen, J. (1973). Free recall of categorized and uncategorized lists: A test of the Jensen hypothesis. *Journal of Educational Psychology, 3,* 304–312.

Koelega, H. S. (1992). Extraversion and vigilance performance: 30 years of inconsistencies. *Psychological Bulletin, 112,* 239–258.

Kranzler, J. H., & Jensen, A. R. (1989). Inspection time and intelligence: A meta-analysis. *Intelligence, 13,* 329–347.

Kumar, D., & Kapila, A. (1987). Problem solving as a function of extraversion and masculinity. *Personality and Individual Differences, 8,* 129–132.

Kyllonen, P. C., & Christal, R. E. (1990). Reasoning ability is (little more than) working memory capacity?! *Intelligence, 14,* 389–433.

Lazarus, R. S., & Folkman, S. (1984). *Stress, appraisal and coping.* New York: Springer.

Leon, M. R., & Revelle, W. (1985). Effects of anxiety on analogical reasoning: A test of three theoretical models. *Journal of Personality and Social Psychology, 49,* 1302–1315.

Logan, G. D. (1985). Executive control of thought and action. *Acta Psychologica, 60,* 193–210.

Longstreth, L. E. (1984). Jensen's reaction time investigations: A critique. *Intelligence, 8,* 139–160.

Loo, R. (1979). Role of primary personality factors in the perception of traffic signs and driver violations and accidents. *Accident Analysis and Prevention, 11,* 125–127.

Mackenzie, B., & Cumming, S. (1986). How fragile is the relationship between inspection time and intelligence: The effects of apparent motion cues and previous experience. *Personality and Individual Differences, 7,* 721–729.

Mackintosh, N. J. (1986). The biology of intelligence? *British Journal of Psychology, 77,* 1–18.

Martin, M. (1978). Assessment of individual variation in memory ability. In M. M. Gruneberg, P. E. Morris & R. N. Sykes (Eds.), *Practical aspects of memory.* London: Academic Press.

Matthews, G. (1983). *Personality, arousal states and intellectual performance.* Unpublished doctoral dissertation, Cambridge University.

Matthews, G. (1985). The effects of extraversion and arousal on intelligence test performance. *British Journal of Psychology, 76,* 479–493.

Matthews, G. (1986).The interactive effects of extraversion and arousal on performance: Are creativity tests anomalous? *Personality and Individual Differences, 7,* 751–761.

Matthews, G. (1987). *Extraversion, self-report arousal and performance: The role of task factors.* Paper presented at meeting of the International Society for the Study of Individual Differences, Toronto.

Matthews, G. (1988). Morningness-eveningness as a dimension of personality: Trait, state and psychophysiological correlates. *European Journal of Personality, 2,* 277–293.

Matthews, G. (1989). Extraversion and levels of control of sustained attention. *Acta Psychologica, 70*, 129–146, 931–940.

Matthews, G. (1992). Extraversion. In A. P. Smith & D. M. Jones (Eds.), *Handbook of human performance: Vol. 3. State and trait*. London: Academic Press.

Matthews, G., & Amelang, M. (1993). Extraversion, arousal theory and performance: A study of individual differences in the EEG. *Personality and Individual Differences, 14*, 347–363.

Matthews, G., Davies, D. R., & Holley, P. J. (1990). Extraversion, arousal and visual sustained attention: The role of resources availability. *Personality and Individual Differences, 11*, 1159–1173.

Matthews, G., Davies, D. R., & Holley, P. J. (1993). Cognitive predictors of vigilance. *Human Factors, 35*, 3–24.

Matthews, G., Davies, D. R., & Lees, J. L. (1990). Arousal, extraversion, and individual differences in resource availability. *Journal of Personality and Social Psychology, 59*, 150–168.

Matthews, G., & Dorn, L. (1989). IQ and choice reaction time: An information processing analysis. *Intelligence, 13*, 299–317.

Matthews, G., & Harley, T. A. (1993). Effects of extraversion and self-report arousal on semantic priming: A connectionist approach. *Journal of Personality and Social Psychology, 65*, 735–756.

Matthews, G., Jones, D. M., & Chamberlain, A. G. (1989). Interactive effects of extraversion and arousal on attentional task performance: Multiple resources or encoding processes? *Journal of Personality and Social Psychology, 56*, 629–639.

Matthews, G., Jones, D. M., & Chamberlain, A. G. (1990). Refining the measurement of mood: The UWIST Mood Adjective Checklist. *British Journal of Psychology, 81*, 17–42.

Matthews, G., Jones, D. M., & Chamberlain, A. G. (1992). Predictors of individual differences in mail coding skills, and their variation with ability level. *Journal of Applied Psychology, 77*, 406–418.

Matthews, G., & Oddy, K. (1993). Recovery of major personality dimensions from trait adjective data. *Personality and Individual Differences, 15*, 419–431.

McCrae, R. R., & Costa, P. T. (1986). Personality, coping, and coping effectiveness in an adult sample. *Journal of Personality, 54*, 385–405.

McCrae, R. R., & Costa, P. T., Jr. (1987). Validation of the five-factor model of personality across instruments and observers. *Journal of Personality and Social Psychology, 52*, 81–90.

McGarry-Roberts, P. A., Stelmack, R. M., & Campbell, K. B. (1992). Intelligence, reaction time, and event-related potentials. *Intelligence, 16*, 289–313.

Morris, L., W., Davis, M. A., & Hutchings, C. H. (1981). Cognitive and emotional components of anxiety: Literature review and a revised worry-emotionality scale. *Journal of Educational Psychology, 73*, 541–555.

Morris, L. W., & Liebert, R. M. (1969). Effects of anxiety on timed and untimed intelligence tests: Another look. *Journal of Consulting and Clinical Psychology, 33*, 240–244.

Morris, N., & Jones, D. M. (1990). Memory updating in working memory: The role of the central executive. *British Journal of Psychology, 81*, 111–122.

Mueller, J. H. (1976). Anxiety and cue utilization in human learning and memory. In M. Zuckerman & C. D. Spielberger (Eds.), *Emotions and anxiety: New concepts, methods and applications*. Hillsdale, NJ: Erlbaum.

Mueller, J. H. (1992). Anxiety and performance. In A. P. Smith and D. M. Jones (Eds.), *Handbook of human performance: Vol. 3. Trait and state*. London: Academic Press.

Myors, B., Stankov, L., & Oliphant, G. (1989). Competing tasks, working memory, and intelligence. *Australian Journal of Psychology, 41*, 1–16.

Navon, D. (1984). Resources—a theoretical soup stone? *Psychological Review, 91*, 216–234.

Necka, E. (1992). Cognitive analysis of intelligence: The significance of working memory processes. *Personality and Individual Differences, 13*, 1031–1046.

Nettelbeck, T. (1973). Individual differences in noise and associated perceptual indices of performance. *Perception, 2*, 11–21.

Nettelbeck, T., & Rabbitt, P. M. A. (1992). Aging, cognitive performance, and mental speed. *Intelligence, 16*, 189–205.

Neubauer, A. C. (1991). Intelligence and RT: A modified Hick paradigm and a new RT paradigm. *Intelligence, 15*, 175–192.

Nichols, S. L., & Newman, J. P. (1986). Effects of punishment on response latency in extraverts. *Journal of Personality and Social Psychology, 50*, 624–630.

Norman, D. A., & Bobrow, D. B. (1975). On data-limited and resource-limited processes. *Cognitive Psychology, 7*, 44–64.

Norman, D. A., & Shallice, T. (1985). Attention to action: Willed and automatic control of behaviour. In R. J. Davidson, G. E. Schwartz, & D. Shapiro (Eds.), *Consciousness and self-regulation: Advances in research* (Vol. 4). New York: Plenum.

Parasuraman, R., Warm, J. S., & Dember, W. N. (1987). Vigilance: Taxonomy and utility. In L. Mark, J. S. Warm & R. L. Huston (Eds.), *Ergonomics and human factors: Recent research*. New York: Springer.

Rabbitt, P. M. A., & Maylor, E. A. (1991). Investigating models of human performance. *British Journal of Psychology, 82*, 259–290.

Rawlings, D., & Carnie, D. (1989). The interaction of EPQ extraversion with WAIS subtest performance under timed and untimed conditions. *Personality and Individual Differences, 10*, 453–458.

Revelle, W. (1987). Personality and motivation: Sources of inefficiency in cognitive performance. *Journal of Research in Personality, 21*, 436–452.

Revelle, W., Humphreys, M. S., Simon, L., & Gilliland, K. (1980). The interactive effect of personality, time of day and caffeine: A test of the arousal model. *Journal of Experimental Psychology: General, 109*, 1–31.

Roberts, R. D., Beh, H. C., & Stankov, L. (1988). Hick's law, competing task performance, and intelligence. *Intelligence, 12*, 101–120.

Rocklin, T., & Revelle, W. (1981). The measurement of extraversion: A comparison of the Eysenck Personality Inventory and the Eysenck Personality Questionnaire. *British Journal of Social Psychology, 20*, 279–294.

Rumelhart, D. E., Hinton, G. E., & McClelland, J. L. (1986). A general framework for paralleled distributed processing. In D. E. Rumelhart, J. L. McClelland, & the PDP Research Group, *Parallel distributed processing: Explorations in the microstructure of cognition. Vol. 1. Foundations*. Cambridge, MIT Press.

Saklofske, D. H., & Kostura, D. D. (1990). Extraversion-introversion and intelligence. *Personality and Individual Differences, 11*, 547–552.

Sarason, I. G., Sarason, B. R., & Pierce, G. R. (1990). Anxiety, cognitive interference, and performance. *Journal of Social Behavior and Personality, 5*, 1–18.

Schneider, W., Dumais, S. T., & Shiffrin, R. M. (1984). Automatic and control processing and attention. In R. Parasuraman & D. R. Davies (Eds.), *Varieties of attention*. New York: Academic Press.

Smith, G. A. (1989). Strategies and procedures affecting the accuracy of reaction time parameters and their correlations with intelligence. *Personality and Individual Differences, 10,* 829–837.

Spearman, C. (1923). *The nature of "intelligence" and the principles of cognition.* London: Macmillan.

Spielberger, C. D. (1966). The effects of anxiety on complex learning and academic achievement. In C. D. Spielberger (Ed.), *Anxiety and behavior.* New York: Academic.

Spilsbury, G. A. (1992). Complexity as a reflection of the dimensionality of a task. *Intelligence, 16,* 31–45.

Spilsbury, G. A., Stankov, L., & Roberts, R. D. (1990). The effect of a test's difficulty on its correlation with intelligence. *Personality and Individual Differences, 11,* 1069–1077.

Stankov, L. (1989). Attentional resources and intelligence: A disappearing link. *Personality and Individual Differences, 10,* 957–968.

Stelmack, R. M., Houlihan, M., & McGarry-Roberts, P. A. (in press). Personality, reaction time, and event-related potentials. *Journal of Personality and Social Psychology.*

Sternberg, R. J. (1981). Intelligence and nonentrenchment. *Journal of Educational Psychology, 73,* 1–16.

Sternberg, R. J. (1985). *Beyond IQ: A triarchic theory of intelligence.* New York: Cambridge University Press.

Sullivan, L., & Stankov, L. (1990). Shadowing and target detection as a function of age: Implications for the role of processing resources in competing tasks and in general intelligence. *Australian Journal of Psychology, 42,* 173–186.

Thayer, R. E. (1989). *The biopsychology of mood and arousal.* Oxford, England: Oxford University Press.

Townsend, J. T., & Ashby, F. G. (1983). *The stochastic modelling of elementary psychological processes.* Cambridge, England: Cambridge University Press.

Vernon, P. E. (1969). *Intelligence and the cultural environment.* London: Methuen.

Wallace, J. F., Newman, J. P., & Bachorowski, J. (1991). Failure of response modulation: Impulsive behavior in anxious and impulsive individuals. *Journal of Research in Personality, 25,* 23–44.

Watson, D., & Clark, L. A. (1984). Negative affectivity: The disposition to experience aversive emotional states. *Psychological Bulletin, 96,* 465–490.

Weinman, J. (1987). Non-cognitive determinants of perceptual problem-solving strategies. *Personality and Individual Differences, 8,* 53–58.

Weinman, J., Elithorn, A., & Cooper, R. (1985). Personality and problem solving: The nature of individual differences in planning, scanning and verification. *Personality and Individual Differences, 6,* 453–460.

Wells, A., & Matthews, G. (1994). *Attention and emotion: A clinical approach.* Hillsdale, NJ: Erlbaum.

Wickens, C. D. (1984). *Engineering psychology and human performance.* Columbus, OH: Merrill.

Zinbarg, R., & Revelle, W. (1989). Personality and conditioning: A test of four models. *Journal of Personality and Social Psychology, 57,* 301–314.

Zuckerman, M. (1991). *Psychobiology of personality.* Cambridge, England: Cambridge University Press.

19

The Relationship of Personality and Intelligence to Cognitive Learning Style and Achievement

Adrian Furnham

Certain topics in psychology have always provoked passionate debate, often because of their sociopolitical implications. Although fashion may dictate which theoretical or methodological approach currently shapes researchers' thinking and experimental work, it is often the implications of the practical application of the findings that cause the most debate.

This handbook looks at the relationships between two such areas of research. The nature of personality and intelligence has provoked considerable discussion in lay, as much as scientific, circles. Some of the issues have been similar; others unique to one particular domain of research. Researchers in both areas have been concerned with the factors making up human personality and intelligence, including biological, social, and cognitive determinants, as well as measurement issues; indeed excellent reviews of these issues can be found in the first section of this book. Issues that are more specific to each area of research include the cross-situational and temporal stability of personality and the cultural determinants of intelligence.

This chapter is concerned with a research issue that has powerful practical implications because it relates to educational outcomes. What is clearly apparent is that both personality and intelligence are multiply determined; furthermore, the relationship between these two variables is far from straightforward. The focus of this chapter, however, is not on personality, intelligence, or the relationship between them but rather on "outcome" measures of the two: specifically, choice of, preference for, or efficiency of cognitive/learning style and method. The terms *cognitive style* and *learning style* have been used synonymously by researchers, though the choice of terms is usually governed by the focus of the variable they examine. Messick (1984) has defined cognitive styles as "characteristic self-consistencies in information processing that develop in congenial ways around underlying personality trends" (p. 61). Guilford (1980) has noted a great disparity of labels and conceptions in the area, however, rendering it difficult to review; he prefers the concept of an "intellectual executive function." Inevitably the complexity of variables in this area means that cognitive learning style (CLS) can be described as an independent, moderator, or dependent variable.

Adrian Furnham • Department of Psychology, University College London, London WC1H 0AP, England.

International Handbook of Personality and Intelligence, edited by Donald H. Saklofske and Moshe Zeidner. Plenum Press, New York, 1995.

A MODEL

Given that it is possible to define, operationalize, and measure cognitive learning styles, the question remains as to how they relate to personality, intelligence, and academic achievement. There has been a plethora of studies on the relationship among personality, learning, memory, and academic achievement, though some correlates have been investigated more closely than others. It has also been acknowledged that many variables moderate these relationships. For nearly 50 years psychologists have been interested in cognitive or learning styles, which they have seen as a central—and powerful—moderator variable. Various models or paths have been suggested, but Figure 1 illustrates some of the more well-established ideas.

The model suggests three things, though each remains hotly disputed. First, personality and intelligence are independent predictors (correlates) of academic achievement (however measured), though most researchers would acknowledge the latter being much more predictive than the former. Second, both personality and intelligence are predictors of a CLS that is itself a moderate of academic achievement. Indeed, many concurrent and construct validity studies relate these styles to traits and ability measures. Precisely how personality and intelligence relate to CLS is, of course, open to debate; some researchers see no necessity for conceiving of a CLS variable at all, whereas others confuse the personality type or dimension with the CLS itself. Third, both teaching (instruction) methods and assessment methods are independently related to CLS and academic achievement in that there may or may not be a fit between a person's preferred CLS and these methods. Despite the attractiveness of this hypothesis, it is difficult to test, and the literature is highly equivocal (Hayes & Allison, 1993).

The model also begs a number of fundamental questions: How are these variables defined and measured? Are there any feedback loops, or bidirectional causality? Are all measures of achievement positively correlated? What is the strength/statistical power of the causative paths? More importantly, perhaps we need to know more about cognitive/learning styles, which are at the heart of the model.

The model in Figure 1, though probably rarely described as such, seems to be implicit in the writings of many educational and psychological researchers.

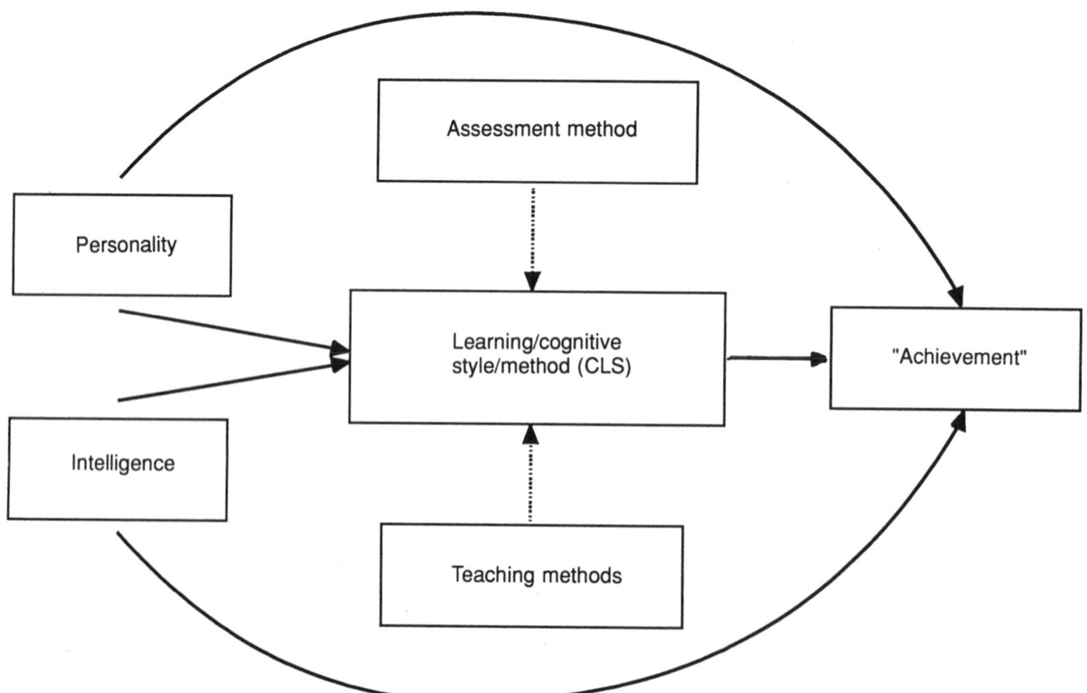

Figure 1. A proposed model for the role of cognitive and learning style.

Educational researchers have been particularly interested in the variables on the right-hand side of the model—namely, how teaching and assessment methods interact with learning styles or preferences to relate to an outcome/achievement variable. A major problem for both the reviewer of this research as well as those interested in testing fit or other theories is the nature of the achievement or outcome variable itself. That is, it is not always certain how reliable, valid, or representative the achievement measure is. It may not be particularly reliable in the sense of either test-retest or interrater reliability; students may behave quite differently on different occasions, and/or those grading the outcomes might not have high agreement with one another. The outcome criterion might not be valid in the sense that it is not an appropriate measure of achievement as demanded by the theory: It may be short- or long-term memory for material, ability to demonstrate a skill, ratings of self-knowledge, or even a measure of satisfaction with the teaching and assessment methods. Knowledge can be assessed by oral examination, written essays, or multiple-choices quizzes, all of which tap into different skills and test information and learning retained in different ways.

Outcome or achievement is no doubt multidimensional, and it is therefore to be expected that CLS and other variables relate to some aspect of the achievement/outcome variable and not others. It behooves the experimenters, however, to specify clearly not only which outcome/achievement measures are thought to be relevant (and which not) but also how the mechanism and process works. Further, if the outcome measure is actually measured only rarely or has poor ecological validity, it may be that the researchers' theory or findings may rarely be observable in the real world. There is often a dilemma for the researcher when selecting an outcome measure: whether to use a convenient, common, but unreliable educational outcome variable (e.g., exam results) or construct a much better, sensitive, and robust measure quite different from those used in the classroom.

For researchers in the areas of personality and intelligence, the relationship between personality intelligence and CLS is also never spelled out very clearly. Those researchers interested in the fundamental structure (or dimensions) of personality and/or intelligence see no need to examine CLS dimensions or styles that they would prefer to incorporate into their models. Similarly, those researchers dedicating to isolating or describing styles that they believe are highly predictive of educational achievement are not particularly interested in relating their concept to grander theories of personality or intelligence. It is usually only after a CLS has been well established and researched that investigators relate it to major theoretical systems in either personality or intelligence, but rarely both. One obvious implication of this model, therefore, is that it provides a scheme whereby pure and applied researcher from various social science disciplines and subdisciplines can come together to share their findings.

There has always been a great debate as to the distinction between cognitive style and ability. Various attempts have been made to draw distinctions between the two (Messick, 1984; Tiedemann, 1989). These include the following:

1. Ability questions refer to *how much* and *what*; style questions to *how*. Ability refers to what kind of information is being processed, by what operation, in what form, how efficiently and so forth. Style refers to the manner or mode of cognition.
2. Ability implies *maximal* performance; style implies *typical* propensities. Ability is measured in terms of accuracy, correctness, and speed of response, whereas style emphasizes the predominant or customary processing model.
3. Abilities are *unipolar*; style is usually *bipolar*. Ability levels range from none to a great deal, whereas styles usually have two different poles with quite different implications for cognitive functioning.
4. Abilities are *value directional*; styles are value *differentiated*. Usually, having more of an ability is considered better than having less, whereas supposed stylistic extreme poles have adaptive value but in different circumstances.
5. Abilities are often *domain specific*; styles cut across domains. Abilities are often specific to various domains (e.g., verbal, numerical, or spatial areas), whereas styles often serve as high-level heuristics.
6. Abilities are *enabling* variables because they facilitate task performance; styles are *organizing* and controlling variables. Abilities dictate level of performance, whereas styles contribute to the selection, combination, and sequencing of both topic and process.

Guilford (1980), however, believes that some cognitive style variables are more like personality traits (e.g., field dependence, scanning), whereas others are more like ability variables. Other researchers have actually used well-established personality tests to define cognitive style, blurring the distinction between personality and cognitive style (Hunt, Krzystofiak, Meindl, & Yousry, 1989; Ruble & Cosier, 1990). This chapter will consider in detail many of the cognitive/learning styles that have been described in the research literature.

COGNITIVE STYLES

The idea that individuals have preferred styles of learning, processing information, and perceiving is not new in psychology. As a consequence, there are a wealth of different conceptualizations going back over 70 years. Messick (1976) listed 19 cognitive-style variables; a cognitive style is usually conceived of as a preference for perceptual organization that includes an individual's self-concept, worldview, typical instrumental responses, and values. According to most researchers in this area, cognitive style determines the mode and accuracy of perception, thinking style, goal-directed behavior, personal belief and value systems, and the focus of attention. Indeed, in their zealousness to emphasize the role of cognitive and learning styles, many have perhaps overstressed their importance or predictive power. Supposedly, cognitive style also influences emotional life—what factors arouse emotions, the kinds of feelings people are likely to experience and their intensity, and how people cope with emotion. Cognitive styles are important in organizing both cognitive and affective data, but most researchers have concentrated more on the cognitive than the affective mechanisms involved. Furthermore, not all have related the CLS to an academic outcome measure.

According to Messick (1984), eight variables represent cognitive style in the narrow sense: broad versus narrow categorizing, cognitive complexity versus simplicity, field dependence and independence, leveling versus sharpening, scanning versus focusing, converging versus diverging, automatization versus restructuring, and reflection versus impulsivity. But this list is not exclusive, as we shall see. Some reviewers have divided this list into "best established" and "other" cognitive styles, reflecting the amount of research done in each area (Guilford, 1980).

This review will consider some of the more important and better-researched learning or cognitive styles. As will become apparent, they have been described by researchers working in very different areas of psychology, despite the fact that they have numerous similarities. Although nearly all those described here may be considered among the more established styles, some (including the first two discussed below) have attracted only modest research attention.

Sharpeners and Levelers

Wulf (1992) noted that the memory for perceived figures undergoes modifications depending on subjects' tendencies either to minimize the differences between figural elements (leveling) or to accentuate them (sharpening). Hebb and Foord (1945) demonstrated empirically that these modifications result from active memory selection and elaboration, not from a passive change in the memory trace. Holzman and Gardner (1960) reported that sharpeners are cognitively more differentiated because they can cope with a wider breadth of stimulus categories and are therefore more adaptive; they are not only cognitively more articulate but also seek excitement (a differentiation of the cognitive motive) rather than security in the pursuit of their goals. Levelers, who have a narrow range of categories, prefer the familiar, are more conforming, and therefore are dominated by considerations of security. Sharpeners are more open to new experience, expend more effort in the pursuit of their goals, and react with more emotional intensity. Levelers blur similar memories, and objects tend to be lost or attended, whereas sharpeners are less likely to confuse similar objects and may even magnify small differences between similar memory traces, thereby exaggerating change and heightening the difference between the present and the past.

Supposedly, although sharpeners probably experience more pleasure, they are also more likely to expose themselves to insecurity, anxiety, and personal danger. Levelers, though "living the safe life," have a smaller repertoire of responses to stress (a less differentiated perceptual structure in that area) and are more vulnerable to the uncertainties of life. Thus this variable has both cognitive and affective consequences. Relatively little research has concentrated on academic or educational correlates of leveling versus sharpening, however, and there remains some doubt as to the validity of the best measure of this variable (Tiedemann, 1989).

Narrow and Extensive Scanners

In a study of attention, Gardner and Long (1962) reported a difference in the scan patterns of individuals attending to a stimulus: Some individuals were wide or extensive scanners, whereas others were narrow scanners. Measuring scanning by photographing eye movements and through the subject's ability to resist the habituating effect of repeated perceptual experience, these researchers found that extensive scanners have more frequent shifts in eye fixations, scan more of the field, and are more resistant to stimulus adaptation. Furthermore, they are more accurate in their estimation of perceptual dimensions. Extensive scanners are supposedly more accurate in the discrimination of other information (e.g., understanding the behavior of others), as well as less impulsive and capable of more enduring motivation effort.

Because extensive scanners process information more accurately, they cope more effectively with anxiety. The propensity to exclusive scanning is associated with meticulousness, concern with detail, and a sharp yet wide-ranging focus of attention (Gardner & Long, 1962). Extreme scanning is related to defense mechanisms of both isolation and projection, suggesting that extensive scanning may serve different purposes under different circumstances or that there may be distinct types of scanning. This style, however, has not stimulated much further research and is not particularly well documented. Certainly how these scanning styles affect achievement, learning, or academic performance has not been investigated.

Psychological Differentiation

Witkin, Dyk, Faterson, Goodenough, and Karp (1962) described a cognitive style, called psychological differentiation, that was to stimulate a great deal of research. Thompson (1988) noted that *field-independent* learners (a) impose organization on unstructured field of knowledge; (b) sample fully from the nonsalient features of a concept in order to attain their relevant attributes and to form hypotheses; (c) prefer active learning situations, including hypothesis formulation; (d) demonstrate a learning curve that is discontinuous, with no significant improvement in learning of a new concept until the appropriate hypothesis is formulated, after which there is a sudden improvement; (e) use mnemonic structures and reorganization of materials for more effective storage and retrieval of information; (f) learn to generalize more readily; and (g) prefer to learn general principles and seem to acquire them easily. *Field-dependent* learners (a) take organization of a field of knowledge as given; (b) use only the most salient features of a concept in the attainment of the relevant attributes and in hypothesis formation; (c) utilize the passive approach to learning; (d) have a learning curve that shows a continuous gradual improvement as relevant cues as sampled; (e) use existing organization of materials in cognitive processing; (f) are less effective in making generalizations; and (g) prefer to learn specific facts and seem to acquire them more.

Again, field dependence/independence has both cognitive and affective features. Furthermore, although the precise details of how dependence or independence may affect academic achievement has not been spelled out, it is not difficult to devise various testable hypotheses. Witkin et al. (1962) reported that subjects differed with respect to their reliance on visual and bodily cues in the judgment of the vertical dimension: Although visual cues were generally dominant, some subjects also used bodily cues as well. These more differentiated subjects were referred to as field independent, and the others as field dependent.

Skeptics have argued that Witkin's rod-and-frame is a technique in search of a theory, in the sense that more research has gone into the measurement tools than the theory they generated. Other researchers have indicated that the measure of psychological independence (i.e., freedom from a restricted perceptual set or modality) is part of a larger class of organization, namely, the articulation or differentiation of the field (Glick, 1968). In general, the less restricted an individual is, the more articulate and differentiated his or her perceptual discrimination will be. Thus set-independent individuals are more accurate and adaptive in their perceptions; because their perceptual structures are more articulated and differentiated, they tend supposedly to be more analytical and to have a wider frame of reference. Witkin (1976) has found a number of developmental and personality correlates of this style.

Tolerance/Intolerance for Ambiguity

Adorno, Frenkel- Brunswick, Levinson, and Sanford (1950), in an attempt to explain Nazi authoritarianism in psychoanalytic terms, came up with the concept of intolerance of ambiguity. Subsequent work has uncovered variables that can be classed as cognitive styles: Rokeach (1960), for instance, used self-report scales to measure tolerance of ambiguity. On the basis of repeated and cross-validated findings, he concluded that people differ in being open-minded or closed-minded. The closed-minded person can be recognized by his or her dogmatism and authoritarianism. Dogmatism is not an either-or property; tolerance and intolerance exist on a continuous scale that can be measured (Furnham & Ribchester, in press).

Intolerance of ambiguity also serves a coping function: The person who is afraid to be alone and worries about the future may seek the certainty of authoritarianism and psychological conservatism. Without explicit leadership and rules in the face of ambiguity, the authoritarian or dogmatic person is unhappy. The open-minded person becomes unhappy with doctrinaire or ideological imperatives. Thus perceptual differentiation determines affect, which may in turn provoke specific behavior to change the affect if it is negative. Rokeach and Kliejunas (1972) point out that situational factors interact with cognitive style to determine the dynamics of behavior. Research into tolerance of ambiguity has excited interest from all areas of psychology (cognitive, clinical, and social) for nearly 50 years (Furnham, 1994; Furnham & Ribchester, in press). To what extent tolerance for ambiguity may be conceived of as a moderator variable, or an integrating vehicle for personality and intelligence variables, is unclear. Certainly it has been conceived of much more as a personality variable than as a cognitive learning style, though quite clearly it could be seen to act as the latter.

Cognitive Consistency

Cognitive consistency has its roots in the cognitive balance theory of Heider (1958). When there is congruence between expectancy and outcome, a state of cognitive balance exists. Heider described a number of balance/imbalance situations in which the subject's expectancy of another's behavior—based on the subject's estimate of the person—is either confirmed or denied. Rosenberg and Abelson (1960) point out that cognitive balance includes an affective component; whether this is positive or negative depends on whether the other person is seen as facilitating one's own goal attainment.

Festinger (1956) described the now well-known and extensively research concept of cognitive dissonance: When individuals find themselves behaving in a way contrary to their beliefs about themselves, cognitive dissonance exists. This discrepant state motivates behavior to remove the dissonance. In trying to make this theory more explicit, Aronson (1972) has added refinements: (a) Dissonance can only occur if the discrepancy exists in an area to which the person has made a commitment (i.e., the person has decided to make this an important issue for himself or herself), and (b) other things being equal, the dissonance is resolved in the direction of maintaining self-esteem. Because people differ in where and when they perceive dissonance, Festinger considered cognitive consistency a cognitive style variable. Investigations into this variable in fact dominated social psychological research from the mid-1960s to the mid-1970s. The links between dissonance and personality and intelligence were never a central focus of research, however, though dissonance reduction was seen to be a common strategy for certain personality types.

Locus of Control

Rotter (1966, 1975) devised an internal–external scale that measures the extent to which an individual attributes the causes or results of his or her behavior to internal or external sources. People with an internal locus of control (i.e., who believe they are masters of their own fate) are described as *instrumentalists*, whereas those with an external locus of control (who believe luck, or powerful others control their destiny) are called *fatalists*. This is perhaps the most popular individual-difference/cognitive style concept ever conceived (Furnham & Steele, 1993). As described by Phares (1976), for example, internally oriented people are more responsible and achievement oriented. Students who fail an examination tend to blame themselves if they are high internals, and to blame outside causes or bad luck if they are high externals. Externals are more subject to anxiety and depression, whereas internals are more likely to use denial (Phares, 1976).

Perhaps the most fundamental difference between internals and externals lies in the ways they seek knowledge about their environment. Feeling that one is in control of the reinforcements that follow behavior should lead to greater efforts to acquire information about one's environment. This seems to be the single most consistent finding running throughout the research literature on locus of control. Seeman (1963) observed that prisoners in a reformatory who expressed internal beliefs were more knowledgeable than externals about reformatory policies and rules, parole regulations, and long-range economic facts that could affect their lives after release. Given that internals are more likely to seek information, be resistant to social influence, and attribute responsibility to themselves and others, one would certainly expect internal–external differences in achievement behavior. A considerable body of research data appears to support this expectation (Phares, 1976; Strickland, 1977). It seems fair to say that internality is directly related to achievement behavior: "Not only do internals appear to work harder at intellectual and performance tasks, but their efforts also appear to be rewarded in that they make better grades and receive more desirable reinforcements by delaying immediate gratification" (Strickland, 1977, p. 240).

There is a distinct tendency for the relationship between achievement and internal beliefs to be stronger in adolescents and children and for the relationship to be more visible in males than in females. In general, which style is more appropriate depends upon the goal to which the behavior is directed; it is also related to other measures (e.g., desire for control; Burger, 1985). Prociuk and Lusier (1975) reported that this cognitive style had generated more research than any other (227 studies in the 1973–74 period alone), a status that remained so 15 years later (Rotter, 1990).

Attribution Style

Attribution style is a personality characteristic that was first introduced by Abramson, Seligman, and Teasdale (1978) and further elaborated by others (Metalsky, Abramson, Seligman, Semmel, & Peterson, 1982). According to the reformulated learned-helplessness model of depression (Abramson et al., 1978) individuals vulnerable to depression differ from the nonvulnerable in the causal judgments they habitually make for good and bad events in their lives (Zemore & Veikle, 1989). Abramson et al. (1978) speculated that a "depressive attributional style" is characterized by the tendency to view aversive events as caused by factors that are internal (in contrast to external), are stable (rather than unstable or temporary), and exert global influences across many domains in one's life (rather than specific or narrow influence in only a few situations). Various measures exist of attributional style (Feather, 1983; Furnham, Sadka, & Brewin, 1992), and attributional style results have been correlated with various personality variables (Mitchell, 1990). Researchers in education have been particularly interested in attribution style, as it has been shown to affect academic performance directly (Ryckman, Peckham, Mizokawa, & Sprague, 1990; van Overwalle, Segebarth, & Goldstein, 1989)—that is, how one attributes the causes of previous academic success and failure has a direct consequence on future academic performance.

Information Gathering and Evaluation

Whetten and Cameron (1984) have reported on the Cognitive Style Instrument (CSI), which is based on McKenny and Keen's (1974) two-dimensional model of cognitive style. The *information gathering* dimension of the model distinguishes a receptive strategy from a preceptive strategy, and the *information-valuation* dimension distinguishes a systematic strategy from an intuitive strategy. Different strategies for taking in, coding, and storing information (information gathering) supposedly develop as a result of certain cognitive filters used by individuals to select the information they pay attention to.

A preceptive strategy emphasizes concepts and generalizations or the relationships among the various elements of data, in gathering information. Preceptive thinkers (who also tend to be convergent thinkers) frequently have preconceived notions about what sort of information may be relevant, and they look at various items of information to find commonalities or consistencies with their preconceptions. The receptive strategy focuses on detail, or on the specific attributes of each element of data, rather than on relationships among the elements. Receptive thinkers (who tend to be divergent thinkers) have few preconceptions about what may be relevant, so they insist on a close and thorough examination of all data. A preceptive strategy focuses on the whole, a receptive strategy on the parts on the whole. A preceptive strategy looks for commonalities and overall categories; a receptive strategy for uniqueness, detail, and exceptions to the general rule.

The second dimension of the model refers to strategies for interpreting and judging information. These strategies supposedly develop as a result of reliance on a particular problem-solving pattern. A systematic strategy approaches a problem from the standpoint of a method or plan with specific sequential steps; there is a focus on appropriate methods and logical progression. People who solve problems systematically conduct an orderly search for objective information. When such people defend their solutions, they emphasize the methods and procedures used to solve the problems. An intuitive strategy, in contrast, approaches a problem on the basis of "gut feel," or an internal sense of how to respond. The problem is often redefined, and approaches are developed through trial and error rather than through logical procedure. Intuitive individuals frequently cannot describe their own problem-solving processes. Problem solutions are often found through seeing analogies or unusual relationships between the problem and a past experience.

A third commonly used dimension of information processing concerns information response—the extent to which individuals are inclined to act or reflect on the information they receive. This dimension separates active strategies from reflection. Individuals employing an active strategy are supposedly inclined to experiment with or to execute a behavior as a result of receiving information. They are doers rather than thinkers, and they are more interested in practical application than in theoretical elegance. Activists feel impatient if a solution or action is not forthcoming when they are confronted with a problem. Conversely, individuals employing a reflective strategy are inclined to ponder information for a longer time before deciding to take action. They tend to observe rather than to participate, and the practical application of information is not nearly so important to them as its meaning and conceptual logic. They are thinkers, not doers.

Thus, Whetton and Cameron (1984) argue that active managers are likely to be more effective when quick decisions are needed and execution and application of information are required. Reflective managers are likely to be most effective with complex or contradictory information that requires in-depth analysis rather than action. McKenny and Keen (1974) and Mitroff and Kilmann (1975) have found that no matter what type of problem they face, individuals use their preferred cognitive style to approach it. Moreover, when given a choice individuals prefer decision situations and problem types that are consistent with their own cognitive style (e.g., individuals scoring high on the systematic strategy prefer problems with a step-by-step method of solution). Henderson and Nutt (1980) have found that differences in cognitive style also produce different decision-making processes in managers. Managers who are more systematic than intuitive, for example, implement more computer-based systems and rational processes than do those who are more intuitive (Mulowsky & Freeman, 1979).

Though there may well be other cognitive style variables that have been identified, described, and documented (and related measures psychometrized), many have simply grown out of the above concepts. They differ in the areas of psychology from which they emerged, the methods for measuring them, and the amount of research that they have attracted. More importantly, few have attempted to compare and contrast these measures to understand where they are conceptually unique or whether the different tests have incremental validity. Clearly many of these concepts overlap, and it is to be expected that the measures correlate positively with each other. Indeed, many small studies that have examined some of these dimensions have frequently reported significant positive correlations (Furnham & Ribchester, in press).

The question remains, however, as to their unique variance and incremental validity—that is, what is unique to each concept. Certainly the way they are conceived and measured is primarily attributable to their subdisciplinary origin in social, clinical, personality, or cognitive psychology. Researchers in the last discipline tend to focus on perception, attention or memory factors and hence conceive of cognitive styles in these terms (Ginter, Brown, Scalise, & Ripley, 1989) whereas the former approaches tend to focus on the inter- and intrapersonal function and consequences of adopting any particular style. Indeed, the area could do with a little conceptual and methodological housekeeping to examine common themes in the myriad of measures that exist. More importantly, the relationship between personality and intelligence/ability and the particular CLS has not always been spelled out. Though some researchers seem to describe a given CLS in personality trait terms, they rarely seem to relate it to well-established traits (e.g., extraversion, neuroticism) or personality systems.

OTHER STYLES

In addition to those discussed above, other styles have been described that have not attracted as much research. These are outlined below.

Category Width

Social and personality psychologists interested in authoritarianism, dogmatism, and rigidity have devised scales to measure these related concepts. Many relate to the concept of category width (Fillenbaum, 1959; Pettigrew, 1958), which entails the consistent preference for inclusiveness as opposed to exclusiveness in establishing the acceptable range for specified categories. This dimension reflects differential tolerances for different types of errors, with broad categorizers tolerating errors of inclusion and narrow categorizers tolerating errors of exclusion. The narrow categorizer is thought to be conceptually conservative, whereas the broad categorizer is thought to be more tolerant to deviant instances.

Cognitive Complexity/Simplicity

Various researchers since Kelly (1955) have noted that some people have preference for complex versus simple ideas. This dimension refers to individual differences in the tendency to explain the environment in a multidimensional and discriminating way. The conceptual system of a cognitively complex individual is highly differentiated (using a large number of distinct dimensions), finely articulated (capable of discriminating the strength of varied stimuli), and flexibly integrated (dimensions being multiply interrelated and organized).

Automatization/Restructuring

This style was first described by Broverman, Broverman, Vogel, Palmer, and Klainer (1964), though it has not attracted much subsequent research, at least under that name. Strong versus weak automatization refers to an individual's ability to perform simple repetition tasks compared to what would be expected of them in this regard from their general ability level. This dimension is considered as a cognitive control variable because of its unipolar and function-specific character. It is conceptualized in ipsative terms. Empirically, relative facility in performing simple automatized tasks has been found to be in opposition to relative skill in perceptual analysis and disembodying, thereby generating an intraindividual bipolarity of automatization versus restructuring that is considered to be a cognitive style. The automatized tendency to respond to the obvious stimulus properties in simple repetitive tasks is, however, dysfunctional on tasks for which the obvious stimulus attributes must be set aside or restructured. Differences between strong and weak automatizers have been noted in regard to occupational level (strong automatizers having higher-status occupations). But Tiedemann (1989) is critical of this cognitive style dimension and argues that it is no more than a behavioral correlate of psychological differentiation (reviewed above).

Convergence and Divergence

Based on his early work on creativity, occupational preference, and ability, Hudson (1966) distinguished between the scientific/convergent and the artistic/imaginative/divergent thinker. This dimension represents the degree of an individual's relative reliance upon convergent thinking (pointed toward logical conclusions and uniquely correct or conventionally best outcomes) as contrasted to divergent thinking (pointed toward variety and quantity or relevant output). Convergence versus divergence has been studied as a manifestation of differences in intelligence versus creativity, with special emphasis on ideational fluency in the production of novel responses as the hallmark of creativity. It remains unclear, however, whether intelligence is correlated with a strong preference for convergent or divergent thinking, partly because it is so difficult to assess the outcome of divergent or creative thinking.

All reviewers of this diverse literature on cognitive style have been highly critical of it (Messick, 1984; Tiedemann, 1989). They have been particularly concerned with the gap between the conceptualization of the various styles, which tends to be rather grand and inclusive, and the empirical testing, which often consists of relative simple laboratory methods of limited reliability and validity. Some dimensions have attracted very little research, whereas others (e.g., field dependence) are seen as a paradigm for research and theorizing (Petzold, 1985).

It is also noticeable from the above review that where styles are related back to personality systems and intelligence models, it is nearly always the former that are favored. Further, the amount of overlap between the two is often taken for evidence of concurrent validity for the CLS, even though it could equally well be taken for evidence of the latter's redundancy. Tiedemann (1989) concluded as follows:

> What needs to be done? In the case of cognitive styles, the gap between conceptual and empirical level is enormous. It cannot be reduced by revising the theory. Accommodating the theory to current operationalizations and eliminating the surplus meaning would mean the abandonment of the cognitive style concept. The heterogeneous operationalizations of the so-called cognitive styles have indeed little in common, apart from the claimed but not achieved assessment of a style dimension.
>
> On the other hand, adequate preference operationalizations of the underlying theoretical construct would mercilessly expose the failure of the whole concept. Competence tests are inadequate measurement devices

> for preference constructs, as shown earlier; however, most style dimensions are operationally defined in this way. Therefore, on the basis of given operationalizations, most cognitive styles can easily be integrated into Guilford's (1980) Structure of Intellect Model. From this point of view within the frame of current cognitive styles research in nearly all cases, it is merely behaviour correlates of different performance dimensions that are accumulated. Attempts to operationalize field dependence using preference measurements have failed in the process of validation. Williams (1975) found no connections between preferences and traditional style tests. Serious doubts seem warranted with regard to the pervasive influence of preferences postulate in the underlying construct.
>
> As a result of this analysis, the cognitive style concept has to be considered a failure on the diagnostic level and, therefore, the empirical level as well. With regard to current findings, serious doubts seem warranted regarding successful operationalizations for future research. Cognitive styles are conceptualized as a high-level heuristics. If heuristics seem inappropriate, then they have to be altered or abandoned. The concept of cognitive style has been theoretically and empirically analyzed for more than 3 decades now. At the moment, nobody can claim that cognitive styles do not exist. But life is short, and so my personal opinion of the state of research into cognitive styles has to be: There is no point in chasing a chimera! (pp. 272–273)

LEARNING STYLES

Another way of conceiving of an individual-difference moderator variable has been not so much cognitive style as learning style. The difference between the two is not always clear. Certainly cognitive style is conceived as in much more general terms, whereas learning style usually refers exclusively to personal preference in the learning of information or skills; hence learning styles are frequently "validated" against academic or knowledge criteria. Once again there has been a proliferation of measures in this area, though here the different measures and theories are much more closely related than was the case with cognitive style. Three of the most common used will be examined below.

The Learning Style Inventory (Kolb, 1976, 1984)

This measure and theory have attracted much more research than any other. Kolb's model combines two bipolar dimensions of cognitive processing: the active-reflective dimension ranges from direct participation to detached observation, whereas the abstract-concrete dimension ranges from dealing with tangible objects to dealing with theoretical concepts. Kolb defined a four-stage cycle of learning that begins with the acquisition of concrete experience, which gives way to reflective observation on that experience. Then theory building or abstract conceptualization occurs, which is put to a test through active experimentation. The cycle then begins again as the experimentation itself yields new concrete experiences. Each stage of the cycle requires different abilities, and the learner must decided which ones to apply in any situation. Because individuals tend to be more skilled in some abilities than others, they are inclined to favor a particular learning style.

In Kolb's model, individuals prefer to gather information either through concrete experience (CE) or abstract conceptualization (AC), then process that information through either reflective observation (RO) or active experimentation (AE). CE includes affective learning skills, whereas RO involves perceptual learning skills. Four learning-styles categories are possible based upon how a person combines preferences in gathering and processing information. Accommodators combine CE and AE, divergers combine CE and RO, assimilators combine RO and AC, and convergers combine AC and AE.

According to Kolb, the greatest strength of the convergent learning style lies in problem solving, decision making, and the practical application of ideas. People with this style seem to do best in such situations as conventional intelligence tests, where there is a single correct solution to a problem. Convergers prefer dealing with technical tasks and problems rather with social and interpersonal issues. The divergent learning style has the opposite strengths of the convergent style, emphasizing concrete experience and reflective observation. The greatest strength of this orientation lies in imaginative ability and awareness of meaning and values. The divergent style is so named because a person of this type performs better in situations that call for generation of alternative ideas and tends to be imaginative and feeling-oriented. Divergers have broad cultural interests and tend to specialize in the arts.

Assimilators prefer abstract conceptualization and reflective observation; the greatest strength of this orientation lies in inductive reasoning, in the ability to create theoretical models, and in assimilating disparate observations into an integrated explanation. This learning style is more characteristic of individuals in the basic sciences and mathematics rather than the applied sciences. In organizations, persons with this learning style are found most often in the research and planning departments. The accommodative learning style has the opposite strengths of assimilation, emphasizing concrete experience and active experimentation. The greatest strength of this orientation lies in doing things carrying out plans and tasks, and in getting involved in new experiences. The adaptive emphasis of this orientation is on opportunity seeking, risk taking, and action. As the style name implies, it is best suited for those situations in which one must adapt oneself to changing immediate circumstances.

Various studies have been concerned with the psychometric properties of the Learning Styles Inventory (Atkinson, 1988; Atkinson, Murrel & Whiters, 1990), and it has attracted a considerable amount of research. For instance, some have tried to distinguish between the learning styles of more versus less successful students (Titus, Bergandi, & Shryock, 1990). Green, Snell, and Parimaneth (1990) investigated the ability of the Learning Style Inventory (as well as an aptitude and interest test) to predict group learning style in a sample of 147 community college students enrolled in a social science course. Inferences drawn from the data suggested that including a learning styles inventory as part of a reassessment package for entering students can provide valuable information for students in making choices of academic goals and careers.

Research by Kolb (1984) clearly links style to academic major and career choices. He found that individuals with certain cognitive styles gravitated toward academic majors that reinforce those styles (e.g., business reinforces active, receptive styles; mathematics reinforces reflective, perceptive styles). Moreover, he discovered that cognitive styles also affect managerial behavior. For example, managers who held high-risk, high-pressure jobs in the trust department of a bank tended to be active and receptive; those in low-risk, low-discretion jobs tended to be reflective and preceptive. Similarly, receptive managers tended to rely on information from other people in their investment decisions, whereas preceptives relied on analytically oriented printed material. Sein and Robey (1991) looked at learning style and the efficacy of computer training methods. They predicted, and found, that convergers and assimilators performed better when trained with an abstract conceptual model (depicting the computer system in terms of synthetic forms, e.g., flowcharts or abstract schematic diagrams), whereas divergers and accommodators performed better when provided with an analogical model (which depicts the computer system in terms of another with which the learner is familiar).

More recently, researchers have turned their attention to the stability of learning style and ability correlates. Pinto and Geiger (1991) found longitudinal stability of learning styles over a year, which suggests that styles are fairly traitlike, but also that they may be fairly difficult to alter. Geiger (1991) examined learning style and student grade-point average and concluded that assimilators are significantly more likely to be top students because they are best at making sense of divergent pieces of information.

The Learning Styles Questionnaire (Honey & Mumford, 1982)

Honey and Mumford (1982), two British researchers, defined learning styles similar to those of Kolb, though their measures have attracted less attention. Activators, the first group, involve themselves fully and without bias in new experiences; their days are filled with activity, and they revel in short-term crisis. They tend to thrive on the challenge of new experiences but are bored with implementation and longer-term consolidation. Reflectors, the second group, prefer to collect data, both firsthand and from others, and ponder experiences from many different perspectives before coming to any conclusions. The third group, theorists, adapt and integrate observations into complex but logically sound theories. They like to think problems through in a step-by-step, logical way; they tend to be detached and dedicated to rational objectivity rather than anything subjective or ambiguous. Finally, pragmatists are keen on trying out theories and techniques to see if they work in practice; they search out new ideas and take the first opportunity to experiment with applications. They are supposedly essentially practical, down-to-earth people who like making decisions and solving problems.

Various studies done in different countries have provided evidence of the reliability and validity of this instrument (Allison & Hayes, 1988; Hayes & Allison, 1988). The similarity between the Kolb (1976) and Honey and Mumford (1982) measures is striking; furthermore, because both seem to be conceived and described in trait terms, it is relatively easy to relate them to established tests. Furnham (1992) related the famous Eysenckian traits (H. Eysenck & Eysenck, 1975) to both learning style measures. He found many predicted correlations, particularly between extraversion and the activist ($r = .52$), converger ($r = .33$), and accommodator (r = .33) learning styles. It therefore seems that established personality traits can account for about 10% to 20% of the variance in learning styles.

The size of the intercorrelations, though, begs the all-important question of incremental validity. The assumption underlying the development of a new instrument, or the adaptation of an old one, is that by so doing one can achieve increased face and predictive validity. In other words, if well-established and theoretically sound personality variables relate closely and coherently to learning style, as suggested above, why not simply measure personality instead of learning style? There remain persuasive arguments for this approach. Parsimony both of theory and measurement would require fewer rather than overlapping measurement instruments. There has been an enormous research endeavor into personality that could inform the learning styles issues (M. Eysenck, 1981); there is little evidence and even less theory concerning the etiology of the learning style types, or of their stability over time. This is not to say that learning style preferences are not important, but whether they need to be conceived and measured while ignoring established personality theory is questionable. Nevertheless, the application of theoretically and psychometrically robust measures to all aspects of behavior is to be welcomed. Clearly, because of the size of the shared variance, there is a relationship between established personality traits and learning style preferences. Hence it may be sensible to use personality tests in addition to, rather than instead of, the learning styles instruments when examining the role of learning.

Adaption-Innovation (Kirton, 1989)

Kirton (1976, 1989) has developed research concerned with an individuals' preferred cognitive strategies relative to change. The learning or cognitive style he described is thought to be related to strategies of creativity, problem solving, and decision making but independent of cognitive capacity, success, cognitive techniques, and coping behavior. These assumptions are not fully supported by the extant data, but the ideas and tests have captured the imagination of applied professionals, who seem obsessed with how people react to change (Kirton & Pender, 1982). Kirton (1976) described a single dimension labeled by the end points: adaptors and innovators. In essence, adaptors have a reference for "doing things better," whereas innovators trade off immediate efficiency to "do things differently." Kirton summarized his position as follows:

1. Both adaptors and innovators need to operate within their own level limits (knowledge, know-how, permitted scope).
2. Adaptors and innovators have different attributes, each of which, depending on the circumstances, could be advantageous or disadvantageous.
3. One set of these attributes come naturally to an individual, the opposing set has to be learnt and exercised as part of an individual coping behaviour. People are at their best when operating in their preferred mode.
4. When coping behaviour is no longer needed, there is a tendency to return to and exploit preferred style.
5. Such (personal adjustment) coping behaviour is extensive in terms of stress.
6. People use other forms of coping behaviour, e.g., change circumstances to suit preference, form part of a team, use intermediaries better able to reach the very different cognitive style of another, use mentors and facilitators. (pp. 34–35)

Kirton's concept and measures have attracted a good deal of research. In a very thorough review, Schroder (1989) looked at adaption-innovation correlates of managerial competency and noted some dramatic differences. He suggested that one's style in this dimension reflects the way competencies are expressed; furthermore, these style differences will produce significantly different effects even if people have equivalent managerial competencies. Schroder suggests that it is highly dangerous to form cohesive homogeneous groups, who set up strong resistances to integration and advocates the use of heterogenous groups, who respond better to change.

There appear to be a number of problems with Kirton's theory and measure: First, whether the concept/measure is unidimensional; second, whether cognitive style in any sense is linked to ability; and third, how unique the trait is. Kirton (1989) reports nine factor analytic studies suggesting that the test is multidimensional, with three factors: sufficiency versus proliferation of originality, efficiency of operation, and rule/group conformity. Goldsmith (1985), in a factor analysis of the Kirton Adaptation-Innovation Inventory (KAI) revealed the scale to have high factorial stability across populations. Three factors accounted for 41% of the variance, yet all the items correlated with self-esteem. These are usually correlated about $r = .3$ which, depending on one's definition of superfactors, would usually mean the existence of three (related but distinctive) traits.

Kirton (1989) maintains that the KAI is a measure of style, not ability. He notes that "by splitting creativity into style or level; cognitive complexity into preference or capacity; confining talent to specific capacity; skill and know-how to learned behavior, it is possible to avoid some of the confusion in the current literature" (p. 26). Goldsmith (1986) provides evidence that the KAI is unrelated to the concept of cognitive complexity. According to him, "These expected negative findings support the notion that level and style may be differentiated across other concepts of cognitive complexity and cognitive style. These findings, however, are limited to two samples of American undergraduates and to the measures of cognitive complexity employed" (p. 466). There is probably insufficient evidence, however, to be sure about this point.

Finally there is the issue of whether the KAI measures a unique trait. Kirton (1989) reports on a very large number of concurrent validity studies, with many correlations with conceptually related measures in excess of $r = .50$. Sensation seeking and intuition (in the Jungian sense) appear to be correlated at least .5, a finding that may suggest considerable overlap between the concepts. Kirton and de Ciantis (1986) found that the KAI correlated with about half of the 16PF dimensions, particularly Q_1 (Conservative Experimenting; $r = .60$, $n = 83$) and G (Expedient Conscientious; $r = .44$, $n = 83$). They argue that 16PF factors are central in describing the personality dimensions underlying cognitive style. One could equally well argue, however, that all the variance accounted for by the KAI may be "mopped up" by the Cattellian (or Eysenckian) dimensions, thereby making the former instrument redundant.

Also, Goldsmith (1985) found KAI scores were significantly negatively correlated with dogmatism, and positively correlated with sensation seeking, risk taking, and innovation. Hence he believed that innovators were risk takers who seem to have greater need for novel stimuli, suggesting powerful evidence of classic extraversion. Goldsmith (1985) found large correlations between the KAI and sensation seeking (.67 and .59), risk taking (.64) and sensing-intuiting (−.62 and .55) in a random sample of 270 adults. Again, it is uncertain whether one could maintain that the KAI accounts for unique variance with correlations this size. Carne and Kirton (1982) earlier found high correlations between KAI total and subscale scores and the Myers-Briggs Type Indicator, particularly for intuition ($r = .44$) and perception ($r = .53$).

APPLIED RESEARCH

Cognitive and educational researchers in particular have been eager to apply the research on learning styles. One area that has recently become very interested in cognitive styles is industrial and organizational (O/I) psychology. In an extensive and comprehensive review, Streufert and Nogami (1989) concluded as follows:

> Recent efforts have begun to view concepts from style and complexity theories as they interact with each other, with abilities and with job content, i.e., as they combined to create more versus less effective actions, for example in managers. This approach has placed style and complexity approaches into the context of other applied research and theory which is not related to concerns with cognitive structure. The effects of this "marriage" has added considerable predictive capacity within the organizational context. . . . (p. 129)

There have been essentially two approaches to applied research. The first has been to discover and describe different cognitive and learning style/preferences exhibited by people (often school or university students) in the process of learning and/or teaching. This usually leads to the development of yet more style concepts. A second approach has been to investigate actual learning behaviors of students and how they relate to outcome measures like academic success. Certainly there seems no doubt that different students have a preference for different teaching methods and seem to do best when taught with them. The particular advantage of the latter research is the ecological validity of the dependent variables. A great deal of applied educational and psychological research has examined cognitive and learning style correlates (predictors) of academic success; for instance, various studies have used Entwistle and Ramsden's (1983) model and measurement tools to examine the relationship between learning style and outcome (Meyer, Parsons, & Dunne, 1990; Speth & Brown, 1990). Others have focused on teachers' beliefs and their students' outcomes (Rose & Medway, 1980). Some have pursued research on studying processes (Christensen, Massey, & Issacs, 1991).

Pask (1976) found that even when students were

required to learn in ways that would lead to understanding, they still showed distinct preferences in the styles of learning they adopted. Some students adopted a holistic style; their learning process involved the use of examples, analogies, and anecdotes in building up an idiosyncratic form of understanding deeply rooted in personal experience and beliefs. Other students performed a serialist style in which they began with a narrow focus, concentrated on details and logical connections in a cautious manner, and looked at the broader context only toward the end. Extreme holists were impulsive, even cavalier, in their use of evidence, tending to generalize too readily and to jump to unjustified conclusions (a tendency Pask referred to as "globetrotting"). Extreme serialists were often too cautious, failing to see important relationships or useful analogies, thus leaving their understanding impoverished through "improvidence."

Pask (1988) also found that those students who had been matched with learning materials of their own style learned faster and more fully than students who had been mismatched. Yet as lecturers and textbooks adopt varying styles of presentation, there seems to be an advantage in everyday studying of being able to switch readily between styles (adopting what Pask describes as a "versatile" style). There is evidence that there are systematic differences in preferred learning styles between students in contrasting academic disciplines (Entwistle & Ramsden, 1983)—science students are more serialistic, and art students more holistic—but it is not clear to what extent students are socialized into a way of thinking characteristic of that discipline, or to what extent students of that learning style are attracted to the subject.

SOME UNRESOLVED ISSUES

Research into cognitive and learning styles has been fragmented, idiosyncratic, and multidisciplinary. The result is a variety of different concepts/constructs; some distinct and others overlapping, investigated in and applied to a wide variety of research settings. There have been few attempts to review the area or invest in a research program that might prevent redundant studies. Riding and Sadler-Smith (1992) have, however, made some attempt to integrate a number of cognitive style measures. They took five of these measures and argued that together they in fact measured just two cognitive dimensions: holistic analytical (where the individual tends to process information as a whole or in parts), and verbal imagery (where an individual is inclined to represent mental information verbally or in images). This higher-order classification of the various constructs and measures is long overdue, but a difficult task.

Most importantly, perhaps, important questions in a number of areas have not been satisfactorily answered. These areas include the following:

1. *Etiology of a cognitive/learning style*. Given that people may have definable, measurable, and relatively stable styles, the question arises as to their origin: Are they biologically based, the result of early learning, neither, or both? This is a fundamental question that must be answered to avoid the frequent tautology found in some trait descriptions. It is, of course, a difficult question to research, and for some domains possibly "too hot to handle." To a large extent, though, etiology determines both how and how much a style may be changed.
2. *Variance accounted for*. Even if styles exist and determine in part the learning (however defined and measured) that takes place, few would argue that they are the only—or even the most important—factor that determines learning. The question then needs to be asked whether the amount of variance accounted for by this factor is so small as to be trivial or indeed a major and central factor, as suggested in Figure 1. (Indeed, the figure provides a path analytic model that could be tested.)
3. *The nature of style as a variable*. If cognitive/learning style is a moderator variable between intelligence, personality, and learning, the precise nature of this relationship needs to be spelled out. Indeed, it is necessary to list all relevant variables that relate to learning and specify how they interact. Despite the centrality of this question to this research endeavor, it has very rarely been asked and never satisfactorily answered. Figure 1 provides an example of a testable model, but others could also be conceived.
4. *The processes underlying style*. So far a great deal of the research in this field has been descriptive and taxonomic, aimed at identifying various styles and their consequences. Less work has gone into describing the mechanism or process whereby the style operates. (In terms of the model presented in Figure 1 con-

siderably less work has done into explaining the arrows than the boxes.)

5. *Style versus ability*. Central to the whole issue of cognitive/learning style is the nature of "style" itself. Usually the distinction between a personality trait and intelligence or ability is that personality measures average or typical behavior, whereas intelligence is seen as maximal performance.

More recently various writers have attempted to reconcile the distinction between personality and intelligence, or cognitive style and ability, by talking about typical intellectual engagement. McKenna (1990) noted that the concept of cognitive style has generated much research, particularly the way students learn; the way teachers learn; the concept of cognitive style matching and the preferences of students for courses, teaching methods, and the like. But McKenna believes that the consistency with which research, for example, has shown field-independent individuals perform more effectively than field-dependent individuals contradicts the style conception and suggests a contrasting interpretation in terms of cognitive ability.

CONCLUSION

Despite considerable pure and applied research dating back 50 years, the study of the relationship between personality and ability (intelligence) to cognitive and learning styles, and hence to some (often rather vague) outcome measure, remains fragmented. Rather than a slow and gradual emergence of an experimental paradigm and the formulation of explanatory models and concepts, we have witnessed the opposite: a balkanization of the field, with researchers developing highly similar eponymous constructs that often overlap. Worse than that, few investigators seem to be up-to-date with the developing, though controversial, fields of personality and intelligence, let alone sophisticated developments in psychometrics. This means that the areas delineated in the model presented earlier are not seen by researchers to overlap; hence they remain largely untested, though there are substantial data for some aspects of the model.

Certainly although "pure" researchers appear somewhat skeptical about the value of this field, researchers in education see the value and, indeed, the implications of this research. The concept of a fit between methods of teaching, learning, and assessment is one that will not go away. It is important, however, to establish robust, reliable, and valid measures of academic achievement, which is often the dependent variable. A recent review by Hayes and Allison (1993) of 17 studies drawn from a variety of educational contexts provided support for the proposition that instructional strategy was differentially effective for students with different learning styles. The authors argued that the inconsistency in the results was primarily attributable to psychometric weakness in the dependent variable of achievement.

A pessimist might argue that despite 50 years of research into cognitive/learning styles, we still know precious little if the above questions have not been answered or even attempted. An optimist, though, might be impressed by the research effort that has gone into this topic, by the proliferation of ideas, and by the evidence already accumulated. Nevertheless, pessimists sound more profound than optimists, and hence most recent reviewers in the field tend to be highly critical of developments in this area (Guilford, 1980; McKenna, 1990; Messick, 1984; Tiedemann, 1989).

REFERENCES

Abramson, L., Seligman, M., & Teasdale, J. (1978). Learned helplessness in humans: Critique and reformulation. *Journal of Abnormal Psychology*, *87*, 32–48.

Adorno, T., Frenkel-Brunswick, D., Levinson, D., & Sanford, R. (1950). *The authoritarian personality*. New York: Harper.

Allison, C., & Hayes, J. (1988). The Learning Style Questionnaire: An alternative to Kolb's inventory. *Journal of Management Studies*, *25*, 269–281.

Aronson, E. (1972). *The social animal*. San Francisco: Freeman.

Atkinson, G. (1988). Reliability of the Learning Style Inventory. *Psychological Reports*, *62*, 755–768.

Atkinson, G., Murrel, P., & Whiters, M. (1990). Career personality types and learning styles. *Psychological Reports*, *66*, 160–162.

Broverman, D., Broverman, L., Vogel, W., Palmer, R., & Klainer, E. (1964). The automatization cognitive style and physical development. *Child Development*, *35*, 1343–1359.

Burger, K. (1985). Computer assisted instruction: Learning style and academic achievement. *Journal of Computer Based Instruction*, *12*, 21–22.

Carne, J., & Kirton, M. (1982). Styles of creativity: Test scores correlations between the Kirton Adaption-Innovation Inventory and the Myers-Briggs Type Indicator. *Psychological Reports*, *50*, 31–36.

Christensen, C., Massey, D., & Issacs, P. (1991). Cognitive strategies and study habits. *British Journal of Educational Psychology*, *61*, 290–299.

Entwistle, N., & Ramsden, P. (1983). *Understanding student learning*. London: Croom Helm.

Eysenck, H, & Eysenck, S. (1975). *The Eysenck Personality Questionnaire*. London: Hodder & Stoughton.

Eysenck, M. (1981). Learning, memory and personality. In H. J.

Eysenck (Ed.), *A model for personality*. Berlin: Springer-Verlag.

Feather, N. (1983). Causal attributions for good and bad outcomes in achievement and affiliation situations. *Australian Journal of Psychology, 35*, 37–48.

Festinger, L. (1957). *A theory of cognitive dissonance*. Evanston, IL: Row and Peterson.

Fillenbaum, S. (1959). Some stylistic aspects of categorizing behavior. *Journal of Personality, 27*, 187–195.

Furnham, A. (1992). Personality and learning style. *Personality and Individual Differences, 13*, 429–438.

Furnham, A. (1994). A content and correlational analysis of tolerance of ambiguity questionnaires. *Personality and Individual Differences, 16*, 403–410.

Furnham, A., & Ribchester, T. (in press). Tolerance of ambiguity: A review of the literature, *Current Psychology*.

Furnham, A., Sadka, V., & Brewin, C. (1992). The development of an occupational attributional style questionnaire. *Journal of Organizational Behavior, 13*, 27–39.

Furnham, A., & Steele, H. (1993). Measuring locus of control. *British Journal of Psychology, 84*, 443–479.

Gardner, R., & Long, R. (1962). Cognitive control of attention and inhibition. *British Journal of Psychology, 53*, 381–388.

Geiger, M. (1991). Performance during the first year of college. *Psychological Reports, 68*, 633–634.

Ginter, E., Brown, S., Scalise, J., & Ripley, W. (1989). Perceptual learning style: The link to academic performance, sex, age and academic standing. *Perceptual and Motor Skills, 68*, 1091–1094.

Glick, J. (1968). An experimental analysis of subject-object relationships in perception. In R. Haber (Ed.), *Contemporary research and theory on visual perception*. New York: Holt.

Goldsmith, R. (1985). A factorial composition of the KAI Inventory. *Educational and Psychological Measurement, 45*, 245–250.

Green, D., Snell, J., & Parimaneth, A. (1990). Learning styles in assessment of students. *Perceptual and Motor Skills, 70*, 363–369.

Guilford, J. (1980). Cognitive styles: What are they? *Educational and Psychological Measurement, 40*, 715–735.

Hayes, J., & Allison, C. (1988). Cultural differences in the learning styles of managers. *Management International Review, 28*, 75–80.

Hayes, J., & Allison, C. (1993). Matching learning style and instructional strategy: An application of the person-environmental interaction paradigm. *Perception and Motor Skills, 76*, 63–79.

Hebb, D., & Foord, E. (1945). Errors of visual recognition and the nature of the trace. *Journal of Experimental Psychology, 35*, 335–348.

Heider, F. (1958). *The psychology of interpersonal relationships*. New York: Wiley.

Henderson, J., & Nutt, P. (1980). The influence of decision style on marketing behavior. *Management Science, 26*, 371–386.

Holzman, P., & Gardner, R. (1960). Levelling and sharpening and memory organization. *Journal of Abnormal and Social Psychology, 61*, 176–180.

Honey, P., & Mumford, A. (1982). *The Manual of Learning Styles*. Maidenhead, England: Honey Press.

Hudson, L. (1966). *Contrary imaginations: A psychological study of the young child*. New York: Schocken.

Hunt, R., Krzystofiak, F., Meindl, J., & Yousry, A. (1989). Cognitive style and decision making. *Organizational Behavior and Human Decision Processes, 44*, 436–453.

Kelly, G. (1955). *The psychology of personal constructs*. New York: Norton.

Kirton, M. (1976). Adaptors and innovators: A description and measure. *Journal of Applied Psychology, 61*, 622–629.

Kirton, M. (Ed.). (1989). *Adaptors and innovators: Styles of creativity and problem-solving*. London: Routledge.

Kirton, M., & De Ciantis, S. (1986). Cognitive style and personality. *Personality and Individual Differences, 7*, 141–146.

Kirton, M., & Pender, S. (1982). The adaption-innovation continuum: Occupational type and course selection. *Psychological Reports, 51*, 883–886.

Kolb, D. (1976). *Learning Style Inventory: Technical manual*. Boston: McBer.

Kolb, D. (1984). *Experimental learning*. Englewood Cliffs, NJ: Prentice-Hall.

McKenna, F. (1990). Learning implications of field dependence-independence in cognitive style versus cognitive ability. *Applied Cognitive Psychology, 4*, 425–437.

McKenny, J., & Keen, P. (1974). How managers' minds work. *Harvard Business Review, 51*, 79–90.

Messick, S. (Ed.). (1976). *Individuality and learning*. San Francisco: Jossey-Bass.

Messick, S. (1984). The nature of cognitive styles: Problems and promise in educational practice. *Educational Psychologist, 19*, 59–74.

Metalsky, G., Abramson, L., Seligman, M., Semmel, A., & Peterson, C. (1982). Attributional styles and life events in the classroom: Vulnerability and invulnerability to depressive mood reactions. *Journal of Personality and Social Psychology, 43*, 704–718.

Meyer, J., Parsons, P., & Dunne, T. (1990). Individual study orchestrations and their association with learning outcome. *Higher Education, 20*, 67–89.

Mitchell, J. (1990). Personality correlations of attributional style. *Journal of Psychology, 123*, 447–463.

Mitroff, I., & Kilmann, R. (1975). On evaluating scientific research. *Technological Forecasting and Social Change, 8*, 163–174.

Mulowsky, G., & Freeman, M. (1979). The impact of managerial orientation on implementing decisions. *Human Resource Management, 18*, 6–14.

Pask, G. (1976). Styles and strategies of learning. *British Journal of Educational Psychology, 46*, 128–148.

Pask, G. (1988). Learning strategies, teaching strategies and conceptual or learning styles. In R. Schmeck (Ed.), *Learning strategies and learning styles* (pp. 48–76). New York: Plenum.

Pettigrew, T. (1958). The measurement and correlates of category width as a cognitive variable. *Journal of Personality, 26*, 59–74.

Petzold, M. (1985). Cognitive styles and eidetic imagery. *Psycholgie in Erziehung Untermicht, 32*, 1–13.

Phares, E. (1976). *Locus of control in personality*. Morristown, NJ: General Learning Press.

Pinto, J., & Geiger, M. (1991). Changes in learning-style preferences. *Psychological Reports, 68*, 195–201.

Prociuk, T., & Lusier, R. (1975). Internal-external locus of control: An analysis and biography of two years of research (1973–1974). *Psychological Reports, 37*, 1323–1337.

Riding, R., & Sadler-Smith, E. (1992). Types of instructional material, cognitive style and learning performance. *Educational Studies, 18*, 323–329.

Rokeach, M. (1960). *The open and closed mind*. New York: Basic Books.

Rokeach, N., & Kliejunas, P. (1972). Behavior as a function of attitude-toward-object and attitude-toward-situation. *Journal of Personality and Social Psychology, 22,* 194–201.

Rose, J., & Medway, F. (1980). Measurement of teachers' beliefs in their control over student outcome. *Journal of Educational Research, 77,* 185–190.

Rosenberg, M., & Abelson, R. (1960). An analysis of cognitive balancing. In M. Rosenberg (Ed.), *Attitude organization and change.* New Haven, CT: Yale University Press.

Rotter, J. (1966). Generalized expectancies for internal versus external control of reinforcement. *Psychological Monographs, 80,* 1–28.

Rotter, J. (1975). Some problems and misconceptions related to the construct of internal versus external control of reinforcement. *Journal of Consulting and Clinical Psychology, 43,* 56–57.

Rotter, J. (1990). Internal versus external control of reinforcement: A case history of variables. *American Psychologist, 45,* 489–493.

Ruble, T., & Cosier, R. (1990). Effects of cognitive styles and decision setting on performance. *Organizational Behavior and Human Decision Processes, 46,* 283–295.

Ryckman, D., Peckham, P., Mizokawa, D., & Sprague, D. (1990). The Survey of Achievement Responsibility: Reliability and validity data on an academic attribution scale. *Journal of Personality Assessment, 54,* 265–275.

Schroder, H. (1989). Managerial competence and style. In M. Kirton (Ed.), *Adaptors and innovators.* London: Routledge.

Seeman, M. (1963). Alienation and social learning in a reformatory. *American Journal of Sociology, 69,* 270–284.

Sein, M., & Robey, D. (1991). Learning style and the efficacy of computer training methods. *Perceptual and Motor Skills, 72,* 243–246.

Speth, C., & Brown, R. (1990). Effects of college students' learning styles and gender on their test preparation strategies. *Applied Cognitive Psychology, 4,* 189–202.

Streufert, S., & Nogami, G. (1989). Cognitive style and complexity: Implications for I/O psychology. In C. Cooper & I. Robertson (Eds.), *International review of industrial and organizational psychology* (pp. 93–143). Chichester, England: Wiley.

Strickland, B. (1977). Internal-external control of reinforcement. In T. Bass (Ed.), *Personality Variables in Social Behavior* (pp. 114–126). Hillsdale, NJ: Erlbaum.

Thompson, M. (1988). *Individualizing instructions with microcomputer produced text.* Presented at the annual meeting of the Association for Educational Communication and Technology, New Orleans, LA.

Tiedemann, J. (1989). Measures of cognitive styles: A critical review. *Educational Psychologist, 24,* 261–275.

Titus, T., Bergandi, T., & Shryock, M. (1990). Adolescent learning styles. *Journal of Research and Development in Education, 23,* 165–171.

van Overwalle, F., Segebarth, K., & Goldstein, M. (1989). Improving performance of freshmen through attributional testimonies from fellow students. *British Journal of Educational Psychology, 59,* 75–85.

Whetten, D., & Cameron, K. (1984). *Development management skills.* London: Scott, Foresman.

Witkin, H. (1976). *Socialization and ecology in the development of cross-cultural and sex differences in cognitive style.* Presented at the International Congress of Psychology, Paris.

Witkin, H., Dyk, R., Faterson, H., Goodenough, D., & Karp, S. (1962). *Psychological differentiation.* New York: Wiley.

Wulf, F. (1922). Uber die verandering von vorstellingen (gedachtins und gestalt). *Psychologische Forsching, 1,* 333–373.

Zemore, R., & Veikle, G. (1989). Cognitive styles and proneness to depressive symptoms in university women. *Personality and Social Psychology Bulletin, 15,* 426–438.

IV

Measurement and Assessment of Personality and Intelligence

20

Measurement and Statistical Models in the Study of Personality and Intelligence

Gregory J. Boyle, Lazar Stankov, and Raymond B. Cattell

INTRODUCTION

Psychological Models: Historical Background

Theorizing about personality and intelligence structure initially was limited to prescientific literary and philosophical "insights" (see Howard, 1993). Among these early psychological approaches. Freudian psychoanalytic theory almost certainly has had the major influence on thinking about human personality during the early 20th century, although psychoanalysis itself has now come under critical scrutiny (see H. J. Eysenck, 1985a; Masson, 1990). Another prominent theorist was Murray, who postulated such "needs" as abasement, achievement, aggression, change, cognitive structure, endurance, nurturance, order, sentience, and understanding. Likewise, Jung's introversion-extraversion theory has been influential. The comparatively subjective models of theorists such as Freud, Adler, Jung, Fromm, Erikson, Horney, Maslow, and Sullivan, however, must now be rejected as scientifically unacceptable. Around 1920, the emphasis changed from clinical premetric speculations to more quantitative and overtly experimental approaches, along with recognition of the ability and personality sphere concepts. The inadequacy of socioenvironmental explanations of personality, though, has been amply demonstrated by Zuckerman (1991). Personality is not solely the outcome of family and social conditioning. H. J. Eysenck (1991) has pointed out that these theories are essentially untestable; they are based on speculative or falsified deductions, and they ignore virtually all the experimental and empirical research conducted this century.

Need for a Taxonomy of Psychological Constructs

Attempts to develop a taxonomy of cognitive abilities and personality traits have been based on the factor analytic[1] research of investigators such as Cattell, Comrey, Guilford, and H. J. Eysenck (see Brody, 1988, 1992; Carroll, 1991; Cattell, 1987a; Ceci, 1990).

Gregory J. Boyle • School of Humanities and Social Sciences, Bond University, Gold Coast, Queensland 4229, Australia. Lazar Stankov • Department of Psychology, University of Sydney, Sydney New South Wales 2006, Australia. Raymond B. Cattell • Department of Psychology, University of Hawaii, Honolulu, Hawaii 96844.

International Handbook of Personality and Intelligence, edited by Donald H. Saklofske and Moshe Zeidner. Plenum Press, New York, 1995.

[1]Factor analysis is a mathematico-statistical procedure that is applied to an intercorrelation matrix with the goal of delineating the underlying (often causal) dimensions (latent traits or factors) responsible for the observed correlations between a larger number of variables.

Investigators sought to measure empirically derived factors representing abilities and personality traits. The assumption of cross-situational stability of personality traits akin to that observed for cognitive abilities (changes in abilities occur throughout the life span), has been questioned by Mischel (e.g., 1984). However, this situationist philosophy has been thoroughly refuted and shown to be superficial (e.g., Boyle, 1985b, 1988c; Cattell, 1983; Conley, 1984; Eaves, Eysenck, & Martin, 1989; H. J. Eysenck, 1991; M. W. Eysenck & Eysenck, 1980; Kline, 1986). In summarizing two studies on this issue, Zuckerman (1991, p. 50) reported that "Persons accounted for almost the same percentage of variance in both studies (28–29%), and persons × situations interactions accounted for another significant portion of the variance (22–23%)." Clearly, empirical and experimental investigation of personality and intelligence necessitates the study of suitable intrapersonal psychological constructs—in other words, cognitive and personality traits, as Buss (1989) pointed out (see also Chapter 22, which discusses facet theory approaches to domain definition).

Role of Scientific Method in Elucidating Ability and Personality Structure

Application of the scientific method to the study of personality and intelligence has now emerged as the dominant mode of investigation (Kerlinger, 1986). A necessary, but not sufficient requirement of theoretically postulated causal relationships is correlation of the interrelated variables. Multivariate correlational analyses include procedures such as multiple regression analysis, path analysis, exploratory (EFA) and confirmatory (CFA) factor analysis, as well as the more sophisticated techniques of structural equation modeling (SEM; Bollen, 1989; Byrne, 1989; Byrne, Shavelson, & Muthén, 1989; Cuttance & Ecob, 1987). Psychometric measures provide an avenue for statistical hypothesis testing. Boyle (1988c) argued that measurement is the sine qua non of scientific investigation; without quantitative measurements, it is simply not possible to test hypotheses and, consequently, to discriminate between competing theories or models of intelligence and personality.

That there is a complex interaction between intelligence and personality cannot be disputed (see Boyle, 1983b, 1987b, 1993a; Brody, 1992; Cantor & Kihlstrom, 1987; Cattell, 1987a; Goff & Ackerman, 1992). Conceptually there may be analogies between personality and intelligence, with both being construed as relatively enduring traits (Cattell, 1983). Intelligence test performance may be affected by personality attributes; likewise, development of intellectual skills may be influenced by personality traits (Cattell, 1987a). Additionally, the interaction between intelligence and academic achievement is affected by personality factors. Anxiety can either interfere with or facilitate performance, depending on the individual's competence or intelligence (Brody, 1992). Thus, in highly intelligent and/or competent individuals, heightened anxiety (e.g., under examination conditions) may enhance performance, whereas for less intelligent and/or less competent individuals, anxiety may have a debilitating impact.

Need for Multivariate Measurement and Experimentation

In measuring personality and intelligence variables, there is a clear-cut need for multivariate rather than univariate measurement (Boyle, 1991b; Horn, 1988; Nesselroade & Cattell, 1988). Intrapersonal psychological structure comprises a wide range of personality traits and cognitive abilities (Boyle, 1983b, 1987d; Cattell, 1979, 1980, 1982b, 1987a), so that multivariate measurement is necessitated. Experimental manipulation or therapeutic intervention may have significant effects on several psychological variables simultaneously, which univariate measurement is unable to monitor successfully (Boyle, 1985b). Multidimensional instruments for measuring intellectual abilities include the Comprehensive Ability Battery (CAB; Hakstian & Cattell, 1982), the Stanford-Binet Intelligence Scale (SB-IV; Thorndike, Hagen, & Sattler, 1986; see Boyle, 1989b), the Wechsler intelligence scales (WAIS, WISC, and WPPSI; Kaufman, 1990; Wechsler, 1991), the British Ability Scales (Elliott, Murray, & Pearson, 1983), the Kaufman Assessment Battery for Children (K-ABC; Kaufman & Kaufman, 1983), and the revised Woodcock-Johnson Psycho-Educational Battery (based on Gf/Gc theory; see Hessler, 1982; Woodcock & Mather, 1989). This multivariate experimental approach has been adopted extensively within the Cattellian school (see Boyle & Cattell, 1984; Stankov, 1980, 1987, 1989; Stankov & Chen, 1988).

Statistical versus Clinical Interpretations of Individual Differences

Clinical and psychiatric diagnoses are notoriously unreliable. Johnson (1986, p. 229) contended that diagnostic clinical ratings of interview data tend to be unreliable and low in validity. There is a clear need for diagnoses based on quantitative psychometric evidence, rather than on subjective observations (which are all too prevalent in various forms of psychotherapy). Countless papers on clinical versus statistical (actuarial) prediction have supported the value of the latter. For instance, the Halstead-Reitan Battery has been one of the most useful tools for the clinical neuropsychological assessment of personality-intelligence interactions in relation to brain functioning. Whereas use of the Halstead-Reitan Battery has been based on a neuropsychological key approach over the past two decades (Russell, Neuringer, & Goldstein, 1970), the Luria-Nebraska Battery has been less popular (Boyle, 1986a).

A major problem in clinical neuropsychology has been inadequate incorporation of personality measures (including mood-state and motivation dynamic trait measures) into research studies and applied clinical assessment. Neuropsychological test batteries have focused predominantly on cognitive aspects of brain functioning. Clearly, various forms of brain dysfunction are also associated with changes (from the normal) in such nonability intrapersonal characteristics as personality, motivation and mood states (Powell, 1979). Zuckerman (1991, p. 169) stated that "personality depends on an intact, functioning brain. . . . General psychiatric disturbance is proportional to the amount of brain destruction." These changes may have a profound effect on an individual's life, irrespective of cognitive functioning. There is therefore an urgent need to incorporate measures of nonability intrapersonal variables into clinical neuropsychological assessment. Use of SEM approaches in the modeling of personality-cognitive interactions should greatly facilitate our understanding of underlying psychobiological mechanisms; however, Zuckerman (p. 171) warned that too much emphasis is currently placed on animal models of human traits, and that the "paucity of human brain research, particularly on limbic systems, preclude[s] definitive statements now on the neuropsychology of personality traits. . . . [The] discovery that functional pathways in the brain are served by particular neurotransmitters has provided a new approach to identifying the circuitry involved in behavioral adaptations."

Cattellian Terminology and Philosophy of Research

Cattell saw the need for a taxonomy of psychological constructs (intellectual abilities, personality traits, dynamic motivation traits, and transitory mood states) somewhat akin to the periodic table of elements in chemistry. Therefore he set out to discover, using the best available factor analytic techniques on comprehensive samples of variables and subjects, the major intrapersonal psychological dimensions. Using concise solutions—even employing topological rotation over and above analytic methods alone to achieve the highest level of simple structure possible (see section on exploratory factor analytic methods below—Cattell produced a taxonomy of abilities, traits, dynamics, and states. As his psychometric instruments have been constructed factor analytically, the scales therein are defined by discrete factors (see Miller, 1988).

To avoid confusion over meaning, Cattell coined several new terms to define his factors uniquely. Unfortunately, nonpsychologists and even many research psychologists unfamiliar with Cattellian terminology have consequently been deterred because of an initial difficulty in knowing what he was talking about. Recently though, the Institute for Personality and Ability Testing (IPAT) has simplified Cattell's terminology in the production of more refined versions of his instruments, so that psychologists can no longer complain that the terminology is obscure and unnecessarily difficult to comprehend.

EXPLORATORY FACTOR ANALYSIS: APPROPRIATE METHODOLOGY

Use of exploratory factor analysis in single-shot studies is potentially problematic (Guttman, 1992). EFA methods are driven by the idiosyncrasies of particular samples and therefore may serve to conflate theory. Romney and Bynner (1992) argued that EFA procedures produce "static" factors that are not sensitive to change; however, this criticism applies only to single-occasion R-factoring, whereas factoring of difference scores across measurement occasions (dR technique; see Boyle, 1987e) and of an individual's scores over many repeated occasions (P technique) has demonstrated the important role of dynamic motivation and transitory mood-state factors. Certain EFA procedures optimize the likelihood of obtaining a valid simple structure solution (see Boyle, 1988c, 1993d; Cattell, 1978; Gorsuch, 1983; McDonald, 1985; Mulaik, 1986). To obtain the best possible factor solution, a number of conditions should be satisfied. These conditions are outlined below.

Sampling of Subjects and Variables

It is necessary to select variables strategically to cover thoroughly the personality and ability domains. The general rule of thumb (see Gorsuch, 1983) is that a minimum 10 subjects per variable is required to obtain accurate factor pattern solutions. Even with 300 subjects, the appropriate factor solution is obtained in only 50% of cases: According to Cuttance (1987), "MacCallum (1985) investigated the process of the exploratory fitting of models in simulated data. . . . Only about half of the exploratory searches located the true model . . . in samples of 300 observations . . . and *his success rate in smaller samples* ($N = 100$) *was zero* . . . the probability of locating the correct model by exploratory methods when sample data are used is even less" (p. 243; italics added).

Consequently, we have to assume that many of the EFA studies reported in the psychological literature are flawed because of inadequate sampling of variables and subjects, particularly in studies of multidimensional personality inventories where many variables are involved (see Cudeck & Henly, 1991). For example, in a recent study of personality-intelligence relationships, Goff and Ackerman (1992) undertook several EFA analyses based on the intercorrelations of combined personality and ability measures, using a sample of only 138 subjects; in view of MacCallum's findings, one would expect their factor solutions to be unreliable and of dubious validity. Indeed, Goff and Ackerman's solutions did not satisfy simple structure requirements, as shown by inadequate ±.10 hyperplane counts (see below). Aside from utilizing appreciably larger samples (500 subjects or more), another avenue is to take a "two-handed" approach, wherein the factor models derived from exploratory methods are subjected to goodness-of-fit testing using CFA methods (e.g., Boyle, Borg, Falzon, & Baglioni, 1995).

Determination of the Appropriate Number of Factors

Every subsequent step in an EFA analysis will be adversely affected if a less than optimal number of factors is extracted. The decision as to number of factors is influenced by several considerations, including various psychometric and objective tests, as well as the degree to which simple structure is attained. Empirical research (Hakstian, Rogers, & Cattell, 1982) has demonstrated the utility of the Scree test. As compared with the criterion of Kaiser-Guttman (K-G) eigenvalues greater than unity, the Scree test is more accurate when there are fewer than about 20 or more than 40 to 50 variables (Child, 1990). The test has been automated both by Barrett and Kline (1982), and separately by Gorsuch and Nelson (1981; see Gorsuch, 1983); use of these algorithms removes the subjectivity in determining the relevant "Scree break." Objective tests for determining the number of factors include, for example, the Very Simple Structure (VSS) method, the asymptotic chi-square statistic, Bartlett's test of equality of the last p-m eigenvalues, and Velicer's minimum average partial (MAP) test (see Loehlin, 1990; Velicer & Jackson, 1990a, b). The rotated factor pattern provides a final index of the accuracy of number of factors. The ±.10 hyperplane count (percentage of variables with trivial factor loadings) provides a quantitative index of the extent of simple structure (Boyle, 1993e; Boyle & Stanley, 1986; Cattell, 1978; Gorsuch, 1983). Use of various tests in conjunction with criteria for over- and underextraction and consideration of hyperplane counts facilitate determination of the appropriate number of factors.

Common Factor Analysis versus Principal Components

Principal components analysis (with unities in the leading diagonal of the correlation matrix) artificially inflates factor loadings as a result of spurious common factor variance (Comrey & Lee, 1992). Principal components analysis is mathematically elegant, but the psychological interpretability of the derived components may be less than optimal. Iteration of communality estimates accords with the common factor model; when the number of variables is greater than about 20, iteration actually makes little difference to the factor solution. Gorsuch (1990, pp. 35–36) suggested that at least two to three iterations need to be carried out.

Convergence of communalities proceeds rapidly for well-defined problems, where a factor solution is reliable. As Velicer and Jackson (1990a) have pointed out, poorly defined factors loading on only a few variables (with small loadings), and/or extraction of an inappropriate number of factors, inevitably results in an excessive number of iterations required to reach convergence. Use of principal components analysis provides no indication of the reliability of the solution, whereas the number of iterations in common factor analysis provides a direct (inverse) index of factor reliability. Principal components analysis is a poor substitute for common factor analysis (Cattell, 1978; Gorsuch, 1983; McArdle, 1990; McDonald, 1985).

There are, however, still some proponents of the short-cut principal components (PCA) method (e.g., Schönemann, 1990; Velicer & Jackson, 1990a). They have argued that PCA avoids the problem of factor indeterminacy and is computationally more efficient. Their argument, though, based on expediency and computational speed, is hardly relevant given modern computing facilities. Moreover, Mulaik (1990, p. 54) asserted that the indeterminacy associated with the common factor model is really just an example of the pervasive indeterminacy that exists throughout all science (see Rozeboom, 1990). Snook and Gorsuch (1989) reported that simulation studies show that PCA gives discrepant results when the number of variables in the analysis is low (see Widaman, 1990). They also reported that component loadings are systematically inflated, as compared with factor loadings. Bentler and Kano (1990) likewise pointed out that common factor analysis is preferable to the PCA approach. Gorsuch (1990, p. 39) concluded that use of common factor analysis "recognizes we have error in our variables, [and] gives unbiased instead of inflated loadings. . . . Use of components is primarily the result of decisions made when there were problems computing common factor analysis which no longer exist and the continuation of its being a ready default on computer programs designed during an earlier era."

Oblique Simple Structure Rotation

In accord with Thurstone's simple structure principles (see Child, 1990, pp. 48–49), a unique *oblique* factor pattern solution is usually desirable. Only when simple structure is achieved is it possible for the resultant factors to have the status of causal determinants (Kline, 1980), although causality cannot be inferred solely on the basis of correlational evidence. Use of orthogonal rotation often fails to achieve simple structure; in fact, an oblique rotation to maximum simple structure will stop at the special orthogonal position in the event that uncorrelated factors are actually warranted. Maximum simple structure is often not attained with analytic oblique rotation alone. In general, the higher the hyperplane count, the better is the simple structure of the factor solution, with ±.10 hyperplane counts of at least 65% to 70% suggesting an adequate attainment of simple structure. Thus, in Goff and Ackerman's (1992) study, an orthogonal factor solution exhibited a hyperplane count of only 20.0%, revealing its invalidity. A corresponding oblique factor pattern solution gave a hyperplane count of 58.5%, in accord with the general superiority of oblique versus orthogonal solutions.

It may be necessary to undertake additional topological rotation via Rotoplot (Cattell, 1978). Studies have shown the efficacy of Rotoplot (Cattell, 1978) to improve the resultant ±.10 hyperplane count (Boyle & Stanley, 1986); nevertheless, the increase is often so slight as not to warrant the extra expenditure of time and effort. Measurement noise attributable to idiosyncrasies of particular samples suggests that the search for simple structure in single-sample data may be problematic and less important than replication and cross-validation of results. Although statistical software exists for the easy use of Rotoplot (e.g., Brennan & Nitz, 1986), more important is the need to test the goodness of fit of proposed factor models via CFA methods.

Testing the Significance of Derived Factors

One can test the significance of derived factors using the Kameoka and Sine tables (in Cattell, 1978). Boyle (1988c) demonstrated that these tables are overly conservative in failing to attribute significance to recognizable factors when other criteria clearly show such factors to be meaningful. Less restrictive use of these tables could provide useful information on the significance of factors derived from exploratory methods. Ideally, the invariance of factors (see Byrne, 1988) should be checked across different samples at both primary and second-stratum factor levels. One approach is to employ Cattell's (1978) congruence and salient variable indices, which provide a more accurate indication of factor invariance than does a simple correlational analysis of factor loadings. Perusal of published factor analytic research in psychology and the social sciences reveals that this level of cross-validation recommended by Cattell has rarely been attempted, let alone achieved.

Role of Factor Analysis in Psychological Test Construction

Use of factor analysis provides important evidence as to construct validity, but this evidence alone is insufficient. In addition to factor validity, predictive validity evidence is essential (e.g., O'Toole & Stankov, 1992). Factor validity is a necessary precondition that at best is suggestive of construct validity (also see section on the examination of MTMM data via CFA techniques). In general, EFA methods support a hierarchical model for both personality traits and intellectual abilities. Romney and Bynner (1992), however, argued that EFA cannot reveal a simplex structure wherein there is a linear ordering of tests, amounting to a conceptual limitation of the common factor model. They suggested that cognitive abilities might be explained more adequately in terms of a dynamic split-simplex model comprising a linear ordering of abilities, rather than resorting to explanations in terms of an underlying common factor (see section below, on the factor analysis of abilities). Stankov and Crawford (1993), though, argued that complexity of a series of cognitive tasks is revealed by the size of their loadings in relation to the general factor, which in turn is defined by these tasks and other cognitive measures. This pattern of loadings may not be related to the linear ordering of tasks per se.

Briggs and Cheek (1986, p. 106) recommended routine application of factor analysis in the construction and validation of new personality scales (factor analysis is superior to the superficial approach of cluster analysis; Boyle, 1985b; Cattell, 1978; McArdle, 1984). Factor analysis is an important aspect of construct validation. For example, Boyle (1987c) administered the Eight State Questionnaire (8SQ) and the Differential Emotions Scale (DES-IV) to a sample of 212 undergraduate students on two occasions and factor analyzed the difference scores (dR factoring; see Boyle, 1987e). Using an iterative principal factoring procedure and oblique simple structure rotation, four higher-order mood-state dimensions emerged. Results suggested that two broad mood-state dimensions are measured within each instrument. The first DES-IV factor loaded on guilt, sadness, hostility, fear, shame, and shyness, representing negative emotionality akin to Eysenck's neuroticism dimension. The second DES-IV dimension was a bipolar factor that contrasted interest, joy, and surprise with anger, disgust, contempt, and guilt. The first 8SQ factor contrasted positive (extraversion and arousal) emotions with negative (depression and fatigue) states, whereas the second factor loaded on several neuroticism states (anxiety, stress, depression, regression, and guilt). Thus each instrument could be simplified internally, enabling more efficient measurement of central mood states. In another example, Boyle (1988a) administered the Profile of Mood States (POMS) and the 8SQ to 289 undergraduates. Higher-order scale factoring of the combined instruments revealed four major state dimensions (neuroticism, hostility/anger, vigor, and extraversion versus fatigue-arousal). These findings provided evidence on the internal structure of the two instruments, showing the relationship of higher-stratum dimensions to primary factors. In ascertaining the construct validity of an instrument, however, factor analysis represents only one approach, along with correlational and experimental analyses.

Aims and Scales of Factor Analytically Derived Measurement Instruments

Although requiring further refinements, the CAQ extends measurement into the abnormal personality trait domain (see Boyle, 1990b; Guthrie, 1985). Part 1 measures the usual 16PF factors, plus another six higher-stratum dimensions (see section on higher-order factors below), whereas Part 2 measures 12 separate factor analytically derived psychopathology scales (Kameoka, 1986), and at least five major abnormal dimensions at the second-stratum level (Boyle, 1987d). The clinical factors are labeled D1 (Hypochondriasis), D2 (Suicidal Depression), D3 (Agitation), D4 (Anxious Depression), D5 (Low Energy Depression), D6 (Guilt and Resentment), D7 (Boredom and Withdrawal), Pa (Paranoia), Pp (Psychopathic Deviation), Sc (Schizophrenia), As (Psychasthenia), and Ps (Psychological Inadequacy).

Two limitations of the current version of the CAQ are (a) insufficient numbers of items (Part 1 has only 8 items in each of the 16 scales, although supplementation with other forms of the 16PF is a viable option, and there are only 12 items per scale in Part 2), and (b) the factor structure of the abnormal trait sphere (CAQ Part 2), which needs to be refined and cross-validated using both exploratory and confirmatory factor analytic procedures on independent samples. The factor analytic basis of the CAQ is deficient because some 45 separate studies of subsets of the combined MMPI and depression item pool were undertaken, rather than a single factoring of item parcels. Emergence of seven separate depression factors is an artifact resulting from inclusion of an excessive number (200–300) of depression items, over and above the MMPI item pool, in the factor analyses. Consequently, Part 2 of the CAQ has dubious factor validity. Kline (1993a) has discussed some of the limitations of nonfactored scales such as the criterion-keyed MMPI. Scales that are not factor valid cannot clarify the causal mechanisms involved in psychopathological processes. In assessing the causal determinants of personality and intelligence, factor-valid scales are undoubtedly a great asset.

In a study of the interbattery correlations of the 14 scales in the High School Personality Questionnaire (HSPQ; a downward extension of the 16PF and the 20 CAB ability measures), no fewer than 50 out of 280 correlations were significant. Only 14 of these correlations would have been expected to be significant by chance alone (at the $p < .05$ level). Though the ability and personality domains are conceptually distinct, it is clear that artistic, mathematical, and verbal skills are associated with various personality traits (see Cattell, 1987a). What are often thought of as different qualities of ability are probably complex combinations of cognitive abilities and personality traits. Studies with the 16PF and HSPQ have shown a significant increase in prediction over that based on intelligence tests alone (e.g., Boyle, 1983b; Boyle, Start, & Hall, 1989). Cattell (1987a, p. 480) reported an average 42% increase by including personality in addition to cognitive ability measures alone. There can be little doubt about the combined role of personality and intelligence in influencing academic learning outcomes.

CONFIRMATORY FACTOR ANALYSIS: ROLE IN VALIDATING PSYCHOLOGICAL TESTS

Exploratory-Confirmatory Factor Analytic Dualism

As noted earlier, a two-handed approach to factor analysis of the personality and ability domains is desirable. Exploratory (EFA) and confirmatory (CFA) factor analyses should be carried out on independent samples, and both sets of analyses cross-validated (see Bryne, Shavelson, & Muthén, 1989). Results from an exploratory analysis enable an empirical test (via CFA) of empirically derived models. Confirmatory methods are conceptually driven and enable statistical model testing, unlike the traditional data-driven, exploratory approaches (see Bentler, 1989; Breckler, 1990; Muthén, 1988). In EFA, the latent variable structure usually is unknown, and the focus is on discovering the main factors underlying observed variables. In contrast, CFA is applicable when the latent variable structure has already been suggested on theoretical, empirical, or other grounds (Byrne, 1989; Marsh & Bailey, 1991). Nevertheless, CFA can produce discrepant results (Bagozzi & Yi, 1990; Millsap, 1990; Williams, Cote, & Buckley, 1989).

A common misconception is that EFA is now superseded by CFA. This view could not be further from the truth: The two procedures are complementary, not competing methodologies (Bentler, 1988). EFA is undertaken to map out the factor structure within a domain, whereas CFA is applied to an independent sample to test the fit of the factors previously located (see Bentler, 1990; Cuttance & Ecob, 1987; MacCallum, 1986; McDonald & Marsh, 1990). This dual approach to elucidation of factors and their verification is the desirable way to proceed.

Congeneric Factor Models

One of the best approaches is to undertake CFA, including congeneric one-factor analyses, via PRELIS (Jöreskog & Sörbom, 1988), followed by LISREL (Jöreskog & Sörbom, 1989). Use of PRELIS is important particularly if any of the variables are noticeably skewed or kurtotic, and when dealing with categorical or ordinal data (as indicated above). A major use of CFA is in the validation of psychological tests. CFA procedures enable assessment of the factor structure of an instrument, as well as the appropriateness of the item content of each scale. Boyle (1990c, 1991c, 1992a; Boyle & Fabris, 1992) has undertaken confirmatory analyses of the SB-IV, 8SQ, Menstrual Distress Questionnaire (MDQ; Moos, 1985), and Holland's (1985) Self-Directed Search (SDS). Likewise, Byrne (1989) has carried out extensive confirmatory factor analyses of the Self-Description Questionnaire (see Boyle, 1993d). Many of the extant instruments have a multidimensional scale structure (e.g., 16PF, CPI, MMPI, MDQ, 8SQ, POMS, DES-IV). What is now needed is a systematic application of confirmatory methods to verify the claims of test authors regarding the dimensionality of existing personality and intelligence test instruments.

Measurement versus Structural Models

CFA involves the measurement part of the full structural equation model (which comprises both measurement and structural submodels; see Cuttance & Ecob, 1987). CFA is applied to either an all-X (exogenous) or all-Y (endogenous) model. According to Byrne (1989, p. 8), specifications are made with respect to "(a) The number of factors (ξ's or η's). (b) The number of observed variables (x's or y's). (c) Relations between the observed variables and the latent factors (λ_xs or λ_ys). (d) Factor variances and covariances (Φ). (e) Error variances (and possibly covariances) associated with the observed variables (Θ_δ or Θ_ϵ)." The measurement model (Jöreskog & Sörbom, 1989) is expressed algebraically as

$$x = \Lambda_x\xi + \delta \text{ and } y = \Lambda_y\eta + \epsilon \quad (1)$$

wherein the observed variables are represented by the x's or y's, and the latent variables by the ξ's or η's, respectively. The δ and ϵ values represent the vector of measurement errors. The corresponding equation for the covariance matrices among the x variables is

$$\Sigma = \Lambda\Phi\Lambda' + \Theta_\delta \quad (2)$$

wherein Λ represents the matrix of latent trait loadings, Φ stands for the matrix of covariances between the latent traits, and Θ_δ represents the matrix of error variances and covariances. A similar equation pertains for the covariation matrices among the y variables. The full LISREL structural equation system among the η and ξ latent variables is represented by:

$$\eta = B\eta + \Gamma\xi + \zeta \quad (3)$$

The vectors η and ξ represent the latent dependent and independent variables, whereas B and Γ represent the coefficient matrices, and ζ represents a random residual vector (involving random disturbance estimates, and errors in equations; see Jöreskog & Sörbom, 1989, p. 3). Thus the full LISREL model (Bollen, 1989) incorporates three separate equations (covering the measurement models for x and y, as well as the structural equation model).

Goodness-of-Fit Indices

The goodness-of-fit (GFI) index assesses the fit of proposed models to empirical data sets. The GFI, which ranges from zero through 1.0, provides an estimate of the variance/covariance accounted for by models. The adjusted goodness-of-fit (AGFI) index (which adjusts the GFI for the number of degrees of freedom) and the root mean square residual (RMR) are two of the most important indices to consider. The RMR provides an estimate of the discrepancy between the predicted and observed covariance matrices. Better models have AGFI indices close to 1, and RMR indices close to zero (values less than 0.05; see Byrne et al., 1989). According to Cuttance and Ecob (1987), "Models with an AGFI of less than .8 are inadequate. . . . Acceptable models would appear to have an AGFI index of greater than .9" (p. 260).

In Boyle's (1990c) study of the SB-IV dimensionality, the scale intercorrelations for all 5,013 subjects (reported in the technical manual) were subjected to a CFA analysis via PRELIS/LISREL. The initial two-stage least squares solution served as the starting point for the maximum likelihood (ML) estimation. The resulting AGFI was .87 (RMR = .05). The total coefficient of determination was .99 for the four SB-IV area dimensions (see Thorndike et al., 1986). Congeneric (one-factor CFA) analyses supported the four area dimensions: For verbal reasoning, the AGFI was .89 (RMR = .03); for abstract/visual reasoning, the AGFI was .99 (RMR = .01); for quantitative reasoning, the AGFI was .99 (RMR = 0); and for short-term memory, the AGFI was .96 (RMR = .02).

Boyle's (1991c) CFA analysis of the 8SQ was undertaken on the polychoric item intercorrelations (see Poon & Lee, 1987), computed via PRELIS across all 1,111 subjects. The resulting AGFI was .71 (RMR = .10), indicating an inadequate fit of the eight-factor model (Anxiety, Stress, Depression, Regression, Fatigue, Guilt, Extraversion, and Arousal). Congeneric analyses provided stronger support for the purported subscale structure (mean AGFI was .93; mean RMR = .04). Exogenous latent trait covariances revealed some measurement overlap of scales.

The CFA item analysis of the MDQ on a sample of 369 female undergraduates (Boyle, 1992a) resulted in an AGFI of .87 (RMR = .06), suggesting a reasonable fit of the proposed eight-factor model. Congeneric analyses suggested that some MDQ scales are stronger than others (mean AGFI = .85; mean RMR = .05).

Boyle and Fabris (1992) undertook a CFA on the Self-Directed Search, or SDS (five variables for each RIASEC theme—Realistic, Investigative, Artistic, Social, Enterprising, and Conventional), on a sample of 401 subjects. The AGFI of .75 (RMR = .08), failed to support the postulated RIASEC model. Congeneric results revealed an inadequate fit for the Realistic theme (AGFI = 0.78; RMR = .09). For the other RIASEC themes, the mean AGFI was .89 (mean RMR = .05). Covariances between exogenous latent traits suggested considerable measurement overlap between RIASEC categories.

Boyle et al. (1994) administered a sources-of-stress inventory to elementary school teachers in Malta; the group of 710 full-time teachers was randomly split into two groups. An EFA on the first subsample produced a five-factor oblique solution; factors were labeled Workload, Student Misbehavior; Professional Recognition Needs; Time/Resource Difficulties; Poor Colleague Relations (see Boyle et al., 1994 for item details). The factor solution exhibited a ±.10 hyperplane count of 54%, indicating better simple structure than for a four-factor solution (hyperplane count 45%). CFA on the second subsample supported the five-factor model (AGFI = .91; RMR = .006). A simple recursive model yielded an AGFI of .93 (RMR = .005), suggesting an acceptable fit. Congeneric factor analyses also provided strong support for each of the hypothesized factors (mean AGFI = .96; mean RMR = .02). Incremental fit indices rho and PNF12 (Mulaik, James, van Alstine, Bennett, Lind, & Stilwell, 1989) enabled comparison of the various models.

What is now needed is the testing of new models of personality and intelligence using SEM techniques, wherein the latent traits are regressed onto each other. Such an approach should throw light onto the nature of ability-personality interconnections and interactions. SEM offers much hope for the development of a far more sophisticated understanding of such psychometric interrelationships than currently exists. With exploitation of SEM methods to their full extent (noting limitations alluded to by Breckler, 1990), psychometrics will undoubtedly become one of the most important and exciting fields of psychological research.

Multitrait-Multimethod Matrices: Analyses of Covariance Structures

An innovative application of CFA has been in the modeling of multitrait-multimethod data (Cole & Maxwell, 1985). Byrne and Goffin (1993) have discussed new approaches to the investigation of multitrait-multimethod matrices (MTMM) involving analyses of covariance structures. These models include Jöreskog and Sörbom's (1988) general confirmatory factor analytic model (CFAGEN), Marsh's (1989) correlated uniqueness CFA model (CFACU), and Browne's (1984) composite direct product (CDP) model. According to Byrne and Goffin (1993), the general CFA model enables "(a) an explanation of the MTMM matrix in terms of underlying latent constructs, rather than observed variables, (b) the evaluation of convergent and discriminant validity at the matrix, as well as at the parameter level, (c) the testing of hypotheses related to convergent and discriminant validity, and (d) separate estimates of variance due to traits, methods, and error, in addition to estimated correlations for both trait and method factors" (p. 69). Schmitt and Stults (1986) have critically reviewed the strengths and weaknesses of traditional MTMM approaches to construct validation. Byrne and Goffin have listed several major difficulties with the traditional MTMM approach. They suggested that researchers should estimate all three of the above covariance structure models, accepting the best-fitting one. As they also pointed out (p. 27), "The imminent availability of fit indices for which confidence intervals have been statistically derived (Steiger, 1989; Browne, 1990) holds great promise for the assessment of such competing models." A comprehensive review of the problems associated with application of CFA and MTMM approaches was provided by Marsh (1989; Marsh & Bailey, 1991). Recently, a method for undertaking multiple group CFA analyses (using the UniMult program) has been devised by Gorsuch (1991), which should be useful in the modeling of MTMM matrices.

STRUCTURAL EQUATION MODELING: TESTING MEASUREMENT AND STATISTICAL MODELS

Combination of Factor Analysis and Multiple Regression Analysis

Structural equation modeling (SEM; Anderson & Gerbing, 1988; Cuttance & Ecob, 1987; Martin, 1987) involves the simultaneous application of factor analysis wherein the latent traits (factors) load on the observed variables (measurement model), and multiple regression analysis of the latent traits on each other (structural model; Byrne, 1988). McArdle (1984) pointed out that contemporary modelers can learn much from Cattell's structural modeling endeavors. SEM combines the factor (measurement) and path (structural) models into a single model wherein each latent trait (factor) is regressed onto the others. It is assumed that for each latent trait, the residual and error terms do not correlate either with the factor or each other; in some instances one might question the validity of this assumption. SEM should facilitate scientific hypothesis testing in contrast to exploratory approaches, which historically have often served to conflate theory rather than discriminating between competing hypotheses.

Boyle (1993b) investigated interrelationships among 8SQ mood states and menstrual cycle symptoms (measured via the MDQ) on a sample of 370 undergraduate women. Factor analytic (EFA) results suggested that 8SQ states loaded on two separate factors—one involving neurotic states (anxiety, stress, regression, and guilt), the other contrasting depression and fatigue with extraversion and arousal. Likewise, the MDQ scales separated into two distinct factors—one loading on psychological scales of negative affect, impaired concentration, and behavior change; the other loading on physical symptoms of autonomic reactions, pain, and water retention. A LISREL SEM analysis tested both recursive and nonrecursive models. For the nonrecursive model, all parameters were identified, and the AGFI was .98 (RMR = .04), suggesting a reasonable fit to the data. This model suggested that psychological and physiological states and symptoms interact in a complex manner.

Advantages of Structural Equation Modeling

SEM has the advantage of being able to estimate the magnitude of error terms, unlike the older approach of path analysis, which relied solely on multiple regression procedures and simply assumed that error terms were zero (see Kaplan, 1990). Structural modeling allows statistical testing of the fit of hypothesized models against actual empirical data sets (Bentler, 1990; Connell, 1987; Tanaka, 1987). Variance associated with measurement noise can be partialed out by removing variables with excessive error and that contribute little valid variance ("noisy" variables). Perusal of standardized regression equations associated with the LISREL two-stage least squares estimation procedure suggests which variables should be deleted; this attenuation of "measurement noise" facilitates testing of postulated models. Structural modeling packages (e.g., LISREL, COSAN, EQS) should be used to investigate the *causal* influence of personality and intelligence variables on behavioral outcomes. Another recent advance has been in multilevel modeling packages (e.g., ML3; see Prosser, Rasbash, & Goldstein, 1991), which, when integrated into SEM packages such as LISREL, should facilitate a much more sophisticated analysis of psychometric models of personality and intelligence.

Assumptions for Valid Use of LISREL

Several conditions must hold for valid use of LISREL in testing the fit of proposed models (see Bollen, 1989; Cuttance & Ecob, 1987; Hayduk, 1987; Marsh, Balla, & McDonald, 1988; Romney & Bynner, 1992, p. 14). Parameters of the model should be determined uniquely—only one solution to the set of simultaneous equations should be found ("identified" model). Second, model parameters should be estimated via an iterative procedure such as maximum likelihood (ML) or such other methods as weighted least squares (WLS) or generalized least squares (GLS). Third, given the assumption of multivariate normality, the residual matrix approximation to zero is tested by a likelihood ratio (chi-square) test. Unfortunately, this test is sample-size sensitive, so that with large samples, virtually all proposed models are rejected, even though large samples are desirable to minimize sampling bias (Cudeck & Henley, 1991). Fourth, modification indices for parameters constrained to zero indicate the reduction in chi-square values when parameter constraints are released. Fifth, for noncontinuous variables, computation of Pearson product-moment correlation coefficients may result in significant bias. PRELIS enables computation of polychoric and polyserial correlation coefficients, as required.

Alternative Structural Modeling Packages

Other structural modeling packages include LISCOMP (used with categorical data; Muthén, 1988), COSAN (used with interval data; McDonald, 1985), EQS (Bentler, 1989), and ProcCALIS (Hartmann, 1990). Statistical testing of proposed models enables some assessment of the causal determinants of various intellectual and personality variables on behavioral outcomes (see Biddle & Marlin, 1987; Mulaik, 1987). SEM merges CFA, multiple regression analysis, and path analysis into a single model, and provides a means of discriminating between competing hypotheses and models, in accord with scientific method. Nevertheless, there are limitations of SEM: As Breckler (1990) pointed out, there are serious flaws in many of the published applications. Even though fit of the desired model is identical for a large number of possible equivalent models, this is seldom acknowledged.

Critique of Structural Equation Modeling Procedures

Several potential difficulties in the application of SEM techniques have been discussed comprehensively by Breckler (1990). Likely problems include (a) computation of feasible parameter estimates when certain parameters are not identified fully; (b) use of the sample-size dependent chi-square test; (c) interpretation of the root mean square residual (RMR) index in covariance units; (d) unrecognized equivalent models that are not tested for their fit; (e) tendency toward reification of latent variables; (f) inaccurate modification indices; and (g) drawing causal inferences when the data provide only suggestive relationships between latent variables. According to Bentler (1988),

> the generative theory may be inappropriate, key variables may be omitted, samples may be biased, ambiguity may exist about causal ordering, measurement may be unrepresentative and inadequate, sampling of variables may be arbitrary, time lags for effects may be unknown, and the meaning of latent variables may be obscure. Furthermore, models may not be tested against independent data . . . inappropriate emphasis appears on confirmatory rather than exploratory data analysis; and . . . SEM tends to be applied subjectively and in a post-hoc manner. Key structural assumptions . . . [such as] linearity and additivity of relations, and the statistical assumptions of independent, identical distributions of observations, random sampling . . . [as well as] large samples and multivariate normality, may not be plausible. (p. 3)

Advantages of SEM techniques have been overemphasized, and the validity of proposed structural models is directly related to the adequacy of the data and the sample employed. Testing of competing models will always be plagued by inadequate empirical data sets (e.g., data collected from rather unreliable measurement instruments). In fact, application of CFA methods to the validation of psychological instruments may be problematic. Often when there are more than three items per scale, the CFA analysis produces suboptimal GFI and AGFI indices; this is related to the unreliability of individual items within such personality instruments or intelligence tests. Even though SEM techniques provide new opportunities for advances in psychological knowledge, these techniques are not a panacea for extracting meaning out of sloppy data. The age-old problem of "garbage in, garbage out" applies equally to all statistical methods, including SEM approaches.

PSYCHOMETRIC TRADITION IN THE STUDY OF PERSONALITY AND INTELLIGENCE

Multivariate Psychometric Model

The multivariate psychometric model is an extension of the traditional trait model into other intrapersonal psychological domains. It is based on the mathematico-statistical technique of factor analysis, which determines the major variables for inclusion within the model. The most elaborate development of the psychometric model for behavioral prediction has been by Cattell and his colleagues, with each of the factor analytically elucidated ability, trait, dynamic, and state dimensions contributing to various versions of the "behavioral specification equation" (e.g., Cattell, 1979, 1980, 1983). Kline (1980) pointed out that (a) factors may in some instances have causal properties; (b) they represent the most important variables, provided variables and subjects are comprehensively sampled; (c) rotation to oblique simple structure facilitates determinate solutions; (d) maximization of the ±.10 hyperplane count (Cattell, 1978) results in simple structure solutions; and (e) marker variables should be included. Kline contended that the psychometric model comprises the most important simple structure factors that have emerged in each of the ability, personality, motivation dynamic, and mood-state domains. Unfortunately, many factor analytic studies (e.g., Costa & McCrae, 1992a; Goff & Ackerman, 1992; McCrae & Costa, 1987, 1989; Zuckerman, Kuhlman, & Camac, 1988) have been plagued by failure to attain maximum simple structure, as advocated by Thurstone (see Child, 1990).

Behavioral Specification Equations

Kline (1980) concluded that the Cattellian psychometric model enables valid predictions of behavior, shows the inadequacy of the situationist argument, and facilitates systematic studies in basic and applied psychological research. Cattell's behavioral specification equations (see below) differ in their complexity, and combine the action of cognitive abilities (A), normal and abnormal personality traits (T), dynamic motivation traits (D), and transitory mood states (S). By definition, for individual *i*, the *a*'s represent behavioral outcomes of the response/performance *j*, whereas the *b*'s represent factor loadings/behavioral indices as a function of the focal stimulus *h* and the ambient situation *k*. This quantitative predictive approach is useful in showing the important role of various intrapersonal psychological variables. Clearly, there is a complex interaction between psychological and situational variables in influencing behavioral outcomes, wherein cognitive abilities, personality traits, motivational dynamics, and transitory mood states all interact with situational stimuli in influencing behavioral outcomes, such that:

$$a_{hijk} = \Sigma\, b_{hjkw}\mathbf{A}_{wi} + \Sigma\, b_{hjkx}\mathbf{T}_{xi} + \Sigma\, b_{hjky}\mathbf{D}_{yi} + \Sigma\, b_{hjkm}\mathbf{S}_{mi} \tag{4}$$

With respect to the first-order personality × intelligence interaction, the multiplicative term is shown below in simplified form:

$$\Sigma\Sigma\, b_{hjkwx} \mathbf{A}_{wi} \mathbf{T}_{xi} \quad (5)$$

A detailed presentation and discussion of more sophisticated versions of these prediction equations, including both multiplicative and nonlinear terms, is provided by Boyle (1988c). Although specification of such behavioral prediction equations is theoretically justified, however, in practice it is nearly impossible to quantify empirically the various factor loadings in most instances.

Factor Analysis of Intellectual Abilities

Because intelligence has been viewed as directly related to efficient neurological functioning, measures such as reaction time (RT) and visual acuity have been regarded as appropriate. This line of research was extended by Spearman, who examined rank-difference intercorrelations (see Boyle & Langley, 1989) between ability measures (Brody, 1992; Jensen, 1991; Snow, Killonen, & Marshalek, 1984; Stankov & Cregan, 1993; Stankov & Myora, 1990). Thurstone's development of multiple factor analysis enabled the structural dimensionality of abilities to be elucidated within the constraints of a hierarchical model (see Carroll, 1984; Cattell, 1982b; Guilford, 1985; Horn & Stankov, 1980; Messick, 1992).

Thurstone delineated several primary ability factors, which he labeled Spatial, Perceptual, Numerical, Verbal Relations, Word Fluency, Memory, and Induction (subsequently extended to 20 primary abilities, as measured in the CAB; see Hakstian & Woolsey, 1985; Kline & Cooper, 1984). At first sight, it appeared that Spearman's general ability factor (*g*), and Thurstone's primary mental ability factors were incompatible (Carroll, 1991; Kranzler & Jensen, 1991). Cattell (1982b, 1987a) resolved this apparent discrepancy by factor analyzing Thurstone's primary mental ability intercorrelations; he found that at the higher-order level, general factors (Gf and Gc) emerged (see Boyle, 1988b; Stankov, 1978, 1983, 1986; Stankov & Chen, 1988; Stankov, Horn, & Roy, 1980). Hence Spearman's and Thurstone's findings were compatible, but represented different levels of the hierarchical structure of abilities. Even though Guilford (1981) accepted that his "Structure of Intellect" (SOI) model was defective and reanalyzed his data using oblique rotation, Brody (1992, p. 34) concluded that the purported factor structure underlying Guilford's model remained seriously defective. In view of the lack of empirical support for Guilford's model, it does not provide a satisfactory alternative to the hierarchical Gf/Gc model.

Alternative structures also may be relevant. For example, Guttman's examination of the rank ordering of correlations suggested simplex, circumplex, and radex structures. Simplex structures follow a linear sequence, whereas in circumplex structures all variables lie on a circle, merging into each other. According to Romney and Bynner (1992), the simplex "is reflected in correlations that decrease from the principal diagonal of the correlation matrix to the corners; the 'circumplex' is shown by correlations that decrease initially and then increase towards the corners of the matrix. A 'radex' comprises circumplexes of tests of comparable complexity and simplexes of tests varying in complexity" (pp. 26–27). Radex theory, involving simplex and circumplex models, may be compatible with personality and intelligence structures.

Bynner and Romney (1986) argued that a split-simplex model, whereby vocabulary skill acts as a determinant of cognitive differentiation, is most appropriate. This suggestion has also received support from cognitive information-processing research into memory (Schwartz & Reisberg, 1992). Brody (1992), and Marshalek, Lohman, and Snow (1983) showed that the factor analytically derived hierarchical model is compatible with Guttman's radex theory. Soldz, Budman, Demby, and Merry (1993) reported that whereas personality disorders can be meaningfully located in circumplex space, application of a hierarchical model enables more appropriate location of several disorders. Cattell (1983) and H. J. Eysenck (1991, 1992) have argued strongly for the importance of hierarchical models (see also Chapter 2). Clark, McEwen, Collard, and Hickok (1993) reported on "the general utility of a dimensional approach to the assessment of personality disorder" (p. 90). According to John, Hampson, and Goldberg (1991), people prefer the highest level of abstraction in hierarchical trait models.

The popularity of hierarchical factor models reinforces the notion of stable traits, whereas simplex and circumplex models suggest that personality disorders are more responsive to therapeutic manipulation (Romney & Bynner, 1992). Disorders that can be modeled via circumplex theory may be more amenable to interpersonal psychotherapy, whereas those modeled by simplex theory might be managed best using cognitive-behavioral therapeutic techniques. Romney and Bynner concluded that "parallelism between the circumplex and hierarchical factor models reflects the parallelism between the radex and hierarchical factor models . . . on abilities" (pp. 55–56). Soldz et al. (1993), however, found that although many personality disorders could be located within the circumplex model, their placement within the hierarchical factor model provided a more accurate representation. In Zuckerman's (1991) view, "the hierarchical model of traits . . . is best because it can encompass both broad and narrow traits. The alternate model of a circumplex is less useful because it is generally limited to a two-dimensional model" (p. xi).

Factor Analysis of Personality Traits

Several investigators (e.g., Cattell, 1983; Comrey, 1980; H. J. Eysenck, 1991; Guilford, 1975) have factor analyzed intercorrelations of personality variables with the aim of locating the major dimensions of human personality. This has resulted in the factor analytic development of several multidimensional instruments, such as the 16PF (see Birkett-Cattell, 1989; Boyle, 1990b), the Comrey Personality Scales (CPS; Comrey, 1980), and the Eysenck Personality Questionnaire (EPQ; see Grayson, 1986). Zuckerman (1991) alluded indirectly to one of the virtues of the 16PF, asserting that "a profile of scores on a multitrait test indicates which traits are salient . . . for a given individual without the need to devise an individualized idiodynamic assessment for every subject" (p. 54). The 16PF (and its junior versions, HSPQ and CPQ; see Schuerger, 1992) has stood the test of critical scrutiny over time in various editions of the *Mental Measurements Yearbooks* and/or *Test Critiques*. The 16PF measures intelligence (Factor B) and 15 normal personality trait factors discerned factor analytically from examination of more than 4000 trait names from the English dictionary. In addition, no fewer than six second-stratum factors have been discerned through factor analyses of the intercorrelations of the 16 scales. This multidimensional self-report instrument was constructed on the basis of a comprehensive assessment of the personality domain, as represented in the trait lexicon (cf. John, Angleitner, & Ostendorf, 1988). Moreover, Cattellian psychology provides one of the few models that actively seeks to integrate the roles of personality and intelligence within the same psychometric instruments (e.g., 16PF/CAQ, HSPQ, CPQ; see also Chapter 23).

Criticisms (e.g., H. J. Eysenck & Eysenck, 1985; Zuckerman, 1991) of attempts to replicate the 16PF primary factors based on item intercorrelations have not taken into account the unreliability of single-item responses. As Cattell (1973), Comrey (1980), and Marsh (1989) have all pointed out, it is essential to utilize more reliable groups of items (Cattell's item parcels; Comrey's FHIDs; Marsh's item pairs). Mershon and Gorsuch (1988) have clearly demonstrated the importance of the 16PF primary factors in accounting for considerably more trait variance than do three or five factors.

Measures of psychopathological traits include the Minnesota Multiphasic Personality Inventory (MMPI and MMPI-2; Friedman, Webb, & Lewark, 1989), the Clinical Analysis Questionnaire (CAQ; Krug, 1980), and the Personality Assessment Inventory (PAI; Morey, 1991; see Boyle, 1993c). H. J. Eysenck (1991, p. 783) pointed out that nonfactorial models such as the MMPI and California Psychological Inventory (CPI; Gough, 1987) inadequately measure personality structure. Eysenck (1985b) argued that it would make sense conceptually to factor analyze the CPI item intercorrelations (although because of item unreliability, an analysis of item parcels would be preferable); the resulting greater conceptual clarity would facilitate testing of psychological theories and models. Factor analytically derived scales are preferred over nonfactored scales, especially in the clinical area, where extreme scores on factors may have etiological, diagnostic, and/or therapeutic implications. Moreover, according to Holden, Reddon, Jackson, and Helmes (1983), *"factor analyses of the entire MMPI item pool . . . fail to support the original scoring keys"* (p. 37; italics added). Helmes and Reddon (1993) provided an even more critical review of the MMPI and MMPI-2 instruments, pointing out that both instruments do not satisfy modern psychometric standards for assessing psychopathology. Because the factor structure of the MMPI does not seem consistent with its purported scale structure, its continued use can only serve to promulgate traditional psychiatric labeling and stereotyping. We hope that reliance on such archaic classifications will decline as we enter the 21st century.

Instruments such as the MMPI, CPI, or Hogan (1986) Personality Inventory (HPI; see Boyle, 1992b) have been constructed using empirical keying or an intuitive-rational approach, leaving doubt as to their scale validity. Soldz et al. (1993) provided evidence that psychopathology is often best viewed as the extremes of normally distributed traits, casting doubt on the validity of discrete diagnostic syndrome categories. The factor analytic evidence does not support the MMPI psychiatric syndrome structure (H. J. Eysenck, 1991; Holden et al., 1983). According to Eysenck (1991), the MMPI includes

> ad hoc scales for arbitrarily chosen traits, without any personality theory in mind. . . . when factor analysed the scales of the MMPI fail to appear as hypothesized, [and] items correlate better with scales they do not belong to than with their proper scales. . . . It is perhaps significant that the personality questionnaire more widely used than any other should violate all the rules laid down by psychometrists for the construction of such instruments; that it should be based on no recognizable or clearly stated theory of personality; and that the resulting scales should be interpreted in terms of highly subjective and scientifically meaningless categories (p. 776).

Hence these instruments, and other non-factor-analytically verified instruments of their ilk, cannot be recommended for use in psychological assessment.

Simplification of the Multivariate Psychometric Model

A possible problem with the Cattellian psychometric model is that there are too many primary factors to be of practical utility for applied psychologists—at least 20 primary abilities, 16 normal personality traits, 12 abnormal personality traits, 8 emotional states, and 10 motivation dynamic traits (cf. Cattell & Krug, 1986). Kline (1980) pointed out that "there are so many primaries that a workable useful model would involve so much testing time that it would not be viable. If a model were to be used for any practical purpose, higher-order factors would have to be used" (p. 324). This preference for more parsimonious models of personality and ability structure has been emphasized also by John et al. (1991). One can reduce the number of dimensions by focusing on second-order factors (see Wiggins & Pincus, 1992; Wiggins & Trapnell, in press).[2] Kline argued for incorporation of the higher-stratum factors from each intrapersonal psychological domain into a more parsimonious model. In this vein, Boyle (e.g., 1985a, 1986b, 1987a, c, d, 1988a, b, c, 1989a) has undertaken a programmatic series of studies into higher-order factors within the framework of the comprehensive Cattellian system, with the aim of producing a simplified and more useful psychometric model. Boyle has delineated several second-stratum dimensions within each of the ability, personality trait, dynamic motivation, and mood-state spheres.

Across all intrapersonal psychological domains, the number of primary factors is considerable, whereas use of 25 to 30 second-stratum dimensions clearly enables greater ease of application. Yet some predictive validity is sacrificed in going from primary to secondary factors, as shown by Mershon and Gorsuch (1988). Although 60 to 70 primary factors are a lot for busy clinicians to consider, (a) the truth of structure and (b) the increasing quality of computer prediction should make it more acceptable to focus on primary factors in some situations, at least.

Higher-Stratum Cognitive Abilities

In accord with Cattell (1982b, 1987a), Horn and Stankov (1980), and Stankov and Horn (1980), the following higher-stratum abilities (Boyle, 1988b) have been labeled: fluid intelligence (Gf), crystallized intelligence (Gc), memory capacity (Gm), perceptual speed (Gps), retrieval capacity (Gr), visualization capacity (Gv), and auditory organization (Ga; see Kline & Cooper, 1984). Abilities can be viewed more easily in terms of this smaller number of secondaries. Gf and Gc offer an excellent example of the experimental verification of factors that H. J. Eysenck stresses. After being delineated as separate factors, it was found that (a) Gf has a sigma of 20 IQ points, instead of 15 for Gc; (b) they follow totally different life courses; (c) brain injury affects them differently; (d) they differ completely in suitability for cross-cultural comparison; and (e) Horn's results show that they differ independently as states from day to day. Cattell's *triadic theory of abilities* suggests that secondary ability factors comprise general capacities (Gf, Gc, Gps, and Gr), provincial powers (corresponding to Gv, Ga, and tactile and kinesthetic capacities), and agencies (corre-

[2]Cattell regards the emphasis on higher-stratum factors as problematic. According to him, the ancient Greeks started with four elements—air, earth, fire, and water—but modern chemists recognize the need for 100 elements. The popularity of three or five factors, like the above analogy, represents an understandable but inadequate view of the world. This has been shown by the recent wide survey of predictions of occupational and clinical performances in which prediction from 16 factors greatly exceeded that from 3 or 5 factors (Mershon & Gorsuch, 1988). One could deduce this also from the Cattell-White formula $V_2 = V_1 V_{12}$, in which the loadings of secondaries on items (and life performances) are products of fractions. Secondaries are relatively less useful tools, except to give situational effects to the primaries (Birkett-Cattell, 1989).

sponding both to Gc and to Thurstone's primary ability factors; see Cattell, 1987a; Woliver & Saeks, 1986).

Higher-Stratum Personality Dimensions

At least five higher-stratum personality dimensions have been verified within the normal trait domain (Boyle, 1989a). Previously Cattell (1973, p. 116) had reported eight second-order 16PF factors from more than 10 separate factor analytic studies, showing that Comrey's (1980) factors are closer to being true secondaries rather than primaries). Criticism of the use of factor analysis in delineating personality structure cannot be justified on the superficial argument that Cattell, Eysenck, and Comrey have all claimed different numbers of factors. This criticism does not acknowledge that each investigator has focused on different levels within the hierarchical trait model. Within the abnormal domain, Boyle's (1987d) research has also suggested an additional six second-stratum dimensions, rather than the single psychoticism factor included in the EPQ. Higher-order psychopathological (CAQ) dimensions were related to schizophrenia, psychopathy, psychotic inadequacy, paranoia, helpless depression, and anxious/agitated depression.

In the most comprehensive, methodologically sound scale factoring to date of the 16PF, using a sample of 17,381 subjects (cross-validated for 9,222 males and 8,159 females separately), Krug and Johns (1986) confirmed at least five second-stratum dimensions in the normal trait domain, leaving little doubt as to their accuracy (they also extracted an intelligence factor, loading on Factor B). These findings also agree with Barton's Central State-Trait Kit (CST; see Cattell, 1973) in showing the importance of the secondary dimensions of extraversion, neuroticism/anxiety, tough poise, independence, and control, and demonstrating the inadequacy of the plethora of less substantial claims based on much smaller sample sizes (e.g., Mathews, 1989; McKenzie, 1988).

Five second-order personality factors have also been reported by several other investigators (see Digman, 1990; Goldberg, 1992). Claims as to their "robustness" (e.g., Costa & McCrae, 1992a) are misplaced, however, as this term applies to departures from underlying statistical assumptions (e.g., multivariate normality, heteroscedasticity). It is thus nonsense to talk about the "robust big five." Doubts about the validity of the big five (or Norman Five) have emerged (Livneh & Livneh, 1989), despite the claims of McCrae and Costa (1987, 1989), and Costa and McCrae (1992a, b, c). As Romney and Bynner (1992, p. 3) asserted, structuring the personality sphere into five broad dimensions provides only one possible interpretation that should not be regarded as irrefutable. Eaves, Eysenck, and Martin (1989), and H. J. Eysenck (1990a, b, 1991), have concluded likewise there is little empirical evidence to support the so-called big five (see John, 1990), proposing that only H. J. Eysenck's (1990a, b) psychoticism (P), extraversion (E) and neuroticism (N) factors are needed. Whereas Eysenck's E and N factors emerge at the 16PF second-stratum level, Krug and Johns (1986) obtained an additional three normal dimensions at the Eysenckian level of analysis. In addition, Eysenck's P factor is represented by at least five abnormal trait dimensions at the CAQ second-stratum level (Boyle, 1987d; see Zuckerman, Kuhlman, & Camac, 1988).

H. J. Eysenck (1992) has criticized Costa and McCrae's (1992a) contention that the big five provide an adequate account of the normal personality sphere, arguing that "the postulation of the 5-factor model is a premature crystallization of spurious orthodoxy" (p. 667). Eysenck suggested that apart from E and N, the remaining three dimensions proposed by Costa and McCrae are essentially primaries that are often intercorrelated highly. He pointed out that Costa and McCrae's work has ignored meta-analytic evidence that disputes their claim, and that they provide no theoretical underpinning or nomological network or any attempt to relate the big give to underlying biological and neurobehavioral mechanisms (see Zuckerman, 1991, 1992). Eysenck (1992) concluded that "outside the narrow circle of 5-factor enthusiasts, research has completely failed to find basic factors similar to A, C or O" (p. 668). Thus both Cattell and Eysenck are in complete agreement that studies of the so-called big five are scientifically unacceptable. Furthermore, as Clark, Vorhies, and McEwen (in press, pp. 33–34) point out, the five-factor model may not account for much of the emotion-related variance involved in maladaptive traits.

Yet, as Zuckerman (1991, p. 12) reported,

> The theory of what was measured by the P scale . . . and the psychometric adequacy of the scale itself were challenged almost immediately. . . . Items in the scale are a mixture of impulsivity; sadism or lack of empathy; aggressiveness; sensation seeking; lack of concern about finances, work or punctuality; uncommon social attitudes . . . and a few, mild paranoid-type items. . . . Items suggesting psychotic delusional thinking . . . were mostly dropped . . . because they were so infrequently endorsed.

Although H. J. Eysenck (1991) has summarized a number of factor analytic studies of the 16PF claiming support for his PEN system, few of these studies have been cross-validated across thousands of subjects (as in the Krug & Johns, 1986, 16PF study). No statistical test (e.g., Bartlett, Scree, Humphreys-Montanelli, VSS, MAP) will, on a personality sphere of variables, permit one to stop at five components in a first-order level factor analysis. One cannot obtain accurate secondaries by prematurely stopping a first-order extraction at the number one "believes" exists, to do so only results in extraction and rotation of pseudo-higher order dimensions. The gradual recognition of more factors is interesting: Spearman, 1; Peabody, 2; Eysenck, 3; Thurstone, 6; Comrey, 8; Sells, 11; and finally Cattell, 16 or more (cf. Cattell & Krug, 1986).

The big five have emerged from suboptimal EFA procedures. The "Little Jiffy" approach generally produces inaccurate factor solutions, which nearly always fail to satisfy Thurstone's principle of simple structure (measured via the hyperplane count). This approach provides only a crude approximation to the actual factors (McDonald, 1985). The big five do not adequately measure the personality trait sphere, in contrast to Cattell's comprehensive measurement covering at least five higher-stratum normal traits (16P/CAQ Part 1), a similar number of abnormal traits (CAQ Part 2), and 28 primary factors (16 normal, 12 abnormal). Cattell's (1987b) depth psychometry approach provides not only a quantitative assessment of personality but a qualitative account of each higher-stratum factor in terms of the loadings on particular primaries. Gough (1987) also tried to measure the personality sphere comprehensively (see also Chapter 22), but his failure to utilize factor analytic methods in constructing the CPI resulted in an instrument with uncertain scale validities (H. J. Eysenck, 1991).

Also there has been undue restriction of trait variance, with only 20 of Cattell's original 36 trait clusters included in analyses resulting ultimately in the construction of instruments such as the NEO-PI devised by Costa and McCrae (1992b, c). Only 56% of the normal trait sphere is covered by the big five, so that claims as to their comprehensiveness are misplaced. Indeed, Tupes and Christal (1961, p. 12) pointed out that "It is unlikely that the five factors identified are the *only* fundamental personality factors. There are quite likely other fundamental concepts involved among the Allport-Odbert adjectives." Likewise, Norman (1963, p. 582) stated that " it is time to return to the total pool of trait names in the natural language . . . to search for additional personality indicators not easily subsumed under one or another of these five recurrent factors." Norman's study was prefaced on that of Tupes and Christal, who reported a partly inaccurate five-factor solution derived from questionable factor analytic procedures (see Boyle, 1988c, for a discussion of factor analytic guidelines). In selecting only 20 of Cattell's original 36 personality rating scales, Norman biased his results in favor of the Tupes and Christal factors by selecting only those scales already known to be loaded most highly by them, admitting that "the four scales with the highest median factor loadings for each of the five factors identified in these earlier analyses were selected" (p. 577).

In contrast, Krug and Johns's second-order 16PF factors were based on (a) comprehensive sampling of the normal trait domain as measured in the 16PF (effectively incorporating all 36 of Cattell's original clusters, not just 20); (b) use of more appropriate factor analytic procedures on extremely large samples; and (c) cross-validation of findings on extremely large samples of males and females separately. Krug and Johns's factors correspond only approximately to the currently popular big-five dimensions (neuroticism, extraversion, openness, agreeableness, conscientiousness), which have an amended measurement basis in the NEO-PI (Costa & McCrae, 1992c). This lack of complete alignment also may be partly attributable to failure to achieve simple structure solutions. Boyle (1989a) showed that these currently popular dimensions correspond only roughly to the more reliable 16PF second-order factors.

The five-factor solution presented by McCrae and Costa (1987) exhibited a ±.10 hyperplane count of only 35.8%, indicating poor simple structure. Likewise, the solution presented by Costa and McCrae (1992a) exhibited poor simple structure (hyperplane count of only 30.3%). Costa and McCrae presented a five-factor solution for the revised NEO-PI that gave a hyperplane count of only 31.3%, again failing to achieve simple structure. In contrast, the factor solution reported by Krug and Johns (1986) gave a ±.10 hyperplane count of 71.4%, suggesting much greater validity of the 16PF secondaries over the NEO-PI factors. Thus the factor analytic basis of the Norman Five and the NEO-PI appears inadequate. According to Costa and McCrae, no fewer than six of the WAIS-R scales exhibit significant correlations with Factor O (Openness). The WAIS-R Block Design and Object Assembly subtests exhibit the largest correlations. Openness may be a hybrid dimension measuring both personality and intelligence variance in an unspecified way. Clark and Livesley (in press) also demonstrated that Openness (Factor O) was neither strongly nor consistently verified.

Because of inadequate sampling of variables and subjects, as well as crude factor analytic procedures employed in construction of the NEO-PI, the resulting factors do not achieve a high level of simple structure. Costa and McCrae (1992a, p. 661) attempted to justify their weak factor solution, contending that "although simple structure has been the guiding principle in factor analysis for decades, we know that personality traits do not necessarily conform to it. . . . Many important personality traits are defined by two or more factors." Yet empirical studies of physical plasmodes (see Cattell, 1978) have demonstrated that factors make sense only when simple structure emerges. Consequently, Costa and McCrae's assertion that simple structure does not matter runs counter to accepted factor analytic principles (e.g., Cattell, 1978; Child, 1990; Gorsuch, 1983; McDonald, 1985).

Costa and McCrae (1992a) argued that competing five-factor models of personality might be viewed as rotational variants of the NEO-PI big five. They reported an orthogonal rerotation of the work of Zuckerman, Kuhlman, Thornquist, and Keirs (1991). Most psychological constructs, however, are correlated to some extent. If the aim of rotation is to achieve simple structure solutions, then oblique rotational procedures should be applied, systematically varying the degree of obliquity and settling on the solution with the highest hyperplane count (see Cattell, 1978; Gorsuch, 1983). Costa and McCrae reanalyzed the Zuckerman et al. data with the aim of supporting the claimed NEO-PI factor structure. Perusal of their rerotated solution, however, indicates that simple structure was not achieved. Not only were there several instances where the same variables exhibited factor loadings in excess of .40 across the five factors, but the hyperplane count was only 30.3%, suggesting the factor solution was not a simple structure one. Although Zuckerman et al. also used orthogonal rotation, their five-factor solution exhibited a hyperplane count of 38.2%. Costa and McCrae's attempt to verify their big five clearly failed, as their factor solution was inferior to that provided by Zuckerman et al. (1991).

None of the studies into higher-stratum personality dimensions compare favorably with the Krug and Johns (1986) 16PF study, which was based on more comprehensive sampling of the normal trait domain and much larger sample sizes (more than 17,000 subjects, as compared with just a few hundred subjects in the Costa & McCrae and Zuckerman et al. studies). Evidently, research extending from the Norman Five to development of the NEO-PI appears deficient both in sampling of subjects and variables and in failure to attain simple structure solutions. As Zuckerman (1991, p. 17) pointed out, "The rallying around the 'five robust factors,' or the 'big five' as their supporters call them, probably reflects disillusion with the . . . Cattell multifactor system and the feeling that Eysenck's big three are not enough dimensions to account for the complexity of personality."

Higher-Stratum Motivation and Mood-State Dimensions

Within the area of motivation dynamics, Boyle (e.g., 1985a, 1986b; Boyle, Start, & Hall, 1989) has delineated several higher-order dimensions as measured in the Motivation Analysis Test (MAT) series of instruments. These instruments are *objective* measures of dynamic motivation traits, and therefore they essentially avoid the problems of response sets associated with item transparency; it is virtually impossible for respondents either consciously or unconsciously to distort their motivation profiles in any systematic way. Theoretically, much of human motivation is at the unconscious level (as measured by the unintegrated or U-components in the MAT instruments), so that comprehensive objective motivation measures are all the more important. Conscious motivation dynamic traits are measured via the integrated (I) components (see Cattell, 1985).

From these EFA studies, however, there is considerable discrepancy as to the specific nature of higher-stratum dimensions in studies of the MAT and School Motivation Analysis Test (SMAT). For the 190-item SMAT (which measures drives labeled Assertiveness, Mating/Sex, Fear, Narcism, Pugnacity, and Protectiveness, and acquired interest patterns labeled Self-Sentiment, Superego, School Orientation, and Home Orientation), Boyle et al. (1989) reported six higher-stratum factors among adolescents. Factor 1 contrasted U-Superego, U-School, and U-Home with U-Mating, and U-Narcism. Factor 2 loaded primarily on I-Pugnacity. Factor 3 loaded mostly on I-School and U-Pugnacity. Factor 4 contrasted I-Home and I-Protectiveness with (U + I) Pugnacity. Factor 5 loaded predominantly on U-School, U-Mating and I-Assertiveness, and Factor 6 contrasted I-Superego and (U + I) Self-Sentiment with U-Fear. The 230-item Children's Motivation Analysis Test (CMAT; a downward extension of the MAT and SMAT instruments) provides measures of six biologically based *ergs* (labeled Narcism, Play, Fear, Pugnacity, Curiosity, and Assertiveness), and four culturally acquired *sentiments* (Home Orientation, Self-Sentiment, Superego, and School Orientation). In accord with the view that motivation dynamics are partly acquired as a function of development, higher-order analysis of the CMAT scale intercorrelations has revealed only four dimensions (e.g., Boyle & Start, 1989).

Because instruments designed to measure fluctuating states collectively cover some 30 to 40 primary mood-state dimensions, elucidation of a smaller set of central state factors would enable greater economy of measurement and administration time. Accordingly, Boyle (e.g., 1985a, 1987c, 1988a) carried out a series of programmatic studies into the higher-order factor structure of transitory mood states, using both single-occasion (R-factoring) and across-occasions (differential dR-factoring) change scores. Boyle (1987c) investigated the higher-stratum mood-state factors discernible from a conjoint dR-factoring of difference scores for the 8SQ and DES-IV instruments. The net result has been elucidation of five to six central mood-state dimensions, which might be labeled Extraversion State, Neuroticism State, Arousal-Fatigue, Hostility, and Curiosity. Cattell (1979, 1980) has proposed an elaboration of his behavioral specification equation, incorporating trait-modulation indices to account for the influence of mood states on behavior. For each mood state within the Cattellian psychometric model, it is assumed that a state liability trait exists on which individuals differ. A modulator expressing the mean stimulation of a given stimulus for a particular state transforms this liability value (i.e., situational indices modulate state liability traits).

Varieties of Psychometric Measurement Media

There are three different kinds of measurement media. The first is life-record (L) data, which include *ratings* of others. L-data are often unreliable and invalid, as the perceptual and idiosyncratic biases of the rater may distort the picture of the individual being rated. Second is *questionnaire* (Q) data, which comprise an individual's self-ratings. Unfortunately, responses to transparent self-report questionnaire items are prone to distortion ranging all the way from inadequate self-insight to deliberate dissimulation ("faking good" or "faking bad"; see Bagozzi & Yi, 1990; Boyle, 1985b). Distortion may also occur because of the influence of response sets such as social desirability (Schmitt & Steyer, 1993). Third is *objective test* (T) data wherein the items constitute nontransparent miniature performance tests (see Cattell & Warburton, 1967, for a compendium of more than 500 such miniature objective test devices). T-data has the advantage that response distortion is minimized, as there is no immediately discernible relationship between item content and corresponding personality or ability factors being measured (Boyle, 1990a; Schuerger, 1986; Schmidt, 1988).

Personality inventories such as the 16PF/CAQ, HSPQ, CPQ, Myers-Briggs Type Indicator (MBTI; Briggs-Myers & Briggs, 1985), CPI, HPI, NEO-PI, MMPI and MMPI-2, CPS (Comrey, 1980), and EPQ (H. J. Eysenck, 1991) have all utilized self-report Q-data. Instruments for measuring intellectual abilities, however, have been based on T-data from the very beginning, starting with Galton's simple RT studies (Jensen, 1991) and extending to the SB-IV and the Wechsler intelligence scales (WAIS-R, WISC-R, WPPSI; see Kaufman, 1990). Factor analytic work has resulted in development of the 16PF, CAQ, MAT, CAB, and O-A Batteries (see Cattell & Johnson, 1986, for a detailed description). Such multidimensional instruments are "hostages" for ability and personality structure theory, enabling empirical measurement of factors (mapped longitudinally as life-course curves) and quantification of heritability estimates (via Multiple Abstract Variance Analysis, or MAVA; see Cattell, 1982b, pp. 89–123), along with experimental investigation of abilities and personality traits.[3] The MAVA method provides a sophisticated analysis of the contributions of genetic and environmental variance. As Kline (1993b) reported, "Jinks and Fulker (1970) indeed describe it as a brilliant one-man attempt to develop a statistics of genetic biometrics" (p. 102).

Motivation/Response Distortion in Personality Questionnaires

It is possible to modify Q-data for response bias using motivational distortion scales, which are built into the 16PF range of instruments (Birkett-Cattell,

[3]Because Cattellian psychometric instruments, are constructed factor analytically, the primary factors (abilities, traits, dynamics, and states) represent underlying causal and psychologically meaningful dimensions, such that the validity of the Cattellian psychometric model (including both the ability and personality submodels) can be measured quantitatively and therefore tested empirically.

1989). On the basis of trait-view theory (Cattell, 1982a, 1992b), however, such modification of scale scores is potentially problematic, and reliance on traditional motivation distortion scales may only serve to add further measurement noise into responses on psychometric instruments. Holden, Kroner, Fekken, and Popham (1992) have shown that when faking good, individuals take relatively longer to respond to socially undesirable Q-data items, and vice versa: "The model predicts that differential test item response latencies should be faster for schema-congruent test answers than for noncongruent responses" (p. 272). Because virtually all personality instruments utilize Q-data, whereas intelligence tests are based on T-data measures, the measurement of personality traits has not yet reached the level of certainty already achieved with intelligence testing (Brody, 1992). Failure to obtain simple structure solutions in factor analytically constructed instruments has only served to confound research findings. Guilford's SOI model and the NEO-PI MMPI, MBTI, HPI, and CPI all fail to satisfy simple structure requirements. The scale structures of these instruments are not well supported factor analytically.

Need for Objective Personality Test Construction

Intelligence tests are based on performance T-data, whereas almost all personality instruments (e.g., CPI, MMPI, CPS, EPQ, 16PF, HSPQ, CAQ, NEO-PI, 8SQ, DES-IV, POMS, MDQ) are merely self-rating Q-data scales. There is an urgent need for construction of multivariate objective personality tests, along the lines of the Objective-Analytic (O-A) Battery (Cattell & Schuerger, 1978) which measures 10 factor analytically derived personality traits (see Gough, 1989). Objective (T-data) tests avoid self-report distortion and rater bias; in an objective personality test, the respondent does not know which particular trait is being measured. Scales measured in the O-A Battery have been labeled using Universal Index Numbers: U.I. 16, Ego Standards; U.I. 19, Independence versus Subduedness; U.I. 20, Evasiveness; U.I. 21, Exuberance; U.I. 23, Capacity to Mobilize versus Regression; U.I. 24, Anxiety; U.I. 25, Realism; U.I. 28, Asthenia versus Self-Assurance; U.I. 32, Exvia versus Invia; and U.I. 33, Discouragement versus Sanguiness. These T-data factors correspond to the second-order 16PF factors, raising questions about the meaningfulness of the primary Q-data trait dimensions. The O-A primary factors correspond to normal and abnormal personality L- and Q-data traits at the second-stratum level. Each factor is measured on seven or eight subtests of 20 to 30 minutes each. According to Bolton (1988), the O-A Battery represents an innovative approach to personality assessment. Given the realities of testing in practical settings, administration of the complete O-A Battery is likely to take appreciably longer than the nominal 5 hours. Some evidence of the predictive validity of the O-A Battery in discriminating between various psychiatric syndromes has been provided (see Schuerger, 1986).

Objective Motivation Measurement

Within the dynamic motivational sphere (measured via the MAT series of instruments), application of the behavioral specification equation yields interesting new indications of total motivation (U + I scores), conflict (U − I scores), derivative scores (e.g., Information-Intelligence), decision theory, and interests not yet experimentally investigated. The role of transitory states is also included, as researched in several studies by Boyle (e.g., 1983a, 1985a, 1987a, b, 1988a). There are various new concepts as models here: for example, vector measurement of interest and learning in the dynamic lattice; matrix calculation of learning in life selections; multiple factoring in the data box combining factors of persons × stimuli × occasions; the vector representation of environment; modulation law of states; assignment of vulnerability indices to tests; factor analytic discovery of states by dR- and P-techniques; the representation of learning gain by vector change; law of structured learning through gain in dynamic structures; and representation and quantification of perception change (construing a contextual emphasis in trait view theory, or "attribution theory"; see Cattell, 1979, 1980, 1982a, 1992b).

ITEM ANALYSIS ISSUES: PSYCHOMETRIC PROPERTIES IN PERSONALITY AND INTELLIGENCE RESEARCH

Reliability: Stability versus Dependability

Reliability of psychometric scales is an important precursor for validity (see Thorndike, 1982). It is consistency as measured over time (test-retest rather than "internal consistency") that provides the most accurate estimation of reliability (see Fernandez, 1990; Fernandez, Nygren, & Thorn, 1991). It is important to differentiate between short-term dependability (immediate test-retest) versus longer-term stability (retest intervals ranging from, say, 1 week to several years), which allows an estimation of measurement error (Cattell, 1973). This distinction is critical in assessing the reliability of state versus trait instruments (Boyle, 1983a). Both dependability and stability estimates should be high (.8 or .9) for trait measures (e.g., CPI, MMPI, HPI, MBTI, EPQ, 16PF, CAQ). For state measures, however, dependability estimates should be high, whereas stabilities should be considerably lower if the scale is truly sensitive to situational variability (Boyle, 1985b). For example, the State-Trait Anxiety Inventory (STAI; Spielberger, Gorsuch, Lushene, Vagg, & Jacobs, 1986) should exhibit high dependability estimates for both sections of the instrument, but stability coefficients should be appreciably higher for trait as compared with state scales. In regard to the O-A Battery, Bolton (p. 378) reported test-retest reliabilities over a 1-day interval ranging from .62 to .93 (median .75), and stability coefficients for retest over 3 to 6 weeks ranging from .61 to .85 (median .71). Concept validities (correlations between scale scores and the pure factors) ranged from .64 to .92 (median .76). Consequently, some of the T-data factors measured in the O-A Battery are less stable than is desirable for measures of enduring personality traits. In comparing the reliability and validity of personality and ability instruments, intelligence tests (T-data measures) exhibit appreciably higher coefficients in both respects than do most personality inventories.

Item Homogeneity: Internal Consistency versus Item Redundancy

Reliability is a function of the length of a scale, in accord with the Spearman-Brown prophecy formula (Crocker & Algina, 1986). In general, longer scales with a larger number of items are more reliable than are shorter scales. The item homogeneity of a scale should not be excessively high; otherwise, "internal consistency" may become "item redundancy," whereby items are virtually paraphrases of each other (Boyle, 1991a). We challenge the commonly held view that item homogeneity should always be maximized. Indeed, Cattell (1978) has indicated that low to moderate item homogeneity is preferable, so that each item contributes to the breadth of measurement of a particular scale. Kline (1986) suggested that item homogeneities in the 0.3 to 0.7 range are most desirable:

> Cattell argues that high internal consistency is actually antithetical to validity on the grounds that any item must cover less ground or be narrower than the criterion we are trying to measure. . . . This is obviously the case, for if two variables were perfectly correlated, one would be providing no new information. Thus maximum validity, in Cattell's argument, is obtained where test items do not all correlate with each other, but where each correlates positively with the criterion. Such a test would have only low internal-consistency reliability. In my view, Cattell is theoretically correct (pp. 2–3, see Cattell, 1982c).

Item Response Theory and Computerized Adaptive Testing

Item response theory (IRT; sometimes termed latent trait theory) has emerged as a result of shortcomings with classical test theory (CTT; see Hambleton & Swaminathan, 1985, pp. 1–4, for a list of limitations). IRT relates item responses to an underlying ability trait, where the probability of a correct response to a given item is a function of the ability level. The probability of a correct response takes the graphical shape of an ogive, which can be defined by up to three parameters (item difficulty—position of curve relative to X-axis; item discrimination—slope of curve; and "guessing" parameter—lower asymptote of curve). If these parameters are known, it is necessary to estimate individuals' ability in terms of their item responses, to select the next item to be presented, and to update their ability estimates constantly. Use of Computerized Adaptive Testing (CAT) enables estimation of an individual's trait from as few as half the usual number of administered items. Individuals receive different numbers and combinations of items depending on their particular responses to items (i.e., their ability levels). CAT is considerably more efficient than standard tests constructed on the basis of classical test theory (see Crocker & Algina, 1986; Wainer et al., 1990). A number of major aptitude and ability instruments have been constructed using IRT methods (e.g., U.S. Armed Services Vocational Aptitude Battery, or CAT-ASVAB; DAT).

With recent developments in IRT it is possible to check the contribution of individual items to total scale scores, enabling decisions as to which items to retain and which to remove. Some items may exhibit significant measurement error. The issue of response bias in relation to scoring formats across items with differing levels of measurement also can be addressed more effectively with IRT than with CTT methods (which include the Spearman-Brown prophecy formula, standard error of measurement, Kuder-Richardson estimates of item homogeneity, and dissatenuation statistics). As pointed out by Hambleton, Swaminathan, and Rogers (1991), CTT measures of item homogeneity or internal consistency (such as Cronbach's alpha coefficient) do not test the adequacy of summed scale scores (see Boyle, 1991a). In contrast to CTT methods, IRT is associated with a number of psychometric advances, including the facility to evaluate items for their bias, difficulty level, and relationships to other items within a scale (Rudy, Turk, & Brody, 1992).

Use of IRT allows scale-free measures to be developed, so that various sets of items with scaling and measurement properties can be incorporated into equivalent versions of a scale. Because item parameters associated with IRT approaches are theoretically sample independent, item banks can be readily formed. Unlike traditional CTT models, IRT models are potentially falsifiable, and the statistical fit of specific items and the total scale score are tested explicitly. IRT methods also handle missing item data well, and they enable tests of the legitimacy of "estimated scales" (Rudy et al., 1992).

It is desirable to employ both CTT and IRT methods, where possible, in the construction of intelligence and psychological tests and instruments. On the assumption of a unidimensional model (ascertained by means of an initial factor analysis), one-, two-, and three-parameter IRT models can be employed. The simplest is the one-parameter or Rasch model, which differentiates between items solely in terms of their "difficulty" levels; however, the practical utility of the Rasch model has been severely criticized by Goldstein (1980). Certain considerations must be taken into account in deciding which model is the appropriate one (see Hambleton & Swaminathan, 1985, pp. 307–308, for a discussion of these issues). An interesting application of the two-parameter logistic model has been the work of Grayson (1986), who investigated latent trait models of dichotomous personality questionnaire (EPQ) data.

More advanced IRT models (e.g., partial-credit models) overcome some of the problems associated with Rasch scaling, but these in turn introduce new variables and therefore the possibility of additional error (Hutchinson, 1991). Use of IRT provides evidence as to the most efficient items in a scale (see Butcher, Keller, & Bacon, 1985, regarding extending adaptive testing to personality instruments). The application of computerized adaptive testing (CAT), and more advanced IRT methods in personality and intelligence assessment, is likely to increase dramatically as we enter the 21st century. As Hambleton and Swaminathan (1985) have pointed out, IRT methods facilitate the equating of test scores, item bank development (sets of items with equivalent item characteristics), detection of biased items, and resulting psychological test construction. In the future, greater emphasis will be placed on developing multidimensional IRT models (Weiss & Yoes, 1990), which will have many implications for the construction of personality and intelligence tests.

Correlation Coefficients with Ordinal or Categorical Data

Another potential problem at the item analysis level is the computation of Pearson product-moment correlation coefficients when variables are ordinal or categorical. These estimates can be significantly biased, as demonstrated empirically by Jöreskog and Sörbom (1988). It is desirable, therefore, to compute polychoric correlations when the data are categorical or ordinal (see Hambleton & Swaminathan, 1985), and polyserial coefficients when ordinal and continuous variables are correlated, to minimize biased estimates (Poon & Lee, 1987). Use of PRELIS (Jöreskog & Sörbom, 1988) enables the simultaneous computation of polychoric, polyserial, and product-moment correlation coefficients as required, depending on the measurement level of each pair of variables being correlated. Because the computation of such correlation estimates is the starting point for many multivariate statistical procedures, it is essential that the best possible correlation estimates be derived in the first instance (Boyle, 1991b). Some of the major statistical packages provide estimates only of the product-moment correlations, thereby reducing the validity of many statistical analyses. Consequently, the resultant measurement error built into computed correlation coefficients will be compounded at every subsequent step in the data analysis procedures.

Statistical Effect Size

One of the difficulties with quantitative analyses of data is the distinction between statistical and practical significance. Although treatment effects may be statistically significant, often these effects are trivial and of little practical or conceptual meaningfulness. This issue is particularly problematic when dealing with multivariate analyses based on data from large samples (many personality and intelligence tests, for example, are multidimensional in structure), as the probability of obtaining statistically significant, but trivial, effects is increased in direct proportion to the number of scales, for example, the CPI comprises 20 trait scales, the CAQ has 28 scales, the PAI includes 22 scales, the CAB measures 20 primary abilities, and the NEO-PI-R includes no fewer than 30 primary scales!

Application of the Bonferroni correction reduces the likelihood of accepting statistically significant but trivial results (Winer, Brown, & Michels, 1991). Another approach is to calculate the corresponding effect sizes for each significant effect. Calculation of effect sizes, rather than merely relying on simple significance test results per se, builds into the analysis the requisite degree of caution necessary to draw useful conclusions regarding the size of treatment effects. Interpretation of multivariate analyses of multidimensional personality and intelligence measures requires careful consideration of whether or not significant statistical effects have any practical or conceptual meaning.

Generalizability Procedures

Generalizability theory (Cronbach, 1990; de Gruijter & van der Kamp, 1990; Shavelson, Webb, & Rowley, 1989) involves a generalization of classical test theory. Whereas true-score theory assumes that error variance is homogeneous and that there is only one true score, generalizability theory differentiates between sources of error, enabling a quantitative estimation of the various error components. Construct interpretation is thereby facilitated by a knowledge of which sources of error are larger than others. This is a critically important issue, as the reliability of personality and intelligence measures must be viewed in the light of likely error rates. Three salient sources of error include situations, occasions of measurement, and actual observations. As a general measurement procedure, generalizability theory involves observation, estimation, measurement, and optimization stages. Unfortunately, application of multivariate generalizability has not received much attention in the literature to date (de Gruijter & van der Kamp, 1990; Webb, Shavelson, & Maddahian, 1983). An interesting application to personality research was undertaken by van Heck (1988), however, wherein the generalizability of L-data and Q-data across situations was investigated.

We have already discussed many of the likely sources of error associated with L-data and Q-data (see section above on the psychometric measurement of abilities and personality traits). Both the situation and the occasion of measurement, however, are subject to situational variability and fluctuation of mood states. Cattell (1979) distinguished between the ambient situation (k) versus the overall global situation (e) as likely sources of error, and he built these sources of variability into the more complex versions of his behavioral specification equation (proposing the notion of modulation theory and state-liability traits). A simplified representation (where the global situation is assumed to comprise the focal stimulus, h, plus the ambient situation) is

$$a_{hijk} = b_{hj1}\mathbf{T}_{1i} + \dots + b_{hjp}\mathbf{T}_{pi} + \dots + b_{hjs1}s_{k1}\mathbf{L}_{1i} + \dots + b_{hjsq}s_{kq}\mathbf{L}_{qi} + \text{uniqueness} \quad (6)$$

where the modulator index is s_{kx} for trait x, i represents the individual, j is the response, s denotes the ambient situation indices, and L represents the individual's liabilities (see Cattell, 1979, pp. 187–196). Fortunately, application of the newer SEM methods via statistical modeling packages such as LISREL, COSAN, and EQS can facilitate estimation of error terms, in personality and intelligence research.

Generalizability theory, as extended into the multivariate context, is related to covariance structure analysis. Both approaches attempt to obtain estimates of variance from the variance-covariance matrix. The underlying assumptions for generalizability studies, however, are generally weaker than those associated with covariance structure analyses (Brennan, 1983; de Gruijter & van der Kamp, 1990).

Test Bias in Personality and Intelligence Research

The purpose of administering intelligence and/or personality tests is to make valid predictions of future behaviors. Culture-fair tests (such as Cattell's CFIT measures, discussed above) go part of the way in facilitating accurate predictions across different societies. By restricting the content of these instruments to that which is common across cultures, however, and relationship of this content to real-life situations and predictive validity may be lowered inadvertently. Consequently, many personality and intelligence tests are significantly biased against one cultural group or another. Use of appropriate norms that pertain to particular groups or subgroups is important if biased interpretation of test scores is to be avoided. As Anastasi (1990) pointed out, "Validity coefficients, regression weights, and cut-off scores may vary as a function of differences in the test takers' experiential backgrounds" (p. 194). Hunter, Schmidt, and Rauschenberger (1984) provided an extensive review of cultural and ethnic effects on predictive validity of standardized psychological test scores. Possible test bias (both slope bias and intercept bias; see Anastasi, 1990, pp. 194–199) has been suggested, particularly in the area of intelligence testing. It has been reported that different cultural groups perform differentially on standardized scales. Nevertheless, according to Anastasi (1990), in the United States, "Comprehensive surveys and critical analyses . . . have failed to support the hypothesis that ability tests are less valid for [different cultural groups] in predicting occupational or educational performance" (p. 197). Furthermore, there is no clear-cut evidence of intercept bias, even when a test exhibits similar validity across cultural or ethnic subgroups (Anastasi, 1990, p. 199; Hunter et al., 1984).

SUMMARY AND CONCLUSIONS

The scientific analysis of personality and intelligence now predominates over the earlier, more subjective philosophical and literary speculations. Classical bivariate experimental designs in psychological research have been unduly emphasized at the expense of more appropriate multivariate experimental designs. In contrast to this univariate approach, the Cattellian school stands out as a major force in the promotion of multivariate experimental methods in both the ability and personality domains. The Cattellian psychometric model, however, incorporates many primary abilities, personality traits, dynamic motivation factors, and transitory mood-state dimensions. Though primary traits measured in instruments such as the 16PF and CAQ are numerous, second-order dimensions are more reliable because of the greater number of items loaded by each secondary. Yet higher-stratum dimensions are less predictive than primary traits. In line with depth psychometry (Cattell, 1987b), however, 16PF second-order factors can be interpreted qualitatively in terms of their unique loadings on each of the contributing primary trait factors.

Krug and Johns's (1986) demonstrated at least five major normal personality dimensions, in addition to intelligence. Other investigations (exemplified in the NEO-PI) suggest a slightly different breakdown of the personality sphere. The so-called big five, however, have a history plagued by inadequate sampling of subjects, variables, and inadequate EFA procedures. Norman's (1963) study, on which the big-five theory is prefaced, was flawed in (a) accounting for just over half the known personality trait variance, and (b) in its use of an inappropriate orthogonal rotation that precluded the possibility of obtaining a simple structure solution. Norman's five-factor solution closely matched that of Tupes and Christal, whose variables were selected to maximize the likelihood of finding the big five. This approach to research is to be abhorred. The currently popular big five provide an inadequate overview of personality trait structure.

Krug and Johns's (1986) more comprehensive factor solution satisfied simple structure requirements (hyperplane count of 71.4%). In contrast, McCrae and Costa's (1987) factor solution for the NEO-PI exhibited a hyperplane count of only 35.8%, and the corresponding hyperplane count for the Zuckerman et al. (1991) study was only 38.2%, raising doubts about simple structure. At the second-stratum level, *at least* five major abnormal trait dimensions also emerge from factor analyses of the CAQ primary trait intercorrelations (Boyle, 1987d).

Although the Cattellian and Eysenckian schools appear to differ with respect to the number of personality trait dimensions, this is more a question of interpretation than an insurmountable barrier. Both Cattell and Eysenck agree on the importance of factor analysis in psychometric research, and both agree on many substantive issues (thus the second-order 16PF dimensions correspond closely with the Eysenckian factors), as H. J. Eysenck (1984) has indicated:

> The major conclusions are surprisingly alike; the only remaining difference is that Cattell attaches more importance than I do to his primary factors. . . . it is unusual to discover such close correspondence between authors so distinct in their methods, procedures, evaluations and premises. . . . The Cattell and Eysenck constructs and theories should be seen, not as mutually contradictory, but as complementary and mutually supportive" (p. 336).

Moreover, as Boyle (1989a) has pointed out

> Arguments against the importance of hierarchical structural models of personality, and against the use of factor analysis in discovering and confirming personality structure, cannot be justified on the superficial assertion that Eysenck, Comrey, and Cattell have proposed different numbers of trait dimensions. This frivolous argument fails to acknowledge that each investigator has focused his attention on different levels within the hierarchical structural model of personality traits. (pp. 1296–1297)

The focus of Boyle's work has been on development of a more parsimonious version of the Cattellian psychometric model, emphasizing second-stratum factors instead of primaries. This not only enhances the practical utility of the model, in line with the Eysenckian emphasis on typological dimensions, but extends greatly the coverage of each of the major intrapersonal psychological domains of abilities, traits, dynamics, and states at the broad Eysenckian level of analysis.

Future psychometric research should also focus on construction of objective personality (T-data) instruments to minimize problems associated with item transparency, response bias, and motivational distortion. Although to date most effort has concentrated on personality inventories, these instruments are highly susceptible to motivation distortion. One objective personality instrument (the O-A Battery) has not received widespread use, partly because of the excessive administration time (at least 5 hours), so that its utility in applied situations has not yet been fully explored. Although the O-A Battery enables objective measurement of personality traits, it has not yet received sufficient usage to clearly assess its psychometric properties. Research into objective (T-data) measures of personality undoubtedly offers much promise for a more scientific approach to personality assessment, taking into account underlying psychobiological mechanisms (see Zuckerman, 1991).

The two-handed approach of EFA followed by CFA on an independent sample is a logical way to proceed. The two approaches serve entirely different purposes, and they are complementary rather than competing methods. A frequent criticism is that EFA yields unstable factors that seldom agree with the results of other investigators. An example is the apparent discrepancy between the Eysenckian and Cattellian personality factors: Eysenck claims 3 major trait dimensions, whereas Cattell examines 16 primary factors, and six secondary dimensions in the normal trait domain alone (clearly, to cover both the normal and abnormal personality trait domains, at least 10 to 12 higher-stratum dimensions are required). It is argued that this difference in number of factors demonstrates the unreliability of EFA methods. This criticism, however, is invalid: Second-order factoring of the Cattellian primaries produces the Eysenckian factors together with several additional trait dimensions at the Eysenckian level of analysis. The Eysenckian model of personality structure accounts only for about 25% to 30% of the variance measured within the comprehensive Cattellian framework; likewise, Comrey's system accounts for only 67 to 80% of the Cattellian variance. The Cattellian and Eysenckian factor analytic results exhibit much convergence, as long as comparisons are made at the appropriate level of the hierarchical structure of personality (i.e., at the Cattellian second-stratum level).

Provided adequate sampling of subjects and variables and appropriate methods of factor analysis are employed (see Cattell, 1978; Gorsuch, 1983; McDonald, 1985) and simple structure is obtained (and verified), EFA is an invaluable tool for mapping out the dimensionality of a domain (CFA can then be used to test the validity of the proposed factors). Even with sample sizes of 300 subjects, the correct (exploratory) factor pattern solution is obtained only 50% of the time; this demonstrates the importance of utilizing large samples when undertaking analyses of multivariate data. Many of the published EFA studies have been defective on various methodological grounds. Often studies have not paid adequate attention to this crucial issue, leading to the false impression that EFA is unreliable because it is "sample driven," whereas CFA is more reliable because it is "conceptually driven." It is nonsense to assume that confirmatory methods are not influenced by the idiosyncrasies of samples.

Aside from the new possibilities for research into personality and intelligence using multilevel modeling packages, the general advantage of SEM models over the older exploratory methods (factor analysis, multiple regression analysis, path analysis) is that psychological dimensions can be modeled *dynamically*, wherein change in one aspect might be viewed as "causing" changes in another. Thus, in regard to cognitive abilities, vocabulary appears to directly affect both verbal, and numerical abilities (vocabulary is a precursor for growth of cognitive skills). According to Romney and Bynner (1992, p. 100), "Personality disorders are more complicated, half . . . lying on a straight line (simplex) and half lying on a circle (circumplex). . . . Personal characteristics, whether they be intellectual, behavioral, or attitudinal, are all amenable to change." Soldz et al. (1993), however, demonstrated that the hierarchical factor model of personality structure is better able to account for personality disorders than is the circumplex model. Therefore it is important to reevaluate the adequacy of the so-called big five, and to appreciate the need for a more comprehensive coverage of the trait sphere than that provided in instruments such as the NEO-PI.

Personality and intelligence tests play a complementary role in the assessment of psychological functioning. Many of the extant instruments, though, have severe psychometric limitations pertaining to their psychometric properties, including basic reliability and validity. Nevertheless, with the advent of modern

CFA, SEM, and multilevel modeling techniques, we can now confidently expect some major advances in psychometric conceptualization, measurement, and statistical models of personality and intelligence.

REFERENCES

Anastasi, A. (1990). *Psychological testing* (6th ed.). New York: Macmillan.

Anderson, J. G., & Gerbing, D. W. (1988). Structural equation modeling in practice: A review and recommended two-step approach. *Psychological Bulletin, 103*, 411–423.

Bagozzi, R. P., & Yi, Y. (1990). Assessing method variance in multitrait-multimethod matrices: The case of self-reported affect and perceptions at work. *Journal of Applied Psychology, 75*, 547–560.

Barrett, P. T., & Kline, P. (1982). Factor extraction: An examination of three methods. *Personality Study and Group Behavior, 2*, 84–98.

Bentler, P. M. (1988, October). Bentler critiques structural equation modeling. *Score*, 3, 6.

Bentler, P. M. (1989). *EQS: Structural equations program manual.* Los Angeles: BMDP Statistical Software.

Bentler, P. M. (1990). Comparative fit indexes in structural models. *Psychological Bulletin, 107*, 238–246.

Bentler, P. M., & Kanno, Y. (1990). On the equivalence of factors and components. *Multivariate Behavioral Research, 25*, 67–74.

Biddle, B. J., & Marlin, M. M. (1987). Causality, confirmation, credulity, and structural equation modeling. *Child Development, 58*, 4–17.

Birkett-Cattell, H. (1989). *The 16PF: Personality in depth.* Champaign, IL: Institute for Personality and Ability Testing.

Bollen, K. A. (1989). *Structural equations with latent variables.* New York: Wiley.

Bolton, B. (1988). Review of the Objective-Analytic Batteries. *Test Critiques, 7*, 374–380.

Boyle, G. J. (1983a). Critical review of state-trait curiosity test development. *Motivation and Emotion, 7*, 377–397.

Boyle, G. J. (1983b). Effects on academic learning of manipulating emotional states and motivational dynamics. *British Journal of Educational Psychology, 53*, 347–357.

Boyle, G. J. (1985a). A reanalysis of the higher-order factor structure of the Motivation Analysis Test and the Eight State Questionnaire. *Personality and Individual Differences, 6*, 367–374.

Boyle, G. J. (1985b). Self-report measures of depression: Some psychometric considerations. *British Journal of Clinical Psychology, 24*, 45–59.

Boyle, G. J. (1986a). Clinical neuropsychological assessment: Abbreviating the Halstead Category Test of brain dysfunction. *Journal of Clinical Psychology, 42*, 615–625.

Boyle, G. J. (1986b). Intermodality superfactors in the Sixteen Personality Factor Questionnaire, Eight State Battery and objective Motivation Analysis Test. *Personality and Individual Differences, 7*, 583–586.

Boyle, G. J. (1987a). Central dynamic traits measured in the School Motivation Analysis Test. *Multivariate Experimental Clinical Research, 9*, 11–26.

Boyle, G. J. (1987b). Commentary: The role of intrapersonal psychological variables in academic school learning. *Journal of School Psychology, 25*, 389–392.

Boyle, G. J. (1987c). A conjoint dR-factoring of the 8SQ/DES-IV multivariate mood-state scales. *Australian Journal of Psychology, 39*, 79–87.

Boyle, G. J. (1987d). Psychopathological depression superfactors in the Clinical Analysis Questionnaire. *Personality and Individual Differences, 8*, 609–614.

Boyle, G. J. (1987e). Use of change scores in redundancy analyses of multivariate psychological inventories. *Personality and Individual Differences, 8*, 845–854.

Boyle, G. J. (1988a). Central clinical states: An examination of the Profile of Mood States and the Eight State Questionnaire. *Journal of Psychopathology and Behavioral Assessment, 10*, 205–215.

Boyle, G. J. (1988b). Contribution of Cattellian psychometrics to the elucidation of human intellectual structure. *Multivariate Experimental Clinical Research, 8*, 267–273.

Boyle, G. J. (1988c). Elucidation of motivation structure by dynamic calculus. In J. R. Nesselroade & R. B. Cattell (Eds.), *Handbook of multivariate experimental psychology* (2nd ed., pp. 737–787). New York: Plenum.

Boyle, G. J. (1989a). Re-examination of the major personality-type factors in the Cattell, Comrey, and Eysenck scales: Were the factor solutions by Noller et al. optimal? *Personality and Individual Differences, 10*, 1289–1299.

Boyle, G. J. (1989b). Reliability and validity of the Stanford-Binet Intelligence Scale (fourth edition) in the Australian context: A review. *Australian Educational and Developmental Psychologist, 6*, 21–23.

Boyle, G. J. (1990a, June). *Integration of personality and intelligence measurement within the Cattellian psychometric model.* Paper presented at the Fifth European Conference on Personality, University of Rome.

Boyle, G. J. (1990b). A review of the factor structure of the Sixteen Personality Factor Questionnaire and the Clinical Analysis Questionnaire. *Psychological Test Bulletin, 3*, 40–45.

Boyle, G. J. (1990c). Stanford-Binet Intelligence Scale: Is its structure supported by LISREL congeneric factor analyses? *Personality and Individual Differences, 11*, 1175–1181.

Boyle, G. J. (1991a). Does item homogeneity indicate internal consistency or item redundancy in psychometric scales? *Personality and Individual Differences, 12*, 291–294.

Boyle, G. J. (1991b). Experimental psychology does require a multivariate perspective. *Contemporary Psychology, 36*, 350–351.

Boyle, G. J. (1991c). Item analysis of the subscales in the Eight State Questionnaire (8SQ): Exploratory and confirmatory factor analyses. *Multivariate Experimental Clinical Research, 10*, 37–65.

Boyle, G. J. (1992a). Factor structure of the Menstrual Distress Questionnaire (MDQ): Exploratory and LISREL analyses. *Personality and Individual Differences, 13*, 1–15.

Boyle, G. J. (1992b). Hogan Personality Inventory. *Psychological Test Bulletin, 5*, 130–138.

Boyle, G. J. (1993a). Intelligence and personality measurement within the Cattellian psychometric model. In G. L. van Heck, P. Bonaiuto, I. Deary, & W. Nowack (Eds.), *Personality psychology in Europe* (Vol. 4). Tilburg: Tilburg University Press.

Boyle, G. J. (1993b). *Relationships between mood states and menstrual cycle symptoms in young, healthy women: A structural modeling analysis.* Unpublished manuscript.

Boyle, G. J. (1993c). Review of the Personality Assessment Inventory (PAI). In J. C. Conoley & J. Impara (Eds.), *Twelfth mental measurements yearbook.* Lincoln, NE: Buros Institute of Mental Measurements.

Boyle, G. J. (1993d). Review of the Self-Description Questionnaire (SDQ-II). *Test Critiques, 10*, 632–643.

Boyle, G. J. (1993e). Special review: Evaluation of the exploratory factor analysis programs provided in SPSSX and SPSS/PC+. *Multivariate Experimental Clinical Research, 10*, 129–135.

Boyle, G. J., Borg, M. G., Falzon, J. M., & Baglioni, Jr., A. J. (1995). A structural model of the dimensions of teacher stress. *British Journal of Educational Psychology, 65*, 49–67.

Boyle, G. J., & Cattell, R. B. (1984). Proof of situational sensitivity of mood states and dynamic traits—ergs and sentiments—to disturbing stimuli. *Personality and Individual Differences, 5*, 541–548.

Boyle, G. J., & Fabris, S. (1992). LISREL analyses of the RIASEC model: Confirmatory and congeneric factor analyses of Holland's Self-Directed Search. *Personality and Individual Differences, 13*, 1077–1084.

Boyle, G. J., & Langley, P. D. (1989). *Elementary statistical methods: For students of psychology, education and the social sciences*. Sydney: Pergamon.

Boyle, G. J., & Stanley, G. V. (1986). Application of factor analysis in psychological research: Improvement of simple structure by computer-assisted graphic oblique transformation. *Multivariate Experimental Clinical Research, 8*, 175–182.

Boyle, G. J., & Start, K. B. (1989). Comparison of higher-stratum motivational factors across sexes using the Children's Motivation Analysis Test. *Personality and Individual Differences, 10*, 483–487.

Boyle, G. J., Start, K. B., & Hall, E. J. (1989). Dimensions of adolescent motivation as measured by higher-order factors in the School Motivation Analysis Test. *Journal of School Psychology, 27*, 27–33.

Breckler, S. J. (1990). Applications of covariance structure modeling in psychology: Cause for concern. *Psychological Bulletin, 107*, 260–273.

Brennan, J. M., & Nitz, L. H. (1986). *Stat 1: A statistical toolbox*. Kailua, HI: Sugar Mill Software.

Brennan, R. L. (1983). *Elements of generalizability theory*. Iowa City, IA: American College Testing.

Briggs, S. R., & Cheek, J. M. (1986). The role of factor analysis in the development and evaluation of personality scales. *Journal of Personality, 54*, 106–148.

Briggs-Myers, I., & Briggs, K. C. (1985). *Myers-Briggs Type Indicator (MBTI)*. Palo Alto, CA: Consulting Psychologists Press.

Brody, N. (1988). *Personality: In search of individuality*. San Diego, CA: Academic Press.

Brody, N. (1992). *Intelligence* (2nd ed.). New York: Academic Press.

Browne, M. W. (1984). The decomposition of multitrait-multimethod matrices. *British Journal of Mathematical and Statistical Psychology, 37*, 1–21.

Browne, M. W. (1990). *MUTMUM PC User's guide*. Unpublished manuscript, Department of Statistics, University of South Africa, Pretoria.

Butcher, J. N., Keller, L. S., & Bacon, S. F. (1985). Current developments and future directions in computerized personality assessment. *Journal of Consulting and Clinical Psychology, 53*, 803–815.

Bynner, J. M., & Romney, D. M. (1986). Intelligence, fact or artefact: Alternative structures for cognitive abilities. *British Journal of Educational Psychology, 56*, 12–23.

Byrne, B. M. (1988). Testing the factorial validity and invariance of a measuring instrument using LISREL confirmatory factor analyses: A reexamination and application. *Multiple Linear Regression Viewpoints, 16*, 33–80.

Byrne, B. M. (1989). *A primer of LISREL: Basic applications and programming for confirmatory factor analytic models*. New York: Springer-Verlag.

Byrne, B. M., & Goffin, R. D. (1993). Modeling MTMM data from additive and multiplicative covariance structures: An audit of construct validity research. *Multivariate Behavioral Research, 28*, 67–96.

Byrne, B. M., Shavelson, R. J., & Muthén, B. (1989). Testing for the equivalence of factor covariance and mean structures: The issue of partial measurement invariance. *Psychological Bulletin, 105*, 456–466.

Cantor, N., & Kihlstrom, J. F. (1987). *Personality and social intelligence*. Englewood Cliffs, NJ: Prentice-Hall.

Carroll, J. B. (1984). Raymond B. Cattell's contributions to the theory of cognitive abilities. *Multivariate Behavioral Research, 19*, 300–306.

Carroll, J. B. (1991). No demonstration that "*g*" is not unitary, but there is more to the story: Comment on Kranzler and Jensen. *Intelligence, 15*, 423–436.

Cattell, R. B. (1973). *Personality and mood by questionnaire*. San Francisco: Jossey-Bass.

Cattell, R. B. (1978). *The scientific use of factor analysis in behavioral and life sciences*. New York: Plenum.

Cattell, R. B. (1979). *Personality and learning theory. Vol. 1. The structure of personality in its environment*. New York: Springer.

Cattell, R. B. (1980). *Personality and learning theory. Vol. 2. A systems theory of maturation and learning*. New York: Springer.

Cattell, R. B. (1982a). The development of attribution theory into spectrad theory, using the general perceptual model. *Multivariate Behavioral Research, 17*, 169–192.

Cattell, R. B. (1982b). *The inheritance of personality and ability: Research methods and findings*. New York: Academic Press.

Cattell, R. B. (1982c). The psychometry of objective motivation measurement: A response to the critique of Cooper and Kline. *British Journal of Educational Psychology, 52*, 234–241.

Cattell, R. B. (1983). *Structured personality-learning theory: A wholistic multivariate research approach*. New York: Praeger.

Cattell, R. B. (1985). *Human motivation and the dynamic calculus*. New York: Praeger.

Cattell, R. B. (1987a). *Intelligence: Its structure, growth, and action*. Amsterdam: North-Holland.

Cattell, R. B. (1987b). *Psychotherapy by structured learning theory*. New York: Springer.

Cattell, R. B. (1992a). Human motivation objectively, experimentally analysed. *British Journal of Medical Psychology, 65*, 237–243.

Cattell, R. B. (1992b). Superseding the Motivational Distortion Scale. *Psychological Reports, 70*, 499–502.

Cattell, R. B., & Johnson, R. C. (1986). (Eds.), *Functional psychological testing: Principles and instruments*. New York: Brunner/Mazel.

Cattell, R. B., & Krug, S. E. (1986). The number of factors in the 16PF: A review of the evidence with special emphasis on methodological problems. *Educational and Psychological Measurement, 46*, 509–522.

Cattell, R. B., & Schuerger, J. M. (1978). *Personality theory in action: Handbook for the O-A (Objective-Analytic) Test Kit*. Champaign, IL: Institute for Personality and Ability Testing.

Ceci, S. J. (1990). *On intelligence . . . more or less*. Englewood Cliffs, NJ: Prentice Hall.

Child, D. (1990). *The essentials of factor analysis* (2nd ed.). London: Cassell.

Clark, L. A., & Livesley, W. J. (in press). Two approaches to identifying the dimensions of personality disorder: Convergence on the five-factor model. In P. T. Costa, Jr., & T. A. Widiger (Eds.), *Personality disorders and the five-factor model of personality*. Washington, DC: American Psychological Association.

Clark, L. A., McEwen, J. L., Collard, L. M., & Hickok, L. G. (1993). Symptoms and traits of personality disorder: Two new methods for their assessment. *Psychological Assessment, 5*, 81–91.

Clark, L. A., Vorhies, V., & McEwen, J. L. (in press). Personality disorder symptomatology from the five-factor perspective. In P. T. Costa, Jr., & T. A. Widiger (Eds.), *Personality disorders and the five-factor model of personality*. Washington, DC: American Psychological Association.

Cole, D. A., & Maxwell, S. E. (1985). Multitrait-multimethod comparisons across populations: A confirmatory factor analytic approach. *Multivariate Behavioral Research, 20*, 389–417.

Comrey, A. L. (1980). *Handbook of interpretation for the Comrey Personality Scale*. San Diego, CA: Educational and Industrial Testing Service.

Comrey, A. L., & Lee, H. B. (1992). *A first course in factor analysis* (rev. 2nd ed.). Hillsdale, NJ: Erlbaum.

Conley, J. J. (1984). Longitudinal consistency of adult personality: Self-reported psychological characteristics across 45 years. *Journal of Personality and Social Psychology, 47*, 1325–1334.

Connell, J. P. (1987). Structural equation modeling and the study of child development: A question of goodness of fit. *Child Development, 58*, 167–175.

Costa, P. T., & McCrae, R. R. (1992a). Four ways five factors are basic. *Personality and Individual Differences, 13*, 653–665.

Costa, P. T., & McCrae, R. R. (1992b). *The NEO Personality Inventory (Revised) manual*. Odessa, FL: Psychological Assessment Resources.

Costa, P. T., & McCrae, R. R. (1992c). Normal personality assessment in clinical practice: The NEO Personality Inventory. *Psychological Assessment, 4*, 5–13.

Crocker, L., & Algina, J. (1986). *Introduction to classical and modern test theory*. New York: Holt, Rinehart & Winston.

Cronbach, L. J. (1990). *Essentials of psychological testing* (5th ed.). New York: Harper & Row.

Cudeck, R., & Henly, S. J. (1991). Model selection in covariance structures analysis and the "problem" of sample size: A clarification. *Psychological Bulletin, 109*, 512–519.

Cuttance, P., & Ecob, R. (Eds.). (1987). *Structural modeling by example: Applications in educational, sociological, and behavioral research*. New York: Cambridge University Press.

Digman, R. M. (1990). Personality structure: Emergence of the five-factor model. *Annual Review of Psychology, 41*, 417–440.

Eaves, L. J., Eysenck, H. J., & Martin, N. G. (1989). *Genes, culture and personality*. London: Academic Press.

Elliott, C. D., Murray, D. J., & Pearson, L. S. (1983). *British Ability Scales* (2nd ed.). London: Nelson.

Eysenck, H. J. (1984). Cattell and the theory of personality. *Multivariate Behavioral Research, 19*, 323–336.

Eysenck, H. J. (1985a). *Decline and fall of the Freudian empire*. London: Viking.

Eysenck, H. J. (1985b). Review of the California Psychological Inventory. In J. V. Mitchell (Ed.), *Ninth mental measurements yearbook*. Lincoln, NE: Buros Institute of Mental Measurements.

Eysenck, H. J. (1990a). Biological dimensions of personality. In L. A. Pervin (Ed.), *Handbook of personality: Theory and research*. New York: Guilford.

Eysenck, H. J. (1990b). Genetic and environment contributions to individual differences: The three major dimensions of personality. *Journal of Personality, 98*, 245–261.

Eysenck, H. J. (1991). Dimensions of personality: 16, 5, 3? *Personality and Individual Differences, 12*, 773–790.

Eysenck, H. J. (1992). Four ways five factors are not basic. *Personality and Individual Differences, 13*, 667–673.

Eysenck, H. J., & Eysenck, M. W. (1985). *Personality and individual differences*. New York: Plenum.

Eysenck, M. W., & Eysenck, H. J. (1980). Mischel and the concept of personality. *British Journal of Psychology, 71*, 191–204.

Fernandez, E. (1990). Artifact in pain ratings, its implications for test-retest reliability, and correction by a new scaling procedure. *Journal of Psychopathology and Behavioral Assessment, 12*, 1–15.

Fernandez, E., Nygren, T. E., & Thorn, B. E. (1991). An open-transformed scale for correcting ceiling effects and enhancing retest reliability: The example of pain. *Perception and Psychophysics, 49*, 572–578.

Friedman, A., Webb, J., & Lewark, R. (1989). *Psychological testing with the MMPI*. London: Erlbaum.

Goff, M., & Ackerman, P. L. (1992). Personality-intelligence relations: Assessment of typical engagement. *Journal of Educational Psychology, 84*, 537–552.

Goldberg, L. R. (1992). The development of markers for the big-five factor structure. *Psychological Assessment, 4*, 26–42.

Goldstein, H. (1980). Dimensionality, bias, independence and measurement scale problems in latent trait test score models. *British Journal of Mathematical and Statistical Psychology, 33*, 234–246.

Gorsuch, R. L. (1983). *Factor analysis* (2nd ed.). Hillsdale, NJ: Erlbaum.

Gorsuch, R. L. (1990). Common factor analysis versus component analysis: Some well and little known facts. *Multivariate Behavioral Research, 25*, 33–39.

Gorsuch, R. L. (1991). *UniMult guide* (Version 1.1). Altadena, CA: UniMult.

Gough, H. G. (1987). *California Psychological Inventory (CPI)* (rev. ed.). Palo Alto, CA: Consulting Psychologists Press.

Gough, H. G. (1989). Review of the Objective-Analytic (O-A) Test Battery. In J. C. Conoley and J. J. Kramer (Eds.), *The tenth mental measurements yearbook*. Lincoln, NE: Buros Institute of Mental Measurements.

Grayson, D. A. (1986). Latent trait analysis of the Eysenck Personality Questionnaire. *Journal of Psychiatric Research, 20*, 217–235.

Gruijter, de D. N. M., & Kamp, van der L. J. T. (1990). Generalizability theory. In R. K. Hambleton & J. N. Zaal (Eds.), *Advances in educational and psychological testing: Theory and applications*. Boston: Kluwer.

Guilford, J. P. (1975). Factors and factors of personality. *Psychological Bulletin, 82*, 802–814.

Guilford, J. P. (1981). Higher-order structure-of-intellect abilities. *Multivariate Behavioral Research, 16*, 411–435.

Guilford, J. P. (1985). The structure-of-intellect model. In B. B. Wolman (Ed.), *Handbook of intelligence: Theories: measurements and applications*. New York: Wiley.

Guthrie, G. (1985). Review of the Clinical Analysis Questionnaire. In J. V. Mitchell, Jr. (Ed.), *Ninth mental measurements yearbook*. Lincoln, NE: Buros Institute of Mental Measurements.

Guttman, L. (1992). The irrelevance of factor analysis for the study of group differences. *Multivariate Behavioral Research, 27*, 175–204.

Hakstian, A. R., & Cattell, R. B. (1982). *The Comprehensive Ability Battery*. Champaign, IL: Institute for Personality and Ability Testing.

Hakstian, A. R., Rogers, W. T., & Cattell, R. B. (1982). The behavior of number-of-factors rules with simulated data. *Multivariate Behavioral Research, 17*, 193–219.

Hakstian, A. R., & Woolsey, L. K. (1985). Validity studies using the Comprehensive Ability Battery (CAB): IV. Predicting achievement at the university level. *Educational and Psychological Measurement, 45*, 329–341.

Hambleton, R. K., & Swaminathan, H. (1985). *Item response theory: Principles and applications*. Boston: Kluwer.

Hambleton, R. K., Swaminathan, H., & Rogers, H. J. (1991). *Fundamentals of item response theory*. Newbury Park, CA: Sage.

Hartmann, W. M. (1990). ProcCALIS: Analysis of covariance structures. In F. Faulbaum, R. Haux, & K. Jöckel (Eds.), *SoftStat '89: Fortschritte der Statistik—Software 2* (pp. 74–81). Stuttgart: Verlag.

Hayduk, L. A. (1987). *Structural equation modeling with LISREL: Essentials and advances*. Baltimore, MD: Johns Hopkins University Press.

Heck, van G. L. M. (1988). Modes and models in anxiety. *Anxiety Research, 1*, 199–214.

Helmes, E., & Reddon, J. R. (1993). A perspective on developments in assessing psychopathology: A critical review of the MMPI and MMPI-2. *Psychological Bulletin, 113*, 453–471.

Hessler, G. L. (1982). *Use and interpretation of the Woodcock-Johnson Psycho-Educational Battery*. Allen, TX: DLM Teaching Resources.

Hogan, R. (1986). *Manual for the Hogan Personality Inventory (HPI)*. Minneapolis MN: National Computer Systems.

Holden, R. R., Kroner, D. G., Fekken, G. C., & Popham, S. M. (1992). A model of personality test item response dissimulation. *Journal of Personality and Social Psychology, 63*, 272–279.

Holden, R. R., Reddon, J. R., Jackson, D. N., & Helmes, E. (1983). The construct heuristic applied to the measurement of psychopathology. *Multivariate Behavioral Research, 18*, 37–46.

Holland, J. L. (1985). *Making vocational choices: A theory of vocational personalities and work environments*. Englewood Cliffs, NJ: Prentice-Hall.

Horn, J. L. (1988). Thinking about human abilities. In J. R. Nesselroade & R. B. Cattell (Eds.), *Handbook of multivariate experimental psychology*. New York: Plenum.

Horn, J. L., & Stankov, L. (1980). Auditory and visual factors of intelligence. *Intelligence, 6*, 165–185.

Horn, J. L., & Stankov, L. (1982). Comments about a chameleon theory: Level I/Level II. *Journal of Educational Psychology, 74*, 874–878.

Howard, R. W. (1993). On what intelligence is. *British Journal of Psychology, 84*, 27–37.

Hunter, J. E., Schmidt, F. L., & Rauschenberger, J. M. (1984). Methodological, statistical, and ethical issues in the study of bias in psychological tests. In C. E. Reynolds & R. T. Brown (Eds.), *Perspectives on bias in mental testing* (pp. 41–99). New York: Plenum.

Hutchinson, T. P. (1991). *Controversies in item response theory*. Sydney: Rumsby Scientific.

Jensen, A. R. (1991). General mental ability: From psychometrics to biology. *Diagnostique, 16*, 134–144.

Jinks, J. L., & Fulker, J. W. (1970). Comparison of the biometrical, genetical, MAVA and classical approaches to the study of human behaviour. *Psychological Bulletin, 73*, 311–349.

John, O. P. (1990). The "big five" factor taxonomy: Dimensions of personality in the natural language and in questionnaires. In L. Pervin (Ed.), *Handbook of personality theory and research* (pp. 66–100). New York: Guilford.

John, O. P., Angleitner, A., & Ostendorf, F. (1988). The lexical approach to personality: A historical review of trait taxonomic research. *European Journal of Personality, 2*, 171–203.

John, O. P., Hampson, S. E., & Goldberg, L. R. (1991). The basic level in personality-trait hierarchies: Studies of trait use and accessibility in different contexts. *Journal of Personality and Social Psychology, 60*, 348–361.

Johnson, R. C. (1986). Personality assessment by observers in normal and psychiatric data. In R. B. Cattell & R. C. Johnson (Eds.), *Functional psychological testing: Principles and instruments*. New York: Brunner/Mazel.

Jöreskog, K. G., & Sörbom, D. (1988). *PRELIS: A program for multivariate data screening and data summarization*. Mooresville, IN: Scientific Software.

Jöreskog, K. G., & Sörbom, D. (1989). *LISREL 7: A guide to the program and applications* (2nd ed.). Chicago, SPSS.

Kameoka, V. A. (1986). The structure of the Clinical Analysis Questionnaire and depression symptomatology. *Multivariate Behavioral Research, 21*, 105–122.

Kaplan, D. (1990). Evaluating and modifying covariance structure models: A review and recommendation. *Multivariate Behavioral Research, 25*, 137–155.

Kaufman, A. S. (1990). *Assessing adolescent and adult intelligence*. Chicago: Allyn & Bacon.

Kaufman, A. S., & Kaufman, N. L. (1983). *Kaufman Assessment Battery for Children (K-ABC)*. Circle Pines, MN: American Guidance Service.

Kerlinger, F. N. (1986). *Foundations of behavioral research* (3rd ed.). New York: CBS.

Kline, P. (1980). The psychometric model. In A. J. Chapman & D. M. Jones (Eds.), *Models of man*. Leicester, England: British Psychological Society.

Kline, P. (1986). *A handbook of test construction: Introduction to psychometric design*. London: Methuen.

Kline, P. (1993a). *The handbook of psychological testing*. London: Routledge.

Kline, P. (1993b). *Personality: The psychometric view*. London: Routledge.

Kline, P., & Cooper, C. (1984a). A construct validation of the Objective-Analytic Test Battery (OATB). *Personality and Individual Differences, 5*, 323–337.

Kline, P., & Cooper, C. (1984b). The factor structure of the Comprehensive Ability Battery. *British Journal of Educational Psychology, 54*, 106–110.

Kranzler, J. H. & Jensen, A. R. (1991). The nature of psychometric "*g*": Unitary process of a number of independent processes? *Intelligence, 15*, 379–422.

Krug, S. E. (1980). *Clinical Analysis Questionnaire manual*. Champaign, IL: Institute for Personality and Ability Testing.

Krug, S. E., & Johns, E. F. (1986). A large scale cross-validation of second-order personality structure defined by the 16PF. *Psychological Reports, 59*, 683–693.

Livneh, H., & Livneh, C. (1989). The five-factor model of personality: Is evidence of its cross-measure validity premature? *Personality and Individual Differences, 10*, 75–80.

Loehlin, J. C. (1990). Component analysis versus common factor analysis: A case of disputed authorship. *Multivariate Behavioral Research, 25*, 29–31.

MacCallum, R. (1985, July). *Some problems in the process of model modification in covariance structure modeling*. Paper presented to the European Meeting of the Psychometric Society, Cambridge, England.

MacCallum, R. (1986). Specification searches in covariance structure modeling. *Psychological Bulletin, 100*, 107–120.

Marsh, H. W. (1989). Confirmatory factor analyses of multitrait-multimethod data: Many problems and a few solutions. *Applied Psychological Measurement, 13*, 335–361.

Marsh, H. W., & Bailey, M. (1991). Confirmatory factor analyses of multitrait-multimethod data: A comparison of alternative models. *Applied Psychological Measurement, 15*, 47–70.

Marsh, H. W., Balla, J. R., & McDonald, R. P. (1988). Goodness-of-fit indexes in confirmatory factor analysis: The effect of sample size. *Psychological Bulletin, 103*, 391–410.

Marshalek, B., Lohman, D. F., & Snow, R. E. (1983). The complexity continuum in the radex and hierarchical models of intelligence. *Intelligence, 7*, 107–127.

Martin, J. A. (1987). Structural equation modeling: A guide for the perplexed. *Child Development, 58*, 33–37.

Masson, J. M. (1990). *Final analysis: The making and unmaking of a psychoanalyst*. London: Fontana.

Mathews, G. (1989). The factor structure of the 16PF: Twelve primary and three secondary factors. *Personality and Individual Differences, 10*, 931–940.

McArdle, J. J. (1984). On the madness in his method: R. B. Cattell's contributions to structural equation modeling. *Multivariate Behavioral Research, 19*, 245–267.

McArdle, J. J. (1990). Principal versus principals of structural factor analyses. *Multivariate Behavioral Research, 25*, 81–87.

McCrae, R. R., & Costa, P. T. (1987). Validation of the five-factor model of personality across instruments and observers. *Journal of Personality and Social Psychology, 52*, 81–90.

McCrae, R. R., & Costa, P. T. (1989). The structure of interpersonal traits. Wiggins circumplex and the five-factor model. *Journal of Personality and Social Psychology, 56*, 586–595.

McDonald, R. P. (1985). *Factor analysis and related methods*. Hillsdale, NJ: Erlbaum.

McDonald, R. P., & Marsh, H. W. (1990). Choosing a multivariate model: Noncentrality and goodness-of-fit. *Psychological Bulletin, 107*, 247–255.

McKenzie, J. (1988). Three superfactors in the 16PF and their relation to Eysenck's P, E and N. *Personality and Individual Differences, 9*, 843–850.

Mershon, B., & Gorsuch, R. L. (1988). Number of factors in the personality sphere: Does increase in factors increase predictability of real-life criteria? *Journal of Personality and Social Psychology, 55*, 675–680.

Messick, S. (1992). Multiple intelligence or multilevel intelligence? Selective emphasis on distinctive properties of hierarchy: On Garner's "Frames of mind" and Sternberg's "Beyond IQ" in the context of theory and research on the structure of human abilities. *Psychological Inquiry, 3*, 365–384.

Miller, K. M. (1988). *The analysis of personality in research and assessment: In tribute to Raymond B. Cattell*. London: Independent Assessment and Research Centre.

Millsap, R. E. (1990). A cautionary note on the detection of method variance in multitrait-multimethod data. *Journal of Applied Psychology, 75*, 350–353.

Mischel, W. (1984). Convergencies and challenges in the search for consistency. *American Psychologist, 39*, 351–364.

Moos, R. (1985). *Perimenstrual symptoms: A manual and overview of research with the Menstrual Distress Questionnaire*. Palo Alto, CA: Department of Psychiatry and Behavioral Sciences, Stanford University.

Morey, L. C. (1991). *Personality Assessment Inventory: Professional manual*. Odessa, FL: Psychological Assessment Resources.

Mulaik, S. A. (1986). Factor analysis and psychometrika: Major developments. *Psychometrika, 51*, 23–33.

Mulaik, S. A. (1987). Toward a conception of causality applicable to experimentation and causal modeling. *Child Development, 58*, 18–32.

Mulaik, S. A. (1990). Blurring the distinctions between component analysis and common factor analysis. *Multivariate Behavioral Research, 25*, 53–59.

Mulaik, S. A., James, L. R., Alstine, van J., Bennett, N., Lind, S., & Stilwell, C. D. (1989). Evaluation of goodness-of-fit indices for structural equation models. *Psychological Bulletin, 105*, 430–445.

Muthén, B. O. (1988). *LISCOMP: Analysis of linear structural equations with comprehensive measurement model* (2nd ed.). Mooresville, IN: Scientific Software.

Nesselroade, J. R., & Cattell, R. B. (Eds.). (1988). *Handbook of multivariate experimental psychology* (rev. 2nd ed.). New York: Plenum.

Norman, W. T. (1963). Toward an adequate taxonomy of personality attributes: Replicated factor structure in peer nomination personality ratings. *Journal of Abnormal and Social Psychology, 66*, 574–583.

O'Toole, B. I., & Stankov, L. (1992). Ultimate validity of psychological tests. *Personality and Individual Differences, 13*, 699–716.

Poon, W. Y., & Lee, S. Y. (1987). Maximum likelihood estimation of multivariate polyserial and polychoric correlation coefficients. *Psychometrika, 52*, 409–430.

Powell, G. E. (1979). *Brain and personality*. Farnborough, England: Saxon House.

Prosser, R., Rasbash, J., & Goldstein, H. (1991). *ML3 software for three-level analysis: User's guide for version 2*. London: Institute of Education, University of London.

Romney, D. M., & Bynner, J. M. (1992). *The structure of personal characteristics*. Westport, CT: Praeger.

Roseboom, W. W. (1990). Whatever happened to broad perspective? *Multivariate Behavioral Research, 25*, 61–65.

Rudy, T. E., Turk, D. C., & Brody, M. C. (1992). Quantification of biomedical findings in chronic pain: Problems and solutions. In D. Turk & R. Melzack (Eds.), *Handbook of pain assessment*. New York: Guilford.

Russell, E. W., Neuringer, C., & Goldstein, G. (1970). *Assessment of brain damage: A neuropsychological key approach*. New York: Wiley-Interscience.

Schmidt, L. R. (1988). Objective personality tests: Some clinical applications. In K. M. Miller (Ed.), *The analysis of personality in research and assessment: In tribute to Raymond B. Cattell*. London: Independent Assessment and Research Centre.

Schmitt, M. J., & Steyer, R. (1993). A latent state-trait model (not only) for social desirability. *Personality and Individual Differences, 14*, 519–529.

Schmitt, N., & Stults, D. N. (1986). Methodology review: Analysis of multitrait-multimethod matrices. *Applied Psychological Measurement, 10*, 1–22.

Schönemann, P. H. (1990). Facts, fictions, and common sense about factors and components. *Multivariate Behavioral Research, 25*, 47–51.

Schuerger, J. M. (1986). Personality assessment by objective tests. In R. B. Cattell & R. C. Johnson (Eds.), *Functional psychological testing: Principles and instruments*. New York: Brunner/Mazel.

Schuerger, J. M. (1992). The Sixteen Personality Factor Questionnaire and its junior versions. *Journal of Counseling and Development, 71*, 231–244.

Schwartz, B., & Reisberg, D. (1992). *Learning and memory*. New York: Norton.

Shavelson, R., Webb, N. M., & Rowley, G. L. (1989). Generalizability theory. *American Psychologist, 44*, 922–932.

Snook, S. C., & Gorsuch, R. L. (1989). Principal component analysis versus common factor analysis: A Monte Carlo study. *Psychological Bulletin, 106*, 148–154.

Snow, R. E., Killonen, P. C., & Marshalek, B. (1984). The topography of ability and learning correlations. In R. J. Sternberg (Ed.), *Advances in the psychology of human intelligence* (Vol. 2). Hillsdale, NJ: Erlbaum.

Soldz, S., Budman, S., Demby, A., & Merry, J. (1993). Representation of personality disorders in circumplex and five-factor space: Explorations with a clinical sample. *Psychological Assessment, 5*, 41–52.

Spielberger, C. D., Gorsuch, R. L., Lushene, R. E., Vagg, P. R., & Jacobs, G. A. (1986). *Manual for the State-Trait Anxiety Inventory-Form Y*. Palo Alto, CA: Consulting Psychologists Press.

Stankov, L. (1978). Fluid and crystallized intelligence and broad perceptual factors among 11 to 12 year olds. *Journal of Educational Psychology, 70*, 324–334.

Stankov, L. (1980). Psychometric factors as cognitive tasks: A note on Carroll's "new structure of intellect." *Intelligence, 4*, 65–71.

Stankov, L. (1983). Attention and intelligence. *Journal of Educational Psychology, 75*, 471–490.

Stankov, L. (1986). Kvashchev's experiment: Can we boost intelligence? *Intelligence, 10*, 209–230.

Stankov, L. (1987). Level I/II: A theory ready to be archived. In S. Modgil & C. Modgil (Eds.), *Arthur Jensen: Consensus and controversy*. London: Falmers.

Stankov, L. (1989). Attentional resources and intelligence: A disappearing link. *Personality and Individual Differences, 10*, 957–968.

Stankov, L., & Chen, K. (1988). Can we boost fluid and crystallized intelligence? A structural modeling approach. *Australian Journal of Psychology, 40*, 363–376.

Stankov, L., & Crawford, J. D. (1983). Ingredients of complexity in fluid intelligence. *Learning and Individual Differences, 5*, 73–111.

Stankov, L., & Cregan, A. (1993). Quantitative and qualitative properties of an intelligence test: Series Completion. *Learning and Individual Differences, 5*, 137–169.

Stankov, L., & Horn, J. L. (1980). Human abilities revealed through auditory tests. *Journal of Educational Psychology, 72*, 19–42.

Stankov, L., Horn, J. L., & Roy, T. (1980). On the relationship between Gf/Gc theory and Jensen's Level I/Level II theory. *Journal of Educational Psychology, 72*, 796–809.

Stankov, L., & Myors, B. (1990). The relationship between working memory and intelligence: Regression and COSAN analyses. *Personality and Individual Differences, 11*, 1059–1068.

Steiger, J. H. (1989). *EzPATH: A supplementary module for SYSTAT and SYGRAPH*. Evanston, IL: SYSTAT.

Tanaka, J. S. (1987). "How big is big enough?": Sample size and goodness of fit in structural equation models with latent variables. *Child Development, 58*, 134–146.

Thorndike, R. L. (1982). *Applied psychometrics*. Boston: Houghton Mifflin.

Thorndike, R. L., Hagen, E. P., & Sattler, J. M. (1986). *Technical manual: Stanford-Binet Intelligence Scale* (4th ed.). Chicago: Riverside.

Tupes, E. C., & Christal, R. E. (1961). Recurrent personality factors based on trait ratings. *USAF ASD Technical Report*, No. 61-97.

Velicer, W. F., & Jackson, D. N. (1990a). Component analysis versus common factor analysis: Some issues in selecting an appropriate procedure. *Multivariate Behavioral Research, 25*, 1–28.

Velicer, W. F., & Jackson, D. N. (1990b). Component analysis versus common factor analysis: Some further observations. *Multivariate Behavioral Research, 25*, 97–114.

Wainer, H., Dorans, N. J., Flauger, R., Green, B. F., Mislevy, R. J., Steinberg, L., & Thissen, D. (1990). *Computerized adaptive testing: A primer*. Hillsdale, NJ: Erlbaum.

Webb, N. M., Shavelson, R. J., & Maddahian, E. (1983). Multivariate generalizability theory. In L. J. Fyans, Jr. (Ed.), *New directions for testing and measurement: Generalizability theory* (pp. 67–82). San Francisco: Jossey-Bass.

Wechsler, D. (1991). *Wechsler Intelligence Scale for Children-III*. San Antonio, TX: Psychological Corporation.

Weiss, D. J., & Yoes, M. E. (1990). Item response theory. In R. K. Hambleton & J. N. Zaal (Eds.), *Advances in educational and psychological testing: Theory and applications*. Boston: Kluwer.

Widaman, K. F. (1990). Bias in pattern loadings represented by common factor analysis and component analysis. *Multivariate Behavioral Research, 25*, 89–95.

Wiggins, J. S., & Pincus, A. L. (1992). Personality: Structure and assessment. *Annual Review of Psychology, 43*, 473–504.

Wiggins, J. S., & Trapnell, P. D. (in press). Personality structure: The return of the big five. In S. R. Briggs, R. Hogan, & W. H. Jones (Eds.), *Handbook of personality psychology*. Orlando, FL: Academic Press.

Williams, L. J., Cote, J. A., & Buckley, M. R. (1989). Lack of method variance in self-reported affect and perceptions at work: Reality or artifact? *Journal of Applied Psychology, 74*, 462–468.

Winer, B. J., Brown, D. R., & Michels, K. M. (1991). *Statistical principles in experimental design* (rev. 3rd ed.). New York: McGraw-Hill.

Woliver, R. E., & Saeks, S. D. (1986). Intelligence and primary aptitudes: Test design and tests available. In R. B. Cattell & R. C. Johnson (Eds.), *Functional psychological testing: Principles and instruments*. New York: Brunner/Mazel.

Woodcock, R. W., & Mather, N. (1989). *Woodcock-Johnson Tests of Cognitive Ability*. Allen, TX: DLM Teaching Resources.

Zuckerman, M. (1991). *Psychobiology of personality*. New York: Cambridge University Press.

Zuckerman, M. (1992). What is a basic factor and which factors are basic? Turtles all the way down. *Personality and Individual Differences, 6*, 675–681.

Zuckerman, M., Kuhlman, D. M., & Camac, C. (1988). What lies beyond E and N? Factor analyses of scales believed to measure basic dimensions of personality. *Journal of Personality and Social Psychology, 54*, 96–107.

Zuckerman, M., Kuhlman, D. M., Thornquist, M., & Kiers, H. (1991). Five (or three) robust questionnaire scale factors of personality without culture. *Personality and Individual Differences, 12*, 929–941.

21

Current and Recurring Issues in the Assessment of Intelligence and Personality

David F. Lohman and Thomas Rocklin

In this chapter we discuss current trends in the assessment of intelligence and personality that we believe have implications for the future of these disciplines. The present, however, is always illuminated by the past; indeed, sometimes it is comprehensible only when seen in the context of antecedent events. Therefore, when possible, we identify some of the threads that tie current controversies to previous debates. Although we believe that the issues we have identified will help shape future developments, we refrain for the most part from specific speculations about the future of intelligence and personality assessment. Our reading of others' past predictions about the future of psychological theory and research is that those that are more than simple extrapolations usually look at best charmingly naive in retrospect.

We present this chapter in three major sections: one focusing primarily on the assessment of intelligence, one focusing primarily on the assessment of personality, and one addressing issues at the intersections of intelligence and personality. The juxtaposition of our discussions of assessment in intelligence and personality illustrates points of both contact and difference between the two domains, which we discuss in a final section. The structures of this chapter reflect our personal, no doubt somewhat idiosyncratic, views of what is important to say about each domain. As it turns out, we find ourselves with a little to say about a lot in the intelligence domain and a lot to say about a little in the personality domain.

CURRENT ISSUES IN THE ASSESSMENT OF INTELLIGENCE

Historical summaries are exercises in story telling (Bruner, 1990). Like all stories, the story of the construct intelligence and of the development of tests to measure it can be told differently by selecting, emphasizing, and juxtaposing events in ways that give new meaning to the whole. Indeed, if Goodman (1984) is correct, there may be as many worlds as there are ways to describe them. Alternative worldviews, however, are not equally defensible. Nor are they equally instructive for the tasks of understanding the present and predicting future trends, because different perspectives on the past entail different interpretations of current events and shape different expectations for the future. For example, some of the characters who

David F. Lohman and Thomas Rocklin • Psychological and Quantitative Foundations, University of Iowa, Iowa City, Iowa 52242-1529.

International Handbook of Personality and Intelligence, edited by Donald H. Saklofske and Moshe Zeidner. Plenum Press, New York, 1995.

would be main players in any story of the development and use of intelligence tests often would not even be mentioned in a discussion of the search for a viable theory of intelligence. More importantly, the former tale would be told differently by one who views mental tests as instruments of cultural oppression than by one who sees them as instruments of social change (see Cronbach, 1975). Similarly, the story of theorizing in the United States about intelligence follows a different plot from the parallel story in the United Kingdom, and the joint Anglo-American tale differs even more from the continental European tale (particularly one that would be told from Germany or Russia).

Indeed, the story of intelligence reads more like a convoluted Russian novel than a tidy American short story. There are general themes, to be sure, but also divers subplots that crop up—some unexpectedly, others at regular intervals. Sometimes a new cast of characters, in mute testimony to Santayana's epigram for those unable to remember the past, unwittingly repeat controversies played out earlier. Others play a variation on this theme and foist old constructs with new names on a generation of psychologists lost in the present. But even when the old reappears, the context has changed, and so the result is never exactly the same.

In this necessarily brief account, we can do no more than point to what we consider to be some of the more interesting paths through this large and variegated forest; other, equally instructive paths could and should be followed. We begin with a thumbnail sketch of the controversy between intelligence as a unitary trait and intelligence as a collection of separate traits. This is a struggle not only of theory and method but also of value: particularly, what criteria to use to arbiter among competing theoretical positions. Should psychological meaningfulness prevail, or should parsimony? Or should it be utility? Test users opted for utility, and in America at least, psychological meaningfulness prevailed over parsimony in the theoretical debate. This, then, is the first major plot. It began with Thorndike, found clearest expression in Thurstone, and culminated in Guilford. The comprehensiveness of Guilford's model, however, was also its most glaring weakness. The next phase in our story describes the emergence of the criterion of parsimony and the subsequent resurgence of "*g*" in the guise of a hierarchical model of abilities. This phase ends—predictably, it would seem—with attempts by Horn (1985), Gardner (1983), and others to reassert the criterion of psychological meaningfulness.

The second plot is the tale of two intelligences—fluid and crystallized—and of how Cattell's (1943) theory moved from a little-noticed hypothesis about adult intellectual development and decline to a central feature of several modern theories of intelligence and the guiding framework for many intelligence tests. The third plot is the search for physiological correlates of intelligence and, in some quarters, of a physiological explanation for intelligence. The siren call of reductionism has seduced others as well, notably cognitive psychologists who sought to understand intelligence in information-processing terms. We discuss the work of cognitive psychologists in some detail because the limitations we note have implications for research on personality, which is the topic of the second section of this chapter. Efforts to reconceptualize intelligence to include affect and conation are deferred to the final section of the chapter, as are speculations about the overlap between the two domains of personality and intelligence.

Meaningfulness, Parsimony, or Utility

From g *to Multiple Abilities*

Early in this century, tests of general intelligence gained ready acceptance in schools and industry (Tyack, 1974) even though the meaning of the construct general intelligence was as hotly debated then as it is today. By the 1930s, though, success of Terman's revision of the Binet scale and of the group-administered tests developed during and after World War I overshadowed disagreement about what intelligence might be. This was the heyday for intelligence testing and for those whose fledgling tests gained a foothold in the burgeoning test market. The dissenting position, however, championed early by Thorndike (see Thorndike, Lay, & Dean, 1909) and Kelley (1928) in the United States and by Thomson (1916) in the United Kingdom, gained a new respectability with the introduction of Thurstone's (1935) methods of factor extraction and rotation. Thurstone, using psychological meaningfulness as a criterion, showed how arbitrary factor axes extracted by his centroid method could be rotated to define a small set of correlated "primary" ability factors, thereby dispensing with *g*. There followed an explosion of factorial studies by Thurstone (1938, 1944, 1949), his students (Botzum, 1951; Carroll, 1941;

Pemberton, 1952), and others, notably Guilford and his coworkers in the Army–Air Force (AAF) Aviation Psychology program (Guilford & Lacey, 1947), decomposing primary abilities into still narrower factors or identifying other factors not previously known.

But it became increasingly difficult to comprehend the whole. Wolfe (1940) attempted an early summary. French (1951) followed with an even more comprehensive review, in which he noted how difficult it was to determine whether factors with different labels were indeed different or whether some with the same labels represented different ability dimensions. He proposed that investigators include common reference or marker tests in their studies, a procedure already followed by Thurstone and the AAF workers in their respective studies. Tests selected as markers showed high loadings on one rotated factor; typically these were homogeneous, speeded tests. Thus Thurstone's criterion of simple structure and the use of marker tests lead to a gradual shift in the type of tests included in factorial investigations: The heterogeneous, complex tasks of Binet and Spearman were replaced by the homogeneous, simple tasks of Thurstone and Guilford. The fractionalization of abilities that occurred during this period would not have been possible without this change in the universe of tasks used to define intelligence.

By the mid-1950s the continued proliferation of factors was making it difficult to summarize existing work or to know where to look for new ability dimensions. Guilford (1956), reviving an earlier suggestion of Thorndike, Bregman, Cobb, and Woodyard (1926), posited a three-facet scheme for classifying existing factors and directing the search for new ones. Although many accepted Guilford's Structure of Intellect (SI) model, a few were openly skeptical. Spearman's (1927) claim that the ability space could be spanned by *g* and four group factors was not much more parsimonious than Thurstone's (1938) claim that seven factors would do the job if psychological meaningfulness were given priority. Indeed, Thurstone explicitly invoked parsimony when he argued that the number of common factors should be relatively small even though the number of ability tests was large, even unbounded (see Guttman, 1958). With the prospect of Guilford's 120 independent abilities, however, hierarchical and multiple-ability theories were not equally parsimonious. McNemar (1964), in a critical review, dubbed the SI model "scatterbrained" and advocated a return to *g* via the hierarchical model of Vernon (1950) and other British theorists. Indeed, Humphreys (1962) had earlier shown how a facet model such as Guilford's could be made conformable with a hierarchical model by averaging over rows and columns to define higher-order abilities, a solution Guilford ignored at the time but accepted 20 years later (Guilford, 1985).

Resurgence of g

Thus the construct of general intelligence was at first embraced by many American psychologists, then cast aside as Thurstone's methods of multiple factor analysis won favor, then rediscovered again in the guise of a hierarchical model of abilities, and most recently challenged once again by those who would extend the domain of intelligence in old and new ways. General and special abilities have thus alternately dominated the field, one ascending while the other declined, one in favor while the other challenged. The loyal opposition has always been close at hand.

Reasons for the recurring rise and fall of different theories of intelligence are many. Those who arrived at different conclusions often started with more or less variegated samples of subjects and tests, used different methods of factor analysis, adhered to different social and political philosophies, or held different personal theories about the nature of human abilities (Fancher, 1985). On this view, then, as long as there is controversy over method or differences in the social, political, and personal philosophies of individuals, there will be controversy about the nature of human abilities. The expectation that one theory will triumph is seen as a holdover from turn-of-the-century logical positivism. Indeed, when competing views alternately gain and lose favor in a discipline, changes that on the short view seem like advances may on the long view look more like traveling in circles. One need not read too much of the history of differential psychology to see much that is old in the new, and so such pessimism is not entirely unfounded. For example, Carroll (1989), after surveying the extant literature, wondered why recent factorial studies of abilities rarely even approached the sophistication and comprehensiveness that Thurstone achieved in the 1930s, or that Thorndike had approximated even earlier.

When rival views persist, it may also signal that each has merit, but important limitations as well (see Hunt, 1986). A hierarchical model that posited both broad and narrow abilities thus seemed to preserve the best of both worlds while uniting them in a common framework. In reality, however, the hierarchical model has enhanced the status of *g* and diminished the status of narrower ability factors. This may or may not be a good thing. Certainly there is less tendency to attribute effects to special ability constructs that could more parsimoniously be attributed to general ability. Parsimony, however, is only one of several criteria that may be used to arbiter such decisions; psychological meaningfulness is perhaps equally important, but has been given less weight of late. Indeed, one could argue that psychological clarity declines as factor breadth increases. In other words, the broadest individual-difference dimension—although practically the most useful—is also psychologically the most obscure. There has never been the sort of handwringing over the meaning of factors such as verbal fluency or spatial ability that routinely attends discussion of *g*.

It is ironic that many latter-day advocates of Vernon's (1950) hierarchical model seem unaware that he never claimed psychological validity for the model or for the factors it specified:

> I do not think it is correct to say that I regard, or have ever regarded, hierarchy as a psychological model. It is . . . simply . . . a convenient way for classifying test performances. . . . *Qua* psychological model, I think it is open to a lot of difficulty because successive group factors do not have any very obvious psychological meaning. Thus, my verbal-educational and spatial-mechanical factors do not represent mental abilities; they are the residual common variance left when one has taken out . . . the *g* factor. Similarly, the minor factors are residuals of residuals. (Vernon, 1973b, p. 294)

Interestingly, Vernon claims that "the same sort of difficulty would arise if we started from oblique primary factors and calculated . . . higher-order factors from correlations between the primaries" (p. 294); however, "Burt's hierarchy is different in that . . . it does owe a good deal to neurological and psychological theory. . . . But then his model is not a straight representation of the correlations of a battery of tests." (p. 294) Thus the theoretical parsimony and practical utility of Vernon's hierarchical model were purchased at the price of psychological meaningfulness.

But there were also practical reasons why the theories of Thurstone and Guilford fell into disfavor. Much to the dismay of defenders and publishers of multiple aptitude test batteries, it was discovered that predictions of course grades from one or more special ability scores was usually no better than predictions from *g* (McNemar, 1964). Even more discouraging was the finding that tests of general abilities were also more likely to interact with instructional manipulations (Cronbach & Snow, 1977). In personnel psychology, Schmidt and Hunter (1977) also touted the virtues of general ability and argued that the importance of special abilities for the prediction of job performance had been grossly overstated by a common failure to attend to sampling variability of small-sample correlations.

There are, of course, dissenters. Horn (1985) argues that "what is called intelligence is a mixture of quite different things—different attributes having different genetical and environmental determinants and different developmental courses over the life span" (p. 268). He argues that, like facial beauty, intelligence is composed of distinctive components; evidence for heritability of the whole does not confer ontological status. In a similar vein, Cronbach (1977) argues that *intelligence*, like *efficiency*, is a word that describes the system. One cannot locate the efficiency of a factory in one of its many departments, because efficiency is not a thing but rather one of many indices that describe the functioning of the whole. Neither Horn nor Cronbach argues that the statistical dimension commonly called *g* lacks utility. Rather, they claim that practical utility does not imbue psychological meaningfulness. These and other critics claim that Thorndike, Thomson, and their followers were more nearly right than were Spearman and his followers. Some would even expand the domain of intelligence tasks to include not only social intelligence, which Thorndike (1920) and Guilford (1956, 1985) recognized, but also to include musical and bodily-kinesthetic abilities (Gardner, 1983). Thus the ongoing battle between advocates of *g* and of multiple abilities is probably the major theme in the story of intelligence. A more recent theme is the tale of two intelligences, which we examine below.

Fluid and Crystallized Abilities

In 1943, Cattell first outlined the theory of fluid and crystallized intelligences. The basic idea was that the construct of intelligence (*g*) was really an amalgam of two separate, albeit highly correlated abilities: fluid intelligence (Gf) and crystallized intelligence (Gc). Although interpretation of these constructs changed importantly between initial proposal of the theory and later tests of it (see Lohman, 1989), Gf came to be interpreted as that aspect of intelligence most closely tied to physiological processes. Gc, in contrast, was thought to reflect the cumulative effect of education and experience, or the result of investing fluid intelligence in particular experiences. It was then a short step to the inference that Gf represented the true intelligence of the individual, whereas Gc represented, at best, wisdom, or more commonly, general verbal knowledge and skills acquired through formal schooling and other tutelage.

The theory received little attention when initially proposed, in part because of Cattell's failure to elaborate and promote it, but also because of the dominance of Thurstone's (1938) and later Guilford's (1956) theories of multiple abilities. In the 1960s, however, Cattell and others (notably Horn) conducted a series of studies that tested the early theory and elaborated it considerably. In keeping with Cattell's original theme, however, the theory was most commonly discussed in the context of the growth and decline of intellectual competence during the adult years.

By the late 1970s the theory had attracted a wider audience. Continued elaboration of the theory by Horn (1985) suggested not 2, but as many as 10 higher-order factors. Other theorists, notably Snow (1981), sought to describe the differences between Gf and Gc in information-processing terms. Sternberg (1985) later incorporated the distinction into his triarchic theory of intelligence.

Testing was not far behind. 1983 saw the introduction of the Kaufman Assessment Battery for Children (K-ABC; Kaufman & Kaufman, 1983). Although primarily advanced as the first intelligence test based on the Das-Luria theory of simultaneous and successive processing, the authors also claimed that the Mental Processing scale (simultaneous plus sequential) measured fluid ability, whereas the Achievement scale measured crystallized ability. In 1986, the Stanford-Binet, which had steadily lost ground to its competitors, was completely revised along the lines of Gf-Gc theory (see Thorndike, Hagen, & Sattler, 1986). Other test publishers, particularly those of the K-ABC and Weschler scales, began to claim conformity with Gf-Gc theory as well. However, the most ambitious attempt to develop a test along the lines of the Horn-Cattell version of the theory came with the revision of the Woodcock-Johnson instrument (Woodcock & Johnson, 1989). This battery contains tests that estimate seven group factors: fluid reasoning (Gf), comprehension-knowledge (Gc), visual processing (Gv), auditory processing (Ga), processing speed (Gs), short-term memory (Gsm), and long-term retrieval (Glm). Scores on one or more tests that estimate each ability can be compared to each other or to scores on a companion achievement battery.

Thus the constructs of fluid and crystallized intelligence have gained considerable popularity in recent years, no doubt in part because they have been interpreted differently by different theorists. Some interpret them as end points on a continuum of cultural loading such as that described by Anastasi (1937), Cronbach (1970), and many others, with Gc tests being more and Gf tests less culturally loaded. This seems closest to Horn's (1985) interpretation that Gc reflects "acculturation learning," whereas Gf reflects "casual learning" and "independent thinking" (pp. 289–290). Others, in keeping with Cattell's (1963) investment theory of aptitude, confer a primary status on Gf. These theorists tend to speak of Gf as the real intelligence, a conclusion supported in part by Gustafsson's (1984) claim that Gf is equal to *g* in a hierarchical model. Critics point out that contrary to expectations of this model, tests of Gf do not routinely show higher heritabilities than tests of Gc. Further, educational interventions (Stankov, 1986) and cohort effects (Flynn, 1987) are typically larger for tests of fluid than for tests of crystallized ability. Indeed, some see fluid abilities as among the most important products of education and experience (Lohman, 1993; Snow & Yalow, 1982). In this view, the idea that Gf is the true or physiological intelligence is nothing more than the long-discredited theory of innate intelligence dressed up in a modern guise. Finally, some see the fluid-crystallized distinction primarily in terms of novel versus familiar problem solving, an idea originally proposed by Stern (1914), discussed at some length by Thorndike et al. (1926), most commonly embedded in discussions of aptitude-achievement discrepancies (Green, 1974; Snow, 1980; Thorndike, 1963), and expressed in information-processing terms by Snow (1981):

> [Crystallized ability] may represent prior assemblies of performance processes retrieved as a system and applied anew in instructional or other . . . situations not unlike those experienced in the past, while [fluid ability] may represent new assemblies of performance processes needed for more extreme adaptations to novel situations. The distinction [then] is between *long term* assembly for transfer to *familiar* new situations vs. *short term* assembly for transfer to *unfamiliar* situations. Both functions develop through exercise. (p. 360; italics in original)

Although not explicitly derived from this theory, attempts to develop curriculum-based assessments can be informed by this view of intelligence. Barnett and Macmann (1992) argue that those who would use tests in professional contexts must answer questions about not only construct validity (i.e., "What can be said with confidence?") but also consequential validity (i.e., "What can be said that might be helpful?") On the second point, they argue that IQ scores have little instructional utility. But what form should instructionally useful tests assume? Lohman (1993) argues that those who would tie such tests firmly to the curriculum would estimate only a part of crystallized intelligence and an even smaller part of fluid intelligence. On this view, then, what are needed are instructionally useful measures of fluid abilities—that is, curriculum-based tests that estimate how well students can transfer their knowledge and skills to novel and open-ended problems.

It is unlikely, however, that this view will ever completely displace intelligence tests modeled after the Binet and its progeny. Most lay persons and many professionals believe that a good intelligence test measures—or ought to measure—the innate potential or capacity of the learner. Such beliefs are reborn with each generation and are difficult to change without inducing an even more naive environmentalism. Nonetheless, continued legal challenges to intelligence testing may force changes in beliefs that are impervious to rational argument. The concepts of fluidization and crystallization of abilities (Snow, 1981) provide a useful way to envision these changes. Thus the tale of fluid and crystallized abilities has many implications: some fully realized, some yet to come. The search for physiological correlates of intelligence is even more open-ended.

Physiological Mechanisms

Advances in neuropsychology have been linked to improved techniques for measuring brain activity, especially for locating regions of the brain that show changes in activation across conditions. Inevitably, each new technique for measuring brain activity has been applied to the task of understanding individual differences in intelligence or personality or both (see, e.g., Matarazzo, 1992). Sometimes the results conform nicely to existing theory, such as when Haier et al. (1992) found that changes in glucose metabolic rate correlated with the amount of improvement subjects showed on a computer game: Of the 8 subjects studied, those who showed most improvement on the computer game showed the greatest reduction in glucose metabolic rate. Such findings conform well with theories of skill acquisition (Anderson, 1983; Shiffrin & Sneider, 1977), although they do not explain how automatization of skills occurs. Nevertheless, most would view such findings as interesting corroboration of psychological theory. Similar examples (e.g., Bullock & Gilliland, 1993) can be cited in the personality literature.

Some have advanced more forceful claims. Harking back to Galton (1869), they have sought to show the physiological basis of individual differences in intelligence. Though few would deny that observed differences in intellectual performance must eventually be grounded in physiological processes, the hope that intelligence or personality can be explained at the physiological level is, as Thorndike et al. (1926) concluded, a measurement pipe dream. Why? Because physiological measures must *always* be validated against behavioral criteria. No one would assess individuals' intelligence or personality using one or more physiological measures that had not shown high correlations with corresponding existing measures of intelligence or personality, or with the criteria such tests predict, no matter how theoretically well-grounded the physiological measures might be. Those who have most assiduously sought physiological correlates of intelligence, in particular, often have another agenda. For example, one goal is to find new measures that show high correlations with the old, but that cannot be criticized for "reflecting only differences in cognitive contents and skills that persons have chanced to learn in school or acquire in a cultured home" (Jensen, 1980, p. 704). More concretely, the goal is to find a culture-free, perhaps even experience-free measure of intelligence. Those who view *intelligence* as a term inextricably bound to value and culture see this as a modern Holy Grail.

Reductionism has always held allure for scientists in all disciplines, but with equal persistence has been challenged by philosophers, such as Dewey (1896) in his early critique of the claim that the reflex arc (or stimulus-response bond) could explain all of human behavior. Today, however, it is not only philosophers who challenge reductionism but cognitive scientists as well. For example, the neurologist Sperry (1993) put it this way:

> The cognitive revolution represents a diametric turn around in the centuries-old treatment of mind and consciousness in science. The contents of conscious experience, with their subjective qualities, long banned as being mere acausal epiphenomena or as just identical to brain activity or otherwise in conflict with the laws of the conversation of energy, have now made a dramatic comeback. Reconceived in the new outlook, subjective mental states become functionally interactive and essential for a full explanation of conscious behavior. Tradi-

tional micro determinist reasoning that brain function can be fully accounted for in neurocellular-physiochemical terms is refuted. (p. 879)

Unfortunately, correlations between physiological indices and IQ scores are often significant and sometimes substantial—especially when samples are small and vary widely in ability, and when the correlations are corrected and massaged in various ways. Reports of such newfound relations usually spread like rumors of gold among impoverished miners. Larger samples, tighter controls, and less massaged correlations, however, inevitably show smaller relationships than initially envisioned. Indeed, the best predictor of correlation in such studies is year of publication: Initial reports of a strikingly high correlation are followed by a succession of ever-lower correlations, which usually stabilize in the $r = .2$ to $r = .4$ range. By then, though, a new candidate has entered the field, usually in the form of a preliminary report from a physiological lab on a handful of subjects, and the cycle begins anew.

Although we reject the view that either intelligence or personality will someday be explicable in purely physiological terms, we see a continued role for investigation of the neurological and even biochemical bases of cognitive functioning. In part this research will be fueled by continued advances in brain imaging techniques. Probably the most useful type of studies will be those that go beyond attempts to locate cognitive functions and instead describe the time course of their action. Even more useful would be studies that show qualitative differences in patterns of brain activity over time among individuals who differ in an ability, personality, or style.

Cognitive Psychology and Testing

New methods for measuring brain activity were but one product of a burgeoning cognitive science. In psychology, the rapid rise of the information-processing paradigm gave new meaning to the perennial call to explain "the process . . . by which a given organism achieves an intellectual response" (McNemar, 1964, p. 881). Cognitive processes were modeled as information processes (Lohman & Ippel, 1993). Ability constructs were investigated by searching for differences in either information encoding, transformation, or storage used by individuals identified as exhibiting high or low levels of some ability (Hunt, Frost, & Lunneborg, 1973), or in the manner in which such individuals solve items on tests taken as markers for particular ability constructs (Sternberg, 1977). The former came to be known as the *cognitive correlates* and the latter as the *cognitive components* approach (Pellegrino & Glaser, 1979). Several summaries of this research are available (e.g., Carroll, 1980; Lohman, 1989; Snow & Lohman, 1989; Sternberg, 1985), which may be consulted for a sampling of empirical findings. Here we discuss four general themes that, in retrospect, have characterized this effort: a focus on latencies, on tasks, on components, and finally on theory-based tests.

Latencies

One of the by-products of information-processing psychology was a renewed interest in response latencies, especially in using them to infer the presence and mode operation of different mental processes. Indeed, the association between information-processing and "reaction time" was so strong that some assumed an information-processing analysis of intelligence meant the study of mental quickness. We now know, however, that *individual differences* in response latencies on tasks overlap only in part with *individual differences* in error rates on those tasks, and that errors tend to show higher correlations with broad ability factors, whereas latencies tend to show higher correlations with narrower ability factors. Therefore information-processing analyses of ability constructs must not assume that speed is the only or even the most important aspect of responding. Nevertheless, a general speed dimension can be identified that shows moderate correlation with general fluid intelligence. A general working memory factor based on error scores has shown such high correlations with general fluid intelligence, though, that Kyllonen and Christal (1990) claimed that reasoning ability was little more than working memory capacity. Thus errors and latencies are not interchangeable aspects of performance. Methodological problems plague attempts to separate these two measures, however, making generalizations difficult (Lohman, 1989).

Tasks

Information-processing psychology has sometimes been criticized for its myopic concern with particular tasks. Attempts to understand abilities in information-processing terms rather naturally focused on how subjects solved tasks taken from the laboratory or adapted from the familiar tests. The result was refreshing, especially for those who had viewed individual differences only from afar through the telescope of factor analysis. Tests that appeared simple often evoked a broad range of complex information processing: For example, facile interpretations of spatial tests that assumed all subjects attempted problems in the same way or even that they used a strategy roughly compatible with their "spatial" label came to be questioned. Most of this task-based research enhanced understanding of such intermediate-level constructs as verbal ability (e.g., Hunt, Lunneborg, & Lewis, 1975), spatial ability (e.g., Pellegrino & Kail, 1982), and reasoning ability (e.g., Sternberg, 1982). What began with parades down Main Street, however, eventually petered out in a hundred side streets. Once again, some began to question whether experimental psychology and differential psychology might be fundamentally incompatible. Most researchers, after a brief flurry of interest, quietly moved on to other topics.

Components

A large part of the difficulty in relating the two domains stems from the widespread failure to understand that constructs are often defined differently in experimental and differential psychology. Consider, for example, the most important (or at least the most studied) construct in each domain: learning in experimental psychology, and intelligence in differential psychology. Learning is defined by changes over trials (or columns in a basic person × item data matrix). Intelligence is defined by variation between persons (or rows in that same matrix). In other words, constructs in experimental and differential psychology (and, analogously, in social and personality psychology) are often defined by partitioning the data matrix in different ways. Failure to appreciate the statistical independence of row and column deviation scores has led to much confusion in attempts to relate these two domains, from Woodrow's (1946) failure to find much relationship between learning on laboratory tasks and intelligence to the efforts of Gulliksen and his students (e.g., Allison, 1960; Stake, 1961) to relate learning rate measures to a Thurstonian model of abilities, as well as the more recent efforts of Sternberg (1977) and Hunt, Frost, and Lunneborg (1973) to correlate scores for component mental processes and ability constructs.

Like earlier learning scores, measures of component processes are defined by subtracting one score from another. Gain scores have an unsavory reputation among psychometricians. Cronbach and Furby (1970) went so far as to argue that investigators should learn to pose their questions in ways that would not require the computation of such unreliable scores. This advice, though reasonable to psychometricians, is astonishing to experimentalists, who (from Donders to PET scan watchers) have defined psychological constructs by differences between the performance of subjects in different conditions. The reliability problem, however, is not what it seems. It is easily shown that if all subjects show the same improvement, then the reliability of the gain is zero, even though one can with complete confidence say precisely what each person gained. The key here is that what interests the differential psychologist is not reliability in some absolute sense, but rather the dependability with which individuals can be rank ordered on the score: If individual variation is small or nonexistent, then people cannot be ranked with confidence on the basis of their gains. It is this unswerving fixation on individual differences that blinds differential psychologists and their technical allies, the psychometricians. Their most cherished methods for evaluating tests and the constructs tests measure begin and end with rank orders of individuals.

The experimentalist, in contrast, has built a psychology of particular tasks. He or she often attempts to generalize treatment effects across situations, but rarely attends to the extent to which these effects generalize across tasks. The differential psychologist knows how to estimate the generalizability of individual differences across tasks, but that is not the same thing. In addition to the generalizability of individual differences across tasks, one can examine the consistency across tasks of treatment effects or even of score profiles (e.g., see Cronbach, 1957; also Cattell, 1966). In other words, the experimentalist should be more interested in covariation of response patterns between rows—not between columns, like the differential psychologist. Unfortunately, because the psychometrician is usually more adept at multivariate statistics, efforts to link experimental and differential psychology usually end up playing by differential rules. Entire research programs attempting to link experimental and differential psychology have risen and then collapsed on the basis of a few between-person correlation coefficients.

But the two disciplines *do* meet, or overlap. Nonindependence of row and column variation shows up in the interaction term. When considering the relationship between learning and intelligence, the most important cause of the interaction is an increase in score variation across trials, or what Kenny (1974) called the fan effect. Statistically, this effect occurs when true gain on the learning task is positively related to initial status on the task. If initial status on the learning task correlates with intelligence, then gains will also show a correlation. There are, of course, other possibilities, but this is the typical scenario. Thus the interaction term is the key. Unfortunately, both differential and experimental psychologists have been taught to minimize the interaction term. Differential psychologists evaluate the dependability or reliability of individual differences by the proportion of the between-person variance attributable to the person variance component (Cronbach, Gleser, Nanda, & Rajaratnam, 1972); a large person variance component and a comparatively small person × item interaction variance component are the goal. For the experimentalist, differences between conditions (or i) are judged relative to the size of the p × i interaction.

In contrast, diagnostic information about how subjects solved tasks is most informative when the interaction term is large. In such cases, the single rank order of individuals or of conditions does not give all of the interesting information. Influential developmental psychologists have long built their psychology around tasks that induce subjects to reveal important, preferably qualitative differences in knowledge or strategy by the type or pattern of responses they give. Furthermore, these differences in knowledge or strategy must then be shown to generalize to other tasks or even to be indicative of broad thinking competencies. Piaget was particularly clever in inventing or adapting such tasks; Siegler (1988) has continued the tradition.

Put another way, the primary contribution of an information-processing analysis of a task or problematic situation is information on how subjects understood that situation or solved that task. Although such analyses usefully inform interpretation of test scores even when all subjects follow a uniform strategy, such analyses are most useful for understanding individual differences when there are interesting differences in the way subjects perceive a situation or solve a task. Most tasks studied by experimental psychologists and most tests developed by differential psychologists, however, are not designed to elicit such qualitative differences in knowledge or strategy or to reveal them when they occur. In fact, they are constructed with exactly the opposite goal in mind. For example, information-processing analyses of mental rotation tell us that a major source of individual differences on such tasks is to be found in the speed and accuracy of the rotation process. Did anyone seriously doubt this? What is news is when we find subjects who do not rotate stimuli, or who persist in rotating them in one direction when rotation in the other direction would be shorter, or when some rotate along rigid axes while others perform a simultaneous mental twisting and turning. These strategy differences are of no enduring interest unless they can be related to more global indices of ability or development, as indeed they have been (e.g., Kerr, Corbitt, & Jurkovic, 1980).

Most research in the past 20 years attempting to relate cognitive and differential psychology has assumed that connections between the two disciplines would be more straightforward. Investigators fitted information-processing models to each subject's data, then estimated component scores for different mental processes (e.g., the slope parameter from the regression of latency on angular separation between stimuli in the rotation paradigm), and then used these process-based parameters as new individual-difference variables (see Lohman & Ippel, 1993, for a critical review). Consistent individual differences, however, will be located in the intercepts of the individual regressions, not in the slopes or other component scores, as commonly assumed. Indeed, individual differences in component scores only succeed in salvaging a portion of the variance typically relegated to the error term. Component scores do not decompose and therefore cannot explain the main effect of individual differences on a task (Lohman, 1994). Thus the intercept, which is the residual or wastebasket parameter in componential models, is actually the locus of individual-difference variance that is consistent across trials, whereas component scores, which capture consistent variation in item or trial difficulty, can only help salvage individual-difference variance from the error term.

Theory-Based Tests

Such complexities complicate but by no means embargo traffic between the two disciplines of scientific psychology. Theory-based tests provide one example. Although researchers occasionally estimated the action of particular mental processes by average latency or total errors on a task, the assumptions of the information-processing paradigm discouraged it. Thus Keating and MacLean (1987) argued that researchers who used total reaction time and error scores on tasks instead of component scores to define "process parameters" had abandoned the fundamental logic of the cognitive-correlates approach. Those whose work was judged in part by its contributions to practice, however, were not as inhibited by paradigms. For example, although the researchers at the Learning Abilities Measurement Program (Kyllonen & Chrystal, 1989) investigated whether scores estimating the action of component processes would add to the prediction of success in military training, the battery of new tests they developed generally used total scores on tasks (except when absolutely mandated by the construct under investigation). Cognitive theory thus contributes to establishing the construct validity of tests not as much through new "process scores" that clarify or enhance nomothetic span (Embretson, 1983) as through theory-based tasks whose internal validity (or construct representation; Embretson, 1983) is more easily defended. Other avenues of contribution are noted below, but first we must consider developments in the understanding and assessment of personality.

ISSUES IN THE ASSESSMENT OF PERSONALITY

We turn our attention now to the assessment of personality. Here, too, we note that the story we tell is one of many possible stories. It is a story with two major plots, each with approximately half-century histories. The first plot, one of insurrection, is motivated by a continuous undercurrent of dissatisfaction with the dominant model for personality assessment: the nomothetic approach. Our sense of this plot is that although it may continue far into the future, it is unlikely to end in successful revolution. The second plot relates, at least loosely, to the controversy between intelligence as a unitary trait and as a collection of separate traits. Here, though, the history starts not with a single trait model but with a confusion of separate traits, and it reaches the present with a growing consensus on a quasi-hierarchical model of the structure of personality differences.

We begin this section in earnest by borrowing an equation from Lamiell (1981). This equation represents a generic description of the process of personality assessment.

$$S_{pa} = \underset{i=1}{\overset{m}{f}} (V_{pi})(R_{ia}) \qquad (1)$$

In the equation, S is a score for a particular person p on an attribute a. V represents a variable for which a measurement on person p is made (there are m such variables for attribute a). V might be an item on a self-report inventory or a rating form, or it might be any other indicator of the underlying attribute.[1] R is a measure of the relevance of variable i for attribute a. Measures of personality have most commonly used unit weights for items, but other schemes are also possible. Finally, we note that the function sign is used loosely here. The function used most often to combine observations is summation, but we allow for any function, including holistic judgment. The current trends we identify in personality assessment and our speculations about the future all relate to the ways in which elements of this simple equation are defined.

One clear trend in personality assessment is a reconsideration of the value of idiographic approaches. The debate over the relative value of nomothetic and idiographic approaches to personality assessment has waxed and waned over the half century or so since Allport (1937) proposed an idiographic science of personality. The most recent incarnation of this debate was fueled in part by controversy that raged in the 1970s and 1980s over the relative roles of personality factors and situational factors (not to mention their interaction) in determining behavior; a general dissatisfaction with logical positivism and logical empiricism (e.g., see Rorer, 1990) has contributed to the field's interest in idiography. In fact, a distressingly large array of issues has come to be subsumed under the heading of this debate. For example, in a recent putatively idiographic study (Pelham, 1993), subjects and their roommates or friends rated themselves on a set of explicitly normative scales. The correlation across scales between each subject and the roommate or friend served as an "idiographic" measure. By the definition of idiography we adopt below, the correlation is not an idiographic measure.

Two issues in particular are often confounded, and they deserve to be distinguished from one another in distinguishing idiographic from nomothetic measurement. Briefly, idiographic and nomothetic approaches differ both on whether a common set of attributes is used to describe all people and also on whether comparisons are made between an individual and others in order to understand that individual's

[1]Our focus, however, will be on indicators (e.g., responses to self-report items or rating scales) that rely on humans as sensitive transducers. This reflects both our pessimism about physiological measures of personality—for all the reasons mentioned in our discussion of intelligence—and the general lack of success in the use of "objective" data (Block, 1977).

personality. When a common set of attributes is employed and meaning is assigned to those scores by comparison to the scores of others, we speak of nomothetic measurement. When a common set of attributes is not used and no such formal comparison to others' scores is made, we speak of idiographic measurement. The combination of a common set of attributes with something else than a comparison to others' scores yields several less familiar measurement paradigms, including idiothetic measurement (Lamiell, 1981). In the sections that follow, we discuss the consequences of choices concerning each of these issues.

The Attributes to be Measured

The first issue distinguishing idiographic from nomothetic measurement rests on a consideration of the particular attributes to be measured. In the classic statement of the idiographic approach, Allport (1937) writes of individuals having different traits (in particular, different *morphogenic* traits; Allport, 1961). Thus the uniqueness that we attribute to individuals arises from the fact that they have unique constellations of traits. For Allport, then, an idiographic approach to personality is one in which the attributes to be measured vary from individual to individual.

In fact, the task of personality assessment begins with the identification of the a's in Equation 1 *for each individual*. Further, all the other elements can differ from person to person as well. The particular variables observed (V) and the relevance assigned to each (R) for one person need not be the same for each individual.

In contrast, nomothetic measurement, which has been the dominant paradigm in personality research for at least the last 50 years, insists on a single common set of attributes. Although the identification of a's is an important task in developing a system for assessing personality (as we will discuss below in the context of the development of the big five), that task precedes the measurement of any particular individual's personality. Once the set of common attributes have been identified or defined, the task of assessing an individual's personality reduces to the task of finding a score (S in Equation 1) that represents the extent to which that attribute characterizes that individual. Here each individual's uniqueness comes from his or her particular location in a multidimensional space defined by the attributes selected for measurement.

In summary, an idiographic description of an individual's personality would specify the structure of that person's traits. The description would identify which traits characterize the individual and what relation each bears to the others. A nomothetic description of an individual's personality would specify the extent to which he or she was characterized by a set of attributes shared by all people. In short, the two approaches differ on the usefulness of using a single vocabulary to describe all people. Although this debate has continued unabated throughout the history of scientific research on personality, it has only recently arisen in research on intelligence in attempts to assess individual differences in knowledge structures (see Snow & Lohman, 1989, for one summary).

Some (e.g., Lamiell, 1981; Rorer, 1989) have argued that the distinction we have just described—between description of the structure of an individual's personality, and description of the ways in which individuals' personalities differ—corresponds to the distinction between personality theory and differential psychology. This leads to the conclusion that the psychology of personality is necessarily idiographic. For reasons upon which we will expand, we reject both of the implied isomorphisms (i.e., we hold open the possibility that nomothetic assessment might be a necessary condition for understanding any truly differential construct and a helpful adjunct for interpreting constructs grounded in other domains).

Assigning Meaning to Measurements

The second issue separating idiographic from nomothetic measurement concerns the way in which meaning is assigned to whatever score is assigned to a person. Equation 1 generates a number, but the meaning of that number emerges only when it is compared to some referent. To say that $S_{pa} = 50$ is not at all informative without more information. In general, meaning can be assigned to the measurement characterizing a particular individual by a variety of comparisons.

How, then, do we assign meaning to the S_{pa} values yielded by a personality measurement procedure? Five quite different approaches have been taken in personality research. The first of these, and the most commonly used, has been the normative statement embedded within the nomothetic tradition. In this approach, whatever score we assign to an individual ultimately derives its meaning from its position in a distribution of scores assigned to relevant others. To the extent that personality is about individual differences, this is an abundantly appropriate approach.

Given our broad experience with people, knowing that a particular individual's extraversion score is greater than the scores of 90% of people to whom that individual can be appropriately compared (e.g., agemates, people of the same sex, people from the same cultural background) is quite meaningful. The key, of course, to understanding a normative score—whether it refers to personality or ability or any other characteristic—is understanding the norming group. To say of someone that "He is not particularly bright" has very different meanings when the comparison is to faculty members at one's university than it does when the comparison is to unselected adults.

Still, the typical normative statement leaves a great deal unsaid, and it may even mislead. For example, one of the arguments against norm-referenced interpretations of interest inventories is that one can obtain a score that suggests real interest in a domain only because one expressed dislike for that domain with less vehemence than others in the norm group. Furthermore, to locate a score within a distribution of scores without specifying anything about the processes that generated those scores is psychologically sterile. In fact, there are at least two kinds of information missing. First, the normative statement provides no information about the items or tasks to which the individual responded in generating the score. Even among those who have built personality scales with almost blind empiricism, item content has sometimes been seen as a clue to the psychological nature of the construct (Gough, 1965). The second kind of missing information relates to the question of *how* the individual responded to the item or task. As we discuss below when we address cognitive styles, individuals may respond in qualitatively different ways, and still receive the same score. More importantly, information about how individuals think and behave in situations that they summarized in a self-rating provides the crucial link between an individual-difference construct and general psychological theory.

This central characteristic of nomothetic assessment, the comparison of an individual's score to those of others, has been criticized by proponents of idiographic and other strategies. To say that the meaning of a S_{pa} value depends on the scores obtained by others is, in some sense, to ignore the uniqueness of the individual. Idiographic proponents (who essentially reject the idea that personality constructs are inherently differential) have instead advocated methods that understand an individual's personality on its own terms. In the classic work of idiography, *Letters from Jenny*, Allport (1965) analyzes his subject's personality without any explicit reference to others at all. In analyzing a large corpus of letters from the pseudonymous Jenny Masterson to a young couple, Allport asked a panel of judges to identify Jenny's traits. Of the 198 traits identified by judges, 185 could be categorized into one of eight categories (e.g., self-centered, aesthetic-artistic). These eight separate traits, then, describe Jenny's personality uniquely and without reference to others.

Or do they? Just as a purely normative description of an individual is only partially satisfying, this purely idiographic description leaves something out. Let us consider what it means to say that Jenny Masterson is self-centered. It might mean any of several things; for a moment, let us focus on the possibility that it means she is more self-centered than most women of her time, culture, and age. This translation makes (partly) explicit an ascription rule (Rorer & Wildger, 1983) that the judges may have used. One very plausible model of how the judges went about their task is that they considered many traits that might describe individuals' personalities. In considering self-centeredness, the judges recognized that Jenny was outstandingly self-centered, and therefore they ascribed that trait to her. In considering other traits, the judges may have felt that Jenny Masterson was unremarkable (i.e., not particularly different from the average woman of her time, culture, and age). Thus they chose not to mention these traits.

The ascription rules for traits differ one from another (Rorer & Widiger, 1983). In some cases, for example, the ascription rule depends on the *number* of times a person engages in a particular behavior. Rorer & Widiger cite the examples of "murderous" and "honest." A single (or perhaps at most two) instances of murder would lead us to describe a person as murderous, even though murder is an atypical act for that person. But, one or two instances of honesty, against a backdrop of general dishonesty, would not lead us to describe an individual as honest. Though the ascription rules for honesty and murderousness may both depend on absolute number of instances, the rules differ substantially in terms of what that number is. Other traits (e.g., nervousness) might depend on *proportion*: A person will be described as nervous if his or her ratio of instances of nervousness to instances of calmness is outstandingly high.

The ascription of the trait "murderous" can, in fact, be better understood when it is combined with knowledge about the base rate of murder in some relevant comparison group. Part of the reason that one or two acts of murder lead us to describe a person as murderous has to do with our knowledge of the meaning of murder in our culture. Another part of the reason, though, has to do with the fact that a score of 1 in this area corresponds to the 99th percentile or beyond. Normative interpretations, done well, automatically incorporate base rates (as well as other characteristics of the distribution). Saying that someone's "honesty" score is in the 80th percentile (with the norm group specified) takes into account the fact that most people are honest most of the time.

In contrast, trait scores are simply summaries of (usually self-reported) behavior over many situations. Those with extreme scores are well-characterized, because they exhibit the behavior in most (or few) of the situations sampled. But what about those with average scores?

> A middling score implies no lack of individuality. Rather, the person's behavior is not organized along the dimension we chose to score. The description "50 percent honest" inevitably is inadequate; *when* is the person honest? . . . A personalized description would replace the general trait dimension with dimensions that describe situations the person sees as calling for an honest act (and the opposite). (Cronbach, 1990, p. 564)

Thus part of the dissatisfaction with the nomothetic approach lies in its inability to capture individuality. But there is more. Those who would make predictions about behavior on particular tasks or in particular situations would like to anchor the scale by sampling from a domain of tasks or situations; if they are even more cognitively oriented, then they would like to understand the cognitions that generated the behavior. In short, what they would like is a theory-based, domain-referenced scale. Indeed, with systematic sampling, one could more likely make statements that further conditioned interpretation by specifying under what class of situations certain behaviors or cognitions were more and less probable. This would not in any way preclude normative interpretations of the same score, nor would it preclude reporting of scores that averaged across classes of situations. But defining the domain of situations—there is the rub.

Neither normative nor idiographic comparisons are completely satisfying. In response to this dissatisfaction, Lamiell (1981) has proposed an idiothetic scheme for personality measurement. The goal of idiothetic measurement is an S_{pa} value for each individual that is interpretable without reference to the S_{pa} value of any other individual; to accomplish this goal, idiothetic measurement begins with a sample of indicators (V_i) from the domain of interest. In Lamiell's (1981, p. 281) example, these are 11 specific behaviors (e.g. drinking beer/liquor, studying/reading) that have been empirically demonstrated to span a dimension of adolescent rebelliousness versus compliance. The scores assigned to each V is zero if the respondent denies engaging in the activity during the past week, and 1 if the respondent admits engaging in the activity during the week. The weights assigned to each variable were determined by a multidimensional scaling study, though in principle there is no reason that unit weights (both positive and negative) could not have been used. The S_{pa} for an individual is given by Equation 1, with the function sign representing summation.

So far, nothing in the idiothetic procedure described by Lamiell is inconsistent with traditional nomothetic practice. The departure comes in the way in which S_{pa} is interpreted. In order to make this interpretation without any reference to any other person, Lamiell proposes the calculation of an I_{pa} score. To compute this score, we first calculate the minimum and maximum S_{pa} values obtainable from this set of V and R. I_{pa} is then calculated as the difference between the observed S_{pa} and the minimum S_{pa}, divided by the difference between the maximum and minimum S_{pa}. In other words, a particular person's score on a particular attribute is interpreted by reference to the items used to measure that attribute.

Though unusual in the personality domain, understanding a score by reference to the items attempted by the respondent is a well-known practice in the ability and achievement domains, where it goes by the name of "domain-referenced testing." A necessary, but not sufficient condition for building a domain-referenced test is that the domain to be measured must be well defined (Nitko, 1984). For example, it is a relatively straightforward matter to define the domain of two-number, two digit addition problems; it consists of all possible combinations of two-digit numbers joined by a plus sign. Obtaining a random sample of this domain is just a matter of randomly generating digits and joining them into addition problems. Assuming that the sample is of adequate size, it is reasonable to make such statements as "The examinee can correctly respond to only 20% of two-number, two-digit addition problems." Further, for at least some purposes, that statement has a clear interpretation (e.g., the examinee has not mastered the skill involved in these problems).

This example raises two issues when translated to

the personality domain. The first is whether the domain of behavior representing any personality trait is sufficiently well-defined to allow for domain referencing. Even in achievement testing, domain-referenced tests are built on domain definitions less well-defined than our example; for example, tests built on the *Taxonomy of Educational Objectives* (Bloom, 1956) may be domain referenced (Nitko, 1984). Still, one has to wonder what definition of rebelliousness-compliance would lead a group of psychologists to generate even substantially overlapping behavior indicators. As we shall discuss below, careful construction of tasks with known characteristics has been relatively rare in personality research, but it would make nonnormative interpretations more meaningful.

The second issue that our achievement example raises is more central to a consideration of idiothetic measurement. Although the interpretation that the examinee had not mastered the class of addition problems we defined is clear, it raises as many questions as it answers, and those questions require other sorts of information. For example, the most basic question of what, if anything, we should do about the examinee's lack of mastery depends on comparisons to others. If the examinee is a kindergartner, we would probably be willing to assume that mastery will increase with maturation and exposure to the normal school curriculum. If the examinee is in the third grade, though, we would probably consider some sort of remedial curriculum. We draw these conclusions from knowledge of what is typical in a group to which the target examinee belongs. We might also find idiographic information of use in interpreting this score; for example, it would be helpful to know something about the importance of performing arithmetic problems to this person.

Just as the 20% correct score is only partially informative, so is knowing only that a hypothetical respondent named Mary receives an I_{pa} of .802 (Lamiell, 1981). The score tells us that she is 80% as complaint as the scale would have allowed her to be. That statement is roughly equivalent to the statement that an examinee passed 80% of the items on a criterion-referenced test.[2] Examination of the items making up the scale would help in interpreting the score. In this case, we see that the most rebellious thing Mary did during the past week was "doing nothing in particular"; on the compliant side, she participated in volunteer work and extracurricular activities. These items have meaning partially because we (implicitly) bring to bear our knowledge of the rates at which adolescents engage in these behaviors. If we knew nothing about adolescents, or did not know that Mary was an adolescent, these statements about her would lose much of their meaning.

So far we have argued that normative, idiographic, and idiothetic measurement depend heavily upon each other for support in assigning meaning to S_{pa} scores. For completeness, we describe two other, less common reference points for interpreting personality scores. The ipsative approach (e.g., Block, 1961) depends upon comparisons between an individual's score on a particular variable and that same individual's score on other variables. For example, we might say that among the varieties of self-concept domains, for a particular individual, academic self-concept is more salient or central than the others. Just as with the other interpretive approaches we have described, this approach captures some, but not all of the information we might like to know about the individual. Some of the missing information is available from normative comparisons. For example, if the individual is a student, we might want to know how common it is for students of the same age to place academic issues at the center of their self-concepts. Ipsative comparisons across norm-referenced scales are problematic, because the shape of the profile depends on the norm group. Absolute scales such as response latency (see e.g., the Riding & Dyer, 1980, study discussed below) avoid this problem, which is one of the reasons why such measures are popular among experimentally oriented psychologists. Domain-referenced scores provide an intermediate case: Profiles change when the domain definition or sampling of elements from it is changed, but not with each new sample of subjects.

Finally, personality scores can be interpreted by comparison to the scores of the same individual at other times. We might, for example, note that a child engaged in many impulsive acts per day at school during the first grade, fewer during the third grade, and even fewer during the fifth grade. Assuming comparability of the measures (a nontrivial assumption in some cases), it makes sense to say that the child is becoming less impulsive. Again, this particular interpretive framework provides only part of the information we might want. For example, in addition to absolute change, we might be interested in relative change.

[2]Indeed, if unit weights were used, it would be even more nearly equivalent. One difference remains. Though it makes sense to talk of a zero point on a skills test (the examinee can do no two-number, two-digit addition problems), it does not make sense to speak of zero compliance. Thus, in general, personality scales cannot logically yield ratio scores.

Probably most children become less impulsive as they mature; is the child we are assessing becoming less impulsive at the same rate as other children? Normative information would help us here.

To summarize, nomothetic, idiographic, idiothetic, ipsative, and developmental approaches each provide useful information in moving from an observed S_{pa} to a meaningful description of an individual's personality. None is uniquely informative; each has something to offer, and so combinations are stronger than any method alone.

The Structure of Individual Differences in Personality: The Big Five

As we mentioned earlier, the prerequisite for nomothetic measurement is the identification of the attributes to be measured. Much of the published literature in personality continues to have a "trait of the month" flavor; that is, various traits become interesting to the personality research community, dominate the literature for a period, and then fade from view. Historical examples might include authoritarianism, manifest anxiety, type A personality, locus of control, depression, and achievement motivation; the current favorites might include self-esteem and self-concept. Clearly, as London and Exner (1978) point out, "there has been no overarching plan or theory, implicit or explicit, guiding the selection of topics for trait researchers" (p. xiv). In fact, these authors acknowledge they were forced to order the chapters of their book *Dimensions of Personality* alphabetically for lack of a better scheme.

The history in personality has been, in one respect, quite opposite to the history in intelligence. Successive descriptions of the structure of intelligence broke *g* into more and increasingly smaller and smaller parts. In contrast, the history of structural descriptions of personality involves creating fewer, broader constructs. The framework that has emerged, generally referred to as the "Big Five," has a very long history (see John, Angleitner, & Ostendorf, 1988). For most of that history, the research leading to this five-dimensional model of the structure of individual difference in personality was ignored by most researchers in the field. We can only speculate about why this is changing, but it seems likely that the commercial availability of a respected measure of the big-five constructs (Cost & McRae, 1992) combined with a mix of empirical results (particularly those demonstrating the generalizability of the model, e.g., Digman & Takemoto-Chock, 1981), effective proselytizing (e.g., John, 1989), and frustration with the lack of cumulation of research results all contributed.

In this section, we will not provide a detailed account of research on the big five; the interested reader is referred to almost any of the excellent papers by John for an overview. Historically important papers in the Big Five literature include those by Norman (1963), Tupes and Christal (1961), and Digman and Takemoto-Chock (1981). Our goals in this section are to characterize the Big Five model of the structure of personality, then illustrate how investigators interested in a particular trait that is not among the Big Five can connect their research to the Big-Five structure, as well as the value of such an endeavor.

The factors identified as the big five emerge from a strand of research rooted in Allport and Odbert's (1936) study of the representation of personality in the English language. The premise behind this research is that language must surely have evolved in ways that allow people to describe each others' personalities (Goldberg, 1981); thus the full range of individual differences in personality is available in language. The basic methodology in these studies of the representation of personality in language has been to select some subset of personality descriptors and then ask respondents to use them (e.g., in the form of rating scales) to rate their own or others' personalities. These ratings are then factor analyzed, and the emerging factors are identified as major underlying traits of human personality.

What traits emerge from such an exercise? Various investigators have proposed various names for the traits arising from their analyses, and these names often seem rather different. As John (1990) points out, this is perhaps not surprising given the very broad nature of the traits. Nonetheless, the names John suggests (see Table 1) convey a sense of the factors better than the traditional roman numerals. As he points out, the first letters of the factor names, somewhat rearranged, allow for the mnemonic device of an OCEAN of personality traits. We (perhaps optimistically) suggest the alternative that the big five may provide a CANOE in which further explorations of the personality wilderness can take place.

Particularly in the context of this chapter, it is worth noting that of these factors, perhaps the least well defined is Factor V, Openness. This is the factor that Norman (1963) originally called Culture; others have called this factor Intellect (Digman & Takemoto-Chock, 1981; Peabody & Goldberg, 1989), among

Table 1. The Big Five Personality Factors

I	Extraversion, energy, enthusiasm
II	Agreeableness, altruism, affection
III	Conscientiousness, control, constraint
IV	Neuroticism, negative affectivity, nervousness
V	Openness, originality, open-mindedness

other names. In a clever study in which judges used the Adjective Check List to describe prototypes of high and low scorers on each of the big-five dimensions (John, 1989), the low end of the fifth dimension was characterized by such adjectives as *narrow interests*, *shallow*, *simple*, and *unintelligent*. The high end of the dimension was characterized by a broad range of adjectives, including *artistic*, *civilized*, *dignified*, *ingenious*, *inventive*, *intelligent*, *original*, *polished*, *sophisticated*, *wise*, and *witty*. Clearly, this factor encompasses a very broad notion of intelligence, as well as a notion of cultural sophistication. To a certain extent, it may simply reflect lay people's naive conceptions of intelligence (Fitzgerald & Mellor, 1988; Sternberg, Conway, Ketron, & Bernstein, 1981).

Just as in the intelligence domain, these broad factors can each be divided into several subtraits. There is, however, an interesting difference between structural models of the personality and intelligence domains. In the intelligence domain, it makes sense to speak of a genuine hierarchical model, with *g* occupying a central position at the top of the hierarchy. It is, in other words, sensible to describe a person as highly intelligent, where *intelligent* is interpreted as a reference to the very broad construct of *g*. In contrast, there is no single central construct at the epitome of the hierarchical model of personality. We have no single term for someone who ranks high in each of the five personality factors. Thus the Big Five model really represents five different, probably partially overlapping hierarchies.

The lexical approach to identifying the dimensions of personality is a thoroughly nomothetic enterprise. One of the goals of a nomothetic science of personality is a common vocabulary for the description of personality, and herein lies the greatest contribution of the Big-Five model. For many years now, the bulk of personality research has been conducted in narrow and isolated domains leading to the development of theories and supporting research of single traits. Though one frequently gets the sense that two traits, each with their own literature and theory, bear some remarkable similarities, there is no clear way to evaluate the validity of this suspicion.

Perhaps now we approach the point at which the field can settle on single set of dimensions to which individual traits can be referenced. If the Big Five model is substantially valid, all personality traits are either included among the Big Five or their components or, more commonly, can be defined in terms of a composite of the Big Five. A recent study by Goff and Ackerman (1992) provides an illustration. The study was designed to investigate the relation between a personality trait the investigators call "typical intellectual engagement" and various aspects of intelligence. The investigators selected well-validated existing measures to span the ability and personality domains, and they also included newly constructed measures of typical intellectual engagement and related personality constructs.

Because they included measures of the big five as marker variables, the authors were able to assess the relation between typical intellectual engagement and each of these dimensions. Typical intellectual engagement was relatively highly related to openness (r corrected for attenuation = .72), but Goff and Ackerman point out that this leaves a substantial portion of the variance in typical intellectual engagement that is not shared with openness. This finding suggests a potential deficiency in the Big-Five model: Here is a trait (with demonstrated interesting relations to intelligence) that lies outside the space defined by the Big Five.

This correlation alone, however, is inadequate to address the distinctiveness of typical intellectual engagement and the Big-Five framework. There are a number of reasons other than unreliability that two measures of the same construct might be less than perfectly correlated (Rocklin, 1994). For our purposes, chief among them is that each measure might be less than perfectly construct valid. Thus, the exercise of justifying a putatively new construct is fundamentally one of construct validation. To see, in detail, what such a effort might look like, the interested reader is referred to the original article (Goff & Ackerman, 1992), a comment (Rocklin, 1994) and a reply (Ackerman & Goff, 1994).

Given the level of acceptance that the big five is gaining, efforts such as Goff and Ackerman's deserve to become the norm for personality research. An early step in the development of a new construct ought to be a thorough investigation of the location of that construct in the space defined by the Big Five. In some cases, investigators may find that the trait they are investigating is well subsumed in one of the Big Five hierarchies; in other cases, they may find that a combination of Big-Five variables are needed to describe the construct in which they are interested. In this case, the investigator has perhaps identified a particularly interesting vector within the Big-Five space. Finding such a vector may be quite valuable. Vernon's point, quoted earlier, that the factors emerging from factor analyses of test batteries have no claim to psychological meaningfulness holds with equal force here. There is no guarantee that the axes of the Big-Five space are psychologically meaningful, and it may well be that the most interesting traits, for some purposes, are just such composites. As in the history of theories of intelligence, there will no doubt always be disagreements about the number of traits and the hierarchical arrangement of those traits. The Big-Five framework, though, holds the promise of at least allowing these disagreements to occur within a common context.

ISSUES AT THE INTERSECTION OF INTELLIGENCE AND PERSONALITY

How shall we conceptualize the domains of personality and intelligence? Are they two intersecting sets? Is one (intelligence) a subset of the other (personality)? Or is each defined by emphasizing the spheres of influence of other constructs, such as conation, affection, and volition? Are both necessarily differential constructs? Or are each admixtures of constructs defined over persons and over tasks/situations? In short, discussion of the overlap between these two domains presumes something about the content and purview of each domain and something else about their relative status. In this section we discuss these issues from several perspectives. Mostly we start from intelligence and seek contacts with personality, but we could have as easily worked in the opposite direction.

Expanding Intelligence to Include Affect and Conation

One recurring theme in the story of intelligence is the attempt to account for those affective, motivational, and volitional aspects of cognition long recognized as central to the development and expression of intelligence but ignored with equal persistence in formal theories of human abilities. For example, in the same symposium (Thorndike et al., 1921) in which Thorndike gave the oft-cited definition of intelligence as "the power of good responses from the point of view of truth or fact" (p. 124), he also noted that

> it is probably unwise to spend much time in attempts to separate off sharply certain qualities of man, as his intelligence, from such emotional and vocational qualities as his interest in mental activity, carefulness, determination to respond effectively, persistence in his efforts to do so; or from his amount of knowledge; or from his moral or esthetic tastes. (p. 124)

Similarly, in the same symposium, Freeman noted that a listing of cognitive traits provides an incomplete model of intelligence, which must also include "The characteristic . . . sometimes called temperament or moral character" (Thorndike et al., 1921, p. 134).

Those actively involved in the administration and interpretation of individual intelligence tests (e.g., Binet, 1903; Wechsler, 1950, 1975) have been the most vocal advocates for inclusion of affect. Indeed, the weight given to such "non-intellective factors" (Weschler, 1943) in the interpretation of intelligence first declined with the introduction of group administered tests, and then again with the introduction of factorial methods of analyzing correlational data. Intelligence as a behavioral style was replaced with intelligence as one or more intellectual powers or latent variables that could be inferred, but not observed.

Messick (1987) notes that one of the major ways in which personality impacts cognition is through the influence of affect:

> One of the prime sources of personality influence on cognition is the pervasive impact of positive and negative affect. The positive affects of interest and surprise, along with . . . intrinsic motivation and curiosity, are critical in the initiation and maintenance of cognitive functioning, in the selectivity and duration of attention, and in the differentiation and integration of cognitive structure. In contrast, negative affects such as fear and anxiety lead to interference and disorganization of function, to disruption and pre-emption of attention, and to dedifferentiation and primitivization of structure. Furthermore, mechanisms of defense against anxiety and negative affects, being not only self-protective but often self-deceptive, introduce distortions of their own into cognitive processing. (pp. 36–37)

Trait–Trait Correlations

Differential psychologists who have recognized the overlap between the domains of intelligence and personality have attempted to explore it in several ways. The simplest has been to search for correlations between ability and personality traits, the most frequently reported of which is the correlation between intelligence and the factor Costa and McCrae (1985) call Openness. A recent example can be found in the Goff and Ackerman (1992) study, discussed above. Following earlier leads of Gough (1953), they hypothesized that intelligence would show stronger correlations with a personality construct called "typical intellectual engagement" (TIE) if abilities were measured as typical rather than maximal performance variables (see Cronbach, 1970). Results indeed showed that measures of fluid ability (presumably an index of maximal performance) showed no correlation with TIE, whereas measures of crystallized ability (presumably a better index of typical performance) did. Also noteworthy are studies that show correlations between patterns of abilities and personality constructs (e.g., see Cattell, 1971). For example, the contrast between spatial and verbal fluency abilities has repeatedly shown correlations with extraversion, with high-fluency–low spatial subjects showing higher levels of extraversion and low fluency–high spatial subjects showing higher levels of introversion (Smith, 1964; Riding & Dyer, 1980). Patterns of abilities, however, are probably better understood as predisposing certain styles of thought, which we discuss next.

Styles

The second approach to understanding the intersection of cognition and affect has been through the study of styles of thought, which Messick (1987) defines as "stable individual differences in the manner or form of psychological functioning" (p. 37). Three major classes of styles are typically distinguished: cognitive, learning, and defensive. Cognitive styles include constructs such as field articulation versus global style, extensiveness of scanning, cognitive complexity versus simplicity, leveling versus sharpening, category width, reflection versus impulsivity, automatization versus restructuring, and converging versus diverging.

A variety of learning styles have also been hypothesized (Weinstein, Goetz, & Alexander, 1988). The most general distinction concerns whether strategies lead to deep versus surface processing during learning (Entwistle, 1987; Snow & Swanson, 1992). Such strategies, however, cannot be understood in isolation from motivation for learning (Ainley, 1993; Biggs, 1987). Further, different subject-matter domains may also require or lead learners to develop different global strategies for organizing their knowledge (Pask, 1976).

Finally, defensive styles refer to "consistent . . . ways of organizing and channeling affect in cognition" (Messick, 1987, p. 51). As such, they are primarily ego protective, "but also serve the important adaptive function of maintaining cognition, in the face of intense affects" (p. 51). Four broad defensive styles have been proposed: Obsessive-compulsive, hysterical, paranoid, and impulsive. In the normal range of personality, these are called rigid, impressionistic, suspicious, and unintegrated cognition, respectively (Messick, 1987).

However appealing style constructs have been to theorists, they have not fared as well empirically (e.g., see Tiedemann, 1989; Vernon, 1973). Surely part of the difficulty is that styles are, by definition, situationally labile in a way that abilities are not. But a larger difficulty stems from the application of an inappropriate measurement model. By definition, styles concern not *how much* but *how*. Further, measures of style should yield scores that are bipolar and value differentiated rather than unipolar and value directed (Messick, 1984). But most measures of cognitive styles have inappropriately followed the ability-factor model, which is better suited to value directional questions about unipolar dimensions that ask "how much." Early mental testers—particularly Binet, but others as well (see Freeman, 1926)—were as much concerned with how children solved problems as with the answers they gave. This concern with process was picked up by developmental psychologists but gradually abandoned by psychometricians, especially with the rise of group-administered tests that could be scored by a clerk (and later by a machine). Tests became increasingly efficient vehicles for identifying those who were more (or less) able, but increasingly uninformative as to what abilities might be (Lohman, 1989). Issues of process were exiled to the murky land of cognitive styles. There, isolated from the mainstream of differential psychology, promising style constructs were gradually ground into traits already known to ability theorists, but by other names. When the redundancy was finally discovered, ability theorists claimed priority, and style theorists were left with the residue. Measurement models developed in cognitive psychology to estimate consistencies in strategies are, in fact, much better suited to the task of measuring "how" (Lohman & Ippel, 1993). Thus one of the more important contributions cognitive psychology might make to measurement would be through improved measures of cognitive styles.

Siegler (1988) reported one example of how this might be accomplished. He administered addition, subtraction, and word identification tasks to two groups of first graders. Performance on each item was classified as based on either retrieval or construction of a response using a backup strategy. Students were then classified in one of three groups depending on the pattern of response correctness overall, on retrieval problems, and on backup strategy problems. Siegler labeled the groups as good, not-so-good, and perfectionist students. Perfectionists were students who exhibited good knowledge of problems but set high confidence thresholds for stating retrieval answers. The distinction between perfectionist and good students thus mirrors the cognitive style dimension of reflexivity-impulsivity. Note, however, that the latter dimension is typically defined by performing a median split on latency and error scores on a figure matching task, then discarding subjects in two of the four cells. Siegler started with a model of strategy use that distinguished between strength of associations (a classic "cognitive" construct) and confidence criterion for stating retrieval answers (a "conative" construct). Further, the hypothesized style dimension was shown by examining response patterns across three tasks commonly used in the classroom.

Another example comes from the work of Riding and Dyer (1980). Children in their study first listened to part of a short story and then answered a series of questions about the passage, all of which required inference. Questions were of two types: those that depended on imagery, and those that depended on semantic elaboration. (For example, the story may have mentioned the fact that someone knocked on the door of a cottage; the question might be, "What color was the door?" There was no right answer, because the color of the door was not specified.) Response latency was recorded. The dependent variable of interest, however, was an ipsative score that compared latencies on semantic and imagery questions. The idea was to identify children who were much quicker to answer one type of question than the other. Correlations were then computed between this ipsative score and the Junior Eysenck Personality Inventory. Correlations with the extraversion scale were $r = -.67$ for boys ($n = 107$) and $r = -.76$ for girls ($n = 107$). Thus children who showed a preference for imagistic processing were much more likely to be introverted, whereas those who showed a preference for verbal elaboration were more likely to be extraverted. Although different in many respects, the Siegler (1988) and Riding and Dyer (1980) studies both show consistent individual differences in strategy preference can, with proper observation designs and measurement models (see Lohman & Ippel, 1993), define style constructs that provide an important bridge between the domains of personality and ability.

Development

A third bridge between personality and intelligence has emerged from the study of cognitive and moral development, particularly in the adolescent and adult years. One of the persistent findings in this literature is that at least some young adults move from an epistemology in which knowledge is viewed as given, absolute, and fixed to one in which knowledge is viewed as constructed, contextual, and mutable (Kitchener, 1983; Perry, 1970). Further, although there is disagreement as to whether this development is best characterized as a transition through developmental stages (Kitchener, 1983; Kohlberg, 1984) or as the acquisition of increasingly complex beliefs about different aspects of knowledge (Schommer, 1990), there is some consensus that the nature of these epistemic beliefs influence not only affective responses to problems but how they are solved.

In education, modes of cognition that Dewey (1933) called reflective thinking have been of particular concern. Philosophers such as Ennis (1991) claim that the development of such modes of reflective thought also requires the development of dispositions such as open-mindedness, caution, and tolerance for ambiguity. Others have attempted to demonstrate specific linkages between modes of reasoning and personality variables. Baron (1982) showed how a Dewean five-phase model of reflective thinking could be linked to decision rules governing the operation of each step, and how individual differences in the implementation of these rules reflected temperamental biases and values of the individual. For example, the phase called problem enumeration is guided by rules concerning the number and type of possibilities to generate; similarly, the phase called evaluation is guided by some rule that specifies when to stop thinking. General biases (e.g., impulsiveness) affect both phases, whereas specific biases (e.g., the standard of excellence imposed on solutions) affect one phase more than another. The model thereby provides one interesting way to conceptualize linkages between cognitive development and personality.

Cognition, Affection, and Conation

Conceptual categories impose arbitrary boundaries on experience. The commitment to a particular set of terms that is required to describe a domain inevitably emphasizes some elements and relationships among elements in that domain while de-emphasizing or even obscuring others. Scientists must thus endeavor, in Bacon's metaphor, "to carve nature at the joints" rather than arbitrarily. Novick (1982) made a similar point, but using the statistical concept of exchangeability:

> The essential scientific process is that of changing our identification of a person [or other element] from a large population to a relevant subpopulation . . . Our success as scientists can be measured by our skill in identifying variables that can be used to define relevant, exchangeable subpopulations. (p. 6)

The concept of exchangeability implies that different groupings are possible and is thus closer to modern constructivist theories of knowledge than is Baron's metaphor. Indeed, some domains are less well-structured than others, and so conceptual categories, no matter how elegant, inevitably miss and may even mislead. In such cases, other perspectives are not only possible but desirable, because they reveal relationships formerly hidden from view (Langer, 1989). Fundamental shifts in conceptual categories, however, are rare in well-studied domains. Vast, socially shared conceptual networks are constructed using these categories. Those who have acquired the crystallized knowledge necessary to participate fully in the conversation rooted in these categories may find it difficult to restructure their knowledge in new ways. Thus this last approach is as unusual as it is challenging. The basic idea is to reconceptualize the domain using Aristotle's categories of cognition, affection, and conation (or knowing, feeling, and willing) rather than the categories of personality and intelligence. Affection includes temperament and emotion; conation includes motivation and volition. Snow and Jackson (in press) suggest that conation lies between affection and cognition, and that it thereby constitutes a significant portion of the overlap between "personality" (affection and conation) and "intelligence" (conation and cognition). Following Kuhl and Beckman (1985), motivation and volition are viewed as forming a continuum within the conative category, a continuum that symbolizes a commitment pathway from wishes to wants to intentions to actions (see Corno & Kanfer, 1993).

The principal advantage of this scheme is that it replaces the broad, fuzzy concepts of "personality" and "intelligence" with narrower concepts that have clearer psychological referents. Neither cognition, affection, nor conation, however, are explicitly differential constructs. Whether these new constructs span the same space as the old constructs depends not so much on the conventional meanings of each term but rather on the measurement models and units of analysis assumed for each. For example, Cantor (1990) argues that attempts to understand the "doing" or process side of personality can be resolved to three types of units: schemas, tasks (which include goal structures), and strategies. Each of these units, though potentially something on which individuals could differ, is not *defined* by such individual differences (see Cervone, 1991, on the issue of units in personality research). Attempts to map them onto individual-difference constructs depend on the psychological univocality of the individual difference construct; thus attempts to link cognition and either ability or personality dimensions are generally easier for narrow-band than for broad-band constructs. Cantor (1990) makes this prediction explicitly: "The [cognitive] approach is probably best applied to show the workings of dispositions such as optimism, self-esteem, or shyness that have an identifiable cognitive-motivational component, and that translate readily into goals and self-regulatory processes" (p. 737).

Ackerman and Goff (1994) make a similar point in reply to Rocklin's (1994) argument that most of effects attributed to their factor of typical intellectual engagement may be more parsimoniously attributed to the big-five openness factor. They noted that although higher-order factors (e.g., openness) often have broader predictive utility, they do not necessarily have more psychological reality than lower-order factors. Thurstone and Guilford repeatedly made the same point in discussions of ability factors. Indeed, as we noted above, psychological clarity of individual-difference dimensions seems to vary inversely with the breadth of the dimension.

The Two Disciplines, Continued

An old adage says, "There are two types of people in the world—those who think there are two types, and those who do not." Differential psychologists have typically put themselves in the latter category and smiled condescendingly on experimental psychologists who, by virtue of inferior statistical training, routinely categorized continuous variables. But perhaps there is something else at work. The trait-factor model of differential psychology applies only when (to use Novick's phrase) all subjects can be considered exchangeable members of the same population who differ at most in the weights assigned to each of the different factors in the model. However, the experimentalist is more interested in units of analysis (e.g., schemas, goals, and strategies) that, though often differing quantitatively, are most interesting when they differ qualitatively. For example, Havighurst (1953) and Erikson (1950) described developmental progressions of qualitatively different life tasks; Norem (1989) described different coping strategies of defensive-pessimists and illusory-glow optimists; Kelly (1955) and later self-concept theorists described qualitative differences in self-schemas.

Thus, part of the incompatibility between experimental and differential psychology may stem from the search for qualitative rather than quantitative differences. But just as performance functions fitted to data averaged over subjects can assume a smooth form unlike that shown by any subject in the sample (Estes, 1956), so too can scores for individual subjects created by averaging over items or situations appear to differ quantitatively when item-level data differ qualitatively. This argues that the measurement models of trait psychology are in a fundamental way inadequate for the task of relating the two domains. Measurement models that represent qualitative differences in knowledge, goals, and strategies are needed (see Lohman & Ippel, 1993). So are tasks that elicit such responses.

Ultimately, the issue resolves to (a) construct definition and (b) construct validation. We previously noted that although constructs in differential psychology are invariably defined by individual differences, constructs in other domains may be defined by changes in performance across conditions, by rules that map scores on to context domains or absolute scales, and in other ways that reflect individual-difference variance incidentally rather than directly (and may even obscure it altogether). Thus attempts to discover the cognitive bases of differential constructs must first attend carefully to issues of construct definition. When constructs are defined by individual-difference variance, then experimental analyses of tests may not tell us much about the source of these individual differences unless people solve the tests in different ways and the experimental analyses can identify them. Similarly, when a construct is defined by condition or stimulus variance, then correlating individual scores on tasks that define the construct with other variables may not tell us much about it either. Logic and argumentation provide better avenues of commerce between these two types of constructs—if commerce there be—than do the statistical methods of either discipline.

The primary contribution of cognitive analyses to the understanding of differential constructs is through the validation, particularly the internal validation of those constructs. Although measurement specialists have long recognized that test validation has both an internal and an external dimension (e.g., Loevinger, 1957), methods for addressing questions about internal validity were meager compared to the sophisticated correlation techniques developed to address questions about external validity. Cognitive psychology has altered this situation through the development of new methods for addressing questions about internal validity, and theories by which to interpret their results (Embretson, 1983; Sternberg, 1977).

According to Shepard (1993), analyses of the internal validity of a test should address two aspects: the expected relationships among dimensions of the construct, and the process believed to underlie test performance. The first aspect encompasses Allport's (1937) concern for idiographic assessment, and thus it is a seminal issue in the validation of personality constructs. The second aspect encompasses the array of techniques that are used to infer (and sometimes provide formal models of) cognitive processes and knowledge structures by which subjects generate their responses on tests or the knowledge they use to answer test questions. Although one can sometimes show statistical relationships between the products of an internal validity study and the construct itself (and other individual-difference constructs), connections are more often logical than statistical. For example, one can support the interpretation of a test score as a measure of spatial ability by showing how well the performance of each examinee is described by models that compare spatial and nonspatial strategies for solving items. There is no easy way to reduce such information to a single number that can be correlated with other variables, nor does the correlation much address the issue of how individual scores can be interpreted. Rather, connections are made through argument, inference, and systematic testing of plausible rival hypotheses.

A more systematic accounting for what sort of variability is represented by different constructs may help us keep track of our constructs and keep in line our expectations for relationships among them. Earlier we discussed how learning and ability scores were defined by different partitionings of a simple person × item data matrix. Personality and style variables complicate the picture. Figure 1 shows a modified version of Cattell's (1966) covariation chart: persons × items (nested within tasks) × occasions (or situations). Differential psychologists typically worry about person main effects (or covariation of person main effects across several tasks). Experimental psychologists are less uniform. Those who follow an information-processing paradigm worry about variation over trials with a particular task. Situationalists, however, worry more about covariation of either task main effects (e.g., delay versus no delay of reinforcement) or person main effects across occasions; they typically emphasize the magnitude of the former relative to the magnitude of the latter. Developmentalists do the opposite. Then there are those who worry about interactions. The point is that any rapprochement between experimental and differential psychology has many dimensions, not just two. Person × situation is not the same as person × items within task.

These sometimes subtle variations in construct definition are reflected in the grammatical categories used by different theorists to describe ability and personality constructs. Thus ability theorists disagree whether intelligence is best characterized as a noun (e.g., a structural property of the brain or at trait possessed in a certain amount), an adjective (e.g., identifying certain types of people), a verb (e.g., denoting certain varieties of cognition or action), or an adverb (e.g., describing the qualities of cognition or behavior, such as its speed or efficiency). Those who search for those cognitive processes and knowledge structures that generate behavior labeled intelligent often assume that some nouns will be needed, but they place the most emphasis on verbs and adverbs (i.e., how and how well one thinks). Those who study social and

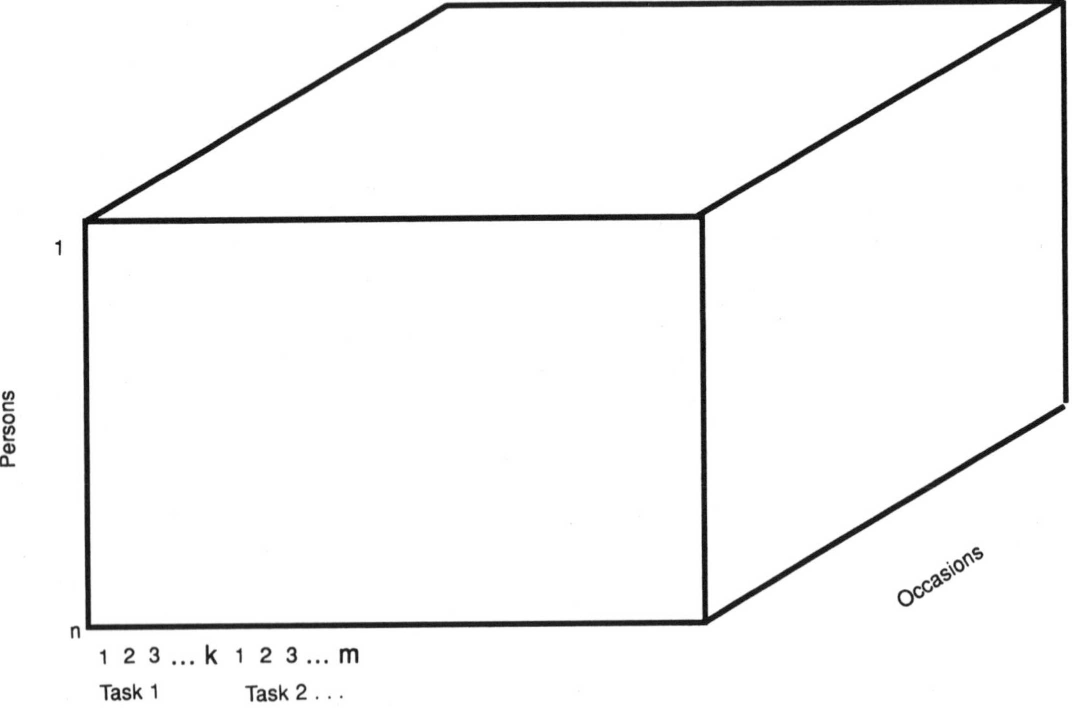

Figure 1. A persons by items (nested within tasks) by occasions covariation matrix. Constructs of interests to experimental, differential, and developmental psychologists may be created by averaging across different facets. Even when given the same name, such constructs can represent quite different sources of variance.

cultural variations in intelligence generally assume that an adjective is needed. Sternberg's (1985) componential and contextual subtheories nicely capture this divergence. In contrast, trait-based theories of personality characterize the domain as a collection of adjectives, and when traits are thought to inhere in the individual, as nouns. The interesting question, though, is whether personality also can be understood using verbs and adverbs. Some (e.g., Cantor, 1990) see this as the wave of the future; others (e.g., Cervone, 1991) are less sanguine about the possibility of a rapprochement between the experimental and differential approaches. If recent attempts to apply cognitive theory to ability constructs are any guide, then bridges will be more difficult to build than initially seems possible. However, careful attention to issues that were insufficiently addressed in ability-process research—particularly those issues we have discussed concerning the definition and measurement of constructs—will surely improve the chances of meaningful progress.

SUMMARY AND CONCLUSIONS

We have discussed much in this chapter—indeed, too much to summarize neatly. At the risk of misleading by omission, we offer the following list of main points.

1. In the domain of intelligence, the controversy over whether intelligence is *unitary or multiple* has a long history, and promises to have an even longer one. In large measure this is because the debate is not only about evidence but also about value such as whether parsimony, utility, or psychological meaningfulness should be given priority. Hierarchical theories offer a compromise, but, as Vernon (1973b) pointed out, may better meet statistical than psychological criteria. We also noted that by emphasizing predictive utility over psychological meaningfulness, such theories have enhanced the status of broad factors and diminished the status of narrower factors. Tests of narrower abilities, however, have never fared as well as tests of broader abilities when utility was the criterion. It is unlikely that new tests will fare better, even though they are more firmly grounded in theory than many of the older classics. Nevertheless, newer tests (such as the revised Woodcock-Johnson) are a boon for researchers and may someday show utility as aptitude variables that interact with instructional or other treatment variables.

2. The *theory of fluid and crystallized abilities* has attracted a wide following. We predict that interest in this theory will continue, for reasons both good and bad. For some, the fluid-crystallized distinction provides a congenial justification for a belief in innate intelligence versus achievement, which is bad. For others, though, the theory has provided a useful way to reconceptualize abilities in terms of cognitive processes and task affordances (Snow, 1992), which is good.

3. *Cognitive psychology* has enormously enriched our understanding of human intelligence and has given us new methods for investigating it. Building bridges between cognitive and differential psychology has proved more difficult than once imagined, however, primarily because researchers have focused on quantitative differences in component process rather than on qualitative differences in solution strategy. Furthermore, we do not believe that broad constructs in either personality or intelligence can be explained as the action of one or more physiological processes, even though we believe that the neuropsychologist has an important place at the table.

4. In the personality domain, the recent consensus over the big five represents an important landmark in the development of the field. Although elaboration and refinement of this system will surely be forthcoming, it provides a useful frame of reference for such discussion. Because of this, studies of ability and personality constructs should include measures of the major dimensions of personality (the big five) and ability (broad group abilities). New individual-difference constructs are often at least partially redundant with constructs already in the catalog. Reference measures also help us interpret results by showing where new scores and constructs are located in this more familiar space. Such studies also allow for the revisions of our understanding of the space by allowing for the identification of inadequacies in existing models.

5. Controversy over the meaning of *nomothetic* scales will likely increase as cognitively inspired research continues, and as more investigators attempt to bridge the gap between purely differential and purely experimental/cognitive approaches to the study of personality. However, both internal and external analyses of performance are needed. External analyses tend to involve normative interpretations of test scores; internal analyses tend to involve ipsative and domain-referenced interpretations. Both are needed, although linkages between them are not as straightforward as some have imagined.

6. *Internal or process-based analyses* tend to be task specific. This is in part an unavoidable consequence of the requirements of such analyses. It is also why experimental psychology is often criticized as a psychology of isolated tasks. For example, it is difficult to say much about how subjects are solving a task unless items or trials are varied systematically along sources of difficulty hypothesized to influence cognitive processes. Process models of heterogeneous tasks are thus impossible unless the analysis focuses on meta-level constructs.

7. *The selection/prediction model* that guided construction of current ability and personality tests is not very informative for decisions about interventions to encourage growth or change. Process-based theories are more informative, but overly optimistic because they rarely examine the extent to which changes in performance transfer outside the bounds of the experimental task or situation. Therefore, new ability and achievement measures are needed that have instructional implications beyond selection. There is already some call for this among school psychologists under the guise of curriculum-based testing. Clinical and counseling psychologists could well use similar measures that described personality constructs in units such as strategies, schemes, and goal structures that have more obvious implications for change. Such measures will be difficult to develop and will likely look very different from today's measures.

8. *Intensive analysis of individual cases* is worthwhile. Perhaps the most interesting analyses will be those of individuals with extreme scores on one or more dimensions of personality or ability. These intensive analyses of individual cases are the most direct way to identify qualitative differences between individuals. They provide avenues both for understanding what it means to be an extreme scorer and for understanding the variety of ways in which one might achieve an extreme score.

9. *The overlap of ability and personality* is more evident when these variables are represented as control processes and strategies than when they are represented as trait dimensions. As Vernon pointed out, a hierarchical model of the traits of ability or of personality can only tell us about the relations among individual differences on tests. These relations have no particular claim to psychological meaningfulness. Further, the research that has led us to consensual descriptions of ability and personality dimensions was almost guaranteed to yield ability factors with little or no relation to personality factors, because of the way in which variables to be factored were chosen. In contrast, variables that describe *what* people do and *how* they do it have much greater potential for coordination. Furthermore, although style constructs have long provided a useful way to conceptualize the intersection between the domains of personality and ability, new categorization schemes (e.g., cognition, affection, and conation) suggest broader overlap than was once imagined.

Now our story is told. Though the plots are diverse and interwoven in ways we have only been able to suggest, they have a promise of happy endings. Current trends in intelligence and personality assessment allow for the hope of a future integrated understanding of the ways (to paraphrase Kluckhohn & Murray, 1953) that each person is like all other people, some other people, and no other person.

REFERENCES

Ackerman, P. L., & Goff, M. (1994). Typical intellectual engagement and personality. *Journal of Educational Psychology.*

Ainley, M. D. (1993). Styles of engagement with learning: Multidimensional assessment of their strategy use and school achievement. *Journal of Educational Psychology, 85,* 395–405.

Allison, R. B. (1960). *Learning parameters and human abilities.* Unpublished report, Educational Testing Service.

Allport, G. W. (1937). *Personality: A psychological interpretation.* New York: Holt.

Allport, G. W. (1961). *Pattern and growth in personality.* New York: Holt.

Allport, G. W. (1965). *Letters from Jenny.* New York: Harcourt Brace Jovanovich.

Allport, G. W., & Odbert, H. S. (1936). Trait names: A psycholexical study. *Psychological Monographs, 47*(211), 1–171.

Anastasi, A. (1937). *Differential psychology.* New York: Macmillan.

Anderson, J. R. (1976). *Language, memory, and thought.* Hillsdale, NJ: Erlbaum.

Anderson, J. R. (1983). *The architecture of cognition.* Cambridge, MA: Harvard University Press.

Barnett, D. W., & Macmann, G. M. (1992). Aptitude-achievement discrepancy scores: Accuracy in analysis misdirected. *School Psychology Review, 21,* 494–508.

Baron, J. (1982). Personality and intelligence. In R. J. Sternberg (Ed.), *Handbook of human intelligence* (pp. 308–351). Cambridge, England: Cambridge University Press.

Biggs, J. B. (1987). *Student approaches to learning and studying.* Hawthorn, Victoria: Australian Council for Educational Research.

Binet, A. (1903). *L'etude expérimentale de l'intelligence* [Experimental studies of intelligence]. Paris: Schleicher Frères.

Block, J. (1961). *The Q-sort method in personality assessment and psychiatric research.* Springfield, IL: Thomas.

Block, J. (1977). Advancing the psychology of personality: Paradigmatic shift or improving the quality of research.In D. Magnusson & N. S. Endler (Eds.), *Personality at the cross-*

roads: Current issues in interactional psychology (pp. 37–63). Hillsdale, NJ: Erlbaum.

Bloom, B. S. (1956). *Taxonomy of educational objectives: Handbook I. Cognitive domain.* New York: McKay.

Botzum, W. A. (1951). A study of the reasoning and closure factors. *Psychometrika, 16*, 361–386.

Bruner, J. (1990). *Acts of meaning.* Cambridge, MA: Harvard University Press.

Bullock, W. S., & Gilliland, K. (1993). Eysenck's arousal theory of introversion-extraversion: A converging measures investigation. *Journal of Personality and Social Psychology, 64*, 113–123.

Cantor, N. (1990). From thought to behavior: "Having" and "doing" in the study of personality and cognition. *American Psychologist, 45*, 735–750.

Carroll, J. B. (1941). A factor analysis of verbal abilities. *Psychometrika, 6*, 279–307.

Carroll, J. B. (1980). *Individual difference relations in psychometric and experimental cognitive tasks* (Report No. 163). Chapel Hill: L. L. Thurstone Psychometric Laboratory, University of North Carolina. (NTIS Doc. No. Ad-A086 057; ERIC Doc. No. ED 191 891).

Carroll, J. B. (1989). Factor analysis since Spearman: Where do we stand? What do we know? In R. Kanfer, P. L. Ackerman, & R. Cudeck (Eds.), *The Minnesota symposium on learning and individual differences: Abilities, motivation, and methodology* (pp. 43–67). Hillsdale, NJ: Erlbaum.

Cattell, R. B. (1943). The measurement of adult intelligence. *Psychological Bulletin, 40*, 153–193.

Cattell, R. B. (1963). Theory of fluid and crystallized intelligence: A critical experiment. *Journal of Educational Psychology, 54*, 1–22.

Cattell, R. B. (1966). *Handbook of multivariate experimental psychology.* Chicago: Rand McNally.

Cattell, R. B. (1971). *Abilities: Their structure, growth, and action.* New York: Houghton Mifflin.

Cervone, D. (1991). The two disciplines of personality psychology. (Review of *Handbook of personality: Theory and research.*). *Psychological Science, 2*, 371–377.

Corno, L., & Kanfer, R. (1993). The role of volition in learning and performance. *Review of Research in Education, 19*, 301–342.

Costa, P. T., Jr., & McRae, R. R. (1992). *Revised NEO Personality Inventory (NEO PI-PR) and NEO Five-Factor Inventory (NEO-FFI) professional manual.* Odessa, FL: Psychological Assessment Resources.

Cronbach, L. J. (1957). The two disciplines of scientific psychology. *American Psychologist, 12*, 671–684.

Cronbach, L. J. (1970). *Essentials of psychological testing* (3rd ed.). New York: Harper & Row.

Cronbach, L. J. (1975). Five decades of public controversy over mental testing. *American Psychologist, 30*, 1–14.

Cronbach, L. J. (1977). *Educational psychology* (3rd ed.). New York: Harcourt Brace Jovanovich.

Cronbach, L. J. (1990). *Essentials of psychological testing* (5th edition). New York: Harper and Row.

Cronbach, L. J., & Furby, L. (1970). How we should measure "change"—or should we? *Psychological Bulletin, 74*, 68–80.

Cronbach, L. J., & Snow, R. E. (1977). *Aptitudes and instructional methods: A handbook for research on interactions.* New York: Irvington.

Cronbach, L. J., Gleser, G. C., Nanda, H., & Rajaratnam, N. (1972). *The dependability of behavioral measurements.* New York: Wiley.

Dewey, J. (1896). The reflex arc concept in psychology. *Psychological Review, 3*, 357–370.

Dewey, J. (1933). *How we think: A restatement of the relation of reflective thinking to the education process.* Boston: Heath.

Digman, J. M., & Takemoto-Chock, N. K. (1981). Factors in the natural language of personality: Re-analysis and comparison of six major studies. *Multivariate Behavioral Research, 16*, 149–170.

Embretson, S. E. (1983). Construct validity: Construct representation versus nomothetic span. *Psychological Bulletin, 93*, 179–197.

Ennis, R. (1991). *Critical thinking: A streamlined conception.* Paper presented at the annual meeting of the American Educational Research Association, Chicago.

Entwistle, N. (1987). Explaining individual differences in school learning. In E. DeCorte, H. Lodewijks, R. Parmentier, & P. Span (Eds.), *Learning and instruction: European research in an international context* (Vol. 1, pp. 69–88). Oxford, England: Pergamon.

Erikson, E. H. (1950). *Childhood and society.* New York: Norton.

Estes, W. K. (1956). The problem of inference from curves based on group data. *Psychological Bulletin, 53*, 134–140.

Fancher, R. E. (1985). *The intelligence men: Makers of the IQ controversy.* New York: Norton.

Flynn, R. J. (1987). Massive IQ gains in 14 nations. What IQ tests really measure. *Psychological Bulletin, 101*, 171–191.

Freeman, F. N. (1926). *Mental tests: Their history, principles and application.* Boston: Houghton Mifflin.

French, J. W. (1951). The description of aptitude and achievement tests in terms of rotated factors. *Psychometric Monographs*, No. 5.

Galton, F. (1869). *Hereditary genius.* London: Macmillan.

Gardner, H., (1983). *Frames of mind: The theory of multiple intelligences.* New York: Basic Books.

Goff, M., & Ackerman, P. L. (1992). Personality-intelligence relations: Assessment of typical intellectual engagement. *Journal of Educational Psychology, 84*(4), 537–552.

Goldberg, L. R. (1981). Language and individual differences: The search for universals in personality lexicons. In L. Wheeler (Ed.), *Review of personality and social psychology* (Vol. 2, pp. 141–165). Beverly Hills, CA: Sage.

Goodman, N. (1984). *Of mind and other matters.* Cambridge, MA: Harvard University Press.

Gough, H., G. (1953). A nonintellectual intelligence test. *Journal of Consulting Psychology, 17*, 242–246.

Gough, H. G. (1965). Conceptual analysis of psychological test score and other diagnostic variables. *Journal of Abnormal Psychology, 70*, 294–302.

Green, D. R. (Ed.). (1974). *The aptitude-achievement distinction.* Monterey, CA: CTB/McGraw-Hill.

Guilford, J. P. (1956). The structure of intellect. *Psychological Bulletin, 53*, 267–293.

Guilford, J. P. (1985). The structure-of-intellect model. In B. B. Wolman (Ed.), *Handbook of intelligence* (pp. 225–266). New York: Wiley.

Guilford, J. P., & Lacey, J. I. (Eds.). (1947). *Printed classification tests.* (Army Air Force Aviation Psychology Research Report No. 5). Washington, DC: Government Printing Office.

Gustafsson, J. E. (1984). A unifying model for the structure of intellectual abilities. *Intelligence, 8*, 179–203.

Guttman, L. (1958). What lies ahead for factor analysis? *Educational and Psychological Measurement, 18*, 497–515.

Haier, R. J., Siegel, B. V., MacLachlan, A., Soderling, E., Lottenberg, S., & Buchsbaum, M. S. (1992). Regional glucose metabolic changes after learning a complex visuospatial/motor task: A position emission study. Brain Research, *570*, 134–153.

Havighurst, R. J. (1953). *Human development and education*. New York: Longmans, Green.

Horn, J. L. (1985). Remodeling old models of intelligence. In B. B. Wolman (Ed.), *Handbook of intelligence* (pp. 267–300). New York: Wiley.

Humphreys, L. G. (1962). The organization of human abilities. *American Psychologist, 17*, 475–483.

Hunt, E. (1986). The heffalump of intelligence. In R. J. Sternberg & D. K. Detterman (Eds.), *What is intelligence? Contemporary viewpoints on its nature and definition* (pp. 101–108). Norwood, NJ: Ablex.

Hunt, E. B., Frost, N., & Lunneborg, C. (1973). Individual differences in cognition: A new approach to intelligence. In G. Bower (Ed.), *The psychology of learning and motivation* (Vol. 7, pp. 87–122). New York: Academic Press.

Hunt, E. B., Lunneborg, C., & Lewis, J. (1975). What does it mean to be high verbal? *Cognitive Psychology, 7*, 194–227.

Jensen, A. R. (1980). *Bias in mental testing*. New York: Free Press.

John, O. P. (1989). Towards a taxonomy of personality descriptors. In D. M. Buss & N. Cantor (Eds.), *Personality psychology: Recent trends and emerging directions* (pp. 261–271). New York: Springer-Verlag.

John, O. P. (1990). The "big five" factor taxonomy: Dimensions of personality in the natural language and in questionnaires. In L. A. Pervin (Ed.), *Handbook of personality: Theory and research* (pp. 66–100). New York: Guilford.

John, O. P., Angleitner, A., & Ostendorf, F. (1988). The lexical approach to personality: A historical review of trait taxonomic research. *European Journal of Personality, 2*, 171–203.

Kaufman, A. S., & Kaufman, N. L. (1983). *Kaufman Assessment Battery for Children*. Circle Pines, MN: American Guidance Service.

Keating, D. P., & McLean, D. J. (1987). Cognitive processing, cognitive ability, and development: A reconsideration. In P. A. Vernon (Ed.), *Speed of information-processing and intelligence* (pp. 239–270). Norwood, NJ: Ablex.

Kelley, T. L. (1928). *Crossroads in the mind of man*. Stanford, CA: Stanford University Press.

Kelly, G. (1955). *The psychology of personal constructs*. New York: Norton.

Kenny, D. A. (1974). A quasi-experimental approach to assessing treatment effects in the nonequivalent control group design. *Psychological Bulletin, 82*, 345–362.

Kerr, N. H., Corbitt, R., & Jurkovic, G. J. (1980). Mental rotation: Is it stage related? *Journal of Mental Imagery, 4*, 49–56.

Kitchener, K. S. (1983). Cognition, metacognition, and epistemic cognition. *Human Development, 26*, 222–232.

Kluckhohn, C., & Murray, H. A. (1953). *Personality in nature, society, and culture*. New York: Knopf.

Kohlberg, L. (1984). *Essays on moral development*. San Francisco: Harper & Row.

Kuhl, J., & Beckmann, J. (Eds.). (1985). *Action control from cognition to behavior*. New York: Springer-Verlag.

Kuhl, J., & Beckman, R. (1993). The role of volition in learning and performance. *Review of Research in Education, 19*, 301–342.

Kyllonen, P. C., & Christal, R. E. (1989). Cognitive modeling of learning abilities: A status report of LAMP. In R. Dillon & J. W. Pellegrino (Eds.), *Testing: Theoretical and applied issues*. New York: Freeman.

Kyllonen, P. C., & Christal, R. E. (1990). Reasoning ability is (little more than) working memory capacity?! *Intelligence, 14*, 389–433.

Lamiell, J. T. (1981). Toward an idiothetic psychology of personality. *American Psychologist, 36*(3), 276–289.

Langer, E. J. (1989). *Mindfulness*. Reading, MA: Addison-Wesley.

Loevinger, J. (1957). Objective tests as instruments of psychological theory. *Psychological Reports, 3*(Monograph Supp. 9), 635–694.

Lohman, D. F. (1989). Human intelligence: An introduction to advances in theory and research. *Review of Educational Research, 59*, 333–373.

Lohman, D. F. (1993). Teaching and testing to develop fluid abilities. *Educational Researcher, 22*, 12–23.

Lohman, D. F. (1994). Component scores as residual variation (or why the intercept correlates best). *Intelligence, 19*, 1–12.

Lohman D. F., & Ippel, M. J. (1993). Cognitive diagnosis: From statistically-based assessment toward theory-based assessment. In N. Frederiksen, R. Mislevy, & I. Bejar (Eds.), *Test theory for a new generation of tests* (pp. 41–71). Hillsdale, NJ: Erlbaum.

London, H., & Exner, J. E., Jr. (Eds.). (1978). *Dimensions of personality*. New York: Wiley.

Matarazzo, J. D. (1992). Psychological testing and assessment in the 21st century. *American Psychologist, 47*, 1007–1018.

McNemar, Q. (1964). Lost: Our intelligence? Why? *American Psychologist, 19*, 871–882.

McRae, R. R., & Costa, P. T. (1985). Updating Norman's adequate taxonomy: Intelligence and personality dimensions in natural language and in questionnaires. *Journal of Personality and Social Psychology, 49*, 710–721.

Messick, S. (1984). The nature of cognitive styles: Problems and promise in educational practice. *Educational Psychologist, 19*, 59–74.

Messick, S. (1987). Structural relationships across cognition, personality, and style. In R. E. Snow & M. J. Farr (Eds.), *Aptitude, learning, and instruction: Vol. 3. Conative and affective process analyses* (pp. 35–76). Hillsdale, NJ: Erlbaum.

Nitko, A. J. (1984). Defining "criterion-referenced test." In R. A. Berk (Ed.), *A guide to criterion-referenced test construction* (pp. 8–28). Baltimore, MD: Johns Hopkins University.

Norem, J. K. (1989). Cognitive strategies as personality: Effectiveness, specificity, flexibility, and change. In D. M. Buss & N. Cantor (Eds.), *Personality psychology: Recent trends and emerging directions* (pp. 45–60). New York: Springer-Verlag.

Norman, W. T. (1963). Toward an adequate taxonomy of personality attributes: Replicated factor structure in peer nomination personality ratings. *Journal of Abnormal and Social Psychology, 66*, 574–583.

Novick, M. R. (1982). Educational testing: Inferences in relevant subpopulations. *Educational Researcher, 11*, 4–10.

Pask, G. (1976). Styles and strategies of learning. *British Journal of Educational Psychology, 46*, 128–148.

Peabody, D., & Goldberg, L R. (1989). Some determinants of factor structures from personality-trait descriptors. *Journal of Personality and Social Psychology, 57*, 552–567.

Pelham, B. W. (1993). The idiographic nature of human personality: Examples of the idiograph, self-concept. *Journal of Personality and Social Psychology, 64*(4), 665–677.

Pellegrino, J. W., & Glaser, R. (1979). Cognitive correlates and components in the analysis of individual differences. In R. J. Sternberg & D. K. Detterman (Eds.), *Human intelligence: Perspectives on its theory and measurement* (pp. 61–88). Hillsdale, NJ: Erlbaum.

Pellegrino, J. W., & Kail, R. (1982). Process analyses of spatial aptitude. In R. J. Sternberg (Ed.), *Advances in the psychology of human intelligence* (Vol. 1, pp. 311–366). Hillsdale, NJ: Erlbaum.

Pemberton, C. (1952). The closure factors related to other cognitive processes. *Psychometrika, 17*, 267–288.

Perry, W. G. (1970). *Forms of intellectual and ethical development in the college years: A scheme*. New York: Holt, Rinehart and Winston.

Riding, R. J., & Dyer, V. A. (1980). The relationship between extraversion and verbal-imagery learning style in twelve-year-old children. *Personality and Individual Differences, 1*, 273–279.

Rocklin, T. R. (1994). The relationship between typical intellectual engagement and openness: A comment on Goff and Ackerman (1992). *Journal of Educational Psychology, 86*, 145–149.

Rorer, L. G. (1990). Personality assessment: A conceptual survey. In L. A. Pervin (Ed.), *Handbook of personality: Theory and research* (pp. 693–720). New York: Guilford.

Rorer, L. G., & Widiger, T. A. (1983). Personality structure and assessment. In M. Rosenzweig & L. Porter (Eds.), *Annual review of psychology* (Vol. 34, pp. 431–465). Palo Alto, CA: Annual Reviews.

Schmidt, F. L., & Hunter, J. E. (1977). Development of a general solution to the problem of validity generalization. *Journal of Applied Psychology, 62*, 529–540.

Schommer, M. (1990). Effects of beliefs about the nature of knowledge on comprehension. *Journal of Educational Psychology, 82*(3), 498–504.

Shepard, L. A. (1993). Evaluating test validity. *Review of Research in Education, 19*, 405–450.

Shiffrin, R. M., & Schneider, W. (1977). Controlled and automatic human information processing: II. Perceptual learning, automatic attending, and a general theory. *Psychological Review, 84*, 127–190.

Siegler, R. S. (1988). Individual differences in strategy choices: Good students, not-so-good students, and perfectionists. *Child Development, 59*, 833–857.

Smith, I. M. (1964). *Spatial ability*. San Diego, CA: Knapp.

Snow, R. E. (1980). Aptitude and achievement. *New Directions for Testing and Measurement, 5*, 39–59.

Snow, R. E. (1981). Toward a theory of aptitude for learning: Fluid and crystallized abilities and their correlates. In M. P. Friedman, J. P. Das, & N. O'Connor (Eds.), *Intelligence and learning* (pp. 345–362). New York: Plenum.

Snow, R. E., & Jackson, D. N., III (in press). Individual differences in conation: Selected constructs and measures. In H. F. O'Neil, J. (Ed.), *Motivation: Research and theory*. San Diego, CA: Academic Press.

Snow, R. E., & Lohman, D. F. (1989). Implications of cognitive psychology for educational measurement. In R. Linn (Ed.), *Educational measurement* (3rd ed.; pp. 263–331). New York: Macmillan.

Snow, R. E., & Swanson, J. (1992). Instructional psychology: Aptitude, adaptation, and assessment. *Annual Review of Psychology, 43*, 583–626.

Snow, R. E., & Yalow, E. (1982). Education and intelligence. In R. J. Sternberg (Ed.), *Handbook of human intelligence* (pp. 493–585). Cambridge, England: Cambridge University Press.

Spearman, C. E. (1927). *The abilities of man*. London: Macmillan.

Sperry, R. W. (1993). The impact and promise of the cognitive revolution. *American Psychologist, 48*, 878–885.

Stake, R. E. (1961). Learning parameters, aptitudes, and achievement. *Psychometric Monographs*, No. 9.

Stankov, L. (1986). Kvashchev's experiment: Can we boost intelligence? *Intelligence, 10*, 209–230.

Stern, W. (1914). *The psychological methods of testing intelligence* (Educational Psychology Monograph No. 13; G. M. Whipple, Trans.). Baltimore, MD: Warwick & York.

Sternberg, R. J. (1977). *Intelligence, information processing, and analogical reasoning: The componential analysis of human abilities*. Hillsdale, NJ: Erlbaum.

Sternberg, R. J. (1982). Reasoning, problem solving, and intelligence. In R. J. Sternberg (Ed.), *Handbook of human intelligence*. Cambridge, England: Cambridge University Press.

Sternberg, R. J. (1985). *Beyond IQ: A triarchic theory of human intelligence*. Cambridge, England: Cambridge University Press.

Sternberg, R. J., Conway, B. E., Ketron, J. L., & Bernstein, M. (1981). People's conceptions of intelligence. *Journal of Personality and Social Psychology, 41*(1), 37–55.

Thomson, G. H. (1916). A hierarchy without a general factor. *British Journal of Psychology, 8*, 271–281.

Thorndike, E. L. (1920). Intelligence and its uses. *Harper's Magazine, 140*, 227–235.

Thorndike, E. L., Bregman, E. O., Cobb, M. V., & Woodyard, E. (1926). *The measurement of intelligence*. New York: Columbia University, Teachers College.

Thorndike, E. L., Lay, W., & Dean, P. R. (1909). The relation of accuracy in sensory discrimination to general intelligence. *American Journal of Psychology, 20*, 364–369.

Thorndike, R. L. (1963). *The concepts of over- and underachievement*. New York: Columbia University, Teachers College.

Thorndike, R. L., Hagen, E. P., & Sattler, J. M. (1986). *The Stanford-Binet Intelligence Scale* (4th ed.). Chicago: Riverside.

Thorndike, E. L., Terman, L. M., Freeman, F. N., Calvin, S. S., Pentler, R., Ruml, B., & Pressey, S. L. (1921). Intelligence and its measurement: A symposium. *Journal of Educational Psychology, 12*, 123–147.

Thurstone, L. L. (1935). *The vectors of the mind*. Chicago: University of Chicago Press.

Thurstone, L. L. (1938). Primary mental abilities. *Psychometric Monographs*, No. 1.

Thurstone, L. L. (1944). A factorial study of perception. *Psychometric Monographs*, No. 4.

Thurstone, L. L. (1949). *Mechanical aptitude: III. Analysis of group tests*. (Psychometric Laboratory Report No. 55). Chicago: University of Chicago.

Tiedemann, J. (1989). Measures of cognitive styles: A critical review. *Educational Psychologist, 24*, 261–275.

Tupes, E. C., & Christal, R. C. (1961). *Recurrent personality factors based on trait ratings*. Technical report, United States Air Force, Lackland Air Force Base, TX.

Tyack, D. B. (1974). *The one best system*. Cambridge, MA: Harvard University Press.

Vernon, P. E. (1950). *The structure of human abilities*. London: Methuen.

Vernon, P. E. (1973a). Multivariate approaches to the study of cognitive styles. In J. R. Royce (Ed.), *Multivariate analysis and psychological theory* (pp. 125–148). New York: Academic Press.

Vernon, P. E. (1973b). Comments on Messick's paper. In J. R. Royce (Ed.), *Multivariate analysis and psychological theory* (pp. 293–296). New York: Academic Press.

Weschler, D. (1943). Non-intellective factors in general intelligence. *Journal of Abnormal and Social Psychology, 38*, 101–103.

Weschler, D. (1950). Cognitive, conative, and non-intellective intelligence. *American Psychologist, 5*, 78–83.

Weschler, D. (1975). Intelligence defined and undefined: A relativistic appraisal. *American Psychologist, 30*, 135–139.

Weinstein, C. E., Goetz, E. T., & Alexander, P. A. (Eds.). (1988). *Learning and study strategies*. San Diego, CA: Academic Press.

Wolfe, D. (1940). Factor analysis to 1940. *Psychometric Monographs*, No. 3.

Woodcock, R. W., & Johnson, M. B. (1989). *Woodcock-Johnson Psycho-Educational Battery-revised*. Allen, TX: DLM Teaching Resources.

Woodrow, H. (1946). The ability to learn. *Psychological Review, 53*, 147–158.

22

Constructing Pers
Intelligence Ins

Methods and Issues

Robert B. Most and Moshe Zeidner

GOALS

The goal of this chapter is to describe methods for developing personality and intelligence measures. By comparing and contrasting the two constructs and how we assess them, we are able to see points of similarity and difference that relate to developing instruments in these two domains. We also want to be very practical and discuss the issues involved in developing personality or intelligence instruments. We will walk through the instrument development process step by step and examine different methods for approaching each step.

We will begin by describing the relationship between the constructs of personality and intelligence. Then we will describe the specific phases of test development. Our goal is for the reader to gain an understanding of how intelligence and personality tests are developed and what the practical issues are in test development.

Robert B. Most • Mind Garden, P. O. Box 60669, Palo Alto, California 94306. Moshe Zeidner • School of Education, University of Haifa, Mount Carmel 31999, Israel.

International Handbook of Personality and Intelligence, edited by Donald H. Saklofske and Moshe Zeidner. Plenum Press, New York, 1995.

THE RELATIONSHIP BETWEEN INTELLIGENCE AND PERSONALITY CONSTRUCTS

Intelligence can be seen as part of the overall structure of human personality and part of the way various personality dimensions fit together to form a coherent whole (Cattell, 1971; Eysenck & Eysenck, 1985; Guilford, 1959). According to this conception, personality is viewed as the superordinate construct, which can be further divided into two complementary categories: noncognitive components (personality motivation, interests, attitudes, needs, etc.) and cognitive components (intelligence traits or factors). This view assumes that because personality deals with the total functioning of the individual, it cannot help but include intelligence as a major component.

An alternative view espoused by David Wechsler (1944), a key figure in intelligence testing, views personality and motivational factors as integral components of the construct of intelligence and therefore part of the construct validity of intelligence tests. Wechsler believes that factors other than intellectual ability (e.g., drive, incentive) enter into intelligent behavior. Accordingly intelligence, or the ability to utilize mental energy in contextual situations, is a manifestation of personality as a whole and cannot be equated with intellectual ability alone. Thus what is needed, accord-

tests from which personality minated but tests in which these tors are clearly present and objec- e.

es

actor analytic research shows that when person- and intelligence measures are analyzed together, e two constructs can generally be differentiated (Mc-Crae, 1987). If so, a question arises: On the basis of which criteria can we differentiate among the two concepts? Table 1 provides a structure for this differentiation.

Trait

Intelligence is unidirectional, whereas personality can be considered bidirectional. It is clear how to set optimal parameters for intelligent behavior. The ideal is to set the value at one end of the parameter, namely, the extreme positive value ("extremely intelligent"). By contrast, a personality trait need not take on an extreme value for it to be set optimally, and midpoint values are often considered as optimal. With personality traits it is difficult to specify what it might mean to say that people are (for example) too sociable, overly impulsive, too rigid, or not aggressive enough.

Intelligence is typically thought of as extending in a single direction, from "little of" to "much of" (Thorndike, 1982). By contrast, personality is generally conceived of as being bipolar. For example, we would conceive of not only an absence of anxiety but also an opposite, which we may label "calm" or "relaxed." The point of neutrality generally lies in the middle—somewhere in between, say, "very anxious," on one hand, and "very relaxed," on the other.

Trait to Item Relationship

In the ability domain, all items are expected to show a monotonically increasing relation with the trait assessed: The higher the person's position on the trait, the higher the chances of answering the item correctly. It would be inconceivable (save for a clerical error, a poor item, a faulty key, etc.) that persons with lower intelligence would show a higher probability of answering an intelligence test item correctly than their higher-intelligence counterparts. By contrast, there is the possibility that personality test items will fail to show a monotonically increasing relation to the bipolar trait (Thorndike, 1982). For example, with respect to the personality test item "I suffer from intrusive and involuntary thoughts once a week," we may get a "no" response from people who seldom have intrusive thoughts, as well as from people who in fact have such frequent and chronic thoughts.

Goals and Optimal Assessment Situation

A major difference between ability and personality measures is in the measurement objectives and the concomitant optimal situations designed to elicit expected responses (Nunnally, 1978). An intelligence test aims at eliciting maximal performance from examinees, and one expects them to give their best effort in solving the problem or engaging the task at hand. Consequently, intelligence is generally measured in

Table 1. Some Relationships Differentiating Personality and Intelligence

Dimension	Intelligence	Personality
Trait	Unidirectional ("little of" to "much of")	Bidirectional (polar extremes)
Trait to item relationship	Strictly monotonic	Not necessarily monotonic
Goals and optimal assessment situation	Test situation requiring maximal performance	Real life situation
Motivation in taking the instrument	High motivation	Tends to vary
Instructions	To do ones' best	To provide a candid response
Criteria for evaluating responses	Veridical criterion	Direction/intensity (no correct response)
Stability of the instrument	Relatively stable	Tends to fluctuate
Reliability of the instrument	Generally high	Varies from high to low
Interpreting results	Relatively straightforward	More open and controversial
Practical utility	Moderate	Low to moderate

evaluative and maximal performance test conditions, with examinees perfectly aware of the evaluative nature of the task and expected to be highly motivated to succeed.

By contrast, a personality measure is designed to gauge a person's typical performance in a real-life situation. Consequently, the examinee is expected to give as frank and as truthful a response as possible, indicating what is typical of his or her feelings or sentiments at a particular moment (state) or in general (trait). Because responses on personality measures are partially under the subject's control and often contaminated by social desirability and other response sets (Baron, 1982; Nunnally, 1978) personality traits are best measured under normal circumstances, and without the subject's awareness.

Motivation and Control in Taking the Instrument

The individual has some degree of voluntary control in modifying personality states and adjusting parameters of personality states. Even personality dispositions are partly modifiable via instruction, as exemplified by the test-anxious person instructed to relax, breath deeply, and think positively when anxious under various testing conditions. By contrast, intelligence is under less personal control and is less amenable to instructions to change or modify behavior. For example, giving a student feedback that he or she has low spatial ability and needs to improve that ability would not be very helpful to that person in adjusting the spatial ability parameter in the desired direction.

Instructions

Intelligence is generally assessed using test conditions involving a set of standard tasks that examinees respond to at a designated time and place (see Zeidner & Most, 1992). Subjects understand they are in an evaluative situation, and they are required to solve problems, define words, draw correct conclusions, and the like. Intelligence has not been profitably assessed by observer ratings (e.g., "How intelligent is Dan?") or self-reports ("How intelligent are you, Dan?").

By contrast, personality researchers have worked most frequently with subjective media (e.g., projective devices), behavioral ratings, and self-inquiry modes of gathering evidence (e.g., inventories). In fact, most measures of personality rely on someone's impression, be it the individual's personal impressions ("I get very anxious when tested") or some other person's impression of the individual being assessed ("He tends to be tense and panicky under test conditions").

Criteria for Evaluating Responses

Whereas a veridical criterion is generally employed in evaluating a response in the intelligence domain (see Nunnally, 1978), behaviors falling under the domain of personality often have no veridical criterion for judging responses. That is, in the domain of intelligence it is possible to determine the correctness of a response. We expect responses to correspond to a correct or valid application or deduction of a rule or principle, be it a logical (e.g., "2, 4, 7, 11; What is the next number in this series?"), semantic (e.g., "What is a parabola?"), or empirical (e.g., "Who was the first president of Israel?") rule. By contrast, it generally makes no sense to speak of a "right" or "good" response on a personality factor; any value judgment in this respect would be purely arbitrary (Catteli, 1971; Thorndike, 1982). Rather than judge personality responses for their correctness at a given level of complexity, they are assessed by the type of sentiments expressed ("I frequently get anxious" versus "I am calm"), and the strength of magnitude of the response ("extremely anxious," "anxious," "somewhat anxious," etc.).

Stability of the Instrument

Whereas theorists generally accept the fact that cognitive traits display considerable stability across situation and over time (Willerman, 1979), the cross-situational consistency of personality traits has been debated (Mischel, 1968), and tests of this hypothesis have yielded inconsistent findings. Some recent studies of personality (see Costa & McCrae, 1986) show promising findings of stability during the adulthood years.

Reliability of the Instrument

It should be noted that dynamic personality variables are more complex and tend to fluctuate more than abilities, which evidence greater stability across time (Cattell, 1971). In fact, the very units of observation in personality assessment (moods, dispositions, emotional states) are quite troublesome for measurement purposes, because they are probabilistic rather than all-or-none phenomena. Thus aggressive people do not always display aggressive traits, and most individuals defined by personality descriptions (e.g., optimistic, impulsive, sociable, honest) do not always possess or display the characteristics ascribed to them (Kleinmuntz, 1982). Though a characteristic trait exists, some personality states may vary appreciably from day to day, thus depressing test-retest reliability coefficients.

Personality measures are generally more susceptible to a wide variety of sources of measurement error (faking, response sets, social desirability). A considerable body of research attests to the lower reliability and validity of personality compared to intelligence measures (see Anastasi, 1986).

Interpreting Results

No one single factor is sufficient to explain an individual's performance on intelligence tests; rather, success or failure results from interactions involving ability, personality and motivational dispositions, task requirements, incentives, and opportunities in the immediate environment, as well as other factors that influence the examinee to engage in various activities. Because subjects are unaware of what is expected of them on most personality tests, interpretations of the test situation may vary considerably from subject to subject, causing considerable ambiguity and further increasing measurement error. Furthermore, in contrast to ability measures, we may not get a typical response on personality measures because the subject chooses not to give it, or because he or she does not have enough self-insight to give it (Thorndike, 1982).

Practical Utility

Both personality and intelligence measures have been used for practical decision-making purposes in a wide array of sectors and settings. Among the various practical uses of personality and intelligence measures are clinical diagnosis, vocational guidance and counseling, school prediction and placement college selection, and personnel selection and placement. The main difference between the two types of measures is that intelligence tests appear more valid and have been more widely used in school prediction and college placement and selection, whereas personality measures have been more used in clinical diagnosis and counseling (Jensen, 1980).

WHAT TO MEASURE

Personality and intelligence each have broad domains of human expression that refer to many distinct aspects of behavioral and interpersonal functioning. The first step in developing an assessment is to define the domain that is to be measured and the uses of the measure (Thorndike, 1982).

Intelligence

Before developing a test of any construct, one should clearly and explicitly express what one wants to test. In our particular case, the label "intelligence" would express our intention in the most general way. We therefore need to begin with delineating notions of intelligence as a psychological construct and get some idea of the kinds of behaviors that would constitute observable and quantifiable instances of intelligent behavior. Indeed, the measurement of intelligence is limited by the clarity with which we are able to define the meaning of the construct.

As a hypothetical construct or trait, intelligence cannot be measured directly but must be inferred by measuring behaviors defined as cognitive or intellectual (Eysenck & Eysenck, 1985). Thus, in assessing intelligence, we cannot compare a person's score directly with any standard objective index of intelligence. Although we may not know what constitutes the stuff of intelligence, we may come to know it by its exemplars and correlates (solving complex logical problems, writing novel computer programs, building a model jet plane, understanding the meaning of rare words, etc.). The lack of precision in defining and observing an inner construct such as intelligence can lead to serious problems in its assessment.

Attempts at deciding on the true definition and nature of intelligence have been largely unsuccessful. At present, there is little consensus among authorities regarding the exact definition of the term, with accounts of intelligence by different writers varied and discrepant. Indeed, there are almost as many definitions of intelligence as researchers proposing them. Despite the lack of consensus among intelligence researchers, though, modern authorities would agree that intelligence may be characterized as follows: it is a multifaceted construct involving distinct kinds of abstract and symbolic problem-solving abilities; it is manifested in the ability to learn or profit from experience or to deal effectively with novel situations in the environment; it grows as people mature and learn; and it facilitates adjustment to one's surroundings (see Kline, 1991).

The intelligence test constructor must identify specific behaviors that represent the construct or define the domain. As pointed out by Jensen (1980), this aspect of intelligence test construction is largely a matter of psychological insight, experience, and the test constructor's particular theory (whether implicit or explicit) on the essential nature of intelligence. One needs to start out with an in-depth understanding and determination of the intelligence domain in order to guide the development of the item pool and facilitate the initial content validity procedures and the construct validity research.

Personality

The definition of personality typically relates to the social world. The measurement of personality often is that of self-reports, which have the utility of predicting a person's social reputation and the manner in which the person is perceived by others (see Hogan, 1991). In this context, *personality* refers to structures or collections of manifest behaviors that would lead others to form concepts about the person. The personality traits are basically concepts inferred from the person's self-reported behavior under various situations. The method used to define a person along the trait dimension relies on their self-reported responses to questions, whereas the criteria for the trait definition is their actual behaviors. Personality assessment is based on the assumption that behaviors as reported are reliably related to actual behavior.

One way of looking at the process is that people behave, and the behaviors are perceived. The perceivers talk about the behavior; the talk is then built into constructs by personologists, who develop personality items to measure the constructs. These are administered to people, and the responses are built into scales that are used to predict behaviors. Thus, because personality is defined by social behavior, there is a circularity to personality measurement. Figure 1 is a schematic of this process.

APPROACHES TO DOMAIN DEFINITION

Following are some methods for defining the domain of intelligence and personality measurements. It is important to have a clear understanding of what is to be measured.

Facet Theory

Facet theory has been used for the specification of the domain of both personality and intelligence constructs. It was developed by Louis Guttman in the 1960s and has considerable potential as a heuristic device for mapping out the domain and specifying the relevant dimensions. The first and perhaps most crucial step in the facet approach is the specification of a

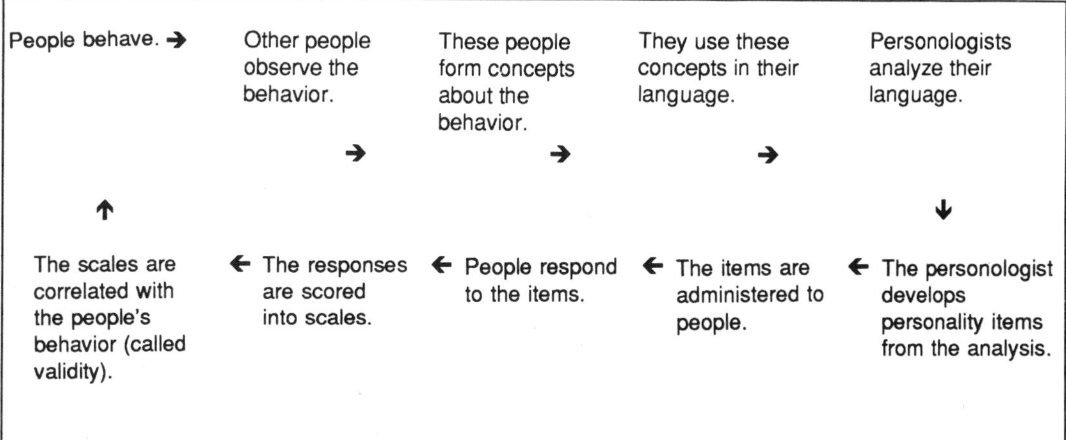

Figure 1. The circular nature of personality measurement.

theoretical framework and the a priori mapping out of the domain and universe of observation. That is, a definitional system for the universe of content and observations on the intelligence or personality domains are specified, most typically in the form of a mapping sentence (to be discussed below).

Intelligence

Guttman and coworkers (Guttman, 1965; Guttman & Levy, 1980, 1991; Schlesinger & Guttman, 1969) have identified three major dimensions or facets of the intelligence domain: language of test presentation of communication (e.g., verbal, numeric, figural), mental operation required by the test (e.g., rule inference, rule application, rule learning), and modality of examinee expression (oral expression, manual manipulation of objects, and paper and pencil). These facets essentially constitute the intelligence domain.

According to facet theory (Guttman & Levy, 1991) an item belongs to the universe of intelligence test items if and only if its domain asks about a rule (be it logical, empirical, semantic, or normative) and the range is ordered from very right to very wrong with respect to that rule. Thus, responses to intelligence tests are interpreted against a veridical criterion, with the range being from perfectly true to not true at all (see Nunnally, 1978). This definition obviously excludes subjective rules such as aesthetic, semantic, or religious guidelines. Furthermore, in contrast to achievement tests, which typically involve rule applications and tasks that are school related, intelligence test items typically require the deduction of an objective rule on tasks that are removed from specific instructional situations (e.g., determining the pattern in the series 3, 7, 15, 31, . . .). A correct response is evidence that the examinee has deduced and used the rule appropriately.

The mapping sentence in Figure 2 delineates these three major facets and the specified observational domain of intelligence (Guttman, 1969; Guttman & Levi, 1991). It is important to point out that tests can vary on other facets as well, including specific content, speededness, and type of memory demanded (recall versus recognition).

Personality

Facet theory is occasionally used in defining the personality domain to develop personality instruments; basically, the method is the same as described above. Dancer (1985) illustrates a definition of the universe for self-esteem items for the Rosenberg Self-Esteem Scale (see Figure 3). This will give a feel for how domains can be mapped by facet theory. Alternatives that are covered in item writing are separated by alternative braces. For example, the respective alternatives item "I feel I have a number of good qualities" would be affective, qualities, beliefs about self, and positive in the range.

Schultz (1966) developed his successful FIRO-B with facet theory method. He carefully mapped all possible combinations of the three constructs, inclusion, control, and affection by four facets:

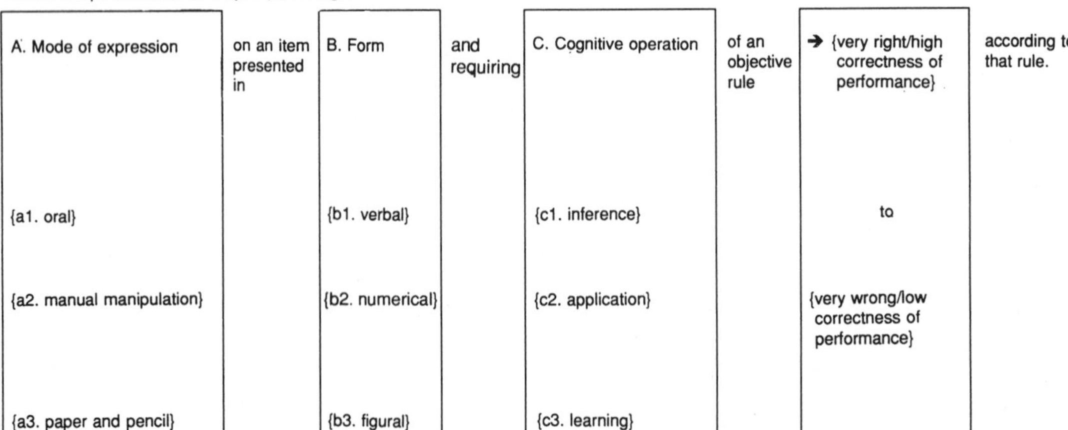

Figure 2. Facet mapping sentence for three major facets and the specified observational domain of intelligence.

An item belongs to the universe of self-esteem items if and only if its domain asks about:

A. Behavior in modality	toward the	B. Criterion of social worth	expressed in terms of assessment	C. Self as evidenced by one's	and the range is ordered from	→ {very positive}	behavior toward social worth.
{a1. cognitive}		{b1. in general}		{c1. actions}		to	
{a2. affective}		{b2. qualities}		{c2. beliefs about self}		{very negative}	
		{b3. performances}					
		{b4. aptitudes}		in some life area			

Figure 3. Facet mapping sentence definition of the universe for self-esteem items for the Rosenberg Self-Esteem Scale.

1. *Observability*: The degree to which the action is observable by others (i.e., *actions* are more observable by others, and *feelings* are more observable by oneself)
2. *Directionality*: The direction of the interaction (either self toward other, other toward self, or self toward self)
3. *Status of action*: Whether the behavior is inclusion, control, or affection
4. *State of relation*: Whether the relation is desired, ideal, anxious, or pathological

Schutz' final instrument measured wanted and expressed inclusion, wanted and expressed control, and wanted and expressed affection.

Folk Concepts to Define the Domain

Personality

One method of defining the domain for personality instruments is to ascertain a set of folk concepts. This is a natural outgrowth from the model in Figure 1, because the personologist studies the descriptions people use to explain behavior. The California Psychological Inventory (CPI; Gough, 1965) is a good example of a personality instrument designed to measure the folk concepts of personality.

> The CPI is a true-false objective inventory scaled for "folk concepts," that is, variables used for the description and analysis of personality in everyday life and in social interactions. It is theorized that such folk concepts, viewed as emergents from interpersonal behavior, have a kind of immediate meaningfulness and universal relevance which enhance their attractiveness as diagnostic concepts.
>
> The system of concepts defined by the 18 scales in the inventory should also be mentioned. Its main property is that it is an "open" system—it can change and grow by the addition or substitution of scales, and if need be can be reduced by the elimination of measures. Its purpose is to reflect social behavior, and in so doing to include a sufficient number of variables so that all major forms of such behavior can be forecast either by one scale or a combination or pattern of scales. (Gough, 1965, pp. 295–296)

Gough (1965) required that scales be "useful" to the practitioner rather than orthogonal or factor pure: "The practitioner in testing seeks variables which permit individuated descriptions of the subject who has been tested, forecasts of what he will say or do, and characterizations of the way in which others will react to him. The greater the range of such information, the more accurate its specification, the greater the value of the instrument which produced it" (p. 294). Since the original 18 scales, he has added two scales, Independence and Empathy, because of the utility of the concepts (and even though Empathy is highly correlated with Psychological Mindedness). Gough did not require his scales to have factor purity because he viewed them basically on their pragmatic value. His goal was to map the concepts that people use when they think of personality in interpersonal relationships, not necessarily to come up with some underlying "truth."

Intelligence

In principle, the conceptual specification of skills of intelligent behavior can be generated from ordinary people's conception of what constitutes intelligent behavior. Thorndike (Thorndike, Bregnan, Cobb, & Woodyard, 1926) was one of the first psychologists to espouse a folk definition of intelligence. Accordingly, he suggested dividing intelligence into three main types: abstract, practical, and social. Thus, a test of intelligence based on a folk view could tap skills such as verbal and numerical ability (e.g., reads widely, speaks clearly and articulately, converses well, displays good vocabulary, works well with numbers), practical problem-solving skills (e.g., facility in manipulating objects, reasons logically, sees relations, sizes up situation well, listens to various sides of an argument), and social competence (e.g., admits mistakes, displays interest in the world at large, sensitive to the needs of other people, is frank and honest with others).

A study of people's lay and expert conceptions of intelligence found that people have well-formed prototypes corresponding to the various kinds of intelligence (academic, social, etc.); that these prototypes are quite similar for experts and lay persons; and that these prototypes are closely related to certain psychological theories of intelligence. In sharp contrast to personality tests, however, folk concepts have not to date been employed in constructing intelligence tests (Sternberg, Conway, Ketron, & Bernstein, 1981).

Lexical Analysis in Personality Domain Definition

A lexical analysis approach (e.g., Goldberg, 1982; Norman, 1963) has attempted to order personality dispositions by probability. By looking at the probability of a personality concept in natural language we can get a measure of how important that concept is to speakers. By combining this approach with statistical methods, the many trait descriptions have been boiled down in various proposed structures of personality. The leading structure currently is the "big five" factor taxonomy (John, 1990).

Systematic Monitoring

To derive an ultimate model of personality we need to know what behaviors individuals manifest in their day-to-day interactions. Craik (1991) is attempting to accomplish this by monitoring people with a video camera and rating their acts. The utility of this, as Buss and Craik (1983a) put it, is that "Systematic monitoring of individual's conduct in everyday settings over standard periods of observation will eventually provide a basis for analyzing the manifested structure of dispositions and for making comparisons between them" (p. 112). Not only does this provide behavioral acts that can be classified into personality constructs, it provides base rates that would allow actuarial prediction of behaviors as a function of personality measurement.

THE NUMBER OF DIMENSIONS IN THE DOMAIN

In both personality and intelligence instruments, the number of dimensions that constitute "intelligence" or "personality" is not merely an academic issue. The number has important practical implications for the operationalization of the construct and the construction of the tests designed to sample and model the domain of discourse (for intelligence, the number of dimensions/abilities assessed, type of tasks most appropriate for assessing specific abilities, specific situations in which abilities are assessed, etc.).

Intelligence

The selection of the various dimensions of intelligence and their components should serve to guide the design of tests and the interpretation of test results. One of the first issues that needs to be addressed relates to the number of dimensions in the domain, as well as the pattern in which the various dimensions are interrelated (Sternberg, 1985). In fact, different psychometric theories of intelligence vary along the considerations of number and pattern. With respect to the number of dimensions, theories may be placed on a continuum ranging from monarchic conceptions (i.e., one major ability that oversees the others) through "oligarchic" conceptions (i.e., several autonomous factors), to an almost anarchical array of dozens of independent factors (the highest count is in Guilford's model, which consists of 150 separate factors).

Narrow Conception

At one extreme, one might imagine a single dimension along which individuals can be rank ordered, or a rather narrow spectrum of abilities constituting the domain (e.g., those related to power of formal abstract reasoning). In fact, the unitary view of intelligence as a coherent entity is deeply entrenched in Western thought (Krechevsky & Gardner, 1991). Thus, intelligence has been commonly construed as a single ability or factor that permeates all forms of intellectual performance and can be brought to bear on any problem-solving situation.

Many theorists (e.g., Eysenck & Eysenck, 1985; Jensen, 1980; Spearman, 1923) posit a general or universal ability factor (denoted as *g*). They believe that the *g* factor permeates all intellectual activity in various degrees. According to this view, to be intelligent is to have an abundance of mental energy, or *g*. Others (e.g., Horn, 1979) propose a two factor model of intelligence; these are described in other chapters.

Broad Conception

At the other extreme, one might conceive of a rather broad conception of the domain, involving additional abilities and more general adaptational skills. Accordingly, a number of researchers (e.g., Thurstone, Guilford, Gardner) have suggested more complex multidimensional approaches to intelligence, and have been open to the idea that the domain consists of several mental facets (Guttman, 1991), dimensions (Guilford, 1967), or factors/vectors (Thurstone, 1938).

Personality

The number of dimensions is also an active topic among personality theorists and instrument developers. One method of finding the number of dimensions is to start with the broadest domain; for example, Cattell (1943) started with 4,500 trait-descriptive terms. This list developed into a set of 35 highly complex bipolar variables. Gough (1965) found that 18 basic scales were sufficient to describe personality, a set that now is 20 scales (Gough, 1987).

Of late there has been a surge of consensus that there are five main domains in personality (John, 1990; Goldberg, 1993). The exact descriptions of the domains vary from researcher to researcher, but basically they are surgency (or extraversion), agreeableness, conscientiousness, emotional stability (versus neuroticism), and culture (or intellect).

Hough (1992) took a very pragmatic approach toward looking for a sufficient set of personality constructs. She used as her criterion the prediction of job proficiency. She examined whether the "big five" taxonomy was sufficient and found that it was not adequate to show good prediction of job proficiency. She added scales of Rugged Individualism (similar to masculinity) and Locus of Control (the amount of control one believes one has over rewards and punishments). She split surgency (extraversion) into Sociability and Ambition. It is important to note that her Ambition scale was the most predictive of job performance. She also found that different scales were predictive for different jobs, which argued for a broader number of scales than just five.

SAMPLING THE DOMAIN

Intelligence

A thorough understanding and specification of the intelligence domain are essential in order to guide the development of the initial item pool, and facilitate initial content validation and construct research, as well as later interpretation of results. In order for intelligence test items to exhibit content validity with respect to the intelligence domain, they should cover all major facets of the domain (exhaustiveness) but exclude irrelevant behaviors (exclusivity). The test constructor should ideally begin by providing a clear and detailed statement regarding the general rationale of the operationalization, specifying the link between the domain and the proposed whole test.

As pointed out by Crocker and Algina (1986), the process by which psychological constructs have been translated into a specific set of items has typically remained private, informal, and insufficiently documented. Typically the test developer will conceptualize one or more types of behaviors believed to manifest the construct and then simply try to "think up" items that require these behaviors to be demonstrated. Unfortunately, this nonsystematic approach can result in the omission of important areas of behavior or inclusion of areas that are relevant to the construct only in the mind of this particular test developer.

Elaborated Definition

Thorndike (1982) suggests employing an elaborated definition of the construct to indicate the testing operations by which the attribute will be assessed. The conception and elaborated definition of intelligence thus would emerge from the whole history of the research dealing with the intelligence construct (e.g., verbal ability, as evidenced by knowledge of common and rare vocabulary items, understanding meaning of written texts, and identifying the best word to fit a particular context).

To broaden, refine, or verify the view of the intelligence construct, one or all of the following activities should be taken:

- *Review of research*: Behaviors that have been frequently studied by others are used to define the construct (vocabulary stock, sentence completion, verbal analogy, etc.).
- *Critical incidents*: Behaviors that characterize the extremes of the performance continuum for the intelligence construct (e.g., outstanding versus very poor school performance).
- *Direct observation* of people engaged in behaviors on the job, in academic settings, or in practical day-to-day problems.
- *Expert judgment* and input from people who have firsthand experience with the intelligence construct (e.g., consultation with clinical child psychologists about which behavior to include in preschool intelligence assessment scale).

Broad versus Narrow Mapping of the Domain

When mapping items onto domains there has been a standard question of whether to define the domain narrowly and write very similar items (which will yield high reliability) or to more broadly and try to sample the whole domain with diverse items (which will increase validity). Humphreys has advocated the broader approach (see Ackerman & Humphreys, 1990), with the breadth guided by how the test is to be used. This advice is important in thinking about how to write items for a domain:

> The test construction process begins with a careful definition of the attribute one is interested in measuring. Items are then constructed and selected for tryout on the basis of two criteria: (a) Each must measure the attribute desired to a useful degree; and (b) Each must differ from the others as much as possible without sacrifice of the central attribute component. Heterogeneity is systematically varied within the limits set by the definition of the attribute.
>
> It is frequently necessary to use small clusters of items that have unwanted variance in common, but the members in the clusters must be kept small and the number of clusters large. Also, if the dominant dimension is not to be unduly affected by a particular source of unwanted or bias variance, that variance must be spread equally among the various sources. It may seem paradoxical, but the larger the number of sources of unwanted variance, the smaller their total contribution to the variance of scores on the test. Such a test is homogeneous with respect to the dominant dimension, but heterogeneous with respect to sources of systematic variance unrelated to the central attribute. Unwanted variance is indirectly controlled by systematic variance of its sources (Ackerman & Humphreys, 1990, p. 234)

Approaches to Domain Sampling

Sampling of items from the domain has generally been conducted in a nonsystematic manner, more often than not based on expertise, intuition, armchair analysis, and trial and error. Facet theory may have considerable potential as a heuristic device for systematically mapping out the domain of intelligence and sampling of items from this domain of discourse. In fact, Guttman (1969) viewed *facets* as an acronym for "facets as assets in the construction of efficient tests systematically." The facet approach to item sampling from the domain is briefly demonstrated below.

As discussed previously (in Facet Theory), construction of a detailed mapping sentence that specifies all relevant content domains is a crucial step in the mapping out of the intelligence terrain. The mapping sentence actually defines the test or test battery that can be developed by specifying the key facets and the corresponding elements belonging to each. This enables the test constructor systematically to build tests that will contain all the elements contained in these facets or subsets of them. As implied in the three-facet mapping sentence presented above, there are three kinds of languages at the disposal of the test constructor for item construction purposes: words, symbols of a more formalized language, and pictures. Furthermore, apart from the language, there are three types of cognitive task operations specified: tasks requiring analytical ability (i.e., in which the subject is required to deduce a rule), tasks requiring rule application (in which the subject needs to apply or operate from the rule that is exhibited), and rule learning. Furthermore, when administering individual tests, the facet of mode of expression may vary and therefore needs to be considered. Because most group tests are paper and pencil, this facet is not relevant in most group testing situations.

Assume we wish to sample items relating to the first two facets specified, that is, the language facet and the cognitive operation facet (holding the third facet, the modality, constant). Because the language facet consists of three elements and the cognitive task facet consists of three elements, we can get a ninefold classification of test items by a Cartesian product of facet elements. Table 2 is the specification table for con-

Table 2. Sample Specifications for Some of the Intelligence Domain

	Language (A)		
Operation (B)	Verbal (a1)	Symbolic (a2)	Figural (a3)
Rule inference (b1)	Verbal reasoning (a1b1)	Numerical reasoning (a2b1)	Figural reasoning (a3b1)
Rule application (b2)	Verbal memory (a1b2)	Symbolic memory (a2b2)	Figural memory (a3b2)
Rule learning (b3)	Verbal learning (a1b3)	Numerical learning (a2b3)	Figural learning (a3b3)

struction of items that would cover the specified domain.

The core of planning an intelligence test is the specification of what contents and processes are to be included in the test. Because creating all possible items would be economically and practically unfeasible in most cases, the accepted alternative is to produce a set of item-domain specifications structured so that items written according to these specifications would be interchangeable. The development of test specifications for intelligence tests generally requires that the test developer attend to two orthogonal properties of items, namely, substantive content and cognitive process or skill (see Robertson, 1992).

Each of the elements in a facet (e.g., verbal, symbolic, figural) is termed a *struct*, whereas the facet profile of a given measure is termed a *structuple*. For example, a numerical item requiring rule application ($x + 1 = 9; x = ?$) would be designated by the structuple or profile a2b2, whereas a symbolic item requiring rule learning (e.g., digit-symbol task) would be designated as a2b3. Thus, any given intelligence task may be classified by the content facets of its structuple or profile.

Given this specification table for the test, the test constructor can proceed systematically to develop items that tap each of the profiles in the cells, amounting to nine profiles in all. For example, using this specification table, verbal reasoning (a1b1) could be assessed by analogy-type items (e.g., cat:kitten :: cow: ___?); numerical reasoning (a2b1) could be assessed by numerical progressions (e.g., 2, 3, 5, 8, ___?); and figural reasoning (a3b1) could be assessed by visual progressions (e.g., − = ≡ =?). Similarly, learning or memory could be systematically assessed by paired associate type items. Thus, subjects could be presented with a series of paired associates in verbal (boy-coat, train-smoke), numerical (68 − 12, 34 − 16, etc.), and figural modes (○ ♦) and asked to provide the second element given the first (see Nevo, 1990).

Personality

Loevinger (1957) had some classic advice for sampling the construct domain. She writes that items should be chosen so as to sample all possible contents which might comprise the trait and to include all known alternative theories of the trait. The content domains "should be represented in proportion to their life-importance." The breadth of the sampling and the relevance to the life-important world of behavior are key concepts for scale development.

In Gough's development of scales, he first clearly defines the intention of the scale. For example, for the Socialization (So) scale, the intention was to "locate individuals and groups along a continuum of asocial to social behavior, and to forecast the likelihood that any person will transgress whatever dividing line his own culture interposes between these two poles of the continuum" (Gough, 1965, p. 296). Because Gough conceives of his scales in terms of role theory, the items for the So scale reflect two content areas: "The first of these more or less directly embodies role-taking ideas, and may be instanced by these items: 'Before I do something I try to consider how my friends will react to it,' 'I often think about how I look and what impression I am making upon others,' and 'I find it easy to "drop" or "break with" a friend' (p. 297).

Act Frequency Approach

The act frequency approach (Buss & Craik, 1983a) provides a method for deriving instrument items or measuring the breadth of a personality concept domain. The act frequency procedure entails two steps: act nominations, and prototypicality ratings. The act nomination instructional set for dominance, for example, was as follows: "Think of the three most dominant females [males] you know. With these individuals in mind, write down five acts or behaviors that they have performed that reflect or exemplify their dominance." This yielded acts such as "I forbade him to leave the room," "I gave advice, although none was requested," "I resisted conceding an argument," and "I walked ahead of everybody else." The acts are then rated by a panel of judges for prototypicality ratings on a 7-point scale with respect to the construct under consideration. Finally, the acts are independently composited into a multiple-act index (from the most central acts, Proto 1, to the most peripheral acts, Proto 4; the four sentences above are indications of dominance from Proto 1 to Proto 4).

ITEM WRITING

Once the domain has been mapped, how the questions are then written is important. There are two basic approaches to writing items for personality and intelligence tests: the rational and the empirical. The differences between rational and empirical techniques are evident not only in the philosophy guiding the construction of the item pool but in a wide variety of other aspects of the test construction process (e.g., method of item analyses, dimensionality of tests, validation). Rather than being two alternatives, however, the two methods could play complementary roles in the process of test construction, with items generated through rational methods and eventually selected on the basis of the joint consideration of internal consistency and external criterion correlations.

Personality

Empirical versus Rational Approaches to Item Writing

In a chapter on developing empirical and rational personality scales, Gough and Bradley (1992) describe how to write personality items for a leadership scale. Their description is especially useful because they contrast the empirical with the rational method.

> The first step would be to examine past writings on the psychology of leadership to see what personal attributes and views concerning interpersonal relationships have been found important. . . . Each of these notions can be translated into self-report items whose relevance to leadership would be obvious.
>
> The test author would probably prepare something like 75 to 100 such items, each one logically linked to a stated notion about the psychology of leadership. Then the pool of items would be administered to a sample of persons as similar as possible in general characteristics to those with whom the scale is eventually to be used. . . .
>
> The number of people needed in the research sample is a matter of judgment. The minimum is probably about 100, but larger numbers are better. . . . The larger the research sample, the more likely generalizations from it will be valid. The next step in a rational analysis is to examine the relationship of each item to the central concept. . . .
>
> Once the set of . . . correlations is available, the researchers scans the list to see if any produced a negative coefficient. This would signify a reversal of function and lead to the item being discarded. Items with very low correlations, even if in the proper direction, would also usually be thrown away. The goal is to end up with from 25 to perhaps 40 items, each having a significant ($p <$ .05) relationship to the total.
>
> A researcher following empirical pathways would begin in the same way—by perusing past work to identify relevant attitudes and dispositions. An initial pool of items would also be drawn up, many quite similar to those formulated by the internal consistency advocate. A difference, however, would occur in that the empiricist would add quite a few other items on the basis of pure hunches or just because they seem to be *ego-syntonic* (an *ego-syntonic* statement is an assertion that the respondents like to endorse or reject). . . . Armed with an experimental pool of, say, 125 items, the empirical researcher would now seek samples to which the preliminary inventory could be given and for which non-test criteria of leadership could be gathered. . . .
>
> The next step for the empiricist is to correlate each of the experimental items with the criterion. . . . Items with statistically significant correlations would be retained, and those with zero or trivial correlations would be deleted. Then the process would be repeated at least once, this time carrying forward only those items that showed promise in the first sample. This cross-validation is essential with the empirical method to guard against purely chance or random correlations that will always occur in any sample. The items that appeared acceptable on statistical ground in both the first and the validational sample would then constitute the empirical scale for leadership potential" (pp. 217–221).

Guidelines for Writing Personality Items

Angleitner, John, and Löhr (1986) classified the most frequently used personality item instruments. A major class includes descriptions of reactions: overt reactions that are publicly observable (e.g., "I often go to parties"); covert reactions that are generally not observable by others (e.g., "I think a lot about myself"); and symptoms or physical reactions (e.g., "I sweat a lot"). Other classes include trait attributions (e.g., "I have good acting abilities"), wishes and interests (e.g., "Sometimes I would really like to curse"), biographical facts (e.g., "I had some trouble with the law when I was younger"), attitudes and beliefs (e.g., "I think the law should be strictly enforced"), others' reactions to the person (e.g., "At parties, I am seldom the center of attention"), and bizarre items (e.g., "Somebody is trying to poison me").

Many authors have provided approximately the same advice on item writing (e.g., Specter, 1992; Strelau & Angleitner, 1991; Thorndike, 1982). Typical suggestions are as follows:

- Start item writing by specifically defining the construct and how it differs from other constructs.
- Read items on other scales of the construct for item ideas.
- Specify the specific manifestation of the trait (i.e., observable behavior, attributions to oneself, wishes or interests).
- Include relevant aspects of the situational context.
- Be clear, short, and concrete.
- Contain a single idea in the item.
- Control reading level.
- Avoid jargon as much as possible.
- Control cultural-specific language.
- Write items that will be understood by subsequent generations.
- Balance favorable and unfavorable items (e.g., "I feel anxious fairly often," "I hardly ever feel anxious").
- Balance keying (e.g., about an equal number of "true" and "false" responses).
- Do not use negatives to reverse meaning (e.g., "I feel anxious," then "I don't feel anxious").
- Control percentage agreement with the item (social desirability).
- If the scale is to be used for selection, write items that will not violate privacy laws.

Intelligence

As discussed for personality tests, a variety of philosophies may be employed in the construction of intelligence test items. In rational or construct-oriented approaches, items are written on the basis of a working theory about intelligence, which is supposed to be reflected in the items; according to criterion-oriented philosophies, items need to show some systematic relation to some external criterion (e.g., age, school achievement, occupational ranking, age).

It is commonly agreed that there really is no well-grounded science or even technology of item writing. In spite of some attempts to mechanize and computerize the task, skills at writing items must be developed through direct experience on a foundation of talent for a particular type of expression. Among the skills are selection of the particular concepts, principles, and skills to be assessed; ingenuity in imbedding these concepts and skills in a particular problem; incisiveness of phrasing problems; and perceptiveness in designing distracters.

One of the first and most important requirements for good item writing is to be clear as possible about the nature of the ability being measured. There is a continuous interaction between the test constructor's conception of the attribute to be measured and the development of formats for test tasks (Thorndike, 1982). For example, if we believe there is evidence for a construct of verbal reasoning, we may choose to measure it by preparing a set of items in the form of verbal analogies, verbal classification, and sentence completion. Analyses of relations among these and other sorts of items will then help us to determine whether these items do, in fact, define a common ability.

Some general principles have been found useful by experts, and their application may make specific item writing easier. Over the years, a wide array of items formats have been invented and tried out, with some gaining more widespread use and recognition then others. These have appeared repeatedly in different tests and seem to be serviceable for measuring significant ability functions. Most test constructors begin by reviewing the familiar formats before searching for something new and different. Jensen (1980) provides a rich and almost exhaustive inventory of both verbal and nonverbal formats available for item construction purposes, and the reader is referred to these illustrations for further information.

The actual writing and polishing of items is a highly skilled undertaking, requiring considerable technical skill, facility of expression, and imagination. The draft should be tried out after being arranged in a guessed approximation of the correct order of item difficulties. One should obtain reactions to the test instructions, examples, what the test appears to be measuring, and identifying items open to criticism. Crocker and Algina (1986) list the following aspects of item construction as important features to keep in mind: (a) accuracy, (b) relevance to test specifications, (c) technical item-construction features, (d) grammar, (e) perceived fairness and unbiased presentation of items, and (f) level of readability.

It has become standard procedure to send items out for judgmental review, wherein items are reviewed by one or more critics to try to identify in advance any deficiencies. Reviewers may relate to a host of concerns such as the following:

- Is the item keyable (i.e., is there only one clearly correct or best answer)?
- Does each item have a certain degree of plausibility (so that a person who does not know the answer might reasonably choose it)?
- Does the item favor of handicap any special groups of examinees?
- Does the item seem fair to both sexes?
- Is the item difficulty reasonable for the level or type of group for which the test is intended?
- Do tasks make too much demand on sensory or motor abilities when these are not the main factor the test purports to measure?
- Is the level of reading difficulty appropriate for the target group?

SELECTING AND PILOTING ITEMS

The methods for selecting and piloting personality and intelligence items are essentially the same and have been described in a number of texts (Crocker & Algina, 1986; Nunnally, 1978; Robertson, 1992; Thorndike, 1982). Both intelligence and personality test items need to be tried out to determine their level of difficulty or popularity and their ability to differentiate between criterion groups (Thorndike, 1982). The tryout also serves the purpose of providing data for additional analyses, checking instructions for test administration, assessing comprehensibility and difficulty of items, assessing scoring procedures, and checking the time limits.

The first tryout should be conducted on a sample of anywhere from 200 to 500 subjects. These subjects should be as similar as possible to the target population with which the test will eventually be used, and covering the range of ages or grades that characterizes those with whom the test will be used (Thorndike, 1982). Tryout samples of about this size provide stable estimates of item difficulty and discrimination indices (Robertson, 1992).

Because the aim is to separate the "sheep from the goats," one should prepare a larger number of items initially than one expects to need in the final set. In the tryout, prepare anywhere from 25% to 400% more than the number of items one wishes to include in the final test (see Golden, Sawicki, & Franzen, 1984; Kline, 1986; Robertson, 1992). The exact number of intended final items depends on a variety of factors (incremental cost of preparing an item, novelty of item format, mode of test administration, etc.). It is highly recommended that there should be a sufficient number of items of moderate difficulty because this ensures a good spread of scores, which in turn increases the test reliability.

Item Selection Criteria

The item data elicited from the tryout are used for an elaborate set of statistical procedures, known as item analysis, designed to secure the operative soundness of the items in the final test. The most effective items from the initial pool are chosen, and items that do not meet pre-established criteria are eliminated. Robertson (1992) identified two main classes of item analysis techniques employed in current test procedures: classical, and modern (or item response theory).

Classical Item Selection

Classical item analysis refers to the standard item statistics used over the past decades, such as difficulty (percentage of examinees passing each item) and discrimination (index of each item's ability to discriminate those having more or having less of a particular ability). The item analytic procedures discussed for cognitive tests are generalizable, with only slight modification, to the construction of personality tests. If agreeing with an item is marked 1 and disagreeing marked 0, the difficulty index (the number who agree divided by the total number of responses) would give an item analytic statistic indicating the "popularity" of the agreement response. Similarly, item discrimination could be calculated as the correlation between the item score and total score.

Modern Item Selection

Modern item analysis, known as latent trait or item response theory (IRT), refers to procedures that have evolved over the last 25 years and have became feasible with the availability of high-speed computers. IRT methods express the probability of success on an item as a function of the examinee's standing on the latent attribute, graphically expressed by an item characteristic curve. Recent advances in the development of latent trait measurement models (Lord, 1980; Rasch, 1960) provide an alternative approach for item selection that is perhaps more accurate than classical methods. These models appear to have considerable promise for scaling of both intelligence and personality test items. Although there is a worldwide trend toward increase in usage of latent trait models, particularly in the United States, only a few recent tests (e.g., the Scholastic Aptitude Test, and the British Intelligence Scale) have been designed to take advantage of the improvements made in test construction by the new latent construct theory methods of scaling. No major personality test has been developed with IRT methods.

It is important to keep in mind that item analysis cannot improve items, and often one needs to pick the least bad from a pretty bad bundle (Butcher, 1968). Item analysis can only analyze the items you enter into the statistics. The key is to have good items to start with then to use item analysis to remove the psychometrically poor ones.

CREATING SCALES FROM THE ITEMS

The Linear Model of Scaling

Experts commonly agree that no one item on an intelligence or personality test battery is a particularly good measure of the scale construct because each item measures a unique source of variance, partly as a result of random error (Crocker & Algina, 1986). In order to arrive at a global index, we typically apply a *linear model* to the subject's item scores. This consists of assigning some numerical value to every correct response (often scored dichotomously as 0 = error, 1 = correct response), treating equal item scores as equivalent (regardless of the nature of test items) and summing scores across single items to obtain a more reliable and accurate index of intellectual capacity. With a large item pool, test items are normally equally weighted (Nunnally, 1978). The *linear model* is the basic rationale behind adding up scores obtained from tests because we assume (and hope to demonstrate) that the items are alike (i.e., functionally equivalent) and correlate in certain predictable ways. In fact, functional equivalence of items is absolutely necessary for using the scoring techniques arrived at in the final index of the construct.

Furthermore, when a large number of item scores is summed, the uncorrelated specific factors cancel out, so that the total score reflects individual differences on the factor common to all items. The sum total of a large number of items would be expected to yield a reliable measure of this general factor.

Assembling Items and the Length of Scales

A variety of approaches have been used for assembling items for purposes of scale formation. Some of these will be briefly mentioned below.

Face Validity

Items are often chosen by a test constructor for a particular scale because they are taken to measure a particular ability (e.g., spatial visualization) or trait (e.g., anxiety) dimension. Though such items may vary in format and difficulty level, they are assumed to measure the same ability. For example, a face-valid measure of spatial visualization could be put together by selecting items that conform to some theory about the construct; that is, they are perceived to require mental rotation of two- and three-dimensional objects in space, with or without reflection. The scale may be based on underlying theory (e.g., of spatial visualization, or what anxiety reactions are expected to be like) or on the impressions of test developers, testees, and other experts.

The Empirical Properties of the Items

Scales may also be identified on the basis of empirical properties of items, particularly as related to the association between the item and an internal or external criterion. Thus items may be chosen for a particular scale because as a cluster they have high internal consistency (e.g., as assessed by Cronbach's alpha), because they correlate highly with total test scores, because they discriminate maximally between two divergent groups (highly intelligent/gifted vs. nongifted children). or because the items show high correlations with an external representation of the intelligence construct (e.g., grade point average).

Factor Analysis

Factor analysis can also be employed with item analytic techniques as a heuristic guideline for selecting the best items to put into specific scales. The common procedure is to choose items that show high loadings on the target factor. Those items intersecting several factors simultaneously, showing no simple loading on the target factor of interest but several small or moderate ones, would be dropped. Regardless of which methodology is employed, the end result of the item analytic procedures is the identification of three basic classes of items (Robertson, 1992): (a) those satisfactory for operational use without further work, (b) those with marginal item statistics that might be salvageable after revision, and (c) those whose item statistics warrants their being discarded.

Factor analysis has been the data reduction method of choice among psychometricians for item scaling purposes, although the results are seldom clear-cut. Accordingly, once we have decided how many dimensions we aim at measuring, factor analysis of the item intercorrelation matrix can help us construct scales to measure these dimensions. Accordingly, items within an item pool that correlate most highly with each target dimension uncovered by factor analysis can be empirically identified and used for purposes of constructing scales to measure the intended dimensions of interest. By employing some criterion factor loading (often set at greater than .30 or .40), sets of items that load on any given factor can be identified as a group of independent scales.

Items that load on the same factor are assumed to relate to an underlying trait that can be represented by a factor score, often represented by the sum total of items loading meaningfully on the designated factor. In order to obtain replicable factors, items sizes of about 200 are advisable (Kline, 1986). Unless the number of subjects is at least 10 times the number of subjects, one may be capitalizing on chance.

In addition, items may be selected based on the empirical clustering of items together following other data reduction procedures, such as cluster analysis and multidimensional scaling. For example, following multidimensional scaling procedures, items that fall in close proximity in the smallest space would be likely candidates to form a scale, as they would appear to measure the same struct of a given facet (see Guttman & Levy, 1991).

Warnings for a Strictly Factor Approach for Finding the Domain

Nunnally (1978) maintains that factor analysis should not be used to construct specific scales. Homogeneous scales should be constructed based on the hypotheses regarding the nature of the ability or trait assessed, with item analysis used to select the most appropriate items for the scale. In order to learn how successful we were, we can apply factor analytic methods to investigate the factor structure of the battery.

Golden et al. (1984) provide a list of warnings to those using a strictly factor analytic method of scale development:

1. One must thoroughly understand the theory that guided the initial item selections or constructions.
2. Each factor method carries a set of theoretical assumptions that guides its meaningful application; thus the test designer must determine which method will create the least distortion on the original data while producing interpretable results.
3. Exploratory (initial) factor analytic solutions may be unstable across groups, and they may not generalize to other samples.
4. The factors may be a function of the characteristics of the sample employed. The presence of subgroups may create dimensions that reflect those a priori group differences.
5. Group characteristics (e.g., age, education, culture, gender differences) may bias responses to create artificial factor dimensions.
6. The factor analysis is a function of the items available for analysis. Thus a cluster of items with similar meaning will create an artificial factor.

Arrangement of Items

Intelligence

Attention should be given to the general arrangement of items from the point of view of ease in applying and scoring the test. It is accepted practice to group intelligence test items with similar content together (e.g., vocabulary items, arithmetic calculations, spatial visualization, mazes, digit coding) and then arrange them within each content category in order of item difficulty. To encourage weaker examinees, tests should start with very easy items that any subject can attempt. Tests should then become gradually more difficult until the last items are only so hard that best subjects get them right. Within the limits of the first two considerations, one should attempt to randomize material as much as possible to cut down on boredom and fatigue. The limited attention span of testees should also be given consideration, and one should not include so many items that the average subject does not have enough time to complete all of them.

Personality

When arranging items for a personality measure, it is important to spread out the items on each scale so that items on a particular scale do not occur sequentially. Gough (1987) distributed what he called "egocentonic" items through the inventory in order to keep the test taker interested through the process of taking 462 items. His Commonality scale is made up of items that are pleasant to respond to; for example, people enjoy responding "yes" to the item "I usually expect to succeed in things I do." Gough distributed these egocentonic items throughout the CPI at times when he thought interest might be flagging.

ESTABLISHING THE RELIABILITY OF THE TEST

Standard Approaches

Reliability, a major quality desired in any test, is a relative and polymorphous concept. In fact, a test actually has no single reliability, with reliability referring to a test's degree of stability, consistency, predictability, accuracy, or generalizability. The reliability of an intelligence test can be assessed from time to time (test-retest), form to form (alternative or equivalent forms) item to item (internal consistency or homogeneity), and scorer to scorer (interobserver or interjudge reliability). See Nunnally (1978) or Crocker and Algina (1986) for specific formula for calculating reliabilities.

The standard approaches to reliability in intelligence and personality measurement are as follows:

1. *Internal reliability*: For example, calculate Cronbach alpha coefficients or item-remainder coefficients (the correlation of each item with the sum of the remaining items).
2. *Test-retest reliability*: For example, readminister the same instrument to the same sample and correlate the scores. Various samples would have different time periods (3 months, 1 year, etc.).
3. *Internal or test-retest reliability* for various types of populations (e.g., samples with low reading level would be expected to have lower internal reliabilities, and samples undergoing developmental changes would be expected to have lower test-retest reliabilities).
4. Provide the *standard error of measurement* (SEM) so that confidence bands can be constructed around the score.

Generalizability

In assessing the reliability estimate, one needs to consider the specific sources of error affecting test performance, the method of reliability estimation, implications of trait stability, and test format, as well as intended usage. Cronbach, Gleser, Rajaratnam, and Nanda (1972), in what is known as generalizability theory, point out that a score may vary not only with the specific test or occasion of measurement but also with a variety of other facets (e.g., specific situation, observer). Thus, if we use a single intelligence test score as if it represented all of the person's capacity across time and situations, we are overgeneralizing from the results, and we need to test the generalizability of the scores systematically across different test facets. Furthermore, Cronbach et al. (1972) identified different types of decisions (e.g., criterion-referenced comparisons, comparison between courses of action, comparison between individual/groups, conclusions about relations between variables), and he proceeded to point out the appropriate error term and type of reliability appropriate for each. The application of generalizability theory methodology, based on the analysis of variance model relating various reliability evaluations to various test applications, has not gained widespread usage among test practitioners. The power of this method has yet to be sufficiently utilized.

Factors That Influence Reliability

Sattler (1988) discusses a variety of factors that can influence test reliability and need to be carefully considered when assessing intelligence tests for particular functions. These include the following:

- *Test length*: The more items on a test, and the more homogeneous they are, the higher the reliability.
- *Test-retest interval*: The smaller the time interval between test administrations, the smaller the chance of change, the higher the reliability.
- *Variability of scores*: The greater the variance of test scores, the higher the reliability estimates is likely to be.
- *Guessing*: The less guessing, the less random the reply, the higher the reliability.

- *Variation within test situation*: The fewer the variations and the more standardized it is, the higher the reliability.

In any event, a test that is reliable for one particular group may not necessarily be reliable for any subgroup or any one individual. How reliable does a test need be for purposes of assessment? It is commonly held that the reliability estimates need to be relatively high (about .90) for clinical decision making and somewhat lower (about .70) for research. A test that does not have adequate reliability should never be used to make decisions about an individual examinee. According to Kline (1986), the minimum satisfying figure for test reliability is .70; below that, the standard error is so large that the interpretation becomes dubious.

In personality measurement, however, some traits can be considered to be more temporal than others. Hence the classifications of state and trait personality (e.g., Spielberger, 1983), where *state* refers the temporary influences and *trait* to enduring dispositions. For example, a state might be a specific situation that invoked anger, whereas a trait might be a person's tendency to get angry in many situations (especially those in which people typically do not get angry). Some traits have greater situational influences than others (e.g., Trickett & Moos, 1970). Thus reliability must be seen in context—state measures are predicted to have lower reliabilities and would not be accurate "state" measurements if they did not.

SAMPLING AND NORMS

Essentially the same procedures are used for norming personality and intelligence tests. In establishing norms, we attempt to relate a raw score (or scaled score) to the performance of one or more reference groups for the purpose of anchoring and giving meaning to test performance. It is commonly agreed among experts that to obtain appropriate norms, the test should be administered to a sample from a reference population (once that has been established and defined) that is as similar as possible to the target population.

The basis upon which most test scores have meaning relates directly to the similarity between the individual being tested and the standardization sample. Thus, if a test was standardized for college students aged 18 to 35, useful comparisons can be made for college students. The more dissimilar the person is from this group, the less useful the test is in evaluating him or her. As Thorndike (1982) pointed out, the normative sample should ideally provide an unbiased and efficient representation of the population, as well as permit an estimate of precision with which the sample does in fact represent the population. For example, in norming an intelligence test to be used for selecting college candidates during their last year in high school, the target group would ideally consist of all 12th graders in the country. It is nearly impossible, though, to list all 12th graders completely and accurately and obtain a random sample. As a result, a number of alternative procedures have been used (e.g., stratified cluster random sampling) to overcome this problem and make the sampling more manageable and feasible (see Thorndike, 1982, for a lucid discussion of the various sampling procedures).

An intelligence test constructor is ordinarily concerned with more general norms: Because the test manual will be used by persons in many different local settings, norms provided must have a general reference. It is also important to point out that there are many possible reference groups with which intelligence scores of an individual might be compared (e.g., age groups, sociocultural and gender groups, college candidates and students, job trainees, local groups, rural areas, regional groups, national groups). Thus the reference group must be developed for special audiences with adequate sizes.

The type of interpretation or decisions we are going to make based on the scores determines the group with which an examinee is compared. If a judgment that is to be based on test scores refers to a local situation (e.g., admission to the educational program of a local city college), then it may be appropriate to use local norms. If the judgment or decision refers to a more general situation (e.g., admission to an Ivy League university or hiring for a nationwide company), then it might be more meaningful to appraise subjects relative to the total cohort.

One needs to keep in mind that no single set of norms can be used in all present or future circumstances, and that the norm must take both individual and group factors into consideration in order to be meaningful. Particular care must be taken in situations where different cultural or language backgrounds will limit exposure to the content domain of the test, thus making the norms inappropriate for culturally different populations.

A variety of criteria may be employed in evaluating the suitability of the norm group. These include the following:

- *Representativeness*: The extent to which the norm group is characteristic of the target population.
- *Sampling*: The inclusion of the various subgroups in the normative group with the representative percentage per subgroup.
- *Recency and timeliness of norms*: The date in which norms were established.
- *Size*: The norm group should be large enough to ensure stability within each representative subgroup. For example, if a test is given to a number of age groups, the norms should contain at least 100 subjects for each age level (Sattler, 1988).
- *Relevance*: It is crucial to consider the relevance of the norms to evaluation of the examinees being assessed.

Psychological tests have typically used "norms of convenience." Many instruments, for example, are normed on college students or an incidental collection of people who may have taken the instrument. When evaluating a test, carefully review the descriptions of the norms in the manual to confirm the representativeness and adequacy of the sampling.

VALIDITY

Validity is the evidence to prove that the scale measures what the author purports it to measure. The mere fact that a test is called an "intelligence" or "honesty" test by its author is not sufficient evidence; one needs empirical evidence to show that the test is indeed valid for the designated purpose. Typically this is done by looking at the items on the scale (face validity), how the scale relates to other measures to which it is similar or dissimilar (convergent and discriminant validity), how it relates to existing samples that relate to the construct (known group validity), how well it predicts current behaviors (concurrent validity), or how well it predicts future behaviors (predictive validity).

Validity refers to the number and range of valid inferences a user can make about a client on the basis of test scores. A test cannot be said to be valid in any abstract sense but must instead be valid in a particular context, for a specific purpose, and with a specific group of people in mind. The type of validation that is most important depends on the inferences to be drawn from the test scores. As Anastasi (1986) points out, almost any data collected in the process of developing a test are relevant to its validity, because they contribute to our understanding of what a test measures. For example, data on internal consistency and retest reliability help to define the homogeneity of the construct and its temporal stability.

Norms can provide additional construct specification, especially if they include normative data for subgroups. Because the interpretive meaning of a test score may continue to be sharpened and refined, validity is a never-ending process. In validating measures, Loevinger (1957) suggested paying attention to the degree to which item content is appropriate to the trait being assessed, the adequacy of domain sampling, structural components, relations among items, and relations between items and external components (item-total, item-criterion relations).

Construct Validity

Construct validity is a continuous process in which new evidence is assembled bearing on the inferences that we can make about a person based on test scores. The assessment of construct validity involves three general steps: (a) conceptualization and careful analysis of the ability or personality trait; (b) consideration of how the construct is manifested in tests, and the ways in which the trait does or does not relate to other behaviors in particular situations; and (c) formal testing of whether the hypothesized relations actually exist. Thus what has come to be designated as construct validity is actually a comprehensive approach that includes the other recognized validation procedures. In fact, test experts have recently come to realize that all questions about test validity actually concern construct validity. This is so because each of the distinct forms of validity helps shed light on the meaning of test scores.

Constructs such as intelligence or personality are ultimately derived from empirically observed behavioral consistencies and are identified and defined through a network of observed relations (Anastasi, 1986). The general logic of construct validity first elaborated by Cronbach and Meehl (1955) stated that in order for a test construct to be scientifically admissible it had to be located in a nomological network. A nomological net consists of statistical and/or deterministic laws that tie observable properties to one another, theoretical constructs to observables, and constructs to one another. The assumption is that in the absence of an infallible criterion measure, one can define a complex psychological phenomenon by showing that its meaning lies in a network of relations among directly observable measures. For example, a measure of intelligence might be validated by showing that it is related to academic achievement, job success, military training ratings, and economic success. A personality trait such as dominance might be validated by nominations to leadership positions, observer ratings of dominant behavior, or instances of taking charge of leaderless groups.

Face Validity

Face validity is a type of "pseudo-validity" (Butcher, 1968), referring to a test that seems to be valid for a particular purpose and group, particularly to the person taking it. This type of validity does not necessarily bear much relation to other forms of validity. There may be some place, however, for face validity in the testing of intelligence or personality, principally to ensure an adequate level of motivation among the respondents. If the questions on a test seem ambiguous, inappropriate, or to measure something else than the construct desired, a likely response is to reduce one's efforts rather than cooperate or work at a maximum level.

Factorial Validity

Factor analysis, both exploratory and confirmatory, has been the method of choice in studying the structure underlying tests (Carroll,1992). In spite of the many problems inherent to the use of factor analysis for studying the structure of abilities, Carroll (1992) believes that for well-designed sets of variables, reasonable and replicable solutions can be discerned. Confirmatory factor methods allow us to specify in advance what one believes on psychological grounds to be a likely factor structure and then to employ one of the available computer programs available to manipulate the data to the best fit.

Criterion Validity

Criterion validity—also called predictive or empirical validity—is determined by comparing test scores with some form of performance or outside measure, whether the measure is taken concurrently (approximately the same time as the test) or predictively (sometime after test scores were derived). Thus predictive validity is commonly regarded as the most convincing type of validity for the effectiveness of intelligence test (Cronbach, 1984).

A main problem confronting criterion validity lies in finding an agreed-upon or acceptable criterion (Smith, 1976); at present we have no infallible or perfectly objective criterion against which to validate scores. Some of the criterion performances that have been employed for validating intelligence tests are scholastic attainment and quality of schoolwork (as assessed by grade point average or observations of teachers and parents), placement in special programs (remedial vs. programs for the gifted), attainment on job training programs, and rudimentary judgments of occupational attainment after leaving school. Criteria in personality test are often observer ratings, supervisor ratings of success on the job, behavior in structured situations, and the like.

Anastasi (1986) suggests that much of the variance among obtained validity coefficients (e.g., when standardized ability tests correlated with performance) may be statistical artifact resulting from small samples size, criterion unreliability, and restriction of range in employee samples. In any case, one should refer to the test manual to assess the similarity between the criteria used for validation purposes and the situation to which one would like to apply the test. It would also be useful to cross-validate psychometric characteristics of the test on a new independent sample of the population with which the test is to be used. Correlating test scores with criterion scores in the original group used in constructing the scores does not produce adequate validity coefficients.

Special Validity Issues in Personality

It is useful to think about the data that can go into validating a personality scale in terms of the following categories (see Block, 1977; Buss & Craik, 1983a): O-data (based upon the reports of observers), L-data (based upon societal life outcomes), T-data (based upon test situations under a controlled experiment model), S-data (based upon self-reports), and A-data (based upon act trends). When thinking about these sources of data, it is useful to remember the practical advice of Kenrick and Funder (1988) for finding predictive validity from trait ratings. They said that the optimum is to

- use raters who are thoroughly familiar with the person being rated,

- make multiple behavioral observations of the individual,
- use traits that are more behavioral and thus publicly observable, and
- make sure that posited behaviors are relevant to the trait.

Act Frequency Approach

Buss and Craik (1983b) show a method of validating and bringing meaning to (as well as contrasting) personality scales. They use their standard method for deriving acts in relation to personality constructs and then look at how self-reported acts of subjects relate to personality scales administered to the same individuals. With this information they yield three indexes: act density, bipolarity, and extensity. Act density shows how well a scale relates to acts that should be associated with that scale. For example, the CPI Sociability (Sy) scale showed many gregarious acts (e.g., "I introduced myself to a new neighbor.") significantly correlated with it, and thus it showed good act density. Density can be considered basic validity evidence.

Act bipolarity is whether an opposing act is also negatively correlated with the scale construct. For example, the CPI Sociability scale (and all the other such scales in the study) did not show an association with many aloof acts. Interestingly, Buss and Craik (1983b) show that scale constructs may not be balanced (bipolar) in their manifestation. Gregarious acts show good bipolarity, whereas aloof acts do not. This can be attributed to the fact that aloofness is more represented by acts that are not performed than those that are exhibited. Gregariousness has a high performance value. Thus, when thinking about scales such as those for sociability, there may be low bipolarity because not being sociable is not a very salient behavior.

Act extensity evidence across scales also shows how "tight" or "loose" a scale is in predicting associated or nonassociated acts. Basically it refers to how broad the scale's manifestation of the construct might be. For example, the CPI Sociability scale shows some relationship to dominant and agreeable acts, as well as a negative relationship to submissive acts.

To Gough (1987), scales must show a utilitarian and pragmatic criterion:

> For instance, does a scale for dominance in fact identify people who are described by others as dominant, strong, self-assured, and resourceful, and in addition do things that can be consensually be classified as dominant? . . . The criteria for the instrumentalist include the degree to which the test classifies people in the way that others classify them, and the accuracy with which scores on the test predict or postdict behavior that is significantly relevant to the purposes put forward for the measure (p. 3)

INTERPRETING TEST SCORES

The issue of test interpretation and the social consequences of test results has long been the center of dispute in the academic community. The interpretation of test scores is intrinsically related to the issue of test validity, because validity relates to the appropriateness of meanings and interpretations assigned to test scores rather than to the test scores themselves (Kane, 1992; Messick, 1989). Various professional organizations have published guidelines for sound test construction and interpretation for examiners: the *Standards for Educational and Psychological Tests* (American Educational Research Association (AERA), American Psychological Association (APA), & National Council on Measurement in Education (NCME), 1985) and the *Guidelines for Computer-Based Test Interpretations* (Committee on Professional Standards (COPS) & Committee on Psychological Tests and Assessment (CPTA), 1986). The reader would do well to refer to these sources to learn more about sound principles of test interpretation.

Intelligence

The data that one obtains from an intelligence test are largely inferential and they depend on the interpretation of the examiner as to what the test allegedly measures, as well as what particular responses are presumed to signify. Though naive test users often take intelligence test scores at face value and treat them as if they were a second-best way to observe behavior, very seldom should they be viewed as samples of intelligent behavior that have some meaningful degree of correspondence to actual behavior (see Hogan & Nicholson, 1988). Even if test scores have predictive significance, their meaning is still a matter for subsequent analysis.

Intelligence Tests as Current Behavioral Repertoire

Intelligence test scores have traditionally been interpreted to represent an individual's basic cognitive capacity or potential, as if the score foretold what level the person would reach if given the opportunity to develop his capacity. As pointed out by Snow (1991), the evidence is necessarily one-sided: Good performance proves that the person does have cognitive capacity, whereas poor performance on tests does not (Snow, 1991).

Cronbach (1984) observed that it is best not to use terms such as *intelligence* and *capacity* in test titles and in communications to the general public. What we are actually testing is present performance. Thus intelligence test scores may perhaps best be viewed as representing the repertoire of cognitive skills and knowledge available to examinee at a given point in time, because no test can accurately assess capacity.

Normative Interpretation Strategy

Traditionally, intelligence test scales have been constructed and interpreted normatively. Scores on a scale indicate an individual's standing relative to the normative population. Thus all descriptions are relative to the population (e.g., an IQ of 130 is high, but 70 is low). The descriptions refer to that reference population (e.g., 130 was a high score in that group of people).

The meaning of scores on normative ability scales is basically more relativistic than acknowledged. Under classical scaling methods, the relative position of a person on an ability scale may change with a different reference population or different set of indicators for the same construct. For example, deviation scores on two measures (e.g., test A = 113, test B = 105) may indicate that the person scores relatively higher on one test relative to the reference population, but it does not necessarily follow that the individual has more of the trait assessed by that test in any absolute sense.

Interpretation in Terms of Reference Factors

According to Matarazzo (1972), the abilities entering into a test are best defined in terms of the reference factors that account for its major variables. Accordingly, examiners will be on the safest ground if they assume that a subject's success or failures are probably caused by strength or weaknesses in the major abilities as defined by the attested factors underlying test scores. Thus factor analysis is important not only for the construction of intelligence tests but also for interpretation purposes and for providing meaning to test scores (Kline, 1986; Sundberg, 1977). For example, a low score on the Vocabulary, Arithmetic, or Similarities test of the WISC-R is best interpreted as the result of limited verbal ability, whereas a low score on the Digit Span test is most appropriately interpreted as being attributable to poor overall memory.

The Whole Context

A simple composite test score should never be used in describing, predicting, or explaining an examinee's behavior. Sound interpretation involves integration of various sources of data and assimilating them into an exposition that describes the examinee's functioning, details specific strengths and weaknesses, and predicts the specific behavioral manifestations one could be expected to see. Thus poor performance on an arithmetic test may be attributable to limited schooling, distractibil:ty, anxiety, or the like rather than low verbal ability. As pointed out by Scarr (1981), intellectual competence is always entwined with motivation and adjustment, and whenever we are measuring a subject's cognitive functioning we are also measuring cooperation, attention, persistence, and social responsiveness to the test situation. Furthermore, the content of particular items may evoke emotional factors, and bizarre responses may be used to interpret items and serve as pathognomic indicators (see Matarazzo, 1972, for numerous illustrations).

Test Interpretation as an Interpretive Argument

When interpreting a test, we are making some of the implications of the score clear. An ability test score always involves an interpretive argument, with the test score as premise. For example, suppose that Bob Ankrum, a fourth grade student, was referred to a school psychologist for testing because of learning problems, and that he scored two standard deviations below the norms on the WISC-R. The first premise in the interpretive argument would be that Bob scores two standard deviations below the normative group (i.e., 98% of the norm group score higher than Bob). A second premise is that students whose WISC-R scores fall two standard deviations below the norm would tend to do poorly under normal class conditions. The concluding statement might be that students who are expected to do poorly under normal class conditions should be assigned to a special remedial class. Thus, based on his low test scores, Bob would be predicted to do poorly in regular class, and the operative decision would be to place him in a remedial class.

The inferences in the interpretive argument above

depend on various assumptions about the relationship between test (scoring two standard deviations below the mean) and nontest behaviors (doing poorly in class), and one must provide evidence to show that the argument is highly plausible. Furthermore, in validating a test one decides on the decisions to be based on test scores (e.g., assignment to special educational programs), specifies assumptions leading from test scores to decisions (poor test performance → poor school performance → need for remedial help), identifies potential competing interpretations (e.g., Bob did poorly on the test because he was extremely anxious, unmotivated, or had problems understanding instructions in English). In the present case, we would need to substantiate the claim that those scoring two standard deviations below average on the WISC-R tend to do very poorly in school, and further, that their achievement can be improved through remedial education. Moreover, because the evidence supporting the premises is largely based on group data, the examiner is often treading on thin ice, as it is unlikely that the personal interpretation and decisions concerning Bob were sufficiently validated.

Profiles as an Aid to Test Interpretation

Clinicians have embraced the suggestion that subtests on conventional tests of intelligence (e.g., the Wechsler tests) profiled themselves into a unique pattern in different pathological conditions or educational categories, or that one of several indices of intersubtest or intratest scatter or unevenness of functioning might also uniquely characterize such different conditions. Hundreds of studies on the use of profile pattern or scatter analysis with the Wechsler tests over the past 50 years, however, failed to produce reliable evidence that such a search would be fruitful. For example, research on the standardization sample for the WICS-R determined that the average child exhibited a substantial amount of fluctuation in subtest performance (varying as much as 7 points on average); learning-disabled children though, showed no unusual amount of scatter that would differentiate them from normal children. This demonstrated the conflict between clinical needs and disappointing empirical results (Matarazzo, 1972).

Although profile analysis may not aid in the assignment of testees to different diagnostic categories, it may be valuable in delineating and interpreting an individual's personal strengths and weaknesses for subjects. This in itself might be useful in individualizing instruction and treatment (Rothlisberg, 1987). Furthermore, Gridley (1987) suggested that a profile analysis may be helpful as a method of generating hypothesis about the origins of intellectual functioning.

Assessment within Context

It should be pointed out that test scores need to be understood within the context of a person's life and ecosystem. Thus assessment of test performance requires appreciation of the possible multiple influences on test scores, interactional influences, and multiple relations (see Zeidner & Most, 1992). This includes the subject's past history and current social, emotional, vocational, and economic adjustments, as well as behavior during the exam. In fact, the kind of life one leads is itself a pretty good test of a person's intellectual ability (Matarazzo, 1972): When a life history is in disagreement with the test results, it is best to pause before attempting classification on the basis of the test alone, as the former is generally a more reliable criterion. Thus interpretation should only be made after examining the relevant information beyond test scores.

Also, no matter how accurate the interpretation of the data, it will be meaningless unless the results can be communicated effectively. Feedback should be given in terms that are clear and understandable to receiver. For example, rather than tell parents their child has an IQ of 115, one may wish to explain that the child is currently functioning among the top 16% when compared to his or her peers and is particularly good in spatial or motor performance and organizing nonverbal material (e.g., piecing puzzles together, building a playhouse).

Personality

To the practitioner using a personality instrument, what the scale means and how it can be used are more important than any of the technical issues. Scale meaning can vary from a reading of the items on the scale to a rich network of correlations with other instruments, descriptive checklists (e.g., an adjective checklist), descriptions from expert interpreters, and correlations with behaviors and experimental studies. Gough (1965) proposes a four-step process for delving into the meaning of a scale:

Step 1. Review of the development of the measure, the procedures and samples used in its construction, its theoretical presuppositions and bases.

Step 2. Analysis of the components of the measure, its items, stimulus materials, and content.

Step 3. Determination of the relationships between the measure and (a) other measures already known and conceptualized, and (b) variables of self-evident importance such as sex, age, status, etc.

Step 4. Specification of the characterological and personological dispositions of individuals who obtain scores defined by the measure itself as diagnostically significant. (p. 297)

Gough adds that in interpreting a scale, "The task for the practitioner . . . is to internalize the content of the scale, and by virtue of this intimate familiarity to enhance the insightfulness of the psychodynamic formulation which is being evolved" (p. 298).

Act frequencies can bring a rich world of meaning into scales. Gough (1987) provides data about act frequencies correlated with the CPI. In an illustration of the Self-Control (Sc) scale, he provides a table of self-reported and spouse-reported acts. The acts related to the Sc scale (e.g., "I really did the dishes after dinner" on the positive correlation end vs. "I told an off-color joke" on the negative correlation end) show how much the scale is related to over- or undercontrol of impulses and the techniques of impression management. High scores tend toward self-denial and repression, whereas low scores tend toward instinctual gratification.

Interpretation by Describing an Individual

A standard method for helping the practitioner learn the meaning of scales is to provide case studies describing an individual and the relationship of that individual's personality to the scales (e.g., see McAllister, 1988). This method is used in a thorough way for the Values and Lifestyles (VALS) types (Holman, 1984). The authors describe their Maslow-inspired types by the usual methods, then go on to describe an individual prototypical of each type and his or her whole life context, history, and orientation. These vignettes are very effective in showing the power and meaning of the VALS scales.

DEALING WITH THREATS TO VALIDITY

The examinee's responses on a test might not be a valid reflection of the measured trait because of a variety of external and personal factors in the test situation. Factors such as misleading or misunderstood instructions, scoring errors, poor health, depressive or anxious mood, illness, daydreaming, or environmental noise introduce an indeterminate amount of error into the testing procedure (Sattler, 1988). Thus unreliable results may be obtained for examinees who are uncooperative or anxious or have difficulty following instructions. Some of the threats to validity are shared by intelligence and personality tests (e.g., anxiety, daydreaming, a noisy testing situation, scoring errors); other factors are unique to each (e.g., coaching or guessing in intelligence testing, and faking good or giving extreme responses for personality tests).

Intelligence

Perceived Bias and Unfairness

A test should be (and be perceived as) fair, and hence not biased in favor of the performance of one group over another. Bias can enter into the test process from a number of directions, including the content of the questions asked, initial stereotypical impressions of the examinee's ability and performance, poor examiner-examinee rapport, and the tester's theory of ability. As Jensen (1980) pointed out, an impressive technology for the study of test bias and the development of multiple indicators of bias has evolved. This is based on the statistical analysis of subgroup differences in such important variables as reliability, construct and predictive validity, factor structure, and item characteristic curves. The perception of bias is often more important than any kind of statistically measured fairness, however, and current ability tests are failing to meet the criterion of perceived fairness. Accordingly, many people remain convinced that cultural or sex bias may invalidate test scores for various sociocultural groups, particularly given the possibility of criterion bias that is shared with the bias of the predictor. (For a more technical and detailed discussion of bias, see Chapter 25.)

Guessing

Whereas guessing is not a major problem on personality tests, it may be on multiple choice intelligence test items. Guessing has the potential of distorting the examinee's response in such cases, reducing both reliability and validity on conventional tests of ability. A good number of formulas have been introduced to correct for guessing (Cohen, Montague, Nathanson, & Swerdlik, 1988; Thorndike, 1982), although these are often based on some questionable assumptions (e.g., that all wrong answers are attributable to guessing, that there are equal chances for options to occur when guessing).

Coaching and Practice

As pointed out by various researchers (e.g., Anastasi, 1990), practice (taking a test without further instruction) and coaching (specific instruction to improve test performance) do make an appreciable difference at the selection borderline. A single practice session can hike scores by about one third of a standard deviation, and when combined with coaching the effects can reach one standard deviation (which is the limit in the improvement). Although coaching may have a smaller effect on natural types of items appearing in individual tests, they may provide some facility in dealing with artificial types of items occurring in most group tests. The only fair solution is to allow a limited amount of practice and instruction on parallel tests to give all potential test takers a reasonable amount of facility.

Personality

Gough (1987) put the problem of threats to validity into perspective:

> In psychological assessment based on self-reports the question necessarily arises of the validity of what a respondent says about self. For instance, one person may furnish a very favorable self-portrait whereas another may stress weaknesses and inadequacies. A third may have lapses of attention in which items are answered in a random or haphazard way. The interpreter of a personality inventory needs to have some way of knowing whether any of these modes of responding have been carried to the point of rendering the protocol unreliable or invalid. (p. 35)

The usual criterion for developing invalidity scales in personality measurement is to ask college students to take the instrument in different frames of mind, such as trying to look as positive as possible or presenting as negative a persona as possible. For a discussion of additional threats to validity in personality measurement, see Kline (1991) and Mischel (1968).

TRAINING TEST USERS

Graduate schools provide courses for instruments measuring intelligence, psychopathology, and brain dysfunction. A professional, however, would require additional learning about nonclinical tests, specific measures, and new tests developed since graduate school. A survey by the British Psychological Society found that most learning about tests came from reading the manual (Tyler & Miller, 1986).

The literature on training (Goldstein, 1993) encourages active participation, feedback, and trainee self-efficacy. Training should begin with simple behaviors that can be mastered easily, then progress to more complex behaviors as trainees become more confident. Also, training should be adapted to the attitudes and prior knowledge of the trainee.

Narrative reports are an effective method for providing good interpretations of tests and for training users in interpreting them. Typically the narrative is developed by an expert interpreter who develops rules for what they might write given particular scores on the scales. The rules are converted into a computer program so that given particular scale scores, particular paragraphs are generated. For more discussion of this resource, see Moreland (1992).

Another effective methods for helping provide good interpretation and training of a personality instrument are short interpretive guides for the test taker. For example, the "Introduction to Type" series (Hirsh & Kummerow, 1990) for the Myers-Briggs Type Indicator (MBTI; Myers, 1987) has proven to be very successful, because it empowers the test taker to learn the constructs actively. It saves the counselor time in describing the instrument, as well as assuring that the descriptions will be accurate.

HOW TESTS CAN BE IMPROVED

Current personality and intelligence tests have many strengths, but they have also been criticized for falling short on a number of counts.

Shortcomings

Intelligence

Sternberg (in press) points out a number of strengths of standardized intelligence tests that explain their popularity and persistence in their conventional form. These include accurate standardization procedures and representative norms, ease of administration and objectivity of scoring, relatively stable scores over time, moderate to high correlations with other tests, reasonable prediction of scholastic achievement, and cost-effectiveness.

Gardner (1992), though, claims that formal intelligence testing procedures are based on a number of questionable practices and assumptions. Accordingly, conventional tests put a premium on instruments that are efficient, brief, and easily administered. Tests also use the same kind of tasks for different age groups under the assumption that development is linear, with young having less of the same kinds of knowledge and skills than older subjects (Gardner, 1992); however, this is not the case.

Furthermore, tests favor individuals who possess a blend of linguistic and logical intelligence and who are comfortable in being assessed in a decontextualized setting under timed and impersonal conditions. Most conventional tests assess only a particular subset of the intelligence domain, being biased heavily in favor of linguistic and logical-mathematical abilities (Gardner, 1992). Individuals strong on this particular combination will receive high scores on most formal tests, even if they are not adept at the domain as a whole. By the same token, individuals weak in either of the verbal or logical facet will fail at other measures because they cannot master the particular format of most instruments.

Because current tests do not exhaust the domain and often lack in "ecological validity," they tend to mask individual strengths and differences on a variety of dimensions (e.g., interpersonal understanding, spatial and practical abilities). Thus experts often fail on "formal" measures of intelligence but can show precisely these skills in the course of ordinary work (e.g., defending rights in a dispute, leadership in a peer group, expertise in football).

In addition, conventional measures do not permit differentiation of difficulty level and speeded aspects of ability (Carroll, 1992), and one should also bear in mind the imperfections of the relative unit of measurement on IQ tests. Neither the original derived IQ nor currently used standardized scores represent the actual amount of intelligence relative to others, and absolute scaling techniques have not yet been successfully employed on a large scale.

An additional shortcoming of standardized tests is that they do not guide prescriptions or remedial activities (Das, 1973). In fact, many assessments are not engaged for the testees' benefit and do not provide enough feedback (e.g., concrete suggestions, relative strengths).

Personality

Hogan and Nicholson (1988) believe that a major problem with personality measures is the tendency for naive researchers to do preliminary validation research but fail to pursue more complicated procedures, with many psychologists unaware of the literature. Additional problems with personality measures considered by Hogan and Nicholson are social desirability; how to interpret and make sense of self-report data; low correlations with physiological measures; and the possibility that relations between personality descriptions only reflect semantic links between words.

Improvements

A number of suggestions have been made on how to improve tests in view of the above shortcomings.

Intelligence

Intelligence testing could be improved by taking the multidimensional structure of ability into account and incorporating the extensive evidence of multiple intelligences or abilities in current tests (Horn, 1979). Test constructors could make efforts to develop a series of shorter, more distinctive, and streamlined subtests, each measuring a homogeneous trait but together covering as wide a range of the intelligence domain as possible.

Furthermore, because many ability tests do not use intrinsically attractive or interesting material, current tests could be improved by making the materials more interesting and having assessment occur in the context of students working on problems and products that engage them (Gardner, 1992). Authentic assessment or contextualized testing procedures, such as those developed by Gardner and colleagues for Project Zero (Gardner & Hatch, 1989), could enhance the ecological validity of current tests. Tests could also be improved by reflecting theoretical developments in the processes used by the individual in performing the test (e.g., planning, attention, coding of information, metacognitive strategies; Das, 1973).

The complaint is sometimes heard that the technology of intelligence tests offers little in the way of novelty over procedures developed in the early years of the century. Current tests could be improved by paying attention to the design of novel and less restrictive forms of test tasks, procedures, and media (Jones & Applebaum, 1989). By moving away from the predominant paper-and-pencil and oral forms of presentation toward task presentation via computers, TV, and movie screens, intelligence testing would reflect recent shifts in the media in communication of knowledge (Horn, 1979). The dynamic character of film, as well as the possibility to control temporal and spatial features of the task, might allow a more comprehensive survey of abilities.

With respect to interpretation, rather than drawing widespread implications from composite scores of a single test, researchers could improve intelligence test interpretation by taking the scatter of scores and the test profile into account. In addition, multifaceted batteries composed of such distinctive subtests would combine information from a variety of sources (e.g., educational, occupational, social, medical) and try to integrate these sources into a whole picture of the individual. Tests could be made more diagnostic and prescriptive by providing sufficient feedback to testees in the form of concrete suggestions for improvement, delineation of relative strengths and deficits, and better guidelines for the intervention and remedial training of low ability individuals (Das, 1973).

Personality

Personality measures seem to be most successful when they are global. The Myers-Briggs Type Indicator and the success of the big-five scales are evidence for the value of a few scales over many. Instruments also succeed to the extent that they can relate personality to applications like personnel selection or team building. The more test users can do in their work with personality scales, the more they will succeed. Finally, successful measures give the test taker a conceptual model of personality. Again the MBTI is an example, because test users can think about interactions between scales, and there is a literature on how the scales should work logically. In fact, there is much less empirical evidence than logical evidence for the MBTI.

There also seems to be a need for specific personality measures (e.g., for impulse control, jealousy, or anger). When test users are dealing with a specific situation such as spousal abuse, they need normative tools to help them put the problem into perspective.

CONCLUSION

Although we have laid out the test construction process in a linear fashion, the actual process is much more dynamic and integrated in reality. Indeed, the process of test revision and refinement is an endless one. The ultimate test for personality or intelligence tests is that they show practical utility in applied settings.

REFERENCES

Ackerman, P. L., & Humphreys, L. G. (1990). Individual differences theory in industrial and organizational psychology. In M. D. Dunnette & L. M. Hough (Eds.), *Handbook of industrial and organizational psychology* (2nd Ed., Vol. 1, pp. 223–282). Palo Alto, CA: Consulting Psychologists Press.

American Educational Research Association (AERA), American Psychological Association (APA), & National Council on Measurement in Education (NCME). (1985). *Standards for educational and psychological tests and manuals.* Washington, DC: American Psychological Association.

Anastasi, A. (1986). Evolving concepts of test validation. *Annual Review of Psychology, 37,* 1–15.

Anastasi, A. (1990). *Psychological Testing* (6th ed.). New York: Macmillan.

Angleitner, A., John, O. P., & Löhr, F. J. (1986). It's what you ask and how you ask it: An itemmetric analysis of personality questionnaires. In A. Angleitner & J. S. Wiggins (Eds.). *Personality assessment via questionnaires: Current issues in theory and measurement* (pp. 61–107). Berlin: Springer.

Baron, J. (1982). Personality and intelligence. In R. J. Sternberg (Ed.). *Handbook of human intelligence* (pp. 308–351). New York: Cambridge University Press.

Block, J. (1977). Advancing the psychology of personality: Paradigmatic shift or improving the quality of research? In D. Magnussen & N. S. Endler (Eds.), *Personality at the crossroads: Current issues in interactional psychology* (pp. 37–63). Hillsdale, NJ: Erlbaum.

Buss, D. M., & Craik, K. H. (1983a). The act frequency approach to personality. *Psychological Review,* 90(2), 105–126.

Buss, D. M., & Craik, K. H. (1983b). Act prediction and the conceptual analysis of personality scales: Indices of act density, bipolarity, and extensity. *Journal of Personality and Social Psychology, 45*(5), 1081–1095.

Butcher, H. J. (1968). *Human intelligence: Its nature and assessment.* London: Methuen.

Carroll, J. B. (1992). Cognitive abilities: The state of the art. *Psychological Science, 3,* 266–270.

Cattell, R. B. (1943). The description of personality: Basic traits resolved into cluster. *Journal of Abnormal and Social Psychology, 38,* 476–506.

Cattell, R. B. (1971). *Abilities: Their structure, growth and action.* New York: Houghton Mifflin.

Cohen, R. J., Montague, P., Nathanson, L. S., & Swerdlik, M. E. (1988). *Psychological testing: An introduction to tests and measurement.* Mountain View, CA: Mayfield.

Committee on Professional Standards (COPS), & Committee on Psychological Tests and Assessment (CPTA). (1986). *Guidelines for computer-based tests and interpretations.* Washington, DC: American Psychological Association.

Costa, P. T., Jr., & McCrae, R. R. (1986). Personality stability and its implications for clinical psychology. *Clinical Psychology Review, 1,* 144–149.

Craik, K. H. (1991, August). *The lived day of an individual: A person environment perspective.* Invited address to the Division of Population and Environmental Psychology at the annual meeting of the American Psychological Association in San Francisco, CA.

Crocker, L., & Algina, J. (1986). *Introduction to classical and modern test theory.* New York: CBS College Publications.

Cronbach, L. J. (1984). *Essentials of psychological testing* (4th ed.). New York: Harper & Row.

Cronbach, L. J., Gleser, G. C., Rajaratnam, N., & Nanda, H. (1972). *The dependability of behavioral measurements: Theory of generalizability for scores and profiles.* New York: Wiley.

Cronbach, L. J., & Meehl, P. E. (1955). Construct validity in psychological tests. *Psychological Bulletin, 52,* 281–303.

Dancer, L. S. (1985). On the multidimensional structure of self-esteem: Facet analysis of Rosenberg's self-esteem scale. In D. Canter (Ed.), *Facet theory: Approaches to social research* (pp. 223–236). New York: Springer-Verlag.

Das, J. P. (1973). Cultural deprivation and cognitive competence. In N. R. Ellis (Ed.), *International review of research in mental retardation* (Vol. 6, pp. 1–53). New York: Academic Press.

Eysenck, H. J., & Eysenck, M. W. (1985). *Personality and individual differences.* New York: Plenum.

Gardner, H. (1992). Assessment in context: The alternative to standardized testing. In B. R. Gifford & M. C. O'Conner (Eds.), *Changing assessments: Alternative views of aptitude, achievement, and instruction* (pp. 77–119). Boston: Kluwer.

Gardner, H., & Hatch, T. (1989). Multiple intelligences go to school. *Educational Researcher, 18,* 4–10.

Goldberg, L. R. (1982). From ace to zombie: Some explorations in the language of personality. In C. D. Spielberger & J. N. Butcher (Eds.), *Advances in personality assessment* (Vol. 1, pp. 203–234). Hillsdale, NJ: Erlbaum.

Goldberg, L. R. (1993). The structure of phenotypic personality traits. *American Psychologist, 48,* 26–34.

Golden, C. J., Sawicki, R. F., & Franzen, M. D. (1984). Test construction. In G. Goldstein & M. Hersen (Eds.), *Handbook of psychological assessment* (pp. 19–37). New York: Pergamon.

Goldstein, I. L. (1993). *Training in organizations: Needs assessment, development, and evaluation* (3rd ed.), Pacific Grove, CA: Brooks/Cole.

Gough, H. G. (1965). Conceptual analysis of psychological test scores and other diagnostic variables. *Journal of Abnormal Psychology, 70*(4), 294–302.

Gough, H. G. (1987). *California Psychological Inventory administrator's guide.* Palo Alto, CA: Consulting Psychologists Press.

Gough, H. G., & Bradley, P. (1992). Comparing two strategies for developing personality scales. In M. Zeidner & R. Most (Eds.), *Psychological testing: An inside view* (pp. 215–246). Palo Alto, CA: Consulting Psychologists Press.

Gridley, B. E. (1987). Measuring adult intelligence. In R. S. Dean (Ed.), *Introduction to assessing human intelligence* (pp. 117–139). Springfield, IL: Thomas.

Guilford, J. P. (1959). Three faces of intellect. *American Psychologists, 14,* 469–479.

Guilford, J. P. (1967). *The nature of human intelligence.* New York: McGraw Hill.

Guttman, L. (1969). Integration of test design and analysis. In *Proceedings of the 1969 Invitational Conference on Testing Problems* (pp. 53–65). Princeton, NJ: Educational Testing Service.

Guttman, L., & Levy, S. (1980). Two structural laws for intelligence. *Megamot, 25,* 421–438.

Guttman, L., & Levy, S. (1991). Two structural laws for intelligence. *Intelligence, 15,* 79–109.

Hirsh, S. K., & Kummerow, J. M. (1990). *Introduction to type in organizations.* Palo Alto, CA: Consulting Psychologists Press.

Hogan, R., & Nicholsen, R. A. (1988). The meaning of personality test scores. *American Psychologist, 43,* 621–626.

Hogan, R. T. (1991). Personality and personality measurement. In M. D. Dunnette & L. M. Hough (Eds.), *Handbook of industrial and organizational psychology* (2nd ed., Vol. 2, pp. 873–919). Palo Alto, CA: Consulting Psychologists Press.

Holman, R. H. (1984). A values and lifestyles perspective on human behavior. In R. E. Pitts & A. G. Woodside (Eds.), *Personal values and consumer psychology* (pp. 35–54). Lexington, MA: Lexington Books.

Horn, J. L. (1979). Trends in the measurement of intelligence. In R. J. Sternberg & K. K. Detterman (Eds.), *Human intelligence* (pp. 191–200). Norwood, NJ: Ablex.

Hough, L. M. (1992). The "big five" personality variables—construct confusion: Description vs. prediction. *Human Performance, 5*(1 & 2), 139–155.

Jensen, A. (1980). *Bias in mental testing.* New York: Free press.

John, O. P. (1990). The "big five" factor taxonomy: Dimensions of personality in the natural language and in questionnaires. In L. A. Pervin (Ed.), *Handbook of personality: Theory and research* (pp. 66–100). New York: Guilford.

Jones, L. V., & Applebaum, M. I. (1989). Psychometric methods. *Annual Review of Psychology, 40,* 23–43.

Kane, M. T. (1992). An argument-based approach to validity. *Psychological Bulletin, 112,* 527–535.

Kenrick, D. T., & Funder, D. C. (1988). Profiting from controversy: Lessons from the person-situation debate. *American Psychologist, 43,* 23–34.

Kleinmuntz, B. (1982). *Personality and psychological assessment.* New York: McGraw-Hill.

Kline, P. (1986). *A handbook of test construction.* London: Methuen.

Kline, P. (1991). *Intelligence: The psychometric view.* London: Routledge.

Krechevsky, M., & Gardner, H. (1991). The emergence and nurturance of multiple intelligences: The Project Spectrum approach. In M. J. A. Howe (Ed.). *Encouraging the development of exceptional skills and talents* (pp. 222–245). Leicester, England: British Psychological Society.

Loevinger, J. (1957). Objective tests as instruments of psychological theory. *Psychological Reports, 3,* 635–694.

Lord, F. M. (1980). *Applications of item response theory to practical testing problems.* Hillsdale, NJ: Erlbaum.

Matarazzo, J. D. (1972). *Measurement and appraisal of adult intelligence* (5th ed.). Baltimore, MD: Williams & Wilkins.

McAllister, L. W. (1988). *A practical guide to CPI interpretation* (2nd ed.). Palo Alto, CA: Consulting Psychologists Press.

McCrae, R. R. (1987). Creativity, divergent thinking, and openness to experience. *Journal of Personality and Social Psychology, 52,* 1258–1265.

Messick, S. (1989). Validity. In R. L. Linn (Ed.), *Educational measurement* (3rd ed., pp. 13–103). New York: Macmillan.

Mischel, W. (1968). *Personality and assessment.* New York: Wiley.

Moreland, K. L. (1992). Computer-assisted psychological assessment. In M. Zeidner & R. Most (Eds.), *Psychological testing: An inside view* (pp. 343–376). Palo Alto, CA: Consulting Psychologists Press.

Myers, I. B. (1987). *Introduction to type.* Palo Alto, CA: Consulting Psychologists Press.

Nevo, B. (1990). The construction of an intelligence test based on the two-faceted model. *Psychologia, 2,* 12–25.

Norman, W. T. (1963). Toward an adequate taxonomy of personality attributes: Replicated factor structure in peer nomination personality ratings. *Journal of Abnormal and Social Psychology, 66,* 574–583.

Nunnally, J. C. (1978). *Psychometric theory*. New York: McGraw-Hill.

Rasch, G. (1960). *Probabilistic models for some intelligence and attainment tests*. Copenhagen: Danish Institute for Educational Research.

Robertson, G. J. (1992). Psychological tests: Development, publication, and distribution. In M. Zeidner & R. Most (Eds.), *Psychological testing: An inside view* (pp. 159–214). Palo Alto, CA: Consulting Psychologists Press.

Rothlisberg, B. A. (1987). Assessing learning problems: How to proceed once you know the score. In R. S. Dean (Ed.), *Introduction to assessing human intelligence* (pp. 207–229). Springfield, IL: Thomas.

Sattler, J. M. (1988). *Assessment of children* (3rd ed.). San Diego, Author.

Scarr, S. (1981). Testing for children: Assessment and the many determinants of intellectual competence. *American Psychologist, 36*, 1159–1166.

Schlesinger, I. M., & Guttman, L. (1969). Smallest space analysis of intellectual and achievement tests. *Psychological Bulletin, 71*, 95–100.

Schutz, W. C. (1966). *The interpersonal underworld*. Palo Alto, CA: Science and Behavior Books.

Smith, P. C. (1976). Behaviors, results, and organizational effectiveness: The problem of criteria. In M. D. Dunnette (Ed.), *Handbook of industrial and organizational psychology* (pp. 745–775). Chicago, IL: Rand McNally.

Snow, R. E. (1991). The concept of aptitude. In R. E. Snow & D. E. Wiley (Eds.), *Improving inquiry in social science: A volume in honor of Lee J. Cronbach* (pp. 249–284). Hillsdale, NJ: Erlbaum.

Spearman, C. E. (1923). *The nature of intelligence and the principles of cognition*. London: Macmillan.

Spector, P. E. (1992). *Summated rating scale construction: An introduction*. Newbury Park, CA: Sage.

Spielberger, C. D. (1983). *Manual for the Strait-Trait Anxiety Inventory*. Palo Alto, CA: Consulting Psychologists Press.

Sternberg, R. J. (1985).*Beyond IQ: A triarchic theory of human intelligence*. New York: Cambridge University Press.

Sternberg, R. J. (in press). Ability tests, measurements, and markets. *Journal of Educational Psychology*.

Sternberg, R. J., Conway, B. E., Ketron, J. L., & Bernstein, M. (1981). People's conceptions of intelligence. *Journal of Personality and Social Psychology, 41*, 37–55.

Strelau, J., & Angleitner, A. (1991). *Explorations in temperament: International perspectives on theory and measurement*. London: Plenum.

Sundberg, N. D. (1977). *Assessment of persons*. Englewood Cliffs, NJ: Prentice-Hall.

Thorndike, E. I., Bregnan, E.O., Cobb, M. V., & Woodyard, E. (1926). *The measurement of intelligence*. New York: Teachers College Bureau of Publications.

Thorndike, R. L. (1982). *Applied psychometrics*. Boston: Houghton-Mifflin.

Thurstone, L. L. (1938). *Primary mental abilities*. Chicago: University of Chicago Press.

Trickett, E. J., & Moos, R. H. (1970). Generally and specificity of student reactions in high school classrooms. *Adolescence, 5*, 373–390.

Tyler, B., & Miller, K. (1986). The use of tests by psychologists: Report on a survey of BPS members. *Bulletin of the British Psychological Society, 39*, 405–410.

Wechsler, D. (1944). *The measurement of adult intelligence* (3rd ed.). Baltimore, MD: Williams & Wilkins.

Willerman, L. (1979). *The psychology of individual and group differences*. San Francisco: Freeman.

Zeidner, M., & Most, R. (1992). An introduction to psychological testing. In M. Zeidner & R. Most (Eds.), *Psychological testing: An inside view* (pp. 2–47). Palo Alto, CA: Consulting Psychologists Press.

23

A Critical Review of the Measurement of Personality and Intelligence

Paul Kline

Intelligence tests cannot be understood without reference to the factor analysis of abilities. Essentially such tests aim to measure the factor (or factors) identified as intelligence. Thus a brief discussion of the factor analysis of abilities is essential in this chapter.

The factor analysis of human abilities effectively began with the famous paper by Spearman (1904) in which the general factor, *g*, was first proposed. It is interesting to note that this concept is still viable, as is shown in the work of Undheim (1981). Nevertheless two of the best-known intelligence tests, the Stanford-Binet and the Wechsler scales, were developed without the aid of factor analysis. It is an impressive testament to the skill of their construction and to the pervasive quality of *g* that these scales are highly *g*-loaded (Jensen, 1980). Indeed, at least until recently they were used as benchmark measures of intelligence.

In the psychometric elucidation of the fields of human ability and personality, however, it is factor analysis that has made advances and understanding possible. Indeed, it will be argued that in many cases, tests that have not been developed by factor analysis have actually hindered and held back progress in psychology, a point that is particularly pertinent to the second section of this chapter on personality measurement.

Paul Kline • Department of Psychology, University of Exeter, Exeter EX4 4QG, England.

International Handbook of Personality and Intelligence, edited by Donald H. Saklofske and Moshe Zeidner. Plenum Press, New York, 1995.

THE FACTOR ANALYSIS OF HUMAN ABILITIES

Although over the years there have been considerable controversies concerning the number and nature of factors of human abilities, there is now a reasonable consensus among most of the leading researchers in the field. What is required is that simple structure factor analyses are obtained, analyses defined by factors with a few high loadings and large numbers of zero loadings. Kline (1993a) contains a simple discussion of how this may be accomplished. Kline (1992b) listed the main ability factors; these are set out in Table 1.

Several important points need to be made about this table. These factors are essentially those of Cattell and his colleagues (fully described in Cattell, 1971), but there is little difference in forms of primary factors from those of other lists (e.g., Ekstrom, French, & Harman, 1976). It is also noteworthy that the most recent and detailed account of the factorial structure of abilities (Carroll, in press) lists these factors as the most important. In the "structure of intellect" model, however, Guilford and his colleagues (e.g., Guilford, 1967) have proposed a huge number of factors, and some psychologists have taken the model seriously. Nevertheless, the work of Horn and Knapp (1973)

Table 1. Ability Factors

Primary factors		Second-order factors	
V	Verbal	Gf	Fluid ability
N	Numerical	Gc	Crystallized ability
S	Spatial	Gv	Visualization
P	Perceptual speed	Gr	Retrieval capacity
Cs	Speed of closure	Gs	Cognitive speed
1	Inductive reasoning	D	Deductive reasoning
Ma	Rote memory	Mc	Motor coordination
Mk	Mechanical ability	Amu	Musical pitch
Cf	Flexibility of closure	Fe	Expressional fluency
Ms	Memory span	ams	Motor speed
Sp	Spelling	asd	Symbol discrimination speed
E	Aesthetic judgement	Mr	Musical rhythm
Mm	Meaningful memory	J	Judgment
01	Originality of ideational flexibility		
FI	Ideational fluency		
W	Word fluency		
02	Originality		
A	Aiming		
Rd	Representational drawing		

showed that there were serious technical problems with this work, and on that account the Guilford factor structure can be ignored.

From the viewpoint of intelligence the most important factors are the second-order factors—especially the two largest, fluid and crystallized ability (G_f and G_c). According to Cattell (1971), these essentially constitute the old Spearman *g*, which, with more efficient rotational procedures, split into two correlated factors. Essentially the claim is that these two factors account for much of the variance in ability, and any theoretical account of human abilities must accommodate g_f and g_c.

Fluid Ability

This is a basic reasoning ability that can be applied to almost any problem, thus accounting for its emergence as a second-order factor. Fluid ability is, like Spearman's *g*, the ability to educe correlates and work out relationships, and it is connected with the total associational neuronal development of the cortex. The population variance of fluid ability has a considerable genetic determination (around 65%), and the environmental determinants appear to spring from within- rather than between-family variables. Scores on fluid ability correlate positively with academic and occupational success, of which it is on average the best single predictor. Kline (1992b) and Jensen (1980) contain detailed information on these points.

Crystallized Ability

This is the factor that loads traditional intelligence tests, especially where the items are verbal. Crystallized ability is fluid ability as it is evinced in the culture. Thus, according to what Cattell (1971) calls investment theory, individuals invest their fluid ability in the skills valued in a particular culture. Consequently crystallized ability would require different tests in different cultures, which is not true for fluid ability.

Because crystallized ability results from the investment of fluid ability, it follows that the two are correlated. At an early age they are highly correlated; as individuals grow and undergo different experiences both in the home and at school, however, this correlation slowly becomes smaller. To some extent, this notion of investment accounts for the social class differences noted in crystallized intelligence, because middle-class children, encouraged by their parents, tend to invest their abilities in skills valued by the culture and schools. This is not always so among children from disadvantaged homes.

INTELLIGENCE TESTS AND THEIR ITEMS

To clarify further the nature of intelligence tests and to avoid repetition in their description, it will be instructive to consider briefly the items used in the best scales. A full description of these can be found in Kline (1992a,b) and Jensen (1980). I shall describe items that load most highly on the two factors.

Matrices. These were used in a famous test, Raven's Progressive Matrices, developed before World War II and still in use (Raven, 1965c). Matrices items load the fluid ability factor more highly than any other type of item, and they clearly reveal the nature of fluid ability and general intelligence. Indeed, as Cattell and Johnson (1986) have shown, almost all the variance in the matrices can be explained by the fluid ability factor and a factor specific to the item form.

Matrices are sequences of diagrams or patterns that have to be completed. Completion requires the ability to work out the relationship between the diagrams and apply the rule to the new case by selecting the correct pattern from a set of possible answers. These items are excellent for test construction because they can be written at any level of difficulty, and there are matrices suitable for 5-year-olds and up to superior adults. The most difficult matrices are solved by only the highest scorers on the fluid ability factor.

Analogies. Analogies are regarded by many workers as being among the best measures of intelligence. Verbal analogies requiring a good knowledge of language load the crystallized ability factor, whereas nonverbal analogies load more highly on the fluid ability factor. Sternberg (1977) has minutely examined analogical reasoning, which he regards as the essence of intelligence. To solve analogies, regardless of format, the subject has to educe the relationship between the first two terms and apply the rule to the second—a good example of intelligence as defined by Spearman.

Series. These items, as the name suggests, consist of a series of patterns, numbers, or words, and the rule linking them has to be educed and applied again to select the correct response from a set of choices. In their pattern form, these items are essentially matrices.

Classification. In these items the subject is required to select the "odd man out" from a set of terms; again, these items may be verbal or nonverbal. To solve these problems, similarities between items have to be worked out such that one term is excluded.

Vocabulary. This item loads higher than any other on the G_c factor. because, although vocabulary must be affected by opportunities to read and hear the language, highly intelligent individuals are able to acquire a bigger vocabulary by being better able to work out the meaning of new words from contexts. Thus all the time the intelligent child is increasing its vocabulary more rapidly than the less intelligent child, and the bigger the vocabulary, the easier it is to increase it.

These are the main types of items used in group intelligence tests. Unless specifically designed to measure only fluid ability, these tests usually measure a combination of fluid and crystallized ability. The use of verbal material will tend to make the test measure crystallized ability, whereas nonverbal items will load on fluid ability. If two brief intelligence test are required, then it is hard to improve upon a combination of matrices and vocabulary items.

Individual Intelligence Tests

The two most famous intelligence tests—the Wechsler scales and the Stanford-Binet test, which have already been mentioned—are not group tests but individual measures. These contain some items and scales different from those above, which were constrained by the fact that they had to be suitable for group testing. These will now be described.

1. *The Wechsler scales.* The first of the Wechsler scales was produced in 1938, and there have been regular updates of them over the years. I shall describe, as the best example of these scales, the Wechsler Adult Intelligence Scale (WAIS; Wechsler, 1986). It should be pointed out that there is also a computer version of the WAIS.

A verbal intelligence, performance intelligence, and overall intelligence score can be obtained from the WAIS. In addition, inferences concerning the profile of scores on the 11 separate scales appear in the manual. These 11 scales fall into two groups—verbal and performance scales. The verbal scales include the following tests:

- *Information* (29 items): This is basically a test of general knowledge.
- *Comprehension* (14 items): This test requires subjects to explain proverbs and solve practical problems.
- *Arithmetic* (14 items): A traditional test of arithmetic problem solving.
- *Similarities* (13 items): In this test subjects have to work out the essential similarity between two things.

- *Digit Span* (17 items): This is a highly interesting test in which subjects are required to repeat strings of digits after they have been read to them, either as heard or backward. Jensen (1980) claims that this scale, especially the backward version, is a good measure of biological intelligence. This view is supported by recent research by Kline, Draycott, and McAndrew (in press) in which a composite measure of digit span and the speed of reading letters (converted to a measure of basic processing speed) loaded highly on a biological intelligence factor.
- *Vocabulary* (40 items): A straightforward vocabulary test that, as Cattell (1971) has shown, always loads highly on crystallized intelligence.

From this description of the verbal tests of the WAIS, it is obvious that the total score on these scales is a measure of crystallized ability, although Digit Span is more a measure of the fluid factor. The performance scales, described, below, are highly useful because they ensure that the WAIS measures fluid intelligence.

- *Digit Symbol* (90 items in 90 seconds): With examples of the pairs of digits and symbols in front of them, subjects have to match the correct digit to a symbol.
- *Picture Completion* (21 items in 20 seconds): Subjects have to recognize within one second what element is missing from each picture.
- *Block Design* (10 items with bonuses for swift completion): In this test, subjects are presented with designs and blocks to make them.
- *Picture Arrangement* (8 items with time bonuses for rapid completion): Each item consists of a set of pictures, which have to be arranged into a sequence such that they tell a story.
- *Object Assembly* (4 items with time bonuses): This test is similar to a jigsaw.

As should be clear these performance tests are of the kind which would be expected to load on fluid ability.

The reliability of the full WAIS scale is high (well beyond .9), and the reliabilities of the verbal and performance scales are only slightly lower. These are highly satisfactory. The reliabilities of the subscales are not so high, however, simply because they are shorter. This has important consequences for interpreting the profiles of scores on the scales, because apparent differences may be within the standard errors of the scale scores.

The test takes about 1 hour to administer to each subject. This is lengthy, but the procedure can be shortened by experienced testers by not giving items that are too easy for the subject. It is possible to give less than the full number of tests, but this reduces the reliability of the scores.

This test is regarded still as a criterion measure of intelligence. Woliver and Saeks (1986) have demonstrated that the performance scales load highly on the fluid ability factor, whereas the verbal score loads crystallized ability. That they do so is a tribute to the clinical intuition of Wechsler, who developed these scales before the two intelligence factors had been clearly differentiated. It would be more sensible, if an individual test were required, to develop a new one with the most recent factorial findings in mind. One could then eliminate the criticism that the verbal scales are highly influenced by educational attainment, especially the arithmetic and information tests.

Nevertheless, the Wechsler scales are highly effective individual tests of intelligence. With the considerable body of research evidence concerning the nature of the scores, it will need an especially good test to replace them.

2. *The Stanford-Binet test* (Terman & Merrill, 1960). This is the second of the individual intelligence tests that were accepted as benchmark measurements of intelligence, at least until the findings of modern factor analysis. The test is a measure of crystallized ability for a range of people aged 4 to 17 years, with a supplement for even younger children. This test is better with children than with adults, for whom there are insufficient discriminating items.

The items in this test are grouped by level of difficulty. Thus at each age level a huge variety of items is provided, including vocabulary, recognition of absurdities, ability to name the days of the week, copying a chain of beads from memory, abstract word definition, building a sentence from a set of words, digit repetition, explanation of proverbs.

The reliability of the IQs at most age levels is beyond .9. For older children, the test takes between 60 and 90 minutes; younger children (below 12) require about half this time. The norms are reasonably large, but inevitably the size of each separate age group is smaller than desirable.

Woliver and Saeks (1986) have an excellent summary of the validity of this test. There is a high correlation (beyond .7) with the corresponding Wechsler scales, and the vocabulary scale of the Stanford-Binet correlates beyond .7 with the whole test. This demonstrates that the test measures crystallized intelligence.

The fact that there is a mixture of items at each age group makes it difficult to compare the scores of a young child and one of, say, 16 years of age. This is because at these ages there is little overlap of item types. As has been argued, there seems little doubt that the overall IQ score of this test is a measure of crystallized ability. It is a disadvantage compared with the Wechsler test, however, that only one overall score can be obtained.

Thorndike, Hagen, and Sattler (1985) have produced a fourth edition of this test, which overcomes some of the above disadvantages. The norms are enlarged, and the items have been grouped into 15 subtests that can be administered separately to obtain four scores: verbal reasoning, quantitative reasoning, abstract visual reasoning, and short-term memory. This seems a better arrangement of the items, but the test must still measure crystallized ability. The Wechsler and the Stanford-Binet tests are classic examples of group intelligence tests. Nevertheless, it would seem more sensible to measure the primary factors separately and derive measures of fluid and crystallized intelligence from them.

3. *The British Intelligence Scale* (BAS; Elliot, Murray, & Pearson, 1983). The BAS was developed to overcome some of the defects of the classical scales. In fact it aims to measure not only intelligence but some of the main factors and cognitive processes, as well as some Piagetian measures. There are 23 scales: speed of information processing, formal operational reasoning, matrices, similarities, social reasoning, block design, letter rotation, cube visualization, copying, matching letter-like forms, verbal tactile matching, immediate visual recall, delayed visual recall, recall of designs, recall of digits, visual recognition, basic number skills, naming vocabulary, verbal comprehension, verbal fluency, word definition, word reading, and conservation. From these scales (from which the tester selects those that appear most relevant), the following broader variables can be measured: intelligence, speed of information processing, reasoning, spatial imagery, perceptual matching, short-term memory, and retrieval and application of knowledge.

Technically, the scale is highly refined. The subscales are reliable and confidence limits for scores are provided, thus making scale comparison less prone to error, and the British norms are extensive. Most of the subscales in the BAS (and their items) are standard fare for measures of intelligence and ability, and there can be little doubt that they are valid instruments. IQ is measured by the following tests: speed of information processing, matrices, similarities, recall of digits, visual recognition, and vocabulary and verbal comprehension. As has been argued, these are standard items for intelligence tests.

In summary, the BAS is a useful individual test of intelligence that is highly similar to the older tests, but with the advantage for the educational psychologist that it can measure other abilities. This is important in practical use.

Group Intelligence Tests

Because the typical items have been described above, the descriptions of these tests can be brief. Furthermore, because a small number of tests are recognized as markers for the *g* factors (see Cattell, 1971), these will be described although in many cases they are relatively old.

1. *Raven's Progressive Matrices* (Raven, 1965b). There are three versions of this test. Standard Matrices are for subjects from 6 to 65 years; the test consists of 60 items in five sets, each set involving different principles of variation and items at all difficulty levels. The Colored Matrices are designed for young children and mentally impaired adults, with 36 items in three sets, whereas the Advanced Matrices (again consisting of 36 items) are for subjects of above average ability.

As Cattell (1971) has shown, Raven's matrices load highly on fluid intelligence. Indeed, the only objection to the test as a measure of this factor is that all the items are of the same kind, thus allowing a confounding with variance specific to matrices items.

The test is highly reliable; although the norms need improvement, it can be regarded as an excellent test of fluid ability. Apart from the difficulty of specific variance, the only other problem concerns the length of the test. As Jensen (1980) has argued, with so few items covering so huge an age range, the level of difficulty between items tends to be large. This leads to some inaccuracy, because difference on only a few items may produce a considerable change in IQ.

This instrument's main use in applied psychology is to predict potential ability in subjects who do not know the language of the culture or who are from deprived backgrounds. In brief, it is an excellent test of fluid ability. Many educational psychologists use Raven's matrices in combination with one of two short vocabulary tests devised by Raven—The Mill Hill and the Crichton Vocabulary Scales (Raven, 1965a,b)—vocabulary being, as has been seen, the highest loading variable on crystallized ability.

2. *The Culture Fair Tests* (Cattell & Cattell, 1959). This test, of which there are three versions, is designed specifically to measure fluid ability. Version 1 is for the age range of 4 to 8 years, as well as retarded adults. This is a difficult test to administer and is in part an individual test. Version 2 is for children aged 8 to 13 years and unselected adults. Version 3 is for high school and college students, as well as superior adults. This is a more difficult form of the second test.

There are four types of items in this test: series, classifications, matrices, and topological conditions. The last is an item form in which there are five boxes, each containing various configurations of circles and squares. Subjects have to indicate into which box a dot could be placed so that it is inside a circle but outside a square.

The evidence concerning the reliability and validity of this test has been fully discussed by Kline (1992a) and Cattell and Johnson (1986). There can be no doubt that it is a reliable and excellent measure of fluid ability with normal and superior adults. With children from disadvantaged backgrounds, with low-intelligence subjects and with subjects from cultures unused to testing, however, the Culture Fair Test is not as useful as might be supposed. This is because, as Jensen (1980) has pointed out, the instructions for the test are difficult and complex.

3. *The AH Series* (Heim, Watts, & Simmonds, 1970, 1974). Over the years Heim and her colleagues have developed a series of intelligence tests measuring fluid and crystallized intelligence. The latest editions are AH2 and AH3 (Heim et al., 1974) for normal subjects over the age of 11 years, and AH6 (Heim et al., 1970), of which there are separate versions for scientists and arts-educated subjects. This AH6 is a high-level intelligence test.

AH2 and AH3 each have three sets of 40 items from which verbal, numerical, and perceptual intelligence scores, together with a total IQ score, can be obtained. The verbal reasoning items are typical: analogies, following complex instructions, and classifications, together with problems concerning family relationships. The numerical items involve series, problems (averages, vehicle speeds), analogies, and the four basic rules. The perceptual test uses similar problems to the above but in diagrammatic form.

From this it is clear that the numerical (N) and vertical (V) scores are typical of crystallized intelligence tests, and the perceptual test is likely to measure fluid ability. This is supported by the correlations of this test with school entrance examinations, and with Raven's matrices. These tests would appear to yield an IQ score similar to that of the Wechsler scales. Needless to say, they are highly reliable.

The high-level tests are essentially difficult versions of the editions just described. The arts version has 30 verbal items, 15 numerical items, and 15 diagrammatic items. The total score must be a mixture of fluid and crystallized ability. The science version, in contrast, has 24 items of each type.

The validity of these tests is not highly attested by the findings in their manual: the science version, for example, correlated only .193 with Raven's matrices. This is partly the result of attenuation caused by restriction of range (always a problem with high-level tests). Despite this, however, these tests would appear to be good choices where group tests of intelligence are required for high-level subjects.

4. *Miller Analogies* (Miller, 1970). This is a high level test of intelligence widely used for graduate entrance examination in the United States. As the name suggests, this test uses verbal analogies as its item form. It is therefore a useful measure of crystallized intelligence, but it is far from ideal because the solutions to some of the analogies demand considerable knowledge.

5. *Watson-Glaser Critical Thinking Appraisal* (Watson & Glaser, 1964). This is a test of crystallized ability designed for graduate recruitment and selection for management. There are five subtests: drawing inferences from facts; recognizing assumptions; drawing deductions from facts; interpretation of statements; and evaluation of arguments. All these are reliable measures. From the nature of the items, this test would be expected to load crystallized intelligence, and this is supported by the correlations with AH5 (an earlier form of AH6, which is discussed above). This test differs from other intelligence tests in that it demands a considerable amount of reading. It is more face valid for high-level jobs than many standard intelligence tests, and this makes the test more acceptable in selection.

These tests are typical measures of intelligence. Despite their age, there is little point in developing new tests, because these load as highly as could be expected on the *g* factors and are highly reliable. To conclude this section, though, I shall mention briefly two unusual measures of intelligence and a new computer-presented test.

6. *Porteus Maze Test* (Porteus, 1965). This test first appeared in 1914 and consists of 28 mazes that subjects have to trace through with a pencil, without stopping and without touching the sides. Norms exist for ages of 3 upward. This test requires no language (except to understand the instructions) and is not dependent on knowledge. It is thus attractive to cross-cultural psychologists, as the references in Porteus (1965) indicate. As Jensen (1980) argues, however, the norms are dubious (being based on small samples), and the reliability of the test is not known. Nevertheless, this test does probably load *g*, because a mazes test (alternative to Digit Symbol in the Wechsler scales) does load the *g* factor. This test might be useful where normal intelligence tests are inappropriate.

7. *Draw-a-Man Test and Goodenough-Harris Drawing Test* (Goodenough, 1926; Harris, 1963). In the original version of this test, subjects were required to draw a man. Drawing skill was not taken into account, but scores depended on accurate observation and the development of concepts of the human figure and its clothing. In the revised version subjects are required to draw pictures of a man, a woman, and themselves. Scoring depends on the developmental features of the pictures.

Jensen (1980) has argued that the revised version of this test probably is a reasonable measure of *g*, because its correlations with the WISC and the Terman scales are similar to the subscales of those tests. It is best used with children below the age of 12, however, because beyond that age scores do not increase with age and variance is reduced. In brief, this instrument is a useful alternative test to a standard measure of IQ.

8. *ABC Tests* (Collis, Irvine, & Dann, 1990). These are tests based upon the cognitive analysis of abilities. A special feature of the scales is that items can be generated at any given level of difficulty by a computer algorithm. The scales test letter checking, symbol rotation, transitive inference, letter distance (subjects have to find which of two letters is the more distant from a third, number distance, alphabet (e.g., A + 1 = B), and odd-man-out (discriminating which item of a series is different).

These tests are too new for a large body of evidence to have accumulated relevant to their validity. There is no doubt that they are reliable, however, and items of a given difficulty level can be generated. A factor analysis of these scales showed that they loaded on a factor separate but correlated (.65) with the intelligence factor (Collis et al., 1990). These measures of ability need further research, but they are potentially of great value because new items can be computer generated.

This description of the items in intelligence tests and some of the tests (both individual and group) that load most highly on the *g* factors indicates clearly the nature of such tests. It is relatively easy to judge the efficacy of any purported test of intelligence in the light of this discussion.

Measurement of Intelligence in Young Children

We have seen that the essence of intelligence, especially fluid intelligence, is reasoning: the education of correlates and the application of the rules educed to new examples. Intelligence tests for young children (2 to 5 years), however, contain items so different that it is by no means certain that the factor they tap is the same. For example, in the Stanford-Binet test, there are items requiring a young child to build a tower of blocks, identify the parts of a body on a doll, copy a chain of beads from memory, and cut paper. However, at the 13-year-old level in the same test, though, the items are to form complete sentences, memorize abstract designs, and make logical inferences from summaries of English. There is no doubt that at the adolescent level the Stanford-Binet is an excellent test of crystallized ability; at the low age levels, the nature of the test variance is less certain.

Other Tests of Ability

In Table 1, 27 primary factors are listed. It might be thought that tests of primary factors would be more efficient in predicting occupational and educational success than would the more broad tests of the second-order *g* factors. Indeed, the construction of aptitude tests is based exactly on this premise, and Thurstone (1947) would certainly have supported such a claim. As has been shown by Kline (1992a), however, the aptitude test functions as a rather inefficient test of *g* simply because all these primary factors are correlated. One test of these primary factors is the Comprehensive Ability Battery (Hakstian & Cattell, 1976).

Other Second-Order Factors

The G_f and G_c factors are the largest second-order factors. Although it is possible to devise tests of the other secondaries, these are so far divorced from tests of intelligence that they are beyond the scope of this chapter.

Conclusions

Performance on a variety of cognitive tasks can be predicted well by intelligence tests measuring the two factors of fluid and crystallized ability. These are pervasive general ability factors. High performers on these factors are good at almost all cognitive tasks. All the evidence summarized by Cattell (1971), Jensen (1980), and Kline (1992b) supports this claim.

THE MEASUREMENT OF PERSONALITY

There are three main types of personality tests: personality questionnaires or inventories (terms I shall use synonymously in this chapter), projective tests, and objective tests. I shall describe and evaluate each type in separate sections of this chapter.

Personality Questionnaires

These, as the name suggests, consist of lists of questions or statements concerning thoughts, feelings, or behavior. Typical items are "Are you keen on punctuality?" (yes/no), and "I always worry about my health" (true/false). Some items are constructed using rating scales (e.g., *strongly agree*, *agree*, *uncertain*, *disagree*, or *strongly disagree*).

Advantages

There are considerable advantages in using personality questionnaires. These are set out below.

It Is Easy to Make Them Reliable. Reliability is an essential characteristic of any psychological test. It has two meanings, referring to the internal consistency of the test and its consistency over time (the test-retest reliability). All good tests must be highly reliable, because in psychometric theory reliability is inversely related to error. The less reliable a test is, the more its variance is error variance. Personality inventories can be made reliable because they eliminate subjective scoring, a major source of unreliability.

It Is Easy to Standardize Them. The meaning of a score on almost all psychological tests is relative rather than absolute. Thus standardization—the setting up of norms for various groups or the whole population—is essential. A score of 10 on a test, for example, is uninterpretable without norms. If 95% of the relevant group score 10 or more, the meaning of the score is quite different than if only 5% score this high.

It Is Relatively Easy to Demonstrate (or At Least Investigate) Their Validity. A test is said to be valid if it measures what it claims to measure. This sounds so banal as to appear unworthy of comment; however, the vast majority of psychological tests are not valid. See Kline (1992a) for a full discussion of this point, which is also shown by perusal of any of the *Mental Measurement Yearbooks*.

It is necessary, therefore, to demonstrate what tests measure. This is far easier to manage with questionnaires that give reliable scores than it is with other forms of personality assessment, which may yield qualitative judgments. In fact, a small number of personality questionnaires, as will be discussed later in this chapter, have some support for their validity.

Personality Questionnaires Are Group Tests, Easy to Administer and Score. These tests can be given to large numbers of subjects at once and can be quickly scored. The considerable amounts of data that can be collected this way allow rigorous evaluation of the validity of the test.

They Are Valuable in Applied Psychology. Because they can be quickly administered and scored, these test are valuable in the educational, occupational and clinical fields. For example, they can be highly useful in hiring selection, where together with ability tests they can yield modest but valuable multiple correlations with job success (Kline, 1993b).

Disadvantages

All these virtues, which are not inconsiderable, have to be considered in the light of the problems and difficulties with personality questionnaires. These will now be examined.

Acquiescence. This is the tendency to agree with items, regardless of content. Obviously, one way to overcome this difficulty when devising the test is to select items endorsed by between 20% and 80% of the trial sample. Furthermore, if some items are keyed "yes" and others "no," at least acquiescence will not entirely destroy the validity of the test.

If a test has demonstrated validity, however, it is difficult to argue that it is contaminated by the response set of acquiescence. That is why it is essential to use only tests that have evidence for validity, rather than those that simply look valid. This face validity has no necessary connection with true validity. Acquiescence can ruin tests.

Social Desirability. This is the tendency to respond to an item because it is socially desirable to do so. Edwards (1957) showed that the endorsement rate for items correlated highly with their social desirability rating, and he developed a test—the Personality Preference Schedule (Edwards, 1959)—in order to overcome this difficulty. This consisted of pairs of items (one of which is selected by the subjects), the members of each pair having been matched for social desirability by previous ratings.

Actually, such elaborate techniques of test construction are not necessary to reduce this response set. If items selected are endorsed by about 50% of the trial sample, it makes no sense to call them socially desirable. Again, if care is taken in writing, items much social desirability can be eliminated. For details of how to write personality test items, readers are referred to Kline (1992a).

Finally it should be noted that if the test has been shown to be valid, the problem of social desirability (like that of acquiescence) must be trivial. There are many tests used in psychology, without much evidence for validity and that are almost certainly contaminated by social desirability.

Tendency to Endorse Extremes. If rating scales are used rather than the more simple yes-no response, some subjects tend to endorse extremes, whereas others almost never use them. These response tendencies can affect validity; however, careful item writing can do much to alleviate this problem.

Personality Inventory Responses Are Easy to Fake. This is mainly important in selection. For example, what salesperson would admit to disliking meeting new people and being shy and at a loss for words? One way to deal with this problem is to claim in the instructions for the test that deliberate distortions can be spotted. This ensures reasonable honesty in all but the psychopathic.

In general, the problems with personality questionnaires are outweighed by the advantages. Not all personality questionnaires, however, are good psychological tests. Indeed, only a few have been shown to be valid, and it is now necessary to examine in a little more detail the validity of personality questionnaires.

To do this it will be necessary to discuss briefly the construction of personality tests. I have dealt with this matter in some detail in Kline (1992a), and I shall restrict myself here to the bare essentials. There are two methods of constructing personality tests, and which one is chosen has profound effects on the nature and validity of the resulting tests.

Criterion-Keyed Tests

In these tests items are selected for the final test if they will discriminate a criterion group from comparable controls. This method of test construction suffers from the difficulty that any criterion group is likely, a priori, to differ from other groups on more than one variable. Thus the resulting test will not be unifactorial, and it will be unclear what it measures. All that one knows about such a scale is that it discriminates one group from another. This lack of necessary psychological meaning is a major difficulty with this type of test. Nevertheless, one of the most widely used personality tests—the Minnesota Multiphasic Personality Inventory (MMPI)—was constructed by this method. Examples of criterion-keyed personality questionnaires are described below.

1. *MMPI and MMPI-2* (Hathaway & McKinley, 1951; Graham, 1990). The original MMPI contains 566 true-false items and has 10 clinical scales: hypochondriasis (*Hs*), psychopathic deviate (*Pd*), paranoia (*Pa*), hypomania (*Ma*), depression (*D*), masculinity-femininity (*Mf*), psychasthenia (*Pt*), hysteria (*Hy*), schizophrenia (*Sc*); and social introversion (*Si*). In addition, more than 200 other scales have been constructed from this item pool using different groups for criterion keying.

There are many problems with the scales of the MMPI, which are fully documented in Kline (1992a). These include poor internal consistency reliability for the scales (with alphas as low as .2) and scales with overlapping items (which render the meaning of factors and correlations unclear). Nevertheless, when the scales are factored only two factors emerge: anxiety and ego strength. At the item level, a study by Costa, Zondeman, Williams and McCrae (1985) on a large sample of normals found nine factors, including neuroticism, psychoticism, masculinity, and extraversion. Three of these correspond to three of the "big five" factors that are claimed to account for much of the variance in personality questionnaires.

What is clear from this discussion is that the MMPI, as originally conceived, is not a reliable or valid test, even though its scales may be useful in discriminating abnormal groups. For this reason the MMPI-2 was produced; however, the changes are disappointingly small, and as I have argued in Kline (1992a), there is little reason to think that there would be much difference from the original. Items that were sexist or referred to sexual preferences, religious beliefs, or bladder and bowel control were replaced. The MMPI-2 is a politically correct version of the MMPI.

2. *The Californian Personality Inventory* (CPI; Gough, 1975).This test is known as the "sane man's MMPI," being an extension and development of the MMPI for normal subjects. Gough constructed the CPI using 178 MMPI items as they stood, adapting 35 others and constructing some originals. In all, the CPI consists of 480 true-false items, selected in the main by their ability to discriminate groups, although a few were constructed using item analysis. The test purports to measure 18 scales: dominance, sociability, social acceptance, responsibility, self-control, good impression, achievement via conformance, achievement via independence, psychological mindedness, capacity for status, social pressure, sense of well-being, socialization, tolerance, communality, flexibility, and femininity.

There are some severe problems with the CPI, although it is extensively used. As is common with tests constructed by the method of criterion keying, there are difficulties with the criteria: For example, the sociability items were selected if they correlated with number of extracurricular activities. There are further problems with the validity studies. To establish validity, biserial correlations were computed between scores and membership of extreme groups. These coefficients are highly volatile, however, all depending on how extreme (in terms of proportions) the groups were.

Another difficulty concerns the lack of independence of the CPI scales. Only four of the scales fail to correlate less than .5 with any other scale, and in the manual to the test Gough claims that the CPI measures four areas of personality: self-assurance, achievement potential, responsible maturity, and interests. No evidence for the validity of these four factors is offered, and it would be strange if scales thus developed just happened to measure them.

Clearly the validity of the CPI is dubious, but it should be noted that McCrae and John (in press) have claimed to find the big-five factors in the CPI. These authors, however, find these factors to be ubiquitous. For all these psychometric reasons, despite its popularity, it is difficult to recommend the CPI.

Recently this test has been updated (Gough, 1987) to introduce a new three vector model. I shall say little about this test, however, because the value of the CPI lies in its body of research findings, which are not applicable to the new test. Any structure that can be found in the CPI is adventitious, because it was constructed by criterion keying. Nevertheless, this new test clearly deserves proper research. Both these examples illustrate the difficulties with criterion-keyed tests. The lack of meaning of the scales and the fact that they can be multifactorial are probably the worst faults. Both these problems, however, mean that their use should be avoided where the emphasis is on understanding and the increase of psychological knowledge. The criterion-keyed test is essentially a pragmatic, empirical device that will discriminate groups and is thus useful for mass screening purposes, but that is all. These tests should be replaced by factor analytic tests.

Factor Analytic and Item-Analytic Test Construction

Factor analysis is in many respects the ideal method of test construction, because it is thus possible to produce a test that measures only one factor. By studying the correlations of such a test with other tests and with external criteria it is possible to establish what that factor is (i.e., to establish the validity of the test).

Because there are technical difficulties with the factor analysis of test items, however, a less complex method has been developed that in many instances gives virtually the same results (Nunnally, 1978). I shall describe this method first.

Item Analysis. In item analysis a set of items is administered to a trial sample, and the correlation of each item with the total score is computed. All items that correlate .3 or more are selected for the test. In addition the P values of each item (the proportion of the sample who put the keyed response) are examined. Only items with P values between 20% and 80% are selected. In this way a unifactorial and discriminating test is developed.

There is a variant on this method in which the alpha coefficient of internal consistency is computed for the whole set of items. The item with the lowest correlation with the total score is then removed, and alpha is recomputed. This process is continued until alpha reaches its highest point and then begins to fall; the set with the highest alpha becomes the test. This method produces almost identical results to the one above.

Item analysis gives highly similar results to factor analysis, except where the item variance is accounted for by two correlated factors, in which case item analysis would produce a mixed test. Because item analysis is so easy to compute, Nunnally (1978) suggests that an ideal procedure is to use item analysis first to remove bad items and then factor the reduced set. This is certainly a practicable and effective procedure. Examples of item-analytic personality tests are given below.

1. *Edwards Personal Preference Schedule* (EPPS; Edwards, 1959). This test has been mentioned because it was constructed in order to eliminate the response set of social desirability. It consists of 225 pairs of forced-choice items (members of pairs matched for social desirability) purporting to measure 15 variables derived from Murray's (1938) theory of needs. This is the theoretical basis of the test. The variables (needs) are achievement, deference, order, exhibition, autonomy, affiliation, intraception, succorance, dominance, abasement, nurturance, change, endurance, heterosexuality, and aggression.

A number of problems with this test make its use of dubious value, although there are many references to it. Although the reliability of the scales is satisfactory, there is little evidence for their validity because most users of the EPPS simply assume it to be so and take the scales at face value. This is unfortunate, because independent evidence in support of Murray's theory of needs is slight.

There are two other problems with the EPPS. First, when statements matched for social desirability are presented as pairs, slight differences between them become exacerbated, thus not eliminating the effects of social desirability. Even more difficult is the use of forced choices, which makes the scores ipsative. Thus each score reflects the relative strength of the need (were it valid) within each individual.

That these are ipsative scores means that the EPPS is not suited to comparing individuals or to constructing norms (although norms have been established). Furthermore, it renders the meanings of correlations between the scales difficult to interpret, and thus factor analyses are quite inappropriate. It should also be noted that scale reliabilities are boosted in ipsative tests.

For all these reasons, the EPPS cannot be recommended as a psychometric instrument. Even as a source of discussion in counseling and guidance the test presents a problem, simply because (despite the fact that it has been much used) there is little evidence for the validity of the scales.

2. *Jackson Personality Research Form* (PRF; Jackson, 1974). There are several versions of the PRF, but in the manual to the test Jackson (1974) suggests that Form E should be used because it is more simple to understand and shorter than the others. It is this version that will be described and scrutinized here.

The PRF consists of 352 self-descriptive items of the true-false format. As with the EPPS, the items were designed to measure Murray's needs. Clearly, therefore, strong evidence of validity must be required for the PRF scales, given the above comments concerning the EPPS.

The standards of test construction in the PRF, given that item analysis rather than factor analysis was used, are about the most rigorous and carefully executed of any personality test. In selecting the items, for example, not only was the biserial correlation of the item with its own scale score taken into account, but so was the biserial correlation with all the other scales. In this way the disadvantage of item analysis versus factor analysis—that items loading two correlated factors might be selected for a scale—was overcome. The effects of social desirability were also minimized by this method.

Naturally, scales designed with such psychometric sophistication are highly reliable for relatively short personality tests. The question of validity, however, is a different matter. As was the case with the EPPS, the scales are assumed to be valid from the nature of the items in them (i.e., they are simply face valid).

I cannot, in a chapter of this length, discuss in detail all the studies of this test that are pertinent to its validity. Kline (1992a) showed that to some extent the factors overlap those of Cattell (discussed below in the section on factor analytic tests), but this is itself a difficulty, as the Cattell factors themselves are not as clear as might be desired (Kline, 1993b). Nevertheless, extraversion and conscientiousness appear to emerge from the factoring of the PRF, and these are two of the big-five factors that are also found in the PRF by Costa and McCrae (1988). From this work it may be concluded that the PRF is a brilliant example of test construction, using item analysis to provide reliable, unidimensional scales. The scales remain unvalidated, however, and their theoretical basis is not powerful.

3. *The Myers-Briggs Type Indicator* (MBTI; Myers & McCaulley, 1985). This test claims to classify individuals into the eight Jungian types: introverted or extraverted feelers, sensationalists, thinkers, and intuiters. (Indeed, the authors of this test have considerably extended this basic Jungian typology into 16 groups, but I shall not consider this complexity here.) The reliabilities of the individual scales are reasonably high, and there is much normative information in the manual: the scores and types of various occupational groups, and large numbers of correlations between the scales and other psychological variables. It should be noted, however, that the items in this scale are ipsative in nature. In terms of information, the manual to this test is outstanding.

Jungian theory (let alone typology of any sort) is not well considered in modern psychology, and so adequate validity studies would be essential for a test such as the MBTI. The continuous scores derived from the MBTI (on which the typology is based) have been examined by McCrae and Costa (1989), who claim to have discerned the ubiquitous big-five factors. The real interest of the MBTI, though, is its purported ability to classify individuals into Jungian types.

There are two separate questions here. First, can the MBTI reliably classify individuals into types? Second, if it can, do these types resemble those of Jung? The typology used in this MBTI depends on scores on the bipolar scales. Thus, if a person is beyond the mean on a scale (e.g., sensing), he or she is classified as that type, and so on with all the scales, thus producing 16 types. It must be pointed out, however, that such classification is not true typology (at least on any one scale), which implies bimodal distributions rather than continuous distributions. There are extensive data in the manual showing the distribution of these types in different occupations. The use of this information is claimed to be for discussion and counseling rather than for selection.

Are these types similar to those used by Jung? Here the evidence is far from clear. Concordance with other measures, claiming to classify into Jungian types but also of unproven validity, is not convincing, and the evidence that the MBTI agrees with the classification of Jungian analysts on extraversion-introversion is interesting. It must be remembered, though, that these analysts may have been using implicit continuous distributions rather than true categories.

The MBTI is a highly interesting test with huge amounts of normative data, and this makes it appealing to occupational psychologists. There is no doubt that it would provide a framework for discussions in the counseling and guidance setting. As a quantitative, psychometric measure, however, its value remains doubtful, despite the number of studies in the manual.

These are probably the best-known personality tests based upon item analysis and psychological theory. The Jackson and Edwards scales are notable for the ingenuity of their construction, whereas the Myers-Briggs is particularly interesting for its typological and Jungian approach. Nevertheless, factor analyses do not support their psychometric use (as distinct from bases for discussions), and it is now necessary to turn to tests developed directly by factor analysis.

Factor Analysis in Test Construction. In this method items are administered to a trial sample and subjected to rotated factor analysis. Selected items have satisfactory P values and load beyond .3 on the factor. This method ensures that tests are unifactorial.

There are technical problems, though, that render this approach to test construction less than perfect. For example, there must be many more subjects than variables; if we are trying out a large number of items, this necessitates a large sample. Another difficulty lies in the choice of correlation coefficient for the item correlations. Many of these are affected by the proportions putting the keyed responses, and such correlations are inevitably unreliable, because an item may be thought of as a one-item test and reliability increases with test length. Some constructors use the unrotated principal-components analysis as their guide to item selection. Because principal-components analysis (by virtue of its algebra) produces a first, large general factor, however, this is unconvincing. All these difficulties mean that factor analysis in test construction can lead to poor tests.

An even more severe problem, fully examined by Kline (1992a), renders much factor analytic test construction futile. Even if the factor analysis is technically sound, the set of items loading on the factor must be identified relative to external criteria. Without this, it may well be that the factor is a bloated specific. Thus factor analysis of tests, in unskilled hands, frequently yields nothing more than a set of items that are essentially paraphrases of each other. The factor, far from being a useful measure, merely indicates that the subjects use English in a standard fashion and recognize certain words and phrases as similar.

Thus in this chapter I shall consider the results

from factor analytic personality inventories where the factors have been identified externally, either (a) by correlations with other tests, (b) by locating them in factor space relative to well-accepted marker factors, or (c) in experimental studies, as has been done with extraversion and neuroticism (Eysenck, 1967). From this discussion, I hope it is clear that a well-validated factor analytic personality test is difficult to impugn on grounds of poor measurement. These are good scientific tools. I shall now briefly describe some of the best-known factor analytic personality inventories; for fuller descriptions, readers are referred to Kline (1992a).

1. *Eysenck Personality Questionnaire* (EPQ; Eysenck and Eysenck, 1975). This test measures three personality factors (extraversion, neuroticism, and psychoticism) and social desirability. It is easy to administer, consisting of 90 yes-no items. The reliability of the scales is high (internal consistency and test-retest reliability), and there are extensive norms, including a general sample of more than 5,000 subjects.

I shall not say much about the validity of these scales, because of all personality tests this has the best-validated set of factors. There is a huge body of experimental findings supporting and explicating the nature of these factors (some of which is described in Eysenck, 1967), as well as considerable factor analytic evidence (summarized in Kline, 1992a, 1993b). It should also be pointed out that there is now an updated version of this test: the EPQR, which has an improved psychoticism scale with a more normal distribution of scores. The EPQ should stand as a marker test for the variables of extraversion, neuroticism or anxiety, and tough-mindedness.

2. *Cattell Sixteen Personality Factor Test* (16PF; Cattell, Eber, & Tatsuoka, 1970). This is one of the most famous personality tests, constructed by one of the great pioneers of the factor analysis of personality. It is a test with a huge body of research into the nature of the factors, much of it summarized in Cattell and Kline (1977) and more recently by Cattell and Johnson (1986).

This test differs from all other factor analytic scales in that the factors were derived from a basis of all descriptive words for behavior. Synonyms were removed, and subjects were rated for all remaining traits. (Thus it could be argued that this set of 16 factors truly does include the full range of personality.) Over the years the characteristics of high and low scorers on the factors, the correlations with other variables, the scores of different occupational and clinical groups, and the heritability ratios of all these factors were collected. Versions of the test are available from the ages of 4 to 5 years and upwards.

Thus these 16 factors are anything but bloated specifics. Furthermore, all these factors, together with ability and dynamic factors were woven into a psychometric, quantitative account of human behavior (Cattell, 1981). Unfortunately, it is by no means clear on reanalysis of these scales that there are in fact 16 factors, although the second-order factors of exvia (extraversion), anxiety, tough-mindedness, and conscientiousness (Factor G) do appear (Kline & Barrett, 1983). These, of course, are similar to the big-five factors of Costa and McCrae, which have already been mentioned. In summary, the 16PF is a brilliant test, but one that is flawed simply because it was produced using simplified techniques of factor analysis (which were necessary because computing facilities were not available). Despite this, it is widely used and found valuable in occupational psychology.

3. *Comrey Personality Scales* (Comrey, 1970). This test measures the eight factors regarded by Comrey as the most important dimensions in personality. These include neuroticism, extraversion, and orderliness; these three factors resemble those of the big five, although this is one of the few tests that has not been factored by Costa and McCrae in their search for these factors.

This test is notable because in an effort to avoid the problems of correlating single items, Comrey factors groups of items to create factored homogeneous item dimensions. These are effectively short scales, and this accounts for the fact that what are usually regarded as second-order factors occur in his list of factors. Comrey also uses a unique method of rotation, and this may result in a failure to reach simple structure. This is an interesting and original test, but it is not clear that these factors are the most salient dimensions of personality.

Conclusions Concerning Personality Questionnaires

From this discussion it can be concluded that personality questionnaires can be made reliable, although there are far more problems in establishing their validity. Most research indicates that there are five second-order personality factors that account for much of the variance in questionnaires. One test, the EPQ, has been extensively validated, and its scales may be used as a criterion for extraversion and anxiety.

Projective Tests

Projective tests essentially present subjects with ambiguous stimuli, which they are required to describe. These responses are then interpreted to provide assessments of personality. Murstein (1963) has claimed that projective tests measure the deepest layers of personality. One of the most famous psychological tests, the Rorschach test (Rorschach, 1921) is projective, being a set of 10 symmetrical inkblots. Projective tests are not much used in scientific psychology, although they are still popular with clinicians. My discussion of projective tests will deal with a number of separate but related issues.

1. Projective tests are idiographic, meaning that they are concerned with what is unique to an individual. This has to be contrasted with personality inventories, which are nomothetic (i.e., concerned with measuring the variables that are common to individuals). It is the emphasis on the unique that makes projective tests appealing to clinicians.

One point deserves to be noted. The term *projective*, as it is applied to tests, bears no relation to *projection*, which in psychoanalytic theory refers to unconscious attribution to others of undesirable traits. The rationale of projective tests is that in interpreting ambiguous stimuli subjects project themselves into them and identify with any human or animal figures. This may be so, but it must also be pointed out that there is no psychological theory supporting this projective hypothesis. In truth, there is no psychological rationale for projective tests other than the assertion that subjects project onto the stimuli their feelings and conflicts.

2. There are many varieties of projective tests. At this point I shall briefly mention a few of the most famous and indicate the nature of the stimuli. The Rorschach, as has been discussed, uses inkblots. The Thematic Apperception Test (TAT; Murray, 1938) portrays human figures in ambiguous situations. Some tests, especially those for children, use animals; the Children's Apperception Test (Bellak, Bellak, & Haworth, 1974) is a good example of this. Other tests (e.g., the House-Tree-Person test; Buck, 1970) require subjects to draw and the drawings are then interpreted. Descriptions of these tests are to be found later in this section.

There are other types of projective tests, which I shall list briefly:

- *Sentence completion.* As the name suggests, subjects are required to complete sentences. Thus, in response to the sentence "All fathers are. . ." the subject who writes *wonderful* is somewhat different from the one who writes *vicious monsters*, or so projective testers believe.
- *Solid objects.* A number of projective techniques use solid objects. Lowenfeld has developed several such tests using dolls, sand, and other miniature objects. Lowenfeld's (1954) Mosaic Test consisting of wooden shapes which can be assembled into objects, is typical of this type.
- *Auditory projective tests.* There are even projective tests consisting of ambiguous sounds; the best-known example is that of Bean (1965).

This wide variety of projective techniques is also attractive to clinicians who want to select a test likely to fit the need of their clients. These projective tests appear far more likely to capture the subtlety and richness of personality than would the often mundane list of items that constitute a personality inventory.

3. Reliability and validity are the main sources of objections to projective tests among scientific psychologists. There is good agreement that they are not reliable, and that there is no strong evidence for their validity. I shall not discuss the detailed evidence here (see Kline, 1992a, 1993b), although it is clear that a main cause of the problem lies in the unreliability of scoring.

4. Vernon (1963) cites many studies indicating that projective test scores are influenced by contextual factors, including the race or sex of the tester, the manner of administering the test, or subjects' views of the nature of the test. It is difficult to argue that projective tests measure the deepest layers of the personality if scores are influenced by such extraneous variables.

5. There problems with the scoring systems for these tests. It has already been pointed out that there is no psychological basis for the rationale of projective tests. Furthermore, the interpretation of responses, once it is accepted that subjects have projected, is dependent on implicit or explicit theories of personality that are certainly not unequivocal. For example the Blacky Pictures (Blum, 1949) are explicitly based on Freudian theory; the Children's Apperception Test, which shows two figures in bed (the primal scene) and a monkey about to lose its tail (castration), has psychoanalytic theory implicit in it. The TAT uses Murray's (1938) theory, and thus many psychologists could not take the results seriously unless they favored such psychodynamic approaches.

6. There have been attempts to develop objective scoring schemes for projective tests. Murstein (1963)

describes several such attempts for the TAT, and Holtzman, Thorpe, Swartz, and Herron (1968) have produced a psychometrically respectable version of the Rorschach.

One objective scoring scheme for projective tests has been extensively examined by the present author. This involves a content analysis of projective test protocols, in which the content is reduced to a set of variables that are either present or absent for each subject. Subjects scoring on these variables are then subjected to multivariate analysis (e.g., Q factor analysis), and the variables distinguishing the groups are examined. Some interesting results have been obtained with this approach (e.g., Holley, 1973), but it is simply a suggestion of what might be done rather than a definitive best method.

Brief Descriptions of Well-Known Projective Tests

I shall describe these tests briefly because, as has been seen, they are not reliable or valid measures in the accepted psychometric sense. Furthermore, their scoring schemes require considerable training to execute, so that no detailed descriptions could be given in a chapter of this length. For further details readers must be referred to Kline (1993b).

1. *The Rorschach test* (Rorschach, 1921). Subjects have to describe the 10 inkblots as they are presented, one at a time, and indicate what each suggests. These responses are recorded together with the response latencies to each card. Then the subjects go through the cards again, explicating and elaborating their responses.

There are many different scoring schemes for the Rorschach, all exceedingly complex, although one of the most recent (Exner, 1986) is the best psychometrically. Some of the scoring categories have high reliabilities, although whether all scorers could reach this accuracy is not beyond dispute. The Exner system requires responses to be coded into eight categories, including content analysis (27 subcategories), populars (has the subject used any of the 13 popular responses) and form quality (a judgment of the reality testing of the subject). The determinants are highly important. Again, I can only give examples; the Exner system is too vast to describe here. If shading of texture is noted, this is held to show a need for affection. When only the form is used, this is interpreted as being related to inspection. Movement in the responses is said to indicate high levels of fantasy.

The objections that have been raised to projective tests in general apply well to the Rorschach. There is a complete lack of theory as to why any of the responses should be so scored (e.g., blackness and depression). The reliability of the judgments is inevitably low, however carefully trained the judges, and despite Exner's huge effort to find empirical support for the interpretations there is no firm evidence for their validity. Furthermore, it is psychometrically unlikely that so many variables could be measured by one test.

Thus, although it is used in clinical psychology and some researchers appear to find it useful, it is difficult to support the use of this test. Indeed perhaps the most telling feature against it is the lack of agreement between the various scoring systems, as is fully discussed in Kline (1992a).

2. *The Holtzman Inkblot Test* (HIT; Holtzman et al., 1961). There are two parallel forms of the HIT, each consisting of 45 cards portraying an inkblot. The subject is asked to give one response to each card, which is followed by a brief inquiry. In all, 22 variables are scored (summed across cards), covering the most important scores on the Rorschach test. Among these variables are reaction time, location, form definiteness, color, shading, and popularity. As might be expected with this format of test, the reliability of scoring (both intra- and interscorer, and test-retest) is high.

Of course, even if the scores are reliable it is important to demonstrate that they are valid. The fact that all scorers can agree a response indicates shading is of no interest per se. Here the evidence is equivocal. The HIT can make discriminations among members of different national and cultural groups, and it can distinguish between normals and schizophrenics. Further, it is clear that the HIT variance is not the same as that of the major personality questionnaires. In brief, this test merits careful investigation, but it cannot be regarded as valid.

3. *The Thematic Apperception Test* (TAT; Murray, 1938). This test was designed by Murray and his colleagues to measure the 19 most important needs and presses in Murray's dynamic system. Many users interpret the responses to the cards either according to psychodynamic theories or their own intuition, however, as Murray himself said this was permissible. He also claimed that his TAT stimuli were only one particular set, and any stimuli that provoked imaginative responses would be suitable for scoring needs and presses and other idiographic variables.

There are 30 stimuli cards in the TAT (together with 1 blank card). These cards are black-and-white portrayals of human figures and are not highly ambiguous, but the whole is sufficiently unstructured to allow imaginative responses. Subjects are requested to say what they think is going on in each picture. Sample pictures are as follows:

- A young boy contemplates a violin on a table.
- A middle-aged woman stands looking through an open door into a room.
- Four men rest on grass.
- A small girl climbs a winding staircase.
- A gaunt man stands, hands clenched, in a graveyard.

Generally, there is not good evidence for the reliability of the TAT. Karon (1981), indeed, claims that this is because scorers are looking for different things, not a claim that gives one much confidence in the test. As regards validity, however, Karon (1981) has argued that it must be established for each user and that failure to find validity indicates that the users—rather than the test—were no good. I would argue that this is true of most projective tests: Generally they are not reliable or valid, but when used by gifted testers such as Murray, useful data can be obtained. This essentially means that such tests are not valuable for scientific work.

There are variants of the TAT, all of which suffer from the same problems as the original. These are the Children's Apperception Test (Bellak, Bellak, & Haworth, 1974), which is a TAT for children aged between 3 and 10 years. There are 10 animal cards and 10 human cards, with human beings in a context as near to the animal version as possible. For example, in one animal card there is a dim cave in which two bears lie side by side, with a baby bear in the foreground; in the human version, the cave is replaced by a tent.

A specifically psychoanalytically scored variant is the Blacky Pictures test (Blum, 1949). Here a family of dogs is portrayed in 10 cards; the family situations are those thought to be salient in psychoanalytic theory. Thus oral sadism is tested with a card showing Blacky biting his mother's collar, and oral erotism is assessed by a card showing Blacky being suckled. This test can be more reliably scored than most other projective tests, because some of the questions are of the short-answer type. As regards validity, this measure, as usual, is equivocal. Freudian theory is so flexible that almost any findings can be regarded as supportive. It is clearly not a useless test and merits cautious research, however, despite the crudity of the drawings.

A more modern variant is the Object Relations Technique (Phillipson, 1955), which uses 12 cards and a blank, all showing highly ambiguous figures. The measure is designed specifically to test modern psychoanalytic object relations theory, which is based on the work of Klein (1948). If this test were shown to be valid, it would be highly useful, because the investigation of modern psychoanalytic theory defies most scientific methods. All the findings in the manual are highly speculative, however, although interesting and suggestive.

4. *House-Tree-Person Test* (Buck, 1970). As has been mentioned, this test requires subjects to draw a house, a person, and a tree. The subjects are then questioned about these pictures, and the results are interpreted. The manual to the test (Buck, 1970) offers no evidence for the interpretative claims, which are imaginative and not a little fantastic; it is used, it appears, on trust. Furthermore the interpretations are based on a mixture of intuition and psychoanalytic theory. For example, if curtains are drawn, the subject is seen as defensive, as is the case if there is a curved rather than straight garden path. Open doors and windows, in contrast, are a good sign that the subject is prepared to be revelatory. Huge feet are supposed to show phallic or castration problems, as is the lack of a chimney or an enormous one (in the true psychoanalytic tradition).

This test is worth some investigation, despite the lack of psychometric information on reliability and validity, simply because it does produce considerable variance in responses. It is also noteworthy that in an objective *g* analysis of HTP responses in criminals, some of the fantastic assertions in the manual to the test received support (Hampson & Kline, 1977).

Conclusions Concerning Projective Tests

The problem with projective tests, as has been made clear, is that there is little evidence for their reliability or validity. In addition, their psychological rationale and the basis of their interpretations are dubious. Because it has also been shown that their scores are influenced by relatively trivial contextual variables, it is curious that they are still used even in clinical psychology. Such use may be attributed to the apparent richness of the data that they provide, in contrast to the triviality of the typical questionnaire; moreover, in the hands of highly skilled testers, they appear to yield insightful material that could not be obtained in any other way. Carstairs's (1957) study of the Rajputs is a good case in point, and Karon (1981) defends the TAT on these grounds.

In brief, it would appear useful to retain projective tests, with all their richness of material, but to develop reliable and validated scoring procedures. If this could be done, projective tests could be powerful tests in the elucidation of personality.

Objective Tests

Objective personality tests are defined by Cattell and Warburton (1967) as tests that can be objectively scored and whose purpose and import is hidden from the subjects. This latter means that they are difficult to fake (although they may be sabotaged), and thus such tests would be useful in selection if they could be shown to be valid. These tests are sometimes referred to as performance tests, but I shall use the term *objective* because this is the terminology of Cattell, who has carried out the most extensive research with them.

First it should be noted that this definition of objective tests also includes projective tests if they are objectively scored and in the compendium of objective tests (Cattell & Warburton, 1967) certain indices from the Rorschach test may be found.

Advantages

If objective tests could be shown to be valid, they would have the following advantages over projective and questionnaire personality tests:

- Because the purpose of the test is hidden from subjects, deliberate distortion is a dangerous procedure. In applied psychology, especially selection, this is highly useful.
- The common response sets of acquiescence and social desirability, the bane of questionnaires, are avoided.
- Objective tests, especially of the physiological variety, might be valuable in cross-cultural research, where the language of questionnaires and the conventions of projective testing can produce problems (Kline, 1993a).

For all these reasons the development of objective tests would appear to be a pressing task for psychometrics, although, unfortunately, little has been done.

Rationale and Validity

In the compendium of these tests, Cattell and Warburton (1967) list almost 700 measures, from which 2,300 variables can be derived. As might be suspected from the definition of objective tests, there is a virtual infinity of possible tests, with much depending on the ingenuity of the tester. As is also clear from the definition, however, having derived the test, we can have no idea of what it might measure.

What is needed, therefore, is a set of principles by which tests might be constructed with a given meaning. Cattell and Warburton (1967) and Kline (1993b) have discussed such principles, the former authors in considerable detail, but it is fair to say that no clear rationale has ever been developed. This is a severe problem, and it is reflected in the fact that the vast majority of objective tests in the compendium are of unknown validity.

Indeed, only one unequivocal statement can be made: No objective test should ever been used unless there is clear evidence of validity. Because these tests are impervious to guesses about their meaning, and because there are no clear principles of objective test construction, demonstrating the validity of these tests is not a simple matter. In principle, construct validity can be demonstrated by rotating to simple structure the scores on objective tests, together with the main ability and personality factors (e.g., extraversion, fluid ability), thus locating the objective tests in factor space and identifying them.

Examples of Objective Tests

To give the flavor of the immense range of objective tests, I shall briefly describe a few from the compendium.

1. Greater number of admissions of frailty or wrongdoing. Notice that the truth or falsity of these admissions is irrelevant; the score is the number endorsed.
2. Greater acquiescence in answering questionnaires. It is interesting to note here that what is regarded as a response set in questionnaire measurement becomes an objective test score.
3. Higher score on a checklist of annoyances. As above, the number is the score, and the truth or falsity of the responses is irrelevant.
4. Little confidence that a good performance could be quickly reached on a number of skills.
5. Faster tapping speed.
6. Faster speed of reading when asked to read normally.
7. Higher speed at reading poetry.
8. Greater preference (on a questionnaire) for

highbrow or sophisticated activities. (Again, the truth or falsity of these claims is not relevant.)

9. Slow line drawing. Subjects have to draw a line as slowly as possible. The scores derived are the length of the line; whether the subject cheated by lifting the pencil or stopping.
10. The fidgetometer. Subjects sit in a chair with electrical contacts at various points that are closed by movement; thus the amount of fidgeting over a given time is recorded. This test well exemplifies the difficulties of faking objective tests: Even if it was realized that the chair recorded movement, is it better to sit still or move a lot?

This list (which excludes physiological measures because these are highly specialized, requiring laboratory facilities) illustrates the strengths and the weaknesses of objective tests as measures of personality. It is difficult to fake these tests because their import is hidden not just from subjects but from most psychologists, even those engaged in assessment. Nevertheless, as has been mentioned, few of the tests in the compendium have evidence of validity.

Cattell collected together the tests with the best empirical support for their validity into a published set of objective personality tests, the Objective Analytic Test Battery (OATB; Cattell & Schuerger, 1978). This test measures 10 variables:

- Ego standards (self-assertion and achievement)
- Independence versus subduedness
- Evasiveness
- Exuberance
- Capacity to mobilize versus regression
- Anxiety
- Realism versus tense inflexibility
- Self-assurance
- Exvia versus invia (extraversion)
- Discouragement versus hope

All variables have seven or eight subtests, making this a long test that is difficult to administer. Tests involved in the OATB include rapid calculation (to measure ego standards), reading comprehension (independence), common annoyances (evasiveness), and comparing letters (capacity to mobilize).

From the examples of the tests that measure the OATB factors, it is strange they are claimed to measure personality. Reading comprehension, for example, is one of the best measures of crystallized intelligence. Kline and Cooper (1984) carried out a construct validity study of the OATB in which it was rotated to simple structure together with the 16PF test and the EPQ (discussed earlier) and the Comprehensive Ability Battery (Hakstian & Cattell, 1976), measuring the main ability factors. The results did not support the validity of the test. In fact, no factors emerged that in any way corresponded to the 10 factors claimed to be measured. Of the factors that did emerge, most were amalgams of personality and ability. It must be concluded that the OATB is not a valid test.

One other objective test battery has been published from the compendium—the Motivation Analysis Test (MAT; Cattell, Horn, & Sweney, 1970). This is a dynamic test measuring, it is claimed, 10 motivational factors: 5 ergs or basic drives (mating, assertiveness, fear, comfort seeking, and pugnacity), and 5 sentiments, or culturally molded drives (self-sentiment, superego, career, sweetheart, and parental home).

In a study of the MAT's psychometric properties by Cooper and Kline (1982), the items did not fit their scales when subjected to item analysis, and the factors that emerged from a simple structure oblique rotation of the test scores made no sense. The battery thus needs considerable further development before it can be used in substantive research. This finding was particularly disappointing because in a previous study in which one subject had completed the MAT for a month and the daily findings were related to the contents of that subject's diary, the scales had appeared to be valid (Kline & Grindley, 1974).

Conclusions Concerning Personality Tests

From this discussion of the three main types of personality tests it is clear that personality questionnaires can be made highly reliable and that there is general agreement that five factors can be found in most of them (the "big five"—extraversion, anxiety, tough-mindedness, conservatism, and conscientiousness). These are the tests most widely used in applied psychology, especially for selection, despite the fact that they are relatively easy to fake.

Even the most keen advocates of the personality questionnaire would be forced to admit, however, that there is something simplistic in reducing the complexity of personality to a few hundred (at most) responses to a set of items. Projective tests cannot be faulted on this count; here responses to ambiguous stimuli are subjected to interpretations of sometimes labyrinthine complexity. This makes them appealing to clinicians, but on the simple psychometric criteria of reliability and validity projective tests are wanting, at least as conventionally scored. Objective scoring schemes may improve this flaw, but may abandon the richness of projective test data in the search for reliability. Clearly, in the case of projective tests, a compromise must be sought that allows the complexity of the responses to be taken into account and yet retains the necessary reliability.

Objective tests have some apparent advantages, especially their resistance to faking and to normal response sets (which may, as has been seen, even be incorporated into the scoring). As yet, however, most have little evidence for validity. This is the next task for personality assessment: to begin the program to develop batteries of valid and reliable objective tests. If this could be done, we would have far more effective personality tests both for the development of personality theory (which is still hopelessly nonquantitative) and for use in applied psychology.

CONCLUSIONS

From this study of intelligence and personality tests, it is clear that the best factor analytic tests measure the fundamental variables accounting for variance in the spheres of personality and ability. That they do so offers powerful opportunities for theoretical and practical advances in psychology. This is the basis of the psychometric model of behavior that has been most elaborately developed by Cattell (see, e.g., Cattell, Eber, & Tatsuoka, 1970). Here we see elaborate multiple regression equations between the 16PF variables and different occupations or clinical psychiatric status. These equations are essentially hypotheses accounting for performance in these jobs. In the full psychometric model, intelligence, other ability factors, and motivational factors would also be included. These findings could be valuable in occupational and clinical psychology. These are practical outcomes for the use of these tests.

On the theoretical level, these findings are interesting because they have to be explained. Research into the nature of all these variables, their physiological basis, and the influence of heredity and environment on their development has already been started by Cattell and colleagues (Cattell, 1981) and by Eysenck (1967). Psychometric theories such as these are in contrast to older accounts of personality because they are based upon sound, psychometric test measurement. Good science is always derived from good measurement, and this is the contribution to psychology from tests of intelligence and personality.

REFERENCES

Bean, K. L. (1965). The Sound Apperception Test: Purposes, origin, standardization, scoring and use. *Journal of Psychology, 59*, 371–412.

Bellak, L., Bellak, S. S., & Haworth, M. R. (1974). *Children's Apperception Test.* Larchmont, CA: Californian Psychological Services.

Blum, G. S. (1949). A study of the psychoanalytic theory of psychosexual development. *Genetic Psychology Monograph, 39*, 3–99.

Buck, J. N. (1970). *The House Tree Person technique: Revised manual.* Los Angeles: Western Psychological Services.

Carroll, J. (in press). *Human cognitive abilities: A survey of factor-analytic studies.* Cambridge, England: Cambridge University Press.

Carstairs, G. M. (1957). *The twice-born: A study of a community of high caste Hindus.* London: Hogarth.

Cattell, R. B. (1971). *Abilities: Their structure, growth and action.* New York: Houghton Mifflin.

Cattell, R. B. (1981). *Personality and learning theory.* New York: Springer.

Cattell, R. B., & Cattell, A. K. S. (1959). *The Culture Fair Test.* Champaign, IL: Institute for Personality and Agility Testing.

Cattell, R. B., Eber, H. W., & Tatsuoka, M. M. (1970). *The 16 factor personality questionnaire.* Champaign, IL: Institute for Personality and Agility Testing.

Cattell, R. B., Horn, J. L., & Sweney, A. B. (1970). *Motivation analysis test.* Champaign, IL: Institute for Personality and Agility Testing.

Cattell, R. B., & Johnson, R. C. (1986). *Functional psychological testing.* New York: Brunner/Mazel.

Cattell, R. B., & Kline, P. (1977). *The scientific analysis of personality and motivation.* London: Academic Press.

Cattell, R. B., & Schuerger, J. (1978). *Personality theory in action: Handbook for the Objective-Analytic (O-A) test kit.* Champaign, IL: Institute for Personality and Agility Testing.

Cattell, R. B., & Warburton, F. W. (1967). *Objective personality and motivation tests.* Urbana: University of Illinois Press.

Collis, J. M., Irvine, S. H., & Dann, P. L. (1990). *The ABC tests: An introduction.* London: Her Majesty's Stationery Office.

Comrey, A. L. (1970). *The Comrey Personality Scales.* San Diego, CA: Educational and Industrial Testing Services.

Cooper, C., & Kline, P. (1982). The internal structure of the Motivation Analysis Test. *British Journal of Educational Psychology, 52*, 228–223.

Costa, P. T., & McCrae, R. R. (1988). From catalogue to classification: Murray's needs and the five factor model. *Journal of Personality and Social Psychology, 55*, 258–265.

Costa, P. T., Zondeman, A. B., Williams, R. B., & McCrae, R. R. (1985). Content and comprehensiveness in the MMPI: An item factor analysis in a normal adult sample. *Journal of Personality and Social Psychology, 48*, 925–933.

Edwards, A. L. (1957). *The social desirability variable in personality research.* New York: Dryden.

Edwards, A. L. (1959). *The Edwards Personality Preference Schedule.* New York: Psychological Corporation.

Ekstrom, R. B., French, J. W., & Harman, H. H. (1976). *Manual for Kit of Factor-Referenced Cognitive Tests.* Princeton, NJ: Educational Testing Service.

Elliot, C., Murray, D. J., & Pearson, L. S. (1983). *British Ability Scales revised.* Windsor, Ontario: National Foundation for Educational Research.

Exner, J. (1986). *The Rorschach: A comprehensive system.* New York: Wiley.

Eysenck, H. J. (1967). *The biological basis of personality*. Springfield, IL: Thomas.

Eysenck, H. J., & Eysenck, S. B. G. (1975). *The EPQ*. London: Hodder & Stoughton.

Goodenough, F. L. (1926). *Measurement of intelligence by drawings*. New York: Harcourt Brace.

Gough, H. G. (1975). *The California Psychological Inventory*. Palo Alto, CA: Consulting Psychologists Press.

Gough, H. G. (1987). *Administrator's guide for the California Psychological Inventory*. Palo Alto, CA: Consulting Psychologists Press.

Graham, J. R. (1990). *MMPI-2: Assessing personality and pathology*. New York: Oxford University Press.

Guilford, J. P. (1967). *The nature of human intelligence*. New York: McGraw-Hill.

Hakstian, A. R., & Cattell, R. B. (1976). *The Comprehensive Ability Battery*. Champaign, IL: Institute for Personality and Agility Testing.

Hampson, S., & Kline, P. (1977). Personality dimensions differentiating certain groups of abnormal offenders from nonoffenders. *British Journal of Criminology*, *17*, 310–331.

Harris, D. B. (1963). *Children's drawings as measures of intellectual maturity: A revision and extension of the Goodenough Draw-A-Man Test*. New York: Harcourt Brace.

Hathaway, S. R., & McKinley, J. C. (1951). *The Minnesota Multiphasic Personality Inventory*. New York: Psychological Corporation.

Heim, A. W., Watts, K. P., & Simmonds, V. (1970). *AH4, AH5 and AH6 tests*. Windsor, Ontario: National Foundation for Educational Research.

Heim, A. W., Watts, K. P., & Simmonds, V. (1974). *AH2/3 manual*. Windsor, Ontario: National Foundation for Educational Research.

Holley, J. W. (1973). Rorschach analysis. In P. Kline (Ed.), *New directions in psychological measurement* (pp. 119–155). Chichester England: Wiley.

Holtzman, W. H., Thorpe, J. S., Swartz, J. D., & Herron, E. W. (1968). *Inkblot perception and personality: Holtzman inkblot technique*. Austin: University of Texas Press.

Horn, J., & Knapp, J. R. (1973). On the subjective character of the empirical base of Guilford's structure of intellect model. *Psychological Bulletin*, *80*, 33–43.

Jackson, D. N. (1974). *Personality Research Form*. New York: Research Psychologists Press.

Jensen, A. R. (1980). *Bias in mental testing*. New York: Free Press.

Karon, B. P. (1981). The Thematic Apperception Test. In A. I. Rabin (Ed.), *Assessment with projective techniques* (pp. 85–120). New York: Springer.

Klein, M. (1948). *Contributions to psychoanalysis 1912–1945*. London: Hogarth.

Kline, P. (1992a). *The handbook of psychological testing*. London: Routledge.

Kline, P. (1992b). *Intelligence: The psychometric view*. London: Routledge.

Kline, P. (1993a). *An easy guide to factor analysis*. London: Routledge.

Kline, P. (1993b). *Personality: The psychometric view*. London: Routledge.

Kline, P., & Barrett, P. (1983). The factors in personality questionnaires among normal subjects. *Advances in Behaviour Research and Therapy*, *5*, 141–202.

Kline, P., & Cooper, C. (1984). A construct validation of the Objective-Analytic Test Battery (OATB). *Personality and Individual Differences*, *5*, 328–337.

Kline, P., Draycott, S., & McAndrew, V. (in press). Reconstructing intelligence: A factor analysis of the BIP. *Personality and Individual Differences*.

Kline, P., & Grindley, J. (1974). A 28 day case study with the MAT. *Journal of Multivariate Experimental Personality Clinical Psychology*, *1*, 13–32.

Lowenfeld, M. (1954). *The Lowenfeld mosaic test*. London: Newman Neame.

McCrae, R. R., & Costa, P. T. (1989). Reinterpreting the Myers-Briggs Type Indicator from the perspective of the five factor model of personality. *Journal of Personality*, *57*, 17–40.

McCrae, R. R., & John, O. P. (in press). An introduction to the five factor model and its implications. *Journal of Personality*.

Miller, W. S. (1970). *Miller analogies test*. New York: Psychological Corporation.

Murray, H. A. (1938). *Explorations in personality*. Oxford, England: Oxford University Press.

Murstein, B. I. (1963). *Theory and research in projective techniques*. New York: Wiley.

Myers, I. B., & McCaulley, M. H. (1985). *Manual: A guide to the development and use of the Myers-Briggs Type Indicator*. Palo Alto, Ca: Consulting Psychologists Press.

Nunnally, J. O. (1978). *Psychometric theory*. New York: McGraw-Hill.

Phillipson, H. (1955). *The object relations technique*. London: Tavistock.

Porteus, S. D. (1965). *Porteus maze test: Fifty years application*. Palo Alto, CA: Pacific.

Raven, J. C. (1965a). *Crichton vocabulary scale*. London: Lewis.

Raven, J. C. (1965b). *The Mill Hill vocabulary scale*. London: Lewis.

Raven, J. C. (1965c). *Raven's matrices*. London: Lewis.

Rorschach, H. (1921). *Psychodiagnostics*. Berne, Switzerland: Huber.

Spearman, S. (1904). "General Intelligence": Objectively determined and measured. *American Journal of Psychology*, *15*, 201–292.

Sternberg, R. J. (1977). *Intelligence, information processing and analogical reasoning: The componential analysis of human abilities*. Hillsdale, NJ: Erlbaum.

Terman, L. M., & Merrill, M. A. (1960). *Stanford-Binet intelligence scale*. New York: Houghton Mifflin.

Thorndike, R. L., Hagen, E. P., & Sattler, J. (1985). *Stanford-Binet intelligence scale: Fourth edition*. New York: Houghton Mifflin.

Thurstone, L. L. (1947). *Multiple factor analysis: A development and expansion of vectors of the mind*. Chicago: University of Chicago Press.

Undheim, J. O. (1981). On intelligence: II. A neo-Spearman model to replace Cattell's theory of fluid and crystallized intelligence. *Scandinavian Journal of Psychology*, *22*, 181–187.

Vernon, P. E. (1963). Personality assessment. London: Methuen.

Watson, G., & Glaser, E. M. (1964). *Critical thinking appraisal*. New York: Harcourt Brace Jovanovich.

Wechsler, D. (1958). *The measurement and appraisal of adult intelligence* (4th ed.). Baltimore, MD: Williams & Wilkins.

Wechsler, D. (1986). *The Wechsler Adult Intelligence Scale*. New York: Psychological Corporation.

Woliver, R. E., & Saeks, S. D. (1986). Intelligence and primary aptitudes. In R. B. Cattell & R. C. Johnson (Eds). *Functional psychological testing* (pp. 166–186). New York: Brunner/Mazel.

24

Personality and Intelligence in the Psychodiagnostic Process

The Emergence of Diagnostic Schedules

R. W. Kamphaus, A. W. Morgan, M. R. Cox, and R. M. Powell

Formal intelligence and personality measures have contributed immeasurably to the psychodiagnostic process. Intelligence measures, for instance, virtually defined the diagnosis of mental retardation for much of this century (Kamphaus, 1993). Similarly, personality measures have been widely used for psychological diagnosis since first being proven useful after World War I, when the Woodworth Personal Data Sheet was found to be practical for the diagnosis of what is currently called posttraumatic stress disorder (Kamphaus & Frick, in press). Today, however, the relationship between intelligence and personality testing and diagnosis is less direct, as diagnostic systems become increasingly behavior based.

This long history of test use and the complexity of issues involved create several potential ways to conceptualize a chapter of this nature. We could review the theoretical relationship between intelligence and personality measures, although theoretical issues are discussed in other chapters. Another approach would involve presenting the range of intelligence and personality measures available and reviewing their psychometric characteristics. Such reviews, however, have been completed in more comprehensive fashion in many volumes (e.g., Reynolds & Kamphaus, 1990).

Our purpose is to focus on the practical enterprise of psychological (or psychiatric) diagnosis and the degree to which popular measures make valuable contributions to the diagnostic process. Few chapters have specifically discussed the interplay of psychometric tests and diagnostic systems; this relationship is a tenuous one, as will be shown in later sections. We think that it behooves the practicing clinician to be aware of the intricacies of this relationship, because the assumptions underlying modern psychodiagnostics and psychometrics are different and yet complementary.

With this rationale in mind, this chapter is organized into three sections. The history of psychodiagnostics is presented first. In the next section, a summary of how personality and intelligence scales are utilized as criteria by formal diagnostic systems is presented, accompanied by a review of research on the use of such measures for the diagnosis of selected child and adult syndromes. The third section presents case studies highlighting the use of these measures for everyday diagnostic practice. In the final portion of the chapter, the contributions of personality and intelligence measures to psychiatric diagnosis are critically evaluated.

R. W. Kamphaus, A. W. Morgan, M. R. Cox, and R. M. Powell • Department of Educational Psychology, University of Georgia, Athens, Georgia 30602.

International Handbook of Personality and Intelligence, edited by Donald H. Saklofske and Moshe Zeidner. Plenum Press, New York, 1995.

HISTORY OF PSYCHODIAGNOSTICS

The histories of diagnostics and psychological assessment are distinct. In ancient times, any phenomenon that was not understandable or controllable (e.g., weather, disease) was considered to be supernatural. This lack of attribution of natural phenomena to scientific events was extended to mental phenomena. In ancient Babylon, for example, each disease was believed to be caused by a specific demon, and the Chinese, Egyptians, Greeks, and Hebrews also practiced similar beliefs at some point in their respective histories (Davison & Neale, 1990).

In the 5th century B.C., Hippocrates, abandoning the traditional Greek belief, introduced the idea that mental illness was caused by natural phenomena rather than supernatural powers. He even classified mental illnesses into three categories: mania, melancholia, and phrenitis (brain fever). Despite Hippocrates's supposition, no further advances were made in the practice of psychological classification for several centuries (Davison & Neale, 1990; Maloney & Ward, 1976).

During the 1600s an English physician, Thomas Sydenham, proposed a classification system that was based on empirical evidence. His proposal differed from the nonsystematic practices mentioned earlier, which were based upon disorders defined loosely by individuals with varying degrees of knowledge concerning mental illness. One of the people influenced by Sydenham's thinking was Wilhelm Griesenger, a German physician, who emphasized that physiological causes should accompany diagnoses of mental disorders. Emil Kraepelin, one of Griesenger's followers, had substantial impact on psychodiagnostic practices. Kraepelin (Davison & Neale, 1990; Pichot, 1990) proposed that a classification system should focus more on the cause, course, and outcome of a disorder than on a conglomeration of symptoms. From this belief arose Kraepelin's multiaxial system of diagnosis, which became the basis for the major classification systems used today (Davison & Neale, 1990; Zaudig, von Cranach, Wittchen, Semler, & Steinbock, 1988).

Diagnostic systems have become increasingly differentiated with the inclusion of multiple syndromes and with the definition of domains of symptoms within syndromes. The creation of intelligence and personality measures has juxtaposed well with this trend toward the assessment of multiple domains (or constructs) in order to make diagnoses.

Major Classification Systems

More uniform psychodiagnostic practices have been developed in this century, resulting in such major classification systems as the *Diagnostic and Statistical Manual of Mental Disorders* (DSM) of the American Psychiatric Association (APA) and the *International Statistical Classification of Diseases, Injuries, and Causes of Death* (ICD) of the World Health Organization (WHO). Although most cultures have abandoned ancient practices and beliefs that mental disorders are caused by supernatural powers, several still adhere to traditional religious and spiritual paradigms in the psychiatric field. A number of cultures have their own classification systems that try to incorporate the DSM and ICD schemes. Examples of these local systems are the French classification system published by the Institut de la Santé et de la Recherche Médicale (INSERM; 1969) which parallels ICD-10 in many areas (Pichot, 1990; Pull, Pull, & Pichot, 1988); the *Egyptian Diagnostic Manual of Psychiatric Disorders* (DMP-1; Egyptian Psychiatric Association, 1979), which was derived from ICD-8 (WHO, 1967), INSERM (1969), and DSM-II (APA, 1968), as well as British, American, and Egyptian tradition and education (Okasha, 1988); and the Chinese Classification of Mental Disorders (CCMD-3), revised in 1984 by the National Professional Conference of Psychiatry (Yu-Cun & Changhui, 1988).

ICD-10

The current ICD-10 has arisen out of a series of revisions from a publication released in 1893, the *International Classification of Disease, Injuries, and Causes of Death* (or the Bertillon classification). In 1891, the International Statistical Congress proposed the development of a nosological system that would be appropriate for worldwide use. This task was given to William Farr, a medical statistician in England and Wales, and Marc d'Espine of Geneva. The resulting *International Classification of Causes of Death* was adopted in 1893 by the International Statistical Institute (ISI) in Chicago. With its first revision in 1899, this system was renamed the *International Statistical Classification of Diseases, Injuries, and Causes of Death* (ICD). Because of the vast increase in knowledge regarding mental disorders, the ICD has been revised ten times, most recently in 1993. A major focus of these revisions has been to develop a system that would be appropriate for international use; input was sought from professionals around the world as part of this effort.

ICD-10 includes categories ranging from mental disorders to accidents, poisonings, and violence and was originally developed to provide a statistical compilation of the causes of morbidity and mortality. Members of the World Health Organization (WHO), who have published the last several revisions, use this system to render data that yields statistics on mortality and morbidity as it pertains to diagnoses from ICD-10. Of the 999 three-digit codings in the ICD-10, only 30 pertain to mental disorders.

DSM-IV

Prior versions of the DSM (and many other systems) have been based primarily on the expert judgment of a relatively small number of clinicians. DSM-IV (APA, 1994) is a major attempt to provide an empirical basis for diagnosis (Widiger, Frances, Pincus, Davis, & First, 1991). Three research methodologies have been used to provide the empirical foundation for DSM-IV (Widiger et al., 1991); these are outlined below.

1. *Literature reviews.* Comprehensive reviews of psychopathology and related research were sought in order to advise the work of committees.
2. *Data reanalyses.* Some existing large data sets were reanalyzed. These data sets were used for testing the applicability of proposed diagnostic criteria (Widiger et al., 1991).
3. *Field trials.* These data collection efforts were used for testing the reliability and validity of proposed diagnostic categories (Widiger et al., 1991).

Because of its foundation in data-based research, DSM-IV could provide valuable guidance for the use of intelligence and personality tests in the diagnostic process. In fact, diagnostic systems such as DSM-IV have profound effects on the use of particular assessment measures for diagnostic purposes by, among other influences, defining the relevant assessment domains for disorders. In some cases, for example, intelligence tests are moot, as the diagnosis is not dependent upon performance in the intelligence domain (e.g., alcoholism). Similarly, personality tests are relegated to second-class status for the diagnosis of some syndromes, as these tests measure domains deemed irrelevant for making the diagnostic decision. An example of the latter scenario is the diagnosis of mental retardation. Personality measures, however, may enjoy increasing utility for making the mental retardation diagnosis as a function of the release of the new American Association on Mental Retardation (AAMR; 1992) diagnostic manual, which includes "psychological and emotional considerations" as an important assessment dimension.

IDEA

Another diagnostic system devised for use with U.S. schoolchildren is contained in the Individuals with Disabilities Education Act (IDEA; 1990). IDEA defines five "syndromes" of severe emotional disturbances that may qualify a child for special education and related services. Emblematic of the influence of the IDEA is the "school form" of the new Devereux Behavior Rating Scale (Naglieri, LeBuffe, & Pfeiffer, 1993). This revision is specifically constructed to assess four of the IDEA categories of severe emotional disturbance, essentially creating a new type of "personality" test. The logical prediction from these examples is that DSM-IV, IDEA, AAMR, ICD-10, and other diagnostic systems will continue to define how intelligence and personality measures will be developed and used for diagnostic practice.

PSYCHOMETRICS AND DIAGNOSIS

Intelligence and personality tests were developed relatively independently of the medical diagnostic nosologies. From their roots in experimental psychology laboratories, psychometric tests were initially devised to measure previously elusive traits in order to define individual differences and make predictions about human behavior (Anastasi, 1988). In essence, psychometric tests are concerned with constructs and traits, whereas diagnostic systems are concerned with disorders.

This distinction between diagnosis and psychometrics is not a minor one. Psychometrics is charged with measuring traits in order to make predictions about behavior (Anastasi, 1988), whereas diagnosis is concerned with classifying medical disorders in order to state symptoms, etiologies, and prognoses (AAMR, 1992). Hence the measurement of intelligence and personality is related to, but not synonymous with, the process of making diagnoses. Similarities in the two enterprises primarily occur when intelligence and personality tests measure traits that are associated with particular disorders (e.g., self-esteem as one of the symptoms of major depression).

Preeminent among the distinctions between diagnostics and psychometrics are the differences inherent in behavioral and psychometric approaches to assessment. Psychological tests emanate from a "nomothetic" approach to assessment and diagnosis, in which an individual's deviance from average is gauged (Cummings & Laquerre, 1990). This method focuses on the assessment of traits on a continuum. Although the early success of intelligence and personality measures in the diagnostic process was impressive, the multiaxial approach commonly used by diagnostic systems has achieved prominence for the diagnosis of most syndromes. The multiaxial approach focuses on tabulating the presence or absence of behaviors in order to make a classification based on quantitative and qualitative data gleaned from numerous sources at various points in time. Shepard (1989) articulates the essential differences in the approaches in the following manner:

> It should be obvious that assessment of emotional disturbance relies almost entirely on clinical judgment. Measurement techniques consist mainly of strategies for collecting direct evidence of behavior patterns. Personality "tests" and measures of self-concept might be relevant, but they are not primary diagnostic indicators. Once a reliable picture of behavior and changes in behavior across situations and time has been established, the process of diagnosis rests on normative comparisons and the ruling out of competing explanations. Formal checklists and observation schedules do not make the clinician more insightful about what behaviors to observe, but they are helpful if they provide a basis for judging how extreme a pattern is in relation to the normal range of individual differences. (p. 565)

The ability of tests to assist in the diagnostic process has been reviewed for decades. The groundbreaking work of Rapaport, Gill, and Schafer (1945–1946) is legendary in this regard. The 1960s and 1970s saw a flurry of work in the diagnosis of child syndromes. Many efforts were made to assess the ability of the Wechsler Intelligence Scale for Children (WISC) to differentiate child syndromes and subtypes of syndromes (Kamphaus, 1993). Emblematic of this effort have been the numerous failed attempts at demonstrating the utility of Wechsler profiles for diagnosing attention-deficit hyperactivity disorder (Kamphaus, 1993). Many examples of the failure of even the best psychometric instruments to reliably differentiate diagnostic groups or subtypes of a disorder can be cited (Kamphaus, 1993).

Diagnostic systems have spurred the design of "tests" that measure the behaviors associated with particular syndromes (e.g., symptom checklists, rating scales, and structured interviews), and these have served to blur further the distinction between assessment and diagnosis. Such measures are unique in the annals of psychometrics in that they resemble traditional trait measures by providing evidence of reliability and certain types of validity, particularly differential validity. The intent of these measures, however, is not to measure a latent trait per se but to provide a systematic means for collecting data regarding the behaviors (symptoms) believed to indicate the presence of a syndrome.

We propose that this new class of assessment instruments be named so as to differentiate these measures from personality and intelligence tests that purport to measure traits. Greater precision in studying the instruments and the traits associated with particular disorders would then be more attainable. Perhaps *diagnostic schedule* is most descriptive; we define a diagnostic schedule as a specialized psychometric method that provides a structured procedure for collecting and categorizing behavioral data that correspond to diagnostic categories or systems (see Table 1). The term *diagnostic* is appealing because these devices emanate directly from diagnostic systems. The term *schedule* is descriptive in the sense that many of these measures are structured devices that provide a systematic method of data collection, yet they do not possess many of the characteristics typical of psychological tests (e.g., homogeneity of trait measurement). Examples of diagnostic schedules that became increasingly popular in the 1980s include behavior problem checklists, behavioral observation coding systems, and structured interviews (Kamphaus & Frick, in press).

We think that it is important to make the distinction between tests and diagnostic schedules because treating these measures as synonymous degrades the quality of both endeavors by drawing attention and resources away from the research efforts needed to improve each procedure. Though the ability of personality and intelligence tests to assist with making diagnoses is of interest, the degree to which such instruments measure their respective traits with precision is of greater potential value for research and associated theory building (Shepard, 1989). Similarly, defining

Table 1. Characteristics of Diagnostic Schedules and Psychological Tests

Diagnostic schedules	Psychological tests
Developed to assist with diagnosis of syndrome (disorder)	Developed to measure a latent trait
Items primarily consist of observable behaviors	Items consist of observable behaviors, subjective feelings, and perceptions
Emphasizes on establishment of differential validity	Emphasis on establishment of construct validity
Attempts to measure syndromes (disorders) that may or may not be stable over time	Attempts to measure traits that tend to possess temporal stability

syndromes based on psychometric test scores constrains the diagnostic process by limiting the search for central symptomatology to test-based data. Furthermore, the utility of combining trait measures for diagnostic purposes, although intuitively appealing, is rarely studied (Thorndike, 1982).

We explore the tenuous relationship between psychometrics and diagnosis for selected syndromes in more detail in the next section, and we describe the typical manner in which tests and diagnostic schedules are used as part of the assessment process of which diagnosis is one function. In addition, we attempt to use examples to define further the nature of diagnostic schedules.

DEFINING THE FUNCTIONS OF ASSESSMENT

The functions (or purposes) of assessment are unfortunately blurred in everyday parlance. Often the purposes of diagnosis, intervention/treatment design, and research are not clearly differentiated, resulting in unnecessary or inappropriate assessment and criticism of the assessment process.

The term *assessment* is usually considered to be relatively generic, referring to the overriding purpose of collecting information (both quantitative and qualitative) in order to conceptualize human behavior. Various components of the assessment process that are of primary interest to the clinician.

One important component of the assessment process is diagnosis: the process of taking a sample of behavior as an indicator of a broader range of human behavior (Anastasi, 1988). In some ways the process of diagnosis can be similar to classification in that the clinician is determining the fit between the samples of behavior taken and a diagnostic template. A template match then allows the clinician to make predictions about treatment, prognosis, course, and so forth. The DSM and other diagnostic systems are concerned with the development of improved templates, which in turn gives clinicians improved algorithms for template matching. Moreover, the DSM has spawned the development of data collection techniques that differ in fundamental ways from the trait-based measures that have dominated traditional psychological assessment.

Testing refers to the formal collection of data that can be quantified. Psychological tests are concerned with sampling behavior in order to make predictions; they use standardized (uniform) procedures for data collection; objectivity is approximated using standardized procedures and statistical methods of test development; and reliability and validity are demonstrated (Anastasi, 1988). A traditionally important aspect of test validity has been the evaluation of the degree to which tests measure a latent trait (or traits) with accuracy.

It is on the issue of trait measurement that psychological tests as traditionally developed and diagnostic schedules diverge. The schedules spawned by diagnostic systems have many of the properties of psychological tests, but some elements that are traditional in psychological assessment are lacking. Whereas standardized procedures are common for interview schedules, for example, norming is relatively rare. Another point of differentiation occurs in the validation process. Traditionally, factorial validity has been central for psychological testing as a means of identifying the latent traits underlying a test. Factor analysis and related techniques for identifying latent traits are less relevant for diagnostic schedules, because the purpose of a diagnostic schedule is to make a diagnosis, not to assess traits (i.e., enduring characteristics of individuals). For this reason, factor analyses of diagnostic schedules have often not produced interpretable results, as will be shown in the next section.

Another important function of assessment is prediction. Again, traditional trait-based measures and diagnostic schedules differ regarding their method of prediction. In traditional personality testing, a trait is measured, allowing the clinician to make predictions about future behavior based on knowledge of the existence of this trait. Diagnostic schedules, however, yield predictive information indirectly through their link with diagnostic systems. The diagnosis, supported by the results of data collected via diagnostic schedules allows the psychologist to access the research base regarding a particular disorder, which in turn allows him or her to make predictions based on knowledge of the course and other characteristics of the disorder (Kamphaus, in press).

Among the multitude of purposes of assessment, others include treatment design, evaluation, research, and placement. This chapter considers only one circumscribed purpose of assessment: the professional's desire to diagnose. The utility of various tests and diagnostic schedules to assist with this process is reviewed next.

DIAGNOSTIC USE OF TESTS AND SCHEDULES FOR SELECTED DISORDERS

In order to examine the use of intelligence and personality tests and diagnostic schedules in the diagnostic process, we have selected four disorders to serve as exemplars of research findings: depression, autism, substance abuse, and schizophrenia. These syndromes were chosen because they have a high prevalence rate and/or large research base, are representative of both child and adult syndromes, and represent a diverse range of conditions. DSM-III-R (APA, 1987) criteria for these disorders were used in many of the studies cited; empirical studies are the focus of our review.

Childhood Depression

Diagnostic Considerations

Childhood depression is typically considered to be a disorder associated with the affective domain of behavior (Semrud-Clikeman, 1990), in contrast to the "cognitive" domain. The criteria for mood disorders presented in DSM-III-R (APA, 1987) make no reference to intellectual functioning in the diagnosis of depression. Hence, if current diagnostic standards are accepted, impairment should be more notable on child personality tests and diagnostic schedules than on intellectual measures. It could be argued that intelligence measures may contribute to the evaluation of merely one symptom of depression (i.e., cognitive impairment), leaving the majority of symptoms to be documented via personality tests, behavior ratings, interviews, observations, and other means.

The core symptoms used by the DSM for the diagnosis of major depression include the following:

- Depressed mood
- Diminished interest in daily activities
- Significant weight loss or weight gain
- Insomnia or hypersomnia
- Psychomotor agitation or retardation
- Fatigue
- Feelings of worthlessness or guilt
- Diminished ability to concentrate or indecisiveness
- Recurrent thoughts of death or suicidal ideation

At least five of these symptoms must be present for a period of at least 2 weeks. Depressed mood or loss of interest in activities must be one of the five symptoms present.

Intelligence Tests

Studies assessing the utility of intelligence measures for making the diagnosis of childhood depression have yielded equivocal findings. Some studies find various aspects of intelligence to be impaired as a result of depression, some find no effect, and still others find an effect so small that the results are unremarkable. In a sample of 5- to 12-year-old children seen at an educational diagnostic clinic, Brumback, Jackoway, and Weinberg (1980) found no differences between depressed and nondepressed children's performances on standardized tests of intellectual functioning. In contrast, Kaslow (1981) found that depressed children in the first and fourth grades showed impaired performance on the Block Design, Coding, and Digit Span subtests of the revised Wechsler Intelligence Scale for Children (WISC-R; Wechsler, 1974), but did not differ from nondepressed children on the WISC-R Vocabulary subtest or the Trail Making Test of the Halstead Reitan Neuropsychological Battery (HRNB; Reitan, 1969).

Additional investigations have led researchers to believe that depressed children show some impairment on many types of intellectual tasks. Bodiford, Eisenstadt, Johnson, and Bradlyn (1988) conducted a study of learned helplessness among depressed children evaluated with a selection of cognitive tasks. The results of this study and others provide evidence of decreased performance speed and increased errors (Kaslow, Rehm, & Siegel, 1984; Kaslow, Tannenbaum,

Abramson, Peterson, & Seligman, 1983; Schwartz, Friedman, Lindsey, & Narrol, 1982).

The relationship between depressive symptoms and cognitive interpersonal problem-solving abilities was investigated by Mullins, Siegel, and Hodges (1985) in children 9 to 12 years old attending a public elementary school. No consistent relationship was found between depression and interpersonal problem-solving skills (as reflected in the number of means stated toward a given story goal and the number of obstacles reported on the way to that goal). Similar findings are reported by Griffin and Siegel (1984) in a sample of adolescents ages 13 to 18. The extent and types of cognitive impairment that could be attributed to depression remains an empirical question.

Personality Tests

The Children's Depression Inventory (CDI; Kovacs & Beck, 1977), a downward extension of the Beck Depression Inventory, is one of the most widely utilized instruments for the assessment of depression in children ages 7 through 17 (Lipvosky, Finch, & Belter, 1989). The CDI is used often in research studies as well as clinical settings (Lipvosky et al., 1989). The CDI is a self-report measure consisting of 27 items that assess cognitive, behavioral, and affective symptomatology of depression (Kazdin, French, Unis, & Esvelt-Dawson, 1983). Item scores range from 0 to 2, with 0 indicating a lack of a symptom and 2 indicating its extreme presence. Administration of the CDI is brief, and it can be completed in group or individual formats.

Test-retest reliability of the CDI is in the .70s and .80s (Kamphaus & Frick, in press). The CDI also correlates with clinician ratings of depression (Kazdin et al., 1983).

The traits underlying the CDI are not well understood, perhaps because the CDI was developed as a diagnostic schedule rather than a personality test. The CDI has been found to measure varying numbers of factors (e.g., Carlson & Cantwell, 1980; Kovacs, 1989; Saylor, Finch, Spirito, & Bennet, 1984; Weiss & Weisz, 1986). These factors have been identified as measuring numerous constructs, including low self-concept (Saylor et al., 1984) and overall distress (Kazdin et al., 1983; Saylor et al., 1984).

The CDI, as noted, is an example of a diagnostic schedule as opposed to a personality test. Some further examples of the distinction between diagnostic schedules and personality tests are presented in Table 2.

Although the CDI produces norm-referenced scores that correlate with other indices of depression and a systematic method for collecting symptomatology, the construct underlying the measure is not well understood. The a priori specification of items to be included in the scale derive from diagnostic systems and are difficult to support with factor analytic research. One could thus question whether depression is a trait, a trait being defined as an enduring characteristic of an individual (Martin, 1984). Depression may in fact be a diagnostic syndrome associated with numerous traits, including negative affectivity (Watson & Clark, 1984) and other temperamental variables. Indeed, constructs such as negative affectivity are the current focus of research efforts aimed at conceptualizing the etiology of depression (Watson & Kendall, 1989).

Though the CDI may be of practical utility for gauging a child or adolescent's views of his or her own symptomatology, the superiority of this method (above and beyond structured interview data, for example) for making the diagnosis of depression is not known (Hodges, 1990). This ability to add to the prediction of behavior or to the accuracy of diagnosis is described aptly by the unresearched "utility" function of a test, or in this case a diagnostic schedule (Thorndike, 1982).

Autism

Diagnostic Considerations

According to DSM-III-R, the diagnosis of an autistic disorder falls under the larger category of pervasive developmental disorders (PDD). The diagnostic criteria for autism include 16 symptoms organized into three categories: reciprocal social interaction, verbal and nonverbal communication and imaginative activity, and activities and interests. The symptoms are ordered so that those listed first tend to be associated with more severe cases and younger age groups. Of the 16 symptoms, 8 have to be evident to make the diagnosis of autistic disorder, and onset must occur prior to the age of 36 months. Other symptoms commonly occurring in cases of autistic disorder include impairments of cognition, movements, responses to sensory input, eating, sleeping, and drinking.

Intelligence Tests

Because many autistic children are also mentally retarded (5% to 30%, according to Yirmiya & Sigman, 1991), the use of an intelligence scale is central to the

Table 2. Examples of Personality Tests and Diagnostic Schedules

Instrument	Author(s)	Population	Evaluation	Format	Product
Personality tests					
Neo-Personality Inventory (NEO-PI)	Paul T. Costa, Jr., and Robert R. McCrae	Adult	Five domains of personality	Paper and pencil	Profile of an individual's personality related to the five domains
Myers-Briggs Personality Inventory (MBTI)	Isabel Briggs Myers and Katherine C. Briggs	Ages 12 to adult	Personality types and interests	Paper and pencil or computer	A description of the person's "type" based on personality factors and interests
Sixteen Personality Factor Inventory (16PF)	Raymond B. Cattell and IPAT staff	Ages 16 to adult	Sixteen primary personality traits	Paper and pencil	Profile of the adult client
Temperament Assessment Battery for Children (TABC)	Roy P. Martin	Ages 3 to 7	Basic temperament of children	Paper and pencil checklist	Description of the child's temperament relative to others of the same age
Diagnostic schedules					
Achenbach Child Behavior Checklist (CBCL)	Thomas H. Achenbach and Craig Edelbrock	Ages 2 to 16	Strengths and behavioral problems of children and adolescents	Paper and pencil checklist	Profile of social skills and behavioral problems and internalizing/externalizing factors
Beck Depression Inventory (BDI)	Aaron T. Beck	Adult	Level of depression	Paper and pencil checklist	Profile of the extent or severity of the individual's depressed mood

Source: Adapted from Sweetland & Keyser (1991).

diagnostic process (APA, 1987). Findings of average or above average intelligence (overall composite IQ scores greater than approximately 70) may call into question the presence of autistic disorder, as such cases have significantly lower probability of occurring.

Lincoln, Courchesne, Kilman, Elmasian, and Allen (1988) reported that those individuals with autism who are regarded as high functioning (IQs greater than 70) have higher scores on performance (nonverbal) tasks, particularly Block Design. Their scores on verbal tasks such as Comprehension tended to be impaired. Similarly, subtests requiring social comprehension (e.g., Picture Arrangement) were also impaired (Yirmiya & Sigman, 1991).

As with any other population, it is important to utilize the correct instruments when assessing autistic individuals. This guideline is of particular importance considering the distinctive behaviors exhibited by persons with autism that may complicate normal testing procedures. Alpern (1967) commented that autistic individuals are testable when the correct instrument is utilized. Although the Wechsler scales are commonly used in these evaluations, Harris, Handelman, and Burton (1990) conducted an examination of the use of the fourth edition of the Stanford-Binet Intelligence Scale (Thorndike, Hagan, & Sattler, 1986) as an instrument for this purpose.

These investigators (Harris et al., 1990) reported that the subjects in their study had the most difficult time with the Absurdities subtest. In contrast, their subjects were most successful with Pattern Analysis (Harris et al., 1990). This report is supported by evidence that the Pattern Analysis subtest measures visual synthesis and visual motor abilities (Delaney & Hopkins, 1987) and that these abilities have been regarded as strengths among autistic children (Rutter & Schopler, 1988). In their report, Lincoln et al. (1988) also found that, on standardized tests, autistic individuals have higher scores on visual-motor and memory tasks and lower scores on verbal tasks.

Though visual-spatial strengths have been documented for this population, this knowledge currently possesses no value in terms of the DSM diagnosis; it is merely of research interest at this time. Similarly, because intelligence test cut scores are not given for this disorder, intelligence measures are also of little practical utility for making the diagnosis of autism. The point is not that intelligence tests should not be used as part of the evaluation process, rather, it is that they have implications for other functions than diagnosis (e.g., research, intervention, and ruling out comorbidity with mental retardation).

Personality Tests

Freeman, Ritvo, Yokota, Childs, and Pollard (1988) found that autistic children have a markedly difficult time with attempts at socialization. A deficit in social skills is reported (Snow, Hertzig, & Shapiro, 1987) as the most tangible diagnostic feature of autism. Autistic children are frequently described as inappropriate responsive or nonresponsive to social stimuli (Snow et al., 1987).

In one study where autistic children were compared to other populations on the Personality Inventory for Children (PIC), the results supported the distinction of autistic individuals as a separate group (Kline, Maltz, Lachar, Spector, & Fischhoff, 1987). These results indicated that autistic children exhibited a more clinically pathological profile when examined for social skills and behavioral qualities (Kline et al., 1987). Their suggestion of future experimentation with larger samples notwithstanding, the evidence presented by these investigators supports the diagnostic process that incorporates resources (e.g., the PIC and other rating scales) that assess socialization problems. Social skills and related inventories may be used to acquire information about reciprocal social interaction in order to document a deficit in this area under the DSM system.

In contrast to the intelligence domain, diagnostic schedules that collect data regarding behavior problems are central to the diagnostic process. Behavior rating scales and observational systems are crucial for documenting the social impairments and communication difficulties associated with autism.

Substance Abuse

Diagnostic Considerations

According to DSM-III-R, persons receiving a diagnosis of psychoactive substance abuse must exhibit either continued use despite knowledge of a problem related to substance abuse, or habitual use in physically hazardous situations. The symptoms must persist for a period of at least 1 month or occur frequently over a longer period of time. The criteria for psychoactive substance dependence for that particular substance must have never been met. No references to intellectual functioning are made.

Intelligence Tests

Frequently, cognitive instruments are utilized when assessing individuals who have a history of substance abuse in order to determine the premorbid intellectual functioning of those individuals (Lezak, 1983). The instrument of choice for this procedure is often the revised Wechsler Adult Intelligence Scale (WAIS-R; Wechsler, 1981). Specifically, the Vocabulary subtest of the WAIS-R is the standard for comparison with other subtests (Lezak, 1983). According to Matarazzo (1972), the Vocabulary subtest correlates highest of all subtests with full-scale IQ.

Sweeney, Meisel, Walsh, and Castrovinci (1989) compared performance on the WAIS Vocabulary subtest with performance on the Similarities subtest (a test that requires the subject to describe how a selection of two items are similar). These investigators discovered that the scores on Similarities were significantly higher than the Vocabulary scores for subjects that were taking part in a detoxification program. Sweeney et al. (1989) duplicated this effect with a second group in this same study, utilizing the WAIS-R; these subjects also demonstrated depressed performance on tests of motor speed, as well as visual and verbal tasks. They concluded that verbal reasoning, assessed by tasks such as Similarities, may be the best representation of the cognitive abilities of these subjects. The verbal reasoning accessed through performance of Similarities incorporates organization of verbal information as well as cognitive flexibility. For subjects such as those in the Sweeney et al. (1989) study, this form of flexibility may be an important contribution to the assessment of cognitive abilities.

Through an effort to evaluate certain contributor variables for the presence of alcoholism, Moss (1989) administered several measures to male subjects who were substance abusers. These instruments included the Psychopathic States Inventory (PSI; Haertzen, Martin, Ross, & Neidert, 1980), the Buss-Durkee Hostility Inventory (BDHI; Buss & Durkee, 1957), and the WAIS-R (Wechsler, 1981). The results indicated that the majority of these patients were impoverished, had achieved a moderate level of education, scored at a lower level on intelligence tests, and had begun abusing substances at an early age (Moss, 1989).

In another report, Meek, Clark, and Solana (1989) offered a similar analysis of the subjects who were substance abusers. They cited Miller (1985), who found that areas of effect on cognitive functioning for this group will be visual motor, memory, and abstract reasoning tasks. In their study of inpatient substance abusers, Meek et al. (1989) utilized the Neurobehavioral Cognitive Status Examination (NCSE; Van Dyke, Mueller, & Kiernan, 1987), a screening test related to the Luria Nebraska Neuropsychological Battery (LNNB; Golden, Purisch, & Hammeke, 1985). Meek et al. determined the presence of deficits in the following areas: visual spatial performance, attention and memory, calculations, abstract reasoning, and comprehension and the improvement on these tasks prior to discharge.

As was the case for the studies of autism, intellectual assessment has been viewed as crucial to obtaining a thorough understanding of the individual's functioning in order to rule out comorbidity, assess response to treatment, suggest the need for additional testing, design interventions, and so forth. In the case of substance abuse, however, the intelligence test does not speak to the issue of diagnosis of the condition directly.

Personality Tests

Frequently individuals who seek treatment for substance abuse are placed in a setting with other psychiatric patients who have an assortment of reasons for seeking treatment. Indeed, according to Kay, Kalathara, and Meinzer (1989), little has been done to distinguish this group on the basis of behavioral characteristics. When comparing substance abusers with other psychiatric patients, these authors discovered that the substance abusers in their sample exhibited more destructive behaviors related to aggression. Furthermore, it was suggested that this group emitted the prevalence of violence and a lack of awareness of social mores (*The Multiple Dilemmas of the Multiply Disabled*, 1986; Vardy & Kay, 1983).

When looking for the possibility of a higher level of both impulsivity and sociability among substance abusers, King, Jones, Scheuer, Curtis, and Zarcone (1990) tried to determine if a relationship exists between level of plasma cortisol and increased scale scores on the Eysenck Personality Inventory (EPI; Eysenck & Eysenck, 1964)—specifically, characteristics such as impulsivity and sociability. These experimenters did not find a significant relationship between level of cortisol among substance abusers and high scores on any of the subscales of the EPI (King et al., 1990). In a case such as this, it may be difficult to determine whether the person has been regarded as impulsive prior to identification as a substance abuser; however, this may be an important consideration.

Diagnostic schedules again predominate for the diagnosis of substance abuse. Many of these schedules are developed by individual clinics and possess little evidence of psychometric adequacy. Diagnostic schedules, however, typically sample the behaviors necessary to make the diagnosis of substance abuse, whereas personality tests serve additional purposes of assessment.

Schizophrenia

Diagnostic Considerations

Schizophrenia is marked by hallucinations, incoherence, catatonic behavior, flat or inappropriate affect, and delusions. In differentiating between schizophrenia and mental retardation, one must ascertain that the behaviors descriptive of both disorders (i.e., low levels of social functioning, oddities of behavior, and impoverished affect) are not the result of communication problems. Another factor to consider is age of onset, because the criteria for a diagnosis of mental retardation state that the symptoms must be present during the developmental phase. It is recommended that "both diagnoses should be made in the same person only when there is certainty that the symptoms suggesting schizophrenia, such as delusions and hallucinations, are definitely present and are not the results of difficulties in communication" (APA, 1987, p. 193).

Intelligence Tests

According to Pernicano (1986), historical psychological research (Klove and Reitan, 1958; Reitan, 1955; Reitan and Fitzhugh, 1971) has revealed a relationship between verbal and performance scores on the Wechsler scales and cognitive deficits. In his study with schizophrenics and other groups, however, Pernicano (1986) did not find a difference that was specific to schizophrenic subjects. It is suggested that the WAIS-R (Wechsler, 1981) be used as an enhancement in the diagnostic process but not as the sole factor (Pernicano, 1986).

In another examination (Roy, Herrera, Parent, & Costa, 1987) of schizophrenic patients that incorporated the WAIS-R, it was discovered that certain aggressive patients had significantly higher scores on subtests such as Digit Symbol and Block Design. Indeed, it was suggested that more violent patients may be more attuned to higher activity tasks such as these performance subtests, whereas less violent patients might fare better on verbal tasks (Roy et al., 1987).

Personality Tests

According to Singh and Katz (1989), schizophrenic patients manifest many complex problems related to personality characteristics. Because of this complexity, a thorough evaluation is mandated for appropriate diagnosis.

A sample of schizophrenic adults was evaluated with the Structured Interview for DSM-III Personality (SIDP; Pfohl, Stangl, & Zimmerman, 1983) and the Millon Clinical Multiaxial Inventory (MCMI; Millon, 1983) for the purpose of detecting personality disorder characteristics (Hogg, Jackson, Rudd, & Edwards, 1990). Results from the SIDP provided evidence of antisocial and borderline personality diagnoses in addition to schizoid traits (Hogg et al., 1990). Furthermore, the MCMI yielded diagnoses of dependent, narcissistic, and avoidant personality disorders (Hogg et al., 1990).

In a study conducted by Curran and Marengo (1990), several personality tests were incorporated to examine the characteristics of catatonic schizophrenia. Instruments included the Incomplete Sentences Adult Form (Rotter & Rafferty, 1950), the Kinetic Family Drawing test (KFD; Burns, 1987), the WAIS-R, the Thematic Apperception Test (TAT; Murray, 1943), the Rorschach, and the MMPI. These experimenters determined the presence of compulsive characteristics, negative features, and avoidance features. It was recommended by the authors that, when using instruments with catatonic schizophrenics, it is helpful to make a careful examination of the items that the patient does not acknowledge, as well as those items that are endorsed (Curran & Marengo, 1990). In this vein, it was understood that schizophrenia may be characterized by personality characteristics that are present as well as those that are significant for their absence (Curran & Marengo, 1990).

Case Studies

In order to delineate more clearly the uses of diagnostic schedules and intelligence and personality tests for diagnosis the following two case studies are presented. An attempt is made to use popular tests and schedules in order to reflect current diagnostic practice in the United States. Furthermore, a child and an adult case are described in order to reflect the diversity of assessment instruments in common usage.

David

David is a 12-year-old fifth grader who was referred by his parents because of school difficulties. He has difficulty writing, according to his mother, who also noted that David has problems sitting still and attending in school. David currently resides with his birth parents and his 17-year-old brother, a high school senior who is doing well in school. David's mother said that the older brother was "hyper" in the early elementary grades, but he began to perform much better in school during sixth grade. Both of David's parents completed 11 years of schooling.

David showed some developmental delays in infancy. His mother recalls being surprised that he "made no noises" until about 3 months of age. He crawled very little. Speech developmental milestones were considerably delayed; he had speech therapy at school for approximately three years. Currently David's grammar is poor, and he has occasional problems with stuttering. David's temperament as a toddler was somewhat difficult: Although he did not exhibit temper tantrums, he did not seem to need much sleep, and he cried excessively. According to his mother, he acts more like a 9-year-old than like his same-age peers.

David's relationships with peers are problematic. He does not have a best friend per se; he frequently fights with playmates and is the victim of considerable teasing by others. He prefers playing with younger children and generally has difficulty forming friendships. He does not have the opportunity to play with many same-age peers in the neighborhood in which he lives. David enjoys sports such as football and basketball; last year he played running back for the football team, but it took him a considerable amount of time to learn the plays. With tenacity, he was able to learn the plays midway through the season.

Behaviorally, David is described by his parents as easily overstimulated at play, having a short attention span, being impulsive, and seeming somewhat unhappy much of the time. They report that he is also overly energetic in play and requires considerable parental attention. He seems uncomfortable meeting new people and generally keeps his feelings to himself. According to his mother, David "is in trouble all the time at school because he can't sit still," and "he talks aloud when doing his match worksheets and other subjects."

David has experienced school difficulties since kindergarten. He was retained in kindergarten because he was "immature." Teachers report that he has difficulty with all academic areas, but particularly reading and spelling. His grades range from Cs to Fs. He has been tested for special education placement, but did not qualify for the learning-disabilities program. His parents report that David has disliked school intensely, especially since the third grade. His father helps David with homework; he says that he works with David for at least an hour every night and in some cases 2 or more hours in order to complete the assignments. He says that David's retention is poor, making this a very frustrating experience for him. He also feels that David's lack of school success adversely affects achievement motivation and academic self-esteem.

David received a neurological evaluation approximately 2 years ago. The neurologist's diagnostic impression from that evaluation was nonspecific. The neurologist did not cite evidence of attention-deficit hyperactivity disorder (ADHD), but she suspected a learning disability. David's psychological evaluation from his school revealed generally below-average cognitive skills and academic achievement. These findings led to the conclusion that David was a slow learner. Subsequent to this evaluation, David has participated in remedial mathematics and reading instruction at his school.

Personality Findings. David shows consistent evidence across evaluations of ADHD on the behavior rating scales that serve as diagnostic schedules. Evidence of symptoms associated with ADHD are longstanding and compelling. The onset criterion is met because David's symptoms of hyperactivity, inattention, and impulsiveness were noted by his parents during the preschool years.

The teacher ratings for the Behavior Assessment System for Children (BASC-TRS) show considerable agreement across academic settings. All teachers provide evidence of hyperactivity, learning problems, and attention problems that are clinically significant. In most cases, these rating scale findings reveal that David possesses these difficulties to a greater extent than at least 98% of the children his age. David also exhibits some elevations on the Atypicality scale of the TRS. Further evidence for the diagnosis of ADHD is provided in the previous psychological report from David's school, where overactivity, impulsivity, and inattention were noted. David's symptoms of ADHD, according to the teacher ratings, are flagrant enough to cause him and his peers considerable difficulty in the classroom. He has difficulty completing his academic assignments and he frequently disrupts others in the class. At this time, David's symptoms of ADHD are the most parsimonious explanation for relative underachievement in reading and spelling.

In this case the behavior rating scales serve as a systematic method for gathering data on the core symptoms of ADHD. David showed evidence of exhibiting all of the core symptoms by age 2, as suggested by DSM-III-R. Above and beyond the collection of symptom information with the diagnostic schedules, historical information is important for making the diagnostic decision. Parental interview data revealed an age of onset in the preschool years, further supporting the diagnosis of ADHD.

In this case personality tests, as traditionally conceived, are noncontributory to the diagnostic decision, although such data may have implications for the other purposes of assessment outlined earlier. In like fashion, the intelligence test results discussed next do not make any contribution to the diagnosis of ADHD, as intelligence test results are not relevant to the diagnostic criteria. Intelligence test results are of some use diagnostically in order to rule out comorbid problems such as mental retardation.

Intelligence Findings. Intelligence test results for David provide clear evidence of intellectual deficits. Evidence of developmental delay is also provided by the BASC-TRS, where David was identified by some teachers as not having adequately developed social skills, leadership abilities, or study skills.

The intelligence tests results suggest the additional diagnosis of borderline intellectual functioning, which in the DSM multiaxial system is a "V" code. Knowledge of delayed intellectual development (which by some diagnostic standards may represent a case of mental retardation) provides important additional diagnostic information in this case in that an additional disorder is indicated.

Behavior Assessment System for Children-Teacher Rating Scales (BASC-TRS). The BASC-TRS is designed to obtain ratings of social competence and behavior problems, as well as the adaptive behavior and school performance of a student. The school-problems scales assess behaviors associated with learning difficulties. In addition, adaptive-skills scales measure the development of prosocial and related skills that foster better adjustment (on these scales, a high score in an indicator of better adjustment).

The BASC-TRS yields T-scores with a mean of 50 and standard deviation of 10. Scores above 70 are considered significantly high. Teacher ratings for David are shown in Table 3.

Differential Ability Scales. Subtest scores of 40 to 60 are considered average as are achievement subtests and composite scores of 85 to 115. David's scores are shown in Table 4.

Table 3. BASC-TRS Scores for David

	T-Scores		
	Teacher 1	Teacher 2	Teacher 3
Hyperactivity	76	83	66
Aggression	55	54	64
Conduct problems	55	55	48
Anxiety	39	35	55
Depression	42	46	53
Somatization	44	44	54
Withdrawal	51	47	51
Atypicality	64	72	64
School problems			
Attention problems	69	71	69
Learning problems	79	81	83
Adaptive skills			
Social skills	40	36	47
Leadership	41	41	43
Study skills	34	33	38

Paul

Paul is a college student who was evaluated to rule out the presence of a learning disability. Paul's grade point average is 2.41 (out of 4). Paul attended technical school for a year before attending university. His verbal SAT score was 540, and his math score was 670.

Paul's father teaches school, and his mother is a minister; both parents have graduate degrees. Paul has two younger brothers and two younger sisters. One sister has graduated from college, and the others are college students. No learning problems were noted for any member of Paul's immediate family.

Paul's birth history and developmental milestones are described as normal. His medical history includes a head injury suffered in a fall from a bicycle when he was in fourth or fifth grade; Paul was unconscious for several minutes following the accident. Paul also broke his leg when he was 5, and had surgery to fuse vertebrae in his neck after an automobile accident at age 17. Paul describes his current health as good.

Paul reports that his family was involved with family counseling when he was in high school. He also received individual psychotherapy briefly in 1990 and then again from 1991 until the present. Paul resumed psychotherapy after he had been discharged from a self-admitted 2-week stay in a general hospital psychiatric unit. An EEG performed last year at the request of his counselor at the mental health center was normal; a CAT scan, also recommended at the time, has

Table 4. Differential Ability Scales Scores for David

Subtests	
Recall of designs	38
Word definitions	31
Pattern construction	37
Matrices	31
Similarities	39
Sequential and quantitative reasoning	31
Composites	
Verbal	75
Nonverbal reasoning	69
Spatial	75
GCA	70
Achievement subtests	
Basic number skills	74
Spelling	69

not been done. Paul reports being depressed since childhood. His current diagnosis from the mental health center is dysthymic disorder and schizoid personality disorder, and he is taking 125 grams of Pamelor daily for depression as prescribed.

Paul's mother reports that he had a short attention span in first grade and difficulties with motivation in third grade. Paul was subsequently placed in the gifted program from 1975 to 1980. In high school Paul struggled with algebra and geometry, and he relates that it took him a long time to read and take tests. Writing papers has proven to be difficult for him at the university: He withdrew from freshman English twice, but finally passed the course on his third attempt. Paul made the honor's list one quarter last year, but had to study extremely hard to do so. Paul believes that he would benefit from having a note taker and untimed tests. His current goals include increasing his knowledge of industrial manufacturing processes, improving his memory, and becoming more motivated and socially adept. He hopes to work as a computer programmer or in construction.

Intelligence Findings

Paul's cognitive functioning was assessed with the WAIS-R, the Bender Test of Visual Motor Integration, the Trail Making Test, the Profile of Nonverbal Sensitivity (PONS), and selected subtests of the revised Woodcock-Johnson Tests of Cognitive Ability (WJ-R) and the Goldman-Fristoe-Woodcock Auditory Skills Test Battery (G-F-W). On the WAIS-R Paul earned a verbal score of 111±5, a performance score of 102±8, and a full-scale score of 107±4. There is a 95% probability that he performed better than 58% to 77% of adults his age.

Paul's profile of individual subtest scores shows a range of ability from low average to superior. Paul has an excellent knowledge of vocabulary (98th percentile). He was able to define words with succinct phrases and precise synonyms; however, he pondered each word for an unusually long time before responding. Paul's response time was also long on Digit Span (84th percentile), a subtest in which he had to repeat sequences of numbers forward and backward. He utilized effective mnemonic strategies, such as grouping and rehearsal, and reported being able to imagine the numbers in his mind before "reading" them. When given oral arithmetic problems to solve, Paul was able to calculate correct answers for most of the questions in 5 seconds or less (Arithmetic, 84th percentile). Paul had more difficulty with a task in which he had to cite reasons for social conventions, describe appropriate social responses, and explain proverbs (Comprehension, 50th percentile). After interpreting one proverb literally, he said that he knew it applied to a life situation but did not know what it (the generalization) was.

Paul's lowest score in the nonverbal cluster of subtests was on Picture Arrangement (25th percentile), a task in which he had to rearrange pictures into a logical story order. Paul made no errors on this timed subtest, but lost points on nearly half of the items because he worked too slowly. He demonstrated skill in analyzing and recreating designs (Block Design, 91st percentile) and was able to assemble three of the four puzzles in a small fraction of the available time (Object Assembly, 25th percentile). During the administration of the WAIS-R, Paul worked with determination and concentration. The only anxiety noted was in his bearing down so hard while copying a code that a clear impression of his pencil marks could be seen on the back of the paper (Digit Symbol, 50th percentile).

The assessment of Paul's auditory and visual processing revealed inconsistencies but no significant strengths or weaknesses in perception, discrimination, or memory. When asked to repeat one-, two-, and three-syllable nonsense words, Paul's occasional errors were in the addition or omission of sounds (G-F-W, 31st percentile). He had difficulty with an auditory closure task requiring him to identify words with sounds missing (WJ-R Incomplete Words, 30th percentile) but accurate perception and memory for sounds in sequence on an auditory synthesis task in which he had to blend sounds to form words (WJ-R Sound Blending, 84th percentile). Paul's ability to remember both sentences (WJ-R Memory for Sentences, 79th percentile) and sequences of unrelated words (Memory for Words, 85th percentile) was in the high-average to above-average range, similar to his mnemonic skill with digits on the WAIS-R. Paul was able to copy geometric figures and designs without errors; he worked extremely carefully and was concerned that his drawings were "nice and neat" and well organized on the paper (Bender, no errors). He also made no errors on a visual discrimination task in which he had to locate matching two- and three-digit numbers in rows of similar looking numbers (e.g., 102, 210, 201, . . . ; WJ-R Visual Matching, 46th percentile). On tasks that demanded a quick perception of a gestalt, such as identifying incomplete and distorted pictures or identifying pictures he had seen briefly from a field of similar pictures, Paul performed less well, though still within the average range (WJ-R Visual Closure, 17th percentile; Picture Recognition, 34th percentile).

Paul was administered the PONS to evaluate his skill in quickly interpreting nonverbal communication, such as gestures, body posture, and tone of voice. His ability to "read" this important component of interpersonal communication was within the average range (30th percentile) although his score was lower than what research has found would be expected of a college student. Paul was equally adept with auditory cues (e.g., vocal inflection) and visual signals (e.g., facial expression). He appeared to interpret messages with a strong negative content (e.g., threatening someone) more accurately than messages that had a milder, more subtle, negative tone (e.g., returning a faulty item to a store).

During the evaluation of his cognitive abilities, Paul demonstrated relative strengths on auditory memory and verbal comprehension tasks, and relative weaknesses on tasks assessing speed of processing and social comprehension. The pattern could indicate cognitive deficits. Instead, though, Paul's success or lack of it on specific tasks appears to be a manifestation of his personality dynamics, which emphasize perfectionism, a preoccupation with details and organization, and indecisiveness. Paul's inflexible, rigid problem-solving approach negatively influenced tasks in which a grasp of the gestalt was needed, as well as those that required him to supply additional information. Paul expressed discomfort at responding to items when he was not absolutely sure of his answer; his overly careful style affected his speed of production significantly on many tasks.

Personality Findings

Behavioral observations were recorded by the clinicians who worked with Paul as a qualitative measure of motivation, work style, problem-solving strategies, and emotional characteristics. The Brief Symptom Inventory (BSI), a self-report measure, was administered to Paul as a measure of symptomatology of emotional distress, depression, and anxiety. The MMPI-2 was administered to Paul as a quantitative measure of his level of emotional adjustment and attitude toward test taking.

Paul was punctual to his assessment appointments and was neatly and casually attired. He was consistently described by the clinicians who worked with him as initially reserved and, although appropriate in answering questions, as maintaining an interpersonal distance throughout the two days of testing. Paul was an active participant whose work effort was described as diligent and efficient. He was noted to stay on task, and he carefully thought out his answers.

Paul appeared detached from the examiners. He was noted to make little eye contact, and he yawned frequently. His physical posture was rigid, and his interpersonal interactions were reserved. He maintained a flat affect throughout the assessment, which could be a symptom of depression or discouragement. His lack of facial expression could also be attributable to his reserved nature; he did not seem to respond to recognize subtle social cues from his examiners. Paul scored above the normal range on the BSI scale utilized to assess emotional distress (Global Severity Index, $T = 66$). Items endorsed suggest distractibility, anxiety, depression, and intrapersonal tension.

Paul's MMPI-2 results produced a Welsh code of 02+−*765*/*843*1:9# F/L:K#. His results suggest that he may have been self-critical and have inadequate defenses in his attitude toward test taking. This finding also suggests that he may have low self-esteem with a low level of insight. His results on the clinical scales suggest tendencies toward social introversion and a low level of self-confidence. Though he is troubled by a lack of involvement with others, his results indicate that he is more comfortable alone. He can be described as hard to get to know, yet sensitive to what others think and overly accepting of authority. He may not display his feelings, resulting in an over controlled demeanor. Although reliable and dependable, he is also conventional and serious. Although he may derive pleasure from productive personal achievement, inflexibility and rigidity in his attitudes and opinions, his cautious approach to problem solving, and difficulty in making even minor decisions appear to interfere with his productivity. A tendency to be anxious, to worry, and to experience guilt feelings exacerbates his difficulties. Paul may make concessions to others in order to avoid confrontation, have somatic complaints, feel frequently like a failure, and be reclusive and appear aloof, thereby maintaining psychological distance from others. A number of these descriptors indicate depression.

Paul appears to lose efficiency in carrying out duties. He may have periods when he feels confused and unable to concentrate. Perfectionism that interferes with completing projects, a preoccupation with details so that the bigger picture is missed, indecisiveness, overconscientiousness and inflexibility, and restricted expressions of affection are indications of an obsessive-compulsive personality disorder.

In summary, the behavioral observations recorded by the clinicians working with Paul during his evaluation are consistent with his BSI and MMPI-2 results. Dimensions of Paul's personality constellation appear to interfere with his interpersonal relationships, work, and academic productivity and success. Individual personal counseling is recommended.

Paul's success or lack of it on other tasks appears to be a manifestation of his personality dynamics. Paul's constellation of personality traits measured by standardized tests and observed during the two-day assessment indicate the diagnosis of obsessive-compulsive personality disorder. He displays the symptoms of perfectionism, a preoccupation with details, a rigid approach to problem solving and insistence on doing things his way, indecisiveness, and restricted expression of affect. These problems are impairing both his social and academic functioning.

In this case interview and BSI results were key to documenting the existence of the five symptoms needed to make a diagnosis of a personality disorder. Although the MMPI was contributory, it did not provide the means to document specifically this range of symptomatology. The instrument that we conceptualize as a diagnostic schedule, the BSI, was central to making the diagnostic decision.

CONCLUSIONS AND FUTURE RESEARCH NEEDS

The relationship between diagnostic systems and popular intelligence and personality tests is a tenuous one. Rarely are measures of psychometrically measurable traits central to the diagnosis of a condition, except perhaps in the case of developmental disorders such as mental retardation. Formal personality tests are useful for the assessment of some domains associated with particular symptoms of psychopathology, such as self-esteem or anxiety. The multiaxial approach to diagnosis, with the associated emphasis on making diagnoses based on current behavioral symptomatology, makes the use of measures of personality traits less useful for differential diagnostic decisions. Measures of psychological traits are useful for defining some individual symptoms of disorders, but more importantly, these technologies are useful for devising treatments, stating prognoses, and research efforts such as studying the risk factors, etiologies, and prognoses of these disorders (Shepard, 1989).

The press to enhance the reliability and validity of DSM diagnoses has created the need for a new brand of "personality" test, which we have tentatively identified and defined as the "diagnostic schedule." Diagnostic schedules typically consists of a list of behaviors rated by a variety of informants. Some test characteristics, such as a norm referencing, are often included for these measures.

Although diagnostic schedules are practical for making diagnostic decisions, such measures have limitations for studying the nature of individual differences or for contributing to other important aspects of the assessment process because they often lack either a clear theoretical basis or evidence of a priori defined traits that can be supported with construct validity evidence. The emergence of diagnostic schedules as the instruments of choice for much of assessment practice is evidence of the profound impact of behaviorally based diagnostic systems on psychometric test development, particularly over the last decade.

The definition of diagnostic schedules requires further specification in order to allow psychometric devices to be properly identified for research and clinical purposes. Some measures—such as the BASC, cited above in the case study of David—appear to assess both traits and disorders, depending on the scales being considered. Relatedly, how would the MMPI be classified, given its roots in the diagnosis of syndromes? If the MMPI were compared to the NEO-PI-R (Costa & McCrae, 1992), a case could be made that the former is actually a diagnostic schedule and not a personality test per se.

The utility of these diagnostic schedules has not been established because of the lack of research studies evaluating the unique contribution that these measures may offer to diagnosis (Thorndike, 1982). Systematic studies of the usefulness of various schedules for making diagnostic decisions could streamline the process of differential diagnosis. Moreover, what does knowledge of diagnosis gained through the use of diagnostic schedules contribute to other aspects of assessment, specifically, treatment implications?

We view psychometric tests and diagnostic schedules as complementary and as having a bidirectional influence on one another. The emergence of the multiaxial behavioral approach to assessment has, however, profoundly influenced psychometric assessment to the point that a new type of hybrid measure, the diagnostic schedule, has emerged as the preeminent methodology for making diagnostic decisions. For diagnostic purposes this may be a reasonable trend. If diagnostic schedules become confused with psychometric tests, however, then the potential for misuse increases. If, for example, psychologists interpret such measures as they would trait measures, statements about chronic disorders may be true, but statements about adjustment disorders would be inappropriate. The examples below are suggestive of the different interpretations warranted by psychometric tests versus diagnostic schedules.

Appropriate conclusions that could be drawn based on diagnostic schedules include the following:

- Tonya suffers from major depression, single episode, severe.
- Tony exhibits nearly enough symptoms to be diagnosed as having conduct disorder.
- Traci has attention problems that are worse than those of 99% of the children her age.

Alternatively, conclusions that could be offered based on psychometric tests include the following:

- Allison shows evidence of poor adaptability to new situations and changes in routine, which puts her at risk for school adjustment problems.
- Patrick's high score on the sensation-seeking scale warrants consideration as part of his vocational counseling and educational planning.
- Maria's somatization tendencies reveal the need for counseling in order to reduce her frequency of emergency clinic visits.

A central difference between these interpretive statements is that those made based on diagnostic schedules are dependent on diagnostic nosologies. A variation of this premise is the third statement, which may result from a norm-referenced behavior rating scale that has a scale devoted to inattention. The interpretive statements made based on psychometric tests, however, can be offered independent of diagnosis. These conclusions are based on the measurement of traits that may or may not represent diagnostic symptoms or signs, yet these conclusions contribute substantially to the assessment process.

The central lesson that we take from this chapter is that we must be exceedingly clear about the role that personality and intelligence tests play (or do not play) in the assessment—particularly the diagnostic—process. As psychologists, we wish to aspire to high levels of assessment practice and ensure that our interpretations are supported by our science (Matarazzo, 1990). Our knowledge of measurement science beckons us to consider the differences between assessment devices carefully in order to ensure that our interpretations have psychometric support. We think that diagnostic schedules represent a relatively new and different class of assessment instrument that has an important but circumscribed purpose as part of the multiple methods used by psychologists in the assessment process.

The role of intelligence and personality measures in the assessment process continues to be substantial because of the link between these measures and the scientific basis of psychological practice. At this point in the development of psychometrics, new methodologies that meld diagnostic systems with psychometrics have proven to be of considerable value for making differential diagnostic decisions.

REFERENCES

Alpern, G. (1967). Measurement of "untestable" autistic children. *Journal of Abnormal Psychology*, *72*, 478–496.

American Association on Mental Retardation. (1992). *Mental retardation: Definition, classification, and systems of support* (rev. 9th ed.). Washington, DC: Author.

American Psychiatric Association. (1968). *Diagnostic and statistical manual of mental disorders* (2nd ed.). Washington, DC: Author.

American Psychiatric Association. (1987). *Diagnostic and statistical manual of mental disorders* (rev. 3rd ed.). Washington, DC: Author.

Anastasi, A. (1988). *Psychological testing* (5th ed.). New York: Macmillan.

Bodiford, C. A., Eisenstadt, T. H., Johnson, J. H., & Bradlyn, A. S. (1988). Comparison of learned helplessness cognitions and behavior in children with high and low scores on the Children's Depression Inventory. *Journal of Clinical Child Psychology, 17*(2), 152–158.

Brumback, R. A., Jackoway, M. K., & Weinberg, W. A. (1980). Relation of intelligence to childhood depression in children referred to an educational diagnostic center. *Perceptual Motor Skills, 50*, 11–17.

Burns, R. C. (1987). *Kinetic house-tree-person drawings (K-H-T-P): An interpretive manual.* New York: Brunner/Mazel.

Buss, A. H., & Durkee, A. (1957). An inventory for assessing different kinds of hostility. *Journal of Consulting Psychology, 24*, 243–249.

Carlson, G. A., & Cantwell, D. P. (1980) A survey of depressive symptoms, syndrome and disorder in a child psychiatric population. *Journal of Child Psychology and Psychiatry and Allied Disciplines, 21*, 19–25.

Costa, P. T., & McCrae, R. R. (1992). *Revised NEO Personality Inventory (NEO PI-R).* Odessa, FL: Psychological Assessment Resources.

Cummings, J. A., & Laquerre, M. (1990). Visual-motor assessment. In C. R. Reynolds & R. W. Kamphaus (Eds.), *Handbook of psychological and educational assessment of children* (pp. 593–610). New York: Guilford.

Curran, V., & Marengo, J. T. (1990). Psychological assessment of catatonic schizophrenia. *Journal of Personality Assessment, 55*(3 & 4), 432–444.

Davison, G. C., & Neale, J. M. (1990). *Abnormal psychology* (5th ed.). New York: Wiley.

Delaney, E. A., & Hopkins, T. F. (1987). *Examiners handbook: An expanded guide for fourth edition users.* Chicago: Riverside.

Egyptian Psychiatric Association. (1979). *Diagnostic manual of psychiatric disorders.* Cairo: Author.

Eysenck, J. H., & Eysenck, S. B. G. (1964). *Manual for the Eysenck Personality Inventory.* London: University of London Press.

Freeman, B. J., Ritvo, E. R., Yokota, A., Childs, J., & Pollard, J. (1988). WISC-R and Vineland Adaptive Behavior Scale scores in autistic children. *Journal of American Academy of Child and Adolescent Psychiatry, 27*(4), 428–429.

Golden, C., Purisch, A., & Hammeke, T. (1985). *Luria-Nebraska Neuropsychological Battery: Forms I and II.* Los Angeles: Western Psychological Services.

Griffin, N. J., & Siegel, L. J. (1984). Correlates of depressive symptoms in adolescence. *Journal of Youth and Adolescence, 13*(6), 475–487.

Haertzen, C. A., Martin, W. E., Ross, F. E., & Neidert, G. L. (1980). Psychopathic States Inventory (PSI): Development of a short test for measuring psychopathic states. *International Journal of the Addictions, 15*, 137–146.

Harris, S. L., Handleman, J. S., & Burton, J. L. (1990). The Stanford-Binet profiles of young children with autism. *Special Services in the Schools, 6*, 135–143.

Hodges, K. (1990). Depression and anxiety in children: A comparison of self-report questionnaires to clinical interview. *Psychological Assessment, 2*, 376–381.

Hogg, B., Jackson, H. J., Rudd, R. P., & Edwards, J. (1990). Diagnosing personality disorders in recent-onset schizophrenia. *Journal of Nervous and Mental Disease, 178*(3), 194–199.

Individuals with Disabilities Education Act. PL (101-475). (1990).

Institut National de la Santé et de la Recherche Médicale. (1969). Section psychiatrie: Classification française des troubles mentaux. *Bulletoin de l'Institut National de la Santé et de la Recherche Médicale*, 24 (2; Suppl.).

Kamphaus, R. W. (1993). *Clinical assessment of children's intelligence.* Needham Heights, MA: Allyn & Bacon.

Kamphaus, R. W., & Frick, P. J. (in press). *Clinical assessment of children's personality and behavior.* Needham Heights, MA: Allyn & Bacon.

Kaslow, N. J. (1981). *Social and cognitive correlates of depression in children from a developmental perspective.* Paper presented at meeting of the American Psychological Association, Los Angeles.

Kaslow, N. J., Tannenbaum, R. L., Abramson, L. Y., Peterson, C., & Seligman, M. E. P. (1983). Problem-solving deficits and depressive symptoms among children. *Journal of Abnormal Child Psychology, 11*, 497–502.

Kaslow, N. J., Rehm, L. P., & Siegel, A. W. (1984). Social-cognitive and cognitive correlates of depression in children. *Journal of Abnormal Child Psychology, 12*, 605–620.

Kay, S. R., Kalathara, M., & Meinzer, A. E. (1989). Diagnostic and behavioral characteristics of psychiatric patients who abuse substances. *Hospital and Community Psychiatry, 40* (10), 1062–1064.

Kazdin, A. E., French, N. H., Unis, A. S., & Esveldt-Dawson, K. (1983). Assessment of childhood depression: Correspondence of child and parent ratings. *Journal of the American Academy of Child Psychiatry, 22*, 157–164.

King, R. J., Jones, J., Scheuer, J. W., Curtis, D., & Zarcone, V. P. (1990). Plasma cortisol correlates of impulsivity and substance abuse. *Personality and Individual Differences, 11*(3), 287–291.

Kline, R. B., Maltz, A., Lachar, R., Spector, S., & Fischhoff, J. (1987). Differentiation of infantile autistic, child-onset pervasive developmental disorder and mentally retarded children with the Personality Inventory for Children. *Journal of the American Academy of Child and Adolescent Psychiatry, 26*(6), 839–843.

Klove, H., & Reitan, R. M. (1958). Effect of dysphasia and distortion on Wechsler-Bellevue results. *Archives of Neurology and Psychiatry, 80*, 709–713.

Kovacs, M. (1989). Affective disorders in children and adolescents. *American Psychologist, 44*, 209–215.

Kovacs, M., & Beck, A. T. (1977). An empirical clinical approach toward a definition of childhood depression. In J. G. Schulterbrandt & A. Raskin (Eds.), *Depression in childhood: Diagnosis, treatment, and conceptual models* (pp. 1–26). New York: Raven.

Lezak, M. D. (1983). *Neuropsychological assessment* (2nd ed.), Oxford, England: Oxford University Press.

Lincoln, A. J., Courchesne, E., Kilman, B. A., Elmasian, R., & Allen, M. (1988). A study of intellectual abilities in high-functioning people with autism. *Journal of Autism and Developmental Disorders, 18*, 505–524.

Lipvosky, J. A., Finch, A. J., Jr., & Belter, R. W. (1989). Assessment of depression in adolescents: Objective and projective measures. *Journal of Personality Assessment, 53*(3), 449–458.

Maloney, M. P., & Ward, M. P. (1976). *Psychological assessment: A conceptual approach.* New York: Oxford University Press.

Martin, R. (1984). *The Temperament Assessment Battery: Interim manual.* Athens, GA: Developmental Metrics.

Matarazzo, J. D. (1972). *Wechsler's measurement and appraisal of adult intelligence* (5th ed.). Baltimore, MD: Williams & Wilkins.

Matarazzo, J. D. (1990). Psychological assessment versus psychological testing: Validation from Binet to the school, clinic, and courtroom. *American Psychologist, 45,* 999–1017.

Meek, P. S., Clark, H. W., & Solona, V. L. (1989). Neurocognitive impairment: The unrecognized component of dual diagnosis in substance abuse treatment. *Journal of Psychoactive Drugs, 21*(2), 153–160.

Millon, T. (1983). *Millon Clinical Multiaxial Inventory manual.* Minneapolis, MN: Interpretive Scoring Systems.

Moss, H. B. (1989). Psychopathy, aggression, and family history in male veteran substance abuse patients: A factor analytic study. *Addictive Behavior, 14,* 565–570.

Mullins, L. L., Siegel, L. J., & Hodges, K. K. (1985). Cognitive problem-solving and life event correlates of depressive symptoms in children. *Journal of Abnormal Child Psychology, 13*(2), 305–314.

Multiple dilemmas of the multiply disabled. (1986). Albany: New York State Commission on Quality of Care for the Mentally Disabled.

Murray, H. A. (1943). *Thematic Apperception Test.* Cambridge, MA: Harvard University Press.

Naglieri, J. A., LeBuffe, P. A., & Pfeiffer, S. I. (1993). *Devereux Behavior Rating Scale–School Form and the Devereux Scales of Psychopathology.* San Antonio, TX: The Psychological Corporation.

Okasha, A. (1988). The Egyptian diagnostic system (DMP-I). In J. E. Mezzich & M. von Cranach (Eds.), *International classification in psychiatry: Unity and diversity* (pp. 55–64). Cambridge, England: Cambridge University Press.

Pernicano, K. M. (1986). Score differences on WAIS-R scatter for schizophrenics, depressives, and personality disorders: A preliminary analysis. *Psychological Reports, 59,* 539–543.

Pfohl, B., Stangl, D., & Zimmerman, M. (1983). *The Structured Interview for DSM-III Personality Disorders (SIDP).* Iowa City: University of Iowa Hospitals and Clinics.

Pichot, P. (1990). The diagnosis and classification of mental disorders in the French-speaking countries: Background, current values and comparison with other classifications. In N. Sartorius, A. Jablensky, D. A. Regier, J. D. Burke, Jr., & R. M. A. Hirschfeld (Eds.), *Sources and traditions of classification in psychiatry* (pp. 7–57). Toronto: Hogrefe & Huber.

Pull, C. B., Pull, M. C., & Pichot, P. (1988). The French approach to psychiatric classification. In J. E. Mezzich & M. von Cranach (Eds.), *International classification in psychiatry: Unity and diversity* (pp. 37–47). Cambridge, England: Cambridge University Press.

Rapaport, D., Gill, M., & Schafer, R. (1945–1946). *Diagnostic psychological testing* (2 vols.). Chicago: Year Book.

Reitan, R. M. (1955). Certain differential effects of left and right cerebral lesions in human adults. *Journal of Comparative and Physiological Psychology, 48,* 474–477.

Reitan, R. M. (1969). *Manual for administration of neuropsychological test batteries for adults and children.* Indianapolis: Author.

Reitan, R. M., & Fitzhugh, K. B. (1971). Behavioral deficits in groups with cerebral vascular lesions. *Journal of Consulting and Clinical Psychology, 37,* 215–223.

Reynolds, C. R., & Kamphaus, R. W. (Eds.). *Handbook of psychological and educational assessment of children.* New York: Guilford Press.

Rotter, J. B., & Rafferty, J. E. (1950). *Manual: The Rotter Incomplete Sentences Blank.* New York: Psychological Corporation.

Roy, S., Herrera, J., Parent, M., & Costa, J. (1987). Violent and nonviolent schizophrenic patients: Clinical and developmental characteristics. *Psychological Reports, 61,* 855–861.

Rutter, M., & Schopler, E. (1988). Autism and pervasive developmental disorders: Concepts and diagnostic issues. In E. Schopler & G. B. Mesibov (Eds.), *Diagnosis and assessment of autism* (pp. 15–36). New York: Plenum.

Saylor, C. F., Finch, A. J., Jr., Spirito, A., & Bennet, B. (1984). The Children's Depression Inventory: A systematic evaluation of psychometric properties. *Journal of Consulting and Clinical Psychology, 52,* 955–967.

Schwartz, M., Friedman, R., Lindsey, R., & Narrol, H. (1982). The relationship between conceptual tempo and depression in children. *Journal of Consulting and Clinical Psychology, 50,* 488–490.

Semrud-Clikeman, M. (1990). Assessment of depression. In C. R. Reynolds & R. W. Kamphaus, *Handbook of psychological assessment of children* (pp. 279–297). New York: Guilford Press.

Shepard, L. A. (1989). Identification of mild handicaps. In R. L. Linn (Ed.), *Educational measurement* (3rd ed.). New York: Macmillan.

Singh, N. N., & Katz, R. C. (1989). Differential diagnosis in chronic schizophrenia and adult autism. In J. L. Matson (Ed.), *Chronic schizophrenia and adult autism: Issues in diagnosis, assessment, and psychological treatment* (pp. 147–180). New York: Springer.

Snow, M. E., Hertzig, M. E., & Shapiro, T. (1987). Expression of emotion in young autistic children. *Journal of American Academy of Child and Adolescent Psychiatry, 26*(6), 836–838.

Sweeney, J. A., Meisal, L., Walsh, V. L., & Castrovinci, D. (1989). Assessment of cognitive functioning in polysubstance abusers. *Journal of Clinical Psychology, 45*(2), 346–351.

Thorndike, R. L. (1982). *Applied psychometrics.* Boston: Houghton Mifflin.

Thorndike, R. L., Hagen, E. R., & Sattler, J. M. (1986). *The Stanford Binet Intelligence Scale* (4th ed.). Chicago: Riverside.

Van Dyke, C., Mueller, J., & Kiernan, R. (1987). The case for psychiatrists as authorities on cognition. *Psychosomatics, 28,* 87–89.

Vardy, M. M., & Kay, S. R. (1983). LSD psychosis or LSD-induced schizophrenia? A multimethod inquiry. *Archives of General Psychiatry, 40,* 877–883.

Watson, D., & Clark, L. A. (1984). Negative affectivity: The disposition to experience aversive emotional states. *Psychological Bulletin, 96,* 465–490.

Watson, D., & Kendall, P. C. (1989). Understanding anxiety and depression: Their relation to negative and positive affective states. In P. C. Kendall & D. Watson (Eds.), *Anxiety and depression: Distinctive overlapping features* (pp. 3–26). San Diego: Academic Press.

Wechsler, D. (1974). *Wechsler Intelligence Scale for Children-Revised Manual.* New York: Psychological Corporation.

Wechsler, D. (1981). *Wechsler Adult Intelligence Scale—Revised manual.* New York: Psychological Corporation.

Widiger, T. A., Frances, A. J., Pincus, H. A., Davis, W. W., &

First, M. B. (1991). Toward an empirical classification for the DSM-IV. *Journal of Abnormal Psychology, 100*, 280–288.

World Health Organization. (1967). *Manual of the international classification of diseases* (rev. 8th ed.). Geneva: Author.

Yirmiya, N., & Sigman, M. (1991). High functioning individuals with autism: Diagnosis, empirical findings, and theoretical issues. *School Psychology Review, 11*, 669–683.

Yu-Cun, S., & Changhui, C. (1988). Principles of the Chinese Classification of Mental Disorders (CCMD). In J. E. Mezzich & M. von Cranach (Eds.), *International classification in psychiatry: Unity and diversity* (pp. 73–80). Cambridge, England: Cambridge University Press.

Zaudig, M., von Cranach, M., Wittchen, H. U., Semler, G., & Steinbock, H. (1988). Schizoaffective psychosis. In J. E. Mezzich & M. von Cranach (Eds.), *International classification in psychiatry: Unity and diversity* (pp. 122–134). Cambridge, England: Cambridge University Press.

25

Test Bias and the Assessment of Intelligence and Personality

Cecil R. Reynolds

The issues of bias in psychological testing have been a source of intense and recurring social controversy throughout the history of mental measurement. In the United States, discussions pertaining to test bias are frequently accompanied by emotionally laden polemics decrying the use of mental tests with any minority group member, because ethnic minorities have not been exposed to the cultural and environmental circumstances and values of the white middle class. Intertwined within the general issue of bias in tests has been the more specific question of whether intelligence tests should be used for educational purposes.

Although scientific and societal discussion pertaining to differences among groups on measures of cognitive or intellectual functioning in no way fully encompasses the broader topic of bias in mental measurement, there is little doubt that the so-called IQ controversy has received the lion's share of public scrutiny over the years. It has been the subject of numerous publications in the more popular press (see Gould, 1981; Jensen, 1980, chapter 1), and court actions and legislation have addressed the use of IQ tests within schools and industry.

Cecil R. Reynolds • Department of Educational Psychology, Texas A&M University, College Station, Texas 77843-4225.

International Handbook of Personality and Intelligence, edited by Donald H. Saklofske and Moshe Zeidner. Plenum Press, New York, 1995.

From Binet to Jensen, many professionals have addressed the problem, with varying and inconsistent outcomes. Unlike the pervasive and polemical nature-nurture argument, the bias issue was until the 1970s largely restricted to the professional literature, except for a few early discussions (e.g., Freeman, 1923; Lippmann, 1923a, b). Of some interest is the fact that one of the psychologists who initially raised the question was the young Cyril Burt (1921), who even then was concerned about the extent to which environmental and motivational factors affect performance on intelligence tests.

Since the 1970s, however, the questions of cultural test bias have burst forth as a major contemporary problem far beyond the bounds of scholarly academic debate in psychology. The debate over bias has raged in both the professional and the popular press (e.g., Fine, 1975). Entangled in the larger issues of individual liberties, civil rights, and social justice, the bias issue has become a focal point for psychologists, sociologists, politicians, and the public. Increasingly, the issue has become a political and legal one, as reflected in numerous court cases and passage in the state of New York (and consideration elsewhere) of "truth-in-testing" legislation. The magnitude—and the uncertainty—of the controversy and its outcome is shown in two highly publicized U.S. federal district court cases. The answer to the question "Are the tests used for pupil assignment to classes for the educably mentally retarded biased against cultural and ethnic minorities?" was yes in California (*Larry P. et al. v. Wilson Riles et al.*; 1979) and no in Chicago (*Parents in Action on Special Education et al. v. Hannon et al.*; 1980), although the overturning of the *Larry P.* finding has since given a consistent nature to the U.S. court findings.

Unfortunately, we are all prisoners of our language. The word *bias* has several meanings, not all of which are kept distinct. In relation to the present issue, the meanings of bias as partiality toward a point of view or prejudice and as a statistical term referring to a constant error of a measure in one specific direction (as opposed to random error) frequently become coalesced. If the latter meaning did not drag along the excess baggage of the former, the issue of bias in mental testing would be far less controversial and emotional than it is. As indicated in the *Oxford English Dictionary*, however, bias as partiality or prejudice can be traced back at least to the sixteenth century, clearly antedating the statistical meaning. Nevertheless, the discussion of bias in psychological testing as a *scientific* issue should concern only the statistical meaning: whether there is systematic error in the measurement of a psychological attribute as a function of membership in one or another cultural or racial subgroup (Reynolds, 1982b). This definition, defined more technically as required later, will be followed throughout this chapter.

THE CONTROVERSY OVER BIAS IN PSYCHOLOGICAL TESTING: WHAT IT IS AND WHAT IT IS NOT

Systematic group differences on standardized intelligence and aptitude tests occur as a function of socioeconomic level, race or ethnic background, and other demographic variables. Black-white differences on IQ measures have received extensive investigation over the past 50 or 60 years. The preponderance of these studies have been reviewed by Shuey (1966), Tyler (1965), Jensen (1980), and Willerman (1979). Although the results occasionally differ slightly, depending on the age groups under consideration, they have not changed fundamentally in the last century. Random samples of blacks and whites show a mean difference of about one standard deviation, with the mean score of the whites consistently exceeding that of the black groups. The differences have persisted at relatively constant levels for quite some time and under a variety of methods of investigation. The exception to this is the reduction of the black–white IQ difference on the Kaufman Assessment Battery for Children (K-ABC; Kaufman & Kaufman, 1983) to about .8 standard deviations on the intelligence portion of the scale, a controversial and poorly understood finding (see Kamphaus & Reynolds, 1987, for a discussion). When a number of demographic variables are taken into account (most notably socioeconomic status), the size of the mean black-white difference reduces to .5 to .7 standard deviations (e.g., Kaufman, 1973; Kaufman & Kaufman, 1973; Reynolds & Gutkin, 1981) but remains robust in its appearance.

Not all studies of racial and ethnic group differences on ability tests show higher levels of performance by whites. Although not nearly as thoroughly researched as black-white groups, Oriental groups have been shown to perform consistently as well as, or better than, white groups (Pintner, 1931; Tyler, 1965; Willerman, 1979). Depending on the specific aspect of intelligence under investigation, other racial and ethnic groups also show performance at or above the performance level of white groups. There has been argument over whether any racial differences in intelligence are real or even researchable (e.g., Schoenfeld, 1974), but the reliability across studies is very high, and the existence of the differences is now generally accepted. It should always be kept in mind, however, that the overlap among the distributions of intelligence test scores for the different races is much greater than the degree of differences between the various groups. There is always more within-group variability than between-group variability in performance on psychological tests. The differences are nevertheless real ones and are unquestionably complex (e.g., Reynolds & Jensen, 1983).

The issue at hand is the explanation of those group differences. It should be emphasized that both the lower scores of some groups and the higher scores of others need to be explained, although not necessarily in the same way. The problem was clearly stated by Eells in his classic study of cultural differences (Eells, Davis, Havighurst, Herrick, & Tyler, 1951);

> Do the higher test scores of the children from high socioeconomic backgrounds reflect genuine superiority in inherited, or genetic, equipment? Or do the high scores result from a superior environment which has brought about real superiority of the child's "intelligence"? Or do they reflect a bias in the test materials and not any important differences in the children at all? (p. 4)

Eells et al. also concisely summarized the hypothesis of cultural test bias as it applied to differences in socioeconomic status (SES):

> If (a) the children from different social-status levels have different kinds of experiences and have experiences with different types of material, and if (b) the intelligence tests contain a disproportionate amount of material drawn from the cultural experiences with which pupils from the higher social-status levels are more familiar, one would expect (c) that children from the higher social-status levels would show higher IQs than those from the lower levels. This argument tends to conclude that the observed differences in pupil IQs are artifacts dependent upon the specific content of the test items and do not reflect accurately any important underlying ability in the pupils (p. 4).

Eells was aware that his descriptions were oversimplifications, and that it was unlikely that all of the observed group differences could be explained by any one of the three factors alone. Loehlin, Lindzey, and Spuhler (1975) concluded that all three factors were probably involved in racial differences in intelligence. In its present, more complex form, the cultural-bias hypothesis itself considers other factors than culture-loaded items, as will be seen below. But the basics of Eells's summary of the hypothesis still hold: Group differences stem from characteristics of the tests or from aspects of test administration. Because mental tests are based largely on middle-class white values and knowledge, they are more valid for those groups and are biased against other groups to the extent that these groups deviate from those values and knowledge bases. Thus ethnic and other group differences result from flawed psychometric methodology and not from actual differences in aptitude (see also Harrington, 1975, 1976).

As is described below, this hypothesis reduces to one of differential validity: Tests measure intelligence more accurately and make more valid predictions about the level of intellectual functioning for individuals from the groups on which the tests are mainly based than for those from other groups. Artifactually low scores on an aptitude test could lead to pupil misassignment to educational programs and unfair denial of admission to college, graduate school, or other programs or occupations in which such test scores are an important decision-making component. This is the issue over which most legal cases have been fought. Further, there would be dramatic implications for whole areas of psychological research and practice if the cultural-bias hypothesis is correct. The principal research of the last century in the psychology of human differences would have to be dismissed as confounded and largely artifactual, because much of the work is based on standard psychometric theory and testing technology. The result would be major upheavals in the practice of applied psychology, as the foundations of clinical, school, counseling, and industrial psychology are strongly tied to the basic academic field of individual differences. The issue, then, is one of the most crucial facing psychology today (Reynolds, 1980c).

In contrast, if the cultural-test-bias hypothesis is incorrect, then group differences are not attributable to the tests and must be caused by one of the other factors mentioned by Eells et al. (1951) or some combination of them. That group differences in test scores reflect real group differences in ability should be admitted as a possibility, and one that calls for scientific study.

The controversy over test bias should not be confused with that over the etiology of any obtained group differences in test scores (see Reynolds & Kaiser, 1990, for a review). Unfortunately, it has often been inferred that measured differences themselves indicate genetic differences, and therefore the genetically based intellectual inferiority of some groups. Jensen has himself consistently argued since 1969 that mental tests measure, to a greater or lesser extent, the intellectual factor *g*, which has a large genetic component, and that group differences in mental test scores may then reflect group differences in *g*. Unless one reads Jensen's statements carefully, it is easy to overlook the many qualifications that he makes regarding these differences and conclusions.

In fact, though, Jensen or anyone else's position on the basis of actual group differences should be seen as irrelevant to the issue of test bias. However controversial, etiology is a separate issue. It would be tragic to accept the cultural-bias hypothesis as true if it is actually false. In that case, measured differences would be seen as not real, and children might be denied access to the educational environment best suited to them. Further, research on the basis of any group differences would be stifled, as would implementation of programs designed to remediate any deficiencies. From our perspective, the most advantageous position for the true white racist and bigot would be to *favor* the best-bias hypothesis. Acceptance of that hypothesis (if false) would eventually result in inappropriate pupil assignment, less adaptive education for some groups, and less implementation of long-range programs to raise intellective performance. In short, inappropriate confirmation of the test bias hypothesis would appear to maintain, not break down, the poverty cycle (Birch & Gussow, 1970).

The controversy is also not over the blatantly inappropriate administration and use of mental tests. The administration of a test in English to an individual for whom English is a second language and whose English language skills are poor is inexcusable, regardless of any bias in the tests themselves. It is of obvious importance that tests be administered by skilled and sensitive professionals who are aware of the factors that may artifactually lower an individual's test scores. That should go without saying, but some legal cases involve just such abuses. In terms of the use of tests to assign pupils to special education classes or other programs, a question needs to be asked: What would one use instead? Teacher recommendations are notoriously less reliable and less valid than standardized test scores. As to whether special education programs are of adequate quality to meet the needs of children, that is an important educational question, but distinct from the test-bias one. This distinction is sometimes confused (e.g., Reschly, 1980).

The controversy over the use of mental tests is further complicated by the fact that resolution of the cultural-bias question in either direction will not resolve the problem of the role of nonintellective factors that may influence the test scores of *individuals* from any group, minority or majority. Regardless of any group differences, it is individuals who are tested and whose scores may or may not be accurate. Similarly, it is individuals who are assigned to classes and who are accepted or rejected. As indicated by Wechsler (1975) and others, nonintellective factors, informational content, and emotional-motivational conditions may be reflected in performance on mental tests. The extent to which these factors influence individual as opposed to group performance is difficult to determine. Perhaps with more sophisticated multivariate designs, we will be better able to identify individuals with characteristics that are likely to have an adverse effect on their performance on mental tests. Basically outside the major thrust of the issue of bias against groups, potential bias against individuals is a serious problem itself and merits research and analysis. Sternberg (1980), who is also concerned about individual performance, observed that research on bias has concentrated on "status variables" such as ethnicity rather than on "functional variables" such as cognitive styles and motivations.

A different aspect of the test-bias hypothesis concerns the effects of practice on performance on the standard aptitude tests used in decisions regarding college and graduate and professional school admissions. Such tests, many of which are produced by the Educational Testing Services (ETS), include the Scholastic Aptitude Test (SAT), Graduate Record Examination (GRE), Medical College Admissions Test (MCAT), and Law School Admissions Test (LSAT). The ETS has consistently maintained that relatively short periods of practice have little effect on performance on these tests, but a dispute has developed around the question of how much effect such practice may have and under what conditions.

This is not the place for a discussion of practice effects per se, but the issue becomes relevant to questions of test bias in the following way: Programs claiming success in raising scores on the ETS-type exams have multiplied in the last few years and have become commonplace in some metropolitan centers. Given the spotty distribution of these programs and their high cost, members of low-SES and rural groups may be effectively excluded from participation in programs that would raise their scores. Thus economic and other factors may result in the scores of members of some groups being lower than they would have been with the benefit of training. The resulting bias, it should be emphasized, would be attributable not to differential validity but to the differential access to programs that help to develop the skills tapped by the tests.

THE NATURE OF PSYCHOLOGICAL TESTING ADDS TO THE CONTROVERSY

The whole issue of cultural bias arises because of the procedures involved in psychological testing. Psychological tests measure traits that are not directly observable, are subject to differences in definition, and are measurable only on a relative scale. From this perspective, the question of cultural bias in mental testing is a subset (though one of major importance) of the problems of uncertainty and possible bias in psychological testing generally. Bias may exist not only in mental tests but in other types of psychological tests as well, including personality, vocational, and psychopathological tests.

Making the problem of bias in mental testing even more complex is the fact that not all mental tests are of the same quality: Like the pigs in Orwell's

Animal Farm, some may be more equal than others. There is a tendency for critics and defenders alike to overgeneralize across tests, lumping virtually all tests together under the same heading. As reflected in the *Mental Measurements Yearbook*, professional opinions of mental tests vary considerably, and some of the most used tests are not well respected by psychometricians. Thus, unfortunately, the question of bias must be answered on a virtually test-by-test basis.

WHAT ARE POSSIBLE SOURCES OF BIAS?

Many potentially legitimate objections to the use of educational and psychological tests with minorities have been raised by black and other minority psychologists. Unfortunately, these objections are frequently stated as facts on rational rather than empirical grounds (e.g., Chambers, Barron, & Sprecher, 1980; Council for Exceptional Children, 1978; Hilliard, 1979). The most frequently stated problems fall into one of the following categories (Reynolds, 1982a):

(1) *Inappropriate content.* Black and other minority children have not been exposed to the material involved in the test questions or other stimulus materials. The tests are geared primarily toward white middle-class homes, vocabulary, knowledge, and values.
(2) *Inappropriate standardization samples.* Ethnic minorities are underrepresented in standardization samples used in the collection of normative reference data. Williams (Wright & Isenstein, 1977) has criticized the WISC-R (Wechsler, 1974) standardization sample for including blacks only in proportion to the United States total population. Out of 2,200 children in the WISC-R standardization sample, 330 were minority. Williams contends that such small actual representation has no impact on the test. In earlier years, it was not unusual for standardization samples to be all white (e.g., the 1937 Binet and 1949 WISC).
(3) *Examiner and language bias.* Since most psychologists are white and speak only standard English, they may intimidate black and other ethnic minorities. They are also unable accurately to communicate with minority children—to the point of being insensitive to ethnic pronunciation of words on the test. Lower test scores for minorities, then, may reflect only this intimidation and difficulty in the communication process, not lower ability.
(4) *Inequitable social consequences.* As a result of bias in educational and psychological tests, minority group members, already at a disadvantage in the educational and vocational markets because of past discrimination and thought unable to learn, are disproportionately relegated to dead-end educational tracks. Labeling effects also fall under this category.
(5) *Measurement of different constructs.* Related to (1) above, this position asserts that the tests measure different attributes when used with children from other than the white middle-class culture on which the tests are largely based, and thus do not measure minority intelligence validly.
(6) *Differential predictive validity.* Although tests may accurately predict a variety of outcomes for white middle-class children, they do not predict successfully any relevant behavior for minority group members. Further, there are objections to use of the standard criteria against which tests are validated with minority cultural groups. That is, scholastic or academic attainment levels in white middle-class schools are themselves considered by a variety of black psychologists to be biased as criteria. (pp. 179–180)

Contrary to the situation in the 1970s, when the current controversy began, research now exists that examines each of the above areas of potential bias in assessment. Except for the still-unresolved issue of labeling effects, the least amount of research is available on the long-term social consequences of testing, although some data are available (e.g., Lambert, 1979). But both of these problems are aspects of testing in general and are not limited to minorities. The problem of the social consequences of educational tracking is frequently lumped with the issue of test bias. Those issues, however, are separate. Educational tracking and special education should be treated as problems of education, not assessment.

MEAN SCORE DIFFERENCES AS TEST BIAS

A popular lay view has been that differences in mean levels of performance on cognitive or ability tasks among groups constitute bias in tests; however, such differences alone clearly are not evidence of test bias. A number of writers in the professional literature have mistakenly taken this position (Alley & Foster, 1978; Chinn, 1979; Hilliard, 1979; Jackson, 1975; Mercer, 1976; Williams, 1974; Wright & Isenstein, 1977). Those who support this definition of test bias correctly state that there is no valid a priori scientific reason to believe that intellectual or other cognitive performance levels should differ across race. What is fallacious, though, is the inference that tests demonstrating such differences are inherently biased because in reality there can be no differences. Just as there is no a priori basis for deciding that differences exist, there is no such basis for deciding that they do not. From the standpoint of the objective methods of science, premature acceptance of either hypothesis is untenable. As stated by Thorndike (1971), "The presence (or absence) of differences in mean score between groups, or of differences in variability, tells us nothing directly about fairness" (p. 64).

Some adherents to the "mean score differences as bias" viewpoint also require that the distribution of test scores in each population or subgroup be identical before one can assume that the test is fair: "Regardless of the purpose of a test or its validity for that purpose, a test should result in distributions that are statistically equivalent across the groups tested in order for it to be considered nondiscriminatory for those groups" (Alley & Foster, 1978, p. 2). Portraying a test as biased regardless of its purpose or validity, though, is psychometrically naive. Mean score differences and unequivalent distributions have been the most uniformly rejected of all criteria examined by sophisticated psychometricians involved in investigating the problems of bias in assessment. Ethnic group differences in mental test scores are among the best-documented phenomena in psychology, and they have persisted over time at relatively constant levels (Reynolds & Gutkin, 1980b, 1981).

Jensen (1980) has discussed the "mean score differences as bias" position in terms of the egalitarian fallacy. The egalitarian fallacy contends that all human populations are in fact identical on all mental traits or abilities; any differences with regard to any aspect of the distribution of mental test scores indicates that something is wrong with the test itself. Such an assumption is totally unwarranted: There are simply too many examples of specific abilities and even sensory capacities that have been shown to differ unmistakably across human populations. The result of the egalitarian assumption, then, is to remove the investigation of population differences in ability from the realm of scientific inquiry. Logically followed, this fallacy leads to other untenable conclusions as well. Torrance (1980), an adherent of the cultural-bias hypothesis, pointed out that disadvantaged black children occasionally earn higher scores on creativity tests—and, therefore, are presumed to have more creative ability—than many white children because their environment has forced them to learn to make do with less and with simpler objects. The egalitarian assumption would hold that this is not true, but rather that the content of creativity tests is biased against white or high-socioeconomic status (high-SES) children.

The attachment of minorities to the "mean score differences as bias" definition is probably related to the so-called nature-nurture controversy at some level. Certainly data reflecting racial differences on various aptitude measures have been interpreted to indicate support for a hypothesis of genetic differences in intelligence and to imply that one race is superior to another. As discussed previously, however, the nature-nurture issue is not an inextricable component of bias investigation. Assertions as to the relative impact of genetic factors on group ability levels step into a new arena of scientific inquiry, with differing bodies of knowledge and methods of research. Suffice it to say that in the arena of bias investigation, mean differences on aptitude or achievement measures among selected groups are not evidence per se that the measures are biased.

Culture-Free Tests, Culture Loading, and Culture Bias

Another area of bias investigation that has been confusing in both the professional (e.g., Alley & Foster, 1978; Chinn, 1979) and lay literature has been the interpretation of culture loading and culture bias. A test can be culture-loaded without being culturally biased. *Culture loading* refers to the degree of cultural specificity present in the test or individual items within it. Certainly, the greater the cultural specificity of a test item, the greater the likelihood of the item's being biased when it is used with individuals from other cultures. The test item "Who was the first president of the United States?" is a culture-loaded item. The item is general enough to be considered useful with children in the United States, but its cultural specificity is too great to allow it to be used on an aptitude measure of 10-year-old children from other countries. Virtually all tests in current use are bound in some way by their cultural specificity. Culture loading must be viewed on a continuum from general (defining the culture in a broad, liberal sense) to specific (defining the culture in narrow, highly distinctive terms).

A variety of attempts have been made to develop a "culture-free" (sometimes referred to as "culture-fair") intelligence test (Cattell, 1979). The reliability and validity of these tests, however, are uniformly inadequate from a psychometric perspective (Anastasi, 1982; Ebel, 1979). The difficulty in developing a culture-free measure of intelligence lies in the test's being irrelevant to intellectual behavior within the culture under study. Intelligent behavior is defined within human society in large part on the basis of behavior judged to be of value to the survival and improvement of the culture and the individuals within the culture. A test that is blind to culture, then, cannot be expected to predict intelligent behavior within a variety of cultural settings. Once a test has been developed within a culture (i.e., is a culture-loaded test), its generalizability to other cultures or subcultures within the dominant societal framework becomes a matter for empirical investigation.

Jensen (1980) admonishes that when one is investigating the psychometric properties of culture-loaded tests across differing societies or cultures, one cannot assume that simple inspection of the content will determine which tests or items are biased against those cultures or societies not represented therein. Tests or items that exhibit characteristics of being culturally loaded cannot be determined to be biased with any degree of certainty unless objective statistical inspection is completed. Jensen refers to the mistaken notion that anyone can judge tests and/or items as being culturally unfair on superficial inspection as the "culture-bound fallacy." The issue of item bias is revisited in some detail later in this chapter.

Labeling Effects

The relative impact of placing a label on a child's behavior or developmental status has also been a hotly discussed issue within the field of psychometrics in general, and bias investigation in particular. The issue has undoubtedly been a by-product of the practice of using intellectual measures for the determination of mental retardation. Although the question of labeling effects is a viable and important one, it requires consideration in bias research only in much the same way as does the ongoing debate surrounding the nature-nurture question. There are some important considerations regarding bias in referral for services, diagnosis, and labeling, however, that no interested student of the diagnostic process in psychology can afford to ignore.

Various studies (e.g., Frame, 1979; Matuszek & Oakland, 1979) clearly indicate that the demographic variables of race and SES do not, independent of other pupil characteristics, influence or bias psychologists' diagnostic or placement behavior in a manner that would cause blacks or lower-SES children to be labeled inaccurately or placed inappropriately (or disproportionately) in special education programs. The empirical evidence, rather, argues in the opposite direction: Black and low-SES children are *less* likely to be recommended for special education class placement than white or higher-SES peers with similar cognitive, behavioral, and emotional characteristics. The data simply do not support Williams's (1970) charge that black children are placed in special education programs on the basis of race or test bias against blacks. When referrals for placement in gifted programs are considered separately from referrals in general, the higher representation of minorities in special education programs can be accounted for by the disproportionately higher incidence of referral among minority student populations (Tomlinson, Acker, Canter, & Lindborg, 1977; Waits & Richmond, 1978).

THE PROBLEM OF DEFINITION

The definition of test bias has produced considerable, and as yet unresolved, debate among measurement and assessment experts (Angoff, 1976; Bass, 1976; Bernal, 1975; Cleary, Humphreys, Kendrick, & Wesman, 1975; Cole & Moss, 1989; Cronbach, 1976; Darlington, 1978; Einhorn & Bass, 1971; Flaugher, 1978; Gordon, 1984; Gross & Su, 1975; Humphreys, 1973; Hunter & Schmidt, 1976, 1978; Linn, 1976; McNemar, 1975; Novick & Petersen, 1976; Petersen & Novick, 1976; Reschly, 1980; Reynolds, 1978, 1982b; Reynolds & Brown, 1984; Sawyer, Cole, & Cole, 1976; Schmidt & Hunter, 1974; Thorndike, 1971). Although the resulting debate has generated a number of selection models with which to examine bias, selection models focus on the decision-making system and not on the test itself. The various selection models are discussed at some length in Hunter and Schmidt (1976), Hunter, Schmidt, and Rauschenberger (1984), Jensen (1980), Petersen and Novick (1976), and Ramsay (1979). The choice of a decision-making system (especially a system for educational decision making) must ultimately be a societal one; as such, it will depend to a large extent on the value system and goals of the society. Thus, before a model for test use in selection can be chosen, it must be decided whether the ultimate goal is equality of opportunity, equality of outcome, or representative equality (these concepts are discussed in more detail in Nichols, 1978).

Equality of opportunity is a competitive model wherein selection is based on ability. As stated more eloquently by Lewontin (1970), under equality of opportunity, "true merit . . . will be the criterion of men's earthly reward" (p. 92). *Equality of outcome* is a selection model based on ability deficits. Compensatory and remedial education programs are typically constructed on the basis of the equality-of-outcome model. Children of low ability or children believed to be at high risk for academic failure are selected for remedial, compensatory, or other special educational programs. In a strictly predictive sense, tests are used in a similar manner under both of these models. Under equality of opportunity, however, selection is based on the prediction of a high level of criterion performance; under equality of outcome, selection is determined by the prediction of "failure" or a preselected low level of criterion performance. Interestingly, it is the failure of compensatory and remedial education programs to bring the disadvantaged learner to "average" levels of performance that has resulted in the charges of test bias now in vogue.

The model of *representative equality* also relies on selection, but selection that is proportionate to numerical representation of subgroups in the population under consideration. Representative equality is typically thought to be independent of the level of ability within each group; however, models can be constructed that select from each subgroup the desired proportion of individuals (a) according to relative ability level of the group, (b) independent of group ability, or (c) according to some decision rule between these two positions. Even under the conditions of representative equality, it is imperative to employ a selection device (test) that will rank-order individuals within groups in a reliable and valid manner.

The best way to ensure fair selection under any of these models is to employ tests that are equally reliable and equally valid for all groups concerned. The tests employed should also be the most reliable and most valid for all groups under consideration. The question of test bias per se then becomes a question of test validity. Test use (i.e., fairness) may be defined as biased or nonbiased only by the societal value system; at present, this value system is leaning strongly toward some variant of the representative-equality selection model. As noted above, all models are facilitated by the use of a nonbiased test. That is, the use of a test with equivalent cross-group validities makes for the most parsimonious selection model, greatly simplifying the creation and application of the selection model that has been chosen.

This leads to the essential definitional component of test bias. Test bias refers in a global sense to *systematic* error in the estimation of some "true" value for a group of individuals. The key word here is *systematic*: All measures contain error, but this error is assumed to be random unless shown to be otherwise. Bias investigation is a statistical inquiry that does not concern itself with culture loading, labeling effects, or test use/test fairness. Concerning the last of these, Jensen (1980) comments as follows:

> Unbiased tests can be used unfairly and biased tests can be used fairly. Therefore, the concepts of bias and unfairness should be kept distinct. . . . [A] number of different, and often mutually contradictory, criteria for fairness have been proposed, and no amount of statistical or psychometric reasoning per se can possibly settle any arguments as to which is best. (pp. 375–376)

There are three types of validity as traditionally conceived: content, construct, and predictive (or criterion related). Test bias may exist under any or all of these categories of validity. Though no category of validity is completely independent of any other category, each is discussed separately here for the purpose of clarity and convenience. (All true evidence of validity is as likely as not to be construct validity, and the other, more detailed divisions are for convenience of discussion.) Frequently encountered in bias research are the terms *single-group validity* and *differential validity*. The former refers to the phenomenon of a test's being valid for one group but not another. The latter refers to a condition where a test is valid for all groups concerned, but the degree of validity varies as a function of group membership. Although these terms have been most often applied to predictive or criterion-related validity (validity coefficients are then examined for significance and compared across groups), the concepts of single-group and differential validity are equally applicable to content and construct validity.

RESEARCH STRATEGIES AND RESULTS

The methodologies available for research into bias in mental tests have grown rapidly in number and sophistication since the early 1970s. Extensive reviews of the questions to be addressed in such research and their corresponding methodologies are available in Jensen (1980), Reynolds (1982b), and Reynolds and Brown (1984). The most popular methods are reviewed below, along with a summary of findings from each area of inquiry. The sections are organized primarily by methodology within each content area of research (i.e., research into content, construct, and predictive validity).

Bias in Content Validity

Bias in the item content of intelligence tests is one of the favorite topics of those who decry the use of standardized tests with minorities (e.g., Hilliard, 1979; Jackson, 1975; Williams, 1970; Wright & Isenstein, 1977). As previously noted, the earliest work in bias centered around content. Typically, critics review the items of a test and single out specific items as being biased because (a) the items ask for information that minority or disadvantaged children have not had equal opportunity to learn; (b) minority children are inappropriately penalized for giving answers that would be correct in their own culture but not that of the test maker; and/or (c) the wording of the questions is unfamiliar, and a minority child who may know the correct answer may not be able to respond because he or she does not understand the question. Each of these three criticisms, when accurate, has the same basic empirical result: The item becomes relatively more difficult for minority group members than for the majority population. This leads directly to a definition of content bias for aptitude tests that allows empirical assessment of the phenomenon: An item or subscale of a test is considered to be biased in content when it is demonstrated to be relatively more difficult for members of one group than for members of another, in a situation where the general ability level of the groups being compared is held constant and no reasonable theoretical rationale exists to explain group differences on the item (or subscale) in question.

One method of locating suspicious test items requires that item difficulties be determined separately for each group under consideration. If any individual item or series of items appears to be exceptionally difficult for the members of any group, relative to other items on the test, the item is considered potentially biased and removed from the test. A widespread approach to identifying biased items involves analysis of variance (ANOVA) and several closely related procedures wherein the group × item interaction term is of interest (e.g., Angoff & Ford, 1973).

The definition of content bias set forth above actually requires that the differences between groups be the same for every item on the test. Thus, in the ANOVA procedure, the group × item interaction should not yield a significant result. Whenever the differences in items are not uniform (i.e., a significant group × item interaction does exist), one may contend that biased items exist. Earlier in this area of research, it was hoped that the empirical analysis of tests at the item level would result in the identification of a category of items having similar content as biased, and that such items could then be avoided in future test development (Flaugher, 1978). Very little similarity among items determined to be biased has been found; no one has been able to identify those characteristics that cause the item to be biased. It does seem that poorly written, sloppy, and ambiguous items tend to be identified as biased with greater frequency than those items typically encountered in a well-constructed standardized instrument. The variable at issue, then, may be item reliability. Item reliabilities are typically not large, and poorly written or ambiguous test items can easily have reliabilities approaching zero. Decreases in reliability are known to increase the probability of the occurrence of bias (Linn & Werts, 1971). Informal inventories and locally derived tests are much more likely to be biased than professionally written standardized tests that have been scrutinized for bias in the items and whose item characteristics are known.

Once items have been identified as biased under the procedures described above, attempts have been made to eliminate the bias by eliminating the offending items and rescoring the tests. As pointed out by Flaugher (1978) and Flaugher and Schrader (1978), however, little is gained by this tactic. Mean differences in performance between groups are affected only slightly, and the test becomes more difficult for everyone involved, because the eliminated items typically have moderate to low difficulty. When race × item interactions have been found, the interaction typically accounts for a very small proportion of variance. For example, in analyzing items on the WISC-R, Jensen (1976), Sandoval and Mille (1979) found the group × item interaction to account for only 2% to 5% of the variance in performance. Using a similar technique with the Wonderlic Personnel Test, Jensen (1977) found the race × item interaction to account for only about 5% of the test score variance. Thus the elimination of the offending items can be expected to have little, if any, significant effect. These analyses have been of a post hoc nature (i.e., conducted after the tests have been standardized), however, and the use of empirical methods for determining item bias during the test development phase (as with the K-ABC) is to be encouraged.

With multiple-choice tests, another level of complexity is added to the examination of content bias. With a multiple-choice question, three or four distractors are typically given in addition to the correct response. Distractors may be examined for their attractiveness (the relative frequency with which they are chosen) across groups. When distractors are found to be disproportionately attractive for members of any particular group, the item may be defined as biased. When items are constructed to have an equal distribution of responses to each distractor for the total test population, then chi-square can be used to examine the distribution of choices for each distractor for each group.

Jensen (1976) investigated the distribution of wrong responses for two multiple-choice intelligence tests, the Peabody Picture Vocabulary Test (PPVT) and Raven's Progressive Matrices (Raven). Each of these two tests was individually administered to 600 white and 400 black children between the ages of 6 and 12. The analysis of incorrect responses for the PPVT indicated that the errors were distributed in a nonrandom fashion over the distractors for a large number of items. No racial bias in response patterns occurred, however, as the disproportionate choice of distractors followed the same pattern for blacks and whites. On the Raven, blacks made different types of errors than whites, but only on a small number of items. Jensen followed up these items and compared the black response pattern to the response pattern of white children at a variety of age levels. For every item showing differences in black-white response patterns, the black response could be duplicated by the response patterns of whites approximately 2 years younger than blacks.

Veale and Foreman (1983) have advocated inspecting multiple-choice tests for bias in distractor or "foil" response distribution as a means of refining tests *before* they are finalized for the marketplace. They note that there are many instances whereby unbiased external criteria (e.g., achievement or ability) or culturally valid tests are not readily accessible for detecting bias in the measure under study. Veale and Foreman add that inspection of incorrect responses to distractor items can often lead to greater insight concerning cultural bias in any given question than would inspection of percentage of correct responses across groups. Veale and Foreman (1983) provide the statistical analyses for their "overpull probability model," along with the procedures for measuring cultural variation and diagramming the source of bias within any given item.

Investigation of item bias during test development is certainly not restricted to multiple-choice items and methods such as those outlined by Veale and Foreman. The possibilities are numerous (see Jensen, 1980, chapter 9). For example, Scheuneman (1987) has used the results of linear methodology on Graduate Record Examination (GRE) item data to show interesting influences on black-white performance when item characteristics (e.g., vocabulary content, one true or one false answer to be selected, diagrams to be used or not used, use of antonym items) are uniformly investigated. Although Scheuneman indicates that future research of this type should reduce the number of variables to address (there are 16 hypotheses), the results nonetheless suggest that bias or content research across groups is a viable way in which to determine whether differential effects can "be demonstrated through the manipulation of relatively stable characteristics of test items" (p. 116).

Scheuneman presented pairs of items, with the designated characteristic of a question format under study present in one item and absent or modified in the other. Paired experimental items were administered in the experimental section of the GRE general test given in December 1982. Results indicated that certain "item elements" (common in general form to a variety of questions) appeared to have a differential impact on black and white performance. For example, significant group × version interactions were seen for one correct true versus one correct false response and for adding/modifying prefixes/suffixes to the stimulus word in antonym items. The question is thus raised as to whether the items showing differential impact are measuring the content domain (e.g., verbal, quantitative, or analytical thinking) as opposed to an aspect of "element" within the presentation to some degree. Scheuneman concludes that more research is needed to establish ways in which more systematic rules and procedures of test construction can be developed.

Another approach to the identification of biased items has been pursued by Jensen (1976). According to Jensen, if a test contains items that are disproportionately difficult for one group of examinees as compared to another, the correlation of "*P* decrements" (the difference in difficulty from one item to the next) between adjacent items will be low for the two groups. Jensen (1974, 1976) also contends that if a test contains biased items, the correlation between the rank order of item difficulties for one race with that for another will also be low. Jensen (1974, 1976, 1977) calculated cross-racial correlations of item difficulties for large samples of black and white children on five major intelligence tests: the PPVT, the Raven, the revised Stanford-Binet Intelligence Scale (Form L-M), the WISC-R, and the Wonderlic Personnel Test. Cross-racial correlations of *P* decrements were reported for several of the scales. Jensen's results are summarized in Table 1, along with the results of several other investigators also employing Jensen's methodology.

As is readily apparent in Table 1, little evidence to support any consistent content bias within any of the scales investigated was found. The consistently large magnitude of the cross-racial correlations of *P* decrements is impressive and indicates a general lack of content bias in the instruments as a whole. As previously noted, some individual items were identified as biased; yet they collectively accounted for only 2% to 5% of the variance in performance differences and showed no detectable pattern in item content.

This method has proved popular with some test publishers who desire to look at the items on a test as a group, even though this approach may be overly sensitive. Using the most recent version of the Detroit Tests of Learning Aptitude (DTLA-3), Hammill (1991) reported correlations of *P* decrements exceeding .90 for all subtests, with most exceeding .95. Similar results have been reported for other aptitude measures. On the 14 subtests of the Test of Memory and Learning (TOMAL), Reynolds and Bigler (1994) report correlations across *P* decrements by gender and ethnicity that all exceed .90, with most again above .95.

Another approach to this question is to use the partial correlation between a demographic or other nominal variable and item score, where the correlation between total test score and the variable of interest has been removed from the relationship. If a significant partial correlation exists, say, between race and an item score after the race–total test score relationship has been partialed, then the item is performing differentially across race within ability level. Bias has been demonstrated at this point under the definition offered above. The use of the partial correlation (typically a partial point–biserial *r*) is the simplest and perhaps the most powerful of the item bias detection approaches, but its development is relatively recent and its use not yet common. An example of its application may be found in Reynolds, Willson, and Chatman (1984).

A common practice in recent times has been a return to including expert judgment by professionals and members of minority groups in the item selection for new psychological and educational tests. This approach was used in development of the K-ABC, the revision of the Wechsler Preschool and Primary Scale of Intelligence (WPPSI-R), the PPVT-R, and a number of other contemporary tests. The practice typically asks for an "armchair" inspection of individual items as a means of locating and expurgating biased components to the measure under development. Because, as previously noted, no detectable pattern or common

Table 1 Cross-Racial Analysis of Content Bias for Five Major Intelligence Scales

Scale	Cross-racial correlation of rank order of item difficulties[a]	
	Black–White[b]	White–Mexican American[b]
Peabody Picture Vocabulary Test (Jensen, 1974)	.99 (.79), .98 (.65)	.98 (.78), .98 (.66)
Raven's Progressive Matrices (Jensen, 1974)	.99 (.98), .99 (.96)	.99 (.99), .99 (.97)
Stanford-Binet Intelligence Scale (Jensen, 1976)	.96	
Wechsler Intelligence Scale for Children-Revised		
(Jensen, 1976)	.95	
(Sandoval, 1979)[c]	.98 (.87)	.99 (.91)
(Mille, 1979 [1949 WISC])	.96, .95	
Wonderlic Personnel Test (Jensen, 1977)	.94 (.81)	

[a]Correlation of *P* decrements across race is included in parentheses if reported.
[b]Where two sets of correlations are presented, data were reported separately for males and females and are listed males first. The presence of a single correlation indicates that data were pooled across gender.
[c]Median values for the 10 WISC-R subtests, excluding Digit Span and Coding.

characteristic of individual items statistically shown to be biased has been observed (given reasonable care in the item-writing stage), it seems reasonable to question this approach to determining biased items. The bulk of scientific data since the pioneering work of McGurk (1951) has not supported the position that anyone can—upon surface inspection—detect the degree to which any given item will function differentially across groups (Shepard, 1982).

Several researchers since McGurk's time have identified items as being disproportionately more difficult for minority group members than for members of the majority culture and have subsequently compared their results with a panel of expert judges. The data have provided some interesting results. Although examples of the failure of judges to identify biased items now abound, two studies demonstrate this failure most clearly. After identifying the eight most and eight least racially discriminating items on the Wonderlic Personnel Test, Jensen (1976) asked panels of five black psychologists and five white psychologists to sort out the most and least discriminating items when only these 16 items were presented to them. The judges sorted the items at a level no better than chance. Sandoval and Mille (1979) conducted a somewhat more extensive analysis, using items from the WISC-R. These two researchers had 38 black, 22 Mexican-American, and 40 white university students from Spanish, history, and education classes identify items from the WISC-R that would be more difficult for a minority child than a white child and items that would be equally difficult for each group. A total of 45 WISC-R items were presented to each judge; these items included the 15 most difficult items for blacks as compared to whites, the 15 most difficult items for Mexican Americans as compared to whites, and the 15 items showing the most nearly identical difficulty indices for minority and white children. The judges were asked to read each question and determine whether they thought the item was (1) easier for minority than for white children, (2) easier for white than for minority children, or (3) of equal difficulty for white and minority children.

Sandoval and Mille's (1979) results indicated that the judges were not able to differentiate accurately between items that were more difficult for minorities and items that were of equal difficulty across groups. The effects of the judges' ethnic background on the accuracy of item bias judgments were also considered. Minority and nonminority judges did not differ in their ability to identify accurately biased items, nor did they differ with regard to the type of incorrect identification they tended to make. The authors' two major conclusions were that "(1) judges are not able to detect items which are more difficult for a minority child than an Anglo child, and (2) the ethnic background of the judge makes no difference in accuracy of item selection for minority children" (p. 6). In each of these studies, the most extreme items were used, which should have given the judges an advantage.

Anecdotal evidence is also available to refute the assumption that armchair analyses of test bias in item content are accurate. Far and away, the most widely cited example of a biased intelligence test item is item 6 of the WISC-R Comprehension subtest: "What is the thing to do if a boy (girl) much smaller than yourself starts to fight with you?" This item is generally considered to be biased against black children in particular, because of the scoring criteria. According to the item's critics, the most logical response for a black child is to "fight back," yet this is a 0-point response. The correct (2-point) response is to walk away and avoid fighting with the child—a response that critics claim invites disaster in the black culture, where children are taught to fight back and would not "know" the "correct white response." Black responses to this item have been empirically investigated in several studies, with the same basic results: The item is relatively easier for black children than for white children. When all items on the WISC-R are ranked separately according to the difficulty level for blacks and whites, this item is the 42nd least difficult item for black children and the 47th least difficult for white children (Jensen, 1976). Mille (1979), in a large-sample study of bias, reached a similar conclusion, stating that this item "is relatively easier for blacks than it is for whites" (p. 163). The results of these empirical studies with large samples of black and white children are unequivocal: When matched for overall general intellectual skill, more black than white children will get this item correct—the very item most often singled out as a blatant example of the inherent bias of intelligence tests against blacks (see also Reynolds & Brown, 1984).

Even without empirical support for its accuracy, a number of prestigious writers support the continued use of the "face validity" approach of using a panel of minority judges to identify allegedly biased test items (Kaufman, 1979; Sandoval & Mille, 1979). Those who support the continued use of this technique see it as a method of gaining greater rapport with the public. As pointed out by Sandoval and Mille (1979), "Public opinion, whether it is supported by empirical findings, or based on emotion, can serve as an obstacle to the use of a measurement instrument" (p. 7). The elimination of items that are offensive or otherwise objectionable to any substantive segment of the population for whom the test is intended seems an appropriate action that may aid in the public's acceptance of new and better psychological assessment tools. The subjective-judgment approach, however, should not be allowed to supplant the use of more sophisticated analyses in the determination of biased items. Instead it should serve as a supplemental procedure, and items identified through this method (provided that some interrater agreement can be obtained—an aspect of the subjective method yet to be demonstrated) as objectionable can be eliminated when a psychometrically equivalent (or better) item can be obtained as a replacement and the intent of the item is kept intact (e.g., with a criterion-referenced measure, the new item must be designed to measure the same objective). The reliability, construct validity, and predictive validity of measures should not suffer any substantial losses for the purposes of increasing face validity.

Researchers such as Tittle (1982) have stressed that the possibility of and need for cooperation between those advocating statistical validity and those advocating face validity in nonbiased test construction are greater than one might think, given the above-cited research. Judgmental analysis allows for the *perception* of fairness in items, tests, and evaluations, and this perception should not be taken lightly. Tittle (1982) argues that "judgmental methods arise from a different, nonstatistical ground. In examining fairness or bias primarily on statistical grounds, we may again be witnessing a technical solution to a problem that is broader than the technical issues" (p. 34). Tests under construction should include definitive information concerning the nonbiased nature of the measure from a statistical standpoint, in addition to support by minority groups or other interested parties who have had the opportunity to inspect the test for the perception of fairness. Cronbach (1980) does not find the issue of fairness as determined by subjective judgment to be outside the realm of test validation: "The politicization of testing ought not be surprising. Test data influence the fortunes of individuals and the support given to human service programs" (p. 100). Tittle (1982) argues that the general field of test development requires greater consensus regarding specific, multidimensional steps taken in formulating "fair" measures, because "fairness" in testing will never be realistically viewed by the public from a unidimensional statistical standpoint.

Considerably less work has been conducted in all areas of bias relative to personality testing, where there would appear to be greater opportunity for cultural, social, and ethnic factors to act to produce bias. Research on item bias of personality measures, though less extensive than with aptitude measures, has produced results similar to those with aptitude measures (see especially Reynolds & Harding, 1983, and Moran, 1990).

Thus far, this section has focused on the identification of biased items. Several studies evaluating other hypotheses have provided data that are relevant to the issue of content bias of psychological tests, particularly the WISC-R. (Although this test is now largely superseded in practice by WISC-III, little data regarding bias are available specifically on this new scale.)

Jensen and Figueroa (1975) investigated black-white differences in mental test scores as a function of differences in so-called Level I (rote learning and memory) and Level II (complex cognitive processing) abilities. These researchers tested a large number of blacks and whites on the WISC-R Digit Span subtest and then analyzed the data separately for digits forward and backward. The content of the digits-forward and digits-backward procedures is the same. Thus, if score differences are attributable only to bias in content validity, score differences across race should remain constant for the two tasks. In contrast, the information-processing demands of the two tasks are quite different, the relative level of performance on the two tasks should not be the same if blacks and whites differ in their ability to process information according to the demands of the two tasks. Jensen and Figueroa (1975) found the latter to be the case. The black-white score difference on digits backward was more than twice the magnitude of the difference for digits forward. Granted, this methodology can provide only indirect evidence regarding the content validity of an instrument; however, its importance is in providing a different view of the issues and an alternative research strategy. Because the Jensen and Figueroa results do not indicate any content bias in the Digit Span subtest, they add to a growing body of literature that strongly suggests the lack of cultural bias in well-constructed, standardized tests.

Another study (Reynolds & Jensen, 1983) examined each of the 12 WISC-R subtests for cultural bias against blacks using a variation of the group × item

ANOVA methodology discussed earlier. Reynolds and Jensen matched 270 black children with 270 white children from the WISC-R standardization sample on the basis of gender and WISC-R full-scale IQ. IQs were required to match within one standard error of measurement (about 3 points). When multiple matching cases were encountered, children were matched on the basis of SES. Matching the two groups of children on the basis of the full-scale IQ essentially equated the two groups for *g*. Therefore, examining black-white differences in performance on each subtest of the WISC-R made it possible to determine which, if any, of the subtests were disproportionately difficult for blacks or whites. A significant *F* ratio in the multivariate analysis of variance (MANOVA) for the 12 WISC-R subtests was followed with univariate *F* tests between black and white means on each of the 12 WISC-R subtests.

A summary of the Reynolds and Jensen (1983) results is presented in Table 2. Blacks exceeded whites in performance on two subtests: Digit Span and Coding. Whites exceeded blacks in performance on three subtests: Comprehension, Object Assembly, and Mazes. A trend was apparent for blacks to perform at a higher level on the Arithmetic subtest, whereas whites tended to exceed blacks on the Picture Arrangement subtest. Although these results can be interpreted to indicate bias in several of the WISC-R subtests, the actual differences were very small (typically on the order of 0.10 to 0.15 standard deviations), and the amount of variance in performance associated with ethnic group membership was less than 5% in each case. The results are also reasonably consistent with Jensen's theory of mental test score differences and their relationship to Level I and Level II abilities. The Digit Span and Coding subtests are clearly the best measures of Level I abilities on the WISC-R, whereas Comprehension, Object Assembly, and Mazes are more closely associated with Level II abilities.

From a large number of studies employing a wide range of methodology, a relatively clear picture emerges: Content bias in well-prepared standardized tests is irregular in its occurrence, and no common characteristics of items that are found to be biased can be ascertained by expert judges (minority or nonminority). The variance in group score differences on mental tests associated with ethnic group membership when content bias has been found is relatively small (typically ranging from 2% to 5%). Even this small amount of bias has been seriously questioned, as Hunter, Schmidt, & Rauschenberger (1984) describe such findings as basically methodological artifacts.

Table 2. Means, Standard Deviations, and Univariate *F*'s for Comparison of Performance on Specific WISC-R Subtests by Groups of Blacks and Whites Matched for WISC-R Full Scale IQ

	Blacks		Whites				
WISC-R Variable	$\bar{X}$	*SD*	$\bar{X}$	*SD*	D^a	F^b	*p*
Information	8.40	2.53	8.24	2.62	−.16	0.54	NS
Similarities	8.24	2.78	8.13	2.78	−.11	0.22	NS
Arithmetic	8.98	2.62	8.62	2.58	−.36	2.52	.10
Vocabulary	8.21	2.61	8.27	2.58	+.06	0.06	NS
Comprehension	8.14	2.40	8.58	2.47	+.44	4.27	.05
Digit span	9.51	3.09	8.89	2.83	+.62	6.03	.01
Picture completion	8.49	2.88	8.60	2.58	+.11	0.18	NS
Picture arrangement	8.45	2.92	8.79	2.89	+.34	1.78	.10
Block design	8.06	2.54	8.33	2.76	+.27	1.36	NS
Object assembly	8.17	2.90	8.68	2.70	+.51	4.41	.05
Coding	9.14	2.81	8.65	2.80	−.49	4.30	.05
Mazes	8.69	3.14	9.19	2.98	+.50	3.60	.05
Verbal IQ	89.63	12.13	89.61	12.07	−.02	0.04	NS
Performance IQ	89.29	12.22	90.16	11.67	+.87	0.72	NS
Full-scale IQ	88.61	11.48	88.96	11.35	+.35	0.13	NS

Note: NS = not significant
[a]White *X* − black *X* difference.
[b]Degrees of freedom = 1, 538.

Although the search for common "biased" item characteristics will continue, and psychologists must pursue the public relations issues of face validity, armchair claims of cultural bias in aptitude tests have found no empirical support in a large number of actuarial studies contrasting the performance of a variety of racial groups on items and subscales of the intelligence scales most widely employed in the United States. Neither differential nor single-group validity has been demonstrated.

Bias in Construct Validity

There is no single method for the accurate determination of the construct validity of educational and psychological tests. Defining bias in construct validity thus requires a general statement that can be researched from a variety of viewpoints with a broad range of methodology. The following rather parsimonious definition is proffered: Bias exists in regard to construct validity when a test is shown to measure different hypothetical traits (psychological constructs) for one group than for another, or to measure the same trait but with differing degrees of accuracy.

As befits the concept of construct validity, many different methods have been employed to examine existing tests for potential bias in construct validity. One of the most popular and necessary empirical approaches to investigating construct validity is factor analysis (Anastasi, 1982; Cronbach, 1976). Factor analysis, as a procedure, identifies clusters of test items or clusters of subtests of psychological or educational tests that correlate highly with one another, and less so or not at all with other subtests or items. It thus allows one to determine patterns of interrelationships of performance among groups of individuals. For example, if several subtests of an intelligence scale load highly on (are members of) the same factor, then if a group of individuals score high on one of these subtests, they would be expected to score at a high level on other subtests that load highly on that factor. Psychologists attempt to determine, through a review of the test content and correlates of performance on the factor in question, what psychological trait underlies performance; in a more hypothesis-testing approach, they will make predictions concerning the pattern of factor loadings. Hilliard (1979), one of the more vocal critics of IQ tests on the basis of cultural bias, has pointed out one of the potential areas of bias in comparisons of the factor analytic results of tests across races:

> If the IQ test is a valid and reliable test of "innate" ability or abilities, then the factors which emerge on a given test should be the same from one population to another, since "intelligence" is asserted to be a set of mental processes. Therefore, while the configuration of scores of a particular group on the factor profile would be expected to differ, logic would dictate that the factors themselves would remain the same. (p. 53)

Although researchers do not necessarily agree that identical factor analyses of an instrument speak to the innateness of the abilities being measured, consistent factor analytic results across populations do provide strong evidence that whatever is being measured by the instrument is being measured in the same manner and is, in fact, the same construct within each group. The information derived from comparative factor analysis across populations is directly relevant to the use of educational and psychological tests in diagnosis and other decision-making functions. Psychologists, in order to make consistent interpretations of test score data, must be certain that a test measures the same variable across populations.

Two basic approaches, each with a number of variations, have been employed to compare factor analytic results across populations. The more popular approach asks how similar the results are for each group; the less popular approach asks whether the results show a statistically significant difference between groups. The most sophisticated approach to the latter question has been the work of Joreskog (c.f., 1971) in simultaneous factor analysis in several populations and now basically represented in the LISREL series of computer programs. Little has been done with this approach, however, within the context of test bias research. Mille (1979) has demonstrated the use of a simpler method (actually developed by Jensen and presented in detail in Jensen, 1980) for testing the significance of the difference between factors for two populations.

As one part of a comprehensive internal analysis of test bias on the 1949 WISC, Mille (1979) compared the first principal-component factor across race for blacks and whites at the preschool, first-grade, third-grade, and fifth-grade levels. This factor, often thought of as a measure of *g*, did not differ significantly across race at any age level. Mille's results with the WISC indicate that factor loadings on *g* are essentially equivalent and that when score differences occur between groups, the differences reflect whatever is common to all variables that make up the test, rather than some personological or moderator variable that is specific to one group.

A number of techniques have been developed to measure the similarity of factors across groups. The two most common methods of determining factorial similarity or factorial invariance involve the direct comparison of factor loadings across groups. The two primary techniques for this comparison are (a) the calculation of a coefficient of congruence (Harman, 1976) between the loadings of corresponding factors for two groups; and (b) the simple calculation of a Pearson product-moment coefficient of correlation between the factor loadings of the corresponding factors. The latter technique, though used with some frequency, is less satisfactory than the use of the coefficient of congruence, because some of the assumptions underlying the Pearson *r* may be violated in the comparison of factor loadings. When one is determining the degree of similarity of factors, a value of .90 or greater is typically, though arbitrarily, taken to indicate equivalent factors (factorial invariance). The most popular methods of calculating factorial similarity produce quite similar results (Reynolds & Harding, 1983), however, at least in large-sample studies.

In contrast to Hilliard's (1979) strong statement that studies of factorial similarity across race have not been reported in the technical literature, a number of such studies have appeared dealing with a number of different tests. The focus here is primarily on studies comparing factor analytic results across races for aptitude tests.

Because the WISC and its successor, the WISC-R, have been the most widely employed individual intelligence tests with school-age children, it is appropriate that the cross-race structure of these two instruments has received extensive investigation for both normal and referral populations of children. Using a large, random sample, Reschly (1978) compared the factor structure of the WISC-R across four racially identifiable groups: whites, blacks, Mexican Americans, and Native American Papagos, all from the southwestern United States. Consistent with the findings of previous researchers with the 1949 WISC (c.f., Silverstein, 1973), Reschly (1978) reported substantial congruency of factors across races when the two-factor solutions were compared (the two-factor solution typically reiterated Wechsler's a priori grouping of the subtests into verbal and performance scales). The 12 coefficients of congruence for comparisons of the two-factor solution across all combinations of racial groupings ranged only from .97 to .99, denoting factorial equivalence of this solution across groups. Reschly also compared three-factor solutions (which typically include verbal comprehension, perceptual organization, and freedom-from-distractibility factors), finding congruence only between whites and Mexican Americans. These findings are also consistent with previous research with the WISC (Semler & Iscoe, 1966). The *g* factor present in the WISC-R was shown to be congruent across race, as was also demonstrated by Mille (1979) for the WISC. Reschly (1978) concluded that the usual interpretation of the WISC-R full-scale IQ as a measure of overall intellectual ability appears to be equally appropriate for whites, blacks, Mexican Americans, and Native American Papagos. Jensen (1985) has presented compelling data indicating that the black-white discrepancy seen in major tests of aptitude reflects primarily the *g* factor. Reschly also concluded that the verbal-performance scale distinction on the WISC-R is equally appropriate across race and that there is strong evidence for the integrity of the WISC-R's construct validity for a variety of populations.

Support for Reschly's (1978) conclusions is available from a variety of other studies of the WISC and WISC-R. Applying a hierarchical factor analytic method developed by Wherry and Wherry (1969), Vance and Wallbrown (1978) factor analyzed the intercorrelation matrix of the WISC-R subtests for 150 referred blacks from the Appalachian region of the United States. The two-factor hierarchical solution determined was highly similar to hierarchical factor solutions determined for the standardization samples of the Wechsler scales generally (Blaha, Wallbrown, & Wherry, 1975; Wallbrown, Blaha, & Wherry, 1973). Vance and Wallbrown's (1978) results with the WISC-R are also consistent with a previous hierarchical factor analysis with the 1949 WISC for a group of disadvantaged blacks and whites (Vance, Huelsman, & Wherry, 1976).

Several more recent studies comparing the WISC-R factor structure across races for normal and referral populations of children have also provided increased support for the generality of Reschly's (1978) conclusions and the results of the other investigators cited above. Oakland and Feigenbaum (1979) factor analyzed the 12 WISC-R subtests' intercorrelations separately for stratified (race, age, sex, SES) random samples of normal white, black, and Mexican-American children from an urban school district of the northwestern United States. Pearson *r*'s were calculated between corresponding factors for each group. For the g factor, the black-white correlation between factor loadings was .95, the Mexican American–white correlation was .97, and the black–Mexican American correlation was .96. Similar comparisons across all WISC-R variables produced correlations ranging only from .94 to .99. Oakland and Feigenbaum (1979) concluded that the results of their factor analyses "do not reflect bias with respect to construct validity for these three racial-ethnic . . . groups" (p. 973).

Gutkin and Reynolds (1981) determined the factorial similarity of the WISC-R for groups of black and white children from the WISC-R standardization sample. This study is particularly important to examine in determining the construct validity of the WISC-R across races, because of the sample employed in the investigation. The sample included 1,868 white and 305 black children obtained in a stratified random sampling procedure designed to mimic the 1970 U.S. census data on the basis of age, sex, race, SES, geographic region of residence, and community size. Similarity of the WISC-R factor structure across race was investigated by comparing the black and white groups for the two- and three-factor solutions on (a) the magnitude of unique variances, (b) the pattern of subtest loadings on each factor, (c) the portion of total variance accounted for by common factor variance, and (d) the percentage of common factor variance accounted for by each factor. Coefficients of congruence comparing the unique variances, the *g* factor, the two-factor solutions, and the three-factor solutions across races all achieved a value of .99. The portion of total variance accounted for by each factor was the same in both the two- and three-factor racial groups. Gutkin and Reynolds (1980) concluded that for white and black children the WISC-R factor structure was essentially invariant, and that no evidence of single-group or differential construct validity could be found.

Subsequent studies comparing the WISC-R factor structure for referral populations of white and Mexican-American children have also strongly supported the construct validity of the WISC-R across races. Dean (1979) compared three-factor WISC-R solutions across races for whites and Mexican-Americans referred because of learning problems in the regular classroom. Analyzing the 10 regular WISC-R subtests, Dean reported coefficients of congruence between corresponding factors of .84 for Factor 1 (Verbal Comprehension), .89 for Factor 2 (Perceptual Organization), and .88 for Factor 3 (Freedom from Distractibility). Although not quite reaching the typical value of .90 required to indicate equivalent factors, Dean's results do indicate a high degree of similarity. The relative strength of the various factors was also highly consistent across races.

Gutkin and Reynolds (1980) also compared two- and three-factor principal-factor solutions to the WISC-R across race for referral populations of white and Mexican-American children. Gutkin and Reynolds made additional comparisons of the factor solutions derived from their referral sample to solutions derived by Reschly (1978; personal communication, 1979), and also to solutions from the WISC-R standardization sample. Coefficients of congruence for the Gutkin and Reynolds two-factor solutions for whites and Mexican-Americans were .98 and .91, respectively. The *g* factor showed a coefficient of congruence value of .99 across races. When Gutkin and Reynolds (1980) compared their solutions with those derived by Reschly (1978) for normal white, black, Mexican-American, and Papago children, and with results based on the WISC-R standardization sample, the coefficients of congruence all exceeded .90. When three-factor solutions were compared, the results were more varied but also supported the consistent similarity of WISC-R factor analytic results across race.

DeFries et al. (1974) administered 15 mental tests to large samples of Americans of Japanese or Chinese ancestry. After examining the pattern of intercorrelations among the 15 tests for each of these two ethnic groups, DeFries et al. concluded that the cognitive organization of the two groups was virtually identical. In reviewing this study, Willerman (1979) concluded, "The similarity in factorial structure [between the two groups] suggests that the manner in which the tests are constructed by the subjects is similar regardless of ethnicity and that the tests are measuring the same mental abilities in the two groups" (p. 468).

At the adult level, Kaiser (1986) and Scholwinski (1985) have analyzed the revised Wechsler Adult Intelligence Scale (WAIS-R; Wechsler, 1981) and reported substantial similarity between factor structures for black and white samples obtained from the WAIS-R standardization data. Kaiser (1986) completed separate hierarchical analyses for all black subjects (n = 192) and white subjects (n = 1,664) in the WAIS-R standardization sample and calculated coefficients of congruence of .99 for the *g* factor, .98 for the Verbal factor, and .97 for the Performance or nonverbal factor. Scholwinski (1985) selected 177 black and 177 white subjects from the standardization sample, closely matched on the basis of age, sex, and full-scale IQ. Separate factor analyses again showed that structures generated from the Wechsler format showed strong similarity across black-white groups beyond childhood and adolescent levels of development.

At the preschool level, factor analytic results also tend to show consistency of construct validity across races, though the results are less clear-cut. In a comparison of separate factor analyses of the McCarthy Scales of Children's Abilities (McCarthy, 1972) for groups of black and white children, Kaufman and DiCuio (1975) concluded that the scales showed a high degree of factorial similarity between the two races. The conclusion, however, was not straightforward; four factors were found for the blacks and three for the whites. Kaufman and DiCuio based their conclusion of factorial similarity on the finding that each white factor had a coefficient of congruence of .85 to .93 with one black factor. One black factor on the McCarthy scales had no white counterpart with a coefficient of congruence beyond .74 (the Memory factor), and the black and white Motor factors showed a coefficient of congruence of only .85.

When investigating the factor structure of the Wechsler Preschool and Primary Scale of Intelligence (WPPSI) across race, Kaufman and Hollenbeck (1974) found much "cleaner" factors for blacks and whites than with the McCarthy scales. The two factors, essentially mirroring Wechsler's verbal and performance scales, were virtually identical between the races. Both factors also appear closely related to the hierarchical factor solution presented by Wallbrown et al. (1973) for blacks and whites on the WPPSI. When comparing factor analyses of the Goodenough-Harris Human Figure Drawing Test scoring item, Merz (1970) found highly similar factor structures for blacks, whites, Mexican Americans, and Native Americans.

In a more comprehensive study employing seven major preschool tests (the McCarthy Draw-A-Design and Draw-A-Child subtests, the Lee-Clark Reading Readiness Tests, the Tests of Basic Experiences Language and Mathematics subtests, the revised Preschool Inventory, and the Metropolitan Readiness Test), Reynolds (1980a) reached a similar conclusion. A two-factor solution was determined with this battery for blacks, whites, males, and females. Coefficients of congruence ranged only from .95 to .99 for the two factors, and the average degree of intercorrelation was essentially the same for all groups, as were eigenvalues and the percentage of variance accounted for by the factors. Reynolds (1980a) again concluded that the abilities being measured were invariant across race and that there was no evidence of differential or single-group construct validity of preschool tests across races or genders. The clear trend in studies of preschool tests' construct validity across race (and sex) is to uphold validity across groups. Such findings add support to the use of existing preschool screening measures with black and white children of both sexes in the very necessary process of early identification (Reynolds, 1979) of potential learning and behavior problems.

As is appropriate for studies of construct validity, comparative factor analysis has not been the only method of determining whether single-group or differential validity exists. Another method of investigation involves comparing internal-consistency reliability estimates across groups. Internal-consistency reliability is determined by the degree to which the items are all measuring a similar construct. To be unbiased with regard to construct validity, internal-consistency estimates should be approximately equal across races. This characteristic of tests has been investigated with blacks, whites, and Mexican Americans for a number of popular aptitude tests.

With groups of black and white adults, Jensen (1977) calculated internal-consistency estimates (using the Kuder-Richardson 21 formula) for the Wonderlic Personnel Test (a frequently used employment/aptitude test). Kuder-Richardson 21 values of .86 and .88 were found, respectively, for blacks and whites. Using Hoyt's formula, Jensen (1974) determined internal-consistency estimates of .96 on the Peabody Picture Vocabulary Test (PPVT) for groups of black, white, and Mexican American children. When children were categorized by gender within each racial grouping, the values ranged only from .95 to .97. On Raven's Progressive Matrices (colored), internal-consistency estimates were also quite similar across race and sex, ranging only from .86 to .91 for the six race-sex groupings. Thus Jensen's (1974, 1977) research with three popular aptitude tests shows no signs of differential or single-group validity with regard to homogeneity of test content or consistency of measurement across groups.

Sandoval (1979) and Oakland and Feigenbaum (1979) have extensively investigated internal consistency of the various WISC-R subtests (excluding Digit Span and Coding, for which internal-consistency analysis is inappropriate) for whites, blacks, and Mexican Americans. Both of these studies included large samples of children, with Sandoval's (1979) including more than 1,000. Sandoval found internal-consistency estimates to be within .04 of one another for all subtests except Object Assembly. This subtest was most reliable for blacks (.95), whereas it was about equally reliable for whites (.79) and Mexican Americans (.75). Oakland and Feigenbaum (1979) reported internal-consistency estimates that never differed by more than .06 among the three groups, again with the exception of Object Assembly. In this instance, Object Assembly was most reliable for whites (.76), with about equal reliabilities for blacks (.64) and Mexican Americans (.67). Oakland and Feigenbaum also compared reliabilities across sex, finding highly similar values for males and females. Dean (1977) examined the internal consistency of the WISC-R for Mexican-American children tested by white examiners. He reported internal-consistency reliability estimates consistent with, although slightly exceeding, values reported by Wechsler (1974) for the predominantly white standardization sample. The Bender-Gestalt test has also been reported to have similar internal-consistency estimates for whites (.84), blacks (.81), and Mexican Americans (.72), and for males (.81) and females (.80; Oakland & Feigenbaum, 1979).

In the review work of Moran (1990) and in a search for more recent work, it is apparent that only a few studies of the differential construct validity of personality tests have been undertaken, despite large mean differences across ethnicity and gender on such popular measures as the stalwart MMPI. A look at the newer MMPI-2 manual suggests gender differences in construct validity but provides no real evidence either way. A few studies of factorial similarity of instruments such as the Revised Children's Manifest Anxiety Scale show little bias and high degrees of similarity by ethnicity and gender (Moran, 1990; Reynolds & Paget, 1981).

Construct validity of a large number of popular psychometric assessment instruments has been investigated across races and genders with a variety of populations of minority and white children and with a divergent set of methodologies (see Reynolds, 1982b, for a review of methodologies). All roads have led to Rome: No consistent evidence of bias in construct validity has been found with any of the many tests investigated. This leads to the conclusion that psychological tests (especially aptitude tests) function in essentially the same manner, that test materials are perceived and reacted to in a similar manner, and that tests measure the same construct with equivalent accuracy for blacks, whites, Mexican Americans, and other American minorities of both sexes and at all levels of SES. Single-group validity and differential validity have not been found and probably do not exist with regard to well-constructed and well-standardized psychological and educational tests. This means that test score differences across race are real and not an artifact of test bias; that is, the tests are measuring the same constructs across these variables. These differences cannot be ignored. As Mille (1979) has succinctly stated, "If this . . . difference [in test scores] is the result of genetic factors, acceptance of the cultural bias hypothesis would be unfortunate. If the difference is the result of environmental factors, such acceptance would be tragic" (p. 162).

Bias in Predictive or Criterion-Related Validity

Evaluating bias in predictive validity of educational and psychological tests is less closely related to the evaluation of group mental test score differences than to the evaluation of individual test scores in a more absolute sense. This is especially true for aptitude (as opposed to diagnostic) tests, where the primary purpose of administration is the prediction of some specific future outcome or behavior. Internal analyses of bias (e.g., in content and construct validity) are less confounded than analyses of bias in predictive validity, however, because of the potential problems in bias in the criterion measure. Predictive validity is also strongly influenced by the reliability of criterion measures, which frequently is poor. The degree of relationship between a predictor and a criterion is restricted as a function of the square root of the product of the reliabilities of the two variables.

Arriving at a consensual definition of bias in predictive validity is also a difficult task, as has already been discussed. Yet from the standpoint of the practical applications of aptitude and intelligence tests, predictive validity is the most crucial form of validity in relation to test bias. Much of the discussion in professional journals concerning bias in predictive validity has centered around models of selection. These issues have been discussed previously in this chapter and are not reiterated here. Because this section is concerned with bias in respect to the test itself and not the social or political justifications of any one particular selection model, the Cleary et al. (1975) definition, slightly rephrased here, provides a clear and direct statement of test bias with regard to predictive validity: A test is considered biased with respect to predictive validity if the inference drawn from the test score is not made with the smallest feasible random error or if there is constant error in an inference or prediction as a function of membership in a particular group. This definition is a restatement of previous definitions by Cardall and Coffman (1964), Cleary (1968), and Potthoff (1966), and has been widely accepted (though certainly not without criticism; e.g., see Bernal, 1975; Linn & Werts, 1971; Schmidt & Hunger, 1974; Thorndike, 1971).

The evaluation of bias in prediction under the Cleary et al. (1975) definition (the regression definition) is quite straightforward. With simple regression, predictions take the form of $Y_i = aX_i + b$, where a is the regression coefficient and b is a constant. When this equation is graphed (forming a regression line), a represents the slope of the regression line and b and Y-intercept. Because our definition of fairness in predictive validity requires errors in prediction to be independent of group membership, the regression line formed for any pair of variables must be the same for each group for whom predictions are to be made. Whenever the slope or the intercept differs significantly across groups, there is bias in prediction if one attempts to use a regression equation based on the combined groups. When the regression equations for two (or more) groups are equivalent, prediction is the same for all groups. This condition is referred to variously as "homogeneity of regression across groups," "simultaneous regression," or "fairness in prediction."

Homogeneity of regression across groups is illustrated in Figure 1. In this case, the single regression equation is appropriate with all groups, any errors in prediction being random with respect to group membership (i.e., residuals uncorrelated with group membership). When homogeneity of regression does not occur, for "fairness in prediction" to occur, separate regression equations must be used for each group.

In actual clinical practice, regression equations are seldom generated for the prediction of future performance. Instead, some arbitrary or perhaps statistically derived cutoff score is determined, below which "failure" is predicted. For school performance, IQs two or more standard deviations below the test mean are used to infer a high probability of failure in the regular classroom if special assistance is not provided for the student in question. Essentially, then, clinicians are establishing mental prediction equations that are assumed to be equivalent across races, genders, and so on. Although these mental equations cannot be readily tested across groups, the actual form of criterion prediction can be compared across groups in several ways. Errors in prediction must be independent of group membership; if regression equations are equal, this condition is met. To test the hypothesis of simultaneous regression, slopes and intercepts must both be compared. An alternative method is the direct examination of residuals through ANOVA or a similar design (Reynolds, 1980b).

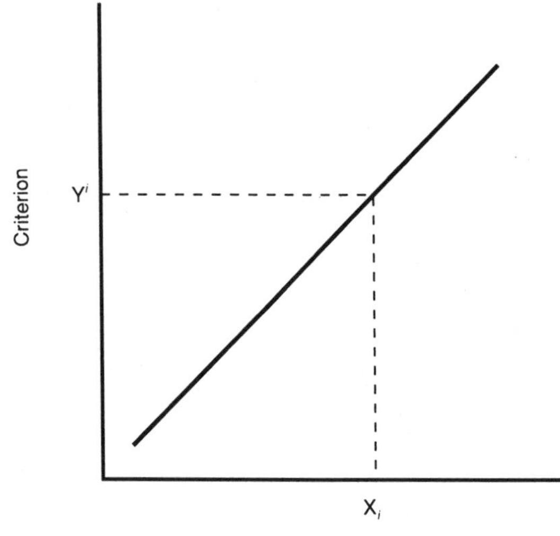

Figure 1. Equal slopes and intercepts result in homogeneity of regression that causes the regression lines for group a, group b, and the combined group c to be identical.

In the evaluation of slope and intercept values, Potthoff (1966) has described a useful technique that allows one to test simultaneously the equivalence of regression coefficients and intercepts across K independent groups with a single F ratio. If a significant F results, the researcher may then test the slopes and intercepts separately if information concerning which value differs is desired. When homogeneity of regression does not occur, there are three basic conditions that can result: (a) Intercept constants differ, (b) regression coefficients (slopes) differ, or (c) slopes and intercepts differ. These conditions are depicted pictorially in Figures 2, 3, and 4, respectively.

The regression coefficient is related to the correlation coefficient between the two variables and is one measure of the strength of the relationship between two variables. When intercepts differ and regression coefficients do not, a situation such as that shown in Figure 2 results. Relative accuracy of prediction is the same for the two groups (*a* and *b*); yet the use of a regression equation derived by combining the two groups results in bias that works against the group with the higher mean criterion score. Because the slope of the regression line is the same for all groups, the degree of error in prediction remains constant and does not fluctuate as a function of an individual's score on the independent variable. That is, regardless of group member *b*'s score on the predictor, the degree of underprediction in performance on the criterion is the same. As illustrated in Figure 2, the use of the common score of Y_c for a score of X overestimates how well members of group *a* will perform and underestimates the criterion performance of members of group *b*.

In Figure 3, nonparallel regression lines illustrate the case where intercepts are constant across groups but the slope of the line is different for each group. Here, too, the performance of the group with the higher mean criterion score is typically underpredicted when a common regression equation is applied. The amount of bias in prediction that results from using the common regression line is the distance of the score from the mean.

The most difficult, complex case of bias is represented in Figure 4. Here we see the result of significant differences in slopes and intercepts. Not only does the amount of bias in prediction accruing from the use of a common equation vary in this instance; the actual direction of bias can reverse, depending on the location of the individual's score in the distribution of the independent variable. Only in the case of Figure 4 do members of the group with the lower mean criterion score run the risk of having their performance on the criterion variable underpredicted by the application of a common regression equation.

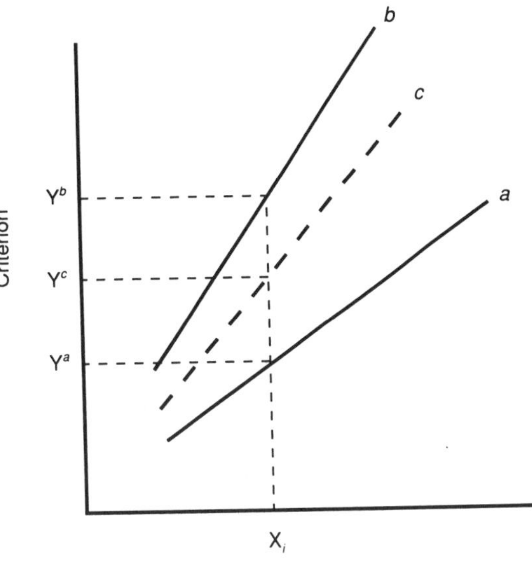

Figure 3. Equal intercepts and differing slopes result in nonparallel regression lines, with the degree of bias dependent on the distance of the individual's score (x_i) from the origin.

A considerable body of literature has developed regarding the differential predictive validity of tests across races for employment selection and college admissions. Little appears in this regard with reference to personality tests (Moran, 1990), however, and this is a major weakness in the literature. Recently, Zeidner (1990) showed similar predictive validity of test anxiety measures (against aptitude test criteria) for Israeli Eastern versus Western college students.

In a review of 866 black-white test validity comparisons from 39 studies of test bias in personnel selection, Hunter, Schmidt, & Hunter (1979) concluded that there was no evidence to substantiate hypotheses of differential or single-group validity with regard to the prediction to job performance across races for blacks and whites. A similar conclusion was reached by O'Conner, Wexley, and Alexander (1975). A number of studies have also focused on differential validity of the Scholastic Aptitude Test (SAT) in the prediction of college performance (typically measured by grade point average of GPA). In general, these studies have

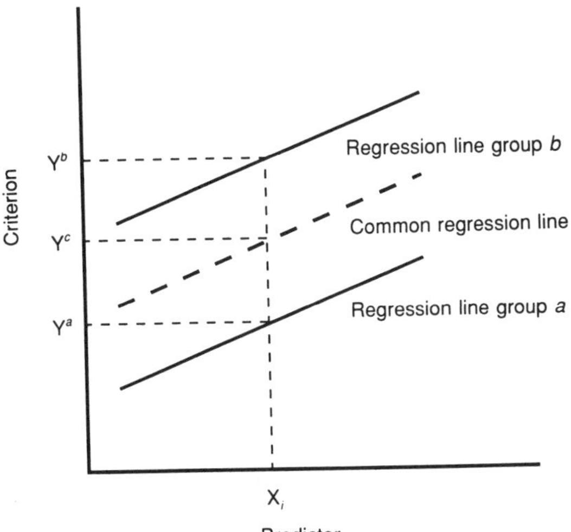

Figure 2. Equal slopes with differing intercepts result in parallel regression lines and a constant bias in prediction.

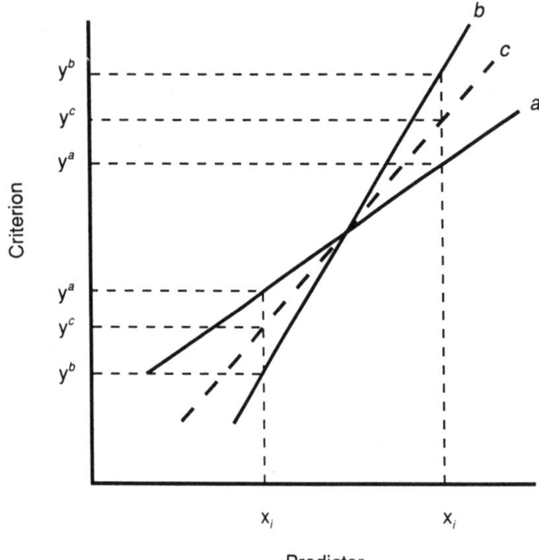

Figure 4. Differing slopes and intercepts result in the complex condition where the amount and the direction of the bias are a function of the distance of an individual's score from the origin.

found either no differences in the prediction of criterion performance for blacks and whites or a bias (underprediction of the criterion) against whites (Cleary et al., 1975). When bias against whites has been found, the differences between actual and predicted criterion scores, although statistically significant, have been quite small.

Reschly and Sabers (1979) evaluated the validity of WISC-R IQs in the prediction of Metropolitan Achievement Test (MAT) performance (Reading and Math subtests) for whites, blacks, Mexican Americans, and Native-American Papagos. The choice of the MAT as a criterion measure in studies of predictive bias is particularly appropriate, because item analysis procedures were employed (as described earlier) to eliminate racial bias in item content during the test construction phase. Anastasi (1986) has described the MAT as an excellent model of an achievement test designed to reduce or eliminate cultural bias. Reschly and Sabers's (1979) comparison of regression systems indicated bias in the prediction of the various achievement scores; again, however, the bias produced generally significant underprediction of white performance when a common regression equation was applied. Achievement test performance of the Native-American Papago group showed the greatest amount of overprediction of all nonwhite groups. Though some slope bias was evident, Reschly and Sabers typically found intercept bias resulting in parallel regression lines.

Using similar techniques, but including teacher ratings, Reschly and Reschly (1979) also investigated the predictive validity of WISC-R factor scores with the samples of white, black, Mexican-American, and Native-American Papago children. A significant relationship occurred between the three WISC-R factors first delineated by Kaufman (1979) and measures of achievement for the white and nonwhite groups, with the exception of the Papagos. Significant correlations occurred between the WISC-R Freedom from Distractibility factor (Kaufman, 1979) and teacher ratings of attention for all four groups. Reschly and Reschly (1979) concluded that "these data also again confirm the relatively strong relationship of WISC-R scores to achievement for most non-Anglo as well as Anglo groups" (p. 239).

Reynolds and Hartlage (1979) investigated the differential validity of full-scale IQs from the WISC-R and its 1949 predecessor, the WISC, in predicting reading and arithmetic achievement for black and white children who had been referred by their teachers for psychological services in a rural school district in the South. Comparisons of correlations and a Potthoff (1966) analysis to test for identity of regression lines revealed no significant differences in the ability or function of the WISC and WISC-R to predict achievement for these two groups. Reynolds and Gutkin (1980a) replicated this study for the WISC-R with large groups of white and Mexican-American children from the Southwest. Reynolds and Gutkin contrasted regression systems between WISC-R verbal, performance, and full-scale IQs and the "academic basics" of reading, spelling, and arithmetic. Only the regression equation between the WISC-R performance IQ and arithmetic achievement differed for the two groups. The difference in the two equations was attributable to an intercept bias that resulted in the overprediction of achievement for the Mexican-American children. Reynolds, Gutkin, Dappen, and Wright (1979) also failed to find differential validity in the prediction of achievement for males and females with the WISC-R.

In a related study, Hartlage, Lucas, and Godwin (1976) compared the predictive validity of what they considered to be a relatively culture-free test (Raven's Progressive Matrices) with a more culture-loaded test (the 1949 WISC) for a group of low-SES, disadvantaged rural children. Hartlage et al. found that the WISC had consistently larger correlations with measures of reading, spelling, and arithmetic than did Raven's matrices. Although it did not make the comparison with other groups that is necessary for the drawing of firm conclusions, the study does support the validity of the WISC, which has been the target of many of the claims of bias in the prediction of achievement for low-SES, disadvantaged rural children.

Reynolds, Willson, and Chatman (1985) evaluated the predictive validity of the K-ABC for blacks and for whites. Occasional evidence of bias was found in each direction, but mostly of the direction of overprediction of the academic attainment levels of blacks. For most of the 56 Potthoff comparisons of regression lines, however, no evidence of bias was revealed.

Bossard, Reynolds, and Gutkin (1980) published a regression analysis of test bias on the 1972 Stanford-Binet Intelligence Scale for separate groups of black and white children. Neither regression systems nor correlations differed at $p < .05$ for the prediction of the basic academic skills of reading, spelling, and arithmetic achievement for these two groups of referred children. An earlier study by Sewell (1979), a black opponent of testing, did not compare regression systems, but also found no significant differences in validity coefficients for Stanford-Binet IQs predicting California Achievement Test (CAT) scores for black and white first-grade children.

A series of studies comparing the predictive validity of group IQ measures cross races has been reviewed by Jensen (1980) and Reynolds (1982a). Both reviewers concluded that the few available studies suggest that standard IQ tests in current use have comparable validities for black and white children at the elementary school level.

Guterman (1979) reported on an extensive analysis of the predictive validity of the Ammons and Ammons Quick Test (QT; a measure of verbal IQ) for adolescents of different social classes. Social class was determined by a weighted combination of Duncan's SES index and the number of years of education of each parent. Three basic measures of scholastic attainment were employed as criterion measures: the Vocabulary subtest of the General Aptitude Test Battery (GATB), the Reading Comprehension test from the Gates Reading Survey, and the Arithmetic subtest of the GATB. School grades in academic subjects for 9th, 10th, and 12th grades were also used to examine for bias in prediction. Guterman reached similar conclusions with regard to all criterion measures across al! social classes: Slopes and intercepts of regression lines did not differ across social class for the prediction of any of the criterion measures by the IQ derived from the QT. Several other social knowledge criterion measures were also examined. Again, slopes were constant across social class, and with the exception of sexual knowledge, intercepts were also constant. Guterman concluded that his data provide strong support for equivalent validity of IQ measures across social class.

As with construct validity, at the preschool level the evidence is less clear and convincing but points toward a lack of bias against minorities. Reynolds (1978) conducted an extensive analysis of predictive bias for seven major preschool tests (the Draw-A-Design and Draw-A-Child subtests of the McCarthy Scales, the Mathematics and Language subtests of the Tests of Basic Experiences, the MRT, the revised Preschool Inventory, and the Lee-Clark Reading Readiness Test) across race and gender for large groups of blacks and whites. For each preschool test, validity coefficients, slopes, and intercepts were compared, with prediction of performance on four subtests of the MAT (Word Knowledge, Word Discrimination, Reading, and Arithmetic) as the criterion measure. Data were gathered on a large number of early achievement tests, and the teachers selected the MAT as the battery most closely measuring what was taught in their classrooms.

Regression systems and validity coefficients were compared for each independent-dependent variable pair for white females (WF) versus white males (WM), black females (BF) versus black males (BM), WF versus BF, and WM versus BM, resulting in 112 comparisons of validity coefficients and 112 comparisons of regression systems. Mean performance on all criterion measures was in the following rank order: WF > WM > BF > BM. The mean validity coefficients (by Fisher z-transformation) between the independent and dependent variables across the 12-month period from pre- to posttest were .59 for WF, .50 for WM, .43 for BF, and .30 for BM. Although the mean correlations were lower for blacks, the 112 comparisons of pairs of correlations revealed only three significant differences, a less-than-chance occurrence with this number of comparisons.

Using the Potthoff (1966) technique for comparing regression lines produced quite different results. Of the 112 comparisons of regression lines, 43 (38.4%) showed differences. For comparisons with race as the major variable (and sex controlled), 31 (55.2%) of the 56 comparisons showed significantly different regression lines. Clearly, racial bias was significantly more prevalent than sex bias ($p < .01$) in prediction. In comparing the various pretests, bias occurred most often with the Preschool Inventory and the Lee-Clark, whereas none of the comparisons involving the MRT showed bias. Though race clearly influenced homogeneity of regression across groups, the bias in each case acted to overpredict performance of lower-scoring groups; thus the bias acted against whites and females and in favor of blacks and males. A follow-up study (Reynolds, 1980b) has indicated one potential method for avoiding bias in the prediction of early school achievement with readiness or screening measures.

Brief screening measures, especially at the preschool level, typically do not have the high level of reliability obtained by such instruments as the WISC-R or the Stanford-Binet. As previously discussed, Linn and Werts (1971) have convincingly demonstrated that poor reliability can lead to bias in prediction. Early screening measures, as a rule, also assess a very limited area of functioning, rather than allowing the child to demonstrate his or her skills in a variety of areas of cognitive functioning. The one well-researched, reliable, broad-based readiness test, the MRT, has failed to show bias with regard to internal or external criteria. Comprehensive and reliable individual preschool instruments such as the WPPSI and the McCarthy scales, although showing no internal evidence of test bias, have not been researched with regard to predictive bias across race. Reynolds (1980b) examined the predictive validity of the seven preschool measures described previously when these were combined into a larger battery, thus increasing the scope and reliability of the assessment.

Because the definition of predictive bias noted earlier requires that errors in prediction be independent of group membership, Reynolds (1980b) directly examined residuals (a residual term is the remainder when the predicted score for an individual is subtracted from the individual's obtained score) across races and genders when the seven-test battery was used to predict MAT scores in a multiple-regression formula. Subtests of the seven-test battery were also examined. Results of a race × sex ANOVA of residuals for each of the MAT subtests when the seven-test battery was employed revealed no significant differences in residuals across races and genders, and no significant interactions occurred. When a subset of the larger battery was submitted to the same analysis, racial bias in prediction did not occur; however, a significant F resulted for sex effects in the prediction of two of the four MAT subscores (Word Discrimination and Word Knowledge).

Examination of the residuals for each group showed that the bias in prediction was again against the group with the higher mean criterion scores: There was a consistent underprediction of performance for females. The magnitude of the effect was small, however, being on the order of 0.13 to 0.16 standard deviations. Thus, at the preschool level, the only convincing evidence of bias in predictive validity is a sex effect, not a race effect. Although females tend to be slightly overidentified through early screening, it is interesting to note that whereas special education classes are more blatantly sexist than racist in composition, it is boys who outnumber girls at a ratio of about 3.5:1 to 4:1. Few, if any, would argue that this disproportionate representation of males in special education is inappropriate or attributable to test bias.

Kamphaus and Reynolds (1987) reviewed the available literature on predictive bias with the K-ABC and concluded that overprediction of black children's performance in school is more common with the K-ABC, particularly its Sequential Processing scale, than with other tests. The effects are small, however, and are mitigated in large part by using the K-ABC Mental Processing Composite. Some bias also occurs against blacks, but when the extensive nature of the bias research with the K-ABC is considered, the results are not substantially different from those with the WISC-R (with the exception of overprediction of black academic performance by the K-ABC Sequential Processing scale).

With regard to bias in predictive validity, the empirical evidence suggests conclusions similar to those regarding bias in content and construct validity. There is no strong evidence to support contentions of differential of single-group validity. Bias occurs infrequently and with no apparently observable pattern, except when instruments of poor reliability and high specificity of test content are examined. When bias occurs, it is most often in the direction of favoring low-SES, disadvantaged ethnic minority children, or other low-scoring groups. Clearly, bias in predictive validity cannot account for the disproportionate number of minority group children diagnosed and placed in EMR and emotionally disturbed (EMH) settings.

CONCLUSION

There is little question that the issue of bias in mental testing is an important one with strong historical precedence in the social sciences and, ultimately, formidable social consequences. Because the history of mental measurement has been closely wed from the outset to societal needs and expectations, testing in all forms has remained in the limelight, subjected to the crucible of social inspection, review, and (at times) condemnation. The fact that tests and measures of human aptitude and achievement continue to be employed in most modern cultures indicates strongly that the practice has value, however, despite the recurring storms of criticism over the years. The ongoing controversy related to test bias and the "fair" use of measures will undoubtedly remain with the social sciences for at least as long as we intertwine the nature-nurture question with these issues and affirm differences among groups in mean performance on standardized tests. Numerous scholars in the field of psychometrics have been attempting to separate the nature-nurture issue and data on mean score differences from the more orderly, empirically driven specialty of bias investigation, but the separation will undoubtedly not be a clean one.

A sharp distinction has developed between the popular press and scientific literature with regard to the interpretation of mental measurement research. The former all too often engenders beliefs that biased measures are put into use for socially pernicious purposes (e.g., Gould, 1981); the latter has attempted to maintain balanced scientific analysis and inquiry in fields (i.e., psychology and education) often accused of courting political, social, and professional ideologies. The former appears to have created confusion in public opinion, to say the least, concerning the possibility of fair testing. The latter—reported in this chapter—has been demonstrating through a rather sizable body of data that the hypothesis of cultural bias on tests is not a particularly strong one at present. In any event, societal scrutiny and ongoing sentiment about testing have without question served to force the psychometric community to refine its definition of bias further, to inspect practices in the construction on nonbiased measures, and to develop statistical procedures to detect bias when it is occurring. We can argue whether the social sciences have from the outset overstepped their bounds in implementing testing for social purposes before adequate data and methods were developed, but the resulting advancements made in bias technology in response to ongoing public inspection are undeniable.

Data from the empirical end of bias investigation do suggest several guidelines to follow in order to ensure equitable assessment. Points to consider include (a) investigation of possible referral source bias, as there is evidence that persons are not always referred for services on the basis of impartial, objective rationales; (b) inspection of test developers' data for evidence that sound statistical analyses for bias across groups to be evaluated with the measure have been completed; (c) assessment with the most reliable measure available; and (d) assessment of multiple abilities with multiple methods. In other words, psychologists need to view multiple sources of accurately derived data prior to making decisions concerning children. We may hope that this is not too far afield from what has actually been occurring in the practice of psychological assessment.

A philosophical perspective is emerging in the bias literature that is requiring test developers not only to demonstrate whether their measures demonstrate differential content, construct, and predictive validity across groups *prior* to publication, but also to incorporate in some form content analyses by interested groups to ensure that offensive materials are omitted. Although there are no sound empirical data to suggest that persons can determine bias upon surface inspection, the synergistic relationship between test use and pure psychometrics must be acknowledged and accommodated in orderly fashion before tests gain greater acceptance within society. Ideally, a clear consensus on "fairness" (and steps taken to reach this end) is needed between those persons with more subjective concerns and those interested in gathering objective bias data during or after test construction. Accommodation along this line will ultimately ensure that all parties interested in any given test believe that the measure in question is nonbiased and that the steps taken to achieve fairness can be held up to public scrutiny without reservation.

Given the significant and reliable methods developed over the last several decades in bias research, it is untenable at this point to abandon statistical analyses in favor of armchair determinations of bias. Test authors and publishers need to demonstrate factorial invariance across all groups for whom the test is designed in order to make the instrument more readily interpretable. Comparisons of predictive validity across races and genders during the test development phase are also needed. With the exception of some recent achievement tests, this has not been common practice, yet it is at this stage that tests can be altered through a variety of item analysis procedures to eliminate any apparent racial and sexual bias.

Bias research in the area of personality testing

must be expanded. Little has been done (see Zeidner, 1990), and this represents a major weakness in the literature. Only recently (e.g., Reynolds & Kamphaus, 1993) have publishers began to give appropriate attention to this problem. Researchers in personality and psychodiagnostics must move ahead in this area of concern.

Acknowledgments. Portions of this chapter are based substantively on a variety of prior works of the author, including Reynolds (1982a, b; 1983; 1991), Reynolds & Brown (1984), and Reynolds & Kaiser (1990).

REFERENCES

Alley, G., & Foster, C. (1978). Nondiscriminatory testing of minority and exceptional children. *Focus on Exceptional Children, 9*, 1–14.

Anastasi, A. (1982). *Psychological testing* (5th ed.). New York: Macmillan.

Angoff, W. H. (1976). Group membership as a predictor variable: A comment on McNemar. *American Psychologist, 31*, 612.

Angoff, W. H., & Ford, S. R. (1973). Item-race interaction on a test of scholastic aptitude. *Journal of Educational Measurement, 10*, 95–106.

Bass, A. R. (1976). The "equal risk" model: A comment on McNemar. *American Psychologist, 31*, 611–612.

Bernal, E. M. (1975). A response to "Educational uses of tests with disadvantaged students." *American Psychologist, 30*, 93–95.

Birch, H. G., & Gussow, J. D. (1970). *Disadvantaged children: Health, nutrition, and school failure*. New York: Grune & Stratton.

Blaha, J., Wallbrown, F., & Wherry, R. J. (1975). The hierarchical factor structure of the Wechsler Intelligence Scale for Children. *Psychological Reports, 35*, 771–778.

Bossard, M., Reynolds, C. R., & Gutkin, T. B. (1980). A regression analysis of test bias on the Stanford-Binet Intelligence Scale. *Journal of Clinical Child Psychology, 9*, 52–54.

Burt, C. (1921). *Mental and scholastic tests*. London: King.

Cardall, C., & Coffman, W. E. (1964). *A method of comparing the performance of different groups on the items in a test* (RB-64-61). Princeton, NJ: Educational Testing Service.

Cattell, R. B. (1979). Are culture fair intelligence tests possible and necessary? *Journal of Research and Development in Education, 12*, 3–13.

Chambers, J. S., Barron, F., & Sprecher, J. W. (1980). Identifying gifted Mexican-American students. *Gifted Child Quarterly, 24*, 123–128.

Chinn, P. C. (1979). The exceptional minority child: Issues and some answers. *Exceptional Children, 46*, 532–536.

Cleary, T. A. (1968). Test bias: Prediction of grades of negro and white students in integrated universities. *Journal of Educational Measurement, 5*, 118–124.

Cleary, T. A., Humphreys, L. G., Kendrick, S. A., & Wesman, A. (1975). Educational uses of tests with disadvantaged students. *American Psychologist, 30*, 15–41.

Cole, N. S., & Moss, P. (1989). Bias in test use. In R. Linn (Ed.), *Educational measurement* (3rd ed.). New York: Macmillan.

Council for Exceptional Children. (1978). Minorities position policy statements. *Exceptional Children, 45*, 57–64.

Cronbach, L. J. (1976). Equity in selection—where psychometrics and political philosophy meet. *Journal of Educational Measurement, 13*, 31–42.

Darlington, R. B. (1978). Cultural test bias: Comments on Hunter and Schmidt. *Psychological Bulletin, 85*, 673–674.

Dean, R. S. (1977). Reliability of the WISC-R with Mexican-American children. *Journal of School Psychology, 15*, 267–268.

Dean, R. S. (1979). *WISC-R factor structure for Anglo and Hispanic children*. Paper presented at the annual meeting of the American Psychological Association, New York.

DeFries, J. C., Vandenberg, S. G., McClearn, G. E., Kuse, A. R., Wilson, J. R., Ashton, G. C., & Johnson, R. C. (1974). Near identity of cognitive structure in two ethnic groups. *Science, 183*, 338–339.

Ebel, R. L. (1979). Intelligence: A skeptical view. *Journal of Research and Development in Education, 12*, 14–21.

Eells, K., Davis, A., Havighurst, R. J., Herrick, V. E., & Tyler, R. W. (1951). *Intelligence and cultural differences: A study of cultural learning and problem-solving*. Chicago: University of Chicago Press.

Einhorn, H. J., & Bass, A. R. (1971). Methodological considerations relevant to discrimination in employment testing. *Psychological Bulletin, 75*, 261–269.

Fine, B. (1975). *The stranglehold of the IQ*. Garden City, NY: Doubleday.

Flaugher, R. L. (1978). The many definitions of test bias. *American Psychologist, 33*, 671–679.

Flaugher, R. L., & Schrader, W. B. (1978). *Eliminating differentially difficult items as an approach to test bias* (RB-78-4). Princeton, NJ: Educational Testing Service.

Frame, R. (1979, September). *Diagnoses related to school achievement, client's race, and socioeconomic status*. Paper presented at the annual meeting of the American Psychological Association, New York.

Freeman, F. N. (1923). A referendum of psychologists. *Century Illustrated Magazine, 107*, 237–245.

Gordon, R. A. (1984). Digits backward and the Mercer-Kamin law: An empirical response to Mercer's treatment of internal validity of IQ tests. In C. R. Reynolds & R. T. Brown (Eds.), *Perspectives on bias in mental testing*. New York: Plenum.

Gould, S. J. (1981). *The mismeasure of man*. New York: Norton.

Gross, A. L., & Su, W. (1975). Defining a "fair" or "unbiased" selection model. *Journal of Applied Psychology, 60*, 345–351.

Guterman, S. S. (1979). IQ tests in research on social stratification: The cross-class validity of the test as measures on scholastic aptitude. *Sociology of Education, 52*, 163–173.

Gutkin, T. B., & Reynolds, C. R. (1980). Factorial similarity of the WISC-R for Anglos and Chicanos referred for psychological services. *Journal of School Psychology, 18*, 34–39.

Gutkin, T. B., & Reynolds, C. R. (1981). Factorial similarity of the WISC-R for white and black children from the standardization sample. *Journal of Educational Psychology, 73*, 227–231.

Hammill, D. (1991). *Detroit tests of learning aptitude* (3rd ed.). Austin, TX: Pro-Ed.

Harman, H. (1976). *Modern factor analysis* (2nd ed.). Chicago: University of Chicago Press.

Harrington, G. M. (1975). Intelligence tests may favor the majority groups in a population. *Nature, 258*, 708–709.

Harrington, G. M. (1976, September). *Minority test bias as a psychometric artifact: The experimental evidence*. Paper presented to the annual meeting of the American Psychological Association, Washington, DC.

Hartlage, L. C., Lucas, T., & Godwin, A. (1976). Culturally biased and culturally fair tests correlated with school performance in culturally disadvantaged children. *Journal of Consulting and Clinical Psychology, 32*, 325–327.

Hilliard, A. G. (1979). Standardization and cultural bias as impediments to the scientific study and validation of "intelligence." *Journal of Research and Development in Education, 12*, 47–58.

Humphreys, L. G. (1973). Statistical definitions of test validity for minority groups. *Journal of Applied Psychology, 58*, 1–4.

Hunter, J. E., & Schmidt, F. L. (1976). Critical analysis of the statistical and ethical implications of various definitions of test bias. *Psychological Bulletin, 83*, 1053–1071.

Hunter, J. E., Schmidt, F. L., & Hunter, R. (1979). Differential validity of employment tests by race: A comprehensive review and analysis. *Psychological Bulletin, 86*, 721–735.

Hunter, J. E., Schmidt, F. L., & Rauschenberger, J. (1984). Methodological, statistical, and ethical issues in the study of bias in psychological tests. In C. R. Reynolds & R. T. Brown (Eds.), *Perspectives on bias in mental testing*. New York: Plenum.

Jackson, G. D. (1975). Another psychological view from the Association of Black Psychologists. *American Psychologist, 30*, 88–93.

Jensen, A. R. (1974). How biased are cultural loaded tests? *Genetic Psychology Monographs, 90*, 185–224.

Jensen, A. R. (1976). Test bias and construct validity. *Phi Delta Kappan, 58*, 340–346.

Jensen, A. R. (1977). An examination of culture bias in the Wonderlic Personnel test. *Intelligence, 1*, 51–64.

Jensen, A. R. (1980). *Bias in mental testing*. New York: Free Press.

Jensen, A. R. (1985). The nature of the black-white difference on various tests: Spearman's hypothesis. *Behavioral and Brain Sciences, 8*, 193–263.

Jensen, A. R., & Figueroa, R. (1975). Forward and backward digit span interaction with race and IQ. *Journal of Education Psychology, 67*, 882–893.

Joreskof, K. (1971). Simultaneous factor analysis in several populations. *Psychometrika, 30*, 409–426.

Kaiser, S. (1986). *Ability patterns of black and white adults on the WAIS-R independent of general intelligence and as a function of socioeconomic status*. Unpublished doctoral dissertation, Texas A & M University.

Kamphaus, R. W., & Reynolds, C. R. (1987). *Clinical and research applications of the K-ABC*. Circle Pines, MN: American Guidance Service.

Kaufman, A. S. (1973). Comparison of the performance of matched groups of black children and white children on the Wechsler Preschool and Primary Scale of Intelligence. *Journal of Consulting and Clinical Psychology, 41*, 186–191.

Kaufman, A. S. (1979). *Intelligent testing with the WISC-R*. New York: Wiley-Interscience.

Kaufman, A. S., & DiCiuo, R. (1975). Separate factor analyses of the McCarthy Scales for groups of black and white children. *Journal of School Psychology, 13*, 10–18.

Kaufman, A. S., & Hollenbeck, G. P. (1974). Comparative structure of the WPPSI for black and whites. *Journal of Clinical Psychology, 30*, 316–319.

Kaufman, A. S., & Kaufman, N. L. (1973). Black-white differences on the McCarthy Scales of Children's Abilities. *Journal of School Psychology, 11*, 196–206.

Kaufman, A. S., & Kaufman, N. L. (1983). *Kaufman assessment battery for children*. Circle Pines, MN: American Guidance Service.

Lambert, N. M. (1979, October). *Adaptive behavior assessment and its implications for educational programming*. Paper presented to the Fourth Annual Midwestern Conference on Psychology in the Schools, Boys Town, NE.

Larry P. et al. v. Wilson Riles et al., C 71 2270 (United States District Court for the Northern District of California, October 1979, slip opinion).

Lewontin, R. C. (1970). Race and intelligence. *Bulletin of the Atomic Scientists, 26*, 2–8.

Linn, R. L. (1976). In search of fair selection procedures. *Journal of Educational Measurement, 13*, 53–58.

Linn, R. L., & Werts, C. E. (1971). Considerations for studies of test bias. *Journal of Educational Measurement, 8*, 1–4.

Lippmann, W. (1923a). A judgment of the tests. *New Republic, 34*, 322–323.

Lippmann, W. (1923b). Mr. Burt and the intelligence tests. *New Republic, 34*, 263–264.

Loehlin, J. C., Lindzey, G., & Spuhler, J. N. (1975). *Race differences in intelligence*. San Francisco: Freeman.

Matuszek, P., & Oakland, T. (1979). Factors influencing teachers' and psychologists' recommendations regarding special class placement. *Journal of School Psychology, 17*, 116–125.

McCarthy, D. (1972). *McCarthy Scales of Children's Abilities*. San Antonio, TX: The Psychological Corporation.

McGurk, F. V. J. (1951). *Comparison of the performance of negro and white high school seniors on cultural and noncultural psychological test questions*. Washington, DC: Catholic University of America Press.

McNemar, Q. (1975). On so-called test bias. *American Psychologist, 30*, 848–851.

Mercer, J. R. (1976, August). *Cultural diversity, mental retardation, and assessment: The case for nonlabeling*. Paper presented to the Fourth International Congress of the International Association for the Scientific Study of Mental Retardation, Washington, DC.

Merz, W. R. (1970). *A factor analysis of the Goodenough-Harris drawing test across four ethnic groups*. Doctoral dissertation, University of Michigan. University Microfilms #70-19.

Mille, F. (1979). Cultural bias in the WISC. *Intelligence, 3*, 149–164.

Moran, M. (1990). The problem of cultural bias in personality assessment. In C. R. Reynolds & R. W. Kamphaus (Eds.), *Handbook of psychological and educational assessment of children* (Vol. 2, pp. 491–523). New York: Guilford.

Nichols, R. C. (1978). Policy implications of the IQ controversy. In L. S. Schulman (Ed.), *Review of research in education* (Vol. 6). Itasca, IL: Peacock.

Novick, M. R., & Petersen, N. S. (1976). Towards equalizing educational and employment opportunity. *Journal of Educational Measurement, 13*, 77–88.

Oakland, T., & Feigenbaum, D. (1979). Multiple sources of test bias on the Bender-Gestalt and the WISC-R. *Journal of Consulting and Clinical Psychology, 47*, 968–974.

O'Conner, E. J., Wexley, K. N., & Alexander, R. A. (1975). Single group validity: Fact or fallacy. *Journal of Applied Psychology, 60*, 352–355.

Parents in Action on Special Education et al. v. Hannon et al., No. 74 C 3586 (United States District Court for the Northern District of Illinois, Eastern Division, July 1980, slip opinion).

Petersen, N. S, & Novick, M. R. (1976). An evaluation of some models for culture fair selection. *Journal of Educational Measurement, 13*, 3–29.

Pintner, R. (1931). *Intelligence testing*. New York: Holt, Rinehart & Winston.

Potthoff, R. F. (1966). *Statistical aspects of the problem of biases in psychological tests* (Institute of statistics Mimco Series No. 479). Chapel Hill, NC: University of North Carolina, Department of Statistics.

Ramsey, R. T. (1979). *The testing manual: A guide to test administration and use*. Pittsburgh: Author.

Reschly, D. J. (1978). Concepts of bias in assessment and WISC-R research with minorities. In H. Vance & F. Wallbrown (Eds.), *WISC-R: Research and interpretation*. Washington, DC: National Association of School Psychologists.

Reschly, D. J. (1980). School psychologists and assessment in the future. *Professional Psychology, 11*, 841–848.

Reschly, D. J., & Reschly, J. E. (1979). Validity of the WISC-R factor scores in predicting achievement and attention for four sociocultural groups. *Journal of School Psychology, 17*, 355–361.

Reschly, D. J., & Sabers, D. (1979). Analysis of test bias with the regression definition. *Journal of Educational Measurement, 16*, 1–9.

Reynolds, C. R. (1978). *Differential validity of several preschool assessment instruments for blacks, whites, males, and females*. Unpublished doctoral dissertation, University of Georgia.

Reynolds, C. R. (1979). Should we screen preschoolers? *Contemporary Educational Psychology, 4*, 175–181.

Reynolds, C. R. (1980a). Differential construct validity of intelligence as popularly measured: Correlation of age and raw scores on the WISC-R for blacks, whites, males, and females. *Intelligence: A Multidisciplinary Journal, 4*, 371–379.

Reynolds, C. R. (1980b). An examination for test bias in a preschool battery across race and sex. *Journal of Educational Measurement, 17*, 137–146.

Reynolds, C. R. (1980c). In support of "Bias in Mental Testing" and scientific inquiry. *Behavioral and Brain Sciences, 3*, 352.

Reynolds, C. R. (1982a). Construct and predictive bias. In R. A. Berk (Ed.), *Handbook of methods for detecting test bias*. Baltimore, MD: Johns Hopkins University Press.

Reynolds, C. R. (1982b). The problem of bias in psychological assessment. In C. R. Reynolds & T. B. Gutkin (Eds.), *The handbook of school psychology*. New York: Wiley.

Reynolds, C. R., & Bigler, E. D. (1994). *Test of memory and learning*. Austin, TX: Pro-Ed.

Reynolds, C. R., & Brown, R. T. (1984). Bias in mental testing: An introduction to the issues. In C. R. Reynolds & R. T. Brown (Eds.), *Perspectives on bias in mental testing* (pp. 1–39). New York: Plenum.

Reynolds, C. R., & Gutkin, T. B. (1980a). A regression analysis of test bias on the WISC-R for Anglos and Chicanos referred for psychological services. *Perceptual and Motor Skills, 48*, 868–879.

Reynolds, C. R., & Gutkin, T. B. (1980b, September). *WISC-R performance of blacks and whites matched on four demographic variables*. Paper presented at the annual meeting of the American Psychological Association, Montreal.

Reynolds, C. R., & Gutkin, T. B. (1981). A multivariate comparison of the intellectual performance of blacks and whites matched on four demographic variables. *Personality and Individual Differences, 2*, 175–180.

Reynolds, C. R., Gutkin, T. B., Dappen, L., & Wright, D. (1979). Differential validity of the WISC-R for boys and for girls referred to psychological services. *Perceptual and Motor Skills, 48*, 868–879.

Reynolds, C. R., & Harding, R. E. (1983). Outcome in two large sample studies of factorial similarity under six methods of comparison. *Educational and Psychological Measurement, 43*, 723–728.

Reynolds, C. R., & Hartlage, L. C. (1979). Comparison of WISC and WISC-R regression lines for academic prediction with black and white referred children. *Journal of Consulting and Clinical Psychology, 47*, 589–591.

Reynolds, C. R., & Jensen, A. R. (1983, September). *Patterns of intellectual performance among blacks and whites matched on "g"*. Paper presented to the annual meeting of the American Psychological Association, Montreal.

Reynolds, C. R., & Kaiser, S. (1990). Test bias in psychological assessment. In T. B. Gutkin & C. R. Reynolds (Eds.), *The handbook of school psychology* (2nd ed., pp. 487–525). New York: Wiley.

Reynolds, C. R., & Kamphaus, R. W. (1993). *Behavior Assessment System for Children*. Circle Pines, MN: American Guidance Service.

Reynolds, C. R., & Paget, K. (1981). Factor analysis of the revised Children's Manifest Anxiety Scale for blacks, whites, males, and females with a national normative sample. *Journal of Consulting and Clinical Psychology, 49*, 349–352.

Reynolds, C. R., Willson, V. L., & Chatman, S. P. (1984). Item bias on the 1981 revision of the Peabody Vocabulary Test using a new technique for detecting bias. *Journal of Psychoeducational Assessment, 2*, 219–227.

Reynolds, C. R., Willson, V. L., & Chatman, S. P. (1985). Regression analyses of bias on the K-ABC. *Journal of School Psychology, 23*, 195–204.

Sandoval, J. (1979). The WISC-R and internal evidence of test bias with minority group children. *Journal of Consulting and Clinical Psychology, 47*, 919–927.

Sandoval, J., & Mille, M. (1979, September). *Accuracy judgments of WISC-R item difficulty for minority groups*. Paper presented to the annual meeting of the American Psychological Association, New York.

Sawyer, R. L., Cole, N. S., & Cole, J. W. (1976). Utilities and the issue of fairness in a decision theoretic model for selection. *Journal of Educational Measurement, 13*, 59–76.

Scheuneman, J. D. (1987). An experimental, exploratory study of causes of bias in test items. *Journal of Educational Measurement, 29*, 97–118.

Schmidt, F. L., & Hunter, J. E. (1974). Racial and ethnic bias in psychological tests: Divergent implications of two definitions of test bias. *American Psychologist, 29*, 1–8.

Schoenfeld, W. N. (1974). Notes on a bit of psychological nonsense: "Race differences in intelligence." *Psychological Record, 24*, 17–32.

Scholwinski, E. (1985). *Ability patterns of black and white adults as determined by the subscales of the WAIS-R*. Unpublished doctoral dissertation, Texas A & M University.

Semler, I., & Iscoe, I. (1966). Structure of intelligence in Negro and white children. *Journal of Educational Psychology, 57*, 326–336.

Sewell, T. E. (1979). Intelligence and learning tasks as predictors of achievement for black and white first grade children. *Journal of School Psychology, 17*, 325–332.

Shepard, L. S. (1982). Definitions of bias. In R. A. Berk (Ed.), *Handbook of methods for detecting test bias*. Baltimore: Johns Hopkins University Press.

Shuey, A. M. (1966). *The testing of Negro intelligence* (2nd ed.). New York: Social Science Press.

Silverstein, A. R. (1973). Factor structure of the Wechsler Intelligence Scale for Children for three ethnic groups. *Journal of Educational Psychology, 65*, 408–410.

Sternberg, R. J. (1980). Intelligence and test bias: Art and science. *Behavioral and Brain Sciences, 3*, 353–354.

Thorndike, R. L. (1971). Concepts of culture-fairness. *Journal of Educational Measurement, 8*, 63–70.

Tittle, C. K. (1982). Use of judgmental methods in item bias studies. In R. A. Berk (Ed.), *Handbook of methods for detecting test bias*. Baltimore: Johns Hopkins University Press.

Tomlinson, J. R., Acker, N., Canter, A., & Lindborg, S. (1977). Minority status, sex, and school psychological services. *Psychology in the Schools, 14*, 456–460.

Torrance, E. P. (1980). Psychology of gifted children and youth. In W. M. Cruickshank (Ed.), *Psychology of exceptional children and youth*. Englewood Cliffs, NJ: Prentice-Hall

Tyler, L. E. (1965). *The psychology of human differences*. New York: Appleton-Century-Crofts.

Vance, H. B., Huelsman, C. B., & Wherry, R. J. (1976). The hierarchical factor structure of the Wechsler Intelligence Scale for Children as it relates to disadvantaged black and white children. *Journal of General Psychology, 95*, 287–293.

Vance, H. B., & Wallbrown, F. H. (1978). The structure of intelligence for black children: A hierarchical approach. *Psychological Record, 28*, 31–39.

Veale, J. R., & Foreman, D. I. (1983). Assessing cultural bias using foil response data: Cultural variation. *Journal of Educational Measurement, 20*, 249–258.

Waits, C., & Richmond, B. O. (1978). Special education—who needs it? *Exceptional Children, 44*, 279–280.

Wallbrown, F. H., Blaha, J., & Wherry, R. J. (1973). The hierarchical factor structure of the Wechsler Adult Intelligence Scale. *British Journal of Educational Psychology, 44*, 47–65.

Wechsler, D. (1974). *Wechsler Intelligence Scale for Children-Revised*. New York: Psychological Corporation.

Wechsler, D. (1975). Intelligence defined and undefined: A relativistic appraisal. *American Psychologist, 30*, 135–139.

Wechsler, D. (1981). *Wechsler Adult Intelligence Scale-Revised*. San Antonio, TX: The Psychological Corporation.

Wherry, R. J., & Wherry, R. J., Jr. (1969). WNEWH program. In R. J. Wherry (Ed.), *Psychology department computer program* (pp.). Columbus: Ohio State University.

Willerman, L. (1979). *The psychology of individual and group differences*. San Francisco: Freeman.

Williams, R. L. (1970). Danger: Testing and dehumanizing black children. *Clinical Child Psychology Newsletter, 9*, 5–6.

Williams, R. L. (1974). From dehumanization to black intellectual genocide: A rejoinder. In G. J. Williams & S. Gordon (Eds.), *Clinical child psychology: Current practices and future perspectives*. New York: Behavioral Publications.

Wright, B. J., & Isenstein, V. R. (1977). *Psychological tests and minorities* (DHEW Publication No. ADM 78-482). Rockville, MD: National Institute for Mental Health.

Zeidner, M. (1990). Does test anxiety bias scholastic aptitude test performance by gender and sociocultural group? *Journal of Personality Assessment, 55*, 145–160.

V

Applications and Clinical Parameters

26

Personality and Intelligence in Industrial and Organizational Psychology

Ruth Kanfer, Phillip L. Ackerman, Todd Murtha, and Maynard Goff

The discipline of industrial and organizational (I/O) psychology focuses on understanding human behavior in the context of work. Since the emergence of I/O psychology as a field of scientific inquiry in the United States at the turn of the century, I/O psychologists have been concerned with a wide variety of topics, including personnel selection and placement, job training, task design, worker motivation, organizational influences on work behavior, and procedures for optimizing job performance and worker efficiency. (For reviews of these and other I/O areas, see Dunnette, 1976; Dunnette & Hough, 1990, 1991, 1992.) From an individual differences perspective, however, two fundamental questions may be proposed to underlie much of I/O theory and research: (a) What roles do cognitive and nonability individual differences play in the determination of job performance? (b) How may individual-difference theories and assessment measures be employed to improve predictions of the fit between an individual and a job?

Ruth Kanfer, Phillip L. Ackerman, Todd Murtha, and Maynard Goff • Department of Psychology, University of Minnesota, Minneapolis, Minnesota 55455.

International Handbook of Personality and Intelligence, edited by Donald H. Saklofske and Moshe Zeidner. Plenum Press, New York, 1995.

To address these questions, I/O psychologists have frequently adopted an interdisciplinary approach that maps theory and research from basic psychology domains (e.g., personality, intelligence) to knowledge about job conditions and requirements. From this coordinated perspective, progress in the basic disciplines and/or the applied domain has often yielded new approaches to workplace issues. For example, in the area of personnel selection, personality measures have long been used as a screening test for detection of potential emotional instability or maladjustment in sensitive, high-stress, or high-security jobs (e.g., police officers, military personnel). More recently, advances in the analysis of job performance have led to increased interest in using modern personality measures to predict ancillary job requirements, such as organizational citizenship and delinquency behaviors (e.g., theft, absenteeism, reliability). Similarly, developments in intelligence theories have most often been used in the context of personnel selection. As societal pressures focus attention on training rather than selection, there is a growing trend toward developing new approaches to job training based upon recent advances in ability theories.

The purpose of this chapter is to review progress in the applications of intelligence and personality theory and survey the current status of these areas in the field of I/O psychology. The first section provides an historical review of developments in I/O personality research from the emergence of the field through the present. The next section describes advances in developments in I/O-related intelligence theory and research from the turn of the century to the present. The third and final section examines enduring issues related to understanding the joint and interactive roles of personality and intelligence in industrial/organizational settings, as well as future trends in the field.

SPECIAL CHARACTERISTICS OF I/O PSYCHOLOGY

It is obvious that in the general population, a wide range of intellectual talent and personality dispositions can be found. I/O psychology, however, does not operate in a vacuum. Demographics of the work force and characteristics of the job environment interact to make personality and intelligence measurement more or less important to industry. For example, when unemployment rates are high and there are substantially larger numbers of applicants than job positions, measurement of personality and intelligence traits can be quite useful in determining the success or failure of such applicants for jobs. When few applicants are available, though, and jobs go otherwise unfilled, the process of selection gives way to the process of recruitment. Under these conditions, the organization often cannot make much use of measures of personality and intelligence, except to weed out only the most seriously unfit potential employees.

Similarly, the conditions of the workplace will also determine the utility of personality and intelligence measures. When a job has particular demands for stable personalities (e.g., police, nuclear power plant operator, airline pilot), detection of abnormal personality is of much greater importance than when performance failure has decidedly less serious public safety consequences (e.g., secretary, salesperson). When jobs require extensive and expensive training (e.g., air traffic controller, airline pilot), intellectual-abilities measures have an obviously greater role in selection than when jobs are at entry level or are suited for unskilled workers (e.g., manual labor, file clerk). The importance of personality and intelligence measures for organizations is thus specific and dynamic, as changes take place in society at large, in the work force, and in the particular organization. It is important to note that the utility of such measurements is not universal, but is affected by these external and internal forces. Our focus in this chapter, however, is on those situations where individual differences in personality and intelligence have an important impact on job behaviors.

HISTORICAL OVERVIEW OF PERSONALITY IN I/O PSYCHOLOGY

Early Developments

Scientific interest and study of personality for I/O purposes began in earnest during the early 1900s (e.g., see Kornhauser, 1922; Young, 1923), with the establishment of the Division of Applied Psychology and the Bureau of Salesmanship Research at the Carnegie Institute of Technology in 1915 and 1916, respectively. The bureau, directed by Walter Dill Scott, was created to promote research aimed at use of scientific methods for selection of salesmen and to produce valid noncognitive measures of personality (defined in terms of character and temperament).

With the entry of the United States into World War I, psychologists were called upon by the military to provide assistance in developing effective selection and placement measures that could be administered relatively quickly to large groups of potential recruits. Work by Yerkes, Otis, and others led to the development and widespread use of group-administered cognitive ability tests (Army Alpha and Army Beta, discussed in greater detail in the next section). As Dunnette and Borman (1979) stated, the use of these tests "marked the beginning of large-scale use of tests and other systematic methods to aid personnel decisions in the world of work" (p. 478).

In addition to testing advances in the intelligence domain, the war brought about the development of the first standardized personality inventory: the Woodworth Personal Data Sheet (also called the Woodworth Test of Emotional Stability). During the war, the Woodworth Personal Data Sheet was administered to recruits for the purpose of screening out (for further psychiatric examination) those who might be susceptible to wartime disorders and thus unsuitable for service (see Franz, 1919; Zubin, 1948). From a different perspective, the Committee on Classification of Personnel (U.S. Adjutant General's Office, 1919) began a program of personality data collection to aid in the process of deciding officer furloughs. In this program, former employers' ratings of officer character traits (e.g., trustworthiness, leadership) were obtained and used as a decision aid.

Although personality tests during the war years were used primarily to screen or detect persons unsuitable for military service (rather than to predict job performance), interest in the use of personality tests for selection and prediction of job performance grew rapidly. As several researchers noted, however, the ultimate success of using personality tests in the industrial arena depended critically on new developments in both theory and measurement methodologies (e.g., see Allport, 1921; Bingham, 1923; Kornhauser & Kingsbury, 1924; Yoakum & Yerkes, 1920). Yoakum and Yerkes (1920), for example, expressed the prevailing view of the field among applied psychologists immediately following the war in this way: "Concerning temperament measurement and classification, there is little to say, for methods at once simple and reliable are not yet available. It is nevertheless obvious that personality attributes are as important as intelligence for industrial placement and vocational guidance" (p. 200).

Post-World War I Developments

The period between World War I and World War II (1919–1939) witnessed a steady expansion of research in the area of personality test development and the use of nonability tests for screening and prediction in industrial settings (Viteles, 1930; Watson, 1932, 1933). By the end of World War I, rating scale methods of personality measurement, popularized by the military and by the Bureau of Salesmanship Research, were being used by several personnel consulting firms and businesses (Kornhauser, 1922). Criticisms of this method were mounting (see, e.g., Allport, 1921; Rugg, 1921, 1922; Thorndike, 1920), however, and these often focused on the reliability and validity of such scales in isolating the target trait from other individual traits being rated (i.e., the "halo" problem). Although research by Furfey (1926), Miner (1917), and Paterson (1923) aimed to improve rating methods for a variety of traits, rating scales soon fell out of favor as predictor measures and became more frequently used as criterion measures for the development of other methods, such as questionnaires (Allport, 1921).

A second family of test methods that received brief attention during the 1920s and early 1930s were the motor expression tests. An outgrowth of the graphology tradition in personality, perhaps the best known of these tests is the Will-Temperament Test, a handwriting test introduced by Downey (1920). Scores on speed, size, disguise, and control of handwriting were used to assess speed, forcefulness and decisiveness of reactions, persistence, perseveration, and care with which reactions were made. Despite early enthusiasm for this test (Collins, 1925; May, 1925) and use of a group-administered version of the test by the Bureau of Personnel Research at the Carnegie Institute of Technology (Ream, 1922), Watson (1933) reported that mounting evidence indicating test unreliability had led to its virtual disappearance from the literature. Recent meta-analytic evidence has further demonstrated the complete lack of validity for graphology measures (Neter & Ben-Shakhar, 1989; Beyerstein & Beyerstein, 1991), but graphology continues to be used for personnel selection in the United States and Europe (see Klimoski & Rafaeli, 1983, and Levy, 1979, respectively).

The emphasis on test methods spawned the introduction of several new paper-and-pencil personality measures designed to asses specific dimensions of personality. Three tests that proved quite popular in the psychological literature were Allport's Ascendence-Submission Test (Allport, 1928), the X-O (Cross-Out) Tests for Investigating the Emotions (Pressey & Pressey, 1919) and the Laird-Colgate Mental Hygiene Inventory (Forms B and C; Laird, 1925a,b). Though these tests were used in a variety of populations for both prediction and detection, widespread interest in the use of this type of self-report inventory for workplace purposes did not appear until the mid-1930s.

The appearance of two new multitrait inventories in the early 1930s—the Bernreuter Personality Inventory (Bernreuter, 1933a,b) and the Humm-Wadsworth Temperament Scale (Humm & Wadsworth, 1933a,b)—spurred two decades of I/O research investigating the potential value of these and other self-report tests in applied settings. The Bernreuter Personality Inventory provided an "all-in-one" measure of four scales (later revised to six scales) that combined items from previously developed scales, including the Allport Ascendence-Submission Test and the Laird-Colgate Mental Hygiene Inventory, along with new scale items (see Goldberg, 1971). The Humm-Wadsworth Temperament Scale, designed to assess several aspects of adjustment based on psychiatric theorizing, was developed using psychiatric criterion methods.

The strong appeal of these tests to applied psychologists was threefold: (a) greater efficiency in personality testing associated with the use of a multitrait inventory, (b) the availability of normative data, and (c) the opportunity to identify more precisely specific traits associated with particular aspects of job performance. In the I/O domain, the Bernreuter Personality Inventory quickly gained prominence for use in business settings (see Kruger, 1938; Pillister, 1936; Maller, 1935; National Industrial Conference Board, 1941). Studies published in the I/O literature during the 1930s and 1940s indicated widespread use of the Bernreuter for predicting performance of salespeople (e.g., Bills & Ward, 1936; Dodge, 1938a,b, 1940), nursing students (e.g., Adams, 1941; Bennett & Gordon, 1944; Garrison, 1939; Rhinehart, 1933), cotton mill supervisors (Harrell, 1940), and aircraft manufacturing supervisors (Sartain, 1946).

Overall, results obtained in studies investigating the validity of the Bernreuter Personality Inventory for predicting occupational performance or behavior problems were disappointing (see Super, 1942). Although Dodge (1940) reported a positive association between the Dominance scale of the Bernreuter Personality Inventory and performance ratings among salespersons, the preponderance of studies reported little evidence for the usefulness of these tests in detection of "problem" employees (Dorcus, 1944) or in prediction of job performance using either achievement/ production or supervisor ratings criteria (e.g., Bennett & Gordon, 1944). As the evidence on these measures accumulated, an increasing number of researchers voiced caution against the use of popular inventories for selection purposes (e.g., Dodge, 1940; Hampton, 1940; Kruger, 1938; Kurtz, 1942).

Three new measures that received substantial attention during the 1940s were the Minnesota Multiphasic Personality Inventory (MMPI; Hathaway & McKinley, 1940, 1951), the Personal Inventory (Shipley, Gray, & Newbert, 1946), and the Cornell Selectee Index (Weider, Mittelmann, Weschler, & Wolff, 1944). As reported by Goldberg (1971), the Cornell Selectee Index provided the equivalent of a World War II update to the Woodworth Personal Data Sheet. Among I/O researchers, many of whom worked with military groups to aid in the development of effective screening techniques during World War II, it was the Personal Inventory and the Cornell Selectee Index that attracted most interest during the latter half of the 1940s.

Reviews of the personality testing field by Ellis (1946) and Ellis and Conrad (1948) suggested that personality studies through the mid-1940s could be broadly organized into five categories, or basic methods used to validate new and existing measures: (a) by using a psychiatric criterion (i.e., comparing scores from a normal group with scores from a diagnosed group), (b) by using a rating criterion (i.e., comparing scores with ratings from peers or supervisors), (c) by examining test intercorrelations, (d) by examining test-retest reliability and response distortion tendencies, and (e) by using a behavior or performance criterion (i.e., comparing inventory scores with subsequent performance). Many tests had been developed using the psychiatric criterion method, with the test intercorrelation method being the next most frequent method used. Reviewing the results of these studies, Ellis (1946) concluded that group-administered paper-and-pencil personality tests "are of dubious value in distinguishing between groups of adjusted and maladjusted individuals, and that they are of much less value in the diagnosis of individual adjustment or personality traits" (p. 426).

As a prelude to their review on the validity of personality inventories in the military, Ellis and Conrad (1948) suggested that personality inventories were more effective when used in the military than in civilian practice. They divided available military studies into two groups: those that employed a psychiatric criterion (i.e., use of tests for screening), and those that employed a performance criterion (i.e., use of test for prediction of performance). In the screening domain, Ellis and Conrad (1948) identified 12 factors that they believed contributed to the relative empirical superiority of inventories for screening purposes in the military compared to civilian practice. Many of these factors (e.g., criterion contamination, criterion overlap) suggested that the more positive results obtained in the military domain reflected inadequacies in civilian validation design rather than effectiveness of the inventory. Ellis and Conrad (1948), however, noted that other factors—such as sample heterogeneity, reduced response distortion (because of more stringent penalties for falsification in the military), specialized design, validation, standardization, and realistic application (screening only)—represent positive features more common in military than civilian test validation research.

Ellis and Conrad (1948) concluded that "personality inventories proved generally ineffective for predicting performance-measures (such as successful completion of a training course)" (p. 421). In support of this conclusion, they noted four problems with studies in this domain: prior elimination of abnormals from the sample, unreliability or invalidity of the performance measures, the relatively small residual variance in performance after accounting for individual differences in aptitude and previous training, and the lack of a priori theorizing about the relationship between personality scores and performance criterion (rather than for use as a screening instrument).

In the applied domain, researchers began to articulate more clearly the problems and promise of using personality inventories in industrial settings. Adams (1941), for example, concisely identified five potential uses of personality tests in industry: "(1) to select from technically competent applicants those who possess the personality characteristics requisite in the jobs to be filled, (2) to diagnose service employees who are maladjusted, (3) to assist in the promotion of qualified employees, (4) to help select personnel in apprentice training programs, especially those designed to train junior executives, and (5) to help prevent the employment of individuals who may prove to be seriously maladjusted" (p. 142). He further argued that tests effective in industry would need to be not only reliable and internally consistent, but also easily administered, simple to score, and able to minimize response-distortion tendencies.

Although there was growing recognition of both the general problems associated with the use of personality measures and the unique difficulties in using such tests in industry, systematic attempts to develop and validate work-related measures of personality were rare. Two early ventures in this direction were made by Jurgensen (1944) and Kornhauser (cited in Kurtz, 1948). In an effort to overcome problems associated with the industrial use of existing personality tests (e.g., tendency for examinee response distortion, the relative importance of the trait for job performance, lack of validation data from industrial settings), Jurgensen (1944) conducted a series of studies leading to the development of the 245-item Classification Inventory. In this empirically based effort, items were selected to minimize social desirability, and preliminary versions of the measure were validated on jobs rather than personality traits.

In contrast to Jurgensen's attempt to devise a general-purpose personality test, the Personality Characteristics test, created by Kornhauser for the Life Insurance Sales Research Bureau in 1932, sought to assess specific personality traits related to performance for life insurance salespeople. As reported by Kurtz (1942), specific traits thought to be associated with life insurance sales performance were identified a priori (e.g., self-confidence), and trait subtests were then constructed and evaluated using a large-scale trait-performance concurrent validation design. Kurtz (1942) reported a positive relationship between the Personality Characteristics test (in combination with a personal history measure) and subsequent sales performance in a sample involving several hundred newly hired life insurance salespeople. In a similar vein, Dodge (1938a,b, 1940) had previously conducted a series of studies seeking to identify the personality traits associated with successful selling.

The systematic use of personality tests for managerial personnel selection and evaluation also began in the 1940s, when the Sears company asked Thurstone to develop a procedure for selection of executives. As described by Bentz (1985), the resulting battery included the Guilford Martin Personality Inventories (later revised and combined with two other Guilford inventories, then published in 1949 as the Guilford and Zimmerman Temperament Survey) as well as ability and interest measures. Hogan, Carpenter, Briggs, and Hansson (1985) reported that the personality measures were used by Sears for the purpose of screening in testing of over 10,000 persons during the 1940s.

As the 1940s drew to a close, I/O research on the use of standardized personality tests for selection and promotion continued at a steady pace (e.g., Abt, 1947; Balinsky, 1945; Challman, 1945; Forlano & Kirkpatrick, 1945; Harrell, 1949; Holmes, 1950; Jensen & Rotter, 1947; Knauft, 1949; Kurtz, 1948; Sinaiko, 1949). At the same time, however, the inconclusive pattern of findings obtained in these studies led to growing controversy over the ultimate usefulness of such tests for selection purposes in industry (e.g., see Barnabas, 1948).

Post-World War II Developments

By the end of World War II, personality testing was firmly established as a topic of central interest to basic and applied psychologists. Rapid advances in personality measurement, particularly with respect to the development of clinically oriented measures, were accompanied by military findings indicating the usefulness of such tests as a screen for detection of potential psychiatric problems among military personnel, particularly when selecting personnel for performance of high-stress or high-security positions.

The widespread use of personality measures in the military during the last part of the war further encouraged their use in civilian industrial settings. Spriegel and Dale (1953) reported that 29% of respondents to a 1947 survey regarding the personnel practices of 325 American companies indicated that their company used personality or interest tests for selection. A follow-up study of 628 companies indicated that this rate had increased to 40% in 1953 (Spriegel & Dale, 1953) and to 56% by the end of the decade (Gross, 1962). Whyte (1954) estimated that about a third of U.S. companies utilized personality inventories in 1952, a figure that swelled to nearly 60% by 1954. For the selection of sales personnel, Cleveland (1948) noted that although research with personality inventories began somewhat later than research with cognitive ability tests, personality inventories received an increasing preponderance of research effort between 1935 and 1945.

The 1950s and early 1960s also witnessed a rapid expansion in research on personality assessment. Biesheuvel (1965) reported that by 1961, 14.4% of the tests listed in Buros's *Tests in Print* purported to assess some aspect of personality. Katzell and Katzell (1962) indicated that "several hundred books, monographs, and articles have been published during the past three years describing the development, application, validity, reliability, and norms of various structured measures of personality" (p. 51). With only a few exceptions (e.g., the Classification Inventory, the Personality Characteristics Test), however, little of the programmatic work on test development was directed toward or occurred in the context of industrial applications. Taylor and Nevis (1961) noted that "by and large, psychological tests are primarily educational and counseling tools. Even among the 114 entries in the section entitled 'Vocations,' relatively few of the entries were developed, standardized, and validated on either employed personnel or job applicants. The same is true to an even greater extent of the 96 nonprojective tests of character and personality" (p. 391).

Ghiselli and Barthol (1953) published the first major review of I/O studies investigating the validity of personality tests for selection purposes in industry. For this review, the authors analyzed validity information from 113 studies utilizing personality inventories in employee selection between 1919 and 1953. To address the question of whether the personality tests might be useful in some occupations but not others, they organized studies into five broad occupational groups. No attempt was made to examine validity coefficients by type of test, trait, or criterion, though Ghiselli and Barthol indicated that they selected only those studies in which the trait appeared to have relevance to the job in question. A summary of their results is provided in Table 1.

Ghiselli and Barthol (1953) reported substantial differences in both the number of studies within each occupational group (ranging from 5 studies for protective workers to 44 studies for foremen), as well as in the effectiveness of personality measures for predicting performance within each occupational group (with mean *r*'s ranging from .14 for general supervisors to .36 for sales clerks and salesmen). The authors noted, with some surprise, that the mean validity obtained in studies of supervisory personnel and foremen was lower than that obtained in studies involving clerical workers, salespeople, or trades and crafts workers. They concluded that though personality inventories did appear to be effective predictors of job performance in some occupations, the effectiveness of such tests varied widely across job category and by study. In conclusion, Ghiselli and Barthol came down on the side of the growing number of I/O researchers who emphasized caution in the use of such tests in industry.

Cautions regarding the use of personality measures in industry continued to appear throughout the 1960s. Two distinct, but related issues began to emerge. The proliferation of inadequately validated personality tests used to meet specific organizational needs, rather than to assess distinct personality traits, made it difficult to evaluate the effectiveness of trait testing for personnel selection (e.g., Dunnette, 1962). Dunnette (1962) and Guion and Gottier (1965), for example, argued that the lack of attention to the theoretical links between the predictor and criterion constructs, along with an often poor understanding of the

Table 1. Weighted Mean Validity Coefficients of Personality Inventories for Various Occupational Groups

Occupation	Mean *r*	Total cases	# of *r*s
General supervisors	.14	518	8
Foremen	.18	6,433	44
Clerks	.25	1,069	22
Sales clerks	.36	1,120	8
Salesmen	.36	927	12
Protective workers	.24	536	5
Service workers	.16	385	6
Trades and crafts	.29	511	8

Source: Adapted from Ghiselli & Barthol (1953).

criterion space, made it difficult to draw substantive conclusions. That is, the existing research environment enabled researchers to assess the potential effectiveness of a particular inventory in predicting job performance (if multiple studies were conducted using the same instrument), but it did not permit generalization to other tests or to the theoretical relationship between specific traits and work behavior.

Another major source of concern for many I/O researchers pertained to the general lack of validation research on measures not created for use in the workplace, as well as to the frequent use of inappropriate validation methodologies when such research was undertaken. Although concerns about methodological issues in determining the validity of a measure had been voiced earlier (e.g., Ellis & Conrad, 1948), I/O psychologists became increasingly concerned about the use of descriptive and concurrent validation methodologies for demonstrating the predictive validity of nonability tests used in industry (e.g., Locke & Hulin, 1962). In addition, greater attention was given to the criterion being used. Katzell and Katzell (1962), for example, noted that although criteria of pathology were being studied vigorously in the personality test literature, there was a noticeable dearth of research using measures of performance as criteria. Because I/O interest focused largely on use of personality tests for prediction of performance, rather than for screening or detection of maladjustment, I/O psychologists could not rely on advances in basic research and would need to conduct validation research using theories of job performance rather than psychopathology or adult development as criteria.

Perhaps because of these problems, reviews on the usefulness of personality inventories after Ghiselli and Barthol (1953) grew increasingly pessimistic in tone (e.g., Locke & Hulin, 1962; Guion & Gottier, 1965). Locke and Hulin (1962) reviewed 18 studies investigating the Activity Vector Analysis (AVA), an 81-item personality measure designed for personnel selection in industry by Clarke (1956) and used by a substantial number of practitioners during the late 1950s. Organizing AVA studies according to the type of validation design used, Locke and Hulin's analysis focused mainly on the methodological issues associated with the various groups of studies. Although several of the studies reported support for the effectiveness of the AVA, Locke and Hulin (1962) argued that all but one study, which yielded inconclusive results, were methodologically flawed. They concluded that the validation studies were not adequate for providing conclusive evidence about whether the AVA predicted job performance.

The most influential review of personality measures in personnel selection during the 1960s was published by Guion and Gottier (1965). In this review of both personality tests and interest measures, the authors examined studies on personality assessment in industry appearing in the *Journal of Applied Psychology* and *Personnel Psychology* from 1952 to 1963. Guion and Gottier included interest measures, such as the Strong Vocational Interest Blank, in the odd belief that both interest and personality measures are used for a common purpose and are difficult to distinguish both theoretically and empirically. Two additional criteria were established for inclusion of a study in the review: (a) that the test had been used for selection in civilian employment settings, and (b) that the test in question had also been examined in at least two other studies within the 12-year period. For each study, only results in which the personality test was examined on its own as a predictor (rather than in combination with other test measures) were considered. Many of the personality measures included in the review were relatively new tests constructed to assess normal personality, including the Guilford-Zimmerman Temperament Inventory, the Gordon Personal Profile, and the Edwards Personal Preference Schedule.

Consistent with the review approach taken by Locke and Hulin (1962), Guion and Gottier (1965) focused their examination of findings largely in terms of type of study design. Among the inventory studies, only 37% used a predictive validity design. Among these studies, 10% reported significant validity coefficients for the measure. Guion and Gottier concluded that "it cannot be said that any of the conventional personality measures have demonstrated really general usefulness as selection tools in employment practice" (p. 140). Echoing conclusions reached in previous reviews, the authors noted the positive findings but placed more emphasis on advocating strong caution in the use of personality tests for personnel selection:

> There is no generalizable evidence that personality measures can be recommended as good or practical tools for employee selection. The number of significance tests resulting in acceptable statements of validity is greater than might be expected by pure chance—but not much. The best that can be said is that in *some* situations, for *some* purposes, *some* personality measures can offer helpful predictions. (p. 159)

A review of the MMPI (Hedlund, 1965) produced similar results. Hedlund concluded that there was a paucity of methodologically acceptable research with the MMPI, and that most of the research produced nonsignificant or negative results. The studies reviewed by Hedlund demonstrated many of the methodological problems highlighted by Locke and Hulin (1962) and Guion and Gottier (1965).

As Guion and Gottier (1965) noted, many studies they reviewed represented what they termed "broadside" studies—that is, studies that correlated every available predictor with every available criterion, regardless of theoretical predictor-criterion relationships (or the lack thereof). Because personality constructs are likely to be differentially associated with performance dimensions in different occupations, effective performance in different occupations is likely to involve different characteristics. If the determinants of performance had been elucidated and considered, many of the correlations that were computed in a broadside design would be *predicted to be negligible* because the personality constructs simply were not relevant for the particular measure of performance in a particular occupation. Broadside studies thus drove down the proportion of correlations showing significant results by including many correlations that were predictably negligible. These correlations can be viewed as evidence of discriminant validity for the personality measures rather than as "misses"; constructs that were not supposed to correlate did not. Considering them misses, as the reviews did, produced artificially poor conclusions. Ghiselli and Barthol (1953) attempted to eliminate studies in which the predictor and the criterion were not theoretically related; Guion and Gottier (1965) did not, a decision that may explain their more pessimistic conclusions.

Guion and Gottier (1965) did eliminate personality measures that were included in fewer than three reports during the 12-year period they studied. Though this had the effect of including only inventories that enjoyed relatively widespread use, it also excluded many studies of "homemade" personality inventories (inventories developed for a specific situation). In general, these required more thought about predictor-criterion relationships and employed a more theoretically driven rationale for selecting items. Also, the homemade inventories tended to measure narrower, more specific traits with better understood relations with the criteria than did the general personality inventories; these narrower traits usually were better matched to the breadth of the criteria. The result, according to Guion and Gottier (1965), was that the homemade inventories fared better than general personality measures.

The I/O reviews on the validity of personality testing for personnel selection indicated good reason for the widespread pessimism about personality assessment in industry. But as Ellis and Conrad (1948) noted in their review of the military personality testing literature two decades earlier, negative findings may result from poor test design, development, and validation rather than from the lack of legitimate predictor-criterion relationships. In fact, many of the critics of modern industrial personality assessment agreed that there was a real need to assess nonability factors and that personality assessment, driven by a rigorous methodological and theoretical concern, could play an important role in personnel selection. Guion and Gottier (1965), for example, noted that "there seems to be a genuine need to predict the kinds of behavior influenced by personality. . . . The fact that personality tests often fail to be able to predict in no way lessens the need" (p. 151). Biesheuvel (1965) stated that "descriptions of job requirements generally abound with attributes that are either partly or wholly noncognitive, such as leadership, supervisory ability, capacity for sustained effort, integrity, sociability, and the like" (p. 300). Guion and Gottier (1965) raise the issue of whether the better prediction for homemade, situation-specific measures reflected the nature of the personality-work relationship or whether general measures of personality, carefully developed, could be as successful: "Is this state of affairs inherent in the nature of the relationship between personality and work, or is it possible that serious, concerted effort might yield more generalized systems of prediction using personality measures? The present writers lean toward the latter possibility" (p. 159).

The widespread use of personality tests for personnel selection in industry peaked during the early 1960s. As the decade wore on, practical problems (e.g., confidentiality, faking), the implications of new civil rights legislation for testing, continuing methodological difficulties in conducting validation research in industrial settings, and the growing situationism debate within psychology about the usefulness of personality constructs appeared as overwhelming problems. As a consequence, the use of personality assessments in industry declined sharply in the 1960s for all but the most sensitive job positions (e.g., police officer, air traffic controller, or nuclear power plant operator), where tests such as the MMPI or 16PF continued to be administered as a preemployment screening device (e.g., see Rosse, Miller, & Barnes, 1991, for a review).

Popular concern that nonability test items invaded individuals' privacy or violated their confidentiality came to a head in the mid-1960s (see Anastasi, 1985; Ridgeway, 1964, 1965). Long-standing scientific criticisms of test developers for use of deceptive or misleading practices when selling tests, inadequate test validation, and the lack of conceptual links between measures and job performance further fueled public disapproval of nonability test usage in industry and led to the development of more elaborate professional standards governing the administration and use of tests (see American Psychological Association, 1970; Anastasi, 1980, 1985, for more thorough reviews).

Another challenge to the use of tests in industry, pertaining to issues of civil rights and fairness, was causing major changes in the field of personnel selection. The Civil Rights Act of 1964, the establishment of the Equal Employment Opportunity Commission (EEOC), and subsequent landmark U.S. Supreme Court rulings laid out the circumstances under which the use of testing for personnel selection would be allowed and the nature of validation evidence organizations would be required to provide in the event of a legal challenge to the use of a test (see Arvey & Faley, 1988, for a discussion). Many companies, fearing the consequences of a long and expensive legal challenge to their selection procedures, simply abandoned preemployment testing in favor of more subjective techniques (e.g., interviews) that were less likely to be challenged (Tenopyr, 1981). As reported by Friedman and Williams (1982), the Prentice-Hall/American Society for Personnel Administrators Survey of 1,339 personnel officers in 1975 and 1976 indicated that 75% of companies had reduced their employee testing during the previous 5 years and that almost 14% had eliminated testing altogether. A similar survey of 196 personnel executives by the Bureau of National Affairs (Miner, 1976) identified the same trend; psychological tests (defined as measures of skill, ability, intelligence, or personality) were used by only 42% of companies in 1976, compared with 55% in 1971 (American Society of Personnel Administrators, 1971) and 90% in 1963 (Bureau of National Affairs, 1963).

At the same time that the applied use of personality assessment was trapped in the midst of public and legal controversy, the theoretical basis of personality assessment came under attack as well. The controversy about the consistency and generalizability of personality traits versus the situational specificity of behavior turned in favor of the situationists in the late 1960s and early 1970s (Anastasi, 1985). In essence, the situationists argued that people's behavior was influenced more by the nature of and forces acting in the situation or environment than by characteristics of the individual (Mischel, 1968, 1969, 1973; Peterson, 1968). Though the issues raised in this debate are beyond the scope of this chapter (e.g., see Hogan, DeSoto, & Solano, 1977; Kenrick & Funder, 1988, for reviews), the implications for the use of personality tests in industry were clear: If situational specificity dominated, then personality tests would be of severely limited utility in predicting behavior across situations and thus job performance.

The 1970s were a relatively quiet period in the history of personality assessment in industry. Reviews of published studies involving the use of personality tests in personnel selection continued to point to the conceptual and methodological problems plaguing research in the area (e.g., Lent, Aurbach, & Levin, 1971; Ghiselli, 1973; Mitchell, 1979). In addition, however, both Lent et al. (1971) and Ghiselli (1973) suggested that previous conclusions about the relationship of personality traits to job performance may have been too pessimistic. Lent et al. (1971) reviewed 406 validation studies published in *Personnel Psychology* between 1945 and 1956 in terms of "significance batting averages" (SBA), which they defined as the ratio of significance frequency ("hits," or correlations whose probabilities of occurring by chance were less than or equal to .05) to usage frequency ("at bats") for a variety of predictors (e.g., individual- and interpersonal-oriented traits). They found that individual character and personality measures demonstrated an SBA of .31 (significantly higher than the results obtained by Guion and Gottier, 1965), whereas interpersonal character and personality measures demonstrated an SBA of .10 (identical to the results obtained by Guion and Gottier). Lent et al. (1971) pointed out that both of these SBAs exceeded the level expected by chance, and further, that both of the SBAs were attenuated by the tendency of researchers to utilize broadside research designs and by criterion unreliability, invalidity, and breadth.

Ghiselli (1973) summarized the published literature from 1920 through 1971 pertaining to the validity of personnel selection methodologies, separated according to occupations and predictors. Ghiselli's results, expressed in terms of the mean validity coefficient weighted according to number of cases, are summarized in Table 2. As he noted, many of the validity coefficients were nontrivial, and personality assessments, like the ability predictors, did again show differential validities across occupations.

Ghiselli stated that for a variety of reasons (e.g., restriction of range in the predictors and criteria, lack of criterion reliability and validity, breadth of criteria), the mean validities he reported should be viewed as *underestimates* of the predictive power of the tests. For example, he estimated that the reliabilities of the criterion measures usually were between .60 and .80 and often as low as .50, seriously limited the observed validity of the predictors. These problems, unrelated to the usefulness of the predictor, also plagued studies reported in other reviews, suggesting that these reviews might also have provided underestimates of the predictive efficacy of the assessments.

In personality psychology during the 1970s, the situationism debate had forced examination of issues such as predictor and criterion breadth, aggregation of items, and test construction techniques (Kenrick & Funder, 1988), and it had led to the creation of more conceptually and theoretically coherent, methodologically sound inventories (Hogan & Nicholson, 1988). In addition, personality research during this time began to coalesce around a five-factor model of taxonomy of personality (Borgatta, 1964; Costa & McCrae, 1988; Digman & Inouye, 1986; Fiske, 1949; Goldberg, 1981; McCrae & Costa, 1985, 1987, 1989; Norman, 1963; Tupes & Christal, 1961; for a more comprehensive account of the nature of the five-factor model, see Digman, 1990). For applied psychologists, the emergence of a common taxonomy of personality provided a critical opportunity for organizing personality constructs and for linking such constructs with job performance constructs.

Table 2. Validity Coefficients for Personality Inventories

Occupation	Performance criterion
Managerial occupations	.21[e]
Clerical occupations	.24[d]
Sales	.31[d]
Protective occupations	.24[c]
Service occupations	.16[b]
Processing workers	.30[b]
Complex machine operators	.24[b]
Bench workers	.50[a]

Source: Adapted from Ghiselli (1973).
[a] $n < 100$
[b] 100 to 499 cases
[c] 500 to 999 cases
[d] 1000 to 4,999 cases
[e] $n > 10{,}000$

REVIEW OF INTELLIGENCE THEORY AND TESTING AND I/O PSYCHOLOGY

Early Research and Applications

In the United States, mass intelligence testing was given its first major tryout during World War I, with mixed success. Hundreds of thousands of U.S. Army recruits were tested with one of two intelligence tests (Army Alpha, the primary instrument, and Army Beta, a nonverbal test for illiterates and nonnative English speakers). The actual number of selection decisions based on these tests, however, remains uncertain (Yoakum & Yerkes, 1920). Individual base commanders showed great variability in their support of the testing enterprise, as well as in their dependence on the tests for selection and classification decisions. Nevertheless, the massive amount of data collected by Yerkes and his colleagues resulted in heightened interest in the use of intelligence tests for selection purposes in industry.

In addition to the widespread administration of group tests of general intelligence during WWI, the U.S. Army developed and administered a number of so-called trade tests essentially specialized tests for particular job knowledge and skills. As Hull (1928) reported, "The tests were designed to separate the men tested into four groups of proficiency: (1) novices, (2) apprentices, (3) journeymen, and (4) experts" (p. 51). According to Hull, the tests fell into three basic categories: verbal and picture tests (both types were paper-and-pencil measurements of job knowledge), and performance tests (generally apparatus-based tests that more or less sampled the skills required by the job).

By the beginning of the 1920s, numerous examples of test construction and administration for prediction of occupational success can be found in the literature (see Viteles, 1932, for a review). The types of applications of ability testing can be divided into two general approaches: the use of general intelligence tests, and the use of specialized aptitude batteries. Adherents of general intelligence tests (basically followers of the Spearman, 1904, doctrine of general intelligence), found valid applications of standard group tests of intelligence in a variety of occupations, including such widely different jobs as secretaries, bookkeepers, machinists, and insurance salesmen (Viteles, 1932).

Other researchers—followers of the group-factor theories proposed by Thomson (1916, 1939), Kelly (1928), and others—found general intelligence tests to be of limited validity in comparison to aptitude, knowledge, and skills tests that were tailored to particular occupations. Two methods for application of ability testing were used by applied psychologists during this period. The first method was to develop tailored test batteries for each occupation after performing the requisite job analysis (which focused on the abilities, knowledge, and skills of the specific job); with this procedure, the investigators would have one test battery for predicting the success of secretaries, another for bookkeepers, another for loom operators, and so on. The second method evolved out of the research efforts by psychologists who focused on finding fundamental abilities and the group factors that underlay such abilities. A number of investigators developed standardized test batteries for a variety of different ability classes, including mechanical abilities (Paterson, Elliott, Anderson, Toops, & Heidbreder, 1930), motor skills (e.g., Farmer, 1927, described in Viteles, 1932), and clerical abilities (e.g., Thurstone, 1919, described in Viteles, 1932). These batteries vastly simplified the application of ability testing in the workplace, as employers no longer needed to perform the lengthy process of job analysis, test construction, and standardization for each specific job. Although employers with large numbers of employees in single occupations often created specialized tests, the simplicity of using the standardized tests resulted in the proliferation of industrial applications through the 1920s and 1930s.

Intelligence Testing during World War II

In the United States during World War II, intelligence theory and research and I/O applications came together in a unified effort that has not been reproduced since. Many prominent psychologists and numerous others who would go on to become prominent in the postwar years coalesced in a number of groups to put ability theory into practice in a highly time-compressed war effort. Ability tests were developed for the selection and classification of thousands of military personnel in the Army, Navy, Army Air Forces, and the Office of Strategic Services (OSS). A full review of these programs is beyond the scope of this chapter, but extensive reviews can be found elsewhere (e.g., Flanagan, 1948; Stuit, 1947). To review the effort briefly, we focus on the program in the Army Air Forces.

The group of psychologists involved in this particular program and their contributions included R. L. Thorndike (selection theory and method), J. Flanagan (critical incidents technique), J. P. Guilford, J. I. Lacey, L. G. Humphreys (development of numerous printed ability tests), A. Melton (development of numerous apparatus tests), J. J. Gibson (motion-picture based spatial ability tests), and P. H. Dubois (classification techniques). Tests were administered to more than 600,000 men in this program; in contrast to the World War I efforts, the tests were used to great effect in selection and classification. Never before had it been feasible to so quickly move through cycles of job analysis, creation of ability tests, evaluation of test validity and reliability, and refinement of procedures. It is not surprising, then, that so much progress in testing methodology and applications was made in the war years.

The postwar result of these investigations was to place intellectual ability test use in personnel decisions much more in the domain of scientific application than it was before the war. Procedures developed during the war for criterion development, statistical methods for evaluating the utility of particular tests, and the tests per se provided the foundation for both basic research and application developments through the 1950s. The proliferation of ability measures (Guilford & Lacey, 1948; Melton, 1948) for example, served as the basis for Guilford's structure of intellect theory (Guilford, 1956), and expanded the coverage of intellectual abilities beyond those specified by Thurstone in the late 1930s (e.g., see Thurstone, 1938; Thurstone & Thurstone, 1941).

Post-World War II Intelligence Testing

The period from the end of World War II through the 1970s had a very different character from previous periods of development and application of intellectual ability tests for industry. No revolutions in approaches occurred; rather, tests were refined and improved in the context of earlier theory and practice. The two approaches that developed during the 1920s—using general intelligence tests for applicant selection, and using specialized batteries of group-factor tests—remained prominent in industrial applications. The major shift in ability testing for industry occurred after the initial publication of technical standards for psychological tests (American Psychological Association, 1954; for the current version, see American Educational Research Association, American Psychological Association, & National Council on Measurement in Education, 1985), because of the validation requirements imposed by the professional associations of psychologists. Industry found it difficult to justify using broad intellectual ability measures for application selection, in that each facet of the intelligence test would need to be demonstrated to be valid for the job in question. As such, there was a decrease in the use of broad ability tests, and an increase in use of test batteries that were tailored to particular group factors of ability (e.g., mechanical abilities, clerical abilities, numerical abilities). This shift in usage was accelerated by U.S. Equal Employment Opportunity Commission (EEOC) rules promulgated during the late 1970s (EEOC, 1978), and several litigations involving the use of ability tests in selection and promotion decisions. The EEOC rules placed validation requirements on industry (that generally proceduralized the guidelines in the APA standards) when adverse impact for protected minorities was found in the organization. Indeed, some organizations (and governmental agencies) abandoned ability testing entirely, rather than defend the use of such tests in court. In a 1975–1976 follow-up survey of manufacturing organizations (the original survey was administered in 1963), a large decline (from 90% to 35%) was found in the use of preemployment psychological tests (BNA, 1976). Fewer than 20 of 300 organizations used tests that obviously provide estimates of general intellectual ability (e.g., Wonderlic Personnel Test, Cattell's Culture Fair Test, SRA Nonverbal Test); the remaining organizations made wise use of specialized ability test batteries (e.g., SRA Clerical Battery, Bennett Mechanical Comprehension, Minnesota Clerical Test, SRA Typing Skills). Thus, regardless of the merits of using general intelligence tests for employee selection, organizations clearly had reduced their overall usage of such tests in favor of either group-factor tests or no ability tests at all.

CONTEMPORARY DEVELOPMENTS FOR INTELLIGENCE IN I/O PSYCHOLOGY

Ability Theory and Selection

Two basic approaches to applying ability theory are most prominent in research and practice today: "validity generalization" and the cognitive or information-processing approach. Each are treated in turn below.

Validity Generalization

The validity generalization approach, most closely identified with the work by Schmidt, Hunter, and their colleagues (e.g., Hunter, 1986; Schmidt & Hunter, 1977; Schmidt, Hunter, & Pearlman, 1981), focuses on the efficiency with which occupational success can be predicted by measures of general intelligence. Schmidt, Hunter, et al. have accumulated a large corpus of data and methodological techniques of meta-analysis to show that general intelligence measures predict job performance as well as ability batteries that are purported to be tailored to specific jobs and organizations. Though some elements of their conclusions remain controversial, one major finding seems irrefutable: With relatively small samples of examinees (e.g., under 300; see Thorndike, 1986), a general ability composite from a test battery has a higher cross-validated prediction efficiency than an optimized regression equation from the same ability battery. Note, however, that this finding may be limited to jobs that are general in scope (e.g., manager, salesclerk), and may not generalize as well to jobs that have more specific demands (e.g., spatial demands in engineering, architecture, air traffic control; verbal demands of authors, editors; clerical speed demands of typists, secretaries, file clerks). That is, when jobs are made up of myriad tasks that require a variety of different abilities, general intelligence is a highly efficient predictor of success. When jobs are more homogeneous in ability demands, particular abilities (spatial, verbal, numerical, perceptual speed) may have greater relative influence in comparison to general intelligence.

From a historical perspective, the position of validity generalization can be thought of as the end of the line of scientific inquiry into the ability determinants of job performance. To the degree that Schmidt and Hunter's perspective is correct, the only useful research on ability-performance relations would be in refinements to measures of general intelligence (which, after nearly 100 years of development, have probably reached an asymptotic level of evolution).

Cognitive/Information-Processing Approach

In contrast to the traditional psychometric approach to intelligence—which is essentially a top-down view, with general intelligence at the top of the hierarchy—the cognitive, information-processing approach is mostly a "bottom-up" view of intellectual ability. Basic research concerning the cognitive approach to intelligence focused first on individual differences in basic information-processing tasks (e.g., encoding, memory storage and retrieval, simple judgments, speed of reaction). In many ways, this approach revisits issues similar to those of early modern psychologists (e.g., J. M. Cattell, 1890; Galton, 1883), though the recent efforts have attacked the issues of individual differences with an array of cognitive theory, modern quantitative techniques, and computer technology. One of the initial issues for this approach was the determination of the fundamental components of individual differences in intellectual abilities (or "elementary cognitive tasks"; Carroll, 1980, 1993).

Although psychologists have focused their attention on these information-processing components of intellectual abilities for 20 years (starting with Hunt, Frost, & Lunneborg, 1973), such attempts have had relatively little impact in applications for selection, for two reasons. The first reason is practical, as it pertains to the logistical difficulties in using the typical computerized measures for assessment of information processing in the I/O domain. In comparison to paper-and-pencil format for traditional employment tests, computers are more expensive, are harder to move from one site to another, require greater upkeep, and so on. These difficulties are similar to those encountered by the Army Air Forces in using "apparatus tests" during WWII (e.g., see Melton, 1948). With the proliferation of personal computers since the 1980s, however, many of these difficulties have diminished, and many organizations have switched from paper-and-pencil to computerized ability tests.

The second reason for the reduced impact of the cognitive/information-processing approach to ability assessment in selection testing is also the reason for the success of the validity generalization approach: Unless jobs are highly specialized and the samples of applicants/incumbents are very large, a general ability composite works as well as any tailored test battery, including tests of basic information-processing components of ability. One reason for this particular result is that broad ability tests successfully sample many different facets of intelligence (e..g, see Humphreys, 1962), whereas information-processing tasks most frequently tap highly specific knowledge, skills, and abilities. Furthermore, there exists a much greater degree of overlap between the breadth of typical job performance criteria and the breadth of general intelligence tests (e.g., see Dunnette, 1963, for a discussion of this issue). Information-processing tasks tap narrow abilities and, as such, can be only reasonably expected to predict relatively narrow criteria.

Notwithstanding these difficulties, research on the information-processing approach to abilities is beginning to have an impact on selection. This approach is seen as particularly promising in the prediction of job performance for highly specialized jobs—those that can be expected to have greater reliance on one set of abilities than others. The cognitive approach has successfully been used in delineating the underlying ability determinants of verbal abilities (e.g., see Carroll, 1993), spatial abilities (e.g., Lohman, 1979, 1987), perceptual speed abilities (e.g., see Ackerman, 1990), and others (for an extensive review, see Carroll, 1993). When job performance can be expected to depend on such abilities, the more precise techniques of ability assessment from this approach will provide the foundation for creation of tailored tests that may be more highly predictive of job performance than general intelligence tests.

This point is especially significant, given the classical problem of bandwidth-fidelity in ability testing (Cronbach, 1990). The bandwidth-fidelity dilemma (or paradox) is that *for a fixed period of testing time*, one can maximize bandwidth (the breadth of the test content) or fidelity (the precision of testing for any construct), but maximizing one criterion comes at the cost of minimizing the other. For broad criteria and jobs with multiple components, the intelligence test works optimally because it has high bandwidth. When criteria are narrow (e.g., typing speed and accuracy for a clerical job), however, tests of greater fidelity (e.g., information processing-based ability tests) will have increased predictive validity.

Ability Theory and Training

A great amount of progress has been made in the past decade concerning the relations between intellectual abilities and individual differences in performance during training. Two theoretical approaches explicitly spell out the expected relations between particular abilities and task performance as skills (Ackerman, 1988) and knowledge are acquired (Kyllonen & Christal, 1989) in the context of practice and training (see Ackerman & Kyllonen, 1991, for a review). The theory proposed by Kyllonen and Christal (1989) specifies four sources of individual differences in the acquisition of knowledge and skills: breadth of declarative knowledge (i.e., knowledge about things), breadth of procedural skills (i.e., knowledge of how to do tasks), capacity of working memory, and speed of processing. When a task allows for transfer of training from previous experience, breadth of declarative knowledge and procedural skills strongly influence performance and learning (e.g., Kyllonen & Tirre, 1988; Kyllonen, Tirre, & Christal, 1991). When a task is novel, however, the critical components of performance over task practice are working memory and processing speed, with working memory capacity most associated with initial task performance and processing speed most associated with performance after practice (Woltz, 1988).

Ackerman's theory segments the ability-performance relations into three broadly defined stages of practice corresponding to Fitts and Posner's (1967) cognitive, associative, and autonomous stages. The theory specifies that general ability and broad content abilities (spatial, verbal, numerical) are most associated with novel task performance (cognitive stage), perceptual speed abilities are most associated with intermediate practiced performance (associative stage), and psychomotor abilities are most associated with performance after protracted practice (autonomous stage). The theory also specifies that only tasks with *consistent* information-processing components will show these three-stage changes in ability-performance relations. Inconsistent information-processing task components (e.g., where novelty or uncertainty prevails), or tasks where the consistency of information processing is not apparent to the subjects, will fail to show changes beyond the cognitive stage of practice (Ackerman, 1988).

The theories make similar predictions for ability-performance relations during practice in several types of tasks. At an intermediate stage of task practice, tests of perceptual speed ability (e.g., tests of substitution, clerical checking, perceptual scanning) and tests of processing speed (e.g., encoding speed, retrieval speed, and response speed), are increasingly associated with individual differences in task performance (Ackerman, 1988; Woltz, 1988). The theories diverge in predicting the determinants of individual differences in task performance at the autonomous stage of skill acquisition. Furthermore, the Kyllonen and Christal theory is more suited to prediction of performance in knowledge-rich tasks (ones that allow for general transfer effects), given the emphasis on previous declarative and procedural knowledge. The Ackerman theory is more suited to prediction of performance in knowledge-impoverished tasks, and for tasks that have substantial motor-processing components.

There are several implications of these theories for I/O applications. One implication relates to the question of optimal criteria for the organization's concerns. That is, these theories specify the abilities that are most associated with individual differences in initial training performance, intermediate training performance, and ultimately, performance on the job. With these theories, an organization can determine which are the critical criteria to predict. When training is long and expensive (or when typical job tenure is short), test constructors can concentrate on the abilities that determine training success. When training costs are less of a concern (or when the organization is more interested in the prediction of individual differences in asymptotic levels of skilled job performance), however, the focus of test construction can be shifted to testing of the abilities that predict long-term skill development and maintenance. The second major implication of these theories is for using ability measures and the design of training methods in an iterative fashion (see Ackerman, 1992, for a discussion of this approach). That is, ability-performance relations may be examined to discover potential causes of trainee failure (e.g., the training material may be especially difficult for trainees of low spatial ability). By modifying the training program (e.g., by creating performance aids such as physical models), the ability demands may be changed or attenuated. As such, selection and training strategies can be continually tuned to optimize the overall cost-benefit function between testing and training.

CONTEMPORARY DEVELOPMENTS FOR PERSONALITY IN I/O PSYCHOLOGY

Interest in personality assessment among I/O psychologists grew steadily during the 1980s. Significant trends in basic and applied domains underlying this renewed interest included the fading of the situationism debate, the emergence of the big-five factor taxonomy of personality and the subsequent focus of applied researchers on personality constructs rather than tests, the further articulation of appropriate construct validation methodologies, and the growing emphasis on the validation of all instruments used for employment decisions. Though reviews of the personality testing literature during the early 1980s remained largely negative (e.g., Schmitt, Gooding, Noe, & Kirsch, 1984), enthusiasm for the potential value of personality tests in industrial/organizational settings during the decade that followed reached a new high, as evidenced by the development of new tests, research on personality-work behavior linkages, and reviews of the literature. The remainder of this section describes recent developments organized into four broad and overlapping areas: (a) taxonomic research, (b) predictor construct developments, (c) other empirical studies, and (d) technical/use issues.

Taxonomic Research

During the past decade, I/O researchers have focused on determining the personality constructs that are important for the performance of particular jobs and identifying predictors that assess these constructs. In contrast to earlier work that emphasized the validity coefficient rather than the predictor or criterion constructs, recent studies tend to employ a construct validation type of strategy. In this multistep approach, researchers begin with job analysis for the purpose of specifying performance traits necessary for job performance or the criterion space. In contrast to the broadside approach discussed earlier, personality constructs are then conceptually linked to performance constructs, and personality measures are validated with respect to both the predictor and criterion constructs in an iterative fashion.

Studies by Borman, Rosse, and Abrahams (1980) and research conducted under the auspices of the U.S. Army Project A team (Hough, Eaton, Dunnette, Kamp, & McCloy, 1990; McHenry, Hough, Toquam, Hanson, & Ashworth, 1990) are representative of this approach. For example, the Army Project A studies involved ability and nonability testing of more than 10,000 personnel. In the Hough et al. (1990) report, analysis of the criterion space was conducted concurrently with investigation of the predictor domain to yield a model of personality–work criterion linkages. A nonability battery, designed to assess six predictor constructs, was developed and empirically evaluated in the context of relationships to a multidimensional set of performance criteria. McHenry et al. (1990) examined the predictive validity of the nonability measures for training and proficiency criteria. Results obtained in both studies indicate that two personality constructs, dependability and achievement, were found to be valid predictors of ancillary job performance criteria (e.g., effort and leadership, personal discipline).

A related approach takes advantage of the big-five factor taxonomy of personality constructs (see e.g., Digman, 1990; Goldberg, 1990). Barrick and Mount (1991), for example, examined the relationship of these five personality dimensions to three job performance criteria among five occupational groups. Using applied studies appearing from 1952 to 1988, Barrick and Mount had raters classify the personality scales used in the research into the various predictor dimensions. Meta-analytic results, summarized in Table 3, indicate that only conscientiousness was substantially related to performance across all occupations and for all types of criteria. In contrast, extraversion was found to be a valid predictor across all criterion types for two occupations (managers and sales).

Another approach to clarifying personality–job performance linkages stems from consideration of the moderating influence of situational strength, or the extent to which demands of the situation constrain variability in employee responses (see, e.g., Adler & Weiss, 1988). Research by Brockner (1985), Peters, Fisher, and O'Connor (1982), and Mowday and Spencer (1981), for example, provides evidence for the moderating influence of situational constraints on the relationship between specific personality dimensions (e.g., self-esteem and achievement motivation) and work performance. At a broader level, Barrick and Mount (1993) examined the role of autonomy as a moderator of the relationship between predictor constructs of conscientiousness and extraversion and an aggregated measure of performance ratings obtained for 146 managers. A Personal Characteristics Inventory (PCI) was developed to provide measures of the five basic personality constructs, and the inventory was then administered to managers. Autonomy, defined in terms of situational pressures, was assessed by employee and supervisor ratings. The results demonstrated support for the hypotheses that autonomy moderated the relationships between conscientiousness and performance as well as extraversion and performance. In addition, however, autonomy was found to moderate the agreeableness-performance relation.

Table 3. Meta-Analysis Results for Personality Dimension–Occupation Combinations (All Criterion Included)

Occupation	Estimated true *r*	Total cases	# of *rs*
Professionals			
Extraversion	−.09	476	4
Emotional stability	−.13	518	5
Agreeableness	.02	557	7
Conscientiousness	.20	767	6
Openness to experience	−.08	476	4
Police			
Extraversion	.09	1,496	16
Emotional stability	.10	1,697	18
Agreeableness	.10	1,437	14
Conscientiousness	.22	2,045	19
Openness to experience	.00	1,364	13
Managers			
Extraversion	.18	11,335	59
Emotional stability	.08	10,324	55
Agreeableness	.10	8,597	47
Conscientiousness	.22	10,058	52
Openness to experience	.08	7,611	37
Sales			
Extraversion	.15	2,316	22
Emotional stability	.07	2,486	19
Agreeableness	.00	2,344	16
Conscientiousness	.23	2,263	21
Openness to experience	−.02	1,566	12
Skilled/semiskilled			
Extraversion	.01	3,888	23
Emotional stability	.12	3,694	26
Agreeableness	.06	4,585	28
Conscientiousness	.21	4,588	25
Openness to experience	.01	3,219	16

Source: Adapted from Barrick & Mount (1991).

Cortina, Doherty, Schmitt, Kaufman, and Smith (1992) used the five-factor taxonomy in an investigation of the effectiveness of two personality inventories (the MMPI and the Inwald Personality Inventory) for predicting a variety of police training and performance criteria (e.g., training grade point average, turnover, probation ratings). Scales from the MMPI and Inwald Personality Inventory were mapped to the five-factor model using a rational classification procedure, and regressions were conducted to evaluate the incremental predictive validity of nonability measures above that provided by a civil-service examination and panel interview used for hiring. The nonability predictors showed the expected pattern of correlations between conscientiousness and the criteria, but showed significant validities for measures of neuroticism as well. Cortina et al. (1992) noted several limitations of the study and suggested further investigations of the linkage between neuroticism and police performance.

Predictor Construct Developments

Guion and Gibson (1988) suggested that narrower, more job-relevant personality measures may be more useful for predicting employee performance than measures that assess broad, personality constructs. In this vein, several new measures have been developed. Gough (1985) reports positive results on the development of a Work Orientation Scale for the California Psychological Inventory, a scale aimed at assessing individual differences in a constellation of attributes such as self-discipline, dependability, and perseverance with respect to work.

R. Hogan and Hogan (1991) have proposed a theoretically and empirically derived network of personality dimensions underlying attainment of status in different kinds of occupations. They argue that different personality factors are important for predicting status or advancement within different kinds of occupations. In conjunction with this conceptualization of a broad theory of personality, R. Hogan (1986) developed the Hogan Personality Inventory. In addition to the basic personality scales (which map roughly onto the big five), J. Hogan and Hogan (1986) developed six work-related scales (published in the Hogan Personnel Selection Series; also see R. Hogan et al., 1985), including service orientation (R. Hogan, Hogan, & Busch, 1984) and managerial potential (J. Hogan, Hogan, & Murtha, 1992). The Index of Managerial Potential scale, for example, is designed to assess individual differences in the constellation of positive, nonability characteristics associated with effective managerial performance (e.g., energetic, confident, ambitious, persuasive). J. Hogan et al. (1992) report positive results from five concurrent validation studies involving school principals, police officers, telephone company managers, and managerial personnel in an insurance company.

Another recent development pertains to assessment of counterproductive behaviors in the workplace, particularly theft. During the past decade, a number of measures have been developed for this purpose (e.g., see Ash, 1991; Sackett, Burris, & Callahan, 1989; Sackett & Harris, 1984, for reviews). Sackett et al. (1989) have organized these measures into two categories: (a) overt integrity tests that ask directly about attitudes toward theft, dishonesty, and illegal acts, and (b) personality-oriented measures that attempt to predict broad performance constructs defined in terms of deviant, counterproductive work behaviors and organizational delinquency. Personality-oriented measures, such as the Personnel Reaction Blank (Gough, 1971) and the Hogan Employee Reliability Scale (J. Hogan & Hogan, 1989) use items similar to those in standard personality measures and tend to be positively associated with high scores on measures of conscientiousness and adjustment. Themes measured by the inventories include trouble/hostility to authority, thrill seeking, conscientiousness/(ir)responsibility, conventionality/good socialization, and hostility/social insensitivity.

Sackett et al. (1989) noted the following recent trends and findings in integrity testing research: (a) a substantial increase in validation research of personality-oriented measures using a variety of objective and subjective criteria thought to be related to the construct of counterproductivity, including measures such as supervisory ratings, grievances filed, and turnover; (b) correlational evidence suggesting a high degree of similarity among the four major personality-oriented tests; (c) substantial correlations between integrity test scores and social desirability scales; and (d) near-zero correlations between integrity test scores and intelligence. Schmidt, Ones, and Hunter (1992) further suggested that personality-oriented measures are more likely to assess the "the extreme lower range of the conscientiousness factor studied by Barrick and Mount (1991)" (p. 640). Although concerns regarding integrity test use in industry remain (e.g., test development and validation often conducted by test publishers, high false positive rates), Schmidt et al. (1992) argued that continued research on personality-oriented integrity tests may significantly contribute to understanding the role of personality in job performance.

Other Empirical Studies

Over the past 10 years, several studies have been conducted to assess the influence of individual differences in specific personality characteristics on specific aspects of job performance. For example, Helmreich, Sawin, and Carsrud (1986) examined the relationship between individual differences in achievement orientation of airline reservation agents using a predictor measure that distinguished three work-related components of achievement motivation and objective criterion measures of time spent on a task. In what they termed the "honeymoon" effect, they found that individual differences in achievement motivation were uncorrelated with training performance but were significantly related to later job performance. Hansen (1989) investigated the influence of distractibility and general social maladjustment in conjunction with demographic variables, job experience, and individual differences in cognitive ability in a cross-validated test of a causal model of industrial accidents. Distractibility and general social maladjustment were assessed by scales rationally developed on the basis of MMPI items designed to measure social adjustment and neuroticism. Hansen found that both personality dimensions were significantly related to the accident consistency.

A second research stream pertains to the continuing use of personality tests in conjunction with other measures to predict long-term managerial/executive performance. Reports by Bentz (1985) and Sparks (1983), for example, document the results of decades-long programs of research conducted in organizational settings, and presented findings that indicate a regular pattern of correlations between the Sociability, Energy, and Ascendance scales of the Guilford inventories and criteria such as compensation and promotability. Bentz (1985) argued that in the domain of executive performance, personality tests have been shown to be useful in both prediction of job progress and job performance.

Technical/Use Issues

An enduring problem in personality testing pertains to the extent to which faking and response distortion may affect the validity of a personality test for predicting performance. Validity results obtained from inventories that are susceptible to faking or response distortion may be adversely affected by the individuals' broader goals (e.g., to avoid military service, to look good to employers). This concern has also been raised in terms of distinguishing between concurrent and predictive validity designs, and as a basis for deemphasizing or omitting concurrent design studies in reviews of the literature.

Several recent studies indicate no important difference between the validity results obtained with concurrent or predictive strategies (Barrett, Phillips, & Alexander, 1981; Bemis, 1968; Lent et al., 1971; Schmitt et al., 1984; Schmitt & Schneider, 1983), thus indicating that the studies utilizing concurrent designs also should be considered.

Hough et al. (1990) examined the effects of faking and response distortion on criterion-related validities of personality constructs assessed by the Army Project A nonability battery. Their findings indicate that although individuals were successful in distorting their responses when instructed to do so, such distortions (with the exception of careless responding) did not substantially influence criterion-related validities. In addition, response validity scales developed to identify different types of response distortion were shown to be generally effective. Hough et al. (1990) noted that their findings of relatively low impact of response distortion in a socially desirable manner on criterion-related validities differ from those of Dunnette, McCartney, Carlson, and Kirchner (1962). Hough et al. (1990) suggested that the difference in findings may be accounted for by several factors, including larger sample size, validation design used (concurrent versus predictive), scoring cutoffs, and sample type (military personnel versus sales applicants). Nonetheless, Hough et al. (1990) recommended that I/O psychologists using personality measures for personnel selection take a conservative approach to this potential problem by continuing to use response validity scales to identify potentially inaccurate descriptions, informing applicants that inaccurate descriptions will be detected, and further examining applicants who show evidence of such distortions.

INTEGRATION OF PERSONALITY AND INTELLIGENCE

Incremental Validity Issues

Given that early uses of personality instruments in selection were typically oriented to detection of psychopathology, and intelligence instruments were used to rank-order applications on ability levels, the two approaches to selection were not positioned to be put into an integrated procedure. That is, when organizations used both intelligence and personality measures for selection, the use of these measures was a two-stage process. The ordering of the tests in the selection procedure was essentially arbitrary; the procedure is well-described as a non-compensatory multiple-hurdle framework. To be selected, an applicant had to have no identified psychopathology and be of high ability in comparison to the rest of the applicant sample. Given the psychopathology orientation of the personality assessment procedures, such an approach seems quite appropriate, although the procedure would eliminate those applicants of very high ability if they indicated any psychopathology.

More recent approaches to the dimensions of normal personality (e.g., the big five) provide the basis for regression predictions of relevant job behaviors. One difficulty, though, is that there is some controversy about the appropriateness of applying linear regression of bipolar scales (such as introversion-extraversion) to unipolar criteria (e.g., job performance)—see, for example, Snow's (1989b) discussion of curvilinear relations among personality, interest, and ability measures.

Given the historical advantage of intellectual ability in predicting job performance, a central question of an integrated approach to personality and intelligence is whether normal personality constructs account for variance in job performance above that accounted for by intellectual ability measures. To answer this question, it is necessary to address the issue of shared variance between personality and intelligence. If the association between intelligence and personality is zero, then any association between personality and job performance can be expected to result in incremental validity in a selection equation. If there is covariance among the constructs, the issue of incremental validity requires a more complicated analysis.

Although the two domains have developed independently, there have been several demonstrations of significant correlations between some personality constructs and intellectual ability measures. Most notable of these associations is the relationship between openness (sometimes called intellect) and general intelligence, which is typically found to be in the neighborhood of r = .30 (e.g., see Costa & McCrae, 1992a; Gough, 1953). More recently, Goff and Ackerman (1992) have shown that openness is related to crystallized intelligence (which includes verbal, information content), and relatively unrelated to fluid intelligence (which includes abstract reasoning). Other elements of the big five generally show negligible correlations with intelligence (Costa & McCrae, 1992b).

With this as background, and acknowledging that this avenue of inquiry has only recently received any formal attention, there have been several studies that have attempted to investigate the incremental validity of personality measures (beyond intellectual ability measures) in predicting job behaviors. By and large, these studies have yet to demonstrate decisively that particular domains of normal personality provide incremental validity in predicting job performance. It is important to acknowledge that these investigations have *not* used the nonlinear approaches advocated by Snow (1989a), but have implicitly assumed that relations between personality constructs and performance are linear throughout the range of responses. Nonetheless, the conclusion of most investigators is that job performance per se is perhaps best left to ability predictors. Rather, personality measures appear to provide significant incremental validity when job behaviors other than direct performance (employee appearance, interpersonal skills, self-confidence, etc.) are under consideration (e.g., see Hakstian, Woolsey, & Schroeder, 1987; McHenry et al., 1990). Although it is premature to render a final analysis of this approach, it seems reasonable to conclude that integrated use of personality and intelligence measures will be most beneficial when ancillary job-related behaviors serve as criteria rather than job performance alone. Whether a *compensatory* approach to integrating personality and intelligence constructs for predicting workplace behaviors can be successfully applied to industry awaits an effort to develop utility models that incorporate all major aspects of job behavior (e.g., performance, appearance, interpersonal relations, absenteeism).

Personality-Ability Interactions

A large number of studies have been conducted since Cronbach (1957) proposed the investigation of aptitude-treatment interactions (e.g., see Cronbach & Snow, 1977, for a review). Nearly all of the applications of aptitude-treatment interaction research have been in the educational domain, however, rather than in the industrial/organizational domain. Researchers have found support for interactions between individual differences in intellectual abilities and outcomes (e.g., school grades) with a variety of different instructional techniques (e.g., low and high structure). Researchers have also studied individual differences in personality characteristics (e.g., trait anxiety, need for achievement) in similar educational contexts. Moreover, several studies have been reported that examine higher-order aptitude-treatment interactions that involve individual differences in both intellectual abilities and personality traits, such as intelligence and need for achievement via conformance or independence (for reviews, see Snow, 1989a; Snow & Yalow, 1982).

Although there are clear implications of these demonstrated aptitude-treatment interactions for education, where many teachers seek to optimize the educational outcomes for classes with a wide range of talent and personality differences, the industrial/organizational domain has been slow to incorporate such findings to industry settings. Rather, the emphasis in industry has continued (at least until recently) to focus on two major themes: developing or finding better selection inventories, and developing improved training programs. Using better selection procedures will result in an overall greater degree of organizational success, whereas improving training programs is expected to result in a reduction of attrition through training failures. Few small organizations have the resources necessary to tailor training procedures to take advantage of aptitude-treatment interactions (although the increased use of computerized training facilities makes individualized training more economically feasible). Furthermore, until recently, organizations still benefited from a "buyer's marker" approach—that is, as was discussed early in this chapter, when the number of job applicants substantially exceeds the number of available jobs, selection procedures are inherently a highly effective means toward maximizing organizational effectiveness.

Many large organizations, however, have discovered that changing demographics have led to a reduction of qualified applications for available jobs (especially for entry-level positions). In addition, when the pool of applicants represents obvious limitations (e.g., illiteracy, or limited prior job experience), organizations end up putting greater emphasis on remedial training. This type of problem has been encountered by the U.S. armed forces, for example, as the demographics have radically changed for 18-year-olds during the past decade. The military has responded to this change in work force by adding more flexibility to training programs so as to allow individuals with lower intellectual abilities additional instruction and practice for the acquisition of job skills. Large organizations (e.g., McDonalds and Burger King) have instituted in-house educational facilities and instructional programs to prepare applications for entry-level job skills. We expect that in the near future, industry will increase attention to aptitude-treatment interactions in both selection procedures and training programs by matching applicant personality/intelligence profiles with available training programs. Such an approach has obvious benefits for both industry and for society at large, in the sense of raising the skill and knowledge levels of a significant portion of the workforce.

SUMMARY AND CONCLUSIONS

Personality Testing

Personality tests have been used by I/O psychologists for the purposes of employee selection and prediction of work behavior in the United States for more than eight decades. During this period, the use of personality tests has repeatedly waxed and waned in association with military and industry needs, conceptual developments and controversies, and legal developments pertaining to testing of all kinds. Unlike that of intelligence testing, the turbulent history of personality testing in industrial and organizational settings cannot be characterized as one in which upward cycles reflect major advances in theory or measurement. Instead, much of the history of personality testing reflects disparate efforts that sustain the general belief that "in *some* situations, for *some* purposes, *some* personality measures can offer helpful predictions" (Guion & Gottier, 1965, p. 159). The enduring use of personality tests among I/O psychologists, despite repeated exhortations for exercising caution and pessimistic reviews regarding the validity of these tests, serves as striking evidence of both the critical need for finding methods to improve "employment fit" and the myriad problems encountered in attempts to address this need in the absence of an integrative, theoretically based approach.

The current picture of the field looks far more promising than it has at any time in the recent past. Personality tests continue to be used, many of dubious value, but the coalescence of research efforts along theoretical lines during the past decade suggests that personality testing practices may be expected to change substantially over the next two decades. Changes in the area may be attributed largely to two forces. First, the emergence of an acceptable taxonomy of personality during the early 1980s has provided applied psychologists with a sorely needed organizational framework for investigation of personality–work behavior linkages. Second, conceptual advances in test validation theory and legal challenges have led to increased use of construct validation strategies that emphasize careful delineation of predictor and criterion constructs. In this perspective, issues such as whether concurrent validation designs provide evidence for predictive validity have given way to more fundamental issues, such as identification of constructs and providing adequate validation of measures purported to assess key constructs.

This "new look" in applied personality research has already borne fruit. Findings obtained by Barrick and Mount (1991) and Project A researchers (Hough et al., 1990; McHenry et al., 1990) provide converging evidence on not only the existence of personality–job performance linkages but, more importantly, on predictor and performance constructs of particular relevance to work settings. Of particular note are findings that indicate a substantial relationship between individual differences in motivational or volitional personality constructs (e.g., conscientiousness, work orientation) and ancillary job performance constructs (e.g., organizational citizenship behaviors and organizational delinquency). Other topics in I/O psychology in which a construct validation approach using nonability test predictors may show promise include leadership and group performance.

It should be noted that the potential benefits of new approaches in applied personality research bear most directly on elucidation of work-relevant personality-performance construct linkages and stimulation of theory development rather than in providing new evidence on the strength of any such linkages. Reviews by Ghiselli and Barthol (1953), Guion and Gottier (1965), Ghiselli (1973), and Barrick and Mount (1991) share one common characteristic; an upper limit of approximately .25 to .30 in mean and estimated true score validity coefficients between broad personality constructs and a variety of performance measures. The stability of these validity coefficients suggests that future research will aim toward refining our understanding of the role of personality in work settings through the development of narrower, work-related personality measures derived from broader personality constructs and clarification of the nomological network of constructs composing the job performance or criterion space (e.g., Hough, 1992). From a practical standpoint, recent findings like those of Barrick and Mount (1991) suggest that the controversy over whether personality tests can be useful for prediction of employee performance is no longer pertinent; the more pressing need at this time is to clarify when, for what, and how they are useful.

Finally, I/O psychologists interested in personnel selection have also more clearly distinguished between personality tests used for preemployment screening or detection of psychological maladjustment and tests used for prediction of workplace adjustment or performance. Interest in clinically oriented personality tests has decreased in direct relation to the development of personality inventories designed and validated on normal and employee populations. (Consistent with this trend, recent developments in integrity testing have focused on predictor constructs derived from the five-factor model and workplace behavior criteria. As such, personality-oriented measures may be regarded as tests for predicting performance rather than for use in screening.) As Butcher (1985) notes, the primary justification for the use of nonability tests in screening-based personnel selection methods is often with respect to public safety or for jobs that have been deemed psychologically sensitive or particularly stressful. Validation efforts in this domain are particularly troublesome because of the need to test all applicants and the sample size needed for detection of relatively few cases. Further, clinical tests may contain items or scales that cannot be easily defended in the courts as job related (for a discussion of this issue in the *Soroka v. Dayton Hudson* case, see Jackson & Kovacheff, 1993). When clinical personality tests are deemed appropriate, however, several studies provide positive evidence for the effectiveness of the MMPI for this purpose (e.g., Dunnette, Bownas, & Bosshardt, 1981; see Butcher, 1985).

Intelligence Testing

Tests of intelligence and intellectual abilities have proved to be both boon and bane to the practice of I/O psychology. Since World War I, millions of job applicants have been subjected to a plethora of ability tests, from tests of general intelligence to trade- and job-skill tests and broad multiple aptitude batteries. Companies have unarguably saved billions of dollars by using ability tests to assure a merit-based selection process. Tests have been used for classification purposes as well, mostly by large companies and governmental agencies. Overall, tests of intellectual abilities are the single most predictive element in employee selection. Such tests are generally more valid than the use of academic and employment credentials—and certainly more valid than the use of personal interviews—in predicting training and on-the-job success. Intellectual ability tests, however, have been the focus of countless critics over the long period of their use. Criticisms have ranged from racial and ethnic bias to the irrelevance of the measures for predicting anything of importance.

As a consequence of these charges, there has been a waxing and waning of industry use of intellectual ability testing during this century. The requirements on industrial use of ability tests have grown exponentially since 1970 in response to AERA/APA/NCME standards and EEOC rules. Companies that have small numbers of employees (or small numbers of employees with similar or identical job titles/functions) have found test validation requirements to be prohibitive, in that the costs of defending the tests exceed the benefits of using them for employee selection. Large corporations and government agencies (especially the armed forces) have generally continued to use ability tests for employee selection, though not without controversy and litigation.

With the exception of the validity generalization movement (discussed earlier), progress in basic research on measurement has offered only a few techniques to ameliorate these obstacles. Procedures for assessing test bias have been developed in the past three decades. Other procedures (e.g., in item response theory) have been used to identify potentially biased test items, so that tests may be modified to reduce racial and ethnic group differences. Such procedures, though, have a limited impact on the legal ramifications of ability test use. For continued use of intelligence testing in industry, the major contribution of basic research on intelligence (e.g., the cognitive decomposition of intellectual abilities, discussed above) will be on increasing the accuracy of predictions for employee performance. A number of developments in the cognitive/information processing approach to intelligence have the promise of accomplishing this goal. As these developments in theory and test development progress, the benefits of testing will outweigh the costs of validation and litigation. Thus the future of intelligence testing in I/O psychology is bright, but not without limits.

Acknowledgments. Support for preparation of this chapter was provided by grants to Ruth Kanfer from the National Science Foundation (NSF/SBR-9223357), and to Phillip L. Ackerman from the Air Force Office of Scientific Research (F49620-93-1-0206).

REFERENCES

Abt, L. E. (1947). The efficiency of the group Rorschach: Testing the psychiatric screening of Marine Corps recruits. *Journal of Psychology, 23,* 205–217.

Ackerman, P. L. (1988). Determinants of individual differences during skill acquisition: Cognitive abilities and information processing. *Journal of Experimental Psychology: General, 117,* 288–318.

Ackerman, P. L. (1990). A correlational analysis of skill specificity: Learning, abilities, and individual differences. *Journal of Experimental Psychology: Learning, Memory, and Cognition, 16,* 883–901.

Ackerman, P. L. (1992). Predicting individual differences in complex skill acquisition: Dynamics of ability determinants. *Journal of Applied Psychology, 77,* 598–614.

Ackerman, P. L., & Kyllonen, P.C. (1991). Trainee characteristics. In J. E. Morrison (Ed.), *Training for performance: Principles of applied human learning* (pp. 193–229). West Sussex, England: Wiley.

Adams, C. R. (1941). A new measure of personality. *Journal of Applied Psychology, 25,* 141–154.

Adler, S., & Weiss, H. M. (1988). Recent developments in the study of personality and organizational behavior. In C. L. Cooper & I. Robertson (Eds.), *International review of industrial and organizational psychology 1988* (pp. 307–330). New York: Wiley.

Allport, G. W. (1921). Personality and character. *Psychological Bulletin, 18,* 441–455.

Allport, G. W. (1928). A test for ascendance-submission. *Journal of Abnormal and Social Psychology, 23,* 118–136.

American Educational Research Association, American Psychological Association, & National Council on Measurement in Education. (1985). *Standards for educational and psychological testing.* Washington, DC: American Psychological Association.

American Psychological Association. (1954). *Technical recommendations for psychological tests and diagnostic techniques.* Washington, DC: Author.

American Psychological Association. (1970). Psychological assessment and public policy. *American Psychologist, 25,* 264–266.

American Society of Personnel Administrators. (1971). Personnel testing. ASPA Survey No. 12. In *Bulletin to Management (BNA Policy and Practice Series).* Washington, DC: Bureau of National Affairs.

Anastasi, A. (1980). Psychological testing and privacy. In W. C. Bier (Ed.), *Privacy: A vanishing value?* New York: Fordham University Press.

Anastasi, A. (1985). The use of personal assessment in industry: Methodological and interpretative problems. In H. J. Bernardin & D. A. Bownas (Eds.), *Personality assessment in organizations* (pp. 1–20). New York: Praeger.

Arvey, R. D., & Faley, R. H. (1988). *Fairness in selecting employees.* Reading, MA: Addison-Wesley.

Ash, P. (1991). A history of honesty testing. In J. W. Jones (Ed.), *Pre-employment honesty testing: Current research and future directions* (pp. 3–20). Westport, CT: Greenwood.

Balinsky, B. (1945). The multiple choice group Rorschach test as a means of screening applicants for jobs. *Journal of Psychology, 19,* 203–208.

Barnabas, B. (1948). Validity of personality and interest tests in selection and placement situations. *Transactions of the Kansas Academy of Science, 51,* 335–339.

Barrett, G. V., Phillips, J. S., & Alexander, R. A. (1981). Concurrent and predictive validity designs: A critical reanalysis. *Journal of Applied Psychology, 66,* 1–6.

Barrick, M. R., & Mount, M. K. (1991). The Big Five personality dimensions and job performance: A meta-analysis. *Personnel Psychology, 44,* 1–26.

Barrick, M. R., & Mount, M. K. (1993). Autonomy as a moderator of the relationships between the big five personality dimensions and job performance. *Journal of Applied Psychology, 78,* 111–118.

Bemis, S. E. (1968). Occupational validity of the General Aptitude Test Battery. *Journal of Applied Psychology, 52,* 240–249.

Bennett, G. K., & Gordon, H. P. (1944). Personality test scores and success in the field of nursing. *Journal of Applied Psychology, 28,* 267–278.

Bentz, V. J. (1985). Research findings from personality assessment of executives. In H. J. Bernardin & D. A. Bownas (Eds.), *Personality assessment in organizations* (pp. 82–144). New York: Praeger.

Bernreuter, R. G. (1933a). The theory and construction of the personality inventory. *Journal of Social Psychology, 4,* 387–405.

Bernreuter, R. G. (1933b). The validity of the personality inventory. *Personnel Journal, 11,* 383–386.

Beyerstein, B. L., & Beyerstein, D. F. (Eds.). (1991). The write stuff: Evaluations of graphology, the study of handwriting analysis. Buffalo, NY: Prometheus.

Biesheuvel, S. (1965). Personnel selection. *Annual Review of Psychology, 16,* 295–324.

Bills, M. A., & Ward, L. W. (1936). Testing salesmen of casualty insurance. *Personnel Journal, 15*, 55–58.

Bingham, W. V. (1923). Psychology applied. *Scientific Monthly, 16*, 141–159.

Borgatta, E. F. (1964). The structure of personality characteristics. *Behavioral Science, 12*, 8–17.

Borman, W. C., Rosse, R: L., & Abrahams, N. M. (1980). An empirical construct validity approach to studying predictor-job performance links. *Journal of Applied Psychology, 65*, 662–671.

Brockner, J. (1985). *Self-esteem at work*. Lexington, MA: Lexington Books.

Bureau of National Affairs. (1963). *Employee selection procedures: Personnel policies forum survey no. 70*. Washington, DC: Author.

Bureau of National Affairs Survey. (1976). *Selection procedures and personnel records: Personnel policies forum survey no. 114*. Washington, DC: Author.

Butcher, J. N. (1985). Personality assessment in industry: Theoretical issues and illustrations. In H. J. Bernardin & D. A. Bownas (Eds.), *Personality assessment in organizations* (pp. 277–310). New York: Praeger.

Carroll, J. B. (1980). *Individual difference relations in psychometric and experimental cognitive tasks* (Technical Report No. 163). Chapel Hill: University of North Carolina, L. L. Thurstone Psychometric Laboratory.

Carroll, J. B. (1993). *Human cognitive abilities; A survey of factor-analytic studies*. Cambridge, England: Cambridge University Press.

Cattell, McK. (1890). Mental tests and measurements. *Mind, 15*, 373–380.

Challman, R. C. (1945). The validity of the Harrower-Erickson multiple choice test as a screening device. *Journal of Psychology, 20*, 41–48.

Clarke, W. V. (1956). The construction of an industrial selection personality test. *Journal of Personality, 16*, 379–394.

Cleveland, E. A. (1948). Sales personnel research, 1935–1945: A review. *Personnel Psychology, 1*, 211–255.

Collins, M. (1925). Character and temperament tests: A preliminary report. *British Journal of Psychology, 16*, 89–99.

Cortina, J. M., Doherty, M. L., Schmitt, N., Kaufman, G., & Smith, R. G. (1992). The "big five" personality factors in the IPI and MMPI: Predictors of police performance. *Personnel Psychology, 45*, 119–140.

Costa, P. T., Jr., & McCrae, R. R. (1988). From catalog to classification: Murray's needs and the five-factor model. *Journal of Personality and Social Psychology, 55*, 258–265.

Costa, P. T., Jr., & McCrae, R. R. (1992a). Four ways five factors are basic. *Personality and Individual Differences, 13*, 653–665.

Costa, P. T., Jr., & McCrae, R. R. (1992b). *Revised NEO Personality Inventory manual*. Odessa, FL: Psychological Assessment Resources.

Cronbach, L. J. (1957). The two disciplines of scientific psychology. *American Psychologist, 12*, 671–684.

Cronbach, L. J. (1990). *Essentials of psychological testing* (5th ed.). New York: Harper & Row.

Cronbach, L. J., & Snow, R. E. (1977). *Aptitudes and instructional methods: A handbook for research on interactions*. New York: Irvington.

Digman, J. M. (1990). Personality structure: Emergence of the five-factor model. *Annual Review of Psychology, 41*, 417–440.

Digman, J. M., & Inouye, J. (1986). Further specification of the five robust factors of personality. *Journal of Personality and Social Psychology, 50*, 116–123.

Dodge, A. F. (1938a). Social dominance of clerical workers and sales persons. *Journal of Educational Psychology, 28*, 132–139.

Dodge, A. F. (1938b). Social dominance and sales personality. *Journal of Applied Psychology, 22*, 132–139.

Dodge, A. F. (1940). What are the personality traits of the successful salesperson? *Journal of Applied Psychology, 22*, 229–238.

Dorcus, R. M. (1944). A brief study of the Humm-Wadsworth Temperament Scale and the Guilford-Martin Personnel Inventory in an industrial situation. *Journal of Applied Psychology, 28*, 302–307.

Downey, J. (1920). Some volitional patterns revealed by the will-profile. *Journal of Experimental Psychology, 3*, 281–301.

Dunnette, M. D. (1962). Personnel management. *Annual Review of Psychology, 13*, 285–314.

Dunnette, M. D. (1963). A note on the criterion. *Journal of Applied Psychology, 47*, 251–254.

Dunnette, M. D. (Ed.). (1976). *Handbook of industrial and organizational psychology*. New York: Wiley.

Dunnette, M. D., & Borman, W. C. (1979). Personnel selection and classification systems. *Annual Review of Psychology, 30*, 477–525.

Dunnette, M. D., Bownas, D. A., & Bosshardt, M. J. (1981). *Electric power plant study: Prediction of inappropriate, unreliable or aberrant job behavior in nuclear power plant settings*. Minneapolis, MN: Personnel Decisions Research Institute.

Dunnette, M. D., & Hough, L. M. (Eds.). (1990). *Handbook of industrial and organizational psychology* (2nd ed., Vol. 1). Palo Alto, CA: Consulting Psychologists Press.

Dunnette, M. D., & Hough, L. M. (Eds.). (1991). *Handbook of industrial and organizational psychology* (2nd ed., Vol. 2). Palo Alto, CA: Consulting Psychologists Press.

Dunnette, M. D., & Hough, L. M. (Eds.). (1992). *Handbook of industrial and organizational psychology* (2nd ed., Vol. 3). Palo Alto, CA: Consulting Psychologists Press.

Dunnette, M. D., McCartney, J., Carlson, H. C., & Kirchner, W. K. (1962). A study of faking behavior on a forced-choice self-description checklist. *Personnel Psychology, 15*, 13–24.

Ellis, A. (1946). The validity of personality questionnaires. *Psychological Bulletin, 43*, 385–440.

Ellis, A., & Conrad, H. S. (1948). The validity of personality inventories in military practice. *Psychological Bulletin, 45*, 385–426.

Equal Employment Opportunity Commission, Civil Service Commission, Department of Labor, & Department of Justice. (1978). Adoption by four agencies of uniform guidelines on employee selection procedures. *Federal Register, 43*(166), 38290–38315.

Fiske, D. W. (1949). Consistency of the factorial structures of personality ratings from different sources. *Journal of Abnormal Social Psychology, 44*, 329–344.

Fitts, P., & Posner, M. I. (1967). *Human performance*. Belmont, CA: Brooks/Cole.

Flanagan, J. C. (Ed.). (1948). *Army Air Forces Aviation Psychology Program research reports: 1. The Aviation Psychology Program in the Army Air Forces*. Washington, DC: Government Printing Office.

Forlano, G., & Kirkpatrick, F. H. (1945). Intelligence and adjustment measurements in the selection of radio tube mounters. *Journal of Applied Psychology, 29*, 257–261.

Franz, S. I. (1919). *Handbook of mental examination methods* (2nd ed.). New York: Macmillan.

Friedman, T., & Williams, E. B. (1982). Current use of tests for employment. In A. Wigdor & W. Garner (Eds.), *National*

Academy of Sciences report on ability testing (Vol. 2). Washington, DC: National Research Council.

Furfey, P. H. (1926). An improved rating scale technique. *Journal of Educational Psychology, 17*, 45–48.

Galton, F. (1883). *Inquiries into human faculty and its development*. New York: Macmillan.

Garrison, K. C. (1939). The use of psychological tests in the selection of student-nurses. *Journal of Applied Psychology, 23*, 461–472.

Ghiselli, E. E. (1973). The validity of aptitude tests in personnel selection. *Personnel Psychology, 26*, 461–477.

Ghiselli, E. E., & Barthol, R. P. (1953). The validity of personality inventories in the selection of employees. *Journal of Applied Psychology, 37*, 18–20.

Goff, M., & Ackerman, P. L. (1992). Personality-intelligence relations: Assessing typical intellectual engagement. *Journal of Educational Psychology, 84*, 537–552.

Goldberg, L. R. (1971). A historical survey of personality scales and inventories. In P. Reynolds (Eds.), *Advances in psychological assessment* (Vol. 2, pp. 293–336). Palo Alto, CA: Science and Behavior Books.

Goldberg, L. R. (1981). Language and individual differences: The search for universals in personality lexicons. In L. Wheeler (Ed.), *Review of personality and social psychology* (Vol. 2, pp. 141–166). Beverly Hills, CA: Sage.

Goldberg, L. R. (1990). An alternative "description of personality:" The big-five factor structure. *Journal of Personality and Social Psychology, 59*, 1216–1229.

Gough, H. G. (1953). A nonintellectual intelligence test. *Journal of Consulting Psychology, 17*, 242–246.

Gough, H. G. (1971). The assessment of wayward impulse by means of the Personnel Reaction Blank. *Personnel Psychology, 24*, 669–677.

Gough, H. G. (1985). A work orientation scale for the California Psychological Inventory. *Journal of Applied Psychology, 70*, 505–513.

Gross, M. L. (1962). *The brain watchers*. New York: Random House.

Guilford, J. P. (1956). The structure of intellect. *Psychological Bulletin, 53*, 267–293.

Guilford, J. P., & Lacey, J. I. (Eds.). (1948). *Army Air Forces Aviation Psychology Program research reports: Printed classification tests*. Washington, DC: Government Printing Office.

Guion, R. M., & Gibson, W. M. (1988). Personnel selection and placement. *Annual Review of Psychology, 39*, 349–374.

Guion, R. M., & Gottier, R. F. (1965). Validity of personality measures in personnel selection. *Personnel Psychology, 18*, 135–164.

Hakstian, A. R., Woolsey, L. K., Schroeder, M. L. (1987). Validity of a large-scale assessment battery in an industrial setting. *Educational and Psychological Measurement, 47*, 165–178.

Hale, M. (1982). History of employment testing. In A. K. Wigdor & W. R. Garner (Eds.), Ability testing: Uses, consequences, and controversies (Part II, pp. 3–38). Washington, DC: National Academy Press.

Hampton, P. (1940). Personality and success in selling. *Personnel Journal, 19*, 108–115.

Hansen, C. P. (1989). A causal model of the relationship among accidents, biodata, personality, and cognitive factors. *Journal of Applied Psychology, 74*, 81–90.

Harrell, T. W. (1949). Humm-Wadsworth Temperament Scale and ratings of salesmen. *Personnel Psychology, 2*, 451–495.

Harrell, W. (1940). Testing cotton mill supervisors. *Journal of Applied Psychology, 24*, 31–35.

Hathaway, S. R., & McKinley, J. C. (1940). A multiphasic personality schedule (Minnesota): I. Construction of the schedule. *Journal of Psychology, 10*, 249–254.

Hathaway, S. R., & McKinley, J. C. (1951). *The Minnesota Multiphasic Personality Inventory manual*. New York: Psychological Corporation.

Hedlund, D. E. (1965). A review of the MMPI in industry. *Psychological Reports, 17*, 875–889.

Helmreich, R. L., Sawin, L. L., & Carsrud, A. L. (1986). The honeymoon effect in job performance: Temporal increases in the predictive power of achievement motivation. *Journal of Applied Psychology, 71*, 185–188.

Hogan, J., & Hogan, R. (1986). *Hogan personnel selection series manual*. Minneapolis, MN: National Computer Systems.

Hogan, J., & Hogan, R. (1989). How to measure employee reliability. *Journal of Applied Psychology, 74*, 273–279.

Hogan, J., Hogan, R., & Murtha, T. (1992). Validation of a personality measure of managerial performance. *Journal of Business and Psychology, 7*, 225–236.

Hogan, R. (1986). *Hogan Personality Inventory manual*. Minneapolis, MN: National Computer Systems.

Hogan, R., Carpenter, B. N., Briggs, S. R., & Hansson, R. O. (1985). Personality assessment and personnel selection. In H. J. Bernardin & D. A. Bownas (Eds.), *Personality assessment in organizations* (pp. 21–52). New York: Praeger.

Hogan, R., DeSoto, C. B., & Solano, C. (1977). Traits, tests, and personality research. *American Psychologist, 32*, 255–264.

Hogan, R., & Hogan, J. (1991). Personality and status. In D. G. Gilbert & J. J. Conley (Eds.), *Personality, social skills, and psychopathology* (pp. 137–154). New York: Plenum.

Hogan, R., Hogan, J., & Busch, C. (1984). How to measure service orientation. *Journal of Applied Psychology, 69*, 167–173.

Hogan, R., & Nicholson, R. (1988). The meaning of personality test scores. *American Psychologist, 43*, 621–626.

Holmes, F. J. (1950). Validity tests for insurance office personnel. *Personnel Psychology, 3*, 57–69.

Hough, L. M. (1992). The "big five" personality variables—construct confusion: Description versus prediction. *Human Performance, 5*, 139–155.

Hough, L. M., Eaton, N. K., Dunnette, M. D., Kamp, J. D. & McCloy, R. A. (1990). Criterion-related validities of personality constructs and the effect of response distortion on those validities. *Journal of Applied Psychology, 75*(Monograph), 581–595.

Hull, C. L. (1928). *Aptitude testing*. New York: World.

Humm, D. G, & Wadsworth, G. W. (1933a). A diagnostic inventory of temperament: A preliminary report. *Psychological Bulletin, 30*, 602.

Humm, D. G., & Wadsworth, G. W. (1933b). The Humm-Wadsworth Temperament Scale Preliminary report. *Personnel Journal, 12*, 314–323.

Humphreys, L. G. (1962). The organization of human abilities. *American Psychologist, 17*, 475–483.

Hunt, E., Frost, N., & Lunneborg, C. (1973). Individual differences in cognition: A new approach to intelligence. In G. Bower (Ed.), *Advances in learning and motivation* (Vol. 7, pp. 87–122). New York: Academic Press.

Hunter, J. E. (1986). Cognitive ability, cognitive aptitudes, job knowledge, and job performance. *Journal of Vocational Behavior, 29*, 340–362.

Jackson, D. N., & Kovacheff, J. D. (1993). Personality questionnaires in selection: Privacy issues and the Soroka case. *Industrial-Organizational Psychologist, 30*, 45–50.

Jensen, M. B., & Rotter, J. B. (1947). The value of thirteen psychological tests in officer candidate screening. *Journal of Applied Psychology, 31*, 312–322.

Jurgensen, C. E. (1944). Report on the "Classification Inventory," a personality test for industrial use. *Journal of Applied Psychology, 28*, 445–460.

Katzell, R. A., & Katzell, M. E. (1962). Development and application of structured tests of personality. *Review of Educational Research, 32*, 51–63.

Kelly, T. L. (1928). *Crossroads in the mind of man: A study of differentiable mental abilities*. Stanford, CA: Stanford University Press.

Kenrick, D. T., & Funder, D. C. (1988). Profiting from controversy. *American Psychologist, 43*, 23–34.

Klimoski, R. J., & Rafaeli, A. (1983). Inferring personal qualities through handwriting analysis. *Journal of Occupational Psychology, 56*, 191–201.

Knauft, E. B. (1949). A selection battery for bake shop managers. *Journal of Applied Psychology, 33*, 304–315.

Kornhauser, A. W. (1922). The psychology of vocational selection. *Psychological Bulletin, 19*, 192–229.

Kornhauser, A. W., & Kingsbury, F. A. (1924). *Psychological tests in business*. Chicago: University of Chicago Press.

Kruger B. L. (1938). A statistical analysis of the Humm-Wadsworth Temperament Scale. *Journal of Applied Psychology, 22*, 641–652.

Kurtz, A. K. (1942). Recent research in the selection of life insurance salesmen. *Journal of Applied Psychology, 25*, 11–17.

Kurtz, A. K. (1948). A research test of the Rorschach Test. *Personnel Psychology, 1*, 41–51.

Kyllonen, P. C., & Christal, R. E. (1989). Cognitive modeling of learning abilities: A status report of LAMP. In R. F. Dillon & J. W. Pellegrino (Eds.), *Testing: Theoretical and applied perspectives* (pp. 146–173). New York: Praeger.

Kyllonen, P. C., & Tirre, W. C. (1988). Individual differences in associative learning and forgetting. *Intelligence, 12*, 393–421.

Kyllonen, P. C., Tirre, W. C., & Christal, R. E. (1991). Knowledge and processing speed as determinants of associative learning. *Journal of Experimental Psychology: General, 120*, 89–108.

Laird, D. (1925a). Detecting abnormal behavior. *Journal of Abnormal Psychology, 20*, 128–141.

Laird, D. (1925b). A mental hygiene and vocational test. *Journal of Educational Psychology, 16*, 419–422.

Lent, R. H., Aurbach, H. A., & Levin, L. S. (1971). Predictors, criteria, and significant results. *Personnel Psychology, 24*, 519–533.

Levy, R. (1979, March). Handwriting and hiring. *Dunn's Review*, pp. 72–79.

Locke, E. A., & Hulin, C. L. (1962). A review and evaluation of the validity studies of Activity Vector Analysis. *Personnel Psychology, 15*, 25–42.

Lohman, D. F. (1979). *Spatial ability: A review and reanalysis of the correlational literature* (Technical Report No. 8). Stanford, CA: Stanford University, School of Education.

Lohman, D. F. (1987). Spatial abilities as traits, processes, and knowledge. In R. J. Sternberg (Ed.), *Advances of the psychology of human intelligence* (Vol. 4, pp. 181–248). Hillsdale, NJ: Erlbaum.

Maller, J. B. (1935). Character and personality tests. *Psychological Bulletin, 32*, 500–523.

May, M. A. (1925). The present status of the Will-Temperament tests. *Journal of Applied Psychology, 9*, 29–52.

McCrae, R. R., & Costa, P. T. Jr. (1985). Updating Norman's "adequate taxonomy": Intelligence and personality dimensions in natural language and in questionnaires. *Journal of Personality and Social Psychology, 49*, 710–721.

McCrae, R. R., & Costa, P. T., Jr. (1987). Validation of the five-factor model of personality across instruments and observers. *Journal of Personality and Social Psychology, 52*, 81–90.

McCrae, R. R., & Costa, P. T., Jr. (1989). The structure of interpersonal traits: Wiggins' circumplex and the five-factor model. *Journal of Personality and Social Psychology, 56*, 586–595.

McHenry, J. J., Hough, L. M., Toquam, J. L., Hanson, M. A., & Ashworth, S. (1990). Project A validity results: The relationship between predictor and criterion domains. *Personnel Psychology, 43*, 335–354.

Melton, A. (Ed.). (1948). *Army Air Forces Aviation Psychology Program research reports: 4. Apparatus tests*. Washington, DC: Government Printing Office.

Miner, J. B. (1917). The evaluation of a method for the finely graduated estimation of ability. *Journal of Applied Psychology, 1*, 123–133.

Miner, M. G. (1976). *Selection procedures and personnel records: Personnel policies forum survey no. 114*. Washington, DC: Bureau of National Affairs.

Mischel, W. (1968). *Personality and assessment*. New York: Wiley.

Mischel, W. (1969). Continuity and change in personality. *American Psychologist, 24*, 1012–1018.

Mischel, W. (1973). Toward a cognitive social learning reconceptualization of personality. *Psychological Review, 80*, 252–283.

Mitchell, T. R. (1979). Organizational behavior. *Annual Review of Psychology, 30*, 243–281.

Mowday, R. T., & Spencer, D. G. (1981). The influence of task and personality characteristics on employee turnover and absenteeism. *Academy of Management Journal, 24*, 634–642.

National Industrial Conference Board. (1941). Experience with employment tests. In *Studies in personnel policy no. 32*. New York: National Industrial Conference Board.

Neter, E., & Ben-Shakhar, G. (1989). Predictive validity of graphological inferences: A meta-analytic approach. *Personality and Individual Differences, 10*, 737–745.

Norman, W. T. (1963). Toward an adequate taxonomy of personality attributes: Replicated factor structure in peer nomination personality ratings. *Journal of Abnormal and Social Psychology, 66*, 574–583.

Paterson, D. G. (1923). Methods of rating human qualities. *Annals of the American Academy of Political and Social Science, 110* 81–93.

Paterson, D. G., Elliott, R. M., Anderson, L. D., Toops, H. A., & Heidbreder, E. (1930). *Minnesota mechanical ability tests*. Minneapolis: University of Minnesota Press.

Peters, L. H., Fisher, C. D., & O'Connor, E. J. (1982). The moderating effect of situational control of performance variance on the relationship between individual differences and performance. *Personnel Psychology, 35*, 609–621.

Peterson, D. R. (1968). *The clinical study of social behavior*. New York: Appleton-Century-Crofts.

Pillister, H. (1936). American psychologists judge fifty-three vocational tests. *Journal of Applied Psychology, 20*, 761–768.

Pressey, S. L., & Pressey, L. W. (1919). "Cross-out" tests, with suggestions as to a group scale of emotions. *Journal of Applied Psychology, 3*, 138–150.

Ream, M. J. (1922). Group will-temperament tests. *Journal of Educational Psychology, 13*, 7–16.

Rhinehart, J. B. (1933). An attempt to predict the success of student nurses by the use of a battery of tests. *Journal of Applied Psychology, 17*, 277–293.

Ridgeway, J. (1964, December). The snoops: Private lives and public service. *New Republic, 151*, 13–17.
Ridgeway, J. (1965, March). Who's fit to serve? *New Republic, 152*, 9–11.
Rosse, J. G., Miller, H. E., & Barnes, L. K. (1991). Combining personality and cognitive ability predictors for hiring service-oriented employees. *Journal of Business and Psychology, 5*, 431–445.
Rugg, H. O. (1921). Is the rating of human character practicable? *Journal of Educational Psychology, 12*, 425–428, 485–501.
Rugg, H. O. (1922). Is the rating of human character practicable? *Journal of Educational Psychology, 13*, 30–42, 81–93.
Sackett, P. R., Burris, L. R., & Callahan, C. (1989). Integrity testing for personnel selection: An update. *Personnel Psychology, 42*, 491–529.
Sackett, P. R., & Harris, M. M. (1984). Honesty testing for personnel selection: A review and critique. *Personnel Psychology, 37*, 221–245.
Sartain, A. Q. (1946). Relation between scores on certain standard tests and supervisory success in an aircraft factory. *Journal of Applied Psychology, 30*, 328–332.
Schmidt, F. L., & Hunter, J. E. (1977). Development of a general solution to the problem of validity generalization. *Journal of Applied Psychology, 62*, 529–540.
Schmidt, F. L., Hunter, J. E., & Pearlman, K. (1981). Task differences as moderators of aptitude test validity in selection: A red herring. *Journal of Applied Psychology, 66*, 166–185.
Schmidt, F. L., Ones, D. S., & Hunter, J. E. (1992). Personnel selection. *Annual Review of Psychology, 41*, 627–670.
Schmitt, N., Gooding, R. Z., Noe, R. A., & Kirsch, M. (1984). Metaanalyses of validity studies published between 1964 and 1982 and the investigation of study characteristics. *Personnel Psychology, 37*, 407–422.
Schmitt, N., & Schneider, B. (1983). Current issues in personnel selection. In K. M. Rowland & J. Ferris (Eds.), *Research in personnel and human resources management* (Vol. 1, pp. 85–125). Greenwich, CT: JAI.
Shipley, W. C., Gray, F. E., & Newbert, N. (1946). The Personal Inventory—is derivation and validation. *Journal of Clinical Psychology, 2*, 318–322.
Sinaiko, H. W. (1949). The Rosenzweig Picture-Frustration Study in the selection of department store section managers. *Journal of Applied Psychology, 33*, 36–42.
Snow, R. E. (1989a). Aptitude-treatment interaction as a framework for research on individual differences in learning. In P. L. Ackerman, R. J. Sternberg, & R. Glaser (Eds.), *Learning and individual differences: Advances in theory and research* (pp. 13–59). New York: Freeman.
Snow, R. E. (1989b). Cognitive-conative aptitude interactions in learning In R. Kanfer, P. L. Ackerman, & R. Cudeck (Eds.) *Abilities, motivation, and methodology: The Minnesota Symposium on learning and individual differences* (pp. 435–474). Hillsdale, NJ: Erlbaum.
Snow, R. E., & Yalow, E. (1982). Education and intelligence. In R. J. Sternberg (Ed.), *Handbook of human intelligence* (pp. 493–585). Cambridge, England: Cambridge University Press.
Sparks, C. P. (1983). Paper-and-pencil measures of potential. In G. F. Dreher & P. R. Sackett (Eds.), *Perspectives on employee staffing and selection* (pp. 349–368). Homewood, IL: Irwin.
Spearman, C. (1904). "General intelligence," objectively determined and measured. *American Journal of Psychology, 15*, 201–293.
Spriegel, W. R., & Dale, A. G. (1953). Trends in personnel selection and induction. *Personnel, 30*, 169–175.
Stuit, D. B. (Ed.). (1947). *Personnel research and test development in the Bureau of Naval Personnel.* Princeton, NJ: Princeton University Press.
Super, D. E. (1942). The Bernreuter Personality Inventory: A review of research. *Psychological Bulletin, 39*, 94–125.
Taylor, E. K., & Nevis, E. C. (1961). Personnel selection. *Annual Review of Psychology, 12*, 389–412.
Tenopyr, M. L. (1981). The realities of employment testing. *American Psychologist, 36*, 1120–1127.
Thomson, G. H. (1916). A hierarchy without a general factor. *British Journal of Psychology, 8*, 271–281.
Thomson, G. H. (1939). *The factorial analysis of human ability.* Boston: Houghton Mifflin.
Thorndike, E. L. (1920). A constant error in psychological rating. *Journal of Applied Psychology, 4*, 25–29.
Thorndike, R.L. (1986). The role of general ability in prediction. *Journal of Vocational Behavior, 29*, 332–339.
Thurstone, L. L. (1938). Primary mental abilities. *Psychometric Monographs, 1.*
Thurstone, L. L., & Thurstone, T. G. (1941). Factorial studies of intelligence. *Psychometric Monographs, 2.*
Tupes, E. C., & Christal, R. E. (1961). *Recurrent personality factors based on trait ratings* (ASD-TR-61-97). Lackland Air Force Base, TX: Aeronautical Systems Division, Personnel Laboratory.
U.S. Adjutant General's Office. (1919). *The personnel system of the United States Army. Vol. 1. History of the personnel system.* Washington, DC: Government Printing Office.
Viteles, M. S. (1930). Psychology in industry. *Psychological Bulletin, 27*, 567–635.
Viteles, M. S. (1932). *Industrial psychology.* New York: Norton.
Watson, G. (1932). Measures of character and personality. *Psychological Bulletin, 29*, 147–176.
Watson, G. (1933). Character and personality tests. *Psychological Bulletin, 30*, 467–487.
Weider, A., Mittelmann, B., Weschler, D., & Wolff, H. G. (1944). The Cornell Selectee Index: A method for quick testing of selectees for the armed forces. *Journal of the American Medical Association, 124*, 224–228.
Whyte, W. H. (1954). The fallacies of "personality" testing. *Fortune, 50*, 117–121.
Woltz, D. J. (1988). An investigation of the role of working memory in procedural skill acquisition. *Journal of Experimental Psychology: General, 117*, 319–331.
Yoakum, C. S., & Yerkes, R. M. (Eds.). (1920). *Mental tests in the American Army.* London: Sidgwick & Jackson.
Young, K. (1923). The history of mental testing. *Pedagogical Seminary, 31*, 1–47.
Zubin, K. (1948). Recent advances in screening the emotionally maladjusted. *Journal of Clinical Psychology, 4*, 56–62.

27

Counseling and the Role of Personality and Intelligence

Norman E. Amundson, William A. Borgen, and Elizabeth Tench

OVERVIEW

It is our intent in this chapter to highlight certain issues pertaining to the areas of personality, intelligence, and environment that are currently of interest in the field of counseling. Vocational development serves as an example of a central counseling focus that illustrates concerns that apply to many counseling endeavors. In particular this discussion centers around the experiences of young individuals as they make their way into the vocational context. Recent studies have demonstrated that this transition period is a time of great flux in an individual's life, and that a successful passage has profound implications for well-being (Amundson, Borgen, & Tench, 1993; Borgen, Amundson, & Tench, 1993; Furnham, 1985; Tiggeman & Winefield, 1984; Warr, Jackson, & Banks, 1982).

This chapter commences with a description of the broad role of counseling in enhancing individual well-being and continues with a discussion of the importance of vocational development in promoting and maintaining such well-being. In subsequent sections, several vocational counseling issues related to personality and intelligence assessment are considered. These issues include the following:

1. Current theory and research of the vocational context require better identification of personality, intelligence, and environmental factors that have may have implications for predicting vocational success and ensuing well-being.
2. These factors, which have previously been considered separately, require interactive rather than independent modeling approaches.
3. Current job market conditions require the restructuring of current models of vocational development.

A recent model that illustrates the increasing awareness of these issues among counselors and counseling researchers is described and is accompanied by a discussion of the relevance and application to counseling practice.

Counseling Commitments and Philosophy

As a starting point it is useful to describe some of the major sets of philosophical concerns and commitments that help to define the discipline of counseling. According to Blocher (1987), the following three propositions underlie the professional counseling enterprise:

> The primary value commitment of the counsellor is to facilitate human development by helping those with

Norman E. Amundson, William A. Borgen, and Elizabeth Tench • Department of Counselling Psychology, University of British Columbia, Vancouver, British Columbia V6T 1Z4, Canada.

International Handbook of Personality and Intelligence, edited by Donald H. Saklofske and Moshe Zeidner. Plenum Press, New York, 1995.

whom he or she works reach their highest level of functioning and to overcome obstacles that might hinder their further growth. Developing human beings can only be fully understood and truly helped within the context of their interactions with the physical, social, and psychological environment. The ultimate goal of counseling is to work with both the client and the environment to facilitate a dynamic and vibrant engagement, or "fit," between the developing person and environment. (p. 11)

The individual, from a counseling perspective, is viewed with reference to both personal development and interactions with the environment. This psychosocial emphasis influences both the theoretical constructs and the practice of counseling.

The Importance of a Career in Counseling

Within the various domains of counseling theory and practice, career counseling stands as a pivotal area of concern, and it is within this context that the concepts of personality and intelligence will be addressed. In approaching the topic from this perspective, particular attention will be given to the issues associated with the post-high school transition.

The most frequently used definition of *career* is that proposed by Super (1976):

> The course of events which constitutes a life; the sequence of occupations and other life roles which combine to express one's commitment to work in his or her total pattern of self-development; the series of remunerated and nonremunerated positions occupied by a person from adolescence through retirement, of which occupation is only one; includes work-related roles such as those of student, employee, and pensioner together with complementary vocational, familial, and civic roles. Careers exist only as people pursue them; they are person-centered. It is this last notion of careers, "they exist only as people pursue them," which summarizes much of the rationale for career guidance. (p. 4)

Counseling directed toward a career theme is concerned with self-understanding, an awareness of the labor market/leisure domains, decision making, and ultimately, self-fulfillment and development through involvement in leisure and work pursuits. Career counselors focus their attention on specific issues such as occupational choice, educational planning, job search, career development, and retirement planning.

Underlying the many elements that constitute counseling foci directed toward the career theme are three essential factors: personality, intelligence, and environmental influences (Amundson, Borgen, & Tench, 1993; Borgen, Amundson, & Tench, 1993). The following sections will illustrate some of the current trends in counseling theory and research.

PERSONALITY, INTELLIGENCE, AND ENVIRONMENT AS INTEGRATED ASPECTS OF COMPETENCE: EXISTING THEORY AND ASSESSMENT

Intelligence has been defined by Sternberg (1985) as an ability to adapt successfully to influences or changes in the environment. The importance of personality, cognitive, and environmental interactions in the constitution of intelligence (as defined in this manner) are illuminated by reference to Sternberg's triarchic theory (1985), which has had a substantial impact on current conceptions of intelligence. Sternberg's theory blends cognitive, personality, and environmental influences and "includes within the realm of intelligence characteristics that typically might be placed in the realms of personality or motivation. . . . For example, motivational phenomena relevant to purpose of adaptive behavior—such as motivation to perform well in one's career—would be considered part of one's intelligence broadly defined" (p. 55).

The triarchic theory comprises three subtheories, described by Sternberg as follows:

> 1. The first subtheory relates intelligence to the internal world of the individual, specifying the mental mechanisms that lead to more and less intelligent behavior. This subtheory specifies three kinds of information-processing components that are instrumental in (a) learning how to do things, (b) planning what things to do and how to do them, and (c) actually doing the things.
> 2. The second subtheory specifies those points along the continuum of one's experience with tasks or situations that most critically involve the use of intelligence. In particular, the account emphasized the roles of novelty and of automatization.
> 3. The third subtheory relates intelligence to the external world of the individual, specifying three classes of acts—environmental adaptation, selection, and shaping—that characterize intelligent behavior in the everyday world. (p. 223)

Sternberg's theory can be applied to the vocational context, where environmental adaptation is critical to success. It can be suggested that personality, cognitive, and environmental influences constitute a triad of factors that interact to produce emotional and behavioral responses to work contexts. There have been many studies that have assessed the manner in which cognitive and personality factors separately index work performance and satisfaction, but very few attempts have been made to define a model that integrates personality, cognitive, and environmental influences (Rosse, Miller, & Barnes, 1991).

The problem of identification and integration of important factors is compounded by additional issues that center around the construct definitions of these elements. Provided that particular personality and intelligence factors are found to be useful predictors of vocational success, there are further clarifications required in the development of new counseling models. These concerns are illustrated by the following examples: (a) whether intelligence can be characterized by a single underlying, stable "*g*" factor or as a multifaceted, possibly mutable entity; (b) whether personality can be adequately represented by stated interests or by static typologies, as is common in many studies of the work context; and (c) how environmental, intelligence, and personality variables interact to influence vocational experiences (Baehr & Orban, 1989; Lent & Hackett, 1987; Lowman & Leeman, 1988; Rosse et al., 1991).

In the following discussion, current work in the areas of intelligence and personality theory and vocational assessment is discussed. The objective is to illustrate that particular elements of these broad areas,when conceptualized in specified ways, are important to contemporary theories that aspire to predict vocational success.

INTELLIGENCE FACTORS

Intelligence as a predictor of vocational success has been studied with a multitude of conceptions and approaches. These approaches have two major underlying themes by which they may be distinguished. The first theme is whether intelligence can be characterized by a single factor, rather than multiple constructs. The second is whether intelligence is a changeable, practical, experience-based phenomenon or a stable, innate entity. Under the rubric of *intelligence* is subsumed all variations of innateness, fixedness, and multidimensionality. The term *ability* is reserved in this discussion to denote a special subset of intelligence characterized by an innate and fixed quantity.

There is a plethora of conflicting theory and findings related to the study of intelligence and vocational success. These conflicts may result from a lack of consensus on how to define intelligence, as well as the failure to consider personality and environmental interactions with intelligence in the study of vocational success.

g versus Multiple Intelligences

Models of g

The importance of intelligence in career selection and job performance has been demonstrated in numerous studies. Many of these studies have focused on the importance of general intelligence or *g* (Hunter, 1986; Gottfredson, 1986) and found links between measures of *g* and vocational success. *g* is an example of an ability conceptualization of intelligence, as the notion of innateness and fixedness underlies most *g* theories. Specific links have been found between *g*, occupational hierarchies, and overall job performance (Gottfredson, 1986; Arvey, 1986). It has been posited that *g* predicts overall job performance better than specific cognitive abilities, but that specific abilities are better predictors of particular job criteria (Arvey, 1986). Hunter (1986) has hypothesized that tailored aptitude composites will not enhance prediction of job performance over *g* predictions because most jobs build on general knowledge rather than specific aptitudes. *g* has also been conceptualized as an executor of specific skills and knowledge (Arvey, 1986).

Models of Multiple Factor Intelligence

Models of social intelligence. There have been several models of intelligence devised—some specifically for the vocational context, and others not—that compete with the concept of a single underlying entity and that may have more explanatory power than *g*. Eysenck (1988) has proposed the division of intelligence into biological, social, and psychometric forms. Gardner's (1983) theory of multiple intelligences is specifically referenced to appropriate career choices. Gardner's theory is a positive view of intelligence, as it entails the underlying notion that each individual has an intelligence profile from which at least one intelligence will be a source of esteem and accomplishment. Several of Gardner's intelligences have significance for a wide range of vocational choices, especially those forms of intelligence that enhance the understanding of the self and of others (intra- and interindividual or social intelligence). Lowman and Leeman (1988) have proposed that social intelligence, which has been determined to be a critical adjunct to new vocational models (Lowman & Leeman, 1988; Rosse et al., 1991), consists of ability (i.e., the individual can identify socially appropriate actions), interests and needs (needs for inclusion, affection, and control), and behaviors (the initiation of structure and consideration for others in leadership). It may be suggested that social intelligence is probably based on perceptual, analytical, and interpersonal skills and is one example of an interaction between intelligence and personality.

Models of practical intelligence. Sternberg and Wagner (1989) have stated that practical knowledge is a better predictor of job success than traditional assessments of intelligence. Similar conceptions of a division between practical intelligence and "cold cognition" have been made by other authors (Baltes, Dittman-Kohli, & Dixon, 1984; Cattell, 1971; Horn, 1970, 1982). Sternberg and Wagner (1989) make the distinction between accumulated experience and practical knowledge, which is proposed to be the result of actions performed upon experiential knowledge, and note that progressions between the two forms of knowing are not always parallel. These authors make the claim that practical intelligence is unrelated to standardized conceptions and measurements of intelligence. This suggestion has important implications for models of vocational success, which are based on assessments made using traditional intelligence tests.

Models of complex intelligence. The notion of cognitive complexity, which is the ability to differentiate and integrate unrelated constructs (Winer & Gati, 1986), has been analyzed in attempts to separate important, distinct aspects of this form of intelligence. The implication is that individuals who possess high levels of cognitive complexity are better able to crystallize vocational choice via more powerful within- and between-category vocational distinctions and comparisons.

Models of intellectual personality. One notion of intelligence that leans toward personality themes is the notion of performance moderated by intellectual environment (Mayer, Caruso, Zeigler, & Dreyden, 1989). These researchers have observed that gifted and average students can be distinguished on the basis of three factors that characterize the intellectual environment: (a) absorption or effortless dissociation from the external world, (b) pleasure or valuing of the thought process, and (c) apathy or anti-intellectual values and low self-esteem about one's own intelligence. This treatment of intelligence reveals the manner in which personality factors may be considered to be intertwined with cognitive factors, as there are certainly both of these elements involved in such characteristic qualities.

Individual intelligence predictors. Many additional intelligence factors thought to predict job performance have been identified. Some of these factors include nonverbal skills, word fluency, vocabulary, closure, flexibility, judgment, and reasoning (Arvey, 1986; Baehr & Orban, 1989). One difficulty with much of the research on intelligence factors is insufficient theoretical basis or explanation for selection of factors under study. It has been noted that occupation-specific assessment enhances prediction, as do assessments of intelligence and personality factors that consider interactions between these factors (Baehr & Orban, 1989; Rosse et al., 1991). Future directions for intelligence and vocational success studies must include more emphasis on justification for predictor selection and more specification of target job contexts.

Stability of Intelligence

The traditional view of intelligence as the single factor ability *g* entails the notions of fixed quantity, innateness, and lifelong persistence of individual differences (Gottfredson, 1986). This view of intelligence is at odds with the conceptualization advanced by authors such as Sternberg (1988), who assert that intelligence is flexible and can be both assessed and assisted. Gottfredson's view implies that stable hierarchies of occupations exist based on the dimension of intelligence and that individuals can be slotted into occupations for which they are innately suited. Sternberg's view is more elastic and subscribes to the notion that individuals can be molded to careers of choice with appropriate assessment and sufficient training. These theoretical distinctions have enormous implications for counseling approaches, in that the counselor can be seen variously as a vocational matchmaker or as a facilitator.

PERSONALITY FACTORS

The study and assessment of personality is a fundamentally important aspect of counseling psychology and has particular relevance to vocational counseling. Much of the difficulty in locating valid predictors of vocational success stems from the lack of theory-driven research in this area (Paunonen & Jackson, 1987). Two other difficulties plague the use of personality predictors of vocational success: First, perceived personality requirements for jobs may not match actual job requirements, and second, personality predictors alone may provide insufficient information to forecast vocational success without considering intelligence factors and environmental influences.

In the following section current research and theory linking personality to vocational success is described. Two major approaches to this research endeavors can be identified as follows: personality as a typology, and personality as a flexible style. In the first case, personality is considered as a trait, and the counselor's task is to wed trait to occupational environment. In the second conception, personality is somewhere between a trait and a state construct that is at least partially amenable to intervention.

Personality as a Typology

Models of Personality as a Trait

The concept of matching individuals identified as particular types to environmentally similar vocations has been a significant tradition in counseling psychology and situates personality at the furthest point from amenability to counseling interventions. This conception of personality is analogous to the innate concept of intelligence put forward by Gottfredson (1986). The work of John Holland (1963, 1973, 1985) is a particularly significant representation of this class of vocational theory. The four assumptions underlying Holland's (1973) theory are as follows:

1. In our culture, most persons can be categorized as one of six types: realistic, investigative, artistic, social, enterprising, or conventional.
2. There are six kinds of environments: realistic, investigative, artistic, social, enterprising, and conventional.
3. People search for environments that will let them exercise their skills and abilities, express their attitudes and values, and take on agreeable problems and roles.
4. A person's behavior is determined by an interaction between his or her personality and the characteristics of his or her environment. (pp. 2–4)

The establishment of congruence between personality and work/education environments is facilitated through competence in self-knowledge and an understanding of the labor market. Job satisfaction depends in part on acquiring a sufficiently good fit between personality characteristics and the environment. An example of the application of Holland's work is found in Holt's (1991) study, in which it was determined that "realistic" individuals value job status over intrinsic job interest, whereas "social" individuals value interest over status.

Models of Static Personal Style

The notion of personal style as a static phenomenon is another example of a trait class approach to the personality domain. The identification of various personal style patterns can be traced back to Hippocrates and his focus on the sanguine, choleric, melancholic, and phlegmatic personality types. A variety of authors (Amundson, 1989; Kunce, Cope, & Newton, 1986; Krug, 1984; Merrill & Reid, 1981) have developed approaches to personal style, with perhaps the most popular being that of Myers and McCauley (1985) and their use of the Carl Jung (1923) typology. According to Jung (1923), personality can be assessed with respect to extraversion/introversion, thinking/feeling, judging/perceiving, and intuition/sensing. Kunce, Cope, and Newton (1991) have reduced the various trait conceptions of personal style to two dimensions of stability/instability and introversion/extraversion. These dimensions find differential expressions in the physical domain (restless/searching), the emotional domain (reserved/quiet) and the cognitive domain (divergent/inquiring). In a manner similar to the approach taken by Holland, these authors posit that personal style can be fitted to job characteristics. It is important to note that assessment of environmental or job characteristics plays a critical role in determining vocational success in these approaches.

Personality as a Flexible Style

Personality has also been conceptualized as falling partway along a continuum of flexibility-fixedness. It is this flexible conceptualization of personality that is currently receiving the greatest interest in counseling research. One of the major reasons for this interest is that certain aspects of style have very important implications for the manner in which personal resources of any kind will be utilized, and the prospect of engendering successful change is most appealing in a counseling context. Several conceptions of flexible style are discussed in this section, including self-efficacy perceptions, decisiveness, and need fulfillment.

Self-Efficacy Perceptions

Self-efficacy perceptions have been defined as beliefs in one's potential for performing behaviors that will achieve a required end result (McAuliffe, 1992). Bandura's work on self-efficacy suggests that the individual approaches a situation with preformulated conceptions about his or her efficacy in a given situation. Self-efficacy is a cognitive motivation derived from internal standards and concerns self-evaluative reactions to one's performances (Bandura, 1977). Judgments of self-efficacy are important determinants of how much effort will be expended by an individual and the length of persistence with difficult tasks. Low self-efficacy is associated with heightened perceptions of future task difficulties (Bandura, 1982). A rapidly growing body of work addresses the notion that self-efficacy perceptions can have powerful effects on resource utilization in the achievement of vocational success. Self-efficacy has been demonstrated to influence career choice and achievements, task persistence, range of careers considered as options, career indecision, agentic behaviors, career exploratory activity, self-appraisal, and perceptions of career-related stress (Betz & Hackett, 1987; Bhagat & Allie, 1989; Blustein, 1989; Brown, Lent, & Larkin, 1989; Lent, Brown, & Larkin, 1986, 1987; McAuliffe, 1992).

Self-efficacy may require separate study in different domains, in different situations, and with respect to both general and specific abilities (Lent et al., 1986). Lent et al. (1987) and Lent and Hackett (1987) have begun to address the issue of combining various personality, intelligence, and environmental factors with considerations of how self-efficacy perceptions interact with these other areas. This model proposes relationships between vocational adjustment and self-efficacy, number of consequences anticipated following a career path choice (cognitive complexity), and the congruence between the individual's interests and interests of others on the chosen field. McAuliffe (1992) has suggested ways in which self-efficacy perceptions can be altered through attributional retraining, recall of successful experiences, researching of evidence that self-beliefs are accurate or inaccurate, restructuring of perceived consequences, and role modeling. McAuliffe also speculates that there may be a generalized form of self-efficacy that renders change between beliefs more accessible.

Career Indecisiveness

Another area of interest pertaining to flexible personal style addresses the notion of decisiveness. Indecisiveness as a habitual response to career issues is distinguished from undecidedness, which is a temporary response to a given problem situation (McAuliffe, 1992; Serling & Betz, 1990). Research on career indecisiveness is typically concerned with assessments of accompanying anxiety. It has been suggested that these coexisting constructs may not be simple dichotomies of decisive–not anxious and indecisive-anxious (Fuqua, Seaworth, & Newton, 1987). Instead, multiple subtypes of these categories may exist, so that an individual may be indecisive but not anxious, or decisive and anxious. Additional personality variables thought to be related to self-efficacy (e.g., locus of control, self-esteem, vocational identity, career salience, fear of commitment, perceived career barriers) that have also been considered have further subdivided categories of indecisive individuals (Lucas & Epperson, 1988; Serling & Betz, 1990).

Routes of Need Satisfaction

Need satisfaction is a major area of personality theory that has been investigated and found to have importance in vocational contexts. McNab and Fitzsimmons (1987) have utilized confirmatory factor analytic techniques to reduce several widely used personal-needs scales to a set of eight basic needs in the work environment: authority, coworker affiliation, creativity, responsibility, security, social service, work conditions, and recognition. Two major studies of youth in transition from high school to work environments (Amundson, Borgen, & Tench, 1993; Borgen, Amundson, & Tench, 1993) determined that similar basic needs require fulfillment even upon initial entry into the work environment. It can be posited that several of these needs are satisfied through different paths, depending on the personality profile of each individual. For example, an introverted individual may satisfy creativity needs through solitary invention, whereas an extroverted individual may choose to fulfill these needs through group endeavors. Alternatively, the two different forms of expression can be applied by either group, which allows the notion of flexible style to emerge.

ASSESSMENT IN COUNSELING

Qualitative versus Quantitative Vocational Assessment

Possibly the most contentious methodological issue in current counseling research is the selection of qualitative or quantitative methods of inquiry, particularly with respect to personality assessment. It appears that although some theorists have determined that the qualitative and quantitative positions are irreconcilable, most researchers have chosen to approach inquiry with a careful blend of both methodologies (Miles & Huberman, 1984).

Qualitative Assessment

Goldman (1992) has articulated a clear rationale for why qualitative assessment is particularly well suited in the counseling field:

- Qualitative assessment usually is more informal and allows for more flexibility on the part of the counsellor in its use, as compared with standardized tests;
- qualitative methods usually do not require the statistical competencies involved in number scores, norms, or data regarding reliability and validity;
- qualitative methods involve the client more actively in the search for self-awareness and can more readily lead directly and immediately into counseling interactions;
- qualitative methods, because they are usually not restricted to pre-set scales and scoring categories, tend to be more open-ended, divergent, and holistic in their interpretation and discussion;
- qualitative methods are especially useful with groups of clients. (p. 616)

Perhaps the greatest problem now facing qualitative inquiry is that the development of rigorous canons of inquiry and methodologies for analyzing qualitative data is still in infancy (Miles, 1979). It may be assumed that qualitative researchers have a set of assumptions, criteria, and rules for determining whether a finding is meaningful. It may be suggested that rapid progress in the utilization and efficiency of qualitative inquiry will be achieved as these guidelines become more explicitly set out in qualitative reports (Miles & Huberman, 1984).

Quantitative Assessment

The term *quantitative assessment* in counseling work denotes the use of standardized tests, experimentally controlled observation, and the use of statistical tools to investigate variables of interest. There are several advantages of quantitative assessment in counseling practice:

- Reliability, validity, generalizability, and replicability of information that is gathered
- Analysis of the laws that govern cause-and-effect relationships
- Reduction of subjectivity of observation
- Potential for systematic variation of variables of interest
- Opportunities for the development and comparison of norms

The advantages of quantitative inquiry are somewhat offset by difficulties in obtaining representative samples and managing to isolate variables of interest for observation and analysis. Indeed, it has been suggested that intense observation of naturally occurring social interactions is required in order to accurately identify meaningful patterns (Miles & Huberman, 1984).

Combining Assessment Methods

Assessment of personality, intelligence, and environmental influences can include both qualitative and quantitative methods, and a treading of middle ground between these two alternatives appears to yield optimal results. Goldman (1992) and Savickas (1992) attest to the importance of not relying solely on quantitative assessment. Research by Holland, Gottfredson, and Baker (1990) has demonstrated how predictive efficiency can be increased by using both qualitative and quantitative assessment with respect to vocational interests and aspirations. Slaney and Mackinnon-Slaney (1990) have illustrated how qualitative methods can be used to extend the focus of career counseling and can lead to a more comprehensive assessment. Savickas (1992) points to the need for understanding how people construe their present abilities, interests, and personality as part of an overall life pattern. It can be suggested that the nature of the problem at hand determines the best method of inquiry, and that skillful blending of the two approaches will yield optimal results.

Assessment of Intelligence

In assessing intelligence, the counseling focus is usually on aptitudes; some of the commonly used standardized measures include the Differential Aptitude Tests (Bennett, Seashore, & Wesman, 1982a,b) and the General Aptitude Test Battery (U.S. Employment Service, 1979). Qualitative assessment of intelligence does not share the rich history that belongs to quantitative assessment. With respect to qualitative assessment measures, the focus is upon levels of competence perceived by the self with respect to various aptitudes. It is often interesting to compare the scores from standardized measures with self-assessments.

Assessment of Personality

There are several different kinds of personality assessment measures used in counseling work that reflect particular theoretical orientations. The variety of assessment tools described below serve as examples of widely used tools that are based on the following theoretical positions: (a) activity-interest-occupation relationships, (b) personality-occupation matching, (c) client-generated vocational information, and (d) interpersonal skills–occupation matching. These different approaches can be classified under the general headings of quantitative and qualitative assessment. The major difference is that whereas intelligence assessment in counseling has traditionally focused on quantitative methodology, personality assessment is at the center of the quantitative-qualitative debate.

Quantitative Personality Assessment

Activity Preference Measures

Much vocational counseling assessment is based on the notion that personality traits can be identified by activity preferences (Broughton, Trapnell, & Boyes, 1991). The Strong-Campbell Interest Inventory (Hansen & Campbell, 1985) for example, includes reference to the Holland personality theme scales as well as to interests. There is currently a debate in counseling assessment work as to whether aspirational statements have more predictive validity than interest inventories (Holland et al., 1990). Despite this debate there are a number of personality tests that have been and continue to be widely used in vocational counseling.

Personality-Occupation Matching Assessment

The most widely used standardized personality test is the Myers-Briggs Type Indicator (MBTI; Myers & McCauley, 1985). The MBTI is based on Jungian theory and classifies individuals into four dichotomous categories: extraversion-introversion, sensation-intuition, thinking-feeling, and judgment-perception. The MBTI has been widely applied to match the interests of individuals with the characteristics of occupations. Studies have demonstrated that different Jungian types are drawn to different occupations (Shultz, 1986). In one study, teachers and social work students showed high levels of intuiting and feeling, whereas police officers and dental students showed high scores on extraversion, sensing, and thinking; these disparate scores reflected differing patterns of interpersonal interaction (Hanewitz, 1978).

Another example of a personality test is the Personal Styles Inventory (PSI; Kunce, Cope, & Newton, 1991). This measure is based on the personal styles model of personality, which uses a circumplex format to align two basic dimensions (introversion-extraversion and the need for stability-change). The scales are tailored to the emotional, physical, and cognitive domains. The PSI is designed for use in evaluating the fit between an individual's personal styles and job roles and expectations. It goes beyond the matching of individual to occupation and can be used to select specific positions within occupations in order to fine-tune the fit. A plethora of similar inventories with specific advantages and disadvantages have been developed by other researchers (Geier, 1977; Krug, 1984).

Qualitative Assessment

Client-Generated Vocational Information

These measures include the following: (a) the Life Line, which is a graphical recording and concurrent counselor-mediated discussion of life events that are meaningful to the individual; and (b) the Vocational Card Sort, which is a process in which the client generates personally relevant vocational categories by sorting through occupational options listed on cards with an ensuing counselor-mediated discussion of vocational interest themes.

Interpersonal Skills–Occupation Matching Assessment

In all of the assessment devices listed above, the constructs being measured are intrapersonal. One measure that is somewhat different was developed by Amundson (1989) for self- and interpersonal development. The Individual Style Survey (Amundson, 1989) includes the perceptions of others as well as self-perception. This is an important adjunct to interest testing as environmental influences, which are part of the triad of factors posited to predict vocational success, become an important part of assessment (Broughton, Trapnell, & Boyes, 1991).

The work cited to this point has focused on the development of assessment measures and procedures to assist individuals in expanding their levels of self-understanding, as well as relating that self-understanding to the world of work. Most of these endeavors have been developed since World War II and have had as an underlying assumption that there existed a stable or expanding labor market. In much of the developed world up to the early 1980s, this assumption was correct. It allowed counselors to assist clients in assessment of personality, intelligence, and other personal attributes and to link those personal characteristics with the job and broader career paths that the characteristics suggested. It has, however, become increasingly clear that for many sectors of the labor force this assumption is no longer valid. For a decade now, various minor and major recessions have reduced or altered labor market demands. These changes have drastically affected people's opportunity to use their abilities or meet their psychosocial needs through paid work (Krannich, 1991).

A RAPIDLY CHANGING LABOR MARKET CONTEXT

As counselors attempt to help people with career decisions and career goal setting they must focus attention on both personal and environmental factors. What has been particularly challenging in recent years has been the rapid pace of environmental change. An important aspect of this change has been the structural changes to the labor market. Some of the changes include increased globalization of markets, increased competitiveness, a shift from manufacturing to service- and information-oriented work, a desire for a more flexible work force with an emphasis upon part-time and contract work, the need for higher levels of education and training, and the inclusion of more women and minority-group workers in response to changing demographic trends (Krannich, 1991). These changes have resulted in considerable economic and social disruption at the individual level and also within both public and private employment sectors.

In response to this fast-moving environmental change, many people have found themselves in a reactive position, unclear about how to proceed. Traditional assumptions regarding education and work no longer seem viable. Higher standards and quota systems in education often restrict opportunity. High levels of unemployment and underemployment also cause concern. Even if one has a college or university degree, there is no guarantee that a suitable job will be available.

Coping within the new economic context requires not only a set of valued skills but also flexibility with respect to planning and personal style, self-confidence, self-efficacy, self-marketing skills, and social support (Herr, 1990). This range of abilities, attitudes, and social involvement is broadly based and reflects a sense of personal competence with respect to achieving a personally acceptable or satisfying occupational or career pattern.

In the sections that follow we present some of the results of studies regarding the transition from high school and youth unemployment. The information from these studies, when viewed from the perspective of the developmental needs of young adults, underscores the points just made regarding the need to reexamine current career counseling paradigms.

The Experience of Young People

The period of late adolescence is often seen as the time when issues related to career preparation and entry are a prominent focus. A look at this age group within the current labor market context clearly illustrates the need to reconsider the place of intelligence and personality variables in career counseling.

Perhaps a place to begin is with the developmental needs of older adolescents and young adults. Havighurst (1952) described work and relationships as two predominant issues, whereas Erikson (1968) focused on the importance of intimacy and commitment to goals. Levinson (1978) cited the importance of changing relationships and exploration in the lives of young adults. Crystallizing vocational choice and exploring it was viewed by Super (1963) as a critical developmental issue to be addressed. All of these theorists refer to the importance of older adolescents and young adults being able to address vocational issues and/or personal relationship issues.

The assumption made is that young people will move from a primary attachment to their parents to experimenting with and consolidating friendships and intimate relationships with peers. The period is characterized by some turmoil and uncertainty as new relationships develop and dissolve. In considering vocationally related issues, the assumption made is that young people will have engaged in self-exploration on their own or with the assistance of family, friends or a counselor. If a counselor is seen, tests of intelligence, personality, and interests are often used as tools in assisting the self-exploration process. The goal of the counseling is to help the young person to develop an expanded awareness of the areas to target in choosing a viable career option.

The premise underlying many of the developmental and career models is that the area of personal relationship development is in a state of flux and change, but that the transition into a job or career area is much calmer and more within the control of the young person involved. In the current context of a rapidly fluctuating labor market, the accuracy of the second part of this premise is open to question. Older adolescents and young adults now face the challenge of trying to meet their personal and career-related developmental needs when both areas are characterized by fluctuations of opportunities, uncertainty, and a diminished sense of personal control. An examination of the experience of young people after they have left high school and when they have become unemployed illustrates the difficulties encountered as they attempt to cope with these uncertainties.

The Transition from High School

Several studies conducted by the authors and others (Borgen & Amundson, 1993; Amundson, Borgen, & Tench, 1993; Borgen, Amundson, & Tench, 1993; Tiggeman & Winefield, 1984; Warr, Jackson, & Banks, 1982) serve as an illustration of (a) the lack of preparation of high school graduates for the current postsecondary education and labor market realities, (b) the amount of personal and vocational turmoil experienced in the first 18 months following high school graduation, and (c) some of the factors that positively and negatively influence these experiences.

The End of Grade 12

In the final month of secondary school, a sample of students from a large urban school district in Vancouver, British Columbia, were asked to rate on a 5-point Likert scale the likelihood of their entering jobs of their choice. Of the 245 who responded, 183 (75%) were certain or very certain that they would attain their first job choice. Students were also asked to write a few sentences regarding their expectations about their career future; these responses were then categorized into themes. Of the 214 who responded, 62% indicated that they expected to be successful and to work in positions that were challenging, rewarding, enjoyable, and personally satisfying. In addition, 10% wrote about the opportunity to make money, and 7% indicated the importance of job stability and security. Only 7% wrote about being worried, being unsure, or having low expectations.

The students were also asked about perceived barriers to reaching their career goals. Of the 195 students who responded, 51% listed concerns about meeting postsecondary education entrance requirements, or being able to compete for postsecondary programs or jobs. Another 24% listed barriers regarding the costs of postsecondary education.

The Postsecondary Experience

After about 18 months, 60 students were interviewed regarding their experience. As part of the interview they were asked about factors that they perceived as helpful or hindering in their post–high school experience. Positive factors mentioned included supportive family and friendship relationships; making money; satisfying leisure activities; personal achievements; education-related success (e.g., being able to enroll in desired courses or receiving scholarships); full-, part-time, or volunteer work; moving into one's own living quarters; travel; and changing seasons (i.e., from winter to spring).

In addition to the positive factors, several negative factors were outlined. These included relationship problems with family, friends, and dates; personal difficulties involving sickness or pregnancy; career confusion; unemployment; financial problems; problems related to work (e.g., underemployment, job insecurity, boring and meaningless jobs); problems involving not being able to get into desired programs and courses; difficulty in adjusting to postsecondary demands and lifestyle; and changing seasons (i.e., from summer to fall or winter).

In terms of the developmental issues cited by Erikson, Havighurst, Levinson, and Super, it is evident that the young adults in the study were attempting to address their career and relationship needs. It is also clear that the personal relationship issues were in flux and acted as both positive and negative influences on their post–high school experience. It is also interesting to note that the career area was an area of turmoil, characterized as a source of both growth and stress. The interviews further illustrated that there is an interaction between career barriers and being able to address personal relationship needs. If a young person is unable to move on to employment or further education, the type and range of peer contact is greatly influenced. This often makes it difficult to gain a sense of growth or expanded independence, which are important aspects of development for young adults.

In summary, then, these young people graduated from high school with a sense of personal optimism regarding their ability to attain their first choice of a job or career area. At that time they also identified possible barriers that they might face in progressing educationally and/or vocationally. Their experiences bore out their concerns regarding sufficient availability of desired jobs or educational opportunities. It seems clear that the assumptions of stable or expanding educational and vocational opportunities and a linear, smooth entry into a career path were not true for this group of young adults.

Other studies conducted by Borgen and Amundson (1987) indicated that young people who became unemployed after high school experienced significant barriers to their career and personal development. These young people also identified positive and negative factors that influenced their experience. These factors were very similar to the ones just cited for the sample in our current study. It would seem that the threats to self-confidence that are often associated with the experience of unemployment for youth and adults (Borgen & Amundson, 1984) are now also being felt by young people during the post–high school transition.

THE ROLE OF PERSONALITY AND INTELLIGENCE IN ESTABLISHING AND MAINTAINING A SENSE OF PERSONAL COMPETENCE

In the preceding sections an attempt has been made to illustrate the following points:

1. Traditional theory and assessment of personality, intelligence and environmental factors in vocational contexts requires revised approaches to combine these factors.
2. Current economic conditions have affected the adequacy of currently used conceptions of vocational progress thereby creating opportunities for the development of contemporarily relevant models of the vocational context.

It may be suggested that a new model that tracks vocational progress through an expression of personal competence achieved by the conjoining of personality and intelligence factors in response to environmental influences will be of great utility in the current economic climate. The following section is an effort to address the issue of personality, intelligence, and environmental interaction in the vocational context by the presentation of a recently developed model of vocational competence that subsumes these three factors. This model of personal competence has been developed by Amundson (1990) and incorporates eight interlocking elements characterized as personal skills through which personality and intelligence are combined in adaptive responses to rapidly changing environmental opportunities. This model demonstrates particular emphasis on adaptability to ongoing environmental change, and it is this focus on the interaction of personality and intelligence in response to change that lends new understanding to vocational development.

Sternberg's (1985) triarchic theory of intelligence has provided a useful starting point from which Amundson's model of vocational adaptation has been developed. This usefulness has been in part the result of Sternberg's emphasis upon practical or social intelligence, which (as noted in preceding sections) has been proposed to be an important element of vocational success. This broad-based approach is too inclusive a concept for some theorists (Eysenck, 1988), but it does fit well within the competence model that follows and the general career counseling domain. In considering personal competence, it is important to recognize that the term *competence* refers to a state of being as well as to a state of doing: A competent person is one who has the capacity (or power) to deal adequately with emerging situations. As Amundson's model is described below, Sternberg's fundamental concept of interaction among personality, intelligence, and environment becomes apparent as a major theme that runs through the eight elements.

A Model of Personal Competence

The following model incorporates eight factors which are proposed by Amundson to enhance vocational success.

Purpose. Motivation, commitment and initiative are triggered by a clear sense of direction and purpose. People are willing to devote themselves fully to tasks when they value what they are doing and see how they can make a positive contribution.

Problem solving. To be effective problem solvers, people must cultivate the ability to abstract information from a wide variety of sources, to consider all aspects of an issue, to think creatively, to make sound judgments, and to construct effective action plans. People who are good problem solvers are able to think clearly under difficult circumstances.

Communication skills. Through communication we express our ideas to one another (verbally, nonverbally, and in written form) and incorporate the ideas of others into our perspective. Good communicators are able to express themselves clearly and succinctly. They are also active listeners and take the time to check what was heard against what was intended.

Theoretical knowledge. The development and maintenance of up-to-date theoretical knowledge requires a foundation of specific facts (procedures) and concepts. A growing knowledge base is dependent on having developed an efficient system of obtaining and organizing information. To maintain this spirit of inquiry and knowledge acquisition, one must be involved in a variety of lifelong learning activities.

Applied knowledge. Practical experience serves to consolidate theoretical knowledge. This experience must be structured in such a way that it contains elements of security, relevance, challenge, and critical reflection.

Organizational adaptability. This capacity focuses on a person's knowledge of written and unwritten societal rules and the ability to maneuver within organizational structures to accomplish goals. People with strength in this area display ingenuity and persistence and are able to bend rules successfully to their advantage.

Human relations. Building and nurturing positive relationships ensures a foundation of emotional and practical support. Relationships can occur at many different levels, each with its own advantages and challenges (e.g., family, peer group, authority figures, clients/customers).

Self-confidence. Self-confidence is based on self-knowledge, self-acceptance, emotional support, and past successes. With a strong sense of personal security, the person is willing to take risks, to persevere, and to learn from the mistakes that are made along the way.

AN EXPANDED VIEW OF CAREER COUNSELING: ENGENDERING COMPETENCE

Applying Existing Theory

Consideration of existing theories of personality and intelligence along with the description of the experience of youths in transition has brought home the point that many extant vocational theories, although providing important contributions to understanding of vocational development, could benefit from contextualization and intertwining. Amundson's theory (1990) is one example of how adaptability to circumstances might be enhanced along with aspects of personality and intelligence. Indeed, several of the components are quite interchangeable under the broad headings of personality and intelligence. The benefits for counselors that will be derived from such contextualization and integration are significant. The description of today's economy implies that the second term in the expression *vocational choice* has increasingly less applicability. The whole notion that the individual can select from a wide range of occupations and simply plug or be plugged into a job is seriously in question. The current economy is that reference system within which all counselors function, apply existing theories, and develop novel conceptions. If extant theories are only occasionally found to be valid in application, it may be in part because revisions are needed in light of current economic conditions. A sense of how the current situation impinges on the usefulness of decontextualized theory may be illuminated by considering how current theories might fare when embedded in applied settings in the context of a slow economy.

Contextualizing Theories of Intelligence

Sternberg's (1985) triarchic theory of intelligence is an example of an elegant theory that might be enhanced by embedding it in the current economic context. This domain specificity is a critical notion, as vocational theory is often developed from models derived in alternative contexts. Sternberg makes reference to the critical use of intelligence by interaction with demanding tasks and situations. Environmental factors such as labor market conditions determine the likelihood of occurrence of such encounters that will ensure the development of intelligence. In a slow economy, the individual may find it difficult to engage in appropriate, development-engendering situations (which most likely present themselves in employment environments). The question of environmental adaptability then becomes a crucial, even primary aspect of any vocational theory. Because conditions have eliminated so many options, the counselor is required to introduce much more significant changes in the client's lifestyle than simply to suggest changes in career direction.

Contextualizing g

Contextualization of vocational theory has profound implications for most theories of intelligence that transcend debates over *g* versus "not-*g*" (Gottfredson, 1986; Hunter, 1986). It is apparent in the current diminishing economy that the simple matching by the counselor of an individual's intelligence level to an occupational hierarchy is increasingly less useful. The nature of labor requirements is changing to include a preponderance of service jobs and a demand for workers who can perform skill-based information-loaded jobs (Ross, 1992). The question may then be asked as to what will become of individuals determined by such theory to fit the middle of the occupational hierarchy. Even within such a humanistic theory of intelligence as Gardner's (1983) theory of multiple intelligences, it may be suggested that particular profiles of intelligences will be more easily matched to the profile of the economy.

The many conceptions of social intelligence (Gardner, 1983; Lowman & Leeman, 1988; Rosse et al., 1991) still do not strongly imply an adaptational component. Instead, such theories have as an underlying theme the notion that a given or matured and completely formed individual capacity for social intelligence promotes adaptation in the vocational context. The same difficulty applies to models that break performance skills into separate components (Arvey, 1986; Baehr & Orban, 1989). These theories do not specify how the individual gathers personal resources to overcome environmental obstacles in order either to mature or to demonstrate such skills. These models leave little room for the counselor to intervene constructively and instead result in the failure of the individual either to find satisfying work or to find work at all.

Contextualizing Flexibility

The notion of flexibility of personal skills (Sternberg, 1985) is a more hopeful and useful view of individual functioning for counselors to employ in an uncertain economy. Sternberg's model indicates that the individual can adapt to trying circumstances and possibly could be adapted to vocational contexts if more specification of how personality factors contribute to overcoming lack of exposure to intelligence-enhancing experiences. In the current economy, personality and adaptability might be considered primary considerations in any vocational theory.

Theories of intelligence must also be contextualized with respect to the environment of the individual. Mayer et al. (1989) have begun to introduce this concept with their model of intellectual environment and the manner in which an individual views, values, and applies his or her own intelligence. Much more theory and research on such self-appraisal and self-recognition is required to tie existing personality theory into performance resulting from either innate or developed intelligence. It is apparent that self-knowledge is a fundamental aspect of adaptation. Counseling psychology,which is based on a long tradition of personality self-awareness, needs now to implement ways in which the individual can best gain access to information that will enhance this process.

Contextualizing Theories of Personality

A contextualized consideration of the relationship between personality and vocational choice has similar ramifications to that of the relationship between intelligence and vocational choice. Vocational theories that conceptualize personality as a stable trait (Holland, 1963, 1973, 1985) or stable style (Kunce et al., 1991; Myers & McCauley, 1985) should be able to provide explanations of how various personality types and their corresponding occupational destinies fare under current economic conditions. Once again, if one subscribes to theories that espouse exclusive stability of personality, the emphasis must be on how such traits allow the individual to adapt to circumstances. Without such a link, the forecast for the psychological and economic well-being of much of the population will be dismal. The counselor's role is also severely limited under the auspices of these kinds of conceptions. It is most likely because of such concerns and feedback from workers in the field that contemporary research is centered on such flexible elements of personal style as self-efficacy perceptions, indecisiveness, and route of need satisfaction (Betz & Hackett, 1987; Bhagat & Allie, 1989; Blustein, 1989; Brown et al., 1989; Lent et al., 1986, 1987; McAuliffe, 1992; McNab & Fitzsimmons, 1987; Serling & Betz, 1990). Such approaches remove the clean lines of diagnostic personality categories but instead allow the consideration of how positive interventions might best be accomplished.

Broadening Career Counseling Definitions

The studies cited, along with several others (Herr, 1992; Herr & Cramer, 1992) and Amundson's model, suggest a broadened definition of career counseling that recognizes the developmental needs of young adults within the context of shifting personal and career opportunities. They also imply a blurring of the distinction between personal and career counseling. The approach that we suggest includes the use of measures to assess intelligence and personality as needed, but these measures are used with a different set of assumptions regarding how the client can translate the information generated into personally relevant knowledge. An evolving counseling model is under development by the authors and includes some of the elements outlined.

Strategies for Developing Multiple Plans

The goal of counseling in this context is to assist the client in using self-knowledge (generated in a variety of ways) not to narrow thinking about career options, but to generate a range of viable alternatives. The studies that we have conducted indicate that many young people leave high school with one plan and a high level of expectation that the plan can be realized. They then become discouraged if the plan does not work and seem to lack the tools to generate another one. We suggest that a part of career counseling now include helping young people to develop lateral thinking skills: the ability to visualize different futures for themselves, as well as to assess options effectively and make decisions within a context of uncertainty (Gelatt, 1989). These activities would assist the clients in expanding their range of competence through the development of a sense of purpose and problem-solving skills more reflective of environmental opportunities.

Self-Advocacy

It is clear that there is now a need to market oneself effectively in order to find a place within post-secondary education and the labor market. Clients need to develop strategies for maneuvering through bureaucracies and networking with a sense of assertiveness and self-efficacy (Bandura, 1986). This would positively influence the development of several components of competence, including communication skills, self-confidence, organizational adaptability, and effectiveness in human relations generally.

Managing Changing Relationships

The developmental theorists already cited and the young people involved in our studies of transition and unemployment have noted the turmoil and excitement that can be generated in developing and changing relationships. The importance of this aspect of development is heightened further within the current context of career uncertainty. Young people may need to rely more heavily on family, friendship and intimate relationships, now that developmental growth opportunities may be more restricted in the career area. In addressing these relationship issues, counsellors can assist clients in developing their human relations competence through the enhancement of a more open approach to communication and problem solving, and the building of self-confidence.

Meeting Basic Needs

Our studies of transition and unemployment (Amundson & Borgen, 1987; Amundson, et al., 1993; Borgen & Amundson, 1987, 1993; Borgen et al., 1993) have indicated that people experience some psychological difficulties when they encounter a downward shift in their ability to meet their needs. Needs have been described variously. Maslow (1968) presented them in a hierarchy from basic needs for survival and environmental stability to higher-order needs for community and mastery. Toffler (1980) categorized needs under the headings of community, meaning, and structure.

Young adults experiencing challenges in meeting their needs through the areas of career and/or relationships may benefit from some counseling assistance. Knowing that some levels of frustration may be expected in such circumstances can be a relief in itself. Counseling focused on the issues related to needs can help to increase competence in the areas of human relations, organizational adaptability, and purpose. Counseling can also provide positive alternatives to need fulfillment through a route other than one's occupation. Our transition and unemployment studies have demonstrated that the two most significant factors that aid transition are financial and activity satisfaction (Amundson & Borgen, 1987; Amundson et al., 1993; Borgen & Amundson, 1987, 1993; Borgen et al., 1993). It appears that if financial concerns are not immediately pressing and the individual can satisfy basic needs through avenues other than occupational ones (e.g., in group social activities), then psychological well-being will not be seriously impaired. This is an example of adaptability to environmental circumstances that lends credence to the notion of contextualization of extant theories of vocational development.

Coping with Stress

Living with two major sets of developmental issues in turmoil and a reduced or altered ability to meet psychological needs can lead to stress. Part of counseling in such cases should involve the identification of the sources of the stress and the discussion and practice of various coping strategies. These may include relaxation techniques, managing self-talk, focusing, and using support systems. These activities will have the effect of enhancing components of competence related to organizational adaptability, human relations, and self-confidence.

Bridging Programs

Part of the difficulty encountered by young people involves lack of hands-on experience regarding the culture of work. Counselors can be of assistance by creating opportunities for work experience or co-op education, and by helping young people to develop and enhance study and job search skills. This can have the effect of relating learning to work and life more generally. It will also help to address competence factors involving applied knowledge and human relations.

Information and Information Access

It has become almost trite to say that we live in the age of information. The task for all of us, including young people leaving high school, is how to turn that information into personally relevant knowledge. Traditionally, career counseling has included awareness of educational, occupational, and organizational information and trends. Within the current context of rapidly changing occupational opportunities, it is crucial also to help clients develop methods to gather and interpret information from a variety of sources (Wurman, 1989). This will assist in the development of competence factors related to theoretical knowledge and human relations.

CONCLUDING COMMENTS

The suggestions above concentrate on helping the individual to enhance existing skills and intelligences, but they retain a primary emphasis on engendering adaptability through personality factors such as responses to stress. Such suggestions can be implemented whether one subscribes to either trait or flexible conceptions of personality and intelligence. These suggestions capitalize on the integration of skills and information available to the individual while also allowing room for adapting to obstacles to need fulfillment through routes other than occupational ones.

The purpose of this chapter has been to review the role and use of intelligence and personality variables in counseling, with a particular focus on career counseling. Often issues related to counseling generally, and career counseling specifically, have focused on the individual and his or her need to have an expanded range of personal knowledge. An example of this focus is seen in the definition of *career* by Super cited earlier. It is within this context that measures of intelligence and personality are often used. We suggest that information regarding these variables continues to be important to clients. We also suggest, however, that career counseling be conceptualized more broadly, because our studies indicate that a greater range of information regarding environmental variables is now crucial. This information can help clients to view their attributes in a new light, make sense of their interactions with their environment and their reactions to those exchanges, and look for new opportunities for personal and career growth with a revised set of expectations.

REFERENCES

Amundson, N., Borgen, W., & Tench, E. (1993). *Post-secondary experience: Factors that aid transition.* Unpublished paper.

Amundson, N. E. (1989). *The Individual Style Survey.* Edmonton: Psychometrices Canada.

Amundson, N. E. (1990). *A model of personal competence.* Unpublished paper.

Amundson, N. E., & Borgen, W. A. (1987). Coping with unemployment: What helps and hinders. *Journal of Employment Counseling, 24,* 97–106.

Arvey, R. (1986). General ability in employment: A discussion. *Journal of Vocational Behavior, 29,* 415–420.

Baehr, M., & Orban, J. (1989). The role of intellectual abilities and personality characteristics in determining success in higher-level positions. *Journal of Vocational Behavior, 35,* 270–287.

Baltes, P. B., Dittman-Kohli, F., & Dixon, R. A. (1984). New perspectives on the development of intelligence in adulthood: Toward a dual-process model of selective optimization with compensation. *Life-Span, Development and Behavior, 6,* 33–76.

Bandura, A. (1977). Self-efficacy: Toward a unifying theory of behavioral change. *Psychological Review, 84,* 191–215.

Bandura, A. (1982). Self-efficacy mechanism in human agency. *American Psychologist, 37,* 122–147.

Bandura, A. (1986). *Social foundation of thought and action: A social cognitive theory.* Englewood Cliffs, NJ: Prentice-Hall.

Bennett, G. K., Seashore, H. G., & Wesman, A. C. (1982a). *Differential Aptitude Tests: Administrators handbook.* San Antonio, TX: Psychological Corporation.

Bennett, G. K., Seashore, H. G., & Wesman, A. C. (1982b). *Differential Aptitude Tests: Technical supplement.* San Antonio, TX: Psychological Corporation.

Betz, N., & Hackett, G. (1987). Concept of agency in educational and career development. *Journal of Counseling Psychology, 34,* 299–308.

Bhagat, R., & Allie, S. (1989). Organizational stress, personal life stress and symptoms of life strains: An inquiry into the moderating role of styles of coping. *Journal of Vocational Behavior, 35,* 231–253.

Blocher, D. H. (1987). *The professional counselor.* New York: Macmillan.

Blustein, D. (1989). The role of goal instability and career self-efficacy in the career exploration process. *Journal of Vocational Behavior, 35,* 194–203.

Borgen, W., & Amundson, N. (1984). *The experience of unemployment.* Toronto: Nelson.

Borgen, W., & Amundson, N. (1987). The dynamics of unemployment. *Journal of Counseling and Development, 66,* 180–184.

Borgen, W., & Amundson, N. (1993). *Transition from high school: An exploratory study.* Unpublished paper.

Borgen, W., Amundson, N., & Tench. E. (1993). *Influences on psychological well-being through the transition from high school to work or further education.* Unpublished paper.

Broughton, R., Trapnell, P., & Boyes, M. (1991). Classifying personality types with occupational prototypes. *Journal of Research in Personality, 25,* 302–321.

Brown, S., Lent, R., & Larkin, K. (1989). Self-efficacy as a moderator of scholastic aptitude: Academic performance relationships. *Journal of Vocational Behaviour, 35,* 64–75.

Cattell, R. B. (1971). *Abilities: Their structure, growth and action.* Boston: Houghton.

Erikson, E. H. (1968). *Identity, youth and crisis.* New York: Norton.

Eysenck, H. J. (1988). The concept of intelligence: Useful or useless? *Intelligence, 12,* 1–16.

Fuqua, D., Seaworth, T., & Newman, J. (1987). The relationship of career indecision and anxiety: A multivariate examination. *Journal of Vocational Behavior, 30,* 175–186.

Furnham, A. (1985). Youth unemployment: A review of the literature. *Journal of Adolescence, 8,* 109–124.

Gardner, H. (1983). *Frames of mind.* New York: Basic Books.

Geier, J. G. (1977). *Personal Profile System.* Winnipeg, Manitoba: Performance Systems International.

Gelatt, H. B. (1989). Positive uncertainty: A new decision-making framework for counseling. *Journal of Counseling Psychology, 36,* 252–256.

Goldman, L. (1992). Qualitative assessment: An approach for counselors. *Journal of Counseling and Development, 70,* 616–623.

Gottfredson, L. S. (1986). Societal consequences of the "*g*" factor in employment. *Journal of Vocational Behavior, 29,* 379–410.

Hanewitz, W. (1978). Police personality: A Jungian perspective. *Crime and Delinquency, 24,* 152–172.

Hansen, J. C., & Campbell, D. P. (1985). *Manual for the SUIB-SCII* (4th ed.). Stanford, CA: Stanford University Press.

Havinghurst, R. J. (1952). *Developmental tasks and education.* New York: McKay.

Herr, E. L. (1990). Emerging trends in career counseling. *International Journal for the Advancement of Counseling, 15,* 255–288.

Herr, E. L. (1992). Counseling for personal flexibility in a global economy. *Educational and Vocational Guidance, 53,* 5–16.

Herr, E. L., & Cramer, S. H. (1992). *Career guidance through the lifespan: Systematic approaches* (4th ed.). New York: HarperCollins.

Holland, J. L. (1963). Explanation of a theory of vocational choice: Vocational images and choice. *Vocational Guidance Quarterly, 11,* 232–239.

Holland, J. L. (1973). *Making vocational choices: A theory of careers.* Englewood Cliffs, NJ: Prentice-Hall.

Holland, J. L. (1985). *Making vocational choices: A theory of vocational personalities and work environments* (2nd ed.). Englewood Cliffs, NJ: Prentice-Hall

Holland, J. L., Gottfredson, G. D., & Baker, H. G. (1990). Validity of vocational aspirations and interest inventories: Extended, replicated, and reinterpreted. *Journal of Counseling Psychology, 37,* 337–342.

Holt, P. (1991). Differential effects of status and interest in the process of compromise. *Journal of Counseling Psychology, 36,* 42–47.

Horn, J. L. (1970). Organization of data on life-span development of human abilities. In L. R. Goulet & P. B. Baltes (Eds.), *Life-span developmental psychology and theory.* New York: Academic Press.

Horn, J. L. (1982). The aging of human abilities. In B. B. Wolman (Ed.), *Handbook of developmental psychology.* Englewood Cliffs, NJ: Prentice-Hall.

Hunter, J. E. (1986). Cognitive ability, cognitive aptitudes, job knowledge, and job performance. *Journal of Vocational Behavior, 29*, 340–362.

Jung, C. (1923). *Psychological types*. New York: Harcourt Brace.

Krannich, R. L. (1991). *Careering and re-careering for the 1990's*. Woodbridge, VA: Impact.

Krug, S. (1984). *The Adult Personality Inventory*. Champaign, IL: Institute for Personality and Ability Testing.

Kunce, J. T., Cope, C. S., & Newton, R. (1986). *The Personal Styles Inventory*. Columbia, MO: Educational & Psychological Consultants.

Kunce, J. T., Cope, C. S., & Newton, R. (1991). Personal Styles Inventory. *Journal of Counseling and Development, 70*, 334–341.

Lent, R., Brown, S., & Larkin, K. (1986). Self-efficacy in the prediction of academic performance and perceived career options. *Journal of Counseling Psychology, 33*, 265–269.

Lent, R., Brown, S., & Larkin, K. (1987). Comparison of three theoretically derived variables in predicting career and academic behaviour: Self-efficacy, interest congruence, and consequence thinking. *Journal of Counseling Psychology, 34*, 293–298.

Lent, R., & Hackett, G. (1987). Career self-efficacy: Empirical status and future directions. *Journal of Vocational Behavior, 30*, 347–382.

Levinson, D. (1978). *The seasons of a man's life*. New York: Ballantine.

Lowman, R. L., & Leeman, G. E. (1988). The dimensionality of social intelligence: Social abilities, interests, and needs. *The Journal of Psychology, 122*, 279–290.

Lucas, M., & Epperson, D. (1988). Personality types in vocationally undecided students. *Journal of College Student Development, 29*, 460–466.

Maslow, A. E. (1968). *Toward a psychology of being* (2nd ed.). Toronto: Van Nostrand.

Mayer, J., Caruso, D., Ziegler, E., & Dreyden, J. (1989). Intelligence and intelligence-related personality traits. *Intelligence, 13*, 119–133.

McAuliffe, G. (1992). Assessing and changing career decision-making self-efficacy expectations. *Journal of Career Development, 19*, 25–36.

McNab, D., & Fitzsimmons, G. (1987). A multitrait-multimethod study of work-related needs, values, and preferences. *Journal of Vocational Behaviour, 30*, 1–15.

Merrill, D. W., & Reid, R. H. (1981). *Personal styles and effective performance*. Radnor, PA: Chelton.

Miles, M. (1979). Qualitative data as an attractive nuisance: The problem of analysis. *Administrative Science Quarterly, 24*, 590–601.

Miles, M., & Huberman, A. (1984). Drawing valid meaning from qualitative data: Toward a shared craft. *Educational Researcher, 58*, 20–30.

Myers, I. B., & McCaulley, M. H. (1985). *Manual: A guide to the development and use of the Myers-Briggs Type Indicator*. Palo Alto, CA: Consulting Psychologists Press.

Paunonen, S., & Jackson, D. (1987). Accuracy of interviewers and students in identifying the personality characteristics of personnel managers and computer programmers. *Journal of Vocational Behavior, 31*, 26–36.

Ross, S. (1992). *Understanding the labor market*. Unpublished manuscript.

Rosse, J. G., Miller, H. E., & Barnes, L. K. (1991). Combining personality and cognitive ability predictors for hiring service-oriented employees. *Journal of Business and Psychology, 5*, 431–445.

Savickas, M. L. (1992). New directions in career assessment. In D. H. Montross & C. J. Shinkmon (Eds.), *Career development: Theory and practice*. Springfield, IL: Thomas.

Schultz, D. (1986). *Theories of personality*. Monterey, CA: Brooks-Cole.

Serling, D., & Betz, N. (1990). Development and evaluation of a measure of fear of commitment. *Journal of Counseling Psychology, 37*, 91–97.

Slaney, R., & McKinnon-Slaney, F. (1990). The Vocational Card Sorts. In C. E. Watkins, Jr., & V. Campbell (Eds.), *Testing in counseling practice* (pp. 317–371). Hillsdale, NJ: Erlbaum.

Sternberg, R. J. (1985). *Beyond IQ: A triarchic theory of human intelligence*. New York: Cambridge University Press.

Sternberg, R. J. (1988). *The triarchic mind*. New York: Viking.

Sternberg, R. J., & Wagner, R. (1989). Individual differences in practical knowledge and its acquisition. In P. Ackerman, R. Sternberg, & R. Glaser (Eds.), *Learning and individual differences: Advances in theory and research* (pp. 267–282). New York: Freeman.

Super, D. E. (1963). *Career development: Essays in vocational development*. New York: College Entrance Examination Board.

Super, D. E. (1976). *Career education and the meaning of work: Monographs on career education*. Washington, DC: Office of Career Education, U.S. Department of Education.

Tiggemann, M., & Winefield, M. (1984). The effects of unemployment on the mood, self-esteem, locus of control, and depressive effect of school leavers. *Journal of Occupational Psychology, 57*, 33–42.

Toffler, A. (1980). *The third wave*. New York: Bantam Books.

U.S. Employment Service. (1979). The General Aptitude Test Battery (GATB). Washington, DC: Author.

Warr, P. B., Jackson, P. R., & Banks, M. H. (1982). Duration of unemployment and psychological well being in young men and women. *Current Psychological Research, 2*, 207–214.

Winer, D., & Gati, I. (1986). Cognitive complexity and interest crystallization. *Journal of Vocational Behavior, 28*, 48–59.

Wurman, R. S. (1989). *Information anxiety*. New York: Doubleday.

28

Intelligence and Personality in School and Educational Psychology

Jeffery P. Braden

Intelligence and personality are fundamental to understanding children's performance in schools. The first practical intelligence test was developed by Binet and Simon for use in Parisian public schools, and schools have remained the primary source for research and application regarding theories of intelligence. Although research regarding personality has generally evolved in clinical settings and then been transferred to schools, educators continue to develop and apply theories and techniques drawn from personality research.

The intersection of intelligence, personality, and schools creates a complex and varied literature. Consequently, I will use a three-dimensional map to organize and describe the research linking individual differences to education and schools. The first dimension of my map comprises the educational applications, or uses, of intelligence and personality. The second dimension comprises the distinction between educational and school psychology. The third and final dimension comprises the psychological domain of the research, which I have arbitrarily dichotomized into emphases on intelligence versus personality. Because these dimensions are admittedly arbitrary, a brief explanation of each is provided to illustrate the ways in which research on intelligence and personality is linked to educational and school psychology.

The first dimension, educational uses of research, is defined by three primary applications. The first is the way in which psychological knowledge is used to distinguish between normal and abnormal deviations in individual differences. The normal/abnormal distinction is important for understanding how constructs of intelligence and personality are applied to schools. Identification of abnormality, and the creation of classes linked to abnormal states, appears repeatedly in discussions of intelligence and personality in schools. Abnormality can be further divided into abnormalities associated with dysfunctional levels of intelligence (e.g., mental retardation) and personality (e.g., sociopathic personality disorder), and "abnormalities" associated with superior functional levels (e.g., giftedness, leadership).

The second educational application is the study of normal differences in intelligence and personality. With respect to intelligence, educators are interested in understanding intraindividual variability in cognitive abilities (i.e., identifying relative strengths and weaknesses within learners), and in methods to enhance cognitive performance (e.g., strategies to improve memory). With respect to personality, educators are interested in developing a prosocial orientation in chil-

Jeffery P. Braden • Department of Educational Psychology, University of Wisconsin-Madison, Madison, Wisconsin 53706.

International Handbook of Personality and Intelligence, edited by Donald H. Saklofske and Moshe Zeidner. Plenum Press, New York, 1995.

dren, motivating children to learn, and adapting instruction to differences in children's temperament.

The third educational use of individual-differences research is the study of educational responses to intelligence and personality. Educators respond to students' intellectual and personality traits by modifying students' intelligence or personality, by accommodating individual differences in personality and intelligence among children, and by selecting and providing alternative placement to children on the basis of the child's personality or intelligence.

The three primary applications of individual differences to education (i.e., abnormality versus normality, normal variations in ability and personality, and educational responses to intelligence and personality) provide but one dimension for organizing the literature on intelligence and personality in educational and school psychology. The second dimension is created by drawing a distinction in orientation between educational and school psychology. Educational psychology is primarily concerned with understanding the psychological factors that influence learning. Consequently, educational psychologists are often concerned with "normal" differences among individuals. In contrast, school psychologists apply psychological research to schools (Lambert & Goodman, 1992). School psychologists are often, but not exclusively, interested in identifying abnormality (e.g., mental retardation, personality disorders). Although this distinction is arbitrary (i.e., there are many educational psychologists concerned with abnormality and educational applications, and many school psychologists who work normal children and who conduct their own research), the distinction between educational and school psychology will serve as a second dimension in organizing this chapter.

The third dimension of the organizing model draws a distinction between intelligence and personality as foci or emphases of research. Although the distinction between intelligence and personality is arbitrary and arguably inappropriate for some topics (e.g., learning styles), the distinction is drawn in this chapter for organizational convenience. Categorizing research by the degree to which it stresses cognitive abilities (i.e., intelligence) rather than affective characteristics (i.e., personality) also reflects a bias latent in educational research. This bias draws an admittedly artificial distinction between cognitive and affective components of learning. The tendency to distinguish between research addressing individual differences in cognitive ability (i.e., intelligence) and individual differences in affective characteristics (i.e., personality) remains, however, and is incorporated into the organization of this chapter.

Together, the primary applications of intelligence and personality research, the distinction between educational and school psychology, and the emphasis on intelligence versus personality form a three-dimensional framework for organizing the remainder of this chapter. This three-dimensional model is illustrated in Figure 1. The chapter begins with the first "cube" in the model, which is the discussion of abnormality in intelligence and personality. Research on abnormality is grouped within this section by its research emphasis (i.e., intelligence versus personality). Within each of these subcategories, the similarities and differences of educational and school psychologists are explored to elaborate the relationships among intelligence and personality in educational and school psychology. This approach is repeated in the sections addressing normal variations in intelligence and personality. The chapter concludes with a discussion of issues for research linking intelligence and personality to education and schools.

ABNORMAL INTELLIGENCE AND PERSONALITY

Abnormal intelligence is defined as extreme variation from the norm. Thus intellectual abnormalities take two forms: abnormally low intelligence, and abnormally high intelligence. Each of these is widely studied in educational psychology, and each is a condition that school psychologists are often asked to identify.

Mental Retardation

Abnormally low intelligence is commonly called mental retardation. The symptoms vary as a function of the severity of the retardation. Some individuals will manifest difficulty in learning school-related competencies (e.g., reading) but otherwise make functional adaptations to society; others will be so profoundly retarded that they have extreme difficulty mastering essential self-help skills (e.g., independent feeding, toilet training, speaking). Consequently, mental retardation is typically subdivided into mild and severe types, with the latter encompassing severely and profoundly retarded individuals. These two types are generally distinguished by additional physi-

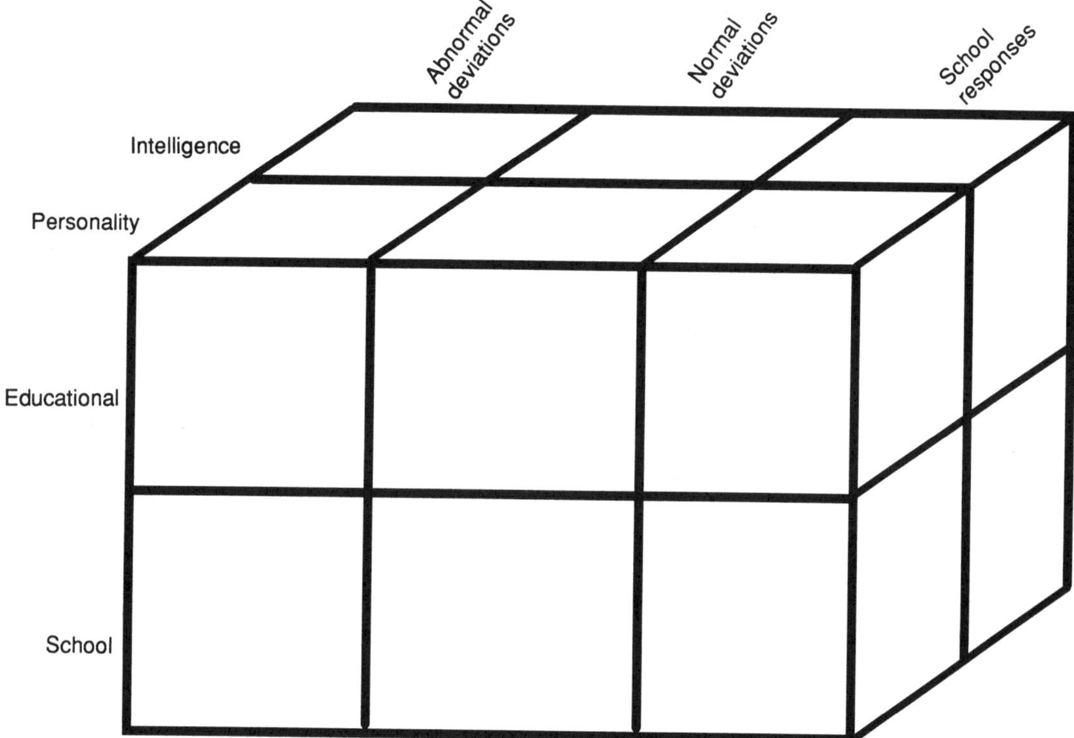

Figure 1. The three-dimensional model for mapping research.

cal anomalies (mild cases typically have none), limited (mild) versus comprehensive (severe) deficits in functioning, and prognosis (60% of mildly retarded individuals achieve social independence as adults, and an additional 20 to 30% achieve partial independence; Reschly, 1990). Although some have argued that mild mental retardation is a phenomenon created exclusively by schooling (i.e., mildly retarded children are often believed to function normally outside school settings), Reschly (1990) states that "contrary to much thought in Western societies, mild mental retardation is recognized in virtually all societies, regardless of geographic location, amount of geographic isolation, or degree of complexity" (p. 421).

Mental Retardation and Learning

Educational psychologists are interested in the relationship between mild mental retardation and learning. Because severely retarded individuals are rarely able to achieve school-related learning, most work in educational and school psychology focuses on individuals with mild retardation. Although people often assume that mentally retarded children have difficulty in all forms of learning, contemporary research suggests that mental retardation affects certain kinds of learning much more than others. The kinds of learning most affected by mental retardation can be described by the content of what is to be learned, the length of time needed to achieve mastery, and the fluency of generalization and transfer of learning.

Certain content can be learned nearly as well by mentally retarded children and their nonretarded peers. This content is generally linked with rote memorization of familiar material (e.g., recall of digit strings) and other tasks involving simple replication of an act (e.g., learning to press a lever when a light goes on; Chi, 1981). Mentally retarded children typically perform less well than nonretarded peers when left to their own devices; however, when given explicit instructions, mentally retarded children perform normally on simple recall tasks. In contrast, complex learning that requires mental manipulation of material (e.g., repeating a string of digits backward) is much more difficult for mentally retarded children. Interventions intended to boost the performance of mentally retarded children on complex tasks generally fail to close the gap between their performance and those of their peers.

Although mentally retarded children can learn to perform simple tasks as well as their nonretarded peers, there is a growing body of evidence that they cannot learn to perform decision tasks as rapidly. Speed of information processing research, which measures the time needed to make meaningful discriminations (e.g., deciding whether *a* and *b* are the same letter), shows that mentally retarded individuals are often as accurate in their discriminations as nonretarded peers but are not able to make the discriminations as rapidly (Vernon, 1981). Thus mild mental retardation may not inhibit the ability to perform normally on simple tasks, but it may significantly inhibit the efficiency with which simple tasks are performed.

The difference in learning between simple and complex tasks has been recognized in some theories of intelligence. For example, Jensen (1973) distinguishes between Level I abilities, which are needed for learning simple tasks, and Level II abilities, which are needed for learning complex tasks; Campione and Brown (1978; Borkowski, 1985) draw a similar distinction between the architectural system (simple processes) and the executive system (complex processes). Mildly retarded children often demonstrate Level I abilities similar to their nonretarded peers, but exhibit significant deficits in Level II abilities. Thus mildly retarded children can be reasonably expected to learn independent living skills, specific vocational skills, and other effective adaptations to society, because many of these skills require only Level I abilities. In contrast, mildly retarded children are unlikely to learn content associated with complex mental activity, such as literacy skills for contemporary society.

The second aspect of learning associated with mental retardation is length of time needed to achieve mastery. Mentally retarded children need more time to achieve mastery of specific criteria than do nonretarded peers (Gettinger, 1984). They require more time in part because they also require more practice trials to achieve mastery than nonretarded peers. This phenomenon has long been recognized in schools, in that mildly retarded children have often been called "slow learners."

The third learning deficit associated with mental retardation is generalization and transfer of learning. Indeed, this deficit is often considered the most intractable—and most important—problem confronting mildly retarded children (Reschly, 1990; Wong, 1989). Generalization refers to the tendency to recognize related stimuli (e.g., all instances of the letter *r*) as equivalent to a specific stimulus (e.g., the letter *r* on the chalkboard in the classroom). Transfer refers to the tendency to apply cognitive strategies learned in one situation (e.g., ask the teacher for help in the classroom) to other situations (e.g., ask the supervisor for help on the job). Nonretarded children spontaneously generalize and transfer learning, requiring deliberate instruction or prompts only on occasion (e.g., when placed in novel settings, when learning unfamiliar material).

In contrast, mentally retarded children require extensive, deliberate instruction to generalize what they have learned, and to transfer patterns of behavior to new situations (Campione & Brown, 1978; Wong, 1989). Thus mentally retarded children are at a relative disadvantage when being taught new skills. Even if they have the prerequisite knowledge and skills, they typically fail to mobilize these to learn new material. They require more frequent, more explicit, and more intense prompts than their nonretarded peers to generalize and transfer learning.

Identifying Mentally Retarded Children in Schools

Not surprisingly, the learning difficulties associated with mental retardation have encouraged schools to identify and serve mentally retarded children. School psychologists are the primary agents who help schools identify mentally retarded children.

For the purposes of identification, mental retardation is defined as "significantly subaverage general intellectual functioning existing concurrently with deficits in adaptive behavior, and manifested during the developmental period" (Grossman, 1983, p. 11). The functional rendering of this definition is (a) a score on a test of intelligence falling two or more standard deviations below the mean, coupled with (b) a similarly low score on a scale of adaptive behavior, which are (c) observed in school-aged children. All three criteria must be met in order for a child to be diagnosed as mentally retarded. Although this definition has been widely accepted (Reschly, 1990), the tripartite definition of mental retardation may be changing. New definitions (American Association on Mental Retardation, 1992) include a fourth criterion, which is the degree to which individuals require additional services to adjust to societal demands. Using this definition, it might be possible for a child to have intelligence and adaptive behavior scores more than two standard deviations below the mean, yet not be considered retarded because he or she does not require extensive modification of the environment to meet social expectations. The new definition for mental retardation has yet to be widely disseminated and accepted, and so it is unclear how the construct of environmental adaptation will be implemented in defining mental retardation.

School psychologists typically use tests of intelligence to establish the first criterion in defining mental retardation. Ordinal scales of development, such as the Bayley Scales of Infant Development (Bayley, 1993) or the Denver Developmental Screening Test (Frankenburg, Dodds, & Fandal, 1975), are often used to diagnose retardation in very young children and in very low-functioning older children and adults. Although ordinal scales do not yield norm-referenced scores for older children and adults, psychologists often use them to describe severe to profound mental retardation (e.g., to derive mental age classifications) and to plan interventions (Sattler, 1988). In cases in which it is not clear whether the individual meets the criteria for mental retardation, school psychologists are more likely to opt for norm-referenced tests of intelligence. These types of intelligence tests include tests in which items are quite similar in content (e.g., the Matrix Analogies Test [Naglieri, 1981a,b]; the Mill-Hill Vocabulary Test [Raven, 1982]), as well as batteries composed of distinct subtests (e.g., the Wechsler Intelligence Scale for Children [WISC-III; Wechsler, 1991]; Woodcock-Johnson Psychoeducational Battery-Revised [WJ-R; Woodcock & Johnson, 1987]). It is generally recommended that psychologists do not rely on a single test of intelligence for diagnosing subaverage general intellectual functioning (Sattler, 1988, chapter 21). Instead, psychologists should use either an intelligence test battery or more than one homogeneous content test.

Psychological professionals also use scales of adaptive behavior to establish whether individuals meet the second criterion of mental retardation. Adaptive behavior scales are usually semistructured interviews with the primary caregiver (e.g., the child's mother) in which questions are asked to elicit information about the child's current performance. Such scales typically comprise communication with others, self-help skills, and knowledge and competence in community settings. Some scales provide criterion-referenced information about levels of performance, but most provide norm-referenced scores indicating the child's performance relative to normal peers. Some adaptive behavior scales (e.g., Vineland Adaptive Behavior Scales; Sparrow, Balla, & Cicchetti, 1984) also include normative comparisons to special populations, such as retarded children in residential settings. Examples of items that might be found on adaptive behavior scales are included in Table 1.

One of the biggest problems confronting school psychologists is differentially diagnosing the effects of mental retardation from the effects of social disadvantages. Because socially disadvantaged children are not provided opportunities to learn information and skills to the same degree as more advantaged peers, they

Table 1. Adaptive Behavior Scale Items by Domain

Communication	Self-help	Community
Looks at caretaker	Rooting reflex	Smiles at parent
Uses two-word sentences (e.g., mama bye-bye)	Expresses needs nonverbally	Reacts to strangers
Follows two-step directions	Uses eating utensils	Names family members
Asks simple questions	Toilet trained	Plays cooperatively with other children
Names letters of alphabet	Dresses independently	Has best friend
Reads simple sentences	States name, address, parent's name on request	Plays rule-based games
Writes simple sentences	Travels neighborhood without assistance	Recognizes various social settings and acts accordingly
Uses telephone	Avoids danger	Dates or engages in courtship rituals
Uses language to resolve conflicts	Gets to work on time	Participates in civic functions (e.g., voting)
Writes business letters	Cooks independently	Acts according to well-defined ethical code
Writes papers, diary, or other complex documents	Manages money to meet housing, food, and other obligations	

often appear to be "retarded" on tests of academic achievement, word knowledge, general information, and social reasoning. Surveys of adaptive behavior (i.e., acquired knowledge within the child's home and community) and culture-reduced tests of intelligence must be used to discriminate limited learning ability from limited learning opportunity. The logic of this process is that average adaptive behavior or average performance on culture-reduced intelligence tests rule out mental retardation; children must be consistently low across all domains before they are diagnosed as mentally retarded. This concept is illustrated in Figure 2, which contrasts the range of performance demonstrated by mentally retarded children against the range of performance demonstrated by socially disadvantaged children.

A case history can illustrate how mental retardation is diagnosed by a school psychologist. The psychological report generated by a school psychologist is included in Figure 3. The report begins by providing general information about the child, followed by the reason for referral to the psychologist, the psychologist's observations and test results, and his or her conclusions and recommendations. Although the report is similar to the kinds of reports generated by school psychologists, there are two important differences. The first is that the report has been shortened for the purposes of illustration. The second difference is

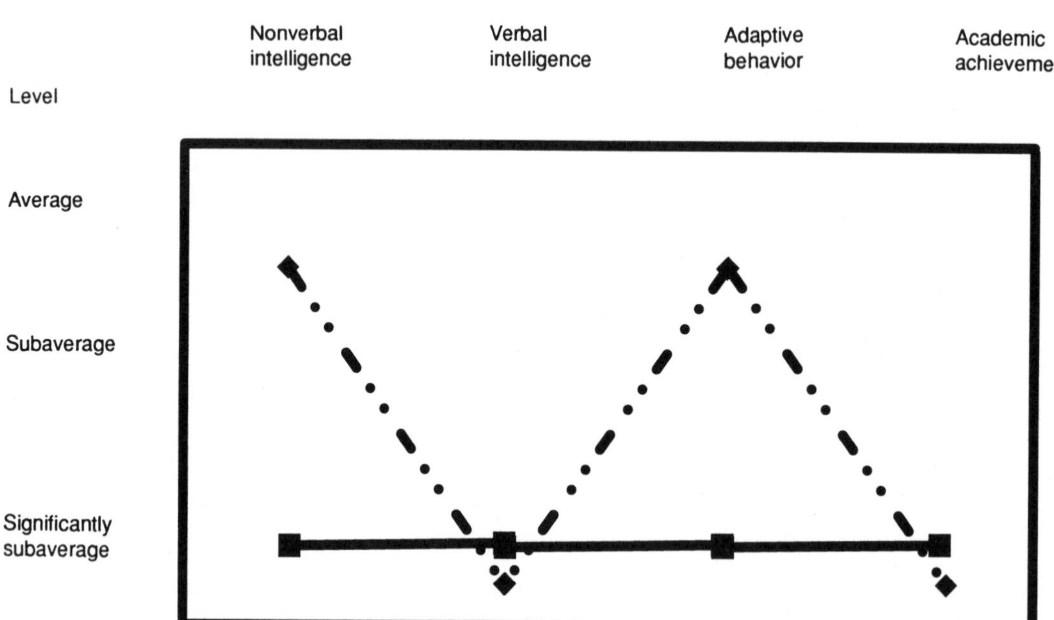

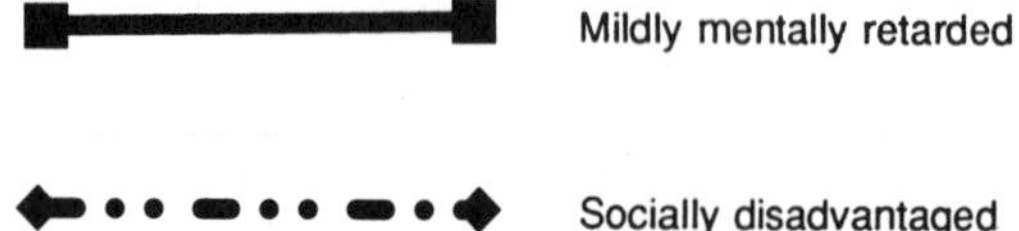

Figure 2. The relative performance of mild mentally retarded and disadvantaged children across assessment domains.

the inclusion of children's drawings to illustrate the information that psychologists use to generate scores and other observations of the child's performance; normally, drawings and other "raw data" are kept separately from the report. It is important to notice that the final diagnosis of mental retardation is consistent with the criteria offered in this chapter (i.e., that the child performs significantly below average on tests of intelligence, adaptive, and academic behavior, and that these delays are evident during the developmental period).

Gifted Intellectual Ability

From a statistical point of view, abnormality exists at both ends of the intelligence distribution. Individuals who fall in the upper range are often called "gifted," because societies generally value and reward intellectually talented people. Thus children who are abnormally advanced in intelligence relative to their peers are perceived as having received a gift, in that they often enjoy a relative advantage over nongifted (or average) peers in meeting scholastic and social demands.

Giftedness and Learning

Virtually all of the relative learning disadvantages experienced by mentally retarded children are reversed in gifted children. Gifted children perform complex learning tasks much more efficiently and fluently than their average peers. Gifted children also require less time to achieve mastery, and they spontaneously generalize and transfer learning to new tasks and settings. About the only characteristic they share with their average and mentally retarded peers is their ability to learn rote information (i.e., gifted, average, and mild mentally retarded children often exhibit similar performance on simple learning tasks). Gifted children are faster, however, and therefore more efficient in making simple, meaningful discriminations (Cohn, Carlson, & Jensen, 1985). Gifted, average, and mentally retarded children make simple, meaningful discriminations with equal accuracy, but they differ with respect to the speed with which such decisions are made. Thus there is an increasing body of evidence suggesting gifted children are "quick," both literally and figuratively.

Gifted children differ most from their nongifted peers on complex learning tasks. Complex learning requires insight, intention, novelty, and links to prior knowledge and skills. Learners derive insight when the material or task to be learned has an organizing principle; gifted children are adept at discerning the principles underlying a particular task, and are quick to use those principles to guide their learning. Intention is deliberate focusing of mental effort in order to sustain learning. Although it is possible to learn by simple association (e.g., operant or respondent conditioning), learning that requires an individual to recognize, plan, execute, and evaluate—in other words, think—is achieved more rapidly and efficiently by gifted individuals. Likewise, gifted children learn material or processes that are novel or new more rapidly and effectively than their nongifted peers. Finally, gifted children are better than nongifted peers at learning tasks related to previous knowledge and cognitive skills. Material that is hierarchically organized (so that learning of step C requires mastery of steps A and B) is more rapidly learned and mastered by gifted children than by nongifted peers. It must be emphasized that gifted children are not better at all types of learning (e.g., they learn randomized lists of nonsense words at about the same rate as nongifted peers), but they often excel at the types of complex learning societies tend to value.

Identifying Gifted Children in Schools

Because gifted children have unusual talents for learning complex information, schools in virtually all countries seek to identify such children for special treatment (see Wieczerkowski, 1986). School psychologists identify gifted children through a three-part assessment process (Cropley, 1989; Sattler, 1988). The first phase of identifying gifted children usually relies on a nomination process, in which children suspected of having exceptional talent are nominated by parents or teachers for additional assessment. In some settings, however, group test data may be used to identify potentially academically talented and gifted students. Individuals who pass the screening process are moved to the second stage of assessment, in which they are given group tests of intelligence. Individuals with high group test scores (typically two or more standard deviations above the mean) move to the third phase of assessment, in which they may be given a test battery by the school psychologist.

The second or third phase of identification may include additional evidence of exceptional intellectual ability, such as leadership traits or other behavior exhibited in school and community settings. These be-

PSYCHOLOGICAL REPORT

Name: Jan
Date of Birth: 10 June, 1986
Age: 7 years 11 months

Date of Examination: 12 April, 1994
Grade: First
Teacher: Ms. Serota

Reason for Referral

Jan was referred because his teacher was concerned that Jan was not progressing in school at a rate typical of other children.

Background Information

Ms. Serota reports that Jan can read only a few words, and often does not recognize letters of the alphabet. He counts to 20, but cannot count beyond 20. He cannot add numbers for sums greater than 10. Jan has attended school regularly for three years, and has received formal reading and math instruction for the last two years. Ms. Serota reports that Jan's delayed progress in school led to his being retained in first grade. Despite repeating the first grade, Jan has not yet mastered basic preacademic and academic skills.

Jan's mother, Ms. X, reports that Jan sat up independently at 12 months, walked at 18 months, began talking at 2 years 4 months, and was toilet trained at 4 years of age. Jan dresses himself in the morning, although he continues to need help with small buttons, zippers, and tying his shoes. He plays with children who are younger, although he gets along well with everyone in the neighborhood.

Observations

I observed Jan in Ms. Serota's class twice, and once on the playground during recess. During the first observation, Jan read aloud with other children in a small reading group. He attended to the children and teacher throughout the session, although he frequently requested help to find his place. He read only a few words aloud when it was his turn to read; other children and the teacher prompted him for words he did not know. During the second observation, Jan worked independently on math. He was given a worksheet of single digit addition to 20 and subtraction below 10. Jan worked without distraction during the 20 minute session, frequently counting out answers on his fingers or counting blocks. During morning recess, Jan played alone in an area off the grass with a toy soldier. Other peers were engaged in games during the recess, but Jan appeared content to engage in isolated play. He neither sought nor was the target of social contact during the recess period.

Assessment Results

WISC-III Verbal IQ: 62
Performance IQ: 68
Full Scale IQ: 62
Draw A Person
Man: 68 Woman: 55 Self: 72 Total: 62

Figure 3. A school psychologist's report on a mildly retarded student.

Vineland Adaptive Behavior Scales
- Communication: 74
- Daily Living Skills: 62
- Socialization: 66
- Composite: 64

Woodcock-Johnson-Revised Tests of Academic Achievement (Grade-based norms)
- Broad Reading: 66
- Broad Mathematics: 78
- Broad Written Language: 70
- Broad Knowledge: 58

Jan's scores on intelligence tests consistently placed in the Mildly Retarded range. This means Jan scores are at or below the first percentile relative to other children Jan's age. Jan's performance in adaptive behavior is similarly low compared with peers. Despite three years of schooling, and repetition of the first grade, Jan's academic achievement in reading, written language, and general knowledge is also at or below the first percentile relative to children with three years of schooling.

Reports from Jan's teacher and mother suggest that Jan maintains a strong prosocial orientation. He is eager to please others and comply with requests and directions. He shows consistent interest in schooling, and works diligently on assignments in and out of class. Jan was eager to please throughout both examination sessions, despite the length of the sessions (more than two hours) and the difficulty of the tasks presented to him. However, Jan occasionally complained that some tasks were difficult, and he readily admitted that he had problems reading, writing, and solving problems. I inferred from his ready compliance with requests, smiles during the testing, and willingness to help pick up test materials that test rapport was good, and that results reflect Jan's best efforts.

Figure 3. *(Continued)*

Impressions and Recommendations

Jan's scores on tests of intelligence, academic achievement, and adaptive behavior are consistent with a diagnosis of mild mental retardation. A meeting including his parents, teacher, and special education personnel should be convened to discuss Jan's eligibility for special education services.

Jan's strengths lie in his prosocial orientation and strong motivation to please others. Although he struggles to acquire and retain academic skills, his motivation for learning and following directions remains high. If appropriately nurtured, this will be an asset that will help him in school and the community. One way to encourage his positive orientation to schooling is to provide instructional demands that are moderately difficult for him so that he can experience success.

Consultation with Jan's teachers is recommended to develop appropriate instructional strategies for helping Jan acquire basic academic skills and community knowledge. Generally, instructional strategies that break down complex tasks into small, incremental steps, with frequent repetition and practice in transferring learning to "real life" settings, are recommended to enhance skill development. Frequent evaluation of Jan's progress and monitoring of educational interventions will help pinpoint strategies of particular value to Jan. Curriculum-based measures (e.g., rates of academic behavior) may be particularly helpful in monitoring Jan's response to instructional programs, especially for basic academic tasks.

Collaboration with Jan's parents and teacher is encouraged to provide consistent expectations and practice of new skills in home and school. Effective, regular communication and planning can insure that gains at home are reinforced and practiced at school, and vice versa.

All of the adults involved in Jan's education are encouraged to consult with the school psychologist regarding appropriate academic and social interventions to help Jan's development. Although Jan's progress in school and community settings may be slower than many other children, there is no reason Jan cannot continue to learn and strive toward independent adult living.

Jeffrey P. Braden, PhD NCSP
Examiner

Figure 3. *(Continued)*

haviors may be assessed informally via interviews, or formally through the use of behavioral checklists (e.g., Scales for Rating the Behavioral Characteristics of Superior Students; Renzulli, Smith, White, Callahan, & Hartman, 1976). In most cases, the operational definition of intellectual giftedness is the complement of the definition for mental retardation—namely, two or more standard deviations above the mean on tests of intelligence and achievement, although supplementary evidence of exceptional skills in adaptive behavior is not universally required (Cropley, 1989).

In certain situations, school psychologists may want to distinguish further among various levels of giftedness. Psychologists who serve selective educational institutions (e.g., selective secondary or postsecondary schools) may need to discriminate among individuals in the top 5%. Standard tests of intelligence are not effective for this purpose, because they have an inadequate psychometric ceiling (i.e., an insufficient number of difficult items). Consequently, school psychologists may use specialized tests for this purpose. Such tests include Raven's Advanced Matrices (Raven, 1962), college aptitude or placement tests that are administered to younger children (Cropley, 1989), and tests developed for private use by selective organizations (e.g., Mensa, 1980).

Abnormal Personality

Extreme variations in personality are also of interest to schools. Unlike intellectual abnormalities, which can be either desirable (i.e., giftedness) or undesirable (i.e., mental retardation), abnormal personality is viewed as an undesirable condition. Deviations from "normality" are defined as maladaptive states, which often become the focus of change in educational settings.

Defining Abnormal Personality

Abnormal personality is usually considered in the context of identifying emotional disturbance in educational settings. In turn, emotional disturbance is a concept derived from clinical psychology and psychiatry. Abnormal personality conditions are defined in clinical taxonomies such as the revised third edition of the *Diagnostic and Statistical Manual of Mental Disorders* (DSM-III-R; American Psychiatric Association, 1987) as a constellation of symptoms or characteristics that lead to disturbances in children's functioning in school, family, or community activities.

Because of its clinical origin and implications, abnormal personality is not commonly studied with respect to its impact on education and learning. Instead, research in educational and school psychology is focused on the treatment and diagnosis of emotional disturbance resulting from abnormal personality. The treatment of emotional disturbance will be considered later in this chapter; its diagnosis will be discussed in the next sections.

Diagnosis of Emotional Disturbance

In order to define the impact of emotional disturbance on children, school psychologists typically investigate three functional domains: intraindividual, peer interaction, and school/community. The tendency to minimize intraindividual disturbance as a criterion, however, has been gaining momentum in educational settings. Many educators prefer to view emotional disturbance in terms of behavior disorders and disregard the notion of personality altogether (Wood, 1990). Despite this trend, there is still a strong influence to incorporate intraindividual emotional disturbance into diagnostic criteria, and so all three functional domains must be evaluated by school psychologists to identify emotionally disturbed children.

Intraindividual Dysfunction. Intraindividual dysfunction is manifested as thought disorder or affective disorder. Thought disorders are reflected in a child's inability to think logically and coherently in a manner appropriate for the child's mental age. Affective disorders are reflected in a child's mood, which can be consistent (e.g., depressed, withdrawn) or volatile (e.g., a cycle of mania followed by depression). Either of these dysfunctions must be chronic and unusual relative to the child's peers to be considered as evidence of emotional disturbance.

School psychologists typically assess intraindividual dysfunction through clinical interviews, structured self-report inventories, or projective techniques. School psychologists frequently interview parents or teachers in addition to the child to determine the severity and longevity of observed problems. Structured self-report inventories are usually modeled on the Minnesota Multiphasic Personality Inventory (MMPI), meaning they are empirically driven instruments that ask the child to endorse items that are "most like" himself or herself. The child's responses are then compared to the response patterns of normal and clinically abnormal groups to identify abnormal personality traits. The Personality Inventory for Children (Wirt, Lachar, Klinedinst, & Seat, 1984) is a good example of this type of inventory.

Finally, projective techniques are used to elicit ways of thinking from children that the child may not be able or willing to verbalize to others. Although classical inkblot approaches may be used, it is more common to use drawing tests and semistructured stimuli for projective assessment of children. The most popular drawing tests invite the child to draw a picture of a person (of a man, a woman, or himself or herself) and then use established scoring criteria to derive estimates of social-emotional dysfunction (e.g., Naglieri, McNish, & Bardos, 1991) and cognitive functioning (e.g., Naglieri, 1988). There are many types of drawing tests that are used to infer intraindividual emotional dysfunction, including the Kinetic Family Drawing and the House-Tree-Person techniques (see Knoff, 1986, for a review of assessment techniques). Semistructured projective tests for children include Make a Picture Story, Childhood Apperception Test, the Educational Apperception Test, and the Blacky Pictures. These tests are composed of drawings or materials depicting situations that are familiar to the child but are ambiguous in nature. The child's response is elicited in order to infer his or her emotional response to familiar situations. Semistructured projective tests are less popular than drawing tests for diagnosing intraindividual dysfunction, but can be used when drawing tests are inappropriate.

Peer Interaction. The diagnosis of disruption or disturbance of peer interactions is shown in a child's abnormal interaction patterns. Abnormal peer interactions often take on one of two forms: those characterized by conflict, defiance, or other aggressive actions; and those characterized by withdrawal, isolation, or other actions that seclude the child from others. Some children swing between these two types of behavioral patterns, creating a hostile isolation from others. The child's age and developmental level must be considered when deciding whether interaction patterns are abnormal. The parallel play typically exhibited by a young child, for example, is abnormal for an adolescent.

School psychologists diagnose abnormal interactions through the use of observations, structured interviews, behavior checklists, and self-report measures. The most popular method for collecting data regarding interpersonal interactions is to use a behavior checklist. A number of checklists are available for use in school settings, most of which request that the child's teacher rate the frequency, severity, or duration of certain behaviors. Such checklists often use a comparative rating system (e.g., asking whether a child exhibits a behavior more frequently, about as often, or less frequently than similar age peers), although others use other anchors (e.g., frequently-sometimes-never or yes-no). Examples of checklists include the Child Behavior Checklist (Achenbach & Edelbrock, 1986), the Connors Parent Rating Scale (Connors, 1985; cited in Sattler, 1988), the Revised Behavior Problem Checklist (Quay & Peterson, 1987), and the Devereux Behavior Rating Scale–School Form (Naglieri, LeBuffe, & Pfeiffer, 1993). Most behavior checklists produce factor scores reflecting different constellations of behavior (e.g., anxious, socially withdrawn, obsessive-compulsive, attention problems) to describe more accurately the type of abnormality exhibited by the child. Behavior scales are also used to infer intraindividual disturbance by virtue of bizarre or unusual behavior observed by others.

School/Community Disturbances. Abnormal relations with the community at large are usually defined for children as problems in school. Because children rarely interact with other community institutions outside the family, their behavior in school reflects their interactions with society at large. The failure to meet social expectations for age-appropriate behavior suggests abnormality. Children with intra- or interpersonal disorders who meet social expectations are not considered emotionally disturbed, although they may be considered odd or eccentric. If a child manifests intra- and interpersonal dysfunction, however, and these difficulties render the child unable to meet school and community expectations for behavior, the child is considered to be emotionally disturbed.

School and community dysfunction is typically assessed with adaptive behavior rating scales. These may be the same instruments used to establish subaverage adaptive behavior in the diagnosis of mental retardation, although many scales include a maladaptive behavior domain. Whereas the adaptive behavior scales will typically ascertain the child's current performance levels in terms of independent living, self-help, communication, and social interaction, maladaptive behavior scales rate the frequency and severity of abnormal behaviors exhibited in school or community settings. The other way to establish a child has failed to meet age-appropriate social demands is to measure academic achievement. If the achievement is lower than expected given the child's age and cognitive abilities, it is possible to infer that the child is experiencing difficulties meeting social and community (i.e., school) expectations for behavior. Formal methods for assessing adaptive behavior, such as the Vineland Adaptive Behavior Scales (Sparrow et al., 1984) or the Scales of Independent Behavior (Bruininks, Woodcock, Weatherman, & Hill, 1984), are often combined with informal methods for assessing adaptive behavior, such as interviews, case history, or observation of the child in natural settings.

Intelligence and Personality as Exclusionary Criteria

Intelligence and personality are the defining characteristics of mental retardation, giftedness, and emotional disturbance. As such, intelligence and personality are primarily *inclusionary* criteria. Intelligence and personality are also used as *exclusionary* criteria, however, in determining some exceptional conditions. In other words, a child may be considered to fall into one of these exceptional categories only if abnormal intelligence or personality can be excluded as causes of the child's difficulties.

Children with learning disabilities have a discrepancy between their current and expected levels of performance. Intelligence tests are typically used to infer expected levels of performance, and personality measures are used to exclude personality dysfunction as a cause of poor performance. Thus children who are learning disabled must exhibit achievement below the level expected from their age and intelligence, and their low achievement cannot be attributable to abnormal personality factors (Wong, 1989). Such distinctions are not always reliably drawn, but most countries that offer special education generally incorporate exclusionary criteria in defining learning disabilities (Opper & Teichler, 1989).

Intelligence and personality are implicitly used as exclusionary criteria in definitions of mental retardation and emotional disturbance. The diagnosis of mental retardation is reserved for cases in which the cause of the child's difficulties is intellectual, not emotional. The distinction is difficult to make in extreme causes of emotional dysfunction (e.g., autism), because the severity of dysfunction makes it difficult to estimate the child's intelligence accurately. Likewise, children who are mentally retarded are rarely diagnosed as emotionally disturbed, even if they exhibit maladaptive behavior. The differential diagnosis of giftedness, mental retardation, emotional disturbance, and learning disability requires the coordination of many psychological measures and judgments. The criteria for differentially diagnosing educational exceptionalities are presented in Table 2.

Although most of the distinctions among disabling conditions are recognized and adopted by Western nations for defining educational exceptionality, criticisms of differential diagnosis are growing. Critics note it is not always possible to discriminate reliably among diagnostic categories. Consequently, many educators prefer to emphasize manifest behavior, and diminish differential diagnosis, when they define educational abnormalities.

NORMAL DIFFERENCES IN INTELLIGENCE AND PERSONALITY

The ways in which normal variations in intelligence and personality influence education are also of interest to educational and school psychologists. Abnormalities of intelligence and personality influence learning, and the study of abnormality can often lead to a better understanding of normal human conditions. It is important to understand how normal variations in intelligence and personality affect education, however, in order to help schools, military and government agencies, and businesses function more effectively.

Normal Differences in Intelligence

There are many theories regarding the nature of intelligence in the normal population. These have been covered in greater detail elsewhere in this volume (see Chapters 2 and 3). A brief review of major theories, though, is needed to identify how educational and school psychologists view the relationship between intelligence and learning.

A cynic once remarked that there are as many theories of intelligence as there are psychological researchers. This is undoubtedly an exaggeration, but it captures the variety and complexity of the field. Based on a comprehensive review of research on intelligence, Carroll (1991) concluded that there are five dominant theoretical paradigms for describing intelligence: unitary theories, dichotomous theories, factor theories, hierarchical theories, and theories of multiple intelligence. Each of these paradigms influences the ways in which educators view individual differences in children's cognitive abilities.

Unitary Approaches to Intelligence

The unitary theory of intelligence dominates most educational psychology research and in school psychology practice. This is odd, not least because unitary theories are known to provide inadequate, incomplete descriptions of intellectual abilities. The no-

Table 2. Diagnostic Criteria for Differential Diagnosis of Educational Exceptionalities

	Performance domains			
Diagnostic category	Intelligence	Academic achievement	Adaptive behavior	Personality
Mental retardation	Subaverage (≤70)	Subaverage (≤70)	Subaverage (≤70)	Not the cause of subaverage scores
Emotional disturbance	Average (>70)	Lower than intelligence	Lower than intelligence	Abnormal relative to peers
Learning disability	Average (>70)	Well below intelligence	Average (>70)	Normal relative to peers
Gifted	Superior (>130)	Superior (>130)	Average or higher	Normal or superior relative to peers

tion of unitary or general intelligence, however, still dominates educational and school psychology. Although Charles Spearman first defined general intelligence in terms of the first unrotated principle factor extracted from a psychometric battery (i.e., *g*), the operational definition for general intelligence is customarily an IQ derived from a single test or a composite derived from an intellectual test battery.

IQs are used widely in educational psychology research as a marker for individual differences in intelligence. Researchers use IQs to estimate or control statistically for the influence of intelligence in their findings. Likewise, school psychologists typically define exceptionality in terms of unitary notions of intelligence. Mental retardation, giftedness, and other exceptionalities that use intelligence as an inclusionary or exclusionary criterion typically assume a composite IQ best represents intelligence. Although the unitary approach to intelligence has been flatly rejected as theoretically inadequate, it continues to be embraced as pragmatically powerful. Composite IQs, inadequate and incomplete as they may be, still have substantial empirical and practical utility for predicting educationally relevant outcomes.

Educational outcomes that are strongly associated with IQ include, but are not limited to, the following (adapted from Jensen, 1980, chapter 8):

1. Intentional learning
2. Hierarchical learning
3. Learning meaningful material
4. Transfer of learning to new situations
5. Insightful learning
6. Learning tasks of moderate difficulty
7. Time needed to master new tasks
8. Age-related learning (e.g., learning to read)
9. Learning in the early stages of skill acquisition
10. College grades
11. Grades in graduate school
12. Years of formal education
13. Parent, teacher, and peer ratings of intelligence
14. Indexes of scholastic achievement (e.g., achievement tests, teacher grades)

Because of the substantial body of research linking differences in educational outcomes to IQ, the unitary approach to intelligence continues to hold a place of prominence in educational and school psychology. The unitary approach to intelligence has been attacked because it provides an insufficient account of cognitive abilities (e.g., Gardner, 1983; Sternberg, 1985), however, and also because of some of the implications that follow from it. For example, the difference in IQ distributions between North American whites and African Americans remains a hotly debated subject, although nearly 25 years have passed since Jensen (1969) suggested the difference was largely intractable and probably genetic in origin.

Dichotomous Approaches to Intelligence

Dichotomous theories reject a unitary or composite view of intelligence in favor of a view that defines intelligence as a function of two relatively distinct types of ability. There are many versions of dichotomous theories (e.g., Jensen's Level I/Level II model, Wechsler's verbal/nonverbal distinction). The fluid/crystallized theory (Horn, 1968, 1985) illustrates the educational implications of two-factor theories. In fluid/crystallized theory, crystallized ability represents the ability to perform and succeed on culturally relevant intellectual tasks (e.g., reading, general knowledge, mathematical reasoning); in contrast, fluid ability represents the ability to perform and succeed on culture-reduced intellectual tasks (e.g., novel problem solving, nonverbal reasoning, figural analogies).

The rise in popularity of the fluid/crystallized approach to intelligence is directly related to the rise in popularity in research on minority and disabled children in schools. Children from the dominant cultural majority typically have approximately equal opportunities to develop both types of intellectual abilities, and so they usually perform about as well on fluid tasks as they do on crystallized tasks. For children from the majority, then, unitary IQs provide simpler and equally (or more) accurate indexes of intelligence. In contrast, children from nondominant minorities, as well as disabled children, often lack opportunities to learn the fundamental knowledge and skills needed to complete crystallized ability tasks successfully. Therefore unitary IQs that combine or rely solely upon crystallized ability tasks will systematically underestimate the intellectual abilities of minority and disabled children.

This insight elicited a substantial body of educational research, which has yielded equivocal outcomes. Research with minority children has shown that non-English-speaking minorities achieve lower scores on crystallized ability tasks (presented in English) than on fluid ability tasks (Jensen, 1980). Native English-speaking minorities (e.g., African Americans), however, often score similarly or even somewhat lower on fluid ability tasks than on crystallized ability tasks (Jensen & Reynolds, 1982). Research with disabled children has been more consistent in supporting the fluid/crystallized dichotomy. For example, deaf children score very poorly on crystallized ability tests, but are equal to their normal-hearing peers on most fluid ability tasks (Braden, 1992, 1994).

Although large differences between crystallized and fluid abilities within an individual can have significant educational implications (e.g., deaf children can learn visual/spatial and novel tasks much easier than they can learn verbally loaded tasks), such differences are unusual. Most children have similarly developed crystallized and fluid abilities. Because of this similarity, the differences in learning among the majority of children are adequately captured in a single intelligence test score. The distinction between fluid and crystallized abilities has influenced psychological assessment practices, however, particularly with minority and disabled children. School psychologists have been sensitized to the need to discriminate between culture-loaded (i.e., crystallized) and culture-reduced (i.e., fluid) abilities (Sattler, 1988). In fact, the recognition that assessment must include more than one type of intellectual ability measure led to legal mandates for the appropriate assessment of children in schools (e.g., U.S. Public Law 94-142 requires children to be assessed in a manner intended to reduce the impact of prior learning opportunities).

Independent Factor Approaches to Intelligence

Factor theories of intelligence are popular in educational psychology primarily because of the link between multiple facets of ability, or aptitudes, and scholastic learning. Since Thurstone's seminal research on factor approaches to intelligence, there has been a tendency to define intellective factors in terms of educationally relevant characteristics (e.g., verbal reasoning, quantitative reasoning), although others (e.g., Guilford, 1967) have described factors in ways that emphasize psychological processes. Factor approaches to psychology are closely allied with learning aptitudes, which are a product of intellectual ability and prior learning opportunities. The research on the measurement of aptitudes has outstripped the literature on the instructional implications of aptitudes, in part because aptitude is quite closely tied to achievement. Individuals with strong achievement in a given domain generally have strong aptitudes, and vice versa, a finding that has led to relatively few pragmatic implications for aptitude measures. One notable exception to this conclusion is the educational research on scholastic aptitude differences between genders: Females score lower than males on college-entry mathematical aptitude tests and are underrepresented in the top-scoring 5% to 10%. This has led to debate regarding the source of this finding (e.g., sex differences, instructional differences, cultural influences).

Intellective factors may also be defined independent of academic subjects. Sternberg (1985) has proposed a triarchic theory of intelligence that includes practical/social, academic, and metacognitive components. The literature on exceptional children was dominated for many years by sensory-based intellective factors, which defined learning aptitude by sensory modality (e.g., "visual" or "auditory" learners). Nonacademic intellective factors have promoted the notion of "learning styles," in which learning is viewed as the interaction between the individual's aptitude (or learning style) and the instruction offered to the individual (or treatment). Support for aptitude-treatment interactions (ATIs) has been more philosophical than empirical. Advocates of ATIs (e.g., Carbo, 1983) argue that instructional outcomes can be enhanced by matching learning aptitudes to instructional practices, whereas critics challenge the concept by noting the lack of empirical support for ATIs (Reschly, 1988).

An example may illustrate the problems associated with nonacademic aptitudes, or learning styles, and instruction. Kaufman and Kaufman (1983) developed an instrument that defines learner aptitudes in terms of simultaneous versus sequential processing abilities. The authors argued that learners who are relatively stronger in simultaneous processing ability will learn best when instruction is presented in a simultaneous fashion (i.e., in a holistic way so that units of information are defined relative to each other, such as in a map), and learners strong in sequential ability will learn best when information is presented in a serial, or successive, fashion. The Kaufmans then developed a program to encourage teachers to match simultaneous and sequential instruction to learner aptitudes (called K-SOS; Kaufman, Kaufman, & Goldsmith, 1984).

The research in support of differential response to instruction, however, is less than compelling. Ayers and Cooley (1986) found outcomes the opposite of those predicted by the K-SOS approach (i.e., "simultaneous learners" learned better in a sequential instructional setting than in a simultaneous instructional setting). Newer research drawn from the same model (e.g., Naglieri, Das, & Jarman, 1990) shows more promising results, in part because the method for discriminating learner styles is more sophisticated and adheres to neuropsychological research. Equivocal or contradictory results have cast a shadow on ATI research, though, and have led some to question its efficacy for educational practices.

Perhaps more than any other approach to intelligence, independent factor approaches to intelligence have stimulated examination of educational curricula. For example, Guilford's (1967) "structure of intellect" (SOI) model of cognitive abilities mapped ability domains untapped by most intelligence tests and not represented in educational curricula. Creativity, divergent production, and other aspects of thinking were virtually absent in traditional curricula, which stress memorization and recall, convergent thinking, and deductive intellectual abilities. Although the SOI model has not been widely accepted or used as a means of assessing intelligence in schools, educational psychologists have used Guilford's work to guide criticism and construction of school curricula.

Hierarchical Factor Approaches to Intelligence

Hierarchical theories of intelligence attempt to combine the robust nature of unitary theories with the greater detail and differentiation afforded by factor theories. The combination of these different approaches yields a model of intelligence in which general ability is superordinate and intellective factors are subordinate. The reason general ability is superordinate is because people generally perform well or poorly across intellective factors (e.g., people who score well on one factor tend to also score well on other factors). Most people are aware of their own relative strengths and weaknesses (e.g., some people have better-developed verbal aptitudes rather than performance aptitudes), however, and so unitary theories of intelligence are insufficient for describing intellectual abilities.

Figure 4 displays a hierarchical model of intelligence derived from Horn and Cattell's fluid/crystallized approach. General ability is the superordinate construct, and the fluid/crystallized factors constitute the second-order factors. First-order factors are subordinate to second-order factors. It is important to remember that factors near the top of the figure subsume a greater proportion of variation among individuals, whereas those toward the bottom of the figure subsume relatively small portions of variation.

Although widely accepted among researchers in intelligence, hierarchical models are still at an exploratory stage of research within educational psychology. Most of the research employing hierarchical models of processing abilities uses factor analysis or other correlational methods to describe the relationships between first-, second-, and third-order factors and scholastic achievement. As yet, there is little experimental research linking hierarchical models of intelligence, specific instructional procedures, and learning outcomes.

The one exception to this statement is the vigorous research on assessment of (dis)abilities, and assessment practices that recommend hierarchical models for interpretation of psychological assessment results (e.g., Sattler, 1988; Woodcock & Johnson, 1987). These recommendations are drawn from correlational and factor analytic studies, as well as studies of hierarchical abilities in various exceptional groups. Based on these findings, which are admittedly correlational, contemporary school psychology practice typically recommends interpretation of intellectual assessment results within a hierarchical factor model.

Multiple Intelligences

Finally, theories of multiple intelligences have begun to influence educational psychology research and practice. Based primarily on the work of Gardner (1983), the theory of multiple intelligences is essentially a typology approach to independent factors. Gardner uses studies of exceptionally talented people to argue that there are eight distinct types of intelligence. Gardner's work has sparked a number of efforts to establish the viability of his model for normal variations in intelligence, and to investigate instructional implications of multiple intelligence models. To date, the research appears to be following a trend similar to that of Guilford's work, in that the primary impact of the theory is to offer new criteria for defining curricular narrowness in the psychological domain. Like Guilford's SOI model, however, the theory of multiple intelligences has yet to provide a practical test of intelligence conforming to the theory.

It is important to note the critical impact that test development has on bringing theories of intelligence into educational psychology research and school psychology practice. First, the development of a test that

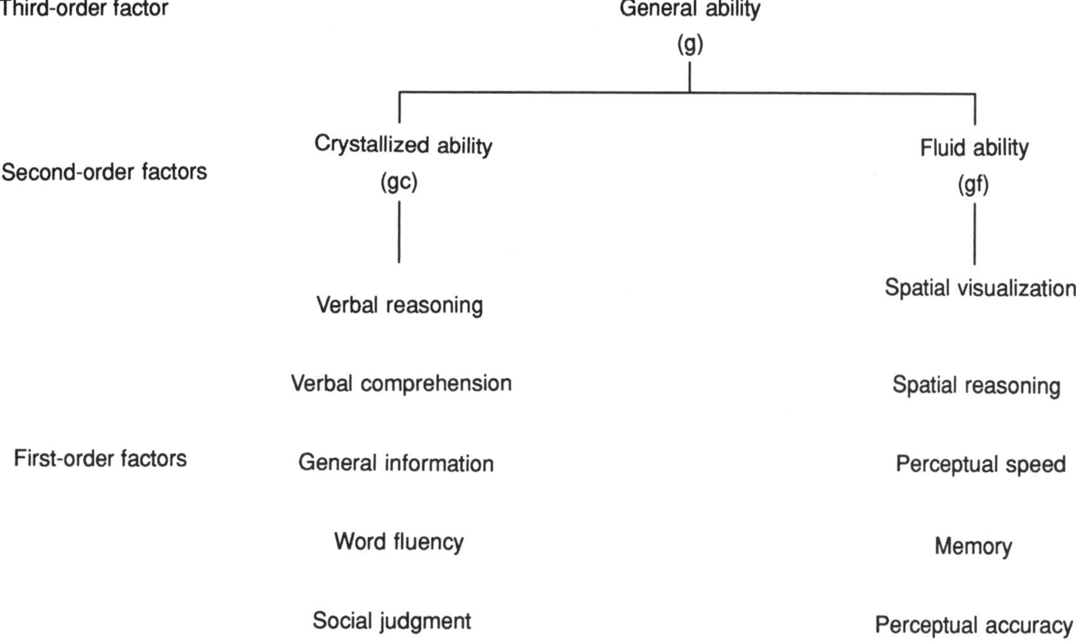

Figure 4. An example of hierarchical organization of intellectual abilities.

performs in a manner consistent with a theory provides a compelling demonstration of theory viability. Although unsuccessful efforts to build a test do not invalidate the theory (e.g., the many unsuccessful attempts to build a flying machine did not invalidate aerodynamic theory), successful construction of a test lends positive support to the theory (e.g., successful powered flight validated the basic principles of aerodynamic theory). Second, development of a test enhances its adoption by other researchers. For example, the Wechsler series of intelligence tests have been used in thousands of research studies, despite its lack of relationship to established models of intelligence. Third, tests are technologies for practitioners such as school psychologists. A practical, well-developed test is powerful and efficient, and thus is more likely to be used than elegant, but impractical, approaches to measurement.

These three aspects of test development may account for the relative popularity and obscurity of some intelligence theories. For example, unitary approaches to intelligence remain popular because (a) tests have been successfully developed that are consistent with the model, (b) these tests are widely adopted and used in research, and (c) the tests are efficient, effective, and practical measures for school use. In contrast, Sternberg's (1985) triarchic theory of intelligence has not yet produced a practical test of intelligence. Therefore it has yet to affect educational psychology research or practice significantly, despite the enthusiasm for the model in theoretical circles. If this relationship continues to hold, the ultimate success of Gardner's multiple intelligences approach may be determined by the development of a practical test for multiple intelligences.

Normal Differences in Personality

The relationship between personality and learning is also studied in educational and school psychology. Generally, normal differences in personality are linked to learning in one of two approaches: the study of motivation, and the study of temperament. Each of these is discussed in the following sections.

Personality and Motivation

Personality differences between children are related to their desire to initiate, sustain, and ultimately complete learning tasks. Although persistence is widely regarded as important to success (e.g., Albert Einstein and Thomas Edison both attributed their success to perseverance rather than intelligence), it is studied less often in educational research—and is less likely to be applied to school psychology practice—than cognitive models of performance. Consequently, educational psychologists have studied the relationship between personality factors and motivation in order to understand better how personality affects learning.

Achievement motivation can be considered to stem from three factors (Weiner, 1992): (a) cognitions, or self-thoughts, before and during the task; (b) structural differences between individuals, or tendencies in how one views and performs during tasks, and (c) environmental factors, especially those relating to consequences for task completion. The thoughts held by children before and during learning include the attributions they make regarding success or failure (i.e., the cause, locus, and controllability of factors leading to success or failure), and their sense of self-efficacy (i.e., their sense of personal ability to succeed in the task at hand). These cognitions facilitate or inhibit instrumental behavior toward learning and success on tasks.

Personality differences have been linked to tendencies, or habits, that children display in achievement settings. There are four general approaches linking personality characteristics to achievement motivation. Perhaps the most popular of these is the need for achievement (often abbreviated nAch), which stemmed from the seminal work of Murray (e.g., 1938) linking environmental demands (presses) to individual tendencies to respond (needs). His work has led need for achievement to be included in many personality tests, including the Thematic Apperception Test, the Edwards Personal Preference Schedule (Helms, 1983), the personality Research Form (Jackson, 1984), and the Sixteen Personality Factor Questionnaire (16PF; Cattell, 1986). Recent research has tended to neglect need for achievement as a personality variable, however, because many of the predictions from nAch theory have not been confirmed despite many attempts to do so (Weiner, 1992).

A second link between personality and achievement motivation is an individual's tendency to ascribe internal or external causes to outcomes such as success or failure. Individuals are said to have an internal locus of control if they attribute causes to events as being within themselves (e.g., ability, effort). In contrast, individuals who attribute causes to events outside themselves (e.g., luck, situational factors) are said to have an external locus of control. Although internal locus of control has been linked with higher levels of achievement and persistence on tasks, the research in this area has also diminished in recent years.

Individual differences in anxiety provide the third link between personality and achievement motivation. Unlike need for achievement and locus of control, research linking anxiety to achievement motivation remains an active and vibrant field of research. Anxiety has been linked to positive and negative achievement outcomes. The link between anxiety and performance is often attributed to the relationship between anxiety and levels of arousal: Low levels of anxiety are believed to represent low levels of arousal, whereas high levels of anxiety are linked to high levels of arousal in the nervous system.

The curvilinear relationship between levels of arousal and performance is described as the Yerkes-Dodson law. Although Yerkes and Dodson originally proposed that the curvilinear relationship linked performance and activation of nervous system components (not arousal per se; Winton, 1987), the principle has been extended to arousal and, in particular, individual differences in anxiety (e.g., Deshpande & Kawane, 1982). This law suggests that low and high arousal states inhibit learning, whereas moderate amounts of arousal are ideal for motivating learning. The relationship between arousal and learning is depicted in Figure 5.

Although anxiety and arousal are not identical concepts, they are strongly related. Consequently, the arousal/performance relationship described in the Yerkes-Dodson law links anxiety and academic performance (i.e.,high and low levels of anxiety are associated with less successful performance and learning than are moderate levels of anxiety). Careful study of this relationship suggests that other personality factors alter the nature of the anxiety/performance relationship. For example, extraversion modifies the anxiety/performance link so that when individual differences in extraversion are controlled, the arousal-performance link assumes a linear relationship (Green, 1984; Matthews, 1985; Matthews & Lees, 1990).

Anxiety is readily measured by a number of personality instruments. Among the most popular is the State-Trait Anxiety Inventory (Speilberger, 1984), which measures peoples' tendency to be anxious (trait) as well as their current temporal anxiety (state). The influence of current anxiety state is partly a function of environmental characteristics (e.g., tests routinely elicit greater anxiety than practice), and partly a function of individual differences in anxiety (e.g.,

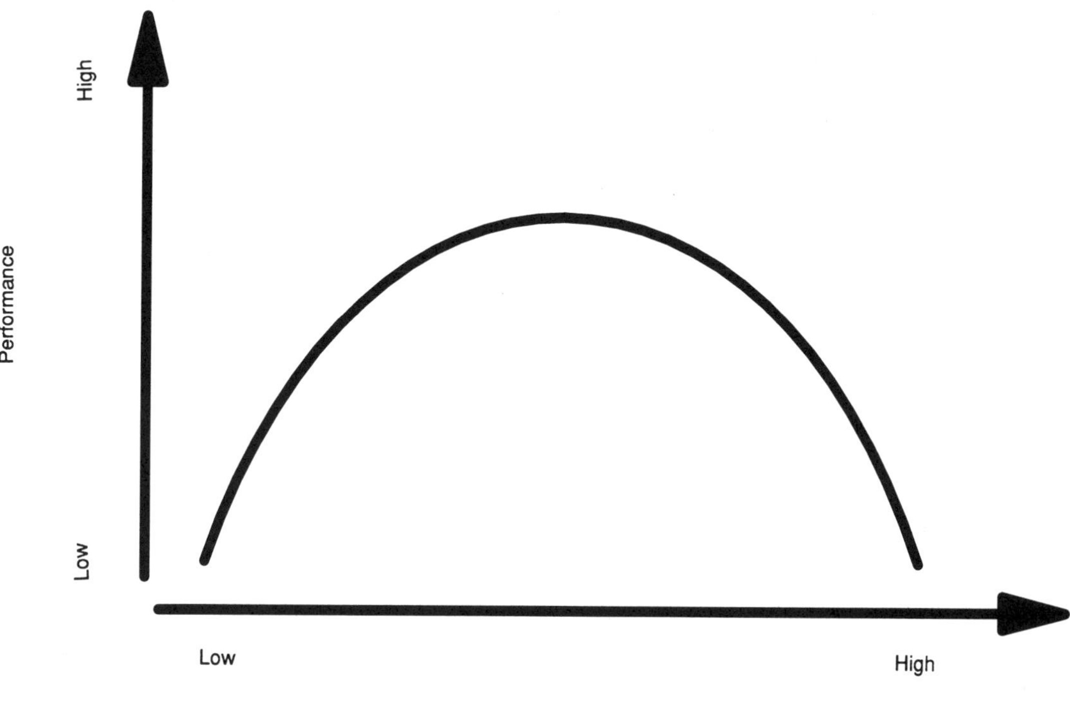

Figure 5. The Yerkes-Dodson law linking performance to levels of arousal.

some people are consistently more or less anxious than others). Thus individual differences in anxiety interact with situational factors to influence learning (e.g., less anxious people may do better in test situations because they are aroused to optimal levels, whereas highly anxious people may experience debilitating levels of arousal in such situations). The study of the role of anxiety on learning is complicated by the relationships among anxiety, situational performance demands, and other factors such as tendency to prepare. For example, test-anxious individuals often study less frequently, and less effectively, than individuals with low test anxiety (Naveh-Benjamin, McKeachie, & Lin, 1987). A more complete review of issues related to anxiety, and other personality characteristics associated with learning (e.g., extraversion), are provided in Chapter 15.

The fourth approach linking personality to achievement motivation is the study of attributional styles. Essentially, this line of research attempts to extend the study of cognitions or thoughts to individual differences. Attributional style is the tendency for an individual to perceive certain factors consistently as the cause of outcomes across situations. For example, children with a pessimistic attributional style tend to anticipate failure and to attribute both failure and success to forces beyond their control; consequently, they view achievement opportunities with trepidation. In contrast, children with an optimistic attributional style tend to anticipate success and to perceive the causes of success or failure to be under their control. Other attributional styles meld attribution, self-efficacy, locus of control, and other features into behavioral composites or personality styles to understand better the link between personality and achievement motivation.

The research on self-concept and achievement motivation represents another effort to link individual differences in cognitions, or thoughts and perceptions, to motivation. Research on self-concept falls into two general categories: research on self-esteem, and research on self-efficacy. Self-esteem is considered to be a global characteristic of the individual that is relatively stable across time and situations, whereas self-efficacy is situation-specific and varies as a function of an individual's perception of personal competence to meet task demands.

The research linking self-concept to academic achievement has been largely correlational. In other words, the modest relationship between a child's self-concept and the child's academic achievement is interpreted as consistent with a reciprocal model of causality. Higher self-concept encourages children to initiate and sustain efforts to learn, whereas low self-concept discourages children from initiating and sustaining tasks in the absence of external rewards. It is also recognized that learning success influences self-concept (i.e., successful learning raises self-concept), however, and so the positive relationship between self-concept and academic achievement is believed to be reciprocal. Generally, self-efficacy for specific types of tasks show stronger relationships to academic achievement than do global measures of self-esteem (Bracken & Howell, 1991).

The connection between personality characteristics, achievement motivation, and instructional practices is not well understood, but there is research showing some important links between personality and instructional practices (Atkinson & Raynor, 1974; Klonsky, 1989). For example, children low in need for achievement often choose tasks that are either extremely easy or extremely difficult, whereas children high in need for achievement select tasks of moderate difficulty. Reward structures, such as intrinsic versus extrinsic reinforcement, interact with personality styles to influence achievement motivation (Weiner, 1992). Although preliminary research has been fruitful in suggesting ways that personality, motivation, and instructional practices interact, the links between these domains are not well defined.

The measurement of need for achievement and self-concept has influenced the practice of school psychology. School psychologists may use personality tests (e.g., the 16PF or Edwards Personal Preference Scale) for assessing the personality and motivational tendencies of secondary students. In contrast, self-esteem measures are often used with younger children to assist with identification of learning problems. Global self-esteem measures, such as the Piers-Harris Self Concept Scale (Piers & Harris, 1984), are most widely used, but the recent advent of multidimensional measures that incorporate global self-esteem and specific self-efficacy ratings for various life roles (e.g., Bracken & Howell, 1991) promise more refined measures of self-concept for school use. There are also many instruments used by school psychologists to measure individual differences in achievement motivation (see Clinkenbeard & Murphy, 1990, for a review of approaches).

Temperament and Personality

Temperament can be described as the constellation of personality characteristics. Indeed, personality research has its genesis in the study of temperament, which was first begun during ancient Western civilizations. Temperament as a personality construct has been revived in part because studies of children have shown early and enduring constellations of behaviors (or temperaments).

The study of temperament and learning is a relatively new area of study for educational psychologists (Keogh, 1989; Kohnstamm, 1990). Although temperament can be approached from physiological, theoretical, or infancy development perspectives, the most common method in educational psychology is to adopt a clinical perspective. For example, temperaments that are characterized by high degrees of physical activity, impulsivity, and aversion to sustained effort are deemed incompatible with traditional school practices emphasizing physical passivity, reflective thinking, and persistence (Martin, 1989). Thus the link between temperament and learning has focused primarily on how temperaments inhibit learning, because the child's temperament conflicts with the demands of the learning situation. There is a substantial body of literature demonstrating how children's temperament interacts with environmental and instructional characteristics to influence performance (Barclay, 1983).

Unfortunately, there are few practical measures of temperament for use in schools. Most temperament measures have been developed in clinical settings and are commonly developed for use with infants. A notable exception is the Temperament Assessment Battery for Children (Martin, 1988), which provides a practical measure of temperament for school use.

Other Applications of Personality to Schools

Two other approaches that incorporate personality into educational research and practice deserve mention. One is the effort to link learners' personality types to instructional practices. For example, personality types from the Myers-Briggs Type Indicator (Myers & Briggs, 1987) have been liked to differential responses to instructional approaches (i.e., an aptitude-treatment interaction) in research on secondary and postsecondary students (e.g., Hudson, Doyle, & Venezia, 1991). The search for personality-type-as-learning-style mirrors the research on aptitude-treatment interactions using factor approaches to intelligence.

The second link between personality and learning comes from research on the role of emotion in human performance. One such link is the role of emotion in the creative process. Russ (1993) and others (e.g., Feist, in press) have shown that emotional states vary across stages of the discovery process. Consequently, it is reasonable to assume that individual differences in emotional state may be linked to discovery and creativity. The research on this subject is still largely retrospective in nature, however, and has not yet generated practical applications to schools.

EDUCATIONAL RESPONSES TO INTELLECTUAL AND PERSONALITY DIFFERENCES

There are three ways in which schools respond to individual differences in intelligence and personality. First, schools and seek to change or modify children's intellectual abilities or personality characteristics. Second, they can accommodate or adjust to individual differences in personality and intelligence. Third, they can select or segregate children based on their intelligence or personality. Each of these educational responses to education shall be addressed in the following sections.

Changing Intelligence and Personality

To some degree, schools are charged with the responsibility to change intelligence and personality. Knowledge changes rapidly as technologies improve; consequently, teaching children ways to think and learn becomes more important than teaching specific information. Conversely, moral development has been the primary impetus for schools since their inception. Both of these charges imply that schools must change, or at least foster, intellectual and personal development.

Efforts to change intelligence and personality have one of two goals. The first goal is to remedy deficient or abnormal intellectual or personal conditions. This goal is usually adopted in special education settings or other settings in which children have already been identified as abnormal, and efforts are made to mitigate or remove the abnormal condition. The second goal is to develop desirable intellectual and personal traits in the general population of schoolchildren. This approach endeavors to enhance cognitive and personal characteristics deemed positive by society.

Remedying Abnormality

The educational research on mentally retardation does more than describe the impact of mental retardation on learning; it also seeks to identify ways to correct learning deficiencies in mentally retarded children. Generally, these approaches seek to teach cognitive strategies that are found in normal children but are lacking in mentally retarded children. Consequently, there is a vigorous research base regarding the effects of teaching metacognitive strategies to mildly mentally retarded children (Wong, 1989). Two examples of work illustrate different approaches to this problem. The work of Campione and Brown (1978) follows from cognitive-behavioral interventions, in which overt instruction is followed by successive fading, cuing, and prompting to enhance strategy generalization. Effects from this approach have shown that remedial interventions are most effective for very specific skills and settings, but are relatively ineffective in producing spontaneous generalization and transfer across widely varying content and settings.

The work of Feuerstein and his colleagues in Israel have claimed more impressive results. Feuerstein (1980) developed a curriculum known as "instrumental enrichment" (IE) to enhance cognitive skills. This curriculum is founded on the assumption that mediated learning experience (MLE) is the proximal cause of individual differences in intelligence. MLE is a process in which caregivers, usually parents, interpose themselves between the environment and the child in order to assign meaning and to control the child's interaction with the environment. IE attempts to provide "saturated" MLE in order to teach retarded children cognitive strategies. IE uses deliberately culture- and context-reduced stimuli in order to enhance transfer of cognitive strategies to other tasks and settings.

Evaluations of IE describe dramatic gains in cognitive skills. More importantly, some IE studies find cognitive gains generalize across time, tasks, and settings. These claims are particularly impressive because Feuerstein generally works with severely retarded children, whereas most other educators work with mildly retarded children. Haywood's extension of Feuerstein's work to children in North America has also shown positive results (e.g., Haywood, Brown, & Wingenfeld, 1990), but neither he nor others have replicated the dramatic gains reported by Feuerstein. Feuerstein's (1979) dynamic assessment model, which was developed to diagnose and remedy cognitive deficiencies, has also been criticized for its lack of scientific rigor (Frisby & Braden, 1992; see Tzuriel, 1992). The search for effective methods to remedy the learning problems of mentally retarded people continues to attract researchers, in part because the learning problems experienced by mentally retarded people have been found to be severe and relatively intractable.

Schools also embrace efforts to remedy abnormal personality states. Such remedial efforts generally fall into one of two dominant philosophies. The first philosophy views abnormal personality states as emotional disturbance and seeks to remedy the disturbance primarily via therapeutic means. Therapies reflect their historical roots in medical treatment, in that they often stress hospitalization or other alternative settings, meetings with a healing professional, and other experiences that reflect a medical setting more than they reflect customary educational practices. Therapies based on ego psychology are an exception to this rule, however, in that ego-oriented approaches often focus on boosting children's academic performance as a means of enhancing ego strength.

The second approach to remedying abnormal personality states adopts a behavioral philosophy. In this approach, abnormal behaviors are viewed as the product of learning history rather than as symptoms of an underlying disturbance. Consequently, interventions to remedy abnormalities assume a strong learning paradigm (which is often operant in orientation). Remedial approaches often begin with a functional analysis of behavior to identify environmental characteristics that may elicit or sustain problem behaviors. Following the analysis, critical individuals in the child's environment are taught how to change the environment to reduce the intensity, duration, and frequency of problem behaviors. Interventions typically target a few specific behaviors, and data are gathered to evaluate and adjust interventions based on changes in the targeted behaviors (e.g., Bergan & Kratochwill, 1990; Kratochwill & Bergan, 1990).

There is also an increasing emphasis to move behavioral intervention programs from secluded, highly controlled settings into the "educational mainstream." This approach stresses inclusion of children, even those with severe difficulties such as autism, into classes with unimpaired peers. In part because of its demonstrated success, and in part because of its compatibility with educational goals to enhance student skills, behavioral approaches have become quite popular for altering abnormal personality or behavioral states (Wood, 1990).

Developing Skills in Normal Individuals

Schools often adopt programs to enhance the intellectual and personal characteristics of students. These programs seek to develop cognitive or personal skills that will generalize to academic and social learning. Indeed, most countries now accept the primary mission of schools to be teaching children how to learn; consequently, teaching children cognitive and social learning strategies is becoming as much a part of some school curricula as teaching them to read and write.

Curricula to enhance cognitive skills come under many labels, the most recent of which is "critical thinking skills." Programs to enhance critical thinking often attempt to teach cognitive operations (e.g., syllogistic thinking) that are to be applied to a wide variety of content (e.g., evaluating a scientific theory or a political argument). Despite the proliferation of programs to enhance cognitive skills, cognitive curricula do not enjoy the organization and refinement of academic curricula (Bangert-Drowns & Bankert, 1990). Some cognitive curricula have their roots in remedial programs. For example, Feuerstein's Instrumental Enrichment technique has been adapted and adopted for use in all Venezuelan schools—and in some schools in the United States—as part of regular instruction. Other cognitive curricula are based on theories of intelligence, and seek to foster intellectual skills in children (e.g., Meeker, 1969, developed a cognitive curriculum on Guilford's Structure of Intellect model of intelligence). The efficacy of approaches to enhance intellectual skills is most clearly demonstrated when the skills are content based; efforts to enhance intellectual skills that generalize across content matter are more controversial with respect to outcomes (Bangert & Kulik, 1982; Bangert-Drowns & Bankert, 1990).

Personality development per se does not enjoy wide popularity in Western countries, although other countries (e.g., China) are more likely to emphasize development of personality traits in educational experiences. Typically, personality development is enhanced to the degree that personality characteristics overlap with moral development goals (e.g., altruism, sensitivity to others' needs). Prosocial characteristics are fostered in schools in the hope that characteristics will maintain into adulthood and enhance citizenship and civic responsibility. The dominant method for teaching such characteristics is through socialization (i.e., creating and maintaining prosocial structures in schools) rather than deliberate, didactic instruction.

There are two exceptions to the conclusion that personality is infrequently a subject of instruction in school. The first exception is found in the increasing emphasis on social skills training in the United States, where recent developments in the assessment and instruction of social skills (e.g., Gresham & Elliot, 1990; Reynolds & Kamphaus, 1992) are being generalized to regular classrooms. The second exception is the emphasis on efforts to prevent later personal and social maladjustment. Such preventive efforts draw heavily on public health models of service delivery, which stress (a) early identification and treatment for individuals at risk and (b) promotion of wellness or health as a means of reducing later difficulties (Hightower & Braden, 1991). Both of these approaches appear to be increasing in popularity, particularly in countries (e.g., the United States) where the primary responsibility for socializing children is shifting from families to schools.

Accommodating Normal Variability in Intelligence and Personality

Grouping Strategies

The accommodation of intellectual and personality differences is a theme that has been more popular in theory than in implementation. Although educators have long recognized that there are substantial differences among students with respect to intelligence and personality, most curricula are uniform, are subject based, and provide few variations to accommodate individual differences among learners. Consequently, grouping or tracking is the most common strategy for dealing with the customary differences in intelligence and personality found in the normal population. This approach clusters children (usually of similar ability, not personality) together and simply changes the rate with which they progress through the curriculum; lower groups or tracks proceed through the curriculum at a slower pace than higher groups.

The grouping or tracking approach to schooling has been hotly debated in recent years. Criticisms include the self-fulfilling prophecy inherent in grouping (e.g., lower-functioning children are given less exposure to complex material, which guarantees they will remain lower functioning), the isolation of children from normal variability, and the relatively poor educational outcomes such groupings produce (e.g., Tesh & Jaeger, 1990). Homogeneous grouping is still widely practiced, however, and some studies find it produces better outcomes than heterogeneous grouping strategies (e.g., Butler et al., 1978; Slavin, 1987).

Judging the relative efficacy of heterogeneous versus homogeneous grouping is complicated by findings of differential effects. For example, some studies show heterogeneous grouping has a positive effect on achievement, but a negative effect on self-image, relative to homogeneous grouping practices. Other research finds the opposite outcome with secondary students: Not only does homogeneous ability grouping improve academic outcomes, but it substantially improves high ability students' attitudes toward learning (Kulik & Kulik, 1982).

Two critical issues are often overlooked in the debate over grouping strategies. The first is the treatment integrity, or the degree to which the school's actions adhere to scientific principles. Programs may be poorly conceived and implemented, which reduces their chances of success despite the ultimate value inherent in the program (Johnson et al., 1983).

The second issue is the basis on which children are assigned to groups. In the United States, assignment to homogeneous groups on the basis of intelligence has been attacked in court and is now rarely practiced (except for identification of gifted and mentally retarded children). In contrast, homogeneous grouping on the basis of academic performance is widely practiced and has been successfully defended in court (Reschly, Klicklighter, & McKee, 1988). Because achievement and intelligence overlap, group assignments based on achievement may differ little from those that would be created by intelligence, except for children who may be intelligent but who have lacked opportunities to learn. In part because of the fear of creating an elitist system based on tests of any kind, the popularity of ability grouping is declining in the United States and other countries, despite some evidence that it produces better outcomes (especially at the secondary level).

Although homogeneous grouping on the basis of ability and performance is widely debated, homogeneous grouping by age is widely accepted among educators. In fact, it is largely unquestioned as an appropriate educational strategy. Individuals of the same age are placed together in "grades" and typically advance through school isolated from older and younger children. Cross-age grouping, based on ability and performance, is more effective than within-age grouping for elementary school students (Gutierrez, 1992). Sadly, cross-age grouping and ungraded elementary schools are rare, whereas homogeneous grouping on the basis of age is rarely questioned.

Altering Curricula

The second major approach to accommodating individual differences in ability is to diversify the academic curricula. If children have multifaceted abilities (or even multiple intelligences), it follows that schools should include more in their curricula than a narrow range of academic subjects and processes. This argument has been echoed by educators for many years and in many ways, but the cry for diversification has generally lost out to cries for going "back to basics" and accountability. This may be in part because curriculum diversification tends to be based not on sound theories of intelligence but rather on exaggerated (and oversimplified) generalizations with only partial research support. For example, Sperry's work on split-brain patients is often cited as the basis for many diverse curricula, from creative thinking to right brain/left brain education. These curricula often have no direct ties to Sperry's research despite claims to the contrary. Nevertheless, attempts to translate research on intelligence into educational curricula continue. Gardner is currently developing a curriculum to complement his theory of multiple intelligences, which may be more successful than previous attempts to diversify the curriculum.

Accommodating Personality Differences

Less attention is devoted to accommodating differences in personality than to accommodating intellectual differences. In part, this is because schools are charged with molding or shaping personalities at younger ages, and in part because the links between personality and achievement are less obvious than the links between intelligence and achievement.

Many secondary schools, however, try to accommodate individual differences in their adolescent students. It is often assumed that personality is less malleable at this point in development, and so individual differences are viewed requiring accommodation rather than change through education. Secondary schools commonly offer a variety of course options ranging from basic life and vocational skills to advanced placement courses in academic subjects (e.g., mathematics, humanities); students are encouraged to select options based on their interests, personality, aptitude, and achievement. Most secondary schools offer comprehensive curricula (i.e., a range of courses spanning vocational to college-preparatory emphases), whereas some schools—usually those in large, urban areas—may offer specialized curricula in a narrowly focused area (e.g., sciences, performing arts). Entry into specialized secondary schools is usually selective, and entry criteria often include measures of prior achievement, personality, and aptitudes.

The goal of most secondary schools is to prepare students for entry into society at large. The decision to pursue work, additional vocational/technical training, or college entry is one that confronts all secondary students. A fundamental assumption of secondary guidance programs is that postsecondary plans are improved when students (and those who advise them) have accurate information about the students' intellectual and personality characteristics. Guidance counselors and school psychologists use personality and aptitude tests to measure individual differences in personality and aptitude. Data are typically sought in two related domains: vocational interests (i.e., what students like to do), and vocational aptitudes (i.e., what they are good at doing).

A number of vocational interest inventories are used in secondary settings to help students identify their vocational interests and match these interests to occupational domains. The Strong Interest Inventory, the Jackson Vocational Interest Survey, the Wide Range Interest Inventory, and the Kuder General Interest Survey are popular examples of vocational and prevocational interest surveys. Students typically respond to items identifying characteristics as most/least like themselves; the completed inventories are returned to school professionals (e.g., counselors and psychologists), who share the results with students. The objective feedback helps students better understand how they compare to others and how their interests compare to those in various occupational categories.

An interesting variation on the traditional vocational interest battery is the Self-Directed Search (SDS), which is an interactive, computer-administered survey of students' preferences in response to specific items. The SDS program generates a description of the student's interests (based on six possible dimensions) and links this description to career domains. Two advantages of the SDS not shared by other interest inventories are the immediate feedback given to the student and the opportunity for the student to explore many different career alternatives. One disadvantage of the SDS is the relatively weak link between results and actual career choices; consequently, school psychologists and counselors who use the SDS are encouraged to consider additional data when advising students on career choices (Levinson, 1990).

Vocational aptitude tests are more frequently used by employers for employee selection than by guidance counselors for vocational guidance. General vocational aptitude batteries such as the General Aptitude Test Battery (GATB), Differential Aptitude Test, or Wonderlic Personnel Classification Test, however, can be used to help students understand how their aptitudes and abilities (a) compare to others and (b) match particular occupations. Vocational aptitude tests with narrower foci (e.g., the Bennett Mechanical Comprehension Test, Minnesota Clerical Test) are occasionally used in guidance programs to provide students information about how their specific vocational abilities compare to those of others in the same field. Once again, it is assumed that accurate information about one's occupational aptitudes will stimulate more realistic personal appraisals and better occupational decisions. Data from aptitude and interest measures are consequently used to guide students toward appropriate secondary school choices (e.g., class selection), and postsecondary options (Kehas, 1989).

Selecting Students by Intelligence and Personality

In addition to changing and accommodating individual differences in these two domains, schools may also select and segregate students according to intelligence and, to a lesser degree, personality. Selection and segregation are practiced for two related, but distinct motives: to identify and treat disabled children, and to identify and enhance gifted and talented children. Each of these selective approaches to accommodating individual differences is widely practiced throughout the world.

Identifying and Treating Disabilities

As has been implied throughout this chapter, schools seek to identify dysfunctional abnormalities in intelligence and personality. Historically, schools tend to progress through three distinct phases in their response to disabled children. The first phase is to exclude disabled children from school, as they may be deemed inappropriate. In the second phase, schools accept disabled children but act as caretakers to relieve the family and society of the "burden" of the disabled child. In the third phase, schools accept exceptional children as legitimate students with legitimate educational needs. Currently, most countries around the world are moving toward or have reached the third phase. The current goal for most schools is to remedy or mitigate the impact of disabilities on children's schooling, and the most popular approach to meeting this goal is to create special programs designed to serve particular disabilities (e.g., mentally retardation, emotional disturbance). Selection into these programs is determined by medical and psychological tests for diagnosing physical and psychoeducational disabilities.

Two controversies surround special programs for severely disabled children. The first is the degree to which special programs are segregated from the regular school program. Segregation falls along a continuum ranging from full inclusion (placing exceptional children in regular classrooms 100% of the time) to a segregated setting (e.g., a residential school physically removed from regular school premises). Most special programs fall between these two extremes, so that disabled children are served part of the time in a special classroom, and part of the time in a regular class setting (Opper & Teichler, 1989). Critics of segregated programs are gaining attention, however, and most countries have attempted to reduce the degree of segregation inherent in special education programs.

The second controversy surrounding special programs is the reliability and validity of psychoeducationally defined disabilities. An increasing number of critics (e.g., Reschly, 1988) are questioning utility of such labels as "learning disabled," "mildly mentally retarded," and "severely emotionally disturbed." Such critics cite limited support for the reliability of diagnoses based on intelligence and personality measures, and note that differential diagnosis of these conditions is not directly linked to differential treatment responses. Those who support the continued use of psychoeducational disability categories note their wide acceptance in the psychological literature and in medical diagnositic systems (e.g., DSM-III-R), as well as the substantial body of research on such conditions extant in the literature. In some ways, the debate over disabling conditions is similar to the controversy in defining emotional disturbance. Critics of the current system favor behavioral, low-inference models of causation, whereas supporters favor cognitive/affective, higher-inference models of causation. At this time, it is not clear how this debate may be resolved.

Selection of Gifted and Talented Students

Selective education for gifted and academically talented children has long been practiced in Western societies. Surprisingly, selective education programs are also popular in socialist countries (Cropley, 1989), despite strong political pressures for educational programs to eschew individual differences in ability (e.g., Martuza, 1986). The reason for selective education programs is straightforward: The gifted individual and society benefit from the development of exceptional abilities and talents. Consequently, special programs have been created in many countries around the world to serve these children. With few exceptions (e.g., China; see Zha Zixiu, cited in Wieczerkowski, 1986), countries consistently define gifted and talented individuals primarily by intelligence and achievement (Cropley, 1989).

There are two issues that are hotly debated by those researching and serving gifted students. The first issue is whether gifted children are best served by an enrichment or an advancement approach to education. The enrichment approach advocates keeping gifted children with their age peers and enhancing their talents through supplementary activities. The acceleration approach advocates moving children into classes that match their ability (typically by advancing them into higher grades or classes with older children). There are findings to support and challenge both practices, and so this debate is likely to continue for the foreseeable future.

The second issue centers on the logistical implementation of programs serving gifted children. Some favor segregated programs, which include gifted children and exclude nongifted peers. Others favor integrated programs, in which gifted children spend a substantial portion of their time with nongifted peers. One approach that uses an accelerated curriculum but keeps gifted children in regular schools is the system of *D-Zug-Klassen* ("express classes") in Germany. Other alternatives to serving gifted children range from after-school, club, and other semiformal activities to enrichment/supplemental programs within regular schools, self-contained classrooms, and even separate schools. Although one might assume that semiformal activities would be most popular within countries with political systems that eschew individual-difference philosophies, this is not the case. The United States is the biggest practitioner of semiformal approaches, whereas separate schools were found in every province of the former Soviet Union (Cropley, 1989).

Because selection into programs for gifted children is viewed as desirable, there is often a substantial focus on selection (and exclusion) procedures. Intelligence tests are the most popular methods for selecting children into programs, although achievement tests are becoming more popular in Western countries for sociopolitical reasons. One alternative to the clique of giftedness created by selective criteria is the revolving-door model proposed by Renzulli, Reis, and Smith (1981). In this model, a larger number of children at the top end of the intelligence or achievement distributions are served by inclusion into special programs for short periods of time; thus they revolve into and out of special programs throughout their school career. This is seen by advocates as a desirable compromise that limits the costs of permanently selecting large groups while eliminating the undesirable consequence of inappropriate rejections. There is no question, however, that there is a strong social value in most countries attached to having one's child identified as gifted, and so selective programs are more popular than alternatives like the revolving-door model.

CONCLUSIONS

The literature describing intelligence and personality in educational and school psychology is too large and varied to be summarized in a single chapter. Three general themes or dimensions that permeate this literature: (a) the emphasis of the research, which is arbitrarily characterized as either cognitive (i.e., intelligence) or affective (i.e., personality); (b) distinctions among the ways in which individual differences are studied and used in education, which include defining abnormality, normal variability in intelligence and personality, and ways in which schools respond to intelligence and personality differences; and (c) the distinction between educational and school psychology. These three themes serve to illustrate how intelligence and personality intersect with educational psychology research and school psychology practice.

Throughout this chapter I have drawn an artificial distinction between intelligence and personality. Although the distinction may be useful as an organizational device, it is ultimately inaccurate and potentially misleading. Intelligence and personality are inextricably bound together. The bond between personality and intelligence is empirical, as demonstrated by correlations among intelligence and personality measures. It is also conceptual: Intellectual processes mediate incoming stimuli and change them into information by assigning meaning. Affective or personality processes also mediate incoming stimuli and alter them by assigning emotion. Consequently these processes interact in reciprocal, recursive fashion.

A brief example may illustrate the bond between personality and intelligence. When children are confronted with a new learning task, their relative success is influenced by their personality and intelligence. Children with a strong sense of self-efficacy, low anxiety, and an internal locus of control will attempt tasks more quickly and persist in the face of failure longer than those whose sense of self-efficacy is low, whose anxiety is high, and who perceive that their efforts have little to do with task success. Likewise, children who are more intelligent than their peers (particularly in intellectual domains associated with crystallized learning ability) are also more likely to succeed than less intelligent peers. The interplay between personality and intelligence influences the probability of success on a new learning task. Brighter children are more likely to have a strong sense of self-efficacy and an internal locus of control. Because they (accurately) perceive themselves to be more likely to succeed on the task, they are more likely to mobilize attributional and motivational processes that lead to success than less intelligent peers. Also, because they perceive the task as less threatening, they are not as likely to be anxious as less intelligent peers. Thus children's personality characteristics interact with intellectual characteristics in promoting or reducing learning.

Although most relationships between personality and intelligence are linear (i.e., desirable personality traits are associated with high levels of intelligence, and vice versa), there are some situations in which personality and intelligence interact in unexpected ways. For example, extraversion and arousal have been found to interact with intelligence and time of day to affect performance (Matthews, 1985). Consequently it must be remembered that personality, intelligence, and situational demands are not independent constructs. These constructs interact in real-life learning situations, and they cannot be neatly separated into "personality" and "intelligence" domains.

There are many issues yet to be resolved—and many more that will continue to demand research—in the effort to link personality and intelligence to education. One critical issue is whether the current popularity of behavioral approaches in the United States (and to a lesser degree Australia and England) will continue to increase in popularity. Perhaps educational practices will eventually reflect the cognitive revolution that has characterized recent research in psychology, but at the present time, the efforts to increase accountability in special and regular education coincide with behavioral approaches to problem definition and intervention. Behavioral approaches generally eschew individual differences as irrelevant and instead stress environmental conditions (e.g., contingency management, instructional rigor) as important factors in learning.

Another critical issue is the general gap, or lack of coherence, between psychological research and educational practices. For example, theories of intelligence have long ago eschewed single-factor theories of intellectual ability, yet many countries still use composite IQs and other unitary-factor concepts to make decisions about mental retardation, giftedness, and related classifications. Furthermore, individual differences in cognitive abilities and personality are inconsistently recognized and addressed by schools. This is particularly unfortunate, because much of the theoretical and practical work in personality and intelligence hopes to improve educational practices.

Three factors may give rise to the lack of coherence between scientific work in personality and intelligence and educational practices. First, the lack of consensus among scientists regarding the essentials of intelligence and personality undoubtedly confuses educators. For example, some renowned researchers promote the value of general, unidimensional ability indexes (e.g., Jensen, 1989), whereas others reject such indexes in favor of qualitatively distinct categories or types of intelligence (e.g., Gardner, 1983). Second, the pragmatic value of research is often less than what is needed in educational settings. For example, personality tests may allow prediction for what will happen in groups of children, but they have limited value for making specific predictions about an individual's behavior (e.g., Mischel, 1968). Third, prevailing educational and social philosophies are often in conflict with scientific findings. An example of this conflict is found in research on the heritability of individual differences. Educators in the United States typically view ability as readily modifiable and largely determined by shared environments, and thus they are not comfortable with the implications of research showing the substantial influence of heredity—and the small influence of shared environment—on traits like intelligence.

Despite problems in transferring research on intelligence and research to educational and school psychology, the links between such research and education will continue be strong. The research linking individual differences in intelligence and personality to learning is simply too powerful to be ignored. Thus educational psychologists will continue to investigate the relationship between personality and intelligence on learning, and school psychologists will continue to apply theories and technologies based on psychological research to help schools adapt, shape, and respond to children's individual differences.

REFERENCES

Achenbach, T. M., & Edelbrock, C. S. (1986). *Child Behavior Checklist and Youth Self-Report.* Burlington, VT: Author.

American Association on Mental Retardation. (1992). *Mental retardation: Definition, classification, and systems of supports* (9th ed.). Washington, DC: Author.

American Psychiatric Association. (1987). *Diagnostic and statistical manual of mental disorders* (rev. 3rd ed.). Washington, DC: Author.

Atkinson, J. W., & Raynor, J. O. (Eds.). (1974). *Motivation and achievement.* New York: Wiley.

Ayers, A. J., & Cooley, E. J. (1986). Sequential versus simultaneous processing on the K-ABC: Validity in predicting learning success. *Journal of Psychoeducational Assessment, 4,* 211–220.

Bangert, R. L., & Kulik, J. A. (1982, March). *Individualized systems of instruction: a meta-analysis of findings in secondary schools.* Paper presented at the annual meeting of the American Educational Research Association, New York. (Document available from the ERIC Document Reproduction Service, ED 220358)

Bangert-Drowns, R. L., & Bankert, E. (1990, April). *Meta-analysis of effects of explicit instruction for critical thinking.* Paper presented at the annual meeting of the American Educational Research Association, Boston. (Document available from the ERIC Document Reproduction Service, ED 328614)

Barclay, J. R. (1983). A meta-analysis of temperament-treatment interactions with alternative learning and counseling treatments. *Developmental Review, 3,* 410–443.

Bayley, N. (1993). *Bayley Scales of Infant Development—Revised.* San Antonio, TX: Psychological Corporation.

Bergan, J. R., & Kratochwill, T. R. (1990). *Behavioral consultation and therapy.* New York: Plenum.

Borkowski, J. G. (1985). Signs of intelligence: Strategy generalization and metacognition. In S. R. Yussen (Ed.), *The growth of reflection in children* (pp. 105–144). Orlando, FL: Academic Press.

Bracken, B. A., & Howell, K. K. (1991). Multidimensional self concept validation: A three-instrument investigation. *Journal of Psychoeducational Assessment, 9,* 319–328.

Braden, J. P. (1992). Intellectual assessment of deaf and hard of hearing people: A quantitative and qualitative research synthesis. *School Psychology Review, 21,* 82–94.

Braden, J. P. (1994). *Deafness, deprivation, and IQ.* New York: Plenum.

Bruininks, R. H., Woodcock, R. W., Weatherman, R., & Hill, B. (1984). *Scales of Independent Behavior.* Allen, TX: DLM Teaching Resources.

Butler, J. M., DeRuzza, D., Wollenberg, J. P., & Handley, H. M. (1987). *Differences in achievement and time-on-task with homogeneous and heterogeneous ability grouping of second graders.* Paper presented at the annual meeting of the American Educational Research Association, Washington, DC. (Document available from the ERIC Document Reproduction Service, ED 289589)

Campione, J. C., & Brown, A. L. (1978). Toward a theory of intelligence: Contributions from research with retarded children. *Intelligence, 2,* 279–304.

Carbo, M. (1983). Research in reading and learning style: Implications for exceptional children. *Exceptional Children, 49,* 486–494.

Carroll, J. B. (1991). *Human cognitive abilities: A survey of factor-analytic studies.* Cambridge, England: Cambridge University Press.

Cattell, R. B. (1986). *The handbook for the 16 Personality Factor Questionnaire.* Champaign, IL: Institute for Personality and Ability Testing.

Chi, M. T. H. (1981). Interactive roles of knowledge and strategies in development. In S. Chipman, J. Segal, & R. Glaser (Eds.), *Thinking and learning skills: Current research and open questions* (Vol. 2). Hillsdale, NJ: Erlbaum.

Clinkenbeard, P. R., & Murphy, S. C. (1990). Measuring student motivation. In C. R. Reynolds & R. W. Kamphaus (Eds.). *Handbook of psychological and educational assessment of children: Personality, behavior, and context.* New York: Guilford.

Cohn, S. J., Carlson, J. S., & Jensen, A. R. (1985). Speed of information processing in academically gifted youths. *Personality and Individual Differences, 6,* 621–629.

Connors, C. K. (1985). *The Connors Rating Scales: Instruments for the assessment of childhood psychopathology.* Unpublished manuscript, Children's Hospital National Medical Center, Washington, DC.

Cropley, A. J. (1989). Gifted and talented: Provision of education, In J. Husen & T. N. Postlethwaite (Eds.), *The international encyclopedia of education: Research and studies* (Vol. 1, pp. 377–384). New York: Pergamon.

Deshpande, S. W., and Kawane, S. D. (1982). Anxiety and serial verbal learning: A test of the Yerkes-Dodson Law. *Asian Journal of Psychology and Education, 9*(3), 18–23.

Feist, G. J. (in press). The affective consequences of artistic and scientific problem solving. *Cognition and Emotion.*

Feuerstein, R. (1979). *The dynamic assessment of retarded performers: The learning potential assessment device theory instruments, and techniques.* Baltimore, MD: University Park Press.

Feuerstein, R. (1980). *Instrumental enrichment: An intervention program for cognitive modifiability.* Baltimore, MD: University Park Press.

Frankenburg, W. K., Dodds, J. B., & Fandal, A. W. (1975). *Denver Developmental Screening Test: Reference manual* (rev. ed.). Denver: University of Colorado Medical Center.

Frisby, C. L., & Braden, J. P. (1992). Feuerstein's dynamic assessment approach: A semantic, logical, and empirical critique. *Journal of Special Education, 26,* 281–301.

Gardner, H. (1983). *Frames of mind: The theory of multiple intelligences.* New York: Basic Books.

Gettinger, M. (1984). Individual differences in time needed for learning: A review of literature. *Educational Psychologist, 19*, 15–29.

Green, R. G. (1984). Preferred stimulation levels in introverts and extroverts: Effects on arousal and performance. *Journal of Personality and Social Psychology, 46*, 1303–1312.

Gresham, F. M., & Elliott, S. N. (1990). *Social Skills Rating System*. Circle Pines, MN: American Guidance Service.

Grossman, J.J. (Ed.) (1983). *Classification in mental retardation*. Washington, DC: American Association on Mental Deficiency.

Guilford, J. P. (1967). *The nature of human intelligence*. New York: McGraw-Hill.

Gutierrez, R. (1992). Achievement effects of the nongraded elementary school: A best evidence synthesis. *Review of Educational Research, 62*, 333–376.

Haywood, H. C., Brown, A. L., & Wingenfeld, S. (1990). Dynamic approaches to psychoeducational assessment. *School Psychology Review, 19*, 411–422.

Helms, J. E. (1983). *A practitioners guide to the Edwards Personal Preference Schedule*. Springfield, IL: Thomas.

Hightower, A. D., & Braden, J. P. (1991). Prevention. In T. R. Kratochwill & R. J. Morris (Eds.), *The practice of therapy with children* (2nd ed., pp. 410–440). New York: Pergamon.

Horn, J. L. (1968). Organization of abilities and the development of intelligence. *Psychological Review, 75*, 242–259.

Horn, J. L. (1985). Remodeling old models of intelligence. In B. Wolman (Ed.), *Handbook of intelligence* (pp. 267–300). New York: Wiley.

Hudson, P. E., Doyle, R. E., & Venezia, J. F. (1991). A comparison of two group methods of teaching communication skills to high school students. *Journal for Specialists in Group Work, 16*, 255–263.

Jackson, D. N. (1984). *Personality Research Form manual*. Port Huron, MI: Research Psychologists Press.

Jensen, A. R. (1969). How much can we boost IQ and scholastic achievement? *Harvard Educational Review, 39*, 1–123.

Jensen, A. R. (1973). Level I and Level II abilities in three ethnic groups. *American Educational Research Journal, 4*, 263–276.

Jensen, A. R. (1980). *Bias in mental testing*. New York: Free Press.

Jensen, A. R. (1989). The relationship between learning and intelligence. *Learning and Individual Differences, 1*, 37–62.

Jensen, A. R., & Reynolds, C. R. (1982). Race, social class and ability patterns on the WISC-R. *Personality and Individual Differences, 3*, 423–428.

Johnson, D. W., Johnson, R. T., & Maruyama, G. (1983). Interdependence and interpersonal attraction among heterogeneous and homogeneous individuals: A theoretical formulation and a meta-analysis of the research. *Review of Educational Research, 53*, 5–54.

Kaufman, A. S., & Kaufman, N. L. (1983). *K-ABC: Kaufman Assessment Battery for Children*. Circle Pines, MN: American Guidance Service.

Kaufman, A. S., Kaufman, N. L., & Goldsmith, B. Z. (1984). *Kaufman Sequential or Simultaneous*. Circle Pines, MN: American Guidance Service.

Kehas, C. D. (1989). Counselor roles. In J. Husen & T. N. Postlethwaite (Eds.), *The international encyclopedia of education: Research and studies* (Vol. 1, pp. 1088–1090). New York: Pergamon.

Keogh, B. K. (1989). Applying temperament research to schools. In G. A. Kohnstamm, J. E. Bates, & M. K. Rothbart (Eds.), *Temperament in childhood* (pp. 437–450). Chichester, England: Wiley.

Klonsky, B. G. (1989). Development of achievement orientation. In J. Husen & T. N. Postlethwaite (Eds.), *The international encyclopedia of education: Research and studies* (Vol. 1, pp. 1–5). New York: Pergamon.

Knoff, H. M. (1986). *The assessment of child and adolescent personality*. New York: Guilford.

Kohnstamm, G. A. (1990). Temperament. In J. Husen & T. N. Postlethwaite (Eds.), *The international encyclopedia of education: Research and studies* (Vol. 2, pp. 660–663).

Kratochwill, T. R., & Bergan, J. R. (1990). *Behavioral consultation in applied settings: An individual guide*. New York: Plenum.

Kulik, C. C., & Kulik, J. A. (1982). Effects of ability grouping on secondary school students: A meta-analysis of evaluation findings. *American Educational Research Journal, 19*, 415–428.

Lambert, N., & Goodman, M. (1992). School psychology. In M. C. Alkin (Ed.), *Encyclopedia of educational research* (pp. 1158–1165). New York: Macmillan.

Levinson, E. M. (1990). Vocational assessment involvement and use of the Self-Directed Search by school psychologists. *Psychology in the Schools, 27*, 217–228.

Martin, R. P. (1988). *Temperament Assessment Battery for Children*. Brandon, VT: Clinical Psychology Publishing.

Martin, R. P. (1989). Activity level, distractibility, and persistence: Critical characteristics in early schooling. In G. A. Kohnstamm, J. E. Bates, & M. K. Rothbart (Eds.). *Temperament in childhood* (pp. 451–462). Chichester, England: Wiley.

Matthews, G. (1985). The effects of extraversion and arousal on intelligence test performance. *British Journal of Psychology, 76*, 479–493.

Matthews, G. D., & Lees, J. L. (1990). Arousal, extraversion, and individual differences in resource availability. *Journal of Personality and Social Psychology, 59*, 150–168.

Martuza, V. R. (1986). Evaluation of reading achievement in Cuban schools: A comparative perspective. *Reading Teacher, 40*, 306–313.

Meeker, M. N. (1969). *The structure of intellect*. Columbus, OH: Merrill.

Mensa. (1980). *The Mensa test*. New York: Author.

Mischel, W. (1968). *Personality and assessment*. New York: Wiley.

Murray, H. A. (1938). *Explorations in personality*. New York: Oxford University Press.

Myers, I. B., & Briggs, K. C. (1987). *Myers-Briggs type indicator*. Palo Alto, CA: Consulting Psychologists Press.

Naglieri, J. A. (1985a). *Matrix Analogies Test: Expanded form*. San Antonio, TX: Psychological Corporation.

Naglieri, J. A. (1985b). *Matrix Analogies Test: Short form*. San Antonio,TX: Psychological Corporation.

Naglieri, J. A. (1988). *Draw A Person: Quantitative scoring system*. San Antonio, TX: Psychological Corporation.

Naglieri, J. A., Das, J. P., & Jarman, R. F. (1990). Planning, attention, simultaneous, and successive cognitive processes as a model for assessment. *School Psychology Review, 19*, 423–442.

Naglieri, J. A., LeBuffe, P. A., & Pfeiffer, S. I. (1993). *Devereux Behavior Rating Scale: School form*. San Antonio, TX: Psychological Corporation.

Naglieri, J. A., McNish, T. J., & Bardos, A. N. (1991). *Draw A Person: Screening procedures for emotional disturbance*. Austin, TX: Pro-Ed.

Naveh-Benjamin, M., McKeachie, W. J., & Lin, Y. (1987). Two types of test-anxious students: Support for an information processing model. *Journal of Educational Psychology, 79*, 131–136.

Opper, S., & Teichler, U. (1989). European Community (EC): Educational programmes. In J. Husen & T. N. Postlethwaite (Eds.). *The international encyclopedia of education: Research and studies* (Vol. 1, pp. 342–347). New York: Pergamon.

Piers, E. V., & Harris, D. B. (1984). *Piers-Harris children's self-concept scale: The way I feel about myself.* Los Angeles: Western Psychological Services.

Quay, H. C., & Peterson, D. R. (1987). *Manual for the Revised Behavior Problem Checklist.* Coral Gables, FL: Author.

Raven, J. C. (1962). *Advanced Progressive Matrices.* London: Lewis.

Raven, J. C. (1982). *Mill Hill Vocabulary Scale: 1982 edition.* London: Lewis.

Raven, J. C., Court, J. H., & Raven, J. (1982). *Manual for Raven's Progressive Matrices and Vocabulary Scales: Section 5A.* London: Lewis.

Renzulli, J. S., Reis, S. M., & Smith, L. H. (1981). *The revolving door identification model.* Mansfield, CT: Creative Learning Press.

Renzulli, J. S., Smith, L. H., White, A. J., Callahan, C. M., & Hartman, R. K. (1976). *Scales for rating the behavioral characteristics of superior students.* Wethersfield, CT: Creative Learning Press.

Reschly, D. J. (1988). Special education reform: School psychology revolution. *School Psychology Review, 17,* 459–475.

Reschly, D. J. (1990). Mild mental retardation. In J. Husen & T. N. Postlethwaite (Eds.), *The international encyclopedia of education: Research and studies* (Vol. 2, pp. 419–423). New York: Pergamon.

Reschly, D. J., Klicklighter, J., & McKee, P. (1988). Recent placement litigation. Part I, regular education grouping: Comparison of "Marshall" (1984, 1985) and "Hobson" (1967, 1969). Part II, minority EMR overrepresentation: Comparison of "Larry P." (1979, 1984, 1986) with "Marshall" (1984, 1985) and "S-1" (1986). Part III, analysis of differences in "Larry P.," "Marshall" and "S-1" and implications for future practices. *School Psychology Review, 17,* 9–50.

Reynolds, C. R., & Kamphaus, R. W. (1992). *Behavior Assessment System for Children.* Circle Pines, MN: American Guidance Service.

Russ, S. (1993). *Affect and creativity: The role of affect and play in the creative process.* Hillsdale, NJ: Lawrence Erlbaum.

Sattler, J. M. (1988). *Assessment of children* (3rd ed.). San Diego, CA: Author.

Slavin, R. E. (1987). Ability grouping and student achievement in elementary schools: A best-evidence synthesis. *Review of Educational Research, 57,* 293–336.

Sparrow, S. S., Balla, D. A., & Cicchetti, D. V. (1984). *Vineland Adaptive Behavior Scales.* Circle Pines, MN: American Guidance Service.

Speilberger, C. D. (1984). *State-Trait Anxiety Inventory: A comprehensive bibliography.* Palo Alto, CA: Consulting Psychologists Press.

Sternberg, R. J. (1985). *Beyond IQ: A triarchic theory of human intelligence.* Cambridge, England: Cambridge University Press.

Tesh, A. S., & Jaeger, R. M. (1990, April). *An evaluation of the effects of "bona fide" homogeneous grouping on the achievement of elementary school students.* Paper presented at the annual meeting of the American Educational Research Association, Boston. (Document available from the ERIC Document Reproduction Service, ED 318752)

Tzuriel, D. (1992). The dynamic assessment approach: A reply to Frisby and Braden. *Journal of Special Education, 26,* 302–324.

Vernon, P. A. (1981). Reaction time and intelligence in the mentally retarded. *Intelligence, 5,* 345–355.

Wechsler, D. (1991). *Wechsler Intelligence Scale for Children* (3rd ed.). San Antonio, TX: Psychological Corporation.

Weiner, B. (1992). Motivation. In M. C. Alkin (Ed.), *Encyclopedia of educational research* (pp. 860–865). New York: Macmillan.

Wieczerkowski, W. H. (Ed.). (1986). *Giftedness: A continuing worldwide challenge.* New York: Trillium.

Winton, W. M. (1987). Do introductory textbooks present the Yerkes-Dodson Law correctly? *American Psychologist, 42,* 202–203.

Wirt, R. D., Lachar, D., Klinedinst, J. K., & Seat, P. D. (1984). *Multidimensional description of child personality: A manual for the Personality Inventory for Children.* Los Angeles: Western Psychological Services.

Wong, B. Y. L. (1989). Metacognition and specific learning disabilities. In J. Husen & T. N. Postlethwaite (Eds.), *The international encyclopedia of education: Research and studies* (Vol. 1, pp. 511–517). New York: Pergamon.

Wood, F. H. (1990). Behavior disorders. In J. Husen & T. N. Postlethwaite (eds.), *The international encyclopedia of education: Research and studies* (Vol. 2, pp. 39–42). New York: Pergamon.

Woodcock, R. W., & Johnson, M. B. (1987). *Woodcock-Johnson Psychoeducational Battery-revised.* Allen, TX: DLM Teaching Resources.

29

Personality, Intelligence, and Neuropsychology in the Diagnosis and Treatment of Clinical Disorders

Margaret Semrud-Clikeman and Phyllis Anne Teeter

Historically clinicians and researchers have utilized theories drawn from research in personality or intelligence or neuropsychology in isolation, with less attention given to the interaction between these three fields in the evaluation of childhood and adult disorders. Although each paradigm provides essential information for understanding disorders, it is likely that used alone, the approaches will miss important information needed for both assessment and the development of appropriate interventions.

Assessment of intelligence and personality variables is an important cornerstone in clinical psychology. The relationship between psychological adjustment and personality characteristics has been demonstrated for both children and adults (Martin, 1988). One of the goals of clinical psychology is to provide a full and comprehensive picture of the individual's functioning. Included in this picture are the client's strengths and weaknesses, as well as how these variables contribute to the client's overall adjustment. Competent clinical psychologists provide a diagnosis not as an end to itself but as to an aid to treatment. As such, diagnosis is integrally related to treatment.

The attempt to understand clinical disorders as "reflections of physically disordered brains, or as behavior patterns to be understood only at a psychological level of analysis" misses important variables contained in either paradigm (Taylor, 1983, p. 239). Achenbach (1990) suggested that childhood psychopathology be conceptualized as a combination of "microparadigms" including the paradigms of neuropsychology, cognitive-behavior, psychodynamic theory, and family systems, which are then formed into a "macroparadigm."

It is likely that an integrated paradigm approach would be useful for conceptualizing not only childhood but adult disorders. The assessment of the client's support system, previous developmental history and behavior, personality style, and neuropsychological deficits is likely to provide a more comprehensive and useful picture for the development of treatment programs.

Evidence is mounting that some diagnoses previously considered to be functional in origin are in fact organically based, with functional and environmental components. Although diagnosis in clinical psychology (or, for that matter, other branches of psychology) is complicated by this relationship, it is also enriched

Margaret Semrud-Clikeman • Department of Educational Psychology, University of Washington, Seattle, Washington 98195. Phyllis Anne Teeter • Department of Educational Psychology, University of Wisconsin-Milwaukee, Milwaukee, Wisconsin 53201.

International Handbook of Personality and Intelligence, edited by Donald H. Saklofske and Moshe Zeidner. Plenum Press, New York, 1995.

in that variables such as brain damage or biochemical differences contribute to diagnoses and treatment. Using a broader brush to paint an intervention picture allows the clinical psychologist to address not only current but also future client needs. Moreover, the clinical psychologist using information from neuropsychology—or the neuropsychologist using knowledge from clinical psychology—can more readily anticipate and appropriately treat the client's difficulties.

Therefore the purpose of this chapter is to present a rationale for the integration of intelligence, personality, and neuropsychological data in developing treatment programs for both children and adults. This chapter is organized into four main sections. First, a brief overview of neuroanatomy and neuropathology, the functional organization of the brain, and a model of the neuropsychology of emotions in adults and children are presented. Second, selected psychiatric disorders in adulthood are reviewed, including schizophrenia, obsessive disorders, and affective disorders. Disorders of childhood are also introduced, including attention-deficit hyperactivity disorder, conduct disorder, depression, and anxiety disorder; these disorders are discussed in light of neuropsychological, intellectual, and personality features. Third, treatment issues are outlined within the DSM-III-R (American Psychiatric Association [APA], 1987) multiaxial paradigm. Finally, therapeutic issues specific to adults and to children are highlighted, with several case studies presented as examples.

NEUROANATOMY AND NEUROPATHOLOGY

Cytoarchitectural mapping of the human brain has been greatly facilitated by modern neuroimaging techniques, including computed tomography (CT) and magnetic resonance imaging (MRI; Tranel, 1992). The cortex is comprised of the right and left hemispheres, with four major lobes: frontal, parietal, occipital, and temporal (see Figure 1). Large bundles of myelinated fibers connect these various intra- and interhemispheric regions. The two hemispheres are connected via several transverse commissures or pathways, including the corpus callosum and anterior commissure, whereas association fibers connect cortical regions within each hemisphere (Reitan & Wolfson, 1985). These pathways allow for rapid communication across cortical and hemispheric regions, for the perception and integration of stimuli, and for the organization of complex output (e.g., emotional responses to stimuli). Dysfunction of these systems can result in a variety of behavioral, intellectual, and personality manifestations (Tranel, 1992).

The frontal lobes are the most anterior cortical structures and are comprised of the primary motor, premotor, and prefrontal regions. Lesions to the primary motor cortex can result in paralysis to the contralateral side of the body; lesions to the premotor cortex can produce more complex coordination problems because this region directs the execution of the primary motor area (Reitan & Wolfson, 1985). Lesions to the prefrontal cortex, with its complex connections to other brain regions (i.e., thalamic, hypothalamic, and limbic areas) often result in affective dissociations, impaired executive functions and judgment, and intellectual deficits (Tranel, 1992). Figure 2 illustrates important anatomical regions involved in these lesions; see Table 1 for a summary of the effects of frontal lobe dysfunction.

The temporal lobe has three major divisions, including the superior temporal gyrus, or Wernicke's areas; the lateral/inferior region, with anterior and posterior areas; and the mesial aspect, with connections to hippocampal and amygdala regions (Tranel, 1992). Although the temporal lobe has primary auditory perception and auditory association functions, it also plays a significant role in memory functions, as well as facial (prosopagnosia) and object recognition.

The parietal cortex is separated from the frontal regions by the central sulcus and from the temporal lobe by the lateral fissure (Teeter, 1986). The parietal lobes play a central role in the perception of tactual information, including the recognition of pain, pressure, touch, proprioception, and kinesthetic sense. Lesions can produce sensory deficits to the contralateral side of the body, as well as other more complex deficits when the temporoparietal and inferior parietal regions are involved (Tranel, 1992).

Finally, the most posterior region of the cortex comprises the occipital lobe (primary visual cortex), which is further divided into dorsal (superior) and ventral (inferior) areas (Tranel, 1992). Lesions to the dorsal or ventral region produce various visual defects (see Table 1 for a summary).

Developmental Variables

Although brain injury in adults frequently produces highly focal damage as indicated above, neuropsychiatric disorders in children are commonly a re-

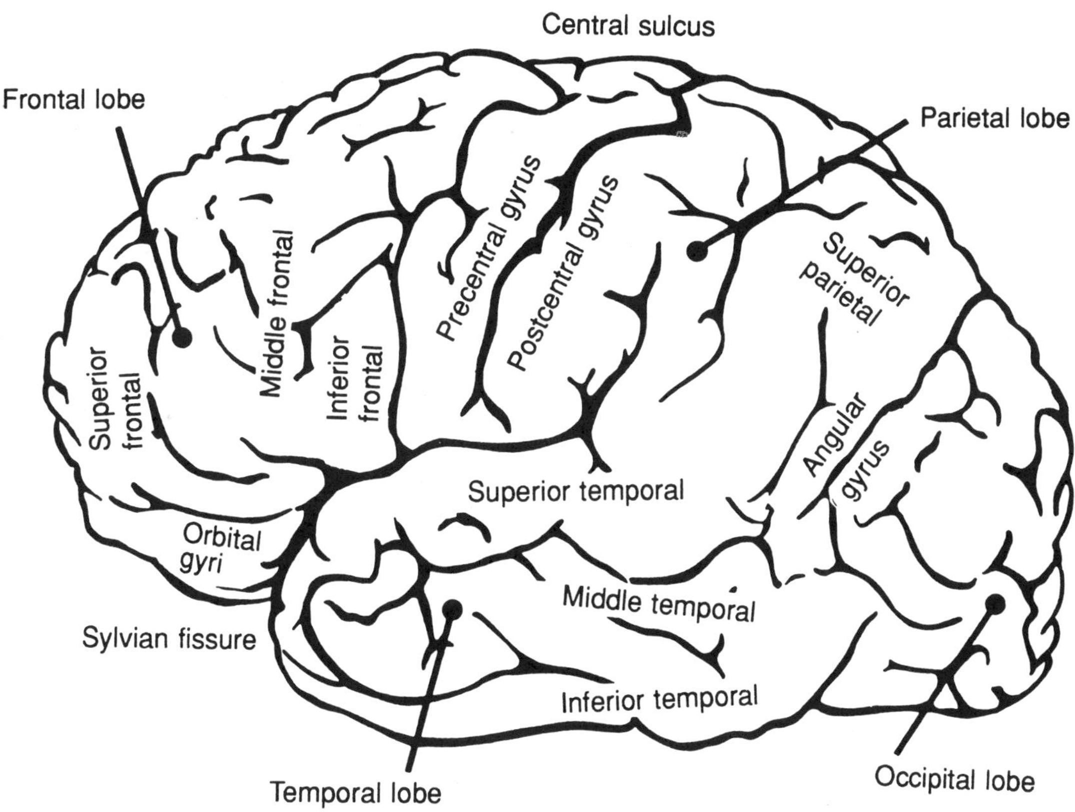

Figure 1. Important neuroanatomical landmarks.

Table 1. Relationships between Site of Injury and Behavioral Sequaelae

Injury site	Neuropsychological behaviors	Psychiatric signs
Frontal lobe		Depression, apathy; possible relationship of frontal lobe to ADHD, OCD, bipolar disorder, and schizophrenia
Motor strip	Paralysis to contralateral side	
Premotor	Complex motor programs disrupted	
Dorsolateral region	Expressive aphasia, problems with repetition	
Prefrontal region	Problems with judgment, reasoning, insight modulation of affect, disinhibition, depression	
Temporal lobe	Auditory perception and comprehension skills, long-term memory, reading difficulty, lowered IQ	Some relationship to depression, apathy, thought disorder-like processes, denial of problems
Parietal lobe	Difficulty with visual-motor integration, kinesthetic sense, inabilty to interpret facial expressions and vocal intonation	Quasi-spatial reasoning, general psychopathology, confusion, problems with social comprehension
Occipital lobe	Visual defects, interpretation of visual information	Obsessiveness, inability to interpret social situations

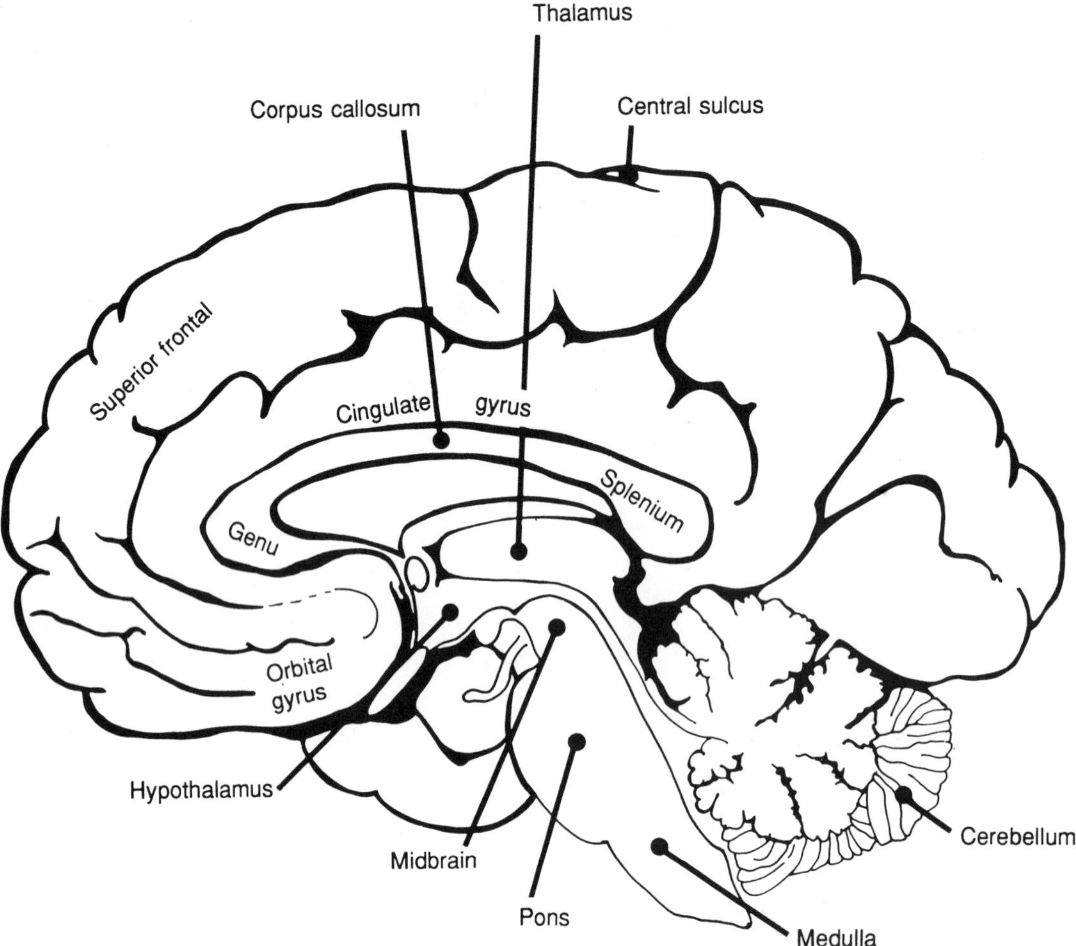

Figure 2. A mid-sagittal view of selected neuroanatomical regions.

sult of neurodevelopmental disorders rather than lesions or degenerative disorders affecting an otherwise healthy brain (Cook & Leventhal, 1992). This finding has generated a great debate on whether early damage to the developing brain has a better prognosis than later damage. Lenneberg (1967) found that the developing brain has the potential for greater plasticity for language acquisition than the more mature brain. Cook and Leventhal (1992), however, argue that most "childhood-onset neuropsychiatric disorders occur because the normal processes of brain maturation do not occur in a sufficiently organized manner. Thus, there is little or no period of normal brain functioning" (p. 640).

Although the brain has a somewhat defined morphology at birth, the myelination of axons, the formation of synaptic connections, and the arrangement of these synapses continues into adolescence and generally corresponds to the development of complex human behaviors. Disorders in childhood (e.g., obsessive-compulsive disorder, attention-deficit hyperactivity disorder, and Tourette's syndrome) may involve abnormalities in the regulation of plasticity. These abnormalities may occur during a period when the brain is apparently overproducing then pruning the axonal-synaptic processes (Cook & Leventhal, 1992). Further disorders in childhood rarely affect an isolated function (e.g., language, motor, or cognitive processes) because interference in the developmental process of one brain region most likely affects the development of other areas as well. (Please see Tranel, 1992, and Reitan & Wolfson, 1985, for a more in-depth review of neuroanatomy and neuropathology.)

A FUNCTIONAL ORGANIZATIONAL APPROACH

One of the directions neuropsychology has taken is an attempt to localize the "brain damage" a client has experienced (Fletcher & Taylor, 1984). Misconceptions can arise as a result of this emphasis. Fletcher and Taylor (1984) suggests that localization rests on the assumption that specific behavioral deficits are direct reflections of brain damage/disease and that these behavioral deficits represent brain impairment on a clearly delineated continuum.

Illustrative of the above concerns is the finding that clients with documented brain damage in the same specific area of the brain do not always show the same type of behavioral deficits (Mesulam, 1985). Though localization of damage is often useful with adults, it is likely that the developing brains of children do not lend themselves as directly to localization (Hynd & Willis, 1988). Because the child's brain continues to develop postnatally in dendritic complexity and synaptic organization, trauma at an early age can disrupt development and have a negative impact on behaviors and abilities that develop at later ages.

Thus the clinician must consider not only the neuropsychological variables normally addressed through an assessment, but also the role development plays in outcome from any type of brain trauma (Boll & Barth, 1981). A functional organization approach would separate the behavioral characteristics of a disorder into variables that form the basis of the disability and those that are correlated with the disability (Fletcher & Taylor, 1984).

For example, in adults with closed head injury, it may well be that variables such as the person's preinjury personality, level of occupational attainment (as a rough measure of intelligence), and support system will affect the severity of the behavior evidenced from the injury. Thus a client who experiences a moderate closed head injury, was relatively successful and emotionally stable prior to the injury, and also had established a good support system may respond readily to treatment. In contrast, a client who had a personality disorder, a problematic employment history, and/or a shaky support system may require additional support in order to profit from rehabilitation. Thus the use of a functional organizational approach is likely to provide a more accurate prediction for treatment success than the use of a neuropsychological, personality, or cognitive assessment alone. In order to elucidate more fully the role of personality and/or emotional functioning in clinical disorders, the following section discusses a possible neuroanatomical basis for emotions.

HEMISPHERIC SPECIALIZATION: A THEORETICAL MODEL OF EMOTIONS

Although much of the research has focused on identifying the specific emotions associated with damage to a particular brain region, more elaborate models are available. Bear (1983) provides a more comprehensive explanation of the relationship between neurocognition and human emotions in adults. Bear's paradigm is based on data from research investigating hemispheric asymmetry using intracarotid anesthetization, electrocortical stimulation, lesion site, neuroendocrine markers, neuropsychological assessment, and clinical observation. The functional asymmetry of the cortex with the right hemisphere is characterized as affective, emotional, concerned, vigilant, spatial, simultaneous/holistic, peripheral, incidental, and impulsive, whereas the left hemisphere is characterized as cognitive, neutral, unconcerned, inattentive, temporal, sequential, analytic, central, intentional, and reflective.

Bear (1983) further details the relationship between temporofrontal (ventral system) and parietofrontal functions and psychological behavior. The ventral temporofrontal systems (inferotemporal visual cortex to limbic structures to orbital frontal structures) play a role in storage of associations between visual and emotional processes, the evaluation of drives, and the development of response strategies. Bear (1983) hypothesizes that damage to temporal or orbital prefrontal regions would interfere with accessing previously learned emotional responses/associations, including social restraints. Without this functional system, an individual may demonstrate aggressive (or sexual) responses to the environment with little or no appreciation for learned consequences. Damage in any part of this functional network may result in discrete emotional and behavioral deficits.

The dorsal parietofrontal system (inferior parietal lobe to limbic system to dorsolateral frontal cortex) plays a role in the activation of emotions, and lesions to this region may result in apathy or neglect. Integrating numerous research results (Dimond, Farrington, & Johnson, 1976; Geschwind, 1965; Heilman, Schwartz, & Watson, 1978), Bear (1983) suggests that the nature of the cognitive processing functions of the left hemisphere may be related to reflective and rigid or stereotypical responding. Conversely, the right hemisphere is particularly suited for incidental learning, with the right dorsal regions adding affective qualities to the cognitive processes in order to arouse emotional responses, recognize threats, and initiate goal-directed responses. The temporofrontal portions of the right hemisphere might be superior for memory functions, discriminating vocal intonations, identifying facial expressions, and decoding and assigning emotional meaning to perceptions (Semrud-Clikeman & Hynd, 1990). A relationship of right parietal and possibly dorsal frontal regions with denial and neglect has been found with adults with right hemispheric damage (Ross, 1981).

Neuropsychological Basis of Emotions in Adults

Most studies investigating the neuropsychological basis of emotions have focused on adults. Research has shown that frontal lobe damage results in numerous psychological problems in adults, including behavioral inflexibility, response inhibition, reduced verbal fluency, and altered personality (Kolb & Whishaw, 1980). Kolb and Whishaw describe two syndromes in adults that have been associated with frontal lobe dysfunction: pseudodepression, which is characterized by signs of apathy, no initiative, few observable emotions, and reduced verbal output; and pseudopsychopathology, which is indicated by immature behavior, little restraint, foul language, high motor activity, and poor social skills. Thus, it appears that frontal lobe dysfunction in adults can produce behaviors that mimic and consequently may be difficult to distinguish from psychopathology.

The relationship between emotions and nonfrontal, posterior brain regions has also been investigated. Although the temporal lobe is the primary auditory cortex, it does serve more than this unitary function. Kolb and Whishaw (1985) indicate that the temporal lobes serve a complex role in the perception and analysis of auditory information, in the integration of sensory input from occipital and parietal cortices, in the storage and retrieval of memory traces, and in the assignment of emotional significance of affective properties to stimuli. Without the affective assignment of emotional significance, an individual would simply respond to information as if it had no particular or specific emotional meaning.

Neuropsychological Basis of Emotions in Children

Although numerous studies have addressed the neuropsychological basis of emotions in adults, similar efforts to understand the neuropsychology of emotions in children are less well articulated. Contributing factors that may confound such studies include maturational changes in the developing brain, the relative importance of environmental influences on development, the influences of onset of injury, and the age-specific difficulties in measuring abilities in children.

The Fletcher and Taylor (1984) model conceptualizes developmental neuropsychology with consideration as to how moderator variables (i.e., including environmental and social factors) influence the basic competencies/deficits and where the central nervous system is viewed as one of several influences. In this model, questions in developmental neuropsychology begin to focus on the sequence in which skills are developed and how these skills change with each developmental stage. Fletcher and Taylor suggest a need to focus on how disabilities interfere with or disrupt normal development, rather than focusing on identifying which brain areas are deficient.

PSYCHOPATHOLOGY FROM A NEUROPSYCHOLOGICAL VIEW

Children with psychopathology have been studied for cognitive and/or neuropsychological patterns related to different types of psychiatric disturbance. Results from recent research suggests that many psychiatric disorders may well have an underlying organic etiology (Dean, 1986). When adults with psychiatric diagnoses have been neuropsychologically assessed using a commonly used battery approach (e.g., Reitan or Luria Nebraska measures), there is a significant reduction in accuracy of diagnosis (Hynd & Semrud-Clikeman, 1990). A further reduction in differential diagnostic accuracy by neuropsychological assessment is often found when process schizophrenics are added to an adult sample (Dean, 1985; Heaton, Baade, & Johnson, 1978). Heaton et al. (1978) concluded in their review of schizophrenia that process schizophrenics and patients with diffuse brain damage show similar neuropsychological profiles.

Similar difficulties in differential diagnosis between functional and organic etiology are found in child and adolescent samples (Dean, 1985, 1986). Hertzig (1982) found roughly one third of her adolescent sample with a history of psychiatric disorder to also be neurologically impaired. Tramontana, Sherrets, and Golden (1980) found 60% of their psychiatric child and adolescent patients to have neuropsychological deficits. The severity of these neuropsychological disorders were found to vary with duration; when the duration of the psychiatric disorder exceeded 2 years, there was a higher probability of neuropsychological disorder. Moreover, the most severe neuropsychological impairments were found on complex cognitive and perceptual tasks in these children. Thus a relationship between chronicity of psychiatric disorders and neuropsychological deficits has been found in both children and adults.

In summary, it is likely that the commonly made distinction between psychiatric and organic syndromes may be faulty. This distinction has been based on the assumption that psychiatric disorders are based on psychosocial influences, whereas organic disorders are directly related to biological influences. With the advent of new technology that allows for the visualization of brain structure and metabolism, we are learning that this dichotomy is not likely to hold up empirically. Mounting evidence suggests that biochemical and structural neurological abnormalities are present in many psychiatric disorders (Andreason, Olsen, Dennert, & Smith, 1982; Semrud-Clikeman, Hynd, Novey, & Eliopulos, 1991; Zametkin & Rapoport, 1990).

Differences in neurochemistry have been found in patients with affective disorders (Jarvik, 1977) and in some forms of schizophrenia (Andreasen et al., 1982). In similar fashion to Fletcher and Taylor's (1984) plea to view childhood disorders along a continuum, Dean (1986) suggests that the "organic-functional distinction for mental disorders" (p. 95) is also better understood as a continuous and not as an all-or-none phenomena. Thus viewing child and adult psychiatric disorders from a combined personality and neuropsychological interface would seem to be most efficient for a comprehensive understanding of these diagnoses. The following section discusses selected psychiatric disorders from this conceptualization.

FRONTAL LOBE DYSFUNCTION

Adults with schizophrenia or obsessive-compulsive disorder have been found to have global frontal dysfunction as well as cognitive impairment (Abbruzzese et al., 1993; Cattaneo et al., 1988). With the advent of new technology that allows for the structure and function of living brains to be analyzed, evidence is mounting that disorders which used to be considered functional in origin now appear to have organic contributions to their pathology.

Schizophrenia

Results from magnetic resonance imaging (MRI) and positron emission tomography (PET) have found structural abnormalities and decreased metabolic activity in the dorsolateral prefrontal cortex in schizophrenics (Andreasen et al., 1982; Berman, Torrey, Daniel, & Weinberger, 1992; Williamson et al., 1989). Moreover, MRI scans with schzophrenics have found diminished hippocampal regions and limbic system structures in the temporal lobe involved in modulation of emotional response and memory.

Berman et al. (1992) correlated structural and functional abnormalities in the brains of schizophrenics involved in cognitive tasks. These researchers found that normal subjects showed increased blood flow in the prefrontal cortex while taking the Wisconsin Card Sorting Test. In contrast, schizophrenic subjects showed less blood flow in the prefrontal cortex and did more poorly on the Wisconsin. Moreover, schizophrenic patients with the smallest hippocampal structures showed the greatest deficit in prefrontal blood flow. This hypoperfusion in the prefrontal cortex is likely attributable to the rich connection system between the hippocampus and the prefrontal cortex.

Studies with children (observed from the first month of life to 3 years of age) who had parents with psychiatric disorders including schizophrenia, bipolar disorder, schizoaffective disorder, and schizoid personality disorder found differences in development (Kozlovaskya & Goryunova, 1988). These children showed abnormalities in motor and sensory development. In addition to deficient motor development, auditory and visual development was also found to be disordered for these children. The authors suggested that these children's disordered psychoneurological development was related to their parent's psychiatric disorders and might in turn affect their later development.

Thus schizophrenics have brains that show altered structures which are not the result of infection or of a progressive disorder. These structures are intimately tied to memory and reasoning skills. Moreover, the more the structures are affected, the poorer the performance on cognitive measures.

Obsessive-Compulsive Disorder

The orbitofrontal cortex is suspected to be involved in obsessive compulsive disorder (OCD). Structural and metabolic differences have been found in the subcortical frontal regions in OCD patients (Garber, Ananath, Chiu, Griswold, & Oldendorf, 1989; Scarone et al., 1992). These areas of the brain correspond to regions thought to be heavily implicated in metacognition. Moreover, Abbruzzese et al. (1993) suggest that although these patients with OCD or schizophrenia show frontal lobe involvement, the neurofunctional pathways may differ between the two disorders.

Affective Disorders

The above hypothesis is further supported by the finding that affective disorder may be related to right frontal and temporal functional differences (Dawson, Klinger, Panagoitides, Hill, & Spieker, 1992; Flor-Henry, 1976). Aberrant right hemispheric brain electrical activity (EEG) has been found in adults (d'Elia & Perris, 1974) and in infants of depressed mothers (Dawson et al., 1992). Neuropsychological assessment has also found deficits on tasks measuring right hemispheric performance in depressed adults and children (Abrams & Taylor, 1980).

Recent studies of the incidence of major depression have found that in conjunction with a genetic disposition for affective disorders, an unknown environmental influence is also at work. In an epidemiological study in Sweden, an increase in bipolar or unipolar depression and suicide was found since 1940 (Gershon & Reider, 1992). This finding was corroborated by studies in Canada, the United States, and Switzerland. These findings suggest a birth-cohort effect with 15- to 19-year-olds born in the 1950s 10 times more susceptible for suicide than those born in the 1930s. Thus children of patients appear to be highly susceptible for these disorders than were their parent's siblings. Gershon and Reider (1992) conclude that "this relation clearly implies an interaction between genes and some environmental factor, which must have been changing continuously over the past few decades. The factor remains a mystery" (p. 129).

Therefore it appears that the affective disorders (unipolar and bipolar depression) show an interaction between environmental and genetic factors. These factors appear to negatively influence not only cognitive measures but also the adaptive functioning of these clients. In summary, studies with adults with diverse psychiatric diagnoses suggest that frontal dysfunction is present both behaviorally and biologically (Abbruzzese et al., 1993; Dean, 1986). Moreover, a genetic predisposition appears to exist in these disorders that interacts with environmental variables and tips the scales for some clients to the development of psychiatric disorders.

Evidence from Childhood Psychopathology

The involvement of frontal dysfunction in psychopathology has been found for children. Kusche, Cook, and Greenberg (in press) studied children with diagnoses of externalizing (i.e., ADD, conduct disorder), internalizing (i.e., anxiety, depression), and comorbid psychopathology. They concluded from this study that children with these disorders all evidenced frontal lobe dysfunction as evidenced by performance on neuropsychological measures. Further frontal lobe dysfunction was felt to be generally related to childhood psychopathology and not specific to any diagnosis.

Therefore it appears that the frontal lobe, which is charged with the regulation of behavior, is heavily implicated in both child and adult "functional" disorders (which may well have an organic as well as a psychiatric basis). The following section discusses different types of psychopathology from a functional organizational approach using data derived from both neuropsychology and personality paradigms. In order to understand more fully the impact of frontal lobe dysfunction in disordered or injured brains, it is necessary to discuss briefly the role of frontal lobes in development.

The Role and Development of Frontal Lobes in Children

Studies have recently focused on the neurodevelopment of cognitive abilities in an effort to determine when specific brain areas become functionally operational in children. These studies have focused on the frontal lobes in children because of the "executive" functions (e.g., planning, flexibility, and self-monitoring) that have been attributed to this area. It also seems necessary to investigate the emergence of the frontal lobes in children, given that the frontal lobes play so prominently in the control of human emotions in adults (Bear, 1983; Grafman, Vance, Weingartner, Salazar, & Amin, 1986).

Some suggest that the frontal lobes of children begin to develop between the ages of 4 and 7 years (Luria, 1973), whereas others hypothesize development begins in adolescence and continues up to about 24 years of age (Golden, 1981). Recent research suggests that children do exhibit behaviors thought to be mediated by the frontal lobes much earlier. Becker, Isaac, and Hynd (1987) found that 10- and 12-year-olds had mastered the capability of inhibiting motor responses, or remembering the temporal ordering of visual designs, of using strategies for memory tasks, and attending to relevant details and ignoring distracting stimuli, all of which are thought to be mediated by the frontal lobes. Six-year-olds had more difficulty inhibiting motor responses and had trouble remembering the order of designs. There appeared to be a developmental shift for 8-year-olds for inhibiting motor response, and although children at all age levels were able to verbalize directions, they were not always able to inhibit perseverative responding until about 8 years. Children in the older age ranges (10 and 12 years) also displayed verbal and nonverbal strategies to aid their performance.

Passler, Isaac, and Hynd (1985) found similarly that children progress through developmental stages showing mastery of some frontal-mediated tasks at 6 and at 8 years, whereas some tasks were not mastered even by the age of 12. These findings suggest that the greatest period of development for frontal lobe functioning occurs between the ages of 6 and 8 with continued growth beyond the 12-year level for more complex skills. Though basic research is useful for building a neurodevelopmental model for children, research with psychiatric populations can provide further information concerning the relationship between personality, intelligence, and neuropsychological functioning.

Executive Functions

One of the main roles of the frontal lobes is to carry out executive functions. Executive functions generally include four basic components: planning, goal formulation, carrying out plans, evaluation of performance (Lezak, 1983). Difficulties with executive functions have been found in children (Moffitt, 1992) and adults (Abbruzzese et al., 1993) with significant psychopathology.

ADHD

Children with executive function deficits are at risk for the development of significant psychopathology. The outcome for children with executive function deficits coupled with attention deficit hyperactivity disorder and conduct disorder has been found to be the poorest compared to any other childhood disorder (Moffitt & Henry, 1989). Moreover, early aggressive tendencies plus neuropsychological delays in early childhood were highly predictive for delinquent behavior in adolescence and criminal behavior in adulthood (Moffitt & Silva, 1988).

Children with attention deficit hyperactivity disorder (ADHD) with hyperactivity, as well as comorbid aggressive behavior, show executive function deficits on measures thought to evaluate planning, inhibition, and divided attention (Gorenstein, Mammato, & Sandy, 1989). Moreover, brain scanning techniques have found lowered metabolism in the prefrontal brain regions on sustained attention tasks in both children and adults with ADHD (Lou, Henriksen, & Bruhn, 1984; Zametkin & Rapoport, 1992). This finding serves to demonstrate that these subjects have brain metabolism differences that are translated into behavioral difficulties. Moreover, because executive function deficits have such a negative impact on day-to-day functioning, it is likely that the brain differences coupled with problematic behavior and difficulty in learning from experience often result in feelings of lowered self-esteem and efficacy.

Children with ADHD plus aggressive behavior have been found to be less popular, more disliked, and more likely to be rejected by their peers (Atkins & Pelham, 1991). In contrast, children with ADHD and withdrawn behaviors are often isolated and seem to lack social skills (Hynd et al., 1991). These children also appear to be a higher risk for mood disorders, including anxiety and depression (Hynd et al., 1991; Milich & Landau, 1989).

Thus children with ADHD with comorbid externalizing or internalizing disorders appear to be at risk not only for poorer academic achievement but also for the development of concurrent psychopathology. Using Fletcher and Taylor's (1984) paradigm of disorders and co-occurring psychopathology, it is currently unclear whether these disorders are mutually independent or whether they are interrelated; that is, it is possible that having one disorder (e.g., ADHD) makes one more vulnerable for the development of another.

Frick and Lahey (1991) suggest that ADHD should be viewed by differentiating primary symptoms from associated problems. This approach is very similar to the suggestion of Fletcher and Taylor (1984) for isolating main symptoms with correlated behaviors. Frick and Lahey (1991) suggest that the variables of inattention/disorganization and motor hyperactivity/impulsivity are the main dimensions of ADHD. Associated behaviors are poor academic achievement, problematic peer relationships, and low self-esteem. It would appear that this paradigm provides a method for understanding ADHD and for devising appropriate treatments. Because this paradigm stresses the heterogeneity of the disorder, the clinical observation that ADHD children and adolescents differ on the number of associated behaviors is supported.

Biederman and colleagues (Biederman et al., 1992; Biederman, Newcorn, & Sprich, 1991) have found that children with ADHD have a tendency to develop affective disorder in about 30% percent of cases. Moreover, children with ADHD tend to have parents and/or siblings who evidence ADHD or mood-based psychopathology. In addition, ADHD continues into adulthood for approximately 50% of subjects. In this case many of these subjects have continuing difficulty with the law, substance abuse problems, difficulty holding a job, and problems with interpersonal relationships (Biederman & Steingard, 1989).

Whether ADHD children of ADHD parents are at risk because of genetic tendencies or whether environmental variables significantly contribute to the development of comorbid disorders is not currently clear. It may well be that a biological predisposition interacts with an unfavorable environment to foster a more severe type of psychopathology.

Head Injury

Adults with executive function deficits often have experienced significant brain trauma, usually through open or closed head injuries from auto accidents. Concentration problems, along with memory difficulties, are the most common symptoms following head injury (Binder, 1986). Moreover, executive function deficits appear to be strongly tied to the degree of social and vocational recovery following injury (Sohlberg & Mateer, 1989). The most common region of damage from open or closed head injury is the frontal lobes, because of their proximity to the cranium: In a car accident, the frontal lobes are thrown forward against the skull from the momentum of the crash. The temporal pole is also susceptible to damage for the same reason.

Intelligence

Damage to the frontal lobes has not been found to adversely affect intelligence (Sohlberg & Mateer, 1989). Difficulty does arise in everyday functioning as the child or adult experiences significant difficulty in organizing and coordinating cognitive processing. Although information storage and retrieval remain intact, attention, motivation, and behavior regulation are often significantly affected. The frontal lobes appear to coordinate information from other parts of the brain. When there is impairment in this region of the brain, difficulties are often seen in setting and meeting goals and in everyday functioning, despite relatively intact intelligence. For example, Luria (1980) found that patients with lesions to the frontal lobes tended to be unable to analyze a problem systematically, see relationships between key variables, and evaluate these relationships. These patients had subsequent difficulty solving problems because of an inability to integrate the problem-solving process. Their solutions were most often fragmentary and derived from hastily scanned data.

Brain Injury and Psychiatric Sequelae in Adults

Grafman et al. (1986) investigated the effects of lateralized frontal lobe lesions to mood alterations in adults with penetrating head wounds to the orbitofrontal, dorsofrontal, and nonfrontal cortices. Individuals with left and bilateral orbitofrontal lesions did not differ from controls when reporting mood states. Right orbitofrontal patients, however, reported feelings of anger, anxiety, and panic reactions; left dorsofrontal subjects reported feelings of anger and hostility. Right frontal subjects also had a higher incidence of psychiatric problems and suffered from depression more often than nonfrontal subjects. Although left orbitofrontal subjects did not report psychological distress, individuals in this group appeared to present themselves in an exaggerated positive light, seemed more interested in philosophical issues, and appeared less concerned about interpersonal problems.

Grafman et al. (1986) further indicate that the right orbitofrontal cortex plays a role in the control of anxiety, whereas injury to the left dorsofrontal cortex may result in anger and/or hostility resulting from the disinhibition of mood states. Moreover, the authors suggest that the intensity of this disinhibition may be partially determined by the magnitude of verbal-cognitive deficits that may affect self-control, verbal mediation, and self-examination of the mood state being experienced (Grafman et al., 1986).

Impairments in frontal lobe functioning following head injury are described by clinicians as a mixture of behavioral and cognitive deficits. Problems include increased emotional lability, decreased motivation, apathy, and disinhibition (Stuss & Benson, 1986). In clients with a past history of a head injury who appear to be depressed or who seem to be highly egocentric, disinhibited, and unempathic, the clinician may wish to evaluate the neuropsychological status of the client (particularly as to social-emotional functioning), as well as looking for the usual cognitive deficits found with frontal lobe damage.

Adults with head injury often cannot adequately solve everyday problems, even though their intelligence is found to be within normal ranges. When faced with a dilemma, they utilize a trial-and-error approach and will often not stop attempting to solve the problem by an approach that has not worked (i.e., they are unable to shift their cognitive set and try another possible solution). It is evident that these types of deficits will negatively influence the persons's adjustment, as well as their ability to adapt their behavior appropriately.

Achenbach's paradigm of looking at all levels of analysis (Achenbach, 1990) is useful in assessing head-injured adults with difficulty in everyday living, particularly when assessing the changes in personality that are often seen. Animal and human studies have found that frontal lobe damage did not change the personality but rather accentuated personality traits and difficulties (Sohlberg & Mateer, 1989).

It is reasonable to speculate that latent traits are disinhibited following a brain injury and expression is given to behaviors that previously would not have been allowed to appear (Jarvie, 1954). The necessary research on premorbid personality functioning and its relationship to functioning following an accident has not been completed at this time.

Judd (1986) has developed a paradigm that describes in psychiatric terms several of the behaviors often seen in patients with head injury. For example, personality and/or conduct disorders seen in patients with head injury are more likely attributable to problems with impulsivity and social disinhibition. For these patients, thought disorders could really be the result of aphasia, anomia, or confusion. The use of personality diagnosis is not helpful for such patients and may actually be counterproductive.

Thus, when clients with neuropsychological deficits and resulting personality and behavioral difficulties are seen for standard psychotherapeutic therapy, it may be extremely difficult for the therapist without additional training in neuropsychology to assist the client (Judd, 1992). Moreover, therapists must be aware of the limitations the client has participating in traditional psychotherapy, given the lack of insight often seen with head injury.

Children

Age plays a role not only in brain development but also in outcome following trauma. A direct relationship has been found between the length of coma following a closed head injury and intelligence. Children younger than 8 years old have been found to have more severe cognitive deficiencies than children over 10 years of age (Brink, Garrett, Hale, Woo-Sam, & Nickel, 1970; Woo-Sam, Zimmerman, Brink, Uyehara, & Miller, 1970). Younger children may well be at higher risk for later cognitive deficits.

Woods (1980) has found that children injured in the first year of life tend to have severe intellectual deficits that are verbally and nonverbally based, whereas children injured after 1 year of age show more lateralized effects. For example, children with left hemisphere damage were found to evidence decreased verbal and nonverbal skills, whereas right hemisphere damage produced impaired nonverbal skills and intact language abilities (Woods, 1980). Left hemisphere damage between the ages of 5 to 12 often produces aphasia that is usually transitory. After age 16, adult-like aphasia is seen with left hemisphere damage (Boll & Barth, 1981). Teachers and parents are often unprepared to deal with the deficits in adjustment seen with children with head injury (Carney & Gerring, 1990).

Reading Deficits

Reading deficits are often a sequelae of some forms of traumatic brain injury (Klonoff, Low, &

Clark, 1977; Schaffner, Bijur, Chadwick, & Rutter, 1980) or neurodevelopmental processes, particularly in the left planum temporale in dyslexic children (Galaburda, 1991). Over time, reading deficits may affect the overall verbal intelligence, vocabulary attainment, and comprehension abilities of children (Stanovich, 1993). Thus, early brain trauma or neurodevelopmental disorders resulting in reading deficits may in effect reduce the overall knowledge acquisition capabilities of young children.

Cognitive psychologists argue that the richness and complexity of the knowledge base that an individual brings to a task allows for more sophisticated, complex learning (particularly later acquisition) and may affect the ease with which cognitive components are executed or employed during certain activities (Kolligan & Sternberg, 1987). Swanson (1982, 1993) asserts that previously acquired or learned information influences a child's ability to encode, process, and utilize new information. Reitan and Davison (1974) have long argued that despite evidence of plasticity, early damage to the immature, developing brain can have serious long-term effects. It may be that the longer the brain is "normal," the greater is its capacity to increase the richness and complexity of the knowledge base, which is ultimately related to new learning. Because brain damage appears to have its greatest effect on new learning (Hebb, 1942), children (who by definition have less accumulated knowledge and experience) would be greatly affected in their attempts for new learning. Moreover, severe deficiencies may not show up until later years, when cognitive flexibility and independent thinking are required for learning and functioning.

Because historically children with head injuries are not seen in a hospital or for rehabilitation (DiScala, Osberg, Gans, Chin, & Grant, 1991), it is possible that many adults with the cognitive, social-emotional, and language impairments often seen subsequent to head injury have been undiagnosed throughout their development. Thus these clients are high risk for continuing difficulty in everyday functioning which may be assumed to personality based but may in fact, be attributable to neuropsychological variables (Boll, 1983).

EXTERNALIZING DISORDER

Children and adolescents with externalizing disorders (i.e., aggression, inattention, overactivity, antisocial behavior) have been found to show differences in academic achievement depending on the combination of behavioral problems and the age of the child. For example, a child with attention-deficit hyperactivity disorder is at higher risk for school learning problems than a child with aggression. In contrast to younger children, a strong correlation exists between delinquent behavior and underachievement for adolescents (Hinshaw, 1992). Moreover, early learning problems have been found to be highly related to later psychopathology (Pianta & Caldwell, 1990).

Intelligence

Conduct-disordered children have been found to have significantly lower intelligence than non-conduct-disordered children (Nieves, 1991; Semrud-Clikeman, Hynd, Lorys, & Lahey, 1993). In fact, a high IQ may serve as a mitigating factor for the development of delinquent behavior in high-risk children (White, Moffitt, & Silva, 1989), as well as for adults (Kandel et al., 1988). A review by Moffitt (1992) found that for adolescent males most studies found language-related deficits, suggesting some involvement of the left hemisphere. This finding has also been detected for adult conduct-disordered males, who tend to have poorer verbal processing and less language lateralization than controls (Hare & Connoly, 1987).

Thus it would appear that a child with a tendency for conduct disorder whose cognitive development is poorer particularly in regard to language skills is at higher risk for developing significant antisocial behavior as an adolescent and as an adult. It is not currently known the contribution each variable makes to the ultimate development of an antisocial personality disorder, or which variables are correlated and which causative. It is important from the point of view of treatment, however, to realize that cognitive and language deficits appear to be significantly related to delinquent behavior. In this manner cognitive and personality variables interact and have a lot to contribute to intervention programs. Early prevention programs are sorely needed to assist in offsetting the development of delinquent behavior in high-risk children.

Conduct Disorder

There have been suggestions that conduct disordered children may possess significant neuropsychological and/or neurodevelopmental deficits. It has long been hypothesized that children with conduct disorders (CD) have poor verbal skills (Witelson,

1987), and Yeudall, Fromm-Auch, and Davies (1982) have suggested that chronic delinquents may show impairment in right frontal regions. Generally studies with delinquents have produced equivocal findings concerning the nature and extent of neuropsychological deficits present. Berman and Siegal (1976) support the notion that some juvenile delinquents are neurologically impaired. In contrast, Appellof (1986) found no differences between nonviolent delinquents and normals on several neuropsychological measures.

Linz, Hynd, Isaac, and Gibson (1988) suggest that these equivocal findings may be a result of different levels of violent and nonviolent behaviors reported in children across studies. Linz et al. investigated aggressive delinquents in an effort to determine the presence of frontal lobe dysfunction in this group. Aggressive delinquents did score poorly on measures of receptive language skills, which may account for their difficulties understanding the consequences and mediating their behaviors appropriately. McBurnett, Hynd, Lahey, and Town (1988) also found that children with conduct disorders did poorly on a word naming task and were generally deficient in expressive language skills. As was earlier suggested, a verbal deficit may negatively influence the development of neural structures, with in turn may affect intellectual development.

Using linear structural equations, Tremblay, Masse, Perron, and Leblanc (1992) found that poor school achievement in middle elementary school and adolescence is predicted by disruptive behaviors in first grade. Although first-grade achievement is related to first-grade disruption and fourth-grade achievement, the relationship between first- and fourth-grade achievement and delinquency at age 14 years diminishes once first-grade disruptive behaviors are controlled. This study clearly shows that the primary focus of intervention needs to be placed on behavioral control rather than on academic acquisition.

INTERNALIZING DISORDERS

Although some believe that internalizing disorders are more closely related than externalizing disorders to brain dysfunction in children (Tramontana & Hooper, 1989), there is a paucity of published research to support this hypothesis. Moreover, internalizing disorders such as depression have been found to co-occur with disruptive behaviors (Semrud-Clikeman & Hynd, 1991). As mentioned previously, approximately 30% to 40% of ADD children also experience depression and/or anxiety disorders (Biederman et al., 1991). Moreover, ADD children have a significantly higher tendency to have parents who have diagnoses of anxiety disorder and/or depression than children with other psychiatric diagnoses or normal children. Thus it is often difficult to obtain a sample of children with only internalizing symptomatology, and research that has done so is rare (Kusche, Cook, & Greenberg, in press).

Depression

As also mentioned earlier, depressive symptoms tend to present with neuropsychological measures that implicate frontal lobe and right hemispheric regions in adults. In a comprehensive review of the depression literature, Brumback (1988) found approximately 50% to 66% of depressed children have deficits on cognitive and sensorimotor measures associated with right hemisphere functioning. Brumback (1988) found a much lower incidence of left hemispheric dysfunction (approximately 10%), with 30% of depressed children showing bilateral dysfunction.

Children with depression have been found to perform more poorly on the Wechsler Intelligence Scale for Children-Revised (WISC-R: Wechsler, 1974) subtests of Block Design, Coding, and Digit Span (Kaslow, Rehm, & Siegel, 1984). These subtests are thought to be sensitive to right hemispheric function (Teeter, 1986). In contrast, these children have also shown average scores on measures that are thought to be sensitive to left hemisphere functioning, such as the WISC-R Vocabulary subtest or Trails A & B (Reitan, 1979).

Similar findings have been obtained with adults with depression. Lower performance than verbal scores on measures of cognitive ability (Kronfol, Hamsher, Digre, & Waziri, 1978), poorer performance on dichotic listening tasks with the right ear (Yozawitz, Bruder, Sutton, Sharpe, Gurland, Fleiss, & Costa, 1979) and deficient scores on digit symbol and paired associate learning (Berndt & Berndt, 1980) have been interpreted as a right hemisphere deficits implicated in adult depression (Kusche et al., in press).

Selected antidepressants such as desipramine have also been found to be clinically helpful for patients with ADHD (Biederman et al.,1991; Brumback, 1988). The efficacy of antidepressants with ADHD as well as depression may relate to Voeller's (1986) suggestion that ADHD may be related to right hemispheric dysfunction. Given the high comorbidity of depressive and anxiety symptoms in children with

ADHD, it is interesting that antidepressants are helpful in treatment suggesting a relationship between depression and ADHD.

Anxiety

Anxiety disorders have not been extensively studied using neuropsychological measures. Anxiety has been found to interfere with academic functioning (Strauss, 1991). performance decrements have been found on WISC-R Digit Span, Arithmetic, and Coding subtests in anxious children (Kaufman, 1979; Strauss, 1991). Children with anxious and dependent behavior who also shows signs of motor clumsiness, associated movements, and/or fine motor delays are at high risk for the development of long-term problems with anxiety and withdrawal (Shaffer et al., 1985).

Anxiety disorders have been found to be highly comorbid with ADD (Biederman et al., 1991) and depression (Brumback, 1988). It is not clear at this point what neuropsychological differences may exist between children with comorbid internalizing and externalizing disorders (e.g., conduct disorder and anxiety or depression) and those with co-occurring internalizing disorders (e.g., anxiety and depression). It is highly likely that these children present different behaviorally as well as neuropsychologically. Further research is needed in this area to determine more fully characteristics unique to each combination of diagnosis.

Kusche et al. (in press) sought to evaluate neuropsychological differences among children with internalizing-only, externalizing-only, and mixed symptoms. They found that although all groups were poorer compared to controls, the mixed-symptom group showed the most severe and widespread deficits. The internalizing-only group was the closest to the control group and showed the least amount of impairment, whereas the externalizing-only group showed moderate amounts of impairment.

The above study also looked at possible cognitive functioning among the three groups. The mixed group had the highest number of children with below-average ability,whereas the internalizing and externalizing groups showed similar scores on an estimated IQ test (WISC-R Vocabulary and Block Design). When all below-average-ability children were removed from the analysis, the clinical groups were similar in ability but below the control group in cognitive ability. Kusche et al. (in press) suggest that a higher IQ may help offset tendencies toward psychopathology. This finding has also been detected for adult samples (Sohlberg & Mateer, 1989).

Summary

From the above review it would appear that a clear demarcation between functional and organic underpinnings for many psychiatric disorders does not exist for children or adults. Many of the disorders appear to implicate frontal lobe dysfunction, with its concomitant deficits in executive function. In addition, many clients with documented brain damage have been found to have increased incidence of significant psychiatric disorder (Rutter, Chadwick, & Shaffer, 1983).

Because deficits in attention, memory, language comprehension, and/or language production negatively affect participation in and benefit from traditional psychotherapy (Parmelee & O'Shanick, 1987), the client with neuropsychological deficits requires specialized treatment in order to come to terms with the difficulties. Without use of a combined neuropsychological/psychiatric point of view, the above behaviors may be attributed to malingering, personality disorder, or oppositional behavior. The following section discusses treatment approaches for clients with neuropsychological dysfunction.

TREATMENT VARIABLES

In working with children and adults with suspected neuropsychological dysfunction, it is important not only to incorporate treatment that addresses the social and emotional difficulties experienced by the client but to also evaluate the need for rehabilitation (for the adolescent or adult) or training (for the child who has never developed the skill to be rehabilitated) as part of the intervention. Moreover, for the adolescent/adult and child, it is important that the support system be assessed and assisted in the intervention.

Before we turn to types of intervention, it is important to discuss briefly diagnostic standards that not only use the primary diagnosis but also look at the effect of this diagnosis on the person's functioning both before and after the difficulties arose. The use of a multiaxial method for diagnosis is important in order to delineate the primary diagnosis as well as the level of stress and both previous and current levels of global functioning.

Multiaxial Perspective

When diagnosing and designing intervention plans, DSM-III-R (APA, 1987) provides guidelines for a multiaxial process. The first three axes are helpful for the diagnostic phase (Axis I, Clinical Syndromes; Axis II, Developmental and Personality Disorders; Axis III, Physical Disorders and Conditions), whereas the last two axes are helpful for the intervention phase (Axis IV, Severity of Psychosocial Stressors; Axis V, Global Assessment of Functioning). Table 2 presents the multiaxial classification system of DSM-III-R. This classification approach allows for the differentiation of various features of child and adult disorders and provides a method for considering mental disorders (e.g., major depression or conduct disorder on Axis I) as well as personality disorders (e.g., obsessive-compulsive or borderline personality disorder on Axis II) that might otherwise go undiagnosed. Personality disorders may significantly affect a treatment plan if ignored. Axis II also allows for the identification of cognitive, academic, or social disorders in children (e.g., specific developmental disorders).

When designing intervention plans for individuals with personality, cognitive or social complications subsequent to brain injury or in conjunction with neurodevelopmental disorders, Axes IV and V are particularly useful. Axis IV provides a method for determining the nature and severity of psychosocial stressors, specified as either acute (onset within last 6 months) or enduring (onset more than 6 months earlier). Types of stressors include school or employment problems, family or marital problems, illness or physical injuries, or abusive or conflictual relationships. Symptoms can be classified on a continuum from mild (e.g., change of school or job) to moderate (e.g., expulsion from school, loss of job), severe (e.g., divorce), or catastrophic (e.g., sexual abuse, death of a loved one). Axis V assesses the overall functioning of the individual (including psychological, social, and occupational) currently and within the past year. The Global Assessment Functioning Scale ranges from minimal symptoms to imminent danger of severely hurting self or others.

Table 2. Examples of DSM-III-R Multiaxial Classification System

Axis I	Clinical syndromes and V codes	
	296.3x	Major depression, recurrent
	312.90	Conduct disorder, undifferentiated type
	V62.30	Academic problem
Axis II	Developmental disorders and personality disorders	
	315.00	Developmental reading disorder
	301.83	Borderline personality disorder
Axis III	Physical disorders and conditions	
	Late effects of viral encephalitis	
	Neurologic disorder associated with dementia	
Axis IV	Severity of psychosocial stressors	
	Psychosocial stressors: change of school	
	severity: 2—mild (acute event)	
	Family factor: divorce	
	Severity: 6—extreme (acute event)	
Axis V	Global assessment of functioning (GAF)	
	Current GAF: 50—serious symptoms	
	Highest GAF past year: 65—some mild symptoms	

Axes I, II, and III emphasize the need to identify disorders from a multiple perspective (i.e., to account for related but not mutually exclusive problems), whereas axes IV and V emphasize the need to assess disorders within the context of the individual's life. DSM-III-R also provides descriptors for several organic syndromes (i.e., behavioral or psychological symptoms with no specified or known etiology) and disorders (i.e., symptoms associated with known etiology). Specific categories of organic disorders/symptoms do not imply that other mental disorders are independent of brain functioning: "On the contrary, it is assumed that all psychological processes, normal and abnormal, depend on brain function" (APA, 1987, p. 98). Thus when we view brain injury or neurodevelopmental disorders within this model, we can more easily identify the associated intellectual, personality, or social features that may accompany a specific disorder. Presumably less information is lost by approaching disorders from a multiaxial model, and the manner in which disorders affect an individual's life functioning can be more readily addressed from this perspective. The use of a multidimensional/multimeasure paradigm for designing treatment plans for clients with neuropsychological difficulties is particularly important for dealing with the social and emotional difficulties. This area of psychotherapy is fairly recent and is in the developmental stage.

Initial Issues

Sensory impairments need to be evaluated before treatment or neuropsychological assessment is begun. Moreover, as mentioned earlier, the predamage personality of the injured adult is important to assess. For children and adolescents with developmental concerns, or adults with suspected past injuries, it is also very important to evaluate temperament and/or personality functioning. Temperamental/personality features such as impulsivity, reactivity, or activity level can contribute to difficulties in learning new behaviors or to higher risk for accidents.

In addition, grief reactions, anger, frustration, and depression need to be addressed when the client first learns of the difficulty now present in his or her life. A parent of a brain-damaged child or an adult with an injury needs time for adjustment and grieving for the lost skills. Children need to come to terms with the fact that they are different from their peers and from how they were in the past. McCabe and Green (1987) found that children who had suffered a brain injury were acutely aware of their lost skills. Because many children and adolescents are developing their sense of self, this development may be forestalled and/or derailed. Motivation and attentional problems may significantly interfere with the acquisition of new learning; perseverative behavior may prevent the child from changing ineffective behavior to a situation at hand. Teachers and parents need to be aware that these "behaviors" are not willful or psychopathological but possibly are related to the trauma.

Moreover, parents of a child with a head injury must also deal with the loss of their "perfect" child. For many parents, a necessary process of grieving must occur before any interventions are begun. It is important to acknowledge these feelings and provide support through family treatment in conjunction with rehabilitation efforts. It is also important for the family systems to reconnect to the client—who may no longer be the same person—after the injury (Martin, 1988).

For example, a 5-year-old girl with a severe head injury was referred to the first author for assessment. Her performance on developmental scales and the Stanford-Binet Intelligence Scale (Fourth Edition) were in the average range. Reports from her parents and teachers indicated a child who had age-appropriate social skills and was well-behaved prior to the injury. Following the injury the child showed more volatility, less ability to tolerate disruptions in routine, and more dependent behaviors. These differences continued 6 months after the injury. No neurological or psychological measures indicated deterioration of cognitive or motor skills; the neurologist felt the child was showing "emotional disturbance" not related to the injury. Therapy indicated severe parental stress and guilt over the injury and some overcompensation as a result of these feelings. The "softer" signs of problems in adjustment that appeared to be emotional in nature, however, were consistent with behavioral change often seen with traumatic brain injury. Treatment proceeded in assisting parents and teachers in training the child in methods of soothing herself, developing self-talk when she felt the need for support, and using training to help with environmental transitions both expected and unexpected.

Thus, for clients with neuropsychological difficulties, it is important to approach the emotional aftermath from a systems approach. Moreover, therapy with clients with neuropsychological disorders needs to proceed somewhat differently from traditional models as a result of disorders of attention, memory, and ability to evaluate one's own behavior. Livingston, Tyler, and Crawford (1988) studied families with head-injured members and found that most were moderately to significantly affected by the member's disorder. In addition, the level of emotional stress has not been found to be predicted by the degree of physical involvement (Brooks, Campsie, Symington, Beattie, & McKinley, 1986). Instead, emotional stress was related to the type of behavioral and emotional deficits rather than to cognitive deficits.

Neuropsychotherapy

Judd (1992) has coined the term *neuropsychotherapy* to describe therapy with brain-injured patients. Neuropsychotherapy involves helping the clients deal with their emotions, personalities, and behaviors following neuropsychological difficulty. This process incorporates behavioral management techniques with an emphasis on helping the client to regain control of his or her behaviors. For children and adolescents, parents and teachers are recruited to assist in teaching appropriate behaviors to the patient, as well as dealing with the myriad emotional and social changes experienced by him or her.

It is particularly important to involve teachers in the treatment, as schools are often not informed about changes in behavior and emotion following head injury. Behaviors that may look like anxiety, low frustration tolerance, depression, or poor motivation may be more related to moderate head injury than to personality variables. Without preparation and assistance, clients with head injuries and other trauma may experience additional unnecessary adjustment problems in school and/or employment.

Neuropsychotherapy provides for intervention within the systems in which the child/adolescent/adult is involved. Therapy needs to address the client's change in emotional reactivity and/or communication; in the case previously described, the child's emotional responses significantly increased. Moreover, she experienced difficulty with brittleness in that she was not able to change with environmental demands.

Clients may also show decreased reactivity. A middle-aged man seen by one of the authors had experienced a whiplash injury; difficulties in motivation, emotional expressiveness, and attention were seen 6 months after the injury. He was thought by his family and fellow workers to be depressed. Neuropsychological assessment showed significant frontal lobe dysfunction, however, and treatment helped him to cope with the change from being a vital participant in life to being a person who described himself "as dragging myself through what I used to like to do." He was referred for assessment and treatment by his wife; he had not recognized these problems himself. One of the goals of treatment was to assist him in increasing his awareness of his deficits, including learning how to be aware of environmental and internal cues to his emotional state.

Judd (1992) suggests that initially the family may need to take on the brunt of the responsibility for retraining. The goal is for the client to assume more of the burden for himself or herself as therapy continues. Cases with demonstrated head injury often require gradual regaining of responsibilities, with the therapist serving as a mediator between the client and his or her family.

For cases that have recovered beyond the point of caretaking, self-awareness is often a problem. The use of videotapes, mirrors, and role-playing exercises to assist in the development of self-awareness have been found to be helpful. Likewise, direct training in self-awareness training and ways to compensate for these deficits can be very useful.

A case seen by the first author illustrates the use of compensation strategies. A woman with a severe head injury who experienced significant attentional and memory was referred for therapy because of anger and severe depression over loss of previous skills. Initial sessions involved discussions of the loss of skills, as well as probing here inability to function as she had in the past. Self-awareness of deficits was particularly important, as she utilized denial of her problems. A journal for detailing problems she experienced was kept and allowed for discussions of the difficulties as well as assisting her in developing compensation. Rather than challenging her defense system, the therapist allowed her to evaluate her behavior through the use of the journal while discussing the disruption in her life. A related tactic was to help her to anticipate problems that might arise in upcoming experiences and situations. Eventually she was able to acknowledge the changes in her life, some of which appeared to be permanent. By providing her with a way of evaluating situations and selecting alternative behaviors, the therapist did not challenge her hope that she would return to her preinjury state or her need to deny problems. Instead, she was able to use the journal to reenact previous experiences in the sessions and evaluate her reactions.

Adults

At times, clients may present what appears to be strictly psychiatric disorders that may be neurologically based. In these instances, behaviors typically described in psychological or psychiatric terms may be a result of slow-growing brain tumor processes. A 32-year-old male seen by the second author was referred because of severe rage and anger control problems, sexual acting out, and emotional dyscontrol. His employment history was remarkable in that he had been frequently discharged from positions; for example, he was discharged from the army because of psychiatric problems related to his severe rage, fighting, and disorderly conduct. In the course of developing a vocational rehabilitation plan, his counselor recommended a neuropsychological and psychiatric consultation. In a routine neuropsychological assessment, frontal lobe signs emerged, and the patient reported an unusual absence of smell. Further neurological examination revealed a brain tumor in the uncus that was impeding on other frontal-limbic structures.

It is apparent from this example that the bidirectional nature of psychiatric-neuropsychological aspects must be considered when treating adults and children. In this instance, an adjustment problem was initially being treated from a primarily psychological behavioral approach, when neurological-neuropsychological approaches were also essential for properly diagnosing and treating this individual.

Treatment with Children

Treatment with children needs to take a developmental perspective and be structured so that it changes with the child's age. As mentioned earlier, the age at which the injury is experienced influences the treatment of the child. Moreover, skills that emerge at later ages may be negatively affected by damaged areas. Because these skills have not yet developed, assessment following injury may not determine a later deficit.

Executive functions that develop fully after age 10 may not evidence damage when assessed at age 5. Therefore, the therapist who works with younger children and their families needs to provide information to the families about these skills and assist in assessing them as they begin to develop. It may well be necessary to provide assistance at various ages in helping the child/adolescent compensate for difficulty experienced later.

Children may also experience more diffuse damage from head injury than adults, suffering more global cognitive, behavioral, and emotional deficits (Pirozzolo & Papanicolaou, 1986). Emotional and behavioral control deficits may affect children's ability to establish boundaries between themselves and others, recognition of others' feelings and motivations, development of empathy, and awareness of identity, all of which are developmental tasks (Lehr, 1990). Children with impulse control difficulties not only experience more negative interactions with their environments but also are at higher risk for psychopathology (Breen & Barkley, 1984). These children also show poorer social skill development.

Therapy may be necessary to assist with social skill development. Social skills may need to be directly taught. The use of role play, puppets, and videotapes may assist in recognition and labeling of emotions. Moreover, the generation of alternative behaviors can be taught as part of the social training. Social skills training programs alone are not successful with these children, as additional work may be needed in basic skills as well as application. Because of attention and memory difficulties, skills need to be reviewed, reinforced, and practiced in many situations in order for children with head injuries to profit from these interventions.

The need for a treatment plan that considers both the school and home environment is apparent from a case referred to one of the authors. An 11-year-old was referred to the second author for comprehensive neuropsychological assessment 3 years after a vehicular accident in which he had sustained a linear fracture to the frontal region medial to the right orbit and was in a coma for an extended period. Neuropsychological examination revealed severe right hemisphere deficits, with relatively intact verbal language abilities. Measures of acquired knowledge were particularly depressed as were tasks sensitive to motor speed, coordination, planning, and sequencing; reasoning and concept formation; and visual-motor integration. Social and psychological behaviors were extremely compromised, with signs of disinhibition, impulse control problems, attentional deficits, perseveration, low frustration tolerance, swearing, and emotional lability. Although overall intelligence was measured in the deficient range, the subtests of similarities and comprehension were within the average range. Despite these difficulties, this child did not quality for special services in the schools and was receiving no assistance in a regular education classroom.

The background and preinjury information of this case revealed a less than optimum situation. The child was placed in a transitional first grade because of concerns about low readiness skills, a lack of interest in learning, and poor self-help skills. The home environment was described as deprived and unstimulating; the child's parents were inconsistent in their ability to follow through on school recommendations. Preinjury formal testing indicated at least average academic and intellectual potential. Following the head injury, academic and behavioral functioning severely deteriorated from earlier measures, except for low average reading achievement. The child made virtually no progress over a 2-year period in math and the content areas of science, social studies, and the humanities. Moreover, the child's behavior was described by his parents and teachers as significantly different than that in preinjury reports. Despite recommendations from several medical teams and the parents, the child was not judged as educationally handicapped under state guidelines.

When the total picture of postinjury deficits was clearly delineated during an arbitration hearing, a new treatment plan was developed. Because of a lack of family stability and emotional/psychological/financial support, the child was placed in a residential treatment center that vigorously addressed his academic, social-emotional, and problem-solving deficits. Although signs of frontal lobe dysfunction remain, the child has made remarkable progress since this treatment change.

CONCLUSIONS

Head injury can affect several types of development. Most often, emotional and behavioral difficulties are found for children/adolescents and adults. Specialized treatment of these disorders needs to be provided in terms of not only cognitive rehabilitation but also therapy for changes in the client's ability to adapt socially and emotionally to his or her environment.

Too often, clients with head injuries (or other disorders) are treated for cognitive problems without emotional support beyond the initial adjustment period. Psychosocial and cognitive factors often interact and in turn affect the person's overall adaptation. Studies assessing long-term adaptation to head injury have found that continuing problems have been found in socialization, work/school environments, and leisure activities for as long as 5 years following injury (Lezak, 1987).

Neuropsychological assessment should be the first step in looking at difficulties in adjustment. Interventions based on such assessment can assist the client in adjustment, and they need to be continued throughout the child's development. Parents and teachers need to be prepared for problems which may occur during development. Few school systems provide inservice training for their teachers in preparation for understanding initial and later problems associated with traumatic brain injury. Given the finding that adults also tend to continue to experience difficulty in adjustment, treatment needs to prepare clients as well as their support systems for long-term difficulties they may experience.

This chapter has attempted to provide a framework for understanding the interrelationship between psychological and neuropsychological aspects of mental disorders. As we have developed the necessary technology to evaluate the living brain, it has become clear that the dichotomy between psychological and organic problems may not be as evident as previously believed. Clients who present with problems of depression, obsessiveness, motivation, attention, and/or memory may have a history of familial psychiatric problems or have experienced trauma. A thorough clinical interview is imperative to rule out possible organic contributions to these disorders. For cases that include a risk for organic contribution to psychiatric problems, neuropsychological assessment would assist in evaluating a client's strengths and weaknesses as well as in planning appropriate treatment.

As discussed earlier in this chapter, treatment varies from standard therapies when organic contributions are present. Treatment with adults and children often includes cognitive rehabilitation, with some support provided during this program. Research has demonstrated, however, that social and emotional difficulties often continue after most rehabilitation programs end. Work with employers, teachers, and social support systems is indicated. Training for teachers, parents, spouses, and relatives of these affected clients needs to be included in any treatment program. Thus a functional organization program would emphasize all of these aspects and provide the client with the most comprehensive program possible.

REFERENCES

Abbruzzese, M., Ferris, S., Bellodi, L., & Scarone, S. (1993). Frontal lobe dysfunction in mental illness. *Psycoloquy, 93*, 1–13.

Abrams, R., & Taylor, M. A. (1980). A comparison of unipolar and bipolar depressive illness. *American Journal of Psychiatry, 137*, 1084.

Achenbach, R. (1990). Conceptualizations of developmental psychopathology. In M. Lewis & S. Miller (Eds.), *Handbook of developmental psychopathology* (pp. 3–13). New York: Plenum.

American Psychiatric Association. (1987). *Diagnostic and statistical manual of mental disorders* (rev. 3rd ed.). Washington, DC: Author.

Andreasen, N. C., Olsen, S. A., Dennert, J. W., & Smith, M. R. (1982). Ventricular enlargement in schizophrenia: Relationship to positive and negative symptoms. *American Journal of Psychiatry, 139*, 297–302.

Appellof, E. (1986). Prefrontal lobe functions in juvenile delinquents (Wisconsin Card Sorting Test). *Dissertation Abstracts International, 46*(9), 3206B.

Atkins, M. S., & Pelham, W. E. (1991). School-based assessment of attention deficit-hyperactivity disorder. *Journal of Learning Disabilities, 24*, 197–204.

Bear, D. M. (1983). Hemispheric specialization and the neurology of emotions. *Archives of Neurology, 40*, 195–202.

Becker, M., Isaac, W., & Hynd, G. W. (1987). Neuropsychological development of nonverbal behaviors attributed to "frontal lobe" functioning. *Developmental Neuropsychology, 3*, 275–298.

Berman, A., & Siegal, A. (1976). Adaptive and learning skills in juvenile delinquents: A neuropsychological analysis. *Journal of Learning Disabilities, 9*(9), 51–58.

Berman, K. F., Torrey, E. F., Daniel, D. G., & Weinberger, D. R. (1992). Regional cerebral blood flow in monozygotic twins discordant and concordant for schizophrenia. *Archives of General Psychiatry, 49*, 927–934.

Berndt, D. J., & Berndt, S. M. (1980). Relationship of mild depression to psychological deficit in college students. *Journal of Clinical Psychology, 36*, 868–874.

Biederman, J., Faraone, S. V., Keenan, K., Benjamin, J., Krifcher, B., Moore, C., et al. (1992). Further evidence for family-genetic risk factors in attention deficit hyperactivity disorder. *Archives of General Psychiatry, 49*, 728–738.

Biederman, J., Newcorn, J., & Sprich, S. (1991). Comorbidity of attention deficit hyperactivity disorder with conduct, depressive, anxiety, and other disorders. *American Journal of Psychiatry, 148*, 564–577.

Biederman, J., & Steingard, R. (1989). Attention deficit hyperactivity disorder in adolescents. *Psychiatric Annals, 19,* 587–596.

Binder, L. M. (1986). Persisting symptoms after mild head injury: A review of post concussive syndrome. *Journal of Clinical and Experimental Neuropsychology, 8,* 323–346.

Boll, T. J. (1983). Minor head injury in children: Out of sight but not out of mind. *Journal of Clinical Child Psychology, 12,* 74–80.

Boll, T. J., & Barth, J. T. (1981). Neuropsychology of brain damage in children. In S. B. Filskov & T. J. Boll (Eds.), *Handbook of clinical neuropsychology.* New York: Wiley.

Breen, M. J., & Barkley, R. A. (1984). Psychological adjustment in learning disabled, hyperactive, and hyperactive/learning disabled children as measured by the Personality Inventory for Children. *Journal of Clinical Child Psychology, 13,* 232–236.

Brink, J., Garrett, A., Hale, W., Woo-Sam, J., & Nickel, V. (1970). Recovery of motor and intellectual function in children sustaining severe head injuries. *Developmental Medicine and Child Neurology, 12,* 565–571.

Brooks, L., Campsie, L., Symington, C., Beattie, A., & McKinley, W. (1986). The five year outcome of severe blunt head injury: A relative's view. *Journal of Neurology, Neurosurgery, and Psychiatry, 49,* 764–770.

Brumback, R. A. (1988). Child depression and medically treatable learning disability. In D. L. Molfese & S. J. Segalowitz (Eds.), *Brain lateralization in children: Developmental implications* (pp. 463–505). New York: Guilford.

Carney, J., & Gerring, J. (1990). Return to school following severe closed head injury: A critical phase in pediatric rehabilitation. *Pediatrician, 17,* 222–229.

Cattaneo, A. M., Biserni, P., Cazzullo, C. L., Locatelli, M., Gambini, O., & Scarone, S. (1988). Neurofunctional assessment of obsessive-compulsive disorder: A comparative and methodological analysis. *Schizophrenia Research, 2,* 57.

Cook, E. H., & Leventhal, B. L. (1992). Neuropsychiatric disorders of childhood and adolescence. In S. C. Yudofsky & R. E. Hales (Eds.), *Textbook of neuropsychiatry* (pp. 639–662). Washington, DC: American Psychiatric Press.

Dawson, G., Klinger, L. G., Panagiotides, H., Hill, D., & Spieker, S. (1992). Frontal lobe activity and affective behavior of infants of mothers with depressive symptoms. *Child Development, 63,* 725–737.

Dean, R. S. (1985). Neuropsychological assessment. In J. D. Cavenar, R. Michels, H. K. H. Brodie, A. M. Cooper, S. B. Guze, L. L. Judd, G. L. Klerman, & A. J. Solnit (Eds.), *Psychiatry.* Philadelphia: Lippincott.

Dean, R. S. (1986). Neuropsychological aspects of psychiatric disorders. In J. Obrzut & G. W. Hynd (Eds.), *Child neuropsychology* (Vol. 2, pp. 83–112). New York: Academic Press.

d'Elia, G., & Perris, C. (1974). Cerebral functional dominance and depression: An analysis of EEG amplitude in depressed patients. *Acta Psychiatrica Scandinavica, 49,* 191.

Dimond, S. J., Farrington, L., & Johnson, P. (1976). Differing emotional responses from right and left hemispheres. *Nature, 261,* 690–692.

DiScala, C., Osberg, J. S., Gans, B. M., Chin, L. J., & Grant, C. C. (1991). Children with traumatic head injury: Morbidity and post acute treatment. *Archives of Physical and Medical Rehabilitation, 72,* 662–666.

Fletcher, J., & Taylor, H. (1984). Neuropsychological approaches to children: Towards a developmental neuropsychology. *Journal of Clinical Neuropsychology, 6,* 39–56.

Flor-Henry, P. (1976). Lateralized temporo-limbic dysfunction and psychopathology. *Annals of the New York Academy of Sciences, 280,* 777–797.

Frick, P., & Lahey, B. B. (1991). Nature and characteristics of attention deficit hyperactivity disorder. *School Psychology Review, 20,* 163–173.

Galaburda, A. (1991). Anatomy of dyslexia: Argument against phrenology. In D. Duane & D. Gray (Eds.), *The reading brain: The biological basis of dyslexia* (pp. 119–131). Parkton, MD: York.

Garber, H. J., Ananath, J. V., Chiu, L. C., Griswold, V. J., & Oldendorf, W. H. (1989). Nuclear magnetic resonance study of obsessive-compulsive disorder. *American Journal of Psychiatry, 146,* 1001–1005.

Gershon, E. S., & Reider, R. O. (1992). Major disorders of mind and brain. *Scientific American,* 127–133.

Geschwind, N. (1965). Disconnection syndromes in animals and man. *Brain, 88,* 237–294.

Golden, C. (1981). The Luria-Nebraska Children's Battery: Theory formulation. In G. W. Hynd & J. Obrzut (Eds.), *Neuropsychological assessment and the school-aged child* (pp. 277–302). New York: Grune and Stratton.

Gorenstein, E. E., Mammato, C. A., & Sandy, J. M. (1989). Performance of inattentive-overactive children on selected measures of prefrontal-type function. *Journal of Clinical Psychology, 45,* 619–632.

Grafman, J., Vance, S., Weingatner, H., Salazar, A., & Amin, D. (1986). The effects of lateralized frontal lobe lesions on mood regulation. *Brain, 109,* 1127–1148.

Hare, R. D., & Connoly, J. F. (1987). Perceptual asymmetries and information processing in psychopaths. In S. A. Mednick & T. E. Moffitt (Eds.), *Biology and antisocial behavior.* New York: Cambridge University Press.

Heaton, R., Baade, L., & Johnson, L. (1978). Neuropsychological test results associated with psychiatric disorders in adults. *Psychological Bulletin, 85,* 141–163.

Hebb, D. O. (1942). The effect of early and late brain injury on test scores, and the nature of normal adult intelligence. *Proceedings of the American Philosophical Society, 85,* 275–292.

Heilman, K. M., Schwartz, H. D., & Watson, R. T. (1978). Hypoarousal in patients with neglect syndrome and emotional indifference. *Neurology, 29,* 229–232.

Hertzig, M. E. (1982). Stability and change in nonfocal neurological signs. *Journal of the American Academy of Child Psychiatry, 21,* 231–236.

Hinshaw, S. P. (1992). Externalizing behavior problems and academic underachievement in childhood and adolescence: Causal relationships and underlying mechanisms. *Psychological Bulletin, 111,* 127–155.

Hynd, G. W., Lorys, A. R., Semrud-Clikeman, M., Nieves, N., Huettner, M. I. S., & Lahey, B. B. (1991). Attention deficit disorder without hyperactivity (ADD/WO): A distinct behavioral and neurocognitive syndrome. *Journal of Child Neurology* (Supplement), 17–25.

Hynd, G. W., & Semrud-Clikeman, M. (1990). Neuropsychological assessment. In A. S. Kaufman (Ed.), *Assessing adolescent and adult intelligence* (pp. 638–748). Boston: Allyn & Bacon.

Hynd, G. W., & Willis, W. G. (1988). *Pediatric neuropsychology.* Orlando, FL: Grune & Stratton.

Jarvie, H. F. (1954). Frontal lobe wounds causing disinhibition: A study of six cases. *Journal of Neurology, Neurosurgery, and Psychiatry, 17,* 14–32.

Jarvik, M. E. (1977). *Psychopharmacology in the practice of medicine.* New York: Appleton-Century-Crofts.

Judd, T. (1986). *Assessment and interventions for major symptoms of brain damage*. Workshop in Managua, Nicaragua.

Judd, T. (1992). *Neuropsychotherapy: Psychotherapeutic techniques for brain injured clients*. Workshop at the Washington State Psychological Association, Seattle.

Kandel, E., Mednick, S. A., Kirkegaard-Sorenson, L., Hutchings, B., Knop, J., Rosenberg, R., & Schulsinger, F. (1988). *Journal of Consulting and Clinical Psychology, 56*, 224–226.

Kaslow, N., Rehm, L., & Siegel, A. (1984). Social-cognitive and cognitive correlates of depression in children. *Journal of Abnormal Child Psychology, 12*, 605–620.

Kaufman, A. S. (1979). *Intelligent testing with the WISC-R*. New York: Guilford.

Klonoff, H., Low, M. D., & Clark, C. (1977). Head injuries in children: A prospective five year follow-up. *Journal of Neurology, Neurosurgery, and Psychiatry, 40*, 1211–1219.

Kolb, B., & Whishaw, I. (1980). *Fundamentals of human neuropsychology*. San Francisco: Freeman.

Kolb, B., & Whishaw, I. (1985). *Fundamentals of human neuropsychology* (2nd ed.). San Francisco: Freeman.

Kolligan, J., & Sternberg, R. J. (1987). Intelligence, information processing and specific learning disabilities: A triarchic synthesis. *Journal of Learning Disabilities, 20*, 8–17.

Kozlovskaya, G. V., & Goryunova, A. V. (1988). Psychological disintegration during the early development of children at high risk for endogenous mental disorders. *Soviet Neurology and Psychiatry, 21*, 26–35.

Kronfol, Z., Hamsher, K. D., Digre, K., & Waziri, R. (1978). Depression and hemispheric functions: Changes associated with unilateral ECT. *British Journal of Psychiatry, 132*, 560–567.

Kusche, C. A., Cook, E. T., & Greenberg, M. T. (in press). Neuropsychological and cognitive functioning in children with internalizing, externalizing, and comorbid psychopathology. *Journal of Clinical Child Psychology*.

Lehr, E. (1990). A developmental perspective. In E. Lehr (Ed.), *Psychological management of traumatic brian injuries in children and adolescents* (pp. 41–98). Rockville, MD: Aspen.

Lenneberg, E. H. (1967). *Biological foundations of language*. New York: Wiley.

Lezak, M. D. (1983). *Neuropsychological assessment* (2nd ed.). New York: Oxford University Press.

Lezak, M. D. (1987). Relationships between personality disorders, social disturbances, and physical disability following traumatic brain injury. *Journal of Head Trauma Rehabilitation, 2*, 57–69.

Linz, T., Hynd, G. W., Isaac, W., & Gibson, D. (1988). Do behaviors attributed to frontal lobe functioning discriminate between aggressive conduct disordered juvenile delinquents? *Archives of Neuropsychology, 1*, 29–35.

Livingston, R., Taylor, J. L., & Crawford, S. L. (1988). A study of somatic complaints and psychiatric diagnosis in children. *Journal of the American Academy of Child and Adolescent Psychiatry, 27*, 185–187.

Lou, H. C., Henriksen, L., & Bruhn, P. (1984). Focal cerebral hypoperfusion in children with dysphasia and/or attentional deficit disorder. *Archives of Neurology, 41*, 825–829.

Luria, A. R. (1973). *The working brain*. New York: Basic Books.

Luria, A. S. (1980). *Higher cortical functions in man* (2nd ed.). New York: Basic Books.

Martin, D. A. (1988). Children and adolescents with traumatic brain injury: Impact on the family. *Journal of Learning Disabilities, 21*, 464–470.

McBurnett, K., Hynd, G. W., Lahey, B., & Town, P. (1988). Do neuropsychological measures contribute to the prediction of academic achievement? *Journal of Psychoeducational Assessment, 6*, 162–167.

McCabe, R. J. R., & Green, D. (1987). Rehabilitating severely head-injured adolescents: Three case reports. *Journal of Child Psychiatry and Psychology, 28*, 111–126.

Mesulam, M. (1985). *Principles of behavioral neurology*. Philadelphia: Davis.

Milich, R., & Landau, S. (1989). The role of social status variables in differentiating subgroups of hyperactive children. In L. M. Bloomingdale & J. Swanson (Eds.), *Attention deficit disorder: Current concepts and emerging trends in attentional and behavioral disorders of childhood* (Vol. 5, pp. 1–16). Elmsford, NY: Pergamon.

Moffitt, T. E. (1992, April). *The neuropsychology of conduct disorder*. Paper presented at NIMH workshop on conduct disorders, Washington, DC.

Moffitt, T. E., & Henry, B. (1989). Neuropsychological assessment of executive functions in self-reported delinquents. *Development and Psychopathology, 1*, 105–118.

Moffitt, T. E., & Silva, P. A. (1988). IQ and delinquency: A direct test of the differential detection hypothesis. *Journal of Abnormal Psychology, 97*, 330–333.

Nieves, N. (1991). Childhood psychopathology and learning disabilities: Neuropsychological relationships. In J. E. Obrzut and G. W. Hynd (Eds.), *Neuropsychological foundations of learning disabilities* (pp. 113–146). San Diego, CA: Academic press.

Parmelee, D. X., & O'Shanick, G. J. (1987). Neuropsychiatric interventions with head injured children and adolescents. *Brain Injury, 1*, 41–47.

Passler, M., Isaac, W., & Hynd, G. W. (1985). Neuropsychological behavior attributed to frontal lobe functioning in children. *Developmental Neuropsychology, 1*, 349–370.

Pianta, R. C., & Caldwell, C. B. (1990). Stability of externalizing symptoms from kindergarten to first grade and factors related to instability. *Development and Psychopathology, 2*, 247–258.

Pirozzolo, F. J., & Papanicolaou, A. C. (1986). Plasticity and recovery of function in the central nervous system. In J. E. Obzrut & G.W. Hynd (Eds.), *Child neuropsychology: Theory and research* (Vol. 1, pp. 10–21). San Diego: Academic Press.

Reitan, R. M. (1979). *Manual for administration of neuropsychological test batteries for adults and children*. Tucson, AZ: Author.

Reitan, R. M., & Davison, L. (1974). *Clinical neuropsychology: Current status and applications*. New York: Wiley.

Reitan, R. M., & Wolfson, D. (1985). *Neuroanatomy and neuropathology: A clinical guide for neuropsychologists*. Tucson, AZ: Neuropsychology Press.

Ross, E. D. (1981). The aprosodias: Functional-anatomical organization of the affective components of language in the right hemisphere. *Archives of Neurology, 38*, 561–569.

Rutter, M., Chadwick, O., & Shaffer, D. (1983). Head injury. In M. Rutter (Ed.), *Developmental neuropsychiatry* (pp. 83–111). New York: Guilford.

Scarone, S., Colombo, C., Livian, S., Abbruzzese, M., Ronchi, P., Locatelli, M., Scotti, G., & Smeraldi, E. (1992). Increased right caudate nucleus size in obsessive-compulsive disorder (OCD): Detection with magnetic resonance imaging. *Psychiatry Research, 45*, 115–121.

Schaffner, D., Bijur, P., Chadwick, O., & Rutter, M. (1980). Head injury and later reading disability. *Journal of the American Academy of Child Psychiatry, 19*, 592–610.

Semrud-Clikeman, M., & Hynd, G. W. (1990). Right hemispheric dysfunction in nonverbal learning disabilities: Social, academic, and adaptive functioning in adults and children. *Psychological Bulletin, 107*, 196–209.

Semrud-Clikeman, M., & Hynd, G. W. (1991). Review of issues and measures in childhood depression. *International Journal of School Psychology, 12*, 275–288.

Semrud-Clikeman, M., Hynd, G. W., Novey, E. S., & Eliopulos, D. (1991). Dyslexia and brain morphology: Relationships between neuroanatomical variation and neurolinguistic tasks. *Learning and Individual Differences, 3*, 225–242.

Semrud-Clikeman, M., Lorys, A. R., Hynd, G. W., & Lahey, B. B. (1993). Differential diagnosis of children with ADD/H and ADD with co-occurring conduct disorder: Discriminant validity of neurocognitive measures. *School Psychology International, 14*, 361–370.

Shaffer, D., Schoenfeld, I., O'Connor, P. A., Stokman, C., Trautman, P., Shafer, S., & Ng, S. (1985). Neurological soft signs. *Archives of General Psychiatry, 42*, 342–351.

Sohlberg, M. M., & Mateer, C. A. (1989). *Introduction to cognitive rehabilitation: Theory and practice*. New York: Guilford.

Stanovich, K. E. (1993). The construct validity of discrepancy definitions of reading disability. In G. R. Lyon, D. B. Gray, J. F. Kavanagh, & N. A. Krasnegor (Eds.), *Better understanding learning disabilities: New views from research and their implications for education and public policies* (pp. 273–308). Baltimore, MD: Brookes.

Strauss, C. S. (1991). Anxiety disorders of childhood and adolescence. *School Psychology Review, 19*, 142–157.

Stuss, D., & Benson, F. (1986). *The frontal lobes*. New York: Raven.

Swanson, H. L. (1982). A multidimensional model for assessing learning-disabled student's intelligence: An information-processing framework. *Learning Disabilities Quarterly, 5*, 312–326.

Swanson, H. L. (1993). Learning disabilities from the perspective of cognitive psychology. In G. R. Lyon, D. B. Gray, J. F. Kavanagh, & N. A. Krasnegor (Eds.), *Better understanding learning disabilities: New views from research and their implications for education and public policies* (pp. 199–228). Baltimore, MD: Brookes.

Taylor, E. A. (1983). Measurement issues and approaches. In M. Rutter (Ed.), *Developmental neuropsychiatry* (pp. 239–248). New York: Guilford.

Teeter, P. A. (1986). Standard neuropsychological batteries for children. In J. Obzrut & G. W. Hynd (Eds.), *Child neuropsychology: Clinical practice* (Vol. 2, pp. 187–228). New York: Academic Press.

Tramontana, M. B., & Hooper, S. R. (1989). Neuropsychology of child psychopathology. In C. R. Reynolds & E. Fletcher-Janzen (Eds.), *Handbook of clinical child neuropsychology* (pp. 87–106). New York: Plenum.

Tramontana, M. G., Sherrets, S. D., & Golden, C. J. (1980). Brain dysfunction in youngsters with psychiatric disorders: Application of Selz-Reitan rules for neuropsychological diagnosis. *Clinical Neuropsychology, 2*. 118–123.

Tranel, D. (1992). Functional neuroanatomy: Neuropsychological correlates of cortical and subcortical damage. In S. C. Yudofsky & R. E. Hales (Eds.), *Textbook of neuropsychiatry* (pp. 57–88). Washington, DC: American Psychiatric Press.

Tremblay, R. E., Masse, B., Perron, D., & Leblanc, M. (1992). Early disruptive behavior, poor school achievement, delinquent behavior, and delinquent personality: Longitudinal analyses. *Journal of Consulting and Clinical Psychology, 60*, 64–72.

Voeller, K. K. S. (1986). Right-hemisphere deficit syndrome in children. *American Journal of Psychiatry, 143*, 1004–1009.

Wechsler, D. (1974). *Manual for the Wechsler Intelligence Scale for Children-Revised*. New York: Psychological Corporation.

White, J. L., Moffitt, T. E., & Silva, P. A. (1989). A prospective replication of the protective effects of IQ in subjects at high risk for juvenile delinquency. *Journal of Consulting and clinical Psychology, 57*, 719–724.

Williamson, P. C., Kutcher, S. P., Cooper, P. W., Gary-Snow, W., Szalai, J. P., Kaye, H., Morrison, S. L., Willinsky, R. A., & Mamelak, M. (1989). Psychological, topographic EEG and CT scan correlates of frontal lobe function in schizophrenia. *Psychiatry Research, 29*, 137–149.

Witelson, S. (1987). Neurobiological aspects of language in children. *Child Development, 58*, 653–688.

Woods, B. T. (1980). The restricted effects of right-hemisphere lesions after age one: Wechsler test data. *Neuropsychologia, 18*, 65–70.

Woo-Sam, J., Zimmerman, I. L., Brink, J. A., Uyehara, K., & Miller, A. R. (1970). Socioeconomic status and post-traumatic intelligence in children with severe head injuries. *Psychological Reports, 27*, 147–153.

Yeudall, L., Fromm-Auch, D., & Davies, P. (1982). Neuropsychological impairment in persistent delinquency. *Journal of Nervous and Mental Disease, 170*, 257–265.

Yozawitz, A., Bruder, G., Sutton, S., Sharpe, L., Gurland, B., Fleiss, J., & Costa, L. (1979). Dichotic perception: Evidence for right hemisphere dysfunction in affective psychosis. *British Journal of Psychiatry, 135*, 224–237.

Zametkin, M. D., Nordahl, T. E., Gross, M., King, A. C., Semple, W. E., Rumsey, J., Hamburger, S., & Cohen, R. M. (1990). Cerebral glucose metabolism in adults with hyperactivity of childhood onset. *New England Journal of Medicine, 323*, 1361–1366.

30

Intelligence and Personality in Criminal Offenders

David J. Baxter, Laurence L. Motiuk, and Sylvie Fortin

The notion that criminal behavior is a product of aberrant cognitive processing or fundamental character defects has a long history, apparent in the early concepts of "moral imbecility" and "moral insanity" popularized in the 1800s. At one point, it was even suggested that mental deficiency was the chief cause of criminal behavior (Caplan, 1965; Pichot, 1978). In contrast, some of the major criminological theories of the past few decades, dominated by a more sociological orientation, have discounted individual psychological factors entirely, viewing crime as an outcome of certain societal forces and inequalities (see Andrews & Wormith, 1989).

Picking a path through the literature on intelligence and personality in offenders is not an easy task. At times, one gets the impression of two camps headed in different directions—on the one hand, criminologists with limited knowledge of psychology or psychometrics, and on the other, psychologists with as limited an understanding of crime and delinquency—and sometimes arriving at quite different conclusions from the same empirical evidence (see Andrews & Wormith, 1989). The literature consists of a rather diverse portfolio of studies of delinquents, psychopaths, and adult criminals, all subsumed under the general category of criminal offenders. Moreover, for virtually every positive finding of intellectual or personality differences between offenders and nonoffenders, there is also a negative finding.

One major reason for this is that many of the studies are characterized by the use of heterogeneous offender groups, groups defined on the basis of rather loose criteria, and inappropriate control or comparison groups often lacking even rudimentary matching procedures. For example, in different studies, subjects have been identified as psychopaths on the basis of psychiatric diagnosis, scores from various personality tests, Cleckley's (1964) criteria, or Hare's (1983) Psychopathy Checklist. The absence of uniformity in measures or operational definitions makes comparing across studies difficult, because it is not at all clear that different studies are examining the same or even a similar population. By the same token, comparing average or below-average IQ delinquents to bright high school students, or incarcerated criminals to hospitalized schizophrenics, would seem to have little potential for advancing our knowledge about crime and delinquency.

Although there is some convergence among the various formulations, psychopathy is not a unitary concept. The syndrome is defined by a list of person-

David J. Baxter • University of Ottawa and Ministry of Correctional Services, Rideau Treatment Centre, Merrickville, Ontario K0G 1N0, Canada. Laurence L. Motiuk • Carleton University and Correctional Service of Canada, Ottawa, Ontario K1A 0P9, Canada. Sylvie Fortin • School of Psychology, University of Ottawa, Ottawa, Ontario K1N 6N5, Canada.

International Handbook of Personality and Intelligence, edited by Donald H. Saklofske and Moshe Zeidner. Plenum Press, New York, 1995.

ality or behavioral characteristics (e.g., lack of anxiety or guilt, egocentricity, lack of empathy), with Cleckley (1964) providing what has become the most influential description. Other writers added emphasis on impulsivity, sensation seeking, and impaired social cognition, and distinguished between the primary or "true" psychopath and the secondary or neurotic psychopath, who shows evidence of psychological distress (see Hare, 1970; Hare & Schalling, 1978; Quay, 1965). There is less agreement on issues of measurement or operationalization (Hare & Cox, 1978). Quay (1965) and Hare (1970) both stress that constructs such as psychopathy are best understood as dimensions, with different individuals exhibiting the symptoms to varying degrees, rather than discrete typologies. This appears to have had limited impact on the research literature, however, where the use of cutoff scores on various measures is still not uncommon.

Whereas psychopathy is defined in terms of behavioral or personality characteristics, delinquency and criminality refer only to antisocial or criminal acts, with no inherent assumptions about underlying traits or causes. Delinquency is defined as behavior that is illegal, immoral, and/or deviant with respect to prevailing societal values and mores. As Wirt and Briggs (1965) observe, these three dimensions of delinquency are somewhat independent: For example, not all delinquent behavior is necessarily either illegal or immoral. Thus interpretation of some delinquency studies is difficult because of the mixing of petty delinquents with more serious criminal offenders. Criminality, in contrast, is defined in terms of contravention of existing laws, so that there is little or no ambiguity at a given point in time as to what constitutes illegal behavior. Nonetheless, criminal acts may include behaviors that are not necessarily offensive to all members of a society or even antisocial (see Fishbein, 1990).

The extent to which psychopathy, delinquency, and criminality overlap empirically is difficult to determine. Rates of diagnosis of psychopathy vary for different settings, but typical estimates are that about 30% of incarcerated criminals are psychopaths and that they are responsible for a disproportionate share of total criminal acts (Hare, 1983; Hare & Jutai, 1983). Nevertheless, it has been noted that there are probably many psychopaths who avoid detection by the criminal justice system, and that many of the most persistent criminals are not psychopaths (Fishbein, 1990; Trasler, 1978). Thus, although research on psychopathy has produced some intriguing findings, implications for the general offender population may be limited.

The persistence or chronicity of antisocial behavior is also a critical factor, particularly in delinquency studies. Certain types of delinquent behavior appear to be rather common among adolescents of varying socioeconomic and ethnic backgrounds, but "only a small minority . . . exhibit serious or persistent involvement" (Tolan & Thomas, 1988, p. 307). Recent research has revealed some important differences between individuals who "drop out" of the delinquent process and those who persist through adolescence into their adult years (Loeber & Stouthamer-Loeber, 1987; Patterson, Capaldi, & Bank, 1991; Patterson, De Baryshe, & Ramsey, 1989; Tolan & Thomas, 1988). The distinction between transient delinquency and persistent delinquency or criminality, however, is rarely acknowledged or addressed in studies of intelligence and personality in offenders.

These issues (i.e., differences in theoretical orientation, the diversity of offender populations, the persistence of criminal behavior, and problems of definition and measurement) permeate the offender research literature to such an extent that synthesis of the major findings is often quite difficult. The reader should keep these points in mind as we consider some of the issues more specifically related to intellectual and personality factors in offenders and attempt to highlight some of the more consistent or replicable findings.

INTELLECTUAL FACTORS

Although some early studies used instruments such as the Binet or the Wechsler-Bellevue Intelligence Scale (see Caplan, 1965), most of the research on intellectual functioning in offenders has employed the original or revised versions of the Wechsler Adult Intelligence Scale (WAIS) or the Wechsler Intelligence Scale for Children (WISC).[1] The Wechsler scales consist of six verbal subtests (Information, Vocabulary, Arithmetic, Similarities, Comprehension,

[1]The abbreviations WAIS and WISC are used here generically to refer to both the original and revised versions of these tests. Several other measures (e.g., the Quick Test, Raven's Progressive Matrices, the Porteus Mazes, the Shipley Institute of Living Scale) have also been used in offender research; they are not reviewed here because of the restricted range of abilities evaluated by the tests or, in some cases, because of questions about their psychometric properties.

Digit Span) and five performance subtests (Picture Completion, Picture Arrangement, Block Design, Object Assembly, Digit Symbol on the WAIS or Coding on the WISC), yielding scores for verbal, performance, and full-scale IQ, each with a mean of 100 and a standard deviation of 15. A few recent studies have used the Multidimensional Aptitudes Battery (MAB; Jackson, 1984); a multiple-choice test. The 10 MAB subtests correlate well with and tap the same dimensions as their WAIS counterparts, though the correlations are better for the verbal subtests than for the performance subtests. Nine of the subtests have the same names as their WAIS equivalents, and the tenth (Spatial) corresponds to Block Design; there is no MAB equivalent for Digit Span. The MAB has the advantage that it can be group administered, making it useful for routine testing with large samples.

The weight of recent evidence suggests that intelligence does play a role in crime and delinquency. The relationship is neither simple nor direct, however, but rather seems to involve an interaction with various situational, demographic, and personality factors. Low IQ tends to be associated with poor school performance, conduct disorders, and other factors that are predictive of delinquency and poor sociobehavioral adjustment (Fishbein, 1990; Hirschi & Hindelang, 1977; Quay, 1987; White, Moffitt, Earls, Robins, & Silva, 1990). Moreover, there is some evidence that high IQ may "protect" high-risk children from some of the developmental factors predictive of delinquency and criminality; conversely, "low IQ may increase vulnerability to delinquency during adolescence even in boys who [are] not antisocial as preschoolers" (White, Moffitt, & Silva, 1989, p. 723). Although IQ is also correlated with socioeconomic status, the protective effect of high IQ is evident even after controlling for this (Hirschi & Hindelang, 1977; Quay, 1987), as well as for the possibility that more intelligent delinquents might simply be more adept at evading detection of their antisocial acts (Moffitt & Silva, 1988; Quay, 1987). Thus, although there is no direct link between low IQ and crime, intelligence appears to function as a moderator variable in children and adolescents, interacting with more directly associated risk factors to determine delinquency outcome.

The focus of more recent research has shifted from global intelligence to specific aspects of intellectual or cognitive functioning. The relevant literature on offenders can be summarized as two broad categories: studies of discrepancies between verbal and performance IQ, and studies of specific subtest scores or patterns.

Verbal-Performance IQ Discrepancies

Wechsler (1958) observed that delinquents and psychopaths, with "occasional exceptions" generally reflecting "some special ability or disability" (p. 176), obtained higher scores for performance than for verbal IQ (hereafter P > V) on the Wechsler intelligence scales. He characterized this as "the most outstanding single feature of the "sociopath" (p. 176). Although numerous studies have observed high frequencies of P > V in various delinquent or criminal populations (Cornell & Wilson, 1992; Lueger & Cadman, 1982; Moffitt & Silva, 1988; Walsh, 1992), there have also been many negative or inconclusive findings (Caplan, 1965; Guertin, Ladd, Frank, Rabin, & Hiester, 1966, 1971).

The P > V sign appears to reflect depressed verbal IQ (VIQ) in delinquents more than differences in performance IQ (PIQ; Andrew, 1977, 1981; Quay, 1987), with the latter generally in the normal range and the former in the low-normal range. Blatt and Allison (1981) suggest that P > V is common in offenders because they are "generally 'action-oriented' people who are unable to establish the delay necessary for dealing with questions requiring thought and concentration and internal elaboration"; they do better on the performance subtests because "they are much more comfortable with tasks requiring manipulation and action" (p. 205).

Part of the reason for the many inconsistencies in research findings is inadequate matching in the criminal and noncriminal samples (Caplan, 1965; Fishbein, 1990). For example, P > V has been shown to be related to ethnicity (De Wolfe & Ryan, 1984), education (Pernicano, 1986), poor verbal or reading skills (Andrew, 1981; De Wolfe & Ryan, 1984), and socioeconomic class (Caplan, 1965). Such factors are unequally represented in delinquent and nondelinquent populations, but many studies have failed to control for this. Pernicano (1986) notes that "individuals with personality disorders have often done poorly at school and may have difficulty in problem-solving, both of which are reflected in poorer scores on Information and Arithmetic subtests and may result in an overall poorer Verbal IQ" (p. 542). Wechsler (1958) himself cautioned that "the significance between a subject's Verbal and Performance score cannot be interpreted *carte blanche* but only after due weight is given to the various factors which may have contributed to it" (p. 160).

Lezack (1983) has also noted that the relative values of verbal and performance IQ are dependent on full-scale IQ, "with a strong tendency for Verbal Scale IQ scores to be higher at the higher Full Scale IQ score levels and for the tendency to be reversed in favour of higher Performance Scale IQ scores when the Full Scale IQ score is very much below 100" (p. 243). Some unpublished data from a sample of adult offenders at Rideau Treatment Center (RTC),[2] a medium-security correctional facility, supports Lezack's observations: For the MAB, we found that the magnitude and direction of VIQ-PIQ discrepancies was significantly correlated with full-scale IQ, as well as with VIQ and PIQ.

Recognizing that offender populations are not homogeneous, some studies have explored the possibility that P > V may be diagnostic only of certain subgroups. Recidivists seem to be more likely than nonrecidivists to exhibit P > V (Haynes & Bensch, 1981; Lueger & Cadman, 1982). They also tend to have lower full-scale IQ (Lueger & Cadman, 1982), however, and both recidivism and P > V are predicted by poor verbal skills (Andrew, 1977, 1981). There is also some evidence that P > V may be more prevalent in violent than in nonviolent offenders (Andrew, 1978; De Wolfe & Ryan, 1984; Walsh, 1987, 1992). Andrew (1977) speculated that low VIQ might result in deficits in verbal inhibition (i.e., inhibitory self-talk), while relatively high PIQ might facilitate physical acting out in these subjects. In a similar vein, Heilbrun (1979) suggested that individuals who are deficient in "internal speech" (reflected in low VIQ) may be more likely to act out feelings of anger and frustration because they are less able to talk themselves out of trouble; consequently, they may be more likely to be involved in violent and "opportunistic" (impulsive) crimes (see Walsh, 1987). Again, however, there are negative findings with respect to P > V and violence (e.g., Tarter, Hegedus, Winston, & Alterman, 1985). In the RTC sample, VIQ-PIQ discrepancy did not differentiate significantly between assaultive and nonassaultive offenders.

[2]Unpublished data from the RTC Assessment Unit database (D. J. Baxter, 1993). The mean FSIQ for this sample ($N = 533$) was 93.11 ($SD = 11.3$, range 70–126; VIQ $M = 90.01$, $SD = 10.6$; PIQ $M = 98.93$, $SD = 13.99$). These values are comparable to those reported for the WAIS in offender samples.

In any case, the P > V sign is probably of limited utility, because it appears that factors such as reading ability or general verbal ability account for as much or more of the variance than PIQ-VIQ discrepancy (De Wolfe & Ryan, 1984; Hodges & Plow, 1990). Guertin et al. (1966) conclude that "VIQ is probably less than PIQ whenever education (especially reading) has been poor, there is long-term social maladjustment, [and] the environmental emphasis has been on 'doing' and not 'thinking' " (p. 402).

Finally, it is important to distinguish between statistical group differences and the actuarial significance of relatively small VIQ-PIQ discrepancies. For the WAIS, Ryan (1984) cautions that a difference of less than 21 points should not be considered abnormal based on frequencies in the standardization sample (see Silverstein, 1985). The average VIQ-PIQ discrepancy in offender groups is on the order of 8 to 10 points, which is less than one standard deviation for the WAIS (Pernicano, 1986) and occurs in about 38% of normal adults (Grossman, Herman, & Matarazzo, 1985). In the RTC sample, the mean discrepancy was 8.9 ($SD = 10.9$), virtually identical to values reported for the WAIS. Fewer than one third of the RTC subjects had discrepancies of 15 or more points, and only 15% had discrepancies greater than 20 points. Similar observations have been made for the WISC (Kaufman, 1976; Quay, 1987).

Recently an anonymous reviewer for a major psychological journal commented, in effect, that the P > V sign was a dead issue. Perhaps it should be. It is still not uncommon to see the issue raised in correctional/forensic assessment reports (including court evaluations), however, and research articles suggesting diagnostic significance for P > V continue to appear in the psychological press (e.g., Cornell & Wilson, 1992; Walsh, 1992). One reason for this may be that, leaving aside for a moment the question of magnitude, when VIQ-PIQ discrepancies occur in offender samples they are almost always in the direction of lower VIQ: In the RTC sample, only 4% had VIQ at least 8 points higher than PIQ. There may be a number of reasons (particularly deficiencies in educational background) to expect relatively low VIQ scores, and hence a P > V discrepancy, in offender populations. This has little value as a diagnostic sign, however, because it occurs with some frequency in nonoffender populations, is by no means present in all offenders, and when present has little information value in itself without inspection of the specific subtest scores producing the lower VIQ (e.g., low Information, Arithmetic, and Vocabulary scores, suggesting academic deficiencies; low Similarities score, suggesting concrete or categorical thinking; or low Comprehension score, suggesting difficulties with social judgment or reasoning).

Patterns of Subtest Scores

Wechsler (1958) described a pattern of subtest scatter that he thought characterized delinquents and psychopaths—relatively high scores on Picture Arrangement and Object Assembly and relatively low scores on Similarities, Arithmetic, and Information. He interpreted this pattern as indicating good social intelligence, on the one hand, and concrete thinking, neglect of information not relevant to immediate gratification of needs, and difficulties with sustained concentration, on the other. There is little empirical evidence for Wechsler's observations, however, or indeed for the existence of any unique pattern characterizing offenders as a whole.

Part of the problem is that such predictions seem to reflect an oversimplified view of offenders. For example, Blatt and Allison (1981) observe that although low Comprehension scores may represent defiance of conventionality, some psychopaths score very high on this subtest, reflecting social facility and glibness; other criminals and psychopaths may show high Picture Arrangement with low Comprehension, indicating "sensitivity to personal nuances but a disregard for social conventionality" (Blatt & Allison, 1981, p. 201). Similarly, Westen (1991), noting that psychopaths can often provide "nearly perfect answers" on the Comprehension subtest, comments that "what accounts for sociopathic behavior is not a lack of knowledge of the rules (e.g., 'People should not steal') but a lack of investment in the rights, feelings, and interests of others" (p. 437). Given the heterogeneity suggested by such observations, it seems unreasonable to expect consistent patterns of Wechsler subtest scores in unselected offender samples.

Nevertheless, there is a possibility that specific offender subgroups may show more consistent subtest patterns. For example, McKenzie, Baxter, and Andrews (1993) administered the MAB to behaviorally defined groups of impulsive and nonimpulsive offenders. They found that impulsives scored lower on Comprehension than nonimpulsives, although there were no significant differences for any of the other subtests, nor for VIQ, PIQ, FSIQ, or VIQ-PIQ discrepancy. Impulsive subjects also did more poorly on measures of interpersonal problem-solving skill (Spivack & Shure, 1974), and Comprehension scores correlated significantly with the problem-solving measures. Thus, in this sample at least, it appears that impulsive criminal offenders exhibit a pattern of test scores consistent with specific deficits in social intelligence rather than general intellectual ability.

A few studies have looked at performance on the Similarities subtest, in light of observations that some offenders display concrete or inflexible thinking that might predispose them toward more impulsive or violent crimes (e.g., Field, 1986). Some studies have found a relationship between lower Similarities scores and violence (Kunce, Ryan, & Eckelman, 1976; Tarter, Hegedus, Alterman, & Katz-Garris, 1983; Spellacy, 1977), whereas others have not (Ryan & Blom, 1979; Shawver & Jew, 1978). For the MAB, McKenzie et al. (1993) found no relationship between Similarities scores and impulsive or violent crimes.

Finally, several studies have examined the WAIS Digit Span subtest or similar measures in psychopaths and violent offenders. The interest in digit-span measures seems to be based primarily on the rather specious rationale that the presumed lack of anxiety in psychopathic subjects should facilitate performance on such tasks (see Andrew, 1982). In fact, there is little evidence either for consistent patterns of digit-span performance in various offender subgroups or for a consistent relationship between these test scores and anxiety (see Guertin et al., 1966, 1971).

Summarizing across studies of offenders, one is most likely to observe relatively low scores on subtests such as Information, Vocabulary, and Comprehension. This, however, is pretty much what one would expect to find in subjects with disadvantaged socioacademic backgrounds. Thus such findings are best interpreted as reflecting disruptions in education resulting from a history of rebelliousness, aggression, student-teacher conflicts, suspensions or expulsions, frequent school changes, and a general lack of interest or motivation regarding academic pursuits. We agree with the general conclusion of Guertin et al. (1966) that "searching for Wechsler signs that will identify lawbreakers regardless of demographics is futile" (p. 391).

Social Intelligence and Problem Solving

Quay (1987) has suggested that poor verbal skills, in addition to explaining most of the variance in VIQ-PIQ discrepancies, "underlie such higher order personality-cognitive functions as interpersonal problem solving, perspective taking, person-perception, and moral reasoning" (p. 115). Thus offenders might be expected to exhibit specific deficits in social intelligence, regardless of IQ (see McKenzie et al., 1993). Problems with social intelligence and problem solving have also been highlighted in conceptualizations of psychopathy and in theories about the etiology of antisocial behavior.

Deficiencies in social interpretation, perspective taking, and interpersonal problem solving have been reported for both delinquents and adult criminal offenders (Arbuthnot, Gordon, & Jurkovic, 1987; Ross & Fabiano, 1985). These deficits have been linked to impulsivity, aggression, and other indices of social maladjustment in children (Dodge & Feldman, 1990; Spivack & Shure, 1974), which in turn are associated with peer rejection and later delinquency (Patterson et al., 1989, 1991). In adult offenders, deficits in at least some of these skills are associated with poor institutional adjustment and recidivism (McKenzie et al., 1993; Tweedale, 1990). Finally, the common measures of social cognition appear to be independent of general intelligence level (Spivack & Shure, 1974; Tisdelle & St. Lawrence, 1986). Generally speaking, the research on social-cognitive deficits in offenders has yielded findings with a relatively high degree of consistency and suggests that specific aspects of social intelligence may be much more important than general intelligence in the etiology of antisocial behavior. From a clinical standpoint, it is worth noting that the Wechsler scales do not specifically evaluate social-cognitive skills, although certain subtests (e.g., Comprehension) are correlated with and may provide some clues to deficiencies in these skills.

PERSONALITY FACTORS

There is a sizable literature on personality measures in offenders, primarily using the Minnesota Multiphasic Personality Inventory (MMPI) and the California Personality Inventory (CPI).[3] In spite of serious methodological deficiencies in many of these studies, the majority have reported significant differences between offenders and various comparison groups (Andrews & Wormith, 1989; Arbuthnot et al., 1987; Gearing, 1979; Quay, 1965, 1987). There are also some indications that combining personality data with, for example, family and academic variables can substantially improve prediction of delinquency (Arbuthnot et al., 1987).

[3]The Eysenck Personality Questionnaire has been quite influential in offender research in Britain and Europe, but it has received limited attention in North American offender research and is not reviewed here (see Trasler, 1978).

The Minnesota Multiphasic Personality Inventory

The MMPI is the most widely used self-report inventory in research or clinical practice, at least in North America. It includes three validity scales (*L*, *F*, and *K*) and eight scales originally devised to target specific diagnostic categories: Hypochondriasis (*Hy*), Depression (*D*), Hysteria (*Hy*), Psychopathic Deviate (*Pd*), Paranoia (*Pa*), Psychasthenia (*Pt*), Schizophrenia (*Sc*), and Hypomania (*Ma*). Two other standard scales, Masculinity-Femininity (*Mf*) and Social Introversion (*Si*), were added later, as well as several supplementary scales that are routinely scored, including Anxiety (*A*), Repression (*R*), Ego Strength (*Es*), and the MacAndrew Alcoholism Scale (*MAC*). The recent revision and restandardization of the MMPI (MMPI-2) has added several new supplemental scales with potential for research and assessment with offenders (Graham, 1990), but as yet there is little published research on these scales.

Current use of the MMPI is based on empirical or actuarial associations between profile configurations and personality/behavior traits. Because most of the clinical scales are not unidimensional, they are usually denoted by their abbreviations or numbers (e.g., *Pd* or Scale 4) rather than the original scale names. For example, *Pd* includes items related to family discord, authority problems, social alienation, and social imperturbability (Graham, 1977). High *Pd* scores are associated with rebelliousness, impulsivity, egocentricity, and anger/resentment, so it is not surprising that the scale is often elevated in offenders. It is also commonly elevated in normal adolescents, athletes, policemen, and men involved in divorce or custody disputes, however, and in fact *Pd* and *Ma* are the most common MMPI elevations in normal young men. Thus *Pd* is by no means a simple measure of criminality or psychopathy. Similarly, the *Sc* scale includes items related to social alienation, a sense of loss of control over emotions and behavior, and unusual sensory experiences, so it is frequently elevated in nonschizophrenic offenders, particularly those with extensive substance abuse histories.

The MMPI research literature is fraught with methodological problems, including serious deficiencies in sampling procedures, adequacy of control groups, and profile interpretation that in some cases approaches misuse of the test (Arbuthnot et al., 1987; Gearing, 1979). Sometimes, one or two scales are extracted from the test and used as stand-alone questionnaires, without regard to the very real possibility that this may result in a substantial change in the testing context and hence in how subjects respond to the individual items. Another problem is the common reliance on univariate analysis of single scales or two-point codes (Graham, 1977, 1990). In clinical practice with the MMPI, the emphasis is more on configural interpretation, where the 3 validity scales and 10 clinical scales are considered conjointly and in combination with other psychometric and demographic data. Interpretations of individual scales do appear to have some validity in the sense that they correlate significantly with psychiatric or behavioral symptomatology (Boerger, Graham, & Lilly, 1974; Hedlund, 1977) and two-point code interpretations probably yield improved diagnostic accuracy over single-scale interpretations (Gynther, Altman, & Sletten, 1973). In effect, however, these approaches discard important—sometimes essential—information elsewhere in the MMPI configuration that may in some cases substantially modify the interpretation and render the "cookbook" conclusions quite inaccurate (see Hedlund, 1977).

A number of individual MMPI scales have been shown to differentiate between delinquents and nondelinquents, or adult criminal offenders and nonoffenders, as well as among various subtypes of delinquents or criminals (Arbuthnot et al., 1987; Dahlstrom, Welsh, & Dahlstrom, 1975; Gearing, 1979; Monachesi & Hathaway, 1969). These include *F*, *Pd*, *Pa*, *Sc*, and *Ma*, with *Pd* and *Ma* being the most frequently studied scales as well as those most consistently differentiating between offender and nonoffender groups. The *Ma* scale in particular correlates significantly with measures of sensation seeking and impulsivity, which are themselves associated with delinquency and criminality (Zuckerman, 1978).

The *F* scale requires special comment. One of the three validity scales, it consists of a number of items that are infrequently endorsed by normals. *F* scores tend to vary across different ethnic groups (Dahlstrom, Lachar, & Dahlstrom, 1986; Graham, 1977, 1990), however, although the magnitude of the differences is rather small and at least partly attributable to socio-academic differences. High *F* scores have also been reported in several studies of offenders (Gearing, 1979); Morrice (1957) suggested that this might reflect the general social deviance characterizing antisocial personality disorder. It has also been suggested (Gynther, 1961; Gynther, Altman, & Warbin, 1973; Gynther & Shimkunas, 1965) that a high *F* score is a valid reflection of hostility and aggression in offenders. In support of this, Hedlund (1977) reported that *F* was significantly correlated with "antiauthority attitudes and acting-out behavior" (p. 745), and there is some evidence that the sum of *F*, *Pd*, and *Ma* scores is related to aggression or violence (Huesmann, Lefkowitz, & Eron, 1978; Mungas, 1984). It is also possible that substance abuse alone may elevate *F* scores (Gynther, 1961; Gynther et al., 1973).

This issue is an important one because of the traditional characterization of high *F* profiles as "invalid" or "fake bad." In clinical practice with offenders, it is not unusual to see high elevations on *F*. In part, this is probably because of item overlap between the *F* scale and *Pd*, *Ma*, and *Sc*, so that elevations on the latter scales will tend to also elevate *F* in a valid profile (Hedlund, 1977). Though high *F* scores may suggest that the *objective* severity of problems or symptoms has been exaggerated, the profile may be nonetheless a fairly accurate portrayal of the offender's *subjective* perceptions of his or her current status—especially where the MMPI has been administered shortly after admission to prison, when subjective distress and overall profile elevations may be at their peaks (Dahlstrom et al., 1975; Gearing, 1979; Pierce, 1972).

Several studies have found differences on the MMPI between first offenders and recidivists, or differences that are predictive of later criminal recidivism (Flanagan & Lewis, 1974; Gough, Wenk, & Rozynko, 1965; Holland & Holt, 1975; Mandelzys, 1979), notably on *Pd*, *Ma*, and sometimes *Mf*. The MMPI also differentiates between offenders exhibiting poor versus good prison adjustment, again on *F*, *Pd*, and *Ma* and frequently on *Pa* and *Mf* (Carbonell, Megargee, & Moorehead, 1984; Pierce, 1972; Sutker & Moan, 1973). Additionally, differences on *F*, *Pd*, and *Ma* have been reported for aggressive/violent versus nonaggressive offenders, as noted above (Huesmann et al., 1978; Mungas, 1984). Thus the MMPI-offender literature can be summarized by noting that the major differences are on scales reflecting distrust, rebelliousness, impulsivity, social alienation, and aggression.

Graham (1977) noted that the MMPI clinical scales can be divided into two categories, with *Pd*, *Pa*, *Sc*, and *Ma* suggesting problems with impulse controls and the six remaining clinical scales suggesting inhibition or restraint of impulses (p. 158). McKenzie et al. (1993) explored this suggestion, using the mean of *Pd*, *Pa*, *Sc*, and *Ma* as an "impulsivity index" that significantly discriminated between behaviorally defined impulsive and nonimpulsive offenders. Moreover, higher scores on the index were associated with poorer institutional adjustment and with a much higher rate of criminal offending. In clinical practice, when the impulsivity scales are elevated and the inhibitory scales are low, a relatively high potential for verbal or physical acting out is suggested. For the reverse pattern one would predict a relatively low potential for acting out, whereas simultaneous elevations in both categories may be associated with episodic aggression.

A similar pattern is suggested in a noteworthy project summarized by Monachesi and Hathaway (1969). This was a longitudinal study that included administration of the MMPI to a total of more than 15,000 ninth-grade students and several follow-up studies conducted up to 10 years later. Profiles categorized according to the highest scale elevation revealed that *D*, *Mf*, and *Si* ("inhibitory" scales) were associated with a low risk for delinquency, whereas *F*, *Pd*, *Sc*, and *Ma* ("excitatory" scales) were associated with a relatively high risk for later delinquency. The remaining clinical scales—*Hs*, *Hy*, *Pa*, and *Pt*—were found to have little or no association with delinquency risk in these studies. Analysis of the frequencies of two-point and three-point codes in the samples against actual versus expected (base) rates for subsequent delinquency showed a delinquency rate above the base rate for certain codes, including Pd-Ma, and conversely, delinquency rates significantly below the base rates for codes such as *D-Pt*.

Finally, several recent MMPI studies have employed cluster analysis. First systematically exploited with offender samples by Megargee and his associates (Megargee & Bohn, 1979), this technique avoids some of the more serious problems of MMPI research by considering the entire profile or configuration, rather than one or two scales in isolation, and by deriving relatively homogeneous subgroups of offenders. Megargee and Bohn identified 10 different MMPI configurations that were found to be associated with significant differences in offense type and severity, adequacy of institutional adjustment, and recidivism. There have since been several replications of the basic findings for the Megargee classification scheme (Motiuk, Bonta, & Andrews, 1986; Van Voorhis, 1988; Zager, 1988). Although there have been some criticisms and/or questions regarding Megargee's specific groups and procedures, the general methodology has also been applied with some success to specific offender subgroups, including sex offenders (Kalichman, 1990; Kalichman & Henderson, 1991) and murderers (Holcomb, Adams, & Ponder, 1985; Kalichman, 1988).

The California Personality Inventory

The CPI is a self-report personality test evaluating normal personality traits rather than psychopathology. It includes two validity scales and 16 "personality" scales grouped into four categories, the two major ones being social poise/social ascendancy (e.g., Dominance, Sociability) and socialization/social responsibility (e.g., Socialization, Responsibility, Self-Control). The CPI has also been recently revised (Gough & Bradley, 1992).

The most frequently studied CPI scale in offender research is the Socialization (*So*) scale (see Megargee, 1972). In general terms, this scale provides a measure of social conformity and the extent to which social values are accepted and internalized, though Rotenberg (1978) has described it as a measure of "social sensitivity, since it actually measures the subject's empathic or role-taking ability" (p. 192). *So* scores are negatively correlated with MMPI *Pd* scores and with psychopathy ratings (Hare & Schalling, 1978). Because the scale was derived independently and only later inserted into the CPI, it is suitable for use as a stand-alone test. Empirically, the scale has differentiated between delinquent or offender groups and various control groups in numerous studies in several countries (Arbuthnot et al., 1987; Quay, 1965; Schalling, 1978). *So* scores in schoolage boys are predictive of later delinquency (Caplan, 1965; Schalling, 1978). The scale also differentiates between recidivists and first offenders (Gough et al., 1965; Hindelang, 1972; Kendall, Deardorff, & Finch, 1977) and predicts adequacy of institutional adjustment among incarcerated offenders (Carbonell et al., 1984; Kendall et al., 1977; Hindelang, 1972). As a research instrument, the *So* scale appears to be one of the stronger univariate psychometric predictors of general criminality and psychopathy (Andrews & Wormith, 1989; Gough & Bradley, 1992; Megargee, 1972; Schalling, 1978).

Critics of the *So* scale have pointed out that the ability of the scale to differentiate between offenders and nonoffenders is neither surprising nor impressive: It was developed using criterion keying precisely to perform that task, and many of the items have to do with past antisocial behavior. Clinically, we have found that the majority of offenders score low on this scale (i.e.,T = score less than 30), indicating undersocialization and defiance of conventionality. The scale is clinically useful or interesting primarily in those exceptional cases where *So* is higher (e.g., 40 to 50), suggesting that socialization deficits are not a significant factor in the criminal behavior of these subjects.

INTERACTIONS BETWEEN MEASURES OF PERSONALITY AND INTELLIGENCE

Although not originally developed for this purpose, the Wechsler scales have come to be used clinically as an adjunct to or component of personality assessment and diagnosis, based on presumed personality correlates or implications of specific subtest scores, configurations, or responses to individual subtest items. The rationale behind this is that "the various aspects of psychological functioning do not exist in isolation; rather, one is always observing and assessing the balance among affects, drives, defenses, and cognitive controls" (Blatt & Allison, 1981, p. 193). Thus "intellectual processes are considered to be [an] integral part of personality" (p. 194). The validity of this approach has been explored in a few studies examining relationships between Wechsler subtest scores and scores on various personality inventories (e.g., MMPI, or CPI), though not specifically with offenders (see Blatt & Allison, 1981; Guertin et al., 1966, 1971).

In light of the psychopathy and social cognition literatures, studies investigating the Comprehension and Picture Arrangement subtests should be particularly relevant. Comprehension is generally viewed as a test of social judgment and practical social reasoning (Blatt & Allison, 1981), whereas Picture Arrangement is said to be a test of social interpretation, social planning and anticipation, cause-effect reasoning, and sequential thinking (Blatt & Allison, 1981; Lezack, 1983; Wechsler, 1958). Individually or in combination, these two subtests have been interpreted as measures of social intelligence and conventionality.

A few early studies reported correlations between Picture Arrangement and Comprehension and scales such as the MMPI Social Introversion (*Si*) scale, but later studies were unable to replicate the findings (e.g., Nobo & Evans, 1986). In the RTC sample, we obtained small negative correlations between *Si* and both Comprehension and Picture Arrangement, but neither MAB scale was related in any meaningful way to type or number of offenses. Moreover, it is not clear why one would necessarily expect to find poorer social intelligence in introverts: Many extraverted offenders appear to be seriously hampered with respect to social reasoning and problem-solving ability (McKenzie et al., 1993; Ross & Fabiano, 1985).

On balance, although the rationale for personality interpretations of Wechsler subtest performance is intuitively appealing, empirical support is far from overwhelming. Despite extensive clinical and research experience with the scales, many of the basic clinical assumptions have yet to be tested in a systematic fashion (Blatt & Allison, 1981). Indeed, it is hard to believe that tests such as the WAIS are *not* related to and affected by some personality factors. Unfortunately, the research literature, as Guertin et al. (1971) have noted, appears to suffer from a fundamental naïveté about the complexity of personality, intelligence, and the instruments devised to measure these constructs. Thus many of the relevant studies to date can be aptly described as overly simplistic tests of oversimplified hypotheses.

The question of how intellectual factors may influence scores on personality measures has also received little attention in offenders. It has been known for some time that some MMPI scales are affected by differences in ethnicity, education, and socioacademic background, including *L*, *K*, *Hy*, *Mf*, and *Si* (Dahlstrom et al., 1975, 1986; Graham, 1977, 1990). In general, there does not appear to be any consistent relationship between the MMPI scales and measures of general intelligence (Dahlstrom et al., 1975), with the exception of *Mf* and *L* (Gynther & Shimkunas, 1966; Thurmin, 1969). In offenders, Panton (1960) found that lower IQs were associated with elevations on *Hs*, *D*, *Pt*, and *Sc*, whereas higher IQs were associated with elevations on *Hy*, *Pd*, and *Ma*. This finding suggests that less bright offenders tend to exhibit symptoms of neuroticism and anxiety, whereas brighter subjects tend to exhibit symptoms consistent with personality disorder. Panton's "lower IQ" subjects, however, were defined as those with IQ scores below 110, so the generality of these results is questionable.

In the RTC sample, IQ scores were significantly correlated with several MMPI scales, but the majority of the correlation coefficients were quite low (less than .20). Subjects with P > V discrepancies of at least 8 to 10 points had significantly lower scores on *D*, *Hy*, *Pd*, and *Mf*, though with more stringent P > V criteria (15 or 20 points) these differences disappeared. Correlations between VIQ-PIQ discrepancy and MMPI scales were low and mostly nonsignificant. Several MAB subtests correlated significantly with various MMPI scales, but again the magnitude of these correlations was quite small. The largest correlation coefficients were obtained for Comprehension (versus *F*, *Mf*, and *Sc*). It is worth noting that with the exception of a weak correlation between *Ma* and Picture Arrangement, none of the MAB scales correlated significantly with *Pd*, *Ma*, *MAC*, or the *CPI So* scale—the scales most likely to differentiate between offenders and nonoffenders.

CONCLUSIONS AND A THEORETICAL-CONCEPTUAL FRAMEWORK

As Fishbein (1990) has observed, "Maladaptive behavior is a function of a cumulative developmental process" and over time early risk factors for delinquency tend to be "compounded by suboptimal environmental and social conditions" (p. 33). A child evidencing early symptoms of maladjustment (e.g., temper tantrums, aggression) for whatever reason creates, in a very real sense, a different social-cognitive-emotional environment than a child who is more cooperative, compliant, or sociable. The negative reactions elicited by antisocial behaviors tend to create a vicious cycle of punishment, rebelliousness, rejection-alienation, low self-esteem, and aggression that affects sociodevelopmental factors at home, at school, and in peer interactions and exacerbates the effects of any cognitive-intellectual deficits or maladaptive personality traits on the socialization process (Fishbein, 1990; Quay, 1987).

Early antisocial behavior, particularly aggression, is predictive of subsequent delinquent and adult criminal involvement, especially for more serious criminal offenses (Loeber & Stouthamer-Loeber, 1987; Stattin & Magnusson, 1989). There is a modest negative correlation between IQ and aggression, but the association between early aggression and later crime is significant even after controlling for this (Huesmann, Eron, Lefkowitz, & Walder, 1984; Stattin & Magnusson, 1989). By middle childhood, aggressive children are maladjusted in a number of ways: "It is rare to find a highly aggressive boy who is not educationally or socially handicapped in many ways. They often are restless and exhibit concentration difficulties, they show low school motivation and underachieve, and they tend to have poor peer relations" (Stattin & Magnusson, 1989, p. 717).

Patterson et al. (1989) hypothesize that the developmental pathway to persistent delinquency begins with an unstable family base—family stressors such as unemployment, marital conflict or divorce, or death; family violence; antisocial behavior in the parents or other relatives; harsh and/or inconsistent disciplinary practices; poor emotional bonding between parents and child; and so forth. Children from these families tend to be "impulsive, mean, and disruptive" in their early social interactions (Hartup, 1989) and to evidence various antisocial behaviors, including interpersonal aggression, as well as various signs of social incompetence. As a consequence, they are rejected by their conventional or normal peers and, by default, are left to associate with other deviant and rejected children who display similar antisocial behaviors (Dodge & Feldman, 1990). This greatly increases the risk for later delinquency and adult criminality. Their antisocial attitudes and behavior patterns become more entrenched as time goes on, in part because of chronic exposure to antisocial values and chronic isolation from more prosocial forces, and in part because over time these attitudes and associations become an integral component of their social identities (Elliott, Ageton, & Canter, 1979; Fortin & Baxter, 1993).

These antisocial, rejected children exhibit a number of deficits in social competence and social cognition, characteristics that persist into their adult years. Whether such deficits are a cause or consequence of the deviant behavior is difficult to determine conclusively, and in all likelihood the relationship is an interactive one (Fishbein, 1990; Quay, 1987). Low IQ seems to be associated with poor interpersonal adjustment even in the preschool years (Quay, 1987; White et al., 1990). White et al. (1990) note that the identification of early antisocial behavior as the best single predictor of later delinquency and the onset of antisocial behavior as early as age 3 suggests the involvement of "components of temperament." In a similar vein, Quay (1965) notes that "temperamental features" may function as the link between low IQ (especially low verbal IQ) and academic failure and antisocial behavior. A child who begins the socialization process with limited intelligence, poor social or cognitive skills, neuropsychological dysfunction, a learning disability, and/or disruptive behavioral or personality traits does so at a considerable disadvantage. This will be compounded by subsequent difficulties in academic adjustment and social relationships, and by isolation or alienation from less disadvantaged peers and association with similarly disadvantaged and rejected peers (Dodge & Feldman, 1990; Fishbein, 1990; Hartup, 1989; Patterson et al., 1989, 1991).

These findings have two important implications. First, *any* form of cognitive impairment or personality trait that influences either interpersonal relationships or academic achievement will tend to increase the risk for persistent delinquency and criminality. Second, problems in interpersonal relationships and/or academic achievement are likely to exacerbate existing deficits or maladaptive traits to produce further distortions or disturbances in personal and interpersonal adjustment. Subsequently, certain lifestyle correlates of delinquency (e.g., substance abuse) may increase the discrepancies between the delinquent's cognitive or social-cognitive functioning and that of his or her more advantaged peers as time goes on.

Criminality is both multidimensional and multidetermined, and the offender population is heterogeneous with respect to a number of critical cognitive and personality variables. Impaired intellectual or cognitive functioning is only one of many risk factors for persistent delinquency or criminality, and criminality is only one of a number of forms of maladjustment that may be related to such impairment. Some of the studies reviewed here have suggested relationships between certain specific cognitive deficits or character traits and specific types of criminal behavior. In most of the existing literature, however, the relationship is ambiguous and equivocal, particularly regarding the question of whether one is a cause or a consequence of the other. We strongly endorse the conclusions of previous reviews (e.g., Arbuthnot et al., 1987; Caplan, 1965; Quay, 1987) that there is little to be gained by additional studies involving comparisons between heterogeneous or vaguely defined offender and nonoffender groups. Rather, future research should be guided by recent theoretical and empirical advances in attempting to clarify how intellectual-cognitive factors and personality factors interact with one another and with other known risk factors in the etiology of antisocial behavior.

Some implications for clinical work with offenders are also indicated. In selecting assessment instruments, the psychologist needs to be aware not only of general psychometric issues but also of issues specific to criminal offenders. Assessment of offenders has several purposes, including identification of treatment needs and goals, evaluating amenability to treatment, screening for potential management problems (suicide risk, protective custody, security issues), estimation of risk to self or others, and determination of supervision requirements (i.e., classification issues). Given that decisions regarding custody alternatives, parole, and so on may rest on the outcome of the assessment, the likelihood of dissimulation must be considered, and thus tests with high face validity or lacking reliable validity indicators should probably be avoided. The MMPI has several characteristics that recommend it for correctional/forensic settings, including the ability to evaluate adequacy of impulse controls, potential for violence, suicide risk, and so forth. We would recommend adding measures of factors specifically related to recidivism (e.g., criminal attitudes scales, recidivism risk scales) to enhance predictions derived from the MMPI.

With respect to intelligence tests, preference should be given to the WAIS or MAB. In most cases, there is little to recommend the use of abbreviated or unidimensional instruments designed primarily to estimate full-scale IQ. As we have seen, specific aspects of intellectual or cognitive functioning in offenders seem to be much more important than global intelligence, and tests that provide only an IQ score probably have little to contribute. Most importantly, clinicians need to move beyond simplistic, single-factor approaches to risk-needs assessment and rehabilitation and to adopt approaches that better reflect the diversity and complexity of criminal offenders and the multifactorial nature of criminal behavior and recidivism.

Acknowledgments. The views expressed here are those of the authors and do not necessarily reflect those of any government office or agency. We thank Arthur Gordon and Moira Tweedale for assistance in the development of this chapter.

REFERENCES

Andrew, J. M (1977). Delinquency: Intellectual imbalance? *Criminal Justice and Behavior*, *4*, 99–104.

Andrew, J. M. (1978). The classic Wechsler P > V sign and violent crime. *Crime and Justice*, *6*, 246–248.

Andrew, J. M. (1981). Reading and cerebral dysfunction among juvenile delinquents. *Criminal Justice and Behavior*, *8*, 131–144.

Andrew, J. M. (1982). Memory and violent crime among delinquents. *Criminal Justice and Behavior*, *9*, 364–371.

Andrews, D. A., & Wormith, J. S. (1989). Personality and crime: Knowledge destruction and construction in criminology. *Justice Quarterly*, *6*, 289–309.

Arbuthnot, J., Gordon, D. A., & Jurkovic, G. J. (1987). Personality. In H. C. Quay (Ed.), *Handbook of juvenile delinquency* (pp. 139–183). New York: Wiley.

Blatt, S. J., & Allison, J. (1981). The intelligence test in personality assessment. In A. I. Rabin (Ed.), *Assessment with projective techniques: A concise introduction* (pp. 187–231). New York: Springer.

Boerger, A. B., Graham, J. R., & Lilly, R. S. (1974). Behavioral correlates of single-scale MMPI code types. *Journal of Consulting and Clinical Psychology, 42*, 398–402.

Caplan, N. S. (1965). Intellectual functioning. In H. C. Quay (Ed.), *Juvenile delinquency: Research and theory* (pp. 100–138). Princeton, NJ: Van Nostrand.

Carbonell, J. L., Megargee, E. I., & Moorehead, K. M. (1984). Predicting prison adjustment by means of structured personality inventories. *Journal of Consulting and Clinical Psychology, 52*, 280–294.

Cleckley, H. (1964). *The mask of sanity* (4th ed.). St. Louis, MO: Mosby.

Cornell, D. G., & Wilson, L. A. (1992). The PIQ-VIQ discrepancy in violent and nonviolent delinquents. *Journal of Clinical Psychology, 48*, 256–261.

Dahlstrom, W. G., Lachar, D., & Dahlstrom, L. E. (1986). *MMPI patterns of American minorities*. Minneapolis: University of Minnesota Press.

Dahlstrom, W. G., Welsh, G. S., & Dahlstrom, L. E. (1975). *An MMPI handbook: Vol. 2. Research applications* (rev. ed.). Minneapolis: University of Minnesota Press.

De Wolfe, A. S., & Ryan, J. J. (1984). Wechsler performance IQ > verbal IQ index in a forensic sample: A reconsideration. *Journal of Clinical Psychology, 40*, 291–294.

Dodge, K. A., & Feldman, E. (1990). Issues in social cognition and sociometric status. In S. R. Asher & J. D. Coie (Eds.), *Peer rejection in childhood* (pp. 119–155). Cambridge, England: Cambridge University Press.

Elliott, D. S., Ageton, S. S., & Canter, R. J. (1979). An integrated theoretical perspective on delinquent behavior. *Journal of Research in Crime and Delinquency, 16*, 3–27.

Field, G. (1986). The psychological needs and deficits of chronic criminality. *Federal Probation, 50*, 60–66.

Fishbein, D. (1990). Biological perspectives in criminology. *Criminology, 28*, 27–72.

Flanagan, J., & Lewis, G. (1974). First prison admissions with juvenile histories and absolute first offenders: Frequencies and MMPI profiles. *Journal of Clinical Psychology, 30*, 358–360.

Fortin, S., & Baxter, D. J. (1993). *Criminal allegiances and criminal identity*. Unpublished manuscript, University of Ottawa.

Gearing, M. L. (1979). The MMPI as a primary differentiator and predictor of behavior in prisons: A methodological critique and review of the recent literature. *Psychological Bulletin, 86*, 926–963.

Gough, H. G., & Bradley, P. (1992). Delinquent and criminal behavior as assessed by the revised California Psychological Inventory. *Journal of Clinical Psychology, 48*, 298–308.

Gough, H. G., Wenk, E. A., & Rozynko, V. V. (1965). Parole outcome as predicted from the CPI, the MMPI, and a base expectancy table. *Journal of Abnormal Psychology, 70*, 432–441.

Graham, J. R. (1977). *The MMPI: A practical guide*. New York: Oxford University Press.

Graham, J. R. (1990). *MMPI-2: Assessing personality and psychopathology*. New York: Oxford University Press.

Grossman, F. M., Herman, D. O., & Matarazzo, J. D. (1985). Statistically inferred vs. empirically observed VIQ-PIQ differences in the WAIS-R. *Journal of Clinical Psychology, 41*, 268–272.

Guertin, W. H., Ladd, C. E., Frank, G. H., Rabin, A. I., & Hiester, D. S. (1966). Research with the Wechsler Intelligence Scales for Adults: 1960–1965. *Psychological Bulletin, 66*, 385–409.

Guertin, W. H., Ladd, C. E., Frank, G. H., Rabin, A. I., & Hiester, D. S. (1971). Research with the Wechsler Intelligence Scales for Adults: 1965–1970. *Psychological Record, 21*, 289–339.

Gynther, M. D. (1961). The clinical utility of "invalid" MMPI F scores. *Journal of Consulting Psychology, 25*, 540–541.

Gynther, M. D., Altman, H., & Sletten, I. W. (1973). Replicated correlates of MMPI two-point code types: The Missouri actuarial system. *Journal of Clinical Psychology, 29*, 263–289.

Gynther, M. D., Altman, H., & Warbin, R. (1973). Interpretation of uninterpretable MMPI profiles. *Journal of Consulting and Clinical Psychology, 40*, 78–83.

Gynther, M. D., & Shimkunas, A. M. (1965). More data on F > 16 MMPI profiles. *Journal of Clinical Psychology, 21*, 275–277.

Gynther, M. D., & Shimkunas, A. M. (1966). Age and MMPI performance. *Journal of Consulting and Clinical Psychology, 30*, 118–121.

Hare, R. D. (1970). *Psychopathy: Theory and research*. New York: Wiley.

Hare, R. D. (1983). Diagnosis of antisocial personality disorder in prison populations. *American Journal of Psychiatry, 140*, 887–890.

Hare, R. D., & Cox, D. N. (1978). Clinical and empirical conceptions of psychopathy and the selection of subjects for research. In R. D. Hare & D. Schalling (Eds.), *Psychopathic behavior: Approaches to research* (pp. 1–22). New York: Wiley.

Hare, R. D., & Jutai, J. W. (1983). Criminal history of the male psychopath: Some preliminary data. In K. T. Van Dusen & S. A. Mednick (Eds.), *Prospective studies of crime and delinquency* (pp. 225–236). Boston: Kluwer-Nijhoff.

Hare, R. D., & Schalling, D. (Eds.). (1978). *Psychopathic behavior: Approaches to research*. New York: Wiley.

Hartup, W. W. (1989). Social relationships and their developmental significance. *American Psychologist, 44*, 120–126.

Haynes, J. P., & Bensch, M. (1981). The P > V sign on the WISC-R and recidivism in delinquents. *Journal of Consulting and Clinical Psychology, 49*, 480–481.

Hedlund, J. L. (1977). MMPI clinical scale correlates. *Journal of Consulting and Clinical Psychology, 45*, 739–750.

Heilbrun, A. (1979). Psychopathy and violent crime. *Journal of Consulting and Clinical Psychology, 47*, 509–516.

Hindelang, M. J. (1972). The relationship of self-reported delinquency to scales of the CPI and MMPI. *Journal of Criminal Law, Criminology, and Police Science, 63*, 75–81.

Hirschi, T., & Hindelang, M. J. (1977). Intelligence and delinquency: A revisionist review. *American Sociological Review, 42*, 571–587.

Hodges, K., & Plow, J. (1990). Intellectual ability and achievement in psychiatrically hospitalized children with conduct, anxiety, and affective disorders. *Journal of Consulting and Clinical Psychology, 58*, 589–595.

Holcomb, W. R., Adams, N. A., & Ponder, H. M. (1985). The development and cross-validation of an MMPI typology of murderers. *Journal of Personality Assessment, 49*, 240–244.

Holland, T. R., & Holt, N. (1975). Prisoner intellectual and personality correlates of offense severity and recidivism probability. *Journal of Clinical Psychology, 31*, 667–677.

Huesmann, L. R., Eron, L. D., Lefkowitz, M. M., & Walder, L. O. (1984). Stability of aggression over time and over generations. *Developmental Psychology, 20*, 1120–1134.

Huesmann, L. R., Lefkowitz, M. M., & Eron, L. D. (1978). Sum of MMPI scales *F*, 4, and 9 as a measure of aggression. *Journal of Consulting and Clinical Psychology, 46*, 1071–1078.

Jackson, D. N. (1984). *Multidimensional Aptitude Battery (MAB): Manual.* London, Ontario: Research Psychologists Press.

Kalichman, S. C. (1988). Empirically derived MMPI profile subgroups of incarcerated homicide offenders. *Journal of Clinical Psychology, 44,* 733–738.

Kalichman, S. C. (1990). Affective and personality characteristics of replicated MMPI profile subgroups of incarcerated adult rapists. *Archives of Sexual Behavior, 19,* 443–459.

Kalichman, S. C., & Henderson, M. C. (1991). MMPI profile subtypes of nonincarcerated child molesters: A cross validation study. *Criminal Justice and Behavior, 18,* 379–396.

Kaufman, A. S. (1976). Verbal-performance IQ discrepancies on the WISC-R. *Journal of Consulting and Clinical Psychology, 44,* 739–744.

Kendall, P. C., Deardorff, P. A., & Finch, A. J. (1977). Empathy and socialization in first and repeat juvenile offenders and normals. *Journal of Abnormal Child Psychology, 5,* 93–97.

Kunce, J. T., Ryan, J. J., & Eckelman, C. C. (1976). Violent behavior and differential WAIS characteristics. *Journal of Consulting and Clinical Psychology, 44,* 42–45.

Lezack, M. D. (1983). *Neuropsychological assessment* (2nd ed.). New York: Oxford University Press.

Loeber, R., & Stouthamer-Loeber, M. (1987). Prediction. In H. C. Quay (Ed.), *Handbook of juvenile delinquency* (pp. 325–382). New York: Wiley.

Lueger, R. J., & Cadman, W. (1982). Variables associated with recidivism and program termination of delinquent adolescents. *Journal of Clinical Psychology, 38,* 861–863.

Mandelzys, N. (1979). Correlates of offense severity and recidivism probability in a Canadian sample. *Journal of Clinical Psychology, 35,* 897–907.

McKenzie, I., Baxter, D. J., & Andrews, D. A. (1993). *Correlates of impulsivity in adult criminal offenders.* Manuscript submitted for publication.

Megargee, E. I. (1972). *The California Psychological Inventory handbook.* San Francisco: Jossey-Bass.

Megargee, E. I., & Bohn, M. J. (1979). *Classifying criminal offenders: A new system based on the MMPI.* Beverly Hills, CA: Sage.

Moffitt, T. E., & Silva, P. A. (1988). IQ and delinquency: A direct test of the differential detection hypothesis. *Journal of Abnormal Psychology, 97,* 330–333.

Monachesi, E. D., & Hathaway, S. R. (1969). The personality of delinquents. In J. N. Butcher (Ed.), *MMPI: Research developments and clinical applications* (pp. 207–220). New York: McGraw-Hill.

Morrice, J. K. W. (1957). The MMPI in recidivist prisoners. *Journal of Mental Science, 103,* 632–635.

Motiuk, L. L., Bonta, J., & Andrews, D. A. (1986). Classification in correctional halfway houses: The relative and incremental predictive criterion validities of the Megargee-MMPI and LSI systems. *Criminal Justice and Behavior, 13,* 33–46.

Mungas, D. (1984). Discriminant validation of an MMPI measure of aggression. *Journal of Consulting and Clinical Psychology, 51,* 313–314.

Nobo, J., & Evans, R. G. (1986). The WAIS-R Picture Arrangement and Comprehension subtests as measures of social behavior characteristics. *Journal of Personality Assessment, 50,* 90–92.

Panton, J. H. (1960). MMPI code configurations as related to measures of intelligence among a state prison population. *Journal of Social Psychology, 51,* 403–407.

Patterson, G. R., Capaldi, D., & Bank, L. (1991). An early starter model for predicting delinquency. In D. J. Pepler & K. H. Rubin (Eds.), *The development and treatment of childhood aggression* (pp. 139–168). Hillsdale, NJ: Erlbaum.

Patterson, G. R., De Baryshe, B. D., & Ramsey, E. (1989). A developmental perspective on antisocial behavior. *American Psychologist, 44,* 329–355.

Pernicano, K. M. (1986). Score differences in WAIS-R scatter for schizophrenics, depressives, and personality disorders: A preliminary analysis. *Psychological Reports, 59,* 539–543.

Pichot, P. (1978). Psychopathic behavior: A historical overview. In R. D. Hare & D. Schalling (Eds.), *Psychopathic behavior: Approaches to research* (pp. 55–70). New York: Wiley.

Pierce, D. M. (1972). MMPI correlates of adaptation to prison. *Correctional Psychologist, 5,* 43–47.

Quay, H. C. (1965). Personality and delinquency. In H. C. Quay (Ed.), *Juvenile delinquency: Research and theory* (pp. 139–169). Princeton, NJ: Van Nostrand.

Quay, H. C. (1987). Intelligence. In H. C. Quay (Ed.), *Handbook of juvenile delinquency* (pp. 106–117). New York: Wiley.

Ross, R. R., & Fabiano, E. A. (1985). *Time to think: A cognitive model of delinquency prevention and rehabilitation.* Johnson City, TN: Academy of Arts and Sciences.

Rotenberg, M. (1978). Psychopathy and differential insensitivity. In R. D. Hare & D. Schalling (Eds.), *Psychopathic behavior: Approaches to research* (pp. 187–196). New York: Wiley.

Ryan, J. J. (1984). Abnormality of subtest score and verbal-performance IQ differences on the WAIS-R. *International Journal of Clinical Neuropsychology, 6,* 97–98.

Ryan, J. J., & Blom, B. E. (1979). WAIS characteristics and violent behavior: Failure to replicate versus failure to generalize. *Journal of Consulting and Clinical Psychology, 47,* 581–582.

Schalling, D. (1978). Psychopathy-related personality variables and the psychophysiology of socialization. In R. D. Hare & D. Schalling (Eds.), *Psychopathic behavior: Approaches to research* (pp. 85–106). New York: Wiley.

Shawver, L., & Jew, C. (1978). Predicting violent behavior from WAIS characteristics: A replication failure. *Journal of Consulting and Clinical Psychology, 46,* 206.

Silverstein, A B. (1985). Verbal-Performance IQ discrepancies on the WAIS-R: Estimated vs. empirical values. *Journal of Clinical Psychology, 41,* 694–697.

Spellacy, F. (1977). Neuropsychological differences between violent and nonviolent delinquents. *Journal of Clinical Psychology, 33,* 966–969.

Spivack, G., & Shure, M. B. (1974). *The problem-solving approach to adjustment.* San Francisco: Jossey-Bass.

Stattin, H., & Magnusson, D. (1989). The role of early aggressive behavior in the frequency, seriousness, and types of later crime. *Journal of Consulting and Clinical Psychology, 57,* 710–718.

Sutker, P. B., & Moan, C. E. (1973). Prediction of socially maladaptive behavior within a state prison system. *Journal of Community Psychology, 1,* 74–78.

Tarter, R. E., Hegedus, A. M., Alterman, A. I., & Katz-Garris, L. (1983). Cognitive capacities of juvenile violent, nonviolent, and sexual offenders. *Journal of Nervous and Mental Disease, 171,* 564–567.

Tarter, R. E., Hegedus, A. M., Winston, N. E., & Alterman, A. I. (1985). Intellectual profiles and violent behavior in juvenile delinquents. *Journal of Psychology, 119,* 125–128.

Thurmin, F. J. (1969). MMPI scores as related to age, education, and intelligence among male job applicants. *Journal of Applied Psychology, 53,* 404–407.

Tisdelle, D. A., & St. Lawrence, J. S. (1986). Interpersonal problem-solving: Review and critique of the literature. *Clinical Psychology Review, 6*, 337–356.

Tolan, P., & Thomas, P. (1988). Correlates of delinquency participation and persistence. *Criminal Justice and Behavior, 15*, 306–322.

Trasler, G. (1978). Relations between psychopathy and persistent criminality: Methodological and theoretical issues. In R. D. Hare & D. Schalling (Eds.), *Psychopathic behavior: Approaches to research* (pp. 273–298). New York: Wiley.

Tweedale, M. (1990). *Interpersonal problem-solving and deterrence: Effects on prison adjustment and recidivism*. Unpublished doctoral dissertation, University of Ottawa.

Van Voorhis, P. (1988). A cross-classification of five, offender typologies: Issues of construct and predictive validity. *Criminal Justice and Behavior, 15*, 109–124.

Walsh, A. (1987). Cognitive functioning and delinquency: Property versus violent offenses. *International Journal of Offender Therapy and Comparative Criminology, 31*, 285–290.

Walsh, A. (1992). The P > V sign in corrections: Is it a useful diagnostic tool? *Criminal Justice and Behavior, 19*, 372–383.

Wechsler, D. (1958). *The measurement of adult intelligence* (4th ed.). Baltimore, MD: Williams & Wilkins.

Westen, D. (1991). Social cognition and object relations. *Psychological Bulletin, 109*, 429–455.

White, J. L., Moffitt, T. E., Earls, F., Robins, L., & Silva, P. A. (1990). How early can we tell? Predictions of childhood conduct disorder and adolescent delinquency. *Criminology, 28*, 507–533.

White, J. L., Moffitt, T. E., & Silva, P. A. (1989). A prospective replication of the protective effects of IQ in subjects at high risk for juvenile delinquency. *Journal of Consulting and Clinical Psychology, 57*, 719–724.

Wirt, R. D., & Briggs, P. F. (1965). The meaning of delinquency. In H. C. Quay (Ed.), *Juvenile delinquency: Research and theory* (pp. 1–26). Princeton, NJ: Van Nostrand.

Zager, L. D. (1988). The MMPI-based criminal classification system: A review, current status, and future directions. *Criminal Justice and Behavior, 15*, 39–57.

Zuckerman, M. (1978). Sensation-seeking and psychopathy. In R. D. Hare & D. Schalling (Eds.), *Psychopathic behavior: Approaches to research* (pp. 165–186). New York: Wiley.

31

Personality and Intellectual Capabilities in Sport Psychology

Gershon Tenenbaum and Michael Bar-Eli

HISTORICAL PERSPECTIVES ON PERSONALITY: FROM TRAITS AND DISPOSITIONS TO INTERACTIONS AND TRANSACTIONS

More than four decades ago, philosophers Dewey and Bentley (1949) argued that there are three phases in the development of theories in each scientific discipline: (a) self-action, in which objects are regarded as behaving under their own power; (b) interaction, in which objects are regarded as being in a causal interaction where one acts upon another; and (c) process transaction, in which objects are regarded as relating to one another within a system. Within psychology, it has long been debated as to which source accounts for most of the variance in human behavior (Houts, Cook, & Shadish, 1986; Kenrick & Funder, 1988; Pervin, 1985). For instance, Ekehammar (1974) differentiated between "personologism" (which advocates stable, intraorganismic constructs as the main determinants of behavioral variance) and "situationism" (which emphasizes situational factors as the main source of behavioral variance). It seemed to Ekehammar that personality psychology was moving toward being governed by interactionism. The latter "can be regarded as the synthesis of personologism and situationism, which implies that neither the person nor the situation per se is emphasized, but the interaction of these two factors is regarded as the main source of behavioral variation" (p. 1026).

Interactionism in fact became the zeitgeist of personality psychology in the late 1970s, especially when combined with cognitive theoretical perspectives (Bem, 1983; Snyder, 1983). Some investigators have proceeded even further in researching personality, toward transactionism. For example, Pervin (1977) stated that too much psychological research had been conducted on the self-action level and suggested that transactionism had a greater potential for investigating complex human behavior, particularly in applied settings (see also Bandura, 1978; Cronbach, 1957). Interactionism, however, still seems to play a major role in current personality psychology (Vealey, 1992).

Sports personality research was characterized in the 1950s and 1960s mainly by the self-action level. The person-situation debate in the personality literature, however, culminated with the interactional perspective as the preferred paradigm in sports personality research. For example, Martens (1975), reviewing the literature from 1950 to 1973, concluded that the interactional paradigm was the direction that sports personality research should take. Martens based his

Gershon Tenenbaum • Department of Psychology, University of Southern Queensland, Toowoomba, Queensland 4350, Australia. Michael Bar-Eli • Ribstein Center for Research and Sport Medicine Sciences, Wingate Institute for Physical Education and Sport, Netanya 42902, Israel.

International Handbook of Personality and Intelligence, edited by Donald H. Saklofske and Moshe Zeidner. Plenum Press, New York, 1995.

conclusion on the premise that situationism was an overreaction to the trait paradigm and that behavior in sports could best be understood by concurrently studying the effects of environmental and intrapersonal variables.

Martens's conclusion did not bring the person-situation debate within sports psychology to an end (Fisher, 1984a; Morgan, 1980a, b; Silva, 1984). Vealey (1989) extended Martens's (1975) review to examine sports personality research from 1974 to 1988. It was found that 55% of the personality literature utilized an interactional approach, compared to 45% that utilized a trait approach. According to Vealey, however, within the interactional category there was a greater trend toward cognitive approaches (35%) as opposed to trait-state approaches (20%). The trait approach in sports personality decreased markedly from 1974 to 1981, whereas the cognitive interactional approach showed a marked increase during this time. The trait-state interactional approach has increased in use from the early 1970s, yet it has not demonstrated the popularity of the trait and cognitive interactional approaches.

In essence, these historical developments reflect the patterns observed for personality research in general psychology. Despite some calls for transactionalism in the sport and exercise domain (Bar-Eli, 1985; Nitsch, 1985), interactionalist approaches still seem to prevail. In this chapter, we will follow these developments. First we discuss the relationship between personality and motor behavior, emphasizing mainly traditional self-acting concepts. Then we emphasize the role of cognitive variables, stressing the relationship between intellectual characteristics and motor behavior. Finally, we briefly introduce some directions for future research in personality within the sports and exercise domain.

PERSONALITY AND MOTOR BEHAVIOR

Sensation Seeking

The construct of sensation seeking was originally proposed by Zuckerman, Kolin, Price, and Zoob (1964). They argued that some individuals prefer extraordinarily high levels of stimulation to moderate levels. Individuals who rank high in sensation seeking are said to search for experiences that are exciting, risky, and novel. For such persons, "living life on the edge" is a personal orientation and a framework for evaluating the worth of prospective endeavors. Zuckerman et al. (1964) argued that human organisms are not necessarily drive or tension reducers, but rather strive for "optimal stimulation." This notion takes into account large individual differences in the need for stimulus reduction and, hence, the concept of sensation seeking.

Zuckerman originally hypothesized that people differed in levels of cortical arousal, but later, he (e.g., Zuckerman, 1979, 1987) refined his theory to suggest that sensation seekers possess stronger orienting responses than other individuals. An orienting response is an individual's first reaction to a new or unexpected stimulus. It is a tendency toward sensory intake, as opposed to defense responses, which attempt to screen out stimuli. Indeed, stronger orienting responses were revealed among sensation seekers (Neary & Zuckerman, 1976). Sensation seekers also demonstrated a link between sensation seeking, brain-wave response (Zuckerman, Murtaugh, & Siegel, 1974) and the production of endorphins (Johansson, Almay, Knorring, Terenius, & Astrom, 1979).

The sports and exercise literature associated with this concept has concentrated mainly on sporting activities selected by sensation seekers. Research in this area has typically used Zuckerman's Sensation Seeking Scale (SSS; see fifth revision in Zuckerman, 1984), which includes the subdimensions of Thrill and Adventure Seeking (TAS), Experience Seeking (ES), Disinhibition (Dis), and Boredom Susceptibility (BS).

The SSS has generally been accepted as a valid assessment tool in sport contexts, particularly with high-risk athletes. Straub (1982), for example, studied 80 male athletes who participated in hang gliding, automobile racing, and bowling. The bowlers scored significantly lower on the total score and two of the four subdimensions when compared with the other two groups. Furthermore, in response to the question "Do you consider your sport to be a high-risk activity?" 67% of the hang gliders, 50% of the auto racers, and none of the bowlers answered positively, though 63% of the hang gliders and 41% of the auto racers reported having been injured at some point in their careers. Similarly, Zuckerman (1983) found auto racers to exhibit unusually high sensation-seeking scores.

Such findings could reflect a need to engage in risky sports activities (Fowler, Knorring, & Oreland, 1980). They could also reflect the fact, however, that sensation seekers are more likely to try a greater number of sports activities (low risk as well as high risk). To clarify this issue, Rowland, Franken, and Harrison

(1986) administered Zuckerman's scale to 97 male and 104 female undergraduate students. Their results indicated that persons scoring high on the scale tend to become more involved in more sports, but that persons scoring low are more likely to remain with one sport for a longer period. In addition, Rowland et al. found a positive correlation between sensation seeking and participation in risky sports. These findings indicate that both increased activity and a desire to get involved with high-risk sports characterize the sensation seeker. In other words, sensation-seeking predicts not only the choice but also the degree of involvement in various sports. Thus it seems that arousal levels that would be excessive for most people are only sufficient to keep sensation seekers from boredom.

Introversion-Extraversion

According to Eysenck (e.g., 1967), there are two superordinate trait dimensions (i.e., "second-order" factors) in personality: introversion-extraversion and neuroticism(emotionality)-stability. These superordinate traits are further subdivided into component traits such as sociability, impulsiveness, activity, liveliness, and excitability, which lead to a person's habitual responses. Eysenck (1967) also suggested a third dimension—psychoticism—strength of superego, which relates to the development of psychopathologies—but this is referred to in the literature far less often than the two other domains.

Eysenck suggested an hereditary biological basis for these superordinate dimensions. Regarding introversion-extraversion, he argued that introverts differ from extraverts in the functioning of the ascending reticular activating system (ARAS), which is responsible for activating/deactivating higher brain portions. Eysenck (1981) later proposed that the base levels of ARAS activation of introverts are higher in comparison to those of extraverts. For this reason, introverts are said to avoid further stimulation, whereas extraverts are induced to seek additional stimulation (because of their lower arousal base levels).

Eysenck's proposal for a neural basis for neuroticism-stability relates to the activity of the limbic system, and the psychoticism-strength of superego is associated with the hormonal system. Extraverts have been found to be more easily conditioned (as well as more highly aroused and reactive) in response to their environment than introverts (Eysenck, 1967; Revelle, Humphreys, Simon, & Gilliland, 1980). Extraverts attend better during short periods, whereas introverts attend more efficiently during the later stages of a prolonged task (e.g., vigilance tasks of prolonged duration; Harkins & Green 1975). The shorter term attention, learning, and performance of introverts may be inferior to that of extraverts, however, despite the former's ability to attend better and longer. According to Gillespie and Eysenck (1980), the learning process of introverts is more easily disrupted by distractions; in addition, when compared to extraverts, they take longer to respond, are more cautious, and are more likely to be stopped in decision processes conducted during attentive tasks.

The Eysenck Personality Inventory (EPI; Eysenck & Eysenck, 1963), made up of 57 yes-no items purporting to measure introversion-extraversion and neuroticism-stability, was first used in sports research with wrestlers at the 1966 world tournament. Specifically, Morgan (1968) found a significant correlation (r = .50) between extraversion and success at that event. Brichin and Kochian (1970) studied Czech females; they found a significant difference in extraversion scores between 81 accomplished athletes and 86 performers of lesser accomplishment. Delk (1973) found a significant difference between 41 experienced male skydivers and the norms of the EPI manual on extraversion scores. Similar results were reported by Kirkcaldy (1980) regarding German athletes.

Fiegenbaum (1981; cited by Eysenck, Nias, & Cox, 1982) compared high-level long-distance runners with 62 regular joggers and 52 control subjects and found that runners scored higher on extraversion than joggers, who in turn demonstrated higher extraversion than the controls. Eysenck et al. (1982) concluded that athletes, both males and females, tend to be extraverts regardless of their expertise level. As Weingarten (1982) states, "most studies on the personality structure of athletes show an abundance of extraverts" (p. 121).

There are, however, some indications (e.g., Spielman, 1963) that extraverts do not easily tolerate repetitious stimuli for prolonged time periods. One would expect extraverts to be attracted mainly to vivid sports disciplines such as football or basketball, which contain various elements of body contact and intensive stimulation. In contrast, introverts will be more attracted to such relatively monotonous sports as rifle shooting, swimming, cycling or cross-country skiing (Weingarten, 1982). As mentioned above, though, athletes in general tend to be more extraverted in comparison to nonathletes (Eysenck et al., 1982).

In summary, introversion-extraversion seems to

be a personality dimension by which top-level athletes can be distinguished from athletes of lower levels, as well as from nonathletes. It remains to be seen, however, whether the typically nontheoretical research in this area will suggest more adequate answers even to practical questions, such as the selection on the basis of this personality dimension (Bakker, Whiting, & van der Brug, 1990). Moreover, much work is needed to illuminate the still-unclear role neuroticism-stability and psychoticism-strength of superego play in the sports and exercise domain.

Anxiety

Spielberger (1989) proposed that anxiety refers to "emotional reactions that consist of a unique combination of: (1) feeling of tension, apprehension, and nervousness; (2) unpleasant thoughts (worries); and (3) physiological changes" (p. 5). This widely accepted definition is interactional in nature, because an anxiety state is caused not only by traits but also by stressors. The latter are viewed as situations that involve some physical and/or subjectively appraised (i.e., psychological) danger or threat (Spielberger, 1989).

Early approaches to anxiety (e.g., Taylor, 1953) conceptualized it as a relatively stable and unchanging construct. Later, researchers such as Cattell (1972) and Spielberger (1972) delineated anxiety into the trait and state components: Whereas trait anxiety represents the relatively stable and unchanging predisposition of a person to perceive situations as threatening, state anxiety is a dynamic variable that relates to the perception of individual and/or environmental factors as stressors.

Early psychometric instruments developed to assess trait anxiety, such as the Taylor Manifest Anxiety Scale (TMAS; Taylor, 1953), have not been widely accepted by sports psychologists. Despite the established construct validity of Spielberger's State-Trait Anxiety Inventory (STAI; Spielberger, Gorsuch, & Lushene, 1970; Spielberger, Gorsuch, Lushene, Vagg, & Jacobs, 1983) and its demonstrated utility in a variety of settings, including sports (Spielberger, 1989), several alternative scales have been developed to evaluate anxiety in this specific context. Martens suggested alternatives such as the Sport Competition Anxiety Test (SCAT; Martens, 1977), the Competitive State Anxiety Scale (CSAI; Martens, Burton, Rivkin, & Simon, 1980), and more recently the Cognitive-Somatic Anxiety Questionnaire (CSAI-2; Martens, Vealey, & Burton, 1990), which conceives anxiety as a multidimensional construct rather than a global one. Although general measures of anxiety proved to be useful in sport and exercise (Hanin, 1986; Morgan, 1984), the trend of developing sport-specific scales is more noticeable (Raglin, 1992). For example, Ostrow's (1990) directory of psychological tests in the sports and exercise sciences includes 14 sport-specific anxiety tests developed between 1977 and 1990, with only three developed before 1986.

Research on anxiety in sports and exercise has been conducted mainly within the framework of two paradigms—namely, the drive and the inverted-U theories. Hull-Spence's drive concept (Hull, 1943; Spence, 1956) and its relationship to motor performance were extensively reviewed by Martens (1971, 1974). Studies in this area were classified according to the criterion of absence or presence of experimental stressors (e.g., electric shock). The absence of stressors was aimed to examine the drive theory's chronic hypothesis, that high-anxiety individuals will respond with greater drive across all situations. The presence of stressors was intended to test the drive theory's emotional reactivity hypothesis (Spence & Spence, 1966), which stated that differences between high- and low-anxiety persons would become more evident in the presence of stressors.

Martens found only a few studies that supported both hypotheses. Accordingly, he recommended the abandonment of the drive theory, advising alternative trait-state conceptions (Martens, 1972). This recommendation is further strengthened by the difficulty of accurately measuring habit strength in nonlaboratory settings, which are typical to the realm of applied sport and exercise. Moreover, most motor behaviors found in this domain cannot be considered simple, and therefore are problematic to test within the framework of the drive theory (Martens, 1974, 1977).

The inverted-U theory is currently viewed as more accountable to the research of anxiety in sports and exercise (Weinberg, 1989). This theory hypothesizes that performance effectiveness will increase as arousal increases to some optimal point; a further increase in arousal will produce performance decrements. Despite the conceptual differences between the terms *arousal* and *anxiety*, several researchers have used anxiety measures to account for arousal (for reviews, see Raglin, 1992; Weinberg, 1989). For example, Martens and Landers (1970) assigned high, moderate, and low trait anxiety (A-Trait) subjects to a motor tracking task involving three levels of stress. They found that subjects in the moderate stress condition performed better than subjects in the high or low stress conditions, and that subjects with moderate A-Trait scores outperformed low and high A-Trait subjects.

Klavora (1978) assessed 924 pregame state anxiety (A-State) values of 95 subjects throughout an interscholastic high school basketball season, controlling individual differences in playing ability by asking coaches to evaluate each player's game performance with regard to the player's regular ability. Klavora's results showed that best performance was usually associated with moderate pregame A-State and that worst performance was quite typical for either extremely high or low A-States. Sonstroem and Bernardo (1982) similarly related pregame A-State responses to performance of 30 college varsity players across three games of a basketball tournament, controlling for individual differences in arousal reactivity. The authors found that median anxiety values were significantly associated with best game performance; moreover, 18% of the game performance variance could be explained by a curvilinear relationship with pregame state anxiety. Thus these studies support the inverted-U hypothesis in both the laboratory (Martens & Landers, 1970) and the field (Klavora, 1978; Sonstroem & Bernardo, 1982).

Fiske and Maddi (1961) discussed the role task characteristics play in varying the range of optimal arousal. These authors proposed that as task complexity increases, optimal arousal range will decrease. Oxendine (1970) extended this proposal and developed a hierarchical classification of sports activities based on their complexity (i.e., degree of fine motor control, effort, and judgment required for performance). Activities such as weight lifting, sprinting, and football tackling and blocking were contrasted with bowling, field goal kicking, and figure skating. The former sports, demanding gross motor activities, require high arousal levels compared to the latter sports, which demand fine motor activities.

This idea was supported by Weinberg and Genuchi (1980), who found low levels of both competitive A-Trait and A-State to be related to better scores achieved across three days of a golf tournament, with golf being considered a task requiring precision and other fine movements. Other studies conducted to test this hypothesis, though, either failed to support Oxendine's hierarchy of motor tasks (Basler, Fisher, & Mumford, 1976), or even contradicted it (Furst & Tenenbaum, 1984). Despite these and other reservations raised against Oxendine (Martens et al., 1990; Neiss, 1988), his conceptualization is still considered influential within sports and exercise psychology (Raglin, 1992). Future research should devote more attention to this important issue.

Future studies on anxiety and sport/exercise performance should also inquire the role of individual differences within the framework of the inverted-U theory. Recent reviews (Gould & Krane, 1992; Raglin, 1992) reveal considerable ambiguity and confusion in the understanding of the range of individual differences among athletes. Hence future research efforts should attempt to clarify this issue within the framework of the inverted-U paradigm.

Cognitive mechanisms such as attention seem to play an important role in explaining the arousal/anxiety-performance curvilinear relationship depicted by the inverted-U function. For example, Landers (1978, 1980) suggested that low arousal is associated with uncritical acceptance of irrelevant cues, whereas high arousal is associated with elimination of relevant cues as a result of factors such as perceptual narrowing (Easterbrook, 1959). In contrast, moderate arousal, which increases perceptual selectivity, causes an optimal elimination of task-irrelevant cues, and thus the curvilinear arousal-performance relationship (inverted-U function) can be observed. A full test of this promising theory, however, has never been carried out (Gould & Krane, 1992).

Bar-Eli, Tenenbaum, and Elbaz (1990) used the constructs of anxiety and attention to explain athletes' aggressive behavior during competition. Early theories of anxiety accounted for individual performance differences by the presence or absence of task-irrelevant responses in subjects' behavioral repertories (Sarason, Mandler, & Craighill, 1952). The cognitive-attentional anxiety theory (Wine, 1980, 1982) conceptualized anxiety in terms of cognitive and attentional processes aroused in evaluational settings. According to this approach, cognitive anxiety misdirects attention from task-relevant cues to task-irrelevant self- or social evaluation cues. Although originally related to test anxiety, this theory applies to other situational contexts (Carver & Scheier, 1988), such as sports (Burton, 1988). According to Bar-Eli et al. (1990), as an athlete's anxiety arises in competition, it is accompanied by a higher probability of task-irrelevant behaviors. Because high levels of arousal tend to instigate and magnify aggressive behavior (Caprara, Renzi, D'Augello et al., 1986; Zillman, 1971), however, it is predicted that the more substantial an athlete's deviation from optimal arousal as a result of high anxiety, the higher the probability that he or she will reveal task-irrelevant behaviors, including "hostile" aggression (aggression that is an end rather than a means; Husman & Silva, 1984). This hypothesis has gained strong empirical corroboration in sport disciplines such as team handball (Bar-Eli et al., 1990), basketball (Bar-Eli & Tenenbaum, 1988, 1989a), and tennis (Bar-Eli, Taoz, Levy-Kolker, & Tenenbaum, 1992).

In conclusion, interactional approaches (e.g., Martens et al., 1990) seem to have a great potential for generating considerable research in sports personality with regard to anxiety-behavior relationship (Vealey, 1992). Future research would also have to test various modifications to the inverted-U hypothesis, which have recently been suggested. For example, Hanin's (1989) "zone of optimal functioning" (ZOF) theory appears to be a good candidate for furthering knowledge (Landers, 1989), probably in combination with Morgan's (1985) "mental health" model (Raglin, 1992). Other unidimensional views of arousal/anxiety, such as Mahoney's (1979) coping model, or multidimensional views such as the psychic energy model (Martens, 1988), reversal theory (Kerr, 1989), the catastrophe cusp model (Hardy & Parfitt, 1991; Krane, 1992), and the psychological performance crisis model (Bar-Eli & Tenenbaum, 1989b) deserve more empirical research to verify their validity for examining the anxiety construct in sports and exercise. Finally, research incorporating psychobiological states (Hatfield & Landers, 1983; Neiss, 1988) might make a substantial contribution, mainly because of its emphasis on the interaction among cognitive, emotional, and physiological variables. It remains to be seen whether transactional approaches (e.g., Hackfort & Schultz, 1989) will in fact realize the promise of replacing interactional approaches in the more distant future, as would have been predicted by philosophy (Dewey & Bentley, 1949).

Motivation

Motivation research in sports and exercise began from typical self-acting approaches to personality. For example, it was argued that a considerable amount of physical and sports activity can be related to the need to fulfill such motives as competence (White, 1959), stimulation and arousal seeking (Ellis & Scholtz, 1978), perceptual augmentation/reduction (Petrie, 1967; Ryan & Foster, 1967), and affiliation (Alderman, 1976). A similar line of research has continued in the form of investigating motives for participation and withdrawal in youth sports. Petlichkoff (1992) analyzed data from a survey that included more than 10,000 young people from 11 cities across the United States. Her results indicated that (a) participation in organized sports declines sharply as youngsters get older; (b) "fun" is the key reason for involvement, and "lack of fun" is one of the primary reasons for discontinuing; (c) winning plays less of a role than most adults would think; and (d) not all athletes have the same motivations for their involvement. These results are in line with previous findings (for reviews, see Gould & Petlichkoff, 1988; Weiss & Petlichkoff, 1989).

In a series of studies, Scanlan and her associates (reviewed in Scanlan & Simons, 1992) offered the construct of sport enjoyment to account for such findings. This approach views enjoyment as a cornerstone of motivation in sports, in close affiliation with constructs such as perceived competence (Harter, 1981) and intrinsic challenge (Csikszentmihaly, 1975; Deci & Ryan, 1980). In contrast to previous research, however, Scanlan's research is much more interactional in nature in that it attempts to identify the sources of enjoyment, which are quite often located in a person's environment (Scanlan & Simons, 1992).

Sports are in essence competitive activities. As defined by Martens (1976), sports competition is "a process in which the comparison of an individual's performance is made with some standard in the presence of at least one other person who is aware of the criterion for comparison and can evaluate the comparison process" (p. 14). To explore the role of personality factors within this framework, McClelland-Atkinson's achievement motivation theory received considerable attention in early literature, with sports psychologists making use of traditional tests to measure its constructs (Fineman, 1977).

Following McClelland, Atkinson, Clark, and Lowell (1953), Atkinson (1964, 1974) extended his theory of achievement motivation. In essence, Atkinson's model uses an interactional approach, which formally specifies the role of personality and situational factors as determinants of achievement behavior. Despite the fact that this theory has been the starting point for much of the achievement research to follow, only a few investigations in sports psychology directly tested its predictions with regards to physical-motor tasks (Healey & Landers, 1973; Ostrow, 1976; Roberts, 1972, 1974; Ryan & Lakie, 1965). Moreover, the results of these studies did not always support the predictions of Atkinson's model.

During the 1970s and 1980s, the cognitive approach gave motivation research a substantial impetus, in particular through Weiner's attribution theory (Weiner, 1974, 1986). Weiner's attempt to insert causal attributions into achievement motivation made the situation and its meaning more important; in contrast, individual differences and personality aspects became less important (Maehr, 1989; Roberts, 1992a). The corpus of work on attribution in sports and exercise has grown in both interest and volume (see reviews by Biddle, 1993; McAuley & Duncan, 1990). Although attribution theory has been a potent force in social sports psychology, some of its weaknesses have become evident when motivation research in sports is considered (Biddle, 1993; Roberts, 1992a), probably because of its strong situationistic, self-acting emphasis.

The future of research on motivation in sports seems to lie in the social-cognitive approach. Several theories suggested within this framework have incorporated cognitive, affective, and value-related factors that mediate the process of choice and attainment of achievement goals. Among these theories, self-efficacy (Bandura, 1977, 1986), perceived competence (Harter, 1978, 1981) and various achievement-goal perspectives (Dweck, 1986; Maehr & Braskamp, 1986; Nicholls, 1984, 1989) have played a major role. Based on such approaches, Roberts (1992a) proposed an integrative framework to portray a dynamic process model of motivation, which gives the demonstration of ability a central role. In this model, factors such as goals of action (competitive, mastery), motivational climate (competitive, mastery), perceived ability (high, low, irrelevant) and achievement behavior (adaptive, maladaptive) are considered in order to integrate dynamically ideas delineated in current views of motivation in sports and exercise (Roberts, 1992b). This model is transactional in nature and, as such, leaves many issues open (e.g., the adequate research methods needed for its complete empirical testing; see Tenenbaum & Bar-Eli, 1992). It reflects, however, the way motivation approaches to personality in sport have advanced from self-acting concepts (stressing person or situation) through interactional or social-cognitive approaches to approaches that attempt to conduct future transactional research in this area.

INTELLECTUAL CAPABILITIES AND MOTOR BEHAVIOR

As depicted in previous sections, testing the personality profile of athletes was quite a popular procedure among sports psychologists, mainly in the 1960s and 1970s. Although intelligence was considered as an inherent personality trait within various instruments (e.g., the MMPI or 16PF), the findings drawn from them on athletes' intelligence were inconclusive and sometimes misleading. This result has led researchers to draw attention to other methods and paradigms that more validly account for intelligent behavior related to skilled motor performance.

Intelligence remains a complex cognitive construct that needs further clarification, particularly when it is applied to a specific field such as motor performance. Does skilled motor performance requires intelligence? If so, what are the necessary intellectual traits? Furthermore, some motor tasks are performed automatically, particularly in situations involving time pressure. Are such actions dependent on any cognitive construct, or can they be performed skillfully independent of intellectual control? These questions are addressed in this section.

Intelligence and Intellectual Requirements in Sport

Intelligence is the capacity to acquire and apply knowledge. Behavior is considered to be intelligent when people are capable of dealing with old and new demands posed by the environment. Intelligence indicates adaptable behavior based upon the capacity to solve problems, and this behavioral effectiveness is directed by cognitive processes and operations (Combs, 1952; Estes, 1982). Fisher (1984b) further argues that intelligent behavior depends heavily on the richness and variety of perceptions processed at a given moment—that is, the brain's capacity to encode (store and represent) and access (retrieve) information relevant to the task being performed. Because tasks vary with respect to unique characteristics and requirements, it is assumed that the nature and integration of the perceptual-cognitive component required for each task is also unique. Moreover, similar tasks may be performed in different situations; therefore, intelligent behavior is dependent on intellectual capacity, the nature of the task, and the situation in which the task and person interact.

Sports proficiency is in essence intelligence (Fincher, 1976) because it involves encoding of relevant environmental cues, processing them, and choosing an appropriate response. Open motor skills, as well as some closed skills, require making decisions in a continuously changing environment; therefore adaptable behavior is required to perform motor skills proficiently. Thus the classical definition of intelligence fits well into the motor domain, although one should consider both the uniqueness of the environment and motor skills in the general schema. An athlete may arrive at the most appropriate decision while performing a motor task, but execute it inefficiently because of motor immaturity. Therefore it is believed that cognitive skills are necessary but not sufficient for a skilled performance.

It may be concluded that intelligent motor behavior consists of a perceptual style that requires the performer to attend to and concentrate on relevant cues and efficiently process the information, using working and long-term memory mechanisms. This enables the anticipation of upcoming events and formation of internal representations of the external environment in time and space. Finally, an organized, indicative, and controlled movement can be chosen and executed (Marteniuk, 1976). These cognitive characteristics are shown in Figure 1.

Information Processing, Knowledge Structures, Experience, and Decision Making

To function efficiently in a dynamic and complex environment with restricted rules requires the athletes to be aware of its complexity and to choose essential cues among many. Thereafter the athlete must identify a cue pattern, activate short-term memory in planning his or her moves, and set up strategies (tactics). These tasks precede any response patterns or retrieval pattern from long-term memory, which are stored so that a preferable solution can be found (Fisher, 1984b).

Several studies examined the motor-perceptual factors that distinguish experienced from inexperienced subjects. It was concluded that experienced subjects utilize the stimuli presented to them more

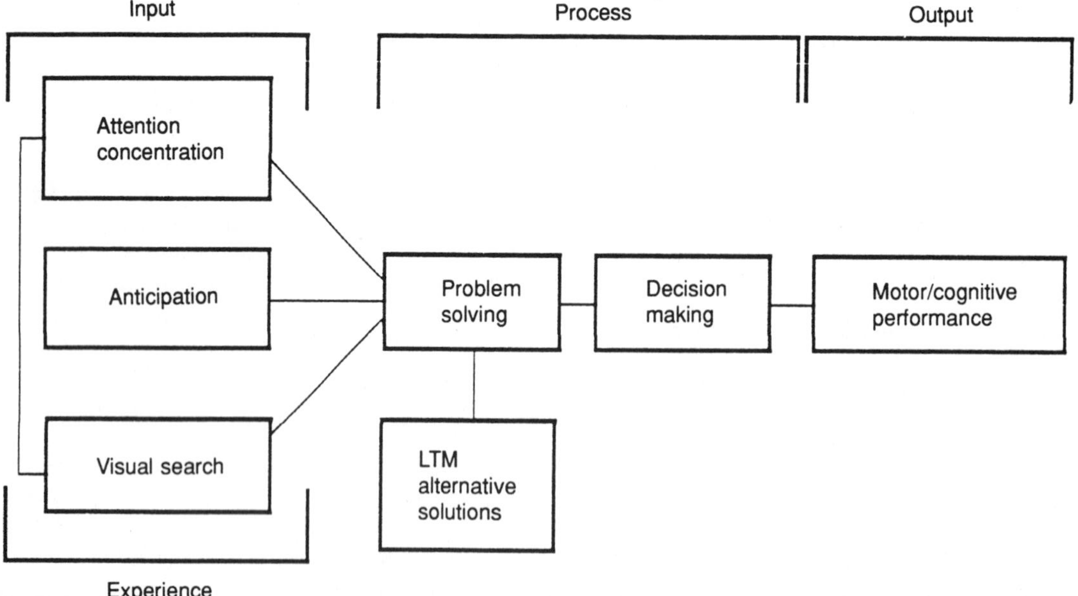

Figure 1. A general model showing how perceptual components such as attention, concentration, visual search of cues, and anticipation of upcoming events that are operated during physical effort and arousal state affect information processing until a motor response is executed (output).

efficiently than inexperienced subjects. Thus the former analyze only necessary information related to performing skills in which time constitutes a determining factor, such as those required in tennis, badminton, and squash (Abernethy & Russell, 1987). Annett and Kay (1956) also maintain that experienced persons examine all the essential information in the early stages of action, whereas the inexperienced person expects information to arrive in the course of events. It follows that experienced players have more time to decide and act.

Encoding information while glancing is usually automatic and dependent on early learning. As one becomes more experienced, qualitative changes in integrative perceptual processing take place without any noticeable change in the encoding processes. Gibson (1969) maintained that an improvement in integration of the information, irrespective of time and space, is actually an increase in sensitivity to the relations among stimuli at the highest level. It is reasonable to assume that experienced athletes integrate information more efficiently than inexperienced ones as a result of more effective matching between newly encoded and stored information (Hochberg, 1982).

According to Abernethy (1987a, b), experience develops more realistic expectations of forthcoming events and, in turn, enhances rapid responses to the occurrence of certain environmental events. Also, the reservoir of options held by the experienced enables skilled judgment as to what is likely to happen in a given situation (Marteniuk, 1976). It seems that experience increases the probability of choosing the correct response, particularly in fast-paced sports. Experience may be perceived not as a chronological variable, but rather as one that confounds a substantial amount of cognitive variables that determine the decision making ability of athletes.

Reaction and Decision Times, Timing Accuracy, and Information Processing

The study of fast-paced ball games (e.g., football, basketball, tennis, hockey) is extensively concerned with reaction time (RT), because the time to detect, process, decide, and respond is very limited. In studies in which the correlation between performance and RT was estimated, the findings are inconsistent. Decision time and choice reaction time (CRT) have been shown to be different in skilled and unskilled athletes (Whiting & Hutt, 1972), and performance quality has been shown to be associated with faster RT (Olsen, 1956). In addition, practice significantly reduces CRT under substantial environmental load compared to CRT under manipulation of information processing load (Conrad, 1962). This reduction in decision time is probably a result of expectations to stimulus-response possibilities, the probability of stimuli to occur, and the sequential dependencies in stimulus presentation (Abernethy, 1987b; Hyman, 1953), all of which facilitate a more rapid response (Abernethy, 1987b).

Abernethy (1991) maintains that in receiving a tennis stroke, a player may have between 500 and 600 ms (if ball speed averages 40–45 ms^{-1}) during which he or she faces uncertainty about the ball direction and speed and must plan an appropriate response. Accordingly, the decision as to what return stroke to play consists of as little as 30 to 50 ms of ball flight information(!). Expert players usually choose the most appropriate strategies among those stored in their long-term repertoire. The research on this topic is concerned mainly with the problem of how much of skilled performance is accounted for by cognitive function (i.e., making the right decisions), motor proficiency (executing the perfect motor skills), or both interactively.

In several sports, the player faces a ball that changes direction on bouncing and then reaches him or her very quickly. It is possible that earlier cues of ball flight and/or other cues are used by experts for more precisely predicting the final location of the ball (Abernethy & Russell, 1984; Adams & Gibson, 1989; McLeod, 1987). The advanced predictions by experts supply them more time to plan the response, so that faster RT is not necessarily required to produce a skillful move. Skilled performers were not found to have faster RTs than less skilled athletes (McLeod & Jenkins, 1991); furthermore, catching performance did not decrease when the last 200 ms of a ball flight were not viewed (Lamb & Burwitz, 1988). It may be concluded that differences in accuracy and other task specificities could not be attributed to RT or CRT but rather to other cognitive characteristics.

A number of studies have shown that some people can use information in less than 20 ms (Carlton, 1981). McLeod and Jenkins (1991) argue that although choice RT in fast-paced ball games is reported to be around 200 ms, it is possible that when the stimulus comes from internal sources rather than external ones, RT might be even faster. The time taken to modify an action on the basis of continuously available and changing visual information is much less than that required to initiate an action when new visual information is given (Lee, Young, Reddish, Longh, & Clayton, 1983). Table tennis players were found to time their shots to coincide with certain aspects of ball flight with a standard duration of 8 ms (Bootsma & van Wieringen, 1988). Ski jumpers approaching the lip of the jump could time their upward thrust with a standard deviation of about 10 ms. Several such examples introduced by McLeod and Jenkins (1991) suggest that within the course of action, very fast movements are produced by athletes. It is assumed that skillful performance is very much dependent upon such timing initations and refinements, rather than RT or CRT per se.

An additional aspect that may be considered a determinant of skilled performance is the *game schema*, a neurological structure in the brain established through long and continuous practice. This structure enables the prediction of similar and familiar events with higher probability than unsimilar and unfamiliar events. Skilled performers may have a clearer schema that may help them to understand, remember, and predict the outcomes of game situations. Consequently their dependence on fast reactions, which are associated with more errors, is reduced (McLeod & Jenkins, 1991).

Whiting (1991) also argues that RT to the onset of visual stimulus is not an influential variant of skilled performance in fast ball games, because actions are not presented in a sudden fashion. Anticipatory skills and the capability to modify continuous actions are more valuable components required in order for an action to be skillful. It is the nature of information processing that mostly contributes to skilled performance, rather than the "hardware" skills.

Recall Capability and Motor Proficiency

In a series of studies (Allard, 1984; Allard, Graham, & Paarsalu, 1980; Allard & Starkes, 1980; Bard & Fleury, 1976; Bard, Fleury, Carriere, & Halle, 1980; Chase & Simon, 1973; Starkes & Deakin, 1984), athletes were asked to scan slides or films and detect, recognize, or recall targets within structured and unstructured situations in sport settings. Chess experts recalled structured but not unstructured (random) chess boards significantly better than their less qualified counterparts following a 5-second exposure (Chase & Simon, 1973). Similar results were obtained with male basketball players (Allard et al., 1980), female field hockey players (Starkes & Deakin, 1984), and volleyball players (Borgeaud & Abernethy, 1987). Although some studies failed to reproduce these results with volleyball players (Allard et al., 1980; Allard & Starkes, 1980), it is believed that long exposure to repeated situations increases the familiarity with the environment and subsequently improves the recall capability of events that occur within this environment.

The relatively few studies carried out on recall of relevant visual information have compared expert athletes to novice or nonathletes after a relatively long exposure (2 to 8 seconds). They have found experts to be superior in the use of strategies that enable the detection of a target within the environmental display (Beitel, 1980; Gentile, Higgins, Miller, & Rosen, 1975), as well as the recall of structured game situations in a variety of sports.

Allard and Starkes (1980) and Starkes and Allard (1983) argue that with time, the organization mechanism is developed to a stage that enables the skilled athlete to better recall the situation and respond appropriately. The findings have shown that the superiority of skilled athletes in recalling specific structured sport situations (but not other situations) is related not to memory capacity but to the use of different encoding and retrieval strategies (Borgeaud & Abernethy, 1987). It was also argued that experts utilize more efficiently the memory representations sensitive to objects in the display (Neisser, 1967; Prinz, 1977, 1979; Prinz & Atalan, 1973).

The studies on recall capability of athletes in the sports domain have not accounted for several variables inherent in real-life situations. In real situations the athlete is required to scan, recall, and process information while performing additional skills (e.g., bouncing a ball, watching the opponents' positions). Parallel actions divert some attention from the playing environment to other sources. Also, athletes are required to attend, recall, process, and respond very fast (i.e., in less than 1 second). The athlete is also exposed to an environment in which the number of stimuli is continually changing in time and complexity. Thus the ecological validity of the findings reported in the literature are to be further examined.

Tenenbaum, Levy-Kolker, Bar-Eli, and Weinberg (1994) studied the recall capability of team handball players while trying to overcome the above-mentioned shortcomings. Conditions that imposed perceptual constraint and time pressure were as similar as possible to real-game conditions, the display contained many players, attention was partially diverted to a secondary task (bouncing a ball), and exposure duration was short (0.5 vs. 1.0 seconds). Surprisingly, in most of the situations, expertise effects were not evident in the recall of either the major features (players and ball) or the minor features (spectators), except for the recall of complex displays. However, skilled athletes do not typically engage in explicit recall of game scenes, but rather use the information based on implicit memory processes during game situations. Also, in real game conditions, perception occurs over time rather than as a result of scanning a frozen image.

Memory Representations and Motor Performance

According to Paillard (1991), the organism-environment interaction enriches the stored representations of the organism's internal and external world events. Cognitive processes refer to the computational transactions that incorporate these stored representations in some kind of internal dialogue. These representations enable the prediction and control of perceptual and motor activities. The perception-action cycle may proceed either directly (via a perceptual schema and an associated motor program already available within an existing sensorimotor unit) or indirectly (through a cognitive computation that enables the recognition of significant features of the situation and the subsequent choice of the appropriate motor strategy).

According to this original view, both perceptual and motor systems trigger the action system to an optimal level in the speed-accuracy trade-off. If the law of minimal energy expense regulates the bioenergetical and biomechanical requirements of motion, the law of minimal attention may dominate the requirements of information processing in monitoring actions. Therefore, expert behavior may be characterized by a lower charge on the attentional system when the latter encounters overwhelming information within a short time. This, however, was not evidenced by Bard, Fleury, and Goulet (in press). Nougier, Ripoll, and Stein (1990) found that experts adopt a consistent strategy by avoiding specific expectations as to the behavior of the opponent and attending in a "state of diffuse alertness." Such a state enables one to expect and anticipate forthcoming events and respond very quickly while reducing the frequency of guessing.

Vision, Semantic and Sensorimotor Processing, and Skilled Performance

Based on his previous works in which temporal and spatial occlusion paradigms were applied, Abernethy (1991) concluded that there is an essential link between perceptual skills and the kinematic evaluation of the action being observed by the athlete. Very skilled and less skilled athletes, however, were similar in their visual search strategies. At the same time, information pickup was quite different among experts compared to novices (Abernethy, 1990b).

It is argued that the expert athlete attends to the most important cue, but at the same time scans other cues. The novice athlete attends to and concentrates on one cue, ignoring the others. The research paradigms applied by Abernethy seem to be insufficiently sensitive to the peripheral visual strategies used by athletes when attending to environmental information.

An additional concern, raised by Mestre and Pailhous (1991), is that when an unpredictable perturbation to the ball's kinematic features was introduced within the 200 ms time range before the ball reached the player, experts exhibited stereotyped motor response patterns. Therefore expertise is not dependent on information-pickup superiority. Abernethy's studies lacked the action component that is critical in von Hofsten's (1987) understanding of the perception-action cycle. Mestre and Pailhous (1991) argue that in the expert's action pattern, the actual role of "advance" visual cues might be to trigger an action program, whereas "late" cues enable motor adjustments. This line of research may shed more light on the relationship between perceptual properties and intellectual behavior in the course of motor activation that requires decision making.

Ripoll, Papin, and Simonet (1983) argue that in open-skill sports, vision has two functions: semantic (identifying and interpreting the environment) and sensorimotor (carrying out the response). Consequently, Ripoll (1991) distinguished between two cognitive substances that should be investigated separately and in combination. The first cognitive field of research is "perceiving-acting": how the environmental cues are organized within the neurological system and transferred to the motor system, and whether the nature of processing is direct or inferential. The second cognitive field is "perceiving-understanding": the visual cues used to identify the environment and the operation related to the process of decision making. Whether these two operations work serially or in parallel, are direct or inferential, are automatic or controlled, and are discrete or continuous remains to be determined.

Studies that used the temporal or spatial occlusion paradigms to examine skilled performance have concluded that expert athletes need less information in order to predict forthcoming events and react appropriately (Abernethy, 1990a). Furthermore, the dynamic organization of the environment through the visual system and attending to specific cues within the environment, are those which contribute to skilled performance (Ripoll, 1991).

According to Ripoll (1991), the expert-novice differences are related to the mode of visual scanning, which is synthetic in experts and analytic in novices. Synthetic visual scanning consists of directing one's gaze so that most of the events can be observed and grouped by one visual fixation. When much information and time pressure are inherent within the situation (open skills like those in fast-paced ball games), a synthetic visual strategy is of great advantage for making decisions. Ripoll (1988a) found that volleyball players who correctly solved the problems presented to them used a holistic scanning process in orienting their gaze, independent of the ball or the players' displacements. Thus searching for particular cues is not a sufficient strategy for skilled performance in open, complex, and dynamic situations. It is preferable to fixate on a point in space where most cues are picked up so that a visual pattern can be formed to plan the motor response.

This confirms Chase and Posner's (1965) argument that visual orientation and visual attention are not necessarily related to each other. This argument was experimentally proven by Ripoll, Kerlirzin, Stein, and Reine's (1991) study of boxers of different skill levels. The skilled boxers displayed three times fewer visual fixations than the less skilled boxers. Thus peripheral vision plays the role of alertness in detecting the relevant cues in a long area of the focal vision (Levy-Schoen, 1972) and enables the integration of cues into dynamic patterns that result in fewer fixations of higher duration (Ripoll, 1991).

Future research in this direction should take into account the different nature of various sports. Sports in which time pressure is inherent in the situation but the opponent is pacing the uncertainty (e.g., basketball) should be contrasted with sports in which uncertainty is conveyed by the physical characteristics of the environment, and response is self-paced (skiing, climbing, gliding, etc.).

Dupuy and Ripoll (1989) investigated the visual and sensorimotor behavior of rock climbers. They concluded that the semantic and sensorimotor processes occur in a serial order. Visual cues in the extrapersonal space are used first to identify the route when the body is immobile; then identification of selected cues and handholds is performed and the appropriate place to reach and catch is selected. Only then is the body displayed. One may conclude that a sensorimotor map is driven from external cues, whereas a semantic map is driven internally by a cognitive map progressively constructed with accumulation of route knowledge. According to Ripoll (1991), in both externally or self-paced situations, the semantic and sensorimotor processing seems to be serially organized. This may be questionable, particularly in situations of substantial time pressure. In such situations decision making is automatic and consists of internal representations that produce responses quite automatically, with no necessity for serial processing.

It is quite reasonable to assume that in order to reach skilled performance in situations inflated with information and constrained heavily by time, the skilled athlete uses heuristic rules to simplify the process of problem solving and decision making (Kahneman, 1973; Norman, 1976). According to Ripoll (1991), these rules consist of synthetic visual behavior, processing general rather than specific information, and eliminating irrelevant cues (thereby focusing on the relevant ones).

Attending to External-Internal Cues and Anticipating Forthcoming Events

In an extensive review of the literature on expert-novice differences in sports, Abernethy (1987b) concluded that the main reasons for the difference in performance between the two skill groups may be attributed to feature detection and pattern recognition of the environment, which leads to advanced anticipatory recognition among experts. This rapid and accurate recognition of the environment develops through many repetitions of similar actions and maneuvers (experience) and guides the sensory system in a manner that enables quick access to knowledge structure, which facilitates anticipation and prediction (Keele, 1982). The expert-novice differences in anticipatory decisions in fast-paced ball games as a function of visual certainty are displayed in Figure 2.

Based on studies which have applied a film occlusion paradigm to games such as soccer, ice hockey, volleyball, tennis, cricket, and field hockey, Abernethy (1987a) postulated that advanced identification is of value to the response selection process, particularly under conditions of great temporal stress. These may be viewed as conditions of uncertainty. Also, a

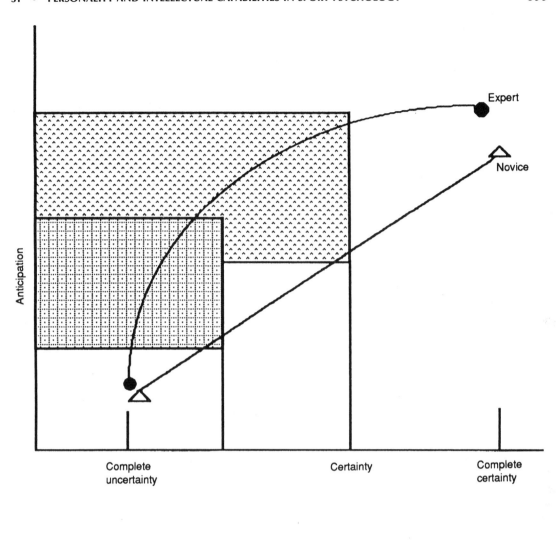

Figure 2. A diagram showing the advantage of skill level (expert vs. novice) in anticipating upcoming events during time of performing motor tasks. Advanced anticipatory skills, particularly under uncertain conditions, enable the athletes to use more time for making decisions.

summary of field studies supports the notion that experts use shorter viewing times and therefore have more time to select their responses (Abernethy, 1987a).

Investigators such as Buckolz, Prapavesis, and Fairs (1988), Abernethy and Russell (1987), and Abernethy (1990a, b) have shown that expert, intermediate, and novice racquet game players appear to attend to similar advance cues, although experts exhibit superior forecasting accuracy as to the final destination of a ball sequence. It is believed that all interpretation of early ball flight information, from shortly prior to ball-racquet contact and on, is processed quite differently by novice, intermediate, and advanced players. That is, anticipation of the final move becomes more accurate, depending strongly on the player's prior knowledge of similar strokes.

In a study by Tenenbaum, Levy-Kolker, Sade, and Liebermann (in press) in which the temporal occlusion paradigm to measure anticipatory skills of tennis players was applied, some contradictory results were obtained. Expert tennis players were not found to differ from intermediate-level players in anticipatory skills. Expert and intermediate-level players were superior to their novice counterparts in only about 50% of the situations. Experts were shown to focus attention on several cues simultaneously at very early stages of their opponent's action initiation, whereas less qualified players usually focused attention on one cue at a time. Of vital importance was the finding that under uncertainty conditions (short exposure to event sequence), novice and intermediate-skill players were more confident in their predictive decisions than experts. Shortly before, at and after ball-racquet contact, however, experts were substantially more confident than the others in their anticipatory decisions. This applied to all the strokes that were examined.

The differences in confidence of anticipatory decisions attributed to skill are of much importance to the understanding of perception-performance relationship. Ball-racquet contact is a stage at which final decisions and error correction take place. Therefore, when confidence in the final stages increases and a qualified solution is determined, a qualified action is executed. Here, in our opinion, are the main differences attributed to skill level of the athletes. The confidence of anticipatory decisions as a function of certainty level and skilled performance is shown in Figure 3.

Attentional Processes and Motor Performance

Nougier, Stein, and Bonnel (1991) make a theoretical distinction between the orientation of attention (Posner, 1980) and the distribution of attentional resources (Navon & Gopher, 1979). Attention is viewed as a combination of facilitations and inhibitions that occur prior to the processing of a signal. When there is too much information to be attended simultaneously, specific processes are necessary to select the most relevant signals with various characteristics (shape, color, texture, etc.). Concentration, vigilance, and preparation may contribute to the efficiency of the internal processes.

Sport activities contain many stages of uncertainty. The extent of uncertainty is determined by the signal-noise ratio (Coombs, Dawes, & Tversky, 1970). Competitors always attempt to hide their intentions from their rivals. Therefore the more attention is oriented toward the relevant cues, the less uncertain is the environment, and probably the more efficient is the process of decision making (Nougier, Stien, & Bonnel, 1991).

Practice of motor skills and tactical operations enhances the automaticity of the attentional process so that a small number of disturbances occur during competitive performance. Attentional processes, however, can also be optional (voluntary and strategic). That is, the expert athlete may initiate unique strategies that help him or her to attend to the relevant cues in the environment and to the intention of the opponent. Furthermore, the skilled athlete can switch from intentional into automatic processes of attentional orientation when necessary. This has been reported by Nougier, Azemar, Stein, and Ripoll (1989) as a typical behavior of expert athletes.

In situations where environmental information has to be processed, the cost-benefit methodology (Posner & Snyder, 1975) was applied quite efficiently. Faster RT at cued locations was termed as "attentional benefit" (facilitation), whereas slower RT at uncued locations was termed "attentional cost" (inhibition; Posner, 1980; Posner, Snyder & Davidson, 1980). The cost-benefit ratio may determine the attentional effect or flexibility (Keele & Hawkins, 1982). Flexibility of attention was defined as the ability of the subject to quickly disengage, orient, and reengage attention on various locations in space. This was believed to be a strong determinant of high-level performance (Keele & Hawkins, 1982). In sports such as tennis, fencing, and ball games, the shift of attention from one cue to the other helps the athlete to determine the probability of the upcoming event and consequently improve his or her performance by decreasing the costs and increasing the benefits of the attentional process (Nougier et al., 1991).

In contrasting expert to nonexpert athletes, Nougier, Ripoll, and Stein (1987, 1990) applied the Posner et al. (1980) paradigm and reported that experts showed reduced costs and benefits (i.e., they were as fast to respond to cued and to uncued locations). Nonexperts were found to exhibit elevated costs and benefits, similar to the regular subjects of Posner et al. (1980). It seems that while performing motor tasks in a skillful manner, athletes learn (consciously or unconsciously) to attend to the relevant signals despite the "noise" that intervenes in their probabilistic choices.

Focal (contracted) and diffuse (expanded) attention modes are also of vital importance in sport.

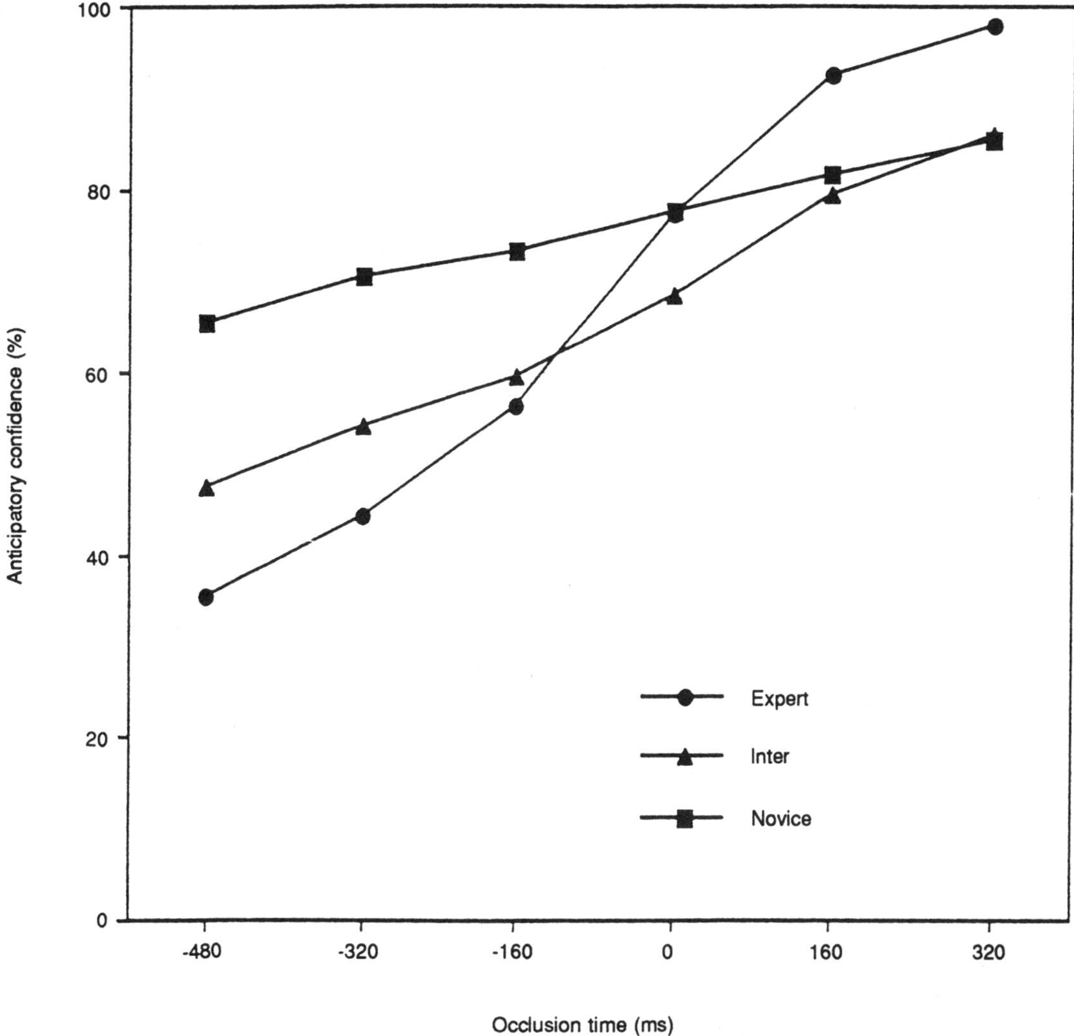

Figure 3. Self-confidence of anticipatory decisions as a function of skill level (expert vs. novice) and certainty condition (visual occlusion time). As visual certainty increases, expert athletes exhibit greater confidence in anticipatory decisions (just prior to motor response). Under uncertain conditions, more confidence is associated with lower skill level.

Nougier et al. (1991) and Nideffer (1976) argue that skilled performance requires one of these attentional modalities, depending on the task characteristics. In archery and shooting, focused attention is preferable (Nougier et al., 1987, 1990), whereas diffuse attention is preferable in table tennis, boxing, and fencing (Ripoll, 1988a, b).

Automatization (Kahneman & Treisman, 1984; Shiffrin & Schneider, 1977) and attentional flexibility (Humphreys, 1981; Keele & Hawkins, 1982; Keele & Neill, 1979) are mechanisms that enable the skilled athlete to perform some skills automatically and at the same time attend to and control more complex situations characterized by a high degree of uncertainty. This is done in a more optimal manner, so that the athlete can simultaneously process several tasks (Nougier et al., 1991).

It is still to be determined how attention is distributed in time and space and how the athlete shifts attention from automatic to voluntary modes before and during engagement in a motor task. These questions should be addressed in each sport separately. An additional field of research involves the eye focus–attention–performance relationship. Is eye focus necessary for attending to the environmental cues? Are expert athletes able to shift attention without altering their eye focus? (Umilta, 1991). We may speculate as to how a skilled performer should act in such situations, but we are uncertain at this stage as to the strategies one should adopt to produce optimal performance.

In addition, Umilta (1991) maintains that voluntary orientation of attention is subjected to interference from the concurrent task and is sensitive to expectations and anticipated events. In contrast, automatic orientation of attention cannot be stopped and does not alter with expectations. It is advisable to compare experts to novices in the two attentional orientation types separately. Significant differences are expected to be obtained in the voluntary type of attention, which is more sensitive to knowledge structure and practice of the athlete.

Castiello and Umilta (1990) reported that as the area of the focused attention decreases, processing efficiency for stimuli located within its borders increases. Thus the ability to control the size of the attentional focus may also be related to skilled performance by maximizing processing efficiency at more relevant locations. It should be examined whether skilled performance is related to the ability to split attention to two or more nonadjacent locations. This ability might prove very helpful for efficient processing and consequently improve decision making through a decrease of uncertainty.

Finally, it is quite acceptable that human beings can process a number of stimuli in parallel; however, only one response is chosen (Umilta, 1991). How is this selection performed? Shallice (1988) suggested two selection processes: contention scheduling (CS), and a supervisory attentional system (SAS). CS is automatic and dependent on the activation threshold of a schemata. Schemata are in mutually inhibitory competition for selection; the one which is triggered is selected to be the response. Some refinements in the election process may occur, however, that are not controlled by CS. It seems that the SAS, which has access to the representation of the environment and the organism's intention, facilitates or inhibits particular action schemata and modulates the CS operation. It is argued that the coordination between CS and SAS is of vital importance to decision making and performance processes in many sports. Whether expert athletes have developed special skills that enable them to switch selection of actions from CS to SAS, and vice versa, remains a subject for future research.

Cognitive and Attentional Styles and Motor Performance

Based on extensive research during the 1940s and 1950s, Witkin et al. (1954) argued that individuals vary in their mode of perception along a continuum from field dependence to field independence. According to Witkin, the perceptual style affects performance in situations that require the separation of an embedded object from its surroundings. Indeed, several studies have demonstrated that field-independent subjects process disembedding problems in an analytical manner, whereas field-dependent subjects tend to solve these types of problems in an intuitive manner (Witkin, Dyk, Faterson, Goodenough, & Karp, 1962; Witkin & Goodenough, 1981; Witkin, Goodenough, & Oltman, 1979). These findings were believed to be reproducible in open and closed skills of motor performance. At the moment, however, one cannot unequivocally proclaim that there is a relationship between cognitive style and sport performance (MacGillivary, 1980; McMorris, 1992).

According to Knapp (1964) and Jones (1972), closed skills consist of physical characteristics such as strength, torque, and technique. Open skills—such as those needed in team handball, basketball, and volleyball, in which a variant sequence of events constantly occurs—require the athlete to continually alter his or her perceptual style (i.e., flexibility of cognitive style). Swinnen, Vandenberghe, and Van Assche (1986) assumed that field-dependent examinees are less successful in a nonstructured learning environment because their information-processing technique does not rely on analysis and construction of the environmental information. In contrast, field-independent examinees utilize organizational techniques in cases where the learned environment is not well determined (i.e., is changing). Furthermore, Jones (1972) extended Poulton's (1957) view of generalized skills and argued that a cognitive style of field dependence imposes perceptual disturbances that are crucial for decision making. Field-independent style enables the counteracting of nonessential stimuli in the environment necessary for decision making and focuses attention on essential information.

The failure to establish a clear relationship between cognitive style and motor performance was attributed mainly to the methodology by which cognitive style was determined (MacGillivary, 1980; McMorris & MacGillivary, 1988), as well as to the fact that the nature of the disembedding differs across sport disciplines. One or two standardized tests are not sufficiently sensitive to detect possible differences among athletes in each particular sport (McMorris, 1992). Most sports demand disembedding to be made in a moving environment, whereas the tests failed to accomplish this requirement. Also, the amount of time in which the performer must make his or her decision is much shorter than that allowed in the test, and the frequency and complexity of the disembedding displays in sports are not well represented in the tests. These shortcomings of the tests are the main reasons for not enabling reliable dissemination of field-dependent from field-independent subjects within specific sport environments.

The cognitive style of field dependence–independence is closely related to the concept of attentional style. Relying on the theories of Easterbrook (1959), Heilbrun (1972), and Wachtel (1967), Nideffer (1976) suggested that attention has two dimensions: width and direction. Width is based on a continuum from narrow to broad (number of stimuli), and direction varies from internal to external.

According to Nideffer (1976), in all sports (individual or team), a unique dimensional integration is required for optimal performance. In general, when the situation is more complex and alters rapidly, an exceptionally focused attention is required from the athlete. When the level of decision making necessitates analyzing or planning, the need for a reflective internal attentional style rises. As a result of an incompatible attentional style, athletes may damage performance. In sports such as soccer, basketball, and tennis, the athlete is expected to alter attentional styles both in width and direction, occasionally quite rapidly. It would seem, therefore, that the ability to alter attentional styles voluntarily is a crucial determinant of an athlete's performance. In such other sports as golf and bowling, the athlete is required to sustain attention on one task for a long time, avoiding disturbing stimuli that would lead to improper decisions.

Athletes with fairly external and narrow attentional styles develop one type of action and remain in this state without initiating any decisions posed by the environmental conditions. Nideffer (1979) argued that anxiety limits the ability to move from one attentional style to another. The narrowing of attention was proven to decrease dual-task type performance (Landers, Furst, & Daniels, 1981). Such tasks are typical in ball games and therefore are believed to be influential in decision making in the course of competition that is mentally and physically demanding. Applying Nideffer's attentional style questionnaire (TAIS) to the sports domain proved in some studies (Kirschenbaum & Bale, 1980; Richards & Landers, 1981), but not all (Aronson, 1981; Landers et al., 1981) that attentional style is a valid component which discriminates between expert and novice athletes.

Perception of Time and Space: Essentials for Controlling Motor Actions

Motor actions are performed in space and time. As such, the perception of time within the space is of vital importance in an environment where external objects are moving, sometimes simultaneously with the performer, and deterministic rules of time are also inherent in the context.

To clarify further the space-time interaction, Laurent and Thomson (1991) distinguish between "movement space" (principle speed and direction) and "approach space" (distance). These two functional spaces are observable in subjects' behaviors when they make adjustments in speed and motion while performing motor tasks. Movements need to be synchronized with the structure of the environment and with the events taking place. Therefore visual timing is primarily important in activities that involve hitting, catching, or intercepting objects (cricket, tennis, football, handball, basketball, etc.). Temporal regulation is also essential in a stable environment (e.g., for jumping, running over irregular terrain; Laurent & Thomson, 1991).

It is quite reasonable that spatio-temporal modulation is also related to anticipation. Catching is a task that requires not only perceiving the speed and direction of the ball, but also predicting its final location in order to execute the skilled response appropriately. In life as well as in sports, most visual regulation is prospective in nature (Lee, Lishman, & Thomson, 1982), regulating the future rather than the present. As such, both timing and prospective control are central features of visuo-motor control (Laurent & Thomson, 1991).

Many of the motor skills involve more complex movements than just running, jumping, or catching. When movements are executed first and adjustments are then required, the organization of movement becomes quite complex. Accuracy of action planning and prospective control is required from the skilled athlete to complete his or her task in a skilled manner.

The degree to which skilled athletes can control time and space in a prospective manner remains to be determined in the future. Research has shown that it is the temporal relationship between the observer and the obstacle, not the spatial relationship, that accounts for appropriate motor functioning (Laurent, 1987; Laurent & Thomson, 1988; Lee, 1980a, b; Lee et al., 1982). The visuo-motor strategies used to perform skilled movement (and essential for optimal development), however, are still unclear.

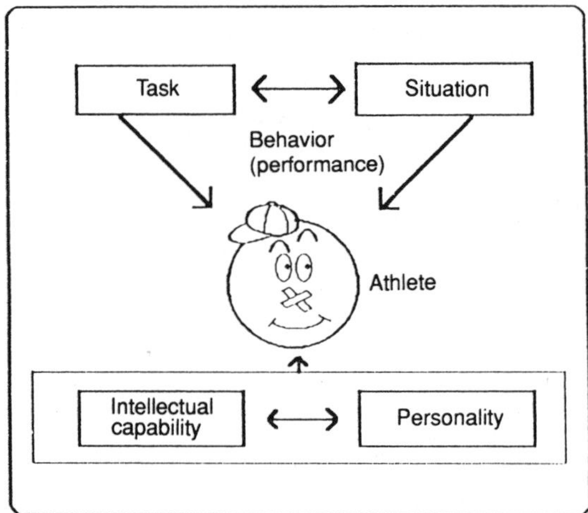

Figure 4. Performance (behavior) of athletes within a transactional system. Sport psychology should implement research paradigms that take into account the interactions among the athletes, the task, and the situation to account for motor performance variability and to gain more ecological validity.

CONCLUDING REMARKS AND FUTURE DIRECTIONS

Sports and exercise psychology is considered a relatively young scientific discipline. Therefore the research of personality and intellectual capability naturally adopted research paradigms and measurement tools from psychology. Common personality inventories were administered to athletes for descriptive purposes as well as to correlate personality with various behaviors and skill performance. The studies on cognitions and perceptions in sports have used similar paradigms to those applied in other settings. Such strategies failed to draw conclusive generalizations as to the relationship of personality traits and intellectual capabilities to behavior and motor performance.

The uniqueness of the milieu of sports and exercise and the nature of the tasks in which the athlete or performer is engaged call for new directions in the domain of exercise and sports psychology. Personality traits and intellectual capabilities should be examined within the transactional context in which performance and behavior are examined interactively in various tasks and situations, as shown in Figure 4.

The transactional approach calls for different research paradigms in the field of sport and exercise with more ecological validity. The psychometric properties of self-report measures of personality traits and states should shift from deterministic approaches to stochastic approaches (e.g., the latent-trait models). Recent developments in this field should also be applied to the field of sports and exercise psychology. Also, the qualitative methods and single case-single subject designs are important approaches that have been neglected in the domain of sports psychology. These applications may contribute much to the understanding of how personality and intellectual capability function in different tasks and situations.

Specific sports personality inventories should be developed. Such inventories may have more potential to distinguish among athletes who differ in personality traits that are relevant to coping with stressful sport demands. Also, specific paradigms are needed to examine possible personality–intellectual capability interactions in sports. For example, simulated decision-making situations may be projected in gradually increasing exposure durations to athletes who differ in anxiety level and attentional flexibility to evaluate their cognitive capacity in such situations. RT and CRT may be added to such paradigms to examine information-processing, encoding, and retrieval processes. Specific paradigms in various sports situations and motor tasks that require cognitive capability when applied interactively with more sensitive methods and tools for measuring personality, have the potential for clarifying how motor tasks are acquired, mastered, and reach perfection.

REFERENCES

Abernethy, B. (1987a). Anticipation in sport: A review. *Physical Education Review, 10*, 5–16.

Abernethy, B. (1987b). Selective attention in fast ball sports: II. Expert-novice differences. *Australian Journal of Science and Medicine in Sport, 19*, 7–16.

Abernethy, B. (1990a). Anticipation in squash: Differences in advance cue utilization between expert and novice players. *Journal of Sports Sciences, 8*, 17–34.

Abernethy, B. (1990b). Expertise, visual search and information pick-up in squash. *Perception, 19*, 63–77.

Abernethy, B. (1991). Visual search strategies and decision making in sport. *International Journal of Sport Psychology, 22*, 189–210.

Abernethy, B., & Russell, D. G. (1984). Advance cue utilisation by skilled cricket batsmen. *Australian Journal of Science and Medicine in Sport, 16*, 2–10.

Abernethy, B., & Russell, D. G. (1987). The relationship between expertise and visual search strategy in a racquet sport. *Human Movement Science, 6*, 283–319.

Adams, R., & Gibson, A. (1989). Moment of ball release identification by cricket batsmen. *The Australian Journal of Science and Medicine in Sport, 21*, 10–13.

Alderman, R. B. (1976). Incentive motivation in sport: An interpretive speculation of research opportunities. In A. C. Fisher (Ed.), *Psychology of sport* (pp. 205–231). Palo Alto, CA: Mayfield.

Allard, F. (1984). Cognition, expert performance, and sport. In M. Whiting (Ed.), *New paths to sport learning* (pp. 22–26). Ottawa: Coaching Association of Canada.

Allard, F., Graham, S., & Paarsalu, M. E. (1980). Perception in sport: Basketball. *Journal of Sport Psychology, 2*, 14–21.

Allard, F., & Starkes, J. L. (1980). Perception in sport: Volleyball. *Journal of Sport Psychology, 2*, 22–23.

Annett, J., & Kay, H. (1956). Skilled performance. *Occupational Psychology, 30*, 112–117.

Aronson, R. M. (1981). *Attentional and interpersonal factors as discriminators of elite and non-elite gymnasts*. Unpublished doctoral dissertation, Boston University.

Atkinson, J. W. (1964). *An introduction to motivation*. Princeton, NJ: Van Nostrand.

Atkinson, J. W. (1974). The mainsprings of achievement-oriented activity. In J. W. Atkinson & J. O. Raynor (Eds.), *Motivation and achievement* (pp. 13–41). New York: Halstead.

Bakker, F. C., Whiting, H. T. A., & van der Brug, H. (1990). *Sport psychology: Concepts and applications*. Chichester, England: Wiley

Bandura, A. (1977). Self-efficacy: Toward a unifying theory of behavioral change. *Psychological Review, 84*, 191–215.

Bandura, A. (1978). The self system in reciprocal determinism. *American Psychologist, 33*, 344–358.

Bandura, A. (1986). *Social foundations of thought and action: A social cognitive theory*. Englewood Cliffs, NJ: Prentice-Hall.

Bard, C., & Fleury, M. (1976). Analysis of visual search activity during sport problem situation. *Journal of Human Movement Studies, 3*, 214–222.

Bard, C., Fleury, M., Carriere, L., & Halle, M. (1980). Analysis of gymnastics judges' visual search. *Research Quarterly for Exercise and Sport, 51*, 267–273.

Bard, C., Fleury, M., & Goulet, C. (in press). Relationship between perceptual strategies and response adequacy in sport situation. *International Journal of Sport Psychology*.

Bar-Eli, M. (1985). Arousal-performance relationship: A transactional view on performance jags. *International Journal of Sport Psychology, 16*, 193–209.

Bar-Eli, M., Taoz, E., Levy-Kolker, N., & Tenenbaum, G. (1992). Performance quality and behavioral violations as crisis indicators in competition. *International Journal of Sport Psychology, 23* 325–342.

Bar-Eli, M., & Tenenbaum, G. (1988). Rule- and norm-related behavior and the individual psychological crisis in competitive situations: Theory and research findings. *Social Behavior and Personality, 16*, 187–195.

Bar-Eli, M., & Tenenbaum, G. (1989a). Observations of behavioral violations as crisis indicators in competition. *Sport Psychologist, 3*, 237–244.

Bar-Eli, M., & Tenenbaum, G. (1989b). A theory of individual psychological crisis in competitive sport. *Applied Psychology, 38*, 107–120.

Bar-Eli, M., Tenenbaum, G., & Elbaz, G. (1990). Psychological performance crisis in high arousal situations—diagnosticity of rule violations and performance in competitive team-handball. *Anxiety Research, 2*, 281–292.

Basler, M. L., Fisher, A. C., & Mumford, M. L. (1976). Arousal and anxiety correlates of gymnastic performance. *Research Quarterly, 47*, 586–589.

Beitel, P. A. (1980). Multivariate relationship among visual-perceptual attributes and gross-motor tasks with different environmental demands. *Journal of Motor Behavior, 12*, 29–40.

Bem, D. J. (1983). Constructing a theory of the triple typology: Some (second) thoughts on nomothetic and idiographic approaches to personality. *Journal of Personality, 51*, 566–577.

Biddle, S. J. H. (1993). Attribution research and sport psychology. In R. N. Singer, M. Murphey, & L. K. Tennant (Eds.), *Handbook of research on sport psychology*. New York: Macmillan.

Bootsma, R., & van Wieringen, P. (1988). Visual control of an attacking forehand drive in table tennis. In O. Meijer & K. Roth (Eds.), *The motor action controversy* (pp. 189–200). Amsterdam: Elsevier.

Borgeaud, P., & Abernethy, B. (1987). Skilled perception in volleyball defense. *Journal of Sport Psychology, 9*, 400–406.

Brichin, M., & Kochian, M. (1970). Comparison of some personality traits of women participating and not participating in sports. *Ceskoslovenska Psychologie, 14*, 309–321.

Buckholz, E., Prapavesis, H., & Fairs, J. (1988). Advanced cues and their use in predicting tennis passing shots. *Canadian Journal of Sport Sciences, 13*, 20–30.

Burton, D. (1988). Do anxious swimmers swim slower? Reexamining the elusive anxiety-performance relationship. *Journal of Sport and Exercise Psychology, 10*, 45–61.

Caprara, G. V., Renzi, P., D'Augello, D., D'Imperio, G., Rielli, I., & Travaglia, G. (1986). Instigation to aggress and aggression: The role of irritability and emotional susceptibility. *Aggressive Behavior, 12*, 78–83.

Carlton, L. (1981). Processing visual feedback information for movement control. *Journal of Experimental Psychology: Human Perception and Performance, 7*, 1019–1030.

Carver, C. S., & Scheier, M. F. (1988). A control-process perspective on anxiety. *Anxiety Research, 1*, 17–22.

Castiello, U., & Umilta, C. (1990). Size of the attentional focus and efficiency of processing. *Acta Psychologica, 73*, 195–209.

Cattell, R. B. (1972). The nature and genesis of mood states: A theoretical model with experimental measures concerning anxiety, depression, arousal, and other mood states. In C. D. Spielberger (Ed.), *Anxiety: Current trends in theory and research* (pp. 115–183). New York: Plenum.

Chase, W. G., & Posner, M. I. (1965). *The effect of auditory and visual confusability on visual memory and search tasks*. Paper presented at the meeting of the Midwestern Psychological Association, Chicago.

Chase, W. G., & Simon, H. A. (1973). Perception in chess. *Cognitive Psychology, 4*, 55–81.

Combs, A. W. (1952). Intelligence from a perceptual point of view. *Journal of Abnormal and Social Psychology, 47*, 662–673.

Conrad, R. (1962). Practice, familiarity, and reading rate for words and nonsense syllables. *Quarterly Journal of Experimental Psychology, 14*, 71–76.

Coombs, C., Dawes, R., & Tversky, A. (1970). *Mathematical psychology*. Englewood Cliffs, NJ: Prentice Hall.

Cronbach, L. J. (1957). The two disciplines of scientific psychology. *American Psychologist, 12*, 671–684.

Csikszentmihaly, M. (1975). *Beyond boredom and anxiety*. San Francisco: Jossey-Bass.

Deci, E. L., & Ryan, R. M. (1980). The empirical exploration of intrinsic motivational processes. In L. Berkowitz (Eds.), *Advances in experimental social psychology* (Vol. 13, pp. 39–80). New York: Academic Press.

Delk, J. (1973). Some personality characteristics of skydivers. *Life Threatening Behavior, 3*, 51–57.

Dewey, J., & Bentley, A. F. (1949). *Knowing and the known*. Boston: Beacon.

Dupuy, C., & Ripoll, H. (1989). Analyse des stratégies visuomotrices en escalade sportive. *Science et Motricité, 7*, 19–26.

Dweck, C. S. (1986). Motivational processes affecting learning. *American Psychologist, 41*, 1040–1048.

Easterbrook, J. A. (1959). The effect of emotion on cue utilization and the organization of behavior. *Psychological Review, 66*, 183–201.

Ekehammar, B. (1974). Interactionism in personality from a historical perspective. *Psychological Bulletin, 81*, 1026–1048.

Ellis, M., & Scholtz, G. (1978). *Activity and play of children*. Englewood Cliffs, NJ: Prentice-Hall.

Estes, W. K. (1982). Learning, memory, and intelligence. In R. J. Sternberg (Ed.), *Handbook of human intelligence* (pp. 170–224). New York: Cambridge University Press.

Eysenck, H. J. (1967). *The biological basis of personality*. Springfield, IL: Thomas.

Eysenck, H. J. (1981). *A model for personality*. Berlin: Springer.

Eysenck, H. J., & Eysenck, S. B. G. (1963). *The Eysenck Personality Inventory*. San Diego, CA: Educational and Industrial Testing Service.

Eysenck, H. J., Nias, D. K. B., & Cox, D. N. (1982). Sport and personality. *Behavior Research and Therapy, 4*, 1–56.

Fiegenbaum, T. (1981). *Persoenlichkeitsmerkmale von Langstreckenlaeufern* [Personality traits of long-distance runners]. Paper presented at a symposium on sports psychology, Munich.

Fincher, J. (1976). *Human intelligence*. New York: Putnam.

Fineman, S. (1977). The achievement motive construct and its measurement. Where are we now? *British Journal of Psychology, 68*, 1–22.

Fisher, A. C. (1984a). New directions in sport personality research. In J. M. Silva & R. S. Weinberg (Eds.), *Psychological foundations of sport* (pp. 70–80). Champaign, IL: Human Kinetics.

Fisher, A. C. (1984b). Sport intelligence. In W. F. Straub & J. M. Williams (Eds.), *Cognitive sport psychology* (pp. 42–50). New York: Sport Science Associates.

Fiske, D. W., & Maddi, S. R. (1961). *Functions of varied experience*. Homewood, IL: Dorsey.

Fowler, C. J., Knorring, L., & Oreland, L. (1980). Platelet monoamine oxidase activity in sensation seekers. *Psychiatric Research, 3*, 273–279.

Furst, D. M., & Tenenbaum, G. (1984). The relationship between worry, emotionality, and sport performance. In D. M. Landers (Ed.), *Sport and elite performance* (pp. 89–96). Champaign, IL: Human Kinetics.

Gentile, A. M., Higgins, J. R., Miller, E. A., & Rosen, B. M. (1975). The structure of motor tasks. In C. Bard, M. Fluery, & J. H. Salmela (Eds.), *Movement: Actes du 7 Canadien en appretissage psycyhomoteur et psychologie du sport* (pp. 11–28). Ottawa: Association of Professionals in Physical Education of Quebec.

Gibson, E. J. (1969). *The ecological approach to visual perception*. Boston: Houghton Mifflin.

Gillespie, C. R., & Eysenck, M. W. (1980). Effects of introversion extraversion on continuous recognition memory. *Bulletin of the Psychonomic Society, 15*, 233–235.

Gould, D., & Krane, V. (1992). The arousal—athletic performance relationship: Current status and future directions. In T. S. Horn (Ed.), *Advances in sport psychology* (pp. 113–141). Champaign, IL: Human Kinetics.

Gould, D., & Petlichkoff, L. (1988). Participation motivation and attrition in young athletes. In F. Smoll, R. Magill, & M. Ash (Eds.), *Children in sport* (3rd ed., pp. 161–178). Champaign IL: Human Kinetics.

Hackfort, D., & Schultz, P. (1989). Competence and valence as determinants of anxiety. In D. Hackfort & C.D. Spielberger (Eds.), *Anxiety in sports* (pp. 29–38). New York: Hemisphere.

Hanin, Y. L. (1986). State-trait research on sports in the USSR. In C. D. Spielberger & R. Diaz-Guerrero (Eds.), *Cross-cultural anxiety* (Vol. 3, pp. 45–64). Washington, DC: Hemisphere.

Hanin, Y. L. (1989). Interpersonal and intragroup anxiety in sports. In D. Hackfort & C. D. Spielberger (Eds.), *Anxiety in sports* (pp. 19–28). New York: Hemisphere.

Hardy, L., & Parfitt, G. (1991). A catastrophe model of anxiety and performance. *British Journal of Psychology, 82*, 163–178.

Harkins, S., & Green, R. G. (1975). Discriminability and criterion differences between extraverts and introverts during vigilance. *Journal of Research on Personality, 9*, 335–340.

Harter, S. (1978). Effectance motivation reconsidered: Toward a developmental model. *Human Development, 21*, 34–64.

Harter, S. (1981). The development of competence motivation in the mastery of cognitive and physical skills: Is there still a place for joy? In G. C. Roberts & D. M. Landers (Eds.), *Psychology of motor behavior and sport—1980* (pp. 3–29). Champaign, IL: Human Kinetics.

Hatfield, B. D., & Landers, D. M. (1983). Psychophysiology: A new direction for sport psychology. *Journal of Sport Psychology, 3*, 243–259.

Healey, R. R., & Landers, D. M. (1973). Effect of need achievement and task difficulty on competitive and noncompetitive motor performance. *Journal of Motor Behavior, 5*, 121–128.

Heilbrun, A. B. (1972). Style of adaptation to perceived aversive maternal control and scanning behavior. *Journal of Consulting and Clinical Psychology, 29*, 15–21.

Hochberg, J. (1982). How big is a stimulus? In J. Beck (Ed.), *Organization and representation in perception* (pp. 191–218). Hillsdale, NJ: Erlbaum.

Houts, A. C., Cook, T. D., & Shadish, W. R. (1986). The person-situation debate: A critical multiplist perspective. *Journal of Personality, 54*, 52–105.

Hull, C. L. (1943). *Principles of behavior*. New York: Appleton.

Humphreys, G. (1981). Flexibility of attention between stimulus dimensions. *Perception and Psychophysics, 30*, 291–302.

Husman, B. F., & Silva, J. M. (1984). Aggression in sport: Definitional and theoretical considerations. In J. M. Silva & R. S. Weinberg (Eds.), *Psychological foundations of sport* (pp. 246–260). Champaign, IL: Human Kinetics.

Hyman, R. (1953). Stimulus information as a determinant of time. *Journal of Experimental Psychology, 45*, 188–196.

Johansson, F., Almay, B. G. L., Knorring, L., Terenius, L., & Astrom, M. (1979). Personality traits in chronic pain patients related to endorphin levels in cerebrospinal fluid. *Psychiatry Research, 1*, 231–239.

Jones, M. G. (1972). Perceptual characteristics and athletic performance. In H. T. A. Whiting (Ed.), *Readings in sport psychiatry* (pp. 96–115). London: Kimpton.

Kahneman, D. (1973). *Attention and effort.* Englewood Cliffs, NJ: Prentice-Hall.

Kahneman, D., & Treisman, A. (1984). Changing views of attention and automaticity. In R. Parasuraman & D. R. Davies (Eds.), *Varieties of attention* (pp. 29–61). New York: Academic Press.

Keele, S. W. (1982). Component analysis and conceptions of skill. In J. A. S. Kelso (Ed.), *Human motor behavior: An introduction* (pp. 143–159). Hillsdale, NJ: Erlbaum.

Keele, S. W., & Hawkins, H. (1982). Exploration of individual differences relevant to high level skill. *Journal of Motor Behavior, 14,* 3–23.

Keele, S. W., & Neill, T. (1979). Mechanisms of attention. In E. Carterette & M. Friedman (Eds.), *Handbook of perception* (Vol. 9, pp. 3–47). New York: Academic Press.

Kenrick, D. T., & Funder, D. C. (1988). Profiting from controversy: Lessons from the person-situation debate. *American Psychologist, 43,* 23–34.

Kerr, J. H. (1989). Anxiety, arousal and sport performance: An application of reversal theory. In D. Hackfort & C. D. Spielberger (Eds.), *Anxiety in sports* (pp. 137–151). New York: Hemisphere.

Kirkcaldy, B. (1980). An analysis of the relationship between psychophysiological variables connected to human performance and the personality variables extraversion and neuroticism. *International Journal of Sport Psychology, 11,* 276–289.

Kirschenbaum, D. S., & Bale, R. M. (1980). Cognitive-behavioral skills in golf: Brain power golf. In R. M. Suinn (Ed.), *Psychology in sports: Methods and applications* (pp. 334–343). Minneapolis: Burgess.

Klavora, P. (1978). An attempt to derive inverted-U curves based on the relationship between anxiety and athletic performance. In D. M. Landers & R. W. Christina (Eds.), *Psychology of motor behavior and sport.* Champaign, IL: Human Kinetics.

Knapp, B. (1964). *Skill in sport.* London: Routledge & Kegan Paul.

Krane, V. (1992). Conceptual and methodological considerations in sport anxiety research: From the inverted-U hypothesis to catastrophe theory. *Quest, 44,* 72–87.

Lamb, K., & Burwitz, L. (1988). Visual restriction in ball-catching: A re-examination of early findings. *Journal of Human Movement Studies, 14,* 93–99.

Landers, D. M. (1978). Motivation and performance: The role of arousal and attentional factors. In W. Straub (Ed.), *Sport psychology: An analysis of athletic behavior.* Ithaca, NY: Mouvement.

Landers, D. M. (1980). The arousal-performance relationship revisited. *Research Quarterly for Exercise and Sport, 51,* 77–90.

Landers, D. M. (1989). Controlling arousal to enhance sport performance. In G. Tenenbaum & D. Eiger (Eds.), *Proceedings of the Maccabiah-Wingate International Congress: Sport psychology* (pp. 7–27). Netanya, Israel: Wingate Institute.

Landers, D. M., Furst, D. M., & Daniels, F. S. (1981). *Anxiety/attention and shooting ability: Testing the predictive validity of the test of attentional and interpersonal style (TAIS).* Paper presented at the annual meeting of the North American Society for the Psychology of Sport and Physical Activity, Boulder, CO.

Laurent, M. (1987). *Les coordinations visuo-locomotrices: Étude comportmentale chez l'homme.* Unpublished doctoral dissertation, Université Aix-Marseille II, France.

Laurent, M., & Thomson, J. A. (1988). The role of visual information in control of a constrained locomotor task. *Journal of Motor Behavior, 20,* 17–37.

Laurent, M., & Thomson, J. A. (1991). Anticipation and control of visual-guided locomotion. *International Journal of Sport Psychology, 22,* 251–270.

Lee, D. N. (1980a). The optic flow field: The foundation of vision. *Philosophical Transactions of the Royal Society of London, B290,* 169–179.

Lee, D. N. (1980b). Visuo-motor coordination in space-time. In G. E. Stelmach & J. Requin (Eds.), *Tutorials in motor behavior* (pp. 281–295). Amsterdam: North Holland.

Lee, D. N., Lishman, J., & Thomson, J. A. (1982). Regulation of gait in long jumping. *Journal of Experimental Psychology: Human Perception and Performance, 8,* 448–459.

Lee, D. N., Young, D., Reddish, P., Longh, S., & Clayton, T. (1983). Visual timing in hitting an accelerating ball. *Quarterly Journal of Experimental Psychology, 35,* 333–346.

Levy-Schoen, A. (1972). Rapport entre mouvements des yeux et perception. In H. Hecaen (Ed.), *Nueropsychologie de la perception visuelle* (pp. 76–92). Paris: Masson.

MacGillivary, W. W. (1980). The contribution of perceptual style to human performance. *International Journal of Sport Psychology, 11,* 132–141.

Maehr, M. L. (1989). Thoughts about motivation. In R. Ames & C. Ames (Eds.), *Research on motivation in education: Vol. 3. Goals and cognitions* (pp. 299–315). New York: Academic Press.

Maehr, M. L., & Braskamp, L. A. (1986). *The motivation factor: A theory of personal investment.* Lexington, MA: Lexington Books.

Marteniuk, R. G. (1976). Cognitive information processes in motor short-term memory and movement production. In G. E. Stelmach (Ed.), *Motor control: Issues and trends* (pp. 175–199). New York: Academic Press.

Martens, R. (1971). Anxiety and motor behavior: A review. *Journal of Motor Behavior, 3,* 151–179.

Martens, R. (1972). Trait and state anxiety. In W. P. Morgan (Ed.), *Ergogenic aids and muscular performance* (pp. 35–66). New York: Academic Press.

Martens, R. (1974). Arousal and motor performance. In J. H. Wilmore (Ed.), *Exercise and sport science reviews* (Vol.2, pp. 155–188). New York: Academic Press.

Martens, R. (1975). The paradigmatic crisis in American sport personology. *Sportwissenschaft, 1,* 9–24.

Martens, R. (1976). Competition: In need of a theory. In D. M. Landers (Ed.), *Social problems in athletics* (pp. 9–17). Urbana: University of Illinois Press.

Martens, R. (1977). *Sport competition anxiety test.* Champaign, IL: Human Kinetics.

Martens, R. (1988). *Coaches' guide to sport psychology.* Champaign, IL: Human Kinetics.

Martens, R., Burton, D., Rivkin, R., & Simon, J. (1980). Reliability and validity of the Competitive State Anxiety Scale (CSAI). In C. H. Nadeau, W. C. Halliwell, K. M. Newell, & G. C. Roberts (Eds.), *Psychology of motor behavior and sport—1979* (pp. 91–99). Champaign, IL: Human Kinetics.

Martens, R., & Landers, D. M. (1970). Motor performance under stress: A test of the inverted-U hypothesis. *Journal of Personality and Social Psychology, 16,* 29–37.

Martens, R., Vealey, R. S., & Burton, D. (1990). *Competitive anxiety in sport.* Champaign, IL: Human Kinetics.

McAuley, E., & Duncan, T. (1990). The causal attribution process in sport and physical activity. In S. Graham & V. Folkes (Eds.), *Advances in applied social psychology: V. Applications of attribution theory* (pp. 37–52). Hillsdale, NJ: Erlbaum.

McClelland, D. C., Atkinson, J. W., Clark, R. W., & Lowell,

E. L. (1953). *The achievement motive*. New York: Appleton-Century-Crofts.

McLeod, P. (1987). Visual reaction time and high-speed ball-games. *Perception, 16*, 49–59.

McLeod, P., & Jenkins, S. (1991). Timing accuracy and decision time in high speed ball games. *International Journal of Sport Psychology, 22*, 279–295.

McMorris, T. (1992). Field independence and performance in sport. *International Journal of Sport Psychology, 23*, 14–27.

McMorris, T., & MacGillivary, W. W. (1988). An investigation into the relationship between field independence and decision making in soccer. In T. Reilly, A. Lees, K. Davids, & W. J. Murphy (Eds.), *Science and football* (pp. 552–557). London: Spon.

Mestre, D., & Pailhous, J. (1991). Expertise in sport as a perceptivo-motor skill. *International Journal of Sport Psychology, 22*, 211–216.

Morgan, W. P. (1968). Personality characteristics of wrestlers participating in the world championships. *Journal of Sports Medicine, 8*, 212–216.

Morgan, W. P. (1980a). Sport personology: The credulous-skeptical argument in perspective. In W. Straub (Ed.), *Sport psychology: An analysis of athlete behavior* (pp. 330–339). Ithaca, NY: Mouvement.

Morgan, W. P. (1980b). The trait psychology controversy. *Research Quarterly for Exercise and Sport, 51*, 50–76.

Morgan, W. P. (1985). Selected psychological factors limiting performance: A mental health model. In D. H. Clarke & H. M. Eckert (Eds.), *Limits of human performance* (pp. 70–80). Champaign, IL: Human Kinetics.

Navon, D., & Gopher, D. (1979). On the economy of the human processing system. *Psychological Review, 86*, 214–255.

Neary, R. S., & Zuckerman, M. (1976). Sensation seeking, trait and state anxiety, and the electrodermal orienting reflex. *Psychophysiology, 13*, 205–211.

Neiss, R. (1988). Reconceptualizing arousal: Psycholobiological states in motor performance. *Psychological Bulletin, 103*, 345–366.

Neisser, U. (1967). *Cognitive psychology*. New York: Appleton-Century-Crofts.

Nicholls, J. G. (1984). Achievement motivation: Conceptions of ability, subjective experience, task choice, and performance. *Psychological Review, 91*, 328–346.

Nicholls, J. G. (1989). *The competitive ethos and democratic education*. Cambridge, MA: Harvard University Press.

Nideffer, R. M. (1976). Test of attentional and interpersonal style. *Journal of Personality and Social Psychology, 34*, 394–404.

Nideffer, R. M. (1979). The role of attention in optimal athletic performance. In P. Klavora & J. V. Daniel (Eds.), *Coach, athlete and the sport psychologist* (pp. 99–112). Toronto: University of Toronto.

Nitsch, J. R. (1985) The action-theoretical perspective. *International Review for the Sociology of Sport, 20*, 263–282.

Norman, D. A. (1976). *Memory and attention: An introduction to information processing*. New York: Academic Press.

Nougier, V., Azemar, G., Stein, J. F., & Ripoll, H. (1989). Information processing and attention with expert tennis players according to their age and level of expertise. In C. K. Giam, K. K. Chook, & K. C. Teh (Eds.), *Proceedings of the 7th world congress on Sport Psychology* (p. 237). Singapore: International Society of Sport Psychology.

Nougier, V., Ripoll, H., & Stein, J. F. (1987). Processus attentionnels et practique sportive de haut niveau. In M. Laurent & P. Therme (Eds.), *Recherches en APS II* (pp. 209–221). Aix-Marseille II, France: Centre de Recherche de l'UEREPS.

Nougier, V., Ripoll, H., & Stein, J. F. (1990). Orienting of attention with highly skilled athletes. *International Journal of Sport Psychology, 20*, 205–223.

Nougier, V., Stein J. F., & Bonnel, A. M. (1991). Information processing in sport and "orienting of attention." *International Journal of Sport Psychology, 22*, 307–327.

Olsen, E. (1956). Relationship between psychological capacities and success in college athletics. *Research Quarterly, 27*, 78–89.

Ostrow, A. C. (1976). Goal-setting behavior and need achievement in relation to competitive motor activity. *Research Quarterly, 47*, 174–183.

Ostrow, A. C. (Ed.). (1990). *Directory of psychological tests in the sport and exercise sciences*. Morgantown, WV: Fitness Information Technology.

Oxendine, J. B. (1970). Emotional arousal and motor performance. *Quest, 13*, 23–32.

Paillard, J. (1991). The cognitive penetrability sensorimotor mechanisms: A key problem in sport research. *International Journal of Sport Psychology, 22*, 244–250.

Pervin, L. A. (1977). The representative design of person-situation research. In D. Magnusson & N. S. Endler (Eds.), *Personality at the crossroads: Current issues in interactional psychology* (pp. 371–384). Hillsdale, NJ: Erlbaum.

Pervin, L. A. (1985). Personality: Current controversies, issues, and directions. *Annual Review of Psychology, 36*, 83–114.

Petlichkoff, L. M. (1992). Youth sport participation and withdrawal: Is it simply a matter of fun? *Pediatric Exercise Science, 4*, 105–110.

Petrie, A. (1967). *Individuality in pain suffering: The reducer and the augmenter*. Chicago: Chicago University Press.

Posner, M. I. (1980). Orienting of attention. *Quarterly Journal of Experimental Psychology, 32*, 3–25.

Posner, M. I., & Snyder, C. (1975). Facilitation and inhibition in the processing of signals. In P. Rabbit & S. Dornic (Eds.), *Attention and performance* (Vol. 5, pp. 669–682). London: Academic Press.

Posner, M. I., Snyder, C. R., & Davidson, B. J. (1980). Attention and the detection of signals. *Journal of Experimental Psychology: General, 109*, 160–174.

Poulton, E. C. (1957). On prediction in skilled movements. *Psychological Bulletin, 54*, 467–478.

Prinz, W. (1977). Memory control of visual search. In S. Dornic (Ed.), *Attention and performance* (Vol. 6, pp. 441–462). Hillsdale, NJ: Erlbaum.

Prinz, W. (1979). Integration of information visual search: The Experimental Psychology Society. *Psychological Beitrage, 25*, 57–70.

Prinz, W., & Atalan, D. (1973). Two components and two stages in search performance: A case study in visual search. *Acta Psychologica, 37*, 218–242.

Raglin, J. S. (1992). Anxiety and sport performance. In J. O. Holloszy (Ed.), *Exercise and Sport Sciences Review* (Vol. 20, pp. 243–274). Baltimore, MD: Williams & Wilkins.

Revelle, W., Humphreys, M. S., Simon, L., & Gilliland, K. (1980). The interactive effect of personality, time of day and caffeine: A test of the arousal model. *Journal of Experimental Psychology, 109*, 1–31.

Richards, D. E., & Landers, D. M. (1981). Test of attentional style and interpersonal style scores of shooters. In G. C. Roberts & D.M. Landers (Eds.), *Psychology of motor behavior and sport—1980* (p. 94). Champaign, IL: Human Kinetics.

Ripoll, H. (1988a). Analysis of visual scanning patterns of volleyball players, in a problem-solving task. *International Journal of Sport Psychology, 19*, 9–25.

Ripoll, H. (1988b). Stratégies de prise d'informations visuelles dans les taches de résolution de problèmes tactiques en sport. In H. Ripoll & G. Azemar (Eds.), *Éléments de neurosciences du sport* (pp. 329–354). Paris: INSEP.

Ripoll, H. (1991). The understanding-acting process in sport: The relationship between semantic and sensorimotor visual function. *International Journal of Sport Psychology, 22*, 221–243.

Ripoll, H., Kerlirzin, Y., Stein, J. F., & Reine, B. (1991). Visual strategies of boxers (French boxing) in a simulated problem solving situation. In *Proceedings of the sixth European conference on eye movements* (p. 83). Louvain, Belgium: Katholieke University.

Ripoll, H., Papin, J. P., & Simonet, P. (1983). Approche de la fonction visuelle en sport. *Le Travail Humain, 46*, 163–173.

Roberts, G. C. (1972). Effect of achievement motivation and social environment on performance of a motor task. *Journal of Motor Behavior, 4*, 37–46.

Roberts, G. C. (1974). Effect of achievement motivation and social environment on risk taking. *Research Quarterly, 45*, 42–55.

Roberts, G. C. (1992a). Motivation in sport and exercise: Conceptual constraints and convergence. In G. C. Roberts (Ed.), *Motivation in sport and exercise* (pp. 3–29). Champaign, IL: Human Kinetics.

Roberts, G. C. (Ed.) (1992b). *Motivation in sport and exercise*. Champaign, IL: Human Kinetics.

Rowland, G. L., Franken, R. E., & Harrison, K. (1986). Sensation seeking and participation in sporting activities. *Journal of Sport Psychology, 8*, 212–220.

Ryan, E., & Foster, R. (1967). Athletic participation and perceptual augmentation and reduction. *Journal of Personality and Social Psychology, 6*, 472–476.

Ryan, E., & Lakie, W. (1965). Competitive and noncompetitive performance in relation to achievement motive and manifest anxiety. *Journal of Personality and Social Psychology, 1*, 342–345.

Sarason, S. B., Mandler, G., & Craighill, P. G. (1952). The effects of differential instructions on anxiety and learning. *Journal of Abnormal and Social Psychology, 47*, 561–565.

Scanlan, T. K., & Simons, J. P. (1992). The construct of sport enjoyment. In G. C. Roberts (Ed.), *Motivation in sport and exercise* (pp. 199–215). Champaign, IL: Human Kinetics.

Shallice, T. (1988). *From neuropsychology to mental structure*. Cambridge, England: Cambridge University Press.

Shiffrin, R., & Schneider, W. (1977). Controlled and automatic human information processing: Perceptual learning, automatic attending, and a general theory. *Psychological Review, 84*, 127–190.

Silva, J. M. (1984). Personality and sport performance: Controversy and challenge. In J. M. Silva & R. S. Weinberg (Eds.), *Psychological foundations of sport* (pp. 59–69). Champaign, IL: Human Kinetics.

Snyder, M. (1983). The influence of individuals on situations: Implications for understanding the links between personality and social behavior. *Journal of Personality, 51*, 497–516.

Sonstroem, R. J., & Bernardo, P. B. (1982). Individual pre-game state anxiety and basketball performance: A reexamination of the inverted-U curve. *Journal of Sport Psychology, 4*, 235–245.

Spence, J. T., & Spence, K. W. (1966). The motivational components of manifest anxiety: Drive and drive stimuli. In C. D. Spielberger (Ed.), *Anxiety and behavior* (pp. 291–326). New York: Academic Press.

Spence, K. W. (1956). *Behavior theory and conditioning*. New Haven, CT: Yale University Press.

Spielberger, C. D. (Ed.). (1972). *Anxiety: Current trends in theory and research* (Vol. 1). New York: Academic Press.

Spielberger, C. D. (1989). Stress and anxiety in sports. In D. Hackfort & C. D. Spielberger (Eds.), *Anxiety in sports: An international perspective* (pp. 3–17). New York: Hemisphere.

Spielberger, C. D., Gorsuch, R. L., & Lushene, R. E. (1970). *Manual for the State-Trait Anxiety Inventory (STAI)*. Palo Alto, CA: Consulting Psychologists Press.

Spielberger, C. D., Gorsuch, R. L., Lushene, R. E., Vagg, P. R., & Jacobs, G. A. (1983). *Manual for the State-Trait Anxiety Inventory (Form Y)*. Palo Alto, CA: Consulting Psychologists Press.

Spielman, J. (1963). *The relation between personality and the frequency and duration of involuntary rest pauses during massed practice*. Unpublished Ph.D. thesis, University of London.

Starkes, J. L., & Allard, F. (1983). Perception in volleyball: The effects of competitive stress. *Journal of Sport Psychology, 5*, 189–196.

Starkes, J. L., & Deakin, J. M. (1984). Perception in sport: A cognitive approach to skilled performance. In W. F. Straub & J. M. Williams (Eds.), *Cognitive sport psychology* (pp. 115–128). New York: Sport Science Associates.

Straub, W. F. (1982). Sensation seeking among high and low-risk male athletes. *Journal of Sport Psychology, 4*, 246–253.

Swinnen, S., Vandenberghe, J., & Van Assche, E. (1986). Role of cognitive style constructs, field dependence-independence, and reflection-impulsivity in skill acquisition. *Journal of Sport Psychology, 8*, 51–69.

Taylor, J. A. (1953). A personality scale of manifest anxiety. *Journal of Abnormal and Social Psychology, 48*, 285–290.

Tenenbaum, G., & Bar-Eli, M. (1992). Methodological issues in sport psychology research. *Australian Journal of Science and Medicine in Sport, 24*, 44–50.

Tenenbaum, G., Levy-Kolker, N., Bar-Eli, M., & Weinberg, R. (1994). Information recall among skilled and novice athletes: The role of display complexity, attentional resources, visual exposure duration, and expertise. *Journal of Sport Sciences, 12*, 529–534.

Tenenbaum, G., Levy-Kolker, N., Sade, S., & Liebermann, D. (in press). Anticipation and confidence of decisions related to skilled performance. *International Journal of Sport Psychology*.

Umilta, C. (1991). Attention in sport: further lines of research. *International Journal of Sport Psychology, 22*, 328–333.

Vealey, R. S. (1989). Sport personology: A paradigmatic and methodological analysis. *Journal of Sport and Exercise Psychology, 11*, 216–235.

Vealey, R. S. (1992). Personality and sport: A comprehensive view. In T. S. Horn (Ed.), *Advances in sport psychology* (pp. 25–59). Champaign, IL: Human Kinetics.

von Hofsten, C. (1987). Catching. In H. Heuer & A. F. Sanders (Eds.), *Perspectives on perception and action* (pp. 33–46). Hillsdale, NJ: Erlbaum.

Wachtel, P. L. (1967). Conceptions of broad and narrow attention. *Psychological Bulletin, 68*, 417–429.

Weinberg, R. S. (1989). Anxiety, arousal and motor performance: Theory, research and applications. In D. Hackfort &

C. D. Spielberger (Eds.), *Anxiety in sports* (pp. 95–115). New York: Hemisphere.

Weinberg, R. S., & Genuchi, M. (1980). Relationship between competitive trait anxiety, state anxiety and golf performance: A field study. *Journal of Sport Psychology*, *2*, 148–154.

Weiner, B. (1974). *Achievement motivation and attribution theory*. Morristown, NJ: General Learning Press.

Weiner, B. (1986). *An attributional theory of motivation and emotion*. New York: Springer.

Weingarten, G. (1982). Psychological disposition toward athletic activity versus psychological development through sport. In E. Gerson (Ed.), *Handbook of sport psychology: Vol. 1. Introduction to sport psychology* (pp. 114–128). Netanya, Israel: Wingate Institute.

Weiss, M. R., & Petlichkoff, L. M. (1989). Children's motivation for participation in and withdrawal from sport: Identifying the missing links. *Pediatric Exercise Science*, *1*, 195–211.

White, R. (1959). Motivation reconsidered: The concept of competence. *Psychological Review*, *66*, 297–334.

Whiting, H. T. A. (1991). Action is not reaction! A reply to McLeod and Jenkins. *International Journal of Sport Psychology*, *22*, 296–303.

Whiting, H. T. A., & Hutt, J. W. R. (1972). The effects of personality and ability on speed of decisions regarding the directional aspects of ball flight. *Journal of Motor Behavior*, *4*, 89–97.

Wine, J. D. (1980). Cognitive-attentional theory of test anxiety. In I. G. Sarason (Ed.), *Test anxiety: Theory, research and applications* (pp. 349–385). Hillsdale, NJ: Erlbaum.

Wine, J. D. (1982). Evaluation anxiety: A cognitive-attentional construct. In H. W. Krohne & L. Laux (Eds.), *Achievement, stress, and anxiety* (pp. 207–219). Washington, DC: Hemisphere.

Witkin, H. A., Dyk, R. B., Faterson, H. F., Goodenough, D. R., & Karp, S. A. (1962). *Psychological differentiation: Studies of development*. New York: Wiley.

Witkin, H. A., & Goodenough, D. R. (1981). Cognitive style: Essence and origins. *Psychological Issues Monograph No. 51*. New York International University Press.

Witkin, H. A., Goodenough, D. R., & Oltman, P. K. (1979). Psychological differentiation in current status. *Journal of Personality and Social Psychology*, *37*, 1127–1145.

Witkin, H. A., Lewis, H. B., Hertzman, M., Machover, K., Meissner, P. B., & Wapner, S. (1954). *Personality through perception: An experimental and clinical study*. Westport, CT: Greenwood.

Zillman, D. (1971). Excitation transfer in communication-mediated aggressive behavior. *Journal of Experimental Social Psychology*, *7*, 419–434.

Zuckerman, M. (1979). *Sensation seeking: Beyond the optimal level of arousal*. Hillsdale, NJ: Erlbaum.

Zuckerman, M. (1983). Sensation seeking in sports. *Personality and Individual Differences*, *4*, 285–293.

Zuckerman, M. (1984). Experience and desire: A new format for Sensation Seeking Scales. *Journal of Behavioral Assessment*, *6*, 101–114.

Zuckerman, M. (1987). A critical look at three arousal constructs in personality theories: Optimal levels of arousal, strength of the nervous system, and sensitivities to signals of reward and punishment. In J. Strelau & H. J. Eysenck (Eds.), *Personality dimensions and arousal* (pp. 217–231). New York: Plenum.

Zuckerman, M., Kolin, E. A., Price, L., & Zoob, I. (1964). Development of a Sensation-Seeking Scale. *Journal of Consulting Psychology*, *28*, 477–482.

Zuckerman, M., Murtaugh, T. M., & Siegel, J. (1974). Sensation seeking and cortical augmenting-reducing. *Psychophysiology*, *11*, 535–542.

32

Intelligence, Personality, and Severe Hypoglycemia in Diabetes

Ian J. Deary

The purpose of this chapter is to describe in detail an area of medical research in which intelligence and personality variables play key, integrated roles. In research on diabetes mellitus, personality and intelligence have been posited as predictors of outcomes related to self-care. Personality and intelligence are also the object of interest as outcome variables in themselves, because there is concern that they might be altered by the illness. The aspect of the illness that much of this interest focuses upon is the phenomenon of severe hypoglycemia, which is described in more detail below. It is largely because the research on personality and intelligence may be centered upon this phenomenon that severe hypoglycemia offers an opportunity to deal with aspects of personality and intelligence in an integrated way as they affect a health-related issue. Moreover, the physiological effects of severe hypoglycemia are relatively well understood and thereby offer a chance to discover the mechanisms that integrate psychological and medical factors in this condition.

Ian J. Deary • Department of Psychology, University of Edinburgh, Edinburgh EH8 9JZ, Scotland.

International Handbook of Personality and Intelligence, edited by Donald H. Saklofske and Moshe Zeidner. Plenum Press, New York, 1995.

MODELS OF ASSOCIATION AMONG PERSONALITY, INTELLIGENCE, AND ILLNESS

The association between personality and intelligence is an underresearched topic. Some of the possibilities for integrating these two major pillars of differential psychology were outlined in one of the few research symposia devoted to the issue (Van Heck, Bonaiuto, Deary, & Nowack, 1994). Although there may be several promising approaches to such integration (e.g., via biological and information processing mechanisms), no overarching explanatory framework has yet been firmly constructed. Therefore, to ask how personality and intelligence may be integrated into research on physical illness may be premature. That is not to say that there is any lack of research on psychological factors in physical illness; in fact, health psychology is experiencing a boom at present. Moreover, much of this research involves cognitive and temperamental variables. It is rare, though, to see such variables integrated around a single medical entity or explanatory construct. Much research is blindly empirical, showing weak associations among medical factors and personological variables where the mechanism of association is obscure or speculative.

An example is research on psychological factors in hypertension, which has attracted both cognitive and personality investigative efforts. Perhaps because common parlance associates high blood pressure with tension, frustration, and anger, there has been much effort to discover the so-called hypertensive personality (Phillips, 1991; later, a similar effort to describe the "diabetic personality" will be seen to have achieved equally little). Early research on hypertensive clinic patients suggesting that they had high levels of neuroticism (Robinson, 1964) was not replicated in community studies (Waal-Manning, Knight, Spears, & Paulin, 1986), and it has been concluded that heightened levels of neuroticism were associated with clinic attendance per se and with receiving the diagnosis of hypertension (Mann, 1986).

Intelligence or cognitive ability-oriented research on hypertension tends not to be integrated with personality research; rather, it emphasizes the contribution to mental impairment made by the illness or the antihypertensive medications (e.g. Deary, Capewell, Hajducka, & Muir, 1991). For example, Starr, Whalley, Inch, and Schering (1993) conducted measurements of blood pressure and cognitive function in a large community sample of disease-free old people, and they found that high blood pressure was associated with cognitive impairment in this sample of the population. This type of study is typical of much health-related psychological research, where cognitive variables are usually cast as dependent variables putatively affected by an illness process or medical intervention. In contrast, personality variables tend to assume the role of independent variables that convey some protection against or risk for a particular illness, or mediate the effects of interventions. This is true of hypertension, and also of the cognitive and personality-based research on HIV infection and AIDS (Egan & Goodwin, 1992).

The particular personality factors that should be further investigated in relation to health risks and outcomes is the focus of much thought. Smith and Williams (1992) understandably consider the applications of well-validated personality dimensions (e.g., the big five) to health research and also make a case for the further study of optimism, hardiness, and hostility. Interestingly, hostility might be related to hypertension (Mann, 1977), and it would appear that hostility is perhaps the key aspect of personality captured in the Type A construct that might be associated with coronary heart disease (Booth-Kewley & Friedman, 1987; Matthews, 1988).

Much of this apparent link between behavior and health, though, might be an artifact. Many studies reporting positive results rely on self-reports of medical status, and Stone and Costa (1990) have suggested that the large body of research into heart disease and Type A personality might have revealed a "distress-prone" rather than disease-prone personality. An exception to this problem of interpretation might be peripheral vascular disease (Deary, 1991). It is possible to assess the degree of blockage or peripheral vasculature objectively, and a small but significant association has been found between peripheral vascular disease and hostility in a large community sample (Deary, Fowkes, Donnan, & Housley, 1994). In the same sample, a significant association was found between hostility and serum triglyceride levels (Fowkes et al., 1992). These effects are not large, however, and their meaning in mechanistic terms has proved difficult to elaborate.

This point brings up the most difficult issue in this area of research. Finding statistical associations between personality and intelligence variables and indices of physical health is hard enough, but to give a reductionistic explanation of such associations is even more challenging, not least because the biological bases of the personality dimensions and human intelligence are largely obscure (but see Zuckerman, 1991, and Vernon, 1993, for reviews of these areas). An additional problem is that personological variables may interact with health in multiple ways that many studies lack the ability to distinguish. A useful discussion of this problem is undertaken by Suls and Rittenhouse (1990), who argue that personality may be construed as a factor inducing physiological hyperreactivity, a constitutional predisposing factor, and a predictor of risky or dangerous behaviors, among other possible relationships.

Given these general remarks and many caveats, I now turn to the central illustrative topic of this chapter.

DIABETES AND SEVERE HYPOGLYCEMIA

Diabetes mellitus is an illness that results from a partial or total lack of insulin, or from its ineffectiveness. Insulin is a hormone that helps metabolizing cells in the body to remove glucose from the bloodstream. Diabetes, therefore, results in high blood levels of glucose (hyperglycemia) with low glucose levels in the cells of the body. Diabetes may be treated with special diets, oral hypoglycemic agents, or injections of animal or human insulin. In this chapter, almost all of the research discussed will deal with problems associated with insulin-dependent diabetes (sometimes called Type 1 diabetes), which typically starts between infancy and young adulthood and requires insulin injections.

The particular interest in insulin-dependent diabetes arises because one of the most common side effects of insulin treatment is hypoglycemia. Because the level of glucose in the blood is dependent upon many factors (e.g., food ingestion, exercise, illness), it is impossible for the patient with diabetes to achieve continuously normal blood glucose levels with insulin injections; therefore, episodes of hyperglycemia and hypoglycemia are common. Most episodes of hypoglycemia are minor and easily self-treated by the ingestion of glucose drinks or sweets. More severe episodes are associated with coma and seizures and have a recognized mortality. Within the medical specialty of diabetes, practitioners and their patients must chart a dangerous course between hyper- and hypoglycemia in the knowledge that insulin injections cannot achieve the subtleties of glycemic control afforded by insulin secreted by a normally functioning pancreas. On the one side, there are the dangers of persistent hyperglycemia associated with deficiencies in renal, vascular, nervous, and visual function; on the other side, there is the threat of hypoglycemia.

The danger associated with hypoglycemia, and the interest it provides for a book concerned with intelligence and personality, is associated with the special metabolic characteristics of the brain. The brain is totally dependent on glucose for normal metabolism and in the absence of glucose is not able to utilize any substitute fuel. Therefore, during hypoglycemia brain function becomes deranged (Deary, 1992). There has recently been an increasing research effort directed toward detailing the effects of hypoglycemia in the short and long term. During acute hypoglycemia, patients suffer some of a recognized set of symptoms (Pennebaker et al., 1981). In addition, there are characteristic hormonal changes associated with low blood glucose levels, and cognitive function deteriorates progressively as levels become lower (Pramming, Thorsteinsson, Theilgaard, Pinner, & Binder, 1986). Although recovery of full cognitive function as assessed by psychometric and reaction time tests might be delayed by an hour or so (Deary, 1992), in all but the most severe cases, apparent recovery of cognitive function is complete after hypoglycemic attacks.

The question of what happens to the brain in the longer term following repeated episodes of severe hypoglycemia has become more important with the knowledge that intensified insulin regimens, aimed at achieving a more physiological blood glucose profile in diabetic patients, increase the risk of severe hypoglycemia by 2 to 3 times (DCCT Research Group, 1991; Reichard, Berglund, Britz, Levander, & Rosenqvist, 1991). If the brain is repeatedly deprived of its sole fuel over several severe hypoglycemic episodes (i.e., attacks in which the patient requires the help of others for recovery), are there lasting effects on intelligence and personality? This question has an obvious clinical importance and provides, in addition, an interesting opportunity for differential psychologists to study the effects of a relatively common and measurable environmental brain insult on important aspects of individual differences.

The focus on severe hypoglycemia in this chapter should not lead the reader to infer that there are no other possible causes of cognitive and temperamental change in diabetes. In fact, diabetes has such a large number of metabolic effects that the problem in assessing previous research, which *has* indicated that diabetic patients perform less well on tests of cognitive ability than matched controls, has been to identify the causes of such change, be they biological or otherwise (Richardson, 1990).

SEVERE HYPOGLYCEMIA AND INTELLIGENCE

Ryan (1988) has described the relatively sound evidence indicating that children with insulin-dependent diabetes underperform on cognitive tests when compared with healthy controls, as well as the likely risk factors in such patients, who show poorer memory, attention, and rates of nonverbal responding. Ryan, however, stated that "relatively few large scale studies have explicitly examined the relationship between cognitive dysfunction and serious episodes of hypoglycemia, particularly when the episodes occur during adulthood and do not necessarily eventuate in a neurologic crisis" (p. 90).

Bale (1973) tested 100 patients with insulin-dependent diabetes and 100 nondiabetic controls on the Walton-Black Modified New Word Learning Test. Patients were under 65 years of age and had been treated with insulin for 15 years or more. Age of onset of diabetes was from 3 years of age. Estimation of history of hypoglycemia was obtained by interview and by checking medical records. Controls were matched for age, sex, and social class. Scores of less than 6 on the Walton-Black test were taken as indicative of brain damage; low scores might be obtained by those who had poor premorbid ability, but this was not considered. Seventeen of the diabetic patients and none of the controls scored less than 6 on the test, and the low scores were not related to age.

Patients with diabetes were then assigned to three groups with different experiences of hypoglycemia: those with a history of hospital admissions for severe hypoglycemia ($n = 33$); those who had been treated at home or in a hospital emergency department for severe hypoglycemia ($n = 44$); and those without a history of severe hypoglycemia ($n = 23$). For the three groups, respectively, the numbers of patients scoring in the "damaged" range of the Walton-Black test were 10, 6, and 1 ($p < .05$). Of the 17 patients with low learning test scores, 15 were tested on the Wechsler Adult Intelligence Scale (WAIS). According to Bale (1973), there was only 1 patient with an "abnormal" verbal-performance difference (performance IQ 28 points lower than verbal IQ). Bale did not analyze the data further, but did provide a table of the verbal and performance IQ scores for the 15 patients tested on the WAIS. The mean difference between verbal and performance IQ was 5 points, indicating that the group as a whole might have suffered some moderate loss of cognitive ability, perhaps as a result of severe hypoglycemia. Loss of cognitive ability led to early retirement in one male.

Bale (1973) concluded that abnormal scores on the Walton-Black test "appeared to be related to the apparent severity of past hypoglycaemic episodes" (p. 340). Some of the difficulties that face present studies in this area are presaged in this early effort. First, there is the matching of controls to diabetic patients. In Bale's study the patients and controls were relatively well matched on demographic variables, but matching for educational experience and premorbid IQ would have been desirable, because the hypothesis is that the diabetic patients (as a result of severe hypoglycemia or some other CNS insult) had fallen from a previous level of cognitive functioning. This is not necessarily straightforward, however, because of the second problem with the study's design: including those patients with childhood onset of diabetes. There seems to be fair agreement on the point that early onset of diabetes results in cognitive underachievement (Ryan, 1988). This poses a problem for the technique of measuring cognitive deficit using premorbid-current IQ differences. The measurement of IQ decrement assumes that there is full cognitive development up to late adolescence. Clearly, for those with organic damage in childhood and early adolescence, full potential is never attained; no measure of so-called premorbid IQ will be able to estimate the ability level they would have attained if there had not been damage in childhood. Further, because ability has some causal effect on the level of education, and possibly also on the level of social class attained through employment, matching for class and education might be matching the diabetic patients with controls whose level of cognitive function is the same only as that to which the former have fallen. Therefore inclusion of diabetic patients with onset of illness in childhood is likely to decrease the likelihood of detecting any cognitive impairment, because attempted matching for premorbid mental ability might lead to patients being matched with controls of lower original cognitive potential.

Moreover, the idea of a "brain damage" level of scoring on a single neuropsychological test is naive. The distribution of most test scores follows a Gaussian curve, and it is arbitrary to designate a given level as abnormal. The main message from Bale's (1973) indicative study is the difficulty of interpretation presented when those with childhood onset of diabetes are included.

This problem is present also in the study carried out by Franceschi et al. (1984), who tested 37 patients with insulin-dependent diabetes and 26 controls matched for age, sex, education, and social class. From the demographic information supplied in the paper it is clear that some of the diabetic patients had the disorder in childhood. All subjects were aged 18 to 35, were right-handed, and had no neurological history. Unlike Bale (1973), who attempted to test the hypothesis that "mild dementia" in diabetes was caused by episodes of hypoglycemia, Franceschi et al. focused on duration and severity of the illness. A number of factors that might be interpreted as causal to any cognitive underperformance in patients with diabetes were mentioned: 17 had mild peripheral neuropathy; 10 had background retinopathy; 32 patients had 2 or more episodes of ketoacidosis; and "hypoglycemic episodes were relatively common but rarely severe" (p. 229). However, none of these is quantified in the study to try to account for individual differences in ability between patients. From a number of tests (including IQ-type tests, concentration and spatial ability tests, and the Wechsler Memory Scale), the only differences between the groups were on total Wechsler Memory Quotient and scores on two of the WAIS subscales; in all instances, diabetics performed at lower levels than controls. There was no relationship between neuropsychological test scores and disease duration or severity, although the latter was estimated using indices of glycemic control (e.g., glycated hemoglobin) and not episodes of hypoglycemia.

Franceschi et al. (1984) determined that patients with insulin-dependent diabetes do suffer specific cognitive impairments, for instance on "global [sic] memory." Their final conclusions, however, were generally positive: "Global intelligence, spatial and visual analysis, psychomotor ability and concentration and attention are preserved in diabetic patients. . . . In diabetic patients there are subtle and selective neuropsychological deficits . . . [which] seemed not to interfere with the patients' jobs or with their everyday life" (p. 230).

Such optimism in accepting the null hypothesis is difficult to defend. The number of subjects gives the study little power, and the problem of the near impossibility of correct matching for premorbid mental ability arises here also. There appears to be little doubt that some of the patients had childhood onset of diabetes. If the diabetic patients had suffered cognitive insults during development and, as a result, had underperformed in education and reached lower levels of social class than some notional original ability level might have indicated was possible, then they were being matched with individuals who were not representative of their true potential. There could be a more significant deficit that is undetected here for both power and matching reasons. The three possible causes offered for the lower scores attained by diabetics on some tests were CNS vascular or metabolic dysfunction or the emotional influence of chronic illness. These variables were not operationalized or quantified, however, and the hypotheses were not tested more specifically.

A more specific hypothesis was tested by Lawson et al. (1984). They suggested that those diabetic patients with peripheral neuropathy might also have CNS neuropathy, and that this might lead to impaired intellectual function. The authors tested 48 patients aged 16 to 60 years with insulin-dependent diabetes. Age of onset ranged from 5 to 60 years. Forty age- and sex-matched controls were also tested. Members of the diabetic group were significantly lower for education experience, though, and the duration of diabetes was very heterogeneous (1 month to 45 years). It would appear unlikely that anyone diagnosed as having diabetes as little as 1 month previously would have had time to develop any brain damage that the disease might cause.

A battery of neuropsychological tests included the Wechsler Memory Scale and some WAIS subtests. In agreement with the studies by Bale (1973) and Franceschi et al. (1984), diabetic patients examined by Lawson et al. (1984) performed more poorly on the memory quotient. There were no differences on IQ scores. In fact, the WAIS performance IQs of the two groups were very similar, but the controls had an 8-point advantage in verbal IQ, which probably reflected their higher levels of education. Although the authors made very little of this result, they found a correlation of .32 between verbal-performance IQ difference on the WAIS and an estimate of peripheral neuropathy within the diabetic group. Lawson et al. (1984) were cautious lest this might be a Type I error, but the method of looking for a potentially causal variable and correlating it with an estimate of IQ decrement within the diabetic group is an interesting and useful methodological alternative to the matched-groups design, and it circumvents many of the problems of finding appropriately matched controls. This interesting result was not considered to be of sufficient import to prevent Lawson et al. from concluding that "cognitive deficit is not a cardinal feature of our clinical population of diabetic patients."

Skenazy and Bigler (1984) began their report by posing the question of whether "borderline sugar states" have a deleterious effect on brain function. They tested 59 Type 1 diabetic patients aged 18 to 47 years, all of whom had an onset of diabetes before age 30: 39 were sighted, and 20 were blind because of retinopathy. Of 44 nondiabetic controls who were tested, 20 had nonneurological physical complaints or illness, and 24 were healthy. The groups were quite closely matched for educational experience, but the healthy control group was markedly younger than the other groups (e.g., 10 years younger than the sighted diabetic group). This degree of age disparity is usually unacceptable in cognitive studies because of the relationship between age and many mental abilities. Neuropsychological tests included the Halstead-Reitan Neuropsychological Test Battery, the WAIS, and the Wechsler Memory Scale. An interview assessed various problems related to diabetes, including the number of severe hypoglycemia episodes.

Skenazy and Bigler (1984) reported that the performance IQ of sighted patients (the WAIS could not be administered to blind patients) with diabetes was lower than that of controls who had other illnesses or were healthy. In agreement with Bale (1973), they found that the diabetes patients had a performance IQ 4.5 points lower than their verbal IQ. Sighted diabetic patients were also poorer than controls on the Trail

Making Test B, but in disagreement with previous studies the diabetic patients did not have impairments on the Wechsler Memory Scale.

Possibly the most interesting results of this study are related to the authors' attempts to correlate specific diabetic problems with performance and verbal IQ scores. There were no significant correlations between onset age of diabetes and IQ measures. Performance IQ correlated at $-.44$ ($p < .04$) with the number of "insulin reactions" and at $-.29$ (ns) with the number of diabetic comas experienced by the sighted diabetic patients. Verbal IQ correlated at $-.05$ (ns) and $-.07$ (ns) with the same two variables. If it is accepted that verbal IQ on the WAIS represents a measure of premorbid IQ and that performance IQ is more representative of current functioning, then these results suggest that the direction of causation is from hypoglycemic episodes to lower IQ rather than the converse. Although the numbers in each group are relatively small and the estimates of hypoglycemia were retrospective, the methods and results reported warranted improvement and attempted replication.

This idea was developed in a study by Wredling, Levander, Adamson, and Lins (1990) where two groups of 17 patients with insulin-dependent diabetes with and without repeated attacks of severe hypoglycemia were tested. The age range was 26 to 72, and the groups were matched for age, onset age of diabetes, duration of diabetes, insulin regimen, neuropathy, retinopathy, education, and employment. The group with a history of episodes of severe hypoglycemia scored lower on two out of five tapping tests, had higher rates of perspective reversal on the Necker Cube Test, had decreased forward digit span, and were slower on the Digit Symbol test. There were no between-group differences on the Trail Making test, however, or on reaction time measures. On a complex maze learning test, the severe hypoglycemia group had a slower processing rate and checking times but solved a greater number of the mazes correctly. The authors concluded from this latter result that the group with a history of hypoglycemia attacks had adopted a more cautious speed-accuracy trade-off function. Their more general conclusion was that severe hypoglycemia may produce permanent cognitive impairment. Although this is a relatively small study and groups were not matched for premorbid IQ specifically, the matching was otherwise very careful, and the results suggest that hypoglycemia might be a specific factor leading to impaired cognitive performance in patients with diabetes.

Overall, there appears to be an indication that there is a modest verbal-performance IQ disparity in diabetic patients after several years of treatment with insulin (Ryan, 1988; Skenazy & Bigler, 1984). Second, there is some evidence for a global or short-term memory impairment when diabetic patients are compared with controls (Franceschi et al., 1984; Lawson et al., 1984; Ryan, 1988; Skenazy & Bigler, 1984). Third, the suggestion that there might be a correlation between cognitive impairment and measures of illness severity is one hypothesis that might be investigated further (Lawson et al., 1984; Ryan, 1988; Skenazy & Bigler, 1984; Wredling et al., 1990).

What methodological considerations can be gleaned from these studies? For reasons stated above, patients with childhood onset of diabetes should be excluded to allow an estimate of full premorbid intelligence to be made. It is probably wise to exclude elderly patients from study because age reduces cognitive function, especially for performance IQ. Patients are unlikely to have suffered any cognitive-impairing effects of diabetes unless they have had the illness for a sufficient length of time; therefore, all diabetic patients in such a study should have been treated with insulin for several years. It is also necessary to have good operational measures of both independent and dependent variables in the study. First, this means having reliable and valid measures of hypoglycemia experience; for the dependent variable, it means having reliable and valid measures of IQ decrement. It is important to ensure that any relationship obtained between the independent and dependent variables is not affected by confounding variables.

Langan, Deary, Hepburn, and Frier (1991) examined the specific hypothesis that experience of hypoglycemia was related to cognitive impairment in insulin-treated diabetic patients. This promised to be more informative than a simple demonstration that a group of diabetic patients score lower on an arbitrary battery of mental tests than do controls. Langan et al. (1991) studied 100 insulin-treated diabetic patients aged 25 to 52 whose onset of diabetes occurred after 19 years. Estimates of the frequency of severe hypoglycemia were made retrospectively using structured interviews. To check the reliability of these reports, 85 patients were reinterviewed about 18 months after the first interview and asked again about their experience of severe hypoglycemia (Deary, Langan, Graham, Hepburn, & Frier, 1992). The Pearson correlation between the two estimates was .76 ($p < .001$), indicating that the ratings of frequency of severe hypoglycemia were reliable. The validity of the interview-derived ratings of frequencies of severe hypoglycemia was checked by undertaking an extensive review of the hospital and general practice records of 47 of the patients who tended to be at the extremes for severe hypoglycemia (i.e., they had experienced either five or more episodes or none at all). This validation exercise indicated that patients were giving very accurate information about their past experience of hypoglycemia.

Estimates of IQ decrement were obtained using the National Adult Reading Test (NART) as a premorbid IQ estimate and revised WAIS (WAIS-R) performance IQ as the measure of current functioning. Estimation of premorbid IQ has progressed a great deal in the last decade or so. From the initial use of WAIS verbal IQ as a premorbid IQ measure, psychologists moved to using a combination of demographic variables to estimate premorbid IQ (Crawford, 1989). More recently the NART has been found to correlate very highly with WAIS-R IQs in young healthy individuals and to have the characteristic of not decreasing with age or even with moderate degrees of dementia (Crawford, Stewart, Parker, Besson, & Cochrane, 1989). Therefore, it has been concluded that the NART offers the best available estimate of a subject's premorbid IQ. At the same time as subjects in the Edinburgh study (Langan et al., 1991) were returning to check the reliability of the severe hypoglycemia estimates, they were retested on the NART and the WAIS-R performance IQ. The correlation between the two estimates of IQ decrement, about 18 months apart, was .78 ($p < .001$; Deary et al., 1992). Therefore, IQ decrement estimates were reliable.

Using these two reliable indicators for the independent and dependent variables, Langan et al. (1991) reported a correlation of $-.24$ ($p < .05$) between the frequency of severe hypoglycemia and IQ decrement. The correlation between severe hypoglycemia frequency and performance IQ was .26 ($p < .02$), whereas the correlations with NART and WAIS-R verbal IQ were .14 and .03, respectively (both nonsignificant). When the confounding effects of age, duration of diabetes, and blood glucose level at the time of neuropsychological testing were removed by partial correlation, the correlation between frequency of severe hypoglycemia and IQ impairment rose to $-.33$ ($p < .001$). The correlation with performance IQ rose to similar levels, whereas the NART and verbal IQ correlations stayed close to zero. This allowed the conclusion that there appears to be a significant association between estimated cognitive impairment and the frequency of severe hypoglycemia. Further, because of the near-zero correlations between hypoglycemia estimates and premorbid IQ, it was possible to rule out the possibility that it was those subjects with lower IQ who were having more hypoglycemia episodes (e.g., it appeared possible that more frequent hypoglycemia was a cause of lower IQ rather than the converse).

The repeat testing of 85 of the original subjects for reliability of the key measures of hypoglycemia and IQ decrement allowed their intercorrelation to be corrected for the slight unreliability of both measures. After correction for unreliability, the correlation between frequency of severe hypoglycemia and IQ decrement rose to $-.40$ ($p < .001$). Langan et al. (1991) also reported significant correlations between severe hypoglycemia frequency and four-choice Hick-type reaction time measures, which were of a similar magnitude to those with IQ decrement, but there were no significant correlations between hypoglycemia estimates and memory, verbal fluency, or Paced Auditory Serial Addition Test scores.

The study by Langan et al. (1991) is the first to answer Ryan's (1988) complaint that "there have been no formal studies that have examined the relationship between hypoglycemic episodes and brain dysfunction in large samples of adults" (p. 92). It was concluded tentatively that episodes of severe hypoglycemia might lead to some reduction in performance IQ and that such episodes should be avoided.

A possibly important criticism of this and other research is that the estimates of severe hypoglycemia, although highly reliable and seemingly valid, were retrospective. Prospective studies of insulin-treated diabetic patients might provide more accurate indices of hypoglycemia episodes and will obviate the need for premorbid IQ estimates by measuring cognitive function directly at different time points. Some limitations of prospective trials, however, may be raised. When individuals are included in a prospective study they might still record episodes of hypoglycemia less than accurately. Moreover, patients might alter their behavior by the fact of being included in a study. Thus a prospective study might fail to examine the natural experience of hypoglycemia in the treatment of diabetes.

Reichard et al. (1991) reported on a prospective study examining the effects of allocating adult subjects with an average duration of diabetes of 17 years to intensive glucose control ($n = 44$) or normal control ($n = 53$). Subjects were asked about the number of hypoglycemia-induced comas they had experienced before the study, and they kept a record of severe hypoglycemia episodes during the study. After 3 years of this prospective study, 25 of the 44 patients on intensified insulin therapy had experienced a total of 102 severe hypoglycemia episodes. In the conventional therapy group, 12 of the 53 patients had experienced a total of 28 severe hypoglycemia episodes. Therefore it is clear that tight control of blood glucose increases the likelihood of severe hypoglycemia. This was also highlighted in a recent report by the DCCT Research Group (1987).

Subjects in the study by Reichard et al. (1991) were given neuropsychological tests at baseline, and 3-year follow-up, and again at 5 years (Reichard, Britz, & Rosenqvist, 1991). Tests used were auditory and visual reaction time, digit span, the perceptual maze test, and the Necker Cube Test. There were no significant differences between the intensified and normal therapy groups at 3 years, and the authors concluded that the increased experience of severe hypoglycemia did not affect the cognitive functioning of the patients. This prospective study does not agree with the conclusions of the studies by Langan et al. (1991) or Wredling et al. (1990), or with some other studies discussed above.

The main limitation of the study by Reichard et al. (1991), however, was their failure to separate their groups on the basis of the key independent variable (Deary & Frier, 1992). Although the patients were divided into intensive and normal treatment groups, the authors were interested primarily in whether severe hypoglycemia resulted in poorer cognitive performance. If their data are studied, it is clear that 19 members of the intensively treated group had no severe hypoglycemia episodes and that 12 of the normal treatment group did have such episodes. Therefore the groups were not separated directly for hypoglycemia experience, and the overlap in this key variable reduces the power of the study. It makes sense to separate the groups by treatment method if one suspects that there are several occult variables across treatment types that might lead to different levels of cognitive performance, but if there is a clear notion that a key variable is involved (in this case, severe hypoglycemia), the groups should be separated on *that* variable and not on an imperfect surrogate.

Another concern is with the relatively small and nonstandard psychometric test battery. The Necker Cube Test and perceptual maze test are not widely used in clinical studies, nor are they well characterized psychologically. Digit span is typically not very sensitive to organic brain insults. A larger, more standard battery (e.g., the WAIS and/or the Wechsler Memory Scale) would have offered more convincing tests of psychological functions. Therefore there is cause to doubt the sensitivity of both the independent and dependent variables used in the study by Reichard et al. (1991), and the null hypothesis should not be accepted too readily (Deary & Frier, 1992).

A study concerned primarily with physical indicators of encephalopathy in Type 1 diabetes was reported by Dejgaard et al. (1990). They found that 40% of long-duration and 5.3% of short duration Type 1 diabetes patients had abnormal brainstem auditory evoked responses. Further, 69% of the long-duration diabetes patients and only 12% of age-matched healthy volunteers had subcortical and/or brainstem lesions on MRI scanning. The long-duration patients were compared with premorbid IQ–matched controls on a number of neuropsychological tests. Although there were no differences on most of the memory tests or on trail making, the diabetic patients were 5 points lower on WAIS performance IQ ($p < .01$). The authors were not able to attribute the impairments found to specific clinical causes. This study adds to the impression gained above that a measure of IQ decrement, or of performance IQ in groups matched for premorbid IQ, is particularly useful in revealing cognitive impairments.

The study conducted by Langan et al. (1991), which found an association between retrospectively estimated frequency of severe hypoglycemia and estimated IQ decrement, did not test controls in addition to the diabetic patients. Although this is not necessary in order to examine the specific hypothesis under test, it is useful to discover whether patients with diabetes have lower cognitive functioning than matched controls even when they have not experienced severe hypoglycemia. This extension of the original study was conducted by Deary, Crawford et al. (1993). The 100 insulin-treated diabetic patients studied by Langan et al. (1991) were matched to 100 nondiabetic healthy controls on age, sex, social class, years of education, and premorbid intelligence. After controlling for premorbid intelligence, the diabetic group members were significantly lower than the healthy controls on both WAIS-R performance ($p = .017$) and verbal ($p = .033$) IQ scores. The difference in overall IQ between the two groups was not large, however, at about 5 IQ points.

Deary, Crawford et al. (1993) further analyzed the difference between the diabetic and control groups. When the effects of severe hypoglycemia were removed statistically from the diabetic group, there was no difference between the two groups in WAIS-R performance IQ. Therefore it was tentatively concluded that repeated episodes of severe hypoglycemia might be causing a slight lowering of performance IQ in adults. Furthermore, removal of the effects of hypoglycemia did not abolish the WAIS-R verbal IQ difference between the diabetic and control groups, leading the authors to conclude that the lower verbal IQ of the diabetic patients might have its cause in some other aspect of diabetes. This might be a result of the social effects of the illness (e.g., time lost in education), though other biological effects (e.g., repeated hyperglycemia), could not be ruled out.

With an association established between severe hypoglycemia and slight decrements in performance IQ, a further investigation on the same group of patients was undertaken to discover which information-processing aspects of intelligence were associated with experience of severe hypoglycemia (Deary, Langan, Graham, Hepburn, & Frier, 1992). Of the original 100 patients (Langan et al., 1991), 85 were retested 18 months later. As stated above, the hypoglycemia interviews and the WAIS-R and premorbid IQ tests were readministered. In addition, a series of information-processing tests related to IQ-type tests were given: the Rapid Visual Information Processing Test (RVIP), the Hick reaction time task, and the Sternberg memory scanning test.

Associations were found between frequency of severe hypoglycemia and some of the information-processing measures. Moreover, several associations were found between current and premorbid intelligence measures and several measures of information-processing efficiency. The results of key interest, however, were those where the same information-processing estimates were associated with IQ decrement estimates and frequency of severe hypoglycemia. This result was found for three information-processing variables: the number of false alarms in the RVIP task, the slope in the Hick task, and the decision time in the Hick task.

The increased false alarm rate associated with more frequent hypoglycemia was interpreted as indicating that subjects had a lowered response threshold and were slightly more prone to detect targets in their absence. Generally it appeared that hypoglycemia and IQ decrement shared an effect on decision-making and response-initiation processes. Frequency of severe hypoglycemia was not associated with time-dependent working memory processes, however, as demonstrated by the fact that there was no association with either the number of target hits in the RVIP task or the Sternberg memory scan measures.

Further analysis of the physiological basis of the intelligence and information-processing decrements associated with severe hypoglycemia was undertaken using single photon emission tomography (SPET; MacLeod et al., 1992). Ten of the subjects studied by Langan et al. (1991) who had experienced five or more episodes of severe hypoglycemia were compared with 10 diabetic subjects matched for age, sex, and premorbid IQ level who had never experienced severe hypoglycemia. In addition, 20 nondiabetic controls were scanned; this allowed the effects of diabetes per se to be separated from the effects of severe hypoglycemia. Regional cerebral blood flow was estimated under resting conditions by SPET scanning after an intravenous injection of ^{99m}Tc-Exametazine. The regional distribution of the isotope (which indicates regional cerebral blood flow differences) was assessed in 12 brain regions derived from a standard neuroanatomical atlas. The group with previous severe hypoglycemia had increased radioisotope uptake in the left frontal cortex, at levels significantly greater than the nondiabetic group or the diabetic group with no previous severe hypoglycemia. Both diabetic groups had significantly increased radioisotope uptake in the right frontal cortex when compared with the nondiabetic control group. Therefore, severe hypoglycemia and diabetes per se appear to have independent and different effects on brain blood flow, especially in the frontal cortex. Although the design of this study did not allow these brain areas to be associated with cognitive changes, the frontal lobe changes have been indicated as a possible biological substrate for the cognitive changes found after repeated severe hypoglycemia and after diabetes per se.

Studies on severe hypoglycemia and intelligence, therefore, appear to have associated severe hypoglycemia specifically with certain changes in fluid intelligence and have begun to trace the putative intelligence changes to their bases in information-processing stages and to their biological origins. An associated research effort examined the impact of severe hypoglycemia on personality and vice versa.

A PSYCHOMETRIC APPROACH TO THE SYMPTOMS OF HYPOGLYCEMIA

As a part of the research undertaken in relation to severe hypoglycemia and personality, it was necessary to have validated indices of hypoglycemia symptoms. During hypoglycemia there are generally agreed to be two groups of symptoms experienced by patients. The first group, autonomic symptoms, are associated with the autonomic reactivity consequent upon low blood glucose levels. These include such symptoms as sweating and palpitation. The second group, neuroglycopenic symptoms, are assumed to be related to the direct effects of low blood glucose upon the cerebral cortex. They include such symptoms as the reduced ability to concentrate and incoordination. In order to relate the experience of these two groups of symptoms to personality variables, however, it proved necessary to validate individual symptoms as belonging to a particular group. In fact, such an exercise had never been undertaken. Research on hypoglycemia had tended to allocate symptoms to particular groupings—autonomic or neuroglycopenic—based upon experimental evidence and physiological assumptions about the origin of the symptoms (e.g., see Berger, Keller, Honegger, & Jaeggi, 1989; Heine, van der Heyden, & van der Veen, 1989; and comments by Frier & Hepburn, 1989; Hepburn & Frier, 1989).

This situation was rather unusual for a psychometric researcher. There was wide agreement among diabetic researchers about the existence of two groupings, or factors of symptoms. Furthermore, there were understood to be known physiological generating mechanisms for the two factors. There was less agreement, however, about some symptoms than about others: for example, hunger was sometimes thought to be an autonomic symptom and at other times considered a neurolglycopenic symptom, and anxiety had an uncertain position. In other words, the underlying biological structure was understood, but there was some difficulty in identifying valid markers for each resultant symptom group—quite the reverse of the usual situation in personality research, where factors are often well indexed by items but where underlying structures are obscure. Additionally, some symptoms were prominent in some subjects and absent in the hypoglycemic responses of others. A method of independent validation was required.

Over a series of three studies, our research group took a psychometric approach to the partitioning of hypoglycemic symptoms to particular groups. Essentially, symptoms were treated as if they were items in a personality inventory, and subjects were asked to indicate whether they suffered them during hypoglycemia or not. The hypothesis tested was that symptoms generated by the same underlying physiological mechanisms would tend to co-occur and would be identifiable as factors in multivariate analyses.

The first investigation obtained details of the symptoms experienced during acute hypoglycemia (blood glucose at or below 2 mmol/l) induced in 55 diabetic and nondiabetic subjects in the laboratory (Hepburn et al., 1991). Symptom ratings on a 7-point scale were collected for each subject at the time of the acute autonomic reaction and subjected to principal components analysis with varimax rotation. Two clear factors emerged. Trembling, anxiety, sweating, warmness, and nausea were grouped together and appeared to represent an autonomic factor. Dizziness, confusion, tiredness, difficulty in speaking, shivering, drowsiness, and inability to concentrate were loaded prominently on a second factor that appeared to be neuroglycopenic.

In a second study, 295 randomly selected insulin-dependent diabetics who were attending an outpatients' clinic were asked to indicate which of a number of symptoms were typically experienced by them during episodes of hypoglycemia (Hepburn, Deary, & Frier, 1992). In this larger study, five factors were identified underlying the symptoms of hypoglycemia. Confusion, odd behavior, inability to concentrate, drowsiness, and difficulty with speaking were grouped as an autonomic factor. Hunger, sweating, trembling, anxiety, and pounding heart formed a clear autonomic factor. Nausea, dry mouth, weakness, and headache formed what appeared to be a factor assessing general malaise during hypoglycemia. The fourth and fifth factors had loadings on only two symptoms each. Additionally, the fourth and fifth factors appeared to be specific aspects of the neuroglycopenic factor. The fourth factor's symptoms were incoordination and difficulty with walking, which appeared to be a motor dysfunction specific factor. The fifth factor had loadings for blurred vision and tingling, which appeared to be related to the sensory aspects of neuroglycopenia. On reviewing the results of the previous study of symptoms (Hepburn et al., 1991) a factor similar to the general malaise factor described above had only just failed to meet the criteria for acceptance. Therefore, at this stage it appeared that a three-factor model of the hypoglycemia symptoms might suffice—autonomic, neuroglycopenic and malaise—and such a model was tested in the next study.

Deary, Hepburn, MacLeod, and Frier (1993) identified 11 symptoms of hypoglycemia that were frequently reported and appeared to be key markers for the three hypothesized factors. Sweating, palpitation, shaking, and hunger were used as markers for the autonomic factor. Confusion, drowsiness, odd behavior, speech difficulty, and incoordination were used as markers for the neuroglycopenic factor. Nausea and headache were used as markers for the malaise factor. Data relevant to only these symptoms from the 295 subjects tested in the study described above (Hepburn, Deary, & Frier, 1992) were reanalyzed; three clear factors emerged with symptoms loading on their designated factors and, in most cases, at very low levels on the other factors (Deary et al., 1994).

Following this finding 303 different insulin-dependent diabetics were asked to indicate which of the 11 symptoms they experienced during episodes of hypoglycemia (Deary, Hepburn, et al., 1993). Their data were analyzed using principal components analysis with varimax rotation, and the same three factors emerged clearly. Between the two groups of 295 and 303 diabetic patients respectively the coefficients of congruence for the autonomic, neuroglycopenic, and malaise factors were .97, .96, and .88 respectively. Confirmatory factor analyses using the EQS Structural Equations package was used to confirm that in both large groups of patients, the three-factor model with the predesignated symptom loadings was the best model for hypoglycemic symptoms. The three-factor model was acceptable for both groups. Further, multisample confirmatory factor analysis was used to test the rigorous hypothesis that all symptom-factor loadings and all residual variance associated with symptoms were equal across the two groups. This hypothesis was confirmed.

In summary, the methods of psychometrics proved useful in identifying key marker items for physiological factors already known to exist. The psychometric solution has produced validated groupings of hypoglycemic symptoms that are associated with physiological mechanisms. Previous discrepancies in the uses of particular symptoms as factor markers have been resolved. The identification of validated autonomic and neuroglycopenic factor markers was essential for some of the later work on personality and severe hypoglycemia, which is described below.

SEVERE HYPOGLYCEMIA AND PERSONALITY

Efforts to find and validate the association between severe hypoglycemia and intelligence and any intellectual decrement had to overcome certain methodological problems. Perhaps the most significant contribution to overcoming these was the recent development of more valid estimates of premorbid intelligence, which allowed estimates of change to be made from cross-sectional data. A similar problem arises with personality, and it proves to be less soluble. If we wish to assess any changes in the main dimensions of personality after severe hypoglycemia, there is no recourse to measures of premorbid personality styles that are directly comparable to current personality functioning.

Before moving on to research that specifically involves the effects of hypoglycemia, it should be noted that there are at least two other areas of diabetic research involving personality. The first is the search for what has been called the "diabetic personality," something that is largely agreed to be a myth (Dunn & Turtle, 1981). No specific personality traits have been associated with diabetes, and the occasional claims to have found diabetic personality profiles appear to produce findings similar to those of other chronic disease groups (Spergel, Erlich, & Glass, 1978). Personality material found in diabetics that has interested psychologists with a psychoanalytic bent, especially bizarre dreams, is probably attributable to nocturnal hypoglycemia (Tattersall, 1981).

The second approach has been to attempt to discover the personality and cognitive correlates of diabetic control. This line of research has arisen because diabetic patients are involved with their own care at unusually technical levels compared to other illnesses. They must decide upon their schedules of glucose testing and insulin injections based upon their food intake, exercise, and state of health. Therefore it has been hypothesized that there might be certain personalities who control their illness better, or that those with higher levels of cognitive functioning might find the many operations involved easier to cope with. One of the main problems with this area of research is in finding an adequately validated measure of diabetic control with which to correlate personological variables. Glucose levels are not adequate; they are transient and may be made to look good by altering records kept at home or by making sure that glucose levels are optimal only at clinic visits. Self-report estimates of compliance with medical regimens and instructions are known to be unreliable, and it is all but impossible to capture the flexibility needed to deviate from instructions when the situation demands.

The most frequently used measure of diabetic control is the biochemical estimate of the percentage of glycated hemoglobin (HbA_1) in the bloodstream. This provides an integrated estimate of the blood glucose levels that the patient has experienced over the last 4 to 6 weeks and, therefore, represents an average of proximity to physiological blood glucose levels. HbA_1 concentrations at levels that indicate good control have been found to correlate with increased age (Brownlee-Dufeck et al., 1987), cognitive maturity and perceived competence in adolescents (Ingersoll, Orr, Herold, & Golden, 1986), increased neuroticism (but not intelligence) in 6 to 16-year-old children (Fonagy, Morgan, Lindsay, Kurtz, & Brown, 1987), and decreased anxiety and depression (Mazze, Lucido, & Shamoon, 1984; Wilson et al., 1986). Others have found that poor control of HbA_1 is associated with introversion, sociability, and curiosity but not neuroticism, anger, or anxiety in a limited sample of adolescents (Lane et al., 1988).

Gordon et al. (1993) reported a correlation of 0.43 ($p < .01$) between neuroticism and glycosylated hemoglobin, a result that is interesting but requires replication. In unpublished research in our laboratory, we examined the association between HbA_1 and Eysenck's extraversion, neuroticism, psychoticism, impulsivity, venturesomeness, and empathy factors and Broadbent's Cognitive Failures Questionnaire scores; we found no significant associations in a group of 57 insulin-dependent diabetic adults. Further, we found no significant correlations between HbA_1 concentrations and intelligence or social class. Older subjects tended to have better HbA_1 concentrations, however, though age explained only 3.5% of the variance in HbA_1 levels. There are few clear results emerging from such research, except to indicate that it is almost impossible to define a valid measure of diabetic control.

Gold, Deary, O'Hare, Reckless, and Frier (1993) attempted to assess changes in personality traits as a result of repeated hypoglycemic episodes. Six insulin-treated diabetic patients who had suffered repeated episodes of severe hypoglycemia were examined. Their spouses were all members of a self-help group and had noticed progressive cognitive and personality changes in their dependents. In all cases it proved possible to verify independently that each patient had suffered multiple episodes of severe hypoglycemia during treatment with insulin. Two caregivers had given up full-time employment to look after their dependents. All caregivers had reduced social involvement because of either a lack of interest or a tendency to tire easily on the part of the patients. Four of the six caregivers reported having become irritable, depressed, and anxious because of the personality—and to some extent the cognitive—changes in their spouses. Three of the caregivers met the criterion for psychiatric caseness on the General Health Questionnaire, an estimate of general, nonpsychotic psychiatric distress.

To gauge the changes in the personalities of these patients who had suffered large numbers of hypoglycemic symptoms, spouses were asked to complete the Eysenck Personality Questionnaire on behalf of their diabetic dependents, indicating "how they appear now" and "how they appeared prior to changing." Significant changes were found in neuroticism (which increased from a mean of 8.8 to 15.5, $p = .05$) and extraversion (which decreased from 10.3 to 2.3, $p = .04$). No changes were found for psychoticism or on the lie scale. Whereas the results show interesting changes, there are problems in their interpretation. The method used to make premorbid and current personality assessments was unusual, and the patients were from a particular group (i.e. those with articulate and able spouses who got together to form a self-help group because of the problems they were facing in caring for diabetic relatives). Therefore response biases might be expected, though one might have expected the psychoticism scale scores to rise if spouses had been overzealous in making the point about the burden of care they were suffering. The results obtained received some support from a Swedish study, which found that diabetic patients who had suffered repeated episodes of severe hypoglycemia had higher anxiety levels and lower levels of happiness than patients with no history of severe hypoglycemia, though the groups did not differ on self-rated neuroticism (Wredling, Theorell, Roll, Lins, & Adamson, 1992).

In summary, this was an attempt to conduct pilot research on an extreme group who had suffered unusually large numbers of attacks of severe hypoglycemia. Nevertheless, it identifies tasks for future research in the area and suggests that severe hypoglycemia might affect personality variables in addition to cognitive factors. It will be interesting to pursue this further, especially to assess whether the effects of hypoglycemia on intelligence and personality act via shared information-processing mechanisms or whether it has several distinct effects on information-processing components.

Other avenues might prove to be more accessible for personality research related to severe hypoglycemia. Hypoglycemia is greatly feared by diabetic patients (Frier, 1993) and there are individual differences in the degree to which patients fear the episodes. A measure of hypoglycemia fear was developed by Cox, Irvine, Gonder-Frederick, Nowacek, and Butterfield (1987) and involves two subscales: a worry scale (which assesses the frequency and severity of hypoglycemia-related concerns) and a behavior scale (which assesses the practical changes that patients make in order to avoid hypoglycemia). Scores on the hypoglycemia fear scale have been related to patients' having greater numbers of psychological symptoms, higher perceived stress, and greater previous experience of severe hypoglycemia (Irvine, Cox, & Gonder-Frederick, 1992).

The hypoglycemia fear questionnaire was used in a recent project that sought to discover the associations among personality, previous severe hypoglycemia experience, fear of hypoglycemia, and awareness of hypoglycemia (Hepburn, MacLeod, Deary, & Frier, 1992). Awareness of hypoglycemia refers to a diabetic patient's ability to be consciously aware of the symptoms related to the onset of an episode of hypoglycemia (Frier, 1993). Awareness of hypoglycemia forms a continuum from total awareness to total unawareness. In total, 305 insulin-dependent patients were tested; 2 had never experienced hypoglycemia and were excluded from further analyses. Thirty-six percent of the patients had experienced some degree of reduced awareness of hypoglycemia for more than 1 year. Patients with reduced awareness had higher neuroticism levels ($p < .01$) and lower extraversion levels ($p < .01$) on the revised short form of the Eysenck Personality Questionnaire. On the hypoglycemia fear scale, patients with some degree of unawareness had higher worry scores ($p < .001$), but their behavior scores were the same as those of the fully aware patients.

The covariance matrix containing extraversion, introversion, previous amounts of severe hypoglycemic episodes, state of awareness, and the hypoglycemia fear worry and behavior scales was subjected to a structural equation modeling exercise in order to discover the causal associations among the variables. Also added were scores representing the number of autonomic and neuroglycopenic symptoms experienced by patients in a typical hypoglycemic episode. The best-fitting causal model, assessed using the method of generalized least squares in the EQS Structural Equations package, is shown in Figure 1.

The most striking result in Figure 1 is the number of causal associations that arise from individual differences in neuroticism. Perhaps not surprisingly, neuroticism is associated with a tendency to worry about hypoglycemia; it is also associated with the tendency to report being unaware of hypoglycemia and to the numbers of neuroglycopenic symptoms experienced in a typical episode. An interesting association is that between neuroticism and the number of autonomic symptoms experienced in a typical hypoglycemic episode. This relatively strong association tends to support Eysenck's suggestion that individual differences in neuroticism might be related to autonomic reactivity, because in the present case neuroticism is associated with a validated scale of autonomic symptoms. Of course, another interpretation of this finding, and of the other neuroticism associations, might be that people with high neuroticism scores are distress prone and will overreport on a large number of medical symptoms (Deary, MacLullich, & Mardon, 1991; Stone & Costa, 1990). Extraversion levels tended to be reduced a little by altered awareness of hypoglycemia, perhaps reflecting a change in social confidence in those who tend not to have warning about the onset of an episode of hypoglycemia.

The model also indicates that there are no direct effects of personality on the number of hypoglycemic episodes experienced in the last year, though there are indirect effects of neuroticism acting via awareness of hypoglycemia and numbers of neuroglycopenic symptoms experienced in a typical hypoglycemic episode. Awareness was the only other predictor of worry about hypoglycemia (apart from neuroticism), indicating that hypoglycemia fear was high in those individuals who had a personality tendency toward negative affect and who were uncertain about detecting a hypoglycemic episode. The only predictor of hypoglycemia-related behavior change was worry, and not actual recent experience of hypoglycemia.

In summary, there is some preliminary evidence to indicate that personality might be altered as a result of severe hypoglycemia, though whether this is true in relation to the more usual experience of many diabetic patients remains to be seen. It would also appear that personality—especially individual differences in neuroticism—plays an important part in the reported symptomatic experience of hypoglycemia, reported changes in hypoglycemia awareness, and in worry about hypoglycemia.

CONCLUSIONS

Severe hypoglycemia is an iatrogenic brain insult that forms a part of many patients' experience of insulin-treated diabetes mellitus. Because its cognitive and neurophysiological effects on the brain may be studied in the acute situation and quantified, it offers a useful model for studying the effects of changes on the

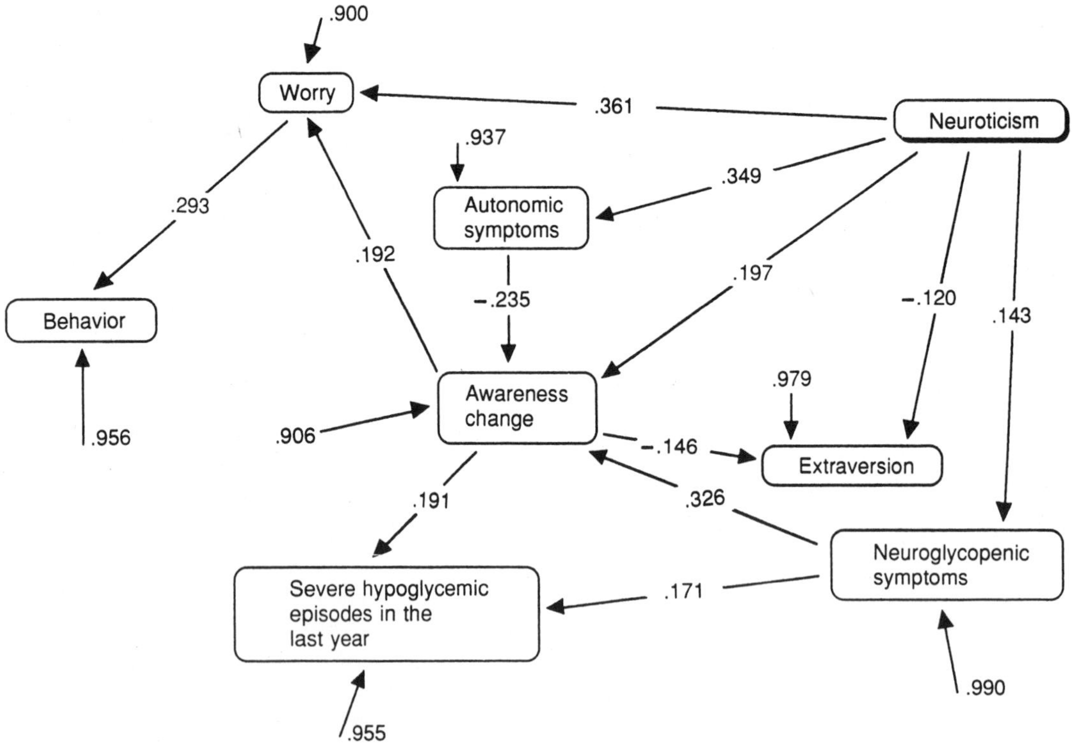

Figure 1. Best-fitting model of the relationships among personality dimensions and self-reported hypoglycemia-related phenomena (including number of episodes in the last year, awareness of episodes, symptoms experienced during episodes, and fear of hypoglycemia).

metabolic environment on brain functions (Deary, 1992). It has proved possible to obtain relatively reliable estimates of patients' previous hypoglycemia episodes and thereby achieve rough estimates of the total extent of brain insult. Such estimates appear to be related to decline in fluid intelligence, and this has been associated further with particular information-processing stages and changes in regional brain metabolism estimated by SPET scanning. Changes in personality dimensions, as rated by spouses, have been demonstrated in severely affected patients. Personality, especially neuroticism, plays an important part in patient-reported hypoglycemic phenomena, particularly the experience of autonomic symptoms, offering some confirmation of Eysenck's hypothesis concerning the biological basis of neuroticism.

Further study of severe hypoglycemia offers a tractable way to link intelligence and personality through brain metabolism and information-processing functions. The effects of severe hypoglycemia on personality and intelligence at the psychometric level may be tracked down in a reductionistic exercise using models of information processing that capture important aspects of individual differences in cognitive ability and personality. Ultimately, functional brain scanning studies offer the possibility of finding which brain areas support individual differences in intelligence and personality and how the functioning in these areas may be affected by reduction in brain glucose levels.

REFERENCES

Bale, R. N. (1973). Brain damage in diabetes mellitus. *British Journal of Psychiatry, 122*, 337–341.

Berger, W. G., Keller, U., Honegger, B., & Jaeggi, E. (1989). Warning symptoms of hypoglycaemia during treatment with human and porcine insulin in diabetes mellitus. *Lancet, 1*, 1041–1044.

Booth-Kewley, S., & Friedman, H. S. (1987). Psychological predictors of heart disease: A quantitative review. *Psychological Bulletin, 101*, 343–362.

Brownlee-Dufeck, M., Paterson, L., Simonds, J. F., Goldstein, D., Kilo, C., & Hoette, S. (1987). The role of health beliefs in the regimen adherence and metabolic control of adolescents and adults with diabetes mellitus. *Journal of Consulting and Clinical Psychology*, *55*, 139–144.

Cox, D., Gonder-Frederick, L., Nowacek, G., & Butterfield, J. (1987). Quantifying fear of hypoglycemia: A preliminary report. *Diabetes Care*, *10*, 617–621.

Crawford, J. R. (1989). Estimation of premorbid IQ: A review of recent developments. In J. R. Crawford & D. M. Parker (Eds.), *Developments in clinical and experimental neuropsychology* (pp. 55–74). New York: Plenum.

Crawford, J. R., Stewart, L. E., Parker, D. M., Besson, L. A. O., & Cochrane, R. H. B. (1989). Estimation of premorbid intelligence: Combining psychometric and demographic approaches improves predictive accuracy. *Personality and Individual Differences*, *10*, 793–796.

DCCT Research Group. (1991). Epidemiology of severe hypoglycaemia in the Diabetes Control and Complications Trial. *American Journal of Medicine*, *90*, 450–459.

Deary, I. J. (1991). Personality. In F. G. R. Fowkes (Ed.), *Epidemiology of peripheral vascular disease* (pp. 217–226). Berlin: Springer.

Deary, I. J. (1992). Diabetes, hypoglycaemia and cognitive performance. In A. P. Smith & D. M. Jones (Eds.), *Handbook of human performance* (Vol. 2, pp. 243–259). London: Academic Press.

Deary, I. J., Capewell, S., Hajducka, C., & Muir, A. L. (1991). The effects of captopril versus atenolol on memory, information processing and mood. *British Journal of Clinical Pharmacology*, *32*, 347–353.

Deary, I. J., Crawford, J. R., Hepburn, D. A., Langan, S. J., Blackmore, L. M., & Frier, B. M. (1993). Severe hypoglycaemia and intelligence in adult patients with insulin-treated diabetes. *Diabetes*, *42*, 341–344.

Deary, I. J., Fowkes, F. G. R., Donnan, P. T., & Housley, E. (1994). Hostile personality and risks of peripheral arterial disease in the general population. *Psychosomatic Medicine*, *56*, 197–202.

Deary, I. J., & Frier, B. M. (1992). Intensified conventional insulin treatment and neuropsychological impairment [Letter]. *British Medical Journal*, *304*, 447.

Deary, I. J., Hepburn, D. A., MacLeod, K. M., & Frier, B. M. (1993). Partitioning the symptoms of hypoglycaemia using multi-sample confirmatory factor analysis. *Diabetologia*, *36*, 771–777.

Deary, I. J., Langan, S. J., Graham, K. S., Hepburn, D., & Frier, B. M. (1992). Recurrent severe hypoglycemia, intelligence, and speed of information processing. *Intelligence*, *16*, 337–359.

Deary, I. J., MacLullich, A. M. J., & Mardon, J. (1991). Reporting of minor physical symptoms and family incidence of hypertension and heart disease—relationships with personality and Type A behavior. *Personality and Individual Differences*, *12*, 747–751.

Dejgaard, A., Gade, A., Larsson, H., Balle, V., Parving, A., & Parving, H. (1990). Evidence for diabetic encephalopathy. *Diabetic Medicine*, *8*, 162–167.

Dunn, S. M., & Turtle, J. R. (1981). The myth of the diabetic personality. *Diabetes Care*, *4*, 640–646.

Egan, V., & Goodwin, G. M. (1992). HIV and AIDS. In A. P. Smith & D. M. Jones (Eds.), *Handbook of human performance* (Vol. 2, pp. 219–242). London: Academic Press.

Fonagy, P., Morgan, C. S., Lindsay, M. K. M., Kurtz, A. B., & Brown, R. (1987). Psychological adjustment and diabetic control. *Archives of Disease in Childhood*, *62*, 1009–1013.

Fowkes, F. G. R., Leng, G. C., Donnan, P. T., Deary, I. J., Riemersma, R. A., & Housley, E. (1992). Serum cholesterol, triglycerides, and aggression in the general population. *Lancet*, *340*, 995–998.

Franceschi, M., Cecchetto, R., Minicucci, F., Smizne, S., Baio, G., & Canal, N. (1984). Cognitive processes in insulin-dependent diabetes. *Diabetes Care*, *7*, 228–231.

Frier, B. M. (1993). Hypoglycaemia in the diabetic adult. In A. Aynsley-Green & J. Gregory (Eds.), *Balliere's clinical endocrinology and metabolism* (Vol. 7). London: Balliere Tindall.

Frier, B. M., & Hepburn, D. A. (1989). Plasma noradrenalin, human insulin, and hypoglycaemia [Letter]. *Lancet*, *2*, 1269.

Gold, A. E., Deary, I. J., O'Hare, J. P., Reckless, J. P. D., & Frier, B. M. (1993). *Changes in personality and cognitive function following recurrent severe hypoglycaemia in patients with type 1 diabetes*. Manuscript in preparation.

Gordon, D., Fisher, S. G., Wilson, M., Fergus, E., Paterson, K. R., & Semple, C. G. (1993). Psychological factors and their relationship to diabetes control. *Diabetic Medicine*, *10*, 530–534.

Heine, R. J., van der Heyden, E. A. P., & van der Veen, E. A. (1989). Responses to human and porcine insulin in healthy subjects. *Lancet*, *2*, 946–949.

Hepburn, D. A., Deary, I. J., & Frier, B. M. (1992). Classification of symptoms of hypoglycaemia in insulin-treated diabetic patients using factor analysis: Relationship to hypoglycaemia unawareness. *Diabetic Medicine*, *9*, 70–75.

Hepburn, D. A., Deary, I. J., Frier, B. M., Patrick, A. W., Quinn, J. D., & Fisher, B. M. (1991). Symptoms of acute insulin-induced hypoglycaemia in humans with and without IDDM: A factor analysis approach. *Diabetes Care*, *14*, 949–957.

Hepburn, D. A., & Frier, B. M. (1989). Hypoglycaemia unawareness and human insulin [Letter]. *Lancet*, *1*, 1394.

Hepburn, D. A., MacLeod, K. M., Deary, I. J., & Frier, B. M. (1992). Fear of hypoglycaemia, personality and hypoglycaemia unawareness in patients with insulin-treated diabetes [Abstract]. *Diabetic Medicine*, *9* (Suppl. 2), S43.

Ingersoll, G. M., Orr, D. P., Herold, A. J., & Golden, M. P. (1986). Cognitive maturity and self-management among adolescents with insulin dependent diabetes mellitus. *Journal of Paediatrics*, *108*, 620–623.

Irvine, A. A., Cox, D., & Gonder-Frederick, L. (1992). Fear of hypoglycemia: Relationship to physical and psychological symptoms in patients with insulin-dependent diabetes mellitus. *Health Psychology*, *11*, 135–138.

Lane, J. D., Stabler, B., Ross, S. L., Morris, M. A., Litton, J. C., & Surwit, R. S. (1988). Psychological predictors of glucose control in patients with IDDM. *Diabetes Care*, *11*, 790–800.

Langan, S. J., Deary, I. J., Hepburn, D. A., & Frier, B. M. (1991). Cumulative cognitive impairment following recurrent severe hypoglycaemia in adult patients with insulin-treated diabetes mellitus. *Diabetologia*, *34*, 337–344.

Lawson, J. S., Erdahl, D. L. W., Monga, T. N., Bird, C. E., Donald, M. W., Surridge, D. H. C., & Letemendia, F. J. J. (1984). Neuropsychological function in diabetic patients with neuropathy. *British Journal of Psychiatry*, *145*, 263–268.

MacLeod, K. M., Hepburn, D. A., Deary, I. J., Ebmeier, K., Goodwin, G., & Frier, B. M. (1992). Variations in regional cerebral blood flow in patients with Type 1 diabetes: Effects of diabetes and a history of recurrent severe hypoglycaemia [Abstract]. *Diabetic Medicine*, *9* (Suppl. 2), S11.

Mann, A. H. (1977). Psychiatric morbidity and hostility in hypertension. *Psychological Medicine*, *7*, 653–659.

Mann, A. H. (1986). The psychological aspects of essential hypertension. *Journal of Psychosomatic Research*, *30*, 527–541.

Matthews, K. A. (1988). Coronary heart disease and Type A behaviors: Update on and alternative to the Booth-Kewley and Friedman (1987) quantitative review. *Psychological Bulletin, 104*, 373–380.

Mazze, R. S., Lucido, D., & Shamoon, H. (1984). Psychological and social correlates of glycaemic control. *Diabetes Care, 7*, 360–366.

Pennebaker, J. W., Cox, D. J., Gonder-Frederick, L., Wunsch, M. G., Evans, W. S., & Pohl, S. (1981). Physical symptoms related to blood glucose in insulin-dependent diabetics. *Psychosomatic Medicine, 43*, 489–500.

Phillips, K. (1991). Essential hypertension. In M. Pitts & K. Phillips (Eds.), *The psychology of health* (pp. 171–186). London: Routledge.

Pramming, S., Thorsteinsson, B., Theilgaard, A., Pinner, E. M., & Binder, C. (1986). Cognitive function during hypoglycaemia in Type 1 diabetes mellitus. *British Medical Journal, 292*, 647–650.

Reichard, P., Berglund, A., Britz, A., Levander, S., & Rosenqvist, U. (1991). Hypoglycaemic episodes during insulin treatment: Increased frequency but no effect on cognitive function. *Journal of Internal Medicine, 229*, 9–16.

Reichard, P., Britz, A., & Rosenqvist, U. (1991). Intensified conventional insulin treatment and neuropsychological impairment. *British Medical Journal, 303*, 1439–1442.

Richardson, J. T. E. (1990). Cognitive function in diabetes mellitus. *Neuroscience and Behavioural Reviews, 14*, 385–388.

Robinson, J. O. (1964). A possible effect of selection on the test scores of a group of hypertensives. *Journal of Psychosomatic Research, 8*, 239–243.

Ryan, C. M. (1988). Neurobehavioural complications of Type 1 diabetes: Examination of possible risk factors. *Diabetes Care, 11*, 86–93.

Skenazy, J. A., & Bigler, E. D. (1984). Neuropsychological findings in diabetes mellitus. *Journal of Clinical Psychology, 40*, 246–258.

Smith, T. W., & Williams, P. G. (1992). Personality and health: Advantages and limitations of the five-factor model. *Journal of Personality, 60*, 395–423.

Spergel, P., Ehrlich, G. E., & Glass, D. (1978). The rheumatoid arthritic personality: A pseudodiagnostic myth. *Psychosomatics, 19*, 79–86.

Starr, J. M., Whalley, L. J., Inch, S., & Schering, P. A. (1993). Blood pressure and cognitive function in healthy old people. *Journal of the American Geriatrics Society, 41*, 753–756.

Stone, S. V., & Costa, P. T. (1990). Disease-prone personality or distress-prone personality? The role of neuroticism in coronary heart disease. In H. S. Friedman (Ed.), *Personality and disease* (pp. 178–200). Chichester, England: Wiley.

Suls, J., & Rittenhouse, J. D. (1990). Models of linkages between personality and disease. In H. S. Friedman (Ed.), *Personality and disease* (pp. 38–64). Chichester, England: Wiley.

Tattersall, R. B. (1981). Psychiatric aspects of diabetes: A physician's view. *British Journal of Psychiatry, 139*, 485–493.

Van Heck, G. L., Bonaiuto, P., Deary, I. J., & Nowack, W. (Eds.). (1994). *Personality psychology in Europe* (Vol. 4). Tilburg, Netherlands: Tilburg University Press.

Vernon, P. A. (Ed.). (1993). *Biological approaches to the study of human intelligence*. Norwood, NJ: Ablex.

Waal-Manning, H. J., Knight, R. G., Spears, G. F., & Paulin, J. M. (1986). The relationship between blood pressure and personality in a large unselected adult sample. *Journal of Psychosomatic Research, 30*, 361–368.

Wilson, W., Ary, D. V., Biglan, A., Glasgow, R. E., Toobert, D. J., & Campbell, R. C. (1986). Psychosocial predictors of self-care behaviours (compliance) and glycemic control in non-insulin-dependent diabetes mellitus. *Diabetes Care, 9*, 614–622.

Wredling, R., Levander, S., Adamson, U., & Lins, P. E. (1990). Permanent neuropsychological impairment after recurrent episodes of severe hypoglycaemia in man. *Diabetologia, 33*, 152–157.

Wredling, R. A. M., Theorell, P. G. T., Roll, H. M., Lins, P. E. S., & Adamson, U. K. C. (1992). Psychosocial state of patients with IDDM prone to recurrent episodes of severe hypoglycaemia. *Diabetes Care, 15*, 518–521.

Zuckerman, M. (1991). *Psychobiology of personality*. Cambridge, England: Cambridge University Press.

33

Personality and Intelligence in the Military

The Case of War Heroes

Reuven Gal

The better part of valor is discretion.
—Shakespeare

INTRODUCTION

Personality Factors in the Military

"How would I behave in a battle?" This, claims British military historian John Keegan (1976), is the central question for any young man training to be a professional soldier. The battlefield is one of the ultimate tests of what will triumph: the situation or the personality; the innate instincts or the acquired skills; the emotions—fear, horror, rage, vengeance—or the cognition, tactics, and intelligence.

Both personality and intelligence factors are critical in the military setting. Whether it is in combat roles or in barrack choirs, most of the demands imposed on the soldier cannot be supplied by acquired skills only, nor are they handled just by automatic drills. The military environment typically requires adjustment to extremely harsh conditions, coping with life-threatening events, enduring adverse situations, surviving dangerous risks, and persisting through sustained efforts. Furthermore, it requires contradictory demands: compliance along with creativity, restraint with audacity, and trust with caution. And for the commanders and officers, the military setting also imposes the need to apply leadership, make critical decisions under stress, impel men (or women) to risk their lives, and solve problems that are at times unsolvable.

Indeed, young individuals who choose a military career as their profession can be identified by several personality characteristics, including conformity, patriotism, acceptance of authority, need for recognition, and leadership (Card, 1977). They also differ from their comparable peers in expressing greater loyalty and commitment to the organization, higher bureaucratic tendencies, and less need to control their own destiny (Card, 1978).

Personality dispositions and intelligence level also play a critical role regarding military assignments and performance. No wonder the military is one of the largest consumers in the world of personality assessment and intelligence testing (Steege & Fritscher, 1991). Back in World War I, American psychologists had already developed the Army Alpha and Beta tests

Reuven Gal • The Israeli Institute for Military Studies, Zikhron Ya'akov, Israel 30900.

International Handbook of Personality and Intelligence, edited by Donald H. Saklofske and Moshe Zeidner. Plenum Press, New York, 1995.

to enable the screening of potential combatants. Based on the research of Binet in France, those group-administered tests were the first tests of general aptitude and intellectual ability and were administered to more than 1.7 million potential conscripts (Zeidner & Drucker, 1988). During World War II, the forerunner of the CIA, the office of Strategic Service (OSS), assessed its candidates against a cluster of mental and emotional requirements typical to its martial demands (emotional stability, effective intelligence, energy and initiative, motivation for assignment, leadership, and security; OSS Assessment Staff, 1948). Not surprisingly, the Israeli Defense Forces (IDF) screen combat-officer candidates against very similar personality factors: sociability, social intelligence, emotional stability, leadership, devotion to duty, decisiveness, and perseverance under stress (Gal, 1986).

In theory, personality factors and individual differences seem to be antithetical to the military: Large organizations, like the military, usually emphasize uniformity and standardization. Yet the extreme diversity, complexity, and demanding characteristics of most military jobs require the selection of the "right stuff" for the right assignment (Hilton & Dolgin, 1991). In fact, the diversity and differentiation in combat roles are at times so large that even specializations among combat aviators (e.g., fighter, bomber, tanker) require different personality profiles (Retzlaff & Gilbertini, 1987). Similarly, one may assume that distinct manifestations of combat performance—such as performing a heroic act under heavy bombardment versus breaking down under the same circumstances—might result from different personality profiles of the combatants involved. The validity of this assumption will be further examined later.

Of particular interest for this chapter is the unique profile of personality and intelligence that characterizes military leaders, namely, commissioned officers or noncommissioned officers (NCOs) in commanding positions. Although the general issue of military leadership is beyond the scope of this chapter (for reviews, see Buck & Korb, 1981; Hunt & Blair, 1985), some specific findings are of relevance. Contrary to the stereotyped (or intuitive) perception of military leaders being assertive, bold, and forceful, several studies have demonstrated quite the opposite. Ross and Offerman (1991), for example, investigated U.S. Air Force officers in their midcareer stages and found that the more charismatic these officers were perceived as being by their subordinates, the higher they were on measures of feminine attributes and nurturing, and lower on measures of masculinity, dominance, and aggression. Roush and Atwater (1992) similarly found that naval officers characterized as "feeling" (as opposed to "thinking") types were also rated higher as charismatic leaders. Feeling types normally concentrate on affective responses of others rather than on impersonal processes and cognition.

Intelligence Factors in the Military

It is commonly assumed (e.g., Stouffer, Devinney, Star, & Williams, 1949) and frequently validated (e.g., Egbert et al., 1957; Eitelberg, Laurence, Waters, & Perelman, 1984; Scribner, Smith, Baldwin, & Phillips, 1986) that more intelligent fighters are better fighters. In the Israeli army, for example, there is a clear linear relationship between conscripts' initial "general quality score" (which is predominantly weighed by intelligence and education level) and their consequent achievements in service (Gal, 1986, pp. 81–82). Similar findings were recently reported by Osato and Sherry (1993) with U.S. Army volunteers; specifically, it was found that "soldiers in the highest third of the IQ distribution enjoyed greater degrees of self-confidence and adaptiveness to change" (p. 59).

In an all-volunteer military, such as that in the United States, distribution of personnel intelligence is determined primarily by the quality of those who volunteer and by their choices of military occupations. In a draft-based system, such as in the IDF, intelligence is a factor in placement and assignment policy. Indeed, within the IDF, the intelligence-scores curve is clearly biased (compared to the overall population) toward the combat roles and combat units (Gal, 1986, p. 85).

Intelligence is obviously a significant ingredient in leadership perceptions (e.g., Lord, DeVader, & Alliger, 1986) as well as in actual leadership behavior (e.g., Fiedler & Garcia, 1987). Fiedler (1992), however, claims that under stressful conditions intelligent individuals may not necessarily function well as nleaders. Among other empirical data, Fiedler derives his conclusion from a dissertation study conducted on a sample of combat infantry officers and NCOs (Borden, 1980). It should be emphasized, though, that the stressful conditions in that particular study involved "stress with boss," rather than stress in combat.

Notwithstanding office-type stress, there is strong evidence in the literature and research that effective leadership requires a high level of general intelligence (Zaccaro, Gilbert, Thor, & Mumford, 1991). Evidently as a result of selection policy, screening procedures, and assignment considerations, officers and commanders in the military are also characterized by higher levels of intelligence.

An important aspect of the intelligent ingredient in leadership behavior comes from a vast body of literature (see review in Zaccaro et al., 1991) indicating that the specific type of intelligence required for leadership performance is *social intelligence*. An accepted definition of social intelligence is "the ability to understand the feelings, thoughts, and behaviors of persons, including oneself, in interpersonal situations and to act appropriately upon that understanding" (Marlowe, 1986, p. 52). Ford (1986), however, suggested that one of the ways individuals can be socially intelligent is through their conformity, which involves "efforts to create, maintain, or enhance the identity of the social units to which one is part" (pp. 125–126). Clearly visible is the relevance to issues of soldiers, bonding, combat units' cohesion, and commanders' roles in building such cohesiveness.

Combat Heroism

Psychological research has long sought to solve the riddle of heroism and bravery under combat conditions. Among the repeated questions addressed are the following: How can feats of bravery on the battlefield be explained? What are the characteristics, if any, of the hero? Are there heroes at all, or is a hero born out of a specific situation? In addition to the academic debate of whether circumstantial or personality factors account for an individual's behavior in extreme situations (e.g., Gal & Israelashwili, 1978; Hallam & Rachman, 1980), these intriguing questions have potential relevance to issues of selection, training, and preparation of men to the extreme demands of battlefield situations.

A number of researchers who have struggled with these and related questions (DeGangh & Knoll, 1954; Gal, 1992; Goodacre, 1953; Larsen & Giles, 1976; Little, 1964; Moskos, 1973; Shirom, 1976; Trites & Sells, 1957) came to the conclusion that the dominant motivating factor for acts of courage can be found in the structure of social relationships within the primary group (i.e., the immediate comrades in the squad, the platoon, or the company). These researchers emphasize factors such as morale, group cohesion, comrade relations, and a sense of mutual responsibility as reasons for a combatant to risk his or her life beyond the call of duty in a combat situation. With regard to the personality predispositions of the particular hero, the relevant traits according to this view are "social" traits such as sociability, loyalty, belongingness, and fidelity.

Egbert and his colleagues (1957, 1958), who conducted the Fighter 1 study, provided additional information concerning the personal characteristics of highly effective combatants. The Fighter 1 study sought to identify the differences between "fighters" (soldiers who had received, or had been recommended for, a decoration for valor in combat or were evaluated by peers as high performers) and "nonfighters" (soldiers who were evaluated by peers as poor performers or admitted themselves as such) among American combat soldiers in Korea. Among the differences revealed in this study, the fighters were found to be more intelligent, more masculine, more socially mature, and more emotionally stability , as well as to have more leadership potential than nonfighters. In addition, the fighters were preferred socially and in combat by their peers, showed better health and vitality, had a more stable home life, had a greater reservoir of military knowledge, and had demonstrated greater speed and accuracy in manual and physical performances (Egbert et al., 1957, p. 4).

An extensive study by Rachman (1978, 1983) conducted on a group of bomb-disposal operators in the British army revealed very similar results. In general, these volunteer combatants, who were frequently called upon to perform highly dangerous tasks, showed an above-average level of mental and emotional stability. Furthermore, in a comparison of those operators who had been decorated for special acts of gallantry to equally competent but nondecorated operators, the decorated operators had obtained exceptionally low scores on the Cattell 16PF Hypochondriasis scale—they reported no bodily or mental complaints whatsoever. Though Rachman's final conclusion is that fear and fearlessness are to some extent personality traits, however, his observation also revealed the important role of "effective training, perceived competence, and high group morale and cohesion" (Rachman, 1983, p. 163). These, in turn, further facilitate fearlessness and heroic behavior.

Likewise, combat heroism is also a behavior arising from unique circumstantial conditions. Systematic analyses of situations leading to acts of heroism have been carried out by researchers who have approached the question from this situational (rather than personality) point of view. For example, Blake and Butler (1976) examined the circumstances that resulted in 207 American soldiers being awarded the Congressional Medal of Honor in Vietnam. The various aspects relating to the heroic acts were factor analyzed into two main categories: lifesaving activities, and war-winning activities. The first category included cases such as rescue attempts, unusually aggressive actions, and smothering hand grenades with one's own body. The second category consisted of activities such as rear defense, refusal of medical attention, and initiation of leadership behavior. Blake and Butler's analysis thus exemplifies an attempt to describe acts of heroism by using situational terms, not personality traits, to characterize those particular acts.

It becomes clear, then, from this literature review that war heroism is an extreme behavior occurring under extraordinary situations. It is also quite evident that those combatants involved in such extreme behavior can be characterized by a series of personality dispositions, mental attributes, and intellectual capabilities. Are these characteristics unique to actual heroes, however, or are they typical of combatants or individuals involved in high-risk activities in general? Lacking in most of the studies in this area is the inclusion of a special control group comprised of individuals who have the same background as the "heroes," and who were exposed to exactly the same battle conditions, but who did *not* perform an act of bravery. Would the heroes be different from these control counterparts? Would they exhibit personality dispositions or mental capabilities that are significantly distinct from their counterparts?

In the following sections I will describe an attempt made to identify such distinctions while utilizing such a control group. I will focus on one of Israel's most extreme war experiences, the 1973 Yom Kippur War. Several investigators studied in depth the psychological reactions of Israeli combatants who had actively participated in this Arab-Israeli war (e.g., Levav, Greenfield, & Baruch, 1979; Lieblich, 1983; Sohlberg, 1976; Yaron, 1983). None of these studies, however, focused on gallant behavior in combat, nor did they analyze systematically personality and intelligence factors of those who had performed extreme feats of heroism on the battlefield. This is, indeed, the goal of the present work.

WAR HEROES: AN ISRAELI CASE STUDY

Subjects and Procedure

Subjects for this study were Israeli soldiers who received bravery decorations at the conclusion of the Yom Kippur War. The procedure for determining the allocation of these awards was as follows: A special committee of senior officers, representing the various services of the IDF, was appointed to examine the information provided by unit commanders regarding exceptional acts of bravery of their soldiers and to carry out a preliminary selection of candidates. The candidates selected for further consideration (if alive) and/or other eyewitnesses were then interviewed by members of the committee. Subsequently, the committee determined whether the acts of bravery met the preestablished criteria for decoration; and, if so, what level of decoration should be awarded.

A total of 283 medal recipients constituted the final group of subjects in this study: all 194 soldiers who, following the war, had received the *Ott Hamoffett* (exemplary conduct medal; third-level award) and all 89 soldiers who had been decorated with the *Ott Ha' oz* (bravery medal; second-level award). Preliminary statistical checks showed no significant differences on several major variables between those awarded the respective medals; thus both groups were combined for the purposes of further analyses. Our sample did not include those few soldiers who had been awarded the highest-level decoration (*Ott Hagvurah*) because they constituted a very small and exceptional group (only 8 soldiers).

As expected, the sampled subjects came from all the different corps of the military and ranged across most military ranks. Three different types of service exist in the IDF:

- *Compulsory service*. This includes all conscripts who are drafted at the age of 18 for 3 years of mandatory service. In practice, about 85% of all the male manpower pool in Israel (with the exception of Arab citizens) go through this compulsory service.
- *Permanent service*. The smallest of the three IDF components, this category comprises career officers and NCOs who have made the military their profession. All higher command positions, including those of reserve units (see below) are designated for permanent-service officers.
- *Reserve service*. This is the largest component of the Israeli armed forces. According to the International Institute for Strategic Studies (1981–1982), approximately 65% of the IDF's strength is made up of reserve soldiers.

Table 1 delineates the distribution of the medalists according to their type of service.

Table 1. Distribution of Medal Recipients According to Types of Military Service

Type of military service	N	%
Compulsory service	80	28.3
Permanent service	90	31.8
Reserve service	113	39.9
Total	283	100.0

Although all the different corps (or branches) of the IDF took active parts in the Yom Kippur war, it was mainly the ground forces (i.e., armor, infantry) that suffered the main impact of this war. The air force, though much smaller in number, was also severely affected, especially during the first days of the war. Table 2 presents the distribution of medalists according to their corps/branches.

Although it is not possible to provide the (classified) information regarding the relative size of each branch, a note should be made about their specific natures. A unique characteristic of the Israeli combat units, especially the armor and infantry corps, is their personnel stability and strong in-group cohesion (Gal, 1986). This is true for both the regular (compulsory) and reserve units. Quite typically, one may find in a reserve armor unit individuals who have served as members of the *same* tank crew throughout several wars.

Table 3 provides the rank distribution of the medal recipients. Again, for classification reasons, information about the distribution of ranks in the total IDF population is not available. It is, however, estimated that the proportion of the officers corps' strength (including both junior and senior officers) within the combat ground units is about 6% (Gabriel & Gal, 1984).

Table 2. Distribution of Medal Recipients According to Branch of Military Service

Branch of service	N	%
Armor	152	53.7
Infantry (including paratroopers)	51	18.0
Air force	22	7.8
Medical corps	18	6.4
Navy	7	2.5
Engineering corps	6	2.0
Ordnance	5	1.8
General staff[a]	4	1.4
Other	18	6.4
Total	283	100.0

[a]Officers with the rank of colonel and above.

Table 3. Distribution of Medal Recipients According to Military Rank

Military rank	N	%
Lower-rank enlisted (private, private 1st class, corporal)	35	12.4
Noncommissioned officers (sergeant, 1st sergeant, regimental sergeant)	67	23.7
Junior officers (2nd lieutenant, lieutenant, captain)	106	37.4
Senior officers (major, lieutenant colonel, colonel)	75	26.5
Total	283	100.0

Measurements

The medal recipients were analyzed with respect to three classes of variables and subsequently compared to two separate control groups (see following section). The three classes of variables were (1) biographical background variables; (2) military aptitude and performance variables; and (3) personality evaluations.

Biographical Background Variables

These included age, physical fitness level (on a scale of 21 to 97, where 97 reflects perfect health), and ethnic origin.

Military Aptitude and Performance Variables

This group of variables included the following:

1. *General Quality Score* (GQS). This is used in the Israeli armed forces as a general selection index and is a composite of four components: intelligence evaluation, level of education, level of command of the Hebrew language, and a motivation index. The GQS index (known in Hebrew as KABA, an acronym for "quality category") has a lower limit of 43 and an upper limit of 56. As a single composite score, it represents a general indication of the individual's military aptitude (Gal, 1986). For the purpose of this study, two components of this overall index were singled out: intelligence and motivation. Hence the following

two indexes (the PPR and the MSI) were analyzed independently.

2. *Primary Psychotechnical Rating* (PPR). This is an intelligence evaluation score ranging from 10 to 90. It is derived from a version of the Raven's Progressive Matrices and an Otis type of verbal test. When compared to a conventional intelligence measurement, a PPR of 90 is roughly equal to an IQ of 135. The PPR constitutes about one third of the General Quality Score.
3. *Motivation-to-Service Index* (MSI). This index, which varies between 8 and 40, reflects the recruit's motivation to serve in the army and his prospects for successfully adjusting to combat units. The MSI is derived from a semistructured interview administered to all recruits before their induction into the army.
4. *Number of military courses.* The number of courses the subject has completed during his military service.
5. *Course scores.* These are the averaged scores obtained by the soldier in the various military courses he has attended. The last two indexes reflect the subject's general level of soldiery.

Personality Evaluations

Ordinarily no personality tests are administered to IDF conscripts, either before or at the time of their conscription. The only time a personality evaluation is made is when candidacy for officers' school is examined. Thus the examination of personality variables and their relationship to the behavior of war heroes in this study included only a subgroup of the medalist sample. Of the original 283 medalists, only those 77 who had files at the central IDF Officers Selection Board (OSB) were included in this analysis. These subjects were either commissioned officers, or at least had been candidates for the officers' school, and therefore had gone through the preliminary examinations for officer candidacy.

The mean scores of seven personality evaluations taken from these subjects' OSB files were computed. These personality evaluations included the following characteristics: sociability, social intelligence, emotional stability, leadership, devotion to duty, decisiveness, and perseverance under stress. Scores on these characteristics were determined by trained psychologists who had conducted in-depth interviews with the candidates and also derived their evaluations from a battery of projective tests (including the TAT and the Sentence Completion Test) administered to the candidates during their OSB procedures. The ranges of possible scores were 1 to 7 for the decisiveness and leadership characteristics, and 1 to 5 for the other characteristics.

Control Groups

Two separate control groups were used in this study. For the biographical background variables and the military aptitude and performance variables, a special pair-matched control group was constructed through a multiphase procedure. First, only those units in which 3 or more combatants had been awarded were identified. Then, for each awarded soldier in these units, a group of matched soldiers were selected who resembled the medal recipient in three aspects: unit served in during the war, rank, and combat position. For example, if a tank gunner had won a medal for his performance in a certain battle in the Golan Heights, a group of tank gunners from the same battalion who had also participated in the same battle (but had not won an award) were identified. Although the number of matched counterparts thus selected varied from 3 to 200 combatants for each medalist, the final control group was made up of groups of three randomly chosen subjects for each subject in the experimental group.[1]

Consequently, the final comparison was made between 51 medal recipients in the experimental group and 153 individuals in the control group. A set of t-tests was administered in order to check the possibility that these 51 medalists were not a random sample of the original 283 subjects in the entire experimental group. The tests indicated that such was not the case.

Because not all the subjects in the pair-matched control group had passed through the Officers Selection Board, a separate control group was needed for the comparative analysis of the personality evaluation. The comparison group was made up of a random sample of 300 soldiers who had passed the OSB examinations in 1975 (Atzei-Pri, 1977). The mean scores of the seven personality evaluations derived from this

[1]This ponderous production was possible through the generous help of the Central Computerized Manpower Division of the IDF.

sample are representative of the population distribution of these variables during the early 1970s.

Results

Biographical Background Variables

The distributions of age and physical fitness level of the subjects, as well as of their countries of birth and origin, were obtained for both the experimental (award recipients) and (pair-matched) control groups. The mean age of both the award recipients and their counterparts, was relatively low, between 24 and 25 years. It should be recalled that more than 70% of the award recipients were reservists (and thus had to be older than 21). No significant difference, however, was found between the age means of the experimental and control groups.

In addition, medal recipients did not differ from their pair-matched controls with regard to their ethnic origin. Because Israel is an immigration state for Jews of all origins, it is usually interesting to look into what differences can be found among various ethnographic groups. Specifically, the comparison between the Western (Ashkenazi, mainly European) and the Eastern (Sephardic, from Asia and North Africa) groups is meaningful. At the time of the Yom Kippur War, each of these two groups constituted about 50% of the population in Israel.

In this study, the 84% of the awarded soldiers were Israeli born ("Sabras"), compared to 75% of the control group. In terms of ethnic origin, most of the medalists (75%) came from Ashkenazi families (62% in the control group) and only 11% were of Sephardic origin (24% in the control group). Though somewhat different, a chi-square test defined this difference (chi-square = 3.83) as not significant.

Although both the experimental and control groups revealed a relatively high level of physical fitness, the awarded soldiers were in significantly ($p < .025$) better physical shape. As Table 4 shows, 90% of the medalists were in the highest physical fitness level, and none were in the lower category.

Table 4. Distribution According to Physical Fitness Level of Experimental and Control Groups

	Experimental group		Control group	
Physical fitness level	N	%	N	%
45–76	—	—	12	8
82–85	5	10	9	6
89–97	46	90	132	86
Total	51	100	153	100

Note: $t = 2.35$; $p < .025$.

Military Aptitude and Performance Variables

The means of five indices related to the subjects' aptitude, intelligence, and military performance are presented in Table 5. Although the PPR and the MSI are the subscores that constitute nearly all of variable 1, the General Quality Score, they are presented separately to enable a more detailed investigation. The means of these three variables, in both the experimental and the control groups, represent very high levels (of general quality, intelligence, and level of motivation, respectively). In comparison to norms derived from the entire military population, the mean GQS of the awarded soldiers is in the 93rd percentile; the medalists' means of the PPR and the MSI fall in the 86th and 95th percentiles, respectively. The mean scores of the three "quality" variables were slightly higher in the experimental group, but they did not differ significantly from the corresponding means in the control group.

The two groups also did not differ with regard to the number of military courses taken during their prewar military service (a mean frequency close to 3 courses per individual in both groups). The level of performance obtained in these courses, however, as reflected in their mean scores, was significantly higher ($p < 0.001$) for the medal recipients (79.9) than for their matched counterparts (74.6).

Personality Evaluations

Table 6 shows the six mean scores of personality evaluations computed for the 77 medalists who had gone through the Officers Selection Board. These scores are compared to a comparable (though not specifically matched) comparison group.

In general, the medalists scored higher in all but one (sociability) of these personality variables. Four of these variables were found significantly different (all at the $p < .001$ level); as the awarded soldiers scored higher than their nondecorated counterparts on leadership, devotion to duty, decisiveness, and perseverance under stress. With regard to the other three personality evaluations—sociability, social intelligence, and emotional stability—the differences between the two groups were not statistically significant.

Table 5. Means of Indexes of Military Background

	Experimental group		Control group			
Variable	Mean	*N*	Mean	*N*	*t*	*p*
1. General Quality Score (GQS)	53.97	29	53.20	136	1.33	NS
2. Primary Psychotechnical Rating (PPR)	71.81	51	69.23	150	0.94	NS
3. Motivation to Service Index (MSI)	29.1	40	28.56	115	0.72	NS
4. Number of military courses	2.93	44	2.82	127	0.40	NS
5. Mean score of courses	79.86	44	74.58	127	3.85	0.001

Discussion

The analysis of the various measures of the Israeli war heroes makes it possible to develop a profile, made up of personality as well as intellectual variables, of a skilled combatant who has performed beyond excellence under extreme war conditions. Note that I do not refer to a profile of a superlative hero. Indeed, based on these findings, the Israeli medal recipients during the Yom Kippur War do not form an unusual or deviant group, either in their personality or in their intelligence level.

In terms of their background and military characteristics, about 40% of the medal recipients were reservists—that is, not professional soldiers, but ordinary civilians called to fulfill their patriotic duty. Although still somewhat under represented compared to their assumed proportion in the total force, these awarded reservists demonstrate that war heroism is not necessarily exclusive to professional warriors.

More than half of the decorated soldiers belonged to the armored units, thus reflecting the basic nature of the Yom Kippur War, which primarily involved intensive tank battles. Within the armor corps group, however, most of the medalists were either tank commanders or members of tank crews, which are normally characterized by very high cohesion (Gal, 1986). Being part of a highly cohesive group was also typical of medalists from the infantry and paratrooper units in this war. Indeed, these latter units had a relatively high rate of recognized heroic behaviors. The important role of high unit morale and cohesion in producing acts of bravery in battle (Rachman, 1983; Stouffer et al., 1949) has been further substantiated in the present study.

The distribution of the medals ranged along the entire scale of military ranks—from privates to colonels. There is, however, a clear overrepresentation of officers (mostly commanding officers) on this list. Officers (both reservists and permanent service corps members) made up about 64% of the entire list of decorations (more than 10 times their proportion in line units). Furthermore, if one adds to this figure the number of decorated NCOs (most of whom also served in junior command positions), one gets essentially an inverted ratio of leaders to led.

On average, the award recipients were relatively young and generally in good shape, thus confirming previous findings (e.g., Egbert et al., 1957, 1958) concerning superior fighters' characteristics. As for socio-

Table 6. Mean Scores of Personality Evaluations

Personality evaluations	OSB medalists group (N = 77) Mean	Comparison group (N = 273) Mean	*t*	*p*
Sociability	3.94	3.96	0.57	NS
Social intelligence	4.06	3.90	0.44	NS
Emotional stability	3.20	3.12	1.02	NS
Leadership	3.31	2.34	6.13	0.001
Devotion to duty	4.19	4.01	4.45	0.001
Decisiveness	3.24	2.34	12.32	0.001
Perseverance under stress	2.94	2.18	11.81	0.001

ethnographic characteristics, it can be concluded from this study that in the Israeli Defense Forces of the 1970s, it was much more likely for Israeli-born individuals of European origin to perform an extraordinary act of heroism on the battlefield than it was for any other (e.g., Sephardic) ethnic group. This phenomenon, which is influenced by demographic fluctuations, is seemingly not in evidence in more recent years (Bar-Haim, 1987).

Of special interest to the present discussion are the findings related to the medalists' intellectual level. Though the awarded soldiers clearly represent a very high-ranking segment among the Israeli soldier population in terms of their general quality, they nevertheless did not differ in these qualities from their matched counterparts. Their mean General Quality Score (a composite score based on their levels of intelligence, education, and motivation) falls in the 93rd percentile of the entire population, but the control group's GQS average also is situated above the 90th percentile. Selecting the best-quality personnel for the combat units of the IDF is a well-established dictum in the Israeli armed forces. Thus high quality (i.e., a mixture of intelligence, education, and motivation level) is apparently a necessary, though not sufficient, prerequisite for valorous conduct in combat. Perhaps it is this "quality," when coupled with high achievements in military training (as reflected in the medalists' superior mean score of military courses), that distinguishes them from their non-decorated peers. Indeed, superior performance in various military tasks was one of the characteristics of excellent fighters among the American combat soldiers in Korea (Egbert et al., 1957, 1958), as well as among British bomb-disposal operators (Rachman, 1983).

The Israeli medalists also demonstrated high (although not extremely high) intellectual ability. The mean score of the intelligence indexes of the medal recipients in the present study is in the 86th percentile of the entire IDF population. Although this finding disproves the frequently made claim that only unintelligent people run conspicuously high risks, it nevertheless does not advocate extreme intelligence as a prerequisite for heroism. This is congruent, to a degree, with some recent claims (Fiedler, 1992) and findings (Borden, 1980) that intelligent individuals may not necessarily function well as leaders under certain stressful conditions.

Finally, though the available data concerning personality characteristics is rather limited, this study provides some indications regarding the role of personality factors in heroic behavior. Using personality evaluations obtained through the IDF Officers Selection Board, it was found that the Israeli medal-awarded heroes of the Yom Kippur War (more accurately, those in the group who were officers or had been officer candidates) were slightly more devoted to their duty, more decisive, and more persevering under stress, as well as more capable of leadership, than their peers of the same population. This finding is at least partially congruent with traditional personality profiles expected from highly demanding martial jobs (e.g., Hilton & Dolgin, 1991; OSS Assessment Staff, 1948).

In three out of seven personality measures available (emotional stability, sociability, and social intelligence), however, no statistically significant differences were found between the medalists and their comparison group. Although these findings are somewhat indistinct (mainly because of an inherent inability to compare the OSB medalist group with a matched nonmedalist control group), they nevertheless specifically controvert those recent studies (Ross & Offerman, 1991; Roush & Atwater, 1992) that emphasize the more social and nurturing aspects of the highly-rated military leaders. Furthermore, recent evidence (Ford, 1986; Zaccaro et al., 1991) suggesting the importance of social intelligence for effective leadership did not receive substantial support in our study.

The present findings, derived from a sample of Israeli decorated combatants, do not contribute significantly to the more general "right stuff" paradigms for specific military assignments (e.g., Hilton & Dolgin, 1991). Even within the four personality evaluations statistically differentiating between the medalist and the nonmedalist groups in our study, the mean differences found were small, and they did not by themselves generate a distinct psychological profile of the combat hero. In contrast, a separate methodological attempt (utilizing a facet analysis), conducted on the same database of medal-winning acts, yielded a series of *situational* characteristics of those battle settings within which the heroic acts occurred (Gal, 1983, 1987). The four most common situational profiles produced by this analysis accounted for about 70% of the analyzed cases. Based on this finding, it was claimed "that when in a given battle a certain combination of conditions occurs, it will increase the likelihood that one or more feats of heroism will emerge" (Gal, 1987, pp. 42–43).

CONCLUSIONS

Neither the situational approach nor the analyses of the individual differences as presented in this work can provide, of course, a precise prediction of the specific individual who will actually carry out an act of heroism in the midst of a given battle. It is appropriate to close this chapter with the conclusion reached by Hallam and Rachman (1980) in their study of heroism, entitled "Courageous Acts or Courageous Actors?": "Presumably the answer is that the determinants of particular acts of courage are a combination of general personality characteristics . . . and of specific situational factors (p. 345).

REFERENCES

Atzei-Pri, M. (1977). *Response frequencies in Officers Selection Board files* (Research Report, Classification Branch), Israeli Defense Forces, Tel Aviv.

Bar-Haim, A. (1987). Patterns of ethnic integration among the Israeli military elite. *Megamot, 30*(3), 276–287.

Blake, J. A., & Butler, S. (1976). The medal-of-honor, combat orientation and latent role structure in the United States military. *Sociological Quarterly, 17*, 461–567.

Borden, D. F. (1980). *Leader-boss stress, personality, job satisfaction and performance: Another look at the interrelationship of some old constructs in the modern large bureaucracy.* Unpublished doctoral dissertation, University of Washington, Seattle.

Buck, J. H., & Korb, L. J. (1981). *Military leadership.* Beverly Hills, CA: Sage.

Card, J. J. (1977). Differences in the demographic and sociopsychological profile of ROTC vs. non-ROTC students. *Journal of Vocational Behavior, 11*, 196–215.

Card, J. J. (1978). Career commitment processes in the young adult years: An illustration from the ROTC/Army career path. *Journal of Vocational Behavior, 12*, 53–75.

DeGaugh, R. A., & Knoll, D. V. (1954). *Attitudes relevant to bomber crew performance in combat* (U.S. Air Force Personnel Training Research Center Bulletin No. 54-18). Randolph Air Force Base, TX. U.S. Air Force.

Egbert, R. L., Meeland, T., Cline, V. B., Forgy, E. W., Spickler, M. W., & Brown, C. (1957). Fighter 1: An analysis of combat fighters and non-combat fighters (HumRRO Technical Report No. 44). Monterey, CA: U.S. Army Leadership Human Research Unit.

Egbert, R. L., Meeland, T., Cline, V. B., Forgy, E. W., Spickler, M. W., & Brown, C. (1958). Fighter 1: A study of effective and ineffective combat performers (HumRRO Special Report No. 13). Monterey, CA: U.S. Army Leadership Human Research Unit.

Eitelberg, M. J., Laurence, J. H., Waters, B. K., & Perelman, L. S. (1984). *Screening for service: Aptitude and education criteria for military entry.* Washington, DC: Office of the Assistant Secretary of Defense (Manpower, Installations, and Logistics) and Human Resources Research Organization.

Fiedler, F. E. (1992). Time-based measures of leadership experience and organizational performance: A review of research and a preliminary model. *Leadership Quarterly, 3*(1), 5–23.

Fiedler, J. E., & Garcia, J. E. (1987). *New approaches to effective leadership: Cognitive resources and organizational performance.* New York: Wiley.

Ford, M. E. (1986). A living systems conceptualization of social intelligence: Outcomes, processes, and developmental change. In R. J. Sternberg (Ed.), *Advances in the psychology of human intelligence.* Hillsdale, NJ: Erlbaum.

Gabriel, R., & Gal, R. (1984, January). The IDF officer: Linchpin in unit cohesion. *Army, 34*(1), 42–50.

Gal, R. (1983). Courage under stress. In S. Breznitz (Ed.), *Stress in Israel.* New York: Van Nostrand Reinhold.

Gal, R. (1986). *A portrait of the Israeli soldier.* Westport, CT: Greenwood.

Gal, R. (1987). Combat stress as an opportunity: The case of heroism. In G. Belenky (Ed.), *Contemporary studies in combat psychiatry.* Westport, CT: Greenwood.

Gal, R. (1992). Unit cohesion. In *International Military and Defense Encyclopedia.* McLean, VA: Pergamon-Brassey's.

Gal, R., & Israelashwili, M. (1978, June). *Personality traits versus situational factors as determinants of individuals coping with stress: A theoretical model.* Paper presented at the International Conference on Psychological Stress and Adjustment in Time of War and Peace, Jerusalem, Israel.

Goodacre, D. M. (1953). Group characteristics of good and poor performing combat units. *Sociometry, 16*, 168–179.

Hallam, R. S., & Rachman, S. J. (1980). Courageous acts or courageous actors? *Personality and Individual Differences, 1*(4), 341–346.

Hilton, T. F., & Dolgin, D. L. (1991). Pilot selection in the military of the free world. In R. Gal & A. D. Mangelsdorff (Eds.), *Handbook of military psychology.* New York: Wiley.

Hunt, J. G., & Blair, J. D. (1985). *Leadership on the future battlefield.* Washington, D.C.: Pergamon-Brassey.

International Institute for Strategic Studies. (1981–1982). *The military balance.* London: Author.

Keegan, J. (1976). *The face of battle.* New York: Viking.

Larsen K. S., & Giles, H. (1976). Survival or courage as human motivations: The development of an attitude scale. *Psychological Reports, 39*, 299–302.

Levav, I., Greenfeld, H., & Baruch, E. (1979). Psychiatric combat reactions during the Yom Kippur War. *American Journal of Psychiatry, 135*(5), 637–641.

Lieblich, A. (1983). Between strength and toughness. In S. Breznitz (Ed.), *Stress in Israel* (pp. 39–64). New York: Van Nostrand Reinhold.

Little, R. (1964). Buddy relations and combat performance. In M. Janowitz (Ed.), *The New Military* (pp. 195–224). New York: Russell Sage Foundation.

Lord, R. G., DeVader C. L., & Alliger, G. M. (1986). A meta-analysis of the relation between personality traits and leadership perceptions: An application of validity generalization procedures. *Journal of Applied Psychology, 71*, 402–410.

Marlowe, H. A., Jr. (1986). Social intelligence: Evidence for multidimensionality and construct independence. *Journal of Educational Psychology, 78*(1), 52–58.

Moskos, C. C. (1973). The American combat soldier in Vietnam. *Journal of Social Issues, 31*, 25–37.

Osato, R. L., & Sherry, P. (1993). Age and IQ effects on army enlisted male CPI profiles. *Military Psychology, 5*(1), 41–61.

OSS Assessment Staff. (1948). *Assessment of men: Selection of personnel for the Office of Strategic Services.* New York: Rinehart.

Rachman, S. (1978). *Fear and courage.* San Francisco: W. H. Freeman.

Rachman, S. (1983). Fear and courage among military bomb

disposal operators. *Advances in Behavior Research and Therapy, 4* [special issue] *3*, 97–173.

Retzlaff, P. D., & Gilbertini, M. (1987). Air Force personality: Hard data on the "Right Stuff." *Multivariate Behavioral Research, 22*, 383–399.

Ross, S. M., & Offermann, L. R. (1991, July). *Transformational leaders: Measurement of personality attributes and work group performance.* Paper presented at the annual meeting of the Society for Industrial Organizational Psychology, St. Louis, MO.

Roush, P. E., & Atwater, L. E. (1992). Using the MBTI to understand transformational leadership and self-perception accuracy. *Military Psychology, 4*, 17–34.

Scribner, B. L., Smith, D. A., Baldwin, R. H., & Phillips, R. L. (1986). Are smart tankers better? AFQT and Military Productivity. *Armed Forces and Society, 12*(2), 193–206.

Shirom, A. (1976). On some correlates of combat performance. *Administrative Sciences Quarterly, 21*, 419–432.

Sohlberg, S. C. (1976). Stress experiences and combat fatigue during the Yom Kippur War—1973. *Psychological Reports, 38*, 523–529.

Steege, F. W., & Fritscher, W. (1991). Psychological assessment and military personnel management. In R. Gal & A. D. Mangelsdorff (Eds.), *Handbook of military psychology.* New York: Wiley.

Stouffer, S. A., Devinney, L. C., Star, S. A., & Williams, R. M. (1949). *The American soldier* (Vol. 2). Princeton, NJ: Princeton University Press.

Trites, D. K., & Sells, S. B. (1957). Combat performance: Measurement and prediction. *Journal of Applied Psychology, 41*, 21–130.

Yaron, N. (1983). Facing death in war: An existential crisis. In S. Breznitz (Ed.), *Stress in Israel* (pp. 3–38). New York: Van Nostrand Reinhold.

Zaccaro, S. J., Gilbert, J. A., Thor K. K., & Mumford, M. D. (1991). Leadership and social intelligence: Linking social perceptiveness and behavioral flexibility to leader effectiveness. *Leadership Quarterly, 2*, 317–342.

Zeidner, J., & Drucker A. J. (1988). *Behavioral science in the army: A corporate history of the Army Research Institute.* Alexandria, VA: US Army Research Institute for the Behavioral and Social Sciences.

34

Personality and Intellectual Predictors of Leadership

Dean Keith Simonton

Contemplate the lives of these historical figures: Moses, Buddha, Mohammed, Pope Urban II, Martin Luther, and Joseph Smith; Alexander the Great, Julius Caesar, and Genghis Khan; Richelieu, Cavour, and Bismarck; Demonsthenes, Cicero, Lincoln, and Winston Churchill; Spartacus, Joan of Arc, Bolívar, Garibaldi, Gandhi, and Martin Luther King; Tiberius Gracchus, Robespierre, Lenin, and Mao; Hammurabi, Kublai Khan, Ivan the Terrible, Queen Elizabeth I, and Louis XIV; Franco, Mussolini, Hitler, and Tojo; Cosimo Medici, Meyer Rothschild, Andrew Carnegie, and Alfred Krupp. Now think about the persons who occupy one of these contemporary roles: president of the United States, prime minister of Great Britain, secretary general of the United Nations, CEO of Ford Motor Company, pontiff of the Roman Catholic Church, Dalai Lama of Tibetan Buddhism, speaker of the U.S. House of Representatives, chief justice of the Supreme Court, governor of the state of California, mayor of Berlin, and president of the American Psychological Association. Finally, to get closer to what some of us may have directly experienced, recall persons whom you have actually known: the manager who supervises your unit at work, the lieutenant who commanded your platoon, the president of your local parent-teacher association, the captain of your college track team, the student body president back in your high school days, the master of your youth club, or the head of the street gang in the old neighborhood.

This is quite a collection of disparate individuals. Some hail from the past, others from the present; some are famous, others infamous, and yet others obscure. Still, they share one thing in common: All were called upon to display leadership. Moreover, many of these individuals were selected by their followers precisely because they were thought to possess the characteristics deemed essential to effective leadership. Presumably not everyone in the population of citizens can claim these desirable traits; otherwise it would make far more sense to pick the leader by lottery, much as was done in the democracy of ancient Athens. But what are these crucial personal assets? Can we psychologists devise reliable and valid measures of the needed attributes? In particular, can we successfully predict who will do best in such positions of power and influence?

My goal in this chapter is to address these questions. In the first part, I will present a historical overview of the key methods and findings. I say "overview" with deliberation: The literature has become so rich that even a book-length presentation cannot hope to review what we have learned in any real detail (see Bass, 1990). As is immediately apparent in the opening paragraph above, leadership can assume a diver-

Dean Keith Simonton • Department of Psychology, University of California at Davis, Davis, California 95616-8686.

International Handbook of Personality and Intelligence, edited by Donald H. Saklofske and Moshe Zeidner. Plenum Press, New York, 1995.

sity of forms. We can speak of political, military, religious, and economic leaders. We can talk about leaders who have made history, and leaders who affect our everyday lives at work and at play. Furthermore, when we consider this diversity in combination with the awesome variety of dimensions on which people may differ, it is obvious that the number of potential prediction equations is virtually infinite!

In the second part, I will examine some of the central issues that make simple answers impossible. The connections between leadership and individual-difference variables, whether the latter be cognitive or dispositional, are extremely intricate. Indeed, one of the recurrent faults of earlier psychological studies of leadership was the failure to recognize many niceties. As will become clear, it is not the dearth of measures that makes the prediction of leadership so difficult. Rather, the problem lies with the complexity of the phenomenon. If I had to identify the single most central lesson to be learned from this whole chapter, it would be this: The days are long past when psychologists could seriously offer us simple equations for predicting leadership.

HISTORICAL OVERVIEW

If we wish to isolate the intellectual and personality factors that predict leadership, we have two methodological options. The most popular choice is the *psychometric* option. Here investigators directly assess leaders (and often their followers as well) on certain abilities, interests, values, motives, and so on. Typically the measurement relies on the administration of standard tests, although occasionally a researcher will have to venture into a new assessment domain. In any case, given that this approach entails the application of mainstream disciplinary techniques, it might seem surprising that this is not the exclusive method in the field. One drawback, however, should be evident: Psychologists can only conduct such inquiries on subjects who are willing and able. Yet many leaders would rather not expose themselves to direct psychological scrutiny. For example, it seems almost inconceivable that candidates for political office would be willing to risk taking a battery of tests simply to satisfy some researcher's scientific curiosity (see Costantini & Craik, 1980). What would happen if the inventory revealed some latent psychopathology? Furthermore, for sheer practical reasons, many leaders could not take the tests anyway. Probably the best excuse imaginable is that the leader may be already deceased.

In circumstances like these, the investigator may resort to an alternative method, the *historiometric* approach (Simonton, 1990b). Here quantitative techniques are applied to archival materials like biographies, written correspondence, public speeches, and televised debates. For instance, the presidents of the United States have been subjected to a tremendous amount of psychological scrutiny: Various content analysis procedures have been applied to oral and written materials, and observer-based personality instruments have been adapted for use with available biographical data (Simonton, 1987b, 1993). Hence, where psychometric studies concentrate on the more everyday forms of leadership, historiometric studies focus on the more historic exemplars. Even so, often the two approaches converge on some compatible conclusions about the prime predictors of leadership.

Psychometric Studies

Anyone who has lectured on leadership has probably talked about the "great-person" theory. This position holds that leaders, and especially the most effective leaders, claim certain traits that set them above the rest of us. Presumably this definitive character entails some combination of intellectual capacities and personality disposition. Although this viewpoint is often associated with the rather rhapsodic argument that Thomas Carlyle (1841) offered in his essay *On Heroes, Hero-Worship, and the Heroic*, nothing prevents us from testing its scientific truth. If this theory has any validity at all, it should be a simple matter of finding those individual differences that correlated most highly with leadership. And certainly psychologists have a well-stocked armory of tests with which to attack this problem. If one just takes a peak of any catalog of available tests (e.g., Buros, 1974), one would probably believe that there must be something among all these choices that would successfully predict leadership. Those who have spent their careers studying this question, however, have often come away with a more pessimistic outlook. In fact, most of us who lectured on leadership in the 1970s and 1980s have probably affirmed that the great-person theory is dead: Neither intellectual capacity nor personality attributes may bear any connection with leadership ability. To appreciate why so many researchers drew this conclusion, we need to recount the history of the field.

First Wave

The earliest empirical study of the personal characteristics of leaders was conducted back in 1904 (Stogdill, 1977). Appropriately enough, the study's author was Lewis M. Terman, one of the pioneers in the development of differential psychology. Using schoolchildren as subjects, Terman made two primary observations. First, children who emerged as leaders in one group were also likely to emerge as leaders in a second group; in other words, leadership functions as a trait that enjoys cross-situational consistency. Second, the leaders could be differentiated from the followers on several measurable characteristics, such as speech fluency. Unfortunately, Terman had not yet devised the Stanford-Binet Intelligence Scale, and therefore he could not report on any IQ contrasts. Even so, Terman's inquiry has become something of a mini-classic in the field (Gibb, 1969b). The closely related questions of cross-situational consistency and demonstrable individual differences became the two dominant themes of most research for the next 40 years.

As the middle of the 20th century approached, the empirical literature had become large enough that a research review was badly needed. Furthermore, as so often happens in the behavioral sciences, the findings often seemed contradictory or confusing, making an integrative summary all the more mandatory. This valuable service was carried out by Ralph Stogdill (1948), one of the key figures in the scientific study of leadership (see also Jenkins, 1947). The resulting paper, "Personal Factors Associated with Leadership," became a true classic in the field; in fact, more than 40 years later it was still thought worthy enough to be reprinted as a separate chapter in a modern compendium of leadership research (Bass, 1990). Over those years, Stogdill's conclusions helped shape a whole generation of attitudes about whether leadership corresponded with individual difference variables. To help readers appreciate the nature of this influence, I will present the general contents and approach of Stogdill's review.

Stogdill's paper surveyed the results of 124 studies published between 1904 and 1947. These studies applied a great range of subject pools and methods. Thus the subjects spanned preschool children, elementary and secondary students, college undergraduates, and adults in various organizational settings, such as military and business. Leadership was gauged according to nomination by qualified observers, selection by associates, occupation of leadership positions, historical eminence, or some other criterion; the psychometric measures included tests of intelligence and personality, questionnaires, rating scales, and interviews. All told, more than two dozen individual-difference variables were scrutinized, although some of these concerned physical attributes like height or age. For each variable Stogdill would tally the number of studies showing a positive relationship, the number finding a negative relationship, and the number indicating no association at all. Regarding the introversion-extraversion dimension, for instance, he found five pros, two cons, and four nulls—and then concluded that this factor bears little connection with leadership.

For those who advocated a great-person view, the net outcome of Stogdill's summary must have been disappointing. Only a handful of variables showed any consistent link with leadership, especially intelligence, responsibility, and social activity. Even when a consistent pattern emerged, the correlation coefficients were often modest indeed. In the strongest case—namely, intelligence—the average correlation across the reviewed studies was only .28. As if this were not bad enough, Stogdill noted that many investigators found the pattern of traits to vary across the specific situations in which leadership was exercised: What would be the right trait for one circumstance might be the wrong trait for another. Although Stogdill also mentioned how some inquiries demonstrated noticeable cross-situational consistency in leadership, this message was often overlooked by later researchers. Indeed, Stogdill's exhaustive review was frequently cited as disproving the great-person theory. Intellectual and personality traits were thought to have minimum predictive power in comparison to situational forces.

Unfortunately, later developments served only to strengthen this pessimistic inference. For example, Mann (1959) published an updated review that was much more focused than Stogdill's, yet drew similar conclusions. Mann's paper looked at what research had to say about the predictive utility of such traits as intelligence, adjustment, extraversion-introversion, dominance, masculinity-femininity, conservatism, and interpersonal sensitivity. For the most part, the median correlations were rather small, and even the highest observed coefficients were frequently unimpressive. The minimal predictive validity was even apparent in a robust variable like intelligence. As Mann (1959) put it, "no correlation reported exceeds 0.50, and the median r is roughly .25" (p. 248). Personal attributes just did not seem to explain much variance in leadership.

To be sure, we could always fault the methods for these poor results (see Gibb, 1969a). Perhaps the psychometric instruments were unreliable, or maybe the gauges of leadership lacked validity. Other studies, however, did not let great-person theorists off the hook so easily. These investigations examined the cross-situational consistency of leadership and found it wanting (e.g., Barnlund, 1962). Individuals who emerged as leaders in one situation were *not* always those most likely to emerge in other situations. If leadership does not even behave in a traitlike manner, it is pointless to search for the personal attributes that distinguish leaders from everybody else (see also Geier, 1967; Murphy, 1941); they may be just like the rest of us!

By the time I was a graduate student in the early 1970s, the situation had replaced the individual as the prime agent behind leadership. Encouraging this replacement was a fashionable trend in personality psychology to cast doubt about the cross-situational consistency of all traits, leadership and otherwise (Mischel, 1968). Behaviors did not reflect an underlying personality that individuals carried with them from place to place, but rather were mostly manifestations of situational demands and constraints. For about a decade, whenever I lectured on leadership before students and lay audiences, I would routinely lament that with the minor exception of intelligence, no individual-difference factor enjoyed any broad predictive usefulness. Leadership is less the result of being the right person and more the consequence of being at the right place at the right time. In the past few years, nonetheless, current work has obliged me to revise my lecture notes. Why?

Second Wave

Several changes in the discipline have prepared the ground for a more sympathetic perspective on individual differences. Three developments are especially important.

First, personality psychologists have reasserted the real stability of character traits (Epstein & O'Brien, 1985). After much controversy and methodological refinements, we now know that individuals are not at the mercy of their social contexts to the extent originally claimed. The environment does exert its influences, naturally, but these are impressed upon persons with a certain stable propensity to behave in one way rather than another. If this holds for a large number of characteristic behaviors, leadership might have personal correlates after all. Hence the current zeitgeist smiles more favorably on an individual-difference perspective.

Second, and perhaps encouraged by the foregoing shift in disciplinary focus, the number of personality traits on which individuals can be assessed has expanded considerably since the earlier literature reviews. many of these new dimensions appear to feature significant relationships with leadership. One example is the recent work on "self-monitoring" (Dobbins, Long, Dedrick, & Clemons, 1990; Ellis, 1988; Ellis, Adamson, Deszca, & Cawsay, 1988; Ellis & Cronshaw, 1992; Garland & Beard, 1979; Wood & Mitchell, 1981; Zaccaro, Foti, & Kenny, 1991). This is the tendency for some persons to manipulate carefully the impression they make on others, a skill and inclination of obvious value to effective leadership (Snyder, 1974). Surprisingly, sometimes these advances would involve taking an old test and teaching it to do new tricks. For instance, the projective Thematic Apperception Test (TAT) has been made to gauge leader motives and other dispositions in ways not originally envisioned by Henry Murray (1938) and his collaborators (e.g., Cummin, 1967; House, Spangler, & Woycke, 1991; Winter, 1991).

Third, certain methods of data analysis have become far more sophisticated over the years. As a consequence, conclusions drawn in earlier studies have been shown to be inadequate by modern standards. I offer two illustrations below.

1. We must not take on face value the early literature reviews concerning the correlation between personal traits and leadership (House & Baetz, 1979). As any psychologist should know, the methodology of research summaries has radically transformed in the past several years. It is no longer acceptable to do simple counts of pros, cons, and nulls. Instead, anyone summarizing the empirical literature should exploit modern meta-analysis techniques whenever applicable (Hunter & Schmidt, 1990). Besides applying more definite qualitative criteria about what published studies to examine, these techniques provide more precise mathematical measures of effect sizes than can be revealed by median or mean correlations.

The value of this methodology was proven in a meta-analysis executed by Lord, De Vader, and Alliger (1986). Beginning with the studies reported in Mann (1959) and then updating the literature with more current publications whenever feasible, the authors applied the meta-analytic technique known as validity generalization. Several traits were shown to predict whether an individual is perceived as a leader by other group members, including intelligence, masculinity-femininity, dominance, adjustment, and extraversion. Not only were the summary coefficients usually higher than those reported in Mann (1959), but the discrepancies became especially big once the correlations were adjusted for attenuation. For example, the "corrected correlations show that intelligence explains four times as much variance in leadership perceptions as do Mann's findings" (p. 405). Finally, the validity generalization procedure divulged that the variation in the correlation coefficients across studies can be explicated largely by methodological contrasts rather than by situational factors. All told, this meta-analysis revives the idea that leaders possess something that the rest of us do not.

2. The next illustration reinforces this inference even more. As noted earlier, another complaint about the great-person theory is that leadership often displays minimal cross-situational consistency. If the same person is the leader in one group but the follower in another, how can we possibly ascribe leadership to the individual? One of the most potent experimental methods for addressing this problem is the *rotational design*. Here the group membership is systematically varied (with or without orthogonal changes in task assignments), and then the leadership of the participants gauged across situations. Although some investigators using this design have reported some cross-situational stability (e.g., Bell & French, 1950; Borgatta, Couch, & Bales, 1954), others have judged that leadership shows negligible consistency (e.g., Barnlund, 1962).

As was the case for the literature reviews, however, statistical approaches to rotational designs have become more powerful in recent years, leaving open the possibility that reanalysis of the earlier data might yield stronger results. That is exactly what happened. When Kenny and Zaccaro (1983) carefully reexamined a study published 20 years earlier (Barnlund, 1962), they found that between 49% and 82% of the variance could be safely assigned to some stable personal trait. Kenny and Zaccaro (1983) did not actually measure the relevant attribute, but they speculated that the underlying factor may "involve the ability to perceive the needs and goals of a constituency and to adjust one's personal approach to group action accordingly" (p. 678). In other words, leadership requires not so much a simple trait as a complex of traits, such as social perceptiveness and behavioral flexibility (see also Kenny & Hallmark, 1992; Zaccaro, Gilbert, Thor, & Mumford, 1991). Nevertheless, the fact remains that the locus of leadership resides inside the personality and not just in the environmental circumstances.

In light of these three developments, we can say with confidence that the psychometric approach to leadership has undergone a renaissance. There definitely exist variations across individuals in the ease with which they assume and perform leadership behaviors. The significance of this revival is reflected in the arrival of the new journal *Leadership Quarterly*, which includes several personality psychologists on its editorial review board. More importantly, this journal announced the 1990s with three special issues devoted to the topic of "Individual Differences and Leadership" (Fleishman, Zaccaro, & Mumford, 1991, 1992a, b). This subject would have seemed rather passé only a decade ago. The resurgence of the psychometric perspective is reinforced by a parallel revival in historiometric methods.

Historiometric Studies

If we think about it a bit, the dismal returns from the early psychometric inquiries did not have to overturn the great-person theory. After all, these investigations almost invariably involved samples of rather ordinary people, like you and me. In Mann's (1959) review, for instance, the subjects were often college students working in small groups that an experimenter had randomly tossed together in a laboratory cubicle. An advocate of great-person position could always argue that this is not the sphere in which the authentic leader operates. Rather, this theory describes the true greats whose names are writ large in the annals of civilization, people like those listed at the onset of this chapter.

This argument does a nice job of circumventing any contradictory findings of the psychometric approach, but it does not do so without presenting problems of its own. For the objection would lack scientific merit unless we had some way to evaluate the personal qualities of these undoubted leaders. How can we do this?

It turns out that there exist two principal alternatives. The first is psychobiography. Back in 1910 Sigmund Freud established the technique of applying psychoanalytic theory to biographical information about a historic personality, in this case Leonardo da Vinci

(Freud, 1910/1964). Later he extended psychobiography to famous leaders, most notably President Woodrow Wilson (Freud & Bullitt, 1967). Since then, psychobiography has become a major enterprise, especially in political psychology (Tetlock, Crosby, & Crosby, 1981). Although still a major force today, numerous scholars do not accept the method as a bona fide scientific approach to the study of leadership (Simonton, 1983b). Aside from objections that many psychologists raise with regard to psychoanalytic theory, the method favors qualitative analyses of single cases. Yet most behavioral scientists prefer a more nomothetic methodology in which quantitative analyses are applied to multiple cases. This quantitative, multiple-case approach is what historiometry is all about.

To help the reader understand the nature of historiometric research, I will again give a little historical perspective on the technique before I recount current advances.

Pioneer Investigations

Historiometrics and psychometrics had common roots. Both grew out of the attempt of Francis Galton to quantify individual differences and then use these measures to predict other human characteristics (Galton, 1883). By the beginning of the 20th century, a body of mathematical techniques had emerged that were collectively styled *biometrics*. Nonetheless, within psychology biometrics soon split into two related modes of analysis: psychometrics and historiometrics. In fact, only a couple of years after Lewis Terman (1904) initiated the psychometric study of leadership, Frederick Woods (1906) began studying it through historiometry. Woods (1909) defined this as a technique where "the facts of history of a personal nature have been subjected to statistical analysis by some more or less objective method," adding that "historiometry bears the same relation to history that biometry does to biology" (p. 703). Woods (1911) explicitly included Galton as among his predecessors in developing this enterprise.

Woods himself published two major historiometric monographs. The first assessed members of European royal families on intellectual and moral character to learn whether these traits are inheritable (Woods, 1906; see Thorndike, 1936). The second evaluated the personal qualities of European monarchs and then showed that these attributes correlated with well-being of the nation of which they reigned (Woods, 1913; see Simonton, 1983a, 1984b). Like most innovative studies, these applications contain many faults. Still, at least Woods illustrated how researchers might gauge the intellectual and personality attributes of historic figures.

Curiously, the first psychologist to follow up Woods's innovation was Lewis Terman. Although he was busy developing the Stanford-Binet, Terman thought that historiometrics could produce IQ scores comparable to those produced by psychometrics. Using the definition of IQ as the ratio of mental age to chronological age, Terman (1917) first tried out this idea on Francis Galton, for whom he estimated an IQ score close to 200. Then nearly a decade later, one of Terman's doctoral students, Catherine Cox (1926), carried out a more ambitious application of the same method. Besides providing IQ scores for 301 historic individuals, including 109 famous leaders, Cox assessed a subset of her subjects on 67 personality traits. Her goal was to show that personal attributes successfully predict the magnitude of success. For example, she showed that the IQ scores correlated .25 with an individual's eminence (see Simonton, 1976; Walberg, Rasher, & Parkerson, 1980). This coefficient remarkably close to the what Mann (1959) said was the median correlation observed in small group research.

Sadly, Cox's (1926) investigation was the high point in this early phase of historiometric research. Although these methods were exploited by some influential figures in differential psychology, such as James McKeen Cattell and Edward L. Thorndike, most of the later work concentrated on creative genius rather than outstanding leadership (Simonton, 1984a). Furthermore, by the time Thorndike (1950) published his own posthumous historiometric study, the technique was practically dead. For the next dozen years or so, few reputable psychologists were willing to move their operations from the laboratory to the library. Perhaps not coincidentally, this is about the same period that saw the great-person theory of leadership languish near death as well.

Contemporary Inquiries

In the past couple of decades, historiometric studies of leadership have become more commonplace. One impetus for this resurgence is the recognition that historic leaders represent the supreme exemplars of the phenomenon. How successful would anyone consider psychologists if they could explain why a college student got high leadership ratings in an experimental group of five strangers but not have the foggiest idea why Franklin Roosevelt is considered a great president, Frederick the Great a phenomenal general, Ignatius Loyola an influential religious leader, or Henry Ford a successful entrepreneur? Hence even some scholars who devote most of their time studying contemporary and more mundane leaders will occasionally sneak a peak at these more conspicuous instances (e.g., Bass, Avolio, & Goodheim, 1987; Bass & Farrow, 1977; House, Spangler, & Woycke, 1991; Spangler & House, 1991; Thorndike, 1950).

But there is another possible reason for this resurgence, an impetus that I believe is even more crucial. After biometrics bifurcated into psychometrics and historiometrics, the alternative strategies did not develop at the same pace. Whereas psychometrics became extremely sophisticated, historiometrics had progressed very little since the days of Woods, Terman, Cox, and Thorndike. Where psychometricians were developing advanced measurement techniques and multivariate data analyses, historiometricians continued to calculate simple correlation coefficients on crude data. In the past several years, however, these two analytical traditions have again converged, with psychometric theory informing historiometric practice (Simonton, 1990b).

Probably the best illustrations of this convergence come from those researchers who have managed to translate psychometric instruments into some historiometric measure. For example, the coding schemes originally created to handle protocols emerging from the Thematic Apperception Test have been adapted for use on the public speeches of eminent leaders (Donley & Winter, 1970; Wendt & Light, 1976; Winter, 1973). David Winter (1987), in particular, has been able to derive meaningful scores on power, achievement, and affiliation motives from the inaugural addresses of United States presidents. A similar transformation occurred to the Paragraph Completion Test, invented to assess people on conceptual complexity (Schroder, Driver, & Streufert, 1967). This has given rise to a method for coding speeches and correspondence for integrative complexity, a measure of information-processing sophistication (e.g., Suedfeld, Corteen, & McCormick, 1986; Suedfeld & Rank, 1976; Tetlock, 1979).

These are all examples of content analysis, one of the most important varieties of historiometric research (Simonton, 1990b). Of course, not all content analyses entail straightforward adaptations of established psychometric techniques. Often an investigator will have to devise a new coding scheme from scratch, using psychometric methods only as guidelines (e.g., Hoffer, 1978; Miller & Stiles, 1986). Moreover, content analysis is not the only way to asses the personal attributes of great leaders. As earlier observed, the early pioneers had already introduced ways to tease out intellectual and personality traits from biographical information. This approach has been developed so that we can now score historic leaders on traits like intelligence, dominance, extraversion, flexibility, persistence, charisma, and morality (e.g., Bass, Avolio, & Goodheim, 1987; Cox, 1926; Etheredge, 1978; House, Spangler, & Woycke, 1991; Simonton, 1983a, 1986c, 1988b; Thorndike, 1936, 1950; Woods, 1906). Needless to say, if we combine the content analytical measures with those derived from biography, psychologists can study important leaders with great thoroughness. The presidents of the United States, specifically, have been assessed on so many traits via such a diversity of techniques that they must surely represent the most exhaustively scrutinized leaders in the history of psychology (for review, Simonton,1987b, 1993).

All of this historiometric measurement would count as mere academic busywork were it not for one central fact: These content analytical and biographical assessments do indeed predict leadership performance as gauged by multiple criteria (Simonton, 1987b, 1990b). For example, measures of power, achievement, and affiliation motivation drawn from presidential inaugural addresses predict general performance ratings, the use of military force during crises, the stance taken in international arms control agreements, the likelihood of administration scandals, and the kinds of appointments made to cabinet positions (Wendt & Light, 1976; Winter, 1987; Winter & Stewart, 1977). In a parallel fashion, these motivational profiles can successfully predict the campaign activities of U.S. presidential candidates as well as the leadership behaviors of politicians elsewhere in the world (e.g., Hermann, 1980; Winter, 1980, 1982). Interestingly, these historiometric relationships between motivation and leadership often parallel quite closely the findings of psychometric research (Winter & Carlson, 1988).

Indeed, this last point can be broadened into the assertion that many central results in historiometric research parallel those found in psychometric inquiries. For instance, individual variation in intelligence often emerges as a significant predictor of historic leadership (Cox, 1926; McCann, 1992; Simonton, 1976, 1984b, 1986b, 1991a, b), just as it does for more everyday manifestations of the phenomenon

(Lord et al., 1986; Mann, 1959; Stogdill, 1948). This convergence on similar conclusions despite the divergence in methods suggests that the great-person theory is not totally off the mark. Intellectual and personality factors do indeed help differentiate leaders from followers, and effective leaders from incompetent leaders—thus justifying this chapter's very existence. Even so, it is no easy task to specify the exact nature of the connections between character and leadership. These difficulties are reviewed below.

CENTRAL ISSUES

Any attempt to predict leadership using personal attributes should confront two questions. First, what are the most appropriate measurements? Second, what are the best predictive models? These two sets of issues form a logical sequence. We cannot begin to formulate the predictive models without first learning what predictor variables must enter the hopper. Furthermore, these two problems cut across both psychometric and historiometric inquiries into leadership.

Measurements

Before we can conduct any empirical research whatsoever, we must first decide: What we exactly are going to measure? What do our measures really mean? The fate of any particular study will often stand or fall on the answers to such questions. This measurement issue divides into four principal dilemmas: Shall our criteria of leadership be global or specific? How broadly should we define our predictors? What is the place of individual and situational predictors in our equations? And to what extent are we assessing individuals on transient states rather than enduring traits?

Global versus Specific Criteria

Those readers who are familiar with the literature on leadership may believe that I have been remiss for not discussing one key point: If we are predicting leadership, how do we measure the criterion in the first place? Often when we converse about leadership in the abstract, we treat it as a global characteristic of individuals. Some people are leaders and others followers, or some leaders display higher levels of leadership than do other leaders. Moreover, the great-person theory encourage us to talk this way. Supposedly, there are special people out there who have what it takes to emerge as outstanding leaders no matter what the specific requirements of a particular leadership role.

The psychometric literature, however, suggests that it is seldom useful to conceive leadership in a so generic a fashion. Instead, frequently leadership in a specific situation must be defined in more narrow terms. The reason for this specificity is simple: The factors that predict one manifestation of leadership may not be identical to those that predict a contrary manifestation. For example, Cattell and Stice (1954) used the 16-Factor Personality Questionnaire (16PF) to predict four forms of leadership in a military setting. The trait profiles that discriminated the leaders from the nonleaders varied according to the specific conception of leadership; none of the 16 factors emerged as a consistent predictor across all operational definitions! So, the end result was separate prediction equations for problem-solving, salient, popular, and elected leaders. And even these results somewhat oversimplify the picture, for Cattell and Stice focused solely on the differences between leaders and nonleaders. They did not derive equations that predict the magnitude of success at a particular type of leadership. Yet the variables that separate leaders from nonleaders (i.e., emergence from the group) need not be equivalent to the variables that distinguish the effective leaders from those less so (i.e., performance within the group).

The necessity to recognize multiple criteria is also apparent in the historiometric literature. This need is especially evident in all the research on presidential leadership (Simonton, 1987b, 1993). Sometimes investigators isolate the predictors of presidential greatness (e.g., Holmes & Elder, 1989; McCann, 1992; Simonton, 1991b; Wendt & Light, 1976; Winter, 1987; Winter & Stewart, 1977); this is a rather global gauge of performance based on the ratings of experts (e.g., Murray & Blessing, 1988; cf. Ballard & Suedfeld, 1988). Other times researchers scrutinize specific performance criteria, such as election performance, legislative success, treaty negotiation, and executive appointments (e.g., Etheredge, 1978; Simonton, 1986b, 1987a, 1988b; Winter, 1987; Winter & Stewart, 1977). The predictors of one narrow criterion may be quite different from those for another criterion, and no predictor emerges for both global and specific criteria. Even worse, even when a predictor is found in more than one equation, that prediction may not go in the same direction. For instance, the affiliation motive correlates with successful negotiation of arms limitation agreements, but it also correlates with having scandals break out in the presidential administration (Winter, 1987). Similarly, whereas intelligence is positively associated with an incumbent's overall greatness rating (McCann, 1992; Simonton, 1991b), it is also negatively associated with the size of the mandate received from voters (Simonton, 1986c).

Broad versus Narrow Predictors

The same careful discriminations that we must bring to bear on the criterion measures we must also apply to the predictors. A good example is intelligence, one of the most frequently investigated variables in the psychometric literature. Yet the proper measurement of this construct is also one of the most controversial questions in the history of psychology. Some consider intelligence to represent some kind of broad information-processing power, such as suggested by the construct of Spearman's (1927) *g* factor (e.g., Jensen, 1992). Others question the existence of any general factor, arguing instead that there are different kinds of intellectual abilities, skills, or components (Gardner, 1983; Guilford, 1967; Sternberg, 1985). Although many empirical studies opt for generic assessments of intellectual capacity, others have argued that this choice contributes nothing to either predictive success or theoretical understanding. For example, outstanding interpersonal or social intelligence may be the central cognitive component of leader emergence and effectiveness (Zaccaro, Gilbert, Thor, & Mumford, 1991). It may be this ability alone that enables someone to exhibit the perceptiveness and flexibility necessary to display leadership in a diversity of circumstances.

The range of possibilities becomes all the more obvious when we switch from intellectual to personality predictors. A common tendency is to use scores on standard personality inventories as predictors of leadership; the Cattell and Stice (1954) paper mentioned earlier is an obvious example. The trait profiles on the 16PF are designed to discriminate individuals in the general population, and they are not tailored for the peculiarities of leader behavior. Even so, many researchers in the leadership area assume that the dispositional differences of most importance are more closely linked with the phenomenon. For instance, in Fiedler's (1967) well-known contingency model, the critical individual factor is how someone feels about his or her "least preferred co-worker" (LPC). This is taken as a gauge of whether a person is oriented toward task performance or social relationships. Even if LPC scores correlate with more fundamental personality traits, it is this more narrow factor that is central in the predictive model. Another illustration of such a more narrowly defined individual-difference variable is the recent psychometric and historiometric research on the transformational versus transactional leadership styles (e.g., Bass, Avolio, & Goodheim, 1987; Hater & Bass, 1988; Yammarino, Spangler, & Bass, 1993). As for the LPC construct, any relationships these styles have with more elementary personality traits may be less important than the immediate associations these styles exhibit with criteria of leader performance.

It would make everything more pleasant if I could generalize this lesson by concluding that the more narrowly conceived predictors always outperform the more broadly defined predictors. But this is not invariably the case. In predicting the performance of U.S. presidents, for example, general predictors derived from the Adjective Check List (Gough & Heilbrun, 1965) or the Thematic Apperception Test (Murray, 1938) can actually do better than assessments of leadership style that more closely match the unique features of the Oval Office (Simonton, 1986c, 1987b, 1988b). Therefore, we can never take it for granted that specialized predictors are superior to generalized predictors. That must be determined on a case-by-case basis

Individual versus Situational Variables

As already noted, opponents of the great-person theory maintained that leadership is totally a function of context, not personal qualities. In line with this stance, an ample number of experimental studies have shown how leadership can sometimes be dictated entirely by such circumstantial factors as seating arrangements (e.g., Howells & Becker, 1962; Ward, 1968). Even in the domain of historic leadership, the situation may be the prime influence. One case in point is the so-called vice-presidential succession effect in American history (Simonton, 1985b), in which those who unexpectedly become the chief executive upon the death or resignation of the incumbent tend to perform less well in the White House. Although observers have often attributed this to the personal attributes of vice presidents, recent analyses show that this effect is probably situational in nature (Simonton, 1985b, 1986c, 1988b). Lacking a direct electoral mandate, such "accidental" presidents simply suffer political liabilities that are not their doing.

Insofar as we wish to predict leadership with any precision, the implication is obvious: We must often include situational variables alongside any individual variables in our prediction equations. This then makes it the psychologist's responsibility to decipher how much explained variance can be attributed to the personal traits and how much to external constraints and opportunities. For example, historiometric studies of military leaders show that both individual and situational factors predict success on the battlefield, with situational predictors having somewhat more influence (Simonton, 1979, 1980; see also Ballard & Suedfeld, 1988; Simonton, 1984b, 1992).

One complication makes this recommendation a bit more difficult to follow in practice: It is not always easy to specify whether a given predictor represents an index of personal qualities uncontaminated by situational inputs. The research on the motivational makeup of the U.S. presidents offers an illustration (e.g., Holmes & Elder, 1989; Wendt & Light, 1976; Winter, 1987; Winter & Stewart, 1977). Using the inaugural address, each president can be assessed on the power, achievement, and affiliation motives. These motive scores can then be correlated with various performance measures, such as the president's willingness to exploit American military might to attain foreign policy objectives. The implicit assumption is that the motive scores represent a stable characteristic of each president, and hence that they constitute pure personality measures.

Yet this postulate is not as safe as it may first appear (Simonton, 1987b). Because the president delivers his inaugural address in a specific political milieu, the motive imagery with which he expresses his ideas may at least partly mirror that more encompassing setting. Thus, when the international scene seems quite volatile and dangerous, the president may sense the need to communicate strength and toughness as a warning to enemies abroad (see McCann, 1990; McCann & Stewin, 1987). When later in the administration the nation's commander in chief is obliged to use troops to respond to some foreign conflict, a spurious relation is set up between the motive score and the leader's overt behavior. After all, that military intervention may merely be the logical conclusion of the political circumstances that existed at the onset of the president's term in office.

I am not claiming that the motive scores are necessarily contaminated by contextual factors, but only that psychologists must be sensitive to the possibility. Furthermore, this precaution can hold for psychometric research as much as historiometric research. Only by using experimental methods can the investigator deliberately divorce the measurement of intellect and personality from the assessment of situational variables.

State versus Trait Indicators

I have just suggested that the need for power may not constitute a completely stable attribute. Instead, a leader's power motivation may fluctuate from one moment to the next, according to other circumstances. Thus this drive may express a transient state as well as an enduring trait. One can spot indirect evidence for this suggestion in the motivation scores published for U.S. chief executives. Those presidents who were elected more than once to the office will have delivered two inaugural addresses, and the motive scores derived from each are never the same (Donley & Winter, 1970). Admittedly, one could dismiss these temporal discrepancies as mere consequences of measurement errors. The reliability coefficients for the TAT assessments were not high enough to guarantee identical scores even if a president's motivational makeup was perfectly constant over the 4-year interval. Even so, we have evidence from another quarter that establishes in a more convincing fashion the necessity of carefully weighing the relative proportion of trait and state in the measurement of a given characteristic.

I noted how the Paragraph Completion Test has been successfully converted into a content analytical scheme that can be applied to the speeches and correspondence of leaders. The outcome are scores on an intellectual inclination known as *integrative complexity*. This is the capacity to examine all the contradictory opinions on an issue and then integrate these diverse perspectives into a single, coherent position. Frequently researchers have treated this measure as a personality trait that predicted effectiveness in military figures, revolutionaries, politicians, and a host of other leadership positions (e.g., Suedfeld, Corteen, & McCormick, 1986; Suedfeld & Rank, 1976; Suedfeld & Tetlock, 1977; Suedfeld, Tetlock, & Ramirez, 1977).

Nevertheless, it is also clear that integrative complexity can function as a more volatile characteristic that may fluctuate within a leader according to circumstances (e.g., Suedfeld & Bluck, 1988; Tetlock, 1981b, 1985). Thus integrative complexity will often decline during times of severe stress (Suedfeld & Piedrahita,

1984; Suedfeld & Tetlock, 1977; Suedfeld, Tetlock, & Ramirez, 1977). Even if certain leaders may have higher baseline levels of integrative complexity, these stressful circumstances may drag information processing down to less efficient levels. A good illustration is the Confederate general Robert E. Lee (Suedfeld, Corteen, & McCormick, 1986). His tendency toward sophisticated thought served him well on the battlefield, for on this trait he surpassed all the generals the Union threw at him until the arrival of U. S. Grant. At the same time, it is clear that Lee's integrative complexity was sizably depressed during the Civil War. Indeed, by the time Lee faced Grant, the military situation going so badly for the Confederacy that Lee's integrative complexity dipped below Grant's, when earlier in the conflict it had been higher. Consequently, the discrepant circumstances probably reversed the contrast between Lee and Grant on this attribute.

Though some scholars may not wish to generalize from a single case, other investigations have found comparable results. Take, for instance, the tendency for liberal legislators to display higher integrative complexity than their conservative colleagues (Suedfeld, Bluck, Ballard, & Baker-Brown, 1990; Tetlock, 1981a, 1983, 1984; see also Tetlock, Bernzweig, & Gallant, 1985). The magnitude of this difference is by no means stable. When liberals form the minority in a legislature dominated by conservatives, the contrast between the two groups becomes more negligible (Pancer, Hunsberger, Pratt, Boisvert, & Roth, 1992; Tetlock, Hannum, & Micheletti, 1984; see also Tetlock & Boettger, 1989). Analogous results have been found in the literature on the authoritarian personality (Simonton, 1990a). As a personal attribute, authoritarianism operates as both trait and state; though it tends to be stable, it is also susceptible to the impact of threatening circumstances (Ertel, 1985).

Therefore, the central lesson remains that we must always determine how much our measures assess stable attributes and how much they tap momentary responses to extrinsic conditions. To the extent that the latter holds, we are not strictly using traits to predict leadership.

Models

Suppose we have resolved the above enigmas of measurement. Judging from the tenor of the empirical literature, many of us might believe that we are practically home free; all that is left to do is to compute correlation coefficients between criteria and predictor variables. The more sophisticated among us might run multiple regression analyses to determine which linear combination yields the most accurate predictions. But these procedures fall short of an optimal strategy. The most commonplace correlation methods presume that we are only interested in predictors whose consequences for leadership are direct, linear, additive, and static. Yet to comprehend fully the individual foundations of leadership, we must allow for less simple-minded predictive models. In particular, we must permit functions that may be indirect, curvilinear, multiplicative, and dynamic.

Direct versus Indirect Paths

Imagine this scenario: A respectable sample of leaders are evaluated on a particular performance criterion. These same leaders also take a battery of psychometric tests that gauge various aspects of cognitive capacity and personality disposition. Given these two sets of measurements, we then calculate the zero-order correlation coefficients between the criterion and these assessments, and discover that several individual-difference variables emerge as potential predictors. We then run a multiple regression analysis, perhaps regressing the criterion scores on all the significant correlates in a stepwise procedure. Usually only a small subset of the initial batch of candidate predictors ends up making a substantial contribution to the explained variance. The remainder apparently lacks predictive utility. Once we control for the predictive power of the significant variables, these superfluous correlates add nothing, right?

Wrong. There are two principal causal interpretations of this scenario. On the one hand, if a zero-order correlate does not become a useful predictor in a multiple regression equation, it may be because this variable has a *spurious* correlation with the leadership criterion (Kenny, 1979). Once the variance this spurious correlate shares with the criterion and the true predictors is subtracted by the multivariate procedure, the correlation disappears. In this case, we can safely conclude that this factor has no explanatory or predictive value. On the other hand, an alternative causal model could hold that this situation reveals that one variable has only an *indirect effect* on the criterion. That is, the excluded correlate has a direct effect on one of the predictors, which then influences the criterion directly. This distinction between spurious and indirect effects is crucial. Indirect effects, unlike spurious effects, bear a causal relationship with leadership.

As such, we can with full justification use indirect-effect variables as predictors whenever the direct-effect variables are unavailable.

Historiometric research on presidential leadership offers an excellent example. Several studies show that the incumbent's power motive predicts whether his administration will receive a high performance rating by experts (e.g., Wendt & Light, 1976; Winter, 1973, 1987). Nevertheless, this motivational inclination is only one of dozens of variables that exhibit significant zero-order correlations with assessed presidential greatness (Simonton, 1986b, c, 1988b). When we try to construct a multiple regression equation that optimally predicts the ratings, the power motive does not emerge as a predictor (McCann, 1992; Simonton, 1986b,c). Nevertheless, some of the key predictors of executive performance are partially associated with power motivation (Winter, 1987; Winter & Stewart, 1977).

We can accordingly infer that a president who rates high in power drive is more likely to have events happen during their administration that lead to more positive evaluations. For instance, power motivation predicts an incumbent's willingness to exploit military force to achieve foreign policy ends (Winter, 1987), and yet wartime presidents tend to be more highly rated than peacetime chief executives (Holmes & Elder, 1989; Kenney & Rice, 1988; Nice, 1984; Simonton, 1991b). Consequently, not only is power motivation central to our understanding of presidential leadership, but in addition this personal factor can serve as a proxy predictor in the absence of the direct antecedents. This latter possibility is not academic either. When a president first enters office, events like military interventions remain in the future, and hence his score on power motivation may be one of the few facts in hand.

We can generalize this point by saying that a variable that fails to enter a multiple regression equation may still have an important place in both explanation and prediction. We cannot automatically exclude a variable without careful consideration of the most plausible causal model. Under certain practical conditions, variables that gauge only indirect effects on a leadership criterion may have considerable predictive usefulness.

Linear versus Curvilinear Functions

When we calculate the zero-order correlations between a leadership criterion and a collection of possible predictors, we are making an implicit assumption about the form of the function connecting dependent and independent variables. We are specifically assuming that the function could be graphed as a straight line in Cartesian coordinates (where the vertical axis indicates the criterion and the horizontal axis the predictor). The correlation coefficient thus gauges the linear relationship. If we use the Pearson product-moment coefficient, for instance, the correlation tells us that if we change the score on the predictor by 1 standard deviation, we predict that the criterion will change by r standard deviations. Moreover, that prediction stays constant throughout the range of scores on the criterion. It follows that the correlation statistic can seriously underestimate the relationship between criterion and predictor whenever the actual function departs from the linear. In the extreme case, the dependent and independent variables might be tied to a curvilinear, U-shaped function. In this situation, the correlation might be zero even if the predictor could account for almost all the variance in the criterion.

Because the bulk of the leadership research has relied heavily on linear measures of statistical association, the empirical literature may seriously underestimate the predictive value of many measures of personal attributes. The role of intelligence in leadership illustrates this predicament quite well. More psychometric studies have probably scrutinized this factor than any other personal attribute, and probably no individual-difference variable has come out as most consistently related to leadership assessments of various kinds (Lord et al., 1986; Mann, 1959; Stogdill, 1948). Even so, the observed correlations are often modest. Yet scrutiny of the scatter plots often reveals that the relation between intelligence and leadership is not linear (e.g., Ghiselli, 1963). Beyond a certain level of intellect, further increases in cognitive capacity can actually inhibit leader effectiveness (Gibb, 1969a; Hollander & Julian, 1970). In fact, a recent formal model predicted that a leader's influence over the group is maximized when his or her intelligence is only about 1.2 standard deviations above the group average (Simonton, 1985a). Much psychometric data supports this theoretical prediction.

Such curvilinear, even nonmonotonic functions can hold for personality traits as well. One study of European absolute monarchs revealed that morality bears a curious U-shaped relationship with leadership, the most effective kings and queens either acting out of high principles or else behaving in an utterly unscrupulous fashion (Simonton, 1984b). Presidential greatness exhibits an analogous pattern: The greatest chief executives are either inflexibility idealistic or flexibly pragmatic, rather than falling some place in the middle (Simonton, 1986b). In contrast, an experiment that examined the impact of personal Machiavellianism in small groups found a curvilinear, inverted-U relationship between scores on this trait and the odds that an individual would emerge as the group's leader (Gleason, Seaman, & Hollander, 1978).

Hence we have enough factual illustrations to suggest that curvilinear functions may be commonplace in the real world of leader behavior. The more common these functions are, the more our simple correlation coefficients may understate the predictive efficiency of intellectual and personality variables.

Additive versus Multiplicative Effects

Testing for curvilinear relationships is a complicated business that need not be discussed here (see Darlington, 1990, chap. 12). I should mention, however, that the most powerful approach in a multiple regression analysis is to introduce both linear and quadratic forms of the same predictor variable. Thus, if leadership is a curvilinear function of intelligence, the latter variable should be accompanied by the same variable squared, or intelligence multiplied by itself. Yet we need not confine multiplicative terms to quadratic functions of a single variable. On the contrary, we can always introduce the product of two different predictors along with the original variables separately. This product or multiplicative term then tests for the occurrence of two-way interaction effects. This is what happens if the impact of one predictor on the criterion varies according to the values assumed by another predictor (and vice-versa, because interactions are symmetrical).

I only mention this possibility because there is ample empirical reason for believing that such interaction effects permeate the literature on leadership (e.g., Ellis & Cronshaw, 1992; McClane, 1991). These effects are of two main types: individual × individual and individual × situational interactions.

Whenever one trait's impact on leadership depends on the values assumed by another trait, we have interaction of the first type. One of the earliest illustrations comes from Catherine Cox (1926), who showed that intelligence alone did not suffice to produce success; rather this intellectual attribute had to be accompanied by motivational determination. Specifically, "high but not the highest intelligence, combined with the greatest degree of persistence, will achieve greater eminence than the highest degree of intelligence with somewhat less persistence" (p. 187). Moreover, more than two personal attributes can enter the multiplicative function, creating three-way and even higher-order interaction effects. For example, modern behavioral genetics suggests that innate leadership ability may require the simultaneous inheritance of a complex of separate characteristics, including self-confidence, assertiveness, dominance, and attractiveness (Lykken, 1982). Another example is recent research suggesting that successful leadership requires a distinctive "motive pattern" that explains more variance than each of the motivational components operating separately as "main effects" (e.g., McClelland & Boyatzis, 1982; Spangler & House, 1991; Winter, 1991). The required configuration entails exceptional power motivation (especially a power drive that amply exceeds the need for affiliation) coupled with sufficient self-control ("activity inhibition") to rechannel the power needs towards more socially constructive ends (see also House & Howell, 1992).

In the second type of interaction, the effect of a personal characteristic may hinge on the external circumstances in which leadership is being exercised, yielding an individual × situational interaction effect. Examples abound in both psychometric and historiometric research. The best-known example in the first methodological domain is probably Fiedler's (1967) contingency model of leadership. This argues that the relationship between leadership style (LPC scores) and leader effectiveness depends on factors that gauge how favorable the situation is to the exercise of leadership (see Peters, Hartke, & Pohlmann, 1985). From the second methodological domain, we can cite a study of presidential leadership that looked at the relationship between the executive's personal flexibility and his legislative performance (Simonton, 1987a). Flexibility only had predictive value when the opposing party controlled the legislative branch, a circumstance in which the ability to bargain, negotiate, and compromise is a premium.

Naturally, interaction effects can simultaneously incorporate both several individual characteristics and several situational factors, yielding even more elaborate predictive models. An example is the *multiple screen model* of Fiedler and Leister (1977). This holds that the relationship between leader intelligence and task performance in a work group is moderated by leader motivation and experience, as well as leader-boss relations and leader-group relations. In other words, the association between an intellectual predictor and a leadership criterion is contingent on two individual variables and two situational variables.

Indeed, if we allow for curvilinear functions along with multiplicative effects, our predictive models can become even more complex. For example, the roughly inverted-U curve that describes the relationship between leader intelligence and effectiveness varies according to the type of leadership required in a given situation (Simonton, 1985a). In particular, the peak of the curve appears at different intelligence levels depending on whether the individual is expected to be a social-emotional specialist who concentrates on maintaining group morale or a task specialist who focuses on getting the job done (see Bales, 1970; Fiedler, 1967).

These further complications aside, the very existence of multiplicative effects has two sobering implications regarding the prediction of leadership. First, if any predictor participates primarily in interactions rather than as an noncontingent effect, then we cannot expect the "validity coefficients" to be very good in the absence of the appropriate product terms. Thus, if the relation between intelligence and leadership depends on several individual and situational characteristics, do not even hope for impressive correlation or regression coefficients. So the many trait-leadership relationships reported in the literature may seriously underestimate the potential predictive power that we would obtain under multiplicative models. Second, if most of the essential predictors of leadership enter into product terms only, we cannot expect leadership ability to be normally distributed in the population (see Burt, 1943). On the contrary, even if all the relevant predictors exhibit normal distributions, the distribution of their higher-order product will be described by an extremely skewed lognormal probability distribution (Simonton, 1984a, chap. 5). Put differently, individuals who "have everything going for them—in the sense that they have high scores on all pertinent individual and situational predictors—should be quite rare. Hence, in predicting leadership, we are inadvertently attempting to predict an extraordinary phenomenon. We should lower our expectations accordingly.

Static versus Dynamic Equations

The foregoing elaboration may have made a few readers a little despondent over the prospects of successfully predicting leadership. Not only must we carefully consider whether the effects are direct or indirect, but we must allow for the possible intrusion of curvilinear and multiplicative terms in our prediction equations. As if these niceties were not enough, I must close with a final admonition: In all likelihood, comprehensive and precise prediction will require dynamic rather than static models. The procedures treated up to this point postulate that leadership is pretty much a static phenomenon. Given a set of circumstances and a set of scores on the relevant personal qualities, we should derive performance predictions that would be as valid today as tomorrow or next year. To be sure, the situation might change for some capricious reason, but this entails only the replacement of one score by an updated score on some contextual factor.

A dynamic model, in contrast, includes time as an integral part of the prediction equation. Both individuals and situations may change in a systematic manner as a function of some temporal measure. For example, leaders may become more conservative, less likely to take risks, and less flexible as a function of age (e.g., Schubert, 1983; Vroom & Pahl, 1971). And groups may go through a regular series of transformations in the process of establishing norms and role expectations (e.g., Tuckman, 1965). Furthermore, the relationship between the leader and the group may undergo systematic changes as well. One example is the "idiosyncratic credit" that accrues to leaders who have served long enough to gain the trust of those led. This asset enables the leader to advance original ideas without threatening the support of followers or subordinates (Hollander & Julian, 1970). The interaction between leader and group can be compared to long-term love relationships that will often experience drastic but predictable shifts as the dyad matures. Whatever the details, we cannot ignore the consequence: The mix of useful predictors may alter so that the optimal prediction equation at time t may differ remarkably from that at time $t + 1$.

Let me offer an illustration drawn from recent work on the interplay between intelligence, experience, job stress, and leader effectiveness (Fiedler, 1992). We must begin by recognizing that a leader has two main resources to draw upon when dealing with the daily problems of guiding a group. On the one hand, the leader can always rely on his or her general problem-solving powers. By this I mean the ability to encode large amounts of information, to find the best representation of the problem, and to employ the optimal heuristics in quest of a solution (Hayes, 1989).

Supposedly, this is gauged by any worthwhile intelligence test. On the other hand, the leader can always lean upon his or her past work experience. Given a sufficient history at a particular job, the leader should be able to recall the procedures that solved similar problems in the past.

These two alternative problem-solving strategies have different advantages and disadvantages. For instance, abstract problem-solving ability is often ineffective under highly stressful conditions, which interfere with efficient information processing. Highly experienced leaders, by comparison, can frequently make almost instinctive, split-second decisions founded on the expertise they have accumulated at their position. Indeed, many studies show that personal intelligence may display a negative relationship with performance in stressful settings but exhibit a positive relationship when the environment is more relaxed—and the pattern for experience is often reversed.

Yet ponder what these two interaction effects tell us. Although both intelligence and experience are attributes of the leader, only intelligence can be viewed as a relatively stable trait. Experience is quite different, for we must consider it to represent a constantly transforming state variable. That transformation, furthermore, is a function of time. In fact, the operational definition of experience is usually the amount of time a leader has occupied a particular position. Therefore, in order to predict leader performance as a function of a trait variable (intelligence) and a contextual factor (job stress), we must incorporate time explicitly into the equation. Not only will the impact of intelligence vary according to the concurrent level of job stress, but its predictive utility will shrink as experience expands over time. For those leaders who have accumulated many years at their current position, intelligence may become an irrelevant variable under even the most tranquil conditions.

In this illustration, time moderates the predictions in a linear way. Nonetheless, dynamic equations may include time in a curvilinear fashion. For instance, many qualities that affect leadership may be described by a single-peaked, nonmonotonic function of personal age (Simonton, 1988a). Situational variables may also assume the form of curvilinear time functions, at times even yielding cyclical patterns. For example, such cyclical processes have often been suggested for presidential leadership (e.g., McCann, 1992; Simonton, 1987b). Cyclical movements imply that the predictive power of a given equation may rise and fall over time. Hence, once we expand our equations to contain dynamic components, computing our predictions can become even more convoluted.

CONCLUSION

I must admit the limitations of this review. I have made no attempt to survey the full richness of the literature. Most obviously, I have not tried to cover all the theoretical perspectives on leadership. Here three omissions are perhaps the most conspicuous:

1. I have not examined the difficult issue of whether leadership is a perceptual rather than behavioral phenomenon. In line with recent developments in social cognition, some researchers have argued that the predictors of leadership are highly informative about how people perceive leaders in terms of categories or schemata, but these predictors may have often relatively little to do with actual leader performance (Eden & Leviathan, 1975; Lord & Maher, 1991; Rush & Russell, 1988; Rush, Thomas, & Lord, 1977; Shamir, 1992). The judgment of political leadership, in particular, may be more in the eyes in the beholder than in those of the actors beheld (Foti, Fraser, & Lord, 1982; Simonton, 1986a).

2. I have not addressed the old debate about whether leaders are born or made. This controversy dates from the days of Francis Galton (1869) and has received new attention in the work of behavioral geneticists (Lykken, 1982). This question has obvious relevance for any program designed to identify and nurture potential talent in leadership areas.

3. I have not looked at how leadership ties in with creativity. Creativity and leadership have been bound together since the time of Galton (1869), Cox (1926), and Thorndike (1950), and theoretical connections continue to be forged today (e.g., Mumford & Connelly, 1991; Simonton, 1984a).

Probably we cannot appreciate why our prediction equations work the way they do without resolving these and other theoretical questions. Resolution of these issues may even help us to refine our predictive skills, in line with Kurt Lewin's (1947) advice that "nothing is as practical as a good theory" (p. 18). Still, we have insufficient space here to do these topics justice.

Indeed, I have not even explored all the technical aspects of prediction. For example, I have not even mentioned the optimal procedures for deriving point and interval estimates. Nor have I touched upon the pros and cons of unit weighting of predictors in the equations. Most seriously, perhaps, I have not delved into how measurement reliability and validity affects multivariate predictions. Because the issues underlying these technical points are not restricted to leadership, the general problems are treated at sufficient length in any standard textbook (e.g., Cohen & Cohen, 1983; Darlington, 1990).

Despite all these constraints, this chapter has still covered considerable territory. It has conveyed some of the key complexities in linking personal attributes to leadership. These include questions about what we must measure and how our measurements should best enter into our predictive models. Once we acknowledge these intricacies, there can be no more excuses for the simplistic studies that too often have dominated the literature. Whether we are looking at historic forms of leadership or more everyday forms of the phenomenon, it is time to get sophisticated. What makes one person a leader and another a follower, or what makes one a better leader than another, is not the kind of matter that can be dispatched by a handful of correlation coefficients. Now that research in this area is apparently on the upswing, and even the great-person theory has received renewed attention, we can look forward to a more sound psychology of leadership. I hope that future psychologists will eventually construct prediction equations that capture all manifestations of the phenomenon and that recognize the phenomenon's inherent complexity.

REFERENCES

Bales, R. F. (1970). *Personality and interpersonal behavior.* New York: Holt, Rinehart & Winston.

Ballard, E. J., & Suedfeld, P. (1988). Performance ratings of Canadian prime ministers: Individual and situational factors. *Political Psychology, 9,* 291–302.

Barnlund, D. C. (1962). Consistency of emergent leadership in groups with changing tasks and members. *Speech Monographs, 29,* 45–52.

Bass, B. M. (1990). *Bass & Stogdill's handbook of leadership: Theory, research, and managerial applications* (3rd ed.). New York: Free Press.

Bass, B. M., Avolio, B. J., & Goodheim, L. (1987). Biography and the assessment of transformational leadership world-class level. *Journal of Management, 13,* 7–19.

Bass, B. M., & Farrow, D. L. (1977). Quantitative analyses of biographies of political figures. *Journal of Psychology, 97,* 281–296.

Bell, G. B., & French, R. L. (1950). Consistency of individual leadership position in small groups of varying membership. *Journal of Abnormal and Social Psychology, 45,* 764–767.

Borgatta, E. F., Couch, A. S., & Bales, F. R. (1954). Some findings relevant to the great man theory of leadership. *American Sociological Review, 19,* 755–759.

Buros, O. K. (Ed.). (1974). *Tests in print: II. An index to tests, test reviews, and the literature on specific tests.* Highland Park, NJ: Gryphon.

Burt, C. (1943). Ability and income. *British Journal of Educational Psychology, 12,* 83–98.

Carlyle, T. (1841). *On heroes, hero-worship, and the heroic.* London: Fraser.

Cattell, R. B., & Stice, G. F. (1954). Four formulae for selecting leaders on the basis of personality. *Human Relations, 7,* 493–507.

Cohen, J., & Cohen, P. (1983). *Applied multiple regression/correlation for the behavioral sciences* (2nd ed.). Hillsdale, NJ: Erlbaum.

Costantini, E., & Craik, K. H. (1980). Personality and politicians: California party leaders, 1960–1976. *Journal of Personality and Social Psychology, 38,* 641–661.

Cox, C. (1926). *The early mental traits of three hundred geniuses.* Stanford, CA: Stanford University Press.

Cummin, P. C. (1967). TAT correlates of executive performance. *Journal of Applied Psychology, 51,* 78–81.

Darlington, R. B. (1990). *Regression and linear models.* New York: McGraw-Hill.

Dobbins, G. H., Long, W. S., Dedrick, E. J., & Clemons, T. C. (1990). The role of self-monitoring and gender on leader emergence: A laboratory and field study. *Journal of Management, 16,* 609–618.

Donley, R. E., & Winter, D. G. (1970). Measuring the motives of public officials at a distance: An exploratory study of American presidents. *Behavioral Science, 15,* 227–236.

Eden, D., & Leviathan, U. (1975). Implicit leadership theory as a determinant of the factor structure underlying supervisory behavior scales. *Journal of Applied Psychology, 60,* 736–741.

Ellis, R. J. (1988). Self-monitoring and leadership emergence in groups. *Personality and Social Psychology Bulletin, 14,* 681–693.

Ellis, R. J., Adamson, R. S., Deszca, G., & Cawsey, T. F. (1988). Self-monitoring and leadership emergence. *Small Group Behavior, 19,* 312–324.

Ellis, R. J., & Cronshaw, S. F. (1992). Self-monitoring and leader emergence: A test of moderator effects. *Small Group Research, 23,* 113–129.

Epstein, S., & O'Brien, E. J. (1985). The person-situation debate in historical and current perspective. *Psychological Bulletin, 98,* 513–537.

Ertel, S. (1985). Content analysis: An alternative approach to open and closed minds. *High School Journal, 68,* 229–240.

Etheredge, L. S. (1978). Personality effects on American foreign policy, 1898–1968: A test of interpersonal generalization theory. *American Political Science Review, 78,* 434–451.

Fiedler, F. E. (1967). *A theory of leadership effectiveness.* New York: McGraw-Hill.

Fiedler, F. E. (1992). Time-based measures of leadership experience and organizational performance: A review of rescarch and a preliminary model. *Leadership Quarterly, 3,* 5–23.

Fiedler, F. E., & Leister, A. F. (1977). Leader intelligence and task performance: A test of the multiple screen model. *Organizational Behavior and Human Performance, 20,* 1–14.

Fleishman, E. A., Zaccaro, S. J., & Mumford, M. D. (Eds.). (1991). Individual differences and leadership: Part I [Special issue]. *Leadership Quarterly, 2*(4).

Fleishman, E. A., Zaccaro, S. J., & Mumford, M. D. (Eds.). (1992a). Individual differences and leadership: Part II [Special issue]. *Leadership Quarterly, 3*(1).

Fleishman, E. A., Zaccaro, S. J., & Mumford, M. D. (Eds.). (1992b). Individual differences and leadership: Part III [Special issue]. *Leadership Quarterly, 3*(2).

Foti, R. J., Fraser, S. L., & Lord, R. G. (1982). The effects of leadership labels and prototypes on perceptions of political leaders. *Journal of Applied Psychology, 67*, 326–333.

Freud, S. (1964). *Leonardo da Vinci and a memory of his childhood* (A. Tyson, Trans.). New York: Norton. (Original work published 1910)

Freud, S., & Bullitt, W. C. (1967). *Thomas Woodrow Wilson: A Psychological study*. Boston: Houghton Mifflin.

Galton, F. (1869). *Hereditary genius: An inquiry into its laws and consequences*. London: Macmillan.

Galton, F. (1883). *Inquiries into human faculty and its development*. London: Macmillan.

Gardner, H. (1983). *Frames of mind: A theory of multiple intelligences*. New York: Basic Books.

Garland, H., & Beard, J. F. (1979). Relationship between self-monitoring and leader emergence across two task situations. *Journal of Applied Psychology, 64*, 72–76.

Geier, J. G. (1967). A trait approach to the study of leadership in small groups. *Journal of Communication, 17*, 316–323.

Ghiselli, E. E. (1963). Intelligence and managerial success. *Psychological Reports, 12*, 898.

Gibb, C. A. (1969a). Leadership. In G. Lindzey & E. Aronson (Eds.), *Handbook of social psychology* (2nd ed., pp. 205–282). Reading, MA: Addison-Wesley.

Gibb, C. A. (Ed.). (1969b). *Leadership: Selected readings*. Baltimore, MD: Penguin.

Gleason, J. M., Seaman, F. J., & Hollander, E. P. (1978). Emergent leadership processes as a function of task structure and Machiavellianism. *Social Behavior and Personality, 6*, 33–36.

Gough, H. G., & Heilbrun, A. B., Jr. (1965). *The Adjective Check List manual*. Palo Alto, CA: Consulting Psychologists Press.

Guilford, J. P. (1967). *The nature of human intelligence*. New York: McGraw-Hill.

Hater, J., & Bass, B. M. (1988). Superiors' evaluations and subordinates' perceptions of transformational and transactional leadership. *Journal of Applied Psychology, 73*, 695–702.

Hayes, J. R. (1989). *The complete problem solver* (2nd ed.). Hillsdale, NJ: Erlbaum.

Hermann, M. G. (1980). Explaining foreign policy using personal characteristics of political leaders. *International Studies Quarterly, 24*, 7–46.

Hoffer, P. C. (1978). Psychohistory and empirical group affiliation: Extraction of personality traits from historical manuscripts. *Journal of Interdisciplinary History, 9*, 131–145.

Hollander, E. P., & Julian, J. W. (1970). Studies in leader legitimacy, influence, and innovation. In L. L. Berkowitz (Ed.), *Advances in experimental social psychology* (Vol. 5, pp. 33–69). New York: Academic Press.

Holmes, J. E., & Elder, R. E. (1989). Our best and worst presidents: Some possible reasons for perceived performance. *Presidential Studies Quarterly, 19*, 529–557.

House, R. J., & Baetz, M. L. (1979). Leadership: Some empirical generalizations and some new research directions. *Research in Organizational Behavior, 1*, 341–423.

House, R. J., & Howell, J. M. (1992). Personality and charismatic leadership. *Leadership Quarterly, 3*, 81–108.

House, R. J., Spangler, W. D., & Woycke, J. (1991). Personality and charisma in the U.S. presidency: A psychological theory of leader effectiveness. *Administrative Science Quarterly, 36*, 364–396.

Howells, L. T., & Becker, S. W. (1962). Seating arrangement and leadership emergence. *Journal of Abnormal and Social Psychology, 64*, 148–150.

Hunter, J. E., & Schmidt, F. L. (1990). *Methods of meta-analysis: Correcting error and bias in research findings*. Newbury Park, CA: Sage.

Jenkins, W. O. (1947). A review of leadership studies with particular reference to military problems. *Psychological Bulletin, 44*, 54–79.

Jensen, A. R. (1992). Understanding *g* in terms of information processing. *Educational Psychology Review, 4*, 271–308.

Kenney, P. J., & Rice, T. W. (1988). The contextual determinants of presidential greatness. *Presidential Studies Quarterly, 18*, 161–169.

Kenny, D. A. (1979). *Correlation and causality*. New York: Wiley.

Kenny, D. A., & Hallmark, B. W. (1992). Rotational designs in leadership research. *Leadership Quarterly, 3*, 25–41.

Kenny, D. A., & Zaccaro, S. J. (1983). An estimate of variance due to traits in leadership. *Journal of Applied Psychology, 68*, 678–685.

Lewin, K. (1947). *The research center for group dynamics*. New York: Beacon House.

Lord, R. G., De Vader, C. L., & Alliger, G. M. (1986). A meta-analysis of the relation between personality traits and leadership perceptions: An application of validity generalization procedures. *Journal of Applied Psychology, 71*, 402–410.

Lord, R. G., & Maher, K. J. (1991). *Leadership and information processing: Linking perceptions and performance*. Boston: Unwin Hyman.

Lykken, D. T. (1982). Research with twins: The concept of emergenesis. *Psychophysiology, 19*, 361–373.

Mann, R. D. (1959). A review of the relationships between personality and performance in small groups. *Psychological Bulletin, 56*, 241–270.

McCann, S. J. H. (1990). Threat, power, and presidential greatness: Harding to Johnson. *Psychological Reports, 66*, 129–130.

McCann, S. J. H. (1992). Alternative formulas to predict the greatness of U.S. presidents: Personological, situational, and zeitgeist factors. *Journal of Personality and Social Psychology, 62*, 469–479.

McCann, S. J. H., & Stewin, L. L. (1987). Threat, authoritarianism, and the power of U.S. presidents. *Journal of Psychology, 121*, 149–157.

McClane, W. E. (1991). The interaction of leader and member characteristics in the leader-member-exchange (LMX) model of leadership. *Small Group Research, 22*, 283–300.

McClelland, D. C., & Boyatzis, R. E. (1982). Leadership motive pattern and long-term success in management. *Journal of Applied Psychology, 67*, 737–743.

Miller, N. L., & Stiles, W. B. (1986). Verbal familiarity in American presidential nomination acceptance speeches and inaugural addresses. *Social Psychology Quarterly, 49*, 72–81.

Mischel, W. (1968). *Personality and assessment*. New York: Wiley.

Mumford, M. D., & Connelly, M. S. (1991). Leaders as creators: Leader performance and problem solving in ill-defined domains. *Leadership Quarterly, 2*, 289–315.

Murphey, A. J. (1941). A study of the leadership process. *American Sociological Review, 6*, 674–687.

Murray, H. A. (1938). *Explorations in personality*. New York: Oxford University Press.

Murray, R. K., & Blessing, T. H. (1988). *Greatness in the White House: Rating the presidents, Washington through Carter*. University Park: Pennsylvania State University Press.

Nice, D. C. (1984). The influence of war and party system aging on the ranking of presidents. *Western Political Quarterly, 37*, 443–455.

Pancer, S. M., Hunsberger, B., Pratt, M. W., Boisvert, S., & Roth, D. (1992). Political roles and the complexity of political rhetoric. *Political Psychology, 13*, 31–43.

Peters, L. H., Hartke, D. D., & Pohlmann, J. T. (1985). Fiedler's contingency theory of leadership: An application of the meta-analysis procedures of Schmidt and Hunter. *Psychological Bulletin, 97*, 274–285.

Rush, M. C., & Russell, J. E. A. (1988). Leader prototypes and prototype-contingent consensus in leader behavior descriptions. *Journal of Experimental Social Psychology, 24*, 88–104.

Rush, M. C., Thomas, J. C., & Lord, R. G. (1977). Implicit personality theory: A potential threat to the validity of leader behavior questionnaires. *Organizational Behavior and Human Performance, 20*, 93–110.

Schroder, H. M., Driver, M. J., & Streufert, S. (1967). *Human information processing: Individuals and groups functioning in complex social situations.* New York: Holt, Rinehart & Winston.

Schubert, G. (1983). Aging, conservatism, and judicial behavior. *Micropolitics, 3*, 135–179.

Shamir, B. (1992). Attribution of influence and charisma to the leader: The romance of leadership revisited. *Journal of Applied Social Psychology, 22*, 386–407.

Simonton, D. K. (1976). Biographical determinants of achieved eminence: A multivariate approach to the Cox data. *Journal of Personality and Social Psychology, 33*, 218–226.

Simonton, D. K. (1979). Was Napoleon a military genius? Score: Carlyle 1, Tolstoy 1. *Psychological Reports, 44*, 21–22.

Simonton, D. K. (1980). Land battles, generals, and armies: Individual and situational determinants of victory and casualties. *Journal of Personality and Social Psychology, 38*, 110–119.

Simonton, D. K. (1983a). Intergenerational transfer of individual differences in hereditary monarchs: Genes, role-modeling, cohort, or sociocultural effects? *Journal of Personality and Social Psychology, 44*, 354–364.

Simonton, D. K. (1983b). Psychohistory. In R. Harré & R. Lamb (Eds.), *The encyclopedic dictionary of psychology* (pp. 499–500). Oxford: Blackwell.

Simonton, D. K. (1984a). *Genius, creativity, and leadership: Historiometric inquiries.* Cambridge, MA: Harvard University Press.

Simonton, D. K. (1984b). Leaders as eponyms: Individual and situational determinants of monarchal eminence. *Journal of Personality, 52*, 1–21.

Simonton, D. K. (1985a). Intelligence and personal influence in groups: Four nonlinear models. *Psychological Review, 92*, 532–547.

Simonton, D. K. (1985b). The vice-presidential succession effect: Individual or situational basis? *Political Behavior, 7*, 79–99.

Simonton, D. K. (1986a). Dispositional attributions of (presidential) leadership: An experimental simulation of historiometric results. *Journal of Experimental Social Psychology, 22*, 389–418.

Simonton, D. K. (1986b). Presidential greatness: The historical consensus and its psychological significance. *Political Psychology, 7*, 259–283.

Simonton, D. K. (1986c). Presidential personality: Biographical use of the Gough Adjective Check List. *Journal of Personality and Social Psychology, 51*, 149–160.

Simonton, D. K. (1987a). Presidential inflexibility and veto behavior: Two individual-situational interactions. *Journal of Personality, 55*, 1–18.

Simonton, D. K. (1987b). *Why presidents succeed: A political psychology of leadership.* New Haven, CT: Yale University Press.

Simonton, D. K. (1988a). Age and outstanding achievement: What do we know after a century of research? *Psychological Bulletin, 104*, 251–267.

Simonton, D. K. (1988b). Presidential style: Personality, biography, and performance. *Journal of Personality and Social Psychology, 55*, 928–936.

Simonton, D. K. (1990a). Personality and politics. In L. A. Pervin (Ed.), *Handbook of personality theory and research* (pp. 670–692). New York: Guilford.

Simonton, D. K. (1990b). *Psychology, science, and history: An introduction to historiometry.* New Haven, CT: Yale University Press.

Simonton, D. K. (1991a). Personality correlates of exceptional personal influence: A note on Thorndike's (1950) creators and leaders. *Creativity Research Journal, 4*, 67–78.

Simonton, D. K. (1991b). Predicting presidential greatness: An alternative to the Kenney and Rice Contextual Index. *Presidential Studies Quarterly, 21*, 301–305.

Simonton, D. K. (1992). Presidential greatness and personality: A response to McCann (1992). *Journal of Personality and Social Psychology, 63*, 676–679.

Simonton, D. K. (1993). Putting the best leaders in the White House: Personality, policy, and performance. *Political Psychology, 14*, 539–550.

Snyder, M. (1974). The self-monitoring of expressive behavior. *Journal of Personality and Social Psychology, 30*, 526–537.

Spangler, W. D., & House, R. J. (1991). Presidential effectiveness and the leadership motive profile. *Journal of Personality and Social Psychology, 60*, 439–455.

Spearman, C. (1927). *The abilities of man.* New York: Macmillan.

Sternberg, R. J. (1985). *Beyond IQ: A triarchic theory of human intelligence.* New York: Cambridge University Press.

Stogdill, R. M. (1948). Personal factors associated with leadership: A survey of the literature. *Journal of Psychology, 25*, 37–71.

Stogdill, R. M. (1977). *Leadership: Abstracts and bibliography 1904 to 1974.* Columbus: College of Administrative Science of the Ohio State University.

Suedfeld, P., & Bluck, S. (1988). Changes in integrative complexity prior to surprise attacks. *Journal of Conflict Resolution, 32*, 625–635.

Suedfeld, P., Bluck, S., Ballard, E. J., & Baker-Brown, G. (1990). Canadian federal elections: Motive profiles and integrative complexity in political speeches and popular media. *Canadian Journal of Behavioural Science, 22*, 26–36.

Suedfeld, P., Corteen, R. S., & McCormick, C. (1986). The role of integrative complexity in military leadership: Robert E. Lee and his opponents. *Journal of Applied Social Psychology, 16*, 498–507.

Suedfeld, P., & Piedrahita, L. E. (1984). Intimations of mortality: Integrative simplification as a predictor of death. *Journal of Personality and Social Psychology, 47*, 848–852.

Suedfeld, P., & Rank, A. D. (1976). Revolutionary leaders: Long-term success as a function of changes in conceptual complexity. *Journal of Personality and Social Psychology, 34*, 169–178.

Suedfeld, P., & Tetlock, P. (1977). Integrative complexity of communications in international crises. *Journal of Conflict Resolution, 21*, 169–184.

Suedfeld, P., Tetlock, P. E., & Ramirez, C. (1977). War, peace, and integrative complexity. *Journal of Conflict Resolution, 21*, 427–442.

Terman, L. M. (1904). A preliminary study of the psychology of the pedagogy of leadership. *Pedagogical Seminary, 11*, 413–451.

Terman, L. M. (1917). The intelligence quotient of Francis Galton in childhood. *American Journal of Psychology, 28*, 209–215.

Tetlock, P. E. (1979). Identifying victims of groupthink from public statements of decision makers. *Journal of Personality and Social Psychology, 37*, 1314–1324.

Tetlock, P. E. (1981a). Personality and isolationism: Content analysis of senatorial speeches. *Journal of Personality and Social Psychology, 41*, 737–743.

Tetlock, P. E. (1981b). Pre- to postelection shifts in presidential rhetoric: Impression management or cognitive adjustment. *Journal of Personality and Social Psychology, 41*, 207–212.

Tetlock, P. E. (1983). Cognitive style and political ideology. *Journal of Personality and Social Psychology, 45*, 118–126.

Tetlock, P. E. (1984). Cognitive style and political belief systems in the British House of Commons. *Journal of Personality and Social Psychology, 46*, 365–375.

Tetlock, P. E. (1985). Integrative complexity of American and Soviet foreign policy rhetoric: A time-series analysis. *Journal of Personality and Social Psychology, 49*, 1565–1585.

Tetlock, P. E., Bernzweig, J., & Gallant, J. L. (1985). Supreme Court decision making: Cognitive style as a predictor of ideological consistency of voting. *Journal of Personality and Social Psychology, 48*, 1227–1239.

Tetlock, P. E., & Boettger, R. (1989). Cognitive and rhetorical styles of traditionalist and reformist Soviet politicians: A content analysis study. *Political Psychology, 10*, 209–232.

Tetlock, P. E., Crosby, F., & Crosby, T. L. (1981). Political psychobiography. *Micropolitics, 1*, 191–213.

Tetlock, P. E., Hannum, K. A., & Micheletti, P. M. (1984). Stability and change in the complexity of senatorial debate: Testing the cognitive versus rhetorical style hypothesis. *Journal of Personality and Social Psychology, 46*, 979–990.

Thorndike, E. L. (1936). The relation between intellect and morality in rulers. *American Journal of Sociology, 42*, 321–334.

Thorndike, E. L. (1950). Traits of personality and their intercorrelations as shown in biography. *Journal of Educational Psychology, 41*, 193–216.

Tuckman, B. W. (1965). Developmental sequence in small groups. *Psychological Bulletin, 63*, 384–399.

Vroom, V. H., & Pahl, B. (1971). Relationship between age and risk taking among managers. *Journal of Applied Psychology, 55*, 399–405.

Walberg, H. J., Rasher, S. P., & Parkerson, J. (1980). Childhood and eminence. *Journal of Creative Behavior, 13*, 225–231.

Ward, C. D. (1968). Seating arrangement and leadership emergence in small discussion groups. *Journal of Social Psychology, 74*, 83–90.

Wendt, H. W., & Light, P. C. (1976). Measuring "greatness" in American presidents: Model case for international research on political leadership? *European Journal of Social Psychology, 6*, 105–109.

Winter, D. G. (1973). *The power motive*. New York: Free Press.

Winter, D. G. (1980). An exploratory study of the motives of southern African political leaders measured at a distance. *Political Psychology, 2*, 75–85.

Winter, D. G. (1982). Motivation and performance in presidential candidates. In A. J. Stewart (Ed.), *Motivation and society: A volume in honor of David C. McClelland* (pp. 244–273). San Francisco: Jossey-Bass.

Winter, D. G. (1987). Leader appeal, leader performance, and the motive profiles of leaders and followers: A study of American presidents and elections. *Journal of Personality and Social Psychology, 52*, 196–202.

Winter, D. G. (1991). A motivational model of leadership: Predicting long-term management success from TAT measures of power motivation and responsibility. *Leadership Quarterly, 2*, 67–80.

Winter, D. G., & Carlson, D. G. (1988). Using motive scores in the psychobiographical study of an individual: The case of Richard Nixon. *Journal of Personality, 56*, 75–103.

Winter, D. G., & Stewart, A. S. (1977). Content analysis as a technique for assessing political leaders. In M. G. Hermann (Ed.), *The psychological examination of political leaders* (pp. 27–61). New York: Free Press.

Wood, R. E., & Mitchell, T. R. (1981). Manager behavior in social context: The impact of impression management on attributions and disciplinary actions. *Organizational Behavior and Human Performance, 28*, 356–378.

Woods, F. A. (1906). *Mental and moral heredity in royalty*. New York: Holt.

Woods, F. A. (1909). A new name for a new science. *Science, 30*, 703–704.

Woods, F. A. (1911). Historiometry as an exact science. *Science, 33*, 568–574.

Woods, F. A. (1913). *The influence of monarchs*. New York: Macmillan.

Yammarino, F. J., Spangler, W. D., & Bass, B. M. (1993). Transformational leadership and performance: A longitudinal investigation. *Leadership Quarterly, 4*, 81–102.

Zaccaro, S. J., Foti, R. J., & Kenny, D. A. (1991). Self-monitoring and trait-based variance in leadership: An investigation of leader flexibility across multiple group situations. *Journal of Applied Psychology, 76*, 308–315.

Zaccaro, S. J., Gilbert, J. A., Thor, K. K., & Mumford, M. D. (1991). Leadership and social intelligence: Linking social perceptiveness and behavioral flexibility to leader effectiveness. *Leadership Quarterly, 2*, 317–342.

Index

ABC Tests, 511
Abilities. *See also* Cognitive abilities; Mental abilities
  academic achievement and, 35
  changed perspectives on, 163
  cognitive style distinguished from, 399–400, 411
  factor analysis of, 428–429, 505–506
  multiple, 448–449, 451
  multivariate research on, 16–17
  personality and, 35, 595–596
  scientific method in elucidating, 418
  triadic theory of, 18, 430–431
Abilities: Their Structure, Growth and Action (Cattell), 5
Abilities tests, 33–34
Ability theory, 588–590
Abnormal intelligence, 622–630
Abnormal personality, 630–633
Absolutist theory, 107
Abstract conceptualization, 406–407
Academic achievement, 35
Acceleration approach, 646
Accommodating learning style, 218–219, 406–407, 408
Accuracy, 341, 343
  composite scores and, 27–28
  strategy selection/application and, 386–388
ACER-AL test, 35
Achievement creativity, 231
Achievement motivation
  classroom learning and, 166
  economic growth and, 118–120
  intelligence and, 310–312
  literacy and, 153
  school/educational psychology and, 638–640
  sports and, 692–693
Achievement tests, 161–162
Acquiescence, 512–513
Acquired immunodeficiency syndrome (AIDS), 37–38, 356, 712
Act frequency approach, 485–486, 495
Action control theory, 166
Action patterns, 132
Activators, 407
Active experimentation, 406–407
Active rehearsal, 378
Active strategy, 404
Activity-centered theories of styles, 218–220
Activity preference measures, 610
Activity Vector Analysis (AVA), 583
Adaptable learning, 176
Adaptation
  information processing and, 391–392
  as learning style, 408–409
A-data, 494
Adjective Check List, 747
Adjustment, 304–307
Adoption studies, 75
  on cross-cultural differences, 111
  on genetic/environmental covariance, 67
  on genetic/environmental interactions, 66
  on intelligence genetic factors, 61–62
  longitudinal, 83, 87–91, 98, 101
  on nonshared environment, 68
  on personality genetic factors, 63–64
Affect, 463–466
Affective disorders, 631, 652, 658
Affective goals, 132, 133
Affective styles, 213
Affirmative action, 52
African Americans. *See* Blacks
Africans, 54, 108, 111, 114
Agencies, 18
Aggression
  cognitive correlates of, 192–193
  cognitive-social theory on, 191–193
Aggression (*Cont.*)
  criminal offenders and, 682
  gender and, 108, 115–116, 120
  intelligence and, 302–304
  social exchange model of, 189
  sports and, 691–692
Aging, 24–25
Agoraphobia, 268
AH Series, 510
Alcoholism, 334–335
Allport, G. W., 4, 11, 205, 251, 456, 458, 461, 467
Allusive thinking, 238
Alzheimer's disease, 335, 356
Ambient situation, 438
Ambiverts, 323, 326, 339–340
Ambulatory depressives, 260
American Association on Mental Retardation (AAMR), 527
American Eugenics Society, 53
Ammons Quick Test, 567
Amphetamines, 242
Amygdala, 652
Analogies, 507
Analysis of variance (ANOVA), 31, 553, 558, 564, 568
Analytic-descriptive style, 210
Anarchic form of mental self-government, 222, 223
Anatomical correlates, 22
Androgens, 116
Anger, 302–304
Anger, hostility, aggression (AHA) phenomenon, 303
Annual Review of Psychology, 4, 10–11
Anthropological perspectives, 33–35, 38
Anthropometry, 54
Antisocial personality disorder, 115, 256–257, 535
Anxiety, 418. *See also* State anxiety; Trait anxiety

Anxiety (*Cont.*)
academic achievement and, 35
attentional tasks/resources and, 376
classroom learning and, 171–172
cognitive processes and, 33
cross-cultural differences in, 114–115
information processing and, 390
intelligence and, 300–302
neuropsychological basis of, 664
school/educational psychology and, 638–639
sensory event-related potentials and, 352
sports and, 690–692
strategy selection/application and, 386–387
Anxiety disorders
cognition and, 267–276
genetic factors in, 68
Appalachians, 55
Approach space, 703
Aptitude, for classroom learning, 165
Aptitude-treatment interactions (ATI), 154, 635–636
Architectural system, 624
Armchair inspection, 555–557
Armed Services Vocational Aptitude Battery (CAT-ASVAB;DAT), 436
Army, U.S., 586–587
Army-Air Force (AAF) Aviation Psychology program, 449
Army Air Forces, 587, 589
Army Alpha test, 578, 586, 727–728
Army Beta test, 578, 586, 727–728
Army General Classification Test, 316
Arousal, 326
anxiety and, 638
creativity and, 242–243
on EEG, 331–333
information processing and, 389, 391
inspection time and, 339–340
sports and, 690–691
time of day and, 310, 342, 344, 372–373, 374, 647
Articulatory loop, 378, 380, 381
Ascendence-Submission Test, 579
Ascending reticular system (ARAS), 689
Ascription rule, 458–459
Asians. *See* Orientals
Assessment. *See also* Intelligence assessment; Personality assessment
of cognitive interference, 286–287
defining functions of, 529–530
of exceptionality, 186-187
in vocational/career counseling, 609–611
Assimilating learning style, 218–219, 406–407
Assimilation-accomodation model, 308
Associative memory, 379
Asymptotic chi-square statistic, 420
Attentional biases, 263–264, 269–272
Attentional processes, 700–702
Attentional resources, 29–30, 375–378
Attentional styles, 702–703
Attentional tasks, 375–378
Attention deficit disorder (ADD)
anxiety and, 664
neuropsychological basis of, 663
Attention-deficit hyperactivity disorder (ADHD), 536–537
depression and, 663–664
neuropsychological basis of, 654, 659–660
Attention direction, 290–291
Attitudes, classroom learning and, 170–171
Attributions, 153, 192, 312
Attribution styles, 403, 639
Attribution theory, 166
Auditory inspection time (IT), 26–27
Auditory organization, 430
Auditory projective tests, 518
Australian aborigines, 108–109
Authoritarianism, 749
category width and, 404–405
intelligence and, 314
intolerance of ambiguity and, 402
longitudinal studies of, 85–86
Authoritarian Personality, The (Adorno et al.), 314
Autism, 531–533
Automatization, 405, 701–702
Autonomic symptoms, 719–721, 723
Averaged evoked potentials (AEPs), 327, 329–336, 337, 340, 343, 344
Avoidant personality disorder, 258–259

Bandura, A., 173, 187, 188, 196, 313
Bandwidth-fidelity dilemma, 589
Baptists, 315
Basic information processing, 370–371
Bayley Mental Development Index (MDI), 88, 98
Bayley Scales of Infant Development, 625
Beck Depression Inventory, 531
Behavioral disorders
cognitive-social theory on, 189–193
learning disabilities and, 193–197
Behavioral repertoire, 136–137
Behavioral specification equations, 427–428
Behavior Assessment System for Children-Teacher Rating Scales (BASC-TRS), 536, 537, 540–541
Behavior categorization, 210–212
Behavior episodes, 126–127
Behavior episode schemata (BES), 127–130
Behavior genetic studies, 82–84
from adolescence to adulthood, 98
in early adulthood, 98–99
in infancy, 97–98
Behavior Problem Checklist-Revised, 632
Belief systems, 312–316
Belongingness goals, 132–134
Bem Sex Role Inventory, 36
Bender-Gestalt test, 563
Bender Test of Visual Motor Integration, 538
Bennett Mechanical Comprehension Test, 588, 645
Bentley, A. F., 687
Berkeley longitudinal studies, 81, 95
Bernreuter Personality Inventory, 579, 580
Beyond I.Q.: A Triarchic Theory of Human Intelligence (Sternberg), 5
Beyond the Pleasure Principle (Freud), 191
Big five personality dimensions, 7, 9, 16, 17, 95, 369, 482
assessment and, 461–463, 469
controversy over, 431–433, 439
creativity and, 234
description of, 96
genetic factors in, 64
history of, 461
industrial/organizational psychology and, 590–591
longitudinal studies and, 99
prediction of job proficiency and, 483
Big three personality dimensions, 95
Binet, A., 49–50, 108, 163, 251, 728
Biochemistry, 22
Biological-cultural interaction theory, 107
Biological determinism
decline of, 51–52
renaissance of, 52–55
Biological intelligence, 10
Biological theory, 107
Biometrics, 744, 745
Bipolar depression. *See* Manic-depressive illness
Birth order, 69
Blacks, 8, 49, 55
biological determinism and, 52
cross-cultural differences in intelligence, 108, 109, 110–111, 112–114
cross-cultural differences in personality, 118

Blacks (*Cont.*)
education and, 75
environmental factors and, 69–70
locus of control and, 312
school/educational psychology and, 634–635
test bias and, 439, 546, 549, 551, 554, 556, 557–558, 560–563, 565–566, 567, 568
Blacky Pictures test, 518, 521, 631
Bonds, 21, 27
Bonferroni correction, 438
Borderline personality, 535
Brain
event-related potentials and, 350–351
glucose metabolism by, 22–23
significance of size, 22, 114
Brain damage, 655, 666, 714. *See also* Head injuries
psychiatric sequelae in adults, 660–661
reading deficits and, 661–662
Brainstem auditory evoked potentials (BAEPs), 360–362
Braodbent's Cognitive Failures Questionnaire, 722
Brief Symptom Inventory (BSI), 539–540
Brigham, Carl C., 50
British Ability Scales (BAS), 418, 489, 509
Broad auditory function (Ga), 17, 18, 19, 30
Broad categorizers, 405
Broad quantitative ability (Gq), 19
Broad speediness function (Gs), 17, 18–19, 26, 27
Broad visualization (Gv), 17, 18, 19, 30
Brown v. Board of Education, 52, 53
Burt, Cyril, 545
Buss-Durkee Hostility Inventory (BDHI), 534

Caffeine, 310, 342, 344
California Achievement Test (CAT), 567
California Psychological Inventory (CPI), 15, 85, 95, 432
act frequency approach in, 495
confirmatory factor analysis and, 423
criminal offenders and, 678, 680–681
factor analysis and, 429
folk concepts and, 481
industrial/organizational psychology and, 592–593
item analysis of, 514
longitudinal studies and, 98, 99
measurement media in, 434
motivation/response distortion in, 435
California Psychological Inventory (CPI) (*Cont.*)
score interpretation in, 498
statistical effect size and, 438
Capability beliefs, 136
Career counseling. *See* Vocational/career counseling
Career indecisiveness, 608
Carlyle, Thomas, 740
Cascade Hypothesis, 24
Categorical data, 437
Category width, 207, 211, 404–405
Cattell, J. M., 744
Cattell, R. B., 5, 6–7, 9, 16, 18, 21, 322, 419, 425, 427, 428, 430–431, 432, 438, 439–440, 448, 450–451, 468, 483, 509, 522, 746, 747
Caucasians. *See* Whites
Cerebral blood flow (CBF), 23
Charcot, J. M., 54
Child Behavior Checklist (CBCL), 212, 532, 632
Child-centered approach, 220
Childhood Apperception Test, 631
Children
cognitive development in, 86–91
criminal offenders and, 682
depression in, 530–531, 663
diabetes in, 713, 714
exceptionality in. *See* Exceptionality
extraversion in, 322–323
intelligence tests and, 511
neuropsychology in, 652–655, 658, 667–668
as basis of emotions, 656
brain injuries, 661, 666
frontal lobe dysfunction, 658–659
schizophrenia and, 657–658
Children's Apperception Test, 518, 521
Children's Depression Inventory (CDI), 531
Children's Manifest Anxiety Scale-Revised, 563
Children's Motivation Analysis Test (CMAT), 36, 433–434
Chinese Classification of Mental Disorders (CCMD-3), 526
Chinese people, 108, 109, 561
Chlorpromazine, 242
Choice reaction time (CRT), 25, 329, 695–696
Chomsky, N., 107
Chunking, 151, 152, 378
Circumplex structures, 428–429
Civil Rights Act of 1964, 585
Civil Rights Commission, 52
Classical item selection, 488
Classical test theory (CTT), 436–437
Classification Inventory, 581
Classification items, 507
Classroom learning, 161–181
experiential states in, 175–176, 178, 179
induced motivational states and, 176–178
intelligence and, 161–165
objective–subjective competence interface in, 173–175, 178, 179
personality and, 165–179
Clinical Analysis Questionnaire (CAQ), 422, 431, 432, 439
factor analysis and, 429
measurement media in, 434
Clinical Assessment Questionnaire (CAQ), 21
Clinical diagnoses, 418–419
Closed-mindedness, 402
Closed skills, 702
Coaching, 499
Cognition, 453
affection and conation and, 466
aggression and, 192–193
anxiety disorders and, 267–276
continuity and change in adulthood, 95
manic disorders and, 266–268
mood disorders and, 260–266
personality disorders and, 253–260
Cognition-centered studies of style, 207–214
Cognitive abilities
AIDS and, 37–38
higher-stratum, 430–431
Cognitive-affective styles, 213
Cognitive-attentional anxiety theory, 691–692
Cognitive avoidance, 273
Cognitive-based interventions, 290–291
Cognitive biases, 263–265
Cognitive capacity, 29–30
Cognitive complexity/simplicity, 405
Cognitive components, 453
Cognitive conceptualization, 195–196
Cognitive consistency, 402
Cognitive controls, 210
Cognitive deficits, 262–263
Cognitive development, 86–91, 465–466
Cognitive dissonance, 402
Cognitive event-related potentials (ERPs), 351, 355–356
Cognitive goals, 132, 133
Cognitive interference, 285–295
assessment of, 286–287
cognitive-based interventions for, 290–291
intelligence and, 295

Cognitive interference (*Cont.*)
social adjustment and, 295
social support-based interventions for, 291–293
test anxiety and, 287–291
Cognitive Interference Questionnaire (CIQ), 286, 292, 293
performance goal orientation and, 294
test anxiety and, 287–290, 291
Cognitive peremptoriness, 293–295
Cognitive performance, 301-302
Cognitive processes, 33
Cognitive psychology, 453–456, 469
experimental, 28–33, 38
Cognitive schemata, 252
Cognitive slippage, 305
Cognitive-social skills, 197–198
Cognitive-social theory, 188–189
on emotional and behavioral disorders, 189–193
on learning disabilities, 193–198
Cognitive-Somatic Anxiety Questionnaire (CSAI-2), 690
Cognitive Style Instrument (CSI), 403
Cognitive Style Questionnaire (CSQ), 343
Cognitive styles, 207–209, 213, 397, 464
ability distinguished from, 399–400, 411
applied research on, 409–410
in behavior categorization, 210–212
defined, 206
literacy and, 154
model for, 398–400
psychopathology and, 252–253
sports and, 702–703
in teaching, 219–220
types of, 400–406
unresolved issues in, 410–411
Cognitive testing, 453–456
Cognitive triad, 190
Colorado Adoption Project (CAP), 87–91, 102
Colorado Childhood Temperament Inventory (CCTI), 97
Coming of Age in Samoa (Mead), 33
Common factor analysis, 420–421
Competence, 130
objective–subjective interface, 173–175, 178, 179
role of intelligence and personality in, 613–614
vocational/career counseling and, 614–617
Competing task paradigm, 29–30
Competitive State Anxiety Scale (CSAI), 690
Complex intelligence, 606
Complexity, 19–21, 30–31
Components, 454–455
Composite direct product (CDP) model, 425
Composite scores, 27–28
Comprehensive Ability Battery (CAB), 326, 418, 511, 522
factor analysis and, 428
measurement media in, 434
statistical effect size and, 438
Computed tomography (CT), 652
Computerized adaptive testing (CAT), 436
Comrey Personality Scales (CPS), 429, 434, 517
Conation, 153–154, 463–466
Concepts, 128
Conceptual differentiation, 253
Conceptual styles, 210–211
Conceptual Style Test (CST), 210
Concrete experience, 406–407
Conduct disorders, 662–663
Confirmatory factor analysis (CFA), 418, 423–425, 440
correlated uniqueness, 425
exploratory factor analysis and, 423
general, 425
goodness-of-fit indices in, 424–425
measurement versus structural models in, 423–424
structural equation modeling and, 426
Confluence theory, 69–70
Congeneric factor models, 423
Congruence, 137
Conjoint measurement theory, 31–32
Connors Parent Rating Scale, 632
Conservative thinking style, 224–225
Conservativism, 47–48, 402, 749
Consortium for Longitudinal Studies, 72–73
Constricted-flexible control, 207, 212
Construct definition, 467–469
Construct validity, 467–469, 493–494
bias in, 559–563
Contention scheduling (CS), 702
Content-specificity hypothesis, 264
Content validity, 553–559
Context beliefs, 136
Contexts, 132
Contingency model, 747, 751
Convergent thinking style, 218–219, 232, 403, 406–407
characteristics of, 405–406
Cooperative-planner approach, 220
Coopersmith Self-Esteem Inventory, 313
Coping, 304–307
Coping intention, 178
Coping styles, 304–305
Cornell Selectee Index, 580
Correlated uniqueness confirmatory factor analysis (CFACU), 425
Correlation coefficients, 437
Cortisol, 534
COSAN, 30, 426, 438
Covariation chart, 468
Cox, Catherine, 744, 751
CPQ, 429, 434
Craniometry, 54
Creativity, 231–244
achievement, 231
arousal and, 242–243
intelligence and, 307–308
manic disorders and, 267
as a mental process, 237–239
nature and definition of, 231–233
personality and, 233–234, 242–243
psychoticism and, 233, 234–237
trait, 231
Criminal offenders, 673–683
intellectual factors and, 674–678, 681–682
personality factors and, 678–682
Criterion-keyed tests, 513–514
Criterion-related validity, 494
bias in, 563–568
Critical thinking skills, 642
Cronbach alpha coefficient, 437, 491
Cronback, L. J., 9
Cross-cultural differences, 107–120
in intelligence, 108–114
in personality, 114–120
in personality tests, 33–34
Crossman's card-sorting task, 25, 26
Crystallized intelligence (Gc), 6–7, 38, 349, 430–431
anxiety and, 33
assessment of, 448, 450–452, 469
attentional tasks/resources and, 375–376
competing tasks and, 30
diabetes and, 22
factor analysis of, 428, 506
gender and, 36
intelligence tests and, 508
personality in, 17–18
pragmatics and, 34
radex model and, 19, 21
school/educational psychology and, 634–635
short-term memory and, 379
temperament test measures and, 323, 325
vitamins and, 22
working memory and, 29
Cultural view, 107, 120

Culture, 155–156
Culture bias, 550–551
Culture-bound fallacy, 551
Culture Fair Intelligence Tests , 16, 33, 510, 588
Culture-fair tests, 438–439, 550–551
Culture loading, 550–551, 635
Curiosity, 308–309
Current selves, 178
C-W Scale, 211
Cyclothymia, 267

Darwin, C., 116
Data gathering, 196
da Vinci, L., 743–744
Decision time (DT), 336–337, 338, 340, 695–696
Declared interests, 49
Decoding, 148, 151
De-differentiation hypothesis, 24
Defensive styles, 464
Deficiency hypothesis, 195–196
Deficit theory, 109, 110–111
Degeneracy, 53–54
de Gobineau, A., 54
Delinquency, 674
Densensitization, 291
Denver Developmental Screening test, 625
Dependability, 435–436
Depression
  attentional tasks/resources and, 376
  attributional style and, 403
  bipolar, *see* Manic-depressive illness
  in children, 530–531, 663
  cognition and, 260–266
  cognitive-social theory on, 190–191
  creativity and, 233, 234
  diabetes and, 23
  environmental factors in, 76–77
  genetic/environmental interactions in, 66
  genetic factors in, 68
  learned-helplessness model of. *See* Learned helplessness
  neuropsychological basis of, 658, 663–664
  pseudo, 656
  unipolar, 234, 658
Depth Psychometry (Cattell), 21
Detroit Tests of Learning Aptitude (DTLA-3), 555
Developmental hypothesis, 188
Developmentalists, 468
Devereux Behavior Rating Scale, 632
Dewey, J., 6, 452, 687
Diabetes, 22–23, 711–724. *See also* Hypoglycemia
Diabetic personality, 712
Diagnostic and Statistical Manual of Mental Disorders (DSM), 190, 526, 529
Diagnostic and Statistical Manual of Mental Disorders-III (DSM-III), 253, 255–256
Diagnostic and Statistical Manual of Mental Disorders-III-R (DSM-III-R), 631
  autism, 531
  childhood depression, 530
  multiaxial process, 665
  substance abuse, 533
Diagnostic and Statistical Manual of Mental Disorders-IV (DSM-IV), 254, 256, 258, 527
  anxiety disorders, 268
  cyclothymia, 267
  manic disorders, 266
  mood disorders, 260
Diagnostic Psychological Testing (Rapaport), 4
Dichorionic twins, 71–72
Dichotomous approaches to intelligence, 634–635
Difference theory, 109–110, 111–112
Differential Aptitude Test (DAT), 322
  gender and, 35–36
  school/educational psychology and, 645
  temperament test measures and, 326
  vocational/career counseling and, 610
Differential Emotions Scale (DES-IV), 422, 423, 434
Differential psychology, 48–50, 454–455
  assessment and, 466–469
Differential validity, 552
Digit Symbol test, 716
Dimensions of Personality (London & Exner), 461
Disabilities, 645–646
Discourse, 148
Disorganizational syndrome, 206
Distractor responses, 554
Divergent thinking style, 218–219, 232, 307, 403, 406–407
  characteristics of, 405–406
Dogmatism, 404–405
Domain-referenced testing, 459–460
Domain sampling, 483–486
Dopamine, 243
Dopamine agonists/antagonists, 242
Double cancellation, 31, 32
Double-threshold hypothesis, 236
Draw-a-Man Test, 511
dR-factoring, 419, 422, 434
Drive theory, 690
Dual-task performance, 375–376, 377
Dubois, P. H., 587
Dunedin longitudinal study, 91–95, 101
Dunn Learning Style Inventory, 219
Dynamic assessment model, 642
Dynamic equations, 752–753
Dyslexia, 148, 662
Dysthymia, 260
D-Zug-Klassen, 646

Ecological validity, 500
Economic growth, 118–120
Education, 75–76
Educational Apperception Test, 631
Educational psychology. *See* School/educational psychology
Educational Testing Services (ETS), 548
Edwards Personal Preference Schedule (EPPS), 515, 583, 638, 640
Egocentric items, 491
Egyptian Diagnostic Manual of Psychiatric Disorders (DMP-1), 526
Eight State Questionnaire (8SQ), 422, 423, 425–426, 434
Einheitspsychose, 234
Einstein, Albert, 148
Electroencephalogram (EEG), 23, 329–336, 339, 340, 368
  affective disorders and, 658
  extraversion and, 331–334, 335–336, 373
  sensory event-related potentials and, 352–353
  short-term memory and, 383
Elementary cognitive tasks (ECTs), 21, 25, 28, 357, 360, 362
Embedded Figures Test (EFT), 209
Emotional disorders
  cognitive-social theory on, 189–193
  learning disabilities and, 193–197
Emotional intelligence, 252
Emotionally exciting teaching, 220
Emotional responsiveness, 136
Emotions, neuropsychological basis of, 656
Empirical style, 213, 214
Encephalopathy, 718
Endorphins, 688
Energic model of styles, 214, 215–218
Enrichment approach, 646
Environmental factors, 59–77
  genetic factors covariance with, 67–68
  genetic factors influenced by, 64–65
  genetic factors influence on, 65–66
  genetic factors interaction with, 66–67

Environmental factors (*Cont.*)
inferred, 74–77
nonshared, 68–71
partitioning of variance and, 59–64
EQS Structural Equations, 426, 438, 721, 723
Equal Employment Opportunity Commission (EEOC), 585, 588
Equality of opportunity, 552
Equality of outcome, 552
Equity goals, 134, 139
Ergs, 434
Eskimo peoples, 111
Ethnocentrism, 108, 116–117, 314
Eugenics, 49–50, 53, 55
Eugenics Record Office, 53
Event-related potentials (ERPs), 329, 341–342, 349–362
amplitude of, 353
brain and, 350–351
brainstem auditory, 360–362
cognitive, 351, 355–356
latency in, 353
sensory. *See* Sensory event-related potentials
Evolutionary psychology perspective, 84–86
Exceptionality, 185–199
assessment of, 186–187
definition and incidence of, 185–186
intelligence and, 186
need for integrative description of, 187
personality and, 186
Exchangeability, 466
Excitation-inhibition equilibrium, 243
Exclusionary criteria, 632–633
Exclusiveness, 405–406
Executive functions
mental retardation and, 624
neuropsychology of, 652, 659–662, 668
Executive style of mental self-government, 221–222
Exner system, 519
Experiential states, 175–176, 178, 179
Experimental cognitive psychology, 28–33, 38
Experimental interventions, 72–74
Experimental psychologists, 454–455, 467–469
Explorations in Personality (Murray), 4
Exploratory factor analysis (EFA), 418, 419–423, 440
confirmatory factor analysis and, 423
determination of factor number, 420
sampling of subjects and variables, 420
significance of derived factors, 421
Exploratory factor analysis (EFA) (*Cont.*)
structural equation modeling in, 425–426
Extensive scanners, 401
External cues, 698–700
Externalizing disorders, 662–663
External locus of control, 312, 402–403, 638
External style of mental self-government, 224
Extraversion, 215, 343, 344, 369–370
academic achievement and, 35
attentional tasks/resources and, 377–378
brainstem auditory evoked potentials and, 360–362
creativity and, 234, 236
criminal offenders and, 681
cross-cultural differences in, 115
EEG and, 331–334, 335–336, 373
event-related potentials and, 341–342
hypoglycemia and, 722, 723
imagistic processing and, 465
influence of Jung's model, 417
information processing and, 372–374, 389, 390–391
inspection time and, 339–340
intelligence and, 309–310, 322–323, 325
learning styles and, 407–408
P300 and, 357–358, 359–360
sensory event-related potentials and, 351–352, 355
short-term memory and, 368, 373, 382–384
sports and, 689–690
strategy selection/application and, 387–389
time of day and, 647
Extrinsic orientation, 311–312
Eysenck, H. J., 4, 5, 7–8, 9, 16, 53, 187, 251, 309, 310, 322–323, 329, 428, 430, 431–432, 439–440, 689, 723, 724
Eysenck Personality Inventory (EPI), 534, 689
Eysenck Personality Questionnaire (EPQ), 15, 74, 323, 343, 431
creativity and, 236, 239
EEG and, 330–331, 332, 333, 334
factor analysis and, 429, 517
hypoglycemia and, 722, 723
inspection time and, 339, 340
measurement media in, 434
Objective Analytic Test Battery and, 522
reaction time and, 337
speed measures and, 28
Eysenck Personality Questionnaire (EPQ) (*Cont.*)
Structure of Temperament Questionnaire and, 324–327
Eysenck Personality Questionnaire-Junior Version (JEPQ), 323, 465
Eysenck Personality Questionnaire-Revised (EPQ-R), 340

Facet theory, 479–481, 484–485
Face validity, 489, 494
Factor analysis, 529
of abilities, 428–429, 505–506
common, 420–421
confirmatory. *See* Confirmatory factor analysis
construct validity and, 559–562
creation of scales and, 489–490
exploratory. *See* Exploratory factor analysis
in personality test construction, 514, 516–517
of personality traits, 429–430
structural equation modeling in, 425–426
Factor B, 322
Factor extraction, 448
Factorial validity, 494, 529
Factor rotation, 448
Faking, 513
Famille nevropathique, 54
Fan effect, 455
Fatalists, 402
Father-absent homes, 69–70
Feed-forward cycle, 273
Feelings, 171–172
Feeling types, 215
Fells Child Behavior Scales, 232
Field dependence-independence, 207, 212–213
description of, 209–210, 401
sport psychology and, 702–703
50-Bipolar Self-Rating Scales (50-BSRS), 17
Fighter 1 study, 729
FIRO-B, 480–481
Flanagan, J., 587
Flexibility, 615
Fluid intelligence (Gf), 6–7, 38, 349, 430
anxiety and, 33
assessment of, 448, 450–452, 469
competing tasks and, 30
composite scores and, 27–28
diabetes and, 22
factor analysis of, 428, 506
gender and, 36
health and, 24
inspection time and, 26

Fluid intelligence (Gf) (*Cont.*)
intelligence tests and, 508
mechanics and, 34
personality in, 17–18
radex model and, 19, 21
school/educational psychology and, 634–635
short-term memory and, 379
single tasks and, 30–31
speed and, 26, 27
temperament test measures and, 323
vitamins and, 22
working memory and, 29
Focused scanning, 255–256
Folk concepts, 481–482
Formal linguistic register, 143, 148
Frames of Mind (Gardner), 5
Free recall, 379–380, 382–383
Free Sorting Test, 210
Freud, S., 54, 191, 743–744
Frontal lobes, 23, 652, 653
dysfunction in, 657–662, 663
F-Scale, 86, 314
Functional inflexibility, 253
Functional literacy, 144, 146
Functional organizational approach, 655

g, 6, 21, 372, 448–449, 605–606, 634, 747
attentional tasks/resources and, 375–376, 377
construct validity and, 561
contextualizing, 615
cross-cultural differences in, 111
factor analysis of, 428
information processing and, 389, 391
models of, 605
resurgence of, 449–450
short-term memory and, 368, 378, 380–381, 384
social policy and, 8–9
strategy selection/application and, 385–386
test bias and, 547
Gain scores, 454–455
Galen, 186
Galton, F., 5, 49, 81, 108, 186, 744, 753
Game schema, 696
Game theory, 8
Garrett, H. A., 53
Garth, T. R., 109
Gates Reading Survey, 567
Gender
aggression and, 108, 115–116, 120
brain size and, 22
intelligence differences and, 35–37
literacy and, 156
personality differences and, 35–37
scholastic aptitude and, 635
Gender (*Cont.*)
social behavior and, 138–140
social intelligence and, 138–140
test bias and, 567–568
General ability. *See g*
General Aptitude Test Battery (GATB), 567, 610, 645
General capacities, 18
General confirmatory factor analysis (CFAGEN), 425
General Health Questionnaire, 722
Generalizability, 438, 491
Generalization, 624, 627
Generalized anxiety disorder, 268, 270
Generalized least squares (GLS) method, 426
General Quality Score (GQS), 731–732, 733, 735
Generative flexibility, 128–129
Genetic factors, 59–77
environmental factors covariance with, 67–68
environmental factors influenced by, 65–66
environmental factors influence on, 64–65
environmental factors interaction with, 66–67
in intelligence, 61–63, 112–114
partitioning of variance and, 59–64
in personality, 63–64
Genetic similarity theory, 117
Genius, 233, 234–237
Germany, 174–175, 180
Gibson, J. J., 587
Giftedness, 185–186, 627–630
classroom learning and, 173
identification of in schools, 627–630
learning and, 627
longitudinal studies of, 83
selective education for, 646
strategy selection/application and, 385
Global situation, 438
Global style of mental self-government, 223
Globetrotting, 410
Glucose, 22–23, 452, 712–713, 720, 721–722
Glycated hemoglobin, 721–722
Goal attainment, 130
Goal establishment, 196
Goal importance, 135–136
Goal orientation
classroom learning and, 166, 169–170
learning, 294
performance, 294
Goddard, H. H., 50
Goldman-Fristoe-Woodcock Auditory Skills Test Battery (G-F-W), 538
Goodenough-Harris Human Figure Drawing Test, 511, 562
Goodness-of-fit indices, 424–425
Gordon Personal Profile, 583
Graduate Record Examination (GRE), 548, 554
Grant, M., 54
Grant, U. S., 749
Graphology, 579
Great-person theory, 740, 741
Gregorc Style delineator, 217
Griesenger, W., 526
Group-factor theories, 587
Grouping strategies, 643–644
Group intelligence tests, 509–511
Guessing, 498–499
Guidelines for Computer-Based Test Interpretations, 495
Guilford, J. P., 4, 5, 6, 7, 9, 17, 428, 448, 449, 450, 451, 587, 636, 642
Guilford Martin Personality Inventories, 581
Guilford-Zimmerman Temperament Survey, 581, 583

Haloperidol, 242
Halo problem, 578
Halstead, W. C., 10
Halstead-Reitan Neuropsychological Test Battery (HRNB), 419, 530, 715
Handbook of Educational Psychology (Berliner & Calfee), 144
Handbook of Human Intelligence (Sternberg), 5
Handbook of Research in Teaching the English Language Arts (Flood et al.), 144
Handbook of Research on Curriculum (Jackson), 144
Handbook of Research on Reading (Barr et al.), 144
Handbook of Research on Teaching, The (Wittrock), 144
Head injuries, 655, 660, 667, 668–669. *See also* Brain damage
Head Start, 72–73
Health issues, 24–25
Hemispheric specialization, 655–656
Hereditary Genius (Galton), 5, 108
Heritability. *See* Genetic factors
Herrnstein, R. J., 54
Hesiod, 119
Hick reaction time task, 717, 719
Hick's law, 25–26
Hidden interests, 49
Hierarchial factor, 19–21, 636
Hierarchial model, 449, 450
Hierarchic form of mental self-government, 222, 223

Higher-stratum cognitive abilities, 430–431
Higher-stratum mood states, 433–434
Higher-stratum motivation, 433–434
Higher-stratum personality dimensions, 431–433
High-level theories, 322, 340–343
High School Personality Questionnaire (HSPQ), 423, 429, 434
Hippocampus, 652, 657
Hippocrates, 186, 526, 607
Historiometric studies, 740, 743–746, 750
Histrionic personality disorder, 257–258
Hogan Personality Inventory (HPI), 429, 434, 435, 593
Holistic style, 410
Holtzman Inkblot Test (HIT), 519
Hopkins Symptom Checklist, 74
House-Tree-Person Test, 520, 631
Hoyt's formula, 562
Humm-Wadsworth Temperament Scale, 579
Humors, 186
Humphreys, L. G., 587
Hyperactivity, 191, 194
Hyperglycemia, 712–713
Hypertension, 711–712
Hypervigilance, 255–256
Hypoglycemia, 711–724
  intelligence and, 22–23, 713–719
  personality and, 22–23, 721–723
  psychometric approach to symptoms, 719–721
Hypoglycemia fear scale, 722–723
Hypomania, 266, 267–268

Ideology, 45–56
  defined, 45–46
  differential psychology and, 49–50
  technology and, 50–51
Idiographic personality assessment, 456–461, 467
Idiosyncratic credit, 752
Imagistic processing, 465
Impulsivity, 303–304, 369–370
  EEG and, 331–332
  glycated hemoglobin and, 722
  inspection time and, 340
  reflectivity versus, 207, 209, 211–212
  speed–accuracy trade-off and, 341
  strategy selection/application and, 387–389
  time of day and, 310, 342, 344, 374
Inactive-learner hypothesis, 195–196
Inclusive fitness, 117
Inclusiveness, 405–406
Incomplete Sentences Adult Form, 535
Incremental validity, 594–595
Independence condition, 31, 32
Independence model, 165
Independent factor approaches to intelligence, 635–636
Index of creativity, 236
Individual intelligence tests, 507–509
Individuality goals, 132–134, 139
Individual Style Survey, 611
Individuals with Disabilities Education Act (IDEA), 527
Induced motivational states, 176–178
Industrial/organizational (I/O) psychology, 409, 577–598
  early developments in, 578
  post-World War I development of, 579–581
  post-World War II developments in, 581–586
  special characteristics of, 578
Infancy, personality and temperament in, 97–98
Inferential-categorical style, 211
Information gathering/evaluation, 403–404
Information integration, 196
Information processing, 28, 367–392
  attentional and cognitive frameworks for, 368–369
  basic, 370–371
  cognitive and adaptational explanations in, 389–391
  depression and, 260–261
  industrial/organizational psychology and, 589
  intelligence and, 162–163, 371–372, 391–392
  psychometric and conceptual issues in, 369–370
  sport psychology and, 694–696
Information response, 404
Innovation, 408–409
Inspection time (IT), 18–19, 327, 336, 338–340
  auditory, 26–27
  information processing and, 371–372
  visual, 26–27
Institut de la Santé et de la Recherche Médicale (INSERM), 526
Institute for Personality and Ability Testing (IPAT), 419
Instructional practices, 640–641
Instrumental enrichment (IE), 641–642
Instrumentalists, 402
Insulin, 712–713
Insulin-dependent diabetes, 712–713, 718
Integrative complexity, 748–749
Integrative goals, 132, 133, 139
Intellectual orientation, 311–312
Intellectual personality, 606
Intelligence
  abnormal, 622–630
  anatomical correlates of, 22
  attempts to raise, 164–165
  attentional tasks/resources and, 375–376
  behavior episode schemata repertoire and, 130–131
  belief systems and, 312–316
  biochemistry and, 22
  classroom learning and, 161–165
  cognitive interference and, 295
  complex, 606
  conduct disorders and, 662
  contextualizing theories of, 615
  coping and adjustment and, 304–307
  creativity and, 307–308
  criminal offenders and, 674–678, 681–682
  cross-cultural differences in, 108–114
  crystallized. *See* Crystallized intelligence
  curiosity and, 308–309
  dichotomous approaches to, 634–635
  emotional, 252
  environmental factors in, 71–72
  event-related potential amplitude and, 353
  event-related potential latency and, 353
  exceptionality and, 186
  as exclusionary criteria, 632–633
  experimental interventions in, 72–74
  fluid. *See* Fluid intelligence
  frontal lobe dysfunction and, 660
  gender and, 35–37
  genetic factors in, 61–63, 112–114
  health issues in, 24–25
  hierarchial factor approaches to, 19–21, 636
  high-level theories of, 322, 340–343
  history of theory and research, 3–11
  hypoglycemia and, 22–23, 713–719
  independent factor approaches to, 635–636
  industrial/organizational psychology and, 588–590, 594–596
  information processing and, 162–163, 371–372, 391–392
  literacy and, 148–153
  longitudinal studies of, 86–95, 99–101
  low-level theories of, 322, 327–340
  in the military, 728–729
  motivation and, 310–312
  motor behavior (sports) and, 693–703
  multiple. *See* Multiple intelligences

Intelligence (*Cont.*)
negative affectivity and, 300–304
neural adaptability and, 353–355
normal differences in, 633–637
P300 and, 356–357, 359–360
personal, 321
personality conceptions integrated with, 131–132
personality trait correlation of, 299–317
practical, 33, 34, 252, 606
psychometric, 322–323
psychopathology and, 251–253
as quantitative variable, 31–33
sensory event-related potentials and, 352–355
short-term memory and, 378–381
social. *See* Social intelligence
speed measures and, 27
stability of, 606
strategy selection/application and, 384–386
temperament test measures and, 323–327
therapy and, 306–307
unitary approaches to, 633–634
vocational/career counseling and, 605–606, 613–614
Intelligence A, 367
Intelligence and Personality (Heim), 321
Intelligence assessment, 447–456
meaningfulness in, 448–450
parsimony in, 448–450
personality in, 463–469
physiological mechanisms and, 452–453
utility in, 448–450
vocational/career counseling and, 610
Intelligence B, 367, 389
Intelligence C, 367, 368, 389
Intelligence constructs, 251–253, 475–478
Intelligence in context, 162
Intelligence research
central position in psychology, 15–16
ideology in, 45–56
Intelligence tests
achievement tests versus, 161–162
autism and, 531–533
bias in, 438–439
characteristics measured in, 478–479
childhood depression and, 530–531
criteria for evaluating response, 477
as current behavioral repetoire, 495–496
dimensions of, 482–483
domain sampling and, 483–485
facet theory on, 480
Intelligence tests (*Cont.*)
folk concepts and, 481–482
goals of, 476–477
group, 509–511
improving, 500–501
individual, 507–509
industrial/organizational psychology and, 586–588, 597–598
instructions in, 477
interpreting results of, 478
item analysis issues in, 435–439
item arrangement in, 490
items on, 507–512
item writing for, 487
motivation and control in, 477
norms in, 492–493
optimal assessment situation and, 476–477
personality tests compared with, 475–478
reliability of, 477–478, 491–492, 508
sampling in, 492–493
schizophrenia and, 535, 537, 538–539
score interpretation in, 495–497
shortcomings of, 499–500
societal changes and, 35
stability of, 477
substance abuse and, 533–534
utility of, 478
validity of, 493–495, 498–499, 508–509
Interaction, 687
Interest, in classroom learning, 170
Internal consistency (reliability), 436, 437, 491, 562–563
Internalizing disorders, 663–664
Internal locus of control, 312, 402–403, 638
Internal style of mental self-government, 223–224
International Statistical Classification of Diseases (ICD), 267, 526–527
Interpersonal cognitive problem solving (ICPS), 188
Interpersonal skills-occupation matching assessment, 611
Interpretive biases, 264, 272–273
Intraindividual dysfunction, 631
Intrinsic motivation, 166
Intrinsic orientation, 311–312
Introduction to Theories of Personality (Hall & Lindzey), 4
Introversion, 215, 341, 343, 344, 369
academic achievement and, 35
attentional tasks/resources and, 377
brainstem auditory evoked potentials and, 360–362
creativity and, 236, 243
Introversion (*Cont.*)
criminal offenders and, 681
EEG and, 331–334, 335–336
influence of Jung's model, 417
information processing and, 391
inspection time and, 339–340
intelligence and, 309–310, 323
P300 and, 357–358, 359–360
sensory event-related potentials and, 351–352
sports and, 689–690
strategy selection/application and, 388, 389
time of day and, 372, 374
verbal elaboration and, 465
Intuitive strategy, 403–404
Intuitive types, 215
Inverted-U theory, 331, 333, 350
leadership and, 752
sport psychology and, 690–691, 692
Inwald Personality Inventory, 592
Ipsative personality assessment, 460
IQ. *See* Intelligence; Intelligence tests
Israeli Defense Forces (IDF), 728, 730–735
Item response theory (IRT), 436, 488–489
Items
analysis, 435–439, 514–516
arrangement of, 490–491
bias, 48–49
creating scales from, 489–491
homogeneity, 436
identification, 379
on intelligence tests, 507–512
redundancy, 436
reliability, 553
writing, 486–488

Jackson Personality Research Form (PRF), 515
Jackson Vocational Interest Survey, 644
Japan, 54, 156
Japanese people, 108, 109, 113, 561
Jensen, A. R., 8, 16–17, 21, 53, 73, 75, 109, 111, 112, 310, 325, 329, 336–337, 338, 498, 547, 550, 551, 552, 553–555, 556, 557–558, 562, 624, 634
Jews, 54, 315
Judicial function of mental self-government, 221, 222
Jung, Carl, 215, 417, 607

Kaiser-Guttman (K-G) eigenvalues, 420
Kanji, 156
Katagana, 156
Kaufman Assessment Battery for Children (K-ABC), 323, 418, 451, 546

Kaufman Assessment Battery for Children (K-ABC) (*Cont.*)
content validity of, 554, 555
predictive validity of, 567, 568
Kent-Rosanoff Word Association Test (WAT), 239
Kinetic Family Drawing test (KFD), 535, 631
Kirton Adaptation-Innovation Inventory (KAI), 217, 408–409
Kluckhon, C., 4
Knowledge acquisition components, 162
Kraepelin, Emil, 526
K-SOS, 635–636
Kuder General Interest Survey, 644
Kuder-Richardson 21 formula, 562

Labeling effects, 551
Lacey, J. I., 587
Laird-Colgate Mental Hygiene Inventory, 579
Language, 107
Language conceptualization, 194–195
Larry P. et al. v. Wilson Riles et al., 546
Lashley, K. S., 9–10
Latencies, 453
Latent inhibition, 241–242
Laughlin, Harry, 53
Law of cognitive structure activation, 262
Law School Admissions Test (LSAT), 548
L-data, 16, 434, 435, 438, 494
Leadership, 739–754
historiometric studies of, 740, 743–746, 750
measurements of, 746–749
models for, 749–753
psychometric studies of, 740–743
Lead exposure, 74–75
Learned helplessness, 190, 312, 403
Learning
giftedness and, 627
mental retardation and, 623–624
Learning Abilities Measurement Program, 456
Learning-centered teaching, 220
Learning disabilities
cognitive-social theory on, 193–198
literacy and, 148
school/educational psychology and, 632–633
Learning goal orientation, 294
Learning intention, 178, 179
Learning Style Inventory (LSI), 218, 343, 406–407
Learning Style Questionnaire (LSQ), 343
Learning styles, 206, 218–219, 397, 464
applied research on, 409–410
literacy and, 153, 154
types of, 406–409
unresolved issues in, 410–411
Learning system, 176
Least preferred coworker (LPC), 747, 751
Lee, R. E., 749
Lee-Clark Reading Readiness Test, 562, 567, 568
Left brain hemisphere, 652, 655–656
Legislative style of mental self-government, 221
Letters from Jenny (Allport), 458
Level I abilities, 16–17, 557, 558, 624
Level II abilities, 16–17, 557, 558, 624
Leveling-sharpening, 207, 212, 400
Lexical access, 151
Lexical analysis, 482
Liberalism, 47–48, 52, 53, 315, 749
Liberal thinking style, 224
Life Line, 610
Life-record data. *See* L-data
Likert scales, 32, 612
Linear model of scaling, 489
LISCOMP, 426
LISREL, 423, 424, 426, 438, 559
Literacy, 143–157
cultural and contextual predictors of, 155–156
defining, 144–145
diversity and constancy in, 146–147
functional, 144, 146
individual differences in, 146
intellective predictors of, 148–153
oral, 143, 144
personality and, 153–155
print, 143, 145–146
sources of diversity in, 147–148
sub-rosa, 155
Little Jiffy approach, 432
Living Systems Framework (LSF), 125, 126, 127, 129, 130, 131, 132, 137, 138
Local style of mental self-government, 223
Locus of control
characteristics of, 402–403
intelligence and, 312
school/educational psychology and, 638
Logical style, 206
Longitudinal studies, 81–102
behavioral development understanding and, 101–102
behavior genetic perspective in. *See* Behavior genetic studies
evolutionary psychology perspective in, 84–86
of intelligence, 86–95, 99–101
Longitudinal studies (*Cont.*)
of personality, 95–99
prediction and, 81–82
theory testing and, 82
Long-term memory, 382, 384
Look-say techniques, 154
Louisville longitudinal twin study, 86–87, 97
Lovibond object-sorting, 238
Low-level theories, 322, 327–340
Luria Nebraska Neuropsychological Battery (LNNB), 534, 656

MacArthur Longitudinal Twin Study (MALTS), 97, 102
McCarthy Scales of Children's Abilities, 562, 567, 568
Machiavellianism, 751
Magnetic resonance imaging (MRI), 652, 657
Make a Picture Story, 631
Malaise, 720–721
Malays, 114
Management goals, 135
Mania, 66, 526
Manic-depressive illness
cognition and, 266–267
creativity and, 233, 234, 243
neuropsychological basis of, 658
Manic disorders, 266–268
Manic episodes, 266–267
Manifest Anxiety Scale (MAS), 10
Mankind Quarterly, 53
Mann, R. D., 741–742, 743, 744
Manual of Learning Styles, 407–408
Marlow-Crowne Social Desirability Scale, 316
Marx, Karl, 47
Matching Familiar Figures Test (MFFT), 211–212
Mathematics, 179, 180–181
anxiety and, 171–172
attitudes toward, 170–171
objective-subjective competence interface in, 174–175
Matrices, 507
Matrix Analogies Test, 625
Matthew effect, 155
Maximum likelihood (ML) method, 426
Mead, Margaret, 33, 116
Meaningfulness, 448–450
Mean score differences, 549–550
Measurement of Adult Intelligence (Wechsler), 5
Measurement of Intelligence, The (Eysenck), 5
Mechanics, 34
Mediated learning experience (MLE), 641

Medical College Admissions Test (MCAT), 548
Melancholia, 526
Melton, A., 587
Memory biases, 264–265, 272–273
Memory capacity (Gm), 430
Memory representation, 697
Menarche, 22
Menstrual Distress Questionnaire (MDQ), 423, 424, 425–426
Mental abilities
  classroom learning and, 172–179
  primary, 8–9, 428, 431, 448
  structure of, 86
Mental energy, 21, 27, 29
Mental health, 305–307
Mental Measurements Yearbook, 512, 549
Mental retardation, 622–627
  autism and, 531–533
  giftedness compared with, 630
  identification of in schools, 624–627
  learning and, 623–624
  phenylketonuria and, 61
  remedies for, 641–642
  schizophrenia distinguished from, 535
  strategy selection/application and, 385
Mental self-government theory, 207, 220–226
Meta-analysis, 18–19
  of leadership qualities, 742–742
Metacognition, 188–189
  behavior and, 197
  classroom learning and, 163, 164–165, 173–174, 178
  literacy and, 152–153
Metacomponents, 162, 385
Meta-comprehension, 145
Metaphoric style, 213, 214
Metropolitan Achievement Test (MAT), 566, 567, 568
Metropolitan Readiness Test (MRT), 562, 567, 568
Mexicans
  cross-cultural differences in intelligence, 113
  test bias and, 556, 560–561, 562–563, 566
Military, 578–579, 580, 581–582, 586–587
  intelligence in, 728–729
  personality in, 727–728
  war heroes in, 727–736
Miller Analogies, 510
Mill-Hill Vocabulary Test, 322, 625
Millon Clinical Multiaxial Inventory (MCMI), 535
Minerals, 22, 73–74
Minimum average partial (MAP) test, 420
Minnesota Clerical Test, 588, 645
Minnesota Multiphasic Personality Inventory (MMPI), 541
  confirmatory factor analysis and, 423
  construct validity of, 563
  creativity and, 233–234
  criminal offenders and, 678–680, 681–682, 683
  exploratory factor analysis and, 422
  factor analysis and, 429–430
  industrial/organizational psychology and, 580, 583–584, 592, 593
  intraindividual dysfunction and, 631
  longitudinal studies and, 98
  measurement media in, 434
  motivation/response distortion in, 435
  problems with, 513–514
  schizophrenia and, 535
Minnesota Multiphasic Personality Inventory-2 (MMPI-2), 429, 513–514, 678
  construct validity of, 563
  measurement media in, 434
  schizophrenia and, 539–540
Mixed model, 165
Mnemonic style, 206
Modeling, 291
Modern item analysis. *See* Item response theory
Modulation theory, 438
Monarchic form of mental self-government, 222
Mongoloids. *See* Orientals
Monoamine oxydase (MAO), 243
Monochorionic twins, 71–72
Mood
  cognitive processes and, 33
  higher-stratum, 433–434
Mood disorders, 260–266
Moral development, 465–466
Morphogenic traits, 457
Morton, S. G., 108
Motivation
  achievement. *See* Achievement motivation
  classroom learning and, 176–178
  higher-stratum, 433–434
  intelligence and, 310–312
  intelligence and personality tests and, 477
  intrinsic, 166
  literacy and, 153–154
  objective measurement of, 435
  personality and, 637–640
  school/educational psychology and, 637–640
Motivation (*Cont.*)
  social intelligence and, 135–136
  sports and, 692–693
Motivational Systems Theory, 125, 138
Motivation Analysis Test (MAT), 433, 434, 435, 522
Motivation/response distortion, 434–435
Motivation-to-Service Index (MSI), 732, 733
Motor expression tests, 578
Movement space, 703
Movement time (MT), 336–337
Multiaxial perspective, 665
Multidimensional Aptitudes Battery (MAB), 675, 676, 677, 681, 682, 683
Multidimensional Personality Questionnaire (MPQ), 64, 85, 95, 98, 99
Multiple abilities, 448–449, 451
Multiple Abstract Variance Analysis (MAVA), 434
Multiple Aptitude Battery, 357
Multiple Dilemmas of the Multiply Disabled, The (Vardy & Kay), 534
Multiple factor analysis, 428
Multiple intelligences
  models of, 605–606
  school/educational psychology and, 636–637
Multiple regression analysis, 418, 425–426
Multiple screen model, 751–752
Multitrait-multimethod matrices (MTMM), 425
Multivariate analysis of variance (MANOVA), 558
Multivariate measurement, 418
Multivariate psychometric model, 38, 427, 430
Multivariate research, 15, 16–17
Murray, H. A., 4
Myers-Briggs theory of psychological types, 214, 215, 216, 217–218
Myers-Briggs Type Indicator (MBTI), 409, 499, 501
  description of, 532
  item analysis of, 516
  measurement media in, 434
  motivation/response distortion in, 435
  school/educational psychology and, 640–641
  vocational/career counseling and, 610

Narcissistic personality disorder, 257
Narrow-band syndromes, 190
Narrow categorizers, 405
Narrow scanners, 401

National Adult Reading Test (NART), 717
National Heart, Lung, and Blood Institute twin study, 95
Native Americans, 108, 113, 114. *See also* Papagos
Natural tempo, 27
Nature of Human Intelligence, The (Guilford), 5
Nature of Intelligence, The (Thurstone), 5
Necker Cube Test, 716, 718
Need for achievement (nAch), 638
Need satisfaction, 608–609
Negative affectivity, 300–304, 370
Negative priming, 239–241, 242
NEO Personality Inventory (NEO-PI), 17, 432–433, 439, 440, 541
  description of, 532
  measurement media in, 434
NEO Personality Inventory-Revised (NEO-PI-R), 95, 438
Network models, 260, 261, 266
  anxiety disorders and, 268–269, 270
  of information processing, 370–371
Neue Anthropologie, 53
Neural adaptability, 353–355
Neural efficiency hypothesis, 23–24
Neuroanatomy, 652–655
Neurobehavioral Cognitive Status Examination (NCSE), 534
Neuroglycopenia, 720–721, 723
Neuropathology, 652–655
Neuropsychology, 9–10, 651–669
  executive functions and, 652, 659–662, 668
  externalizing disorders and, 662–663
  functional organizational approach in, 655
  internalizing disorders and, 663–664
  multiaxial perspective on, 665
  psychopathology in, 656–657
Neuropsychotherapy, 666–667
Neuroticism, 369
  academic achievement and, 35
  attentional tasks/resources and, 376–377
  brainstem auditory evoked potentials and, 361
  creativity and, 234, 236, 243
  cross-cultural differences in, 115
  EEG and, 331
  environmental factors and, 76–77
  event-related potentials and, 341–342
  experimental interventions and, 74
  genetic factors in, 68–69
  health and, 24
  hypertension and, 712
  hypoglycemia and, 722, 723, 724
Neuroticism (*Cont.*)
  information processing and, 389, 390, 391
  intelligence and, 305, 323, 325
  P300 and, 358, 360
  sensory event-related potentials and, 352
  short-term memory and, 381–382
  sports and, 689, 690
  strategy selection/application and, 386–387
New Left, 53
New look, 207, 209, 213
New Right, 53
New structure of intellect model, 17
Niche selection, 63
Nomothetic assessment, 456–461, 469, 528
Nonshared environment, 68–71
Normative statements, 457–459, 460, 461
Normative test score interpretation, 496
Norms, 492–493
Norms of convenience, 493
Nutrition, 73–74, 76

Objective Analytic Test Battery (OATB), 434, 435, 436, 440, 522
Objective motivation measurement, 435
Objective-subjective competence interface, 173–175, 178, 179
Objective test data. *See* T-data
Objective tests, 521–522
Object Relations Technique, 520
Oblique simple structure rotation, 421
Obsessive-compulsive disorder, 259, 268, 274–275, 654, 658
Occipital lobes, 652, 653
OCEAN, 461
O-data, 494
Oddball paradigm, 356–357, 359–360, 362
Oligarchic form of mental self-government, 222
On Heroes, Hero-Worship, and the Heroic (Carlyle), 740
On-Line Motivation Questionnaire, 178
Open-mindedness, 402
Openness, 461–462, 464
Open skills, 702
Optimism, 302
Oral literacy, 143, 144
Ordinal data, 437
Orientals, 54
  brain size in, 22
  cross-cultural differences in intelligence, 108, 109, 111, 113, 114
  cross-cultural differences in personality, 115, 118
  test bias and, 546
Osborn, Frederick, 53
Otis Higher Test C, 36
Overinclusiveness, 237–242
Overpull probability model, 554
Oxford Happiness Inventory (OHI), 326–327

P300, 355–356, 362
  intelligence and, 356–357, 359–360
  personality and, 357–358, 359–360
Paced Auditory Serial Addition Test, 717
Panic disorder, 268, 274
Papagos, 560, 561, 566
Paragraph Completion Test, 745, 748
Paranoid personality disorder, 255–256
Paranormal beliefs, 314–315
Parental loss, 68–69
Parents in Action on Special Education et al. v. Hannon et al., 546
Parietal lobes, 652, 653
Parsimony, 448–450
Partial correlation, 555
Partitioning of variance, 59–64
Path analysis, 84, 418, 426
Pavlov, I., 10, 243, 324
P decrements, 554–555
Peabody Picture Vocabulary Test (PPVT), 554, 555, 562
Pearson, K., 50
Pearson product-moment coefficient correlation, 323, 324, 426, 560, 750
Peer interaction, 631–632
PEN system, 431–432
Perceived control
  classroom learning and, 168–169
  intelligence and, 312
Perceiving-acting, 697–698
Perceiving-understanding, 697–698
Perceptual-clerical speed, 27
Perceptual speed (Gps), 430
Perfectionists, 465
Performance components, 162
Performance effectiveness, 302
Performance goal orientation, 294
Personal agency beliefs, 136, 188
Personal Characteristics Inventory (PCI), 591
Personal intelligences, 321
Personal Inventory, 580
Personality
  abilities and, 35, 595–596
  abnormal, 630–633
  academic achievement and, 35
  accomodating differences in, 644–645
  AIDS and, 37–38
  anatomical correlates of, 22

Personality (*Cont.*)
classroom learning and, 165–179
cognitive interference and, 292–293
contextualizing theories of, 615–616
creativity and, 233–234, 242–243
criminal offenders and, 678–682
cross-cultural differences in, 114–120
in crystallized intelligence, 17–18
environmental factors in, 72
exceptionality and, 186
as exclusionary criteria, 632–633
experimental interventions and, 74
as a flexible style, 607–609
in fluid intelligence, 17–18
gender and, 35–37
genetic factors in, 63–64
health issues in, 24–25
higher-stratum dimensions of, 431–433
high-level theories of, 340–343
historical perspectives on, 3–11, 687–688
hypoglycemia and, 22–23, 721–723
industrial/organizational psychology and, 590–596
information processing and, 391–392
intellegence conceptions integrated with, 131–132
intelligence construct and, 251–253
literacy and, 153–155
longitudinal studies of, 95–99
low-level theories of, 322, 327–340
in the military, 727–728
motivation and, 637–640
motor behavior (sports) and, 688–693
multivariate research on, 16–17
nature and organization of, 125–130
normal differences in, 637–641
P300 and, 357–358, 359–360
psychometric intelligence and, 322–323
psychopathology and, 251–253
as a quantitative variable, 31–33
scientific method in elucidating, 418
sensory event-related potentials and, 351–352, 355
speed measures and, 27, 28
structure of, 95–97
temperament test measures and, 323–327
three levels of measurement, 165–167
as a typology, 607
vocational/career counseling and, 606–609, 613–614
Personality (Guilford), 4
Personality: A Biosocial Approach to Origins and Structures (Murphy), 4
Personality: A Psychological Interpretation (Allport), 4
Personality assessment, 456–463
assigning meaning to measurements, 457–461
attributes measured in, 457
idiographic approach to, 456–461, 467
intelligence in, 463–469
nomothetic approach to, 456–461, 469
qualitative, 610–611
quantitative, 610
vocational/career counseling and, 610–611
Personality Assessment Inventory (PAI), 429, 438
Personality Assessment System (PAS), 5
Personality-centered studies of styles, 214–218
Personality Characteristics test, 581
Personality constructs, 475–478
Personality disorders, 253–260
Personality in Nature, Society and Culture (Kluckhon & Murray), 4
Personality Inventory for Children (PIC), 533, 631
Personality-Occupation Matching assessment, 610
Personality Preference Schedule, 513
Personality questionnaires, 512–517
advantages of, 512
criterion-keyed, 513–514
disadvantages of, 512–513
motivation/response distortion in, 434–435
Personality research
central position in psychology, 15–16
ideology in, 45–56
Personality Research Form, 638
Personality states
leadership and, 748–749
personality traits distinguished from, 300
test reliability and, 492
Personality tests. *See also* Objective tests; Personality questionnaires; Projective tests
autism and, 533
bias in, 438–439
characteristics measured in, 479
childhood depression and, 531
criteria for evaluating response, 477
cross-cultural differences in, 33–34
dimensions of, 483
domain sampling and, 485–486
facet theory on, 480–481
folk concepts and, 481–482
Personality tests (*Cont.*)
goals of, 476–477
improving, 501
industrial/organizational psychology and, 596–597
instructions in, 477
intelligence tests compared with, 475–478
interpreting results of, 478
item analysis issues in, 435–439
item arrangement in, 491
item writing for, 486–487
lexical analysis and, 482
motivation and control in, 477
need for objective construction of, 435
norms in, 492–493
optimal assessment situation and, 476–477
reliability of, 477–478, 491–492
sampling in, 492–493
schizophrenia and, 535, 536–537, 539–540
score interpretation in, 497–498
shortcomings of, 500
stability of, 477
substance abuse and, 534–535
types of, 512–523
utility of, 478
validity of, 493–495, 499
war heroes and, 732, 733, 734
Personality Through Perception, 208
Personality traits, 476
classroom learning and, 178
factor analysis of, 429–430
intelligence correlates of, 299–317
leadership and, 748–749
models of, 607
personality states distinguished from, 300
test reliability and, 492
Personal State Questionnaire (PSQ), 326–327
Personal Styles Inventory (PSI), 610
Personnel Reaction Blank, 593
Personologism, 687
P factor, 431
Phenylketonuria, 61
Phobias, 274
Phonics, 154
Phrenitis, 526
Physiological mechanisms, 452–453
Piaget, J., 10, 308
Piers-Harris Self Concept Scale, 640
Pioneer Fund, 53
p-m eigenvalues, test of equality of, 420
Porteus Maze Test, 511
Positron emission tomography (PET), 23, 657

Potthoff technique, 567
Practical intelligence, 33, 34, 252, 606
Practice, for tests, 499
Pragmatics, 7–8, 34
Pragmatists, 407
Preceptive strategy, 403
Prediction
  longitudinal studies and, 81–82
  psychodiagnosis and, 529–530
Predictive validity, 549, 563–568
Predictor constructs, 592–593
PRELIS, 423, 424, 437
Prenatal events, 66
Preschool Inventory-Revised, 562, 567, 568
Primary mental abilities, 8–9, 428, 431, 448
Primary Mental Abilities (Thurstone), 5
Primary Psychotechnical Rating (PPR), 732, 733
Primary-secondary task paradigm, 29–30
Principal components analysis, 420–421
Print literacy, 143, 145–146
Problem solving, 137
  aggression and, 192
  criminal offenders and, 677–678
ProcCALIS, 426
Processing deficiencies, 192
Processing efficiency, 302
Process transaction, 687
Profile of Mood States (POMS), 422, 423
Profile of Nonverbal Sensitivity (PONS), 538, 539
Profiles, 497
Progesterone, 116
Project A, 594, 596
Projective tests, 518–521
Proportion, 458
Propositions, 128
Provincial powers, 18
Pseudodepression, 656
Pseudopsychopathology, 656
Psychodiagnosis, 525–541
  of autism, 531–533
  of childhood depression, 530–531
  classification systems for, 526–527
  history of, 526–527
  psychometrics and, 527–529
  of schizophrenia, 535–540
  of substance abuse, 533–535
Psychological constructs, 417–418
Psychological differentiation, 401
Psychological tests
  confirmatory factor analysis and, 423–425
  exploratory factor analysis and, 421–422
Psychometric intelligence, 322–323
Psychometrics, 427–435
  behavioral specification equations in, 427–428
  hypoglycemia and, 719–721
  information processing and, 369–370
  item analysis issues in, 435–439
  in leadership studies, 740–743
  meta-analysis and, 18–19
  psychodiagnosis and, 527–529
  variety of media for, 434
Psychomotor-poverty syndrome, 206
Psychopathic States Inventory (PSI), 534
Psychopathology, 249–278
  intelligence and, 251–253
  neuropsychological basis of, 656–657
  pseudo, 656
Psychopaths, 5, 673–674
Psychopathy Checklist, 673
Psychoticism
  brainstem auditory evoked potentials and, 361
  creativity and, 233, 234–237
  EEG and, 331, 332
  glycated hemoglobin and, 722
  intelligence and, 305–306, 323
  P300 and, 358
  sensory event-related potentials and, 352
  sports and, 689, 690
P technique, 419
Public Law 94-142, 635

Q-data, 16, 434–435, 438
Qualitative personality assesment, 610–611
Qualitative vocational assessment, 609–610
Quantitative personality assesment, 610
Quantitative variables, 31–33
Quantitative vocational assessment, 609–610
Queensland Test, 33
Quick test, 316

Race. *See also* Cross-cultural differences; specific ethnic, racial groups
  brain size and, 22
  intelligence and, 109–110
  r-k characteristics and, 117–118
Race Psychology (Garth), 109
Racial hygiene, 50
Racism, 51–52, 53
Radex model, 19–21, 428–429
Radical cultural relativism hypothesis, 34–35
Rapaport, D., 4, 5, 238
Rapid Visual Information Processing Test (RVIP), 719
Rating scale methods, 578
Rational style, 213, 214
Raven's Advanced Progressive Matrices (APM), 323
  giftedness and, 630
  inspection time and, 340
  reaction time and, 338
  temperament test measures and, 325
Raven's Progressive Matrices, 16, 23, 32, 322, 507
  construct validity of, 562
  content validity of, 554
  cross-cultural differences and, 114
  EEG and, 329, 335
  extraversion and, 310
  items on, 509–510
  P300 and, 356
  predictive validity of, 566–567
  strategy selection/application and, 385
Reaction time (RT), 18–19, 325, 327, 336–338, 339, 343
  cross-cultural differences in, 113
  diabetes and, 22
  EEG and, 329, 331
  Hick's law and, 25–26
  information processing and, 371–372
  short-term memory and, 383
  sports and, 695–696
  strategy selection/application and, 387–388
Reaction to Tests Questionnaire (RTT), 286–287, 289
Reading, 144, 145–146
Reading deficits, 661–662
Reality-distortion syndrome, 206
Reassuring, 290–291
Recall capability, 696–697
Receptive thinkers, 403
Reductionism, 452–453
Reference factors, 496
Reflective thought, 6, 342, 404, 406–407, 465
  impulsivity versus, 207, 209, 211–212
  stages of, 340–341
Regression equations, 564–568
Relational style, 210–211
Relativist theory, 107
Reliability, 435–436, 477–478
  factors influencing, 491–492
  of intelligence tests, 477–478, 491–492, 508
  internal, 436, 437, 491, 562–563
  of personality questionnaires, 512
  of personality tests, 477–478, 491–492
  of projective tests, 518

Reliability (*Cont.*)
test–retest, 491
Religious conservatism, 315
Reorganization, 378
Representative equality, 552
Resource acquisition goals, 134
Restructuring, 405
Retrieval capacity (Gr), 430
Revolving-door model, 646
R-factoring, 419, 434
RIASEC model, 424
Right brain hemisphere, 652
affective disorders and, 658
depression and, 663
specialization of, 655–656
Right-Wing Authoritarian (RWA) scale, 85
Rigidity, 404–405
r-k characteristics, 117–118
Rockefeller, N., 148
Rod-and-frame technique, 401
Rod and Frame Test (RFT), 209
Rorschach test, 6, 518, 519, 535
Rosenberg Self-Esteem Scale, 480
Rotated factor pattern, 420
Rotational design, 743
Rote learning, 623, 627
Roth-Jensen apparatus, 25–26
Rotoplot, 421

Safety goals, 135
Sampling, 420, 492–493
domain, 483–486
Satisficing, 126
Scales, 489–491
Scales for Rating the Behavioral Characteristics of Superior Students, 630
Scales of Independent Behavior, 632
Scanning, 253, 255–256, 401
Schema theory, 260–261, 266, 268–269, 270
Schizoaffective illness, 234
Schizophrenia, 52, 254, 266
cognitive styles in, 206
creativity and, 234, 236–239, 240, 242, 243, 244
frontal lobe dysfunction and, 657–658
genetic/environmental interactions in, 66–67
genetic factors in, 65
intelligence and, 305, 306
mental retardation distinguished from, 535
nonshared environment and, 70
psychodiagnosis of, 535–540
Schizotypal personality disorder, 254–255
Scholastic Aptitude Test (SAT), 303, 489, 548, 565–566
School/educational psychology, 621–648
abnormal intelligence and, 622–630
abnormal personality and, 630–633
accomodating personality differences, 644–645
altering curricula, 644
developing skills in normal individuals, 642–643
grouping strategies and, 643–644
identifying and treating disabilities, 645–646
normal intelligence differences and, 633–637
normal personality differences and, 637–641
remedying abnormality and, 641–642
School Motivation Analysis Test (SMAT), 433
School segregation, 52
Scoring
interpretation in, 495–498
of personality questionnaires, 512
of projective tests, 518–519
Scree test, 420
Scripts, 128–129
S-data, 494
Sears, R. R., 10–11
Self-action, 687
Self-assertive goals, 132, 133, 139
Self-concept
intelligence and, 312–313
school/educational psychology and, 639–640
Self-control, 189, 190, 302
Self-Description Questionnaire, 423
Self-determination goals, 134, 139
Self-Directed Search (SDS), 326, 423, 424, 644–645
Self-efficacy, 250
aggression and, 192
classroom learning and, 166, 167–168, 174
intelligence and, 313–314
school/educational psychology and, 639–640
vocational/career counseling and, 608
Self-esteem, 639–640
Self-monitoring, 250, 742
Self-referenced cognitions, 173–174, 175, 178–179
about subject areas, 169–171
about the self, 167–169
feelings and, 171–172
Self-regulation
classroom learning and, 163, 164, 174
cognitive-social theory and, 189, 191
literacy and, 153, 154
Self-worth theory, 166
Semantic encoding, 151
Semantic network model. *See* Network models
Semantic processing, 697–698
Semantics, 7–8
Sensation seeking, 688–689
Sensation Seeking Scale (SSS), 688–689
Sensing types, 215
Sensorimotor processing, 697–698
Sensory event-related potentials (ERPs)
intelligence and, 352–355
personality and, 351–352, 355
Sentence Completion Test, 732
Sentence completion tests, 518
Sentiments, 434
Sequenced Inventory of Communication Development (SCID), 98
Serialist style, 410
Series, 507
Serological imbalances, 22
Serum uric acid (SUA), 22
Sex hormones, 116, 191
Shadowing, 375–376
Sharpening. *See* Leveling-sharpening
Short-term acquisition and retrieval (SAR), 17, 18, 19, 30
Short-term memory, 367, 368–369, 373, 375, 378–384, 391
intelligence and, 378–381
resource limitations of, 380
Shuey, A., 53
Sibling Inventory of Different Experiences (SIDE), 70, 72
Signal detection, 255
Significant batting averages (SBA), 585
Simple phobias, 268
Simplex structures, 428–429
Simultaneous learners, 635–636
Single cancellation, 31
Single-group validity, 552
Single photon emission tomography (SPET), 719, 724
Single tasks, 30–31
Situationalists, 468
Situationism, 687
Sixteen Personality Factor Test (16PF), 15, 16, 17, 21, 431–432, 433, 439
academic achievement and, 35
confirmatory factor analysis and, 423
cross-cultural replication of, 33
description of, 532
factor analysis and, 429, 517
industrial/organizational psychology and, 584
intelligence and, 326
Kirton Adaptation-Innovation Inventory and, 409
leadership and, 746, 747

Sixteen Personality Factor Test (16PF) (*Cont.*)
measurement media in, 434
motivation/response distortion in, 434–435
Objective Analytic Test Battery and, 522
school/educational psychology and, 638, 640
social intelligence and, 34
war heroes and, 729
Skill-related processes, 136–137
Slave systems, 378
Social adjustment, 295
Social behavior, 125–140. *See also* Social intelligence
domains of, 132–135
gender and, 138–140
processes contributing to effective, 135–138
Social cognition hypothesis, 195
Social desirability, 315–316, 513
Social determinism, 52, 53, 55
Social disadvantages, 625–626
Social encoding capabilities, 137
Social engineering, 50
Social exchange model of aggression, 189
Social goals, 132, 139–140
Social intelligence, 33, 321. *See also* Social behavior
contextual processes and, 137–138
criminal offenders and, 677–678, 681
described, 34
gender and, 138–140
in the military, 729
models of, 605–606
motivational processes and, 135–136
psychopathology and, 252
skill-related processes and, 136–137
Social learning theory, 312
Social phobias, 268, 274
Social planning capabilities, 137
Social policy, 8–9
Social relationship goals, 132–134
Social responsibility goals, 134
Social support-based interventions, 291–293
Social task goals, 132, 133, 135, 139
Societal changes, 35
Sociobiology, 52, 116
Socioeconomic status
cross-cultural differences in intelligence and, 112–113
test bias and, 547, 550, 551
Sociological perspectives, 33–35, 38
Solid objects tests, 518
Soroka v. Dayton Hudson, 597
South Sea Islanders, 109
Span memory, 379
Spearman, C., 8, 111, 428, 587, 634, 747
Speech, 145–146
Speed, 25–28, 341, 343, 344. *See also* Broad speediness function
g and, 372
strategy selection/application and, 386–388
Spencer, H., 116
Spider phobias, 274
Split-brain patients, 644
Sport Competition Anxiety test (SCAT), 690
Sport psychology, 687–704
attentional processes and, 700–702
attentional styles and, 702–703
cognitive styles and, 702–703
decision making and, 694–695
experience and, 694–695
external cues and, 698–700
information processing and, 694–696
knowledge structures and, 694–695
memory representation and, 697
motivation and, 692–693
perception of time and space in, 703–704
recall capability and, 696–697
semantic and sensorimotor processing and, 697–698
sensation seeking and, 688–689
vision and, 697–698
SRA tests, 588
Stability, 435–436, 477
of intelligence, 606
Standard error of measurement (SEM), 491
Standardization, 512, 549
Standard social science model, 84–85
Standards of Educational and Psychological Tests, 495
Stanford-Binet Intelligence Scale, 451, 741
brain injury and, 666
children and, 511
confirmatory factor analysis and, 423, 424
content validity of, 555
exploratory factor analysis and, 418
fluid and generalized intelligence in, 18
items on, 508–509
longitudinal studies and, 88
measurement media in, 434
predictive validity of, 567, 568
State anger, 303
State anxiety, 268, 269, 274, 638
attentional biases and, 271–272
sports and, 691
State-liability traits, 438
State-Trait Anxiety Inventory (STAI), 436, 638, 690
Static equations, 752–753
Static personal style, 607
Statistical effect size, 437–438
Statistical interpretations, 418–419
Sternberg memory scanning test, 719
Stogdill, R., 741
Strategy selection/application, 384–389
Strelau Temperament Inventory (STI), 323–326, 337, 339
Stress, 76–77
classroom learning and, 166
coping styles and, 304–305
integrative complexity and, 748–749
vocational/career counseling and, 617
Stressful life events, 82
String measures, 329, 330, 332–333, 334, 335, 353, 362
Strong-Campbell Interest Inventory, 610
Strong Interest Inventory, 644
Strong Vocational Interest Blank, 583
Stroop test, 370
Structs, 485
Structuples, 485
Structural equation modeling (SEM), 418, 419, 425–427, 440
advantages of, 426
critique of, 426–427
Structural instability, 253
Structured Interview for DSM-III Personality (SIDP), 535
Structure of intellect (SOI) model, 7, 17, 307, 428, 435, 449, 636, 642
Structure of Temperament Questionnaire (STQ), 323, 324–327
Subject-centered teaching, 220
Subjective organization goals, 132, 133
Sub-rosa literacy, 155
Substance abuse, 533–535
Suicide, 66, 658
Superiority goals, 134, 139
Superstition, 314–315
Supervisory attentional system (SAS), 702
Swaps tests, 30–31, 32–33
Swedish Adoption Study of Aging, 62, 68
Sydenham, T., 526
Syntactics, 7–8
Syntality factors, 34
Syntax, 148
Systemic strategy, 403
Szasz, T., 187

Talented students, 646
Task goals. *See* Social task goals

Task-oriented approach, 220
Tasks, 453–454
Task value, 169
Taxonomy
of human goals, 132, 133
of psycholgoical constructs, 417–418
research in, 591–592
Taxonomy of Educational Objectives (Bloom), 460
Taylor, J. A., 10
Taylor Manifest Anxiety Scale (TMAS), 690
T-data, 16, 434, 435, 436, 440, 494
Teaching styles, 219–220
Temne, 111
Temperament, 97–98, 640
Temperament Assessment Battery for Children (TABC), 532, 640
Temperament test measures, 323–327
Temporal lobes, 652, 653, 656
Terman, L. M., 50, 83, 251, 741, 744
Terminal drop, 24
Tertiary storage and retrieval (TSR), 17, 18
Test anxiety, 171
attentional tasks/resources and, 376
cognitive interference and, 287–291
cognitive peremptoriness and, 293–294
cognitive performance and, 301–302
intelligence and, 300–302
strategy selection/application and, 386–387
Test bias, 438–439, 498, 545–570
in construct validity, 559–563
in content validity, 553–559
controversy over, 546–549
in criterion-related validity, 563–568
definition problem in, 551–552
labeling effects of, 551
mean score differences as, 549–550
possible sources of, 549
in predictive validity, 549, 563–568
Test of Memory and Learning (TOMAL), 555
Testosterone, 191
Test-retest reliability, 491
Tests in Print, 582
Tests of Basic Experiences, 562, 567
Test users, training of, 499
Texas Adoption Project, 64, 98
Thematic Apperception Test (TAT), 118, 518
description of, 519–520
leadership and, 742, 745, 747, 748
schizophrenia and, 535
school/educational psychology and, 638
war heroes and, 732
Theorists, 407
Theory-based tests, 455–456
Theory testing, 82
Therapy, 306–307
Thinking styles, 205–226, 464–465
activity-centered theories of, 218–220
cognition-centered studies of, 207–214
nature and definition of, 206
personality-centered studies of, 214–218
Thinking types, 215
Thorndike, E. L., 448, 451, 452, 463, 483, 492, 550, 744
Thought disorders, 631
Thought Occurrence Questionnaire (TOQ), 286, 288, 290
Three factor theory of personality, 322
Thurstone, L. L., 5, 6, 428, 431, 432, 448–449, 450, 451, 635
Time of day, 310, 342, 344, 372–373, 374, 389, 647
Timing accuracy, 695–696
Tolerance for unrealistic experience, 207, 209, 212
Tolerance/intolerance for ambiguity, 401–402
Tourette's syndrome, 654
Trail Making Test, 538, 715–716
Trait anger, 303
Trait anxiety, 268, 269, 274, 638
attentional biases and, 271–272
intelligence and, 300
sports and, 690–691
Trait creativity, 231
Trait to item relationships, 476
Trait-trait correlations, 463–464
Transfer, 624, 627
Transmarginal inhibition (TI), 324
Triadic reciprocality, 188
Triadic theory of abilities/intelligence, 18, 430–431
Triarchic theory of intelligence, 604, 615
Triplet Numbers test, 30–31, 33
True-score theory, 438
Truth-in-testing legislation, 545–546
Tubal ligation, 50
Twin studies, 75
on educational influences, 76
on environmental factors in intelligence, 71–72
on environmental factors in personality, 72
on intelligence genetic factors, 61–63
longitudinal, 86–87, 95, 97, 98–101
on nonshared environment, 68, 70, 71
on personality genetic factors, 63–64
schizophrenia and, 65
on stress, 77
Type A personality, 130, 712
Type 1 diabetes. *See* Insulin-dependent diabetes
Typical intellectual engagement (TIE), 462, 464

Unidimensional unfolding, 32
Unipolar depression, 234, 658
Unitary approaches to intelligence, 633–634
Unitary functioning, 126, 131
United Nations Educational, Scientific and Cultural Organization (UNESCO), 109
Universalist theory, 107
Utility, 448–450, 478
UWIST Mood Adjective Checklist (UMALC), 372

Validity, 493–495
construct. *See* Construct validity
content, 553–559
criterion. *See* Criterion-related validity
dealing with threats to, 498–499
differential, 552
face, 494
factorial, 494, 529
incremental, 594–595
of intelligence tests, 493–495, 498–499, 508–509
of objective tests, 521
of personality questionnaires, 512
of personality tests, 493–495, 499
predictive, 549, 563–568
of projective tests, 518
single-group, 552
Validity generalization, 588–589, 743
Values and Lifestyles (VALS) types, 498
Vasectomy, 50
Verbal elaboration, 465
Verbal input register, 379–380, 381
Verbal-performance IQ discrepancies, 675–677
Versatile style, 410
Very Simple Structure (VSS) method, 420
Vice-presidential succession effect, 747
Vicious circles, 253
Vigilance, 377, 386
Vigorous Adapted Development, 34
Vineland Adaptive Behavior Scales, 625, 632
Vision, 697–698
Visual inspection time (IT), 26–27
Visualization capacity (Gv), 430
Visuospatial scratchpad, 378, 381
Vitamin C, 23

Vitamins, 22, 73–74
Vocabulary, 148, 151
Vocabulary items, 507
Vocational Card Sort, 610–611
Vocational/career counseling, 603–618
  assessment in, 609–611
  intelligence factors in, 605–606, 613–614
  personality factors in, 606–609, 613–614

Walton-Black Modified New Word Learning Test, 713–714
War heroes, 727–736
Watson-Glaser Critical Thinking Appraisal, 510
Wechsler, D., 5, 251, 548, 675
Wechsler Adult Intelligence Scale (WAIS), 5, 8, 418
  anxiety and, 300
  criminal offenders and, 674–675, 676, 677, 681, 683
  EEG and, 329, 330–331, 335
  extraversion and, 309, 323, 384
  histrionic personality disorder and, 257
  hypoglycemia and, 714–716, 718
  items on, 507–508
  longitudinal studies and, 95
  temperament test measures and, 325
  therapy and, 307
Wechsler Adult Intelligence Scale-Revised (WAIS-R), 251, 432
  construct validity of, 561–562
  depression and, 262
  EEG and, 332
  fluid and generalized intelligence measures in, 18
  hypoglycemia and, 717, 718–719
  inspection time and, 340
  measurement media in, 434
  obsessive-compulsive disorder and, 259
  schizophrenia and, 535, 538
  substance abuse and, 534
  temperament test measures and, 325
Wechsler Bellevue-I (WB-1), 5
Wechsler Intelligence Scale for Children (WISC), 418
Wechsler Intelligence Scale for Children-Revised (WISC-R) (*Cont.*)
  construct validity of, 559, 560–561
  criminal offenders and, 674–675
  EEG and, 335
  predictive validity of, 566–567
  psychodiagnosis and, 528
Wechsler Intelligence Scale for Children-III (WISC-III)
  content validity of, 557
  mental retardation and, 625
Wechsler Intelligence Scale for Children-Revised (WISC-R), 323, 342
  anxiety and, 664
  childhood depression and, 530
  construct validity of, 560–561, 562–563
  content validity of, 553, 555, 556, 557–558
  cross-cultural differences and, 108
  depression and, 663
  fluid and generalized intelligence in, 18
  longitudinal studies and, 88, 92, 93
  measurement media in, 434
  predictive validity of, 566, 568
  radex model and, 19
  score interpretation in, 496–497
Wechsler Memory Scale, 714, 715–716, 718
Wechsler Preschool and Primary Scale of Intelligence (WPPSI), 418
  construct validity of, 562
  fluid and generalized intelligence in, 18
  measurement media in, 434
  predictive validity of, 568
Wechsler Preschool and Primary Scale of Intelligence-Revised (WPPSI-R), 555
Wechsler scales. *See also* specific scales
  criminal offenders and, 675–677, 678
  items on, 507–508
  patterns of subtest scores on, 677
  Stanford-Binet test and, 508–509
  verbal-performance discrepancies on, 675–677
Weighted least squares (WLS) method, 426
Well-being system, 176
Wells, H. G., 50
Whites
  brain size in, 22
  cross-cultural differences in intelligence, 108, 109, 114
  cross-cultural differences in personality, 115, 118
  environmental factors and, 69–70
Wide Range Interest Inventory, 644
Wide Ranging Achievement test, 76
Will-Temperament Test, 579
Wilson, Woodrow, 744
Wisconsin Card Sorting Test, 657
Wisdom, 33, 34
Witkin Group Embedded Figures Test, 36
Wonderlic Personnel Classification Test, 553, 555, 556, 588, 645
Woodcock-Johnson Brief Scale, 323
Woodcock-Johnson instrument, 451
Woodcock-Johnson Psycho-Educational Battery-Revised (WJ-R), 418, 469, 625
Woodcock-Johnson Tests of Cognitive Ability-Revised (WJ-R), 538, 539
Woods, Frederick, 744
Woodworth Personal Data Sheet, 525, 578
Working memory, 29, 151, 152, 301, 378, 380
Working memory placekeepers (WMPs), 29, 32
Working self-concept, 178
Writing, 144, 145–146

X-O (Cross-Out) Tests for Investigating the Emotions, 579

Yerkes, R. M., 50, 579
Yerkes-Dodson law, 638
Yoakum, C. S., 579
Yom Kippur War, 730–735

Zeitgeist model, 47, 53, 54–55
Zone of optimal functioning (ŹOF) theory, 692